HANDBOOK
OF
SOUTH AMERICAN INDIANS

JULIAN H. STEWARD, *Editor*

Volume 3

THE TROPICAL FOREST TRIBES

Prepared in Cooperation With the United States Department of State as a Project
of the Interdepartmental Committee on Scientific and Cultural Cooperation

COOPER SQUARE PUBLISHERS, INC.
New York • 1963

SMITHSONIAN INSTITUTION
BUREAU OF AMERICAN ETHNOLOGY
BULLETIN 143

Published by
COOPER SQUARE PUBLISHERS, INC.
59 Fourth Ave., New York 3, N. Y.
Library of Congress Catalog Card No. 63-17285

Printed in the United States of America
by SENTRY PRESS, New York, N. Y. 10019

21240

LETTER OF TRANSMITTAL

SMITHSONIAN INSTITUTION,
BUREAU OF AMERICAN ETHNOLOGY,
Washington, D. C., June 1, 1945.

SIR: I have the honor to transmit herewith a manuscript entitled "Handbook of South American Indians. Volume 3. The Tropical Forest Tribes," edited by Julian H. Steward, and to recommend that it be published as a bulletin of the Bureau of American Ethnology.

Very respectfully yours,

M. W. STIRLING, *Chief.*

DR. C. G. ABBOT,
Secretary of the Smithsonian Institution.

CONTENTS

ILLUSTRATIONS

PLATES

FIGURES

MAPS

PREFACE

Conciseness is possible only when data are fully understood. Representation of cultural forms no less than of physical objects may be accomplished in a few incisive strokes if the outlines are clearly perceived, but when they are blurred or invisible the only recourse is to set down all fragments in the hope that further knowledge or study may reveal the true forms. Prolixness in the present volume is inevitable. Despite the comparative uniformity of the Tropical Forest cultures and their environments, the descriptions have required at least twice the space of the far more complex Andean cultures. This is explainable by the inadequacy of sources. Not over half a dozen of the hundreds of tribes have been described with the completeness demanded by modern ethnology. Information is largely from random travelers' observations— mention of a lip plug here, a cultivated plant there, a house type elsewhere. Compilation of all the information from the many scattered sources leaves the tribal pictures overloaded with minutiae, usually of dress, ornaments, and weapons, while the essential outlines of the cultures are not even suggested. The authors have, therefore, presented their data in some fullness rather than select or suppress detail in favor of broad patterns that can only be guessed and that, therefore, may prove to be fictitious. This emphasis on detail has led to division of the area into a large number of small groups—in some cases, individual tribes—with a consequent repetition of the commoner culture elements. At the same time, it gives the impression of capricious distributions and of bewildering variety, for detached elements continually appear without any apparent relationship to the culture contexts. Further field work in archeology, linguistics, and ethnology, all desperately needed in the area, and comparative studies of existing data should go far toward permitting a synthesis of these data in terms of ecological, historical, and configurational factors.

It was the original plan to include in Volume 3 all the Tropical Forest and Savanna tribes of southern and eastern Brazil, the Amazon, the Guianas, lowland Venezuela and Colombia, the Antilles, and Central America. It has become evident, however, that the tribes of Venezuela north of the Orinoco River and of the northern portions of Colombia differed from the peoples of the Amazon in many important respects. The Antilles, especially before the *Carib* invasions, shared some of the distinctive Venezuelan culture. Central America, though having greater similarity to the Tropical Forests than to the adjoining Andean or Mexican cultures, was strongly influenced by the latter. In view of these cultural relationships, it has seemed desirable to reserve Central America, Northwestern South America, and the Antilles for a separate volume, which will be the fourth of the Handbook. The present volume, therefore, includes only those Tropical Forest and Savanna peoples south of the Orinoco River.

When preparation of this volume began, the culture areas were so imperfectly known that it was impossible to use them as a basis for planning and assigning articles. Their determination had to await a comparative study of the finished articles. Contributors were, therefore, requested to describe the tribes or regions that they knew from previous experience or for which they had access to the literature. The articles are arranged in major areas, corresponding to the five parts of the volume. But these are only in part culture areas. (Compare map 1, showing the coverage of these parts, and map 8, the culture areas.) Haphazard as the arrangement of articles may appear in hindsight, they place on record sufficient detailed data with information on the sources to provide guides to the essential facts about all the tribes. They are not exhaustive, however, and do not presume to supersede all previous works. Lowie's Introduction gives some hint of the richness of material to be found in original sources, and works such as Nordenskiöld's comparative studies contain abundant material not recorded here.

The articles differ widely in scope. Some, especially those on the *Guaraní,* the *Tupinamba,* the Montaña, the Juruá-Purús region, and the Guianas, represent a general survey of the literature and are broadly synthetic. Others, such as that on the Uaupés-Caquetá and Nimuendajú's large number of short articles on tribes south of the lower Amazon, are based upon much original field work as well as upon the literature. Still others, for instance the *Tenetehara,* the *Tapirapé,* the *Carajá,* the *Nambicuara,* and the *Tucuna,* are essentially original reports of field work done by the authors of these articles. In general, tribes which are little-known through existing literature are treated most fully.

Lowie has provided a general view of the Tropical Forest cultures in his Introduction, utilizing articles in this volume and various primary sources, such as Koch-Grünberg, Roth, and Nimuendajú, according to their adequacy in describing the different features of the culture. The Introduction is not a summary of the present volume, but rather a composite picture, with variations and their distributions noted only for the more important features.

At the end of the volume, the editor has attempted to group the tribes described in tentative culture areas. This is based essentially on the material of the present volume. It shows some of those groups of elements which give the cultures their local character.

This volume is written largely from the point of view of the aboriginal Indian, not because of any prejudice with respect to acculturation but because the anthropology of the area has traditionally been oriented in this direction. As Indians lived in an independent and primitive state in this area long after they were subdued elsewhere—a half million or more wild Indians still inhabit the less accessible portions of it, some of them not yet contacted by Whites—anthropology naturally has directed its attention to recording the pre-Columbian cultures so richly represented. As Indians became absorbed into the national populations, losing their cultural identity, they passed from the purview of anthropology. It is true that the changes in native culture wrought by missionary teaching, steel tools, Old World domesticated plants and animals, and other factors incident to the coming of the Whites and even of the Negroes are noted from time to time. But preoccupation with the aboriginal continues, and the very interesting processes of the Indian's assimilation of European culture have not been expressly reported. Though acculturation in this area is not so compelling a practical problem as in areas such as the Andes, where the Indian culture is still a matter of some national concern, it is no less important scientifically, for distinctive processes are represented.

Bibliography.—The bibliography of the tribes covered in this volume has been presented with a fullness commensurate with the need, for space prohibits inclusion of all items submitted by contributors. Where full bibliographies have been published previously, the present volume includes only sources actually cited in the articles, but where no large bibliographies are in print, every item submitted is included. The bibliographies are limited to literature cited in the case of the Montaña, covered by Tessmann (1930); the tribes of eastern Bolivia, published by Métraux (1942); and the *Tupinamba,* also given by Métraux (1928 a, b). For the remaining tribes and regions, all items are included here, thus affording unusually complete bibliographies which probably omit only very rare or local sources and an undetermined amount of archival material.

A rich and virtually untapped source of information is the museums. The contributors have undertaken no museum research, believing that this should wait until after the war when there will be more time and easier transportation and when such European collections as remain may be studied.

Tribal locations.—Because an unusually large number of tribes is covered in this volume, the location of each by the nearest degree of latitude and longitude is given as an aid to finding them on the map.

ACKNOWLEDGMENTS

To the many contributors to the third volume of the Handbook the editor wishes to express deepest gratitude. Their fine cooperation in helping solve the many technical problems of coordinating the various articles has enormously lightened the task of preparing the volume. Special thanks are due Dr. Robert H. Lowie, Dr. Curt Nimuendajú, and Dr. Alfred Métraux for their generous assistance in the scientific editing of many articles besides their own, and to Dr. Gordon Willey and Miss Ethelwyn Carter for their consistent devotion to the innumerable chores necessary to the work.

We are also grateful to the Central Translating Division of the Department of State and to the Strategic Index of the Americas for assistance in translating many articles written in Portuguese.

Illustrations have been drawn from many sources. The American Museum of Natural History, New York; The University Museum, Philadelphia; the Museo Etnográfico de la Facultad de Filosofía y Letras, Buenos Aires; the Museu Paraense Emilio Goeldi, Belém do Pará; the National Geographic Magazine, Washington, D. C.; and the Museo de Ciencias Naturales, Asunción, Paraguay, have generously permitted the Handbook to utilize photographs from their large collections. Special mention must be made of the large series of excellent photographs of the *Yagua* and *Witoto* Indians furnished by Dr. Paul Fejos of the Viking Fund, New York City. Other individuals who have kindly furnished photographs are Albert W. Stevens, H. E. Anthony, Llewelyn Williams, G. H. H. Tate, C. B. Hitchcock, Claude Lévi-Strauss, M. W. Stirling, Max Schmidt, Charles Wagley, James Sawders, Curt Nimuendajú, Irving Goldman, Batista Venturello, and T. D. Carter.

JULIAN H. STEWARD, EDITOR.

CONTRIBUTORS TO VOLUME 3

OF THE

HANDBOOK OF SOUTH AMERICAN INDIANS

FRANCISCO DE APARICIO, *Museo Etnográfico de la Facultad de Filosofía y Letras, Buenos Aires, Argentina.*

EDUARDO GALVÃO, *Museu Nacional, Rio de Janeiro, Brazil.*

JOHN GILLIN,[1] *Department of Sociology and Anthropology, Duke University, Durham, N. C.*

IRVING GOLDMAN,[2] *Coordinator of Inter-American Affairs, Washington, D. C.*

ALLAN HOLMBERG,[3] *Rubber Development Corporation, Washington, D. C.*

DONALD HORTON, *Columbia Broadcasting System Television, New York, N. Y.*

PAUL KIRCHHOFF, *Escuela Nacional de Antropología, Instituto Nacional de Antropología é Historia, México, D. F.*

CLAUDE LÉVI-STRAUSS, *Ecole Libre des Hautes Études, New School for Social Research, New York, N. Y.*

WILLIAM LIPKIND, *Office of War Information, Washington, D. C.*

ROBERT H. LOWIE, *Department of Anthropology, University of California, Berkeley, California.*

BETTY J. MEGGERS,[4] *Museum of Anthropology, University of Michigan, Ann Arbor, Michigan.*

ALFRED MÉTRAUX,[5] *Smithsonian Institution, Washington, D. C.*

CURT NIMUENDAJÚ,[6] *Museu Paraense Emilio Goeldi, Belém do Pará, Brazil.*

JULIAN H. STEWARD,[7] *Institute of Social Anthropology, Smithsonian Institution, Washington, D. C.*

CHARLES WAGLEY, *Department of Anthropology, Columbia University, New York, N. Y.*

1948.
[1] Present address: Institute for Research in Social Science, University of North Carolina, Chapel Hill, N. C.
[2] Present address: United States Department of State, Washington, D. C.
[3] Present address: Institute of Social Anthropology, Lima, Perú.
[4] Present address: Department of Anthropology, Columbia University, New York, N. Y.
[5] Present address: Department of Social Affairs, United Nations.
[6] Deceased.
[7] Present address: Department of Anthropology, Columbia University, New York, N. Y.

MAP 1.—Areas of South America covered by Volumes 1, 2, 3, and 4 of the Handbook of South American Indians. Diagonal hachure, Marginal Tribes, Volume 1; stipled, Andean Civilizations, Volume 2; white, tribes of the Tropical Forests, Volume 3; vertical hachure, areas covered by Volume 4. These are not culture areas (see map 8).

VOLUME 3.   THE TROPICAL FOREST TRIBES

THE TROPICAL FORESTS: AN INTRODUCTION

By ROBERT H. LOWIE

The Tropical Forest area centers in the Amazon region, but the traditional "Tropical Forest" culture by no means coincides with the geographical region indicated.   In Im Thurn or Koch-Grünberg we constantly encounter the contrast between selva (pls. 1, *bottom*; 3) and savanna (pl. 4, *center*) without commensurate cultural differences.   We must also reckon with cases of Forest peoples who migrated into new territories, retaining basic traits, yet losing others for environmental reasons and borrowing still other features from their new neighbors.   The Chiquitos-Mojos peoples form a good illustration.   The Tropical Forest complex is marked off from the higher Andean civilizations by lacking architectural and metallurgical refinements, yet outranks cultures with the hunting-gathering economy of the *Botocudo* or with the moderate horticulture of the *Apinayé* (*Ge* stock).   At the core of the area the diagnostic features are: the cultivation of tropical root crops, especially bitter manioc; effective river craft; the use of hammocks as beds; and the manufacture of pottery.

The very wide distribution of certain traits in the area is correlated with navigation.   Thanks to their mobility, the canoeing tribes were able to maintain themselves in the midst of boatless populations, to travel with ease over periodically inundated tracts, and to diffuse their arts and customs over enormous distances.   The combination of this technological factor with natural conditions has produced the extraordinary leveling of culture ("acculturation" in German parlance) in this area.   As Nordenskiöld (1930 a, p. 1 f.) has stressed, northeastern Bolivia looks close to Perú on a map, but is separated by immense silvan barriers and by unnavigable watercourses, so that cultural differences obtrude themselves.   On the other hand, the Orinoco and Amazon Basins are linked by the Casiquiare (pl. 5, *center, left,* and *bottom*).   Accordingly, earthenware decoration in Santarém may precisely duplicate details from the Lesser Antilles (ibid., 16 f.) ; and the *Macushí* of Guiana no less than the *Maué* of the Tapajóz River sling a girl's hammock near the roof when she attains puberty.   (Roth, 1915, p. 311 ; Spix and Martius, 1828–31, 2:1,318; Bates, 1892, 2:405 f.)

In so vast a territory, inhabited by diverse stocks, regional variations are naturally not effaced. Enclaves of ruder tribes impressed early travelers, as when Bates (1892, 1:316, 327 f.) noted the isolated *Mura* of the lower Madeira River as nonhorticultural fishermen (but see p. 258) and the *Arara* as boatless nomads who grew no manioc (pp. 226, 230). On the other hand, significant traits—say, fish drugging, urucú and genipa paint, the couvade—have passed far beyond the traditional bearers of the Tropical Forest mode of life. Nor are features common to simpler tribes and to manioc-growing canoers necessarily derived from the latter; in specific instances the reverse may hold (Métraux, 1928 b, p. 194; 1928 a, p. 168 f.).

Linguistically, we have to deal primarily with three major families, the *Arawakan,* the *Cariban,* and the *Tupí-Guaraní.* The *Arawakans* were spread over the Antilles in 1492 and had recently entered the southern tip of Florida; in the Antilles, they had been overrun by *Cariban* invaders; in Guiana members of this family were their neighbors. The *Mehinacú* of the upper Xingú River, the *Mojo* of Bolivia, the *Paressí* of the Mato Grosso, the *Tereno* of the Chaco, the *Goajiro* west of the Gulf of Venezuela, and various groups of the Purús and upper Ucayalí Rivers are all *Arawakan.* The *Tupí-Guaraní* are equally far-flung: the majority live south of the Amazon, including the *Auetö* of the Xingú headwaters and the *Guaraní* of the Paraná-La Plata region; but we find them also on the coast of Brazil, north of the Amazon (*Oyampi, Emerillon*), on the Ucayalí River (*Cocama*), and even near the Andes (*Chiriguano*). Of lesser, but still considerable range, are the *Caribans,* who turn up near the Xingú sources (*Bacaïri*), but most typically jostle *Arawakans* in Guiana and the West Indies.

Two other families are the *Tucanoan (Betoya)* in the Vaupés (Uaupés)-Yapurá-Rio Negro district and the *Panoan,* whose representatives live on the Ucayalí, the Javari, the upper Juruá, and the Madeira Rivers. The *Tucano* of the Caiarí-Vaupés River are typical of the *Tucanoans;* the *Conibo* on the Ucayalí River and the *Chacobo* Indians west of the Mamoré-Guaporé confluence, of the Panoans. The *Witoto,* between the upper Yapurá and the Putumayo Rivers, form a distinct linguistic family. "*Miranya,*" like "Digger Indian" in the United States, designates no fixed unit, but various unrelated tribes ranging between the Caquetá and the Putumayo Rivers (Koch-Grünberg, 1921, p. 393; also, this volume, p. 155). The *Yuracare* along the upper reaches of western affluents of the Mamoré River in eastern Bolivia are a linguistically isolated Forest people.

CULTURE

SUBSISTENCE ACTIVITIES

Agriculture.—The distinctive achievement of the area is the domestication and cultivation of tropical root crops (see Sauer, Handbook, vol. 6)—

bitter and sweet manioc, sweet potatoes, cara, and arrowroot—of which the poisonous bitter manioc is most important, though it is not known to all tribes.   Seed crops are secondary, but virtually all tribes grow several varieties of maize.   In the marginal region of the Guaporé River, maize and peanuts are the staples, manioc becoming secondary (p. 372). Indeed, the *Nambicuara* follow a seasonally alternating pattern, raising manioc and other crops during the rains, but otherwise practicing a hunting-gathering economy with the usual sexual division of labor (pp. 362–363). Native American fruits, particularly palms, are widely cultivated, but have spread greatly since the Conquest, as have bananas, sugarcane, and other Old World crops.   Indigenous cultivated plants also include dyes, fish drugs, coca (near the Andes), tobacco, cotton, and arrow canes or reeds.   The domesticated plants and their distributions are given in the following list.

Cultivated plants of the Tropical Forests[1]

Name	Occurrence and use
Food Plants	
*Manioc, cassava (*Manihot utilissima*) :	
Sweet variety (*aypi*) : yuca, macaxeira, macaxera.	Aboriginal throughout the Tropical Forests.
Bitter variety : mandioca, maniva, maniveira.	Aboriginal to the Guianas, south to the *Guarani* and *Tupinamba,* southwest to the *Mojo* and *Caripuna,* little in the Juruá-Purús region; west to the *Tucano* and *Tucanoans,* except the *Encabellado,* but none among other tribes of Perú and Ecuador.
*Sweet potato, camote (*Ipomoea batatas*).	Aboriginal throughout the Tropical Forests and Savannas.
*Yam, cara, carahu (*Dioscorea* sp.).	The true yam is an old world domesticate, but wild species of *Dioscorea* occur in Brazil, some of them perhaps domesticated, especially cara, grown throughout the Amazon Basin.
*Yautia, malanga, mangareto, mangará (*Xanthosoma sagittifolium*).	Various native species, being the American equivalent of taro. Brazil, Guianas.
*Arrowroot (*Maranta arundinacea*).	Brazil, Guianas; recent in the Uaupés-Caquetá region.
Maize (*Zea mays*).	An aboriginal staple throughout the Tropical Forests, most tribes having many varieties.
*Cashew, cajui (*Anacardium occidentale*).	Aboriginal to Brazil. *Anacardium microcarpum* bark is used for canoes.
*Peanut (*Arachis hypogaea*).	Aboriginal throughout Tropical Forests.
*Kidney bean (*Phaseolus vulgaris*).	Aboriginal; probably widely distributed but rarely identified with certainty in the Tropical Forests.

---

[1] Starred items are discussed in "Cultivated plants of Central and South America," by Carl Sauer, in Volume 6 of the Handbook, and their identifications conform with Sauer's.

Name	Occurrence and use

Food Plants—Continued

*Lima bean (*Phaseolus lunatus*). — Aboriginal among *Tupinamba, Maué, Apiacá,* and probably many other tribes.

*Jack bean (*Canavalia ensiformis*). — Rarely identified but probably of wide native distribution in Brazil.

*Squash (*Cucurbita*). — Sauer (vol. 6) gives *Cucurbita maxima* as the aboriginal Andean species, which probably occurs also in Brazil, and *C. moschata* as the species of northeastern Brazil.

*Papaya, mamoeiro (*Carica papaya*). — An aboriginal fruit occurring among all these tribes though perhaps spread somewhat since the Conquest. The fruit is called papaya or manão.

*Surinam cherry (*Eugenia unifora*). — Aboriginal fruit of eastern South America.

Lucuma obovata. — Aboriginal fruit of Brazil.

*Guayaba, guava (*Psidium guajava*). — Probably recently introduced to the Uaupés-Caquetá area and elsewhere.

*Pineapple (*Ananas sativus*). — Probably aboriginal throughout the Tropical Forests.

*Banana (*Musa paradisiaca sapientum*). — Probably Old World Origin (see vol. 6), but not a staple throughout the Tropical Forests.

*Plantain (*Musa paradisiaca normalis*). — Doubtful whether native America. Brazil, Montaña.

Inga. — Montaña; Uaupés-Caquetá region.

*Sicana (*Sicana odorifera*). — Aboriginal in Brazil, Paraguay. An unidentified species was grown in eastern Perú.

*Avocado, abacate (*Persea americana*). — Aboriginal (?) in Guianas; eastern Perú.

*Pepper, ají (*Capsicum*). — Aboriginal, throughout the Tropical Forests.

*Arracacha (*Arracacia xanthorrhiza* or esculenta). — Aboriginal root plant; *Mojo*.

Hualusa (*Colocasia esculenta*). — Upper Guaporé River. Recent (?) among *Tacanans*.

Castor oil, mamona (*Ricinus communis*). — Upper Xingú River.

*Chonta or pejibaye palm (*Guilielma gasipaes*). — Aboriginal in Amazon. This supplies both food and a widely used bow wood.

Bacaiuva palm (*Acrocomia* sp.). — Upper Xingú River.

Pupunha palm (*Guilielma gasipaes*). — Juruá-Purús Rivers.

Caimito (*Chrysophyllum cainito*). — Eastern Perú

Pepino (*Solanum muricatum*). — Eastern Perú

Cacabo (*Xanthosoma* sp.). — Eastern Perú

*Cacao (*Theobroma cacao*). — Aboriginal in America, but probably post-Conquest in Tropical Forests, where wild species were widely gathered.

Name	Occurrence and use
Food Plants—Continued	
Frutas de lobo (*Solanum lycocarpum*).	Upper Xingú River.
Mangabeira (*Hancornia speciosa*).	Upper Xingú River. Supplies latex for coating balls.
Mamona (*Ricinus communis*).	Upper Xingú River.
Narcotics	
*Coca (*Erythroxylon coca*).	Aboriginal in northwestern portion of Tropical Forests and northern Montaña; Uaupés-Caquetá; *Ipurina.*
Tobacco (*Nicotiana tabacum*).	Aboriginal to most but not all tribes of the Tropical Forests.
Plants used in manufactures	
*Cotton (*Gossypium barbadense* and *G. hirsutum*).	Both species are aboriginal in the Tropical Forests, but the distinction is rarely recorded.
*Urucú, achiote, bixa (*Bixa orellana*).	Berry used for red dye. Aboriginal throughout Tropical Forests.
*Genipa, genipapo, jenipapeiro (*Genipa americana*).	Fruit eaten; used for black dye. Aboriginal throughout Tropical Forests.
*Calabash, cujete (*Crescentia cujete*).	Aboriginal probably throughout the Tropical Forests.
Gourd (*Lagenaria siceraria*).	Aboriginal among many Tropical Forest tribes.
Reeds, caña de Castilla, tacuapi (*Arundo donax*).	*Guarani.* Arrow shafts.
Uba cane (*Gynerium sagittatum*).	Aboriginal on the upper Xingú River. For arrow shafts.
Rhamnidium sp.	Shrub. Seeds used for beads. *Guarani.*
Coix lacryma-jobi.	Shrub. Seeds used for beads. *Guarani.*
Razor grass (*Scleria* sp.).	Aboriginal on the upper Xingú River. Sharp blades used for shaving.
Drugs and Poisons	
Nissolia sp.	Herb used for snake bites, *Guarani.*
Barbasco (*Lonchocarpus nicou*).	A fish poison: Montaña and probably elsewhere (see p. 518).
Clebadium vargasii.	A fish poison: Montaña and probably elsewhere (see p. 518).
Tephrosia (*Tephrosia toxicaria*).	A fish poison: Montaña and probably elsewhere (see p. 518).

A few tribes of the area, such as the *Shirianá, Waica,* and *Guaharibo* and the *Macú* of the Rio Negro formerly had no farming, but have recently adopted it from their neighbors. On the other hand, the *Guayaki* and the *Mura* have abandoned cultivation since the Conquest and subsist solely on hunting and gathering.

The manner of clearing the forest for typical slash-and-burn agriculture (pls. 8, *top;* 111, *top;* 126) is described on pages 99 and 825. The men make the clearings, the rest of the work devolves on the women, who plant, weed, harvest, and prepare the food. The *Chiriguano,* under Andean influence, have in the main masculine tillage.

To prepare bitter manioc, the tuber is peeled, washed, and grated on a board set with spines or stones (pls. 89, *bottom;* 90, *bottom;* 111, *bottom*), the resulting pulp being typically crammed by handfuls into a cylindrical basketry press (tipití) with an upper and a lower loop (pls. 90, *top;* 111, *center*). The upper loop is hung from a projecting house beam, while a strong pole is passed through the lower and put under the fulcrum made by tying a stick to a house post at an acute angle. A woman sits on the free end of the pole, thus extending the container and diminishing its diameter. The poisonous prussic acid thus squeezed out through the interstices of the basketwork is allowed to drip into a vessel. The purged pasty mass is shaken out as a snow-white; nearly dry mass, which is pounded in a mortar and passed through a sifter, falling on a mat. The resultant starchy whitish powder is either (*a*) baked on a clay grid into thin flat cakes, "beijú," or (*b*) prevented from consolidation by stirring, thus yielding an accumulation of small, dry crumbs, "farinha" pellets, like those of white bread. Of a morning an *Aparaí* woman may prepare 30 beijú—the weekly household supply; well-baked and dried, these will keep for a long time, as will the pea-sized pellets, so that both products provide serviceable traveling fare. (Speiser, 1926, p. 146; Roth, 1924, pp. 217, 277 ff.; Im Thurn, 1883, p. 252. Further details on manioc preparation will be found on pp. 102, 200, 413, 450, 666. 772–773, 829.)

Naturally, the processes varied somewhat locally. On the upper Amazon it was possible to plant manioc on the earthy banks without the necessity for a clearing (Bates, 1863, p. 210), and the period of maturation is variously given as 9 months, 10 months, or even 2 years. (P. 692; also Roth, 1924, p. 216; Im Thurn, 1883, p. 251; Koch-Grünberg, 1921, p. 334.) The basketry press obviously presupposes earlier developmental stages, such as are noted among the *Witoto* and on the upper Purús River, where muscular effort is required to wring the poison by hand out of a plaited sack. This may represent an earlier technique (Métraux, 1928 a, pp. 104, 114 f.). It should be noted, however, that boiling is probably sufficient to drive off the prussic acid.

The aboriginal implements included hafted stone celts for chopping trees, hardwood shovels, and pointed dibbles (Roth, 1924, p. 214; Koch-Grünberg, 1921, p. 334). The spade appears in the periphery subject to Andean influence (*Chiriguano*).

Collecting.—Collecting wild fruits is naturally less important at the core of the area than among marginal tribes, such as the *Nambicuara,* the *Sirionó,* the *Shirianá,* or the *Macú.* Nevertheless, a fairly long roster of wild species whose fruits and nuts are widely exploited for food appears in the following list.

Useful wild plants of the Tropical Forests[1]

Name	Occurrence and use
Drugs and Poisons	
Assacú, possumwood or sandbox tree (*Hura crepitans*).	Widely used for drugging fish.
Ayahuasca, cayapi, yagé, huni, hayac-huasca (*Banisteriopsis caapi, B. inebrians,* and *B. quitensis*).	A strong drug, used especially among tribes of the upper Amazon.
Borrochera.	See Ayahuasca.
Campa.	See Floripondia.
Cayapi.	See Ayahuasca.
Cunambí (*Clibadium surinamense*).	A small tree, the leaves of which are used to drug fish.
Curare, curarí.	A deadly poison, used generally for blowgun darts, made from a liana, *Strychnos toxifera*.
Curupa.	The leaves of *Mimosa aracioides*, powdered and taken as snuff or as an enema for magical and therapeutic effects.
Datura.	See Floripondia.
Floripondia, huanto, campa, datura, borrochera (*Datura arborea*).	A strong intoxicating drug, used especially among tribes of the upper Amazon.
Guayusa (*Ilex* sp.).	An anesthetizing drug, used in eastern Ecuador.
Hayac-huasca.	See Ayahuasca.
Huanto.	See Floripondia.
Huni.	See Ayahuasca.
Niopo.	See Parica.
Parica, yupa, niopo.	The seeds of *Mimosa acacioides*, powdered and taken as snuff for a stimulant.
Phyllanthus conami.	A fish drug.
Yagé.	See Ayahuasca.
Yoco (*Paullinia yoco*).	A stimulating drug, used in Colombia.
Timbó (*Paullinea pinnata* or *Serjania* sp.).	Fish drug.
Yupa.	See Parica.
Foods and Manufactures	
Achua palm.	See Burity.
Almecega (*Tetragastris balsamifera*).	Resin used for lighting.
Ambaíba.	A mulberry tree of the genus *Cecropia*, yielding various products.
Anajá, palm (*Maximiliana regia*).	The shoots yield a fiber used in the manufacture of mats, baskets, screens, and hats.
Andiroba, Brazilian mahogany (*Carapa guianensis*).	The seeds contain oil used by the natives for insect bites and lighting purposes.

---

[1] The present list includes principally the plants mentioned in the present volume. A more thorough study of the wild-plant resources will be found in Volume 6 of the Handbook.

Name	Occurrence and use
Foods and Manufactures—Continued	
Angelim (*Andira* sp.).	Dugout wood.
Aratazeiro.	Anonaceae. Bow wood.
Arrow reed (*Gynerium saccharoides*).	Arrow shafts.
Assaí (*Euterpe oleracea*).	A very common palm from the fruit of which a beverage of the same name is made.
Attalea humboldtiana.	Palm with an edible fruit.
Attalea spectabilis.	Palm with an edible fruit.
Araucaria brasiliensis.	A pine with an edible nut in *Guaraní* country.
Babassú palm (*Orbignya speciosa*).	Widely distributed on the uplands, supplying an important edible oil from the hard kernels of its prolific fruit.
Bacaba palm (*Oenocarpus bacaba* and *O. distichus*).	Abundant througout the Amazon Valley, supplying cooking oils from the nuts and a drink similar to assaí from the pulp of the fruit.
Bactrix marajá.	Palm with an edible fruit.
Balsa.	See Palo de balsa.
Brazil nut, Pará nut (*Bertholletia excelsa*).	Important food.
Burity, murití, mirití, achua palm (*Mauritia flexuosa* and *M. vinosa*).	Edible fruit and pith; fibers used for cordage, clothing, hammocks, and roofing; trunk contains edible beetle larvae.
Bussú palm (*Manicaria saccifera*).	The leaves, resembling those of a banana tree, make an excellent, durable thatch.
Cabacinho	A variety of cacao fruit.
Cajú (*Anacardium occidentale*).	Edible fruit.
Cajueiro.	The tree, *Anacardium occidentale*.
Camayuva cane (*Guadua* sp.).	Used for arrow shafts.
Carayuru.	Pigment from leaves of *Bignonia chica*.
Carludovica trigona.	Basket material.
Castanha.	A Brazil nut or cashew nut. Castanha de Pará—*Bertholletia excelsa,* a castanha or Brazil nut. Castanha sapucaia—*Lecythis paraensis,* a nut from the sapucaia; a paradise or cream nut.
Catizal.	See Paxiuba.
Cedar (*Cedrela angustifolia*).	Tree used to make dugout canoes.
Cumarú (*Coumarouna odorata*).	A tree which yields the tonka bean, a source of vanillalike flavoring.
Cupuassú (*Theobroma grandiflorum*).	A plant very closely related to the cacao tree, whose pulp is used as a flavoring or as a preserve, with seeds yielding a white fat similar to cocoa butter.
Curauá.	A plant of the Bromeliaceae family whose leaves supply fibers used for the manufacture of hammocks and cordage.

Name	Occurrence and use

Foods and Manufactures—Continued

Curuá piranga.

(1) A widely distributed palm (*Attalea spectabilis*) bearing oil-producing seeds; (2) a palm (*A. monosparma*) whose leaves are used for thatch.

Embira (*Couratari* sp.).

The fiber is used for making hammocks, cordage, bowstrings, etc.

Euterpe oleracea.

A palm with an edible fruit.

Greenheart (*Nectandra rodioei*).

Seeds eaten.

Guaraná (*Paullinia sorbilis, P. cupana*).

P. sorbilis seeds used as medicine; *P. cupana,* to flavor a beverage.

Hymenaea courbaril.

Resin used as pot glaze.

Iacareva (*Calophyllum* sp.).

Dugout wood.

Itaúba.

Common name of three species of trees of the Lauraceae family (*Ocotea megaphylla, Silvia itauba,* and *Silvia duckei*) whose wood is excellent for making boats and canoes.

Jabotá (*Cassia blancheti*).

A tree, the bark of which is used to make canoes.

Jatahy.

A tree, the bark of which is used to make canoes.

Jauary (*Astrocaryum jauary*).

One of the most common palms on the low várzeas, the folioles of which are used to make lightweight hats, the skin of the petiole to weave mats, sieves, manioc tipitís, hammocks, etc., the fleshy part of the fruit being used as an edible oil.

Jerimú, jerimum.

The fruit of the serimuzeiro tree (abobora in the southern States).

Manga (*Mangifera indica*).

A mango, the fruit of the mango tree.

Masaranduba (*Mimusops excelsa*).

A tree yielding an edible fruit.

Mirití.

See Burity.

Moronobea coccinea.

The gum of this plant is made into a glue.

Murití.

See Burity.

Nibi (*Carludovica*).

A vine, used for basketry material.

Oenocarpus sp.

A palm with an edible fruit.

Palo de balsa (*Ochroma* spp.).

A very light wood used for making rafts, often called "balsas."

Pará.

Brazil nut.

Pau d'arco (*Tecoma* sp.).

Bow wood.

Paxiuba, pashiuba palm, barrigon (*Iriartea ventricosa*).

The bark used for bedding and wall covers, the trunk for canoes, bows, flutes, etc. An unidentified species, called catizal, provides thorns for manioc graters.

Leopardwood (*Brosimum aubletii*).

A bow wood.

Name	Occurrence and use
Foods and Manufactures—Continued	
Pequí, pequiá, piquiá (*Caryocar villosum*).	These species are the largest in the Amazon Valley, attaining a diameter of more than 5 meters at the base of the trunk. Oleaginous seeds (50 percent oil) are contained within the roundish fruit, which is 45 percent oil; the cooked seeds are edible.
Protium heptaphyllum.	Rosin used for lighting.
Siriva palm (*Cocos* sp.).	Wood used for clubs.
Tabebuia longipes.	The gum used as adhesive.
Tauari.	See Embira.
Tucumã.	Any of several commercially important palms which yield textile fibers, and in some cases also edible fruits used for making wine; specifically, *Acrocomia officinalis, Bactris setosa,* and especially *Astrocaryum tucuma,* the tucumã palm, the leaves of which furnish excellent coarse fibers used in manufacturing rope, hammocks, hats, etc., and the nuts of which are used as blunt arrowheads and as beads.
Urucurí palm (*Attalea excelsa*).	
Vismia guianensis.	Rosin used in pot glaze.

Under the head of collecting also falls the gathering of such animal food as mollusks, caterpillars, larvae, and ants, some of which are treated as delicacies or relishes. Wild honey is easily secured from the virtually stingless species of the Meliponinae in the Orinoco region and is everywhere a favorite food. The *Guayaki* largely subsist on honey, fruits, and other parts of the pindo palm and on the grubs of beetles.

Hunting.—The relative importance and the purpose of hunting vary locally. Game, especially the peccary, is usually sought for food, but many species are taboo to various tribes. The *Carajá* hunt primarily to obtain feathers, while the *Mojo* are most interested in stalking the jaguar in order to win honors. Hunting is generally of secondary importance among the tribes of the major rivers, who obtain their protein more readily from fish, turtles, turtle eggs, and manatee than from forest game.

Dogs are used in the chase, but were aboriginally absent in many tribes. As for hunting techniques, the Guiana Indians manifest virtually all the tricks adaptable to their fauna. They imitate the call of the tapir, deer, monkeys, and birds to allay their suspicions; stalk deer; fire the savanna grass and encircle large game in communal drives; dig out armadillos from their burrows; or lie in ambush, screened by a shelter built on the ground or in a tree. On the Orinoco River the manatee is harpooned from a canoe paddled by the hunter's wife, while on the Amazon it is caught in a net and killed by driving a wooden plug up its nostrils. (See also pp. 258, 517, 827.) Among the *Mojo,* as in México, Chiriquí, Haiti, and on Lake Maracaibo, ducks are familiarized with the sight of floating calabashes so that a swimmer wearing a headgear of calabash shell may catch the birds with his bare hands (p. 413; also Nordenskiöld, 1931 b, p. 43). The Indians also use various snares, traps (pls. 72; 112, *bottom;* figs. 52, 62), deadfalls, and blinds (pl. 114, *bottom*); some of these devices may be due to Negro influence.

The distinctive hunting weapon of the region is the blowgun (pls. 7, *left;* 73; 74; 110, *top*); it is conspicuous in the western tribes of the Guianas, on the upper Amazon, and in adjoining districts, and it appears as far south as the *Pawumwa* of the Guaporé River and in the gallery forests of the Province of Mojos. In many of these localities, however, it is recent, and it never reached the *Tupinamba* nor the tribes of the lower Madeira, Tapajóz, Xingú, and Tocantins Rivers. Its diffusion seems clearly to have been from the north or northwest, and, although availability of materials for its manufacture may have conditioned its local occurrence, its wide post-Columbian spread, as Nordenskiöld has suggested, may have hinged on that of curare. Curare is the deadly poison which makes the slim darts effective and led various tribes to supplant their earlier spear throwers and bows with blowguns (Nordenskiöld, 1924 b, pp. 57–64, map 7; also, this vol., pp. 33, 355). So rapidly and widely has the blowgun spread that Stirling (1938) has even suggested its post-Conquest introduction to the New World.

The blowgun is used solely for hunting, never for warfare.

The blowgun may consist of two complete tubes, one within the other; or of an inner tube within a case of two split halves; or of a single tube composed of two split halves each carefully grooved and tightly strapped together. The length may be anywhere from 8 to 10 feet (2.4 to 3 m.) or even 16 feet (4.8 m.). A sudden puff of breath applied to a small truncate mouthpiece forces out the dart, which is usually of palmwood the thickness of a knitting needle, from 9 to 16 inches (23 to 40 cm.) in length, and tipped with the poison. Curare may kill the quarry within a few minutes. A good marksman will strike his target at a distance of 120 feet (36 m.). The noiselessness of the procedure enables the natives to shoot from its perch one bird or monkey after another; which explains their preference of the blowgun to firearms. Quivers are variously made: the Aiarí River Indians make a basketry tube about 17 inches (43 cm.) long and constricted toward the middĺe, the bottom being of wood or a piece of calabash. The lower part is externally coated with pitch, the rest with a finer plaitwork which displays the black and red meander patterns typical of the regional basketwork and also painted on pottery. Elsewhere, a section of bamboo is used.

Since neither the requisite wood or cane nor the poison is of general occurrence, the blowgun and its accessories are traded over considerable distances.

However, the presence of the blowgun does not exclude the bow, which serves against larger quadrupeds even in the center of the blowgun area. Tropical Forest bows are notable for their great length—those of the *Sirionó* are 9 feet (2.8 m.) long with arrows to match—perhaps necessitated by the common use of palmwood, especially chonta. The material for the stave varies locally, however; leopardwood (*Brosimum aubletii*) is traded between Brazil and Guiana. Among a few tribes, the median cross section is circular, but among most it is semicircular or flat.

The bowstring is of wild-plant fibers, particularly tucum. Arrows nearly everywhere have cane shafts and five types of heads: (1) A large, lanceolate bamboo blade (pl. 6, *left, bottom*); (2) a jagged, rodlike point of hardwood, bone, or a sting ray, often with additional barbs; (3) a blunt knobbed head for stunning birds; (4) several diverging points for impaling fish; and (5) harpoon heads for aquatic game. Additional types of limited distribution are whistling arrows, with a hollow nut on the tip, and incendiary arrows. Stone, being unknown throughout most of the area, is rarely employed for heads.

To make an arrow in the Guianas, the barbed tip formerly was fixed in a slot tediously prepared by first drilling holes adjoining one another with a deer-horn tool, with which the intervening material was removed. Wedged in this groove, the bone was fastened with twine and cement. The shaft is of arrow reed (*Gynerium saccharoides*), sometimes specially grown for the purpose. It is two-feathered if intended for the air, unfeathered for shooting fish.

Poison is employed on arrow points much less commonly than on blowgun darts. Sometimes curare is used, sometimes other ingredients.

As for the release, the Aiarí River Indians hold the nock of the arrow between the thumb and index, the other fingers merely pressing against the palm of the hand. This primary release is noted for the Guianas, where Roth, however, also observed the string pressed upon by the index finger alone. The *Arawakan Baniva* (upper Orinoco River) draw their bows with their feet; and on the upper Rio Negro, a nocturnal fish-hunter pulls his string and the extra short shaft with his mouth while holding his bow in his left hand and a torch in his right (Koch-Grünberg, 1921, p. 246).

Recently, thrusting spears of wood tipped with lanceolate iron points are used against peccaries and jaguars on the upper Rio Negro. Anciently, the metal heads may have been preceded by quartz or jasper equivalents, such as occur archeologically in northwestern coastal British Guiana.

Domesticated animals and pets.—Dogs are found among nearly all the Tropical Forest tribes, but their aboriginal distribution is open to question, despite their pre-Columbian occurrence in the Andes and the Antilles. Failure of the early chroniclers to mention them casts doubt on their antiquity in the Amazon area, but their general importance to the chase mitigates the conclusiveness of this negative evidence. At least in the Guianas and vicinity, the dogs seem to be cross-bred from the indigenous ones and European imports. The *Nambicuara,* however, obtained theirs from the Rondón expedition.

Several tribes exhibit incipient stages of beekeeping. The *Paressi* keep bees (*Trigona jati*) in gourd hives (p. 351); the *Macuna* and the *Menimehe,* in a section of a hollow log tied to a house beam, and hanging 6 feet (2 m.) above the ground (Koch-Grünberg, 1921, p. 385; Whiffen, 1915, p. 51). (For American distribution, see Nordenskiöld, 1930 c, pp. 196–210.)

The Muscovy duck (see Handbook, vol. 6) was kept under domestication by the *Guarani,* and probably by the *Tupinamba,* the *Mojo,* and the Montaña tribes.

Pigs and chickens were widely adopted from Europeans, and, in the grasslands of the Province of Mojos, cattle. The *Mojo* had many cattle, but the *Maropa* were better herders (p. 443).

As pets, the Indians keep all sorts of birds and beasts, including monkeys and agoutis. Women often suckle young mammals as they would their own offspring.

Fishing.—Both nonhorticultural populations like the *Mura* of the lower Madeira River (p. 258; also Bates, 1892, p. 327) and many northwest Brazilian manioc growers were above all fishermen, and even elsewhere within the area the relevant processes were important. Of these, drugging was probably the most productive (pl. 109, *top*). Over a hundred narcotic species are known to have been applied, many of them in the Amazon-Orinoco region. (See Handbook, vol. 5; also Killip and Smith, 1931.) Perhaps the most graphic account is by Spix and Martius (1823–31, 3:1063–1065), which states that large quantities of timbó tendrils were crushed and carried in boats along the surface of the water, causing the fish to become dizzy and to leap up or drift unresistingly till they could be shot or picked up by hand.

Another widespread practice is to shoot fish with bows and arrows, (pls. 6, *right;* 109, *bottom*), a technique extended with detachable heads (harpoon arrows) to turtles (pl. 48, *bottom*). Fish spears (pl. 6, *top, left*) are also commonly used.

Nets with sinkers had a very restricted distribution in pre-Columbian South America, and are lacking in our area, owing, no doubt, largely to the many trees and branches in the rivers that would render them useless. But dip nets (pl. 101, *center*) are widespread, especially on the upper Amazon, where they are made of tough tucum fiber.

Basketwork is used in various ways to entrap fish. In very shallow water or mud an open-mouthed basket is thrown over the fish, which are extracted by hand through the orifice. Widespread is the use of creels and basketry traps.

Weirs (pl. 89, *top*) and stone dams, combined with bailing out water from the enclosed area or with drugging, are often constructed with great care.

In contrast to the Andean hooks of copper and gold, the fishhooks of the Amazon-Orinoco—if present at all—were of bone, wood, or spines. In *Witoto* mythology there is a reference to a naturally barbed hook made of a bat's elbow (Preuss, 1921, 1:71). Bait, which is also used to lure fish within arrow range, consists of berries, seeds, ants, spiders, etc.

(For Fishing, see Roth, 1924, pp. 189–201; Koch-Grünberg, 1921, pp. 242–257; Nordenskiöld, 1924 b, pp. 86–102, maps, 8–11; 1922, pp. 131–133.)

The habits of fish in the upper Rio Negro country locally necessitate an adaptive nomadism. Though the Indians of the Caiarí-Vaupés district with its abundant supply throughout the year can afford stability, the minor streams elsewhere dry up from December to March, so that the fish retreat to the main rivers and the natives must follow suit, exploiting one locality after another until even larger species ascend the tributaries. For the 3-month migratory period the Indians provide themselves with basketfuls of large dried manioc cakes.

Food preparation.—The preparation of manioc cakes and pellets has already been sketched. After the starchy sediment of the expressed juice has settled, the water is poured off and boiled for several hours with peppers, being thus thickened into "cassarip." This somewhat acid broth may receive additions such as meat, small fish, or even ants. All animal food is boiled with water or cassarip, yielding the characteristic "pepper pot," meat being thus boiled daily by way of preserving it.

Typical is the baking and smoke-drying of meat or fish, which would rapidly spoil in the humid climate, on a "babracot," i.e., a three- or four-legged stage (fig. 1, *d, e;* pl. 117, *bottom, right*). On the Orinoco, sun-dried fish are pulverized without removal of the bones, mixed with water, and reduced to a paste. In the same region a turtle would be placed in a pit in the ground and covered with sand, a big fire being lit on top. In Guiana and on the Amazon quantities of turtle eggs are placed on frames and dried over a slow fire or in the sun. The oil is extracted by trampling the eggs in a canoe and skimming it off the top. It is used for anointment, cooking, and lighting, and is a favorite article of barter.

For mealing there are wooden pestles and mortars, the latter being sunk into the ground in Guiana and elsewhere so that only a few inches project above ground (pl. 8, *bottom*). The pestle, which has an ill-defined head, is here used with a grinding rather than stamping movement.

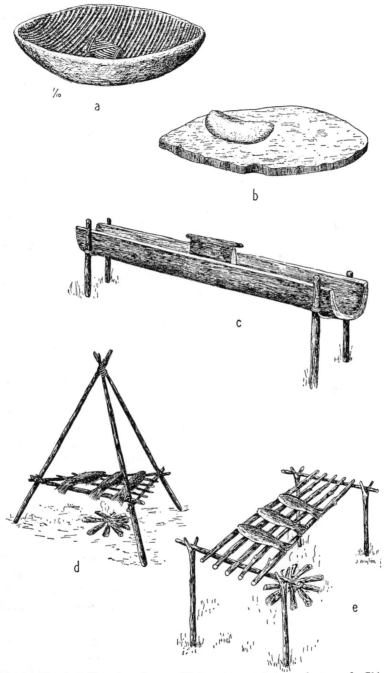

FIGURE 1.—Tropical Forest crafts. *a, Mojo* pottery grinder and mano; *b, Chimane* wood slab and stone mano; *c, Chacobo* wooden trough and block for food grinding; *d, Bacaïri* babracot; *e, Chacobo* babracot. (After Nordenskiöld, 1924 b, maps 16, 15.)

The former use of stone querns, pestles, and mortars is proved by museum specimens in British Guiana (Roth, 1924, pl. 82). Nearer the Andes, a wooden grinding trough (fig. 1, *c*) is used instead of the mortar, but a flat stone slab (fig. 1, *b*) is employed by the *Chimane*. Pottery grinders (fig. 1, *a*) have been found archeologically in the Province of Mojos.

Women boil food, men bake or broil it.

For griddles, naturally split slabs of granite and gneiss have been used even in recent times. More commonly the stoves are of clay and rest on blocks of the same material (pl. 90, *center*). Pots are similarly put either on stones arranged tripod-fashion or on three clay cylinders.

Salt, though comparatively rare, is imported from other regions or obtained directly from saline incrustations in the savanna and from the ashes of certain palms (Roth, 1924, p. 221 et seq.).

There are usually two main meals, in the morning and evening, respectively. Husband and wife in general eat separately.

Geophagy occurs in the area, e.g., commonly in the Juruá-Purús region. The *Caripuna* of Bolivia eat a salty earth.

VILLAGES AND HOUSES

Dwellings and other structures.—The mode of settlement varies. Some houses are designed to accommodate single families, others to hold many families (pls. 30, *top;* 81, *bottom;* 126). One structure of either type may constitute a village, or several may be scattered in near proximity to one another or grouped to form a compact hamlet (pl. 106, *bottom*).

Possibly a thousand *Yuracare* are spread over an enormous silvan tract, along the Chimoré River and other affluents of the Mamoré River, one or two families living by themselves, often miles from their neighbors. The primeval forest virtually starts at the rear walls of their dwellings, which are usually on sites affording at least provisional security from periodic inundations. Characteristic of many groups in the culture area is the large communal house of, say, 20 to 70 residents (*Yecuana* and *Guinau*); *Tupari* (Guaporé River) houses are said to shelter up to 35 families. A *Tupinamba* village consists of 4 to 8 houses, each accommodating 30 to 200 families. Often a single structure, or a pair of this type, accommodates the entire population (Aiarí River). Here, too, safety from the annual overflowing of the banks determines the choice of a site, which is also selected for proximity to potable creek water and for the fertility of the soil. Elsewhere other motives occur, such as security from attack or even availability of potter's clay (in Surinam), some *Carib* tribes allegedly clinging to the edge of savannas for the latter reason. The *Palicur* put up small clusters of habitations on safe forested islands rising from the savanna or on the savanna itself. Waterways connect one hut with another, but become unnavigable or even dry in midsummer, so that visitors must cross series of long logs embedded in the mud. Along the Amazon River, Carvajal observed in 1542 that the houses formed an almost continuous village.

Genuine villages are not wholly lacking even where normally the people live in one or two houses. Thus, the *Macushi* developed an original hamlet of two dwellings into an aggregation of 12, ranged in two streets, though this enlarged settlement, partly due to missionary influence, was reserved for festive use. The *Guarani* set four or eight rectangular houses round a central square plaza, with a double or even triple stockade enclosing the hamlet. Palisades are also attested for the *Tupinamba* (figs. 6, *top;* 11, *top;* 12, *left*), the *Guarani, Tupi-Cawahib,* and for some of the Guiana *Arawak* and *Carib* tribes.

The two main types of dwellings differ according to their round or oblong group plan. Nordenskiöld (1924 b, 3 :24 et seq.) suspected the aboriginal character of rectangular houses outside the Andean region. Unquestionably right in contending that many native groups rapidly adopted the rectangular plan of White neighbors, he seems to have gone too far, for (Friederici, 1925, p. 53) there are sundry unexceptionable early references to oblong houses, e.g., near the Yapurá confluence.

As a matter of fact, several types must be distinguished. The *Palicur* anciently occupied beehive huts with walls and roof merging; a low entrance was closed at night in order to exclude mosquitoes. Another form, shared by *Arawakan* and *Cariban* groups, has palm-leaf thatch covering two rows of elastic rods bent over to yield a pointed arch. Widespread (*Taulipáng, Wapishana,* early *Mojo,* etc.) is a conical roof on a cylindrical substructure, which either remains unenclosed or is walled with bark, wood, leaves, or mud, all these variations sometimes occurring within the same tribe. When small, such huts have a single, low entrance; otherwise there will be two doors on opposite sides, reserved for men and women, respectively. An important variant results when two or even three posts connected by a small ridge pole take the place of the single post terminating in the apex of the cone. The ground plan thus grows somewhat elliptical. However, one or even both gables may be made straight instead of rounded. Thus, there is a genetic tie between the circular and the rectangular forms. Indeed, on the Vaupés River, where Wallace saw houses semicircular in the back but otherwise parallelograms in outline, Koch-Grünberg found a wholly rectangular ground plan. Some of these houses are immense, one described by Wallace being 115 feet (34.5 m.) long, 75 feet (22.5 m.) wide, and 30 feet (9.1 m.) in height and regularly inhabited by about 100 persons, with three or four times that number on festive occasions. The doors are regularly on the gable sides.

Among the simplest habitations of the area are those of the semi-nomadic *Nambicuara,* who most of the year content themselves in the wind-screens (pl. 37, *center, left*), resorting to palm-thatched beehive huts (pl. 37, *top, left*) during the rainy season, and of the *Pirahá*, who make only temporary, flimsy shelters.

Pile dwellings are found among various tribes, especially in Guiana and vicinity, not only on the coast or in the swampy *Warrau* country, but also far in the interior, on dry and even hilly terrain. Koch-Grünberg (1923 a, 3: 23) and Nordenskiöld (1920, p. 4 f.) suggest that these structures are survivals from a period when their builders inhabited swampy or coastal districts. Granaries on piles occur among the *Chiriguano*.

The impermanence of settlement in a particular locality is usually owing to the exhaustion of the soil, but also to disease and death, especially that of a chief. Hence, the population of a tract cannot be directly determined by the number of house sites.

Furniture.—From the time of Columbus' second voyage the hammock (pls. 101, *right;* 107, *bottom*), first noted in Santo Domingo as a regular contrivance for sleeping, has loomed as diagnostic of the Forest culture at its core, contrasting with the marginal *Nambicuara* custom of sleeping on the ground and the platform bed of the *Ge* and of the Montaña (figs. 88, 91, 102). The hammock has, however, spread widely within historic times, being adopted for repose during the day rather than for sleeping at night (p. 833). It is made of cotton, ite (*Mauritia*), tucum, and other materials.

Another household article is a low stool or bench carved from one solid block (pl. 93, *bottom;* figs. 19, 122), frequently in the shape of an animal. The height may be over 1 foot (30.5 cm.) but sometimes does not exceed 3 inches (8 cm.). Special decorations appear on the shaman's settee. Simpler are the plain tripod stools cut from a root or a forked branch with little alteration of the natural growth.

Utensils comprise gourd bottles for drinking water and larger ones for fermented beverages; calabashes; wooden troughs in the west; various clay vessels; mats; diverse baskets and basketry strainers (pl. 117, *bottom, left*). The finer treasure baskets rest on crossbeams, which may also support drinking gourds in bunches, carrying baskets, etc., sometimes suspended from hooks. The only illumination is from the family fireplaces at night and from whatever light penetrates the narrow entrance but for special occasions torches are made from a lump of rosin glued to the tip of a firebrand.

Three stones or clay cylinders serve as a tripod for the cooking vessels in the Orinoco and Vaupés River country.

ENGINEERING WORKS

Roads.—True roads are often wanting in the forest region, where the traveler breaks branches to guide him. Between Berbice and Essequibo the trail was barely 12 inches (30.5 cm.) wide and marked by notches in the trees. In descending walls of rock, crude ladders are sometimes made of rungs lashed to poles. Leaves and spars provide a sort of causeway over swampy or muddy ground. The *Mojo* or their predecessors built up long causeways, each paralleled by a ditch or canal (p. 416). In *Palicur* country the waterways become unpassable in midsummer, hence long tree trunks are laid end to end in the mire to afford transit.

In the upper Rio Negro country the Indians frequently pass from one river to another by following traditional trails affording an easy portage. Thus, the Tiquié River is connected with the Papury and even with the Yapurá River (Koch-Grünberg, 1921, pp. 171–172).

Bridges.—Bridges are simple, typically consisting of a tree of suitable height chopped to fall across the water and provided with a handrail. The *Guaharibo* build more complex bridges (p. 863).

DRESS AND ORNAMENTS

Clothing.—Originally the natives mostly went naked (pl. 6), as early 17th-century observers noted for both sexes along the Oyapock River. A penis sheath or other cover, rather accentuating than removing the impression of nakedness, is widespread   (Nordenskiöld, 1924 b, p. 147 et seq., map 19). Among the *Cubeo* and their neighbors in the Caiarí-Vaupés region, women wear a tiny rectangular apron suspended from a cord of white beads (pl. 104). The men content themselves with a perineal band of red bast. On the lower Apáporis River a wide and long girdle of white bast is wrapped tight around the abdomen and fastened with a black strip of bast (pl. 104) ; and a girdle-cord supports a kilt of narrow bast strips descending to the feet. Usually part, and sometimes all, of the strips are pulled through between the legs and secured behind under the girdle, but those who wear the bast jock-strap customary on the Caiarí River allow the kilt to hang down unconfined (Koch-Grünberg, 1921, pp. 271, 380).

When traveling over rocky tracts, savanna dwellers quickly make for themselves sandals from the bases of *Mauritia* leaves, the string being from the fiber of the leaves of this palm. More durable, but harder are equivalents of deer and tapir hide.

The paucity of clothes markedly contrasts with the profusion of bodily decoration.

Probably owing to Andean influence, the tribes of the western periphery of the area wear more complete garments—the cushma of the Montaña (pl. 49, *bottom*) and the tipoy of Bolivia.

Featherwork.—Feather crowns were mainly of two types, according to whether the frame was fixed vertically or horizontally like the brim of a European hat, with the feathers inserted between its double edges and projecting in the same plane (Roth, 1924, p. 429 et seq., pl. 137). The foundation of the vertical type is a ring-shaped band with projecting rim above and often below also; this band is basketwork, typically twilled. The feathers, fixed in rows on cotton twine, were woven into a cotton band tied behind and supported in upright position by a cotton fillet sewed to them in front. The *Mojo,* anciently noted for feather mosaics that realistically represented animals and men, still make impressive feather crowns (Nordenskiöld, 1924 b, p. 205 f.; 1922, pls. 27, 28).

There are likewise feather frontlets, collars, and cloaks for men (see pl. 123); and at festivals the participants have small feathers or down glued on their body (Roth, 1924, p. 425).

The *Chiriguano* came to supplant feather ornaments with frontlets of Andean type displaying metal plaques.

Tattoo.—Complete tattooing is not widespread, but seems authenticated for the *Cariban Trio,* the *Yuracare, Shipaya,* and the *Mundurucú* (p. 275; also Spix and Martius, 1823–31, 3: 1312). The last had half ellipses on the face, with many parallel lines descending over the chin to the chest, which was ornamented with diamonds while the back also bore designs. But forearms of *Wapishana* and *Taulipáng* women have been tattooed in recent decades, and facial tattoo with conspicuous curvilinear patterns, often of fishhook shape, was common. The pigment, sometimes mixed with honey, was injected with a palm spine, the lancetlike fang of a certain fish, or a fishbone. Among the *Tupinamba* and many other tribes both sexes tattooed.

In the Roraima region tattoo is associated with puberty and has magical significance.

Nordenskiöld (1919 a, p. 120) has suggested that tattoo and genipa paint are negatively correlated.

Painting.—Body and face paint (pls. 85, 86, 88) are widespread, the most common pigments being red urucú derived from the seeds of *Bixa orellana* and bluish-black genipa from the fruit of the *Genipa americana;* both species are cultivated by the natives. These pigments occur beyond the Tropical Forest culture, being popular among the *Ge* and traded into the Chaco. Another widely diffused pigment is carayuru, obtained by fermenting the leaves of *Bignonia chica* or boiling the water in which they are soaked. Genipa designs remain indelible for 9 days and more, which has led travelers to confound them with tattooing. Pigments may be applied for prophylactic as well as esthetic purposes (Roth 1924, p. 88 et seq.).

In the Roraima country the designs vary greatly and, apart from facial decoration, are executed by the women. Elaborate geometrical patterns appear, but also realistic representations of birds and mammals, as well as highly conventional forms of dubious significance (Koch-Grünberg, 1923, 3: 40–45). The *Guarani* and *Yuracare* apply body paint with a stamp (fig. 66, *a, c, d*).

Miscellaneous ornaments.—An indefinite number of decorative devices occur, some being shared with other regions. Besides finger rings suspected of Negro or White origin and the feather decoration (p. 19), there are labrets for the lower lip (as many as a dozen among the *Mayoruna* (pl. 51), whence their name, *Barbudo*) ; nose sticks; earplugs; crowns and frontlets; necklaces and chest ornaments of teeth, claws, or seeds; armlets of palm leaf, bark, beaded string, or cotton; bracelets of bark, feathers, or seeds; belts of basketwork, cotton bands, fruit shells, or hair; and leg ornaments. The calves of *Carib* women's legs are thrown into relief by pairs of tight-fitting bands of woven cotton around the knees and ankles respectively, as noted on Columbus' voyages. (See pl. 38.)

Along the Rio Negro affluents, men generally wear quartz cylinders as neck pendants. These cylinders, about 4 to 6 inches (10 to 15 cm.) long and an inch (2.5 cm.) in diameter, are worn from a cord of palm fiber on which glossy, black seeds have been strung. (Roth, 1924, pp. 412–49; Koch-Grünberg, 1921, pp. 205 f.)

Ornaments of gold and silver were reported from the Amazon (p. 694) and from tribes in contact with the Andean civilizations. So was artificial deformation of the head (p. 694).

TRANSPORTATION

Carrying devices.—For carrying minor utensils there are various pouches, such as a small bark sack for coca and paint and a flat mat satchel. On the Apáporis River the men carry their fire apparatus, scarifying implement, and sundries in a rectangular bag knitted of palm-fiber string (Koch-Grünberg, 1921, p. 384). Throughout most of the area both sexes transport heavy loads in a basketry knapsack resting against the back and supported by a plaited tumpline passing above rather than across the forehead (pl. 121, *top, right*) ; the bearer relieves the pressure by thrusting his arms through lateral loops, which may be temporarily used to the exclusion of the head band in order to rest the neck and head. The carrying net, so popular in the Chaco, is generally lacking but appears among the *Guarani* in the extreme south, where, however, skin bags seem to have preceded it.

Infants are carried in a cotton baby sling made after the same pattern as hammocks. The sling passes over the mother's right shoulder (pl. 26, *left*) and is pushed rearward by a woman when working in her plantation so that the child is then supported on her back.

Boats.—Transportation by water is diagnostic of the culture at its core, especially in contrast to the *Ge* of eastern Brazil (Handbook, vol. 2), but many tribes living either between navigable rivers or on small streams at the headwaters of the main rivers lacked any craft. Thus, the *Shirianá, Waica, Guaharibo,* and Curicuriarí River *Macú,* many tribes of the upper

Napo and Putumayo Rivers and elsewhere along the eastern slopes of the Andes, the *Maué,* and the *Nambicuara* had no canoes. They crossed watercourses on logs or by swimming; some of the tribes constructed rafts. Many tribes which aboriginally lacked canoes, having kept away from rivers to avoid the strong, hostile tribes living along them, adopted canoes when White penetration brought peace to their country, and when steel axes became available to facilitate canoe construction.

In general, Indians not only utilized natural waterways, but also skillfully dragged their craft over rapids. Further, where the several tributaries of a river or the affluents of distinct systems approach one another, the natives have established traditional land routes or portages to eke out the connection by water. Finally, the Casiquiare River (pl. 5, *top, right* and *bottom*) links the upper Rio Negro, hence the Amazon, with the Orinoco River. Given the Indians' skill in coping with swift water and other obstructions, one easily understands the wide diffusion of many traits characteristic of the area not merely over the mainland, but even to the Antilles. Amazing similarities between these islands and interior districts (Santarém) have been emphasized by Nimuendajú, Nordenskiöld, and Palmatary (1939).

The crafts used include simple rafts, often made of very light balsa wood (pl. 71; fig. 95, *a*), dugouts (fig. 67), and bark canoes (figs. 56; 95, *b;* 123).

After felling and rough-hewing a tree for a dugout, the Indians originally applied fire at the top, gradually burning out the wood to an even thickness, then filling the hollow with water, and at the same time keeping up a gentle fire outside. In order further to widen the boat, they might insert crossbeams (pl. 94. *top*). A typical specimen measured 33 ft. (10 m.) in length, 21 in. (53 cm.) in width, and 14 in. (35 cm.) in depth. On the Guiana coast, dugouts had a plank added along the side to form a gunwale. On long journeys a tent is added to protect the goods. Such substances as the bruised sapwood of the Brazil-nut tree (*Bertholletia excelsa*) serve for calking. Square sails of cotton, palm-leaf matting, or laths split from the leaf stalk of *Mauritia* were customary.

Bark canoes (pls. 6, *right;* 27; 32) occur among some tribes of the Amazon Basin and the Guianas, where they are generally restricted to shallow water on the upper reaches of the streams. On the Berbice River the Indians generally make a single piece of the purpleheart (*Peltogyne purpurea*) bark into a canoe, and other trees are used elsewhere for the same purpose. A "wood-skin" of this type, which may be as long as 25 to 30 ft. (7.5 to 9.1 m.), holds 3 men with their baggage. Easily capsized, this craft has compensatory advantages—floating where an ordinary dugout could not pass, and being easily carried on the head over a portage.

In very shallow water the Indians pole their boats; otherwise they propel them with paddles having leaf-shaped or circular blades and usually a crescentic handle.

MANUFACTURES

Bark cloth.—One center for bark cloth lies in northwestern Bolivia (Nordenskiöld, 1924 b, p. 208 et seq., maps 28 and 30); another among the *Tucanoans, Záparoans, Jívaro,* and *Arawak* of the upper Amazon. The industry characterizes none of the three major stocks of our area, but rather such marginal groups as the *Witoto* (pl. 83), *Tucano, Campa, Yuracare,* and *Chacobo.* The inner layer of the *Ficus* bark usually provides the material, which is beaten out with a grooved mallet. (See pl. 94, *bottom; p. 779.*) Among the *Yuracare* this craft is vital, producing men's and women's shirts, which are stamped with painted designs; baby slings; pouches; and mosquito nets. Bast shirts are also typical of masculine dress among the *Chacobo* (Nordenskiöld, 1922, pp. 60, 94, 95). The *Tucano* use bark cloth for mummers' masks and costumes and for images (pl. 64).

Basketry.—The *Shirianá, Waica, Curajá,* and *Guaharibo* make only twined baskets, perhaps a survival of the earliest technique. (For twining technique, see pl. 95, *bottom, right.*) Twilling (pl. 95, *bottom, left*) and latticework (fig. 2) are very widespread. For Guiana are recorded such

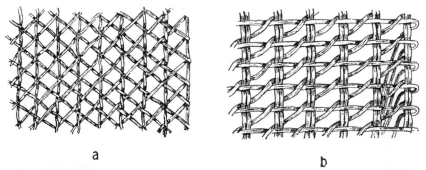

a   b

FIGURE 2.—Tropical Forest basketwork of lattice type. *a,* Common hexagonal weave of Amazon Basin; *b,* special lattice weave of Mato Grosso. (After Nordenskiöld, 1924 b, map 27.)

additional techniques as checker, wrapping, and imbrication. (Koch-Grünberg, 1921, pp. 340–342; 1923, 3: 80–85; Roth, 1924, pp. 137–143, 281–380; Gillin, 1936, p. 51 et seq.) Vines, palms, and other tropical species furnish ideal materials for this industry. The nibi vine (*Carludovica trigona*) is split in half, then the convex outer surface is split off from each piece, yielding a flat, ribbonlike, flexible, and tough strip, which is scraped with a knife.

Basketry articles (pl. 22) include mats, satchels, trays, creels, oblong basketry boxes with lids, two-piece telescoping containers, carrying baskets (pl. 6, *left, bottom*) manioc presses, and fans. Some utensils are in openwork, others closely woven, but in either case they can be waterproofed with broad leaves or pitch, the latter attested for Amazonian tribes by Acuña (1641).

It is noteworthy that basketry is a masculine industry.

The remarkable esthetic effects attained in basketry are treated under Art (p. 39).

Weaving and cordage.—Since major garments are as a rule lacking, loom work includes mainly hammocks, baby slings, anklets, fillets, waist bands, and the like. (See Roth, 1924, pp. 92–118, 381–411.) Complete clothing—the tipoy, cushma, and, in some tribes, the poncho—is woven only near the Andes. In the eastern part of our area, cotton predominates, though not to the exclusion of other materials. It is grown somewhat less on the upper Amazon and its tributaries; in the Rio Negro region, it is either lacking or little cultivated, and a term for the species is absent from the *Arawakan* dialects there (Nimuendajú, personal communication). Even among tribes which cultivate cotton, there is sometimes a preference for wild fibers, which often better withstand heat and moisture. Favorite materials for thread are the fibers of burity palm (*Mauritia flexuosa*), from which a very fine cloth called cachibanco is made; jauary palm (*Astrocaryum jauary*); curauá (Bromeliaceae); embira (*Couratari* sp.); tucum (the fiber of several palms called tucumã); *Cecropia;* and other wild species. On the upper Tiquié River, men make balls of tough cordage and trade them to alien tribes against curare.

True loom weaving has a high, though incomplete, correlation with cotton. Probably the distinctive type, called "cincture," or vertical loom (M. Schmidt, 1914, 4: 214), is one consisting of two uprights perforated top and bottom to permit the insertion of cross beams around which the parallel warp threads are looped, the anterior and posterior ones being separated by a movable rod, while a thinner stick divides the even and odd threads (during the process of manufacture). When the fabric is complete, it forms a ring. (Fig. 3; pl. 115, *top;* also Nordenskiöld, 1919 a, p. 204 et seq.; 1920, p. 174 et seq.). This loom is found in the Guianas, west to the Rio Negro, and south to the *Yuracare* of Bolivia. As it is common to several linguistic families, including the *Cariban,* Max Schmidt's characterization of it as *"Arawak"* seems premature. Bordering the Andes, many tribes use a horizontal loom, the "belt loom" being most common. One end of the loom is attached to a tree or house post, the other to the weaver's belt.

Lacking a loom, tribes such as the *Tucanoans, Witotoans,* and most of the *Tupi* including the *Tupinamba,* finger weave, producing a twined fabric. Netting is restricted to the southern tribes. On the upper Xingú, netted hammocks and carrying bags as well as fish nets occur along with a twined and a true weave.

FIGURE 3.—Loom for manufacture of thick hammocks. Upper Río Negro country, Colombia. (After Koch-Grünberg, 1906 a.)

Pottery.—Pottery is general, but by no means universally manufactured, earthenware being widely exported from centers of production. The Eastern *Nambicuara* completely lack the industry, and their congeners make very coarse ware. To some extent the industry naturally depends on the availability of good clay. The view that the *Arawakans,* unless checked by lack of such material, are uniformly the donors remains an improbable hypothesis (Linné, 1925, pp. 162–169). In eastern Perú, for example, *Arawakan* ware is definitely inferior to *Panoan* or *Tupian* (pp. 577–578), and there is at present no basis for assigning the advanced Marajó and Santarém ceramics to the *Arawakans.* It is only in a few centers, such as the upper Rio Xingú country, that the *Arawak* have a monopoly of pottery making; and if the *Arawak* introduced elaborate wares to eastern Bolivia, there is no proof that they did so elsewhere.

As a rule, women make earthenware, but among the *Yecuaná* and *Guinau,* the industry is wholly masculine (Koch-Grünberg, 1923 a, 3: 347).

For tempering, the use of sand, shell, and pounded sherds is rare within the area. Very distinctive, on the other hand, is the addition of the ashes from siliceous bark (Amazon Basin, Orinoco, and Guiana), reasonably assumed to have supplanted the earlier, less effective use of sand. The proportion of bark and clay varies, presumably with the consistency of the clay, which on the banks of the Amazon would be unserviceable without a siliceous admixture. The Amazon and its affluents form the center for the addition of burnt and crushed sponges found on the roots of riparian trees, the spicules greatly strengthening the material, as proved by Santarém ware (Linné, 1925, pp. 29–59).

Coiling (pl. 62, *bottom, left*), the most widespread technique, is illustrated by the Rio Negro tribes. A vessel is coiled, smoothed with a bit of gourd, and finally polished with a pebble, which is often highly prized (Koch-Grünberg, 1921, p. 344). The potter next dries her vessel for several days indoors and then for an equal period in the sun. For firing, she inverts the pot in a shallow pit, where it rests on a few stones, surrounds it with light wood topped with dry bark, and exposes it to a strongly concentrated fire.

Slip seems restricted to the Marajó-Santarém region and the Montaña. Varnish, made of rosin, e. g., from *Vismia guianensis,* or a copal, e. g., from the courbaril tree (*Hymenaea courbaril*), is applied in the Amazon Basin, and especially by the modern *Carib* in Guiana. Thus, the Barama *Carib* use a certain juice, mildly re-heating the vessel so that the gum melts and seeps into the pores. This also creates a glazed appearance, which vanishes with use. The Içana *Arawak* sprinkle powdered rosin or the milk of a tree over the painted designs, which thus assume a glossy varnish on firing. (Pp. 155–159; also Linné, 1925, pp. 141–154; Koch-Grünberg, 1921 p. 345; Roth, 1924, p. 133.)

Painted pottery is best developed on the Guiana littoral, on Marajó Island, on the Tapajóz River, in the upper Rio Negro region, and in the Montaña and Yungas (pls. 15–18, 52; figs. 16, 17, 36, 60, 73–75, 111, 112). The *Chiriguano* de luxe ware is outstanding for its painted decoration of Andean type, whereas utensils merely bear fingerprint decoration. Negative painting on vessels from Rebordello, on the lower Amazon, is noteworthy (Linné, 1925, p. 136). Painted vessels naturally are reserved for special use—storage, chicha containers, vessels for serving guests, and the like. Utility ware is generally plain and is decorated, if at all, with incisions and fingernail impressions. Modeled ware is found mainly on the lower Amazon, e. g., Marajó (pp. 155–159), where its high development surpasses what might be expected of the historic tribes. It also occurs on the Paraná River (pl. 9).

The craftsmanship in our area is indicated by the variety of forms, especially of nonutilitarian types. Cooking pots and water containers are widespread. Roasting pans, with elevated margin, and plates are well-developed in the northwest Amazon region. Vessels of unusual size are seen in chicha jars; these range from 3 to 4 feet (1 to 1.3 m.) in diameter and height in the Montaña, to 3 feet (1 m.) high and 7 to 10 feet (2 to 3 m.) in diameter on the Rio Negro, where manioc-pulp bowls even attain a diameter of 10 to 14 feet (3 to 4 m.). The modern *Palicur*, though no longer capable of the fine urns of their ancestors, still make roasting pans for manioc flour, large drinking vessels, either conical-bottomed or with annular stand, double drinking vessels with a connecting bar, and a variety of clay toys representing turtles and other species (Nimuendajú, 1926, pp. 41–47). The coast of Guiana and northern Brazil generally abounds in oddly shaped effigy vessels and in grotesque appendages of vessels (Roth, 1924, pp. 134–136).

Amazing similarities in detail prove connections between Antillean and Santarém pottery (Nimuendajú reported in Nordenskiöld, 1930 a).

Gourds.—Calabashes (*Crescentia*) and gourds (*Lagenaria*) are of general importance as dippers, drinking cups, and storage vessels. In the Guaporé River and upper Xingú region, where pottery is crude, calabashes abound and are decorated either with incised or pyrographic designs. The Barama *Carib* have hemispherical cups and containers closed except for perforations of the neck or shoulder. The fruit is picked when completely ripe, the shell cut according to the intended purpose, and the pap removed, sometimes after loosening it by boiling the whole gourd. The calabash is then dried indoors or in the sun until tough and hard. The gourd may be coated with the juice applied to pottery but lacks decoration. As a precaution against the entrance of insects, one gourd is inverted over the mouth of another or the opening is plugged with clean grass (Gillin, 1936, p. 49). Other Guiana Indians, as well as Amazon and Rio Negro tribes, sometimes embellish gourds in painting or incised lines. The halved calabash of the Rio Negro tribes is polished brown on the outside, varnished black within, and sometimes bears incised decoration on the rim or the entire outer surface (Koch-Grünberg, 1921, p. 347; Roth, 1924, pp. 301–03). Pokerwork, though ascribed to the *Kepikiriwat, Tariana, Macushi*, and *Wapishana*, seems rare (Nordenskiöld, 1919 a, p. 225 f.). *Chiriguano* gourds are artistically embellished with painted, incised, or pyrographic designs.

Miscellaneous.—Fire making is generally by drilling (pl. 117, *top;* fig. 54). Various materials serve as shaft and hearth; and the Pomeroon *Arawak* have a compound shaft, the point from the fruit pedicel of a palm being too short so that it has to be tied to a longer stick. Moss, the debris from ant collections, cotton, etc., serve as tinder. To save effort the Indians keep fires burning, even carrying smoldering timber on an earthen hearth during boat trips. The *Witoto* facts are dubious, one authority denying to them any fire apparatus, another crediting them with a percussion technique, still another with drilling. Fires are activated with woven (pl. 47, *top*) or feather fans (fig. 78, *a*).

For illumination the Guiana tribes have candles of rubber or cotton thread drawn through melted beeswax, or substitute gum and comparable materials (Roth, 1924, pp. 69–72).

Rubber is probably derived from *Sapium* and *Hevea* species. Apart from use in ball games, it serves for the manufacture of rings and enema syringes. The *Cayenne* Indians boil the latex, then cover clay molds with several coatings of the boiled rubber, incise designs on it, dry it carefully over a fire, blacken it in the smoke, and finally break the molds (Roth, 1924, pp. 83–85; Nordenskiöld, 1930 c, pp. 184–195).

The Guiana Indians procure a glue from the gum of *Moronobea coccinea*, cutting into the trunk to make a yellowish gum exude, which is mixed with beeswax and powdered charcoal. It is either allowed to run as a semiliquid into a hollow bamboo or to harden at the bottom of a pot. This material serves to fasten arrow points, wax threads, and fishing lines, calking, etc. The whitish resin of *Mimusops globosa* also helps attach different parts of an arrow and the stones of cassava graters. Feathers are glued to the body with various gums and balsams, which are also remedies for sores and other ills.

In much of the area the lack or rarity of stone leads to the use of substitutes. Arrowheads are of wood, bone, and sting-ray spurs, the occasionally reported stone points being highly suspect. In Guiana, knives are sometimes of quartz and perhaps other stones, but there and elsewhere, they are typically of bamboo, fish teeth, etc. Scrapers are of snail shell, the lower jaw of an agouti, slivers of rock removed in celt-manufacture, etc. The preparation of the highly prized quartz cylinders worn by men in the western part of our area is very exacting. The material is obtained from the depths of the forest along the Tiquié River; percussion with another quartz roughly shapes the rock, which is then ground on sandstone and polished with fine sand or pumice imported from the Amazon via the Yapurá River. Months are required for this labor and for the ensuing perforation. The Indian, holding the cylinder with his feet, twirls a pointed palmwood drill on the quartz, adding fine white sand, but no water. At the commencement of the perforating process, the smooth, round quartz is tipped with a lump of pitch until the pit is deep enough to prevent slipping out. Several shafts are worn out during the process, having to be constantly resharpened (Koch-Grünberg, 1921, pp. 205 f.).

The most important stone tools, however, are the celt and the grooved ax (pls. 70, *top;* 118, *e;* fig. 45). They are made either by grinding down fragments broken from rocks or by grinding down water-worn pebbles of suitable contour. In the Apáporis River country, the Indians obtain diabase blades ground by nature so as to be almost ready for use and requiring only the slightest supplementary grinding (Koch-Grünberg, 1921, p. 374). Roth distinguishes elongate, curved celts with a cutting edge at each extremity; small straight-edged blades with butt trimmed for hafting; larger specimens with truncate butts and rounded cutting edges; and narrow flattened celts with markedly pointed butts. The grooved axes have a notch above and below, ranging widely as to width; the butt may be either very convex or rather squat and square.

The hafting technique is far from clear. In the rare cases amenable to direct observation the celt is fitted into an opening cut to correspond to its base and secured with resin. Roth (1924, pp. 72–79) surmises that the blades are often held in the hand; that the grooves of the axes may be intended merely for the twine employed; and that the blunter ax may conceivably be fastened by a withy bent double and fixed with gum and twine.

SOCIAL AND POLITICAL ORGANIZATION

Mode of settlement, matrimonial arrangements, and government are all closely interrelated and separable only for purposes of exposition.

Settlement.—In many of the tribes the settlement consists of one or a few communal houses (maloca). Such arrangements imply some measure of communism, e. g., the joint use of a fireplace for beer manufacture or of a large trough for grinding maize. The population bears no constant ratio to the number of houses: a two-hut hamlet on the Aiarí River harbored some 40 persons, whereas other single maloca settlements on this river had a numerical strength ranging from 10 to 100. If necessary, each could accommodate twice or even four times as many (Koch-Grünberg, 1921, pp. 42, 45). A *Mangeroma* (Juruá-Purús) house was found to have 258 residents; some *Tenetehara* and *Tupinamba* dwellings had nearly 1,000 persons.

In several districts (e. g., *Tapirapé, Carajá, Mundurucú, Chacobo*) a men's club house is set off from the family dwellings.

Matrimonial residence.—In the western part of the area, patrilocal residence predominates along with local exogamy. Koch-Grünberg (1921, pp. 114 f., 211, 309) would have us believe that *Tucanoans* and neighboring *Arawakan* invariably take wives from other tribes, a *Siusí* girl marrying a *Huhuteni* or *Kaus* suitor, a *Bara* girl a *Tuyuca* man. It seems more probable that custom merely prescribes taking a bride from another settlement, irrespective of its linguistic affinity. Goldman (p. 780) found the *Tucanoan Cubeo* to acquire wives outside the village, members of which formed an exogamous, patrilineal sib. Certainly Preuss's *Witoto* "stämme" (1921, 1:11, 153 et seq.) suggest localized clans (Steward's "patrilineal bands," Gifford's "lineages") rather than "tribes" in ordinary parlance.

In the Guianas, matrilocal residence prevails, coupled with bride-service. However, there are notable exceptions and qualifications. The *Palicur* have no fixed rule and regard an independent household as ideal (Nimuendajú, 1926, p. 82). The *Aparai,* in contrast to fellow *Caribans,* are definitely patrilocal (Kirchhoff, 1931, p. 119). Frequently, the matrilocal rule is reversed for the chief and his eldest son (ibid., pp. 125, 190), as also holds for the *Bacaïri* (M. Schmidt, 1905, p. 437). Avuncular marriage for girls (see below) would leave both spouses in their natal village.

Matrilocalism may be temporary (*Macurap* of the Branco River), or permanent. It cannot be considered a specifically *Arawakan* trait. Though the *Locono* exhibit it, it is lacking among the *Wapishana.* Of non-*Arawakans,* the isolated *Warrau,* the *Cariban Tamanak, Macushi, Taulipáng, Rucuyen, Galibi, Kallinago,* and the *Tupian Sirionó, Guayaki,* and *Chiriguano* are temporarily or permanently matrilocal.

Marriage rules.—Premarital license may be consistent with strict feminine chastity in wedlock (Roth, 1924, p. 560; Nimuendajú, 1926, p. 81).

Monogamy is reported for the *Palicur* as early as 1729. Elsewhere polygyny is often either a chief's prerogative (Caiarí River) or is actually practiced mostly by chiefs and shamans, notwithstanding permissive polygyny for others (Roth, 1924, p. 685 et seq.). Polygyny is most commonly sororal (*Trumai*). Simultaneous marriage with a woman and her daughter by another husband crops up sporadically, being orthodox among Kuliseu River tribes, the *Rucuyen,* and sundry *Caribans.*

Bride-service was frequent. Its obligations might be temporary, as among the *Tenetehara* (p. 143) or continue indefinitely, as among the *Tupinamba,* who, however, mitigated the husband's lot if he gave his daughter in marriage to her mother's brother (p. 112). In northwestern Brazil the groom offers presents to his parents-in-law, but the bride brings a dowry.

Preferential kin and affinial unions are varied and widespread. The *Cubeo* prefer cross-cousin marriage together with brother-sister exchange, so that the symmetrical form of the custom is indicated. Cross-cousin marriage is also orthodox among the *Nambicuara,* whose nomenclature reflects the practice; the *Cashinawa;* the *Wapishana;* and various *Caribans* of whom the *Aparai* favor the patrilateral, others the symmetrical type.

The occurrence of avuncular marriage, sororal polygyny, and stepdaughter marriage have been noted.

Position of women.—The discordant evidence presumably reflects local differences: some sources describe women as their husbands' slaves, others as their companions, and among the *Palicur* they set the tone. (Koch-Grünberg, 1921, pp. 353 f.; Roth, 1924, pp. 683 f.; Nimuendajú, 1926, pp. 78 ff.) Since the *Palicur* are patrilineal, the status of women is obviously not a simple function of the rule of descent. Nor is it clearly correlated with particular linguistic families.

Kinship usages.—Mother-in-law avoidance occurs among the *Arawak, Carib,* and *Warrau* of Guiana: a man must not remain in his mother-in-law's dwelling, nor talk with her, nor even look at her (Roth, 1924, p. 685; 1915, p. 344; Kirchhoff, 1931, p. 150). In the same region a man and his wife's father may converse on ordinary topics, but the wife serves as go-between in the conveyance of instructions (Roth, 1915, p. 200). Among the *Tupinamba* a newly wed man and his father-in-law display mutual bashfulness (Kirchhoff, 1931, p. 183).

Among the *Shipaya* a lifelong bond of solidarity is sometimes created between two individuals on the occasion of a ceremony.

Unilateral and bilateral units.—Instead of unilateral types of unit many tribes have territorial groups embracing both blood-kinsfolk and outsiders—especially in-laws—who have come to join them. This type of unit is Kirchhoff's "extended family" (Grossfamilie).

However, unilateral systems are not rare, but not one of the three major stocks presents a uniform social organization. It is true that the *Caribans* present no authenticated case of exogamy with matrilineal descent, which in some tribes is indeed precluded by avuncular marriage (*Tamanac* and *Macushi*); most of them seem to have loose extended families, but patrilineal reckoning may occur in some cases. Of the *Arawakans,* the *Locono* and the *Goajiro* (Handbook, vol. 4) have each a large number of matrilineal clans, which probably holds for the Antillean congeners. On the other hand, the western *Arawakans* lack the trait, and even in the east the *Palicur* have seven patrilineal clans (Nimuendajú, 1926, pp. 22 et seq., 86, 132) ranged in moieties. Of the *Tupians,* on the Rio Branco, the *Arua* have matrilineal, the *Makurap* patrilineal descent, the latter also holding for the *Witoto* and the *Mundurucú,* which latter have exogamic moieties divided into clans. The *Tupinamba* may conceivably have had a patrilineal organization, but certainly not matrilineal clans in view of the orthodoxy of avuncular marriage.

Turning to other stocks, the *Jabuti* (Rio Branco), the *Tucanoans* (*Cubeo*), and the *Tucuna* are patrilineal.

Besides the *Palicur* and *Mundurucú,* the *Kepikiriwat* (Gi-Paraná River) also have moieties, but apparently only for ceremonial ball games. Only the *Mundurucú* moieties are definitely known to be exogamous (p. 277); on the other hand, the feature belongs to the three *Cubeo* phratries. The nameless *Cubeo* phratries own land and unite periodically for a men's initiation ceremony and for the recital of origin myths (pp. 780–781). The *Palicur* moieties have separate cemeteries and are named "lower" and "upper," respectively.

At least partly totemic clan names appear in the *Cubeo, Palicur,* and *Tucuna* schemes. *Cubeo* and *Tucuna* clans own each a set of personal names.

How far we can speak of totemism apart from the above mentioned cases of totemic names, is not certain. One *Palicur* clan traces its descent from a sloth, others from a bird, wild Bromelias, and the earth, respectively; but some of the designations are untranslatable. ʹAmong the *Cubeo,* again, it was not the totemic clan eponyms that were once taboo, but the eponyms associated with the sets of personal names owned by clans.

Political organization.—Commonly each settlement is autonomous, so that the headman merely controls fellow-residents, but some tribes are said to have paramount chiefs (*Yuruna*). In the matrilocal but clanless tribes, a headman might exert much influence by controlling as dependents his daughters' husbands. Indeed, in the *Guayaki* hordes, the father of several daughters who have attracted suitors into fixed matrilocal residence becomes ipso facto the headman. As a rule, however, greater authority belongs to chiefs in unilaterally organized societies. A *Palicur* chief, e. g., welcomes strangers, organizes communal enterprises, and smooths over internal difficulties. But though a chief represents his people, arranges festivities, and leads economic undertakings, he owes hospitality to his tribesmen and probably is never despotic by virtue of his office.

Succession follows distinct patterns. In the Rio Negro region (*Siusi*) a headman is followed first by his several brothers and only after their death by a son. The *Palicur* disregard heredity, the incumbent selecting as deputy and successor the ablest and most popular tribesman. Elsewhere (*Yuruna*) the oldest son normally succeeds his father; failing male offspring, a *Witoto* chief may choose as his successor a son-in-law, thus contravening the normal patrilocal rule.

Where sources speak of accession by ordeals (Roth, 1924, pp. 568–573), a purely titular distinction seems invloved: the successful candidate does not supersede the chief in office, but gains in status. The tests in part coincide with those imposed at puberty.

In some tribes (e. g., *Quijo, Nambicuara*) a chief is usually a shaman.

As for differences in rank, the status of sons-in-law was often inferior in matrilocal societies, but hardly enough so to warrant speaking of an inferior caste, though in some tribes the same term designates a serf and a son-in-law (e. g., Guiana *Carib,* p. 849). Rather different is the case of whole tribes dominated by others. Thus, the originally nomadic *Macú* are well enough treated by economically superior neighbors, but somewhat as might be pet animals. The *Tucano* send *Macú* slaves to get game, fish, or wild fruits and assign menial tasks to them. A master will dole out kashiri or an occasional cigar to his drudge, but bars him from dances; and no *Macú* would intrude into a conversation unasked. Different again is the *Chiriguano* polity. This offshoot of the *Guarani* conquered the economically advanced *Chané,* thus creating an upper class that in various districts lords it over from 5 to over 10 times their number of serfs (p. 467). A stratification is suggested for the ancient *Manasí* of Bolivia: hereditary chiefs, priests, shamans, "captains," and commoners (p. 389).

Property and inheritance.—Individual property rights are recognized, even children being credited with them (M. Schmidt, 1905, p. 438; Roth, 1924, pp. 632, 701). But this does not bar communal ownership of certain goods, such as weirs and general sharing in the yield (e. g., p. 000; Koch-Grünberg, 1921, p. 257). In Guiana land is cleared by communal labor (Kirchhoff, 1931, pp. 141, 157). Since settlements shift with exhaustion of the soil, inheritance of land is immaterial, but fishing rights are sib-owned among the *Cubeo* (p. 781) and on the upper Xingú (p. 324). As for other property, most tribes burn or bury a deceased person's chattels. A *Trumaí* nephew inherits certain songs from his mother's brother. Among the *Siusí* the son is the sole heir; failing issue, the dead man's brother or other kinsman takes his place.

Trade.—Local specialization and the mobility of expert boatmen favored wholesale trading notwithstanding the lack of fixed mediums of exchange. *Acawai* peddlers make long journeys in Venezuela, Brazil, and Guiana. Even such necessities as cassava graters and blowguns are often manufactured in particular distributing centers. Credit is an established concept, payment being often deferred for months.

That *Arawakans* have created all useful goods is unproved. The isolated *Otomac* are famous for their pottery; the *Cariban Arecuna* spread cotton and blowguns; the *Warrau*, their boats; the *Pebans, Macushi,* and *Tucuna*, blowgun poison. Intertribal trade was greatly developed on the upper Xingú River, with formalized procedure (pp. 338–339). The extent of commerce is indicated by the presence of Andean objects of gold, silver, and copper as far east as the upper Paraguay River.

WARFARE

Weapons.—Bows and arrows have already been described under Hunting (p. 12). Some of the fighting arrows are poisoned. Roth rightly wonders at the infrequent use of curare in warfare (blowguns with their curare-poisoned darts were never used), but the *Yahuna* are said to smear it on palm spines attached to their wrists and elbows in preparation for a hand-to-hand encounter (Koch-Grünberg, 1921, p. 362). Spears are common in western rather than in eastern Guiana; they are long, pointed, and firehardened staves of wood, but there is some evidence of prehistoric stone spearheads. In Yapurá and Apáporis River country there are poisoned lances, which are wanting in the Caiarí region; they serve both in war and the chase. These weapons are always united in sheaves of seven; each poisoned tip, inserted in an incision of the shaft and wrapped with bast, is stuck into a separate compartment of a common case for the septet. The arrangement resembles that for poisoned arrows on the Aiarí River (Koch-Grünberg, 1921, pp. 64, 88, 371 f., 396).

Clubs with wrist-loops are common, especially the flat, paddle- or swordlike type (macana, fig. 78, *e–h*). These are large, at times requiring the use of both hands to wield them. A block type, distributed at least from Cayenne to the Orinoco, is made of the hardest, heaviest woods worked into sharp-cornered square ends; sometimes a celt is cemented into a lateral groove (fig. 27). A curious dagger-club tapers to a sharp point at one end, to a blunt one at the other, with the grip in between; it is driven through the ear into a fallen enemy's brain. Other clubs resemble a spatula. The clubs are often elaborately ornamented with basketwork wrapping and engraved designs.

Shields vary greatly in make and shape, but most commonly are circular, of tapir hide. Wickerwork equivalents, occasionally covered with tapir hide, also occur in the Montaña, the Uaupés-Caquetá (pl. 103, *center*), and the Mojos-Chiquitos area, and they persist as dance regalia on the Rio Negro. For the *Cayenne* Indians, an early recorder describes and figures an oblong shield of very light wood, painted with various designs.

Psychology of Warfare.—Some tribes, such as the *Yagua* (p. 735) are reckoned as peaceable, others—notably the *Carib* and *Tupi*—as militaristic. The historic conflict of *Cariban* and *Arawakan* groups in the Antilles is also exemplified by the hereditary enmity of *Galibi* and *Palicur;* and the *Arawakans* of Içana region are traditional enemies of the *Cubeo,* but it would be a grave error to suppose that alignment universally followed linguistic lines. To the contrary, warfare was more common within families, e. g., between *Jívaro* villages, between the *Panoan Conibo* and *Cashibo,* or between *Nahukwa* groups.

Revenge seems to have been the foremost motive for warfare, but the *Parintintin* fought mainly for sport and the *Tupinamba* to gain prestige and to acquire victims to be eaten. The craving for glory also figured largely, as indicated by the use of trophies, e. g., among the *Jívaro* (p. 624) and, on the Orinoco River, by the recital of coups. The *Paressi* are unique in their wars of conquest. Another motive was the capture of individual enemies, a factor greatly intensified by European instigation.

Organization and tactics.—The decision to make war usually takes place at a council in combination with a drinking-bout. The Suriname *Carib* then paint themselves, dance special dances to arouse the jaguar spirit, and undergo magical rites to ensure success. Some tribes summon their fellows by signal drums or by blowing conchs. Several groups are credited with having specially appointed commanders-in-chief and with carrying provisions along. Among the *Mundurucú,* women accompany and assist their warrior husbands.

Open warfare is far less common than nocturnal and matutinal surprise attacks. In attacking a palisaded village, the aggressors often shoot arrows tipped with lighted cotton to set fire to the thatched roofs. Widespread protective measures include the barring of avenues of approach with sharp hardwood stakes and coltrops, both often poisoned, and the stakes frequently set in the bottom of a concealed trench. The use of automatically-released blowguns hidden by the trail (Juruá-Purús) and of irritating fumes from burning peppers is more restricted.

Treatment of prisoners.—Slavery has already been mentioned. Captive women were usually taken in marriage and children reared as ordinary tribal members, but the cannibalistic *Tupinamba,* though taking captives, always killed and ate them sooner or later.

Trophies.—Nearly all warring tribes take human trophies of some kind, most frequently heads, though the *Parintintin* do not disdain arms and legs. The most famous trophies are the *Jívaro* shrunken heads (pl. 63 and p. 625). In some cases, scalps alone are sought, e. g., in Suriname, where the women wear them as ornaments, the *Yecuaná* using the hair for belts. The *Yuruna* and various Montaña tribes prefer the skull. A common practice is to make flutes of the victim's long bones and necklaces of his teeth.

The *Mundurucú* cut an enemy's head off with a cane knife, remove the brains, eyes, tongue, and muscles, then dry the skull, wash it with water, saturate it with urucú oil, and expose it to the sun. When hard, it receives an artificial brain of dyed cotton, eyes of pitch, teeth, and a feather hood for decoration (fig. 28; pl. 23, *left*). Henceforth, the victor regularly carries it with him by a rope. (Spix and Martius, 1823–31, 3:1314).

Cannibalism.—Although our word "cannibal" is derived from a designation of the *Carib,* many *Arawakan* and *Tucanoan* tribes also practiced anthropophagy. Several tribes in Guiana closely resembled the *Tupinamba* in their relevant procedure; they hospitably entertained a prisoner for some time, beginning to taunt him as the fatal hour of his execution approached, then tortured him, and finally crushed his skull with a sword-club. This was followed by the cooking and eating of his flesh, some of the bones being made into flutes. (See figs. 12–14.) *Shipaya* cannibalism is linked with the cult of Kumãpári.

(For the whole section, see Roth, 1924, pp. 144–173, 578–601.) Endo-cannibalism is described under Death (p. 38).

LIFE CYCLE

Birth.—Isolation of the woman during childbirth is customary. Among the *Siusi,* e. g., the woman in labor remains in her hammock within the house, assisted by the female inmates, while the men all depart. The navel string and afterbirth are buried on the spot (Koch-Grünberg, 1921,

p. 116). For 5 days the mother remains secluded in her division of the dwelling, where her husband keeps her company; during this period neither parent may work, wash himself, or eat anything but flat manioc cakes and peppers lest the infant take harm. The seclusion is ended by the father's recital of the names of fish and game animals henceforth permitted to the parents, followed by a joint bath by them and the infant. On that day the father's father bestows a name on the child, usually drawing upon the animal kingdom. The *Cubeo* (p. 787) conform to the *Siusí* rule in this respect, but widely depart from it in other details. Here the expectant mother—not her husband—abstains from the flesh of all quadrupeds for a month before the birth. The delivery may occur in the house or in a special hut or in the woods, but with the assistance of all women. The husband's mother cuts the navel cord with razor grass and immediately buries it with the afterbirth. Of twins of different sex the female, and otherwise the junior infant, is invariably killed. Several hours after a birth the shaman arrives for a conjuring ceremony. Confinement in the young couple's part of the house lasts for 5 days, then all the furniture is moved out of the house prior to the newborn child's first bath, and on the following day a kinsman of the father brings cooked fish, thereby terminating the fast. Eight days after the delivery a great drinking spree is held, to which the parents invite all their kin, and it is then that a name is conferred (Koch-Grünberg, 1921, pp. 310 f.).

In these instances the couvade, which has a very wide distribution, is at best adumbrated. In Guiana the couvade appears in classical form, i. e., natal and prenatal prescriptions and restrictions on the father equal or surpass the mother's, the rationale usually being the infant's welfare. A *Palicur* father is supposed to be everywhere accompanied by the child's spirit, for whom he must carry a miniature bow and arrow lest he himself fail in the hunt; and if he is obliged to enter the woods at night he must carry a sling over his left shoulder for the infant's spirit. Were the man to make incisions in certain trees, the tree-spirit would cause the child's abdomen to grow large like the tree's (Nimuendajú, 1926, p. 83). The Suriname *Carib* forbade the father to hunt or undertake any heavy work; everywhere he had to avoid thorny places on the road, and if he crossed a river by a tree trunk, he would set up a sort of miniature bridge for the child's spirit (Roth, 1924, pp. 695 f.). The *Galibi* subjected the father to the same flogging and scarification tests characteristic at puberty, the idea being to transfer to the child the valor shown. The *Macushi* prohibit both parents to scratch themselves with their fingernails, instead of which they employ the midrib of the kokerite palm (Roth, 1915, pp. 320–324).

There seems to be no support for Max Schmidt's view (1917, pp. 61–64) that the couvade was a potent mechanism for creating an economically subordinate social class. The custom is not confined to matrilocal peoples, as he assumes, but has a wide distribution irrespective of the rule of residence; and its implications are very clearly of the magico-religious order.

Puberty.—Some sort of puberty ordeal is widespread, being obligatory for both sexes before marriage especially in the Guianas, as among the *Carib* and *Warrau*. The principal tests are fasting, exposure to ant bites, scarification, and flagellation. A Pomeroon *Arawak* girl must abstain from meat at her first menses and eat very little fish with small manioc cakes; her *Warrau* sister neither eats, speaks, nor laughs for 2 or 3 days. *Maué, Apinayé,* and *Arapium* boys were exposed to ants, as was customary among various Guiana tribes (see pl. 118, *d*), which latter commonly inflicted severe gashes on adolescents of both sexes. Boys or girls, or both, were flogged among the *Macushí*, the *Marauhá*, and *Araycú* (west of Ega), and tribes of the lower Içá River. Very common is the suspension of a girl in a hammock raised to the highest part of the hut so as to expose her to the smoke. This custom, linked with fasting and other taboos, seems to be in part of upper Amazonia the equivalent of the boys' flogging. The *Taulipáng* combine all the austerities described: A youth is whipped and gashed, the incisions being smeared with magical substances, and exposed to ants, besides being obliged to forego the meat of game and flesh of large birds and big fish for a whole year. This trial is invariably collective, and none of the candidates may utter a cry of pain lest the ceremony be nullified for all celebrants. However, the primary object of the performance is, according to Koch-Grünberg, not a mere test of fortitude, but a magical enhancement of the youths' skill in hunting and fishing; and consequently it may be repeated for like purposes in later life. A *Taulipáng* girl, when coming of age, is exposed to ants, tattooed, and whipped; throughout her first period she remains in her hammock partitioned from the rest of the hut, observes a rigid diet, and is obliged to use a special scratcher for her head. This last taboo also applies to mourners of either sex. At the next four or five menstrual periods the prohibitions are somewhat relaxed, but the girl must not visit the plantation, seize knives or axes, blow on a fire, or talk loudly lest her health suffer. The *Siusí* (Rio Aiarí) cut a girl's hair, paint her with genipa, restrict her food, and wind up with a major carousal. The *Tupinamba* shave the girl's head and scarify her, and the *Guaraní* cut her hair, while among the *Parintintin* and some Montaña tribes she is deflowered. The *Nambicuara* isolate her for several months outside the village, where she receives ritual food, a bath terminating the period of seclusion. (See Koch-Grünberg, 1923 b, pp. 121–131, 168; 1921, pp. 115, 220; Roth, 1915, pp. 308–313; Spix and Martius, 1823–31, 3 :1185 f., 1314 f., 1318, 1320 f; Bates, 1863, 2 :405 f.)

Initiation of boys into a men's tribal society has a limited distribution. The *Tucanoans* initiate boys to the ancestor cult, (the so-called "Yaupary" cult), requiring them to take snuff and revealing to them the secret megaphone and trumpet which represent the voices of the ancestors (p. 783). The *Witotoans* (p. 760) and *Tucuna* (p. 718) seem similarly to initiate boys to the secret trumpets. South of the Amazon, there is no cult, except possibly in the Mojos-Chiquitos area where again there are secret musical instruments. Preparation of boys for manhood starts at a tender age, when they receive their first labrets (*Tupinamba*), take parica snuff (*Mura*), have their teeth stained (*Cashinawa*), sleep in the men's house (*Mundurucú*), are tonsured (*Carajá*), or experience other formal stages of growing up.

Death.—In the disposal of the dead divergent procedures exist, sometimes even with the same tribe. The most widespread practice is to bury the corpse in their huts. Usually care is taken to prevent direct contact with the earth by erecting a palm-leaf shelter or some equivalent device.

The posture is sometimes vertical, in other cases sitting, the latter position being also employed in *Rucuyen* cremation. Almost all the upper Xingú burials are in recumbent position with the head toward the east. Funeral deposits are common, but not universal. Often, especially after the death of a distinguished man, the house is abandoned. The *Cashinawa* destroyed a deceased person's possessions.

Cemeteries occur, as among the *Palicur;* and Humboldt records an assemblage of nearly 600 skeletons of the extinct *Ature,* each in a separate basket, the bones having been variously dyed for this secondary disposal some months after primary burial in damp earth, followed by scraping. Urns near the baskets also held bones, presumably those of one family. (See also pl. 119, *bottom.*) Such secondary urn burial was widespread, especially among *Tupian* tribes.

In some cases there are dietary taboos. The discarding of ornaments and the cutting of the hair are widespread mourning practices. There is often restriction on remarriage during the period. Lamentations are kept up between death and the final ceremonies. Among the *Cubeo,* they continue for 5 days in harmony with the mystic number of the upper Rio Negro country.

A remarkable secondary procedure characterizes the *Tapajó, Cubeo, Arapium,* certain *Panoans,* and some other groups. The cremated corpse or the exhumed bones are burnt to ashes, which are mixed with festive brew, and drunk with the beverage (e. g., pp. 254, 556; also Nordenskiöld, 1930 a, p. 12; Palmatary, 1939, p. 5 f.; Koch-Grünberg, 1921, p. 316; Roth, 1924, pp. 642, 660).

In the Guianas, the closing mortuary solemnities might take place about a year after the death, but the exact date apparently hinged on whether the deceased person's manioc crop sufficed for supplying the wherewithal for a carousal. These festivities involved not only drinking, singing, and dancing, but also in some tribes (*Arawak, Warrau*) mutual flagella-

PLATE 1.—**Brazilian and Paraguayan landscapes from the air.** *Top, left:* Shifting agriculture in the forests of Maranhão, Brazil. *Top, right:* Tebicuary River meandering across grassy plains of southern Paraguay, *Guarani* country. (After Rich, 1942, Nos. 34, 136.) *Bottom:* A jungle delta in the Province of Maranhão, Brazil. (Courtesy Albert W. Stevens and the National Geographic Magazine.)

PLATE 2.—**The Peruvian Montaña.** (*Top*, Courtesy Grace Line; *bottom*, after Johnson, 1930.)

PLATE 3.—**Ecuadorean and Brazilian jungles.** *Top:* Giant ferns, Ecuador. (Courtesy H. E. Anthony and the National Geographic Magazine.) *Bottom:* Along the lower Solimoes River, Brazil. (Courtesy American Museum of Natural History.)

PLATE 4.—**Landscapes of Venezuela and the Guianas.** *Top:* Beyond Suapure, Venezuela, showing abrupt change to densely wooded ranges. The tonka bean is the most characteristic tree. (Courtesy Llewelyn Williams.) *Center:* *Atorai* country, British Guiana. (Courtesy University Museum, Philadelphia.) *Bottom:* The ledge (dark diagonal line) approach to the summit of Roraima, British Guiana. (Courtesy G. H. H. Tate and the National Geographic Magazine.)

PLATE 5.—**Venezuela rivers.** *Top, left:* Upper Orinoco. *Top, right:* Casiquiare River. *Center, left:* Upper Orinoco. *Center, right:* Rio Negro, the Brazilian-Venezuelan border. (Courtesy Llewelyn Williams.) *Bottom:* Casiquiare River, showing typical cut banks and river vegetation. (Courtesy G. H. H. Tate and C. B. Hitchcock.)

PLATE 6.—**Tropical forest hunters and fishers.** *Top, left:* Spearing fish on the upper Xingú. (Courtesy University Museum, Philadelphia.) *Bottom, left: Nambicuara* hunter with carrying basket. (Courtesy Claude Lévi-Strauss.) *Right: Apalakiri* man in bark canoe shooting fish. (Courtesy University Museum, Philadelphia.)

PLATE 7.—**With blowgun and gun in the tropical forest.** *Left: Yagua.* (Courtesy Paul Fejos.) *Right: Jivaro.* (Courtesy Matthew W. Stirling.)

PLATE 8.—**Tropical forest agriculture and food preparation.** *Top:* A collective garden cleared by "slash-and-burn" technique. On the Pimenta Bueno River. (Courtesy Claude Lévi-Strauss.) *Bottom: Yaulapiti* women crushing manioc. (Courtesy University Museum, Philadelphia.)

tion. with a special whip. The dances might include animal mimicry of the type performed at other celebrations. A kind of masquerade, but with exposed faces, occurs among the *Rucuyen;* the performers, wearing a towering headgear and a long bark fringe from the neck downward, successively crack a long whip. But full-fledged masked dances as a mortuary ritual characterize the upper Rio Negro, where butterflies, carrion vultures, jaguars, etc., are all represented by the costumes and the actors' behavior (p. 789). Koch-Grünberg (1921, pp. 78–85, 314 f.) surmises that the purpose is to conciliate the spirit of the dead, to ward off evil demons, and to foster success in hunting and farming. Women attend these performances, but only as spectators (Roth, 1924, pp. 638–665).

ESTHETIC AND RECREATIONAL ACTIVITIES

Art.—In the absence of detailed preliminary studies only a sketchy treatment can be attempted.

As Max Schmidt has indicated, twilling produces parallel diagonal effects, whose combination may yield distinct decorative designs, such as concentric diamonds or concentric squares (M. Schmidt, 1905, p. 334 et seq.). Such textile designs are often secondarily transferred to other media; they may be painted on the face, body, or pottery, incised on house-posts and walls, engraved on dance implements and weapons, and worked in beads (pl. 102, *right*). According to Koch-Grünberg, (1921, pp. 341, 347), the primary textile patterns include zigzags, meanders, series of right angles, etc. However that may be, neither definitely curvilinear nor naturalistic forms can be derived from a textile technique. Thus, variants of a spiral motif are prominently painted on the ceramics of the Brazilian-Guiana litoral. Here also appear characteristic pairs of overlapping, though not actually interlocking hooks; these couples are variously arranged, in four or five-fold vertical series partitioned into panels; in concentric circles on the inside of the vessel, etc. (Roth, 1924, pls. 27–29). Again, the remarkable array of clubs from Guiana and Brazil published by Stolpe (1927, pls. 1, 2, 16 et passim) reveals, indeed, some patterns conceivably of textile origin, but many circles, scrolls, scallops, and sundry combinations of curvilinear with rectilinear figures. There are also unequivocally realistic representations of a quadruped and a group of birds (Stolpe, 1927, p. 4, fig. 9; p. 12, fig. 4, *a*). Far less faithful to nature are the numerous human forms, some of them so conventionalized as to warrant conjecture that they may have sprung from some geometrical figure, with secondary amplification and reading in of a likeness to the human forms. Yet even here no specifically textile model is indicated. Most interesting among these quasi-realistic club decorations are twin figures in juxtaposition and either distinct or joined so that adjacent arms or other parts of the body coalesce (Stolpe, 1927, pls. 9, 10). Realistic forms also appear painted or drawn in charcoal on the bark covering of house walls or on house posts, a masculine torso in full dance regalia being an ever recurrent sample. Such decoration of posts is confined to the upper Caiarí (Vaupés) River and the neighboring Aiarí River (Koch-Grünberg, 1921, p. 348 f.) ; at times the rear of the same pillars bears the picture of a giant snake. On the lower and middle Xingú a maze pattern is painted on the body or incised on utensils (Shipaya).

The masks of the Kaua, pieces of bast sewed over flexible rods, are painted to simulate various beasts, small red circles and many black ones being intended to suggest the spots of the jaguar's skin. The Cubeo have bark-cloth masks representing anthropomorphic legendary beings, such as demons and giants, as well as deer, sloths, snakes, butterflies, etc. (Pl. 98; also, Koch-Grünberg, 1921, pp. 73, 323–327, pl. 4; cf. also the Tucuna bark-cloth animals, pl. 64.) The upper Xingú has many, well-made masks (p. 342). Carved, wooden masks are used by several tribes (pl. 44; figs. 40–42).

Plastic work attains considerable heights in clay (fig. 36), wax (pl. 102; fig. 23), and wood (figs. 30, 31, 37). The effigy pottery and the accessories of earthenware vessels, grotesque and extravagant as they tend to be, indicate much dexterity and sophistication. A Palicur turtle in clay is admirably faithful to nature (Nimuendajú, 1926, p. 48), and the wax figurines of great anteaters, peccaries, and tapirs by the Taulipáng (Koch-Grünberg, 1923 b, p. 126) are certainly creditable. In wood, the benches or stools carved from a single block, with an animal's head at one end and its tail at the other (fig. 37), are noteworthy samples of native skill. Caiman, beetle, jaguar, and snake heads are among those realistically portrayed. Doctors' seats are as a rule specially decorated (Roth, 1924, p. 273 et seq.; Nimuendajú, 1926, p. 61). The Cubeo perform certain dances, holding wooden figures of fish, birds, and lizards. On the Apáporis River the masks of the Opaina are topped by a cylindrical two-winged headgear of very light wood, both the body and the lateral projections being profusely painted (Koch-Grünberg, 1921, p. 397, pl. 12).

Ceramic art has been mentioned (p. 26).

Games.—Many scattered tribes from the Mojos-Chiquitos area and the Guaraní to the Uaupés-Caquetá region and the Guianas played a ball game, many using a special rubber ball.

Another widespread ball game (Yecuana, Taulipáng, Bacaïri, Macushi etc.) is shuttlecock, played with maize husks (fig. 49, c) struck with the flat of the hand. A similar game is popular among young men on the Caiarí (Uaupés and Ariarí Rivers (p. 889). The Kepikiriwat propel the ball with their heads and stake arrows on the issue of a game.

Other athletic sports include true wrestling and a curious contest (Warrau, p. 879), in which each player tries to push back his opponent or throw him by pressure of a special form of shield against his adversary's. Foot races in the savannas over distances of 10 to 20 miles are popular among the *Macushí,* who recognize champion runners. This sport is combined with a drinking bout and wrestling: The beverage brewed is stored in a house and the would-be winner has to force an entry against guards trying to prevent his ingress. A dance follows (Roth, 1924, p. 478 f.)

Boys from an early age practice archery, shooting small birds, and organizing sham battles and hunts. In Guiana there are also diving and other water sports. Children of both sexes imitate the economic activities of adults. They also mimic animals to the accompaniment of songs and model clever wax figurines. Girls play with wooden dolls made by their fathers. *Macushí, Carib,* and *Siusí* boys walk on stilts (fig. 115, *right*). Tops (Guianas, upper Xingú, Montaña, etc.) are spun by youngsters, each trying to upset his opponent's; and there are likewise humming tops and buzzers. In several tribes either the children themselves or their elders often make the rejects of plaitwork into elaborate toys representing such objects as rattles and balls or animals, like fish and fleas.

Cat's-cradle figures exist in great profusion (e.g., Roth, 1924, pp. 488–550). The Andean dice game was played by *Chiriguano.*

Dances.—Irrespective of magico-religious connections, the dances of the area have various social associations and functions. They are probably always linked with singing and drinking bouts; they serve to maintain friendly relations with neighboring tribes; and they offer opportunities for barter, gossip, amatory dalliance, and the settling of quarrels. To invite outsiders, the chief sends messengers with mnemonic cords having a knot for each day until the opening of the festivity, a device also employed on other occasions. Major enterprises may draw together not far from a thousand persons among the *Taulipáng,* with possibly 200 active performers. The dances follow one another in a sequence that is presumably fixed at least in particular tribes. In Guiana the humming-bird dance takes precedence: a company of decorated young men have to fight their way through the ranks of their comrades to the covered liquor-trough, where women try to pour pepper into their eyes, the victor receiving the first drink and every one then capering round the trough. Very popular are dances in mimicry of animals, the performers sometimes impersonating a whole troup of monkeys or a herd of peccaries. Women take part in some dances, but are excluded from others, at least as active performers.

Some dances involve no special paraphernalia; others are characterized by a profusion of ornaments and accessories. In the parishara of the *Taulipáng* a kind of masquerade is worn, a plaited headgear partly covering the face and a long fringe descending to the feet, as in the *Rucuyen* funeral performance. The costume wearers blow wooden tubes with gaily painted figurines at one end, while in the other hand they carry a long staff with pendent deer dew claws or seed capsules at the top. The dancers form a long Indian file, each bending his knees, stamping his right foot, advancing a step, flexing the upper part of the body, then dragging the left foot forward. Each division has a song and dance leader. The staff is struck against the ground in rhythmic unison with the steps. When the performers, starting from the savanna, have reached the village, women and girls join, each placing her right hand on her male partner's left shoulder, or both hands on her neighbor's shoulders on both sides. Now an open ring develops and the performers move forward and backward, to the right and the left, uttering shouts after each figure. During the dancing and the intermission women or girls offer calabashes of drink to the performers.

Some dances are connected with mythological tales and may envisage magical effects in fishing and hunting. The *Apapocuva Guaraní,* haunted by fear of an impending world catastrophe, tried throughout the historic period to escape destruction under the leadership of shamans who were to guide them through sacred dances to an earthly paradise (p. 94). (Koch-Grünberg, 1923 b, p. 154 et seq.; Roth, 1924, pp. 470–483; Nimuendajú, 1914 c.)

Music.—(For general treatment, see Izikowitz, 1935.)

Although stringed instruments—musical bows and violins—undoubtedly occur in the area, their aboriginal character is strongly suspect. There is no reference to them in the earliest post-Columbian literature and the terms applied to these chordophones are in the main clearly derived from Spanish or Negro vocables. It is also noteworthy that, as in Africa, the bow is usually played by striking the string with a stick (Izikowitz, 1935, pp. 201–206).

As to membranophones, the European military drum gained considerable distribution in the historical period, but the general use of Spanish designations again casts doubt on the pre-Columbian occurrence of these instruments in Amazonia, though Roth does not consider the argument conclusive. (Nordenskiöld, 1930 a, p. 165; Roth, 1924, p. 467; Izikowitz, 1935, p. 193.)

On the other hand, percussion idiophones are well represented. Noteworthy in view of Mexican, Pueblo, and California occurrences is the use of a plank foot drum by the *Rucuyen* and at *Arawak* funeral ceremonies (Roth, 1924, pp. 468 f., 649; Izikowitz, 1935, pp. 11–13). Equally significant is the presence of the tomtom ("hollow-log drum"), in eastern Ecuador and in the Orinoco and Rio Negro districts, generally for signaling, as among the *Witoto* (pls. 81, *top; 99, top*). Typically, it is carefully hollowed out from a tree trunk so as to leave a narrow slit. In use it is generally suspended from posts. A unique adaptation of this occurs among the *Mangeroma* (p. 679). The widespread, two-headed skin drum (pl. 62) is probably of European origin. Of jingling idiophone appendages the deer-hoof rattle is noteworthy, being reported from the Roraima region (Izikowitz, 1935, p. 39). More important are rattles, those from gourds (Lagenaria) being shaken by the natural grip, while the round calabash (*Crescentia*) fruits are fitted to a handle. These instruments are often the special property of medicine men, though children may use basketry imitations (pl. 118, *f, g*). They occur far beyond the Tropical Forest area, as does the time-marking ground pounder—Métraux's "baton de rhythme," Izikowitz's "stamping tube"— which seems to have spread far to the south through *Tupi-Guarani* influence. Most frequently a bamboo tube (*Witoto*, pl. 83, *bottom, right; Cubeo*, pl. 96; and Roraima Indians), it is made of *Cecropia* wood in the Rio Negro region (Métraux, 1928 a, pp. 215 f., 225; Izikowitz, 1935, pp. 151 et seq.).

Aerophones are likewise conspicuous. Trumpets assume many forms: there are two- and three-bellied clay vessels with narrow mouthpieces (Orinoco, Guiana); long tubes of spirally wound bark, varying in size (Orinoco River, Vaupés River, *Wapishana*, etc., pl. 39; fig. 100) and in the Rio Negro territory strictly concealed from women; similar wooden instruments (pl. 101, *left*); conchs (Guiana); *Lagenaria* gourds (*Wapishana*); and combinations of a trumpet with a resonator of gourd or other material (fig. 46, *left*). Whether the clarinets found in and near Guiana are aboriginal, is as yet not clear. The wind instruments technically definable as flutes, include, among others, clay and wooden whistles (fig. 49, *a, b,*); quenas or notched flutes (Montaña); bone flutes (fig. 48); nose flutes (*Nambicuara*, pl. 36, *top, right;* Guiana); and panpipes (pls. 36, *bottom, left;* 79). The last-mentioned occur throughout the Tropical Forest and appear in ancient Peruvian graves. Similarity of pitch in Melanesian and South American panpipes led Von Hornbostel to argue for their transmission to the New World, but Izikowitz (1935, pp. 378–408) regards the question as still open.

Narcotics.—Although widely spread and generally cultivated in our area, tobacco has competitors that locally overshadow it. In the northwest, coca chewing and on the middle Amazon, parica snuffing make it recede into the background. Among the *Tuyuca*, guests receive both a cigar and coca. *Witoto* councilors chew coca, but also swear oaths by licking their fingers after dipping them in a sirupy mess of boiled tobacco leaves.

Coca (*Erythroxylon coca*) appears only along the eastern slope of the Andes, except in Colombia, where it spreads eastward in the Uaupés-Caquetá region. Spix and Martius (1823–31, 3: 1169 f., 1180) found no wild samples anywhere in Brazil, and did not strike any plantation before reaching Ega. In the west, however, enormous quantities are consumed, travelers of the Caiarí (Uaupés) district taking a few small

sackfuls of coca in lieu of all other provisions for a march of a day and
a half (Koch-Grünberg, 1921, pp. 174 f., 204). Only the men—the main
consumers—tend, harvest, and prepare the plant. They roast and pound
the leaves up, mix the powder with the ashes from *Cecropia* leaves, and
store the combination in a bast bag into which a long rod is inserted and
secured by tying the container together. By tapping the rod, the user
makes the powder ooze out of the bast, collecting it in a calabash, from
which he can dip it up with a spoon or a leaf. Travelers sling calabashes
with coca powder over the left shoulder and suck out the stimulant with
a hollow bone. The unfamiliarity of the Chiquitos-Mojos Indians with
coca is noteworthy in view of their Andean contacts.

In some tribes (*Arecuna*) women never smoke, in others both sexes
and even children indulge freely. On the upper Amazon, Spix and
Martius (1823–31, 3: 1180) found that tobacco is most frequently used
by shamans, who blow the smoke on their patients (p. 50). Bates
(1863, 2: 407) mentions an extraordinary medicinal use: an old Ega
Indian cured a tumor due to the grub of a gadfly by stupefying the
insect with strong tobacco juice, thereby causing it to relax its grip and
facilitating its removal. This is paralleled among the *Chacobo,* who
grow tobacco for this exclusive purpose (Nordenskiöld, 1922, p. 182.).

In Guiana tobacco is smoked only in the form of cigarettes, the bark
of certain trees providing the wrapper. The *Tuyuca* and *Cubeo* (pl. 103,
left) circulate giant cigars 8 to 10 inches (20 to 25 cm.) long—clamped
between the two tines of a forklike holder. Several Guiana tribes chew
tobacco, mixing it with salt or the ashes of an aquatic plant (*Mourera
fluviatilis*), which are kept in little gourds with a stick projecting through
the stopper. In the Montaña, consumption of tobacco was formerly restricted largely to shamans, but is now more general.

Parica (yupa, niopo) snuff, made of the seeds of *Mimosa acacioides,*
likewise has a considerable distribution, being popular on the lower
Amazon (*Maué, Omagua*), and the Yapurá, as well as sporadically on
the Caiarí (Uaupés) River. In the Guaporé River region a shaman
blows snuff composed of crushed angico, tobacco leaves, and bark ashes
into his patient's nose. The *Witoto* put one branch into the mouth, the
other into one nostril, a puff of breath propelling the powder into the
inner portions of the mucous membrane. These people also have an
X-shaped combination of two bones, by which two friends may simultaneously blow snuff into each other's nostrils (fig. 106). Parica evokes
sneezing and extreme exhilaration to the point of frenzy, followed by
depression and stupor. It may figure largely at festivals (Spix and
Martius, 1823–31, 3: 1074 f.). Parica is taken as an enema with a syringe
in the Juruá-Purús region, and among the *Mura* (p. 263).

In the northwest Amazon region, cayapi (*Banisteriopsis caapi* and
other species; see p. 7), is a favorite stimulant, served as an infusion

at festivals, such as the *Tucano* tribal society's dance, in order to induce delightful hallucinations, which have been compared to those due to hashish. All things appear to be huge and gorgeously colored, there are visions of motley-tinted snakes and of erotic experiences. Some partakers fall into a deep sleep, awakening with severe headache. On novices the brew acts as an emetic. Women never drink cayapi, the preparation of which is wholly a masculine task. The men pound up the roots, stems, and leaves of the shrub into a greenish-brown mass, which is washed with water, squeezed dry, and again pounded and washed. The resulting substance, not unlike cow dung in appearance, is strained through a double sifter into the bellied cayapi urn, which is covered with leaves and placed outdoors. It has two horizontal handles and two perforations with a connecting suspension cord. Though never washed, the vessel is now and then repainted with the same yellow designs on a dark-red background. (See also, Koch-Grünberg, 1921, pp. 189 ff., 200 f., 219 f., 373.)

Other stimulants, largely restricted to southeast Colombia and tropical Ecuador, are floripondia (*Datura arborea*) and yoco (*Paulliniayoco*). (See p. 7.)

Peppers (*Capsicum*) are used by the *Macushi* as a stimulant, crushed peppers and water being poured into the nostrils to cure headache. In the Pomeroon district *Capsicum* enemas are in vogue.

Intoxicating drinks.—Fermented beverages are lacking on the upper Xingú and among many *Tupian* tribes, but for large sections of the area the drinking spree, as an end in itself or an accompaniment of all serious occasions, is diagnostic, especially in contrast to the *Ge*. A variety of beverages are prepared, of which the narcotic cayapi has already been described. Manioc forms the most common base of fermented drinks, generically called chicha, but may be only one of several ingredients.

The preparation of chicha is illustrated in the Rio Negro region, where it is called cashiri. The Indians mix the particles of toasted manioc cakes in a trough with fresh water, fermentation being accelerated by the addition of chewed beijú. The chewing is done mainly by women, who carefully knead the mass together with leaves of a certain tree. The trough, tightly covered, is allowed to stand indoors by a fire maintained overnight, yielding a sweetish, harmless brew. Two days' fermentation is required for intoxicating effects, which a woman achieves by squeezing the brown gruel through a basketry strainer into a pot, from which she or her husband serve guests. Sometimes the mass, after being set fermenting, is kept wrapped up in the trough of a large pot, to be strained with water when an occasion for use arises. Sweet potatoes, maize, and the fruits of the pupunha and of other palms may all be substituted for manioc (Koch-Grünberg, 1921, p. 39 f.), to which in modern times sugarcane juice is frequently added.

The Barama *Carib* makes cashirim by grating and squeezing cassava, then putting it into a large pot with water, into which they spit chewed portions of thin manioc cakes. The mixture is then placed in the household trough and fermented for 3 days, when it acquires the alcoholic content of weak beer. For another chicha, called paiwari, these Indians thoroughly toast manioc cakes; small fragments of these are put into a pot filled with water and bits of chewed cake are added, as for cashirim, before removal to the trough. The toasting produces a distinctive cereal-like taste which Gillin compares to rye toast soaked in weak beer; it obviously allies the brew to Rio Negro cashirim.

In other parts of the area, a great variety of starchy crops and of wild fruits are made into chicha, but distillation is unknown except to the *Quijo,* among whom it is undoubtedly a post-Columbian acquisition.

RELIGION, SHAMANISM, AND MEDICINE

High Gods and tribal heroes.—Roth's denial (1915, pp. 117 ff.) of any notion of a Supreme Being in the Guianas is not literally correct. According to an early author quoted by him, the Sun is regarded as an outstanding deity by some Orinoco tribes, and the Moon by others; the Barama *Carib* conceive of a primeval starter of the universe (Gillin, 1936, p. 155); and the *Witoto* deity (Preuss, 1921, pp. 25 et seq., 166), notwithstanding the curiously abstract statements about his primeval doings, is even more definitely a creator and maintainer of the world. The *Apapocuva Guarani* speak of Our Great Father as the creator, and his sons figure as heroes. Nevertheless, generally a Supreme Being, if present, recedes in religious consciousness before other beings.

Among these, tribal heroes loom large, at least in myth. They appear either as lone figures, pairs, or trios. Thus, the *Yahuna* tell of Milomaki, a boy who suddenly appeared from the east and sang so beautifully that everyone came to hear him. But when his auditors came home and ate fish, they all fell dead, so their kinsfolk burnt the boy on a pyre. His soul rose to the sky, however, and out of his ashes grew the pashiuba palm, whose wood the people made into large flutes that reproduced the wondrously fine tunes sung by the boy. These instruments—taboo to women and small boys, who would die if they saw them—the men still play when fruits are ripe, and they dance in honor of Milomaki as the creator of all fruits (Koch-Grünberg, 1923 b, p. 386 f.). The *Cubeo* tell of Hömänihikö, whose mother drowns while big with him. He crawls out of her womb when a carrion vulture pierces her abdomen. Flying on the bird's back, the wonder-working infant transforms his own grandmother from a serpent into human shape, avenges his father's death by shooting the jaguar responsible for it, and kills all manner of the then quasi-human beasts, birds, and insects. Although two brothers of the hero are mentioned, he alone figures as the national ancestor. One of his brothers, however, Kuai, is considered the inventor of masquerade dances and their costumes; the other, dwelling in a large stone house, presides over the souls of the dead.

According to our authority, Kuai is originally an *Arawakan* character, the son of Yaperikuli, the national hero of the tribes of that stock in the Rio Negro region. He is credited with the rock-drawings seen in *Tariana* territory; and on the Aiarí River a large human rock-engraving is interpreted as Kuai, after whom the *Siusí* name their sacred flutes, taboo to women, which are blown at a festival celebrated when certain palm fruits have ripened. Successive flagellation of the dancers till their blood streams from their wounds characterizes this ceremonial, which is also named Kuai (Koch-Grünberg, 1923 b, pp. 69, 121, 261).

Typical twin myths are known from the Xingú River (*Bacaïri, Shipaya*), the *Tupi-Guarani* tribes, the *Warrau,* and the *Cariban* tribes. In the Guiana form, the Sun renders a woman pregnant with twins, then leaves her. She follows in his tracks, guided by one or both of the unborn children, whom she affronts so that advice is no longer forthcoming. As a result, she strays to the Jaguar house, where she dies (*Warrau*) or is killed (*Carib*). Either the Jaguar or Frog, his mother, extracts the twins by a Caesarean operation; they get fire for mankind (*Warrau*), avenge and restore their mother (*Carib*), and finally reach their father, where they turn into stars (*Carib*). In the *Macushi* variant, one of the twin brothers is carried off by a crane, but the other develops into a culture hero, teaching the Indians useful things as he travels about (Roth, 1924, pp. 130–136).

It is not clear how generally the tribal heroes are prayed to or otherwise worshiped, but *Cubeo* supernaturalism centers in the cult of the clan ancestors and in shamanism. The former is associated with the boys' initiation, at which the novices learn about sacred musical instruments, taboo to women, and are whipped to make them grow. Males bathe to the sound of sacred horns when seeking strength. Widespread among *Tupian* tribes is a mythological character—Our Great Father of the *Guarani*—associated with an afterworld of happiness. Among both the *Tupinamba* and *Guarani,* this god became prominent in a strong messianic cult (pp. 90, 93–94, 131).

Thunder is the principal deity of the *Nambicuara* and reveals himself to shamans; less frequently, to other adult males. He is an important deity, but definitely not a Supreme Being for the *Guarani.*

Animism.—Animism is very strongly developed. The *Taulipáng,* who credit even plants and animals with souls, attribute no less than five to mankind. Only one of these goes to the land of spirits after the death of the body, three turn into birds of prey, the fifth remains with the corpse and bears the same name as a demon who causes eclipses. The surviving soul goes to the sky via the Milky Way; it is waylaid by dogs, which destroy it if its owner abused his dog on earth, other souls being allowed to join their tribesmen.

Widespread notions typical of primitive belief elsewhere crop up here too. Thus the *Cubeo* hold that the soul leaves the body in dreams and in sneezing. Great significance is attached to dreams.

Fundamental to the entire area are bush spirits, which are variously conceived but universally feared, so that a common function of the shaman is their control. The Barama *Carib* recognize five distinct categories with a controlling master within each, the classes being associated, respectively, with the forest and land generally; the air; the water; the hills; and miscellaneous places or things, such as houses and industries. Each group is symbolized by a stone of a distinctive color or texture, supposedly represented by small pebbles in the rattle of the shaman through whom the spirits are approached. In addition, the Barama *Carib* recognize other supernatural beings definitely in any of the major categories. The bush spirits are generally mischief makers, causing the mishaps of daily life; water spirits figure as on the whole benevolent, but wreck travelers who venture to utter certain tabooed words while in a boat. (See also Roth, 1924, pp. 179 f., 245 f., 252.)

The *Taulipáng* have a well-defined belief in certain beings as lords or "fathers" of whole classes of beasts, etc. Thus, a fisherman must pray to the master of fish to let him have a catch. Supernatural beings, including animals, are supposed to be really anthropomorphic, but capable of shifting their shape by donning an appropriate covering. Thus the "father of game animals," who is also identified with the rainbow, turns into a large snake by putting on a mottled skin, as does the "father of fish"; and the jaguar correspondingly transforms himself from human guise by clothing himself in his skin (Koch-Grünberg, 1923 b, pp. 176–189). Generically similar notions appear in the masquerade dances of the *Siusi* and the Cubeo, whose demons are identified with the costume worn by the performers, though the spirits themselves are visible only to the medicine men, not to the lay spectator.

The conflict of good and evil spirits is well illustrated at *Palicur* festivals, where each decorative feather on a dancer's headgear is the seat of a supernatural guardian, and the feathered staffs bounding the ceremonial square warn the protectors against the advent of demons, who bump against the cord connecting the posts. Moreover, the pole erected as a path to heaven is topped with a dance rattle bearing two of the spirit feathers and is further guarded by half a dozen feathered staffs at its foot (Nimuendajú, 1926, pp. 66 f., 87 f.).

Shamanism.—Probably a temple cult with priests as distinguished from shamans is restricted to the Mojos-Chiquitos region. On the other hand, shamans—though not shamanistic procedures—are reported as lacking among the *Sirionó*. On the lower Xingú, the shaman intermediates between living people and the gods and souls of the dead, but curing is a secular function.

The shaman often socially overshadows the chief, for the spirit world is most commonly approached through him only. Occasionally, but rarely and probably only in some tribes, women practice. A son often inherits his father's profession, but this is by no means a universal rule. The shaman is primarily a doctor and detector of sorcerers, but may also act as master of ceremonies (e.g., *Guaraní,* p. 92; *Palicur*), counselor in warfare, prophet, finder of lost goods, name giver, depository of tradition, weather maker, etc. A prospective shaman undergoes a long period of training under his father or teacher, during which he diets, is instructed, acquires familiar spirits, and receives in his body various magical substances or objects regarded as the source of his power and, when projected into victims, as the cause of disease. He is also given tobacco in various forms and other stimulants, especially in the northwest Amazon region, such as *Datura* and ayahuasca. In some tribes, the shaman receives his magical substance from a spirit, in others from his tutor. For a few tribes, the practitioner is stated to control one or more familiar spirits (e.g., *Tenetehara, Tapirapé,* pp. 147, 177). In the western Amazon, he is associated with the jaguar (p. 682). There is no evidence that shamans of this area manifest epileptic or other abnormal tendencies, but trances, usually induced by drugs, are not uncommon.

The magical substance is usually a quartz crystal in Guiana, a "thorn" or "arrow" in the region of the western Amazon and upper Xingú. During his initiation, the neophyte gains immunity to and control of those substances, which he is supposed to take into his body.

The foremost insignia of the shaman—widespread, though not universal—are the gourd rattle, the crystal, a carved and painted bench, and a doll whose position during treatment indicates whether a patient is to recover. The doll is reported from parts of Guiana. The *Taulipáng* medicine man shakes a bunch of leaves instead of the rattle so used by doctors from Guiana to the Caiarí (Uaupés) River. The bench seems most characteristic of Guiana. Crystals turn up in Guiana, on the Orinoco, and in the upper Rio Negro region, whither they may have been imported from the Orinoco (Koch-Grünberg, 1923 b, p. 208). On the Guaporé River the shaman's insignia are a snuffing tube, a board for mixing snuff, and a mystic feathered stick. Among the powers widely claimed by shamans is the ability to transform themselves into jaguars. A *Cubeo* shaman's soul enters a jaguar when he dies, thus separating itself from other people's spirits, which join the clan ancestors.

Palicur doctoring is in most ways typical (Nimuendajú, 1926, pp. 91 et seq.). The shaman invariably works in complete darkness under a mosquito net—the equivalent of a special palm-leaf compartment anciently used. Putting on a feather diadem, he rises, bids all present farewell since his soul is about to start on its journey, and crawls under the net, an assistant passing in to him the animal-shaped bench and a basket holding the shamanistic paraphernalia. The doctor sits down, removes from his basket the dance rattle and a root whose odor the spirits like, for which reason he grates away particles of it and sprinkles them on his hair. The assistant next hands him a lighted cigar. Soon groans, whistling, and singing become audible, the glowing tip of the cigar is seen floating downward from the ceiling of the mosquito net, and a resounding footstep signalizes the entrance of the first spirit into the medicine man's body. His own soul has left to summon the friendly spirits, including those of the dead. Each of these sings his own chants to the music of the rattle, all spectators joining. After 5 to 10 minutes of singing, the spirit converses with the assistant. Those present question the visitant about their own affairs. At last there arrives one spirit considered expert in the treatment required, and him the assistant consults. This continues for hours until the last spirit leaves, as indicated by the soaring cigar tip. The shaman crawls out of his compartment. Another procedure is to bring the patient, too, under the net. In actual treatment the doctor undresses the sick man, shakes his rattle all over the body till he strikes the seat of the malady, then summons his patrons against the causes of the disease, which may precipitate a noisy conflict. If the powers of evil conquer, the doctor admits his failure and casts about for a more competent colleague. Extraction of the disease by suction is also reported, but not reckoned essential. A cured patient regales his savior with a dance and drinking-festival, which is naturally directed by the successful doctor.

Some of these traits, even apart from the sucking technique, have a wide distribution. The insistence on darkness, for example, occurs among the Pomeroon *Arawak* and *Carib*. Certain *Palicur* features are elaborated elsewhere: The *Siusi* shaman massages out of the patient five sticks as the agents of the disease and not merely puffs a cigar, but blows the smoke on the patient—a prevalent practice throughout the Tropical Forests (pl. 120, *center*)—and himself swallows the smoke; again, the *Taulipáng* shaman drinks tobacco juice to expedite his soul to the sky. Ventriloquism seems highly developed by the *Taulipáng;* a Northwest Brazilian specialty is pouring cupfuls of an aromatic infusion over the patient's head and body (Koch-Grünberg, 1921, pp. 97 f., 113). The Montaña and northwest Amazon doctor extracts needles or thorns as pathogenic agents (pp. 532, 703).

Fees are often contingent on a cure. In recent times a *Taulipáng* healer is usually compensated with European goods. A *Cubeo* receives urucú, pottery, bows, or hammocks. The *Palicur* express their appreciation by a feast.

The nonmedical duties of a *Palicur* shaman are illustrated during festivals, when he consecrates feathers, dance rattles, and carved settees by blowing smoke on them, thereby causing spirits to enter these objects, whence they are expelled at the close of the ceremony (Nimuendajú, 1926, pp. 95, 98 f.)

Bad shamans may practice magic or summon spirits to harm personal enemies, but most tribes deal severely with such sorcerers. Alleged witchcraft is a usual incentive for murder, and consequently the most common cause of warfare, as it initiates a series of reprisals.

Soul-loss as a cause of disease has been recorded from few tribes—e.g., *Cocama, Omagua, Coto,* and *Itonama*—but it is a concept that would escape superficial observation.

Kanaima.—(Gillin, 1936, pp. 99 f., 149–152; Roth, 1915, pp. 346, 354 et seq.; Koch-Grünberg, 1923 b, pp. 216–219.) This term and its equivalents in Guiana designate (*a*) a certain evil spirit; (*b*) the man possessed by it or otherwise driven to devote himself to a work of vengeance; (*c*) the procedure followed by the avenger, including the poison or other means employed. In any case, the concept denotes the most malevolent antisocial behavior. Among the Barama *Carib,* the prospective kanaima is regarded as joining a cult, learning from its headman the arts of entering houses unseen, benumbing one's victims, and inflicting incurable ailments. Kanaimas are accordingly outlawed, killing them being a meritorious deed. The *Taulipáng, Tucanoan, Witotoan, Jívaro,* or *Campa* belief in jaguar shamans merges in the kanaima concept, for the kanaima often dons the jaguar pelt in order to alarm and kill people. Contagious magic is likewise imputed to these individuals; they enclose a victim's spittle in a bamboo container and, by working magic over it, destroy the expectorator. Hostile tribes are often regarded as kanaimas.

Medicine.—(Roth, 1924, pp. 702–714.) Apart from supernatural treatment, a shaman may employ techniques open to the laity. Prominent among Guiana remedies are emetics, e.g., the bitter bark of the wallaba tree (*Eperua* sp.), of which two or three drams are boiled in a quart of water, a few spoonfuls making an effective dose. Purgatives include the root of *Cephaelis ipecacuanha.* In Guiana enemas are made from a turtle, jaguar, or other mammalian bladder attached to a reed nozzle; and rubber syringes characterize tribes on the Amazon. Vapor baths occur: while the patient rests in his hammock, red-hot stones are thrown into a large vessel of water under him (*Macushí, Guinau*); or water is thrown on large heated stones so as to envelop him in the steam. *Rucuyen* women take such vapor baths after confinement. Bleeding is frequently used for fatigue, stiffness in the limbs, and other ailments. Ant bites serve as counterirritants in cases of rheumatism and fever, the patient sometimes rolling himself in an ant's nest. Many domestic remedies against fevers, diarrhea, dysentery, and other afflictions consist of decoctions or infusions of the inner bark of certain trees. Guaraná, a hard substance made from the pounded seeds of *Paullinia sorbilis,* is prepared by the *Maué,* who have a virtual monopoly of it, and widely traded as a medicine against diarrhea and intermittent fevers; it is grated and then mixed with water

(p. 252). For sting-ray wounds the Indians of the lower Amazon apply a poultice of mangrove bark mixed with palm oil. The sticky gum of *Eperua* serves as a plaster for wounds. For snake bite the wound is cut out and sucked, but some tribes also administer antidotes in the form of infusions; on the Essequibo River, the decoction of a certain root was both drunk and poured upon the wound. On the upper Amazon, *Cyperus* roots were attributed many therapeutic and magic virtues.

Magic and ritual practice.—The machinations of witches and sorcerers have already been noted, with the occasional practice of contagious magic. The Indians of the Guaporé River (p. 378) believe in an invisible fluid which shamans may introduce, for good or evil, into food or human bodies. Impersonal supernaturalism is prominent in the prescriptions and taboos incident to birth and other critical situations. (See Life Cycle, p. 35.) The belief in a sympathetic bond between related individuals extends beyond the couvade in the general rule in Guiana that a patient's whole family must share his dietary restrictions (Roth, 1915, p. 352), a notion shared by some *Northern Ge.* A principle akin to sympathetic magic also appears in the use of certain varieties of caladia to attract particular animals and fish because of some fancied similarity: A "deer" caladium is supposed to suggest horns and the coloring of the fur in its venation, an "armadillo" caladium resembles the animal in having small projecting ears, etc. (Roth, 1915, p. 281 f.).

Taboos are innumerable. To mention only a few, chosen for their comparative interest, Guiana tribes will not tell spirit legends in the daytime nor utter a person's name in his presence; a hunter never brings his kill home, but leaves it for the women to fetch. The *Arawak* abstain from eating after nightfall lest they be transformed into animals; during the couvade, *Macushi* parents must substitute a special scratcher for their fingernails (Roth, 1915, pp. 193, 294–295, 304, 323). Of these, the last-mentioned recurs as far south as the *Yahgan,* and the name-taboo is equally pronounced among the *Siusi* and *Cubeo* (Koch-Grünberg, 1921, pp. 117, 311). Some taboos, such as the story-telling one and the prohibition of women from seeing the instruments sacred to a spirit (Koch-Grünberg, 1921, pp. 119, 322) on pain of automatic death are, of course, associated with animistic notions.

Of positive prescriptions may be cited the talismanic application of red body paint, scarification, and the ever recurrent flagellation.

Of extraordinary interest are the magical formulae of the *Taulipáng,* which the discoverer, Koch-Grünberg (1923 b, pp. 219–270) aligns with *Cherokee* and *Hupa* equivalents in North America. They are the property of laymen on equal terms with shamans and serve mainly to cure or impose bodily afflictions. These spells are linked with brief tales expounding how ancestral beings introduced various ills into the world, which can be removed with the aid of beasts or plants somehow associated with the malady. Thus, intestinal worms are overcome by declamation of a formula in which two dogs are addressed, for dogs suffer from these worms without dying from them.

A number of ritual and semiritual practices are found in the area, entering various contexts. The ant ordeal, associated especially with boy's puberty in the Guianas and among several *Tupian* tribes south of the Amazon, is used by the *Mura* to insure fishing success. Flagellation enters the Vaupés-Caquetá boy's initiation into the ancestor cult and the *Macushi* girl's puberty rite, but the *Mura* whip children to increase manioc yield and adults to give them strength, the *Chébero* flog pubescent girls, and the Guiana *Arawak* whip one another at a funeral ceremony to drive away evil spirits. In the Montaña, several tribes put pepper in the eyes of hunters for clear vision and strength, but the Pomeroon *Arawak* take pepper in enemas as a curative. Similarly, the several kinds of snuff and tobacco in various forms were taken for many purposes.

Ceremonialism.—Ceremonials connected with the life cycle—birth, puberty, initiations, and death—are most pronounced and have been mentioned. Many tribes, especially the *Tupians*, had rites concerned with subsistence activities, some even resembling harvest ceremonies. Of this type are *Mundurucú* festivals for maize and manioc growth and for hunting and fishing success, when a shaman makes offerings to fish skulls; the *Guarani* and *Tapirapé* harvest ceremony; the *Tenetehara* honey festival to protect growing maize; the *Cashinawa* dance to influence the maize spirit; the *Camayura* hunting and fishing ceremony; and the *Trumai* manioc ceremony.

In the Rio Negro country the mystic significance of the number five is conspicuous. A funeral festivity opens 5 days after the burial and continues for 5 days, as does a mother's post-natal seclusion; youths initiated by flagellation are subject to 5-month dietary taboos; an accepted suitor spends 5 days in his prospective father-in-law's house; the lament over the dead lasts 5 days; a shaman extracts 5 sticks (Koch-Grünberg, 1921, pp. 98, 107, 113, 116, 196, 263, 308, 310, 314, 322, 329). Elsewhere there is no such unequivocal preference, yet the *Taulipáng* believe in 5 human souls, make the shaman's apprentice drink a bark infusion for 5 nights, and have sporadic references to 10 and other multiples of five (Koch-Grünberg, 1923 b, pp. 170, 189, 203, 205).

The major festivals on the upper Rio Negro seem to fall into two main categories: (*a*) those associated with musical instruments taboo to women; (*b*) performances by mummers. The costumes and dances (p. 41) characteristic of the second type are at least sometimes linked with a memorial service in honor of a recently deceased tribesman. Their object is said to be complex—appeasement of spirits by their impersonation and promotion of fertility by phallic dances (Koch-Grünberg, 1921, pp. 82 et seq., 324 et seq.). All sorts of animals may be realistically mimicked. The other type of performance, the "Yurupary" dance of the Lingua Geral, may be regarded as the basis of a men's tribal society (but see p. 704). The sacred instruments symbolize the spirit to whom the ceremonial is dedicated, and flogging of the novices is a prerequisite to entrance (Koch-Grünberg, 1921, pp. 120 f., 130, 135 f., 198 ff., 217 ff., 263, 314 f., 322, 372). The *Mundurucú* tell a myth about a pristine matriarchate, the women making their spouses do all the work while themselves lived in the club house and played wind instruments. Once, however, the men detected them in the act, took the flutes away from them, and reversed the relative status of the sexes (Kruse, 1934, 1: 51–57). This tale is obviously very similar in essence to the Fuegian story of a great revolution depriving women of the ascendancy they enjoyed as possessors of masks.

In the *Shipaya* feast of the dead, the souls enter the shaman's body. Among the same people, Kumãpári, father of twin heroes and identified with the jaguar, is the center of a cult which involves cannibalism.

MYTHOLOGY AND LITERATURE

Under the head of Religion, Shamanism, and Medicine (p. 46), certain hero myths have been indicated. For lack of preliminary work, it is impossible to offer a comparative tribal study, let alone one on the literary styles. The culture hero, whose main contribution to mankind was domesticated plants, is universal in the area, as indeed elsewhere. In some tales he is also the Creator; associated with him is a trickster, often his brother. For the *Witoto* we have a useful roster of themes, but Preuss's bias in favor of lunar interpretations mars his presentation. However, he shows the prevalence of stories revolving about the elopement of either spouse and the urge for vengeance (Preuss, 1921, 1: 115 et seq.).

In view of the nature of the available material, it is merely feasible to list a number of important motifs. Some of them have an extremely wide range, far beyond the Forest area, as demonstrated in Koch-Grünberg's popular collection (1927).

Remarkable is the *Witoto* story of the incestuous nocturnal lover whom his sister identifies by painting him (Preuss, 1922, pp. 107, 331). A still closer analogy to the *Eskimo* tale, however, occurs among the *Shipaya* on the Iriri River, a tributary of the Xingú River, where the brother is identified with the moon, as he is by the *Canelo* of eastern Ecuador, the *Warrau* and *Arawak* of Guiana. (Nimuendajú, 1919–20, vols. 14–15, p. 1010 f.; Karsten, 1935, p. 522; Roth, 1915, p. 256.)

A motif of pan-American interest that occurs in many distinct settings is the rolling skull. In the *Cashinawa* version, a decapitated man's skull rolls after his own kin, transforming itself into the moon and also creating the rainbow and menstruation (Capistrano de Abreu, quoted by Koch-Grünberg, 1927, p. 232 et seq.). The motif, known from the Chaco, occurs among such people as the *Warrau* and the *Shipaya* (Roth, 1915, pp. 129; Nimuendajú, 1921–22, p. 369). Its African occurrence raises the recurring problem of possible Negro influence (Weeks, 1913, p. 208), which arises also concerning the tale of the perverted message that brings death to mankind (Juruá-Purús).

The magical flight, though rare in South America, is attested for the *Mundurucú* and the *Carajá* (Koch-Grünberg, 1927, pp. 203, 227).

Sharpened-Leg, the man who whittles down his leg and attacks his companion with it, figures in *Warrau* and *Carib* lore (Roth, 1915, pp. 195 f.), as well as in *Shipaya* (Nimuendajú, 1921–22, p. 370) and *Ge* tradition.

The ascent to the sky by an arrow-chain is related by the *Guarayú* in the Madeira drainage (Koch-Grünberg, 1927, p. 283), as well as by the *Jívaro, Tupinamba, Cumana,* and *Chiriguano.* The division of people in climbing from the sky to the earth or from the underworld to our earth because of a stout individual blocking the passage is common to the *Warrau, Carajá, Mundurucú,* and several tribes of the Montaña. This certainly recalls the North American *Mandan-Hidatsa* story of the pregnant woman breaking the vine that led from a cave to the upper world. The North American thunderbird also turns up (*Chiriguano*).

Among more generic themes found within the area may be cited the suitor's tests, the deluge, the destruction of the world by fire, and etiological animal tales, the requisition of fire, and the Amazon women.

LORE AND LEARNING

Economic and technological pursuits involve considerable empirical knowledge, which is likewise displayed in the sportive mimicry of the animal dances. Intricately tied up with their practical occupations is the Indians' star lore. In Guiana, at least, the year is divided not into lunar months but into seasons defined, above all, by the regular succession of the stars and constellations in certain positions in the sky. The Pleiades are of special importance, their rising from the east or disappearing in the west marking the advent of the wet and dry seasons and especially indicating the proper time to commence agricultural operations. The various stars are also associated with game, fish, and plants in season. The year, in short, is determined by the reappearance of the Pleiades and is subdivided according to the appearance of other constellations, which are correlated with the abundance of economically significant animals and plants. The rainy and the dry season bear distinctive designations, and their advent is foretold by special observations—on the size of the young turtles, the croaking of the rain frog, etc.

To indicate the number of days before some such event as a feast, the Guiana host (or party of the first part) sends to the guest (or partner) a knotted string, of which he retains a replica. Each morning the two men concerned untie one knot, the knotless cord being supposed to correspond to the day of arrival. The *Palicur* substitute for the cord a bundle of rods suspended from a reed, turning down both ends of each stick every day (Nimuendajú, 1926, p. 94). This device strikingly resembles North American *Choctaw* practice.

Distances are reckoned by the number of nights required for the journey.

Remarkable geographical knowledge and cartographic skill are evidenced by the maps of the *Taulipáng,* who are accustomed to outline their itinerary on the ground and to indicate the shapes of mountains by an accumulation of sand. Native sketchers will recite the names of rivers and their affluents in order, marking waterfalls, and defining the appearance of peaks (Koch-Grünberg, 1923 b, pp. 90, 118; pls. 34, 35). Similar maps, including an astronomical star chart, are made in the Rio Negro region (Koch-Grünberg, 1921, pp. 160, 213). (Roth, 1924, pp. 715–720; see also upper Xingú, p. 348.)

ETIQUETTE

A *Taulipáng* never enters a strange house unbidden, but remains standing at the entrance until asked to enter. A speaker is never interrupted; on official occasions a long oration is merely punctuated by polite interjections on the auditor's part. In such situations neither interlocutor looks at the other, both staring fixedly into space—a usage rather common among South American tribes (Koch-Grünberg, 1923 b, p. 111 f.). On the Caiarí River, any one leaving on a specific errand, such as going to hunt or farm or even to ease himself, announces the fact to the other inmates, who encourage him to go about his business (Koch-Grünberg, 1921, p. 280 f.).

Commonly men and women eat separately. Hands are carefully washed before and after meals. At a party it is inadmissible to refuse a drink, for such an act evokes suspicion.

The etiquette regulating kinship behavior and the procedures at ceremonial situations have been considered under appropriate heads (Roth, 1924, pp. 235–239, 620–631).

The widespread weeping salutation also appears in this area (*Guaraní, Yuruna*).

BIBLIOGRAPHY

Acuña, 1641; Bates, 1863 (1892); Friederici, 1925; Gillin, 1936; Im Thurn, 1883; Izikowitz, 1935; Karsten, 1935; Killip and Smith, 1931; Kirchhoff, 1931, 1932; Koch-Grünberg, 1906 a, 1921, 1923 a, 1923 b, 1927; Kruse, 1934; Linné, 1925; Mangelsdorf and Reeves, 1939; Métraux, 1928 a, 1928 b; Nimuendajú, 1914 c, 1919–20, 1921–22, 1926, 1930 b; Nordenskiöld, 1912, 1917 c, 1919 a, 1920, 1922, 1924 a, 1924 b, 1930 a, 1930 c, 1931 b; Palmatary, 1939; Preuss, 1921, 1922; Roth, 1915, 1924; M. Schmidt, 1905, 1914, 1917; Setchell, 1921; Speiser, 1926; Spix and Martius, 1823–31; Stirling, 1938; Stolpe, 1927; Weeks, 1913; Whiffen, 1915.

Part 1. The Coastal and Amazonian Tupi

THE ARCHEOLOGY OF THE PARANÁ RIVER

By Francisco de Aparicio

INTRODUCTION

At the beginning of historic times various groups of native peoples lived along the lower Paraná River, from its confluence with the Paraguay to the Delta. Some of these peoples were island dwellers and navigators; others lived along the banks of the river and were adapted to both a riverine and terrestrial life. Still others were land hunters who, perhaps, came only seasonally to the river to fish. The latter do not concern us here, but the first two groups, the island peoples and those who lived permanently along the Paraná littoral are considered here as typical inhabitants of the Paraná.

GEOGRAPHICAL SETTING

At its confluence with the Paraguay, the Paraná River turns south to form the lower Paraná. In this southward course its width varies from 1 to 2½ kilometers (⅝ to 1½ miles) in the north and gradually widens toward the south. The great volume of alluvium which the river carries has resulted in the formation of numerous islands at the Delta which are dissected by small streams. Ramirez, in referring to these islands, said that: "There were so many that they could not be counted." They are a characteristic feature of the Paraná Delta landscape, and they offered, in the past, exceptionally advantageous sites for the dwellings of native peoples.

The banks of the Paraná are quite irregular in appearance. The left margin, from Corrientes to Diamante, where the formation of the Delta begins, is in some places high and falls sharply to the river, forming steep bluffs 30 meters (about 100 ft.) in height. At other places the decline from the high ground to the river is more gradual. These gradual slopes usually form the transitional terrain between the river and the typical monte country of the region. The right margin of the Paraná, on the other hand, is low. A flooded zone, of 10 to 40 kilometers (about 6 to 25 miles) in width, borders the river down to the city of Santa Fé.

57

From there, to the confluence of the Carcarañá, the Coronda subsidiary defines the edge of the firm land that rises only a little above the ordinary level of the waters. South of the Carcarañá, the river bank rises to high cliffs; and these highlands, in some places, continue inland for a short distance. This same topography continues down the Plata to the vicinity of Buenos Aires. The Indians occupied these highlands, and undoubtedly it was on the heights that the conquistadors had their first contact with the natives, as the flood plains were nearly always inaccessible.

The lower Paraná has numerous left tributaries, the most voluminous of which is the Iberá draining a large basin. The other tributaries flow from the western watershed of the Argentine Mesopotamia. These rivers were good locations for primitive communities, but archeological evidence indicates that they were occupied only near their mouths. On the right bank, the Paraná receives two tributaries which were of great significance in the life of the pre-Columbian populations. These are the Salado, which crosses the country from the border of the Puna de Atacama to Santa Fé, and the Carcarañá, which descends the Sierra de Comechingones. According to the geographical information which the Indians of Sancti Spíritu supplied to the explorer Cabot, it is evident that these two rivers, and especially the Salado, must have served as important routes of native commerce. Typical Paraná cultures had, however, penetrated only a few kilometers up the Salado, and no remains of the Paraná type have ever been discovered on the Carcarañá. In the northern part of the Province of Santa Fé, the rivers that run parallel to the Paraná before entering it duplicate its general environmental conditions.

The Delta embraces approximately 200 kilometers (125 miles) of the lower course of the Paraná. This extremely low region is intersected by a great number of streams, and it is subject to the tides of the Río de la Plata, which inundate it periodically. During these floods only a few small, unusually high areas remain above the waters. On such areas are found the remains of the indigenous peoples of the region.

The shores of the Paraná are covered, for the most part, with monte (shrub vegetation) of a Mesopotamian type. The abundance of the flora varies considerably according to the latitude or to which river bank is involved. A hydrophyllic vegetation thrives in the insular region of the Delta, the most common species being the willow (*Salix humboltiana*), the ceiba (*Erythrina crista-galli*), and the yatay palm (*Cocos yatay*), the last a conspicuous tree the fruit of which was used by the Indians. In general, the insular landscape is characterized by swamp and aquatic vegetation of extraordinary exhuberance.

The rich Paraná flora afforded the Indian refuge and materials for shelter, but it yielded no important food element. The fauna, however, abundantly satisfied almost all the needs of the early inhabitants.

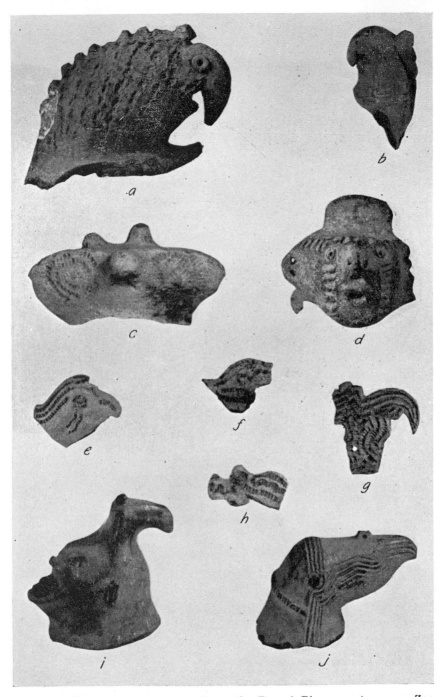

PLATE 9.—**Plastic representations from the Paraná River country.** *a-c*, Zoomorphic handles, Malabrigo; *d*, human-head handle, vicinity of city of Paraná; *e-h*, silhouette rim attachments; *i*, *j*, free representations of birds. (*a* and *c*, Approximately ½ actual size; *b* and *d*, approximately ⅔ actual size; *e-h*, approximately ⅓ actual size; *i* and *j*, approximately ⅕ actual size.) (Courtesy Museo Etnográfico de la Facultad de Filosofía y Letras, Buenos Aires.)

PLATE 10.—**Paraná River area sherds.** *a-e,* Incised lines with notched or punctated interiors ("drag-and-jab" technique); *f, g,* sherds of the insular delta complex. (Courtesy Museo Etnográfico de la Facultad de Filosofía y Letras, Buenos Aires.)

ETHNOGRAPHIC CONSIDERATIONS AND CONCLUSIONS

A brief analysis of the archeology of the Paraná demonstrates three distinct archeological complexes: two in the region of the Delta, and a third which is found along both shores of the river above the Delta. The accounts of the early European discoverers of this country indicate that the Indians whom they encountered belonged to different tribes or "nations." In interpreting the written sources by comparing them with the archeological evidence, it becomes clear that there were three outstanding aboriginal groups.

The first of these were the *Querandí,* who lived in the territory of Sancti Spíritu: The "people of the country," as Ramirez called them. Oviedo y Valdés (1851–55) says that they were inland dwellers, and Sebastian Cabot (*in* Medina, 1908) affirms that their territory extended to the foot of the mountains. They occasionally reached the coast, and this explains why their name was given to the creek at whose mouth the Portuguese explorer Lópes de Sousa set up two landmarks bearing the coat of arms of his king. Later, Mendoza, according to Ulrich Schmidel (1903), encountered the *Querandí* in the region where the Port of Santa María de Buen Aire was situated. These Indians, in spite of their presence on the coast, cannot be considered as typical inhabitants of the Paraná and are not treated in this paper. Undoubtedly, they did not form a tribe, properly speaking, but were a band or a group who, a little after the second founding of Buenos Aires, are no longer mentioned but became confused with the other Indians of the plains and were included under the general name of "Pampas."

The second important group were the *Guaraní,* who inhabited some of the islands and navigated the Paraná, "because they were the enemies of all the other nations," says Ramírez. The *Guaraní* left behind cemeteries with urn burials and other types of characteristic remains. Finally, the chroniclers mention a series of people who lived along the banks of the river: *Carcarai, Chana, Begua, Chana-Timbú, Timbú, Mocoretai, Camarao, Mepene.* All of these peoples were, evidently, small bands belonging to a larger group, the third major group of the area. The archeological evidence found along the shores of the Paraná verifies the testimony of the conquistadors who, although they gave many names to these people, left no doubt that culturally they were fundamentally uniform. To these people can be assigned the dominant archeological complex of the Paraná, characterized by the ceramic representations and accompanying other remains (Aparicio, 1928–29).

The sites, other than those of the *Guaraní,* which have been found on the "cerritos" (small elevations) of the Delta cannot yet be assigned to any of the people mentioned in the early literature. All that is known of these people is confined to the archeological materials themselves. These materials differ both from the Paraná complex of the ceramic plastic representations and from those of the *Guarani* sites. It is very possible that when the remains from some of the sites of the right margin of the Río de la Plata are better known that these will prove to have a close relationship with those from the Delta "cerritos."

HISTORY OF ARCHEOLOGICAL INVESTIGATIONS

The excavation of the "Túmulo Prehistórico de Campana," made around 1877 by Don Estanislão S. Zeballos and Pedro P. Pico (1878), began archeological research along the Paraná and was also the first systematic investigation of an Argentine archeological site. Several years later, in 1893–94, Ambrosetti found fragments of decorated pottery in Entre Ríos and a handsome collection of plastic representations in pottery from the site of Goya. Further field work was not attempted along the Paraná littoral until Frenguelli and the present author discovered important sites on the Malabrigo River. Other minor discoveries were also made by Frenguelli, by the author, and by Antonio Serrano.

The Delta of the Paraná is known from the works of L. M. Torres (1913) and from the recent excavations of the North American, Samuel K. Lothrop.

The bibliography relative to Paraná archeology includes important works of other authors—Ameghino, Lafone Quevedo, Outes, and Torres. These are, however, monographic treatments of selected themes and are based upon rapid exploratory trips, occasional discoveries, or library research. The present brief synthesis is based, for the most part, upon the personal investigations carried out in the lower Paraná region by the author. These investigations are only partly published.

ARCHEOLOGICAL SITES

SITES ALONG THE PARANÁ

Campana and Goya are the classic sites of the Paraná littoral. The first was studied with surprising care for the period in which the excavations were made (1877). The investigators stated, with regard to the nature of the mound:

We established *a priori* that this monument was a tumulus similar to those found in the different territories of Europe and the Americas. Its material consists of decayed vegetal substances and Quaternary deposits. Taking the form of an ellipse, its major diameter measures 79 varas [approximately 220 feet, or 70 m.]; the lesser diameter was 32 varas [approximately 90 ft., or 30 m.]; and its greatest height was 2½ varas [approximately 7 ft., or 2.2 m.] above the surrounding ground. [Zeballos and Pico, 1878.]

Zeballos defined the mound, on the basis of its general appearance, as a tumulus comparable to the earth monuments of other continents. At about the same time, some similar sites had been discovered by reliable amateurs in the lowlands of southern Entre Ríos. The coincidence of these discoveries was commented upon by Ameghino, shortly after this, leading to the supposition of the existence of a culture or "a people of the tumuli."

At Goya, Ambrosetti made very rapid and superficial observations, and his descriptions do not give a clear idea of the conditions under which he discovered the material which he describes. However, judging from investigations in many other sites along the Paraná, it is evident that Ambrosetti was investigating a site quite typical of the region. These sites are always found on the banks of the river or of its tributaries, and are situated on high ground above the zone of inundations. The cultural remains are always found at a very slight depth, immediately below the humus. They consist of potsherds, apparently scattered intentionally, hearths, remains of food, and human bones coming from secondary inhumations. The writer has noted sites of this type in Corrientes, in the vicinity of the city of Paraná, near Diamante and Victoria, in Gaboto and other places along the right bank of the Coronda, and in various localities north of the city of Santa Fé. A site of the same type, but located on low ground in the insular region, is Las Tejas, explored by Antonio Serrano, in the vicinity of the Lake of Coronda.

The better-known sites of the Paraná are, however, those of the right bank of the Malabrigo River. They are located upon a series of hills that extend a short distance from the edge of the river. Frenguelli remarks that, taking into account the "characteristic alignment [of these hills] upon the edge of a fluvial valley, and the nature and homogeneity of the materials that compose them," they must be interpreted "as ancient aeolian accumulations [sand dunes] more or less affected by later weather action, that shaped them in the form of hills, which are likely places, in these regions, for the refuge of indigenous populations" (Frenguelli and Aparicio, 1923). In all of the mounds explored, artifacts and human skeletal remains have been found at only a very slight depth in the sand.

SITES OF THE DELTA

In the insular region and the bordering lowlands of the Delta, a country subjected to periodic flooding or tidal action of the estuary of the Rio de la Plata, locations of aboriginal dwellings were limited to only a few elevated places, which are referred to today as "cerritos," or little hills. In them are found cultural refuse and human burials. Because of their appearance, as small mounds rising above the surrounding lowlands, these "cerritos" have been considered by some authorities, especially Torres, as true tumuli that were deliberately constructed by man. However, Lothrop, who has explored one of these "mounds," believes that their artificial elevation is the inadvertent accumulation of detritus left by human occupation. Outes, who explored a site of this type in Mazaruca, also tends to this latter view:

Mazaruca, as with the great majority of the other burial places in more or less isolated elevations, is a relatively consolidated sand dune. Some of these dunes are covered by a cap of humus, deep enough to be considered the product of the slow transformation of the coarse quartz sand which forms the underlying material of the dune, and to which has been added continuously detritus carried by floods and the decomposed organic matter from the rank vegetation that covers the surface ot the marsh. [Outes, 1912.]

The author has had occasion to investigate a similar site in "La Argentina," in the region of Mazaruca, and concurs with Outes (Aparicio, 1928). It is unfortunate that a comprehensive study of the geological nature of the "cerritos" has not yet been made.

CULTURAL REMAINS

THE PARANÁ LITTORAL

Plastic representations.—The sites along the shores of the Paraná are characterized by modeled pottery figures or plastic representations, with which are associated quantities of potsherds, plain, incised, and, in a few cases, painted. By and large, however, the materials, which are almost exclusively ceramics, are of rather poor quality and of monotonous uniformity.

All of the plastic representations are hand-made, and knowledge of molds was lacking. All of the figures conform to a definite art style which distinguishes them from comparable pottery representations found in other American areas.[1] The native artists of the Paraná interpreted the regional fauna with surprising talent and sensibility. They were sometimes able to reproduce nature with a masterly realism; in other instances, they modified the form until they achieved stylizations of a disconcerting audacity. Both types of depiction are usually complemented by incised decoration which is purely geometric and in no sense zoomorphic characterizations.

The plastic representations, in some cases, were adornos on pottery vessels, serving either as handles or simply as added ornaments. The figure handles are bulky and are attached to the vessel walls; the purely decorative adornos are silhouette forms which appear to have been added to the rims as an extention of the vessel wall. In both cases, the figures have the same paste, firing, finish, etc., as the vessels of which they form a part.

---

[1] Attention has often been called to the analogies existing between the plastic representations of the Paraná and of the Amazon and other regions of the continent. Nordenskiöld in studying this problem contrasted a series of schematic drawings. As in such schemes, the sculptures have lost all stylistic quality, and the resemblances of one with the other are therefore surprising. However, anyone who has seen an appreciable quantity of plastic representations of the Paraná and of the Amazon, and who has some artistic sensibility, would not hesitate to declare the analogy to be of theme and not of style.

The function of the separate or free figures can only be conjectured. They differ from the attached figures in being larger and usually solid rather than hollow, as is the case with the latter.

At the sites of Malabrigo, Resistencia, Campana, and Goya, the figures are almost exclusively of the attached type. In sites of the river country of Santa Fé, between San José del Rincón and Gaboto, and in those along the banks of the Paraná between the city of Paraná and the Delta (such as Las Tejas), the free figures have been found in greater abundance. As there is a fairly adequate bibliography upon this subject, only a few typical examples of the plastic representations will be illustrated and discussed here. Plate 9, *a,* a handle figure from Malabrigo, is a magnificent example of interpretative realism. Although executed in a slovenly manner and free of all technical preoccupation, it unites surprising elements of expression and life. The beak is exaggerated in its dimensions but faithfully portrayed; the fierce expression of the eye and the tufted crest give the head a singular dynamism and exceptional vitality. The decorations of the piece have been executed with a marked lack of prolixity. They consist simply of a series of parallel rows of punctations that run perpendicular to the tufted crest and cover both sides of the face. Below, and at the sides of the beak, this simple ornamental feature is repeated in smaller size. Another handle representation from Malabrigo (pl. 9, *b*) is a good example of extreme stylization. Although this head has the same general characteristics as the last, the artist's intent was obviously different. His interest was not in achieving sincere realism, but in producing a graceful and elegant formalism, which he accomplished with admirable simplicity by portraying a beak of disproportionate size and a long undulant crest which extends down the back of the head. The crest plays an important decorative role, complementing two grooved projections at the sides of the head. Ornamentation is limited to some parallel zigzag lines. This particular specimen is almost completely covered with red ocher.

The great parrots were the preferred subjects of the native sculptors of the Paraná littoral, and representations of them constitute an overwhelming majority of known specimens. Other birds and animals were also portrayed. Plate 9, *c,* another handle specimen from Malabrigo, is a beautiful example of an owl. The artist has retained only features necessary to the characterization: Eyes, "horns," and beak. He has represented them with great ease and assurance.

The artists made human representations much less often than animals, and with less success. An example of accentuated human realism is the little head (pl. 9, *d*) from the vicinity of the city of Paraná.

No intact vessel has yet been discovered with two figure handles attached, but the great number of rim sherds with such attachments leaves little doubt that such handles were used on vessels, e. g., figure 4, a nearly complete specimen from Las Tejas, Santa Fé. The handles on this piece are of an exceptional type, as the zoomorphic figure has been depicted as an entire body rather than by the usual practice of simply showing it as a head (Aparicio, 1925).

FIGURE 4.—Paraná River vessel with zoomorphic handles. (Courtesy Museo Etnográfico de la Facultad de Filosofía y Letras, Buenos Aires.)

The silhouette rim attachments which the author first discovered and published some years ago, are definitely in the artistic style of the Paraná plastic representations (pl. 9, *e-h*). The silhouettes have been made by cutting out the outline of the animal which is being represented from a flat piece of clay. The surfaces of the figures are then treated somewhat in the manner of relief sculpture, in some cases to augment the characterization intended, and in others simply to decorate the figures. [Aparicio, 1923.]

Various examples of separate or free representations, either complete or fragmentary, have been examined by the author. Plate 9, *i*, can be considered typical. Artistically, it is contemptible. The heavy modeled parrot is scarcely recognizable. The head reproduced in plate 9, *j*, though of unusual beauty, is no doubt a similar piece. Although the subject has been drastically conventionalized, the essential characteristics—beak, crest, and throat—enable one to recognize it immediately as a royal condor. The head is covered with incised decoration, which, as usual, is disconnected and seems to lack design plan.

Pottery.—Plastic representations are always found in association with plain, incised, and painted potsherds. Some instances of combined painting and incision have also been noted. Various ornamental combinations have been made with incised lines, but these have not yet been systematically analyzed. These decorative combinations show some similarity to comparable pottery decorations from other primitive cultures. However, the exact nature of these incised decorations, and the manner in which they have been executed, is characteristic of the Paraná littoral. Incision was made in the soft paste by a small pointed instrument which effected a series of successive impressions, or a groove with a notched interior. These notched grooved lines ("drag-and-jab") vary considerably, depending upon the size and shape of the instrument used. Plate 10, *a-e,* shows a random selection of such sherds. At a glance one can see the identity of the pottery decorations with those found on the plastic representations.

In addition, pottery decorated with incised lines and separate punctations is not lacking. Pottery may also have the most elementary sort of decorative treatment: fingernail impressions and finger-and-fingernail impressions in various combinations. These latter types are, nevertheless, in the minority, and they cannot be considered as typical manifestations of the culture. (See concluding section of *Guaraní* influences.)

The people of the Paraná littoral apparently had the custom of intentionally destroying their pottery and other ceramic artifacts. Because of this, very few complete specimens are now extant. The sherds, however, reveal that there were various vessel forms, some small and carefully made, others large, coarse, and without decoration. There is only one good example of a vessel of the finer ware; but there are, perhaps, a dozen of the large coarse vessels. These latter are usually subglobular in shape. All complete vessels have been brought together in a special monograph (Iribarne, 1937).

Miscellaneous ceramic objects.—Exceptionally, in some sites, pipes, pendants, and spindle whorls have been found.

Nonceramic objects.—Artifacts of stone or bone are extremely scarce. In Malabrigo, the stone industry can be considered nonexistent; in Goya, four worked stone artifacts and several bolas were found; in Campana, Zeballos and Pico mention the finding of 150 pieces of worked and polished stone. Unfortunately, this last material was lost and there is no description available. However, the exceptional lithic representation at Campana can be satisfactorily explained if it is realized that the site lies on the periphery of the Paraná littoral culture. This stone artifact complex was probably the result of contact with neighboring peoples.

Bone artifacts are similar to stone artifacts in their occurrence. Their presence at Campana, again, must be explained by the geographical location of the site.

THE PARANÁ DELTA

The Delta culture of the "cerritos."—Although the general aspect of the Delta sites is more or less uniform, the contents of these sites is variable. Some sites contain urn burials accompanied by a very characteristic artifact complex. Other sites have direct inhumations accompanied unspecialized ceramics and bone artifacts. The latter correspond to sites already mentioned, with the exception of Arroyo Malo explored by Lothrop (1932).

The sites with the direct inhumations and the nondistinctive archeological content, represent the insular culture of the "cerritos," presumably the remains of the ancient occupants of the Delta. In addition to being little specialized, and lacking in definitive characteristics, the pottery and artifacts from the "cerritos" are very scarce. Skeletal remains, on the other hand, are quite abundant. The potsherds that have been found show very simple line and punctate combinations. They differ, significantly, from those attributed to the peoples of the *Guaycurú* family, and, even more strikingly, from the well-known *Guaraní* ceramics. In plate 10, *f, g,* are shown sherds from the sites of the insular Delta complex. (Cf. with pl. 10, *a-e.*)

A stone industry is very poorly represented in these Delta sites. Those artifacts found probably were trade pieces received from neighboring peoples. Artifacts of bone and horn, such as awls, punches, and points, although not highly specialized or differentiated, are the most typical.

Guaraní influences.—Various sites of the Delta are characterized by great funerary urns. Despite the fact that investigations at only one such site have been fully published (Lothrop, 1932, Arroyo Malo), the artifact complex associated with this culture of the urn burials is well known and is attributed to the *Guaraní* peoples. The distribution of *Guaraní* finds is very extensive, allowing comparisons with similar discoveries made in relatively remote regions, such as the upper Paraná and the upper Paraguay Rivers. In addition, they are also found throughout the entire geographical area to which we have been referring in this paper. Sometimes these *Guaraní*-type finds are found by themselves; in other instances they are found as intrusions into archeological strata of other cultures.

The *Guaraní* funerary urns have peculiar forms. The surfaces are plain or fingernail marked, or, more rarely, they are completely or partially painted with polychrome decorations (fig. 5; pls. 11, 12). Fragments of pottery are also found in association with the burial urns. These suggest vessels of different forms and uses which have been decorated in a similar manner to the funerary vessels.

There are also typical stone artifacts in association with the above pottery. These are polished axes and lip plugs of various forms.

BIBLIOGRAPHY

Ambrosetti, 1893, 1894; Ameghino, 1880–81; Aparicio, 1923, 1925, 1928, 1928–1929; Cabot (*in* Medina, 1908); Frenguelli and Aparicio, 1923; Iribarne, 1937; Lafone-Quevedo, 1909; Lothrop, 1932; Outes, 1912; Oviedo y Valdés, 1851–55; Schmidel, 1903; Torres, L. M., 1913; Zeballos and Pico, 1878.

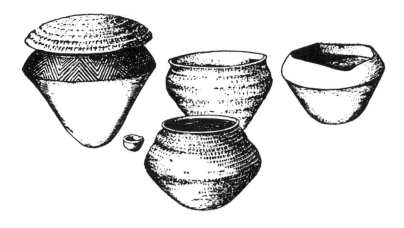

FIGURE 5.—*Guaraní* pottery from the Paraná Delta. *Top:* Painted, fingernail-marked, and plain wares. *Bottom:* Painted urn (height, 18 inches (44.5 cm.)). (Courtesy Museo Etnográfico de la Facultad de Filosofía y Letras, Buenos Aires; and after Lothrop, 1932, pl. 10.)

THE GUARANÍ

By ALFRED MÉTRAUX

TRIBAL DIVISIONS

The area inhabited by the *Guaraní* (map 1, *No. 1*; see Volume 1, map 7) has shrunk considerably since the 16th century. Today the *Guaraní* who have preserved their cultural identity form isolated islands in Paraguay and southern Brazil. The subtribes mentioned by Spanish conquistadors and missionaries have disappeared, and the names which designate modern *Guaraní* groups are fairly recent and appear in the literature only in the 18th century. Therefore, it is necessary to deal with ancient and modern *Guaraní* as if they were separate entities. The *Guaraní* language, however, is still spoken by Mestizos, or acculturated Indians, in most of the territory where it was used at the time of the Conquest. The rural population of Paraguay is often called *Guaraní*. Therefore, in order to avoid confusion between these modern civilized *Guaraní* and their primitive contemporaries, we shall always refer to the latter as *Cainguá*.

Guaraní of the 16th and 17th centuries.—The *Guaraní* were first known as *Carijó* or *Cario*, but the name *Guaraní* finally prevailed in the 17th century. At this time, the *Guaraní* were the masters of the Atlantic Coast from Barra de Cananea to Rio Grande do Sul, (lat. 26°–33° S., long. 48°–52° W.) and from there their groups extended to the Paraná, Uruguay, and Paraguay Rivers.

Guaraní groups, called by the early chroniclers "Guaraní de las islas," *Chandris,* or *Chandules,* lived in the 16th century on the islands of the Río de la Plata, and on the southern side of the Paraná Delta from San Isidro to the vicinity of the Carcarañá River (lat. 34° S., long. 58° W.) There were some *Guaraní* enclaves along the Uruguayan shore, at Martín Chico, and from San Lazaro to San Salvador. Pottery vessels of unmistakable *Guaraní* origin have been found near San Francisco Soriano and Concordia in Uruguay, on the island of Martín García and at Arroyo Malo, between the Luján River and the Paraná de las Palmas River.

On the eastern side of the Uruguay River, the borderline between the *Charrua* and the bulk of the *Guaraní* nation ran near Yapeyú. On the western side, the *Guarani* occupied all the land from Yapeyú to the Paraná River (Serrano, 1936, p. 121). From the junction of the Paraná and Paraguay Rivers, *Guarani* villages were distributed continuously up the eastern side of the Paraguay River and up both sides of the Paraná River. They reached north to the Mbotetey (Miranda) River (lat. 20° S.,), and east probably to the Serras de Amambay and Maracayú. The *Guarani* were especially numerous in the Paraná Basin and in the Province of Guairá. There were also countless settlements along the tributaries of the Paraná River, the boundary between the *Tupinakin* and *Guarani* being approximately the Tieté River. The *Guarani* extended south to the Province of Tapé (today, Serra Geral).

Although *Guarani* was the generic name of this widespread people, the Spaniards in the 16th and 17th centuries distinguished local tribes by special names. Around Lagoa dos Patos, the *Guarani* were called *Arechane* (lat. 32° S., long. 51° W.) ; from the Apa River to the Mbotetey (Miranda) River, *Itatin* (lat. 22° S., long. 57° W.) ; in the Serra Geral and Rio Grande do Sul, *Tapé* (lat. 30° S., long. 52° W.) ; around San Estanislao and San Joaquín, *Tobatin;* on the Ypané River, *Guarambaré* (lat. 23° S., long. 56° W.) ; and on the Ivahy (Ivahyete) River, *Taioba.* Tribes with a different language and culture, such as the *Caingang,* or with a different culture, such as the *Guayaki,* were scattered among the *Guarani.*

In the second half of the 17th century, the *Northern Guarani* or *Itatin,* were driven south by the *Mbayá-Guaicurú,* a Chaco tribe.

Modern Guaraní tribes.—Since the 18th century, the *Guarani* groups who had remained independent and had not been collected in missions have been distinguished from the Christianized *Guarani* by the name *Cainguá* (*Kaa-thwua, Kaingua, Cayuá, Monteses*), which means "Inhabitants of the Forest."

About 1800, the *Cainguá* (*Caagua*) inhabited the headwaters of the Iguatemí River, extending north toward the upper Miranda River to Cerro Pyta in the Cordillera de San José near the headwaters of the Ypané River. They also lived near the Jejuí-guazú (Jejuí) and the Aguaray-guazú Rivers and in the vicinity of the cities of Curuguaty, San Joaquín, and San Estanislao (Azara, 1904, p. 407).

The *Cainguá* proper lived on the Ypané River, the *Carima* in the Serra Maracayú (lat. 23° S., long. 54° W.), and the *Taruma* east of the Yhú River (lat. 24° S., long. 56° W.).

The Indians who at the end of the 18th century lived on the right side of the Paraná River between the Guarapay and Monday Rivers and on the left side of the Paraná River from Corpus to the Iguassú River, were known as *Guayana* (lat. 26° S., long. 56° W.). A group of these *Guayana* still exists at Villa Azara on the stream Pirá-pyta. These *Guarani*-speaking *Guayaná* should not be confused with the ancient

Guayaná of São Paulo and Paraná, who were *Caingang* Indians (Azara, 1904, p. 406).

Modern *Cainguá* (*Caaiguá*) are divided into three groups:

(1) The *Mbyá* (*Mbwiha, Ava-mbihá, Caayguá, Apyteré, Baticola*), who occupy the forested spurs of the Serra de Maracayú (lat. 25°–27° S., long. 55° W.) and the region around Corpus in the Argentine territory of Misiones. Groups of *Mbyá* (or *Cainguá*) are even more widely scattered in Mato Grosso and in the States of Paraná and Rio Grande do Sul.

(2) The *Chiripá,* who live south of the Jejuá-guazú River and are also reported on the right and left sides of the upper Paraná River, along the Yuytorocaí River and north of the Iguassú River (lat. 25° S., long. 54°–56° W.).

(3) The *Pañ'* (*Terenõhẽ*), who live north of the Jejui-guazú River.

Of these three groups, the *Mbyá* have remained the closest to their ancient *Guaraní* culture; the *Chiripá* are the most acculturated.

There are also several groups of *Cainguá* or *Guaraní* in Brazil. The *Apapocuva* (lat. 24° S., long. 54° W.) regard themselves as distinct from the Paraguayan *Cainguá* although they are closely related to them. Before they started in 1870 trekking east in search of the Land-Without-Evil (see below, p. 93), they lived on the lower Iguatemí River, in the southern tip of the State of Mato Grosso. In 1912, 200 still lived on the Iguatemí River; about 200 in the reservation of Araribá, in the State of São Paulo; 100 on the Rio das Cinzas, in the State of Paraná; about 70 in Potrero Guazú, in Mato Grosso; and about 40 at the mouth of the Ivahí River. The *Tañyguá,* who also made this trek, resided on the Paraná River near the Iguatemí River (lat. 23° S., long. 54° W.). After a long migration which took them to the Atlantic Coast, they became established on the Rio de Peixe and the Itariry River, where a few of them still remained in 1912.

The ancient habitat of the *Oguauíva,* from which they migrated toward the Ocean in 1830, was situated near the Serra de Maracayú (lat. 24° S., long 54° W.). In 1912, 100 *Oguauíva* lived in the reservation of Araribá, and 40 near the coast.

The other *Cainguá* groups who, according to Nimuendajú (1914 a, p. 293), lived in southern Brazil about 1912 were: The *Cheiru,*[1] near the mouth of the Iguatemí; the *Avahuguai,* on the Dourados; the *Paiguaçu,* on the Curupaynã River (Mato Grosso); the *Yvytyiguá,* opposite the Serra do Diabo, in the State of Paraná; the *Avachiripá,* on the left side of the Paraná (State of Paraná); the *Catanduva Jatahy,* in the same State.

The *Apapocuva, Tañyguá, Oguauíva,* and *Cheiru* are regarded as *Guaraní* whereas the *Avahuguai, Paiguaçu, Yvytyiguá, Avachiripá,* and

---

[1] There are also *Cheiru* in Paraguay near the Guaira Falls.

Catanduvá are designated in Brazil under the generic term of *Caiuá* (*Kayguá*).

The *Ivaparé* (*Aré, Shetá*), erroneously called *Botocudo* or *Notobotocudo* because of their wooden labrets, are a *Guaraní*-speaking group living on the Ivahy River, near the Ranharanha (Ariranha) Cachoeira (lat. 24° S., long. 53° W.). These Indians have abandoned farming, and roam in the forests like the *Guayaki* (Borba, 1904, Loukotka, 1929).

At present most of the *Cainguá* groups are in constant contact with the Mestizos and Whites, and many *Cainguá* work as peons in the estancias, in the maté or lumber camps. With the earned money they buy clothes, tools, food, pots, sugar, and salt. Consequently, they have abandoned weaving and even their native ware. On the other hand, they still cultivate the same plants as their ancestors.

Population.—Nimuendajú (1914 a, p. 293) estimated in 1912 the total number of the Brazilian *Cainguá* at about 3,000.

Sources.—Information on the ancient *Guaraní* is scanty and fragmentary, but can be supplemented by our better knowledge of their descendants, the numerous *Cainguá* tribes of Paraguay and southern Brazil. Moreover, from all available evidence, ancient *Guaraní* culture appears to be basically like that of their neighbors and kinsmen, the coastal *Tupí*.

Most of the data on the ancient *Guaraní* used in this chapter come from the "Comentarios de Alvar Nuñez Cabeza de Vaca" (see Pedro Hernández, 1852), Schmidel (1903), Ruíz de Montoya's (1892) "Conquista espiritual," and the "Cartas anuas de la Compañia de Jesus" (1927–29). Del Techo (1673, 1897) and Lozano (1873–75), who often have been regarded among our best authorities on the *Guaraní,* obtained most of their data from Jesuit reports (Cartas anuas).

The earliest description of the *Cainguá* appears in Dobrizhoffer (1874). Azara's (1809, 1904) often-quoted passages on the *Guaraní* should be used with caution. Rengger (1835) in the beginning of the 19th century and Vogt (1904), Ambrosetti (1895 b), and Vellard (1939 a) in recent times have contributed good information on the material culture of the Paraguayan *Cainguá*. On the *Cayuá* of Southern Brazil, we have a monograph by Von Koenigswald (1908). The outstanding sources on the modern *Guaraní,* or *Cainguá,* are a monograph by Nimuendajú (1914 a) on the religion and mythology of the *Apapocuva-Guaraní,* and a series of studies by Father Franz Müller (1934–35) on the Paraguayan *Cainguá*.

Pablo Hernández's (1913) monumental work is the most complete modern source on the history and organization of the Jesuit missions. Cardiel's (1900) "Declaración de la verdad" and Muratori's (1754) "Nouvelles des missions du Paraguay" are excellent 18th-century treatises on life in the missions.

ARCHEOLOGY OF THE GUARANÍ AREA

Many archeological finds have been made in the area formerly inhabited by the *Guaraní,* but only a few systematic investigations have ever been undertaken of ancient sites or cemeteries. The attribution of some of the remains unearthed in former *Guaraní* territory is often uncertain because the *Guaraní* seem to have been late comers in the regions where we find them in the 16th century. They were preceded by people of different prehistoric cultures, some of which, such as the *Caingang,* have survived up to the present. The main problems center around classification of stone implements, which cannot always be easily distinguished from those produced by the early non-*Guaraní* population. Pottery, however, leaves little or no margin for doubt. The aboriginal occupants of Paraguay or southern Brazil had either no ceramics or else only a very crude ware. *Guaraní* ware presents the following features: A corrugated decoration produced by thumb impressions on the soft clay, linear designs in red and black on a whitish background, and the use of large conical chicha jars as funeral urns (pls. 11, 12).

There is a striking resemblance between the pottery of the ancient *Tupinamba* of the coast (Netto, 1885; Ihering, 1904) and that of the *Guaraní* of Paraguay. The modern *Chiriguano,* descendants of *Guaraní* invaders from Paraguay, still make chicha jars almost identical in shape and decoration to those which are so often unearthed in their home country. Moreover, typical *Guaraní* vases have been found associated with rosin labrets, a lip ornament still worn by modern *Cainguá.*

Direct, or primary, urn burial was the usual form of interment among the *Guaraní* and persists among the *Chiriguano* of Bolivia. Archeology has amply confirmed the statements of early writers. The corpse was forced with the limbs flexed into a jar and covered with another vessel.

Ihering (1895, 1904), Mayntzhusen (1912), Ullrich (1906), Kunert (1890, 1891, 1892), Kunike (1911), Meyer (1896), Ambrosetti (1895 b), Vellard (1934), and Linné (1936) have described isolated finds. Max Schmidt (1932) has given a list of recent discoveries and has attempted to make a classification of the rich archeological material in the Museum of Asunción. Pottery of unmistakable *Guaraní* origin has been collected on the islands of the Paraná Delta (pl. 11, *top, center*). They have been published and discussed by L. M. Torres (1913) and Outes (1917, 1918). Lothrop (1932, pp. 122-146) has given us a careful description of the results of his investigation in a *Guaraní* cemetery at Arroyo Malo, a small tributary of the Luján River, east of El Tigre, in the Province of Buenos Aires. Serrano (1936) has dealt with *Guaraní* archeology in connection with his study of the ancient native cultures of Uruguay.

The ware found in areas historically occupied by *Guaraní* tribes consists mainly of funeral urns, large plates or vessels used as lids for these urns, and some pots which formed part of the funerary equipment.

Funeral urns, which originally were chicha jars, are of two main types: (1) those decorated on the upper part with rows of corrugated impressions or markings produced either with the fingers or with a stick, and (2) painted ones.

The urns of the first category usually have a conical shape with a bulging upper part and a low outflaring or direct rim (pl. 11, *bottom, left*). Those of the second type are usually biconical with a flat or rounded bottom and a direct rim which often presents a median ridge (pl. 12, *a*). The height of the urns normally varies between 40 to 70 cm. (16 to 28 in.) and their diameter between 46 to 76 cm. (19 to 50 in.). A few specimens are one meter (3 ft.) high.

Smaller vessels are (1) undecorated, (2) covered on their entire outer surface by fingernail marks (pl. 11), (3) painted (pl. 12), and (4) painted on the inside and decorated with fingernail marks or corrugated impressions on the outside.

Several nail-incised vessels were found by Ambrosetti (1895 b) on the Alto Paraná and by Lothrop (1932, pp. 134–135) at Arroyo Malo, near Buenos Aires, and at Paraná-Guazú.

Most of the specimens of small ware known up to the present are shallow bowls, or bowls with inverted rims. Some painted specimens have a characteristic biconical shape with a flat bottom. A few globular pots with outflaring rims seem to have been used in cooking. A single specimen with a tubular neck has been published by Vellard (1934, fig. 8, *3*).

Some of the funeral urns and wide bowls found by Lothrop at Arroyo Malo are covered with a grayish slip and are adorned with red paint on the exterior.

The decoration of the polychrome urns and bowls consists generally of red lines on a whitish background, but sometimes white patterns have been traced on a red background. Often the red designs are underscored by black strokes or bordered by incisions. On a few specimens coarse red patterns have been applied directly on the surface of the vessel. The motifs are always geometrical. They may be described as sigmoid curves, labyrinths, Greek frets, and elaborations of the chevron. A few vessels are decorated with plain red bands on a white background.

Many urns show on their lower portions striations resulting from the use of corn husks in the smoothing process.

Guaraní vessels are, as a rule, without handles, though, according to Mayntzhusen (1912, p. 465), they may occur in a few instances. Some vessels were suspended through holes in the rim or through lateral prominences.

At Arroyo Malo were found some clay "hemispheres," or lumps decorated with incised patterns. Lothrop (1932, p. 143) calls them fire dogs, that is to say, supports for pots, a hypothesis completely unconfirmed. No object of that type has been found in any other *Guarani* region.

A fragment of a double vessel found at Arroyo Malo suggests a type of bowl used by the *Chiriguano,* though these modern vessels are obviously copied after European yerba maté containers. An effigy vessel collected at Arroyo Malo is definitely alien to *Guarani* culture as known through archeology.

Crude stone drills, knives, hammers, and arrow-shaft polishers are listed by Mayntzhusen (1912, p. 463) among the stone objects he picked up from refuse heaps on the upper Paraná River. He also mentions quartz lip plugs. Simple neolithic stone axes without any groove have been found in *Guarani* sites of the upper Paraná River, on the island of Martín García, and at Arroyo Malo. Lothrop (1932, p. 145) describes two fragmentary bolas from Arroyo Malo. One is well made with a broad groove; the other is roughly shaped with a narrow groove. Outes (1917, fig. 28) figures also a grooved bola obtained at Martín Garcia. The bola was not a *Guarani* weapon and its use seems to have been limited to the *Guarani* of the Delta.

Hammerstones, roughly shaped by abrasion and including some pitted ones, have come to light in the excavations of Arroyo Malo.

The bone artifacts which Mayntzhusen claims to have collected on ancient sites of the Paraná River include needles, weaver daggers, spatulae, fishhooks, and flutes. He also discovered perforated shell disks and some human or animal teeth which were parts of a necklace.

THE CONQUEST

No mineral wealth has ever been exploited in Paraguay, but metal objects found among the aborigenes of this country in the 16th century brought about the conquest of the entire basin of the Rio de la Plata. The gold and silver, which members of the Solis expedition obtained from the *Guarani* and other Indians of this region, had come originally from the *Inca* Empire. At the end of the 15th century, probably under the reign of Inca Yupanqui, bands of *Guarani* had crossed the Chaco to raid the peaceful *Chané* along the *Inca* frontier and even attacked tribes directly under *Inca* rule. Some of these *Guarani* bands settled in the conquered territories; others returned loaded with loot. Groups, small and large, followed the first invaders and renewed their assaults against the "people of the metal." The number of metal objects which reached Paraguay and the Rio de la Plata in this manner must have been considerable for, from the beginning of the Conquest, regions which actually had nothing to entice the Spaniards were the object of their most violent covetousness. These regions became the gateway to El Dorado.

The first positive information on the "Sierra de la Plata" or "Tierra rica" was obtained by Alejo García, who, with a few other white men, joined a *Guaraní* raid against the *Inca* border. He wrote of his discovery to his companions who had remained in Santa Catarina. When Sebastian Cabot landed at Pernambuco in 1526, he had been told of gold and silver in the region of the Rio de la Plata. Later, in Santa Catarina he obtained more detailed information from Alejo García's companions and heard that "near the sierra there was a white king, dressed like a Spaniard," and that Garcia and his companions had seen mines and had spoken with the Indians who lived near the sierra and "wore silver crowns on their heads and gold plates hanging from their necks and ears and attached around their belts." With his letter, García had sent specimens of the metal. Convinced that they had reached El Dorado, Sebastian Cabot abandoned his intended journey to the East Indies and decided to ascend the Rio de la Plata, where he was assured he could "load a ship with gold and silver." Cabot sailed the Paraná and then the Paraguay River to its junction with the Pilcomayo River. Ramirez, in his famous letter recounting the Cabot expedition, says that, "the *Guaraní* Indians of the region of Santa Ana wear many ear pendants and pendants of gold and silver," and that a brigantine's crew saw the same things somewhat upstream. Through an interpreter, the Spaniards learned that the *Chandule,* who were Indians of the same tribe living 180 miles (60 leagues) up the Paraguay River, "traded gold to the Guaraní for beads and canoes." The *Chandule,* who were probably the *Guaraní* of the region of Itatí, had much metal, "according to the Indians, because women and children went from their settlements to the mountain and brought back the aforesaid metal" (Ramírez *in* Medina, J. T., 1908, p. 456).

The Cabot expedition was a failure, but the reports about the Sierra de la Plata, the *Caracara* Indians (i.e., the *Quechua* Indians of Charcas), and the silver and gold of the *Guaraní* were avidly received by the Spaniards and led to the expedition of Adelantado Pedro de Mendoza. In 1536, Mendoza sent Juan de Ayolas up the Paraguay River to find a route to the land of the *Caracara.* Ayolas ascended the Paraguay River to the Port of Candelaria, at lat. 19° S., whence, led by a former slave of García, he crossed the Chaco through the land of the *Mbayá,* and reached the *Caracara.* Like Alejo García, he returned "with 20 loads of gold and silver," but, on reaching the Paraguay River, he and his companions were massacred by the *Payagua* Indians (1538). A year earlier, Juan de Salazar de Espinosa had founded the city of Asunción. The *Cario* (*Guaraní*), who understood the aim of the Spaniards and who hoped to make them allies in their raids, were extremely friendly to the Spaniards, and provided them with food and women. Henceforth, the *Guaraní* served as auxiliaries and porters in all Spanish expeditions, whether to the Chaco or to the Andes. When Alvar Nuñez Cabeza de Vaca fought the *Mbayá-Guaicurú* in 1542, he was assisted by 10,000

Guarani, who gathered at Tapuá. Two thousand *Guarani* accompanied Domingo de Irala in 1548 and even more followed Nufrio de Chaves in 1558.

The *Guarani* later resisted the ruthless exploitation of which they were victims (for example, the revolts of Tabaré and Guarambaré), but they lacked the determination and unity shown by other tribes so that their revolts were easily crushed. Later *Guarani* rebellions were often led by native messiahs, the most famous of whom was Obera (end of the 16th century), who promised the Indians supernatural support and convinced them that the happiness of native times would be restored after the final expulsion of the White men.

From the outset, the conquistadors, like the European colonists on the coast of Brazil, were strongly attracted by the beauty of the *Guarani* women—who readily yielded to their solicitations—and took native wives or mistresses. As some of these were daughters and sisters of local chiefs, the alliances proved useful to the Spaniards, for the Indians felt obliged to support and serve their new relatives. The Spaniards lived scattered in small ranches around Asunción, surrounded by harems (some with 20 to 30 women), and by their wives' relatives.

The young colony came to consist of a rapidly growing Mestizo population, without which it would have been abandoned soon after the Conquest of Perú. The system of encomiendas, introduced in the middle of the 16th century, had the usual dire effects on the native population. Forced to work for their masters and often ill-treated, the Indians died by the thousands. At the end of the 16th century, there remained within a radius of 21 miles (7 leagues) around Asunción, only 3,000 Indians. The region of Tapuá, north of Asunción, which had been covered with ranches, was practically abandoned. The disappearance of the natives, however, was compensated by the constant increase of the Mestizos, or "mancebos de la tierra," whose lawlessness is often stressed by Spanish chroniclers. These descendants of early Spaniards and *Guarani* form the main element in the million or so people of modern Paraguay, so that their language is still spoken in rural Paraguay, in the Argentine territory of Misiones, and in the State of Corrientes. Even in cities, such as Asunción, part of the population still uses the language of their *Guarani* ancestors.

The missions.—Unlike the *Guarani* under the Spanish encomiendas, that portion of the tribe which occupied the upper Paraná River and the Uruguay River basin was subject to Jesuit missions for about two centuries (1608–1767). Their post-Conquest history, therefore, is identical with that of the missions. The first Jesuits (Juan Solano, Manuel de Ortega, and Tomas Filds) arrived in Asunción in 1588. Two of these fathers went to the region of El Guairá, a territory defined on the west by the Paraná River, on the north by the Tieté River, on the south by the Iguassú

River, and in the east by a vague line drawn by the treaty of Tordesillas. Here, the Spaniards had founded two cities, Ciudad real del Guairá (1554) and Villarica. The two Jesuits visited numerous Indian villages, baptizing children and moribunds, but they did not establish any permanent mission. In 1609, the King of Spain, at the request of Hernandarias de Saavedra, Governor of Paraguay, granted the Jesuits permission to conquer the 150,000 *Guarani* Indians of El Guairá, by "means of doctrines and by the preaching of the Gospel."

The first Jesuit mission in Paraguay was San Ignacio Guazú, founded north of the Paraná River, but the first establishments of El Guairá (Nuestra Señora de Loreto and San Ignacio-mirí on the Pirapo River), which were to become so prosperous, were created in 1610 by Fathers José Cataldino and Simon Maceta. The apostle of the *Guairá* was the famous Antonio Ruíz de Montoya, founder of 11 missions between 1622 and 1629 and author of the great classic of *Guarani* language, the "Arte, vocabulario, tesoro de la lengua Guaraní" (1876). In another book, "Conquista espiritual . . . del Paraguay" (1892), he reports his adventures and successes and the ruin of the missions. In 1630, the flourishing missions of El Guairá were destroyed by the raids of slave hunters from São Paulo, the dreaded mamelucos, who attacked the missions and captured all whom they did not slaughter. In a few years, they are said to have killed or enslaved 300,000 *Guarani* Indians. From 1628 to 1630 they took 60,000 Indians from the Jesuit missions to São Paulo. In 1631 Ruíz de Montoya evacuated Loreto and San Ignacio, the two last missions to survive in El Guairá, and took the people in a heroic anabasis from El Guairá to the Paraná River. Twelve thousand Indians began this forced migration but only 4,000 survived its vicissitudes.

The northern territory of the *Guarani*, between the Paraguay, Mbotetey (Miranda), and Jejui-guazú Rivers and the Sierra de Amambay, was called the Province of Itatin after one of its local *Guarani* subtribes. The Jesuits founded four missions here in 1631, but in 1632 these were all destroyed by the mamelucos from São Paulo. Later, two new missions were founded in the same area.

The same year the Jesuits entered the mountainous region in the Brazilian State of Rio Grande do Sul, which forms the divide between the basins of the Uruguay and the Jacui Rivers. This was formerly called Tapé, but today only a branch of the mountain system is known as Sierra de los Tapes; the remainder is known as Sierra de San Martín and Cuchilla Grande. From 1632 to 1635, the Jesuits founded 10 "reducciones" here. The renewed assaults of the mamelucos in 1638 forced the Jesuits to evacuate the missions of Tapé, a region that was forever lost to Portugal. After these last inroads, the *Guarani* Indians received guns and, on two occasions—at Caazapá-guazú and at Mbororé (1639 and 1640)—they defeated the mamelucos. From 1687 to 1707, eight new missions were founded which, together with the others, formed the 30 cities of the so-called "Paraguayan State of the Jesuits."

The Jesuit expansion was resisted by certain *Guarani* shamans, chiefs, and especially messiahs, who seem to have been very numerous in this period of hardship and misery. Meanwhile, the Jesuits were persecuted by the encomenderos, who could not tolerate the loss of so many Indians to the missionaries. The southern missions of Yapeyú and La Cruz were often molested by the incursions of the *Yaró, Mbohane, Minuane,* and *Charrua* Indians. Several expeditions of *Guarani* were led by Spanish officers against these wild tribes.

The first blow to the Jesuits was the treaty of 1750 between Spain and Portugal, by which Philip VI yielded to Portugal seven Jesuit missions on the eastern side of the Uruguay River (San Borja, San Nicolas, San Luís, San Lorenzo, Santo Angel, San Miguel, and San Juan) in exchange for the colony of Sacramento. The Indians refused to abandon their villages and resisted by arms the forced expulsion. Both Spain and Portugal had to send armies, which defeated the Indians in 1756. Three years later, the Tratado de Límites was abrogated and the seven towns were returned to the Jesuits, but in the meantime they had been partially destroyed and the Indian population, estimated at 30,000 a few years before, had considerably decreased.

The year 1767, when all Jesuits were expelled from South America, is a fateful date in the history of the South American Indians. The Indians who had been under Jesuit rule dwindled or disappeared altogether. Tribes left their missions to return to the bush; Indians in Jesuit colonies reverted to barbarism and regions previously explored again became geographical blanks on the map.

The new charter which Don Francisco de Paula Bucareli y Ursua drafted for the missions after the expulsion of the Jesuits differed from the previous system only in minor points. The so-called communistic feature of the Jesuit regime and the restrictions on commerce were maintained, but none of the more progressive aspects of the plan, such as the foundation of a University, were ever applied. Control of the missions was given to Franciscans, assisted by lay administrators. The results were baleful. The missions were invaded by colonists who robbed the Indians of their lands and destroyed the cattle and maté plantations. The fields were abandoned and the handicrafts forgotten through lack of teachers. The Indians were forced to work for the Whites and were victimized by the local authorities. Many continued to live on their plantations but others returned to the forests. Those who remained in the missions were completely demoralized by alcoholism and the bad example of the colonists. The wars of independence and the later national wars completed the decadence and the ruin of the missions. In 1801 the seven towns in Uruguay were given back to Portugal; in 1817 the dictator, Francia, ordered the destruction of the five missions south of the Paraná River. The 15 missions between the Paraná and Uruguay Rivers were abandoned during the war of 1816–18. The *Guarani* who were not slaughtered settled in small villages, often near the ancient missions. In 1848 the dictator of Paraguay, Carlos Antonio Lopez, suppressed Bucareli's regime and forced the 6,000 *Guarani* who still occupied missions to live in ordinary villages like the remainder of the Paraguayan population. The last vestiges of the Jesuit system disappeared after that date.

The Jesuit missions of Paraguay have been the subject of considerable controversy concerning their alleged communistic organization.

CULTURE

SUBSISTENCE ACTIVITIES

The early *Guarani* seem to have been proficient horticulturists, perhaps superior to their modern descendants, the *Cainguá,* who are said to be unable to subsist entirely on the output of their small fields. Like the *Tupinamba,* the *Guarani* supplemented their diet with all kinds of wild fruits, and with game and fish.

Farming.—The whole community, among both ancient and modern *Guarani,* cooperated in clearing a large field by the slash-and-burn method in a thick forest and then subdivided it into family plots. Planting and sowing were regulated by the course of the Pleiades. The main agricultural tool was the digging stick. After five or six years of cultivation fields were considered exhausted and were abandoned.

Most plants typical of the Tropics, except cayenne pepper, were raised by the *Guarani* and are still grown by their descendants, the *Cainguá* and the Paraguayan Mestizos. Manioc, mainly the sweet species, and maize are the staples. The *Cainguá* cultivate manioc, maize (5 varieties), several varieties of sweet potatoes, beans, mangara (*Xanthosoma* sp.), a tuber called carahu (*Dioscorea* sp.), a leguminosea called mbacucu, peanuts, pumpkins, bananas, papayas, and watermelons. They also grow an herb (*Nissolia* sp.) for curing serpent bites, and two shrubs (*Rhamanidium* sp., and *Coix lacryma-jobi*), the seeds of which serve as beads. The *Pañ'* and *Chiripá* raise tacuapi reeds, or caña de Castilla (*Arundo donax*), for their arrow shafts. The *Cainguá* are very fond of sugarcane, which is for them a delicacy.

Gathering wild foods.—The *Guarani* of the southern Brazilian plateau consumed great quantities of pine nuts (*Araucaria brasiliensis*), which are abundant in that region.

The modern *Cainguá* subsist far more than did their ancestors on wild plants, especially pindo palms (*Cocos romanzoffiana*). This tree not only provides them leaves for making baskets, but also with vitamin-rich terminal shoots, with juicy fruits, oily nuts, and pith which the Indians eat in times of want. They also gather the fruits of other palms, such as *Acrocomia mokayayba, A. totai, Cocos yatay, Attalea,* and of several trees and other plants, including *Carica, Annona,* araza, ihwa-imbé (*Philodendron bipinnatifidum*), mburucudyà (*Passiflora edulis*), wild oranges, etc.

The *Cainguá* relish honey, which is for them an important food resource. The *Apapocuva* have taken the first steps toward domesticating bees. When they gather honey, they spare several combs so that the bees can return to the same place another time. They also acclimatize swarms of bees to their villages. The fat of butterfly larvae (Phalaenidae and Morphidae) and of beetles (tambu, *Calandra palmarum*[2]) is part of *Cainguá* diet. They fell some trees for the purpose of developing the larvae in the decayed wood.

Hunting.—Because the *Cainguá* prefer meat to any other food, their main concern when they move their village is to choose an area with abundant game. They make great use of traps. These are of two types: dead falls, which crush the game; and spring snares with automatic release, for birds and even for large quadrupeds, like tapir or deer. Traps and pitfalls are often located at places where animals enter fenced fields. The *Cainguá* capture parrots in a noose at the end of a pole. They have dogs trained for hunting, especially for jaguars.

Lower jaws of jaguars are kept as trophies suspended in front of huts.

Fishing.—Fishing is of secondary importance. It is reported that the ancient *Guarani* angled with wooden hooks; those living on the Coast used tucumã fiber nets. Although modern *Guarani* are well provided with iron hooks, they still shoot fish with bows and arrows, force them into baskets placed in the openings of stone dams, or poison them in calm water with the juice of a Sapindaceae (Vogt, 1904, p. 204).

Domesticated animals.—The only domesticated animal in pre-Columbian times was the Muscovy duck. Today they have dogs, chickens, and many other European farm animals.

Cooking.—The food of the rural population of Paraguay is largely a heritage of the ancient *Guarani*. The most popular dishes prepared with maize are chipas—cakes made of maize flour—mbai puy, maize mush, abati pororo, boiled maize, and guaimi atucupé—maize dough wrapped in leaves and cooked under the ashes. The *Cainguá* have about 12 recipes for preparing maize. Maize flour baked in a green bamboo joint is a *Cainguá* specialty.

Manioc tubers are generally boiled or roasted. They are also sliced, dried in the sun, and pounded into a flour with which the *Cainguá* make wafers. Flour for wafers is also prepared by the *Cainguá* with tubers soaked in water or mud for 8 days, and then dried in the sun and ground. Manioc starch is also extracted by grating the tubers—today on a tin grater—and washing the mass in water.

---

[2] *Rhynchophorus* sp., according to Strelnichov.

They crush the pith of the palms in a mortar, strain it through a sieve, and dry it in the sun.

Meat is more often broiled on a spit than on a babracot. Broiled fish and game are sometimes ground into powder (piracui).

Cainguá do not use salt. Instead they season their food with the ashes of a tree (*Machaerium angustifolium*).

Wooden mortars are generally made of a long log hollowed at one end, but some have the grinding pit on the side. Flour is strained through beautifully plaited sieves, identical to those of Guiana, although Paraguay is the southernmost limit of their distribution. When the *Cainguá* have no pottery at hand, they boil food in green bamboo joints. They serve food in wooden dishes or in calabashes of various sizes and shapes.

VILLAGES AND HOUSES

A typical *Guarani* village consisted of four to eight large rectangular houses—some about 50 m. (165 ft.) long—grouped around a square plaza. Each house had a vaulted or gabled roof which rose from the ground and was supported on a ridge pole that rested on a row of posts dividing off the quarters of each individual family. The roof was thatched with grass, palm leaves and, in certain regions of the coast, with pieces of bark. There was a door on each side of the house. Villages were fortified with a double or triple stockade and a series of moats, bristling with half-buried spears.

The vaulted hut has survived only among the *Pañ'*. Other *Cainguá* now build either a gable roof resting on the ground and thatched with tacuapi grass, or palm leaves, or a gabled house with vertical wattle-and-daub walls (4 to 6 m., or 13 to 20 ft., long; 3 to 4 m., or 10 to 13 ft., wide). Grass thatching is sewn to the structure with large wooden needles. Of all the modern *Guarani* only some *Cainguá* of Brazil still lived in communal houses 50 years ago. These houses were 25 to 50 feet (7.5 to 15 m.) long and were grouped in villages surrounded by a thorn hedge or a palisade.

Household furniture.—The aboriginal cotton or palm-fiber hammock is now being supplanted by the platform bed or sleeping mat. Four-legged benches, which are often carved out of a single log in animal shapes, are still fairly common. Utensils and foods are stored on shelves suspended from the roof or are hung on wooden hooks or on bent deer feet.

DRESS AND ADORNMENT

Clothing.—Most of the *Guarani* went entirely naked, although in certain regions, it seems, women wore either a loincloth or a cotton dress (the tipoy), a sacklike garment covering the body from the breasts to the knees which was eventually adopted universally through missionary influence. The southernmost *Guarani,* who lived in a harsh climate, followed the example of the *Charrua* and wore skin cloaks. In some *Caingua* groups, men wear a loincloth (hence the name *Chiripá*); in others they pass a piece of cloth between the legs and tuck it under a belt of human hair or fibers (hence the name, *Baticola,* "crupper"). Today cotton ponchos are sometimes worn by men.

Ornaments.—The distinctive lip ornament of ancient and modern *Guarani* is a long T-shaped stick made of jatahy rosin; labrets of stone or bone were exceptional.[2a] Women hang triangular shell pendants from their ears. In the 16th century, men wore huge shell-disk necklaces, which have often been discovered in archeological sites. A few privileged individuals suspended on their chest pendants of silver or copper plates which had reached Paraguay from Perú.

At ceremonies, modern *Caingua* men wear feather wreaths, cotton sashes fringed with feathers, or seed necklaces with feather tassels. Pairs of these necklaces are crossed over the chest. Children's and women's necklaces are strung with pyramidal wooden beads, wooden or bone pendants carved into human or animal forms, seeds, small gourds, fish vertebrae, pendants made of toucan skin, and other objects.

Feather cloaks, formerly worn by famous chiefs, are no longer seen, but feather bracelets and diadems are still used by shamans or participants in religious ceremonies. On some headdresses, feathers were mounted on a woven frontlet, a technique suggesting Andean influence. Feather garlands were sometimes tied on top of the head in the form of rudimentary bonnets. The *Mbyá* wear bracelets, garters, and anklets of human hair. Belts of hair are worn only by men. Finger rings of palm fruits or iguana tails seem now to have become fashionable.

The circular tonsure of the ancient *Guarani,* still used by some *Caingua* groups, did not extend to the forehead, as among the *Tupinamba,* but was similar to that of Franciscan monks.

Painting.—The use of urucú for body paint is widespread, but that of genipa seems to be limited to the Brazilian *Caingua.* Other groups substitute for it the juices of several plants or a mixture of charcoal and honey or wax. Traditional facial designs are dots and stripes, sometimes applied with bamboo stamps.

The ancient *Itatin* rubbed ashes from bones of birds of prey or swift animals into cuts made in their skin to improve their dexterity in archery.

TRANSPORTATION

Boats.—The ancient literature rarely mentions dugout canoes though they must have been common on the Paraguay and Paraná Rivers. The Paraguayan *Caingua* live on streams that are unsuited to boats and consequently make only a few dugouts or bamboo rafts, mainly for crossing

---

[2a] Today labrets have fallen into disuse.

rivers. They propel these craft with poles. The *Cayuá* of Brazil, who reside near larger streams, are good boatmen and travel a great deal in large dugouts, 8 to 12 feet (2.5 to 3.5 m.) long.

Carrying devices.—Goods are carried in cylindrical or rectangular twilled baskets, reinforced with a wooden frame. *Pañ'* carrying baskets are relatively extensible and are made of intertwined pindo leaves, the midribs strengthening the whole structure. Carrying nets made of bark strips were clearly introduced with the maté industry. The *Guaraní* skin bag is certainly older than the net and appears to be an article that originated locally or was borrowed from tribes to the south.

Babies are ordinarily carried in a sling, straddling their mothers' hips, but they may be transported in baskets or in skin bags.

MANUFACTURES

Basketry.—The *Guaraní* weave temporary baskets of the pinnae of pindo palms, the midrib serving to reinforce the rim. More permanent containers are made of twilled fabrics of tacuarembo strands. They are ornamented with black, geometrical motifs.

Spinning and weaving.—Thread is made of cotton carded with a bow, or of *Bromelia,* nettle (*Urera grandifolia*), and palm (*Acrocomia totai*) fibers.

Cotton is spun with a drop spindle and woven on a vertical loom with a circular warp. Cloth is generally white with alternate brown and black stripes, dyed with the bark of *Peltophorum dubium* and *Trichilia catigua.* The technique of darning weft strands through warp elements attached to a vertical loom, though it has been observed in modern times, was probably an early practice abandoned when true weaving became general, probably through *Arawak* influence.

Pottery.—*Guaraní* ceramics are known through archeological finds in São Paulo, Rio Grande do Sul, near Asunción in the Argentine territory of Misiones, and on the island of Martín García. The largest specimens are funeral urns, which also served as beer containers. Small dishes and bowls have a white interior slip which bears sigmoid figures, curves, triangles, mazes, and "grecques." The large jars and ordinary ware have continuous rows of thumbnail or other impressions over their entire surface. The *Cainguá,* who have practically given up pottery, make only a ware that is decadent in quality and shape. Bowls with a flaring base ("compotera" types) may perhaps be a survival of a pre-Columbian type.

Leather work.—The *Cainguá* carry their small possessions in skin bags.

Weapons.—*Cainguá* bows are made of palm wood, guayaihwi (*Patagonula americana*), or ihvira payú, ihvira pepé (*Holocalyx balansae*). They are 6 to 8 feet (2 to 2.5 m.) long, circular or oval in cross section, and entirely or partially wrapped with guembé bark (*Philodendron* sp.)

or covered with a basketry sheath in the center. A small bulge at each end made of wrapped bark strips prevents the fiber bowstring from slipping. Archers wear wrist guards of human hair or of cotton (*Chiripá*). The main types of arrowheads found in the tropical area are used by the *Cainguá:* Lanceolate taquara heads; tapering sticks, plain or barbed on one or both sides; and conical wooden plugs for stunning birds.

The war arrows of the ancient *Guaraní* were often tipped with human bones.

The arrow shafts are made either of the native tacuati reed (*Merostachys argyronema*) or more commonly of the imported tacuapi, or caña de Castilla (*Arundo donax*).

The feathering is of the Eastern Brazilian, or arched type. The pellet-bow is widely used by young *Cainguá* boys to shoot birds or small rodents. [3] The missiles are small clay pellets.

Cainguá clubs are either swordlike with cutting edges or plain sticks with a square cross section and a basketry sheath around the handle. Sometimes they taper into a point. The *Guaraní* were acquainted with the sling but found little use for it in their forested habitat.

The *Guaraní* warriors whom the Spaniards fought in the 16th century carried shields, often decorated with feathers. This defensive weapon has not been reported since the 17th century.

SOCIAL AND POLITICAL ORGANIZATION

Among the ancient *Guaraní,* the social unit was probably the large extended patrilineal family—perhaps the sib. Sometimes as many as 60 families lived under the same roof. Each community had a chief, but the actual power was often in the hands of a shaman. Many of the great *Guaraní* leaders who resisted the Spaniards in the 17th century were shamans endowed with divine prestige. Some ancient chiefs extended their influence over a fairly wide area. A general council of chiefs and adult men decided community and district affairs and elected war chiefs who commanded obedience during expeditions.

All *Apapocuva-Guaraní* chiefs, for at least a hundred years, have been shamans who have reached the highest rank within their profession. Like the ancient chiefs, they have been credited with supernatural power and with miracles performed on behalf of their people.

A *Guaraní* chief was succeeded by his eldest son unless there was some stronger member of the family. However, an eloquent man distinguished in warfare might become chief. Persons dissatisfied with their headman might secede and start a new settlement under another leader. Chiefs of *Cainguá* communities in Paraguay have a Spanish title and carry a stick as symbol of their office. Fifty years ago, a few villages were administered as in Jesuit times, by a cacique mayor and cacique menor, a sargento, and

---

[3] For a good description of the *Guaraní* pellet-bow, see Azara, 1809, 2:67.

a cabo (Vogt, 1904, p. 203). Today the number of Indians under the authority of a chief vary from 20 to about 100.

The members of the ancient *Guaraní* communities built the houses of their chiefs and tilled their fields and harvested their crops (Ruíz de Montoya, 1892, p. 49).

Law and order.—It is only about modern *Caingúa* communities that there is some information on justice and law. Thieves are detected by shamans, who touch each suspected man on the chest near the heart. If the fingers leave a red mark, the man is guilty. A stolen wife must be returned with a present. In case of murder, if the criminal's relatives do not pay the wergild to prevent a feud, the offended family takes the punishment into its own hands.

Etiquette.—Among ancient *Guaraní,* when a guest entered a hut, he was surrounded by women who wailed and enumerated the deeds of his dead relatives. The guest covered his face with his hands and shed a few tears. The amount of crying and wailing was proportionate to the importance of the visitor (Ruíz de Montoya, 1892, p. 52).

LIFE CYCLE

Birth and naming.—Even in modern days, a pregnant woman must avoid any food that might make her child abnormal. After childbirth, the father lies in his hammock until the infant's navel cord falls off, refraining from activities thought harmful to the baby. The *Apapocuva* believe that babies are reincarnated dead people, hence one of the shaman's first tasks is to identify the returning spirit and, by means of his supernatural power, to obtain a magic substance to be rubbed into the child's body. Infant baptism, though Catholic in many respects, is permeated by ancient rites and beliefs. Names refer to mythical beings or to sacred objects associated with the place on the horizon from which the soul is supposed to have come. Children may be very closely identified with the deities of the Upper World, and those from the west, the abode of Tupã, may receive a miniature of the bench symbolic of their divine namesake. In case of danger, especially if a person is sick, his name is changed and a new ceremony of baptism is performed (Nimuendajú, 1914 a, pp. 302–303).

Boys' initiation.—A *Caingúa* boy undergoes something of an initiation rite when, prior to puberty, his lower lip is perforated for the insertion of a labret. After a group of boys has been somewhat anesthetized with beer, a specialist perforates each boy's lower lip with a wooden or deer-horn awl and prays to Tupã that the labret may protect its wearer against death. For the three following days the initiates eat only maize mush. After their initiation they drop the infantile "u, u" (yes) for the adult masculine "ta."

Girls' puberty.—Among ancient *Guaraní,* at her first menstruation, a girl was sewn in her hammock and remained there for 2 or 3 days. Her hair was cut short and, until it grew to its former length, she had to forego meat and to work hard under the supervision of an older woman. For modern *Cainguá* also, coming of age is a critical period which calls for many ritual observances; the girl is secluded for 3 weeks behind a screen in a corner of the house and eats only a few foods, which must be lukewarm. She must not talk, laugh, lift her eyes from the ground, scratch herself, or blow on the fire. She must also listen to advice concerning her future life as a wife and a mother. Before she resumes normal activities, a shaman washes her with a special decoction.

Marriage.—There is little information on marriage in ancient times. Girls were married soon after puberty. Child betrothal is reported among the *Guaraní* of the Paraná River. In some cases little girls were given to grown men, who lived with their child wives, probably in the house of their future parents-in-law.

Child betrothal is reported among modern *Cainguá,* but the girls remain with their parents, who receive presents from their prospective sons-in-law. The preferred form of marriage seems to have been between cross-cousins and between a maternal uncle and his niece. Union with a mother and her daughter and sororal polygyny can be inferred from allusions in the Jesuitic literature. Only chiefs and influential shamans seem to have been able to support several wives. Some powerful caciques are said to have had from 15 to 30 wives. The levirate is stated by Ruíz de Montoya (1892, p. 49) to have been observed by chiefs. Today residence is patrilocal.

Death.—So strong is the hope for reincarnation that a dying *Apapocuva* (Nimuendajú, 1914 a, p. 307) accepts death with great fortitude. He sings medicine songs while women wail and the shamans chant, shaking their rattles in farewell to the departing soul.

Among the ancient *Guaraní,* as soon as a man had breathed his last, his wives and female relatives gave the most violent demonstrations of grief, often injuring themselves by flinging themselves to the ground from some elevation (Ruíz de Montoya, 1892, p. 52).

The ancient *Guaraní* put their dead into large chicha jars and covered them with a bowl. These funeral urns were buried up to the neck (Ruíz de Montoya, 1892, p. 52).[4] Modern *Cainguá* bury their dead directly in the ground with arms and legs flexed against the body or lay them with their possessions in a wooden trough or hollowed tree trunk.

Both ancient and some modern *Guaraní* bury their dead in the hut, which is immediately abandoned. The *Cainguá* of Paraguay inter the

---

[4] Ruíz de Montoya, 1892, p. 52: " . . . muchos enterraban sus muertos en unas grandes tinajas, poniendo un plato en la boca para que en aquella concavidad estuviese mas acomodada el alma aunque estas tinajas las enterraban hasta el cuello."

corpse in the bush and build a miniature hut on the grave. They burn the dead man's house and sometimes the whole settlement. For a short time they bring food to the grave and keep a fire burning upon it. Secondary interment is reported for the *Mbyá* chiefs. A dead person's name is taboo.

As among the *Tupinamba*, visitors and members of the community were received with tears and expressions of sorrow. These manifestations of grief took place probably only if somebody in the village had died. (See Etiquette, p. 86.)

According to the *Apapocuva,* after death a soul first attempts to reach the Land-Without-Evil where "Our Mother" resides, but even if it passes the demon Anäy unscathed, other souls may detain it until its reincarnation. Those who have suffered a violent death or leave behind a beloved person or have been frustrated and are reluctant to go to the hereafter, are likely to haunt the familiar places of life until they are expelled or are reincarnated in a newborn baby. Children's souls are the only ones that can easily reach the Land-Without-Evil (Nimuendajú, 1914 a).

CANNIBALISM

Cannibalism, although never attributed to modern *Cainguá,* was an honored practice among the ancient *Guarani.* Its ritual seems to have been the same as among the *Tupinamba* (p. 119). The prisoner was well treated and was given a wife; but finally, after many months and even many years of captivity, he was ceremonially sacrificed on the village plaza. Like the *Tupinamba*, the *Guarani* prisoner pelted his tormentors with stones and boasted of his great deeds and of those of his people. Children were urged to crush the victim's skull with small copper axes and to dip their hands in his blood, while they were reminded of their duties as future warriors. According to Ruíz de Montoya (1892, p. 51), everyone who touched the corpse with his hand or with a stick and everyone who ate a morsel of it assumed a new name.

ESTHETIC AND RECREATIONAL ACTIVITIES

Art.—Decorative art among the *Cainguá* is limited to the simple geometrical patterns of basketry work, and to the motifs painted on pottery, incised or burned on gourds. Lozenges are one of the favorite designs; anthropomorphic or zoomorphic themes are exceptional.

Games and toys.—Small children show certain skill at modeling men or animals of wax, clay, or palm leaves. Their favorite recreations are wrestling, racing, hide-and-seek, tug-of-war, shooting, and dancing. The toys mentioned by our sources are noise-producing tops and buzzing disks.

The ancient *Itatin,* i.e., the *Guarani* north of the Apa River, played games with rubber balls. These ball games were still popular in some Jesuit missions until the 18th century.

Today the *Cainguá* play with a maize-leaf shuttlecock, which they throw at each other and try to keep in the air as long as possible.

Musical instruments.—Among the ancient *Guarani* and among their modern descendants, the gourd rattle and the stamping tube are the most sacred religious instruments. In the *Apapocuva-Guarani* tribe, rattles are handled only by men. Their "voice," i.e., their sound, is believed to be endowed with sacred power. Shamans are capable of shaking rattles according the most varied rhythmic patterns. The stamping tube is a bamboo section closed at one end, trimmed with feathers, and engraved with checkerboard designs. It is an instrument reserved to women who pound it against the ground to produce a dull thud which marks the cadence of their dances.

The flutes of the ancient *Guarani* were often made of the long bones of their slain enemies. There is no information in our sources about their other musical instruments.

There are few types of musical instruments among modern *Cainguá*. The *Pañ'* and *Chiripa* have musical bows which they play either with their fingers or with a fiddle bow. The transverse flute with six stops and a blowhole was adopted by *Mbyá* men in post-Columbian times. A curious type of panpipe used only by women has been reported among modern *Cainguá*. It consists of five bamboo tubes of different sizes which are not bound together, but are simply held with both hands. Spanish drums and guitars are now supplanting native musical instruments.

Narcotics.—Yerba maté, or "Paraguay tea," though now characteristic of Paraguay and used daily by the *Guarani*, who sip it through a reed from a small gourd, is scarcely mentioned in the old literature. The aboriginal *Guarani* seem to have regarded it as a magic herb taken only by shamans. Modern *Cainguá* collect maté in the forest and prepare it in their villages, drying the leaves for a whole night on a platform over a fire.

Tobacco was smoked in the form of cigars or in pipes. Clay pipes have been found archeologically, and the *Cainguá* still used them not long ago. Like some *Chiriguano* pipes, those of the *Cainguá* had their bowls ornamented with a sort of crest.

Like the *Tupinamba* and other Brazilian tribes, the *Guarani* celebrated all the main events of life with drinking bouts: The return of a successful hunting or fishing expedition, harvest, and the execution of a prisoner. Their favorite beverage (kaguiai) was prepared mainly with maize but also with sweet potatoes and more rarely with manioc. Fermentation was activated by the addition of chewed corn or leaves of caa-tory (*Physurus* sp.). Modern *Cainguá* prepare mead, which may be quite strong.

RELIGION

The great personages of *Apapocuva-Guarani* mythology deserve the title of gods though they remain aloof from the affairs of this world. Creators and Transformers, they continue to exist and men yearn to live in their company. Some day they will destroy the world which they have created and shaped. The most majestic deity is the Creator, Ñanderuvuçú, Our Great Father, who now resides in a dark region which he lights with the glimmer of his chest. His wife, who was also the first woman, Ñandeçy, Our Mother, has her abode in the west in the Land-Without-Evil. According to Vellard (1939 a, p. 169), the main deity of the *Mbyá* is Ñamandu who lives in the east and gives life to the world. Tupã is the deity of the west. The north belongs to Yahira, the god of vengeance and death. Vellard (1939 a, p. 171) quotes prayers to Ñamandu in which he is asked for game or for good health, but there is no evidence of a cult of the Creator among the *Apapocuva*.

The *Pañ'* and *Mbyá*, who in the past have certainly been subject to Jesuit influences, recognize Tupã as the Creator and High God. Among the *Apapocuva*, whose ancient traditions seem unimpaired, Tupã, son of Ñandeçy, is a secondary nature deity, the personification of the thunder. He is a short man, with woolly hair, who causes a storm every time he crosses the skies in his wooden trough in the company of Thunder Birds. The original nature of this secondary god, promoted to an exalted position among acculturated *Guarani,* is still present in the memory of his worshippers, who refer to him as "The Great Thunder," "The Great Noise," or "Master of Thunder." Under him, minor Tupã are respectively lords of the rain, hailstorm, lighting, and thunder (*Pañ'*). A stock of traditional prayers which these Indians address to their God whenever in need of help betrays Christian influences.

Certain rites observed by the *Apapocuva* and even by the ancient *Guarani* can be interpreted only as worship of the sun, whom the *Apapocuva* call "Our Father." Sun is given as the Son of Our Great Father or of Tupã.

Animism.—According to the *Apapocuva*, two souls coexist in every man. One, called ayvucué, comes from the mansion of some deity in the west, zenith, or east, and enters the body immediately after birth. This soul is identified with a peaceful disposition, gentleness, and a craving for vegetables; but the temperament of a person is conditioned by the animal soul (acyiguá), which he harbors in the nape of his neck. Patient and friendly people may have a butterfly soul; whereas a jaguar soul makes a man cruel and brutal. Unrest, violence, malice, and lust for meat are generally ascribed to the acyiguá.

Dreams are experiences of the soul and are paid great attention, especially by shamans, who derive their supernatural knowledge and power from them.

PLATE 11.—**Fingernail-marked Guaraní ware.** *Top:* Sherds from Martín García, Argentina. *Center:* Vessels from Arroyo Malo, Paraná Delta. *Bottom:* Vessels from Paraguay. Funerary urn at left. (*Top,* after Bruzzone, 1931; *center,* after Lothrop, 1932; *bottom,* courtesy Max Schmidt.)

PLATE 12.—**Guaraní and other pottery from Paraguay.** *a, b,* Painted; *c,* plain; *d, e,* probably *Mbayá-Guana* incised ware. (Courtesy Max Schmidt.)

After death the two souls separate; the ayvucué generally tries to reach the Land-Without-Evil, but may linger dangerously near his former home. The animal soul, too, is likely to turn into a fearful ghost. To drive the ayvucué away, the shamans organize a dance in which two opposite groups of dancers, by running to and fro and passing each other at full speed, so confuse the soul that it is lost in a maze. The shaman then is able to deliver it to Tupã, who takes it to the Land of the Dead. The animal soul has to be attacked with weapons and exterminated like a dangerous animal (Nimuendajú, 1914 a, p. 305).

The *Caingua* feel themselves surrounded by spirits or demons, who appear in human or animal forms. They are the masters or the protectors of animals, plants, trees, water places, and winds. These genii, if offended, can be harmful.

Ceremonials.—Among the *Apapocuva-Guarani*, any trouble, any anxiety felt by the community or the shaman, or even the prospect of a collective enterprise stimulates a ceremonial dance. The performers stand in a line, the women on one end, jumping up and down on the same spot and pounding their stamping tubes; the men on the other end, shaking their rattles, slightly stooping, knees bent, throwing their feet forward and backward in a rapid tempo. The shaman faces the dancers and walks, runs, or bounces in front of them brandishing his rattle. Each woman in turn performs a solo dance in front of the line of the men, and sometimes she may invite a man to dance opposite her (Nimuendajú, 1914 a, p. 347).

Great emphasis is placed on orientation; the dancers always face the east and, when the entire line revolves, it invariably moves north, west, and south, describing a perfect ellipse. Dancers often hold ceremonial clubs, trimmed with basketry sheaths. The shaman carries a ritual stick. Dances take place in special fence-enclosed huts, which open toward the east and serve as storehouses for the ritual paraphernalia.

The most important *Apapocuva* ceremony is celebrated by the whole tribe just before harvest. Cultivated plants, wild fruits, and game are exhibited near candles and, after 4 days of ritual dancing, are sprinkled with holy water. The assistants at the ritual are also baptized on the same occasion. The object of the festivities, which are characterized by a spirit of harmony and pleasant cheerfulness, is to guard men and food from evil influences. The *Caingua* offer cakes made with the first ripe maize to Tupã.

SHAMANISM

No amount of training can make an *Apapocuva-Guarani* a shaman if he has not been supernaturally inspired with magic chants. To every adult male or female sooner or later a dead relative reveals a chant, which the recipient eagerly teaches to the rest of the community. Its possession confers a certain immunity against accidents. A shaman is a man who owns a great many magic chants, which he uses for the common good of his people. He must also be capable of leading a ceremonial dance, of playing the rattle gourd in the different modes, and of performing the rites befitting certain circumstances. The main test of his skill is offered by the harvest dance, which can be successfully organized only by full-fledged shamans. By his "voltes" and jumps, the shaman endeavors to make his body "light." He must also have frequent dreams, because they give him superior knowledge and insight into the future.

The ancient *Guarani* and even many modern groups assign disease to the intrusion of an object into the body. The *Apapocuva* visualize the source of the illness as an invisible substance that the shaman sees after he has chanted for several hours. The treatment's aim is to extract that substance and to endow the patient with magic power.

Legends and historical traditions both attest the extraordinary prestige enjoyed by some shamans of old who were leaders of their tribes. After receiving their inspiration, these great men retired into the wilderness, where they lived on celestial food. By constant dancing some *Apapocuva-Guarani* shamans gradually subjugated their animal soul, strengthening their ayvucué, or peaceful soul, until they could fly toward the heavenly Land-Without-Evil.

Among ancient *Guarani* great medicine men worked miracles by their chants. With their saliva they caused death. They were strong enough to drag a whole tribe across a large river. They claimed absolute control of all natural phenomena, including stars. After their death, their bones, kept as relics in luxurious hammocks hung in special huts, were worshiped and consulted as oracles. Ordinary shamans added to their prestige by sleight of hand.

Shamans are not only responsible for the religious life, but also interfere in the administration of justice. Whenever a succession of misfortunes is imputed to witchcraft, the shaman unmasks the sorcerer, who is savagely killed. The shamans' political power derives, naturally, from their prestige and from the fear which they inspire. Usually, witchcraft is blamed on a neighboring tribe. Sorcerers kill their victims by practicing witchcraft on their exuviae.

MYTHOLOGY

The high-sounding names of the main characters in the *Apapocuva-Guarani* mythology tinge it with a solemnity quite foreign to the versions of the same motifs collected elsewhere.

The story of the creation is told in impressive terms. At the beginning there was darkness, and the Eternal Bats fought in the night. Our Great Father found himself and created the earth, which he propped on the Eternal Cross. With him was a companion, Our-Father-Who-Knows-Everything. Our Great Father made a woman, Our Mother, whom he generously shared with his subordinate. Our Mother conceived the Twins, Our Elder Brother, and Our Younger Brother, the former by the Creator. and the latter, who was weak and stupid, by the Creator's companion. From that point the *Apapocuva* version follows more or less the *Tupinamba* sequence of motifs. The mother is killed by the Jaguars, on which the Twins later take their revenge. Our Great Father's Son manifests his superiority by always taking the initiative in any adventure and by repairing the blunders of his younger brother. The Twins are secondary culture heroes who complete the work of the Creator. Our Elder Brother steals fire from the vultures on behalf of mankind and teaches the medicine dances to the Añan, who in turn train the men. Our Elder Brother still resides in the zenith taking care of mankind in a very indefinite way. He will participate in the final destruction of the world by removing one of the props on which it lies.

In a *Pañ'* myth, fire is acquired by the Celestial Rhea.

The Añan demons, who are the constant victims of the practical jokes played by the Twins, are purely folkloric characters, with the exception of a single Añan who devours the souls of the dead when they pass by his hammock.

The *Aré* have a myth about a flood (Borba, 1904, pp. 61–64) from which a single man escaped by climbing on top of a palm tree. The sapacuru birds created land again by dropping piles of earth into the water. The man was taken on a raft to a place where many women were bathing. He took a woman for himself, and their descendants are the *Aré*.

Cosmology.—The Sun, as a deity, is called Our Father and is distinguished from the material light and heat which he produces. Sun and Moon are sons of the Creator; the Moon was smeared with genipa when he had homosexual relations with his brother.

Eclipses are caused by the Eternal Bat—according to the ancient *Guarani,* by the Celestial Jaguar—which gnaws the Sun or the Moon. The *Apapocuva* have a very pessimistic outlook on the future of the world; they are firmly convinced that its end is near. Very soon Our Great Father will set the earth on fire, unleashing the Eternal Bat and the Blue Jaguar which will destroy the stars and mankind.

The *Pañ'* identify the Milky Way with the Celestial Rhea; when the bird will have finished eating two heaps of food (Magellanic Clouds) it will devour mankind (Lehmann-Nitsche, 1936–37).

MESSIANIC AND REVIVALISTIC MOVEMENTS

From the period of European Conquest to the present day, the *Guarani* have been periodically stirred up by religious crises similar to messianic revivals in other parts of the world. Either a prophet would start a religious and political evolution by announcing the end of Spanish rule and the approach of a new golden age; or else some tribe would leave its territory in quest of the Land-Without-Evil. According to missionary accounts, shamans often represented themselves as the Lords of the Universe and preached a holy war against the intruders. These messiahs performed rites and expressed ideas that, like the redeemer concept, included many borrowings from Christianity.

During the last century, three *Guaraní* groups, the *Apapocuva,* the *Tanyguá,* and the *Oguauíva,* fearing an imminent destruction of the world announced by their shamans, desperately attempted to reach the Land-Without-Evil, where there is abundance of all good things and eternal life. Since most authorities located the paradise somewhere in the east, beyond the sea, these migrations were directed toward the Atlantic Coast. In 1910, a group of *Apapocuva* sought to lose weight through dancing, so as to fly over the ocean.

This great hope, which has so deeply influenced the destiny of these Indians, is based on a myth which describes the first destruction of the universe by fire and water. A shaman forced his people to dance day and night so as to open the way to the heavenly country. Modern *Guaraní* often tried to emulate this act, irrespective of repeated failures, which they blamed on ritual mistakes or on the use of foreign foods. The leaders of these movements were always famous shamans surrounded by an aura of mystery.

BIBLIOGRAPHY

Ambrosetti, 1895 a, 1895 b, 1896; Azara, 1809, 1904; Baldus, 1929; Bertoni, 1920, 1922; Blanco, 1931; Bode, 1918; Borba, 1904; Cardiel, 1900; Cartas Anuas, 1927–29; Charlevoix, 1757; Comentarios de Alvar Nuñez Cabeza de Vaca (see Pedro Hernández, 1852); Dobrizhoffer, 1784; Fishbach, 1929; Hernández, Pedro, 1852; Hernández, Pablo, 1913; Ihering, 1895, 1904, 1906; Jarque, 1900; Koenigswald, Von, 1908; Kunert, 1890, 1891, 1892; Kunike, 1911; Lehmann-Nitsche, 1936–37; Linné, 1936; Lothrop, 1932; Loukotka, 1929; Lozano, 1873–75; Mayntzhusen, 1912; Medina, J. T., 1908; Métraux, 1927, 1928 a, 1928 b, 1932; Meyer, 1896; Moreno, 1926; Müller, 1934–35; Muratori, 1754; Netto, 1885; Nimuendajú, 1914 a; Outes, 1917, 1918; Ramírez *in* J. T. Medina, 1908 (*also* Ramírez, Luis, 1888); Rengger, 1835; Ruíz de Montoya, 1876 (1640), 1892; Schmidel, 1903; Schmidt, M., 1932; Serrano, 1936; Strelnikov, 1928; Techo, 1673, 1897; Torres, L. M., 1913; Ullrich, 1906; Vellard, 1934, 1937, 1939 a; Vogt, 1904.

THE TUPINAMBA

By Alfred Métraux

TRIBAL DIVISIONS

Tupinamba.—This name is applied here to all the Indians speaking a *Tupi-Guarani* dialect, who in the 16th century were masters of the Brazilian shore from the mouth of the Amazon River to Cananéa, in the south of the State of São Paulo (map 1, *No. 1*; see Volume 1, map 7). Though linguistically and culturally closely related, these Indians were divided into a great many tribes that waged merciless war against one another. Most of these groups were given different names by the Portuguese and French colonists, but the term *Tupinamba* was applied to the tribes of such widely separated regions as Rio de Janeiro, Bahía, and Maranhão. Because these are the best-known tribes, we shall, for convenience, apply to all of them the term *Tupinamba;* we shall, however, carefully distinguish each subdivision when defining its geographical position.

Coastal tribes.—From north to south we have:

Tupinamba.—Occupying, along with small infiltrations of *Teremembé* (Handbook, vol. 1, p. 573), the whole coast between the Parnahyba (Parnaíba) and the Pará Rivers at the end of the 16th century (lat. 1°–4° S., long. 42°–48° W.). Approximately 12,000 lived on the Island of Maranhão in 27 villages. In three other districts, Tapuytapera, Comma, and Caité, there were about 35 villages, with a total population of approximately 27,000. There were also numerous villages along the Pindaré, Mearim, and Itapecurú Rivers. On the Pará River their last villages were far upstream, near the Jacundá and Pacajá Rivers.

Potiguara (Potivara, Cannibals, Cannibaliers).—A large tribe on the coast between the Parnahyba (Parnaíba) and Paraiba (Parahyba) Rivers. On the mainland, they reached the Serra de Copaóba and the Serra da Ibiapaba. (Lat. 5°–8° S., long. 36°–38° W.)

At the end of the 16th century, the *Potiguara* were expelled from the region of the Parahyba by the Portuguese allied to the *Tabajara,* but many villages of Ceará accepted the Portuguese rule. Cruelly treated by Pero Coelho in 1603, they banded with the Dutch and waged war against the Portuguese until 1654. At that time, the survivors of the tribe who had not fled into the bush were placed in missions by the Jesuits. The *Potiguara,* in spite of their former alliance with the French and the Dutch, became loyal allies of the Portuguese, whom they accompanied in many expeditions. They were rewarded by grants of lands. Their names disappear in the 18th century (Studart Filho, 1931, pp. 91–99).

Caeté (Caité).—On the Atlantic shore between the Paraiba and the São Francisco Rivers (lat. 8°–11° S., long. 36° W.).

Tupinamba.—On the Atlantic shore from the São Francisco River to Camamú, in the south (lat. 11°–15° S., long. 37°–39° W.).

Tupinikin (Tupiniguin, Margaya, Tuaya).—Occupying only a narrow strip of the coast from Camamú to the São Mateus (Cricaré) River, perhaps reaching Espírito Santo in the south (lat. 16°–21° S., long. 39°–40° W.).

Timimino (Tomomyno).—In the south of the State of Espírito Santo and on the lower course and islands of the Paraiba River (lat. 22° S., long. 41° W.). The *Timimino* were constantly at war with the *Tupinamba* of Rio de Janeiro.

Tupinamba (Tamoyo).—Masters of the coast from Cabo de São Tomé to the Bay of Angra dos Reis and even perhaps to Cairoçú Point (lat. 23°–24° S., long. 42°–45° W.). Their inland limits are unknown, but it is likely that they had villages on the upper Parahyba River.

Ararape.—This name is given by Cardim to the *Tupinamba* of the hinterland of Rio de Janeiro.

Tupinakin (Tupiniguin, Tupi, Tabayara).—These southern neighbors and bitter enemies of the *Tupinamba* of Rio de Janeiro were the early inhabitants of the modern State of São Paulo. They were on the coast from Angra dos Reis to Cananéa. They had villages on the Serra Paranapiacaba and in the vast region between the modern city of São Paulo and the Tieté River. (Lat. 24°–26° S., long. 45°–48° W.) Some groups probably lived near long. 50° W.

Inland tribes.—The following tribes lived in the sertão, i.e., the region inland from the Brazilian coast:

The name *Tobayara* is without any doubt a derogatory term meaning enemy. Because it was given by many *Tupi* tribes to their hostile neighbors, and because different tribes appear in the literature under the same name, there is much confusion. *Tobayara* has been applied to: (1) the *Tupi*-speaking Indians east of the Mearim River, State of Maranhão; (2) the Indians of the Serra da Ibiapaba; (3) the *Tupi*-speaking Indians living west of the *Potiguara* tribe; (4) the *Tupi* Indians of the Pernambuco region; (5) the first *Tupi* invaders of Bahía; (6) Indians in the State of Espírito Santo; (7) the *Tupinakin* of the State of São Paulo. All seven of these Indian groups lived inland and were called *Tobayara* by the *Tupinamba* of the coast. Because most of these *Tobayara* are also known under other names, we shall restrict *Tobayara* to the *Tupi*-speaking Indians of Maranhão (lat. 4° S., long. 42° W.).

Tabayara (Tobajara, Miari engüare, Miarigois).—Their native territory was the Serra Grande of Ceará (Serra da Ibiapaba), where they extended to Camocim. Attacked by Pedro Coelho at the beginning of the 17th century, the inhabitants of 70 of their villages migrated to the region of Maranhão. They settled on the upper Mearim River, where they were known to the French as "Indians of the Mearim" (*Miarigois*). The emigrants disappeared as a result of their wars against the French and the *"Tapuya"* and of smallpox epidemics. In 1637, the *Tabayara* allied themselves to the Dutch to wage war against the Portuguese of Maranhão. Their Christianization was undertaken about 1656, but was soon interrupted by a rebellion which lasted until 1673. Then again the Jesuits established missions among them. Their name appears in official documents until 1720.

Tupina (Tobayara, Tupiguae).—Scattered in the woods from north of the São Francisco River to the Camamú River in the south (lat. 11°–15° S., long. 37°–42° W.). Their eastern neighbors were the *Caeté*, the *Tupinamba*, and the *Tupinikin*.

Amoipira.—A detached branch of the *Tupinamba*, living in the hinterland of Bahía on the left side of the São Francisco River (lat. 7°–14° S., long. 39°–43° W.).

Tupinamba tribes that are mentioned in the literature but cannot be localized exactly are: The *Viatan*, formerly living in the region of Pernambuco but exterminated by the *Potiguara* and the Portuguese; the *Apigapigtanga;* the *Muriapigtanga* in the vicinity of the *Tupina;* the *Guaracaio* or *Itati*, enemies of the *Tupinikin;* the *Araboyara*, and the *Rariguora*, whose names only are known.

HISTORICAL MIGRATIONS OF THE TUPINAMBA

The various descriptions of the *Tupinamba* culture, though concerned with Indians as widely apart as those of the Maranhão region and of Rio de Janeiro, harmonize in the smallest details. Such uniformity among groups scattered over an enormous area suggests a comparatively recent separation. This view is fully supported by historical traditions and events that occurred after European colonization. The *Tupi* tribes seem to have dispersed from a common center at a relatively recent date. Their migrations ended only in the second half of the 16th century. The earlier inhabitants of the Brazilian coast from the Amazon River to the Rio de la Plata were a great many tribes ambiguously called *"Tapuya"* by the *Tupinamba* and the Portuguese. At the time of the discovery of Brazil they had been pushed into the woods but still remained near the coast waging war against the *Tupinamba* invaders, whose intrusion was so recent that they had not had time to exterminate or assimilate the former masters of the coastal region. Many *"Tapuya"* had remained in possession of the shore, forming ethnic islands among the *Tupi*-speaking tribes (Handbook, vol. 1, pp. 553–556; map 1, *No. 18;* map 7). The *Teremembé* wandered along the coast of Maranhão. The *Waitaka* of

Espírito Santo and the *Wayana* (*Goyana*) of São Paulo are listed among the Coastal Indians by our sources. *Tupinamba* tradition held that the non-*Tupi*-speaking *Quirigma* were the first inhabitants of Bahía, and that the *Aenaguig* preceded the *Tupinikin* in their habitat. The *Maraca* of the hinterland of Bahía were an enclave among *Tupinamba* tribes.

The only invasions historically recorded are those which took place in the regions of Bahía, Pernambuco, Maranhão, and Pará. The first migration of the *Tupinamba* (in a wider sense) to the coast is that of the *Tupina* (known also as *Tobayara*). They drove the "*Tapuya*" from the seashore, but later were forced to relinquish their conquests to the *Tupinamba* proper and settled in the hinterland. A branch of the *Tupinamba* that had been warring against the "*Tapuya*" did not reach the coast in time and remained on the São Francisco River, where they were known as *Amoipira*. The *Tupinikin* of Pôrto Seguro migrated from the north and may have been the southern wing of the same *Tupinamba* invasion.

The region of Maranhão was settled in the second half of the 16th century by *Tupinamba* from Pernambuco, where they had been defeated and driven back by the Portuguese colonists.

Several typical messianic outbursts took place in the second part of the 16th century when the various *Tupinamba* tribes were forced to yield ground to the Portuguese and were being either wholly outrooted or enslaved. Here, as elsewhere in the New World, these crises were prompted by shamans or prophets who announced the return of the mythical ages and the disappearance of the white scourge. Following a deeply engrained tradition among the *Tupi* tribes, these prophets exhorted them to depart for the "land-of-immortality" where the Culture hero had retired after his earthly adventure. In 1605, a party of *Tupinamba* led by a prophet, whom they worshiped as a deity, left the region of Pernambuco to invade the territory of Maranhão, which then was held by the French. The invaders were defeated by the *Portiguara* and the French at the Serra da Ibiapaba. Earlier, a group of *Potiguara* also set out on a journey to look for the Earthly Paradise, at the prompting of a shaman who pretended to be a resurrected ancestor.

About 1540, several thousands of *Tupinamba* left the coast of Brazil in quest of the "land-of-immortality-and-perpetual-rest" and, in 1549, arrived at Chachapoyas in Perú. As they mentioned having passed through a region where gold was abundant, their reports induced the Spaniards to organize several expeditions to discover El Dorado (Métraux, 1927).

The *Tupinambarana*, discovered by Acuña (1891) on the Amazonian island that bears their name, were also *Tupinamba* of Pernambuco who had deserted their home country to escape Portuguese tyranny. They traveled up the Amazon River, thence up the Madeira River, finally coming in contact with Spanish settlements in eastern Bolivia. Vexed by the Spanish colonists, they returned down the Madeira River to its mouth and settled the island of Tupinambarana. In 1690 they seem to have been on the decline, for the *Guayarise* had moved into their territory (Fritz, 1922, p. 72).

CULTURE

SUBSISTENCE ACTIVITIES

Farming.—The *Tupinamba* drew a large part of their subsistence from farming. Manioc, especially the poisonous variety, was their staple; second in importance was maize, five varieties of which were cultivated, one of them being particularly useful to travelers because it remained tender for a long period.

Other crops listed in early sources are: Cara (*Dioscorea* sp.), mangara (*Xanthosoma mafaffa*), taiá (taioba, *Xanthosoma* sp.),[1] sweet potatoes, lima beans, kidney beans, pumpkins (*Cucurbita moschata*), peanuts, pineapples, and pepper. Bananas were grown on a large scale soon after the discovery of Brazil. Sugarcane and sorghum (*Sorghum vulgare*) were also eagerly adopted from the first White colonists. Several trees, such as cashews and papayas, may have been cultivated in the fields and near the huts.

The *Tupinamba* grew several nonfood plants: gourds, calabash trees, tobacco, cotton, urucú, and probably genipa.

The *Tupinamba* cleared farm land in the forests near their villages, felling the trees with stone axes and burning them a few months later. The ashes served as fertilizer. Women did all planting and harvesting. At the beginning of the dry season, they set out manioc cuttings and sliced tubers, and planted maize and beans in holes made with pointed sticks. They did no other work except some occasional weeding. They allowed bean vines to climb on charred tree trunks but sometimes added sticks as auxiliary props. To increase the cotton yield, they thinned the trees twice a year. Only the women who had planted peanuts might harvest them, a task which entailed special ceremonies.

Collecting wild foods.—The *Tupinamba* supplemented their diet with many wild fruits and nuts, such as jucara, mangaba (*Hancornia speciosa*), cashew (*Anacardium occidentale*), sapucaia (*Lecythis ollaria*), araça orguave (*Psidium variabile*), mocujes (*Couma rigida*), araticús (*Rollinia exalbida*), hoyriti (*Diplothemium maritimum*), jaboticaba (*Myrciaria cauliflora*), acajá (*Spondias purpurea*), pindo palm (*Orbignya speciosa*), and aricuri (*Cocos coronata*), etc. The *Tupinamba* discovered the watery, edible roots of the imbú tree (*Spondias tuberosa*) by the sound made when striking the ground with a stick. Like the Chaco Indians, they ate the fruits and roots of caraguatá (*Bromelia* sp.).

The *Tupinamba* were fond of the iças, or tanajuras ant, with a fat abdomen, which they roasted and ate. Women lured these ants from

---

[1] There is, however, apparently some confusion between mangara (*Xanthosoma mafaffa*) and taioba.

their recesses with magic spells. They also collected hundreds of guara (*Eudocimus ruber*) eggs and roasted them on babracots in order to keep them as a food reserve. These tribes eagerly sought honey, not only for its food value but because the wax was important in their industries. They gathered quantities of oysters (*Ostrea rhizophorae*), which occur abundantly along the coast where they cling to the roots of mangrove trees. Many people relied even more on sea food than on game. Whole villages went to the seashore during certain months to gather oysters, which they ate or preserved by smoking them on babracots. Many of the sambaquís (shell mounds) of the Atlantic Coast (see vol. 1, p. 401) are formed of *Tupinamba* kitchen refuse.

Hunting.—The chase was a major masculine occupation; Indians wishing to eulogize their country declared that it abounded in game—deer, wild pigs, monkeys, agouti, armadillos, forest hens, pigeons, etc. But recorded hunting methods are neither numerous nor elaborate, and collective hunting is mentioned only in connection with certain ratlike rodents, which were surrounded by a party of men and forced into a previously dug ditch, where they were clubbed to death. Most hunting was carried on by individuals or by small groups of men.

The hunting weapons were bows and arrows. Long bows were generally made of hard black wood—pao d'arco (*Tecoma impetiginosa*), ayri palm (*Astroearyum ayri*)—or of jacaranda or sapucaia. The front part was convex, the string side flat. The stave was sometimes partially covered with a basketry sheath and trimmed with feathers. The bow-string was of cotton or tucum fiber (*Astrocaryum campestre*), sometimes painted green or red. The arrows had four main types of head: (1) a lanceolate bamboo (taquara) blade with sharp edges for killing large animals; (2) a simple tapering piece of hard wood, which was barbed for most arrows; (3) a head like the last but tipped with a bone splinter, a fish bone, or a spur of a sting ray that formed a barb; (4) a wooden knob to stun birds and monkeys. Fishing arrows will be mentioned later.

Arrow shafts were made of straight reeds (*Gynerium sagittatum*) without knobs. The feathering was of the "East Brazilian," or tangential type: Two feathers with their barbs cut off along one side were laid spirally against the shaft and fixed with cotton thread at their extremities. The terminal nock seems to have been reinforced with a wooden plug.

The *Tupinamba* quickly learned to train the dogs, which they received from Europeans soon after the Discovery, to hunt game, especially agouti. They beat jaguars from the bush with packs of dogs.

Caimans, which were eaten with relish, were first shot with arrows and then killed with clubs. Small animals, such as lizards, were caught almost exclusively by children.

Blinds, traps, and snares.—Large blinds for watching and shooting birds were built in treetops.

Jaguars and tapirs were caught in concealed pit falls dug across their
main paths. A more elaborate jaguar trap consisted of an enclosure of
strong poles. In entering it, the animal stepped on a contrivance that
caused a heavy log to fall and crush him. Jaguars also were captured by
means of spring snares. A noose attached to a bent pole—the spring—
was laid open on the animal's path. If the jaguar stepped near it, his
weight caused a trigger to fall which allowed the pole to spring upright
and pulled the noose up around one of his paws. The jaguar was then
shot with arrows, whereupon apologies were made to its carcass lest it
take revenge on its murderers. Small traps, snares, and nets were employed to catch small mammals and birds. Parrots were lassoed with a
noose on the end of a pole.

Fishing.—Living by the ocean and on numerous rivers along the
Brazilian coast, the *Tupinamba* had access to large supplies of sea food.
During certain times of the year they lived almost exclusively on fish.
After the rainy season, the *Tupinamba* of Maranhão left their villages for
several weeks to camp (fig. 6, *bottom*) along the shore near shallow
lagoons that swarmed with fish. Enormous quantities of parati fish
(*Mugil brasiliensis*) were also caught in August while swimming upstream
to spawn. This month was, therefore, a propitious time for war expeditions, the rivers yielding a reliable supply of food. Shoals of fish were
driven into empty canoes by striking the water with sticks. Fish, if
numerous, were also dipped out with sieves and gourds, especially at
night when attracted by torchlight. Men armed with fish nets formed a
barrier against which fish were driven by striking the water. Rivers and
coves were often closed with weirs made of branches or with dams of
stones. Fishermen standing on the dam scooped up the fish with dip
nets. Funnel-shaped baskets were placed in running water at narrow
passages where the fish would be forced to enter them and be caught. The
Tupinamba were skillful at shooting fish either with arrows tipped with
several hardwood prongs or with harpoon arrows. They also killed fish
by poisoning calm waters with the juices of several creepers, such as
timbó *(Dahlstedtia pinnata)* and the tingui *(Tephrosia toxicaria)*. Native hooks, which disappeared rapidly after European contact, were made
of thorns; fishlines, of tucumã *(Bactris setosa)* fibers. The *Tupinamba*
were said to be such good swimmers that they could even dive and catch
fish with their hands.

Domestication.—Pets, numerous in any village, were mainly birds and
a few such animals as wild pigs, agouti, monkeys, and even armadillos
and caimans. Certain birds, such as ducks, a kind of turkey, and pigeons,
may actually have been domesticated. These ducks, however, were not
eaten lest their flesh cause a person to become slow. Tame parrots were
taught to speak and became an important article of trade with Europeans,
but also had a certain economic value in native culture, for they were

plucked every year, and their feathers were made into ornaments. The *Tupinamba* changed the natural colors of the feathers of green parrots by "tapirage." By rubbing with the blood of a frog *(Rana tinctoria?)* the sores left by plucking the birds, they caused the new feathers to grow yellow or red. These Indians eagerly received domesticated fowls brought to them by Europeans and unquestionably aided their diffusion in eastern South America. They never ate these fowls, but plucked them, especially the white ones, as they did native birds. The feathers were dyed in a decoction of Brazil wood *(Caesalpinia echinata)*. When the *Tupinamba* received their first dogs from the Portuguese, they called them "jaguars." They grew so fond of them that the women carried the puppies like babies. The *Tupinamba* also kept European pigs, but did not care for their flesh.

Food preparation.—Poisonous manioc required lengthy preparation before consumption. The tubers were peeled with shells and grated on rough-surfaced stones or on special graters, i.e., boards in which stone chips or fishbones were imbedded at close intervals. The poisonous juice was extracted by squeezing the manioc in a long basketry tube (tipití). Afterward, the pulp was sifted and made into flour ("hard flour") by constant stirring while it roasted in a large pottery platter. For wafers (beijú), the mass simply was spread in a more or less thick layer on the same utensil.

Another kind of flour ("water flour") was made from tubers which had been soaked in running water for many days until they began to decay. They were then crushed by hand, strained in the tipití, and passed through a sieve. The pulp was baked as before. A flour called carimã was obtained from tubers that were rotted, soaked in water, smoked on a babracot, pounded in a wooden mortar, and carefully sifted. The famous war flour was a combination of "water flour" and carimã baked for a long time until dried and well roasted. This flour, which would keep for more than a year, was carried by travelers and warriors in waterproof satchels plaited of palm leaves.

Aypi, or sweet manioc, could be eaten directly after boiling or roasting, but was cultivated mainly for brewing mead. It was also made into various kinds of flour. The juice of both species of manioc, if left in the sun for a while, deposited its starch, which was baked and eaten. Other tubers, such as sweet potatoes, cará, mangara, and taiá, required a less elaborate treatment, being either boiled or roasted. Maize, mainly consumed in the form of flour, was also roasted or boiled. Peanuts were broiled and roasted. The name "mingao" designated any mush made of manioc or other flour. Mangara and taiá leaves were eaten as greens.

Meat and fish were roasted or boiled. The broth was often mixed with manioc flour. Small fish, wrapped in leaves, were cooked under ashes. Any surplus of game or fish was dried and smoked for about 24 hours on a huge babracot, a rectangular four-legged grill or platform made of sticks, under which a slow fire burned. Another method for preserving meat and fish was to pound it into a sort of pemmican or flour.

Condiments comprised mainly several species of pepper and occasionally a grass called nhamby (coentro do sertão, *Eryngium foetidum.*). Salt was obtained by evaporating sea water in ditches dug near the shore or by boiling it in large pots. It was also made by boiling lye made of palm-wood ashes. Salt and ground pepper were generally mixed, and every morsel of food was dipped in this powder before being eaten.

The *Tupinamba* ate in silence, all squatting on the ground around a big dish, except the head of the extended family, who lay in his hammock. They were expert at throwing into their mouths manioc flour, which accompanied every dish. Many persons washed before and after every meal.

VILLAGES AND HOUSES

Tupinamba villages consisted of from 4 to 8 huge communal houses built around a square plaza, where the social and religious life of the community centered (fig. 6, *top*). Houses varied in length from about 50 to 500 feet (15 to 150 m.), the average being about 250 to 300 feet (75 to 90 m.), and in width from 30 to 50 feet (9 to 15 m.). The height was about 12 feet (3.5 m.). Thirty families, that is, more than 100 people, could live in a dwelling; some houses even had as many as 200 occupants.

Houses were constructed on a rectangular ground plan. The roof was arched or vaulted, apparently descending to the ground, thus also forming the side walls—hence the frequent comparison in the ancient literature to overturned boats. The structure was thatched with leaves of pindo palm, patiaba, or capara (*Geonoma* sp.) artfully sewn or woven together so as to be entirely waterproof. There was a low door at each end and one or sometimes two on the side. In the interior, the quarters of each family were marked off by two wall posts. The family hammocks were suspended from additional posts. Possessions, such as calabashes, pots, weapons, and provisions, were stored in the rafters or on small platforms. Each family kept a fire burning day and night in its compartment. The center of the hut was left free as a communal passageway. The head of the extended family, his relatives, and slaves were accommodated in the middle or in some other privileged part of the long house. Hammocks, carved benches, and pottery of all sizes and shapes comprised the usual household equipment.

Villages were located on hilltops, where the air was not too stifling. Those exposed to enemy attacks were fortified with a double stockade (fig. 6, *top*), having embrasures for archers. The access to the village was defended with pitfalls and caltrops.

The *Tupinamba* shifted their villages when the house thatching began

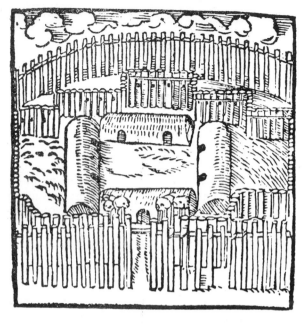

FIGURE 6.—*Tupinamba* palisaded village (*top*) and camp (*bottom*).
(After Staden, 1557.)

to rot or when the soil of their cultivated clearings was exhausted. They did not remain in one place more than 4 or 5 years. A new village was generally built near the old one and retained the same name.

DRESS AND ORNAMENTS

In daily life men and women were entirely naked, except that adult men, especially old men, wore a penis sheath of leaves. Young men contented themselves with a ligature round the prepuce.

Feather ornaments.—In contrast to this lack of dress, ornaments were numerous and showy. On their heads men wore high diadems made of the tails of parrots or other bright birds or bonnets of small feathers fastened in the knots of a cotton net. The feather fabric was so compact that it suggested velvet. Some of these bonnets fell down in the back like long, narrow capes (fig. 7, *left*). The most spectacular feather orna-

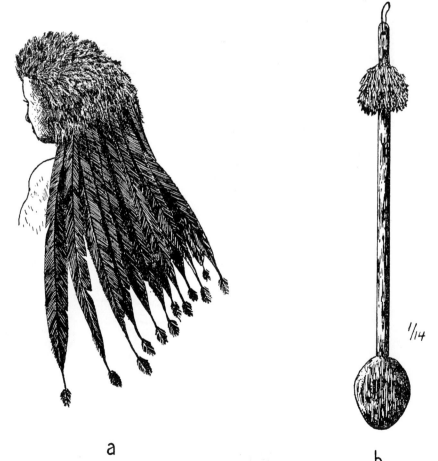

a

b

FIGURE 7.—*Tupinamba* headdress and ceremonial war club. (*b*, Approximately 1/14 actual size.) (Redrawn from Métraux, 1928 a.)

ments were long, wide cloaks composed entirely of red feathers of the guara (*Guara rubra*). Necklaces, bracelets, and anklets were also made of bright feathers. Many feather ornaments, especially cloaks, have found their way to European museums. The best feathered specimens were collected by the Dutch in their early Brazilian possessions, and are now in the National Museum of Copenhagen. For festive occasions or

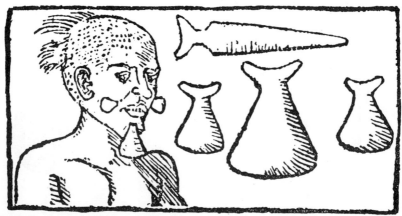

FIGURE 8.—*Tupinamba* dress. *Top:* Warriors with ceremonial club and feather-plume decoration. *Bottom:* Labrets. (After Staden, 1557.)

for war, men suspended on their buttocks an ornament of ostrich plumes in the "form of a large round ball to which feathers were attached" (figs. 8, *top*; 9, *left*).

The love for feathers was so great that men and even women glued them to their heads with wax or sprinkled chopped feathers all over their bodies, which they had previously coated with gum or honey. Often they substitued particles of red or yellow wood for feathers. They also pasted with wax on their temples patches of toucan skin covered with yellow feathers. Feathers, after use, were carefully collected, cleaned, and stored in bamboo tubes sealed with wax.

FIGURE 9.—*Tupinamba* ceremonial objects. *Left:* Warrior's feather plumes worn on hips. *Right:* Ceremonial club and cord. (After Staden, 1557.)

Necklaces and garters.—Chiefs and important men had necklaces of round or square shell (*Strombus pugilis*) beads so long—some were 30 feet (9 m.) in length—that they had to be coiled a great many times round their necks. Others had strings of black wooden beads (*Astrocaryum ayri*). Warriors displayed necklaces strung with the teeth— sometimes as many as 2,000 to 3,000—of their victims. Women used similar necklaces, but ordinarily wore them wound around their arms. Certain women's bracelets are described as a careful assemblage of small pieces of shell imbricated like fish scales. Belts of shell beads are also mentioned in the literature. A most precious male heirloom was a crescentic pendant 6 inches to 1 foot (15 to 30 cm.) long, consisting of well-polished bone and shell plates worn suspended round the neck by a cotton thread.

Men and women wore one or two broad cotton garters under the knee, men trimming theirs with feathers. In the region of Bahía, these garters were bound tightly around little girl's legs to make the calves bulge in later life.

Hairdressing.—Neither sex tolerated any hair on the body. They either pulled it out with their fingers, or shaved it with a bamboo splinter or a quartz knife. With the same instrument men shaved their foreheads back to the level of the ears. Women generally allowed their hair to hang loose down their backs, but, when at work, they tied it up over the head in a knot or divided it into one or two bundles wrapped with a cotton fillet. Combs were made from a fruit with long spikes. The only cosmetic was oil extracted from several fruits, generally those of palm trees (uucuúba, *Myristica sebifera*). The natives washed their hair with a root or the skins of the *Sapindus divaricatus* fruit, which makes suds when soaked in water and squeezed between the fingers.

Labrets.—When a *Tupinamba* boy was 5 or 6 years old, his lower lip was pierced, and henceforth he wore in the hole either a plain wooden plug or a conical bone stick or a shell. Later in life he substituted a green or white stone (beryl, amazonite, chrysoprase, chalcedony, quartz, or crystal) shaped like a **T** or a large button. A few men, generally chiefs or medicine men, perforated their cheeks for similar ornaments, some wearing as many as seven (fig. 8).

Ear ornaments.—Women inserted in their ear lobes a shell cylinder long enough to reach their shoulders or even their breasts. Men wore thin bone sticks, similar to bone labrets, in their ears. Some men also wore small bone or wooden sticks through the wings of the nose.

Tattooing.—Both sexes were tattooed. Charcoal or certain plant juices were rubbed into wounds made with a rodent's tooth or a shell. A man's body was covered with capricious designs, which were extended each time he killed a man in war or sacrificed a prisoner. Judging from a contemporary drawing, such tattooing marks formed regular geometrical patterns, not unlike designs on pottery. Women were tattooed only at puberty.

Painting.—On every important occasion, such as a drinking bout, a funeral, or the slaughtering of a prisoner, men and women painted their bodies. The favorite pigments were black, made of genipa, and red, made of urucú. Black and red paint, alone or alternating, covered large surfaces of the body, especially the lower limbs. Men and women entrusted themselves to skillful artists, generally women, who traced on their persons artistic and capricious patterns consisting of checkers, spirals, waves, and other elements similar to those painted on pottery. Blue and yellow, though less common, were used on the face in combination with the two other pigments.

TRANSPORTATION

Carrying devices.—Heavy loads, such as crops, were carried on the back in elongated baskets that were open on the top and outer side. These were suspended from the forehead by a tumpline.

Children were carried straddling the hip, and supported by a sling manufactured like a small hammock.

Boats.—The *Tupinamba* had three types of watercraft: (1) Dugouts, (2) bark canoes, (3) rafts. Dugouts were hollowed out of huge logs by the laborious process of burning and scraping the charred wood away. The *Tupinamba* of Bahía could finish a canoe in a few days by using the ubiragara tree (*Ficus doliaria* or *Cavanillesia arborea*), which has a soft inside. Large dugouts were manned by 30 to 60 men.

To build a bark canoe, they erected a platform around a suitable tree, peeled the bark off in one large piece, and heated it to bend it "in front and behind, but first lashed it together with wood so that it did not stretch." This craft, sometimes 40 feet (12 m.) long, held from 25 to 30 persons. Like the dugouts, these canoes were used for raids along the coast.

The *Tupinamba* paddled their canoes standing up. The blades were lanceolate in shape, the handles without cross bars or knobs. The *Caeté* navigated the São Francisco River, and even along the coast as far as Bahía, on huge rafts or balsas made of reed bundles tied up with creepers and connected with transverse sticks. Such rafts could easily transport 10 to 12 Indians.

Fishermen sat on small rafts (piperi), made of four or five thick round pieces of light wood bound together with creepers, and propelled them with a flat stick.

MANUFACTURES

Miscellaneous tools.—Trees were felled with stone axes. Ax heads were hafted with a withy bent double around their butts and held fast with bast. Stone chisels, similarly hafted, served for carving. Rodent teeth and wild pig tusks, "bound between two sticks," served for boring. Shells or bamboo splinters were employed as knives. They polished bows with the rough leaves of mbaiba (*Cecropia adenopus*).

Basketry.—Basketry included sieves, fire fans, containers of different types, and perhaps also fish traps. Temporary baskets were made of plaited palm leaves. Those intended for longer service were manufactured of creepers (*Serjania* or *Paullinia*) split into thin strips, which were twilled, yielding geometrical patterns when the strips were black and white.

Spinning and weaving.—Cotton threads were spun with a spindle— a stick with a flat, circular wooden whorl. Women rolled the spindle along the thigh to set it in motion and then dropped it. Ropes were twisted of cotton and other fibers; or were sometimes plaited for ceremonial use.

The *Tupinamba* knew only the simplest technique of twined weaving, which was used for the fabric of the hammocks. The warp strands were wrapped horizontally around two vertical posts and twined together with double wefts. Some fabrics were woven so tightly as to appear to be true woven cloth.

Pottery.—*Tupinamba* pottery was highly praised by early voyagers, but the few extant specimens do not show unusual technical or artistic skill. Bowls, dishes, and vases had simple forms: round, oval, and even square (fig. 10). They were often painted on the inside with red and black linear motifs on a white background and were also glazed with resin (for instance, the resin of the icica, *Protium brasiliense*). The most conspicuous pots were huge jars, with a capacity of about 14 gallons (50 liters), for storing beer. These and cooking pots often were decorated with thumbnail impressions made in the wet clay, an embellishment typical

FIGURE 10.—*Tupinamba* and *Guarani* pottery. *a, b, d, e, Tupinamba*; others, *Guarani*. (Redrawn from Métraux, 1928 a.)

of many *Tupi* tribes. Pottery was baked in a shallow pit covered with fuel. The best pot makers were the old women. Tradition had it that a pot which was not baked by the person who modeled it would surely crack.

Fire making.—Fire was generated by a drill and activated by a fire fan. Torches were sticks of ibiraba wood, which burned steadily once the end fibers had been unraveled.

Weapons.—See Hunting (p. 100).

Calabashes.—Halved gourds served as dishes and bowls. The interior was generally smeared with genipa and the exterior with a yellow varnish. Small containers or mortars were made of the shell of the sapucaia fruits.

SOCIAL ORGANIZATION

From existing documents, we can only surmise the type of social organization prevailing among the *Tupinamba*. Like many Guiana Indians, they lived in large communal houses, whose occupants were related either by blood or by marriage and were probably the members of a patrilineal extended family. A man's brother's daughter was regarded as his daughter, but his sister's daughter was his potential wife. The children of a woman of the tribe by a captive father were regarded as members of the enemy group and were consequently eaten by their mother's relatives. The children of a tribesman were always full-fledged members of the community irrespective of the mother's status.

Marriage.—The preferred marriages were between cross-cousins and between a girl and her mother's brother, or in case there were none, the mother's nearest male relative. The maternal uncle carefully supervised the conduct of his future bride if he did not wish to take advantage of his marital claim, and had to be consulted if his niece wanted to marry another man. If the husband were not the girl's mother's brother, he became his father-in-law's servant. He had to assist him in all economic activities, such as house building, opening clearings, hunting, fishing, and fuel gathering. He also had to accompany him on the warpath, carry his burdens, and supply him with food and shelter. To gain the favor of his in-laws, the bridegroom would assume the responsibility of revenging the death of any of his affinal relatives and offer a prisoner he might have taken to one of his brothers-in-law, who would kill the captive, thereby increasing his prestige by a change of his name. A hard fate it was indeed for those who had few relatives and were, therefore, compelled to live with their in-laws. "Marriage," says Thevet (1575), "costs the man a great deal of work and pain." Suitors, according to Soares de Souza (1851, p. 311), worked 2 or 3 years before they acquired their wives; and after this they had to settle with their in-laws and remain in their service.

Marriage, in its initial phase at least, seems to have been strictly matrilocal, but the general tendency for any man was to liberate himself from his subordinate position by settling with his wife in his parents' long house. Chiefs could do away with matrilocalism and take their wives home; a man related to a powerful family could buy his liberty with presents and favors bestowed on his in-laws; and any man might also gain his freedom by marrying his daughter to his wife's brother.

A widow generally married her husband's older brother or one of his close relatives who had avenged her husband's death, if it had occurred in battle, or who had taken a prisoner to "renew" the deceased spouse's grave and wear his ornaments, in case of a natural death. (See p. 120.) The second husband was expected to be as valiant as the first.

Once redeemed from his bondage, a man could take other wives and often did at the request of a wife eager to share her tasks with them. The first wife always retained a preeminent position, however, and enjoyed the right to hang her hammock next to that of her husband. Each wife of a polygynous man "had her separate lodging in the huts, her own fire and root plantation, and that one with whom he (the husband) cohabited for the time being, gave him his food, and thus he went the round of them" (Staden, 1928, p. 146).

A man could also have wives scattered in different villages. Polygynous wives were given to surprisingly little jealousy and quarreling, though they often included women of other villages who had been captured in war.

A young man unable to find a marriageable girl or lacking a mother or sister to cook for him did not hesitate to take some aging woman as first wife, whom he would discard when he could obtain a more suitable mate. Warriors of renown and famous medicine men had no difficulty in acquiring new wives, who were readily given to them by their fathers or brothers. Some chiefs had as many as 30 wives. Polygyny was thus a mark of prestige and a source of wealth. Matrimonial ties were easily broken by either spouse, sometimes for reasons that appear to us trifling. The divorced woman, if young, would remarry. An adulteress was not severely punished unless her husband was a great chief; but if a captive or without a family to revenge her, she might be killed. The guilty partner was unmolested, lest his kin start a feud.

Prestige.—A man with several daughters attained considerable authority and prestige because he had under him both his sons-in-law and his daughters' suitors. Men who had changed names often, having killed several enemies in battle or sacrificed captives on the village plaza, acquired great prestige and influence in the community.

Slaves.—Though, with few exceptions, all prisoners, male or female, were eventually eaten, they were kept long enough in the community to be considered a special class within *Tupinamba* society. Possession of a prisoner was an envied privilege. One who enjoyed it did not hesitate to make the greatest sacrifices to keep his charge happy and in good health. A man would starve rather than deprive his captive of food, and usually gave him a daughter or sister as a wife. Lacking a close female relative, the captor would ask a friend to give him a woman for the purpose, a request sure to be granted, for conjugal ties with a prisoner were regarded as honorable. In certain cases the prisoner was married to the widow of a warrior killed before his capture and was allotted the deceased's hammock and ornaments. The relations between a prisoner and his new wife were identical with those of any other married couple and were supposed to last forever, the woman being just as attached to her temporary husband as in normal wedlock. These prisoners' wives, it is said, had the responsibility of preventing their husbands from running away, but the statement is to be accepted with reserve. Some authors report cases of women who grew so fond of their husbands that they escaped with them.

Female captives were often taken as secondary wives or concubines by their masters, but sooner or later they were ritually sacrificed unless they belonged to an influential man who had become fond of them. If their masters did not care for them, they were allowed to have sexual relations with whomever they wished. The skulls of female captives who died a natural death were crushed.

Prisoners were kindly treated and regarded their masters, whose quarters they shared, as relatives. The *Tupinamba* were heartbroken to see Europeans mistreat the prisoners they had sold to them. They would come from far away to visit them, and would hide and protect any of their former slaves who escaped.

Prisoners had fields for their maintenance and were free to hunt or fish. They were welcome at the feasts and drinking bouts. It seems, however, that, like a son-in-law or a brother-in-law, they were obliged to work for their masters. They were, moreover, reminded of their servile condition by a few restrictions and humiliations. They could not make a present or work for anybody without their masters' consent. They were forbidden to enter a hut through the thatched wall, though other people might do so. They must, under pain of death, avoid amorous relations with a married woman. If they fell sick, they were immediately sacrificed. Further, at any time they could be the target for the most violent insults and abuses. A woman who refused to accept willingly the sacrifice of children she had by a prisoner, was severly censured, and her family shared her disrepute.

POLITICAL ORGANIZATION

Each long house had a headman who was under the village chief. Some villages had two or even three or four chiefs, if we may rely on Claude d'Abbeville's census of the Maranhão region. Some chiefs extended their power over a whole district and commanded a great many villages. Rank was determined by war prowess (capture and ceremonial execution of prisoners), magic power, oratorical gifts, and wealth.

Soares de Souza writes:

The chief must be a man of courage. He has to belong to a large family and to be well liked by its members so that they are willing to help cultivate his plantations, but even when he opens a clearing with the assistance of relatives, he is the first to put his hand to the task. [Soares de Souza, 1851, p. 325.]

The authority of chiefs, undisputed in war time, was subordinated to the sanction of a council in peace.

This council was composed of the elder men and famous warriors, who met on the village plaza for any important decision. The chief spoke first, and then each councilor in turn gave his opinion, while the others, according to their rank, sat in their hammocks or squatted on the ground smoking huge cigarettes.

Each morning the headman of a hut assigned everybody a task and delivered a speech encouraging the people to go to work and follow the good example of their ancestors.

Chieftainship was inherited by the son or the brother of the deceased chief, if he had the required qualifications.

Social control and justice.—Social control over the individual's behavior was very strong. Great stress was put on the smoothness of manners and gentleness, any outburst of anger being looked on with abhorrence. People shunned the company of temperamental persons. If an Indian felt incapable of controlling his feelings, he warned those present, who immediately tried to calm him down. When a serious quarrel broke out in a village, the individuals involved went to the extreme of burning their own houses, challenging their adversaries to do likewise. Under the influence of anger, these Indians were prone to commit suicide by eating soil.

Blood revenge was a sacred duty. When a homicide might involve two allied groups in a feud, the relatives of the murderer often did not hesitate to kill him, lest the peace be disturbed.

The cooperation of neighbors or relatives in any joint enterprise was rewarded by a drinking party organized by the beneficiaries. A hunter or a fishermen, upon returning home, shared his catch first with the headman of the long house and then with the members of his household. The *Tupinambas'* generosity and willingness to share anything they had are often stressed by the old sources. Anybody could, without asking for permission, use utensils belonging to some housemate.

ETIQUETTE

Guests were greeted with tears. As soon as a visitor entered a hut he was surrounded by the women of the house, who showed their sympathy by friendly gestures and started to cry, intermingling their laments with chants in which they alluded to the dead members of the community and to other mournful subjects. The guest had to pretend that he was shedding tears. When the crying had ceased, the male hosts, who had affected indifference, turned toward the newcomer and welcomed him. Any member of the community who had been absent, even for a short time, was received with weeping when he returned. Chiefs were greeted with tears even if they had only walked to their nearby fields.

The mournful manifestations by which a returning traveler was greeted were actually the reenactment of a funeral rite with which the absent person or the guest was associated.

LIFE CYCLE: BIRTH, PUBERTY, DEATH

Birth.—When a woman felt the first pangs of childbirth, she squatted on a flat piece of wood that leaned against the wall, or directly on the ground. Women neighbors surrounded her but gave little assistance. If the delivery was difficult, the husband pressed on her stomach. In case of a male infant, the father cut the umbilicus with his teeth or between two stones and took him up from the ground in token of recognition. The mother or some close female relative performed the operation on female babies. The mother's brother took the baby girl in his arms, thereby claiming her as his future wife. After the baby was washed, its father or the midwife flattened its nose with the thumb, an operation repeated later during infancy by the mother.

The father took to his hammock and lay in it for several days, receiving the visits of his friends, who expressed their sympathy for his plight. The couvade lasted until the dry navel cord fell off. During this period the father had to refrain from eating meat, fish, and salt. Even after the confinement, he was not allowed to do any hard work lest he cause some harm to the infant. For a baby boy, claws of ferocious animals, a small bow and arrow, and a bundle of grass symbolizing his future enemies were attached to his little hammock, which was suspended between two war clubs. A little girl was given capivara teeth to make her teeth hard, a gourd, and cotton garters.

In the postnatal period, the father performed several magic rites to make the child successful during his life. Thus, he would have a male baby's sling caught in a trap as if it were some game. He would shoot at the sling with the miniature bow and arrows or throw a fishing net over it. When the navel cord was dry, he sliced it into small pieces and tied each to one of the main house posts so that the child would become the progenitor of a numerous family. If the father were absent or dead, the same rites were performed by the mother's brother or some close maternal relative. Food taboos were imposed on the mother during the same period.

Naming.—The choice of a name, a serious matter, was discussed at a special meeting. Generally, the child received the name of an ancestor, a custom that is probably connected with the *Tupinamba* belief that children were reincarnated ancestors.

Childhood.—Boys were gradually weaned at the age of 4 or 5 years (some authors say 6 to 7) and girls a year later. From early infancy children were given solid food in the form of maize, which the mother masticated into a pap and passed from her mouth into the baby's. Children, male and female, remained in close contact with their mothers until the age of 8. Little boys, meanwhile, were encouraged to practice archery and to train themselves for war and hunting. Early voyagers report unanimously that children, though never scolded, were well disciplined. Little is known about early education. To stop their babies from crying, mothers put cotton, feathers, or a piece of wood on their heads. To accelerate a child's growth, they rubbed it with their hands. Every morning one of the headmen went around the village scratching the legs of the children to make them obedient. Naughty children were threatened with the man with the scratcher.

At the age of 4 or 5, young boys had their lower lips pierced for a labret. The operation was a festive occasion attended by the members of the community and inhabitants of other friendly villages. The child was expected not to flinch during the operation, thus showing his fortitude. Thereafter, boys tied up their prepuce with a cotton thread.

Girls' puberty.—A girl underwent a series of severe ordeals at her first menstruation. With her head carefully shaven, she had to stand on a whetstone while geometric designs were cut on her back with a sharp rodent tooth. Ashes of a wild gourd rubbed in the wounds left indelible tattoo marks. This scarification had to be endured without crying. Then the girl lay in her hammock, concealed from sight, and observed a strict fast for 3 days. She must not touch the ground with her feet nor leave the hammock until her second menstruation. Meanwhile, if she had to go outside the hut, she was carried on her mother's shoulders. At her second menstruation, she received additional tattoo marks on the breasts, stomach, and buttocks. Henceforward, she might work but was not permitted to leave the house or to speak. Only after the third period was she free to go to the fields and resume her normal occupations.

Adulthood.—After puberty, girls could indulge freely in sexual practices until marriage. Any girl who lost her virginity had to break a string she wore around her waist and arms after her first menstruation. Premarital chastity was expected of a girl betrothed to a chief and brought up in his house from childhood. Chiefs' infant brides, however, might stay at home until coming of age. No young man could marry or even have sexual relations, according to Cardim (1939), before he had killed one or two prisoners, for the sons of a man who had not shed the blood of his enemies were thought to be cowardly and lazy. This restriction on a young man's sexual life could be obviated, perhaps long before he had been to war, if his father or uncle gave him a prisoner to sacrifice. Men married at about the age of 25.

After 40 a man was an "elder" and did no hard work. He spoke in council. Very old men were respected and treated courteously.

Death.—A sick person who seemed doomed to death was ignored and abandoned. But at the moment of his last breath his relatives surrounded him and displayed the most spectacular forms of grief. They threw themselves on his body or on the ground and burst into tears. Ritual laments and shedding of tears were restricted to women, especially old women, and occasionally old men. The head of the extended family or the women of the long house praised the deceased by stressing his courage at war and his hunting or fishing skill. These funeral orations were interrupted by sighs and cries.

In general, the *Tupinamba* were in such haste to bury their dead that often the dying man was still alive when placed in the earth (fig. 11, *top*). The grave was dug by the deceased's nearest male relatives. The corpse was wrapped in a hammock or tied by cords in a foetal position and squeezed into a big beer jar that was covered with a clay bowl. Some food was placed in the grave and a fire was built in its vicinity to keep bad spirits away. The head of a family was buried in the long house under the quarters he had occupied during life, but there were many exceptions to this rule, according to the age and preferences of the dead man. If the corpse were buried in the open, a small hut was erected upon the grave. Urn burial, though common, was not always practiced. When buried directly in the earth, the body was protected against direct contact with the soil by lining the grave walls with sticks.

Female mourners cut their hair, whereas men let theirs grow on their shaven foreheads. Both sexes painted their bodies black with genipa. Mourning women wailed for many days after a burial and went at times to the grave to ask the whereabouts of the departed soul. Other women of the community who visited them assisted in their ritual laments. The mourning period lasted 1 to 6 months and was strictly observed by the parents, siblings, children, and wife of the deceased. No widow could remarry before her hair had reached the level of her eyes. Before resuming normal life, each mourner entertained his family and friends at a drinking bout with much singing and dancing, at which time widows and widowers cut their hair and painted themselves black.

After death the souls of gallant warriors killed in battle or eaten by their enemies went to a beautiful land in the west where they enjoyed the company of the mythical "grandfather" and of their dead ancestors. They lived there happily and made merry forever. Access to this paradise was forbidden to cowards and to women, except the wives of renowned warriors.

FIGURE 11.—*Tupinamba* burial and cultivation. *Top:* Burial ceremonies within a pali-saded village. *Bottom:* Planting and harvesting of manioc. (After Staden, 1557.)

WAR AND CANNIBALISM

Religious and social values of high importance clustered around war and the closely connected practice of cannibalism. Prestige and political power were derived mainly from the ritual slaughtering of prisoners, which was so far reaching in its influence that it even affected sexual life. The *Tupinamba's* excessive interest in ritual cannibalism contributed toward keeping the different tribes and even local communities in a constant state of warfare and was one of the chief causes of their ready subjection by Europeans. Their mutual hatred of one another, born of a desire to avenge the insult of cannibalism, was so great that the *Tupinamba* groups always willingly marched with the White invaders against their local rivals. Their bellicose disposition and craving for human flesh loom large in many aspects of their culture, such as education, oratory, poetry, and religion. The rites and festivities that marked the execution of a prisoner and the consumption of his body were joyful events which provided these Indians with the opportunity for merrymaking, esthetic displays, and other emotional outlets.

The *Tupinamba* went to war only with the certainty of victory, which they derived from the interpretation of dreams and from ritualistic performances such as dancing and reciting charms. When marching toward the enemy, they paid special attention to any omen and to dreams. The slightest bad omen was sufficient to stop the expedition: once a party of warriors that had almost taken a village retreated because of a few words uttered by a parrot.

Besides arrows and bows, *Tupinamba* weapons included a hardwood club with a shape unique in South America. It consisted of two parts: a long, rounded handle and a flattened, round, or oval blade with sharp edges. The only defensive weapon was a shield of tapir hide. Warriors donned their best feather ornaments and painted their bodies. Men of importance were followed by their wives, who carried hammocks and food for them. The advancing army was accompanied by musical instruments. Whenever possible, they used canoes to avoid long marches. The chief always headed the column, which was disposed in one line. Scouts reconnoitered the country. At night the warriors camped near a river and built small huts in a row along a path.

The proper time to assault the enemy village was chosen cautiously. As a rule, they stormed it at night or at dawn, when least expected. When prevented by a stockade from entering a village immediately, they built another palisade of thorny bushes around the village and started a siege. One tactic was to set fire to the enemy houses with incendiary arrows. Sometimes they slowly moved their fence close to the opposite wall so that they could fight at close range.

The *Tupinamba* fought with courage and determination but without much order as they did not obey any command during the battle. They opened the attack by shooting arrows (fig. 12, *left*), hopping about with great agility from one spot to another to prevent the enemy from aiming or shooting at any definite individual. Amid ferocious howls, they rushed against their opponents to strike them with their clubs, trying to take prisoners, one of the main purposes of the war. Because it was difficult to seize an enemy without the assistance of several persons, it was an established rule that the prisoner belonged to the first man to touch him. When a man was disarmed, the victor touched him on the shoulder and said, "You are my prisoner." Thereafter, the man was his slave. Those who remained in possession of the battlefield would roast the corpses and bring back the heads and the sexual organs of the dead.

The long set of cannibalistic rites and practices began immediately after the capture of a prisoner. On the way home, the victorious party exhibited their captives in friendly villages, where they were subjected to "gross insults and vituperation." The latter retaliated by expressing their contempt for their victors and their pride at being eaten as befitted the brave.

Before entering their masters' village, the prisoners were dressed as *Tupinamba,* with foreheads shaven, feathers glued to their bodies, and a decoration of feather ornaments. They were taken to the graves of the recently deceased of the community and compelled to "renew," that is, clean them. Later they received the hammocks, ornaments, and weapons of the dead, which had to be used before they could be reappropriated by the heirs. The reason for this custom was that touching the belongings of a dead relative was fraught with danger, unless they were first defiled by a captive.

When the prisoners were taken into the village, women flocked around them, snatched them from the hands of the men, and accompanied them, celebrating their capture with songs, dances (fig. 12, *right*), and references to the day of their execution. They forced the prisoners to dance in front of the hut where the sacred rattles were kept.

After this hostile reception, the prisoners' condition changed for the better. Their victors often gave them to a son or some other relative, who had the privilege of slaughtering them and acquiring new names— one of the greatest distinctions which a *Tupinamba* coveted. The prisoners were also traded for feathers or other ornaments. In many cases, the only outward sign of the prisoner's status was a cotton rope tied around his neck, which, according to some sources, was a symbolical necklace strung with as many beads as he had months to live until his execution. The captives were in no way hampered in their movements; they knew perfectly well that there was no place to which they could escape, for their own groups, far from welcoming them, would even have killed any member who attempted to return. On the other hand, to be killed

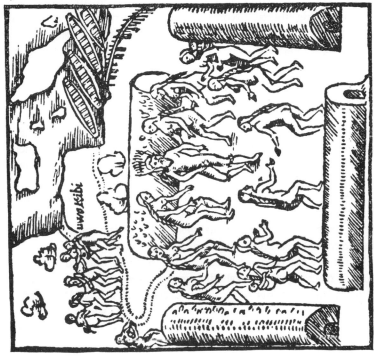

FIGURE 12.—*Tupinamba* warfare and cannibalism. *Left:* Attacking a palisaded village. *Right:* Dance around the newly captured prisoner. (After Staden, 1557.)

ceremonially and then eaten was the fate for which any brave longed once he had lost his liberty. Nothing would have reminded a prisoner of his impending death if, on certain occasions, he had not been exhibited in public and again exposed to jeers and provocations. At drinking bouts, portions of his body were allotted beforehand to the carousers, each of whom—in the victim's presence—learned the part he was to receive at the ceremonial execution.

The village council chose the date of execution and sent invitations to friendly communities. Preparations for the sacrifice started a long time in advance. Certain accessories, like the plaited rope with which the victim was fastened, required a long time to make. Great quantities of beer also had to be brewed for the occasion.

The prisoner feigned indifference toward these signs of his threatening fate. In certain villages he was tied up, but then he indulged freely in all sorts of mischief to revenge his death. The rites observed in these cases started after the arrival of the guests and lasted 3 to 5 days.

On the first day the cord was bleached and artfully knotted, the prisoner was painted black, green eggshells were pasted on his face, and red feathers were glued on his body. The executioners also decorated their own persons with feathers and paint. Old women spent the first night in the hut of the captive singing songs depicting his fate. On the second day they made a bonfire in the middle of the plaza, and men and women danced around the flames while the prisoner pelted them with anything he could reach. The only ceremony of the third day was a dance accompanied by trumpets. The day before the execution the prisoner was given a chance to escape but was immediately pursued. The person who overtook and overpowered him in a wrestling combat adopted a new name, as did the ceremonial executioner. The ritual rope was passed round the prisoner's neck, the end being held by a woman. The prisoner was then given fruits or other missiles to throw at passers-by. Festivities began that night. The prisoner was often requested to dance. Apparently he did so without reluctance and took part in the general rejoicing as if he were merely a guest. He even regarded his position as enviable, for "it was an honor to die as a great warrior during dancing and drinking." The prisoner spent the remainder of his last night in a special hut under the surveillance of women, singing a song in which he foretold the ruin of his enemies and proclaimed his pride at dying as a warrior. His only food was a nut that prevented his bleeding too much. The same night the club to be used for the sacrifice received special treatment. It was decorated, like the prisoner himself, with green eggshells glued on the wood, the handle was trimmed with tassels and feathers (figs. 7, *right*; 9, *right*) and finally, it was suspended from the roof of a hut, women dancing and singing around it during the entire night (fig. 13, *left*).

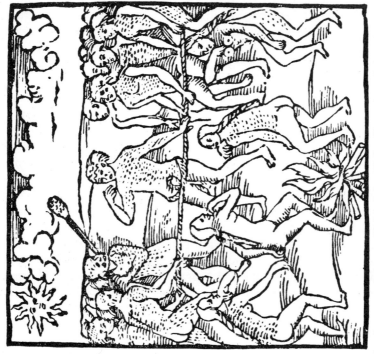

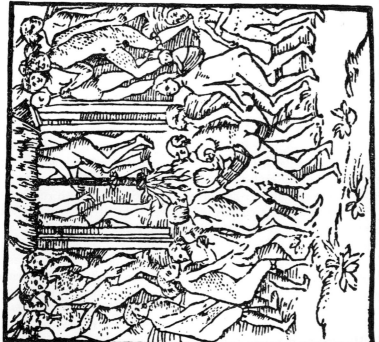

FIGURE 13.—*Tupinamba* cannibalistic ceremonies. *Left:* Singing and dancing around the sacrificial club. *Right:* Execution of the prisoner. (After Staden, 1557.)

The following morning the prisoner was dragged to the plaza by some old women amid cries, songs, and music. The rope was taken from his neck, passed round his waist, and held at both ends by two or more men (fig. 13, *right*). Again he was allowed to give vent to his feelings by throwing fruits or potsherds at his enemies. He was surrounded by women who vied in their insults. Old women, painted black and red, with necklaces of human teeth, darted out of their huts carrying newly painted vases to receive the victim's blood and entrails. A fire was lit and the ceremonial club was shown to the captive. Every man present handled the club for a while, thus acquiring the power to catch a prisoner in the future. Then the executioner appeared in full array, painted and covered with a long feather cloak. He was followed by relatives who sang and beat drums. Their bodies, like that of the executioner, were smeared with white ashes. The club was handed to the executioner by a famous old warrior, who performed a few ritual gestures with it. Then the executioner and his victim harangued each other. The executioner derided the prisoner for his imminent death, while the latter foretold the vengeance that his relatives would take and boasted of his past deeds. The captive showed despondency only if his executioner, instead of being an experienced warrior, was merely a young man who had never been on the battlefield. The execution itself was a cruel game. Enough liberty was allowed the prisoner to dodge the blows, and sometimes a club was put in his hands so that he could parry them without being able to strike. When at last he fell down, his skull shattered, everybody shouted and whistled. The position of the body was interpreted as an omen for the executioner. The prisoner's wife shed a few tears over his body and then joined in the cannibalistic banquet.

Old women rushed to drink the warm blood, and children were invited to dip their hands in it. Mothers would smear their nipples with blood so that even babies could have a taste of it. The body, cut into quarters, was roasted on a barbecue (fig. 14), and the old women, who were the most eager for human flesh, licked the grease running along the sticks. Some portions, reputed to be delicacies or sacred, such as the fingers or the grease around the liver or heart, were allotted to distinguished guests.

As soon as the executioner had killed the victim, he had to run quickly to his hut, which he entered passing between the string and the stave of a stretched bow. Indoors he continued running to and fro as if escaping from his victim's ghost. Meanwhile his sisters and cousins went through the village proclaiming his new name. On this occasion, the male and female relatives of his generation also had to take new names. The members of the community then rushed into the killer's hut and looted all his goods, while the killer himself stood on wooden pestles, where the eye of his victim was shown to him and rubbed against his wrist. The lips of the dead man were sometimes given to him to wear

FIGURE 14.—*Tupinamba* cannibalism. (After Staden, 1557.)

as a bracelet. However, his flesh was strictly taboo to the killer. **After** this the executioner had to recline in a hammock until the hair on his shaved forehead had grown again. During seclusion, he entertained himself by shooting miniature arrows at a wax figure. For 3 days he might not walk but was carried whenever he needed to leave the hut. He also avoided several foods, especially condiments. His return to normal life was celebrated by a big drinking bout, at which the killer tattooed himself by slashing his body in different patterns with an agouti tooth—the more tattooing marks a man could exhibit the higher was his prestige. Even after the feast he was subject to a few more restrictions before he was again a full-fledged member of the community.

The same rites were practiced if, instead of a man, a jaguar had been killed. Later, when the *Tupinamba* could no longer sacrifice their war prisoners, they would open the graves of their enemies and break the skulls with the same ceremonies. The heads of dead enemies were pinned to the ends of the stockade posts.

ESTHETIC AND RECREATIONAL ACTIVITIES

Dances.—Ceremonial dances are described as a monotonous but energetic stamping on the ground by a group of men standing in a circle, with their bodies bent slightly downward and their hands hanging by their sides or laid on their buttocks. The dancers remained on the same spot, except for occasional steps forward and backward and for rotation. Sometimes they shook their heads and made rhythmical gestures with their arms. Dancers were accompanied by songs, the time being marked by shaking rattles or jingling dry fruits that the dancers wore tied round their legs. The rhythm was also given by beating drums or by pounding the ground with a wooden tube. As a rule, men danced separately from women, whose movements are said to have been more violent and exaggerated than those of the other sex. Profane dances were distinguished by a greater freedom of motion and by their orgiastic character. Men and women lost control of themselves, and their dances consisted of wild jumping and running to and fro.

Songs.—*Tupinamba* songs have received much praise. Singers started softly and then gradually sang louder and louder. Cardim says,

They keep among themselves differences of voices in their consort: and ordinarily the women sing the treble, the counter and tenor. [Cardim, 1939, p. 155.]

The songs were started by a choirmaster who sang a couplet; the refrain was repeated by the whole group. The words of these songs refer to mythical events, especially to wars and the heroic deeds of the ancestors. The numerous and graceful allusions to nature were similes. Good composers enjoyed such prestige that if taken prisoner they were released even by their bitterest enemies.

Musical instruments.—When carousing or expressing strong feelings collectively, the *Tupinamba* blew trumpets or played flutes. The trumpets were conch shells with a perforated hole, or a wooden or bamboo tube, on one end of which a calabash served to amplify the sound. Flutes were made of bamboo or of the long bones of slain enemies. Drums, made of a piece of wood hollowed by fire, were small. Rattles have been mentioned above. The time of the dances was beaten with a stamping tube, a thick bamboo stick 4 to 5 feet (1.2 to 1.5 m.) long that was pounded on the ground. On their feet the dancers wore jingles made of fruit shells of *Thevetia ahouai* (Métraux, 1928 a, pp. 214–217).

Narcotics.—Smoking was one of the favorite pastimes in daily life as well as on ceremonial occasions. Tobacco leaves were dried in a hut, then wrapped in a leaf to form a huge cylindrical or conical cigarette. Long tubular bamboo pipes were used exclusively by shamans in magical performances. Stone pipes, found in several points of the Brazilian coast, perhaps belong to another culture anterior to that of the *Tupi*.

Alcoholic beverages.—All social events were occasions for drinking bouts, at which great quantities of beer were consumed. The preparation of large amounts of fermented beverages for these feasts was a heavy task for the women, and was one reason for the polygyny of chiefs. Liquors were made from different plants: sweet manioc, maize, sweet potatoes, mangabeira (*Hancornia speciosa*), cashew, Jaboticaba (*Myrciaria cauliflora*), pineapples, bananas, and also beijú wafers and honey. Manioc beer, the favorite drink, was prepared as follows: The roots, cut into thin slices, were first boiled, then squeezed and partly chewed by young girls. The mass, impregnated with saliva, was mixed with water and heated again over the fire. The liquid was afterward poured into huge jars, half buried in the ground, covered with leaves, and left 2 or 3 days to ferment. A fire was built around the jars to warm the beverage before serving it. Each extended family manufactured its own liquor. When a bout was organized, drinkers went successively to each hut, exhausting the available supply. The women served the liquors in huge calabashes. Old men and guests of honor were served first by the host's closest female relatives. Drinking was always the occasion for riotous merrymaking. Men and women, painted and covered with their more showy ornaments, danced, shouted, whistled, played musical instruments, talked excessively, and brawled. These orgies lasted for 3 or 4 days, during which nobody ate or slept much.

RELIGION

Supernatural beings.—The supernatural powers, by whom the *Tupinamba* felt themselves surrounded, may be classified into two groups: (1) individualized spirits, generally malevolent, which we may call demons or genii; (2) ghosts. The latter, by far the more numerous, differed from the former in having a much more impersonal nature.

The demon of Thunder, Tupã, a secondary character in the early mythology, had as his main function to go "from east to west causing thunder, lightning, and rain." After White contact, this simple demon was promoted to the rank of the Christian God and as such still survives among the *Tupi*-speaking Mestizos.

The bush was peopled by a number of greatly feared demons, who are still active in the folklore of modern Brazil. The most famous of these were Yurupari, Añañ, and Kuru-pirá. Yurupari and Añañ were synonyms, employed respectively by the northern and southern *Tupinamba*. Missionaries and travelers, however, often confused them with ordinary ghosts; they either refer to them rightly as single demons or use these names collectively to designate the whole host of spirits. Just as Tupã was identified with God, Yurupari was equated to the Devil. The Caboclos of Brazil describe him as a goblin, an ogre that haunts the forests and is generally malicious. The same confusion arose about Añañ, who at one time is called a bush spirit and at another, some ghost. Kuru-pirá, scarcely mentioned by the early sources, is the hero of countless tales among the present-day *Tupi*. He is depicted as a goblin with upturned feet, figures as the protector of game, and is rather ill-disposed toward mankind. Other spirits, such as Makashera, Uaiupia, Taguaigba, Igpupiára, and Mbae-tate (will-o'-the-wisp), are scarcely alluded to in the literature.

The world as conceived by the *Tupinamba* was the abode of innumerable ghosts who could be met everywhere, but especially in the woods, in all dark places, and in the neighborhood of graves. These supernatural beings were often harmful: they caused disease, droughts, and defeat. The *Tupinamba* often complained of being attacked and tormented by them. Some ghosts took the form of awe-inspiring animals, such as black birds, bats, and salamanders. Others, more tenuous, changed colors. These spirits were particularly obnoxious in the dark but could be driven away by the fire kept burning all night in *Tupinamba* quarters. No Indian would travel after sunset without a torch or a firebrand lest he be harmed by the evil spirits. So great was their fear of these that they even asked White people to settle in their village in order to keep the spirits in check.

Ceremonialism.—Many details point to cults centering around the supernatural beings described above, who were symbolized by small posts sometimes provided with a cross bar from which painted images were suspended. Small offerings, such as feathers, flowers, or perhaps food, were deposited near them. Spirits were also represented by calabashes painted with human features. Such figures often appeared in the ceremonies of shamans, who burned tobacco leaves in them and inhaled the smoke to induce trances. Maize kernels were put in the mouths of these sacred effigies, which had movable jaws so as to imitate mastication. The grains thus consecrated were sown in the fields, and were expected to produce a good crop. The rattles (maracas), which were highly sacred objects profusely decorated with paintings and feather tufts, are difficult to differentiate from these idols. There is a single statement that seems to indicate that the *Tupinamba* also worshiped wax images kept in special huts.

Rattles were the accessories of all ceremonial activities (fig. 15), but seem to have been used only if previously consecrated by a shaman, who attracted a helpful spirit into them. Every year the villages were visited by shamans (called pay) endowed with power to cause all the rattling maracas chosen by them to speak and grow so powerful that they could grant whatever was required of them. All rattles were presented to the shamans, who conferred upon them the "power of speech" by fumigating them and uttering charms. Then the shamans exhorted the owners of the rattles to go to war and take prisoners to be devoured, for the "spirits in the rattles craved the flesh of captives."

These rattles, after the ceremony, became sacred objects taboo to women. They were placed in a sort of temple and received offerings of food when asked to grant a favor. The spirits who had taken their abode in the rattles advised their owners and revealed future events to them. After a victorious expedition, they were thanked for their assistance.

Shamanism.—The intermediaries between the community and the supernatural world were the shamans. All the chiefs or old men were more or less conversant with magic, but only those who had given some evidence of unusual power were regarded as real medicine men. Their reputation depended mainly on the accuracy of their prophecies and the success of their cures. Those who had achieved fame were known as karaï or pay-wasu, "great medicine men." When a man was about to obtain great magical power, he would shun people, go into seclusion, fast, and then return to announce that he had come in close touch with the spirits. The shamans were rain makers, diviners, and, above all, healers. They had at their service a familiar spirit, sometimes in animal shape, who would follow them and even perform menial tasks for them. The medicine men relied on these spirits when requested to accomplish some difficult task, for instance, to gather rain clouds. They also consulted them as to the issue of some important enterprise or about distant events. The shaman sought interviews with the spirits after 9 days of continence, shutting himself up in a secluded cabin and drinking beer prepared by young virgins. Questions were asked the spirits by the community, but the "whistled" answers were given to the shamans. Some medicine men traveled to the land of the spirits, where they had long talks with the dead.

Shamans as a rule were men, but a few women could prophesy after they had put themselves into a trance, and some old women, said to be possessed by spirits, practiced medicine.

A shaman's breath was loaded with magic power that was greatly reinforced with tobacco smoke. Often the shaman was asked to transfer part

of his "virtue" to the body of some client or disciple. Persons favored
in that way started to tremble. General confessions of transgressions were
imposed by shamans on women in circumstances that are not explained.
Ritual lustrations also were performed by medicine men.

FIGURE 15.—*Tupinamba* shamans wearing feather cloaks and carrying rattles.
(After Métraux, 1928 a.)

The shamans, once recognized as such, enjoyed considerable prestige,
being addressed with respect even by chiefs. Wherever they traveled they
were welcomed with fasts and rejoicing. They inspired such fear that
nobody dared gainsay them or refuse their requests. Some shamans rose
to political power, exercising unchallenged authority in their communities
or even in large districts.

Medicine.—To cure sick people, shamans resorted to the classic methods
of sucking and blowing tobacco smoke over the body of the patient. They
extracted objects considered the cause of the ailment. Female shamans
removed the disease by sucking a thread which had been put in contact
with the patient's body. Medicinal virtues were attributed to genipa paint,
which was used freely for many diseases. Headaches and fevers were
treated by scarification. Wounded people were stretched on a barbecue,
under which a slow fire was lighted, and roasted until their wounds dried.
A great many medicinal herbs are enumerated in early descriptions of

the Brazilian coast, but it is stated only rarely whether the plants actually were used by the Indians for medical purposes, or whether they had been adopted by early European colonists, who were extremely eager to discover miraculous virtues in the Brazilian flora.

Revivalism.—In the years that followed Portuguese colonization of Brazil, the *Tupinamba* were stirred by religious crises that have some analogy with the revivalistic or messianic movements occurring in other parts of the world, especially among some North American tribes. Prophets or messiahs arose among them promising a golden age in which digging sticks would till the soil by themselves and arrows would kill the game without intervention of hunters. The Indians were assured of immortality and eternal youth. The followers of the messiahs gave up their usual activities, dedicated themselves to constant dancing, and even started mass migrations to reach the mythical land of the culture hero. Several of the late *Tupinamba* migrations were caused by the urge to enter the promised land as soon as possible. The leaders of these religious movements were in many cases deified. Certain traits of their personality suggest that they represent a new type of wonder-worker, who had been influenced both by the early traditions of their tribes and by Christian ideas preached to the Indians by the Catholic missionaries. Similar crises occurred in modern times among the southern *Tupi* of Paraguay and Brazil. A comparison between the ancient and the modern messianic outbursts shows remarkable similarities.

These beliefs were closely associated with the cosmology. The *Tupinamba* established a correlation between the eclipses and the end of the world, which marked the beginning of a new era of peace and happiness. Whenever an eclipse occurred, the men chanted a hymn hailing the mythical "grandfather," and the women and children moaned, throwing themselves to the ground in the utmost despair.

MYTHOLOGY

Important fragments of *Tupinamba* mythology have come down to us through the French friar, André Thevet (who visited Brazil in 1555). The main characters are represented by a set of culture heroes listed under the names of Monan, Maira-monan, Maira-pochy, Mairata, and Sumé, all of which may well be synonyms for a single figure: the Tamoi or Mythical Grandfather. The culture hero, Monan, though an exalted creator, does not rank strictly as a god because he was not worshiped. Even his creative activities are not all-embracing; he made "the sky, the earth, the birds, and the animals; but neither the sea nor the clouds" nor, apparently, mankind. Closely associated with him was Maira-monan, who is probably the same Monan with the epithet Maira (Europeans were also called Maira). Thevet calls him the "Transformer" because he was fond of changing things according to his fancies. Maira-monan, described as a great medicine man living in seclusion and fasting, was a benefactor of mankind, on whom he bestowed agriculture. Tradition has it that he changed himself into a child who, when beaten, dropped fruits and tubers. According to another version, he initiated a young girl into the practice of agriculture. As a lawgiver he introduced social organization and imposed severe taboos, including the prohibition of eating slow-moving animals. For unknown reasons, ungrateful people plotted his death and, after several unsuccessful attempts, burned him on a pyre. The bursting of his head originated Thunder, and the fire of his pyre, Lightning. There is no doubt that Maira-monan and Sumé, who is often mentioned as the originator of agriculture, are the same culture hero. Owing to a vague similarity of name, Sumé was regarded by early missionaries as the fabulous apostle Saint Thomas (S. Tomé), the supposed bringer of Christianity to the Indians long before the discovery of America. Petroglyphs or natural fissures in rocks suggesting footprints were attributed to Saint Thomas and were presented as evidence of his extensive travels.

The twin cycle, so common in South American mythology, is closely connected with the personality of the culture hero, Maira. The main episodes of the myth are as follows: Maira deserts his wife, who is pregnant. She sets out in quest of her lost husband and is guided in her journey by the unborn child. Having been refused one of his requests, the child grows angry and remains silent. The mother is lost and arrives at the house of Sarigue (Opossum, subsequently a man), who sleeps with her and makes her pregnant with a second child. Continuing her search for her husband she is misled to the village of Jaguar (also a man), who kills her and throws the twins on a heap of rubbish. They are saved by a woman, who brings them up. They demonstrate their supernatural origin by growing very rapidly and feeding their foster mother abundant game. Remembering, or learning, that Jaguar and his people killed their mother, they take revenge by luring them to the sea and changing them into actual beasts of prey. Then they start again in search of their father. Finally, they find him, but he does not want to acknowledge them as his children before a trial of their origin. He orders them to accomplish difficult tasks. They shoot arrows into the sky and each arrow hits the butt of the other, thus forming a long chain. They pass between two constantly clashing and recoiling rocks. The twin begotten by Opossum is crushed to pieces, but his brother undergoes the ordeal successfully and brings him back to life. The same fate befalls Opossum's son when he tries to steal the bait of the demon Añañ, but again Maira's son revives him. After they have gone through these several ordeals, both are recognized by Maira as his children.

There are two versions of the destruction of the world. The first cataclysm which befell the earth was a big fire set by Monan, which he himself put out by flooding the universe. The flood explains the origin of the rivers and of the sea, which is still salty because of the ashes.

Arikut and Tamendonar were brothers. The latter, a peaceful man, was gravely insulted by Arikut, who threw at him the arm of a victim he was devouring. Tamendonar caused a spring to flow so abundantly that the water covered the surface of the earth. Both brothers escaped and repopulated the universe.

In the cosmogony collected by Thevet, a tale has been incorporated which was and is still very popular among South American Indians (*Chiriguano, Mataco, Toba, Uro-Chipaya*, Indians of Huarochiri). Maíra-pochy (the bad Maira), a powerful medicine man or more probably the culture hero himself, appears in the village disguised as an indigent and dirty man. He makes the daughter of the village chief pregnant by giving her a fish to eat. Later, when all the most handsome men of the region vie with one another to be recognized as the father of the child, the baby hands Maira-pochy a bow and arrows, thus acknowledging him as his father. Maira-pochy shows his supernatural power by raising miraculous crops. He transforms his relatives-in-law into many different animals.

LORE AND LEARNING

The division of time among the northern *Tupinamba* was based on the appearance and disappearance of the Pleiades above the horizon. The ripening of cashews was also used for reckoning time. Dates of future events were calculated with knots or beads on a cord.

A complete list of the *Tupinamba* constellations has been recorded by Claude d'Abbeville. Most of them were named after animals. Eclipses were explained as attempts of a celestial jaguar (a red star) to devour the moon.

BIBLIOGRAPHY

Abbeville, 1614; Acuña, 1891; Anchieta, 1846, 1876–77; Ayrosa, 1943; Cardim, 1939; Denis, 1851; Enformação do Brazil, 1844; Fritz, 1922; Hoehne, 1937; Léry, 1880; Magalhães de Gandavo, 1922; Métraux, 1927, 1928 a, 1928 b; Nieuhoff, 1682; Pinto, 1935–38; Rocha Pombo, 1905; Soares de Souza, 1851; Staden, 1928 (1557); Studart Filho, 1931; Thevet, 1575, 1878 (*see also* Métraux, 1928 b); Vaas de Caminha, 1812–13; Vasconcellos, 1865; Yves d'Evreux, 1864. For further *Tupinamba* references, see Métraux, 1927, 1928 a.

THE GUAJA

By Curt Nimuendajú

HISTORY

The *Guajá* are called *Wazaizara* (wazaí, an ornament of small tufts of feathers stuck with wax in the hair, plus zara, "owner") by the *Guajajara* and *Tembé*, and *Aiayé* by the *Amanayé*. *Guajá* is the Neo-Brazilian form of gwazá.

The tribe is rarely mentioned in literature. In 1774, Ribeiro de Sampaio (1825, p. 8) mentions the *Uaya* among the tribes of the lower Tocantins. A list of the tribes existing in 1861 in the region along the road from Imperatriz to Belém mentions the *Ayaya* as "wild; very few of them are tame, but are timorous and therefore are pursued and killed by the others" (Marques, C. A., 1864). According to the report of F. C. de Araujo Brusque (1862, p. 12), the *Uaiara* (*Guajará*) at times appeared on the upper Gurupí River but did not have a fixed residence.

The author obtained the following information among the *Tembé* of the Gurupí in 1913–14 and among the *Guajajara* in 1929:

The *Guajá* wandered without fixed living places through the jungles between the Capim and upper Gurupí Rivers and between the latter and the Pindaré River, northward to about lat. 3° 40' S. (map 1, *No. 1*; see Volume 1, map 7). In 1910 or 1911 a small group of them committed small thefts in the fields at the mouth of the Gurupí Mirim River. The *Tembé* tracked them to the headwaters of the Gurupí Mirim. Although armed with powerful bows and arrows, the *Guajá* there surrendered meekly to their pursuers, who took them to the village. Here the captives soon died of intestinal ills attributed to the *Tembé's* cooked and seasoned food. The language of the two tribes was so similar that they understood each other with ease. In 1943, the botanist Ricardo Fróes met a group of them on the upper Carú, a left tributary of the Pindaré River.

CULTURE

The *Guajá* did not have any agriculture whatever, but at times stole from the plantations of the *Tembé, Guajajara,* and *Urubú*. When caught, they were killed or at least beaten and imprisoned.

135

The *Guajá* built only temporary shelters, or merely camped under trees, sleeping on leaf beds on the ground.

Some *Guajá* bows and arrows were procured in 1913 by a punitive expedition against the then hostile *Urubú* Indians, who had massacred a *Guajá* camp. The weapons were carelessly made but were very large, the bamboo arrowheads being perhaps the largest known.

In 1913, the *Guaja* still used stone axes.

BIBLIOGRAPHY

Brusque, 1862; Marques, C. A., 1864; Ribeiro de Sampaio, 1825.

THE TENETEHARA[1]

By Charles Wagley and Eduardo Galvão

INTRODUCTION

The *Tupí-Guaraní*-speaking people of northeastern Brazil, commonly called *Guajajara* and *Tembé,* are generally mentioned in the literature as two independent tribes but are really a single group calling themselves *Tenetehara.* By this name they distinguish themselves from the *Urubú* (also *Tupí-Guaraní*), the *Timbira* (*Ge*), and the Neo-Brazilians of the same region.

The *Guajajara-Tenetehara* (map 1, *No. 1*; see Volume 1, map 7) inhabit the region drained by the Mearim, Grajaú, and Pindaré Rivers in the state of Maranhão (lat. 3°–5° S., long. 4°–6° W.); the *Tembé-Tenetehara* (map 1, *No. 1;* see Volume 1, map 7) live along the Gurupí, Guamá, and Capim Rivers in the State of Pará (lat. 2°–3° S., long. 7°–9° W.). The *Guajajara-Tenetehara* now number more than 2,000, but the *Tembé-Tenetehara* are estimated at only 350 to 400. For convenience, we shall refer to these people by the name they give themselves, *Tenetehara,* rather than by the tribal names, *Guajajara* and *Tembé,* by which they are best known in the literature. No important differences of culture or language are known to exist between the *Tembé-Tenetehara* of the State of Pará and the *Guajajara-Tenetehara* of the State of Maranhão.

The region inhabited by the *Tenetehara* is dense tropical rain forest rich in hardwoods, rubber, copaiba (*Copaifera* sp.), and various palms, especially the babassú palm (*Orbignya* sp.), whose leaves and nuts are so important in *Tenetehara* economic life. There is little seasonal variation in temperature in the region, yet there are two definite seasons: the rainy season lasting from December through June, and a dry season from July through November.

The present summary is based on field work done by the authors for 5 months during 1941–42.

[1] The field research on which this article is based was made possible by the Museu Nacional, Rio de Janeiro, Brazil.

HISTORY

The *Tenetehara* seem to have inhabited this general region since pre-Columbian times, and they have been in contact with western culture in one form or another for more than 300 years. As early as 1615, an expedition led by La Ravardière on the upper Pindaré River encountered Indians whom he called *Pinariens* and who were probably *Tenetehara* (*Guajajara*) (Métraux, 1928 a). One year later, Bento Maciel Parente speaks of killing many *Tenetehara* (*Guajajara*) when he traveled up the Pindaré River with 45 Portuguese soldiers and 90 Indian followers (probably *Tupinamba*) in search of gold.

In the middle 17th century, the Jesuits made three separate expeditions up the Pindaré River for the purpose of bringing *Tenetehara* down the river and placing them in mission villages on the Island of Maranhão. Two expeditions, one led by Father Francisco Velloso and Father José Soares, and the second led by the Jesuit Superior, Manoel Nunes, in the middle of the 17th century, were partially successful and founded several mission villages on the lower Pindaré, among them Itaquy. The third expedition, led by the Jesuit José Maria Garconi, returned with a large number of *Tenetehara* and placed them in the mission village called Cajupé on the lower Pindaré. Later, however, when the Jesuits moved their mission village farther down river to Maracú (the present town of Vianna), the majority of these missionized *Tenetehara* returned to the upper Pindaré in fear of their enemies, the *Gamela*. In consequence, the Jesuits established a new mission on the upper Pindaré at the mouth of the Carú River. Besides these religious missions, however, it is probable that the *Tenetehara* were in contact with Portuguese adventurers who wandered in this general region hunting Indians as slaves.

By the middle 18th century, the *Tenetehara* are mentioned as inhabiting also the Grajaú and Mearim Rivers, west of the Pindaré. At the same time Gustavo Dodt mentions them (*Tembé*) along the banks of the Gurupí River. In 1840 the provincial government of Maranhão established the Colony of São Pedro do Pindaré for the Indians of the region, with but little success. The Colony of Januario, established higher up the Pindaré in 1854, was more successful, having a population of 120 *Tenetehara* almost 20 years later. From the last half of the 19th century until the present, there has been a steady advance of Neo-Brazilians into *Tenetehara* territory, especially along the courses of the Mearim and Grajaú Rivers. Except for several sporadic uprisings, the *Tenetehara* have always lived at peace with Neo-Brazilians, and there has been a mutual interchange of culture within the region. Today iron tools, clothes, myths of Iberian and African origin, and many other elements of frontier Neo-Brazilian culture are integrated elements in *Tenetehara* life.

CULTURE

SUBSISTENCE ACTIVITIES

Farming.—Like the extinct coastal *Tupí* groups, the *Tenetehara* are extensive agriculturists. They cultivate principally maize, both bitter and sweet manioc, cará, (*Dioscorea* sp.), squash, peanuts, beans, and bananas. At present, they also have large plantations of rice, which they raise primarily to sell to their Neo-Brazilian neighbors.

Annually from July to November, great areas of forest are cleared for gardens, and the dry vegetation is burned toward the end of November. The gardens are planted throughout December. All *Tenetehara* use steel axes, hoes, and bush knives obtained by trade from Neo-Brazilians.

PLATE 13.—**Tenetehara boys.** *Top:* Boys dressed for puberty ceremony. *Bottom, left:* Boy decorated for puberty ceremony. His father led the song and his mother danced. *Bottom, right:* Portrait of young man. (Courtesy Charles Wagley.)

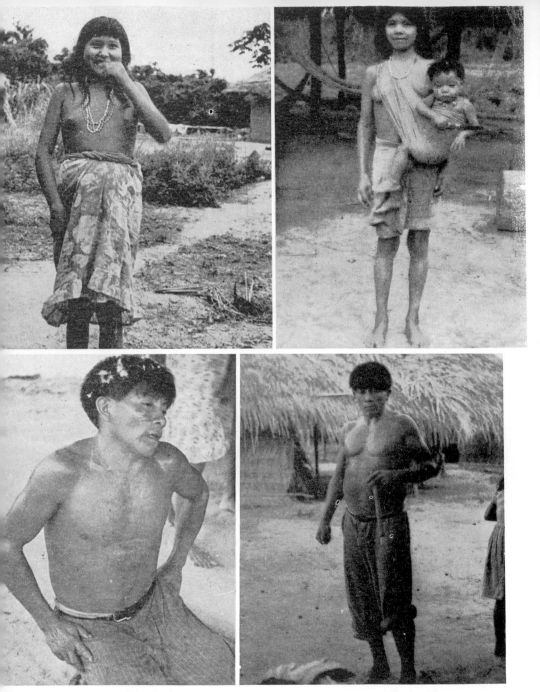

PLATE 14.—**Tenetehara women and shaman.**   *Top, left:* Girl just before puberty ceremony.   *Top, right:* Woman and child.   *Bottom, left:* Shaman possessed by familiar spirit.   *Bottom, right:* Shaman smoking long tobacco cigar and holding in his hand an object drawn from a sick patient.   (Courtesy Charles Wagley.)

Formerly, only women planted and harvested cotton and peanuts, while the cultivation of manioc, maize, and other plants was the exclusive occupation of the men. Today, however, men plant the entire garden, including cotton and peanuts, and women help now and again in light garden tasks. Similarly, the preparation of manioc flour and the carrying of drinking water were exclusively female tasks which a man would have been ashamed to perform; at present both sexes perform them equally.

Gardens are said to be individually owned, yet most commonly an older man makes a garden aided by his real and adopted sons, his nephews, and his sons-in-law. The garden, while used by all in common, is said to be the individual property of the head of the family.

Wild foods.—Hunting is practiced not only to add meat to a basically vegetarian diet, but also to collect animal skins for sale to Neo-Brazilian traders. Tapir (*Tapirus terrestris*), deer, both the white-lipped and collared peccary, monkeys, agouti (*Dasyprocta,* gen.), and various forest fowls are the principal animals hunted. Peccary hides bring especially good prices at Neo-Brazilian villages, and the *Tenetehara* use the money to buy trade goods, such as clothes, salt, and gunpowder.

Today the favorite means of hunting is with muzzle-loading shotguns. Yet, lacking money with which to buy guns, many men of each village still hunt with the bow and arrow.

Fishing is done by ordinary hook and line acquired from Neo-Brazilians. Fishing by poisoning drying pools with timbó (*Serjania* sp.) is known but seldom practiced.

Collecting babassú palm nuts and copaíba oil has acquired extreme importance in modern *Tenetehara* economic life, especially on the Mearim, Grajaú, and Pindaré Rivers. These products, like rice and furs, can be sold in order to buy manufactured articles, such as clothes, guns, fishhooks, and salt.

HOUSES AND VILLAGES

At present, the *Tenetehara* houses in the Pindaré and Grajaú River regions have a rectangular floor plan with hip-roofs. Both walls and roofs are covered with babassú palm leaves. This house form is perhaps Neo-Brazilian, yet people do not remember any other type. In 1924 E. H. Snethlage (1931) found the *Tenetehara* houses on the middle Mearim River of the same type as those of the Neo-Brazilians of the region, and even in the last century, Gustavo Dodt described *Tenetehara* (*Tembé*) houses on the Gurupí River as straw-roofed with clay adobe walls (Dodt, 1873, p. 194), definitely of Neo-Brazilian type. Snethlage speaks of houses covered with bark, but considered this type of roof temporary, explaining its use by the lack of palm leaves in certain districts.

A village generally has two rows of houses with a wide street between them. Larger villages may have three, four, or more rows. The size of

Tenetehara villages varies greatly. According to a recent census made by the Serviço de Protecção aos Indios, the villages of the Pindaré and Grajaú ranged from 35 to more than 800 persons each. Houses are generally occupied by a matrilineal extended family, although many hold only a simple family (man, wife, and young children). Extended family residences are not subdivided by inner walls, but each simple family uses a portion of the house space, having its separate cooking fire around which it hangs its sleeping hammocks. Gourds filled with drinking water, baskets with manioc flour, metal utensils, and other belongings are hung on the upright supports against the walls. Sometimes high platforms are made near the roof for the storage of maize, manioc, hides, farming instruments, etc.

Snethlage (1931) saw a large ceremonial house, which was much larger than the dwellings in the village of Colonía on the Mearim River. It was situated at the end of the village street. On the Pindaré River, the ceremonial house is no longer erected, but formerly it was built for the Honey Feast (see p. 146) and destroyed afterward. It seems to have been but a larger shelter without walls, in which both men and women danced.

CLOTHING

Formerly, the *Tenetehara* were nude. Men tied the prepuce over the glans penis with a piece of palm fiber (Lago, 1822, p. 85). Today they have adopted clothes from the Neo-Brazilians; women always wear skirts and men wear shirts and pants, only occasionally stripping down to a loincloth for heavy work in the gardens. It is now a matter of prestige to have new or better clothes than other people.

MANUFACTURES

Basketry.—Basketry is still woven by the *Tenetehara,* especially in the villages of the upper Pindaré River. A split flexible creeper is used principally. Round sieves for straining manioc flour, square baskets with woven geometric designs, and the flexible tipití for squeezing the poisonous juice from bitter manioc are the most common objects of this class.

Weaving.—Native cotton is used almost entirely for string hammocks. The string is wound horizontally around two vertical posts driven into the ground; double vertical strands are twined at a distance of about 2½ inches (7.5 cm.) apart.

Gourds.—Eating utensils are made from round gourds. The gourds are first boiled, then allowed to dry thoroughly, cut in half, and the interior mass scraped out. The interior is stained black with genipa and frequently the outside is decorated geometrically with incisions or lines of black genipa dye. Frequently, only a hole is cut in a gourd, and it is used as a jug for drinking water or wild honey.

Ceramics.—The pottery which Snethlage noted in 1924 (Snethlage, 1931) was simple and generally undecorated, but some vessels had incised designs.

Today pottery making has been completely abandoned, at least on the Pindaré and Grajaú Rivers. The *Tenetehara* use metal utensils purchased from Neo-Brazilians.

Weapons.—Bows average 3 feet (1 m.) in length; the belly is convex, the inside flat. Bows are generally made of pau d'arco wood (*Tecoma conspicua*), and the bowstring of twined tucum (*Bactris* sp.) fibers. Arrows are comparatively short, averaging only about 3 feet (1 m.) in length. Nowadays they have steel points made from old bush knives and bits of metal purchased from Neo-Brazilians and worked cold. Arrow shafts are of reed (*Gynerium sagittatum*, a grass).

SOCIAL AND POLITICAL ORGANIZATION

Each *Tenetehara* village is politically autonomous. Inter-village relations are maintained by means of visits for ceremonials and for trade, and by intermarriages.

Since the time of the Jesuits, each village has had a secular chief (capitão in Portuguese) appointed by some authority outside the tribe (e.g., Jesuit missionaries, the Colonial, Imperial, and Republican Governments, and at present the Serviço de Protecção aos Indios). In general, this chief is only an intermediary between the Indians and the Neo-Brazilians. He is generally but one of several leaders or heads of the extended families which make up a village. However, the respect that he is accorded by outsiders frequently increases his prestige in the eyes of the villagers.

Each family leader unites about him a large number of kin, either in his own house or in contiguous houses. He may have several young men living with him whom he calls "son" and as many young women whom he calls "daughter" (own daughters, real or classificatory brother's daughter, or wife's real or classificatory sister's daughter) as possible. Because marriage is matrilocal and sons-in-law must work in the gardens of their fathers-in-law at least for a year or two, these "daughters" attract followers for the family leader. According to his individual capacity, the family leader attracts large extended families more or less permanently around him.

Extended family groups cooperatively plant large gardens. Frequently, the leader sells all marketable products, such as skins, rice, and babassú, produced by the entire group, and proportions the results of the sales among the individual families. A village generally has four, five, or more extended families and their leaders, who while not constituting a formal village council, ultimately decide public questions.

Childbirth.—During his wife's pregnancy, a *Tenetehara* man must observe elaborate restrictions in his diet and in his hunting activities. He may not kill or eat jaguars, falcons (*Falconoidea*), ant eaters (*Tamandua tetradactyla*), wildcats, parrots, or various other animals and forest fowls. The purpose of these taboos is to protect the fetus from the "spirit" of the animal killed or eaten. This "spirit" (piwara) enters the unborn child, either causing physical abnormalities or giving it some undesirable attribute of the animal. For example, the spirit of the enormous beaked toucan (*Ramphastos toco*) may cause the child to be born with a large nose; the father who kills a jaguar during his wife's pregnancy may expect to have an insane child.

A new series of taboos begins for both parents at childbirth. Sexual relations are prohibited for parents until the "child is hard," that is, until it begins to have some control over its muscles, 5 or 6 months after the birth. For a week to 10 days, both parents may eat only manioc flour, small fish, and roast maize, and must drink only warmed water. Until the child is weaned, certain meats, such as macaw, white-lipped peccary, and tapir are forbidden to both parents. Breaking any of these taboos arrests the development of the infant and may cause its death.

Puberty.—Formerly, adolescents of both sexes were isolated for 10 days or more in separate huts built especially for the occasion. On the 10th morning, entrails of the agouti were stretched across the door of the hut, and the adolescent had to break these in order to leave. Today boys are seldom isolated at all before their puberty ceremony, and girls may be isolated only by a palm-leaf screen within the family dwelling or they may simply lie in their hammocks in one corner of the room. Even today the girl ends her isolation by breaking the entrails of the agouti stretched across the door, and is chased by the young men of the village when she runs to the stream or pool for a bath.

Formerly, a father examined his son's penis after the isolation period, and, if there were signs of masturbation, the boy was whipped with a vine rope.

The puberty ceremony is for both sexes (see pls. 13, 14). Boys are painted red with genipa, and falcon breast feathers are glued on their breasts and arms (pl. 13). Frequently, the boys carry a wand consisting of about 30 to 40 tail feathers from the red macaw stuck into a wooden handle. Girls are simply painted black over their entire bodies and sometimes white falcon breast feathers are glued to their hair.

The puberty ceremony begins at dawn and lasts 24 hours. It consists mainly of general singing and dancing led by the grandfather of one of the adolescents. Shamans play an important role, calling their familiar spirits and falling into trances under the influence of the spirits (see p. 147). At dawn, after the night of group singing everyone feasts on large quantities of meat, the result of hunting during previous days by all men of the village. At this time the young people are formally given permission to eat of such meats as peccary, guariba monkey, wild goose, and various forest fowls, all of which until now were prohibited to them. Because of this feast, the Neo-Brazilians of the region call the *Tenetehara* puberty ceremony the Festival of Roasted Meat (Festa de Moqueado).

Marriage.—Marriage takes two general forms: Frequently, a young man marries a preadolescent girl, moving to her parents' house and waiting until after her puberty ceremony to consummate the marriage; or a girl's father finds her a husband after her puberty ceremony. In either case, residence for the couple is matrilocal for at least a year after sexual relations begin and generally until the birth of a child. There seem not to be any special marriage ceremonies. After becoming a parent, a young man of initiative may break away from his father-in-law and set up his own household.

Monogamy is the general rule, yet there are cases of family leaders with two and even three wives. In such cases, the wives are usually close relatives; in several instances, they were a widow and her daughter by a previous marriage.

Death.—Antonio Pereira do Lago, writing in the 19th century, reports that the *Tenetehara* buried their dead in the family dwelling, and that the house was destroyed when a second death occurred. At present, burial is in a cemetery, always just outside the village; the body is wrapped in a mat made of babassú palm (*Orbignya* sp.) leaves, or it may be placed in a wooden box similar to that used by local Neo-Brazilians. A low roofed shelter is frequently built over the grave; such grave shelters were noted by Dodt on the Gurupí in the last century.

ESTHETIC AND RECREATIONAL ACTIVITIES

Art.—Native art forms are represented today only by a few items, such as decorated basketwork, incised and painted gourd receptacles, and feather head bands. Wands are made by sticking innumerable tail feathers of the red macaw into a wooden handle.

Music.—The *Tenetehara* are very fond of music. They have not only retained their native music, but have borrowed the Neo-Brazilian music of the region. Singing native songs, however, is still the most popular pastime and the outstanding esthetic of the *Tenetehara*. There are frequent informal reunions called žingareté (to sing much) in the evenings throughout the year, when people sing secular songs for recreation. Such songs last for the greater part of the night, people leaving and joining the group from time to time. Ceremonies are basically singing festivals and each has its particular set of songs. To sing such ceremonial songs out of season would bring supernatural reprisal. The songs of the Honey

Festival are considered the most beautiful by the *Tenetehara*. They are believed to have been learned in mythological times by a young *Tenetehara* shaman when he visited a festival of the animals at the Village of the Jaguar; the songs are those sung by individual animals on that occasion.

Shamans are obliged to have a large repertoire of songs; a group of songs is attributed to each supernatural being, and the shaman must know those of his familiar spirits. A good voice is a prerequisite for shamanism. At shamanistic sessions (p. 147), the shaman sings as he "calls" the spirit, and the spirit sings through him after he is possessed (pl. 14, *bottom, left*); the audience joins the shaman in the refrain of the songs. Shamanistic sessions are well attended, because they give people a chance to come together to sing.

In all group singing both men and women sing, the latter in a higher key, much as among the *Tapirapé* and as described for the *Tupinamba*.

Musical instruments.—Gourd rattles always accompany singing, but they are not sacred, as among the coastal *Tupi*. A trumpet with a bamboo stem and a cow's horn resonator is used during the Honey Festival; during aboriginal times, a gourd resonator was used in place of the cow's horn.

Dancing.—Frequently, during informal singing, the *Tenetehara* keep time to the music by stamping with one foot on the ground. During lively shamanistic sessions and during ceremonies, both sexes dance. Commonly, they simply stamp in one spot, with a heavy beat on one foot. During the Maize Festival, they move in a large circle with a skipping step; on other occasions, a line of men faces a line of women and the two lines advance and retreat from each other. A possessed shaman dances in a manner indicative of the supernatural possessing him; for example, when possessed by the guariba monkey spirit, he postures in imitation of the monkey, and when possessed by the toad spirit, he hops about like a toad.

The *Tenetehara* also frequently hold Neo-Brazilian dances, when men and women dance in couples to waltzes, "sambas," and local folk tunes. For these dances, many young *Tenetehara* have learned to play bamboo flutes and skin drums. Sometimes a Neo-Brazilian is hired to play the accordion for dancing.

Games.—No aboriginal games were noted among the *Tenetehara*. Boys play tops and marbles in the same manner as the Neo-Brazilian children of the region.

Narcotics.—Hashish (*Cannabis indica*), or diamba, as it is called locally, is in widespread use in the region of the Pindaré, Mearim, and Grajaú Rivers, both by the *Tenetehara* and Neo-Brazilians. On the Pindaré River, it is used in long cigarettes made from leaves of the plant rolled in a thin sheet of bark of tawari tree (*Couratari* sp.).

Native tobacco plays an important role in *Tenetehara* religious life, being used by the shamans in the treatment of illness and in all their other activities (pl. 14, *bottom, right*).   It is smoked in long funnellike cigars, about 12 inches (30 cm.) long, wrapped in cane bark.   Smoking of tobacco or hashish is also a general pastime.

There are no indications that the *Tenetehara* have known any alcoholic beverages other than those which they now purchase from the Neo-Brazilians.

RELIGION

Tenetehara supernatural beings (karowara, their generic name) may be conveniently divided into three groups: culture heroes, forest spirits, and ghosts, the last being spirits of the dead and spirits of animals.   All except the culture heroes are malignant and make the world so generally dangerous that the Indians must constantly have recourse to their shamans for protection.

Culture heroes.—*Tenetehara* culture heroes are not active supernatural beings in their modern relations to mankind, but in myths they are culture bringers and creators. (See Mythology, p. 147.)   Among them, Maíra and Tupan are the principal creators of culture.   It is quite possible, however, that the importance of Tupan has been overemphasized by missionaries who identified him throughout Brazil with the Christian God. Tupan was simply the "demon of Thunder" among the coastal *Tupí* (Métraux, 1928 b).

Forest spirits.—Maranaüwa is the owner of the forest and of the animals inhabiting it, especially of white-lipped peccaries, and he punishes *Tenetehara* men who needlessly and wantonly kill this species.   Maranaüwa may be identified as Corropira or Kuri-pira of other *Tupí* groups and of Neo-Brazilian folklore.

Üwan, the spirit which controls the rivers and water life, is given two other descriptive names: Üpóre (ü, water; póre, inhabitant) and Üžáre (ü, water; žare, owner).   This supernatural being is identified by local Neo-Brazilians as the "Mother of Water," a character of Brazilian folklore.   Üwan is described by the *Tenetehara* as a spirit who is always malignant, and who causes illness.

Zuruparí is a forest demon which attracts hunters and leads them astray until they are lost and then kills them.   This spirit corresponds to Yuruparí, or Zuruparí, of Neo-Brazilian folklore.

Ghosts.—Wandering ghosts (ažang) are the souls of people who died from sorcery, who broke incest taboos during their life, or who died by slowly wasting away.   The modern *Tenetehara* explain that the souls of people who die by other means go to the "home of Tupan," a Christian explanation.

The ažang wander through the forests or near the cemeteries and abandoned houses.   They can transform themselves into animals which appear to hunters, frightening them and causing them to lose arrows shot at them by mistake. The *Tenetehara* are very frightened of ažang, especially at night; they always avoid passing near a cemetery or an abandoned house.

The spirits of dead animals (piwara) mainly enforce restrictions on diet and on hunting, such as those imposed upon a man during his wife's pregnancy and his child's early infancy and upon preadolescent children. If a father of a young child, for example, kills a macaw, the spirit of the macaw may make the child ill if he is not treated by a shaman sufficiently strong to control this spirit. Deer, monkeys, forest fowls, toads, tapirs, and many other animals have such spirits.

CEREMONIALS

Besides the puberty rites, two ceremonies are still held by the *Tenetehara* of the Pindaré and Grajaú River region: The Honey Festival (žemuči-hawo and the Maize Festival (awačiwähuhawo). The first takes place during the dry season, and the second accompanies the growth of maize during the rains from January through March. The Maize Festival is basically a song feast and dance, which provides a background for shamanistic performances. Shamans invoke their familiar spirits in order to protect the growing maize.

The Honey Festival takes place during the last days of the dry season and lasts but a few days. Preparations for it, however, require months, because the *Tenetehara* must collect wild honey for it throughout the dry season. Generally, 20 to 30 gourd containers, each holding one to two liters of honey, must be filled. Each night or so during these months, the people of the village gather and sing "to bless the honey." Formerly, the containers of honey were hung to the rafters of a special ceremonial house built for the occasion; nowadays, they are stored in any available empty house. When sufficient honey has been collected, the leader of the ceremony sends out invitations to nearby villages. During the ceremony, the *Tenetehara* dance in a large circle. The songs refer to the original honey feast held by animals in mythical times (Nimuendajú, 1915). The honey is mixed with water and consumed by the dancers; when the honey is gone, the ceremony terminates.

SHAMANISM

In spite of more than 300 years of sporadic contact with missionaries, shamanism continues to be a very active element of *Tenetehara* religious life. In fact, with the decline of native ceremonial life under Neo-Brazilian influence, the activities of the shamans (pažé) absorb most of modern *Tenetehara* religious activity. Like the *Tupinamba* shaman, pay, the *Tenetehara* pažé is a man of great prestige in his community. At present, each village has no less than two or three shamans and some large villages have six or seven; in addition, numerous young men are learning the art. There are few *Tenetehara* who do not attempt during their youth to become shamans.

Tenetehara shamans cure illness by removing the disease-causing objects through sucking or massaging (pl. 14, *bottom, right*). During the cure, the shaman dances and sings, beating time with a rattle and calling his familiar spirits. Men and women of the village join him in the chorus. Now and again, he gulps and swallows smoke from his large tubular cigar, eventually becoming definitely intoxicated. Suddenly, he staggers backward, grasping his chest to show that his spirit has possessed him. A shaman must be able "to call" (be possessed by) the same piwara, or spirit, that has caused the illness in order to be able to extract the object. He approaches the patient and sucks or massages out the extraneous object (ümae), i. e., a piece of stone, bone, or wood.

A shaman shows by his actions which spirit has possessed him (pl. 14, *bottom, left*). If it is a deer spirit (aropohá piwara), he may eat manioc leaves; if ghosts (ažang), he drinks uncooked tapioca flour mixed with water; and if any familiar spirit, he frequently rubs the lighted end of his cigar over his bare chest and arms without being burned. Several informants told of *Tenetehara* shamans who swallow burning coals from a fire while possessed by the spirit of the kururu toad (*Bufo* sp.). Sneth-lage (1927, p. 132) also observed this. On occasions, the familiar spirit is "too strong" for a shaman, and he falls unconscious, remaining extended upon the ground for an hour or more until the spirit leaves him.

The power of a *Tenetehara* shaman depends upon the number of familiar spirits he can "call." Commonly, shamans have five or six such familiar spirits. Because üwan, the owner of water, frequently causes illness, this spirit is most frequently called in cures. At present, on the Pindaré River, there are no shamans who count among their familiar spirits the toad spirit (kurura piwara), the forest demon, Maranaüwa, or the jaguar spirit (žawara piwara). So powerful are these three spirits that no modern shamans dare "call" them. A shaman spends many years learning "to call" his various familiar spirits by singing and acquiring the power to withstand them when possessed. He sometimes visits many villages to learn from other shamans and to acquire a larger number of familiar spirits.

MYTHOLOGY

In *Tenetehara* mythology, two culture heroes stand out, Tupan and Maíra. The figure of Tupan has probably been emphasized by missionary influence; he appears as a creator and protector. Maíra, however, is clearly a native culture creator. He is the donor of fire, which he stole from the vultures, hiding it in a stick of urucú wood so that the *Tenete-hara* might use this soft wood to make fire. Maíra also brought manioc and maize to the *Tenetehara*. Maíra was the father of the Maíra-üra, who was born after his father had abandoned his mother. While wandering in search of Maíra, her husband, this woman conceived a second time when she stayed one night in the house of Mukwüra. From these two unions were born the twins Maíra-üra (üra, son) and Mukwüra-üra. A detailed myth is told of the adventures of these twins in their search for Maíra.

The *Tenetehara* also tell various cycles of animal stories. One cycle deals with the difficulties of the Gamba (*Didelphis* sp.) in arranging a satisfactory husband for his daughter and of how he is followed when trying to imitate the various animals. For example, the girl marries the wood tick, and Gamba, dissatisfied with his new son-in-law, tries to imitate the wood tick by floating to the ground on a leaf from a tree top, but falls hard to the earth. There is also a long cycle in which the tortoise has a trickster role. Other stories recount the Rolling Head and the Festival of the Animals. Modern *Tenetehara* legends include a large series that are of Iberian and Africo-Brazilian origin.

BIBLIOGRAPHY

Barbosa Rodrígues, 1872; Bettendorf, 1910; Dodt, 1873; Froes Abreu, 1931; Kissenberth, 1912; Lago, 1822; Lopes, 1934; Marques, C. A., 1870; Métraux, 1928 a. 1928 b; Moraes, 1860; Nimuendajú, 1915; Plagge, 1857; Ribeiro, 1841; Leite, 1943; Snethlage, E. H., 1927, 1931 a; Wagley, 1942, 1943 a.

THE ARCHEOLOGY OF THE AMAZON BASIN

By Betty J. Meggers

INTRODUCTION

The Amazon has its source in the Andes close to the Pacific and flows northeast 4,000 miles to empty into the Atlantic at the Equator. A dozen large tributaries flow into it at intervals, draining four-tenths of the continent. At the mouth of the Rio Negro the valley is about 200 miles wide, but between the Tapajóz and Xingú Rivers it narrows to 50 or less. Below and above these points the uplands retreat sharply from the river and the valley widens abruptly. Above the Madeira River the forests are just out of water and are inundated long before the river attains its maximum flood level. The natural vegetation of the valley and the uplands is selva, except for scattered savanna lands north of the river and on the Island of Marajó.

In this immense area archeology has made little progress. Here there are none of the large imperishable buildings which mark sites of former human habitation for the archeologist in Perú, and the virgin forest effectively obscures all lesser clues on the surface. The discovery of a site often awaits an accident such as occurred at Santarém when a cloudburst washed out the streets and revealed quantities of pottery. In the more open country on Marajó Island and in the Mojos area of Bolivia, the existence of mounds makes the task somewhat easier.

Stone is scarce in most of the valley and was not a major item in the material culture. Few stone tools, mainly polished axes and celts, have been recovered. The perishable objects which took their place have not survived. Metal tools are rare and were acquired by trade from the Andes and later from the Europeans. As a result, pottery is almost all that the archeologist can hope to find.

Attempts have been made to link the archeological remains with known Indian groups. Many of the earlier writers attributed the elaborate pottery to the *Carib,* whose presence had been recorded along the lower Amazon. The tendency of the later writers has been to favor the *Arawak,* whose high cultural level and widespread migrations are offered as an explanation for the similarities noted from southern Brazil to the Antilles. The question has not yet been settled to the satisfaction of all, however.

149

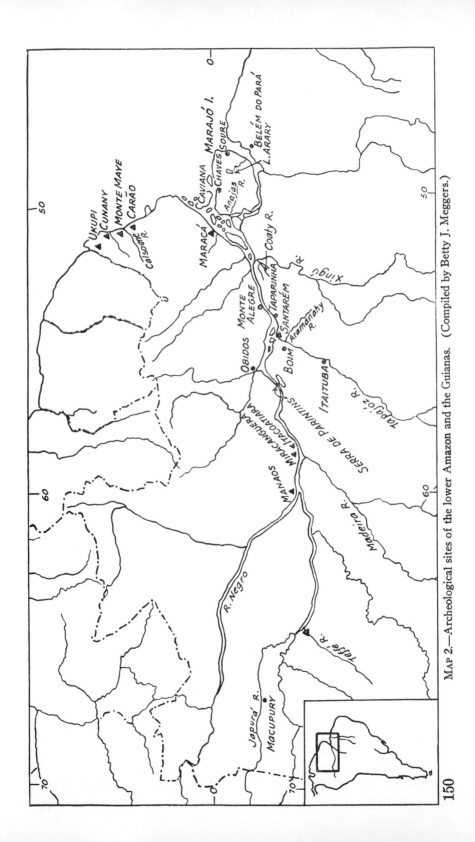

MAP 2.—Archeological sites of the lower Amazon and the Guianas. (Compiled by Betty J. Meggers.)

150

SOURCES

The written sources leave much to be desired. The early work was done largely by men trained in other fields, and it is difficult to know what reliance to place upon their conclusions. The more recent publications are for the most part general summaries or descriptions of collections in museums. An exception is Linné (1928 b), who describes some of the sites excavated by Nimuendajú in Northeast Brazil. Except for Palmatary on Santarém, Métraux on the Upper Amazon, and Goeldi on Cunany, the following sources deal mainly with Marajó: Angyone Costa (1934), Farabee (1921 a), Goeldi (1900), Hartt (1871, 1876, 1885), Holdridge (1939), Joyce (1912), Lange (1914), Linné), (1925, 1928 a, 1928 b), Métraux (1930 a), Mordini (1934), Netto (1885), Nordenskiöld (1930 a), Palmatary (1939), Penna (1877–78), Steere (1927), Torres, H. A. (1929, 1930, 1940), and Uhle, M. (1923).

The largest and most representative museum collections of Amazon pottery are in the Museu Paraense Emilio Goeldi, Belém, Brazil; the Ethnographical Museum, Göteborg, Sweden; and the University of Pennsylvania Museum, Philadelphia, Pa. The Musée du Trocadéro, Paris, has a collection from the Middle Amazon, and the American Museum of Natural History in New York one from Pacoval on Marajó Island.

ARCHEOLOGICAL REGIONS

In this article, the Amazon has been divided for convenience into four areas: Marajó Island, Northeast Brazil, the Santarém region, and the Middle Amazon. The sites in Northeast Brazil (map 2)—Caviana, Maracá, and Cunany—have been grouped together on the basis of a few traits which they have in common and by which they differ from Marajó and Santarém. These are the absence of mounds, with the burial urns placed directly in the ground or in caves, the presence of anthropomorphic funerary urns, the interment of two or more individuals in a single urn, and similarities in the pottery. The urns from these sites show very marked differences in form and detail which indicate the maintenance of distinct local styles in spite of close areal proximity and contemporaneity.

Marajó Island is characterized by the presence of mounds containing burial urns and domestic pottery including tangas, and by a distinctive style of decoration in which painted and incised designs are prominent. At Santarém, both mounds and burial urns are absent. Vessels of unusual shapes, often resting on caryatids and ornamented with bird and animal figures in full round, are characteristic.

A hundred and fifty miles up the Tapajóz River and above the Serra de Parintins on the Amazon, burial urns again appear. The latter area, which we have called the Middle Amazon, includes sites at Miracanguera, Manáos, and Teffé. This area is little known and no accounts of excavations have been published. A comparison of two anthropomorphic urns from sites in the area over 500 miles apart shows a similarity in style. Other fragments are reminiscent of Santarém and Marajó. The upper reaches of the Amazon are virtually unknown archeologically.

The general culture-subsistence pattern for the Amazonian area was probably quite uniform. Agriculture was supplemented by hunting, fishing, and gathering. The high development of the ceramic art, as well as the amount of labor which would have been required to build the stone walls along the coast and the mounds on Marajó, presupposes relatively large communities and indicates an economic and social organization advanced enough to permit the expenditure of large amounts of time and effort on projects unprofitable from the point of view of subsistence. The presence of greenstone objects on Marajó believed to originate from somewhere in the vicinity of Obidos is evidence of widespread trade connections. Early explorers on the Amazon reported that the pottery of Santarém was an important item of barter, and the discovery of a clay bird head on the Island of Carriacou in the Antilles identical with those found at Santarém substantiates their statements. The stone works along the coast are presumed to be evidence that an advanced type of religion was practiced there.

Chronological relationships are uncertain. At Caviana and Maracá objects of European origin have been found in association with the pottery, indicating that these cultures were flourishing in post-Columbian times. Cunany is also dated as contemporary with the Conquest. At Carão on the Mayacaré, however, no objects of European origin or showing European influence have been discovered. Although no objects of European manufacture have been found on Marajó, the reports of travelers on the lower Amazon in the 17th century indicate that fine pottery was still being made there at that time. Nordenskiöld (1930 a, pp. 33–34) has suggested the possibility of arriving at a chronology by comparison with the Andean area, where a relatively precise time sequence has been established. The extension of this method to the Amazon cultures, however, awaits detailed study of the whole region. At present, it is impossible to say what the actual relationships are.

The pottery from Santarém presents a problem because it differs so markedly from that in the rest of the valley. It approaches the pottery of the Antilles in some respects, and the use of the caryatid, of the tripod, and of frogs in jumping position as ornaments are characteristics reminiscent of Central America.

The descriptions given in this account must be recognized as tentative and incomplete. A description of the archeology of the Amazon is largely a story of problems unsolved and work still to be done. To date, this area has attracted the interest of few trained archeologists. The written sources offer few details of the sites and circumstances of discovery of the pottery, and even these are often contradictory.   Another difficulty is that the Amazon Valley has never been mapped in detail.   As a result many of the places referred to in the early literature cannot be found on a map. The pottery in museum collections is not accompanied by any information about its excavation and, although attempts have been made to draw conclusions from its study, much more could be gained by a few sessions in the field.   Nimuendajú has engaged in some explorations in recent years, and the publication of his findings should contribute substantially to our knowledge.

Mounds.—Since 1870, Marajó Island has been the classic spot in Amazon archeology. Located in the mouth of the river just south of the Equator, it has an area of 14,000 square miles and an elevation of about 3 feet (1 m.) above river level in the dry season.   At this time of the year all but a few of the larger rivers are dry and water is scarce.   The opposite situation occurs in the wet season, when the greater part of the island is flooded.   The north central section is rendered uninhabitable by the presence of immense swamps.   In the west are dense forests.   Across most of the remainder of the island stretch the level campos, broken here and there by clumps of trees and by artificial mounds.

These mounds have proved a fertile field for the archeologist.   More than 100 are known, and these are usually located on river banks or at the edges of lakes or swamps.   Some were evidently used only as dwelling sites.   Others served both as house substructures and for burial purposes.   It has not been determined whether any were used exclusively for burial.   Although these mounds have long been known, few of them have been located on a map or described in any detail.   None have been scientifically excavated.   No conclusions have been reached about their relative age.   There is disagreement as to whether or not stratification is present.   Opinion is also divided on the question of intentional zoomorphic shape.

The most famous of the mounds is Pacoval in Lake Ararí.   It was first described by Hartt in 1871, and since then it has been visited repeatedly. It is located close to the east shore of the lake immediately south of the Igarapé das Almas.   It is oblong and divided into two parts, the main mound and a small one at the north end of it and separated from it by a channel.   The north-south length is about 90 m. (290 ft.), the width about 38 m. (125 ft.), and the height about 4 m. (13 ft.) when the water level is low.   Steere (1927) was able to distinguish three strata showing differences in pottery design and other ornaments, with the best examples in the lowest level and the poorest at the top.   Penna (1877) confirmed this sequence on his visit and concluded that these represented phases of a declining civilization.   Derby (*in* Hartt, 1885, p. 22) however states that "all the objects, plain as well as ornamented, were encountered near the surface and in the middle and lower parts of the mound so that it does not seem possible to establish divisions in the deposit." Although stone objects are rare, pottery is abundant here as in most of the mounds. Penna (1877, p. 53) speaks of pottery as covering the ground like a great mosaic. Lange (1914, p. 321) was able to collect over 3,000 specimens in the course of a week.

Pottery similar to that from Pacoval is found at Ilha dos Bichos, a mound of about half an acre in extent which rises 5 to 8 m. (about 16 to 26 ft.) above the plain along Araří River north of Cachoeira. This was examined by Steere in 1870, and he distinguished two layers of occupation separated by a layer of earth. Burial urns were visible at different levels in the ravines which had been washed in the sides of the mound.

Along the Anajás River is a group of mounds known as Os Camutins. Derby (in Hartt, 1885, pp. 23–25) describes four in some detail and states that his informant mentioned 12 in a distance of 1½ miles (about 2.4 km.), all but one on the east side of the river. The majority are in the narrow zone of trees along the bank but at least two are farther off on the plain. The principal mound has a length of approximately 210 m. (680 ft.), a width of 80 m. (260 ft.) at the base, and a height of about 13 m. (42 ft.) above the level of the surrounding plain. It is covered with vegetation, and the slopes have been eroded into ravines. On the west side of the river is a large excavation which appears to have furnished the earth for the construction of the mounds. Derby states that,

the pottery encountered in the largest mound of the Camutins is of the same character as that from Pacoval. From what I could observe it appears that the large jars are more frequently painted than incised, contrary to what is observed at Pacoval. The predominant shape is large, depressed and globular, while at Pacoval smaller sub-cylindrical and conical forms are more common. These observations are insufficient as a basis for a distinction and all the principal shapes are represented in both sites. Fragments of tangas are extremely abundant, but no complete ones were found. The majority are red in color and undecorated, although I saw some painted like those from Pacoval. [Hartt, 1885, p. 25.]

Monte Carmelo is located near the source of the Anajás River. Fragments of pottery are exposed here from the river bed to the summit. Three stratified layers were observed by Holdridge (1939). The top and bottom ones contained quantities of simple, red pottery both incised and plain. Between these two was a layer containing the highly developed incised, sculptured, and painted ware which is characteristic of the highest development on Marajó.

Teso de Severino was described by Mordini (1934, pp. 63–64). This mound is located near the Igarapé de Severino, a tributary of Lake Araří. It has been completely leveled and is marked only by a ring of old trees which outlines its former extent. The pottery here is more

PLATE 15.—**Amazonian pottery from Counany.** Red-on-yellow ware. (After Goeldi, 1900, pls. 1, 2, 3.)

PLATE 16.—**Amazonian burial urns from Márajó.** *a*, Modeled bichrome with white slip (height approximately 3 ft. (92 cm.)). *b*, Two modeled urns, both with inverted bowl lids and found superimposed. These represent a double burial with cremated remains in small urn and entire body in larger one. (Total height approximately 4 ft. 7½ inches (1.41 m.).) *c*, Modeled champlevé urn with white paint filler in designs (height approximately 1 ft. (30 cm.)). *d*, White-slipped incised (height approximately 1 ft. (30 cm.)). (Courtesy University Museum, Philadelphia.)

PLATE 17.—**Amazonian pottery from Marajó.** *a,* Platter-bowl with annular base, white-slipped with some interior painting. *b,* White-slipped and incised urn (height 9 inches (23 cm.)). *c,* Unslipped incised (height 8 inches (20 cm.)). *d,* Interior of white-slipped, incised and red zoned bowl (greatest diameter 17½ inches (44.5 cm.)). (*a–c,* Courtesy University Museum, Philadelphia; *d,* courtesy American Museum of Natural History.)

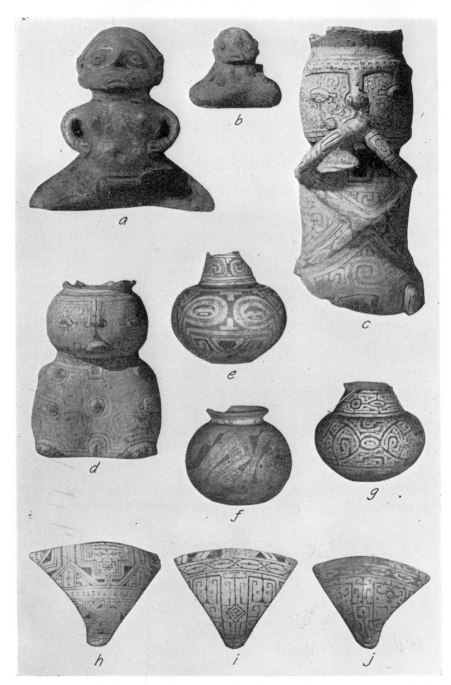

PLATE 18.—**Amazonian pottery from Marajó and Santarém.** *a, b,* Hollow figurines, Santarém. (Larger, approximately 5 inches (13 cm.) high.) *c, d,* Marajó effigy burial urns, incised white, red retouched decoration. (Respective heights, 14 inches (35.5 cm.) and 8⅜ inches (21 cm.).) *e,* Marajó red on white (height, 9 inches (23 cm.).) *f,* Marajó incised white, red retouched (height, approximately 8 inches (20 cm.).) *g,* Marajó red and black on white (height, 7⅞ inches (19.5 cm.).) *h–j,* Tangas, or women's pottery "fig leaves." (*a, b,* Courtesy University Museum, Philadelphia; others, courtesy American Museum of Natural History.)

advanced in design and technique than that from Pacoval. The clay is finer and better fired, the workmanship more careful, and the vessels are partly covered with a kind of glaze probably produced by the resin of jutaisica. Tangas found here are decorated with complicated stylized anthropomorphic motifs. The characteristic frieze of vertical and diagonal lines with the intervening spaces painted a solid color found on tangas from Pacoval, does not occur here.

Santa Izabel, located on the plain northwest of Lake Arari, has also been leveled to the surface of the plain. Penna (1877, p. 51) describes the artifacts as inferior in number and extent to those of Pacoval, but as rivaling the ceramics of the latter in choice of material and perfection of designs, painting, and relief.

Fortaleza was visited by Farabee. The mound

had been built up artificially and then used as a village site. Apparently the people had cremated the remains of their dead and buried the ashes in small urns in the floor of their houses. These urns were beautifully decorated with incised lines or paint or both. Many plates, small bowls, cooking pots, and seats were found buried with these urns. [P. 145.] Four other mounds in the vicinity were excavated but nothing of value was found. They had been used as house sites only, as was indicated by the presence of ashes and fragments of pottery. [Farabee, 1921 a, p. 144.]

Larenjeiras is located northeast of Lago Guajará. It is 5 m. (15 ft.) in height and covers over 2 acres. Pottery of all types is abundant.

These brief accounts represent practically all the definite information that has been published about the mounds. A dozen more are mentioned by name and vaguely located but not described at all. Mordini (1934, p. 62) cites Serra, Teso do Gentios, Menino Deus, and Panellas in the area enclosed by the Ganhão and Cururú Rivers and Lakes Mututi and Asapão. These and a group of seven small mounds on the road from Cajuliros to Faz Café are oval and oriented in an east-west-direction. Pacoval do Cururú, Mataforme, and Ananatuba, also oval, are oriented north-south.

Pottery.—In general, pottery shapes are varied but the paste appears to be constant. The basic clay is light gray which turns orange-red in firing. Sand admixture is rare. The texture varies from coarse to medium, depending on the size and number of particles of pounded sherd used as temper. In some cases these are large enough to retain traces of the original white slip. Manufacture was by the coiling method, and overlapping layers are visible on the interiors of some of the figurines. Firing was done in a kiln and was sufficient to change the color of the paste only on the surface, except in cases where the walls were thin.

The following classification of wares based on surface finish was made by Junius Bird after an examination of the collection from Pacoval at the American Museum of Natural History. These were probably not all contemporary but lack of documentation makes it impossible to establish the chronological sequence.

Plain ware.

Incised plain ware. Both fine and broad incised lines occur, sometimes combined with punctate marks (pl. 17, *c*).

Incised white. The surface is covered with a white slip and decorated with fine incised lines (pls. 16, *d;* 17, *b*). The color of the slip varies from white through cream to orange as a result of variations in firing.

Incised white, red retouch. Like the preceding except that the incised design is accented in places by the addition of red paint to the incisions (pls. 17, *d*; 18, *f*).

Red champlevé. Red slipped ware in which the background or field of the design has been cut back from the original surface and roughened.

Red champlevé, cream paint in cuts. The design is produced by the same technique as in the preceding. A contrast is made between the cut-out parts and the rest of the design by the addition of a light-colored paint to the cuts (pl. 16, *c*).

Double-slipped champlevé. Here the red slip was applied over a white slip and shaved off in the cut-out areas. The use of a double slip produced the same contrast as the preceding method but eliminated the rough surface caused by the presence of tempering granules in the paste.

Incised plain ware, white paint inlay. The designs are applied in bands around the rim and are composed of finely incised lines and a deeply gouged background which were filled with white paint.

Painted ware. Painted decoration was used by itself or in combination with incised and relief ornament (pls. 16, *a, b;* 18, *e, g–j*). Red and brown paint were used separately or together on a light-colored slipped surface.

Two other types occur in the collection at the Museum of Anthropology, University of Michigan:

Incised red. The decoration is in simple geometric patterns of broad incised lines which go through the slip to the orange paste surface to produce a two-color design.

White champlevé. The incised lines and indented areas show the orange original surface while the intervening areas have a white slip.

Nonfunerary pottery is abundant and varied in form. Water jars with narrow mouths are common at Pacoval. Handles, which are present on some, are of two types: two protuberances or lugs placed below the rim, and handles perforated for the insertion of a cord. Large plates or dishes are common but are usually recovered only as fragments. Bowls vary in shape from deep flat-bottomed ones with sloping sides to shallow concave ones. Some are circular, others oval. The former have level rims, and the rims of the latter rise to a high point at the ends and slope downward to the center of the long sides. Decoration on this type is painted or incised, and relief ornament is sometimes found on the rim. Some are decorated both on the interior and exterior and others on the interior only. An unusual form is a bowl with a flaring annular base and an extremely broad concave horizontal rim, so broad that it almost triples the diameter of the vessel (pl. 17, *a*). The interior is painted red or brown on a white or cream slip. The exterior is usually unslipped and undecorated. Of problematical use is the so-called "offertorio" of the older writers. It is a flat or slightly concave disk on a slightly flaring annular base. A few are oval. The usual size is about **17** cm. (6¾ in.) in diameter and **7** cm. (2¾ in.) tall. Some, however, are only half this large. They are un-slipped and the surface of the disk is covered with incised patterns. In the case of the smaller vessels these design areas are often cross-hatched An anthropomorphic face in low relief is often used as decoration on the side. Anthropomorphic and zoomorphic vessels are rare (pl. 18, *c, d*).

Jars of several shapes have been called funerary urns. One has the form of two truncated cones joined together at a point about one-fourth of the distance from the bases of the vessels (pls. 16, *d;* 17, *b*). Another type has a globular body with a flat bottom and a cylindrical neck with an everted lip (pl. 16, *c*). In a third type the body is also globular, but the neck has the shape of a short truncated cone joined to the body at its base (pl. 18, *e, g*). The height of all these rarely exceeds 60 cm. (24 in.). Much larger are the urns with anthropomorphic faces in relief on the neck (pl. 16, *a, b, c*). These may be as much as 95 cm. (37 in.) tall with a rim diameter of 75 cm. (28 in.). They have globular bodies which taper down to an extremely small flat base only about 18 cm. (5 in.) in diameter. The neck joins the body at a pronounced shoulder and terminates in a widely flaring rim. The greatest diameter of the body is only a little more than that of the rim. Two anthropomorphic faces in low relief adorn the neck, one at front and one at back. A small human figure often occupies the intervening space at each side. The body of the vessel is covered with painted decoration in large curvilinear patterns.

Figurines.—Figurines, or "idolos," are variations of the seated type found in many parts of South America. The larger ones are hollow (fig. 16, *right*). The legs are separated and rounded at the end. Often there is a ridge across the base of the tip to represent the foot, which is left smooth or marked with three to eight toes. Arms are shown at the sides, raised, or only suggested by a protuberance or lateral extension at each shoulder. Heads differ in shape and detail, but almost invariably the nose and eyebrows are joined to form a **Y** or **T**. The sex is usually indicated and is, in a majority of cases, female. In addition to these separate figurines, many anthropomorphic and zoomorphic heads are found which once were part of the relief and molded decoration of vessels. These are generally solid. Some show traces of slip and decoration, while others have the orange-red color and rather rough surface of the unslipped clay.

Tangas.—Tangas, which are found in abundance, are thought to have been worn by the women as a pubic covering (pl. 18, *h–j*). They are triangular in shape, about 15 cm. (6 in.) long and 12 cm. (5 in.) wide at the upper edge. The upper edge is convex and the other two are con-cave. The inner surface is concave and the outer convex. There is a small pierced hole, 1 to 2 cm. from each corner, for the insertion of a cord for attachment to the body. Many show grooves where the friction of the cord has worn away the clay. The clay used is always very fine, and

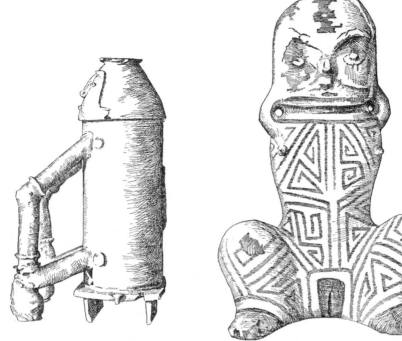

FIGURE 16.—*Maracá* and *Marajó* pottery. *Left: Maracá* urn (height, approximately 2½ ft. (75 cm.)). *Right: Marajó* hollow figurine (red-on-white) (height 24 cm. (9½ in.)). (After Nordenskiöld, 1930 a, pl. 18 and Frontispiece.)

the objects themselves are often exceedingly thin.   Both surfaces are smoothed and usually slipped either red or white.   The outer surface in the latter case is decorated with great care and beauty in a symmetrical pattern.   Mordini (1934) noted that the majority of the tangas found at Pacoval show consistently the same border pattern across the top.   This was not found on tangas from Teso de Severino.   Tangas with dark red slip and no decoration are found at Camutins.

Decorative styles.—Holdridge (1939, p. 74) states that

while there are slight regional differences in the pottery designs and manner of execution, there is a general identity of artistic motives and technic that points to an island-wide cultural integrity.   The most complicated designs found in the Chaves pottery can be duplicated satisfactorily in a piece from Soure.

This continuity of style makes it possible to list a few very characteristic features.   One of the most common geometrical motifs in painted, incised, or relief decoration is the spiral which occurs in many variations, single and interlocking.   Also characteristic are stylized representations of the human face which occur in almost an infinite variety and produce a symmetrical design used on tangas as well as on funerary urns and other vessels.   The **T** is another design element often used.   The sides of funerary urns sometimes show an **H**-like motif in relief. Relief decoration was usually confined to the rim except on the larger vessels, where anthropomorphic and zoomorphic heads in the round were used as decoration on rims and as appliqué on the sides. These as well as the figurines show conventional treatment both in modeling and painting. The most characteristic facial feature is the joining of the eyebrows and nose in a **Y** or **T**. Zoomorphic heads sometimes have coffee-bean eyes and are generally more crude than the anthropomorphic heads. Characteristic of the latter are a double protuberance to indicate the ear, a protuberance on the top of the head, and conventional painted outlines of eyebrows, eyes, nose, mouth, and ears.

Burial.—Secondary urn burial was practiced throughout the island. The urns were buried in the mounds and the most richly decorated were sometimes placed inside cruder ones for protection. A shallow bowllike cover was inverted on top (pl. 16, *b*). At Camutins, the large urns contained whole bodies placed in seated position while the small urns held the ashes of cremated individuals (Farabee, 1921 a, p. 145).

When the urn was placed in the grave, the bottom of the hole was dug to fit it, so that all of the smaller pieces of pottery placed with the dead were deposited at the side of the neck on the shoulder of the urn. [Ibid., p. 146.]

NORTHEAST BRAZIL

Caviana.—Caviana is an island about 50 miles long lying in the mouth of the Amazon north of Marajó. At a cemetery in the southeast of the island, Nimuendajú (Linné, 1928 b) excavated a group of funerary urns. These had been buried directly in the ground. They are of several types and show diversity in the technical skill of the makers as well as in the shape and style of the decoration of the vessel. An urn 33 cm. (13 in.) tall with the mouth at the side and a tiered profile was found at Apany. A similar vessel from Pará was described by Joyce (1912). Both are crudely made and have appliqué decoration of lumps of clay. A more advanced type is a semicylindrical urn with a stylized human figure outlined in low relief on one side. A third type has painted decoration reminiscent of that found on pottery from Ukupi and Cunany. A seated anthropomorphic urn illustrated by Nordenskiöld (1930 a, pl. 20) resembles those from Maracá. The features are in low relief, and the painted decoration is red and gray.

Glass beads, metal knives and axes, and small brass bells from European trade were found with the urns and establish their origin as post-Columbian. Small objects, possibly ornaments, of greenstone were also found.

In the urns, the smallest bones were placed at the bottom, the large ones at the sides, and the skull on top. A single urn sometimes contained the remains of more than one individual. Occasional anthropomorphic urns have two faces, and Linné (1928 b, p. 79) postulates that such an urn was destined to contain two skeletons.

Although its geographical position is that of a link between Marajó and Brazilian Guiana, culturally Caviana is most closely allied with the mainland. The differences which exist between it and Marajó are striking. The only features which are common to both are secondary urn burial and the custom of painting the bones red. The absence of mounds, the anthropomorphic character of the urns, and the style of relief and painted decoration indicate stronger affiliations between Caviana and the coast to the north. Nimuendajú (Linné, 1928 b) has explained this by the theory that the inhabitants of Caviana, the *Aruã*, immigrated from Brazilian Guiana and returned there when the pressure of the Europeans became too strong.

Maracá.—This site has been known since 1870. It is located on a small tributary of the Maracá River which flows through Brazilian Guiana and empties into the Amazon almost at the Equator. There are no mounds. The pottery was found in natural grottos at the edge of a plain close to the river. Funerary urns are abundant, and the majority are in the form of a human being seated on a bench. The trunk, arms, and legs are cylindrical (fig. 16, *left*). The head which forms the cover is about 18 cm. (7 in.) high and has a flat top covered with small knobs. The features of the face are made by ribbons of clay and are enclosed at top and sides by a relief stripe. The sex is either male or female. These figures often have painted ornaments, and Nordenskiöld (1930 a, p. 20) reports that the calf of the leg is swollen, indicating perhaps that binding was practiced by the people. One of these urns was ornamented with green, blue, and white glass beads attached to the arms and spine. These date from the 17th-century European trade contact and indicate the manufacture of these urns in the post-Columbian period. Zoomorphic urns in this same tubular style have also been found in the caves.

The paste is coarse and composed of clay mixed with sand. Cariapé (a vegetal temper) does not appear to have been used. The workmanship is crude; the vessel walls are thick and irregular, and the surface is rough. Paint was restricted to the ornaments mentioned above, and the surface of the vessel as a whole exhibits the tan to orange-brown color produced by firing. Firing was not thorough enough to bake the walls through, and the interior retains the original dark gray color.

According to Penna (1877), these urns contained entire skeletons. The bones were arranged with the pelvis at the bottom, the rest of the bones along the sides, and the skull on top.

Cunany.—The Cunany site on the coast of Brazilian Guiana was discovered by Coudreau in 1883 and described in detail by Goeldi in 1895 (1900). The funerary urns were found in artificial subterranean galleries. Goeldi offered the hypothesis that the ancestors of the builders lived in an area where caves occurred naturally and were used as repositories for burial urns. Their descendents, accustomed to this situation and finding no natural caves in this new area, constructed substitutes. Fragments of pottery identical with those from Cunany were found recently by Nimuendajú (Linné, 1928 b) in a cave of Mont Ukupi near the Arucará River. If Goeldi's hypothesis is correct, these later discoveries may be of greater age. Linné (1928 b, p. 73) states that it is possible to detect some evolution in the painted decoration. The Cunany urns are believed to be post-Columbian or contemporary with the Conquest.

The paste is gray or bluish in cross section. The amount of sand is small and large amounts of crushed sherds were used as temper, especially in the thick-walled vessels. A microscopic examination showed no admixture of ashes of caraipé or of sponges. Firing was sufficient to bake the thin-walled vessels but those with thick walls show a poorly baked center. Fine white clay was used as a slip.

A variety of forms are found, almost all of which are divided into horizontal zones by the more or less sharp changes in plane of the vessel wall, by relief bands, or by changes in design motif. Shapes include large jars with globular bodies and straight necks; jars with small bases, constricted necks and wide rims, often with anthropomorphic facial features in low relief (pl. 15, *d, g*); bowls with vertical sides and flaring rims (pl. 15, *b, f*); rectangular vessels with flat bottoms and outward flaring sides (pl. 15, *c, e*); and oval "boat-shaped" vessels on a cylindrical pedestal (pl. 15, *a*).

Ornament is painted and relief. Painted designs are red on a yellowish slip. The rim and base are sometimes painted solid red. Frets, spirals, steps, commas, and a rambling three-line design are typical geometrical motifs. The corners are occasionally ornamented with a row of vertical notches. Relief decoration includes the outline of a human face on the rim and of the human body on the body of the vessel, and anthropomorphic and zoomorphic figures in the round jutting out from the sides of bowls and rectangular vessels.

All of the vessel shapes listed above except the large jars with globular bodies and straight necks were recorded by Goeldi as having contained traces or fragments of human bones.

Rio Calsoene.—On high points along the coast of Brazil north of the Amazon, as for example on the Calsoene River and on the tributaries of the Cunany River, rows of stones have been found. The largest of these is located on the Estancia José Antonio on the north bank of the lower Calsoene River. It is 100 m. (325 ft.) long but has been damaged in many places. One hundred and fifty stones of all sizes are visible above ground. The largest measures 2 m. (6½ft.) by 70 cm. (26½ in.) by 25 cm. (9¾ in.), and has an estimated weight of 600 kilograms (1,323 lbs.). These stones must have been brought from a considerable distance, an enormous task with primitive methods of hauling and transportation. Excavations made by Nimuendajú (Linné, 1928 b) show that these rocks were not placed over graves. Little pottery was found in the vicinity, and much of that was in a fragmentary state. A vessel with a wide mouth was covered with a large stone slab and protected by two stones at the sides. A few other similar objects have been discovered in the ground. To explain these structures we must resort to speculation, but it seems probable that they had a religious purpose.

Ilha de Carão.—Ilha de Carão is located in a swamp at the mouth of the Mayacaré River. On it is a mound about 10 meters (33 ft.) long and 2.2 meters (6 ft. 8 inches) high. It is stratified into three distinct layers. The lowest, composed of ashes, is 70 cm. (26½ in.) thick and covered with a thick layer of potsherds. These appear to be mainly from platters as much as 80 cm. (30½ in.) in diameter. They show incised decorations as well as traces of red and white paint. The second stratum is about 50 cm. (19½ in.) thick and composed of gray dirt. On top is a layer of yellow clay 1 meter (3 ft. 3 in.) thick. Some stones belonging to the same category as those described from the Calsoene River had been set up on the summit. Pottery fragments in the two upper layers were so badly disintegrated that only sherds from a few small vessels were preserved.

The three layers of the mound do not appear to correspond to three different cultures. While the thick debris of the lowest level may be the product of an independent ancient population, it must be recognized that the differences of technique, decoration, etc. are not great enough to furnish absolute proof for this hypothesis. The pottery of the two upper layers appears to belong to a single period, although some vessels are buried deeper than others. [Linné, 1928 b, pp. 75–76.]

This mound was apparently constructed prior to European contact since no object of European origin or showing European influence has been found associated with it.

SANTARÉM

Distribution.—The lower Tapajóz River is the center of another culture type. Evidence was meager until the summer of 1922 when a cloudburst washed out the streets of Santarém and uncovered stone tools and a great quantity of pottery. Much was saved through the efforts of Nimuendajú, and a subsequent survey by him has made it possible to outline the boundaries of the complex. It extends up the Tapajóz to Aramanahy and is represented by numerous inland sites on the right bank. On the left, there is a site at Boim. To the east, remains are common as far as Taperinha and scattered to the eastern limit at Bocca de Coaty on the Jaraucú River, a tributary of the lower Xingú. The western limit is Serra de Parintins and there are numerous sites on both banks of the Arapiuns River, a tributary entering the Tapajóz northwest of Santarém, and in the region of Lago Grande de Villa Franca.   North of the Amazon there are some sites around Monte Alegre, but Nimuendajú found nothing between here and Obidos (Palmatary, 1939, pp. 4–5).

Ceramics.—The pottery of this area is perhaps the most remarkable in the Amazon Valley.   The paste is light gray in cross section and light tan on the surface.   Santarém pottery is notable for its unusual shapes and profusion of modeled bird and animal ornament (fig. 17).   Many vessels show traces of red paint and some of a white slip.   Among the principal forms are: (1) A six-lobed vessel resting on a flaring annular base or small caryatid.   The neck is tall and narrow and flares out in one or more places to form a flange or series of flanges.   At two opposite sides of the body, the lobe is extended outward and upward and terminates in a stylized bird head with the beak curved downward in a loop.   Other decoration consists of animals modeled in the round, geometrical relief patterns, and lightly incised geometrical designs.   (2) A bowl supported on a caryatid with an hour-glass-shaped base.   The bowl has a vertical rim which is decorated with an incised pattern.   At the widest diameter modeled ornament is attached.   (3) A bowl with almost vertical sides, a flat bottom, and a concentric, or trough rim.   The two edges of the trough are connected at four regular intervals by a wide loop.   (4) A tall jar with a narrow base.   The greatest diameter is about one-fourth of the distance from the base and above this the sides slope inward to the rim.   The height is about 34 cm. (12½ inches).   There is little or no relief and no incised decoration.   (5) A jar with a globular body and a short vertical neck with a wide mouth.   The base is flat or slightly pointed.   Decoration is relief or incised.   (6) Numerous small vessels in four-lobed and other exotic shapes.   (7) Effigy vessels in seated positions with globular bodies.   Two illustrated by Palmatary (1939, figs. 3–4) are covered with painted geometrical figures in red and black on a light-colored background.   (8) Seated figurines (pl. 18, a, b).   These are hollow and larger on the average than those found at Marajó.   The top of the leg slopes downward toward the tip.   The hands are placed at the side, on the leg, or on the chest.   Numerous anthropomorphic and zoomorphic figures and heads are found which were part of the ornament of vessels.   These are generally small and solid.   Anthropomorphic heads, whether figurines or part of the applied decoration of vessels, show various conventional traits: a headdress resembling a diadem, an oblong nose, and ears indicated by a double prominence or with the lobe pierced for the insertion of an ornament.   The eyes are commonly coffee-bean or a horizontal ribbon of clay, although there are numerous other types (Palmatary, 1939).   Zoomorphic heads are abundant and represent a great variety of animals and birds.   Some of the most common of these appear to have been conventionalized and conform rigidly to the con-

FIGURE 17.—Santarém pottery. (After Palmatary, 1939, figs. 2 and 7.)

vention in modeling and decoration. The jaguar has a wide-open mouth, the agouti has its front paws drawn up under the chin, birds have down-curved beaks, etc. Almost all have the round-rimmed protuberant type of eye.

Burials.—In spite of a diligent search, no burials have been discovered in this area. The explanation probably lies in the method of disposing of the dead which was described by Heriarte in the 17th century (Nordenskiöld, 1930 a). The body was left exposed until the flesh had decayed away. The bones were then pulverized and the powder mixed with chicha, which was drunk.

THE MIDDLE AMAZON

Miracanguera.—Miracanguera extends about 5 miles (8 km.) along the north bank of the Amazon opposite the mouth of the Madeira River. According to Nimuendajú, it has been ravaged by flood waters. Penna, writing in 1877, reported that most of the clay objects were found isolated from each other. The material is a fine clay slightly reddish-gray in color. It contains no sand. A white slip was used and there are traces of red paint. Some of the remains indicate a high degree of development of the ceramic art, but were too fragmentary for description. Penna's conclusion was that the ceramics of this area were inferior to those from Santarém and the lower Amazon.

A funerary urn from Itacoatiara, just down the river, is illustrated by Netto (1885, Est. VA). The round bottom rests on a short pedestal. The sides slope inward slightly at the neck and then flare out to the rim. A bowlike cover fits perfectly over the top. The exterior is covered with a white slip. On one side of the neck is an anthropomorphic face with the features in low relief.

Manáos.—The city of Manáos is located on the north bank of the Amazon near the mouth of the Rio Negro, about 900 miles (1,440 km.) above Belém. Although it has been known as an archeological site since the end of the last century, we still have to rely largely on the descriptions of early travelers for information. There are a few articles in museums but these are accompanied by no information about their source.

The funerary urns were buried just below ground level. Steere (1927, p. 25) visited Manáos in 1870 and "on the parade ground of the Brazilian troops stationed there, I saw the rims of several burial urns which were being worn down by the bare feet of the soldiers." Marcoy (quoted by Métraux, 1930 a, p. 174) describes the urns:

These vessels, made of a coarse paste of an obscure red-brown color, are at the level of the ground. Their height varies from 70 cm. (26½ in.) to 1 m. (3 ft., 3 in.) ; the diameter of the mouth is about 40 cm. (15½ in.). Crude designs, lozanges, zig-zags, chevrons, billets are painted in black on their sides. Some have a cover, but the majority are open and empty.

Métraux has described the collection at the Musée du Trocadéro in Paris. Only one piece is intact, a bowl on a flaring annular base. The decoration is in low relief. There are many fragments including a rim sherd with a flat vertical handle ornamented with lines ending in volutes.

The color of the clay is rose-gray. There are numerous heads of birds and animals that were used as ornament on vessels.

Teffé.—Pottery discovered at the mouth of the Teffé River shows similarities both with Santarém and with Marajó. The extension of the eyebrows to form the nose so common on Marajó occurs here. The zoomorphic heads are similar to those from Santarém, and there are other striking resemblances between the pottery of the two areas.

Japurá.—Farther west, above Macupury on the Japurá River, a burial urn containing badly-preserved bones was discovered. It is 42 cm. (16¼ in.) tall and 37.5 cm. (14¾ in.) at the largest diameter. The domelike cover is 23 cm. (9 in.) in diameter and fits the mouth of the vessel exactly. The features of the anthropomorphic face on the neck are in relief and are enclosed by an incised line which runs across the forehead and perpendicularly down the sides, ending in a relief volute on each side below the level of the mouth. The urn is covered with a white slip and decorated at the largest diameter with a red band 6 cm. (2⅜ in.) wide.

BIBLIOGRAPHY

For bibliographic references, see page 151.

THE TAPIRAPÉ

By Charles Wagley and Eduardo Galvão

INTRODUCTION

Isolated from other *Tupí-Guaraní*-speaking people, the *Tapirapé* live in Central Brazil, west of the Araguaya River and north of the Tapirapé River, a western tributary flowing into the Araguaya near the northern tip of the Island of Bananal (lat. 2° S., long. 52° W.). According to tradition, the *Tapirapé* lived for a time on the banks of the Araguaya and Javahé Rivers with the *Carajá*. They quarreled, and the *Tapirapé* moved west to their present territory (map 1, *No. 1;* see Volume 1, map 7). At the beginning of last century, five *Tapirapé* villages formed a line stretching northward into *Cayapó* country beginning at a point a few miles back from the Tapirapé River about 150 miles from its mouth. The *Tapirapé* have always been at war with the *Cayapó,* except for a brief period. Each of these villages contained at least 200 individuals with a total *Tapirapé* population of about 1,000. Since 1900, however, there has been a terrific reduction of *Tapirapé* population.

In 1939, there was only one remaining *Tapirapé* village situated about 20 miles north of the Tapirapé River with a total population of 147 people. This decline in population is basically due to disease (smallpox, respiratorial diseases, etc.) acquired either directly from Neo-Brazilians or from the *Carajá,* who are continually in contact with Neo-Brazilians. *Tapirapé* groups have been also massacred on several occasions by both the *Carajá* and *Cayapó.*

The *Tapirapé* have had but few contacts, however, with Neo-Brazilians. Except for the demoralizing effect of depopulation, their culture has been little modified. Although stories are told of Neo-Brazilian hunters visiting the *Tapirapé* in 1909, the first registered contact with them was in 1912. During that year, Señor Mandacurú, leading an expedition of the Brazilian Indian Protection Service, visited the village nearest the Tapirapé River. In 1914, the Dominican priests visited the *Tapirapé.* From that date on, the Dominicans returned each year or so to a camp on the Tapirapé River for 3 or 4 days at a time and were met by the *Tapirapé,* to whom they distributed trade goods. About 1934, a Protestant missionary, Frederick Kiegel, made several trips, staying 2 or 3 months in a *Tapirapé* village. In 1935, the first trained ethnologist, Dr. Herbert Baldus, resided several months with the *Tapirapé,* and in 1939–40, Wagley spent 12 months with them making the study on which this article is based.

CULTURE

SUBSISTENCE ACTIVITIES

The region inhabited by the *Tapirapé* is one of dense tropical forest; yet near the Tapirapé River and parallel to its small tributaries, there are great strips of semiarid savanna country characterized by scrub growth and groups of burití palms. These plains are flooded during the excessive rains from October to April, and they are arid during the latter part of the dry season (May through September).

Farming.—The *Tapirapé* make great clearings in the forest for their villages, traveling occasionally to the savanna country for hunting. Their large gardens guarantee them an economy of abundance. They plant several varieties of both sweet and poisonous manioc, four varieties of maize, pumpkins, beans, peppers, cará (*Dioscorea* sp.) and yams, peanuts, squash, several varieties of bananas and beans, cotton, and papaya.

Each year, from June to September, the men clear away the forest for their gardens. Clearing is frequently done individually; frequently also it is done cooperatively by the men's ceremonial moiety groups in a work festival (apačirú). When communally prepared, the large clearings are afterward divided into individual garden lots. Gardens are, thus, generally individual property; now and again, however, a younger man plants together with an older man (his father-in-law) or a close relative. When clearing is done by apačirú, plots are allocated for ceremonial moiety leaders, who use the produce during the harvest feast (kaô) at the end of the rainy season. Vegetation and tree trunks, cut down during the dry season and left to dry, are burned in September. Just after the first rains of October, planting is begun. All crops are planted without order or division within the garden plot, and weeds are never cleared away as the garden grows. All gardening is done by men except the planting and harvesting of peanuts and cotton, which is done entirely by women.

Harvest takes place as the various crops ripen. Maize planted in late October or early November ripens in January; in April and May squash, cará, beans, etc. begin to ripen. Manioc is harvested as needed throughout the year. All food from the gardens is said to belong to the wife once it is brought into the house.

Garden plots are planted for 2 years and then abandoned. The second year only manioc is generally planted in the plot. Yet each year a new plot is cleared from virgin forest and thus each gardener has generally two current garden plots—one newly cleared and a second-year plot planted with manioc. The lack of virgin forest on high ground for garden clearings within accessible distance to the village, as well as the fear of the spirits of recent dead, force the *Tapirapé* to move their village site each 4 or 5 years to a new site.

Manioc is by far the most important *Tapirapé* crop, as manioc flour is the basis of their diet. Different from other *Tupi* groups, however, the

Tapirapé do not use the tipití (the long woven tube in which the water is squeezed from poisonous manioc), but squeeze poisonous manioc with their hands. The pulp is then spread out on a platform in the sun to be thoroughly dried. The flour is toasted in a clay pot over a very hot fire.

Wild foods.—Meat is a definite luxury to the agricultural *Tapirapé*. Monkeys, armadillos, forest fowls, cuati (*Nasua* sp.), and both kinds of peccary (*Tayassus tajacu* and *T. pecari*) are occasionally killed in the forest at any time during the year. The hunting and fishing season, however, is from June through October, when the savanna country is dry. The savannas are extraordinarily rich with game. Plains deer, wild pigs, peccary, and wild duck, and geese near the drying swamps are plentiful.

Fish are shot with the bow and arrow and stupefied with timbó (*Paullinea pinnata* or *Serjania* sp.) in the almost dry streams and lakes. The village is almost deserted in September and October, after garden sites have been cleared and before planting. Men, women, and children move out to the plains country near the Tapirapé River and set up a temporary camp. They collect turtle eggs and kill turtles in the river. They gather piqui fruit (*Caryocar vellosum*), andiroba (*Carapa guyanensis*), and other wild fruits, and, from October through November, they find wild honey both on the savanna and in the forest.

Hunting is done with the bow and arrow, but a club is used to finish the kill, especially wild pigs or jaguars.

HOUSES AND VILLAGES

The houses of a *Tapirapé* village form an oval around a large ceremonial men's house (tākana), which is forbidden to the women. Both the large men's house, approximately 20 by 65 feet (6 by 20 m.), and the residential houses, averaging 13 by 33 feet (4 by 10 m.), have a quadrangular floor plan with arched roofs made by bending flexible poles and tying them together over a roof beam (pl. 19, *bottom, left*). The walls and the roof are covered with leaves of buriti palm and wild banana.

In the surviving village, called Tampitawa, there were nine residential houses, each housing from four to eight simple families. Each family occupies a determined sector of the house where they cook, keep their belongings, and hang their sleeping hammocks. Household utensils, such as baskets, pots, hammocks, and gourds, are owned by the women of each simple family. Houses, though built by men, are said to be the property of the women of the house. The house frame is constructed cooperatively by all the men of the house. Each man covers the portion to be used by his wife and children.

Ideally, residence is matrilocal, and the house is inhabited by a group of closely related women and their husbands. The household leader is generally the husband of the oldest woman of the group (see p. 172). Owing perhaps to great depopulation and the accumulation of refugees from many villages in the one village, many combinations of relatives now form residential groups.

DRESS AND ORNAMENTS

Both sexes are nude. Men tie the prepuce over the glans penis with a palm fiber. Both men and women pull out pubic, axillary, and all facial hair. Even eyebrows are considered ugly. Men wear cotton string ligatures around their legs, just below the knee. Men, and sometimes women, wear large cotton wrist bands crocheted directly on to their arms. Young boys and girls sometimes wear similar ornaments on their ankles; these ornaments are painted with a thick coat of red urucú dye and have round cuffs, often 2 to 3 inches (5 to 7.5 cm.) wide. Necklaces of beads given by Neo-Brazilians are highly valued and used almost to excess. Men paint their feet and the calves of their legs red with urucú; both men and women trace a multitude of patterns on their body with black genipa dye.

Men have their lower lip pierced and wear a small wooden lip plug. Two years or so after women have begun sexual life, patterns in the form of a three-quarter moon are made on their faces by scarification with a paca (*Cuniculus paca*) tooth knife. Charcoal and plant juices are rubbed into the wounds to leave dark blue designs.

TRANSPORTATION

The *Tapirapé* do not have canoes. All cargoes are carried by the men in a carrying knapsack made from buriti-palm fibers strapped to their backs.

MANUFACTURES

Weaving.—Hammocks are made by women from native cotton spun on wooden spindles. The technique used is the simple twine weaving used by the *Tupinamba* and other *Tupi* groups.

Ceramics.—At present, the art of ceramics is declining. Pottery is usually for cooking, and is made by women. Sometimes it bears incised geometrical decorations.

Gourds.—Gourds are decorated with geometric incisions.

Basketry.—The most highly developed basketry techniques among the *Tapirapé* are woven and twilled. Two types of baskets are flexible and nonflexible ones; both are of buriti fiber. They generally have a quadrangular base and a narrow, round top, and are used mostly to store manioc or maize flour. Flat, round baskets are used as cotton containers or flour sifters. They are usually ornamented with motifs originating in the weave itself; frequently the finished basket is smeared with black genipa and odd strands are scraped off, giving a negative decorative effect.

PLATE 19.—**Tapirapé ceremonies and house construction.** *Top, left:* Youth in preparation for puberty ceremony. The large, heavy diadem of macaw feathers will be supported by the lock of hair wrapped in cotton cord. *Top, right:* Shaman wearing dangerous ceremonial headdress during Thunder ceremony. He is intoxicated by tobacco and in a trance state. *Bottom, left:* Construction of men's house. *Bottom, right:* Dance masks representing the "Crying Spirit," one of many forest spirits who are said to come to stay for a time in the men's ceremonial house. (Courtesy Charles Wagley.)

Weapons.—Bows have a circular cross section and average about 6 feet (2 m.) in length. The arrows are of cane about 5 feet (1.6 m.) long with heads of bone, hardwood, and the spur from the sting ray (*Potamotyrgon histrix*). They have brilliant feathers, sometimes the red and blue feathers of the red macaw. Clubs are made of several polished hardwoods and are sometimes decorated near the handles with woven strands of cane fibers.

SOCIAL ORGANIZATION

Three distinct social groupings are basic in *Tapirapé* social organization: men's ceremonial moieties, feast societies, and the kinship groups.

Ceremonial moieties.—All *Tapirapé* men belong to one of the patrilineal ceremonial moieties. Each of these moieties is further divided into three age grades. There are consequently two groups of youths (those up to 15 years of age); two groups of men of warrior age (15 to 40 years); and two groups of older men (40 to 60 years). Each group bears the name of a bird, the word "wirã" (bird) being the generic name for the group. These age groups (Baldus, 1937, p. 96, calls them "work groups") function as units in hunting and in clearing garden sites at the cooperative work festival; parallel groups also dance against each other in various ceremonials and reciprocally feast each other. Each moiety owns half of the men's house, and its portion is subdivided into sections owned by the three age grades. The warrior age group of each moiety has a "walking leader" for hunting excursions and communal work, and a "singing leader" for ceremonials. As a man becomes elderly, he entirely drops out of the "bird" groups and is no longer affiliated, as he cannot take part in their economic and ceremonial activities. At present, the *Tapirapé* are so reduced in number that, lacking older men, younger men pass prematurely into the older men's age grade in order to retain the necessary balance for ceremonials.

Feast groups.—Both men and women are divided into eight feasting groups called tãtáupawã (literally, "fire all to eat") Men belong to their fathers' feast group and women to their mothers'. Feast groups are not only nonexogamic, but people prefer to marry within their own group so that husband and wife may attend feasts together. These groups carry the names of the mythological heads of the original eight households of the first *Tapirapé* village. They unite at various times throughout the year for ceremonial meals. The feasts take place at traditional spots in the village plaza, at times when there is an abundance of honey, maize, or meat from the hunt. Each member brings his contribution. Baldus (1937, p. 88) calls these "eating groups," and emphasizes that they are consumers' groups providing a means of distributing food when more is available than a family can eat. Today only six groups meet for feasts, two being extinct for lack of members.

Kinship.—Kinship is more important in furthering solidarity among the *Tapirapé* than either the moieties or the feast groups. *Tapirapé* kinship is bilateral, its chief principle being that all cousins, whether cross- or parallel-cousins, no matter how distant, are considered brothers and sisters. Children of people calling each other siblings are also called siblings. Mother's sisters are called mother, and father's brothers, father. Mother's brothers and father's sisters are distinguished by special terms. Similarly, a man's brothers' children are considered his sons and daughters, and a woman's sisters' children are her children. Children of a man's sisters or a woman's brothers are given special terms.

The wide inclusiveness of kinship affiliation makes it possible for an individual to call the majority of his fellow villagers—and in former days many people in other villages—by terms of close relationship.

An older man of some prestige gathers around him by adoption as many "daughters" or as many of his wife's "daughters" as possible. By the marriage of these "daughters," he attracts a group of younger men within his household who contribute constantly to his larder through the hunt and garden activities. At present, only three of the nine houses in the village were formed in this way, but reduced numbers, we were told, forced various combinations of relatives to share a household.

LIFE CYCLE

Childbirth.—Although aware that pregnancy is brought about by sexual intercourse, the *Tapirapé* believe that conception takes place when a shaman, serving as intermediary, brings a "child spirit" to the woman. Thunder, night, monkeys, wild pigs, and various fish and insects are supposed to contain child spirits.

When the woman is certain that she is pregnant, she tells her husband. They both paint their bodies with genipa and cover their hair with urucú. During the first few days of pregnancy, no restraints are imposed upon the child's parents, but as birth approaches, all sexual contact must cease. All men who have sexual relations with a woman during her pregnancy are considered fathers of the future child, together with the real father.

At childbirth the woman is assisted by her mother and sister and by two male relatives. The husband retires to his hammock and is forbidden to partake of any liquid refreshment.

Infanticide is practiced because it is considered bad to have more than three children, or two children of the same sex. The fourth child, or third of the same sex, of one mother is buried in a hole dug inside the residence for the afterbirth.

On the day after birth, a male child has his lower lip perforated. Until the child is weaned, the parents must refrain from sexual relations and must not eat salt, sugar, honey, or the meat of various animals and forest fowls. Both boys and girls also are restricted in their meat diet. A son and sometimes a daughter of important people may be treated as a favorite child, being given special attention and education and being highly decorated during various ceremonies in which such children are central figures. Treatment as a "favorite child" brings prestige throughout one's whole life.

Puberty.—When a boy is about 12 years old, he ties his prepuce over the glans penis. His hair is cropped close to his head, and his entire body is painted black with genipa. He substitutes a short mother-of-pearl lip plug for the long bone one worn by young boys. During this time, the boy must sleep in the men's house. His arms and legs are scratched from time to time deep enough to draw blood, so that he will grow strong.

When he is about 14 years old, his hair is allowed to grow and is tied at the nape of his neck. His hair is not cut for a year or two in preparation for his puberty ceremony, which is considered the most important event in a man's life. On the appointed day, the boy is richly ornamented, the main ornament being a large diadem principally of red macaw feathers set in a heavy block of wood (pl. 19, *top, left*). This diadem is supported by the hair and weighs well over 10 pounds. For 24 hours the boy is forced to dance continually under the weight of excessive decoration to prove his endurance.

During a girl's first three menstrual cycles, a geometric pattern is traced with genipa on her body. During this time, she must refrain from sexual relations. There is no special puberty ceremony for girls. Girls are usually already married at puberty, especially at present with the lack of women.

Marriage.—Formerly there was some intervillage antagonism, and people preferred to marry within their own village. Despite such antagonism and the fact that villages were 2 to 3 days' walk apart, considerable intervillage visiting occurred, and genealogies show that intervillage marriage was not rare. Today, with refugees from all villages in the one village, antagonisms and local village patriotism exist only in the memory of older people.

Men marry immediately after the initiation rites, and the women, at least in modern times, at any time after the age of 7 or 8 years. People do not marry cousins who are called "brother" and "sister" of close connection, but marriage with those of distant relationship is not infrequent. Monogamy is the absolute rule.

Because the population has declined and men outnumber women, marriage rules have been somewhat altered. All women have husbands, and there are now about 10 young men waiting for 7- or 8-year old girls. There are also marriages between men and very young pre-adolescent girls; these are brought about because the men are greatly dependent on the women's work. In such cases, the husband goes to live in his wife's house, where his mother-in-law helps the girl work for him.

Until the first child is born, marriage bonds are rather weak, but henceforth the marriage is comparatively stable. There are, however, frequent cases of adultery, and a guilty woman who is found out is thrashed by her husband. When a marriage is dissolved, the man leaves the house, which is considered the wife's property, although built by him.

Upon a man's death, his widow remains in the house. After about 2 months of free sexual relations, she chooses a new husband.

Death.—The *Tapirapé* believe that death is brought about by sorcery and never by natural causes. Frequently, when the relatives of the deceased enjoyed sufficient prestige, they kill the shaman whom they suspect.

As soon as it is certain that the sick man will die, mourning begins in the form of a wailing dirge by both men and women. The men dance around the hammock of the dying or dead man, while the women remain seated on the ground. Burial takes place on the day after death. The corpse is stretched out on the hammock. Its feet and head are decorated with urucú dye, and its face is painted black with genipa. The grave is dug in the dead man's house under the place where his hammock was usually hung. The body is buried in the hammock, which is set up in the grave between two poles. All contact with the earth is avoided. Personal possessions of the deceased are buried with him, except that all feather ornaments and bows and arrows are burned.

Five days after the funeral, the relatives walk in file to the ceremonial hut, where they leave the spirit of the dead man. The wailing goes on for many days, sometimes months, and always takes place at sunset. Close-cropped hair is a token of mourning for both sexes.

ESTHETIC AND RECREATIONAL ACTIVITIES

Art.—Obvious esthetic pleasure is derived from skillfully done basketwork; a good workman will destroy a basket which is not turning out well, even though it would serve as a receptacle. Great use is made of highly colored feathers; feathers are both tied and stuck with rosin and wax on to the object to be decorated. Elaborate geometric designs are painted on children's bodies with genipa. The incise work on gourds is also especially striking.

Musical instruments.—Gourd rattles are frequently used to keep time to singing. No sacred powers are attributed to rattles. During the shamanistic ceremony (p. 177), a bamboo trunk is pounded against the ground in time to the music.

Music.—By far the most important *Tapirapé* pastime is singing. A man with a good voice and a large repertoire of songs is much admired by the community. All ceremonies are, basically, singing festivals. Each ceremony during the year has a large set of specific songs: those to be sung by the shaman during the shamanistic "battle with Thunder" (p. 177);

those for group singing during the harvest ceremonies and the ceremony of kawi (p. 176); those for the masked dancers during the dry season; and a very large number of songs specifically for the "Big Sing" (monikahô) during the latter part of the rainy season. During this period (approximately March through April), singing takes place throughout each night from sundown to sunrise. On these occasions, the singing leader and the men of one of the moieties introduce the verse of each song and the refrain is then taken up by the men of the other moiety and the women of the tribe. Women sing in a higher key than the men and, generally, a phrase behind the men. The songs of the masked dancers, each representing a supernatural being, differ stylistically from those used on other occasions in being sung in a falsetto tone, in a manner similar to that of the neighboring *Carajá*. Many such songs have been admittedly learned from the *Carajá*.

Dancing.—Both men and women dance as they sing. In general, the *Tapirapé* dance bending slightly forward, stamping out the time of the music with one foot. Dancing differs greatly, however, according to the occasion. During the harvest ceremonies, men dance in a line, side by side, each man's wife dancing directly behind him. During the group singing of the "Big Sing," the men dance in moiety groups facing each other, and women dance behind the moiety group of their husbands. On one occasion during this time, men dance with women, side by side, with a curious skipping step.

Games.—Men's moieties run foot races against each other after the communal work festival (p. 168); they race in a straight line across the village plaza. Wrestling takes place at one wet-season ceremony, and, now and again, throughout the year as sport. The *Tapirapé* explain, however, that the *Carajá* are better wrestlers and that it is more properly a *Carajá* sport. In wrestling, opponents stand face to face, grasping each other about the neck, and attempt to force or to trip the other to the ground. During one festival, men, one from each moiety at a time, compete by throwing blunt-headed spears at each other. Gambling games are unknown.

Stimulants.—Native tobacco, though used for leisure-time smoking, is principally a stimulant and medicine. A *Tapirapé* will not travel without a supply of tobacco to blow smoke over his tired body at the end of the day, in order to take out soreness and tiredness. Tobacco is necessary to shamans in all their activities. They blow tobacco smoke over the patient in curing (p. 177), and, to induce dreams and a trance, they swallow large gulps of smoke until they become intoxicated and nauseated. When people have seen ghosts, shamans fumigate them with tobacco smoke, in order to drive away the ghost's influence. Shamans fumigate new maize, the first honey of the season and, sometimes, fresh meat to drive out possible supernatural danger. This native tobacco is smoked by laymen in short tubular wooden or clay pipes and by shamans, in tubular clay pipes, sometimes 12 inches (30 cm.) long.

The *Tapirapé* do not routinely plant tobacco as other crops. Occasionally, it is transplanted from scattered patches around the gardens and village to near the houses or gardens, but usually the patches merely seed themselves. A person who discovers a new patch, hastily surrounds it with a low fence to show his ownership of it.

No alcoholic beverages are known to the *Tapirapé*. Beverages made from manioc and maize are prepared as a food and are not allowed to ferment.

RELIGION

Tapirapé religion is based on the belief in two kinds of supernatural beings—disembodied souls of the dead, and malignant forest spirits of many kinds—both designated by one generic term, ančunga (spirit or shadow).

The ančunga iünwera, human spirits or ghosts (aña or anhanga among the *Tupinamba*), live in abandoned villages and frequently come near to the villages of the living "because they are cold" and try to warm themselves close to the houses. The *Tapirapé* are afraid of meeting them and try not to go out at night, when the ghosts most frequently appear.

Souls of the dead continue to live for an undetermined period of time, then die and are transformed into animals. Anyone who hears the croak of a kururú frog (*Pipa pipa*) knows that it is the soul of a leader. A pigeon is the soul of a common man; a paca, that of a woman. The souls of the shamans have a different fate; they go to join Thunder.

In addition to the souls of the dead, there is a large number of malignant beings, also called ančunga, who dwell in the forest. They are very dangerous and kill as many *Tapirapé* as they find. Waré, a legendary hero and a great shaman, had the distinction of killing many ančunga, among whom were the awakú anká, by setting their long coarse hair on fire. The mumpíanká were beings who killed men in order to drink their blood. Some of these forest spirits have become domesticated by the *Tapirapé,* thanks to the powers of their shamans. Several times the *Tapirapé* men dance with masks representing the visiting spirits (pl. 19, *bottom, right*).

Rites.—The real ceremonial season is the rainy season, when the people are thrown together because they can neither farm nor hunt. Mask dances celebrate the visits of the various spirits (ančunga) to the men's house during the dry season. At the end of the rainy season the harvest ceremonial (kaô) and the ceremony of kawi (a souplike beverage made of sweet manioc or of maize) are held.

In the first few months of the rainy season, when the maize crop is threatened by electrical storms and by the first heavy rains, the shamans are called upon to fight Thunder.   This, the important *Tapirapé* ceremony, lasts for 4 days, and is the high point of shamanistic activity.

Kanawana, the Thunder, lives on distant Maratawa surrounded by the souls of dead shamans and by the topü (probably equivalent to the *Tupinamba* word, "tupan"), small anthropomorphic beings whose bodies are covered with white hair.

The topü travel through space in their canoes (half gourds), the sound of which produces the noise of the storm.   The arrows which the topi shoot cause lightning.   During the ceremony, the shamans, completely intoxicated by the tobacco and stimulated by the unceasing dancing and singing, fall into a trance (pl. 19, *top, right*) during which they travel to Thunder's house in order to fight him.   Thunder sets the topü against the shamans, who, wounded by the arrows of "Thunder's creatures," fall into unconsciousness.

SHAMANISM

The *Tapirapé* can visualize the supernatural world through the reports of the dreams of their shamans, whose power grows in proportion to their ability to dream.   A dream is a voyage, during which the soul frees itself of the body and travels through space.   In these dreams the shamans travel to regions which are entirely unknown to the living, and in general are inhabited by spirits.   With their powers, the shamans succeed in taming some of the spirits, who then become their familiar spirits.   The power and prestige of the shaman (pančé) depend on the number of his familiar spirits.

The *Tapirapé* speak of battles between shamans wherein each calls out his familiar spirits against the other while dreaming.   More often, a shaman sets his familiar spirits upon laymen and kills them.   A shaman may also kill his victim during a dream by throwing a malignant object, usually a piece of bone or a worm, into his body.

The victims of sorcery appeal to friendly shamans, who attempt to cure them by extracting the malignant object by suction, massage, and blowing tobacco.   When many deaths occur simultaneously and the *Tapirapé* suspect a certain shaman of having caused them, they do not hesitate to kill him.   One man recalled that during his lifetime 10 shamans suspected of sorcery had been killed.   He himself had killed a shaman whom he suspected of having killed his brother.   In spite of the constant suspicion surrounding them, the shamans do not employ mechanical techniques or sympathetic magic in sorcery.

The shamans make great use of tobacco, which is essential for healing and dreaming.   They smoke it in large tubular clay pipes.   Cures usually take place at dusk.   The shaman squats by the patient's hammock and smokes for a long time, becoming intoxicated and blowing the smoke from the pipe over the patient's body.   He then massages the patient, rubbing toward the extremities of his body. If he fails to extract the malignant object in this fashion, he sucks it out, swallows it, then vomits it up.

At one time, during an epidemic of fever, a shaman used a different method. He prepared a mixture of honey and water, and, after much smoking, spewed it out over the patients and on the houses where there were sick people.

Besides healing, the shamans must protect the people against dangerous spirits (ančunga); they call forth "children's spirits" without which there can be no conception; they prevent wild animals from harming the *Tapirapé* during great hunting or fishing expeditions; and they increase the number of peccaries in the woods. It is also believed that they divine the future in their dreams.

The prestige of shamans is such among the *Tapirapé* that almost all leaders of communities as well as of ceremonial moiety groups and household heads are shamans. As shamans receive payment for successful cures, they accumulate many possessions which they redistribute at a yearly ceremonial. Liberality is essential to prestige in this society where avarice is particularly despised.

MYTHOLOGY

Tapirapé myths fall into two categories: legends telling of the deeds of ancestral heroes, and tales of animals. In the latter, the tortoise (*Testudo tabulata*) is noted for his shrewdness in his dealings with the other animals of the jungle. These stories follow the general *Tupi* pattern.

Among the various *Tapirapé* heroes are Apüwenonu and Petura. The former descended from heaven and lived with the *Tapirapé*. He taught them to plant and harvest cotton, manioc, and maize. When he was old, Apüwenonu returned to heaven and changed himself into a star.

Petura stole fire from the buzzards and brought light to the *Tapirapé*, who until then had not seen day. It is also told of Petura that he stole hatchets and knives from the emu and gave them to the *Tapirapé*.

Txawanamü is famous for a series of songs which tell of his adventures among the mythical ampúawa, enemies of the *Tapirapé*, who made him die a lingering death. Wančina, a great shaman, had his whole house, including his family and belongings, transported to heaven by Kanawana, the Thunder. Waré was another shaman who killed many dangerous forest spirits.

BIBLIOGRAPHY

Baldus, 1935, 1937; Bigorre, 1916, 1917; Métraux, 1927; Wagley, 1940 a, 1940 b, 1943 b.

THE CARAJÁ[1]

By William Lipkind

TRIBAL DIVISIONS AND TERRITORY

The *Carajá* are a river people who since pre-Columbian times have held as the central portion of their territory the inland Island of Bananal, which is formed by the great fork of the Araguaya River (lat. 8°–17° S., long. 48°–52° W., map 1, *No. 1*; see Volume 1, map 7). They must be regarded as an independent linguistic family for the present; their language displays no convincing similarities to any other recorded South American language.

The term *"Carajá"* is used to designate the entire people as well as the largest of the three tribal divisions; the other two are the *Shambioá* and the *Javahé*. The *Carajá* proper have 20 villages on the western or main branch of the Araguaya River, widely spread from Leopoldina south of Bananal clear down to the end of the Island. The *Shambioá,* now nearly extinct, have only two villages left, a little way below Conceicāo. The eight villages of the *Javahé* lie on the eastern or minor branch of the Araguaya River and on the small streams within Bananal. The general location and the relative sizes of the three groups have remained the same since the earliest times.

The native names give some notion of intergroup attitudes. All three groups regard themselves as a single people and use a name meaning "we" to distinguish themselves from other tribes. The *Carajá* proper are called the "great people" by the other two groups. The *Shambioá* are the "companion people." The *Javahé* are called by a name which is used generally to mean "Indian" and bears the pejorative connotation "backwoodsman" or "hick." There is a possible analysis which makes it the "old people" but, even if this etymology is correct, the word no longer has that meaning.

Dialectical differences are slight and other differences not very great, with the *Shambioá* occupying a middle position culturally between the other two groups. This account is based on field work with the *Carajá* proper and refers to the other groups only where they exhibit important differences.

---

[1] The present description of the *Carajá* is based on the author's field work during 1937, done under the auspices of the Department of Anthropology, Columbia University.

ARCHEOLOGY

Large circular hollows in the ground are found at various points in *Carajá* territory, always in the close vicinity of a stream. By tradition these are ancient cemeteries; of old, they say, people did not mourn at a funeral but held a feast in the hollow. One of these hollows located on the height above the river bank at Fontoura is 18 m. (about 58 ft.) long, 15 m. (about 50 ft.) wide, and 1½ m. (5 ft.) deep at its center. The mound forming the northern side was excavated, disclosing two lines of burials with associated pottery, bone labrets, and beads.

The pottery is very similar to modern *Carajá* pottery and the labrets are exactly like those now in the possession of the *Carajá*. The cemetery cannot, however, definitely be identified as *Carajá*. The present-day *Carajá* cemetery is different in location and ground plan. There is now secondary urn burial, and in the first burial the bodies are laid at right angles to the river rather than parallel as were those disclosed by the excavation. Still, the remains show even less resemblance to the *Ge* and *Tupí* peoples in the neighborhood. The question must be left open for further archeological study.

HISTORY

Since the earliest times, the *Carajá* have been at war with their *Ge* and *Tupí* neighbors. The sole exception is the *Tapirapé*, with whom at one time the *Javahé* maintained close and friendly relations. The *Shambioá* were the first to come in contact with the Neo-Brazilians early in the 17th century. Contact with the *Carajá* proper must have begun shortly after the founding of Santa Anna by Bartholomeu Bueno in 1682. The *Carajá* are on good terms with the Neo-Brazilians, trading skins and fish for clothing, beads, knives, axes, guns, sugar, and salt.

Population.—According to the census made by the author in 1939, the *Carajá* number 1,510, divided as follows: *Carajá* proper, 795; *Javahé*, 650; *Shambioá*, 65. These figures should be contrasted with Castelnau's (1850–59) count in 1845 of 2,000 *Shambioá* in four villages, and his estimate of a total of 100,000 *Carajá*, and with Krause's (1911) estimate of 10,000 *Carajá* in 1908.

CULTURE

SUBSISTENCE ACTIVITIES

Farming.—Clearings are made in the thick forest along the watercourses. Gardens must be so located as to be accessible by canoe in the dry season and yet not flooded in the rainy season. The scarcity of such land results in some of the plots being several miles distant from the village. Proximity to fishing grounds is generally held to be more important. The work of clearing is begun in May at the beginning of the dry season. Maize is planted in September, when the first rains come, and manioc shortly after. There is little cultivation beyond weeding. The basic crop is manioc, both the sweet and bitter varieties being cultivated, with maize next in importance. Four varieties each of sweet and bitter manioc and 10 varieties of maize are cultivated. Other crops are: Five varieties of potatoes, two varieties of cara, four varieties of watermelon, three varieties of squash, four varieties of beans, and ten varieties of bananas, as well as peanuts, urucú, tobacco, cotton, calabashes, sugarcane, yams, peppers, pineapples, and papayas. Men do all the work with a little assistance in harvesting and weeding from older women. The *Javahé* are more industrious farmers than the other *Carajá,* cultivating extensive plantations.

Collecting.—A large number of vegetable products are gathered for use as food, medicine, and raw material for manufacture, but only a few are of great importance. The babassu and the burití palms, used for food and textile materials, are among the most valuable. The taquara reed is sought after for arrows. Turtle eggs are a significant item of food during the dry season. Honey is indispensable for feasting.

Hunting.—Although the *Carajá* are passionate hunters, very few of the animals available in the region are eaten. Only the peccary is really sought and constitutes a sizable item in the larder. The other animals that are eaten—the cutia, coati, woodsdeer, monkey, iguana, and a few birds, such as the mutum, jao, and jacu—are killed when encountered but are not eaten by everyone. Peccaries are hunted in a communal drive, the most favorable time being shortly after the beginning of the rainy season when large droves are trapped on islands.

The chief purpose of hunting is to get feathers, and the most desirable birds are the various parrots, herons, the male stork, and the flamingo. The nesting of valuable birds is carefully watched, and the young are stolen and tamed. Feathers stored in small baskets almost constitute a currency, because they are readily negotiable at all times and maintain a stable value.

The principal weapons are the bow and club. The bow, made of a variety of woods but with a preference for juari when available, is round in cross section and about 6 feet (2 m.) long. The arrow is preferably of taquara reed and variously tipped with wood, animal bone, or fish bone. Clubs are beautifully fashioned of heavy hardwood, decorated with delicate carving, and are swung and thrown with equal skill. The lance is now used only for ceremonial purposes.

Fishing.—Fish is the most important food supply. Trapping and drugging fish with timbo is a communal affair; individuals fish with the bow and arrow. There is occasional night fishing, with spearing by torchlight. The pirarucu is killed by harpoon. The hook and line is little used, and apparently was borrowed recently from the Neo-Brazilians.

Food preparation.—Manioc is peeled, grated, squeezed out by hand, and cooked into a soup. When the soup cools, it is masticated for a few minutes, then allowed to stand for a while. The resulting fermentation is not allowed to continue long enough to produce an intoxicating drink. This soup, along with a similar soup made of maize, is a daily staple. Manioc and ground maize are also made into cakes, but this is a holiday variation of diet rather than the staff of life as in other regions. The standard methods of cooking meat, fish, and vegetables are boiling, roasting on a spit, roasting on a grate, and roasting in the embers. Occasionally, some vegetables are baked in hot sand. Maize is the only food that is stored. On platform shelves at the top cf their rainy-season houses, the *Javahé* pile a supply of maize dried on the cob sufficient to last throughout the dry season.

HOUSES AND VILLAGES

The permanent or rainy-season village is erected on a high bank overlooking the river. One or two rows of houses face the river, and the men's house, about 50 feet (15.2 m.) back, faces down river. All the space between the men's house and the family houses is kept perfectly clean and constitutes the dancing plaza of the village. The surrounding clearing extends only a few yards in all directions. All neighboring forest which must be traversed in hunting or gathering is threaded by well-marked trails. A path leads down from the center of the village to the main port where women, married men, and children bathe, and married men land their canoes. Another path cuts diagonally down from the men's house to the bachelor's port where the young men bathe and visitors to the masked dances land their canoes.

The house is rectangular in ground plan with supported horizontal ridge poles (fig. 18). Saplings are sunk into the ground at the sides and

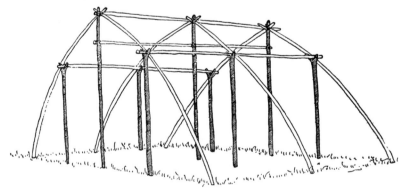

FIGURE 18.—*Carajá* house frame. (Redrawn from Ehrenreich, 1891 b, fig. 3.)

bent over to the ridge pole at the top, where they are firmly tied with bast. Then the whole structure is tightly thatched with successive overlapping layers of palm frond tied to the saplings (pl. 20, *top*). The entrance is a small rectangular opening at the bottom, through which one crawls after pushing aside a door of plaited palm. Every married woman in the family cooks at her own fireplace, which consists of two lumps of hardened clay. Mats used for sleeping and sitting are spread over the entire floor. Wooden stools (fig. 19) may also be found. Bows, arrows, and rattles

FIGURE 19.—*Carajá* wooden stool. (Redrawn from Ehrenreich, 1891 b, fig. 13.)

are shoved into the wall thatch. Baskets, used for storing such things as tobacco, urucú, and feathers, are hung by a string from the ridge poles. Large baskets containing vegetables lie on the ground next to the thatch.

The dry-season house is identical in form but smaller and of flimsier construction. Thatching is looser and the walls are thatched only about halfway to the ground, the north and west sides often being left completely open. The dry-season village is generally constructed on a long beach and, as the site grows dirty, is moved along the beach. The ground plan of the dry-season village is identical with the rainy-season village.

DRESS AND ORNAMENTS

The most prominent facial decoration is a blue-black circular scarification about an inch in diameter over each cheekbone. The ears of infants are pierced and an ornament consisting of a small polished capybara tooth with a feather attached is inserted. A common ear ornament for children is a mother-of-pearl disk with a cut feather fringe set on a blackened thin rod. In a perforation of their lower lips, men wear wood or bone labrets of a variety of shapes (pl. 21; fig. 21, *a*), each assigned to a different age grade; old men use simple wooden plugs.

Men wear their hair long, winding it round a plaited cotton rope reddened with urucú. Women wear their hair about shoulder length.

Armlets crocheted of cotton are worn at the wrists and just above the elbow; similar ornaments are worn just below the knee and at the ankle. These are worn particularly by children and are supposed to aid growth.

Young men wear large armlets almost 12 inches (30 cm.) long crocheted of cotton with hanging fringes.

Women wear a bark-cloth girdle, which is wound round the body and under the crotch and looped over, hanging down in front. Feather head-dresses of a number of different designs are worn by men on festal occasions. Men tie the prepuce with a firmly wound string and wear a string belt.

Elaborately decorated woven belts with hanging ema feathers are worn for wrestling matches. Bird down is glued on the shoulders, arms, and legs. Body painting is very elaborate, and designs covering the entire body are carefully executed with genipa. Urucú is spread generally, with accents on the cheekbones, the nose, and the upper arm.

TRANSPORTATION

The *Carajá* manufacture elongated dugouts, neatly adapted to landing and freeing their craft among the sandbanks.

MANUFACTURES

Bark cloth.—Bark cloth is made of *Apeiba* bast, soaked, beaten with flat stones, and dried until it becomes very soft and white.

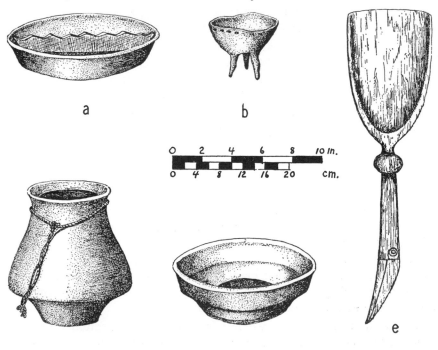

a   b

c   d

e

J. Anglim

FIGURE 20.—*Carajá* manufactures. *a–d,* Pottery; *e,* wooden scoop. (Redrawn from Ehrenreich, 1891 b, figs. 5 and 14.)

Basketry.—The *Carajá* excel in the variety and solidity of their plait-work, which includes burden baskets, strainers, shoulder bags, bottles, elliptical feather cases, and boat-shaped containers for suspension. Twilling and twining are the dominant techniques (pl. 22).

Textiles.—The *Carajá* produce some taffetalike fabrics, but in 1775 Pinto da Fonseca found them using cotton solely for fish nets and bowstrings, so that he himself introduced a loom and taught the women how to work it.

Featherwork.—In contrast to their *Ge* neighbors of Eastern Brazil, the *Carajá* are outstanding for featherwork. They make wide-meshed and close-meshed caps with feathers tied to the intersection of the interlaced splints and arranged into rosettes, diadems of feathers stuck into radially mounted cane tubes, and other types of ornaments (pl. 21).

Axes.—Stone axes figure in old *Carajá* petroglyphs and have been found by many travelers in the area. They were used for adzing, chopping, and warfare, and as chief's badges. Iron axes have rapidly replaced them.

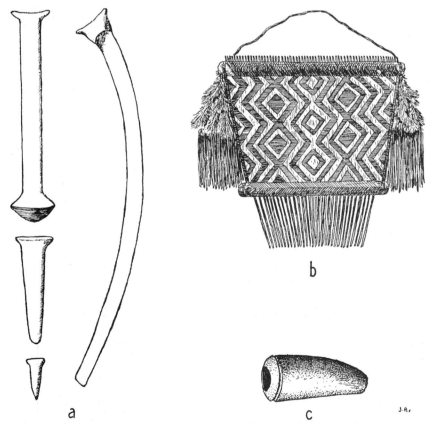

a   c

FIGURE 21.—*Carajá* manufactures. *a,* Labrets; *b,* comb; *c,* pipe. (Approximately ⅓ actual size.) (Redrawn from Ehrenreich, 1891 b, figs. 2, 9, and 4.)

Weapons.—The *Carajá* use bows and arrows (pls. 20, *bottom, left;* 21, *left* and *center*), and their mythology indicates aboriginal use of the spear thrower for hunting monkeys. Recently, they have used a spear thrower of the upper Xingú River type for sport.

Pottery.—Pottery vessels include several forms of plain ware (fig. 20).

SOCIAL AND POLITICAL ORGANIZATION

The kinship structure may be described as double descent. Both lines are important, the greater emphasis falling on the mother's line, and both lines serve different functions. Village citizenship, adoption, and the closest affectional ties are reckoned in the mother's line. Moiety membership and the offices of chief, priest, and food-divider are patrilineally inherited.

The fundamental unit of social organization is the village. Every village has one or more ioló, children of chiefly line, designated by the chief for preferential treatment by the members of the village. The chief names the ioló who is to succeed him or, if he fails to do so, the village makes the choice at his death. Girls of chiefly line are similarly chosen for preferential treatment; each of them is known as the "hidden woman." There is some indication that women functioned as chiefs in former times, but today there is no woman chief. The chief has no coercive powers but directs the village by recognizing the will of the majority in such matters as the selection of camp and garden sites and the announcement of a move at change of season. His principal function is to act as peacemaker, and people readily submit to his adjudication. Because of the importance of religious ceremonials, the priest and the shaman frequently exercise more authority than the chief. When all three offices are vested in a single individual, his authority may be considerable, but it is kept in check by the right of a discontented person to move at any time to another village.

Within the village the important unit is the household. Residence being matrilocal, a household consists of sisters, their husbands, children, and the husbands of grown daughters. Marriage is restricted to one's own generation, the preferred mate being a cousin on the mother's side. There is no sanction but ridicule against wrong marriages, and there are many cases of cross-generational marriage. Marriage is predominantly monogamous, but a few instances of polygyny and one of polyandry were encountered. The avunculate is very important and involves many social and especially ceremonial duties. Cooperation in the household is close and in the village fairly close. In addition, villages are grouped together in ceremonial units, generally consisting of three or four neighboring villages, which celebrate important feasts jointly. This ceremonial unit acts as an insurance group when a village's crop fails or its fish supplies grow scarce. Beyond this, the only intervillage ties

PLATE 20.—**Carajá house and physical types.** *Top:* House. (Courtesy University Museum, Philadelphia.) *Bottom, left:* Warriors. *Bottom, right:* Girls. (After Ehrenreich, 1891 b.)

PLATE 21.—**Carajá types.** (Courtesy University Museum, Philadelphia.)

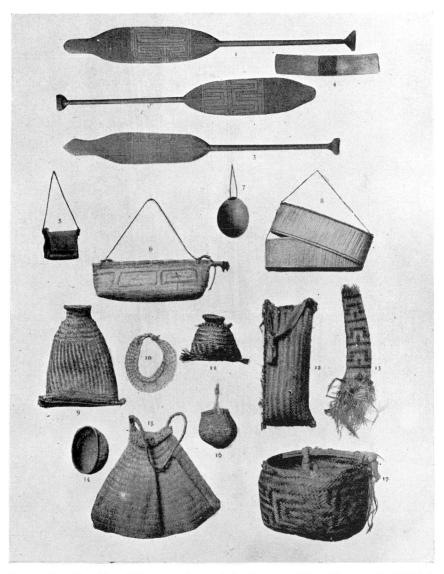

PLATE 22.—**Carajá paddles, gourds, and basketry.** (After Ehrenreich, 1891 b.)

are the product of intermarriage and formal friendship. Intervillage feuds are common and are restrained only by the religious community, sanctuary being granted at all religious ceremonials.

ETIQUETTE

All dealings with visitors are conducted according to elaborate formal patterns. The language is rich in formal appellations, exclamations, and honorific phrases. The most remarkable feature is that women are permitted to behave with perfect freedom, whereas men, until they become fathers, behave with a shy and deferential modesty resembling but exceeding that of the Victorian maiden. Normal relations between members of the same village are formal and dignified; only in the men's house or on fishing and hunting trips is the behavior of men relaxed enough to permit horseplay and casual joking.

LIFE CYCLE

Childbirth and Childhood.—The child gets two sets of names, one male and one female, as soon as the mother is known to be pregnant. These are one's own names given by grandparents of both lines. Taboos in regard to diet and behavior are required of both parents before and after birth. There is a well-developed couvade based on the notion of an intimate connection between the infant and its father. Babies are nursed until they turn to other food of their own volition; sometimes ridicule is used as a sanction against particularly recalcitrant children. No intercourse is allowed during the period of lactation. Babies are carried on the hip, and sleep with the mother until weaning, when they are paired off with other children or with a grandparent. The girl child wears no clothing until weaned and then receives a fringed belt.

Puberty and initiations.—At menstruation, a girl's cheeks are scarified and she assumes the girdle.

A boy passes through a first initiation at about the age of 8 or 9, when his lower lip is pierced and a small bone labret inserted. A couple of years later, he passes through a second initiation, when his hair is cut short to a tonsure, his entire body is stained black with genipa, and he assumes the penis cord. When his hair has grown out to shoulder length, it is put up in a braid, and he attains full status as a young man.

The next change of status for both boys and girls occurs at marriage, when, for the first time, they take on the responsibilities of regular work. Teknonymy is a matter of pride and follows the birth of the first child. The name is retained permanently thereafter, even though the child should die. At about 45 both parents discard their ornaments and accept the status of old age. All the above age grades are named and involve differential behavior and dietary observances.

Death.—At death, the soul becomes a wild ghost if the person has been violently killed and a regular resident of the village of the dead if he has suffered a quiet death. A shaman's soul is translated to the skies. Mourning puts an end to all religious ceremonies and is celebrated by self-laceration, the destruction of property, and daily keening. There is separate burial in formal cemeteries for those who died quietly and those who died violently. The corpse is wrapped in a mat with his weapons and ornaments, and the mat is hung in a shallow grave covered by poles (fig. 22). Food and drink are provided for a short period. After the next change of season, the bones are exhumed and placed in a family urn.

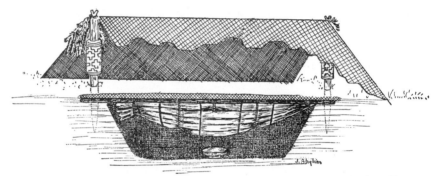

FIGURE 22.—*Carajá* burial. (Redrawn from Ehrenreich, 1891 b, fig. 16)

WARFARE

The *Carajá* are good fighters and have maintained themselves since prehistoric times in a territory surrounded on all sides by warlike enemies. Their usual tactics are waiting outside an enemy village at night and attacking at dawn. In defense, they run to the nearest water, where they are unbeatable. They use the bow and arrow and club, and are skilled wrestlers. They cut off a foot bone of a dead enemy and carry it back to their village; this places them in control of the ghost, who now becomes a caretaker of the village and is impersonated in a special dry-season ceremony. At one such ceremony there were two *Tapirapé* ghosts, three *Chavante,* one *Cayapó,* and one Neo-Brazilian. Present-day warfare is largely with the *Chavante,* the *Cayapó,* and the *Canoeiro.* Now and then a Neo-Brazilian may be killed by stealth to avenge a personal grievance. No captives are taken except women and small children, who are treated as full members of the group.

ESTHETIC AND RECREATIONAL ACTIVITIES

Art.—Decorative art is confined to woven designs on baskets and mats, feather ornaments, elaborate masks with superimposed feather designs,

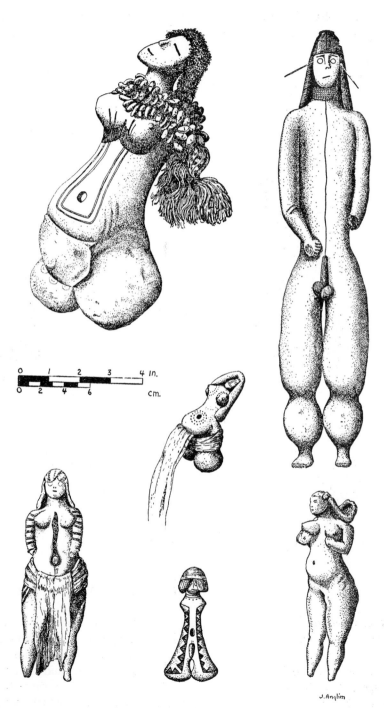

FIGURE 23.—*Carajá* wax and clay dolls. (Redrawn from Ehrenreich, 1891 b, pl. 12.)

small clay dolls (fig. 23), delicately carved clubs, body paint designs, and a little painting and incising of pottery.

a   b

FIGURE 24.—*Carajá* masks. (Redrawn from Ehrenreich, 1891 b, figs. 18, 22.)

Music and dances.—The major art of the *Carajá* is music. A large number of elaborate dances with complex songs, each dance having a separate song style, make up the chief body of the music. These are all religious. In addition, there are some secular dances, and songs are interspersed in the tales. Musical instruments are very few, there being only a rattle accompanying the singers and a small flute which is used as a toy.

Games.—Of numerous games, the most important is a formal wrestling match which is an indispensable part of most religious ceremonies and of all intervillage visits.

Narcotics and stimulants.—Like the other tribes in this region, the *Carajá* have no alcoholic beverages. They smoke tobacco in short cylindrical pipes (fig. 21, *c*). They are heavy smokers, some of the children beginning before they are weaned.

SUPERNATURALISM

Cults.—*Carajá* religion consists of two distinct cults: a cult of the dead and a mask cult (fig. 24). The cult of the dead, which is under the direction of the priest, has for its object the placation of ghosts by a periodical ceremonial which comes to its climax in several large calendrical feasts. The most important of these feasts is the Big House Feast, which is celebrated shortly after the beginning of the rainy season. All the villages which comprise a ceremonial unit come to the one village where the feast is conducted. There is a great mass of ceremonial addressed to various classes of ghosts, but the central portion of the ceremony is the impersonation of animal ghosts. Another important feast, already mentioned, occurs at the height of the dry season and is directed toward the control of enemy ghosts. Two other feasts held in the dry season are chiefly for the entertainment of the ancestors.

The mask cult is concerned with the worship of another class of supernaturals. It consists of an elaborate routine of feasts, interrupted only by death. In these feasts, conducted by the shaman, the supernaturals are impersonated in the complex dances mentioned above.

The two cults are independent of each other and are both strictly men's cults. Any women intruding upon the secrets of the cults is subjected to gang rape and remains a wanton thereafter.

Shamanism.—A shaman is trained by apprenticeship to an older shaman. A certain amount of medical lore is taught but the essence of the training is learning how to communicate with supernaturals in a state of trance.

There is a considerable amount of sorcery. The main technique is bottling a supernatural being into a small image and then directing it into the body of the victim. As almost all deaths are interpreted as the result of sorcery, feuding is continual.

BIBLIOGRAPHY

Castlenau, 1850–59; Ehrenreich, 1891 b; Krause, 1911.

THE TURIWARA AND ARUÃ

By Curt Nimuendajú

THE TURIWARA

LANGUAGE, TERRITORY, AND HISTORY

Turiwara ("those of the Turí"—the meaning of Turí is unknown) is the name used by this tribe and by the *Tembé* (map 1, *No. 1*; see Volume 1, map 7). The *Amanayé* say *Turiwá* or *Turiwã*.

The *Turiwara* language is a *Tupian* dialect of the *He-* group, and scarcely differs from the *Urubú* dialect, which has suggested the possibility that the two tribes are local divisions of one people. That there is a river named Tury in the present habitat of the *Urubú*, and that an *Urubú* group is called *"Turiwara"* is no proof of this possibility. Because the *Urubú* migrated to the Tury River, from Maranhão, only at the beginning of the 20th century, whereas the *Turiwara* had left Maranhão half a century earlier, the *Urubú* band named *Turiwara* can have no connection with the *Turiwara* tribe.

The first record of the *Turiwara* language is a list of personal names and their explanations compiled by Meerwarth (1904), who, however, confused forms of the Lingua Geral with those of the *Turiwara* dialect. The only published vocabulary consists of 103 words (Nimuendajú, 1914 c).

In the 18th century, a tribe named *Turiwara* was noted on the lower Tocantins (Ribeiro de Sampaio, 1812, p. 8; Villa Real, 1848, p. 431). (Lat. 4°S., long. 48°W.) It spoke *Tupian,* judging by the names of their two chiefs in 1793: Tatahi (tatá-i, "little fire") and Areuanajú (arawaná = a fish, *Ichnosoma* sp. + yu, suffix for persons' names).

According to *Tembé* tradition, the *Turiwara* crossed the Gurupí River from the present State of Maranhão shortly after the *Tembé,* probably between 1840 and 1850. In 1862, they lived in three villages on the Capim River below the Acarajuçaua Rapids: Suaçupepora with 30 persons, Cauaxy with 15, and Cariucaua with 60. In 1871, the Pracateua Mission (Assumpção) was founded on the Capim River with 500 (600?) *Tembé* and *Turiwara.* The following year, the murder of the missionary to the *Amanayé* put an end to the Christianization (see p. 200). (Cunha, 1852, p. 82; Brusque, 1862, p. 12; Cruz, 1874, p. 47; Souza Franco, 1842.) This evidently prompted the *Turiwara* to move from the Capim River mission to the Acará Grande River, where, in 1868, a large part of the tribe had already been established near Miritipirange (Gama Malcher, 1878, p. 102). In 1885, there were 100 *Turiwara* here, and 71 more on the left bank of the Acará Pequeno (Baena, 1885, p. 28). In

1899, Meerwarth (1904), the sole source of ethnographic information about the *Turiwara,* visited the tribe on the Acará Grande River. They lived then in 8 places below the Grande Rapids. In 1914, they numbered about 100, and all were on the Acará Grande. In 1942, only 14 survived (Arquivos da Inspectoria do Serviço de Protecção aos Indios).

The *Turiwara* were, according to Meerwarth, visited from time to time by merchants (regatões), mostly Portuguese, traveling in canoes. The merchants cheated the Indians outlandishly (Meerwarth, 1904).

CULTURE

Farming.—Manioc, cotton, urucú, and some bananas and oranges were cultivated.

Houses.—The house was a long, rectangular building with gabled roof and ridge pole. It had no walls.

Clothing.—The *Turiwara* wore clothes of civilized origin, but most of the time they went about with the upper portion of their bodies unclothed.

Transportation.—Houses were connected by overland paths. For river travel, the *Turiwara* had dugout canoes of the "casco" type, which were hollowed and the side walls spread more widely apart by heating inside and out over a fire and stretching. This is also the Neo-Brazilian type. Some canoes had shields fore and aft. The paddle had a crutch handle.

Manufactures.—Meerwarth (1904) lists manufactured objects: Pans for flour making, baskets woven of timbo, carrying baskets woven of liana with straps for hanging from the head and other straps for hanging from the shoulders, painted and unpainted pottery, beautiful hammocks of cotton dyed with urucú, gourds (*Lagenaria*) for holding water and others for beverages, braziers which at night they put under their hammocks for warmth, bows and arrows for fishing, rifles for hunting, bush knives, and iron axes. The women made the hammocks and pottery. The men hunted, fished, helped with flour making, and cut wood.

Social Usages.—The *Turiwara* were monogamous, though a chief formerly had several wives. A girl's father or, if she had no father, her older relatives gave her in marriage without consulting her wishes. The *Turiwara* practiced the couvade.

Meerwarth (1904) lists a series of men's and women's names which, without exception, were nicknames, not true surnames, and referred to the person's favorite food or to some amusing physical or mental peculiarity.

Accompanied by loud monotonous singing and the music of taboca flutes and clarinets (*toré*) made of the trunk of Cecropia, groups of *Turiwara* danced slowly, always singing the same refrain.

BIBLIOGRAPHY

See *Amanayé* bibliography, page 202.

THE ARUÃ

TERRITORY, LANGUAGE, AND HISTORY

In the 17th century, the *Aruã* (*Arouen, Aroua*) occupied the northeastern part of Marajó Island (for Marajó archeology, see this volume, pp. 153–159), the islands of the estuary of the Amazon including Caviana, and perhaps part of the mainland on the left bank of the estuary. Later, they withdrew in part to Brazilian Guiana and the adjacent region of French Guiana. This zone consists almost entirely of lakes and floodlands.

Viñaza (1892) mentions no less than seven works in and on the *Aruã* language, written in the 18th century. Fr. Joaquim da Conceição wrote two religious texts; Fr. João de Jesus, a religious text and a grammar; and Fr. Boaventura de Santo Antonio, a grammar. All these have been lost. In 1877 in the village of Afuá (Marajó), Penna (1881) compiled a vocabulary given by the last *Aruã* of the place, a shaman of about 75. Penna thought the language was *Cariban*, but it is clearly *Arawakan*, though quite different from that of the true *Arawak* of the Guiana Coast and of the *Palicur*. In 1926 on the Uaçá River, the present author found no one who spoke the *Aruã* language. Two old Indians, however, gave a list of 30 vocables.

O'Brian del Carpio (ms.), who entered the estuary of the Amazon in 1621, was the first to mention the name *Aruã*. On Sipinipoco Island (i.e., Sapanapok or Caviana, or else one of the adjacent islands?) he learned the language which "they themselves called Arrua." Laet's map (1899) made 4 years later is the first to record an Arouen Island (i.e., Curuá or another one near it?). At the same time, Des Forest (1899) mentions near Cabo do Norte several *Arouen* villages of "Indians who wear their hair long like women." Later writings and maps distinguish Joanes Island (i.e., Marajó) and the Aruans Island or Islands.

The *Aruã* appeared for the first time in the history of Marajó in 1643 when a ship was wrecked on the Pará River. Father Luiz Figueira and other passengers reached the coast of Marajó, where they were killed and devoured by the *Aruã* (Moraes, 1860). Berredo (1905, 2:66), however, who likes to emphasize the "barbarity and ferocity" of the Indians, states that Figueira and others were drowned, and that nine others reached Marajó Island, where six of them were killed, but he does not say eaten, by the *Aruã*. It seems that the *Aruã* and the other tribes on Marajó Island were always hostile to the Portuguese of Belém, although they maintained friendly relations and commerce through the estuary of the Amazon with other nations, especially the Dutch. Father Antonio Vieira (1735–46, 1:135–136) emphasizes several times that the blame for this hostility lay with the Portuguese. By 1654, the *Aruã* and *"Nheengayba"* threatened the vicinity of the city of Belém itself (Berredo 1905, 2:95), and an expedition was sent against them. (See also Bettendorf, 1910, p. 112.)

These tribes rejected all offers of peace and pardon, and, although Berredo stated that the war was ended with the "fatal annihilation of the barbarians," another armed expedition was in preparation 4 years later. Meanwhile, in 1652, Father Antonio Vieira had succeeded in having the laws sanctioning Indian slavery abolished. He informed the Indians of this and succeeded in making peace before the expedition went afield. Among the tribes which in 1659 solemnly made peace on the Mapuá River and on Marajó were the *Aruã* and their chief Piyé (Peyhé), whose village was in Rebordello, on the eastern point of Caviana Island (Vieira, 1735–46, 1:135, 151–169). The war was over and Christianization began, but the *Aruã* and other Marajó Indians began to migrate to Guiana. The following century is marked by this migration and by the Portuguese effort to prevent it.

The peace had but a limited effect, probably because the Jesuits, after a popular uprising in 1661, were compelled to stop enforcing the laws of 1652. In 1698, a number of the *Aruã* were declared "undesirable on the Northern coast because they were too friendly to the enemy" (the Dutch) and were expatriated to Maranhão (Bettendorf, 1910, p. 663).

In 1701 there was another great conflict with the *Aruã* of Marajó Island, who were established in three villages near the mouth of the Paraguary (Soure) River by Fr. José de Santa Maria. In the absence of the missionary, they were ill-treated by the residents of Belém and by the governor himself, Fernão Carrilho, and left their villages. Upon his return, the missionary and Fr. Martinho da Conceição went up the Paraguary River (Rio de Soure) to repair the damage, but the Indians killed them. The following year, a punitive expedition of 60 soldiers and 200 Indians captured some 200 *Aruã*. The murderers of the two priests were executed in Belém. (Southey, 1862, 5:90; Berredo, 1905, 2:399; Rocha Pombo, 1905, 6:338.) The same year the *Aruã* of Ganhoão (north coast of Marajó) were transferred to the village of the Aroaquis on the Urubú River, in the present State of Amazonas. With *Aruã* from the Cabo do Norte, another village was founded near Belém (Caiá or Monsarás?), but the missionary was not able to prevent the escape of the Indians (Annaes da Bibliotheca . . . I, Nos. 79, 85).

Twenty years later, the *Aruã* who had escaped to Guiana and obtained French support, took the offensive against the Portuguese under a chief named Koymará (Guayamã, Guamã). They attacked the Portuguese settlements and for one year occupied the village of Moribira, 45 kilometers north of Belém. (Rio-Branco, 1899, 2:53, 90, 101; Guajará, 1896, p. 166; Coudreau, H., 1886–87, 1:220.) These hostilities lasted at least until 1727.

From 1738 to 1744, Father Lombard gathered the *Maraón* and *Aruã*, fugitives from the Portuguese missions, in the Ouanari mission, French Guiana (Coudreau, H., 1895, p. 274). In 1743, Barrère recorded the presence of *Aruã* to the south of Mineur River (Amapá Grande?), stating that they had outstanding ability as seamen. From 1784 to 1798, the Portuguese depopulated the entire coast between the Amazon and the Oyapock, taking the fugitive Indians to Pará. As trade invariably attracted the Indians to the French, it was essential that the Portuguese depopulate a zone between Pará and Cayena (Coudreau, H., 1886–87, 1:224). Despite great dangers, however, a large part of the prisoners returned in their fragile canoes to their refuge in Guiana. It was probably at this time that part of the *Aruã* settled on the Uaçá River. The persecutions stopped in the 19th century.

The Indians in Marajó disappeared during the first half of the 19th century. In 1793, *Aruã* were transferred from Chaves (north coast of Marajó) to the lower Tocantins, where the village of Murú was founded for them between the present Patos and Alcobaça (Almeida Pinto, 1906, p. 188). Rebordello counted 279 Indians in 1816, but the last *Aruã* of Marajó and neighboring islands disappeared, probably in consequence of the revolt of the Cabanos, 1834–36. A nucleus of *Aruã* and *Galibí*, however, settled in Uaçá, completely under French influence. With them were also some *Maraón, Palicur,* and *Itutan,* and French Creoles, Chinese, Arabs, and Brazilian Mestizos. In 1854, Father Dabbadie refers to 80 *Aroua* on the Uaçá River, and in 1891 H. Coudreau (1886) mentions 100. In 1925, when the present author spent some time among the 160 Indians of the Uaçá River, the *Aruã* component was much more reduced than the *Galibí*. There was no longer any vestige of the other Indian components, and the only language used was French Creole.

CULTURE

When the *Galibí* and the *Aruã* gathered on the Uaçá River, they probably brought very little of their own original culture, for both had been influenced for nearly a century by the missionaries and other civilized people. In consequence, they were greatly influenced by the *Palicur,* a still relatively strong and intact tribe who had become their neighbors. The little Indian culture that they still possess is practically identical to that of the *Palicur.* Otherwise, their culture is adopted from the French Creoles of Guiana and, to a lesser degree, from the Brazilians. The Serviço de Protecção aos Indios maintains a station among them.

There is nothing in the literature on the original culture of the *Aruã.* The paleoethnological (archeological) material in the urn cemeteries of the region do not lead to any precise conclusion. On Caviana Island, stronghold of the *Aruã* during the last phase of their ethnic existence, the author investigated five urn cemeteries in 1925. Three of these contained glass beads and other European objects. In historic times, only the *Aruã* are known to have inhabited the island, but the style of urn is very different in the three sites mentioned, and there is no certainty as to which one belongs to the *Aruã*. Only one thing is common to all: secondary burial in urns.

BIBLIOGRAPHY

Almeida Pinto, 1906; Annaes . . .; Ayres de Cazal, 1817; Baena, 1839, 1885; Barrère, 1743; Berredo, 1905; Bettendorf, 1910; Coudreau, H., 1886–87, 1893; Forest, 1899; Guajará, 1896; Laet, 1899; Lettres édifiantes et curieuses, 1838 (1780–83); Lombard, 1928; Moraes, 1860; Nimuendajú, 1926; O'Brian del Carpio, ms.; Penna, 1881; Rio Branco, 1899; Rocha Pombo, 1905; Southey, 1862; Texeyra, 1640; Vieira, 1735–46; Viñaza, 1892.

THE AMANAYÉ

By Curt Nimuendajú and Alfred Métraux

LANGUAGE, TERRITORY, AND HISTORY

The names *Amanajó, Manajó,* and *Manaxó* were used in Maranhão, in Piauhy, and on the lower Tocantins; *Amanagé* in Pará. *Mananyé* is the name given by the *Turiwara; Manazewa* by the *Tembé.* The self-denomination, *Manayé* or *Amanayé,* has uncertain meaning, but may be *Guaraní,* amândayé, an "association of people," or amanajé, "alcoviteiro" (Platzmann, 1896). In order to conceal their identity, some groups assumed the name of *Ararandewá* (*Ararandewára, Ararandeuara*), "those of the Ararandéua [River]," and *Turiwá* (*Turiwara*), the name of a neighbor tribe.

On the *Amanayé* language there have been published only two small vocabularies, both in 1914: Lange's and Nimuendajú's. It is the most distinctive of the *Tupí* dialects of the *He-* group. As far as can be ascertained from the vocabularies, there is no difference in the grammar.

The *Amanayé* (map 1, *No. 1;* see Volume 1, map 7) always occupied the upper Pindaré, the Gurupí, and the Capim Rivers, the middle Mojú River, and the central part of the right bank of the lower Tocantins below the mouth of the Araguaya, and were found only rarely away from this region (lat. 4° S., long. 48° W.).

They are first mentioned in 1755 when they made an agreement with the Jesuit P. Daniel Fay (Tray? Tay?), of Acamá (Monção), a *Guajajara* village of the Pindaré River. They had evidently had previous contact with civilized people, for they avoided all Whites except the Jesuits.

According to Ribeiro de Sampaio (1812, p. 9), in 1760, a large band of *Amanayé* moved peacefully southeast to the Alpercatas River, and settled near the village of Santo Antonio. By 1815 there were only 20 of this group, and they were mixed with Negro blood. The last mention of this village was in 1820 (Francisco de N.S. dos Prazeres, 1891, p. 132). A part of this band evidently continued its migration in 1763 across the Parnahyba River into Piauhy (Alencastre, 1857, p. 6), but its subsequent fate is not known.

In 1775, the *"Amanajoz"* are listed among the tribes of the lower right Tocantins (Ribeiro de Sampaio, 1812, pp. 8, 9), and, in 1798, they were seen to the east of the Surubijú River (Mendes de Almeida, n.d., p. 104). In 1845, the *"Amananiú"* were mentioned as inhabitants of part of the Mojú River by Saint-Adolphe. In 1854, they had a village on the Pindaré above the *Guajajara* village of Sapucaia (Marques,

1864), but by 1872 the village had been moved to the Tucumandiua, a western tributary of the Gurupí River (Dodt, 1873, p. 132). In 1862, the *Amanayé* had two villages with 60 people on the Ararandéua River, western tributary of the Capim River, which has subsequently been their center.

In 1872, Fr. Candido de Heremence began to convert the *Amanayé*, *Tembé* and *Turiwara* of the Capim River. With 200 *Amanayé*, he founded the Anauerá Mission (São Fidelis) on the left bank of the Capim River, below the confluence of the Ararandéua and the Surubijú Rivers. The *Turiwara* and *Tembé*, being hostile to the *Amanayé*, were established together farther downstream. The next year, the *Amanayé* killed Fr. Candido and a Belgian engineer, Blochhausen, because during a trip the latter dealt severely with the *Amanayé* crew and injured the chief's son. (Souza Franco, 1842, p. 22; Cruz, 1874, p. 47; Moreira Pinto, 1894; Nimuendajú, unpublished notes.) Reprisals against the *Amanayé* for these murders drove them to take refuge in the region of the Ararandéua River. Today some of them still avoid contact with the civilized people. Others appeared later under the name of *"Ararandewára"* or *"Turiwara"* to conceal their identity.

In 1889, the surviving *Anambé* and *Amanajó*, almost wiped out by epidemics on the Arapary, lived by the last rapids of the Tocantins River (Ehrenreich, 1892, p. 149).

In 1911, Inspector L. B. Horta Barboza, of the Serviço de Proteccão aos Indios, found four *Amanayé* villages with more than 300 inhabitants on the left bank of the Ararandéua River. In 1913, another, more primitive part of the tribe, calling itself *Ararandewára*, was visited by Algot Lange on the upper Mojú River, at approximately lat. 4° S. He has published the only description of the *Amanayé* (Lange, 1914).

During several decades at the end of the 19th century and the beginning of the 20th, the most important person among the *Amanayé* of the Ararandéua River was a mulatto woman named Damasia, wife of a member of the tribe. In 1926, Nimuendajú saw a small group of *Amanayé*, who called themselves *Ararandewá(ra)*, in Mundurucú at lat. 3°55′ S. They had a plantation on the Mojú River. In 1942, only 17 persons, mostly Mestizos, survived in the group headed by Damasia's son (Arquivos da Inspectoria do Serviço de Protecção aos Indios, Para, 1942). These people stated that another group lived away from all contact with the civilized people, on the Igarapé do Garrafão, a left tributary of the Ararandéua River. In 1943, Nimuendajú found a small group of *Amanayé*, who had been living for several decades, in contact with Neo-Brazilians, on the upper Cairary, a tributary on the left bank of the lower Mojú. They called themselves *Turiwa(ra)*.

CULTURE

Subsistence.—The *Amanayé* cultivated manioc, cotton, and tobacco in forest clearings. One clearing measured 1,000 by 1,300 yards. These Indians also hunted, especially turtles, which were abundant. Turtles not consumed at once were kept in small corrals.

Dogs and chickens were introduced by the White man.

Manioc was prepared in a special hut; the tubers were crushed in a trough made of the mirití palm trunk, pressed through a coarse-meshed fiber sifter, then kneaded into balls which were allowed to ferment on a platform. Subsequently, the paste was squeezed in the cylindrical tipití, or manioc squeezer, after which the dry pulp was crushed and spread on

a hot clay pan with slightly upturned edges. Brazil nuts might be added
to manioc flour to improve its taste.

Dwellings.—The *Amanayé* village that Lange visited had 26 houses "of
a very low order, some not having a proper roof, built around a small area
of bush cleared forest." The only furniture was small cotton hammocks.

Clothing.—*Amanayé* men wore nothing but a short cotton string tied
around the praeputium, while women wore only a narrow loincloth.

Men's ornaments included little wooden sticks in the lower lip and turkey feathers stuck in colored cotton bands around the head. Women wore
"garter-like cotton bands below their knees and on their ankles; . . .
some of the youngest maidens insert ornaments made of the ivory nut in
their ear lobes" (Lange, 1914).

Boats.—Dugout canoes, 35 feet (10.6 m.) long, and 5 feet (1.5 m.)
wide, were made of trees felled in the forest and dragged to the water on
rollers by means of creepers.

Manufactures.—Manioc squeezers were plaited of strong m`miriti` palm
and tucum fibers. Cotton spindles had a rounded wooden disk. The loom
was "a simple square frame made of four sticks about 2 feet [0.6 m.]
long, tied together with fiber or ordinary bush-cord to form a square"
(Lange, 1914). Cloth, like hammocks, was loosely twined with a double
weft. Loincloths were stained red with urucú.

The only pottery mentioned is the clay manioc pan.

Weapons.—Bows were large—one being 8 feet (2.4 m.) long and 4
inches (10 cm.) in diameter—and notched at each end for a curauá fiber
bowstring. Arrows were tipped either with a bamboo blade or with a
sharp rod with a few barbs on each side. Occasionally, a small nut which
produced a whistling sound was fastened near the tip. Arrow feathering
was either of the eastern Brazilian arched or of the Xingú sewn type.

Stone axes, used until recently, had carefully ground, quadrangular
heads of diorite with a notch running along the face near the butt. The
head was inserted in the split end of a shaft of pao d'arco and lashed
with heavy fibers, then covered with the black gum from the jutahy tree.

Fire making.—Fire was made with a fire drill. Two men working
together could make a fire in 2 minutes.

Social and political organization.—Lange observed an *Amanayé*
chief whose weak personality suggested that he must have inherited
his position. Lange gives no other information on political or social
organization.

Prior to marriage, young men proved their fortitude by plunging an
arm into a braided fiber cylinder that was closed at both ends and filled
with tocandeira ants.

Musical instruments.—The *Amanayé* had a drum that is unusual in
this area: A long, hollow emba-uba tree trunk was suspended from a

horizontal branch by a thin, tough bush rope. While one man beat the drum with a stick, "another, probably a shaman, danced around it" (Lange, 1914).

Tobacco.—Tobacco was smoked in huge cigarettes, 1 foot (0.3 m.) long and ½ inch (1.2 cm.) thick, wrapped in tauarí bark. These were passed around, each man taking a few draughts in turn.

Drinks.—The *Amanayé* drank a fermented beverage (probably of cassava) called cachiri.

BIBLIOGRAPHY

(Amanayé and Turiwara)

Aguiar, 1851; Alencastre, 1857; Arquivos da Inspectoria . . . , 1942; Baena, 1885; Brusque, 1862, 1863; Cruz, 1874; Cunha, 1852; Daniel, 1840; Dodt, 1873; Ehrenreich, 1892; Francisco de Nuestra Señora dos Prazeres, 1891; Gama Malcher, 1878; Lange, 1914; Marques, 1864; Meerwarth, 1904; Mendes de Almeida, n.d.; Moreira Pinto, 1894; Nimuendajú, 1914 c, unpublished notes; Platzmann, 1896; Ribeiro, 1848 (1870); Ribeiro de Sampaio, 1812; Serviço de Protecção aos Indios, 1942; Souza Franco, 1842; Villa Real, 1848.

LITTLE-KNOWN TRIBES OF THE LOWER TOCANTINS RIVER REGION

By Curt Nimuendajú

INTRODUCTION

This article will deal with the *Pacajá, Anambé, Tapiraua, Kupē-rób* (*Jandiahí*), *Jacundá, Paracanã,* and *Miraño*. These tribes, most of them *Tupí*-speaking, are now virtually extinct (map 1, *No. 1*; see Volume 1, map 7).

THE PACAJÁ

Pacajá (*Pacajara*) means in *Tupí*, "master (*yára*) of the paca" (*Coelogenys paca*). According to Bettendorf (1910, pp. 97, 111), the *Pacajá* used the Lingua Geral.

TERRITORY AND HISTORY

This tribe appears to have centered in the basin of the Pacajá de Portel River. It may also have lived in the lower Tocantins River and the lower Xingú River where a right tributary is named Pacajá (de Souzel) River. (Lat. 2° S., long. 52° W.)

In 1613, an expedition of French from São Luiz do Maranhão and their allies, the *Tupinamba,* passed the Pacaiares River in a campaign against the *Camarapin.* Later, Father Yves d'Evreux (1864) makes a passing mention of the *Pacajá.* In 1626(?), Benito Maciel Parente (1874) mentioned them with the *Yuruna* and other tribes between the Pacajá and "Parnahyba" (Xingú) Rivers. In 1628, the *Pacajá* were "appeased" (Berredo, 1905, 1: 229, 231) by Pedro da Costa Favella on his expedition to the Tocantins (Pacajá?) River. Bettendorf (1910, p. 97) recounts with some exaggeration that at their first meeting the *Pacajá* and the *Tupinamba* annihilated each other. In 1639, the *Pacajá* are mentioned by Acuña (1682, p. 139) as inhabitants of the Pacajá River. Between 1656 and 1662, an ill-fated expedition went in search of mines on the Pacajá River, and the Jesuit Father João de Souto Mayor, who accompanied it, died (Berredo, 1905, 2: 115). It resulted, however, in the *Pacajá* entering a Jesuit mission (Arucará or Portel?), from whence a large part escaped again to their own land. The others were sent to distant missions (Bettendorf, 1910, p. 98; João Daniel, 1841, p. 182). In 1763, the *Pacajá* are mentioned for the last time by De São José (1947, p. 490) as one of the 13 tribes constituting the population of 400 in the village of Portel.

In 1889, Ehrenreich (1891 a, p. 88; 1892, p. 149) was told of the existence of savage *Pacajá* at the headwaters of the Uanapú and Pacajá Rivers near Portel, a statement not subsequently confirmed.

Acuña (1682, p. 139) and Bettendorf (1910, p. 97) considered the *Pacajá* brave and warlike. P. Sotto Mayor (1916) accuses them of cannibalism. In warfare, they eat the enemy which they kill by hand, and keep the skulls as trophies. Some 100 years later, João Daniel (1841) describes them as "very soft and lazy" (i. e., for work in the mission). The women wore short skirts and the men short trousers, which they might have adopted from the runaway slaves who settled at the headwaters of the Pacajá River (?). They were a canoe people; at their encounter with the *Tupinamba,* they came "in over 500 canoes"—evidently an exaggeration.

THE ANAMBÉ

HISTORY AND TERRITORY

The *Anambé* ("anambe" in the Lingua Geral is applied to a considerable number of species of birds, *Cotingidae*) were, by contrast to the *Pacajá,* a modern tribe, which appeared and disappeared during the past century.

The *Anambé* language, according to Ehrenreich's vocabulary, was a *Tupi* dialect of the *He-* group, very similar to the *Tembé-Guajajara* and *Turiwara.* If the texts of legends in the Lingua Geral published by Magalhães (1876) were, as he says, dictated by *Anambé,* this tribe was bilingual, and at the time did not use its own language.

The *Anambé's* (lat. 4°–5° S., long. 50°–51° W.) first contact with the civilized people was in 1842 (Brusque, 1862, p. 12). In 1852, they appeared on the left bank of the Tocantins River (Cunha, 1853, p. 18) ; they numbered 600. Another group lived in the village of Tauá at the headwaters of the Cururuhy, a tributary of the upper Pacajá River, but it was in contact with the first byway of the Caripy River, a tributary of the Tocantins a little above Alcobaça. A village of 250 *Curupity* (?) and *Anambé* on the upper Pacajá River was at war with the *Carambú* (Brusque, 1862, p. 12). In 1874, this village was reduced to 46 persons. The following year 37 of them died of smallpox, and the 9 survivors joined their fellow tribesmen on the Tocantins River.

In 1889, Ehrenreich found a remnant of four completely civilized *Anambé* in Praia Grande, at the end of the Tocantins rapids. Moura (1910, p. 106) mentions *Anambé* in 1896 and shows a picture of two men. The supposed *"Anambé"* seen by H. Coudreau in 1897 were *Arara.* The tribe is today completely extinct.

THE TAPIRAUA

The *Tapiraua* (tapiíra, "tapir"), or *Anta,* lived west of Itaboca Falls in 1889 (Ehrenreich, 1891 a, 1892).[1] Each time they came to the shore of the Tocantins, they were driven back by gun shots. They still used stone implements.

In 1896 or 1897 (Moura, 1910, p. 192), two *"Tapiri,"* or *Anta,* appeared a few kilometers below Timbozal. They had short hair and their

---

[1] The distance from the Tocantins is given as 3 to 4 days' travel (Ehrenreich, 1891 a, p. 88), and as 1 day's travel (Ehrenreich, 1892, p. 148).

ears were pierced by tiny holes, but they lacked tattoo. This tribe is not subsequently mentioned by name, but it may possibly be the same as the *Kupē-rób*.

THE KUPĒ-ROB

Apinayé tradition relates that a tribe called *Kupē-rób* (Kupē, "Indians," i.e., non-*Timbira*, plus rób, "jaguars") or, in Portuguese, *Cupe-lobos*, lived below them on the Tocantins River (lat. 5° S., long. 50° W.), and that the *Apinayé* occasionally attacked them to obtain European-made white beads before the *Apinayé* had begun to trade with the civilized people. The *Kupē-rób* perhaps are identical with the *Jandiahi* who, in 1793, lived below Itaboca Falls (Villa Real, 1848, p. 426), and, in 1844 (Castelnau, 1850, p. 113), lived on the west shore near Itaboca Falls. At the later date, they were hostile to the *Jacundá* and to the Christians, and only rarely were met by travelers. Baena (1870) mentions their habitat as Lake Vermelho, at lat. 5°10' S., west of the Tocantins and below the mouth of the Araguaya. In 1849, Ayres Carneiro (1910, pp. 78–79, 81, 84, 90–91) found famished and lean *Cupe-lobos* on the Canhanhá beach, near the Igarapé do Pucuruhy, lat. 4° 10' S., where they were persecuted by the *Apinayé*. In 1896, this tribe appeared peacefully in the Rebojo de Bacury, a little above Itaboca Falls, hunting and fishing, and using apites (labrets?) of glass (?) or worked stone (Moura, 1910, pp. 160, 193). Above Timbozal (a little above the mouth of the Pucuruhy River), they had an old village site.

H. Coudreau (1897 b, p. 43 and map) had a report in 1897 of unidentified Indians on the upper Igarapé do Bacury. The year before these Indians had come in contact with the civilized people. They were at first peaceful but soon became hostile.

In 1922, eight wild Indians appeared on Volta Grande, on the left bank of the Tocantins. Both sexes had their hair cut all around, and wore a little stick through the ears. The men had their foreskin tied with an embira string, and the woman wore a band of the same material. The children were carried in a sling under the arm. The belly of the bow was flat, the outer side, convex. The bow string was made of curauá (*Bromelia*) and the arrows had flush feathering. A hammock was made of fibers.

One of the men, taken to Belém seriously ill, gave the author a list of 16 words. The language was *Tupí* of the *He-* group, definitely distinct from Ehrenreich's *Anambé* and from *Amanayé*. As the material culture of these people did not correspond to that of the *Paracanã*, it is possible that they were the *Kupē-rób* survivors. Also, it is possible that the Indians who occasionally came peaceably to the post of the Serviço de Protecção aos Indios on the Pucuruhy River were not *Paracaña*, as supposed, but *Kupē-rób*. The people at the post noted that they called certain plants and animals by *Tupí* names, similar to those of the Neo-Brazilians. In 1942, unknown Indians were again seen in the Igarapé do Bacury, and it may be that the tribe still exists around there.

THE JACUNDÁ

At the end of the 18th century and during the first half of the 19th century, the *Jacundá* lived on the Jacundá River, which empties into the Tocantins from the right below Itaboca Falls (lat. 4° 27' S., long. 49° W.). The name designates a fish (*Crenicichla* sp.). Meneses' diary (n. d., p. 175) ascribes to these Indians "red eyes, just like those of a certain fish by the same name."

The only record of the *Jacundá* language is the names of two chiefs of 1793: Uoriniuera, which is a *Tupian* word (warinikwéra, "old war"), and Claxira, which is contrary to *Tupí* phonetics. A map of Brazil of 1846 states: "Jacundá, tractable people who speak the Lingua Geral" (Niemaeyer, 1846).

The *Jacundá* were first mentioned by Villa Real (1848, pp. 424–426, 432) in 1793, when they lived at the headwaters of the Igarapé Guayapí (Jacundá River?) and occasionally appeared on the eastern bank of the Tocantins. Another igarapé (water passage) above Itaboca Falls was also inhabited by the *Jacundá*, who had a port at its mouth. According to Villa Real, the *Jacundá* had two chiefs. Meneses (1919, p. 175) mentions the *Jacundá* in 1799 on the Igarapé of Jacundá, and Ribeiro (1870, p. 37) mentions them in 1815 among the tribes of the Tocantins River. According to Castelnau (1850), they lived in 1844 on the right bank of the Tocantins, above Itaboca Falls, and were hostile to the *Jundiahi* (*Kupē-rób?*) of the opposite bank and to Christians, who rarely saw them. In 1849, they were said to be peaceful.

In 1849, Ayres Carneiro (1910, p. 45) saw 30 to 40 *Jacundá*, including women and children, on the Ambáua beach, a little above the present Alcobaça, on the right side of the river, but they fled into the jungle. Henceforth, their name disappears, and, since 1859 the *Gaviões*, a *Timbira* tribe of the *Ge* group (Handbook, vol. 1, p. 477), has occupied their region (Gomes, 1862, p. 496). Ehrenreich, however, mentions the *Jacundá* in 1889, 30 years after they had probably become extinct.

THE PARACANÁ

HISTORY

In 1910, an unknown tribe of savage Indians appeared on the Pacajá River above Portel. Their repeated attacks on the *Arara-Parirí* caused the latter to abandon their territory on the Iriuaná River, a left tributary of the Pacajá, and to take refuge with the Neo-Brazilians on the lower Pacajá. The *Parirí* called this tribe *Paracaná* (lat. 4°–5° S., long. 50°–51° W.). Perhaps it was the same tribe that, under the name of *Yauarití-Tapiiya*, was hostile to the *Anambé* of the Pacajá River during the last century (this volume, p. 204). At first they were at peace with the Neo-Brazilians, and at times helped them pass Cachoeira Grande Fall of the Pacajá River.

According to information obtained from the *Pariri* in 1914, the *Paracanã* call thunder, "tumpô" (*Tupi,* tupã), and water, "i" (*Tupi,* i). The *Paracanã* language is, therefore, possibly a member of the *Tupian* family.

During the 1920's, the *Paracanã* began to appear on the left bank of the Tocantins, above Alcobaça. They were pretentious and demanding, and, though they used no weapons, they frightened the residents away and pillaged their houses. After 1927, they became openly hostile toward the civilized residents. They would come shooting arrows, and every year they killed people, but they did not mutilate the bodies nor take trophies. Civilized people attributed this hostility to the entrance of nut gatherers into the regions west of the Tocantins. After one of these attacks, the head of the Alcobaça Railroad ordered a punitive expedition, which surprised and killed the *Paracanã* in their camp. This incited the *Paracanã* to attack even within sight of Alcobaça and to extend their raids north to Juana Peres and the upper Jacundá River. During the last two years, however, their raids on the Tocantins side have for an unknown reason ceased completely.

While on the Pacajá, these Indians were always known as *Paracanã,* a name given to them by the *Pariri.* It was wrongly believed on the Tocantins that they were *Asurini* from the Xingú River.

CULTURE

Clothing and ornaments.—The *Paracanã* cut the hair around the head and wore a wooden peg through the lower lip. Several items of apparel are among 142 *Paracanã* objects in the Museu Paraense Emilio Goeldi. There are short cotton women's skirts, 18 inches (45 cm.) long, made with a twined weave, the weft elements a finger's breadth apart. The warp runs all the way around each garment, the cloth being tubular, like that produced by the *"Arawak"* loom. Some strings of red cotton threads are probably pectoral ornaments. There are necklaces of black tiririca (*Scleria* sp.) seeds, alternating with fine tubular bones. A child's (?) headband is made of close-looped cotton string with a strip of Neo-Brazilian cloth and 15 macaw tail feathers carelessly attached. A comb is made of 12 teeth bound with thread between two pairs of sticks; the wrapping is not ornamental. Jingles, probably worn below the knee or on the ankle, are made of piquí (*Caryocar* sp.) nuts hung on cotton thread.

Basketry.—A rectangular basket of the "jamaxim" type for carrying objects on the back has the outer side and the top end open. The side against the carrier's back and the bottom have a twilled weave and black zigzag designs; the outer sides have a fine, open octagonal weave, the strips running in four directions.

Weaving.—A hammock 58 inches (1.8 m.) long, is woven of twined cotton strings and of strings taken from hammocks stolen from Neo-Brazilians. The weft elements are 3 to 4 inches (7 to 10 cm.) apart.

Weapons.—Arrows have camayuva shafts, 54 to 66 inches (1.4 to 1.7 m.) long, and sewn feathering which is bound with fine thread and frequently decorated with small toucan feathers. Three types of heads are: (1) Lanceolate bamboo blades, 24 inches (70 cm.) long and about 2 inches (5.5 cm.) broad at the widest point. These are smeared with black paint on the concave side and a few specimens bear a crude black design on the convex side. Just behind the point, some arrows have a palm coconut, about 1½ inches (4 cm.) in diameter, perforated with a row of as many as nine holes around it. (2) Bone points, either without barbs or with a barb on one or both sides. (3) Plain, rodlike wooden points. The bow is of paxiuba wood, very wide (5 cm., or 2 in.), flat (1 to 2 cm. thick), similar to the *Asurini* bow. It is about 159.5 cm. (62 in.) long. The ends are cut with shoulders, to hold the cord, 5 cm. and 11.5 cm. respectively from the ends.

Fire.—Torches are made of cotton cords or of Neo-Brazilian cloth, and are impregnated with beeswax.

Musical instruments.—A set of panpipes has 8 tubes, ranging from 5½ to 10 inches (12 to 26 cm.) in length and 5 to 12 mm. in diameter and held together by two parallel ligatures of Neo-Brazilian cotton.

THE MIRAÑO

Rivet (1924, p. 689) places a *Tupí* tribe of *Miraño* Indians "between the Acará and Capim Rivers at the headwaters of the Bujarú." On the map of the State of Pará by Santa Rosa, the "Indios Miranhios" appear on the left margin of the Capim River, at lat. 2°30′ S. There was never any tribe by this name, however. Among the *Tembé* there was a large family called "Miranya." The present author found members of this family in the Indian village of Prata as late as 1916. Since the place where the *Miraño* was supposed to be settled coincides almost exactly with the old *Tembé* village of Mariquita, it is probable that the so-called *Miraño* were in reality *Tembé*.

According to Métraux (1928 a, p. 22), *"Amiranha"* is a synonym of *Jacundá*. The *Amanayé* of the Ararandéua River spoke to the present author in 1913 about a tribe called *Mirán,* but they could not tell him where they were settled.

BIBLIOGRAPHY

Acuña, 1682; Ayres Carneiro, 1910; Baena, 1870; Berredo, 1905; Bettendorf, 1910; Brusque, 1862; Castelnau, 1850; Coudreau, H., 1897 b; Cunha, 1853; Daniel, 1841; Ehrenreich, 1891 a, 1892, 1895; Gomes, 1862, Maciel Parente, 1874; Magalhães, 1876; Meneses, 1919; Métraux, 1928 a; Moreira Pinto, 1894; Moura, 1910; Niemaeyer, 1846; Nimuendajú, 1939; Ribeiro, 1870; Rivet, 1924; São José, 1847; Sotto Mayor, 1916; Souza, 1874; Villa Real, 1848; Yves d'Evreux, 1864.

LITTLE-KNOWN TRIBES OF THE LOWER AMAZON [1]

By Curt Nimuendajú

THE ARACAJÚ

In 1668–69, an expedition, led by Major J. de Almeida Freire, started out along the Tocantins River against the *Poqui* Indians, who lived 8 days' march from its banks. On the way back, the expedition passed the *Aracajú* and brought back many bows and arrows, "with some wide and long shields, covered with beautiful feathers" (Bettendorf, 1910, p. 32). (Lat. 4° S., long. 52° W.)

In 1679, P. Jodoco Peres, of Jaguaquara (north side of the Amazon, above the mouth of the Parú) sought the *Aracajú* who were "in the wilds of the Tocanhapes," i.e., the right side of the lower Xingú, south of the Amazon. In 1680, P. Antonio de Silva went by way of the bayou (Pacajá de Souzel River) and the backwoods of the Tocanhapes, and brought some 400 Indians down to the Indian village of Cussary (in front of the present Monte Alegre, on the right side of the Amazon). Shortly thereafter, in 1681, however, Bettendorf tells about being received by the chiefs of the *Aracajú* in Jaguaquara, where these Indians had made a large house, which they abandoned because the land there was very poor for agriculture (Bettendorf, 1910, pp. 324, 335, 337). By 1681, therefore, the *Aracajú* were no longer in Cussary, south of the Amazon, but in Jaguaquara, on the northern side. It seems that they settled on the Parú River, where their presence is mentioned in 1702, when the Commissary of the Capuchins, Fr. Jeronymo de São Francisco, transferred Indians from five tribes, among them the *Aracajú,* to the new Indian village of the *Aroaqui* on the Urubú River (Ferreira, 1841).

Martius found in 1820 that the *Aracajú* and *Apama* comprised the population of Almeirim (Spix and Martius, 1823–31, 1:324). The few *Aracajú* still at liberty lived on the Parú River in small isolated Indian villages. Although at peace with the Brazilians, they could rarely be persuaded to live among them. They were rather dark Indians, with no distinguishing characteristics. Their weapons were not poisoned. They were constantly at war with the *"Oaiapis"* (*Wayapí*) of the upper Jary and Iratapurú Rivers and with the *Cossari* of the Araguaya River. Subsequently, no further mention is made of them.

Martius, who tends to explain all names by the Lingua Geral, interprets *Aracajú* as uara-guaçú, "great people." He considers "wara" to be a substantive, meaning "man" or "people," whereas it is really a personal ending. The vocabulary (1863, p. 17) which he collected in Gurupá also calls forth the following remarks: Of his 53 words, 24 are clearly *Tupi*

---

[1] Map 1, *No. 1*; see Volume 1, map 7.

and 21 no less clearly *Carib,* while 8 cannot be definitely identified. The *Tupi* words belong to the Lingua Geral, not to some special dialect, and, therefore, probably do not represent the tribe's original tongue but the language which they learned at the mission. The *Carib* words are not identical with those of the *Aparai,* as Rivet thought (1924, p. 660), though they have greater resemblance to the dialects north of the Amazon than to those of the south (e.g., *Arara,* etc.). Because the *Aracajú* came from the south of the Amazon, one reaches the conclusion that these *Carib* words also do not represent the original *Aracajú* language, but that they were acquired through contact with some *Carib* tribe after they lived north of the Amazon, and that their own original tongue has been lost entirely.

THE APOTÓ

In the *Aparai* language, apotó means "fire," and thus Araujo Amazonas and Ignacio Accioly write the name of a tribe which is also called, probably by a mistaken transcription, *Apanto* and *Apauto.* The few references to this tribe are all based on that of Christóbal d'Acuña in 1639 (1682), wherein he states that four tribes lived on the Cunurizes (Nhamundá) River, the first having lent its name to the river on the mouth of which it lived, and the second, above the mouth, being the *Apotó* tribe "which speaks the Lingua Geral." This is all that is known about these Indians.

THE PAUXÍ

Three sources give slight information about a tribe or tribes called *Pauxí.*

(1) The *Pauxí* (pauší, paushi, undoubtedly a *Carib* word meaning "mutum," *Cracidae* sp.; cf. *Pausiana,* a *Carib* tribe on Caratirimani River), according to Bettendorf (1910), spoke the Lingua Geral. It was settled in the region of the Xingú River. Between 1658 and 1660, the Jesuit, P. Salvador do Valle, brought more than 600 of this tribe to the Indian village of Tapará, on the right side of that river, almost at its mouth. There is no further notice of them.

(2) The "Fort of the Pauxis" was founded in 1697 on the left bank of the Amazon, where the present-day Villa de Obidos is situated, and Pauxis is today still the name of a lake just below this village. Near this fort there were two small Indian villages which, in 1758, were combined with another from farther away in the Villa de Obidos (Moraes, 1860, p. 508), but nothing further is known of the tribe or tribes which lived there. P. Fritz (1922), in 1690, speaks of the tribe of the *"Cunurizes"* (map of 1691) exactly on the spot where the fort was to be built 6 years later.

(3) When O. Coudreau (1901) mapped the "Cuminã" River (Erepecurú) in 1900, a descendant of fugitive slaves living on this river informed her that a tribe of Indians called *Pauxí* (pronounced pauší, paushi) lived

in the headwaters of the Agua Fria, Penecura, and Acapú Bayous, right tributaries of the Erepecurú River, a little above its mouth. According to this information, the tribe had first lived in Obidos, but before the coming of civilized people, it retreated to the Erepecurú River, then to the mouth of the Penecura River, and, finally, to the headwaters of this river. After 1877, its relations with the fugitive slaves had been broken. From the same informant, Coudreau obtained a list of 38 words. The language is *Carib,* but it differs from the dialect of the *Kasuenā* (*Cashuená*) of the Cachorro River, their nearest neighbors, and from that of the *Pianocotó* of the upper Erepecurú (Coudreau, O., 1901, pp. 132–133). The *Pauxí* no longer exist.

BIBLIOGRAPHY

Acuña, 1682; Berredo, 1905, vol. 1; Bettendorf, 1910; Coudreau, O., 1901; Ferreira, A. R., 1841; Fritz, 1691, 1922; Martius, 1863; Moraes, 1860; Rivet, 1924; São José, 1847; Spix and Martius, 1823–31, vol. 3.

TRIBES OF THE LOWER AND MIDDLE XINGÚ RIVER

By Curt Nimuendajú

GEOGRAPHIC BACKGROUND

The Xingú Basin, as far south as lat. 7° S., is exclusively characterized by Amazonian virgin forest, whose wealth of rubber and nuts attracted the attention of civilized man. From that latitude south or upstream, savannas appear, becoming more and more predominant southward, until the forest is reduced to a narrow border along watercourses, sometimes even encroaching upon the river banks.

It is rolling country. The "Morro Grande" of the Xingú River rises to some 975 ft. (300 m.) above the level of the river. The watercourses are interrupted by rapids and the Xingú River beyond Volta Grande is one of the most difficult rivers in Brazil to navigate. Over long stretches the bed of the river is filled with enormous rocks cut through by channels full of rapids. The Iriri River is of similar type.

The tribes (map 1, *No. 1*; see Volume 1, map 7) of this region may be classified according to these geographical features into three groups.

(1) Canoeing tribes restricted to the Xingú, Iriri, and Curuá Rivers: *Yuruna, Shipaya, Arupai.*

(2) Tribes of the central virgin forest: *Curuaya, Arara, Asurini,* and, formerly, *Tacunyapé.*

(3) Savanna tribes that only temporarily invade the forest zone: *Northern Cayapó,* which were dealt with in Lowie's paper on "The *Northwestern* and *Central Ge*" (Handbook, vol. 1, pp. 477–517).

CULTURAL SUMMARY

Farming, with manioc the staple crop, was the basis of subsistence among all these tribes except perhaps the *Arara,* who were less clearly horticultural. Caimans, turtles, honey, and Brazil nuts were outstanding wild foods. The *Yuruna, Shipaya,* and *Tacunyapé* built large communal dwellings in isolated places for fear of attack. Excellent canoemen, the *Yuruna* and *Shipaya* lived along the rivers, whereas the other tribes kept to the forests. Houses were furnished with wooden stools and hammocks. Dress included breechclouts (?) (*Curuaya*), women's wraparound skirts, and men's penis covers (*Yuruna* and *Shipaya*), and women's

213

aprons (*Tacupyapé*). Ornaments were the usual Tropical Forest types: feather headdresses, arm and leg bands, necklaces, ear sticks, nose pendants (*Arara*), and lip plugs (*Curuaya*). Among manufactures, which suffered because of much nomadism enforced by warfare, were: Cotton textiles (*Yuruna*); ceramics, which are usually plain; incised gourds (*Shipaya*); and stone axes. The bow and arrow was the main weapon.

The sociopolitical unit was the village, seemingly patrilineal in organization and in descent of chieftainship. There was little polygyny and family ties were very strong. Intertribal relations involved intermittent warfare, with cannibalism ascribed to the *Yuruna* and *Shipaya* and trophies more general. The latter include skulls (*Yuruna, Shipaya, Curuaya*), bone trumpets (*Yuruma*), tooth necklaces (*Shipaya*), and scalps (*Arara*).

These tribes drank much fermented liquor, but had no drunken brawls. The *Yuruna* smoked tobacco in cigarettes. Musical instruments include panpipes; shaman's gourd rattles; gourd horns; gourd, wooden, and human-skull trumpets; bone flutes, clarinets, and whistles. The predominating art motif is the maze; sculpture reproduced mythical personages.

Shipaya and probably *Yuruna* religion was based on a cult of the jaguar demon, who was the patron of war and cannibalism, and a feast of the dead, in which men and women drank chicha. The *Tacunyapé* had a similar feast. The shaman, in the capacity of priest, served as intermediary between people and demons and souls. As medicine man, he cured, without the aid of supernatural spirits, by sucking, massaging, and blowing cigarette smoke to remove the disease-causing substance.

LINGUISTIC AFFINITIES

Of the tribes on the lower and middle Xingú, the *Arara* stand apart as *Cariban*. Their speech is so close to *Yarumá* (Paranayuba River, a tributary of the right bank of the upper Xingú) as to permit the hypothesis of a common ancestral tribe, the *Arara* turning north, the *Yarumá* south, perhaps separating under *Cayapó* pressure (Ehrenreich, 1895).

All other tribes are *Tupi*. To be sure, there is not the slightest record of *Asurini* speech, but an English missionary conversant with *Guajajara* who spoke with a young *Asurini* woman captured by the *Górotire* commented on the resemblance of her tongue to the language familiar to him. Accordingly, *Asurini* may be reckoned as probably *Tupi*. About the remaining languages we can be more positive.

Martius (1867) and Lucien Adam (1896) challenge the *Tupi* relationship of *Yuruna*, which is accepted by such competent authorities as Bettendorf, Von den Steinen, and Brinton. Closer study leads me to the provisional conclusion that *Yuruna, Shipaya, Manitsauá*, and perhaps *Arupai* form a special division of impure *Tupi* languages. Lexical *Tupi* elements in *Yuruna* are conspicuous, though often obscured by alterations so that correspondences are proved only by comparison with *Shipaya* and *Manitsauá* equivalents. Contrary to Adam's assumption, there are also important grammatical features of *Tupí* type, though less numerous than might be inferred from the large percentage of *Tupí* vocables. However, the *Yuruna* group does differ greatly from *Tupí* proper, especially in the pronominal system. The present author tentatively recognizes four components: (1) A *Tupí* foundation, even anciently modified by strong influences due to (2) *Arawak,* and in lesser degree to (3) *Carib* languages; to these must be added (4) recent loans from the Lingua Geral.

Shipaya differs so little from *Yuruna* as to permit, with some trouble, mutual intelligibility. Some two dozen words differ radically; otherwise regular shifts appear:

Yuruna		Shipaya
pi	=	si
pe	=	se, si
bi, be	=	zi, ze
c	=	t
za	=	ya
bi	=	dyi

Thus, we have:

Yuruna	Shipaya	English
pinapa	sinapa	comb
pe	se	in (post-position)
abi	azí	back
abí	adyí	Indian
ca	ta	to go
za	ya	name

The grammatical divergences are insignificant: The imperative differs; the negative ka of *Shipaya* corresponds to *Yuruna* poga and teha; *Yuruna* regularly forms the future with the auxiliary verb ca (to go), whereas *Shipaya* has recourse to adverbs.

The *Arupaí* spoke *Yuruna.* They are in no way connected with the *Gurupá* of the Tocantins River and the *Urupá* of the Gy-Paraná.

Curuaya resembles *Mundurucú* as closely as *Yuruna* does *Shipaya.* In some cases it preserves primitive *Tupí* forms better than *Mundurucú.*

The *Tacunyapé,* according to the Jesuits, spoke the Lingua Geral, whereas Von den Steinen credits them with a *Tupí* dialect appreciably distinct from *Yuruna.* The present author found no *Tacunyapé*-speaking Indians, but three Neo-Brazilians, formerly resident in the area and during the last 20 years of the last century in close contact with the tribe, dictated 34 words and phrases, probably badly garbled. Though diverging considerably from the standard Lingua Geral (final t's!), their *Tupí* relationship is beyond doubt.

PREHISTORIC PEOPLES

Not only along the Xingú River and its larger affluents, the Iriri and Fresco Rivers, but also along the smaller tributaries and subtributaries, are found vestiges of a vanished population, whose culture differed from that of the tribes found in the 20th century. The impression is that these tribes formerly occupied all of the jungle region of the Xingú Basin. These vestiges comprise:

(1) Dwelling sites found on points of solid land jutting out to the edge of the water and easily recognized by their "black earth," a cultural layer containing fragments of pottery and stone instruments.

The pottery can be distinguished at first sight from that of present-day tribes. On the lower Xingú and lower Iriri Rivers it is rich in plastic adornment, recalling somewhat the pottery of the Monte Alegre region or even of the *Tapajó*. The pottery of the middle Xingú River and its affluents is plainer, with little plastic or engraved ornamentation, and is not uniform. On the Igarapé das Flechas River, a tributary of the upper Curuá River, two small stone statuettes were found, one representing a beetle, the other a man.

(2) Cemeteries. In the same "black earth" are found burial remains. In the streets of Porto de Moz and Altamira, there may be seen the mouths of urns covered by other vessels; Panellas, a little above Altamira, owes its name to such findings. In Porto Seguro, at lat. 7° 10′ S., on a permanent island of the Xingú River, funeral urns are found, and among them superficially buried skeletons, lying stretched on their backs. Because of their size, all these urns could have served only for secondary burials.

The presence of funeral urns distinguished the culture of the Xingú Basin from that of the neighboring *Tapajó* and its affiliates.

(3) Petroglyphs. Along the Itamaracá and Cajituba Falls of the Volta Grande do Xingú, at Caxinguba (lat. 5° 20′ S.), and along the lower Pacajá and upper Iriri, the figures of men, of animals, and of unknown meaning are engraved on the surface of the smooth rocks. The most important are those at Itamaracá, already known to the first Jesuit missionaries in the 17th century, and one in Pacajá.

(4) Monoliths. In a stony stretch of the Xingú River, at lat. 7° 20′ S., are eight more or less vertical small stone pillars, which are from 1 to 2 meters (3¼ to 6½ ft.) in height and are roughly broken off but not carved. There can be no doubt as to their artificial origin.

(5) At various points of the middle Xingú and of the lower Iriri Rivers, there may be found about 50 piles of small stone blocks on the slabs of the falls.

Stratification.—Downstream from Volta Grande, these remains must, at least in part, be ascribed to the tribes which were encountered by the first explorers. Above this point, however, there is a hiatus between the prehistoric and historic peoples. The Indians of today know nothing of their origin. When the *Yuruna, Shipaya, Arupai,* and other tribes appeared, the sedentary potters no longer existed, probably having been annihilated by the expanding *Northern Cayapó,* who, coming from the open country of the south, spread throughout the Xingú Basin. When the *Tupí* tribes appeared, they found the *Cayapó* already there, for their traditions always make them coexistent, no story accounting for their appearance. These *Tupí* tribes, with the exception of the *Curuaya,* the westernmost tribe, succeeded in penetrating and inhabiting these regions— incidentally, with great difficulty—only because they were excellent boatmen and occupied the islands of the great rivers, while the *Cayapó* made only very primitive craft, which they used exclusively to cross the rivers.

HISTORIC TRIBES

These populations disappeared, and no chronicler has left us any information of ethnographic value about them. The chart of Joannes de Laet (1899), dated 1625, shows the presence of *Apehou* on both sides of the mouth of the Xingú River; in the *Tupí* language of the *"He-"* group, *Apehou* means "man" (apiháw). After 1639, the Jesuits began to establish themselves on the Xingú River, but no one knows what Indians composed their missions. The first missionary, Luiz Figueira, preached in 1636 in *Tabpinima* (the modern *Itapinima?*) to Indians "who were not well versed in the Lingua Geral," i. e., *Tupí-Guaraní,* and founded the Xingú mission later called Itacuruçá and today known as Veiros. Shortly after, five more missions were established. Old chronicles and maps (Heriarte, 1874 [written in 1662]; Samuel Fritz, 1922 [map of 1691]; Bettendorf, 1910 [written in 1699]) refer specially to three tribes: the *Coani,* the *Guahuara,* and the *Guayapí.* The last two spoke the Lingua Geral. These three tribes probably inhabited the western side of the river. At that time the Paraná of Aquiquy, an offshoot of the Amazon that flows into the Xingú, a little above Porto de Moz, was known as the "Coanizes River." The *Guayapí* were settled for a time at the beginning of Volta Grande; in 1763, they and the *Yuruna* were still reported at Freguezia de Souzel. Most of this tribe, however, seems to have emigrated earlier to the north of the Amazon River, probably by way of Jary, and established themselves on the Oyapock River, where they are mentioned after 1729. The *Guahuara* tribe in 1688 had 22 villages in the interior of the central forests (sertão). From Bettendorf one gets the impression that this tribe is identical with the *Curabare* or *Curuaya.*

In the 19th century, writers no longer spoke of Indians on the lower Xingú River, because the survivors had fused with the semicivilized population which spoke the Lingua Geral.

THE YURUNA

Synonyms.—*Juruna, Juruûna, Juruhuna, Geruna* (from the *Tupí-Guaraní*, yurú, "mouth," plus una, "black") ; self-designation and *Shipaya, Yudya* (meaning?) ; in *Curuaya, Parawa-wad* (paráwa, "blue macaw," plus wad, "people") ; in *Arara, Paru-podeari* (parú, "water") ; in *Cayapó, No-irén* (no, "water").

History, territory, and number.—The first reference to this tribe is found in a memorial written by Maciel Parente (1874) in 1626: ". . . the island between the Pacaja branch [of Portel] and the Parnahyba [Xingú] . . . where are situated the provinces of the Pacajaras [Pacajá], Coanapús [Anapú], Caraguatas [?], and Juruhunas." (Lat. 5°–6° S., long. 53° W.)

Afterward, during the entire 17th century, we learn only of the more or less vain attempts to reduce the *Yuruna* to the secular or clerical regime. The chronology of these happenings is, however, very doubtful. An expedition from São Paulo descending the Xingú was attacked on one of the islands of the river ; only two tame Indians escaped, the rest being killed. An expedition commanded by the Captain-General of Gurupá, João Velho do Valle, composed of 100 musketeers and 3,000 tame Indians, was driven back with heavy losses. In 1655 or 1657, the Jesuits were able to settle two large divisions of the tribe in villages in Maturú (Porto de Moz) ; this work was, however, interrupted by the first expulsion of the order in 1661. Later (1665?) the Jesuits took some *Yuruna* and *Tacunyapé* to the villages of the lower Xingú, but the majority returned to the plains. In 1666 (?), the *Yuruna* defeated another party. Between 1682 and 1685, the *Yuruna* and *Tacunyapé* defeated an expedition of tame Indians and *Caravare* (*Curuáya*) led by Gonçalves Paes de Araujo, inflicting great losses. Then the *Yuruna* started out in 30 war canoes to attack the civilized population. In 1691 or 1692, the Jesuits failed in an attempt to reopen relations, the *Yuruna* killing every one sent out to them.

According to Father José de Mello Moraes (1860), the *Yuruna* were settled in four small villages on islands of the Xingú, 30 leagues from its mouth. As he sets the distance between the mouth and the first falls at 40 leagues, the *Yuruna* were still 10 leagues below those falls. These tribes must have early abandoned this place, however, retreating to above the falls of Volta Grande, where the Jesuits (in the middle of the 18th century?) also had the mission of Anauerá or Tauaquéra, a little above present-day Altamira. The missionaries were finally expelled by the Indians, who were dissatisfied with their strictness.

During the following 150 years, there is no record of the tribes above Volta Grande, which seem to have been left to themselves, protected by the dangerous falls and by their reputation as ferocious cannibals ; as late as 1831, their attacks were feared above Souzel. In 1841, the Vicar of this village, Torquato Antonio de Souza, made a new attempt to establish a mission in Tauaquéra, which, after a few years, seems to have been abandoned.

In 1843, the *Yuruna*, by that time completely tame, were visited by Prince Adalbert of Prussia, guided by Father Torquato. At that time they lived in nine small villages between Tauaquéra and a point 1 hour above Piranhaquara. There was no village in Volta Grande, but the *Yuruna* paid friendly visits in Souzel and knew a little *Tupí-Guaraní*. Father Torquato reported their number as 2,000, which would average 222 to each village ; possibly 200 would come nearer to the truth.

In 1859, the Government of the Province of Pará initiated again the catechization of the tribes above Volta Grande ; however, the first attempt was a failure. At this time the number of *Yuruna*, in three villages, was calculated at 235. This mission was kept up until about 1880, with, it seems, little success. In a fairly detailed report by President Carlos de Araujo Brusque (1863), apparently based on information given by the missionary, the total number of *Yuruna* in that year was 250.

When Von den Steinen descended the Xingú in 1884, this mission was no longer in existence. Two hundred and five *Yuruna* inhabited five villages between "Pedra Preta" (lat. 4° 40′ S.), above Piranhaquara, and lat. 8° 30′ S., a little below Pedra Seca. These Indians still maintained their independence, and their original culture was almost intact. The civilized population had not yet reached the mouth of the Iriri.

When H. Coudreau visited the Xingú in 1896, the situation of the tribe was completely changed. The 150 *Yuruna,* except for a group which had fled a little beyond Carreira Comprida, had fallen into servitude to the rubber gatherers, whose authority was extended to above the mouth of the Triumph River. Another small group, led by Tuxáua Muratú, lived in Cachoeira Jurucuá, in Volta Grande. The two largest groups, working for Raymundo Marques in Pedra Preta and the Gomes Brothers in Caxinguba (lat. 5° 20′ S.) were composed, respectively, of 15 and 30 persons.

In 1910, a rubber-plantation owner crossed Carreira Comprida and settled a little below *Pedra Seca.* The *Yuruna* refugees there came under his authority, tried to flee upriver, but were pursued with firearms. Later, impelled by poverty and by the attacks of the *Cayapó,* part of them returned, but in 1916 they once more fled to the upper Xingú never to return. They settled near the mouth of a tributary of the left bank, a little above the Martius Falls, where they were still found in 1928 by G. M. Dyott's expedition. They number about 30 Indians. Probably there are also survivors in Volta Grande of Tuxáua Muratú's family.

THE SHIPAYA

Synonyms.—*Juaicipoia, Jacipoya, Jacipuyá, Javipuyâ, Acipoya, Achupaya, Achipaye, Axipai, Chipaya.* Self-designation and *Yuruna*: *Shipáy* (shipá, bamboo for the arrowheads, plus -i, suffix of the collective plural of persons). In *Arara*: *Chipáy.* In *Cayapó*: *No-irén* (*Yuruna*). In *Kuruaya*: *Paráwawad* (*Yuruna*).

Physically, culturally, and linguistically, the *Shipaya* are the closest relatives of the *Yuruna,* being in many respects indistinguishable.

History, territory, and number.—The *Shipaya* (lat. 5° S., long. 55° W.) were first made known to civilization by the Jesuit priest, Roque Hundertpfund, who (in 1750?) went up the Xingú and the "River of the *Jurunas*" (Iriri), on a preaching tour of the *Curibary* (*Curuaya*) and *Jacipoya* (*Shipaya*). Whereas the *Yuruna* had for more than two centuries maintained themselves on a constant defensive against civilized people, the *Shipaya* had until after 1880 remained quietly in their own region without contacts with the civilized world. Kletke (1857), Brusque, and H. Coudreau mentioned them, but did not visit them. The first scientist to have direct and lengthy contact with them was Emilia Snethlage, in 1909, and especially in 1913. In the latter year she set the total number of *Shipaya* at several hundred, an estimate perhaps too high, since in 1918 only about 80 individuals were left. Today there may be only about 30, scattered in Largo do Mutum and Pedra do Cupim on the lower Iriri, and, mingled with a few remaining *Curuaya,* in Gorgulho do Barbado, on the lower Curuá, at about lat. 6° 30′ S.

From remote times the *Shipaya* inhabited the islands of the Iriri River, from the mouth of the Curuá downstream. They never settled farther up, for fear of *Cayapó* attacks. Later, about 1885, the *Cayapó* forced them to evacuate their settlements at the great falls of the Iriri, between lat. 4° 50' and 5° S. and to take shelter in the Curuá, settling in the Gorgulho do Barbado, which they only temporarily abandoned in 1913, after a bloody encounter with the rubber tappers. Since then they have always been divided into two local groups: on the lower Iriri and on the Curuá.

THE ARUPAÍ

This tribe is only known through information given by other Indians, as it became extinct before direct contact with civilized people. Prince Adalbert von Preussen in 1843 heard of them as enemies of the *Yuruna.* Brusque's report (1863) refers to them as *Urupaya,* and devotes a small chapter to them, which I quote here, since it is the only literature on this tribe.

This is a relatively numerous tribe, and although peaceable and relatively free of bad habits, it is extremely distrustful and suspicious in its relations with individuals of other nations. Its habits and customs are the same as those of the Tucunapeuas, with whom they have close bonds of friendship and trade. Since the Tucunapeuas from time to time meet the caravans which go up the Xingú River in search of natural products, it is they who obtain from these caravans objects which they trade to the Urupayas in exchange for canoes, cotton thread, hammocks and chickens. The Tucunapeuas, as intermediates in this trading, charge their neighbors a higher price for the objects they sell them—principally agricultural tools and beads highly prized for ornaments. In general Indians as soon as they come into contact with civilized man and learn the use of firearms, do everything in their power to get hold of these. The Urupayas, however, although acquainted with firearms through the Tucunapeuas, are so terrified by them, that they will not go near an armed man. They preserve a tradition from generation to generation about an ancient encounter with men who shot at them, causing a great slaughter, and this has instilled in them a great horror for firearms. They inhabit the most remote islands of the Xingú that anyone knows of. They cultivate manioc, cotton, and urucú. They are graceful, have beautiful bodies, and a beautiful color, and they are clever and industrious. They obey a "tuxaua" (chief) called Juacuá. [Brusque, 1863.]

Since at that time the Xingú was already known at least as far as the mouth of the Fresco River, the *Arupaí* must have lived still farther up. Approximately, lat. 7° S., long. 53° W.) Also *Shipaya* tradition places them on the Xingú, just above the *Yuruna.* A *Shipaya* band, which anciently migrated to the upper Xingú, fought with this tribe. According to another tradition, they received a few *Shipaya* who paid them a friendly visit. Finally, during a feast, they were taken by surprise by the *Yuruna.* The men were killed or captured to be eaten afterward; the women and children were made prisoners. Some escaped upstream, into the sertão, and were never heard of again. The tribe no longer existed when Von den Steinen descended the Xingú in 1884.

The name *Arupaí* is derived from *Shipaya* "arupá" or "aguayé" (*Eichhornia* sp.) plus "i," suffix of the collective plural for persons.

THE CURUAYA

Synonyms.—*Kuruaya, Caravare, Curibary, Curuari, Curiveré, Curubare, Curabare, Curuahé, Curierai, Curuara, Curuaye, Curiuaye, Curueye, Curiuaia,* and *Curuaya.* Self-designation: *Dyirimáin-id* (?). In *Shipaya, Kiriwai* (kiri, "parokeet," plus wa, "master," plus "i," suffix of the collective plural). In *Yuruna, Kiriwéy* (idem). In *Mundurucú, Huiaunyan; Wiaúnen,* linguistic variant.

History, territory, and number.—Between 1682 and 1685, the *"Caravares"* are mentioned for the first time. At that time a certain Gonçalves Paes de Araujo, who lived among the tribe, went up the Xingú with a few Portuguese, some tame Indians, and *Caravare.* The party fell into an ambush of *Yuruna* and *Tacunyapé,* who killed one Portuguese, all of the tame Indians, and 30 *Caravare.* The latter, "showing an insuperable courage and spirit rarely found among savages," managed to cover the retreat of the Portuguese and to get them back safely to their own lands, although Gonçalves Paes was severely wounded. Bettendorf says that the *"Curabares"* spoke the Lingua Geral and had 20 villages in the sertão. An attempt by Father João Maria Gersony to settle them down on the Xingú (before 1688?) failed because of the influence of a Portuguese named Manoel Paes (the same as Gonçalves Paes?), who employed them in the extraction of cloves (*Dicypellium caryophyllatum*). After Paes had been killed by the Indians, the *Curabare* offered to go down by the Tapajóz River. This seems to indicate that they were already at that time established between the Xingú and the Tapajóz, although much farther north than at the end of the 19th century. (Lat. 7° S., long. 55° W.)

Father Roque Hundertpfund (about 1750) went up the Iriri River on a 9-day preaching tour to the *Curibary* (*Curuaya*) and *Jacipoya* (*Shipaya*). After a 9-day journey upstream, the priest was still a long way from the mouth of the Curuá River, as it takes 18 days of rowing to get to the Curuá from the Xingú. This proves again that the *Curuaya* formerly lived farther to the north. They were mentioned several times during the 19th century, but only through information given by the *Yuruna* and the *Tacunyapé.* According to H. Coudreau, who had no direct contact with them, the tribe in 1896 inhabited the forest on the left bank (?) of the Curuá River. The traditions of the tribe, however, only mention excursions to the west of the Curuá, where they had bloody encounters with the *Karuziad* (*Mundurucú*). The so-called, *"Parintintin,"* who until 1883 attacked the Neo-Brazilians of the Jamaxim River, and who as late as 1895 went through the "seringaes" of the Crepory and Caderiry Rivers, were probably none other than bands of *Curuaya.*. This would also explain their having objects of civilized origin when they first met the civilized people of the Iriri and Curuá Rivers. Beyond a doubt they themselves consider as their own territory the tributaries of the right bank of the Curuá River from lat. 6° 30′ S. to 8° 50′ S. (the bayous Curuazinho, Bahú, and Flechas), where they were found in the 20th century. When the *Shipaya* fled from the *Cayapó* in 1885, retreating to the Curuá River, they came into contact with them. By the time E. Snethlage—the only scientist to visit them in their own territory—saw them in 1909 and 1913, they were already restricted to the Igarapé da Flecha, and greatly influenced by the *Shipaya*. In 1913, they had two "malocas" on the bank of the Flecha; a third maloca 12 km. away from the bayou, on the west side; and numbered about 150. In 1919, they numbered about 120 and inhabited, in small groups of one to four houses, the tributaries of the left bank of the upper Igarapé da Flecha, at lat. 8° 30' S. About a dozen of them lived among the *Shipaya* on the lower Iriri, and scattered among Neo-Brazilians. Up to this time the *Cayapó* had respected the *Curuaya* territory, but from 1918 on they began to extend their incursions to the Curuá River, and in 1934 they attacked and scattered the *Curuaya*. The largest group of the *Curuaya* took the road from the mouth of the Riozinho do Iriri to the Tapajóz; other groups scattered along the middle Iriri. The remainder, except for a few who stayed on the Iriri, live together with the last of the *Shipaya* near "Gorgulho do Barbado" on the lower Curuá. In all, there are perhaps less than 30 of them.

THE TACUNYAPÉ

Synonyms.—*Taconhapé, Tacoyape, Taguanhape, Tacuañape, Tacunhapé, Taconhapê, Taconhapez, Tucunapeua, Peua.* From the *Tupí*, takúnya, "penis," plus "pe," péwa, "small and flat." In *Yuruna, Tacunyãpé.* In *Shipaya, Tacunyãpé.* In *Kuruaya, Eidum,* "honey-eater" (eíd).

History, territory, and number.—In the second half of the 17th century, the west bank of the Xingú above Volta Grande was known as the "side of the *Jurunas*," and the Iriri as "River of the *Jurunas*," while the east bank was known as the "side of the *Taconhapés*." (Lat. 4° S., long. 53° W.) The "River of the *Taconhapés*" was probably the present Pacajá, a tributary of the Xingú.

In 1662–63, the Jesuits first tried to catechize the *Tacunyapé*, but three-fourths of the Indians who had already descended the river returned to the sertão, because the agreement made with them had not been kept. In 1667, again a number of *Yuruna* and *Tacunyapé* were taken down to the Veiros mission, but these, too, soon fled back to their own lands. The third attempt was made, shortly afterward, it seems, by Father Pedro Poderoso. He traveled up the Xingú for 15 days, and, having passed the painted stones (of Itamaracá Falls), he arrived at the landing place and village of the *Tacunyapé*, where he was well received. The Indians who had already been taken downstream the first time refused to listen to any arguments, but many of the others followed the priest. Having been illtreated by the captain-general of Gurupá, however, they returned to the sertão and never turned up again. When, in 1682, Father Antonio da Silva went to the "River of *Taconhapés*" in order to bring down the tribe of *Aracajú*, he made no mention of the *Tacunyapé*.

In 1685, they joined with the *Yuruna* in the attack against Gonçalves Paes and his *Curuaya*, as well as in the subsequent revolt. Father Samuel Fritz's map (1691) places the *Tacunyapé* on the right bank of the Xingú, below the "Pacaya River," under lat. 3° S. In 1692, Father José María Gersony once more succeeded in gathering together a large number of Indians of various tribes in Veiros, but, again, the intervention of the captain-general of Gurupá destroyed the project, transferring the Indians to Maturú (Porto de Moz) and other places.

In the 18th century, the Jesuits succeeded in settling *Yuruna* and *Tacunyapé* in the Tacuana (Tauaquéra) mission, a little above present-day Altamira, and in 1762 and 1784 the *Tacunyapé* are mentioned as among the Indians settled at Portel.

That part of the tribe which succeeded in keeping its independence seems to have retreated to the middle of the Curuá region; that would also explain their friendship with the *Curuaya*. *Shipaya* tradition says that the *Tacunyapé* joined them on the Iriri, having come from the upper Curuá, and settled near them, on an island a little below the mouth of the Rio Novo. Trouble with the *Cayapó* obliged them to return to their former settlement on the Xingú. There they were defeated in 1842 by the *Yuruna,* losing 10 men. A year later Prince Adalbert found their village, one day's journey above Tacuana, abandoned, and was unable to find where the tribe had taken refuge. In 1859, the *Tacunyapé* reappeared in large numbers (500?), and the Government of Pará decided to settle them in a new mission, which was kept up for some 15 to 20 years. In 1863, the fevers prevalent on the Xingú had reduced them to 150. In 1884, Von den Steinen found 70 individuals, living on an island at lat. 3° 30′ S., and the rest of the tribe in that region became extinct within the next 15 years. In 1894, H. Coudreau still found about 40, but that year the smallpox decimated them, and by the end of the century the rest had succumbed to measles and catarrh. In 1919, the writer became acquainted with a single survivor, who, reared among the *Shipaya,* had never learned the language of his tribe.

The *Tacunyapé* became extinct without ever having been studied. We have merely scattered references to them in the writings of missionaries and of travelers who never stayed among them.

Character.—The *Tacunyapé* were considered the most tractable Indians of the entire region. They received the Jesuits courteously; the chiefs and people went out to meet them and made them sit in beautiful hammocks. They were industrious, honest, and intelligent. It is noteworthy that, while other tribes were continually at war one with another, the *Tacunyapé* were permanently at peace with the *Curuaya, Shipaya, Arupai,* and *Arara.*

THE ARARA

Synonyms.—*Apeiaca, Apiacá, Apingui, Pariri.*   Self-designation: *Opinadkóm, Opinadkom* (?). In *Yuruna* and *Shipaya, Asipá* ("prop" or "support," on account of their tattooing design). In *Curuaya, I-amitug* (i, "their," plus ambi, "upper lip," plus tug, "pierced"). In *Cayapó, Kubẽ-nyóe* (kubê, "Indian," plus nyóe, "woodpecker [?]").

History, territory, and number.—In 1853, there appeared for the first time on the lower Xingú an unknown wandering tribe which the Neo-Brazilians henceforth called *Arara,* no one knows why. Ehrenreich without further proof considered them identical with their namesakes in the Madeira region, and even with the *Yuma,* remnants of which tribe still inhabit the headwaters of the Paraná-pixuna, tributary of the right bank of the Purús, at lat. 7° S.

The *Yuruna* informed me that these Indians formerly lived in a bayou, a tributary of the right bank of the Xingú, at the height of Carreira Comprida, perhaps the present-day Igarapé da Fortaleza (lat. 7° 30′ S.). From there they had been dislodged by the *Cayapó.* The latter, not the *Suyá,* are the *"Autikas"* to whom the *Arara* make reference.

In 1861 and 1862, these *Arara* of the Xingú descended below Volta Grande, where they were in peaceful contact with rubber tappers for some time. At that time they numbered 343, not counting children. In December 1862, they made a surprise attack upon the crews of two canoes of *Yuruna,* their capital enemies, killing two and wounding others. A short time later they disappeared.

In 1884, Von den Steinen saw a captive of this tribe among the *Yuruna* of the fifth village. At this time the *Arara* lived in the lands to the west of the Xingú, from the mouth of the Iriri down. The inhabitants of one *Arara* village, who had lived for a short time with their friends, the *Tacunyapé,* had died off.

In 1894, H. Coudreau, too, was unable to find the tribe. About this time the *Arara* disappeared from the left bank of the Xingú, and gathered at the headwaters of the Curuatinga, main branch of the Curuá River, which flows into the Amazon above Santarém, where they were cruelly persecuted by rubber tappers. Perhaps because of these persecutions, they began to work away from the left bank of the lower Iriri. In 1897 they killed six rubber tappers in Nazareth, thereafter disappearing from that bank for good. In 1914 there was still a dwelling with a small clearing of theirs at the headwaters of the Curuatinga. The relations between these *Arara* and the *Shipaya* were usually bad, with bloody fights and kidnapping of each other's children.

A short time afterward the few surviving *Arara* moved upstream on the Iriri, toward the lands on the left bank. In 1917 they vainly tried to make peace with the rubber tappers a little above São Francisco. In 1918 vestiges of these *Arara* were seen on the west bank of the Curuá do Iriri, at lat. 7° 30' S., after which no more was heard of them.

Another band of *Arara*, which numbered about 30 in 1917, settled on the right bank of the Pacajá do Xingú River, at lat. 3° 40' S. They worked for Neo-Brazilians of the Pacajá River, who also used them in warring against the *Asurini*, as happened twice about 1922. There may possibly be some isolated survivor of this group. There probably is still a small group of *Arara* on the upper Anapú, whose upper course approaches the Pacajá do Xingú.

Western Arara.—In 1869, the first bands of this tribe, numbering about 500 persons, appeared peaceably on the western bank of the lower Tocantins, lat. 3° S., and were followed by other smaller groups. They seemed to live to the west of the Trocará Mountains. "Authorities" identified them as *Miranya* or *Apiacá*. In 1873, Bishop D. Macedo Costa took some of them to the capital. In 1889, Ehrenreich observed some of the survivors who were scattered through the settlements along the left bank of the Tocantins, almost as far as Cameta. In 1896, Ignacio Moura mentions a Captain Peter of this tribe, with his family, who served as a guide in official prosecutions of hostile Indians. He is probably the same man H. Coudreau saw the following year, who lived with from 12 to 15 individuals in the Igarapé Ararinha, a little below Breu Branco. Coudreau calls these Indians *Anembé,* but the tattoo he describes and the name of the chief make it seem probable that they were *Arara.* Today none are left.

In 1910 or 1911, another band of *Arara* Indians appeared under the name *Pariri.* They were fleeing from the *Paracanã,* a tribe probably of *Tupi* speech living between the tributaries of the Tocantins and the Pacajá de Portel, from Cachoeira Grande on upstream. The *Pariri* had settled on the Iriuaná, a tributary of the left bank of the Pacajá de Portel. As the *Paracanã* attacks did not let up, the rest of the tribe was obliged to take refuge with the Neo-Brazilians of the region. In 1926 there were still a half dozen of them; in 1932, there remained only a boy and a girl in the last stages of tuberculosis.

There is probably still another band of *Arara* on the Pacajahy River, tributary of the left bank of the upper Pacajá de Portel. The *Pariri* called them *Timirém* or *Cimirem* (red). In 1913 or a little earlier, they came into brief contact with some rubber tappers, after which nothing more was ever heard of them.

THE ASURINÍ

Synonyms.—*Asurini* (from the *Yuruna*, asóneri, "red"), *Assurini, Assurinikin*. In *Yuruna, Surini*. In *Shipaya, Adyí kaporurí-ri* (adyí, "savage," plus kaporurí, "red," kaporurí-ri, "very red"). In *Curuaya, Nupánu-pag* (nupánu, "Indian," plus pag, "red"). In *Arara, Nerimá* (?). In *Cayapó, Kubē-kamreg-ti* (kubé, "Indian," plus kamrég, "red," plus ti, "augmentative").

Territory, history, and number.—The *Asuriní* appear for the first time in 1894, when they attacked a Neo-Brazilian at Praia Grande, above the mouth of the Pacajá do Xingú. In 1896 they twice attacked passing canoes in Passahy (lat. 3° 40' S.) and again at Praia Grande. In that year an armed band of 30, among them the *Tacunyapé* chief, Ambrosio, pursued the attackers, but did not dare to attack their village. Not long after this event Ambrosio was killed and torn to pieces by the *Asuriní*. By that time they were known to have settled between the Xingú and its tributary, the Pacajá. Toward the south they reached the boundary of Morro Grande (lat. 5° S.), with their principal village in the Igarapé Ipixuna (lat. 4° 40' S.), 5 days above its mouth. From then till the present, the *Asuriní* have remained absolutely inaccessible, almost annually attacking whatever rubber tappers venture into their territory. By 1917 their attacks on the right bank of the Xingú had almost completely ceased, but their hostilities against the civilized population of the Pacajá had increased. About 1922, the latter twice furnished the *Arara* with arms and munitions for a war of extermination against the *Asuriní*, but with doubtful success. At least part of the *Assuriní* remained at the headwaters of the Branco River, tributary of the left bank of the Pacajá (lat. 4° S., more or less), and in 1932 they killed a Neo-Brazilian well beyond the former limits of their territory, at the mouth of the Igarapé de Bom Jarbim (lat. 5° 30' S.).

In 1936, the *Górotire-Cayapó*, in their northward expansion, attacked and defeated the *Asuriní*, as proved by the great number of *Asuriní* arrows and ornaments in their possession when, a year later, they made peace with the Neo-Brazilians. Survivors probably still exist today between the Xingú and Pacajá and preserve their hostile attitude. The truth of the matter is that until today no one has tried to pacify them.

H. Coudreau learned that the *Asuriní* were known as "Deer Indians" on the Tocantins, where they were peaceable, whereas those on the Xingú were hostile. However, nobody ever heard of a tribe of that name on the Tocantins—not even Coudreau himself, when surveying that river in 1897. The erroneously named *"Asuriní"* of the lower Tocantins are *Paracaná*, who, since about 1926, have plagued Neo-Brazilians on the left bank, between lat. 3° S. and 3° 40' S. Father Wilhelm Schmidt's guess that they are a *Carajá* subtribe is inadmissible.

CULTURE

SUBSISTENCE ACTIVITIES

In clearings along the river, the *Yuruna* and *Shipaya* raised manioc, maize, potatoes, cara, bananas, sugarcane, cotton, pepper, tobacco, gourds, urucú, and genipa. From the manioc they made fermented flour toasted in clay ovens set on three stones. According to Emilia Snethlage, the *Curuaya* cultivated chiefly bananas, manioc, and other tubers in clearings hidden in the forest far from their homes. When visiting the *Tacunyapé*, Father Pedro Poderoso was given roasted ears of maize, Brazil nuts, and cakes of pounded maize which had been wrapped in leaves and cooked under hot ashes. The *Tacunyapé* cultivated manioc and cotton. The *Asurini* also were farmers.

The *Arara* were less clearly horticultural. After their defeat and dispersal by the *Cayapó,* they became nomadic for some time, with unfavorable consequences to their material culture, which originally may well have been of a higher type before contact with Neo-Brazilians. When the *Arara* first appeared on the Tocantins River, turtles formed their only medium of exchange; Neo-Brazilians, therefore, deny that they had any knowledge of farming. Perhaps some of the bands had really given up planting altogether, but at the headwaters of the Curuá do Norte was found one of their farm clearings; moreover, they owned objects made of cotton and, like their congeners both north and south of the Amazon, they had words for "maize," "tobacco," "potatoes," "manioc," and "beijú."

Hunting and gathering were more important to the *Curuaya* than to the *Shipaya* but fishing was less important. The *Curuaya* fished with a drug made from a liana. The *Yuruna,* though expert canoemen, did little fishing and, dreading to go inland, did little hunting. The *Shipaya* say that 10- or 12-year old *Tacunyapé* boys were expert hunters, never in danger of becoming lost in the forest.

Caimans and turtles were major foods of the *Curuaya*. For the *Yuruna,* "tracajás" (a turtle species) and their eggs, even when containing embryos, were an important food. Other foods included various wild roots and Brazil nuts (*Bertholletia excelsa*). The *Yuruna* also collected the "uauaçu" nut (*Orbignya speciosa*). The *Curuaya* had great skill in obtaining wild honey.

The *Yuruna* and *Shipaya* cooked in pots set on three stones over the fire. They cooked fish without first cleaning it. Utensils included pots, gourds, cylindrical wooden mortars, which sometimes had a separate conical base, a pestle with a head on each end, large canoe-shaped wooden vessels, and spatulate bases of "anajá" palm leaves (*Maximiliana regia*) used as basins. They ate together, everyone sitting around the gourd which held manioc flour and the pot in which fish, hot with pepper, had been cooked.

The only domesticated animals possessed by the *Yuruna* were dogs and chickens. In Von den Steinen's time, 1884, they were not yet in the habit of eating either chickens or eggs. In their huts the *Yuruna* kept a great number of wild fowls and animals.

DWELLINGS AND VILLAGES

Constant fear of being attacked by the *Cayapó* and other hostile tribes forced the *Yuruna* to build their dwellings almost exclusively on the rocky islets of the rapids, where they were safe from the *Cayapó*, who had no skill in handling canoes. In 1843, the largest *Yuruna* village consisted of six dwellings. In 1884, the seven different villages had eight, two, seven, three, one, three, and two dwellings, respectively. The *Shipaya* had an even stronger tendency to isolate their dwellings and, although houses were sometimes quite near one another, more than two were never built in the same place. The *Shipaya* of the Curuá River inhabited the right bank, which up to 1918 had not yet been invaded by the *Cayapó*. On the Iriri River their houses were mostly built on the rocky islands among the rapids and only exceptionally on the solid ground of the left bank, which was less exposed to *Cayapó* attacks than the right bank. The *Tacunyapé* seem originally to have been a forest- not a river-dwelling people, but after their return from the Iriri to the Xingú River they, like the *Yuruna, Shipaya,* and *Arupai,* began to live on the islands. The *Curuaya* of the 17th century were known as forest dwellers. In contrast to the *Yuruna* and *Shipaya,* genuine boatmen who never strayed far from the islands and banks of the Xingú and Iriri Rivers, the *Curuaya* avoided the banks of the large rivers. The central maloca visited by Emilia Snethlage in 1913 consisted of five houses, grouped irregularly around an open yard.

The typical *Asurini* house was a long, rectangular, tent-shaped structure without side walls; one found at the headwaters of the Branco River was 180 palmos, i.e., 128 feet (39.4 m.) in length.

The *Yuruna* had two principal types of dwellings. One type had a rectangular or square gable roof, the rafters being set right on the ground and curved toward the top. Details are lacking. The other type was a rectangular hut, the roof of which came close to the ground, with ridge pole and perpendicular walls. The first of these dwellings was probably the original type. The roof was well-made with "uauaçu" or "anajá" palm grass. The largest house visited by Von den Steinen measured 24 by 24 m. (78 by 78 ft.), and 6 m. (20 ft.) in height; others were only 2 by 4 m. (6½ by 13 ft.). Inside there was always a sort of loft, formed by a scaffolding of poles, to store food supplies, weapons, and utensils. Sometimes this scaffolding hung from the roof.

Shipaya dwellings were similar to those of the *Yuruna.* In 1913, Snethlage found the remains of a big, oval-shaped "maloca." The *Tacunyapé* house Von den Steinen saw in 1884 was "in *Yuruna* style." The original *Curuaya* house seems to have been elliptical, with a row of central posts and two lateral rows on either side, decreasing in height. There seems not to have been any space between the walls and roof; flexible rafters covered with straw gave the houses the look of "long hayricks rounded at the top," in Snethlage's description. At each end was a door closed with a rush mat.

Yuruna, Shipaya, and *Asurini* household furniture consisted of benches cut out of one piece of wood (fig. 25), with a circular or oval seat and two sides forming legs, mats woven of palm leaves, baskets with oval

FIGURE 25.—*Yuruna* wooden stool. (Drawn from specimens, Museu Paraense Emilio Goeldi, Belém.)

lids made of "uauaçu" fiber, and cotton hammocks in which the Indians slept at night and sat during the day. The *Arara* north of the middle Iriri River in 1917 made palm-fiber hammocks. *Curuaya* dwellings were not very clean, and all their utensils were dirty and carelessly made. Their hammocks were small and made of palm fibers; the technique used is not known, but they were not woven. Their benches were crudely made and painted. Prince Adalbert speaks highly of the order and cleanliness of *Yuruna* dwellings.

DRESS AND ADORNMENT

When still entirely free, *Arara* men and women were completely naked. In 1913, the *Curuaya* of the central malocas still were naked, but those of the river malocas dressed like the *Shipaya,* that is, men wore a belt of glass beads and covered the prepuce with a straw sheath, while women wore a woven loincloth. *Yuruna* and *Shipaya* women wrapped lengths of woven gray cloth around their waists; these were open on one side and reached almost to their ankles. Von den Steinen's prints show some women also wearing a kind of cape with wide stripes, apparently made the same way. Besides a belt, which seems originally to have been of cotton, men wore only the truncate cone of dry "uauaçu" fiber of the *Cayapó* and *Bororo* type which covers the male organs. This was the *Yuruna* style in 1884; 12 years later, their dress was more or less Neo-Brazilian (Coudreau, H, 1897 c). *Tacunyapé* women in 1884 were wearing aprons of material bought from civilized people.

Yuruna, Shipaya, and *Curuaya* men's hair hung loose almost to their waist, except when women parted it for them, making a pigtail which they tied with a gray twist of fibers. On their foreheads, where the hair-part started, there was a small circular red spot made with the pollen of sororoca (*Ravenala guianensis*). The *Curuaya* often wore bangs. The women also parted their hair in the middle, allowing it to hang loose behind or tying it in a loose knot. The *Arara* wore their hair, which was brown and wavy, long behind; women's braids often reached their knees. The *Asurini* cut their hair ear-length. These tribes combed their hair with small one-sided combs made from stems.

The *Yuruna* made beautiful headdresses of green feathers and diadems of parrot and macaw feathers covered with small black feathers at the base. The feathers were fastened between two bamboo hoops held together by an elastic net about an inch wide. The *Shipaya* and *Curuaya* made men's diadems of cotton ribbons with feathers, sometimes fastened to straw hoops; those of braided straw in the shape of a hat brim with a tail of feathers or straw were used by both sexes. The *Górotire-Cayapo*, a *Ge* tribe (Handbook, vol. 1) were found to have feather ornaments taken from the *Asurini:* beautiful diadems made of various overlapping tiers of feathers mounted on cotton ribbons.

Yuruna men wore cotton bands 2 to 2½ inches (5 to 6 cm.) wide around their upper arms and ankles; these were crocheted on by women. At festivals, the anklets were often of beads. Narrower bands were also worn by men just below the knees. Boys and men wore a very tight beaded belt, preferably blue, from 4 to 6 inches (10 to 16 cm.) wide. Both sexes from early childhood wore strings of heavy beads around their necks and bandoleer-style, crossing in front and behind. Necklaces were made of worked peccary teeth. The *Shipaya* and *Curuaya* made similar bead ornaments, but showed more artistry in embroidering armbands and forehead bands with beads. In 1913, the *Curuaya*, owing to their relative isolation, still wore more seed and nut than bead necklaces.

Arara ornaments in the museum at Pará include: A diadem of parrot and japú feathers, the base of which is covered with small feathers; a braided cotton forehead band with small red feathers ending in two long strings; necklaces of black seeds and bones; a pair of cotton arm bands; a pair of bracelets of armadillo tail; and a necklace of armadillo claws.

The *Yuruna* and *Tacunyapé* anointed their bodies with a vegetable oil for protection against mosquitoes. They kept the oil in small round gourds decorated with painted or engraved maze designs. *Asurini* warriors stain their bodies with urucú, whence their tribal name. The *Yuruna, Arara, Pariri,* and *Shipaya,* but not the *Curuaya,* tattooed the face. Until 1843 one could observe the characteristic *Yuruna* tattooing to which this tribe owed its name in the Lingua Geral. Both men and women made a black, vertical line down the middle of the face, from the roots of the hair to the chin, and running around the mouth. This tattooing was made by incising with animal teeth and rubbing in genipa stain, the person's social importance being indicated by the width of the stripe. According to André de Barros, the chiefs' faces were all black; Mello Moraes says that the "most distinguished" persons generally had three stripes, the lateral ones being narrower. The width of the middle stripe is given as from 1½ to 2½ inches (3.8 to 7 cm.) by various authors. The tattooing was usually done in childhood. The *Shipaya* had ceased to tattoo before permanent contact with Neo-Brazilians. The *Arara* tattooed at puberty with genipa, making two vertical lines from the eye down to the curve of the lower jaw. The *Pariri* tattooed with charcoal of rubber.

Yuruna men and *Shipaya* and *Curuaya* men and women pierced their ear lobes. Ordinarily, they wore nothing in their ears but for festivals they inserted a long red macaw tail feather, with small feathers hanging from its point and surrounding the base. These feathers were kept in tubes trimmed with small "mutum" feathers. The *Arara* pierced the nasal septum as well as the earlobe. *Curuaya* women wore a stone tembeta in the lower lip.

TRANSPORTATION

The *Yuruna* and *Shipaya* "uba" canoes are well adapted to the rough water of the rapids. They are made of hewn cedar logs, usually hollowed out by means of fire. The cross section is U-shaped, and there is a sort of rectangular platform at bow and stern. Von den Steinen gives the follow-ing dimensions of a *Yuruna* canoe: Length, 30 feet (10.6 m.); maximum width, 3 feet (95 cm.); depth, 1¼ feet (39 cm.); thickness, 1 inch (25 mm.); platform at the bow, 1 foot 10 inches by 1 foot 5 inches (57 by 44 cm.); platform at the stern, 3¼ by 3 feet (1 by 0.9 m.). (Steinen got the measurements of the platforms reversed!). These canoes can easily carry 10 people without baggage. They usually have an awning of rush mats from the middle to the rear, fastened to arched poles. The boats are punted by means of poles and steered by a paddle about 4½ feet (1.45 m.) long. The handle of the paddle, which ends in a somewhat convex cross bar, measures 2 feet (62 cm.); the blade widens toward the blunt end, and sometimes bears the painted maze design.

It seems established that the *Arara* had no form of canoe when first met. They lived on and roamed over dry land, only exceptionally appearing on the banks of the great rivers. The *Asurini* also lacked canoes. The *Curuaya*, living in the heart of the forests, paid little attention to boating. Their original canoe was made of jutahy bark. Later, they made this type only in emergency and constructed crude imitations of the *Shipaya* masterpieces.

Among devices for land transportation, the Museum at Pará has an *Arara* carrying bag of interlaced cords made of palm fibers.

MANUFACTURES

Weaving.—Since the Jesuit period, *Yuruna* women have been famous for their skill in spinning cotton "as fine as hair." They wove hammocks on bamboo frames, measuring 6½ by 9¾ feet (2 by 3 m.). Two threads guided by a little piece of wood were passed horizontally through the vertical threads of the warp; the weaving technique is not clearly described but the product was unquestionably cloth. In order to tighten or separate the horizontal threads, they used a small toothed wooden instrument.

Pottery.—*Yuruna* pottery was simple (fig. 26, *b, d*), without painted or plastic decorations, except for the occasional addition of two small excrescences on diametrically opposite sides of the vessel edge. The principal form, used to hold water and fermented drinks, is a round jar with a short neck. *Shipaya* ceramics are coarser than those of the *Yuruna*.

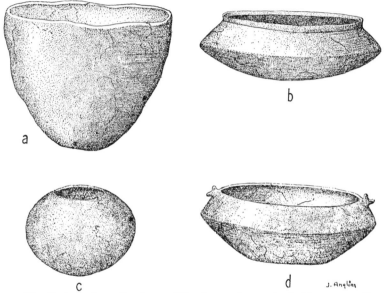

FIGURE 26.—Pottery from the lower Xingú. *a, Arara; b, d, Yuruna; c, Curuaya.* (All 2/9 actual size.) (Drawn from specimens, Museu Paraense Emilio Goeldi, Belém, and Nimuendajú and Snethlage collections.)

Huge vessels 2¼ feet (69 cm.) in diameter and equally high are used for fermented drinks. Exceptional pots were painted inside and outside. *Curuaya* pots resemble those of neighboring tribes, but the ware is inferior and vessels are small and plain. The characteristic form is a small, globular jar (fig. 26, *c*), apparently made in imitation of the capsule of the Brazil-nut tree. *Arara* pottery is very crude (fig. 26, *a*).

Miscellaneous.—The *Shipaya* made "half-gourds" (cuias) from the cuieté and *Lagenaria*. These are painted black inside and outside and sometimes have maze designs. The decorations are sometimes incised on the shell of the green fruit.

Other containers include an *Arara* vessel for dye made of the dorsal carapace of a turtle and a rectangular palm-straw basket with a lid and upright sides.

The *Yuruna* made candles of little wooden sticks wrapped in cotton and soaked in oil.

Weapons.—The principal weapon was the bow and arrow. The club was known only to the *Shipaya* and to the *Asurini* (fig. 27, c). The *Shipaya* attached a short cylindrical club to the wrist by means of a loop. A club of

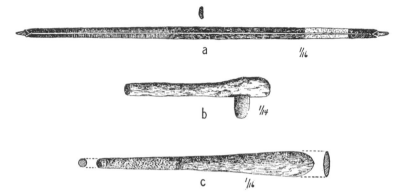

FIGURE 27.—*Asurini* weapons. *a*, Bow; *b*, hafted stone ax; *c*, wooden club. (Drawn from specimens, Museu Paraense Emilio Goeldi, Belém, and Estevão collection.)

the *Asurini* in the Pará Museum is 2¾ feet (85 cm.) long, the handle covered with fibers of two colors interwoven with little skill, the end rounded and flattened, the blade 3 inches (8.5 cm.) wide by 1 inch (2.5 cm.) thick, and both edges cut. The blade is slightly curved, almost like a machete. The cudgels found in the possession of the *Yuruna* were apparently of *Cayapó* origin.

The *Yuruna* bow was of black wood, rectangular in cross section, over 6½ feet (2 m.) long, and notched at the ends to hold the cord. *Curuaya* and *Shipaya* bows were similar. The *Arara* made powerful bows 4⅓ feet (1.3 m.) long with a flattened elliptical cross section about 1½ inches (4 cm.) wide. *Asurini* bows (fig. 27, *a*) in the C. Estevão Collection in Pará are made of paxiuba palm, 5⅓ to 5½ feet (1.62 to 1.67 m.) long. They are distinguishable from all other South American bows by their exaggerated width, 2½ to 3 inches (6 to 7 cm.); the maximum thickness is ½ inch (1 cm.). The ends are notched to hold the cord, one end of which has a ring to slip over the lower tip of the bow. The upper half or third of the bow is almost always wound with dark and white cotton threads, while the lower part is sometimes covered with hawk down glued on.

Yuruna, Curuaya, and *Shipaya* arrows are made of camayuva (*Guadua* sp.) and have bridged feathering. The *Asurini* and *Arara* used sewed feathering. The most common point is a lanceolate blade of bamboo or bone. *Asurini* arrows in the C. Estevão collection range from 4 feet 1

inch to 5 feet 1 inch (125 to 157 cm.) in length. The shaft is of camayuva;
the heads are: (a) of bamboo, 1 foot (32 cm.) long by 1½ inches (4 cm.)
wide; (b) of bone, 6 inches (15 cm.) long by ¾ inch (1.6 cm.) wide, with
a lateral barb; (c) of wood, imitating (a) and (b), or of square or triangular cross section; (d) with four sharp wooden points. The feathering
is sewed. The feathers, usually a hawk and a macaw feather, are very long,
up to 1⅓ feet (40 cm.). The point where they are tied on is sometimes
decorated with four overlapping rows of short feathers, glued on, three
rows of yellow feathers, one row of red. The shaft of the arrow, in the
space between the vanes, is sometimes covered with an interweaving of
very fine black and white fibers or cotton threads of two colors with an
equally ornamental effect. Some arrows have a "tucumã" nut inserted at
the point where the head is fastened into the shaft. This nut makes no
sound and apparently serves only to keep the arrow from penetrating too
far. The *Shipaya* used a fish arrow having a long cylindrical point of
paxiuba palm wood and an incendiary war arrow with a piece of jutahy
resin in the slit end.

The *Arara* used a lance with a long bamboo point.

An *Arara* ax which I observed in 1917 north of the middle Iriri River
had a stone head, with only the cutting edge polished. The head was held
in a cavity in the thickest part of a wooden handle by means of wax and
string lashing. A similar *Asurini* ax in the *Pará* museum has the head
fitted so nicely into the cavity that an adhesive and lashing are unnecessary
(fig. 27, b).

The *Arara* made a chisel of a hafted agouti tooth.

SOCIAL AND POLITICAL ORGANIZATION

In 1913, the *Curuaya* still had a village chief, although an intelligent interpreter who had a monopoly on their communication with Neo-Brazilians enjoyed much greater prestige. Emilia Snethlage believes that chieftainship originally passed from father to son. By 1913, the *Curuaya* were
becoming rubber collectors; by 1919, they were mere serfs of a Neo-
Brazilian boss.

A certain solidarity united the *Shipaya* as against other tribes, but there
was no tribal organization. From the beginning of the 20th century they
seem no longer to have had chiefs (i-áma; i, reverential prefix) and nothing is known of their ancient functions. On war expeditions an experienced man was chosen ad hoc to take command.

The *Yuruna* were divided into villages, each composed of a number of
families (patrilineal?). A comparison of Von den Steinen's and H.
Coudreau's data indicates that these families or communal households
were probably relatively stable. Chieftaincy descended from father to
son; the war leader, however, was not the village chief but a medicine man.

Until shortly before Von den Steinen's expedition there seems to have been a supreme chief of the tribe, who lived at Piranhaquara.

Among the *Shipaya,* monogamy is the rule; bigamy a rare exception. Divorce is uncommon. The couples usually live in perfect harmony and treat each other on equal terms. Both men and women participate in religious ceremonies. Children are treated with an almost exaggerated tenderness, and are rarely given away to civilized people. Infanticide is considered a sin that provokes the anger of the god Kumãpári, who expressly forbade it. Formerly, there existed a relationship of solidarity very formally entered into by two individuals, maĩtumas, of their own free will. The alliance was sealed at the time of the zetábia ceremony in front of Kumãpári's statue. The two maĩtumas were never to quarrel, should converse with each other respectfully, and should help each other during the remainder of their lives. As long as the *Shipaya* kept their identity as a tribe, they were known for their honesty.

Among the *Yuruna,* polygyny (of the chiefs?) was practiced, a man having up to three wives. Since the 17th century, the *Yuruna* have been proverbially jealous of their wives; the uprising of 1666 was due to the abuses of the chief of the expedition in this respect. Von den Steinen noted the harmony prevailing between spouses. Parental love is proved by the breaking of relations with the mission when the missionary sent some children as hostages to Belém. One day Von den Steinen's expedition had to stop and camp long before the scheduled hour in order to prepare the food for the *Yuruna* guide's little daughter, who was feeling hungry. Naughty children were not beaten, but their parents treated them with ostentatious contempt until they mended their ways. Von den Steinen observed that on a canoe trip a father left his disobedient little daughter at the edge of the river, forcing her for a while to follow the canoe on foot with great difficulty.

The old reports describe the *Yuruna* as brave and warlike, and both sexes as hard workers. The women spun and toasted flour even during drinking sprees. Brusque's record (1863), however, calls them lazy, indolent, and thievish. Von den Steinen found them affable, given to laughter, not thievish, and willing to help with the work. He observed the weeping salutation which lasted about a minute and did not provoke tears. When subsequently talking to the host, the visitor stood beside him without looking at him, but staring straight into space. Visitors announced their arrival by blowing a horn.

Among the *Curuaya,* monogamy was the rule; bigamy was rare, according to Emilia Snethlage, chiefly because of poverty and the lack of women, although polygyny was the theoretical ideal. Families are apparently patrilineal. There were indications of the couvade.

There are no reports of intratribal conflict, but all these peoples were intermittently at war with their neighbors, though the *Shipaya* and *Arara* remained at peace with the *Tacunyapé*. In the 17th century, the *Curuaya* are mentioned as enemies of the *Yuruna* and *Tacunyapé;* in 1843, as enemies of the *Yuruna, Shipaya,* and *Piapáy*. The *Asurini* and *Tacunyapé* were at war recently. The implacable enemy of all these tribes was the *Northern Cayapó*, who, during the 18th century, made the *Yuruna* seek shelter in the rocky islands of the rivers and cut off all communications between the *Yuruna* and the tribes of the upper Xingú River until the beginning of the 20th century. We have already seen how the *Curuaya* succumbed to the *Cayapó* in 1934. The *Shipaya* had also been constantly menaced by the *Cayapó* and earlier by the *Mundurucú* and the now extinct *Piapáy*. The *Shipaya* had been alternately at peace and at war with the *Yuruna, Arupaí, Curuaya,* and *Arara* but finally effected an alliance with the *Yuruna* and *Curuaya,* and, despite occasional flare-ups, intermarried and lived together with them. When at peace with the *Yuruna, Shipaya* groups sometimes settled among them on the Xingú. Von den Steinen's vocabulary of the language of the "upper" *Yuruna* is almost pure *Shipaya,* and Coudreau's map shows an old *Shipaya* maloca near that of the *Yuruna* of Jurucuá Falls at Volta Grande.

The *Tacunyapé* were never at peace with the *Cayapó*. The *Cayapó,* while pursuing the *Shipaya,* attacked them at the time when they lived on the Iriri, and a *Tacunyapé* raid against their assailants failed. A strange episode is told about this expedition; the chief of the *Tacunyapé,* mortally wounded by an arrow, requested that one of his warriors divide his body at the waistline with a big knife, so as to have to carry only the upper part of his body in the retreat to their village, leaving the nether part on the battlefield.

Cannibalism.—Since the 17th century, the *Yuruna* have been accused of cannibalism, and the 18th-century *Shipaya* were known as cannibals. The other tribes did not eat human flesh.

Father João Daniel, whose tendency to exaggerate makes him an untrustworthy witness, states that the *Yuruna* kept human fat in kettles for seasoning their food. He also cites cases of these Indians killing people in order to prepare provisions for a trip. The writer also doubts some stories told by the *Shipaya* about such customs of the *Yuruna*. It is probable, however, that cannibalism really existed among the *Yuruna,* more or less under the same conditions as among the *Shipaya*.

Father João Daniel (around 1750) called the *Shipaya* "warlike, cruel, and cannibalistic as these *Yuruna*," and doubtless before closer contact with Neo-Brazilians (around 1885), they were cannibals. Their last victims may have been the *Cayapó* during the conflicts which resulted in the abandonment of the tribal dwellings on the middle Iriri. (See above.) Except for a few cases where vengeance was the motive, cannibalism always took the form of a sort of communion with their national god, Kumãpari, now transformed into the jaguar with an avowed man-eating propensity. Through his medicine man, he used to manifest his desire to eat the flesh of the *Shipaya's* enemy. The tribe then organized an expedition against one of the hostile tribes, the main purpose being to take one of its members alive. The prisoner was taken to the maloca, where he was very well treated. Beverages were prepared, and after the guests had arrived, the prisoner was killed by arrows in the yard, then scalded, quartered, and the pieces cooked or roasted on a rustic grill (moquém). A large pot full of human flesh and drink was then covered with rush mats and placed near the caves for Kumãpari. Of those attending the feast "whoever wished" also ate of the enemy's meat. The killer was not subject to the purification prescribed for nonritual killing.

War trophies.—Trophy taking was more common than cannibalism. The *Yuruna* kept the skulls of their slain enemies. In the uprising of 1686, "they carried as a standard the head of a certain Sergeant Antonio Rodrigues, whom they had killed." Sometimes these skulls served as resonators for their war trumpets. They made flutes of the enemies' bones and used the teeth to decorate their ear lobes. The *Shipaya* decapitated a slain foe, carefully picked the flesh from the skull, fastened the maxillary on with wax, and filled the orbits with wax, placing small bone disks in their centers. The killer hung the trophy in a basket from the ridge pole of his dwelling. He extracted the teeth and made them into necklaces for himself and wife or used them to decorate earplugs. The *Arara* took the following trophies: The scalp (fig. 28, *c*), including the ears, stretched in a hoop; the skin of the face (fig. 28, *b*), similarly stretched and trimmed with tassels of beads, with a loop of beads for hanging; the skull (fig. 28, *a*), cleaned and decorated with two macaw tail feathers inserted behind the zygomata and with cotton fluff; and the teeth made into necklaces (fig. 28, *d*). It is reported that they stripped off the entire skin of one of their dead enemies. The *Curuaya* took trophy heads. In 1919, they told me that they had carefully preserved the skulls of the *Shipaya* killed in their last conflict with them, and that until recently they had danced with them.

ESTHETIC AND RECREATIONAL ACTIVITIES

Drinking festivals.—The *Yuruna* attached great importance to a drink, malicha, made from manioc, fermentation of which was produced by women chewing part of the mass. Sometimes bananas were added. It was allowed to ferment in a canoe set up in the festival house and covered with banana leaves. Drinking parties often lasted for days. During such

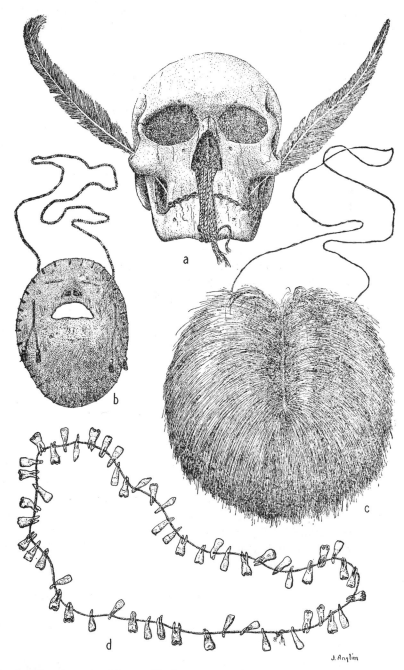

FIGURE 28.—*Arara* trophies. *a*, Skull, ornamented; *b*, skin of human face with open mouth; *c*, human scalp; *d*, human-tooth necklace. (Drawn from specimens, Museu Paraense Emilio Goeldi, Belém.)

an occasion, Von den Steinen saw a gaudily adorned personage who alternately played the pari-tadada and sang, and also served drinks to the others. The *Yuruna* are not quarrelsome when they drink; they sing and talk to themselves, walking up and down, and pay no attention to one another.

From early times, the *Shipaya* too were considered heavy drinkers. At any celebration, even a religious one, enormous quantities of fermented drink were never lacking. The *Shipaya* never became belligerently drunk, but behaved like the *Yuruna*. After contact with Neo-Brazilians, however, they became sadly addicted to rum. The *Curuaya* were also passionately fond of fermented drinks.

The *Yuruna* smoked tobacco in cigarettes rolled in the thin skin of the taurí (*Couratari* sp.).

Musical instruments.—*Curuaya* musical instruments include small panpipes, bone flutes, and two kinds of the "toré" clarinet.

Yuruna musical instruments were: The gourd rattle (maracá), with a plume of macaw tail feathers at the tip; a signaling horn made of a gourd; a horn of thick bamboo with lateral opening for blowing and with loops and tassels of feathers; the same with sounding box made of a gourd or a human skull; small panpipes; a bone flute; Von den Steinen's "bassoon," pcrhaps corresponding to the *Shipaya* "takari" (Karl G. Izikowitz's "toré clarinet"); a great wooden trumpet (pari-tadada) used at drinking sprees with lateral opening for blowing and a bamboo reed from 5.7 to 6.1 feet (175 to 187 cm.) in length.

Shipaya dancing and music were always linked. Some dances imitated certain animals in pantomime. During their sprees, they would walk up and down in pairs or alone, singing and playing the flute with an unearthly din.

Besides the large flutes for the "zetábia" ceremony and the whistles for the dance of souls, the *Shipaya* had the same instruments as the *Yuruna:* a bone flute, panpipes, a signal horn, a large conical wooden trumpet, painted with the maze design (pari-tadada), a small four-holed flute, and the "takari." This last requires four players, for it has a scale of four notes and each player has only one note to play. The melody results from each player's playing his note as required. The quartette forms a circle, each person holding the "takari" with his right hand, and placing his left on his neighbor's shoulder. While playing, they slowly move round and round.

The gourd rattle, identical with the *Yuruna* form, is also used only by the medicine man.

Art.—The *Yuruna* and *Shipaya* (fig. 29) used the maze design on their engraved gourds, but the former did not paint it on their bodies witn genipa, generally limiting themselves to stripes on their forearms and legs, so that, artistically, body decoration was much inferior to that of the *Shipaya*. *Yuruna* artists were generally women. There are numberless variations of the maze motif with which they cover objects and especially the body. Frequently, these body designs, used on festive occasions, are so fine and intricate that they can only be seen at close range. Besides the maze motif, there are also curvilinear patterns.

The most important *Shipaya* sculptural products, statues of mythological personages, do not show great development in this type of work. Little figures of armadillos and other animals are carved from a palm nut (*Bactris* sp.) and made into necklaces. Wooden spoons sometimes appear in artistic and original forms, the handle ending in the form of a clenched

FIGURE 29.—*Shipaya* painted decorations. (Drawn from sketch by Curt Nimuendajú.)

fist, etc. In 1896, H. Coudreau found in an abandoned *Shipaya* tribal house a number of small carved, wooden figures representing animals, a canoe, and other objects. These were well done. (See figs. 30, *a, d, f;* 31, for similar *Yuruna* specimens.).

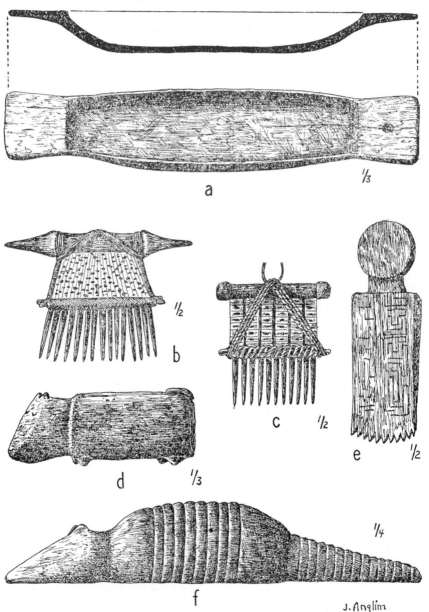

FIGURE 30.—Lower Xingú wood carvings and manufactures. *a, d, f, Yuruna* carved toys (?); *b, c, Yuruna* and *Arara* wood and cord combs; *e, Yuruna* carding comb. (Drawn from specimens, Museu Paraense Emilio Goeldi, Belém.)

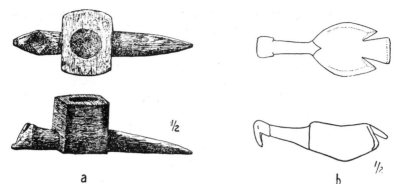

FIGURE 31.—*Yuruna* carved wooden toys (?). (Drawn from specimens, Museu Paraense Emilio Goeldi, Belém.)

RELIGION AND SHAMANISM

The principal figure in *Shipaya* religion is the god Kumāpari, son of another god of the same name, and father of Kunyarima, whose uterine brother was Arubiatá. Kumāpari stole fire from the tapir hawk and created man from arrow-reeds, making the *Shipaya* first of all, whence his title of Sekárika (Our Creator). The brothers carry out a series of difficult tasks, by order of Kumāpari, who in these episodes bears the title Marusawa (*Tupi:* morubisawa, "chief?"). In these adventures Kunyarima gives proof of intelligence and courage, while Arubiatá tries in vain to imitate him, always failing and saved only through his brother's intervention. Kumāpári, angry with all men, goes away down the Xingú, to the north, where, at the end of the world, sky and earth meet. At first of human shape, he now has the form of an old jaguar. He has turned into the god of war and cannibalism, and is the object of a real cult. Consecrated to Kumāpari were: medicine men to whom he would directly manifest himself; their helpers; and the god's wives, who never married men and had certain religious duties.

Sometimes Kumāpari or the two brothers ordered statues (upasi) to be made: cylindrical posts with human heads carved and painted on them by the demon's wives. A ceremony (zetábia) would take place in front of the statues with two large flutes of thick bamboo, held by these women.

Among the many other gods or spirits of the earth and sky, the most important are the terrible Apu-sipayá (Jaguar of Heaven), the aquatic demon, Paí, and the Great Snake, Tobí, from whose ashes sprang all cultivated plants. Respect for these spirits, the help they can give men, and fear of their anger and malevolence constitute, together with magic and the worship of souls, *Shipaya* supernaturalism.

The soul is composed of two parts: the āwá, which after death turns into a specter that frightens but does not kill people; and the isāwi, which inhabits certain large rocks or hills inside which it lives a life similar to that of the living. Jointly, all the isāwi are called i-ánāi (i, reverential prefix, plus ánā, plus i, suffix of the collective plural).

From time to time, the i-ánāi again desire to be among the living and advise the medicine man, who then orders an i-ánāi kariá (feast of the souls of the dead). The ceremonies only take place at night and last 8 or more nights. One by one, the souls enter the medicine man in order to dance and drink with the living. The medicine man appears from the interior of a dark house bringing the jugs of fermented drink, which are wrapped up closely in a rectangular cape of heavy coarse cotton, woven in the "double thread" technique. These threads are covered with cotton-wool, so that the cape resembles a sheep's fleece. The cape is fastened to a hoop worn on the head, and from which hang thick black fringes hiding the wearer's face. A wreath of parrot feathers decorates the head, and the bottom of the cape is bordered with wing and tail feathers of the mutum, which touch the ground. The wearer is completely covered, suggesting a white pillar. The soul is summoned with shouts and the music of two flutes, a single and a double one, fastened together with a thread. It then enters the circle formed by women and men, who welcome it with laughter. In a nasal voice, the soul sings a short verse several times, following the circular dance of the others, then disappears into the house, yielding its place to another soul. This ceremony ends with a great drinking orgy. Throughout the celebration the participants refrain from sexual intercourse. The souls of those recently dead never appear on such occasions. The festival ends with the medicine man's ceremonially restoring to each participant his isāwi, of which the souls had deprived him, for its loss would spell death.

The medicine man is, above all, the intermediary between the laity and the gods, the spirits, and the souls of the dead. The prerequisite for the profession is a tendency toward dreams and visions, a good teacher subsequently instructing the tyro how to develop and use his gift.

Magic, that is, the art of curing and of causing illness, as well as of securing special advantages, is a secular science. It is in no way connected with the spirits and the souls of the dead, although exercised by the medicine man, who heals by sucking and massaging, removing harmful influences from the patient's body, and transferring them to a green branch (compare *Yuruna*); he also blows tobacco smoke over the patient.

The *Yuruna* believed in the god the Shipaya call "Kumāpári," with whom some of their medicine men had direct communication, and also in the culture hero Kunyarima. One of their ceremonies, observed by Von den Steinen, is in every detail identical with the *Shipaya* Dance of Souls (i-ánāi Kariá). The souls, like those of the *Shipaya,* lived in certain large rocks, safe from high water, such as Pedra Preta, Pedra de Caxinguba, and Pedra Seca, to which due reverence was given. What

Kletke says about a benevolent diety and a malevolent deity seems not trustworthy.

The medicine man cured by violent massaging, forcing the pathogenic substances from the body into green branches, which were then carefully taken outdoors. Meanwhile, the patient remained lying in his hammock.

At a *Curuaya* feast, E. Snethlage saw two posts carved with human faces similar to the *Shipaya* statues. It is not known whom they represented. The medicine man's hammock was hung between these posts, and behind them was the canoe with the fermented drink. In the *Curuaya* mythology there are two pairs of brothers, Wítontim and Áizau, whose parents are called Karu-pia and Imíriwon, and Kabi-sáu (kabi, "sky") and Zaizu-sáu (zaizu, "armadillo"). The significance of the so-called "karuara" (in the Lingua Geral), cotton tufts hanging from the ceiling in small vases or baskets, is not certain. Emilia Snethlage says that they contained pathogenic substances the medicine man, an important person in the village, extracted from the body of patients. In his house there was a room walled with bark and closed to visitors, in which he effected his cures. Snethlage assumes an astral cult, a supposition the writer was unable to confirm.

Nothing is known concerning animism or burial practices.

The *Shipaya* say that the *Tacunyapé* celebrated the dance of souls. The cape worn for the dance was of palm fiber, closed all around, with an opening for the head. The souls of the dead came from the forest to participate in the drinking, but did not sing or dance with the living.

Shipaya and *Yuruna* dead were interred inside the house, the hammocks of the closest relatives being hung near the burial. Later, the bones were removed, cleaned, and put away in a basket, which was hung under the ridge pole. The writer does not know what was finally done with them. The closest women relatives cut their hair as a sign of mourning.

BIBLIOGRAPHY

Adalbert von Preussen, 1849, 1857; Adam, 1896; Bettendorf, 1910; Brusque, 1863; Coudreau, H., 1897 c; Daniel, 1841; Ehrenreich, 1891 a, 1895, 1897 a; Fritz, 1922; Heriarte, 1874; Kletke, 1857; Krause, 1936 b; Laet 1899; Macedo Costa, 1875; Maciel Parente, 1874; Martius, 1867; Meyer (*see* Krause, 1936 b); Moraes, 1860; Moura, 1910; Nimuendajú, 1914 b, 1921–22, 1923–24, 1929 b, 1930 a, 1932 a, 1932 b, mss.; Snethlage, 1913, 1920–21; Snethlage and Koch-Grünberg, 1910; Steinen, 1886.

THE MAUE AND ARAPIUM

By Curt Nimuendajú

THE MAUE

INTRODUCTION

Territory.—The *Maué* territory, a region of solid land, was bounded by the lower Tapajóz, the Amazon, the bayou of Uraria, the bayou of Ramos, lat. 5° S., and long. 58° W. (map 1, *No. 1*; map 4). On the banks of the Tapajóz River and the bayous, the tribe lived only temporarily under the influence of civilized people.

Bettendorf (1910) does not mention the name *Maué,* but writes of *Andirá* and *Maraguá* in the region where the *Maué* are mentioned a little later. These two groups are probably local *Maué* subdivisions. The *Andirá* undoubtedly inhabited the Andirá River, which up to the present time is a *Maué* region.

History.—The Jesuits came into contact with these tribes after the Mission to the *Tupinambarana* was founded in 1669. In 1698, the *Andirá* welcomed P. João Valladão as a missionary. It is impossible to locate the *Maraguá* accurately, but they were on a lake between the Andirá and the Abacaxy Rivers, probably on the lower Mauhés-assú, which widens out to form a sort of lake. They had three villages, near one another (Bettendorf, 1910, p. 36). In 1692, after they had killed some White men, the Government declared "just war" against them, which was unsuccessful, as the Indians were forewarned and scattered, only a few offering any resistance. In 1696, the Jesuits took up residence among the *Maraguá,* 100 of whom were transferred in 1698 to the village of Guamá, near Belém. The *Maraguá* are not mentioned in the 18th century.

The *Mabué* (*Maué*) appear for the first time on P. Samuel Fritz's map (1691) of the Amazon, which places them just west of the Tapajóz, at lat. 3° 30' S., the present habitat of the *Maué.* The *Maraguá* were south of the Amazon, opposite the Trombetas River, and the *Andirá* on a water course which might have been the Ramos Bayou.

According to Father João de São José (1847, p. 101), in 1762 the *Mague* lived below the falls of the Tapajóz River, 4 leagues (about 11 miles) inland. The São José (Pinhel) and Santo Ignacio (Boim) Missions on the Tapajóz were settled with *Mague.* In 1762, the Indians of the latter mission killed the director of the village. When they also murdered some merchants, the governor, Ataida Teive, in 1869 forbade any commerce with them hoping to starve them into submission (Nunes Pereira, 1939). After the Brazilians and *Mundurucú* made peace, some of the latter joined some *Maué* in settling a little below the present city of

Mauhés, where Martius (1867) saw them in 1819. In 1832, another bloody conflict took the lives of some civilized men (Souza, A., 1870, p. 86). In 1823, the village of Itaituba was founded on the Tapajóz River with *Maué,* and in 1828 there were 400 of them settled there.

The *Andirá* mission flourished from 1848 to 1855 under Father Pedro de Ciriana, despite conflicts between the missionary and the Parintins authorities. In 1849, it had 507 *Maué;* in 1851, 570; and in 1852, 665, not counting a large number of civilized people. In 1855, the missionary's place was taken by a parish priest (Tenreiro Aranha, 1852, p. 32; Correa de Miranda, 1852, p. 128; Coelho, 1849, p. 784; Wilkens de Mattos, 1856, p. 128).

In 1862 there were 4 villages in the Tapajóz region with 3,657 *Maué* (Souza, A., 1870, p. 25). At the beginning of the 20th century, all but one of these villages on the tributaries of the Tapajóz were destroyed by the rubber gatherers of Itaituba, who took possession of the land. As a result, the *Maué* took sides openly with the Amazon forces in the armed conflict of 1916 between this State and Pará.

In 1939, Nunes Pereira (1939) estimated that there were 2,000 to 3,000 *Maué* in the Andirá region, a figure which may have been a little high.

An adequate study has not been made of the *Maué.* Martius did not live with them very long.

Reports on *Maué* character, based on direct observation, are generally favorable. Bates (1863) called them "invariably friendly to the Whites"; Katzer (1901) found them always friendly, unusually intelligent, quick to understand, and capable of clear expression. The present author regarded them as suspicious and inclined to lie though not to thieving, and as peace-loving and gay. Nunes Pereira (1939) found them skillful and peace-loving.

Language.—The *Maué* language is known through six vocabularies. (Coudreau, H., 1897 a; Katzer, 1901; Anonymous, ms. b; Nimuendajú, 1929 a, 1929 b; Koch Grünberg, 1932.) Fundamentally, it is *Tupí,* but differs from the *Guarani-Tupinamba.* The pronouns agree perfectly with the *Curuaya-Mundurucú,* and the grammar, insofar as the material permits analysis, is *Tupí.* The *Maué* vocabulary, however, contains an element that is completely foreign to *Tupí* but which cannot be traced to any other linguistic family. Since the 18th century, the *Maué* language has incorporated numerous words from the Lingua Geral.

Ethnographical sources.—Barboza Rodrigues (1882 b) visited the *Maué* in 1872, but his information lacks confirmation in some particulars. The present author made a brief visit in 1923 to the more civilized *Maué* on the Mariacuã River. The most recent and detailed information is that of Nunes Pereira in 1939.

CULTURE

SUBSISTENCE ACTIVITIES

Farming.—The *Maué* have always had remarkable interest in agriculture, but lost much of it with the development of the rubber industry. They grow manioc, potatoes, cara (*Dioscorea*), beans, and lima beans:

nowadays, they also cultivate rice and coffee, which they prepare and drink in the Brazilian manner. They still plant their old fruit trees, and they grow kitchen and medicinal herbs on platforms. They also cultivate a few Old World fruit trees. To plant root crops, they use a clean turtle skull to pull the earth over the cuttings, believing that this will increase production. At planting and harvesting times, the owner of a field organizes a feast to reward his helpers.

Hunting.—The *Maué* are good hunters, though hunting is not an important activity. Today many of them use fire arms, but in Martius' time, they would refuse any game killed with guns or with dogs, leading one to believe that originally dogs were as foreign to them as fire arms. Martius was informed that the *Maué* acquired blowguns and poisoned blowgun darts from their neighbors to the west, but this was not confirmed by any other author. Nunes Pereira mentions some practices believed to influence hunting: They pluck the breast and neck feathers of hunted fowl, burn them, and rub them on their guns; they wash their guns and dogs with an infusion from a marsh plant called "jasmin de lontra"; a gun will be lucky if a cipó snake is allowed to decompose inside the barrel, and it will be unlucky if it comes into contact with a pregnant or menstruating woman. The *Maué* do not use game traps or lures of any kind.

Fishing.—They take fish with weirs, a special single-headed arrow poisoning the water with a drug called timbó and, nowadays, fishhooks. That they do not eat the large river fish but utilize only the smaller fish of creeks and forest pools (Martius, 1867) supports the assumption that they have habitually avoided the large rivers.

Wild-food gathering.—Martius states that the Maué roamed the forest in search of palm fruits of various kinds, Brazil nuts, and piquí fruit. They eat winged female sauva ants, which they take at swarming time, roast, and pound with manioc flour. They also eat termites roasted in banana leaves. Spix and Martius (1823–31, 3:1,318) state that they introduced a slender stick into the anthill so that the insects took hold of it and were thus conveyed to the mouth. They also eat a species of batrachian.

VILLAGES AND HOUSES

According to Martius, the *Maué* lived in round single-family houses. Their recent settlements consist of one or more huts, which are usually rectangular with a gable roof and overhanging eaves but without walls. These are well thatched with leaves of the caraná palm. The kitchen is generally in a separate hut, where the manioc flour is made. Nunes Pereira mentions "rooms" in the *Maué* houses, and also a "dance house" and the "house of menstruating women."

The main pieces of furniture are wooden benches carved out of a solid block of wood. Cotton hammocks are twined, and the ends of the warp are attached to special cords (sobrepunhos), which extend beyond them to form loops, by which the hammock is suspended (Nimuendajú, ms.).

Nothing is known regarding aboriginal *Maué* dress. These Indians quickly adopted their present clothing from the Brazilians, although many still are naked from the waist up. They did not disfigure or tattoo themselves. Martius was told, however, that some persons pierced the lower lip and inserted a small piece of wood in it. No authors mention body painting.

The aboriginal *Maué,* a sedentary and agricultural people, lived inland from the rivers, and were not a canoeing people. São José states that "they usually do not know how to swim." Cerqueira e Silva (1833, p. 273) says that they will not ford the Curauahy River, preferring to take a great deal of trouble to make swinging bridges of vines. This may be explained by their aversion to water. Martius stated that they used canoes, some of the "ubá" type hollowed out of guananí logs and others made of jutahy bark. They are poor canoeists even today, but they have a few canoes which are either acquired direct from the civilized population or else, like their paddles, are rough imitations of those used by the Whites. On the other hand, they make long treks on foot, with the heavy basket (jamaxim) on their backs, showing admirable endurance.

Basketry.—From palm leaves and creepers, the *Maué* make baskets with and without lids, sieves, strainers, fans, carrying baskets, hats, and brooms. Some baskets with lids are made of red and black strips. These articles are generally sold to civilized people.

Pottery.—The only earthenware objects made today are pans to dry out the manioc flour; no reference to other types occurs in the literature. Scattered about in old dwellings in the *Maué* territory may be found plain black sherds.

Gourds and calabashes.—Gourd containers lack ornamentation, but calabashes sometimes are fire engraved on the green exterior.

Weapons.—The bow, flat on the belly and convex on the outside, is made of a red wood and has specially made points to hold the ambauva (*Cecropia* sp.) cord. Martius says *Maué* bows were a useful article of trade. The arrows have arched feathering. The points are of: (1) bamboo, rather small and lance-shaped; (2) bone, forming a barb; (3) iron, for hunting tapir; (4) wood, bilaterally serrated; and (5) for fishing, an iron nail forming a barbed point. The *Maué* also have little arrows for children, with a small crosspiece of sticks at the end. They have no arrows with wooden plugs and do not use pellet bows. There are no reports of clubs.

SOCIAL ORGANIZATION

According to Martius, the *Maué* were divided into "hordes"; he cites 12 of these, giving their names in the Lingua Geral. Some of them, however, may not belong to the *Maué* tribe.

According to Nunes Pereira, the *Maué* believe themselves to be descended from the animals or plants that lend their name to each "nation" (i.e., Martius' "hordes"). We have no details or confirmation on this score.

Families are patrilocal.

Maué chiefs enjoy remarkable authority even today, and there seems to be a hierarchy of officials. Succession is patrilinear. There used to be a special burial ceremony for chiefs.

Carefully preserved in the choir of the chapel of the Indian village of Terra Preta, Nunes Pereira found an article which resembles a club, but which the author calls a "magic paddle." It is made of dark wood, 45 inches (1.1 m.) long, 4 inches (11 cm.) greatest width, and 18 inches (45 cm.) thick, narrowing toward the end, which resembles a top. The larger half is ornamented on both sides with carved rhombs, points, and bands, one of which bears an ornament derived from a basketry motive. It was made by the third predecessor of the present chief and has been transmitted to each. The designs allegedly refer to the tradition of the tribe, but no explanation of them is given. The *Maué* call the object "porantin."

LIFE CYCLE

Pregnancy and childbirth.—During pregnancy, both parents are obliged to observe a strict diet of ants, fungi, and guaraná dissolved in water. To let their blood at this time, many cut their arms and legs with a rodent's tooth or a toucan's bill set into a handle, starting profuse hemorrhages. Into these wounds they rub the ashes of burned genipa fruit (Martius, 1867). To facilitate childbirth, the woman's hips are bathed beforehand in the ashes of paca skulls or of birds' eggshells mixed with water. After the birth, the parents' first food consists of fungi and two kinds of ants (sauva and maniuara). The mother has a postpartum rest period of a month, and the father goes on a diet of porridge (mingau) and guaraná. The first food taken after this period is inambú *Tinamus* sp.) flesh (Nunes Pereira, 1939).

Children are carried in a sling hung around the neck. It is made of raw fibers, the ends being tied with a black string. São José (1847) states that the *Maué* practiced infanticide and abortion. Before puberty, girls wear colored bands on their arms and below their knees.

Puberty.—At their first menstruation, girls retire to a hammock hung to the rooftree. They maintain a rigorous diet until the end of the second menstruation, taking only manioc cakes (beijú), fish, and water (Martius, 1867). Nunes Pereira states that they are fed fungi, which their parents bring them, and that, at the end of this period, they eat inambú and toucan flesh. The author fails to explain whether the "house of menstruating women" which he saw was used only for the first menstruation, or for all. In some Indian villages, the same author says, women retire to the "room of unmarried women" during menstruation.

All authors establish some relation between boys' puberty and the Celebration of Tucandira. The *Maué* told the present author that the application of tucanderas (stinging ants), though highly recommended at any time of life, is necessary in boyhood, especially if a youth were somewhat retarded in his physical development, and in old age, when strength began to fail, and in cases of weakness. Nunes Pereira was informed that boys of 6 and young men of 20 (?) were stung. The ceremony, however, has not been witnessed, except by Barboza Rodrigues, who was present for 2 days. His description lacks confirmation on some points. He states that it was celebrated annually in the main hut by convocation of the chief. Everybody brought drinks and barbecued meat. The ants, benumbed by having been left in water overnight, were caught in the mesh of a textile which was used to line a flattened or cylindrical "glove," artistically woven from strips of fibers and adorned with macaw and royal hawk feathers. Everybody gathered in the chief's yard, the women seated in a circle within the circle of men. The chief in the center held the "gloves." The singing began, and the chief shook his rattle (maracá) while the others played bambu flutes and drums. After blowing tobacco smoke on the ants, the chief put the glove on one of the young men, who danced, yelling and howling, inside the circle, amidst the applause of the crowd, until a woman or the chief took the glove off him. After this, everyone moved on to the nearest house and repeated the ceremony. According to Barboza Rodrigues (1882 b), a boy had to endure seven applications of ants, but their sequence, and the relation between them and marriage was not explained.

Martius reports that a cotton sleeve containing ants was first applied to boys between 8 and 10. When they began to cry and scream, the spectators drew them into a noisy dance, until they fell exhausted. Then their stings were treated by older women with the juice of the manioc leaf, and, as soon as they felt better, they had to try to draw their bows. This ceremony was repeated until the age of 14, when a boy could bear it without flinching and was considered ready to marry. According to

Martius (1867), the *Maué* counted their age by the number of applications, but the words, in the Lingua Geral, which he gives in this connection—jübir jepe, jübir mocoim, etc.—only mean "one turn, two turns," etc. (jebyr, "turn").

Marriage.—Today the *Maué* are monogamous, but formerly polygamy was permitted. There is no special marriage ceremony (Nunes Pereira, 1939). The candidate asks the girl's parents for their consent and it is given after long deliberation, even if she has not yet reached puberty. The couple settle in their own hut.

Married women are excluded from dances. All women are forbidden to have any contact with persons outside the tribe and to use the Portuguese language, a prohibition which is not always observed nowadays.

Death and burial.—Today the *Maué* bury in cemeteries, more or less in Christian fashion, but they still place the deceased's personal belongings in the grave. The family observes a fast (Nunes Pereira). Formerly, the dead were buried inside their house, in a sitting position. Martius states that at the death of a chief, the tribe was obliged to go on a diet of ants and guaraná for a month. During the first 2 weeks of this time, the chief's dead body, stretched out and tied to laths, was dried between fires; then it was buried, in a sitting position propped up with stones and sticks in a round hole. The hole was not filled with earth, and at the end of the month the body was taken out and exposed for a day. The whole tribe danced around the body, weeping so that their tears ran into their mouths and were swallowed. In the evening the body was buried in the same place and position, and the celebration continued all night with dancing and drinking. In one instance, when a chief died during a trip, his companions severed his body in two below the ribs, dried the halves, and brought them back to the village.

WARFARE

The *Maué*, though brave, were less warlike than the *Mundurucú*, with whom they warred until the second half of the 18th century. According to Barboza Rodriguez (1882 b), the *Maué* who took part in the last fight between the two tribes had lines of black tattooing on the thorax, similar to that of the *Mundurucú*. They sometimes took prisoners of war. They used the skulls of slain enemies as drinking vessels, and their long bones as flutes. Before fighting, they took guaraná (Martius, 1867).

ESTHETIC AND RECREATIONAL ACTIVITIES

Ornaments.—The *Maué* were formerly famous for articles made of feathers, which were important commodities in their trade. Martius mentions scepters and head and neck ornaments. The feather art has disappeared, with the exception of some feather ornaments on the instrument used during the Celebration of Tucandira. The *Maué* still wear necklaces of small figures carved out of the hard nut of certain palms

Musical instruments.—Drums are heavy cylinders of wood, with one end covered with leather. They are laid horizontally and played with the hands. The *Maué* also use violins and caracachas, which are serrated bambú cylinders scraped with a small stick.

Drinks and narcotics.—The *Maué* are very fond of a drink made from dried cakes of manioc flour (the arobá or paiauarú of Neo-Brazilians).

Since the *Maué* were first mentioned by Bettendorf (1910, p. 36), they have been famous for their cultivation and preparation of guaraná *(Paullinia sorbilis)*, of which they enjoyed the monopoly. The fruit is roasted in an oven, pounded in a mortar, and made into hard, cylindrical rolls. A little is grated off by means of a stone, and the powder is dissolved in water in a gourd. This drink is called capó. People in groups take it many times a day. The head of the house drinks it first and then it is passed from right to left among the others. The *Maué* believe that guaraná brings them luck in any transactions, that it gives joy, and that it is a stimulus to work, preventing fatigue and hunger.

In planting, the seeds are carefully chosen, as are later the young plants. A medicine man goes through a ceremony over the ground when it is ready for planting, and there are celebrations with dancing and drinking. Formerly, the *Maué,* enjoyed a considerable trade in guaraná, but by the end of the last century, it had decreased with the rise of the rubber industry, and today the greater part of the guaraná for commercial purposes is produced by Neo-Brazilians of the region.

The *Maué* explained to Nunes Pereira that guaraná constitutes a protection or charm for them: That it brings rain, protects their farms, cures certain diseases and prevents others, and brings success in war and in love, especially when there are two rivals for the affections of one woman. To the present author, they recommended it as well as parica for its magic effects against storms.

Parica, made from the seeds of *Mimosa acacioides,* is now little used. The seeds are roasted and finely pulverized in a carefully made, shallow basin of a red wood, and the powder is dried on a flat piece of wood "or of porcelain" (Spix und Martius, 1823–31, 3:1,318). The Indians use two long tubular bones to sniff the powder up into both nostrils simultaneously, or they rolled a piece of banana leaf into a tube (Ratzel, 1894, 1:509). There is a statement by Martius (1867, p. 411) which could be interpreted as meaning that the *Maué* also used parica as a clyster.

RELIGION

Today all *Maué* are baptized and have chapels in their villages with images of the saints, which they worship on their own account with litanies, imitating the Christian service in Latin. These services end in dancing and drinking. In these celebrations, they use musical instruments.

Regarding their former religion, Martius (Spix and Martius, 1823-31, 3:1,331) was informed that there were vestiges of a belief in a god and in the power of evil demons.

SHAMANISM

Nunes Pereira (1939) speaks of shamans of great reputation who carry out ceremonies designed to bring about an excellent harvest of guaraná. All guaraná plantations must be "blessed" by the shaman. Some shamans cure diseases; others are evil magicians who cause them. The *Maué* greatly fear sorcery, and attribute all deaths to witchcraft, even if the supposed spell was cast over a year previously. Their reluctance to take medicine furnished by civilized people is prompted by their fear of spells. All shamans work with an assistant. Today they take a strong manioc drink (tarobá) to stimulate them to action. Magic is exercised by the shaman, but everybody knows something about medicinal plants and animal products. Uaciri-pot, the chieftain and shaman, who probably lived in the first half of the last century, had the power of capturing the "mother of sickness" in the plaza by means of conjurations, magic gestures, and lines drawn upon the ground.

MYTHOLOGY

Two legends are recorded (Nunes Pereira, 1939). In the first, the true timbó (a fish drug) and the false timbó originated from the legs of a buried child who had been killed by a spell cast by the fish; water was invented by these same fish. In the second, guaraná originated from the eyes of a boy who was born of the contact of a girl with a little snake, and who was killed by his uncles. From the buried body, several animals were born. The boy was finally resurrected and became the first *Maué*.

THE ARAPIUM

In the 17th and 18th centuries there lived to the west of the lower Tapajóz, a tribe of Indians called *Arapium* (Fritz, 1691, (see Volume 1, map 7) *Arapiyú*), lat. 2° 30′ S., long. 55° 30′ W., which the Jesuits gathered at the beginning of the 18th century in the Cumarú Mission (Villa Franca) at the mouth of the Arapiuns River. Both Martius (1867) and Métraux (1928 a) considered them to be the same as the *Maué*. The only ethnological data regarding them are the following, from João Daniel (1841, pp. 168-71, 478), who saw them:

Girls undergoing their first menstrual period were secluded and made to fast. After the fast, the girl was bled from head to foot with a cutia tooth. She then negotiated a marriage with the first young man she saw.

Before marrying, a young man had to place his arms in long gourds full of sauva ants (*Atta* sp.) to show his courage. A drinking feast concluded the ceremonies.

A dead man's flesh was eaten by his relatives. Old women pulverized his bones and mixed them in drinks.

The *Arapium* held celebrations in honor of the new moon. They went out when it first appeared and stretched out their arms, hands, and fingers, as if asking for health and strength.

Of these cultural features, only the girls' menstrual seclusion and fasting and the young man's ant ordeal are found also among the *Maué*. The others differ from *Maué* customs, proving that the *Arapium* were most likely an offshoot of the *Tapajó* tribe. The present author, exploring the Arapiuns River in 1924, found many old Indian dwelling places where the pottery, with its plastic ornamentation, was very different from that found in the region of the *Maué*, being much more similar to that of the *Tapajó*. After 1762, when the *Arapium* were last mentioned as living in Obidos and on the Arapiuns River, there is no further information regarding them.

BIBLIOGRAPHY

Almeida Serra, 1869 (1779) ; ms. b; Barboza Rodrigues, 1882 b; Bates, 1863; Bettendorf, 1910; Cerqueira e Silva, 1833; Coelho, 1849; Correa de Miranda, 1852; Coudreau, H., 1897 a; Daniel, 1841; Florence, 1841(?) [1825–29]; Fritz, 1691; Furtado, 1858; Katzer, 1901; Koch-Grünberg, 1932; Martius, 1867; Métraux, 1928 a; Monteiro Baena, 1843; Nimuendajú, 1929 a, 1929 b; ms.; Nunes Pereira, 1939; Ratzel, 1894; Ribeiro de Sampaio, 1825; São José, 1847; Souza, A., 1870; Souza, C., 1874; Souza Franco, 1842; Spix und Martius, 1823–31; Tenreiro Aranha, 1852; Wilkens de Mattos, 1856.

THE MURA AND PIRAHA

By Curt Nimuendajú

THE MURA

TRIBAL LOCATION AND HISTORY

From the beginning, these Indians have been known as *Mura* (pro·nounced *Murá* by their neighbors, the *Torá* and *Matanawí* of the Madeira River). Their name for themselves, however, according to Barboza Rodrigues (1892 b, p. 38), is *Buhuraen,* and according to Father Tastevin (1923 a), *Buxwaray* or *Buxwarahay.* In the author's vocabularies. the following forms are given as self-designations: *Bohŭra* (Manicoré River); *Bhŭrai-ada,* meaning "Mura language" (Manicoré River), and *Bohurai; Bohuarai-arasé,* "*Mura* language"; *Nahi buxwara araha,* meaning "that one is *Mura*"; *Yane abahi araha buxwarái,* "we are all Mura."

The *Mura* were first mentioned in 1714 in a letter by P. Bartholomeu Rodrigues (*in* Serafim Leite, 1943), who located them on the right bank of the Madeira River, between the *Tora* and the *Unicoré,* between lat. 6° and 7° 40′ S. They were hostile toward the Jesuit mission founded in 1723 or somewhat later above the mouth of the Jamary River, and, because of this hostility, the mission was transferred farther down the river in 1742. Their unfriendly attitude was the result of a treacherous act committed by a Portuguese trader who had kidnapped some of the *Mura* and sold them as slaves.

For over 100 years, beginning in the early 18th century, the *Mura* were a terrible scourge. The first expedition up the Madeira River into Mato Grosso, under the leadership of Major João de Souza, had bloody encounters with the *Mura* and threw the Indians back with great losses. The *Mura* then avoided open battle and resorted to ambush for which they became famous.

In 1749, when João Gonçalves da Fonseca's expedition had several encounters with them, the *Mura* were established on a lake on the right bank of the Madeira River, opposite the "mouth of the Autaz" (Madeirinha, a little above Borba). By 1768 they had passed to the region north of the Solimões (Cudajaz) River, but before this date they had extended to the lower Purús (Moraes, 1860, p. 535). Upstream, however, they did not go beyond the mouth of the Jamary River.

It seems, therefore, that the original habitat of the *Mura* was on the Madeira River, below the falls and near the mouth of the Jamary River; and that, after they had become a warrior tribe and were aware of the effectiveness of their tactics, they spread out downstream on the Madeira River and as far as the Purús River, and from the latter as far as the Cudajaz River, which is almost opposite (lat. 3°–7° S., long. 50°–63° W.; map 1, *No. 1*; map 4). Evidently this expansion was not a move to draw away from the *Mundurucú* invasion, who at that time, 1768, were merely mentioned on the Maués River. The expansion of the *Mura* was facilitated by the fact that they found the country only sparcely inhabited; the numerous old sedentary tribes had succumbed to the "avenging troops" and to the mission system. Their weak remnants, lacking any initiative and pride against servitude, and concentrated in a few villages, did not have the power to resist the attacks of savages conscious of their superiority as warriors. It seems that the Autaz region from then on began to be the center of the *Mura*, and it remains so today. That the *Mura* had been preceded in the Autaz by other tribes of higher culture is proved by the archeological remains found there by Tastevin (1923 a) and the present author. These include a great number of hardwood fishweirs, anthropomorphic urns of the Miracanguéra type, jade objects, etc.

About 1774, the warlike expansion of the *Mura* had reached its climax, and the desperate Neo-Brazilians demanded their extermination as the only means for avoiding the complete downfall of Amazonas (Ribeiro de Sampaio, 1825). At this time, Ribeiro de Sampaio mentions the *Mura* in the following places: Silves, Madeira River (Borba), Autaz, Uaquirí (?), Manacapurú, Purés River, Cudajaz, Mamiá, Coary River, Catuá, Caiamé River, Teffé River, Capucá, Yauató, Fonte Boa, Japura River, Amaná, Manaus, Jahú River, Uinini River, and Carvoeiro. Other authors add Obidos, Moura, Barcellos, Nogueira, Alvarães, Maripí, Ayrão, Poiares, and Abacaxys. The *Mura* were attacked in these places every year by Government forces. These punitive expeditions, in spite of the resulting bloodshed, were not effective, and the *Mura* continued to show their animosity. In 1784, however, the *Mura* unexpectedly made peace with the Whites. In July, five *Mura* appeared peacefully in Santo Antonio de Maripi, on the lower Japurá River and were followed later by many more. Other *Mura* presented themselves in Teffe, Alvarães, and Borba. In the latter place, where in 1775 an Army outpost had been created for the protection of the residents and travelers against their hostilities, their number grew in 3 years to more than 1,000. 1786, the *Mura* of the Cudajaz came to terms, and by the end of the same year the whole tribe had made peace and started to settle down in permanent villages.

The reason for their peace overtures was, perhaps, the gradual weakening of the tribe by epidemics, by the adoption of foreign elements, and, particularly, by the relentless war that the *Mundurucú* waged against them. The latter, crossing from the Madeira River westward, butchered the *Mura* in Autaz without, however, dislodging them permanently from a single one of the many places that they had occupied. Even after the pacification, the *Mura*, according to Martius, spread farther out upstream on the Solimões to beyond the Tabatinga frontier. The latest establishments, about which there is some information, were on the Jandiatuba River, a little below São Paul de Olivença and in the region of the lower Amazon in Mura-tapera, now called Oriximiná, on the Trombetas River, some 35 km. (22 miles) above the mouth.

In the beginning of the 19th century, relations with the Whites seemed to have been generally good; at least Canon André Fernandes de Souza, who mentions them at that time, does not speak of recent hostilities. According to him, the *Mura* were the only natives respected by the civilized people. Later, however, the *Mura* resumed their hostilities on the Madeira River.

During the "Cabanagem," a revolt that evolved into a general uprising of the Indian, Negro, and Mestizo servants against their White masters, the rebels won the adherence of the *Mura* who, together with them, robbed, killed, and burned. Together with the rebels, they were defeated and massacred, 1834–36. Friction between the *Mura* of the Madeira and the civilized people continued for a long time after the revolt. The report by Governor Tenreiro Aranha in 1852 contains many complaints against members of this tribe, who committed horrible crimes against defenseless people. The governor sent reinforcements to the military outpost in Mataurá, commissioned a well-armed river patrol, and appropriated the amount of 1,308 milreis for mission work. None of these missions (São Pedro, Crato, Manicoré) lasted long. The last acts of hostilities on record on the Madeira refer to the killing of a soldier and two slaves of the Crato missionary by the *Mura* of the Capanã in 1855. Later, the *Mura* gathered on Onças Island for the purpose of attacking travelers.

The author of "Illustração" (Anonymous, ms. a) estimated the number of *Mura* at 60,000 at the time of the pacification. This number is no doubt too high, as is 30,000 to 40,000 given by Martius in 1820 (Spix and Martius, 1823–31, vol. 3). Estimates based on the report of Albuquerque Lacerda showed that the *Mura* did not exceed 3,000 in 1864. In 1926, the present author counted 1,390 inhabitants occupying 26 *Mura* huts on the Madeira, Autaz, and Urubú Rivers. The total number might have been 1,600.

The *Mura* never expanded very much on land. Even during the time of their greatest extension, they always sought the low floodlands of the shores of the Amazon-Solimões River and its tributaries, and similar lands on the Rio Negro and Japurá, Solimões, Madeira, Purús, and Amazon Rivers. They settled only where they could move about in canoes, choosing spots where they could build their villages, plant their crops, and hunt. Throughout their known history, they can be characterized as a canoeing and fishing people.

The *Mura* are today so much crossed with Neo-Brazilians that it is impossible to determine their original physical type. Truly Negroid types, however, are rare. In the area of Yuma Lake, the author found, in 1926, a relatively large percentage of individuals of Indian type, characterized by an arched nose and receding chin. When the *Mura* made peace in 1784, they had already absorbed many foreign ethnic elements from people who had sought refuge among them or who had been captured by them. Large groups of other tribes, such as the *Jumana* and *Iruri*, were with the *Mura* at that time. The *Jumana* belonged to the *Arawakan* family, and both the *Jumana* and *Iruri* had a more advanced culture than the *Mura*. We do not know the influence of these foreign elements on *Mura* culture.

LANGUAGE

After their pacification, the *Mura* began to adopt the Lingua Geral, but at the time of Martius' trip, this language was little used. In 1850 they could speak it, but used the *Mura* language among themselves. Later they substituted Portuguese for the Lingua Geral, and now the majority of the groups use Portuguese. Some groups still speak the Lingua Geral among themselves, but only occasional individuals know the *Mura* language. In many groups it has disappeared completely.

Martius' contention that most of the words of the *Mura* language are of *Tupian* origin has remained unsubstantiated. Even the number of elements adopted from the Lingua Geral is strangely small. Most noticeable are the regular use of the first and second singular, personal pronouns, and first person plural of Lingua Geral.

According to most linguists (Ehrenreich, Chamberlain, Rivet, Loukotka), the *Mura* language is isolated. The fact mentioned by the present author that the *Matanawi* language has a scant half-dozen words in common with the *Mura* does not mean that the two languages should be considered, as by Rivet (1924, p. 673) and Loukotka (1939, p. 154), as members of the same family. Only the following vocabularies have been published: Martius (1867, 2:20), Nimuendajú and Valle Bentes (1923), and Nimuendajú (1925, 1932 b).

CULTURE

SUBSISTENCE ACTIVITIES

Farming.—The *Mura* practiced farming before their pacification, but only on a small scale. According to Fonseca Coutinho (1873), they had large manioc and maize fields on the Autaz River. Moreover, A. F. de Souza (1870) mentions mandioca plantations of the *Mura* on the Matupiry, a tributary of the Madeira River, at the beginning of the 19th century. The author of "Observações addicionais" (Anonymous, ms. a, pt. 2) says that they did not plant anything, but looted the crops of others to make a fine manioc flour. This, however, presupposes that they already had pans, sieves, and tipití baskets. This, together with the Jará ceremony (see below), suggests that they were acquainted with manioc and its preparation. Very likely at war time they found it more convenient to steal tubers than to plant them.

Hunting and fishing.—The gathering of wild fruit was also important in their economy, but above all the *Mura* were fishermen. Their skill was admired not only by the civilized people but by their Indian neighbors, such as the *Catawishi*, who were also fishermen. The *Mura* caught turtles under water by hand, and after harpooning pirarucú *(Arapaima gigas)* and manatee, they pursued them between obstacles of aquatic plants and fallen trees. The importance of the harpoon here suggests that they had been acquainted with this weapon for a long time. In order to bring a dead manatee aboard their canoes, they swamped the craft so as to push it under the floating animal and then floated it again by emptying it.

They knew the use of the babracot, but preferred to roast their meat buried in the ashes or on a spit.

HOUSES AND VILLAGES

The *Mura* build their houses in small groups of two to five, which sometimes are scattered far apart along the shore of a lake or river. They rarely live in isolated huts. According to Tastevin (1923 a), five or six families live in a hut, but the author noted that this occurs only in exceptional cases, each family usually having its own hut. These houses are not as poorly made as it has often been stated, and many of them do not differ from the huts of the poorer Neo-Brazilians of the region. The area surrounding the houses is not generally kept clean.

Judging from a drawing in Martius' Atlas, the original *Mura* hut seems to have been dome-shaped, with the rafters reaching to the ground and thatched with vertical palm leaves.

The anonymous author of "Observações addicionais" (Anon., ms. a, pt. 2) states that as a rule their real home is their canoe, and the present writer noticed in 1926 that the *Mura* of the Juma River slept on a platform in the canoe.

It seems probable that formerly the *Mura* slept on platforms such as those described by Father Tastevin (1923) and not in hammocks.

The early writers report that the *Mura* hammocks consisted only of three cords, a central one to support the weight of the body and lateral ones to maintain the equilibrium. This is obviously a satire of their indolence. Other information is more plausible. Ferreira states that in 1875 their sleeping hammocks were made of fibers of inner tree bark. Alfred R. Wallace (1853) says that they were made of three strips of embira, and Martius that they were made of a piece of bark (innerbark) shaped like a canoe. Bates (1863, p. 305) describes a *Mura* hammock as a "rudely woven web of ragged strips of the inner bark of the mongúba tree" (*Bombax* sp.). Later it seems that the *Mura* imitated the hammocks of neighboring tribes and of the Neo-Brazilians. Father W. Schmidt (1913) mentions a tucum hammock of the *Mura* in the Museum of Vienna, and the author saw two hammocks on the Juma River made of jauary (*Astrocaryum* sp.) fibers.

DRESS AND ORNAMENTS

Both sexes were completely naked, although one of Cavina's water colors (Ferreira, n. d., pl. 3[1]) shows an apron of twisted embira or burity fibers which is suspended from a belt and the upper part of which appears braided; the upper border is ornamented with a band of white zigzags over a red background. The ears and septum were pierced and pieces of cane passed through the holes. The upper lip was perforatd above the corners of the mouth, while the lower lip was perforated in the center. In these holes the *Mura* inserted animal teeth or wooden pegs. According to Ferreira, the lip ornaments are of stone found in pirarucú brains; in the paintings, they are small, whitish, and somewhat three-lobed. They wore their hair trimmed along the forehead at the level of the eyebrows and long behind. It was usually disheveled.

They painted themselves with urucú and with a black pigment. Sometime they smeared themselves with mud as a protection against insects.

---

[1] Ferreira, who was a member of the first expedition to encounter the *Mura*, described this plate as follows: "Um dos gentios Muras que pelo meiado do mez de Novembro do anno proximo passado de 1786 aportaram no logar de Ayrão."

Mura canoes were formerly made of tree bark and were 6.6 m. (about 22 ft.) long, 1.1 m. (3.25 ft.) wide, and 44 cm. (17 in.) deep. The ends were tied up with creepers. These craft carried four or five people. The original type of paddle is unknown. When not in use, the canoes were kept submerged so as to be hidden from any enemy and so that they would not dry up and crack. The fire-hollowed dugout, at first stolen from the Neo-Brazilians and later made by themselves, finally replaced bark canoes.

MANUFACTURES

Mats and basketry.—The *Mura* used large mats on their beds and in their canoes, and smaller ones to sit on. Carrying baskets were made of two interwoven palm leaves.

Pottery and gourds.—According to Martius, the *Mura* had pottery, but he does not say if they made it. The present writer has never seen any ware made by them. He did, however, see gourds which had been dyed black on the inside and crudely carved on the outside.

Weapons.—The only weapon was the bow and arrow. The bow measured 2.7 m. (9 feet) according to João Daniel (1841, p. 168) and 2 m. (6 feet) according to Southey (1862, 6:248–249). The back is strongly convex, the belly only moderately so. W. Schmidt (1913) describes the feathering as radial and cemented. Fishing arrows lacked feathering. War arrows were formerly tipped with lanceolate bamboo heads 33 cm. (13 in.) long and 10 cm. (4 in.) wide, with two large barbs on each side. Now they have iron heads. The author found arrows made of a single piece of paxiuba on Lake Sampaio. An arrow figured by Therese von Bayern (1897, pl. 2, fig. 4) has arched feathering and is tipped with a rod notched along the side. The *Mura* in Covina's picture is armed with two arrows, each with a broad wooden point that has four or five pairs of barbs, and, protruding beyond this point, another lanceolate point of bamboo.

SOCIAL AND POLITICAL ORGANIZATION

When the *Mura* made peace in 1786, they were divided into many groups, each numbering 45 to 150 persons and having its own chief. The 26 groups visited and counted by the author in 1926 averaged 53 persons and ranged from 15 to 120. Chieftainship was formerly hereditary, but carried little authority. According to the author of "Illustração," (Anonymous, ms. a) the *Mura* rendered to the chief "respect and obedience as to a father." A tuft of yellow and black feathers tied to the forehead might have been a distinctive chief's ornament (Martius, 1867). After the pacification, the principal chief of the *Mura* lived at Amatary, on the left bank of the Amazon, somewhat above the mouth of the Madeira River.

Each family head had his private fishing ground which he would defend against any poacher. In quarrels over fishing groups, disputants fought each other with the clubs, which a *Mura* always carried in his canoe to stun the fish after they are caught.

LIFE CYCLE

Pregnancy and childbirth.—During a woman's pregnancy there are no restrictions on her husband. Formerly, during childbirth, the woman would sit on a "log of a certain wood burned all over its surface as charcoal." Such logs were carried in the canoe, so that a trip might not be interrupted by childbirth ("Observações addicionais," Anonymous, ms. a, pt. 2). After childbirth, the father stays at home. He fasts for 5 days and the mother for a longer period. The size of the fish which the father may eat increases as the baby grows. Until the child can walk, the father may not hunt and eat his kill lest during his absence the boto (*Sotalia brasiliensis*) and the jaguar come invisibly and take revenge by killing the child. The author learned that if the father were to hunt a caiman, boto, otter, or anhima (*Anhima cornuta*) before the child could walk, these animals would steal the child's shadow. Herndon and Gibbons (1853–54, vol. 1.) mention cases of infanticide, but the present writer was impressed by the kind treatment of children.

Puberty.—From the beginning of the first menstruation until the end of the second menstruation, the girl is confined in a corner of the hut where she lies in her hammock.

The passage from childhood to adulthood was marked by a ceremony in which boys were permitted for the first time to take parica snuff. (See p. 263.) The boy was also flagellated (p. 264).

Marriage.—The aboriginal *Mura* had only one wife "whom they loved with tenderness and guarded with savage jealousy" ("Observações addicionais", Anonymous, ms. a, pt. 2; see also Spix and Martius, 1823–31, vol. 3). It seems that the *Mura* later became polygynous. Spix and Martius (1823–31, vol. 3) and Wallace (1889) stated that every man had two or three wives, who were kept in abject servitude. They were acquired as prizes in boxing matches between the girl's suitors, which were fought as soon as she had reached puberty. In earlier times, murder of wife stealers was sanctioned; later, such offenders were less severely punished.

Present-day *Mura* still feel honored if a person whom they esteem courts an unmarried daughter, and they allow the girls of the tribe a great deal of liberty. Today a request for marriage is made by the young man to the girl's parents, who sometimes demand of him some service. The marriage is concluded without any formality and, according to Tastevin, is easily dissolved. Marital fidelity is not strictly observed.

Funeral rites.—Formerly, a person was buried with all his possessions wherever he happened to die. At the beginning of the present century, the *Mura* of Murutinga (Autaz) still erected a small hut over the tomb, even in Christian cemeteries, and placed food, drink, and the weapons of the deceased on the grave. The mangoes which grew in the cemetery were reserved for the dead.

WARFARE

For half a century the *Mura* waged unceasing war against the civilized Indians and the Neo-Brazilians. According to Martius, they declared war against occasional enemies by planting arrows, head upward, in the ground in the territory of the rival tribe. Attacks were made silently. They ambushed canoes near rapids where travelers were forced to draw near the shore, watching the approach of their victims from the tops of sumaúma trees (*Ceiba pentandra*). They also ambushed enemies on the paths leading to the plantations. In the onslaught, they did not pay any attention to age or sex. They mutilated the bodies, but did not bring home any trophies, and they have never been seriously accused of cannibalism. According to Ribeiro de Sampaio (1825), they took prisoners to enslave them, but it is more likely that they incorporated them in the tribe. At the time of the pacification, the most important *Mura* chief was a civilized Indian, who had been captured as a child and reared by Whites. His mother, also a captive, acted as an interpreter during the peace negotiations.

By the end of the 18th century, the *Mura's* most feared enemies were the *Mundurucú*, who had come from the region of the Tapajóz River, sailed down the Canumã and Abacaxys Rivers, and established themselves on the Madeira River at Tobocal near the mouth of the Aripuanã River. It is probable that the *Mura's* defeat by the *Mundurucú* contributed greatly to their pacification. According to Martius, the *Mura* feared the *Mundurucú* so much that they did not even resist when the latter came for their women.

ESTHETIC AND RECREATIONAL ACTIVITIES

Musical instruments.—The *Mura* used a kind of clarinet, commonly called toré, made of a thick bamboo, and a five-hole bamboo flute. The latter was used for transmitting messages about a great variety of matters (Marcoy, 1866, and Anonymous, ms. a).

Dances and songs.—The dance witnessed by Martius was an imitation of the Neo-Brazilian dance, and the songs which accompanied it were in the Lingua Geral. The dances in vogue in Tastevin's time (1923 a) are identical to those of the *Mura's* civilized neighbors. Southey (1862, 6:348), however, speaks of an original dance in which the Indians were arranged in two lines. Those of one line were armed with bows and arrows; the Indians of the other line were painted, and blew on long bamboo flutes. A man led the dance with grotesque gestures. In 1926, the *Mura* of the Juma River performed a nocturnal circle dance accompanied by the toré clarinet, and by songs about the sloth (*Bradypus* sp.) After the dance, the men gathered on one side of the ring and women on the other to bleed each other with sharp pirarucú and tambaquí fishbones.

Narcotics.—Parica, made from the roasted seeds of the parica tree (*Mimosa acacioides*), is the most powerful narcotic used by the *Mura*. It was taken either as a snuff or as an enema. As a snuff, it was blown into the nostrils by means of a tube 1 foot (31 cm.) long made of tapir bone or a bird's leg bone. The powder was kept in a large bamboo tube and the doses measured out with an caiman tooth. It caused a general state of excitement and exaltation with auditory hallucinations, and a condition of feverish activity which ended with prostration or unconsciousness. According to Martius, individuals who were over-excited by the narcotic and suffocated died on the spot. "Observações addicionais" states that on the morning following a narcotic spree, the bodies of persons were often found shot with arrows or stabbed with knives. These murders were not considered as crimes and were blamed on the parica.

Parica taken as an enema by means of a rubber syringe had a similar but weaker effect. The participants in groups of ten sat in circles while old women held a vase containing the liquid and passed the syringe from hand to hand. To increase the effect, the enema was accompanied by singing, "Hé! Hé!" (Marcoy, 1866). The drunken men danced and threatened each other with weapons, which the women always tried to remove from the parica house. Present-day *Mura* still snuff parica but take less of it than before. A bamboo tube is used for the purpose (Nunes Pereira, personal communication).

The ancient *Mura* prepared manioc chicha. Today they have acquired two dangerous vices which have contributed to their moral and physical degradation: rum, from the White; and liamba (hashish), from the Negroes (Tastevin, 1923 a, p. 517). A large part of the payment which they receive for their services is rum and liamba, in exchange for which they are willing to surrender to the Neo-Brazilians their last bit of food. Then they spend day after day in a state of torpor, unable to work.

RELIGION

Little is known about *Mura* religion with the exception of a few ceremonies and magico-religious practices. Today the tribe is Christian, but its adherence to the Church lies only in the knowledge of a few saints, the ceremony of baptism, and the celebration of some feasts.

The Parica feast.—Martius denies that parica was taken at puberty initiations and links it instead to the ripening of the parica seeds. Marcoy (1866) says that anyone who had parica would invite others to the parica house, an open shelter built for the purpose and forbidden to women. The great parica feast was preceded by a hunt which lasted one week. The feast began with flagellation, after which came libations of a non-alcoholic beverage made with the fruit of the acahy palm. Then parica was taken, first in the form of snuff and afterward as an enema. The feast ended with a dance which lasted 24 hours. Marcoy's description of the feast contains obvious inaccuracies.

Martius gives second-hand information about this ceremony. The feast was celebrated every year and lasted for 8 days. It began with the drinking of cauim and other intoxicants. Then pairs of men flagellated each other with a long leather thong of tapir and manatee hide. This continued for several days. Afterward the partners kneeled in front of each other and blew parica powder into each other's nostrils by means of a tapir bone tube. (See Martius, 1867, fig. 63.)

Punishment rites.—The flagellation rite was also practiced during the full moon, its purpose being to increase one's strength. One man would hold the victim with his arms outstretched while the old man who performed the flagellations in the puberty ceremonies would whip him with a few lashings on the arms and legs.

After burning the brush for planting, the *Mura* performed a flagellation ceremony in order to increase the output of manioc. They brought in a pile of whips made of jará palm (*Leopoldina pulchra*), and the men surrounded the houses, seizing all the grown children, whose parents could not interfere. Each was held by two men, and forced to lean forward. A very old man sang, danced, and finally whipped the children's backs with the jará whips.

In order to make young boys successful in fishing, the *Mura* take them to a tucandeira ant's nest and force them to expose a hand to the sting of the ants.

Shamanism.—In Wallace's time, 1850, *Mura* shamans were highly regarded as men of great ability. They were feared and their services were always well paid. The shamans observed by Tastevin and the present author are faithful counterparts of the Neo-Brazilian shamans of that region, and have no aboriginal features.

Ornaments and preparations with magic power have been reported among the Juma River *Mura*. A caraipérana (Rosaceae) seed necklace offers protection against grippe and headaches. A necklace made of "tears of Our Lady" wards off eye disease. Painting the face with urucú protects against chickenpox. Juparana leaves were used against malaria. According to Spix and Martius (1823–31, vol. 3), the *Mura* used a monkey penis as a charm against fever.

MYTHOLOGY

Some fragments of *Mura* cosmogony have been collected by Father Tastevin (1923 a) and the author. Heaven is a world, somewhat like the earth, where souls live and die and where the fearsome thunder resides. There is also a nether world, which is an aquatic region. The moon is female during 14 days, when women have greater vigor, and male during a like period, when men are especially strong.

The waters of the earth are connected to those of heaven; when there is a flood on the earth, the waters ebb in heaven, and vice versa.

The coal sack near the Southern Cross is a manatee carrying on its back a fisherman (Alpha and Beta Crucis of the Southern Cross), whose canoe was upset by the fish, while his companion (Alpha and Beta of Centaurus) is getting ready to throw the harpoon. The lightest part of the Milky Way is foam worked up by the manatee in the water.

The origin of the rainbow is explained as follows: A woman carried in her womb two snakes that would climb trees, bring her fruits, and return into her. Her husband killed them, and they went up to the sky, where they became the upper and lower rainbows. The rainbow is also conceived as the mouth of a large snake through which souls enter heaven. So as to obtain free passage, a coin is placed in the mouth of the deceased. If the latter is very poor, a fig is used instead. The master of the rainbow snake is called kaái tuhúi.

The following are some *Mura* myths:

The flood.—Men escaped the rising flood in canoes and found a high rock, where they gathered, subsisting on the animals which also had taken refuge there. After the deluge had passed, they could not find their way home until a shaman took them there.

The great fire.—There was once a world conflagration, from which only one family escaped. The man had dug a deep cave, provided it with 30 pitchers of water, and erected a house of wood and straw inside it. He closed the entrance with stone. The fire passed above the cave, and it was intensely hot in the pit. Two weeks later, the stone was still hot, and the family did not emerge until the stone was cool enough to move. The earth was deserted and had no water or plants. The man built a hut, but he worried because only 10 pitchers of water remained. Then the Holy Ghost came with drums and flags, and the Indian obtained water from him. He got fish from Saint Anthony, palm trees from Saint John, and manioc from Saint Peter. The last ordered him to lie down on his back and when he turned around he saw that the manioc had already grown a foot. On the left bank of the Amazon near Manaos the dry and stunned vegetation bears witness to the great fire.

The prisoners of the pigs.—A newly married man went pig hunting. When he killed a sow, the aroused animals forced him to climb a tree. They dug up the roots of the tree, and when it fell they carried him away.

The pig's mother, a small red animal, kept him with her. When they went past uixu, burity, and biribá trees they asked him whether he ate these fruits, and he answered that he did. The pigs then assumed a human shape. He had to sleep among them. When he arose, they did the same and grunted and sniffed. After 2 months, he managed to escape by climbing a tree and jumping from branch to branch. He carried away the pig's flute. After he had returned home, he invited his wife, his brother, and brother-in-law to hunt pigs. While they remained in the canoe, he blew twice on his flute. Soon a large herd of pigs came running toward him, and he killed as many as he wanted. His other brother returned from a trip and inquired how he obtained so many pigs. Then the brother took the flute and, saying that the other was a fool for having allowed the pigs to take him prisoner, he went ashore, blowing the flute. The pigs killed him and took the flute back.

THE PIRAHÁ

TRIBAL LOCATION, HISTORY, AND LANGUAGE

The *Pirahá* (*Pirianaus, Piaarhaus, Piraheus, Piriahaí, Piriaha, Piriahã, Pinyaha, Iviridyarohú,* "lords of fiber rope," i.e., armbands, *Ivirapa-pokú,* "long bow," and *Tapii,* "strangers") is a subtribe of the *Mura,* which speaks a distinct dialect. It has evidently always occupied its present habitat between lat. 6°25′ and 7°10′ S., along the lower Maicy River and at Estirão Grande do Marmellos, below this river's mouth.

The *Pirahá* have remained the least acculturated *Mura* tribe, but they are known only through a short word list and unpublished notes obtained by the author during several brief contacts in 1922, when efforts were being made to pacify the *Parintintin.*

The dialects of the *Pirahá* and *Mura* of Manicoré are mutually intelligible, and differences in these dialects appearing in the author's vocabulary may be partly attributable to informant difficulties. In a few instances, the *Mura* "r" becomes "g" in the *Pirahá* dialect.

The *Pirahá* are mentioned by Ferreira Penna (1853) in 1853, by Orton (1875, p. 470) in 1873, and by Barboza Rodrigues (1892 b) in 1885, the last describing them as the fiercest of all the *Mura.*

In 1923, they numbered around 90. In 1921, the "Serviço de Protecção aos Indios" established a center to give them aid but, apparently content with their present state, these Indians have shown little inclination to acquire European culture. Except for a few implements, they show almost no sign of any permanent contact with civilized people. They showed no interest in the utensils and clothing given them by the Serviço de Protecção aos Indios. Neither did they steal. In fact, no two tribes offer a more striking contrast than the *Pirahá* and their neighbors, the

Parintintin. The latter were active, clever, greedy for new things, ambitious, and thieving.

In general, the author found the *Pirahá* dull and unresponsive. Their sullenness made field research among them difficult. Their indifference and aloofness is probably more apparent than real, and seems to stem from their deep resentment at seeing their old enemies, the *Parintintin,* being favored by the governmental authorities, whereas they, who had never been hostile to the Neo-Brazilians, were treated with much less regard.

The vocabulary collected among them never exceeded 71 words. The *Pirahá* appeared to be completely indifferent as linguistic informants. In spite of several decades of contact with Neo-Brazilians, their knowledge of Portuguese and of the Lingua Geral never exceeded a dozen words.

THE YAHAHI

Barboza Rodrigues (1892 b) divides the *Mura* into *Pirahens (Pirahá), Burahens,* and the *Jahaahens (Yahahi),* giving for the location of the last the Solimões River. The *Torá* and *Maranawí,* who inhabit the lower Marmellos, call the *Yahahi* a subtribe of the *Mura,* which they say used to live on the Branco River, a tributary of the right bank of the upper Marmellos. The last survivors of the *Yahahi* joined the *Pirahá.*

CULTURE

SUBSISTENCE ACTIVITIES

The *Pirahá* grew maize, sweet manioc (macaxera), a kind of yellow squash (jurumúm), watermelon, and cotton. They were also excellent hunters and fishermen. The only aboriginal fishing technique observed among them was shooting fish with an arrow; however, they used fishhooks obtained from civilized people. They ate Brazil nuts and wild fruit, and they liked honey mixed with water. They did not drink rum.

DWELLINGS

The dwellings of the *Pirahá* were rudimentary and badly constructed. Some were merely a poorly thatched roof covering a rude platform which served as a floor. As the huts were built on the beach slopes, the downhill ends of the flooring poles rested on a horizontal pole supported on two forked posts, while the uphill ends were stuck in the sand of the slope. On this platform were strewn one or more straw mats. The palm leaves of the roof were thrown at random over a still lighter framework, resting on four small forks about 5 to 6½ feet (1½ to 2 m.) above the first. The rain beat in everywhere as there were no walls. Similar, but larger, huts were sometimes placed side by side in twos or threes. In the summer, one saw huts in little groups on the beaches of the Maicy River; in the winter, the Indians lived on land not subject to floods. On one small inland farm, a better constructed, open, gable-roof hut was noted.

DRESS AND ORNAMENTS

The men wore a belt of raw fibers with fringe down the front, covering and holding the penis up against the abdomen. The women, at least in the camps, were nude. The women's ears and the lower lips of some of the men were pierced. The young women, from puberty until marriage, wore two fiber strings, sometimes braided, across the shoulders. Over the biceps the men wore fiber bands with long fringe. The women had necklaces of seeds and animal teeth. Though they had rustic wooden combs, their hair was always more or less unkempt. They did not remove the body hairs. In spite of their river habitat, the *Pirahá,* especially the children, were very dirty and untidy. Use of urucú and genipa body paint was rare.

MANUFACTURES

Miscellaneous.—The *Pirahá* made pouches with handles, baskets of babassú straw, gourds for holding water, gourds with painted black interiors, and spoons made of monkey skulls. They made two types of straw fans, one rectangular and the other in the shape of a fish. There was no pottery. The Indians usually slept on a platform, but sometimes, to escape the mosquitoes, they lay in their canoes, tying them to a branch on the bank. Very rarely, one saw a netlike fiber hammock, in which they rested during the day.

Weapons.—The only *Pirahá* weapon was the bow and arrow; it was powerful but less carefully made than those of the *Parintintin.* The arrows had radial feathering, tied at intervals. A jawbone with tusks was used to smooth the bow and the wooden arrow shaft. On the edge of the bamboo arrow point a cutia's tooth was set in a handle.

WARFARE

The *Parintintin* and the *Pirahá* were constantly at odds. In both tribes there were a number of Indians who bore scars of wounds from this fighting. Their hostile encounters usually took place in the summer when the *Pirahá* went up the Maicy River, sometimes as far as the Maicy Fork, looking for tracajá (turtle, *Podocnemis*) eggs in *Parintintin* country. Likewise, the *Parintintin* attacked the *Pirahá* in their camps on the lower Maicy River almost every year. Unlike their enemies, the *Pirahá* were not cannibals and did not take trophies from the bodies of the slain enemies. They did, sometimes, take prisoners. Thus in 1916 or 1917 they captured a *Parintintin* woman and child and sold them to the civilized people of the lower Marmellos River. Long ago the *Pirahá* seem also to have had some bloody battles with the *Matanawí*, but to all appearances they managed to get along peaceably with the *Torá*.

ESTHETIC AND RECREATIONAL ACTIVITIES

No musical instruments were seen among the *Pirahá*. A group of *Pirahá* who were camped near the Brazilian Government Center held a dance from the rising to the setting of the full moon. Holding hands and singing in unison, men and women formed a circle and danced in an open space. Starting slowly, they accelerated until they were running. This was repeated all night long. One of the men wore around his head a cord with short feathers of many colors; others had yellow grains of mumbaca palm trees (*Astrocaryum mumbaca*) hanging over their ears as ornaments. At a certain time, all were served a warm gruel of the jurumúm (squash) in a large gourd, made by roasting the plant in ashes and crushing it with the hands in water.

BIBLIOGRAPHY

Albuquerque Lacerda, 1864; Anonymous, ms. a; Barboza Rodrigues, 1892 b; Bates, 1863; Daniel, 1841; Fernandes de Souza, 1870; Ferreira, ms.; Ferreira Penna, 1853; Fonseca, 1880–81; Fonesca Coutinho, 1873; Herndon and Gibbons, 1853–54; Leite, 1943; Loukotka, 1939; Marcoy, 1866; Martius, 1863, 1867; Monteiro Noronha, 1862; Moraes, 1860; Nimuendajú, 1924, 1925, 1932 b; Nimuendajú and Valle Bentes, 1923; Nunes Pereira, 1939; Orton, 1875; Ribeiro de Sampaio, 1825; Rivet, 1924; Schmidt, W., 1913; Southey, 1862; Sousa, A., 1870; Spix and Martius, 1823–31, and Atlas; Tastevin, 1923 a; Therese von Bayern, 1897; Wallace, 1853, 1889.

THE MUNDURUCU[1]

By Donald Horton

TERRITORY AND NAME

The *Mundurucú* are a *Tupí*-speaking people in the southwestern portion of the State of Pará and the southeastern corner of the State of Amazonas, Brazil (map 1, *No. 1;* map 4; lat. 5°–8° S., long. 56°–60° W.). When first encountered by Europeans in the late 18th century, the *Mundurucú* were a warlike people, aggressively expanding their territory along the Tapajóz River and adjacent areas. Their expansion reached its limits at the beginning of the 19th century, when they were defeated by the Neo-Brazilians. Since then their territory has dwindled; remnant settlements are located on the Canumá and several of its tributaries (Abacaxis, Paracury, Apucitáua), in the municípios of Maués, Parintins, and Jurití, and on the Cururú River (a southeastern tributary of the Tapajóz). The principal settlements are located along the middle Tapajóz River and especially on its southeastern tributary, the Río de Tropas (between lat. 6° and 7° S., and long. 56° and 57° W.). Communities formerly established on the lower Tapajóz between the Rio de Tropas and the Amazon have been absorbed or wiped out by Neo-Brazilian settlers.

Kruse (1934) distinguishes four regional groups of the *Mundurucú:* The Tapajóz River group, living on both sides of the Tapajóz between the Rio de Tropas and the Cururú River; the Madeira River *Mundurucú,* on the Secudury, a tributary of the Canumá; the Xingú River *Mundurucú,* known also as the *Curuaya,* on the uppermost left tributary of the Igarapé de Flecha, itself an eastern tributary of the middle Rio Curuá do Irirí; and the Juruena River *Mundurucú,* known also as the *Njambik-waras.* Nimuendajú (personal communication) regards the name "*Madeira Mundurucú*" as unsuitable, since the rivers on which this group is located do not flow into the Madeira; he also believes that the *Curuaya,*

---

[1] The writer is indebted to Dr. Curt Nimuendajú, who through personal knowledge of the *Mundurucú* and familiarity with literary sources not available to the writer, was able to provide additional information on the distribution and history of the tribe which has been utilized in the present account.

Where the literature clearly indicates that a custom is no longer practiced, the past tense is employed; otherwise the account is given in the present tense even though it is probable that much of the culture so described no longer persists.

though related linguistically to the *Mundurucú,* are to be regarded as an independent tribe (this volume, p. 221), and that the *Njambikwara* (see *Nambicuara,* p. 361) are not properly classified as *Mundurucú* on any basis.

Martius (1867) reported a group related to the *Mundurucú,* known as the *Guajajara,* who were settled on the Gurupí River near Cerzedello in 1818. The writer has found no further reference to this name in the literature dealing with the *Mundurucú.* (The *Guajajara-Tembé* are a tribe near the east coast of Brazil, page 137.)

According to native tradition, the *Wiaunyen,* at the headwaters of the Mutum River, should be classed as a subtribe of the *Mundurucú.*

The *Mundurucú* refer to themselves as *Weidyénye* (our own, our people) (Kruse, 1934). *Mundurucú (Munduruhú, Mundurucú, Mondurucú, Mundrucú, Moturicú,* etc.) is the name applied to them by the *Parintintin,* in whose language it denotes a species of ant (Strömer, 1932). A nickname widely used by Neo-Brazilians is *Paiquizé (Paikyce)* (Martius, 1867) or *Paikise,* meaning "father knife" or "head-cutter." They are sometimes called *Caras Pretas* ("black face"), in reference to their facial tattooing. (See Kruse (1934), who gives an extensive list of names used by other tribes to designate the *Mundurucú.*)

POPULATION

In 1887, Martius estimated the *Mundurucú* at 18,000 to 40,000, but Strömer believes that, on the basis of known settlement sites, a maximum population of 10,000 at the period of Contact is indicated. Tocantins (1877) listed 21 villages with populations ranging from 100 to 2,600 and a total population of 18,910. According to Campana, there were at the turn of the century about 1,400 individuals in 37 communities in the Tapajóz area. The largest village had 700 inhabitants, and the smallest less than a dozen. Strömer (1932) found 19 settlements with a total of 1,200 to 1,400 inhabitants in 1931, and fewer still in 1937. Both Campana's and Strömer's figures refer only to the population of the main area of concentration. Kruse gives a population of 950 for the Tapajóz group and 800 for the Canumá group.

HISTORY

The first reference to the *Mundurucú* was published in 1768 when Monteiro Noronha[2] listed the *"Maturucú"* among the tribes on the Mauées River. In 1769, according to Manoel Baena (1885), the *Mundurucú* began to move northward along the Tapajóz River, forcing out or exterminating the *Jaguain (Javaim, Hy-au-ahim),* a warlike, cannibalistic tribe then occupying the middle Tapajóz. A *"Mondruci"* settlement a day's journey below the mouth of the Arinos was reported by Almeida Serra in 1779. The *Mundurucú* reached and made unsuccessful attacks upon

---

[2] The writer has not seen all of the sources mentioned in this sketch of *Mundurucú* history; the material here summarized has been in part provided by Dr. Nimuendajú (personal communication).

Santarém and *Gurupá* in 1780 and again in 1784. They attacked the *Mura* in the Madeira River region and a few years later dispersed their southern neighbors, the *Parintintin* (*Cawahiwa*). Their next expedition, involving an army of some 2,000 warriors, is said to have crossed the Xingú and Tocantins Rivers and to have reached the western limits of Maranhão Province. The expedition is said to have been defeated and turned back by the *Apinayé* (see Strömer, 1937), but according to Nimuendajú, it may be doubted that the *Mundurucú* actually went so far east. A Neo-Brazilian punitive force fought a 3-day battle with them on the Rio de Tropas (ca. 1794). Peace was established in 1795 or 1796.

Except for minor conflicts with neighboring tribes, the *Mundurucú* abandoned warfare and gradually relinquished the great territory they had seized. Missions were established on the Tapajóz in 1799 and on the Madeira in 1811. By 1885, the *Mundurucú* still living on the Madeira River had been sufficiently acculturated to be described as "civilized" (Hartt, 1885). A few of the villages of the Tapajóz region are said to preserve as much of the old culture as can survive without military organization, warfare, and head hunting (Strömer, 1932).

The site of the tribe prior to its northward drive along the Tapajóz is not definitely known. Kruse (1934) believes that they lived adjacent to the *Apiacá* in Mato Grosso; Martius (1867) thought that language and customs pointed to an origin still further south. It is Nimuendajú's opinion (personal communication), however, that the *Mundurucú* were originally located on the Río de Tropas, where their principal settlements are found today and where the punitive expedition of 1794 found their chief military strength. *Mundurucú* legend attributes their origin to the town of Necodemus in this area.

CULTURE

SUBSISTENCE ACTIVITIES

The *Mundurucú* subsist partly on horticulture and partly on hunting, fishing, and gathering. Tocantins' (1877) list of plants cultivated by them includes two species of manioc, sweet potato, pineapple, sugarcane, various peppers and beans, and several species of bananas. Other authors mention cotton, tobacco, and genipa. Tocantins names some 30 noncultivated plants utilized in *Mundurucú* economy. Martius (1867) says that this tribe formerly gathered wild rice along the Madeira and Irariá Rivers. They eat ants, larvae, and honey.

Some of the *Mundurucú* now have cattle. Though they do not use these as food, they will eat the meat of domestic animals if it is offered them.

In the aboriginal culture, wild fowl were kept in cages to provide plumage for the featherwork described below.

The *Mundurucú* are said to show great affection for their dogs. Women suckle puppies; when a dog dies it is given the same form of burial as a human being.

There are no published descriptions of *Mundurucú* hunting techniques, but accounts of hunting rituals indicate that tapirs, peccaries, hares, deer, and agoutis are hunted. One ritual simulates the use of a runway of stakes to trap peccaries. Intensive hunting occurs during the summer, when many families occupy temporary huts in the brush.

Barbed arrows are used more commonly than hook and line in fishing. Strömer's vocabulary (1932) includes references to basket traps and weirs. Fish and crocodiles are drugged with poison from twigs and leaves of the timbó.

Food preparation.—Cooking is women's work. Dishes mentioned in the literature include roasted sweet potato, banana mush, manioc broth, cará fruit soup, and a dish consisting of Brazil nuts which have been washed, soaked in water, smoked, crushed, and roasted. Meat is roasted on a babracot of green sticks or on a slanting spit. Strömer's vocabulary includes a word for manioc press and a phrase meaning "roasting house for manioc meal." Mortar and pestle are reported. Beverages are made from wild beans, cacao, and manioc meal mixed with honey and water. The *Mundurucú* had no native alcoholic beverages.

They raise tobacco and smoke it in the form of cigars wrapped in tauari bark.

VILLAGES AND HOUSES

Tocantins and Farabee imply that the dwellings are arranged around ιne periphery of an open village plaza in the center of which is the men's house. Bates, however, mentions a settlement of 30 houses scattered for a distance of 6 or 7 miles along a river bank; and Martius (Spix and Martius, 1823–31, vol. 3) speaks of houses arranged in rows in a forest clearing.

The men's house (ekça) occupied by the warriors, is a prominent feature of the village. Tocantins describes one 100 m. (325 feet) long, covered with thatch and open on one of its long sides. A photograph of a men's house in Farabee (1917 a) shows a rectangular structure, smaller and more crudely built than the dwelling house, with a gable roof and incompletely enclosed sides. The warriors slung their hammocks from posts inside it during the winter and from a series of posts set in three parallel rows and united by cross beams, in the village plaza, during the summer. Although warfare is no longer an important aspect of *Mundurucú* life, the men's house still serves as a men's work place and as a dwelling for the unmarried men. Women are not permitted to enter it.

The dwelling house (ekqa, "big house") photographed by Farabee is a long, rectangular, windowless structure with a high thatched roof and low walls. The men's door is in the center of the long side facing the men's house; the women's door is directly opposite. Strömer describes the house as a long, rectangular building with a roof sloping to the ends and sides, and with rising peaks at each end of the roof crest, but in a later publication (1937) he speaks of the house as "dome-shaped." In the 1850's, Bates found that most of the dwellings had conical roofs and walls of framework filled with mud. The roof was covered with palm thatch, and the eaves extended halfway to the ground. Martius also reported conical roofs.

Within the house each family has its own partitioned quarters and a fire-place or stone manioc oven (Tocantins, 1877). How many families usually occupy a single house has not been reported.

CLOTHING AND ADORNMENT

The only item of *Mundurucú* clothing mentioned in the literature is the three-cornered penis cover suspended from a cotton cord, but there are several descriptions of the ceremonial feather garments for which this tribe is famous. Many authors consider the *Mundurucú* to have been the most expert featherworkers in South America within the historic period.

Featherwork.—Featherwork includes aprons, capes (attached to head-dresses), caps, diadems, belts, girdles, bandoliers, arm bands, and leg bands. The feathers used in this craft were at least in part obtained from birds kept in captivity; red, blue, green, and yellow feathers were carefully sorted by color and size and stored in baskets or in palm-stem cylinders. Martius was told that the *Mundurucú* were able to cause their parrots to grow yellow plumes by plucking their feathers and rubbing frogs' blood into the wounds.[3] The feathers are attached to a net fabric. Tail feathers, arranged in parallel rows, are used in capes and pendants; rosettes of small feathers, bound at the quills, are attached to the base net to cover the attachments of long feathers; imbricated breast feathers may be used to cover the surface of a fabric or to sheathe a cord. Decorative effects are produced by simple alternation of colors.

A characteristic feathered staff is described as a stem of cane or wood about 3 feet (1 m.) long and 2 or 3 inches in diameter. The shaft is either covered with long feathers laid flat against it or sheathed with fine breast feathers. At the upper end a dense band of rosettes forms a projecting collar; a free cluster of long plumes may project from the head of the staff. The feathers are attached with wax and cotton thread. These objects are highly valued and when not in use are carefully stored in cylindrical containers. Their significance has not been reported; Martius merely says that when he approached a *Mundurucú* village, staff-bearers came to meet him.

Tattooing and painting.—The *Mundurucú* tattooing designs consist of fine, widely-spaced parallel lines applied vertically on limbs and torso; bands of lozenges across the upper part of the chest; occasional parallel horizontal lines, and cross-hatchings. Around each eye is tattooed a single-line ellipse; curved lines are drawn around the mouth. Lines converging toward the ears across the cheeks give the appearance of wings spread across the face. (For illustrations of *Mundurucú* tattooing, see the sketches by Hercules Florence (Steinen, 1899).)

---

[3] Nordenskiöld (1924 b, p. 207) says of this custom, which has been reported from other South American tribes, that the color change actually occurs, but zoologists attribute the change to dietary factors.

Hartt and Martius both mention tattooing combs of palm thorns, but Tocantins states that the operation is performed with an agouti tooth. The skin is slashed and genipa juice is rubbed into the wound. Genipa is also used as a paint to color areas enclosed by tattooed lines. Both sexes are tattooed but there are slight differences in design for each. The operation begins when the subject is about 8 years old and proceeds gradually over a period of years. It is seldom completed before the subject has reached the age of 20.

Hairdress.—The aboriginal hair style was the same for both sexes. The hair was cut just above the ears and at the nape of the neck. The crown of the head was shaved but a short, circular tuft was left above the center of the forehead.

MANUFACTURES

Baskets, ropes, and netting.—Baskets are woven of creepers, straw, and twigs. Ropes and cords are made of plant fibers and cotton thread. Women beat the raw cotton with sticks to separate the fibers and twist the thread with the aid of some sort of spindle. Cotton thread is used in knitting net fabrics for featherwork, and in making hammocks. Fibers from the outer surface of murití palm leaves are sometimes used in making hammocks.

Ceramics.—Pottery vessels, made by women, are modeled directly from a mass of clay and are said to be of poor quality.

Weapons.—The following weapons have been mentioned but not described: Bows, arrows of reed and of wood, poisoned war arrows, unpoisoned hunting arrows (Martius, 1867), spears with bamboo blades, javelins, wooden knives, hafted (stone?) axes, and war clubs. A cotton bandage was wrapped around the knuckles of the bow hand to protect it from the bowstring. Katzer (1901) has published illustrations of a number of flat, polished stone ax heads, of oval or nearly quadrangular shape, with lateral notches; these were found archeologically in *Mundurucú* territory. He reports that the *Mundurucú* still make such stone objects, but keep them merely as valuables or as children's toys.

TRADE

Despite hostility between the *Mundurucú* and their neighbors, they traded their featherwork extensively. They are said to have depended on an unidentified northern source for arrow poison. After the advent of the missions, manioc meal, sarsaparilla, and other forest products were exported to Santarém in considerable quantities (Martius, 1867).

SOCIAL ORGANIZATION

According to Kruse (1934), the Tapajóz River *Mundurucú* have a patrilineal sib and moiety system. There are 34 sibs whose members are related to eponymous plants and animals. Sib ancestors are embodied in large ceremonial trumpets called "kaduké," which women are forbidden to see upon pain of lifelong unhappiness. Certain sibs are "related." but the nature of the relationship has not been specified. The sibs are grouped in exogamous moieties: a red moiety of 15 sibs and a white moiety of 19 sibs. A list of the sib names is given by Kruse (1934). In *Mundurucú* tradition these sibs were once warring tribes; their pacification and organization into the present tribal society is attributed to the culture hero.

Polygyny is practiced by men of rank. Younger wives are sometimes solicited voluntarily by the elder wife. Martius reports the levirate. He also states that if a marriageable girl's father dies, and she finds no suitable husband, her mother's brother is obliged to marry her. It is perhaps corroborative evidence of this type of marriage that in the kinship terms given in Strömer's vocabulary, a woman addresses her brother and son-in-law by the same term (tapo).

Patrilocal residence is indicated by Martius' report (1867) that a woman guilty of adultery may be expelled from the house and return to her own family. According to Hartt (1885), each family's section of the communal house is identified by the family's color painted on the post of the partition. No further information about this color symbolism is given.

Each communal house is said to have its house chief and its shaman. Above house chiefs and shamans in rank are war chiefs, chiefs of sub-tribes (regional groups or moieties?), and a chief shaman. Bates (1892) is the only writer who mentions a paramount tribal chief. Farabee (1917 a) makes an obscure reference to differences in class between war chiefs and "civil" chiefs (house chiefs?). He also states that the sons and daughters of war chiefs intermarry.

MILITARY ORGANIZATION AND WARFARE

The central military institution was the group of warriors living in the men's house. This house and the village were constantly guarded by a patrol whose leader gave signals by means of a trumpet or flute. When a war expedition was being planned, a pledge stick was passed among the warriors by the war chief. A warrior pledged himself to join the expedition by cutting a notch in the stick. When the war party got under way, absolute authority was vested in its leader.

War was generally waged during the summer dry season. Whenever feasible, each warrior was accompanied by his wife or sister, who carried his equipment, prepared food, strung hammocks, aided him if he were wounded, and assisted in the preliminary preparation of trophy heads. The women, according to most authors, took no part in the actual fighting.

though Martius reports that women participated in the battle to the extent of recovering arrows shot by the enemy and delivering them to their own warriors. He even asserts that the women "cleverly catch the arrows of the enemy in flight" (Spix and Martius, 1823–31, 3: 1,313). The usual method of attack was to assault the enemy village at daybreak and to fire the huts by means of incendiary arrows. During the fight, the war leader stood behind his warriors directing the attack. Assistants signaled his orders on their trumpets. Women and children of the enemy were taken prisoner; the women were later married by *Mundurucú* men, and the children were adopted. But enemy warriors were killed and their heads taken as trophies.

A *Mundurucú* warrior who had fought bravely but because of a wound had failed to obtain a head, received in compensation a cotton belt from which hung teeth removed from enemy heads. Such a belt might also be given to the widow of a warrior killed in battle (pl. 23, *right*), and her possession of it entitled her to be supported by the community. When a warrior had been wounded, his name was not spoken for a year; during this time he was considered to be dead. At the end of the year, a feast was given to reinstate him in the community.

Trophy heads were dried and colored with urucú or genipa; the brain cavity was filled with cotton and a carrying cord was laced through the lips (pl. 23, *left*). *Mundurucú* trophy heads were not shrunken. (Koseritz (1885) and Barbosa Rodrigues (1882 a) were both in error on this point.)

Strömer believes that the *Mundurucú* were cannibalistic, basing his belief on a passage in native text which seems to imply that some part of the trophy head was eaten. Kruse (1934) denies that the *Mundurucú* were in any way cannibalistic; Nimuendajú (personal communication) doubts the credibility of Strömer's informants on this subject.

LIFE CYCLE

Birth and naming.—According to Martius, the father keeps to his hammock for several weeks after the birth of a child and there receives the visits and solicitude of his neighbors. Immediately after its birth, the child is given a totemic name. Other names are added as the child grows older. If a man performs a heroic deed in hunting or warfare, his heroism will be commemorated by an additional name. When children reach their 8th year, their tatooing begins, and a boy takes up residence in the men's house.

Puberty and marriage.—Martius (1867) says that a girl at her first menstruation is required to undergo a long period of fasting "while exposed to the smoke in the gable of the hut."

A girl may be betrothed while still quite young to a mature warrior. Though she remains with her parents and the marriage is not consummated until she reaches puberty, the prospective husband assumes the responsibility of providing food for her and her parents. A younger man **may** obtain a wife by giving several years' bride service in the household of the girl's parents.

Death and burial.—An "executioner" was pointed out to Martius, whose duty it was to despatch the fatally ill and the senile. Attribution of this custom to the *Mundurucú* is said to be widespread among neighboring tribes.

When a death occurs, the maternal relatives of the deceased cut their hair, blacken their faces, and conduct a prolonged wailing for the dead. The corpse, wrapped in a hammock, is placed upright with flexed knees in a cylindrical grave under the floor of the dwelling. Grave goods consist of ornaments and other small objects. Skeletons of men of high status are exhumed and burned after the flesh has decayed; the ashes are buried in jars.

When a warrior is killed on a distant battlefield, his head is taken back to the village and put on display with his ornaments, trumpet, and weapons. After a feast in honor of the deceased, the head is suspended from the neck of his mother, widow, or sister, and his fellow warriors pledge to avenge his death. During this ceremony the shaman is isolated in a special hut where he blows the sacred trumpet (kaduké). The ceremony is repeated at yearly intervals, terminating with the fourth performance, when the head is finally buried in the house of the deceased.

RELIGIOUS CEREMONIES

At the beginning of winter, the *Mundurucú* perform a ceremony which on alternate years invokes success in hunting and in fishing. The shaman, isolated in a special hut, propitiates the guardian spirits of game animals and fish. A ventriloquistic dialogue in which the voices of the animals are heard proceeding from the hut informs the people of the shaman's success in obtaining the favor of the spirits. Offerings are made to the skulls of animals and fish. The ceremony is directed by a feast leader who is both a prominent warrior and a good singer. Tocantins (1877) reports a similar annual ceremony to propitiate the spirits of maize and manioc.

Farabee (1917 a) describes a feast held at the first full moon in May to celebrate the first hunt following the birth of the April litters of peccaries. After a feast in which young peccaries are eaten, there is a dance in which the performers imitate a herd of peccaries. Children run among the dancers like young peccaries while the older people imitate the sound of peccaries feeding; a dancer representing an old boar protecting the herd wrestles with another dancer who plays the part of a jaguar. The boar succeeds in holding off the jaguar while the herd of peccaries escapes.

In another dance the peccaries are pursued by hunters and their dogs. The peccaries take refuge in a hole in the ground. The hunters then simulate the construction of a trap by standing with legs astraddle to represent an alley of stakes; the peccaries try to escape between the lines of stakes and are killed by a hunter at the end of the alley.

An abbreviated description of a peccary festival is given by Strömer (1932). This is a hunting ceremony in which the skulls of animals play a role. Sexual intercourse is performed ritually by the participants. At one point in the ceremony, the performers dance on a heap of peccary hair while they sing an invocation of success in peccary hunting.

At a special men's festival in honor of the sib ancestors the sacred trumpets are blown. At the conclusion of the ceremony, a special beverage is poured through the trumpet into a cup and drunk by the participants. The ceremony, performed by men alone since women are not permitted to see the trumpets, is said to propitiate the sib ancestors and to obtain their good will toward their descendants.

At the tree festival a tree is set up in the center of the dwelling house; the participants stand around it while the shaman smokes tobacco and invokes on the house the protection of Karusakaibö, the creator god.

SHAMANISM AND SORCERY

The shaman determines the most favorable time for war parties, exorcises evil spirits, takes a leading part in ceremonies, cures the sick, detects sorcerers, and intervenes to terminate eclipses of the sun. Illness is believed to be caused by the intrusion of a worm into the patient's body, or by sorcery. The shaman cures the intrusion by blowing smoke on the patient's body and sucking out the worm. When many deaths or much sickness occur the malevolence of a sorcerer is suspected; the shaman detects the sorcerer and informs the chief of his identity. The chief appoints two warriors to follow the sorcerer until they have a favorable opportunity to kill him. Some hints as to the technique of sorcery are given in Strömer's vocabulary. He records the word, yamain, meaning "to cut off the head and set it back again," and the word, yakut, "hole in the earth in which to bury the head"—both with reference to the practice of sorcery.

Sorcery is said to be virtually the sole cause of homicide among the *Mundurucú*. Adultery is punished by the expulsion of the guilty persons. When two men become antagonistic, one of them takes his hammock and goes to live in the men's house of another village.

MYTHOLOGY

The creator god and culture hero of *Mundurucú* mythology is Karusa-kaibö (Caru-Sacaibê (Tocantins, 1877)); Karusakaibe (Kruse, 1934);

Karusakaibu (Farabee, 1917 a). His wife, Sikrida (Strömer, 1932);
Chicridha (Tocantins, 1877), is a *Mundurucú* woman. Korumtau
(Carutau (ibid.)) is his eldest son and his second born is Anukaite
(Hanu-Acuate (ibid.)). Karusakaibö's companion and helper is Daiiru
(Rayru (ibid.)), an armadillo.

Conflict between Karusakaibö and his sons and companion is a recurrent theme in several myths reported by Strömer and Tocantins. In one
story, Anukaite is seduced by his mother. Karusakaibö learns of the
incest and in anger pursues his son. Anukaite delays his flight to have
sexual intercourse with several importunate women whom he meets on
the way; his father overtakes him and transforms him into a tapir. The
insatiable women are transformed into fish.

On another occasion the offenders are Daiiru and Korumtau. Their
offense is not explained clearly in the account (Strömer, 1932) but appears to involve an improper relationship between Korumtau and some
peccaries, for which Daiiru is partly responsible. Again the guilty are
pursued by Karusakaibö; to evade his father, Korumtau transforms himself successively into a peccary, a cricket, a bird, and a monkey. Once he
is wounded by an arrow shot by the pursuing father, but the armadillo
draws the arrow from the wound. The animals of the forest give aid by
warning of the father's approach. Finally, the two fugitives throw themselves into a body of water and escape.

The *Mundurucú* origin myth tells of the emergence of mankind from
under the ground. According to one version (Farabee, 1917 a), Karusakaibö had made the world but had not created men. One day Daiiru, the
armadillo, offended the creator and was forced to take refuge in a hole in
the ground. Karusakaibö blew into the hole and stamped his foot on the
earth. Daiiru was blown out of the hole by the rush of air. He reported
that people were living in the earth. He and Karusakaibö made a cotton
rope and lowered it into the hole. The people began to climb out. When
half of them had emerged, the rope broke and half remained underground,
where they still live. The sun passes through their country from west to
east when it is night on the earth; the moon shines there when the earth
has moonless nights. According to another version of the tale (Tocantins,
1877), the creator stamped his foot at the site of the village of Necodemos;
White people, Indians, and Negroes emerged from a fissure in the ground.
The creator tattooed the *Mundurucú* like himself; the Whites and Negroes
scattered. Karusakaibö then showed the *Mundurucú* how to raise manioc,
maize, cotton, and other plants and how to utilize them. It was he who
traced the petroglyphs now found on certain cliffs in the region of
Necodemos. Another origin-of-agriculture myth is given in a text gathered by Strömer (1937).

Kruse (1934) reports a myth in which the women are said to have
once been in possession of the men's house, while the men lived in the

dwelling house. The men did all the work, including such women's tasks as fetching firewood, providing manioc, and baking manioc meal. The woman ruler of the tribe and two companions found three sacred trumpets and secretly practiced playing on them in the forest. When the men discovered the secret, they took the trumpets away from the women. The women were sent to the dwelling house and were forbidden to look again upon the trumpets, while the men took possession of the men's house.

Both Strömer (1932) and Farabee (1917 a) report a myth which tells that the sun once fell upon the earth and destroyed its inhabitants by fire. Five days after the fire, the creator sent a vulture from the sky to see if the earth had cooled, but the vulture remained to eat the bodies of men who had been killed. After 4 days a blackbird was sent, but it remained to eat the charred buds of the trees. Four days later, the creator sent a dove, which returned with earth between its claws. Then the creator came down and recreated men and animals of white potter's clay.[4]

LORE AND LEARNING

A few miscellaneous cosmological beliefs were obtained by Farabee: Karusakaibö created the sun by transforming a young man who had red eyes and long white hair. The moon is a transformed virgin with white skin. The rain spirit makes thunder by rolling a pestle in a mortar. The constellations are men and animals in a great savanna. An eclipse of the sun is due to a great fire which sweeps over its surface. A powerful shaman once ascended to the sun and put out the fire. Now, when an eclipse occurs, the shaman sends his yakpu to clear the sun. The yakpu (a fragment of meteoric iron) falls to the earth as a ball of fire. After it cools, the shaman puts it away until the next eclipse.

BIBLIOGRAPHY

Baena, 1885; Barbosa Rodrigues, 1882 a; Bates, 1892; Campana, 1904–06; Chandless, 1862, 1870; Coudreau, H., 1897 a; Farabee, 1917 a; Hartt, 1885; Hörschelmann, 1918–20; Katzer, 1901; Koseritz, 1885; Kruse, 1934; Martius, 1867; Nimuendajú, 1938; Nordenskiöld, 1924 b; Spix and Martius, 1823–31, vol. 3; Steinen, 1899; Strömer, 1932, 1937; Tocantins, 1877; Wood, 1868–70.

---

[4] For texts of some of the myths given in condensed form above, see Strömer (1932); for other myths, not included in this account, see Strömer (ibid.) and Tocantins (1877). Farabee (1917 a) also gives three animal fables which he attributes to the *Mundurucú*.

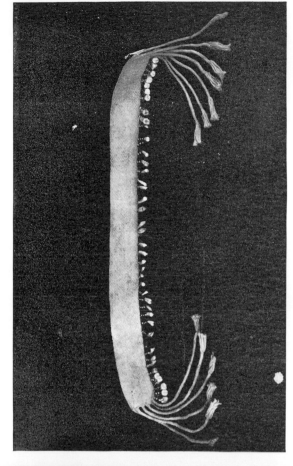

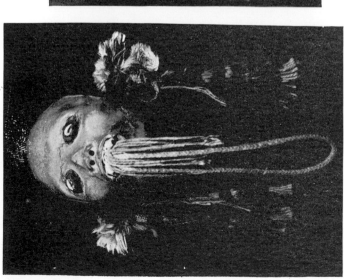

PLATE 23.—**Mundurucú artifacts.** *Left*: Prepared human head with animal teeth set in eye sockets and a suspension cord hanging from the mouth. (Courtesy Museo Etnográfico de la Facultad de Filosofía y Letras, Buenos Aires.) *Right*: Belt of human teeth, woven by widow of a warrior killed in combat. (Courtesy Museu Paraense Emilio Goeldi, Belém.)

THE CAWAHIB, PARINTINTIN, AND THEIR NEIGHBORS

By CURT NIMUENDAJÚ

THE OLD CAWAHIB

Cawahíb (*Kawahíb, Cawahíwa, Cabahiba, Cabaiva, Cauhuahipe, Cahuahiva*) is the 18th- and early 19th-century name of a people who later split into some six groups or tribes, among them the *Parintintin* and the *Tupí-Cawahíb* (pp. 299–305). (Lat. 10° S., long. 58° W.; map 1, *No. 2;* map 3.)

In the 18th century, a tribe named *Cabahiba* lived on the upper Tapajóz River, between the confluence of the Arinos and Juruena Rivers and the mouth of the São Manoel River. Information about this tribe is scanty, partly because it never lived on the banks of the great river, unlike its neighbors, the *Apiacá*. The oldest reference to it, in 1797, appears in an anonymous manuscript (1857) with the laconic entry, "Cabahibas—Lingua Geral: situated below [the Apiacás], near the said confluence [Arinos and Juruena]." Subsequently, when the tribe may no longer have existed as a unit in that region, it is mentioned by writers who evidently based their statements on older data. The *Cabahiba* are not mentioned on the upper Tapajóz by any of the travelers of the first three decades of the 19th century who wrote on the *Apiacá,* but they are noted in other territory. The following is quoted from a list which Castelnau (1850–59, vol. 3) compiled in 1844, but which evidently refers to the situation at the beginning of the century: "The Cabaivas cultivate considerable plantations to the west of the Juruena, but they are located much farther from the river than the nations mentioned before (Tamepugas, Urupuyas, Macuris, and Birapaçaparas)." Manoel Ayres Cazal (1707, p. 256) mentions them in 1817 in the same manner, "To the north of the latter (Appiacás) live the Cabahybas who speak the same language."

In 1819, some *Apiacá* informed Canon Guimarães that the *Cauhuahipe* (*Cawahíb*) lived on the Paramutanga (paraná-mitán, "red river," i.e., "Sangue River"), a tributary of the Juruena, and that they used silver ornaments. Melgaço in his "Apontamentos" (1884) locates them approximately in the same region, on the Campos dos Pareceis, between the Arinos and Juruena Rivers. Another *Apiacá* told Castelnau in 1814

283

that the *Cahuahiva* lived among the tribes along the Juruena, but were driven from the river shores by the *Apiacá*. There is no further mention in the literature of the name *Cabahiba,* but V. P. Vasconcellos' expedition down the Sangue River in 1915 (Rondón, 1916) found unknown and hostile Indians on its lower portions. The behavior of these Indians suggested that they were a *Tupí* tribe, as Rondón believed, and not *Nambicuara,* as Vasconcellos thought.

As the name *Cawahíb* gradually disappeared from the writings about Mato Grosso, *Parintintin* began to appear in Pará at the beginning of the 19th century. *Parintintin* (pari, "non-*Mundurucú* Indian," rign-rign, "fetid") is the name given the *Cawahíb* by the *Mundurucú,* its mortal enemies and neighbors to the north.

The *Mundurucú* originally were concentrated in the region of the Rio das Tropas, but, since 1750, they have expanded mainly at the expense of the *Cawahíb*. The *Mundurucú,* according to their tradition, expelled the *Parintintin* from the Cururú River Basin. They continued to persecute them until the beginning of the 20th century, and no doubt caused them to split into six isolated groups between the São Manoel-Paranatinga and the Madeira Rivers. It has been established that two of the most important of these, the *Parintintin* of the Madeira River and the *"Tupí"* of the Machado, call themselves *Cawahíb*. Two others, one at the headwaters of the Machadinho River and the other in the interior between the upper Tapajóz and São Manoel Rivers, do not, judging by the few known words of their language, differ from the other groups. Historic and ethnographic data indicate that the fifth, that on the Sangue River, is probably also a *Cawahíb* group. Of the sixth, on the upper Bararaty River, it is known only that they are hostile to civilized people and that they occupy a part of the former territory of the old *Parintintin;* it is just barely possible that they form part of the *Cawahíb* tribe.

THE PARINTINTIN

TERRITORY, LANGUAGE, AND HISTORY

Names of the *Parintintin* are: Self-designation, *Cawahíb; Cawahiwa* (kab, káwa, "wasp") ; in *Mundurucú, Pari-rign-rign,* "fetid Indians"; in *Maué, Paritín,* from the *Mundurucú* term designating all hostile Indians; in *Mura* of the Autaz River, *Wáhai*; in *Mura* of the Madeira River, *Toepehe, Topehẽ* (from *Mundurucú* taypehe=penis?) ; in *Pirahá Toypehé;* in *Torá, Toebehé* (from the *Mura*) or *Nakazeti,* "fierce"; in *Matanawi, Itoebehe* (from the *Torá*) or *Tapakará;* and in the Lingua Geral of the past century, *Yawaretá-Tapiiya,* "Jaguar Indians."

Until 1922, the *Parintintin* occupied the region between the Madeira River, the Amazonian parts of the Machado and Marmellos Rivers, and the right tributary of the latter, the Rio Branco.

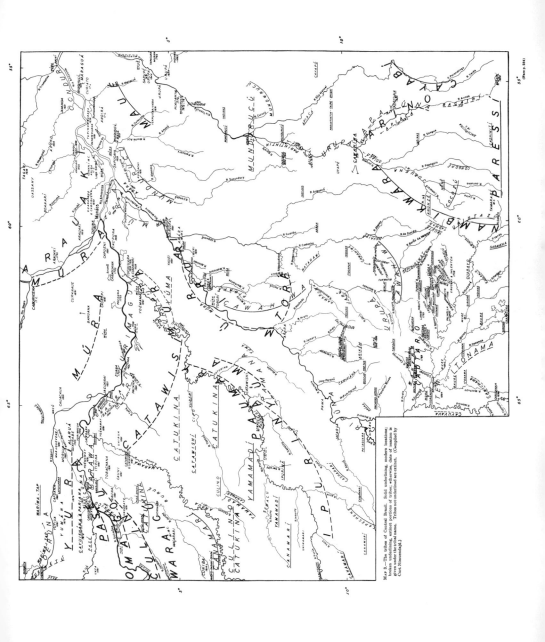

Map 3.—The tribes of Central Brazil. Solid underlining, modern locations; broken underlining, extinct portions of tribes; otherwise, date of session is given under the tribal name. Tribes not underlined are extinct. (Compiled by Curt Nimuendajú.)

The *Parintintin* language is pure *Tupí,* and differs from the upper Machado *Tupí* only in some phonetic variations. In the *Parintintin* vocabulary compiled by Severiano da Fonseca (1880-81) in 1878, only a few words can be identified, the remainder being incomprehensible. In 1922, García de Freitas (1926) took the first vocabulary of 127 words, and in December 1922, the present author (Nimuendajú, 1924, p. 262) collected a vocabulary of 328 entries.

In 1922, the number of *Parintintin* was estimated at 250. García de Freitas (1926) gave a total of 500 for that year, but included two adjacent groups. The existence of one of these is in doubt, and the number of the other may be less than the author thought. At present, the *Parintintin,* excluding the *Apairandé,* who still keep aloof, number about 120. They are divided into three groups: (1) That on the Igarapé Ipixuna, a tributary of Lake Uruapiára; (2) the Tres Casas settlement; and (3) the Calama group. The members of the last two are rubber gatherers (García de Freitas, 1926).

Parintintin were first mentioned as a cannibal tribe in the Madeira region in 1829 (Castelnau, 1850, 3: 164). They occupied territory that belonged previously to the *Torá, Mura* and *Pirahá.* The earliest report of *Parintintin* hostilities known to the present author was in 1852. Since then, the *Parintintin* have probably made at least one assault each year on the civilized people, who were always more or less the losers. They became the scourge of the Madeira.

Cruel guerrilla warfare dragged on for long decades. Punitive expeditions by the Neo-Brazilians, or by the *Mundurucú* under the orders of the latter, did not improve matters. Colonel Rondón instigated an attempt to pacify the *Parintintin,* but his emissary fell into a pitfall and was seriously injured. In 1922, after several ineffectual attacks, the *Parintintin* made their first contact with the personnel of the Serviço de Protecção aos Indios at the Station on the Maicy River, a tributary of the Marmellos River on the left bank. Since then, the tribe has not again attacked the civilized people on the Madeira River. It has, however, suffered great losses from disease acquired through contact with civilization. Part of the survivors went into service under the rubber workers on the Madeira River, and another part remained peacefully on the Igarapé Ipixuna.

CULTURE

SUBSISTENCE ACTIVITIES

The *Parintintin* practice extensive agriculture. They have a variety of maize so tender that it may be eaten raw. They also grow sweet manioc, sweet potatoes, bananas, papaya, urucú, and cotton. Formerly, they did not know tobacco or beans, not even by name.

They are good hunters, though fishing is of greater importance. Tapir is their favorite game, and they relish monkeys but fear losing their arrows on them. To catch birds, they set out sticks covered with the viscous milk of guananí (*Tomorita* sp. ?) (Nunes Pereira, 1940, p. 36). They eat batrachians.

The *Parintintin* take fish with weirs placed across the outlets of lakes, and with bows and arrows shot from their canoes. In suitable places, a fisherman awaits his chance on a platform built on a limb overhanging the river. Frequently, these Indians make decoys—full-size figures of fishes carved of tree bark and painted with charcoal—and hold them underwater by a long, slender rod stuck into the river bank. They lack fishhooks.

The *Parintintin* have no domesticated animals and even fear small dogs, but they keep large numbers of wild birds.

They roast maize in ashes or pound it in a mortar. They wet the flour and make it into balls the size of a fist, which are baked in embers and again crushed in the mortar. The dry flour thus prepared is eaten dry with meat or fish, or it is cooked as a porridge. The *Parintintin* also make flat cakes (beijú) roasted in embers. Their mortar is the vertical, cylindrical type. The pestle is a long, slender stick. When traveling, they carry small portable mortars.

HOUSES AND VILLAGES

The huts are open rectangular sheds 20 m. (about 65 ft.) or more long and 6 m. (20 ft.) high. The roof sometimes extends beyond the hut to form a veranda. Inside, at irregular intervals between the uprights, there are horizontal poles from which the hammocks are hung. The hammocks are small because the Indians sleep doubled-up on their sides. A fire always burns inside.

The huts are grouped at random, with no more than four in each settlement.

DRESS AND ORNAMENTS

A man's complete costume consists of four pieces. (1) The penis sheath is worn by all Indians. It is made of at least 12 overlapping leaves of arumã (*Ischnosiphon ovatus*), partly held together by two stitches. The edges are doubled, so as not to chafe the skin, and the whole piece before being put in place is rectangular in shape. The piece is wrapped around the whole penis to form a cylinder, the edges meeting on the underside. It is tied with a piece of cotton thread around the upper end and another at the head of the penis. To remove the sheath for urinating or washing, the threads are untied. No Indian over 12 years old may go about without this sheath ("kaá"). Penis sheaths of exaggerated length (up to 40 cm.) are doubtless the basis for the legend of a tribe whose members, like the *Parintintin* kaá, hang to their knees. The *Mundurucú* called this tribe the "Taipe-sisi." (2) Some men wear a narrow belt of embira, tied in front so that its short fringes hang over the pubis. (3) All men wear one or more belts, each made of several rings of buriti stalks which are firmly joined in front but hang loose behind, partly covering the buttocks. (4) Arm bands are described below.

Boys 8 to 12, who do not yet use the penis sheath, wear under their burití belts two fringed embira aprons, one over the other. Smaller children go about completely naked or wear a small belt of burití stalk.

Sometimes people wrap embira around the ankles as protection against snakes.

Women have no clothing, but generally tie a cotton thread below the knee and another above the ankle.

Soon after birth, the earlobes of both sexes are pierced. Ordinarily nothing is worn through the hole, but some men put a little stick through, or, on special occasions, a little bamboo stick, the end of which rests on the shoulder, or a feather tuft.

Feather ornaments, used exclusively by men and older boys, are not showy. They comprise feather diadems and neck feathers. The diadems consist of a wide band of feathers of different colors, covered at the base by a narrower band of black feathers. The whole is mounted on a double ring of burití stalks, with a circular elastic net made of cotton threads. The neck pieces are made of straw, feather tufts, cords, light sticks covered with fine feathers, and macaw tail feathers, from the points of which fine feathers or human hair are hung. Another ornament exclusively for men is a babassú straw armband, 3 cm. (1.2 inches) wide, decorated with small feathers glued to it and with tufts and long strings of feathers. Other ornaments are made of embira, with long fringes, or of tubular bones. Children wear necklaces of a great variety of materials and a characteristic ornament consisting of two teeth of a large mammal, e. g., jaguar, peccary, or tapir, symmetrically tied or merely held by a string. The only women's ornament is a string of beads of tucumã and of bone.

The *Parintintin* are always well-groomed and keep their hair combed. Eyebrows and lashes, but not body hair, are plucked. Both sexes cut their hair in a circle, so that bangs fall a little above the eyebrows and the top of the ears are covered. Some women wear their hair long, tied with a cotton thread behind. Hair trimmings are carefully collected to avoid their use in witchcraft. Combs are small and one-sided, the teeth being held between two pairs of sticks by a cotton wrapping.

Tattooing is done with genipa dye. On men, it consists of three lines from each ear, one to the upper lip, one to the corner of the mouth, and one to the chin, with lines encircling the mouth, and a fishtail design at each corner of the mouth. Women have a rectangular Greek fret on the chin, the same length as the mouth with a wide line on each side from the fret to the ear. They also have a fine line over the eye and a horizontal line extending from the corner of the eye. Practically all men have a jaguar tattooed on the inside of the forearm and a pacú

(*Prochilodus* sp.) on the outside. Commonly the left side of a man's back, from the shoulder blade down, has two vertical rows of 10 to 15 rectangles of solid color. Other tatooed figures vary considerably from one individual to another.

As pigments for body paint, the *Parintintin* use clay for white, urucú for red, genipa for dark blue, and burnt Brazil nuts for black, the last restricted to men. Women prefer urucú, with which they sometimes paint themselves from head to foot. For warfare and for welcoming a guest, which is done by simulating an attack, men paint a band 3 fingers wide from one ear to the other, across the mouth. They also paint their forearms and trace horizontal stripes or irregular spots on either side of their chest and thighs. Some smear black on themselves without design. Certain warriors go into combat entirely covered with white, presenting a ghostly appearance.

TRANSPORTATION

The *Parintintin* canoe is made of a section of "jutahy" bark (*Hymenaea*), with raised edges. It is reinforced by long poles along the sides, by inside cross pieces, which serve as seats, and by liana ties at the ends and from side to side. The bottom of the canoe is covered with a mat made of sticks. These craft are 5 to 7 m. (about 16½ to 23½ ft.) long and 0.5 meter (1½ ft.) wide. In spite of their crude construction, they can travel at a high speed. It seems that formerly the *Parintintin,* like the *Apiacá,* used only thick bamboos split in half as paddles, but later they stole so many paddles from the civilized people that they rarely used their original type.

MANUFACTURES

Basketry.—The *Parintintin* have few baskets, except temporary ones woven of green palm leaves. The best are made of babassú straw, with a round bottom. Fire fans are pentagonal, the larger ones being used also as mats when sitting by the fire (apparently the *Parintintin* have no benches). Sieves for maize flour are bowl-shaped.

Spinning and weaving.—The spindle used for cotton has a small button on top of the shank and a jabotí (*Testudo tabulata*) shell whorl with incised decoration. The *Parintintin* may formerly have woven slings for carrying children, but at the time of their pacification, all were made of stolen cloth or of embira. Hammocks are made of cotton, and are twined; the interval between the weft elements varies greatly. Separate strands are not added at the ends to form suspension loops (sobrepunhos); instead, the long, strong warp strands of tauarí (*Couratari* sp.) fibers are gathered into a bundle which is doubled back to form a loop.

Pottery.—No clay pot was ever seen among the *Parintintin,* but this tribe knows the *Tupí* name for pot (nyaepepó, a word formed with nyaé, "clay"), so that the ceramic art must have been lost only recently.

Gourds.—The only vessels are made of calabashes and gourds. The latter were made with a narrow orifice for water containers, and with a wide opening and a suspension cord for holding small items. Calabashes are blackened inside, but lack exterior decoration. Cracks are repaired by sewing with thread.

Weapons.—The main weapon is the bow and arrow. The bows are made of pau d'arco (*Tecoma* sp.) and are over 2 m. (6 ft.) long, with a semicircular cross section, and the belly side flat or slightly concave. The string is three-ply of embira or tauarí (*Couratari* sp.). In shooting, the bow is held diagonally, the upper end slightly to the right. Children's toy bows are either round or semicircular in cross section.

Arrows are of three types: (1) A fishing arrow, of wild cane (*Gynerium*), approximately 2.5 m. (8½ ft.) long, without feathering and with one to three heads barbed with iron nails; (2) a small game arrow, used only occasionally in fishing or warfare, 1.5 m. (4½ ft.) long, with a slender shaft of camayuva (*Guadua* sp.), with tangential (arched) feathering, and tipped with a wooden rod, which is serrated on one side or cut with a series of fine overlapping cones; (3) a large game and war arrow, with a heavy camayuva shaft and a lanceolate bamboo head 40 cm. (16 in.) long. The last may have a barb on each side of the proximal end, two pairs of barbs, a powerful continuous row of teeth on one side, or no barbs at all. The point is extremely sharp, and the edges are made razor-sharp by means of an instrument consisting of a cutia (*Dasyprocta aguti*) tooth attached to a handle. Now and then the hafted end of the point has a beautiful fabric of black and white hairs of the peccary (*Tayassu tajacu*). Arrow feathers are generally of mutum (*Crax*) and royal sparrow hawk, and are 30 cm. (12 in.) long, flush and unspiralled; the wrappings are covered with fine throat feathers of the toucan. The 10 or 12 intermediate ties consist of very fine threads.

On two occasions the *Parintintin* used plain round sticks, 1.5 m. (4½ ft.) long, as clubs and discarded them afterward. They use bamboo daggers with sharp blades like arrowheads and the internodal end as the handle. These are the original knives which they used for various purposes, including cutting their hair.

Fire.—Fire is made with a hand-rotated drill and a hearth which has three slightly concave surfaces. The drill penetrates one of the lateral surfaces through to the bottom surface, where the accumulated powder ignites. Lacking this apparatus, an arrow shaft and bamboo arrowhead are used. Charred cotton serves as tinder.

Moieties.—The *Parintintin* are divided in two exogamic, unlocalized patrilineal moieties: Mitú (*Mitua,* mitu) and Kwandú (*Harpia harpyja,* royal hawk). It is inconceivable to them that there could exist any person, even a foreigner, who was neither a Mitú nor a Kwandú.

For a warlike people, it is strange that the *Parintintin* at the time of the pacification had no chiefs except family heads, whose authority was not absolute. During combat, warriors acted in unison only until the first round of arrows was discharged, after which each did what he pleased and fought if he had courage, or else ran off.

Property.—At the time of the pacification, the majority of the *Parintintin* were admittedly incorrigible thieves who employed all sorts of tricks to steal the property of others openly or by stealth. Even within the tribe, individuals stole from one another, trusting their fellow tribesmen much less than the personnel sent to pacify them. This tendency was noticeable even among children.

Modesty.—By the standards of civilized people, men behaved quite decently, although some individuals enjoyed obscene gestures and sayings. Women and girls, however, behaved with complete decency, and never made their nudity obvious. The men are ashamed to uncover their penis and, when bathing, turn their backs to others as they remove the casing to wash the member. They practice their physiological acts out of sight of others.

Names.—Nothing is known about the manner of naming. People change their names frequently. They do not hesitate either to tell their own names or to ask those of others. Some names of men are: Tawarí (*Couratari* sp.?), Mohangí (mohán, "medicine"), Mboavaím (mbo, active particle, avá, "man," im, negative), and Wiratíb (wirá, "bird," tib, "be").

War.—Before the pacification in 1922, the *Parintintin* lived in constant struggle with everyone outside the tribe. They had not the slightest respect for the life and property of others. For young people, who in general were turbulent, presumptuous, and disrespectful, war was not a deplorable necessity, but a favorite sport.

The *Parintintin* attacked at any season and time of day or night, though most war was waged in summer. War parties never exceeded 20 men. With their bows ready, they would pounce upon the enemy without the slightest notice and with incredible speed, taking advantage of any open path which permitted unobstructed maneuvers. After their first round of arrows was sent through the enemies' straw huts, they burst out with war cries and discharged more rounds. The terrified inhabitants, seeking to escape, often ran directly into the arrows. Those who fell were promptly pierced by a stream of arrows, tramped upon, and beheaded. The victims occasionally saved the situation with firearms, but often the *Parintintin* won in spite of such defense. If they did not win on the first attempt, however, they withdrew immediately.

Whenever possible, the *Parintintin* carried away their victims' heads and sometimes arms and legs. On the way home, they strewed the trail with caltrops made of bamboo arrowheads removed from the shafts, and, at the entrance of their villages, they dug carefully camouflaged pitfalls, bristling with bamboo points. The *Parintintin* never reared captive children.

Warriors, especially young ones, decorated themselves for battle with beautiful feather crowns of vivid colors and with long neck feathers. Many painted themselves black with charcoal from chestnuts or with white clay.

At the time of their pacification, the *Parintintin* were fighting only the Neo-Brazilians and the *Pirahá*.

Cannibalism.—For a long time after the pacification, the *Parintintin* did not deny that they were cannibals. The latest case of cannibalism occurred in 1924 when they killed a family of *Pirahá* (García de Freitas, 1926, p. 70 s.). They saved a piece of the victim's flesh for the representative of the Serviço de Protecção aos Indios, who saw them at that time dancing with the roasted and shriveled hand of their victim.

Trophies.—The *Parintintin* were passionate head hunters. The victims' heads were defleshed and cooked to remove every bit of flesh and to loosen the teeth. The teeth were made into a necklace that was given to one of the warriors. The skull was washed, tied with embira strips, and provided with a cord loop by means of which it was held over the left shoulder during dances. When visitors arrived, the warriors performed with the skulls. Immediately after the war greeting (see below), each warrior mimicked the struggle with the enemy whose skull he carried. He then ran back and forth in front of the visitors, singing a war song, during which he was followed by two young people who presented gourds filled with honey and water to the visitors. The trophy and the gourds were then placed in the front, and everybody shouted and shot arrows at the trophy. Then followed dances around the trophy, accompanied by bamboo flutes. Finally, others danced with the trophy, reciting their own deeds.

According to García, it was the custom to sacrifice prisoners in the plaza, killing them by means of a special spear (more probably a pointed club was used).

ETIQUETTE

When Indians from some other group approached, the inhabitants of the hut hastily put on their war paint, while chewing charcoal, and received the visitors with gestures and shouts of, "Let me kill!". They shot arrows over the heads of the visitors and uttered war cries. Then the household head went forward, put his hand on the shoulder of the first visitor to come to him, stamped his foot, and shouted a long speech of welcome in his ear. After this, they accepted the visitors and removed their war paint.

Birth.—When a child is born, its father and relatives utter war cries and shoot arrows.

Childhood and puberty.—Children are usually well treated, but occasional brutal treatment was observed. When their fringed aprons are replaced for the first time by penis covers, boys go into the jungle to hunt and bring home their kill. Before the penis casing is put on, mandibles (not stings) of tucandeira ants are applied to them. Then the youths approach the house, where they are greeted with war cries, and arrows are shot (García de Freitas, 1926, p. 68).

A girl's first menstruation is announced by war cries and arrow shooting. According to García de Freitas, girls 10 to 12 years of age are publicly deprived of their virginity, in spite of their objections; in one case, two Indians traded their sisters for this ceremony. The faces and bodies of young people, especially young men, bear the marks of bites and scratches received in amorous encounters, for it seems that before marriage there is much liberty for both sexes.

Marriage.—Marriage is arranged by the parents. The groom sometimes receives the bride while she is still a little girl and rears her. After a long time with his first wife, a man may take another, but García noticed only three cases of bigamy in the whole tribe. Young men have a certain aversion to marriage because of the work entailed by family life. During the pacification period, no man ever showed disrespect toward his wife, but a woman was seen to grasp her husband by his hair and slap him, while he merely hid his face. On overland trips, the husband carries his wife's as well as his own basket of goods, and on water he alone paddles the canoe.

Before their pacification, the *Parintintin* accorded old people little consideration.

Burial.—The body is painted with urucú, decorated with a feather diadem, wrapped in the hammock with its legs drawn up and its hands placed between the thighs, and buried in a square grave, 1.5 m. (4½ ft.) deep, in the house. Before the open grave, the possessions of the deceased are distributed among his friends and relatives, but his war arrows are broken and burned. The grave is filled and the earth beaten down with the feet and smoothed with water. Mortars and heavy tree trunks are placed over the grave to protect it against the evil spirit. The women cry much, and the men maintain an attitude of sorrow.

Art.—The best *Parintintin* pictorial art is tattooing. Crude figures of animals and people are sometimes cut on flutes and horns. Wood carvings are crude and at times of monstrous ugliness.

Music and dancing.—A triumphal dance, held after receiving some object, consists of eight steps forward, a half-turn, and eight steps back, etc., and always ends with two double tones on the panpipes and a war shout. It is accompanied by improvised singing.

The *Parintintin* dance in a circle to the bamboo clarinet (toré). Each man keeps his arms around the shoulders of the man next to him and dances in this position, jumping with both feet together. Women occasionally take part in it, passing slightly hunched under the arms of the men.

Musical instruments.—The bamboo flute is 1.5 m. (5 ft.) long. The panpipes have 7 to 15 pipes. A bamboo flute, one finger thick and closed on one end by an internode, has a rectangular opening on side for the mouth and another near the open end for the fingers. Other flutes are double, connected by the common internode in the middle. Signal trumpets are made of thick bamboo and are blown through a side opening. A child's toy consists of a whistle made of the skull of an acoutí-purú (*Sciurus* sp.) with all openings, except the foramen magnum, plugged with wax.

Narcotics.—The *Parintintin* formerly did not know tobacco, and at first it was so repellent to them that they would not go near a person who was smoking.

Nunes Pereira (1940) mentions the invention of cauim, or chicha, by the wife of the culture hero, Bahirá, who toasted maize, chewed it up, put it in a gourd with water and honey and let it ferment many days.

RELIGION

According to García de Freítas (1926), the *Parintintin* sang to the Sun. The song lasts the whole night, until sunrise, during which time they drink only chicha, being forbidden to eat. They regard the moon as the protector of crops, believing that it waters them at the right time.

Ghosts that cause nightmares are sent to "heavenly mansions" by means of chants. They are carried there by the Kaihú spirit (macaco coatá, *Ateles* sp.)

MYTHOLOGY

Some *Parintintin* myths have been transcribed by Nunes Pereira (1940), but they seem incomplete and contain some mistakes. The principal character is the culture hero, Bahirá, the equivalent of the *Apiacá* Bairy and the *Tupinamba* and *Tembé* Maira. Undoubtedly, Bahirá had a companion, like most culture heroes, but Nunes Pereira assumed him to be a different character according to the occasion. The character called an "Indian" by the same author is none other than Azon of the *Tembé* and Anyãi of the *Apapocuva-Guaraní,* as proved by the episode in which Bahirá fools him during the fishing party and the scalping. Some of Bahirá's adventures are based purely on *Tupí* themes, e.g., the theft of fire from the vultures. The motif of the pursuing devil, who was killed tossing a cluster of anajá (*Maximiliana regia*) on his head, occurs also among the *Shipaya.* The story of the man who is imprisoned on a tree or in a cliff near the nest of a bird is known to the *Tembé* and to various *Ge* tribes (*Apinayé, Canella, Sherente, Cayapó*). The story of the prisoner who later changed into a sparrow hawk and took revenge on his malefactor is also found among the *Tembé.*

Some *Parintintin* motifs are entirely lacking in the folklore of other *Tupí* tribes. Thus, the exchange of excrements by which the ant-eater deceives the jaguar, belongs to *Caingang* and *Bacaïri* folklore. The tale of the hero, who is made invulnerable and, changed into a fish, escapes with the arrows shot at him, occurs among the *Sherente, Camacan,* and *Mashacali.* The story of the fish which are caught by the hero and changed into people, and the theme of the mosquitoes originating from the stomach of a mutum (*Crax* sp.) are motifs of the *Tucuna* folklore.

INDIANS OF THE ANARI RIVER REGION

TERRITORY AND HISTORY

In 1914 or 1915, a band of unknown Indians appeared on the upper Anarí River, a left tributary of the lower Machado River, at lat. 9° 40′ S., on lands previously inhabited by the then almost extinct *Jarú.* The band had come from the left branch of the Branco River, a tributary of the Jamary, where it had lived peaceably until friction developed with rubber collectors. In reprisal for an attack, the Indians' village and farms were destroyed, and the group fled to the Preto River region, but, failing to get along with the rubber gatherers there, it moved on to the headwaters of the Agua Azul and Limãozinho Rivers, tributaries of the Madeirinha, and to the Carmelo and Jandahyra River regions. Here they founded three villages. In 1916, they were established on both banks of the upper Machadinho River. Rubber gatherers of the Preto River drove them out of the Carmelo region, but in turn were attacked. Attempts to pacify these Indians began in 1916 but all failed (Horta Barbóza, 1916, pp. 9 f., 26, 32), and, to the present date, 1942, the tribe has maintained its hostile attitude.

The cultural data below indicate that the Indians of the upper Anarí River constitute another group of *Cawahíb.* The name *Bocas Pretas,* "black mouths," given them by Neo-Brazilians suggests that they have black tattoo marks around the mouth, like the *Parintintin* of the Madeira River.

CULTURE

In 1916-17, Captain Horta Barboza gathered a few ethnographic data. These Indians grew maize, manioc, arrow-root, and cotton, but no bananas. One village consisted of nine huts and two large open sheds. There were baskets containing maize, and utensils for preparing meal. The Indians would not accept tobacco, but picked up other gifts that were put out for them. They had pots, a toré-type clarinet, 32 to 40 inches (80 to 100 cm.) long, and hammocks made of wild fibers with small cross twines. The tribe attacked with arrows, giving war cries, and they strew caltrops on the paths. Six words were collected from a captive girl.

THE "PARINTINTIN" BETWEEN THE UPPER TAPAJÓZ AND SAO MANOEL RIVERS

In the triangle between the upper Tapajóz and São Manoel Rivers, below lat. 10° S., there seems to be a tribe called *Tapanyuna* which has been hostile until very recent times. Coudreau and the Franciscans of the Cururú Mission refer to them as *"Parintintin."* Information given H. Coudreau in 1895 by the *Mundurucú*, who were then at war with this tribe, showed that it lived 2 or 3 days' travel above the Seven Falls of the São Manoel River. Father Hugo Mense (personal correspondence) describes them as tall, slender, handsome, long-haired Indians who are cannibals but good pilots. The Mission's published report, "Lose Blätter vom Cururú" (n. d.), contains 21 words which Mense obtained from a captive. The language is very similar to that of *Cawahíb*. Until the 1920's, the tribe still made attacks in the region of the São Tomé River and other right tributaries of the upper Tapajóz. Today it is no longer mentioned.

Another mysterious tribe of the same region is the *Taipe-shishi* (a *Mundurucú* name meaning "large number"), called *Taipö-chichí* by Father Hugo Mense, *Raïpe-chichi* or *Aïpo-sissi* by H. Coudreau (1897 a), *Taypeheh-shishi* by Father Albert Kruse, and *Takai-mbucwú* by the *Apiacá* (according to Kruse, *Takóï-mbukú*, "long penis"). A missionary report found in the Arquivos da Inspectoria do Serviço de Protecção aos Indios in Belém links the tribe to the *Tapanyuna,* probably using this name in the modern sense, but Kruse identifies it as *Parintintin.* The name can only refer to the exceedingly long penis sheath (16 in., or 40 cm.) worn by the *Parintintin,* or at least, by those of the Madeira River. The *Apiacá* informed Koch-Grünberg (1902) that this tribe wore their hair long, like Mense's *"Parintintin,"* a feature which distinguishes them from the Madeira *Parintintin* and relates them to the *Cayabí.* The *Taipe-shishi* are probably the *Parintintin* who live in the region between the upper Tapajóz and São Manoel Rivers, and both names are synonyms designating a group of the *Cawahíb* tribe.

INDIANS OF THE SANGUE RIVER REGION

Information which Father Guimarães (1865) received from the *Apiacá* in 1819 put the *"Cauahipe"* on the Paramutanga (Sangue) River, a tributary of the Juruena. Melgaço (1884) says they were between the Juruena and the Arinos Rivers, and an *Apiacá* told Castelnau in 1844 that the *"Cahuahiva"* had been driven inland from the Juruena River by the *Apiacá*.

In 1915, an expedition of the Commission of Stragetic Telegraph Lines from Mato Grosso to the Amazon, led by Lieutenant F. P. Vasconcellos, was attacked by Indians on the lower Sangue River. These Indians were strong and well built. They used bark canoes, grew manioc and bananas, and had hammocks. The men wore fiber aprons, but the only woman seen was nude. Both sexes wore necklaces and bracelets, and had their faces painted white and three white and black lines painted on the wrists. Their arrows had an arched feathering (Rondón, 1916, pp. 259–270).

Vasconcellos (in Rondón, 1916) classified this tribe as *Nambicuara*, but Rondón correctly related it to the *"Parnauat"* (*Tupi* of the Machado River), for it is probably another offshoot of the *Cawahíb*.

INDIANS OF THE BARARATY RIVER REGION

In Castelnau's list of tribes (1850–59, 3 : 104) compiled from early 19th-century data, he says that the *Parintintin* lived from Todos os Santos Falls, lat. 8° S., to a little above the mouth of the São Manoel River. In 1895, the *Mundurucú* who lived in the region of the Bararaty River (a left tributary of the upper Tapajóz, about 6 miles above the São Manoel River) stated that about 8 days' travel from the mouth and above some falls, lived the *Pari-uaïa-Bararaty* tribe (Coudreau, H., 1897 a). About 1920 these Indians assaulted rubber collectors of this same region, but today they are no longer mentioned.

This may have been another *Cawahíb* group which remained more or less in its original location.

THE "PARINTINTIN" BETWEEN THE JAMAXIM AND CREPORY RIVERS

Friar Pelino de Castovalva, missionary to the *Mundurucú* in Bacabal, in a report prepared in 1876, refers to the appearance of a band of *"Parintintin"* in the vicinity of the mission (right bank of the Tapajóz, lat. 6° 25' S.). The Indians attacked a rubber gatherer at the mouth of the Jamaxim River, and killed a woman, whose head they carried away. The mission *Mundurucú* pursued them and captured several, but they continued their bloody attacks, especially in the Jamaxim River region, until 1883.

H. Coudreau alone has ethnographic data on this group, and he obtained them from a third party in 1895. Every year during the summer the tribe peaceably passed through the rubber forests on the Crepory and Caderiri Rivers, withdrawing in the winter to the interior of the forests between the Xingú and Tapajóz Rivers. The Indians wore their hair long, went completely nude, and had only a little tattooing on their faces. Their language was so similar to that of the *Mundurucú* that they could make themselves understood without the use of the Lingua Geral.

If, instead of tattooing, this tribe painted, the description given Coudreau fits only the *Curuaya* (pp. 221–222), which, from time immemorial, has lived to the east of the Curuá River, a left tributary of the Iriri River. *Curuaya* tradition recounts long excursions made in remote times to the west, where they fought with the *Karuziat* (*Mundurucú*). It seems reasonable, therefore, to suppose that the so-called *"Parintintin"* of the right tributaries of the middle Tapajóz were really wandering groups of the *Curuaya*. These *"Parintintin"* ceased their assaults at exactly the time that the *Curuaya* entered into permanent and peaceful contact with the Neo-Brazilians of the Iriri River. Moreover, neither the *Curuaya* nor the missionaries to the *Mundurucú* mention any other tribe in that territory, and Dr. Emilia Snethlage, going overland in 1909 from the Curuá to the Jamaxim River and descending the latter, found no definite signs of the presence of Indians.

BIBLIOGRAPHY

(Cayabí, Tapanyuna, and Apiacá and Cawahíb, Parintintin, and their Neighbors)

Ayres Cazal 1807 (1707) ; Barboza Rodrigues, 1875 a ; Castelnau, 1850–59, vol. 3 ; Castro and França, 1868 ; Chandless, 1862 ; Costa Pinheiro, 1915 ; Coudreau, H., 1897 a ; Dengler, 1928 ; Dyott, 1929 ; Farabee, 1917 a ; Florence, 1941(?) ; Fonseca, 1880–81 ; García de Freitas, 1926 ; Grubb, 1927 ; Guimarães, 1865 ; Hoehne (see Costa Pinheiro, 1915) ; Horta Barbóza, 1916 ; Katzer, 1901 ; Koch-Grünberg, 1902 ; Krickeberg, 1922 ; Langsdorff (see Florence, 1941(?)) ; Lose Blätter . . . (*see* Missionarios Franciscanos, n. d.) ; Martius, 1867 ; Melgaço, 1884 ; Meyer, 1898 ; Missionarios Franciscanos, n. d. ; Nimuendajú, 1924 ; Nunes Pereira, 1940 ; Oliveira Miranda, 1890 ; Peixoto de Azevedo, 1885 ; Rivet, 1924 ; Rondón, 1916 ; Rossi, 1863 ; São José, 1847 ; Schmidt, M., 1903, 1905, 1929 a ; Schmidt, W., 1913 ; Serviço de Protecção aos Indios, 1942 ; Souza, A., 1916 ; Steinen, 1886, 1940 ; Telles Pires (see Oliveira Miranda, 1890) ; Tenan, n. d. ; Tocantins, 1877 ; Vasconcellos (see Rondón, 1916).

THE TUPI-CAWAHIB

By Claude Lévi-Strauss

TRIBAL DIVISIONS AND HISTORY

The *Tupi-Cawahib* are not mentioned in the literature prior to 1913–14, when they were discovered by General Candido Mariano da Silva Rondón, who headed the Brazilian Military Commission. Little information about them is contained in the reports of the Commission (Missão Rondón, 1916; Rondón, 1916).

The *Tupi-Cawahib* declined rapidly in population within a few years. The 300 individuals who comprised the *Takwatip* clan in 1915 were reduced in 10 years to only 59 persons—25 men, 22 women, and 12 children. In 1938, there were only 5 men, a woman, and a small girl. Thirty years ago, the entire *Tupi* group probably included from 2,000 to 3,000 persons; now only 100 or 150 of them are alive. Epidemics of grippe, during 1918–20, are largely responsible for the decline in population. Several cases of paralysis of the legs, observed in 1938 (Lévi-Strauss, n.d. a), suggest that poliomyelitis may have reached this remote region.

According to the linguistic and historical evidence presented by Nimuendajú (1924, 1925), the *Tupi-Cawahib* and *Parintintin* are the remnants of an ancient *Tupi* tribe, the *Cabahiba*. Since the 18th century, it has often been stated that the *Cabahiba* had once lived in the upper Tapajóz Basin. The language of the *Tupi-Cawahib* closely resembles that of the *Parintintin,* and both are related to the language of the *Apiacá* of the Tapajóz River. After the destruction of the *Cabahiba* by the *Mundurucú,* the *Tupi-Cawahib* settled on the Rio Branco, a left tributary of the Roosevelt River (lat. 10°–12° S., long. 61°–62° W.) From the Rio Branco they were driven to their present territory on both sides of the Machado (or upper Gi-Paraná) River, from the Riosinho River in the southeast to the Muquí and the Leitão River in the north and the northwest. These three waterways are small tributaries of the Machado River. The native groups mentioned by both Rondón and Nimuendajú (1924, 1925) are clans with special geographical localization. According to Nimuendajú's informant, the *Wirafëd* and *Paranawát* (*Paranauad*) were settled on a tributary of the right bank of the

299

Riosinho River. The *Takwatib Eriwahun* (Nimuendajú), or *Takwatip* (Lévi-Strauss), who had once lived on the Tamuripa River, a right tributary of the Machado River, halfway between the Riosinho and the Muquí Rivers, were brought by General Rondón to the Rio Machado, where they lived until 1925, when the last six members of the group joined the Telegraphic Post of Pimenta Bueno. The *Ipotewát,* mentioned by Rondón, are no longer an autonomous unit. According to information recorded in 1938, they were then living on the upper Cacoal between the Riosinho and Tamuripa Rivers. Living downstream were the *Tucumanfét.* The *Paranawát,* mentioned by Rondón and Nimuendajú, lived on the Rio Muquí in 1938. They numbered about 100 individuals and had refused to have any contact with White people. When the remnants of the previously unknown *Mialat* were discovered in 1938 on the upper Leitão River, there were only 16 members of the group (Lévi-Strauss, n.d. a). The now extinct *Jabotifet* were formerly settled between the upper Cacoal and Riosinho Rivers.

CULTURE

SUBSISTENCE

Farming.—The *Tupí-Cawahíb* cultivate gardens in large clearings near their villages and hunt game in the dense forest. They raise: both bitter and sweet manioc; five kinds of maize—a white one with large kernels, a dark red variety, a kind with white, black, and red kernels, one with orange and black kernels, and a red "chiné"; small, broadbeans; peanuts; hot peppers; bananas; papayas; cotton; and calabashes. Digging sticks and stone axes were formerly used for preparing and tilling the fields.

Wild foods.—The *Tupí-Cawahíb* gather several wild foods. To facilitate the collection of Brazil nuts, which are abundant in the region, they clear the forest around each tree. They collect two kinds of cacao beans which are eaten raw and several kinds of berries. To harvest the small pyramidal seeds of an unidentified tall forest grass (awatsipororoke), the natives tie several of the stems together before the ears are ripe, so that the seeds will fall together in small heaps.

The tapir, peccary, forest deer, great anteater, and numerous kinds of monkeys (pl. 25, *left*) and birds are hunted. Wild bees are killed in the hive by closing the entrance with a pad of leaves of an unidentified poisonous tree, and the honey is collected in coarse containers of bark or leaves. Fish are shot with arrows or drugged with a saponine-rich vine that is used in dams constructed of branches and mud in shallow places in rivers. When the *Tupí-Cawahíb* were first observed by the Whites, they kept chickens in conical sheds made of sticks set in the ground in a circle and tied together at the top. There was no dog in the *Mialat* village discovered in 1938.

Food preparation.—Game is singed and smoked in the skin, either intact or in pieces. Babracots are about 5 feet (1.5 m.) high and are constructed on four posts. Game is smoked for 24 hours; during the night, an attendant takes care of the fire. The babracot for drying beans is made of several branches placed on transverse sticks, which are supported on the prongs of a three-forked branch.

Maize chicha (ka-ui) (pl. 24, *left*) is made by drying the kernels and grinding them in a mortar with a few Brazil nuts or peanuts for seasoning. The coarse flour is mixed with water in large bowls, and small children spit saliva in the gruel. After the chicha ferments a few hours, it is put on the fire, and is kept just below the boiling point for 2 or 3 hours. Fresh gruel is constantly added to compensate for the evaporation. The beverage is drunk as soon as it is cold or during the next 2 or 3 days.

Manioc tubers are grated and roasted in large plates. Popcorn is made of maize and of the wild seed, awatsipororoke. Pama berry seeds are eaten roasted. In contrast to the neighboring *Nambicuara*, the *Tupi-Cawahib* are fond of highly seasoned foods. They cook hot peppers and broadbeans in a stew. A kind of salt is prepared by burning acuri palm leaves, sifting the ashes, and washing them with water. Both the water, which is dark brown and bitter, and the ashes, which form a gray astringent powder, are used as condiments.

HOUSES

When Rondón discovered the *Tupi-Cawahib*, their square huts had no walls; the gable roof of palms was supported on posts set in the ground. Hammocks were swung from the posts. In 1915 the *Takwatip* village comprised about 20 houses, each from 12 to 18 feet (3.5 to 5.5 m.) long, arranged in a circle about 60 feet (18 m.) in diameter. Two large houses in the center of the circle, each from 36 to 42 feet (11 to 12.5 m.) long, were occupied by the chief, Abaitara, and his wives, children, and court. Cages for harpy eagles and huts for fowls were in the open space of the circular plaza. There were no fortifications surrounding the village. Quite different was the *Mialat* village discovered in 1938. Of the four square houses, each about 30 feet (9 m.) long, situated in a row, two were used for living quarters and two for food storage. The roof frame was supported by posts, irregularly spaced and set back under the projecting roof, so that the house resembled a square mushroom. The storage quarters had no walls. Each of the other two houses was surrounded by a continuous palisade about 6 feet (2 m.) high, which gave the appearance of a wall but actually did not support the roof, as there was an opening a few inches wide between the lower edge of the roof frame and the top of the palisade. The palisade, which had loopholes (pl. 25, *right*) for shooting arrows, was made of longitudinal sections of palm trunks, fastened edge to edge, the convex surface turned outward. The exterior was decorated with jaguars, dogs, harpy eagles, snakes, frogs, children, and the moon painted in urucú paste.

Platforms were built along the paths leading to the villages as lookouts from which the moves of hostile groups could be observed (Rondón, 1916).

Tree trunks were used to bridge small waterways.

DRESS AND ORNAMENTS

According to Rondón (1916), men wore a garment of woven cotton resembling drawers. In 1938, *Tupí-Cawahíb* men were naked, except for a small conical penis sheath made of the two halves of a leaf plaited and sewed. Women wore a short, cylindrical skirt of woven cotton string, which reached half-way to the knees (pl. 26). Modern *Tupí-Cawahíb* women tattoo their faces with a sharpened deer bone and genipa, applying a geometrical design on the chin and two large symetrical curved stripes on the cheeks, running from the chin to the ears. Men used to paint themselves with genipa or urucú dye when monkey hunting (Rondón, 1916). Both sexes wear bracelets, earrings, necklaces, and rings made of mollusk shells, nutshells, wild seeds, game teeth, and deer bones cut in rectangular plates (pl. 26). For ceremonies, men wear a cap without a top made of a large band of woven cotton, over which feathers are stuck. The chief wears a heavy tuft of feathers hanging down his back. Both sexes pluck their pubic hair and eyebrows, using the thumb nail and a half shell. "Eyebrows wearer" is the derogatory equivalent of "civilized." Woven cotton bands are worn around the ankles, the arm, and the wrists.

TRANSPORTATION

The *Tupí-Cawahíb* made canoes of the bark of large trees (Rondón, 1916). A baby straddles its mother's hip, supported by a cotton sling (pl. 26, *right*).

MANUFACTURES

Spinning.—Spinning is done by women. A *Tupí-Cawahíb* spindle consists of a small stick, with a round wild seed for the whorl. It is very light and is used more for winding thread in balls than for spinning.

Textile arts.—Cotton armlets and anklets are woven by women on primitive vertical looms. Women's skirts are woven and small hammocks are netted with cotton string, and carrying sacks are woven with tucum string.

Basketry.—The *Tupí-Cawahíb* weave flat sieves and baskets of bamboo strips and palm leaves, and fire fans of palm leaves, often decorating the fans with feathers. An ingenious rucksack for carrying large objects or animals is made by knotting two palm leaves together.

Pottery.—The earthenware seen in 1938 consisted of hemispherical bowls, large ones for preparing chicha and small ones for individual meals, and large, circular plates for roasting flour. None were decorated. Informants, however, speak of a purple dye obtained from a wild leaf which was used in former times for painting geometric designs.

Weapons.—*Tupi-Cawahib* bows are about 5 feet 8 inches (1.7 m.) long and are made of a black palm wood. The section is circular and the ends are carved to form a knob and shoulders for fastening the string. The grip is wrapped with cotton. Arrows are of three types: those tipped with a large bamboo splinter, for hunting mammals; those with a blunt point, for bird hunting; and arrows which have short feathers and four to seven bamboo points arranged as a crown around a small ball of string, for fishing. Feathering is flush and tied (Arara type), flush and sewed (Xingú type), or arched (eastern Brazil type). Arrow poison is unknown. When shot, the arrow is grasped between the first and middle fingers, which also draw the string, or else it is held between the thumb and finger, and the string drawn with the other three fingers.

To defend the paths leading to their villages, the *Tupi-Cawahib* set pointed rods or stakes obliquely into the ground, either singly or fencelike. The stakes are from 1 foot (30 cm.) (Lévi-Strauss, n.d. a) to 4 feet (1.2 m.) (Rondón, 1916) in height, so as to impale the foot or the body, and are hidden under foliage taken from the surrounding forest.

Other implements.—Boxes for holding feathers are made of hollowed sections of acuri palm trunks; a longitudinal segment serves as a cover. A manioc grater consists of a wooden board with embedded palm thorns. Spoons and containers are made of calabashes. Ordinary combs and small-tooth combs are of the composite type. Drills and knives are made of iron pieces fastened onto sticks with wax and wrapper cotton.

SOCIAL AND POLITICAL ORGANIZATION

The *Tupi-Cawahib* are divided into several patrilineal sibs, each localized in one or more villages occupying a defined territory. There is a strong tendency toward village exogamy, which is regarded less as a binding rule than as a means of insuring good relations between neighboring sibs. Endogamic marriages are possible, although infrequent. Residence seems to be patrilocal, although contrary practices have been recorded. Consequently, the majority of individuals in any village belong to one eponymic sib, but are nevertheless associated with a few people belonging to different allied sibs. Besides the four group names mentioned by Rondón (1916) and Nimuendajú (1924), no less than 15 new sib names were recorded in 1938 (Lévi-Strauss, n.d. a). As this list is certainly incomplete, the ancient sib organization must have been complex. In addition to sib divisions, each village was divided into two age classes, "the youths" and "the elders." The function of these age classes seems to have been mostly ceremonial.

Chieftaincy is hereditary, passing from the father to son. In former times, the chief was attended by a hierarchy of officials. He possessed judicial power and imposed the death sentence, the convicted person being bound and thrown into the river from a canoe. When the Rondón Commission first met the *Takwatip* chief, Abaitara, he was apparently extending his domination over a large number of sibs and trying, by means of successful wars, to establish his hegemony over others.

WARFARE

Rondón mentions the decapitation of enemies killed in warfare, but does not state that head trophies were prepared.

LIFE CYCLE

Childbirth.—A couvade is observed, during which both parents eat only gruel and small animals. Nuts of all kinds are forbidden them.

Marriage.—The *Tupí-Cawahíb* practice marriage between cross-cousins and between a maternal uncle and his niece. In the latter case, an adult man may betroth a baby girl, who remains under his care and to whom he gives presents until they marry. Although marriage is generally monogamous, a chief may have several wives, usually sisters, or a woman and her daughter. To compensate for the shortage of women thus created, the chief lends his wives to bachelors and to visitors, and fraternal polyandry, associated with the levirate, is practiced within the group. In a polygynous family, one wife has authority over the others, regardless of the differences of age or of previous family relationship.

The existence of homosexuality is not openly acknowledged, but a word meaning "passive pederast" is commonly used as an insult.

Death.—The deceased at the time of Rondón's visit was buried inside his hut under his hammock, which, with his weapons, ornaments, and utensils, was left undisturbed. Mourners, i. e., relatives, cut their hair (Rondón, 1916).

ESTHETIC AND RECREATIONAL ACTIVITIES

Art.—Painting on house walls has already been mentioned.

Narcotics.—Strangely enough, the *Tupí-Cawahíb* do not cultivate or use tobacco. (For chicha, see p. 301.)

Games.—Children play with crude toys made of plaited or twisted straw. In a disk game, "the youths" are matched against "the elders"; each age group alternately shoots its arrows at a rolling wooden disk thrown across the plaza by a pitcher. In another archery contest, they shoot arrows at a dummy representing a man or an animal. There is a belief that to shoot at a wooden dummy may bring death; to avoid the risk, the dummy is made of straw.

Dance and music.—Festivals were given by the chief, who assumed the title, "Owner of the Feast." Festivals were preceded by hunting expeditions to obtain small animals, such as rats and marmosets, which were smoked and strung together to be worn as necklaces. During the feast, men playfully carried a flute player on their shoulders.

In 1938, the *Mialat* chief entertained his people several times with a musical show in which songs alternated with dialogue. He himself played the numerous roles of the comedy, humorously enacting the adventures of several animals and inanimate objects which were mystified by the japim bird. Each character was easily recognized by a musical leitmotif and a special register of the voice.

Musical instruments.—The main musical instruments were pottery trumpets (Rondón, 1916), panpipes with 13 pipes, short flageolets with 4 holes, whistles, and gourd rattles. A clarinet without stops was made of a piece of bamboo about 4 feet (1.2 m.) long; a small piece of bamboo in which a vibrating strip was cut formed the reed.

MAGIC AND RELIGION

We have no indication of the magical and religious beliefs of the *Tupi-Cawahib*. The chief is certainly endowed with shamanistic powers: he treats patients and improvises songs and dances in order to tell and enact his dreams, which are considered to have a premonitory significance. At the end of his musical show, he may become delirious and try to kill anyone in sight.

Although nearly all the sibs have animal or vegetable names, totemism does not seem to exist, for the eponymic plants or animals are freely eaten.

Even today, the *Tupi-Cawahib* capture great harpy eagles, rear them carefully in large square cages, and feed them game, such as birds and monkeys. It is likely that this custom has a magical or religious background, though nothing positive is known in this respect.

BIBLIOGRAPHY

Lévi-Strauss, n. d. a; Missão Rondón, 1916; Nimuendajú, 1924, 1925; Rondón, 1916.

PLATE 24.—**Tupí-Cawahíb village life.** At *left*: Making maize beer. (Courtesy Claude Lévi-Strauss.)

PLATE 25.—**Tupí-Cawahíb village life.** *Left:* Stripping off a monkey skin. *Right:* Painted house wall with a loophole. (Courtesy Claude Lévi-Strauss.)

PLATE 26—Tupí-Cawahíb mothers and children. Typical carrying band for children. (Courtesy Claude Lévi-Strauss.)

THE CAYABI, TAPANYUNA, AND APIACA

By Curt Nimuendajú

THE CAYABI

INTRODUCTION

These Indians call themselves *Paruá,* but since their contacts with Europeans they also use the name *Cayabí.*

Language.—There is practically no difference between the *Tupí* dialect spoken by the *Cayabí* and that of the *Camayurá.* Rivet (1924, p. 659) and Grubb (1927, p. 118) mistakenly place them in the *Cariban* family, probably because of some *Bacaïri* words which they used when they were encountered by A. Pyrineus de Souza's expedition.

Tribal divisions and history.—Among the Indians met by Antonio Peixoto during his expedition to the Paranatinga River were perhaps *Cayabí.* The *Mundurucú* who accompanied the expedition called them *Parabitata* (*parir,* "non-*Mundurucú* Indians," bi; "lip," tatá?). However, unlike the *Cayabí,* these Indians used rafts made of embauva trunks.

The name *Cayabí* appears for the first time in Castelnau's report (1850–59, 2:306) on the Tapajóz region (map 1, *No. 1;* map 4). In 1848, the *Cayabí* figure in a list of tribes as indomitable Indians living near the Salto de Paranatinga. In 1884, Von den Steinen (1886) found among the Paranatinga *Bacaïri* two *Cayabí* women who had been captured during their childhood by a party avenging a murder and the abduction of a child. Hostilities between the *Cayabí* and the Whites began with the advance of the rubber collectors into the region of the Paranatinga River. It is not unlikely that in 1899 some *Cayabí* lived, as Herrmann Meyer heard from the *Auetö* of the Culisseu River, on the Steinen River, the westernmost tributary of the Xingú River. In 1900, they were visited on the Paranatinga River by a Salesian missionary, Father Balzola. The vestiges which Max Schmidt found in 1901 on the headwaters of the Ronuro and Batovy Rivers and identified as *Cayabí* were more likely *Cayapó,* who were later reported in that region by Dyott in 1928 and Petrullo in 1931. In 1901, a skirmish took place between the *Bacaïri* and *Cayabí,* and an expedition sent by Orlando Bruno and Co. found *Cayabí* near the mouth of the Rio Verde, on the Paranatinga River. In 1910, the *Cayabí* killed their long-time director, M. F. Valois Velho, and the same year a punitive expedition killed many of them and captured children.

In May 1915, an expedition led by Lt. Pyrineus de Souza down the Paranatinga-São Manoel River, between lat. 12° 40′ and 11° 30′ S., had numerous encounters with *Cayabí*. The Indians remained friendly so long as the expedition had tools to offer. As Pyrineus de Souza encountered groups of 100 Indians in some places and 200 in others, the total number of the tribe can be estimated at about 1,000.

In 1927, Max Schmidt had brief contacts with six *Cayabí* Indians who had come to get gifts at the Serviço de Protecção aos Indios post located above the móuth of the Verde River, on the Paranatinga River.

After 1936, the *Cayabí,* at first under the name of *Makiri,* began to appear peaceably at the mouth of the São Manoel-Paranatinga River. The missionary, Father Albert Kruse, took a short vocabulary from those who stopped at the *Mundurucú* mission of Cururú. In 1941, another post of the Serviço de Protecção aos Indios was founded on the right bank of the São Manoel River, at about lat. 8° 55′ S. According to the reports of the Arquivos da Inspectoria de Indios of Pará, 90 Indians appeared at the post in 1941, and 42 in 1942 and settled down somewhat above the post. Meanwhile, the mortality among these newcomers was very great.

CULTURE

SUBSISTENCE ACTIVITIES

A. Pyrineus de Souza (1916) saw large cultivated fields and received from the Indians green maize with long and slender ears, cara, batata rouxa (sweet potatoes), and crushed peanuts, which the Indians ate with tapioca. The Indians made balls of meal wrapped in sororoca leaves. From manioc they prepare a highly fermented and very sour drink.

In the forest, the Indians obtain many Brazil nuts which are especially important to them. They also eat barbecued and almost rotten deer meat and ducks broiled with entrails and feathers.

HOUSE AND VILLAGES

The huts of the upper region of *Cayabí* territory are generally located in the fields, away from the rivers. On the banks are only small fishing shanties. Farther down the river, however, Pyrineus de Souza found dwellings along the river banks.

In the houses were nets, gourds, small baskets, and shells, the last used as knives and carried hanging from the neck.

DRESS AND ORNAMENTS

Both sexes go about naked. From early childhood, males tie the foreskin with a thick cotton string, which they always wear in public and remove only to urinate.

Both sexes have the earlobes pierced for the insertion of pieces of wood, the tips of deer horns, or bamboo tubes, 3 to 4 inches long (7.5 to 10 cm.) decorated with tufts of feathers. On the wrists and below the knees, men wear woven cotton bands. Women wear these bands only below the knees, but they also use a belt consisting of several tight strings of threaded beads made of palm nuts.

For festive occasions men wear luxurious feather caps and headdresses. The caps are made of feathers and feather tufts mounted on a cotton net. Some men wear headbands of jaguar, monkey, or coati skin.

Some women pull out their eyebrows, eyelashes, and pubic hair. Men wear their hair long, tied at the neck. Women sometimes cut theirs at the level of the ears and comb it over the forehead. Hair is cut with a shell.

The *Cayabí* paint themselves and dye their hair with urucú. Two wide parallel strips tattooed with genipa at the mouth level for men, and a single stripe on the cheek with vertical lines around the mouth for women, is perhaps a tribal characteristic, according to L. Tenan (n.d.).

TRANSPORTATION

The canoes are made of cashew tree bark (cajui, *Anacardium microcarpum*). The prow and stern are the same, and both are tied with a tough vine. The Indians paddle standing up.

WAR

The Pyrineus de Souza expedition was attacked by the *Cayabí* when it had no more gifts. Before starting hostilities, an important member of the tribe sang and harangued the expedition. Warriors did not wear any special ornaments. They attacked by showering the enemy with arrows amidst loud shouting.

A *Cayabí* arrow described by Max Schmidt is 5 feet 3 inches (1.6 m.) long with a shaft made of camayuva (*Gadua* sp.), radial sewed feathering, and a bone point set so as to form a barb. The bow is flat on the cord side and convex on the outside. These Indians also fought with large thick clubs. According to the *Bacaïri, Cayabí* clubs are made of bacayuva wood. They are carefully carved, flat, about 5 feet (1.5 m.) long, and have a string loop.

The *Cabayí* are said to have held a monopoly on stone axes, which caused conflict with the *Bacaïri* when the latter descended the Paranatinga River. The hostility between the two tribes is old, but was preceded by a period of peace. The *Cayabí* are also accredited with cannibalism. According to L. Tenan (n.d.), they decapitated a slain enemy and cooked the head, eating the meat and making a trophy and musical instruments of the skull. In their attacks against civilized people, they sometimes took children captives.

BIBLIOGRAPHY

See *Cawahíb, Parintintin,* and Their Neighbors, bibliography, page 297.

TAPANYUNA

By 1747, at the time of the João de Souza's expedition, the *Arino* lived on the right bank of the Arinos River and on the upper Tapajóz River, from the territory of the *Macuari* (i.e., *Bacaïri*) at about lat. 11°50′ S., to that of the *Uarupá* on the Haravan River (São João da Barra at lat. 8°55′ S.). The name *Arino* then disappears and its place is taken by *Tapanyuna* (map 1, *No. 1;* map 4).

Tapanyuna is not an *Apiacá* word, but a Lingua Geral term which means "negro." Martius consequently thought that these people were fugitive slaves, but actually the name refers to the black paint they habitually wore.

From the documents which Castelnau compiled (1850–59) on the Arinos River in the first half of the 19th century, the *Tapanyuna* lived on the right side of the Arinos River from *Bacuri* (*Bacaïri*) territory to the Juruena River and on the left side of the Arinos from the *Bacuri* to the *Apiacá* (lat. 11° S.). No other source mentions the *Tapanyuna* on the left side of the Arinos River.

In 1812, the *Apiacá* warned Castro and França (1868) of a tribe which lived upstream on the right bank and used clubs. Three days later, they encountered three canoes which differed from those of the Apiacá, and they saw some fishing baskets. More details on the *Tapanyuna* were gathered by Guimarães (1865) from the *Apiacá* in 1819.

According to the *Apiacá*, there were three tribes on the Peixe River: First, the *Tapanhona*, on the river bank above the falls; next, the *Tapan-honauhum* (perhaps it should be *Tapii-un-uhu*, "large *Tapanyuna*") inland from the river bank; and third, the *Timaoana* (*Cayabi, Timauán, Tapanyuna*), the last of the tribes of the Peixe River. The first were tall, heavy-set, and warlike. They usually protected their dwellings with thorns or sharp stakes and with pitfalls all around. They used bows and arrows, and wore macaw and royal sparrow hawk feathers in their pierced ears. The *Tapanhonauhum* used bows and arrows and clubs, and were also warlike. They painted black circles on their faces, and adorned their pierced ears with multicolored feathers. The *Timaoana,* of average height, were cannibals, and painted their faces from forehead to neck. They used the same weapons as the preceding tribes. The women wore gold ear ornaments and beads. After 1820, only the *Tapanyuna* are mentioned. Métraux was correct in regarding the *Tapanhonauhum* and *Timaoana* as mere local subdivisions of the *Tapanyuna*.

In 1820, Francisco Lopes da Sá (see *Apiacá,* p. 312) reached a *Tapanyuna* village where he found only women and children. On his return he tried to get to the headwaters of the Peixe River, but was stopped by 500 (?) *Tapanyuna* warriors.

According to the tribal list of the Arquivos da Directoria de Indios of Cuyabá, the *Tapanyuna* numbered 800 people in 1848 and were hostile to the *Apiacá* and to the Whites, whose canoes they attacked. In 1895 H. Coudreau (1897 a) obtained meager information about a tribe which lived on the Tapanhuna River (Peixe River) and which spoke the same language as the *Apiacá*. They were said to lure travelers on the Arinos and upper Tapajóz River to their settlements and then to riddle them with arrows.

Another list of tribes, compiled by Castelnau (1850–59), mentions only the *Tapaiunaçú* (*Tapanhonauhum*), a noncivilized, agricultural tribe living near the *Nambicuara,* and the *Tamauanga* (*Timauán*) who, like the former, were a hostile but industrious tribe. In 1892, the *Tapanyuna* (or perhaps the *Parintintin*) looted and fired the *Apiacá* village in the vicinity of the São Florencio Falls. In 1893 or 1894, a small group of *Tapanyuna* (or of the *Parintintin* ?) was massacred by the *Mundurucú* on the Furna Islands where they were gathering Brazil nuts. In 1895, they fatally wounded the first Mato Grosso state collector, García Junior, at the mouth of the Arinos River.

In 1915, Lt. Pyrineus de Souza was warned by the *Cayabi* in the Paranatinga region that downstream there lived some wild Indians who painted their bodies and faces black and who might attack him with arrows and devour him. At a tributary of the left bank (about lat. 11° 15′ S.), he found vestiges of the tribe: two small huts which differed from those built by the *Cayabi,* being constructed of poles cut with iron tools and covered with sororóca leaves. There were babracots for broiling meat and fish, and many fishbones around. A path led into the interior.

After 1910, rubber workers along the tributaries on the right bank of the upper Tapajóz were sometimes attacked by hostile Indians. Those at São Tomé they called *Tapanyuna*. It is probable, however, that these were not the *Tapanyuna* from the Peixe River, but Indians who were known formerly as *Parintintin*. In the *Mundurucú* vocabulary prepared in 1912, Hoehne (*in* Costa Pinheiro, 1915) uses the word *Paridindin* as a synonym for *Tapanhuna,* proving the confusion in the naming of these two tribes, a confusion completed by the increasing tendency to identify the *Tapayuna* with the *Nambicuara* on the other bank of the Tapajóz River.

The only known objects of this tribe are a stone ax reproduced by Coudreau, H. (1897 a, p. 91) and a rectangular wooden shield figured by Krickeberg (1922, 1:276). The latter is such a cultural anomaly that its being attributed to the *Tapanyuna* is very doubtful.

BIBLIOGRAPHY

See Cawahíb, Parintintin, and Their Neighbors, bibliography, page 297.

APIACA

INTRODUCTION

These Indians have always been called *Apiacá*. The *Cayabí* refér to them as *Tapii-tin,* "the white foreigners."

History.—The *Apiacá* are mentioned for the first time in itineraries of 1791 and 1805 published by Castelnau (1850–59, 3: 93). However, it is possible that they were one of the five tribes found on the Arinos River by João de Souza in 1747. In 1812, they established peaceful relations with the expeditions of Miguel João de Castro and Antonio Tomé de França. In 1818, Antonio Peixoto de Azevedo took seven *Apiacá* to Cuyabá, and in the following year the *Apiacá* chief, Severino, and 14 others visited that city. From them, José da Silva Guimarães (1865) obtained information for a memoir on their customs. Their tales about great mineral riches caused Father Francisco Lopes de Sá to undertake an unsuccessful expedition using *Apiacá* guides in quest of gold and diamonds.

In 1828, the tribe was visited by the Langsdorff expedition and the artist, Florence (1941 ?), left a good description and excellent sketches of these Indians.

Castelnau (1850–59, 2:313) met some *Apiacá* in Diamantino and obtained a vocabulary.

Until 1848, the *Apiacá* (map 1; *No. 1;* map 4) inhabited the region between the junction of the Arinos and Juruena Rivers, from the 11th parallel northward. Their villages were located on the left bank of the Arinos River and on the right bank of the Juruena River, but both banks of the rivers were frequented somewhat beyond their junction. The Juruena River settlements had never been visited and all the descriptions refer only to the *Apiacá* on the Arinos River.

The *Apiacá* were very numerous. Records, probably from the beginning of the 19th century, mention bands of 200 to 300 archers each year and a total of 16,000 persons. In 1812, Castro and França (1868) found about 500 people in one settlement, 250 of whom were warriors. In 1819, Guimarães (1865) mentions a village with 1,500 inhabitants. The Arquivos da Directoria de Indios of Cuyabá gives their number at 2,700 for 1848.

In 1862, Rossi (1863) mentioned *Apiacá* on the left bank of the Arinos River, but Chandless (1862) located them above Salto Augusto. Their number was then declining. Barboza Rodrigues (1875) found the *Apiacá* in three villages a little above and below Salto Augusto. Under pressure by the Neo-Brazilians, a large part of the tribe had migrated to the São Manoel River, and became the *Pari-bi-teté* (a *Mundurucú* name meaning "non-*Mundurucú* painted lip Indians"). Twenty years ago, this tribe inhabited the upper course of the Apiacá River, a left tributary of the São Manoel, but it has since disappeared. In 1895, Coudreau, H., (1897 a) found its remnants (100 individuals) living in five huts between Salto São Simão and São Florencio. They were already dependent upon the Neo-Brazilian rubber gatherers. The men and some of the women dressed in civilized fashion, and there was evidence of some Negro mixture.

Katzer (1901) published notes on the tattooing and language of the *Apiacá* found at Itaituba. In the same year, Max Schmidt collected a vocabulary from an *Apiacá* in Rosario, Mato-Grosso, which was published by Koch-Grünberg (1902) with a compilation of all the linguistic and historical data known on these Indians.

With the establishment in 1902 of the Collectoria estadoal do Mato Grosso, the Indians fell on evil times. A great many were killed in reprisal for an attack they made against the collector's office. The situation changed only when José Sotero Barreto took the survivors under his protection and gathered them at the Collectoria. In 1912, there still lived 32 *Apiacá* (Costa Pinheiro, 1915, p. 75). In 1916 they were visited by Farabee (1917 a), who found them mixed with Negroes.

Today the *Apiacá* no longer exist as a tribe. Only a few individuals live at the Collectoria at the mouth of the São Manoel River and in the Franciscan missions on the Cururú River.

Language.—The *Apiacá* language differs very little from *Camayurá,* a *Tupí-Guaraní* dialect spoken on the lower Culisseu River, from *Cayabí* of the São Manoel River, or from the dialect of the *Cawahíb* (*Parintintin* of the Madeira River and *Tupí* of the Alto Machado). *Apiacá* is pure *Tupí* and the difference between it and *Tupinamba* is somewhat greater than between *Tupinamba* and *Guarani*. Soon after their first contact with the Neo-Brazilians, their language received several elements of the Lingua Geral.

CULTURE

SUBSISTENCE ACTIVITIES

Farming.—The *Apiacá* cultivated extensive tracts of land and, according to ancient travelers, their fields stretched beyond sight.

Planting was probably women's task and not a masculine activity, as stated by Guimarães. The *Apiacá* raised bitter and sweet manioc, maize, cara (*Dioscorea*), yams, sweet potatoes, magorito, peanuts, beans, lima beans, pumpkins, cotton, and, already in 1848, watermelons. Tobacco is not mentioned and was apparently unknown.

Wild foods included the Brazil nuts.

Domestication.—Florence (1941 ?) mentions that in a single village he found 80 tame macaws and a falcon in a thatched stick cage. Early sources mention no domestic animals, not even dogs. In 1820, however, Florence found dogs, pigs, chickens, and ducks. By 1848, the *Apiacá* sold fowls to travelers.

Hunting and fishing.—According to the "Nova navegação" (Anonymous, 1856), the *Apiacá* did not eat any kind of fowl; of mammals they only ate peccaries, tapirs, and capybaras.

They caught fish in baskets set at the bottom of weirs across the mouths of streams.

Food preparation.—Maize was crushed in a cylindrical mortar with a pestle 12 feet (3.6 m.) long. Roasted fish were crushed, bones and all, to make a flour. The *Apiacá* kept this and manioc flour in woven bags.

HOUSES

Originally, the *Apiacá* lived exclusively on the river shores in settlements which, with rare exceptions, consisted of a single house, large enough to accommodate hundreds of people. These huts were rectangular with rounded ends, and were covered with a thatched roof of ubim or sapé which rested on straight or arched rafters, and descended to within 1.50 m. (about 5 ft.) of the ground. The walls were made of paxiuba palm or of castanha bark. There was a main door of jatobá bark at each end, and several other doors in the long side walls. The living quarters where the Indians hung their hammocks extended on both sides of the hut, leaving the intervening space entirely free. Above the hammocks were platforms for storing maize and other foods. The house was surrounded by a large, carefully weeded clearing.

Hammocks were made of cotton, either in a net technique or of coarse fabric (Castro and França, 1868, p. 112).

DRESS AND ADORNMENT

Men tied to the foreskin a little sheath of pacova leaves with a ligature that forced the penis inside and covered it entirely. Women were entirely naked.

Some individuals of both sexes wore narrow woven cotton bands below the knees and on the ankles. The use of tight garters four inches (10 cm.) wide decorated with small feathers and of bands with long fringes on the forearms was restricted to men. Both sexes wrapped thick cotton threads around their ankles and wrists. Chiefs adorned their heads with white tufts. To make diadems, feathers were sometimes interwoven in a cotton fabric. On the forehead stood five long macaw tail feathers, with two shorter hawk feathers on each side and yellow japu feathers beyond. Men carried a kind of scepter made of six macaw tail feathers with their bases covered with down.

Both sexes had their ears pierced for the insertion of peccary teeth, small wooden pegs, or feathers. They seem to have inserted feathers through the nasal septum. Men wore long necklaces strung with the teeth of cutia and other small animals. Chiefs used a large, shiny, white collar of shell and large belts of black beads and human teeth. Women's necklaces were made of tucum nuts ground into shape on a stone and perforated with a fish tooth, and interspersed with human teeth, which were their husbands' war trophies. Some men wore belts of animal teeth; others, belts woven of cotton and dyed with urucú, with tassels at both ends. These tassels were tied together and hung over the genitals.

Men cut their hair along the forehead and above the ears. Women wrapped their hair with a cotton fillet so that it formed a horizontal tuft. They did not pluck their eyebrows or eyelashes.

Men were tattooed by women who used tucum thorns. The pattern consisted of three lines extending from each ear, one to a little below the nose, one to a corner of the mouth, one to the chin. At the age of 14, the tattooing was completed with a rectangle around the mouth, a symbol indicating that the wearer could eat human flesh. The designs tattooed on the body are said to have illustrated their war and hunting deeds. According to Florence, these included parallel right angles on their chest and abdomen, and crude representations of animals, fish, men, and women on their arms and legs. A young man had the figure of a jaguar (?) on his right arm and a man on his left. The women's tattooing was done after marriage, and consisted only of a rectangle on the chin, with a band running to the ears.

The *Apiacá* smeared their body with urucú mixed with babassú oil. Some people painted the lower part of the body with genipa; others painted only the arms. A common motif was a line from the hair to the tip of the nose. Women painted their legs and hips with vertical stripes and rows of dots between the lines.

TRANSPORTATION

Settlements were connected by paths, though in "Nova Navegação" (Anonymous, 1856) it is stated that only water ways were used. Canoes were made of a large piece of jatoba (*Hymenaea* sp.) bark held open by crosspieces and having at each end a fold tied with cipó creepers. Such craft could carry up to 38 persons. They were propelled with thick bamboos split in half and about 6 feet (2 m.) long. The Indians paddled standing. The *Apiacá* were the best pilots for the rapids of the Tapajóz River.

Loads were carried overland in conical baskets about 60 to 70 cm. (24 to 28 in.) high.

MANUFACTURES

Basketry.—The *Apiacá* used strips of creeper to weave baskets, trays, sieves, and hourglass-shaped supports for vessels, the last similar to those of the Uaupés River region (p. 776).

Ceramics.—The ceramic ware consisted of pots, pans, and dishes. Some vessels had a biconical shape and were decorated with series of parallel right angles on the upper part.

Weaving.—The *Apiacá* wove hammocks, armbands, and flour bags, but there is no description of the loom.

Weapons.—*Apiacá* bows had a flat belly, a rounded back, and shoulders cut to hold the string. Arrow feathering was of the arched tangential and radial tied types. The point of an arrow in one of Florence's prints has three pairs of powerful barbs. Three Indians portrayed by Florence carry spears from 5 feet to 5 feet 4 inches (1.5 to 1.6 m.) long with bamboo points 8 inches (20 cm.) long and 2 to 3 inches (5 to 7.5 cm.) wide. A long tuft hangs just below the point. Two such spears, used apparently for some ceremonial purpose, are covered from the head to within 16 inches (40 cm.) of the butt, with short feathers arranged in blue, red, black, and yellow bands.

War clubs were short. The use of the macana, indicated by Martius (1867, 1 :203), is doubtful.

SOCIAL AND POLITICAL ORGANIZATION

The *Apiacá* lived in communal huts (malocas), each constituting a settlement with one or more chiefs. The population of these huts was not stable, however, for a man might at will join any settlement within the tribe. According to "Nova Navegação" (Anonymous, 1856, p. 103), the chief bore the title of procró, an obviously truncated word. Under normal conditions, he exercised his office unobtrusively, since perfect equality reigned among all. But when foreigners arrived and in war time, he assumed great authority. His importance is evidenced not only by his distinctive ornaments (feather diadem, shell pendant, belt), but also by the inaugural ceremony which accompanied his taking of office. The chief of the nearest settlement made him sit in the hammock of his deceased predecessor, and presented him with a ceremonial lance and a feather diadem, amidst songs and dances. The office was transmitted from father to son, or, if there were no direct heir, to the nearest relative. Chiefs alone could have as many as three wives.

The *Apiacá* showed kindness to one another and never struck a person, even in fun. Homicide was an unpardonable crime. The greatest punishment which an *Apiacá* could inflict upon an offender was to taunt him publicly with his faults. The guilty and even his kin felt extremely humiliated and debased.

According to Florence, crops were planted and harvested in common. There was cooperation in hunting and in fishing, wherein canoes, traps, and other devices were used. Only weapons and ornaments were private property.

The *Apiacá* were hospitable, though they received unknown visitors with furious shouting and warlike demonstrations. The chief, with all his ornaments, advanced toward the visitor and ordered him to lie down. This done, he dragged him out of the canoe, gave him a hammock in the hut, and offered him chicha. Then they introduced their wives and children to their guests. They gave supplies and feather ornaments to their European visitors, asking for iron tools in return. Although perfectly honest among themselves, their eagerness to get iron tools caused them to steal from the Whites as early as 1819. They would even break up supply boxes to remove the nails.

LIFE CYCLE

Childbirth.—After childbirth, the mother was confined for only a day. Children were brought up in an environment of love.

Puberty.—During menstruation women frequently took cold baths in the house, and they lined their hammocks with leaves of sororoca.

Marriage.—The *Apiacá* married at the age of 14. The bride was given publicly to the groom; chiefs' weddings were celebrated by a feast. Monogamy prevailed, though secret polygyny is mentioned by Castelnau and Coudreau. Chiefs were entitled to several wives. Divorce was easy and was often followed by remarriage. This, however, caused deep resentment in the families concerned. Some unions are said to have been lasting. In case of divorce, the children were allotted to the father.

The sexual act was surrounded with secrecy, but not when visitors were given women in exchange for tools.

Death.—A person was buried in his own house under his hammock amidst cries and fearful shouts. He was placed in a squatting position in a shallow grave, the head only 8 inches (20 cm.) under the ground level. Soil was piled about 16 inches (40 cm.) high over the grave. A widow or widower would lie in his hammock over the grave, his face painted black and his hair closely cropped, eating only a maize mush until the exhumation of the bones which, according to the "Nova Navegação" (Anonymous, 1856), occurred only after a year had elapsed. The bad smell emanating from the tomb was endured as a courtesy to the dead. With tears and praise of the deceased, female relatives unearthed his remains, carefully handing them to tearful assistants who placed them in a basket. The basket was then wrapped in a new hammock and hung from the house rafters in front of the place where the deceased lived. After the hammock had rotted away, the bones were buried again in the grave from which they had been removed. From then on, the dead was forgotten.

It seems that the *Apiacá* were at war with all their neighbors. Until the end of the past century, their worst enemies were the *Tapanyuna* on the right side of the Arinos River and later on the upper Tapajóz River. They fought with them whenever they went to the Rio do Peixe to get material for making stone axes. On the Juruena River, their enemies were the *Nambicuara*. To the north, below the confluence of the Arinos and Juruena Rivers, their enemies were the *Cawahíb* (*Cabahíba*), whom they had driven to the interior of the jungle and to whom they referred since 1819 as the inhabitants of the Para-Mutanga (paraná-mitan, "Red River," or Sangue River), a tributary of the Juruena River. Other hostile tribes mentioned by Castelnau (1850–59) were the *Mutonihuen* (*Matanawí* (?) to the northwest, in the Aripana River Basin) and the *Sitihuava* (?). By 1848, the *Apiacá* were on the defensive against the *Tapanyuna* and the *Nambicuara*. Early sources recount no hostilities between the *Mundurucú* and the *Apiacá,* but the former told Gonçalves Tocantins in 1875 that they had been warring against the *Apiacá* since before 1789. Tocantins (1877) also says that the *Mundurucú* pursued the *Apiacá* in the middle of the last century, forcing the latter to move to Salto Augusto. These data are quite uncertain.

The *Apiacá* waged war not for material gains but only to avenge past affronts, the memory of which the old folks kept alive in their tales. The people would ask the chief for war, and he would take the necessary steps. Formerly, the *Apiacá* would march every year with 200 to 300 warriors against some tribe.

The *Apiacá* set out on war expeditions after harvest but only if their shamans predicted a favorable outcome. Upon the chief's request, neighboring villages always gave their cooperation. Each warrior took his own supplies, and extra supplies were carried in case of need. The chief carried his lance, and two aides carried his bow and arrows. During the campaign, the chief held the title of "satá" (? tatá, "fire"), and everyone obeyed him. He gave the signal for camping and made the fire (by friction ?), from which others took their firebrands. After bathing and eating, he gave the signal for setting up the hammocks and retiring. Trusting in their scouts who had explored the region during the day, the warriors slept without sentries. Next day, to allow the scouts time to get a head start and to hunt, the men bathed and resumed the march when the sun was high. Toward the evening, the column joined the scouts, who reported what they had seen and gave the chief the product of their hunt.

The *Apiacá* preferred to wage war by ambuscade, but if they came unexpectedly in contact with the enemy they fought bravely.

It is well established that the *Apiacá* practiced cannibalism, even as late as 1848. They quartered the bodies of those killed in battle, irrespective of sex, and roasted them. The prisoners led to the village were eaten with elaborate ceremony by all the people of the village. The children were captured and brought up together with the tribe's own children. At the age of 12 or 14, the young captives were sacrificed ceremonially within the circle of the gathered tribe. The children's foster fathers broke their skulls by striking them behind with a club. The bodies were roasted and eaten during an all-night feast. The *Apiacá* were unwilling to sell the captive children at any price ("Nova Navegação," Anonymous, 1856, p. 100). Castelnau (1850-59) states that a young woman prisoner might be spared for 4 or 5 years before she was sacrificed. He also says that only boys having a rectangle tattooed around the mouth at puberty were permitted to eat human flesh. The boys were urged to partake of the flesh that it might instill in them a spirit of courage.

MUSIC AND DANCE

The musical instruments mentioned in our sources are drums, rattles, and bamboo trumpets "emitting unharmonious sounds."

Dancers formed two concentric circles, the inner consisting of men who held a bamboo trumpet in one hand and rested the other on their neighbor's shoulder. They turned to the right and to the left alternately. The women formed another circle on the outside, holding hands and sticking their heads under the left arms of the men and accompanying the dance by hopping. A similar dance is performed by the *Parintintin* of the Madeira River.

RELIGION AND SHAMANISM

According to Castelnau (1850–59) and Guimarães (1865), the *Apiacá* believed in a god who was Creator of the sky and of the earth and expressed his wrath by thunder and lightning. They worship him inwardly and pray to him. In the "Nova Navegação" (Anonymous, 1856), the name of the *Apiacá* god is given as Bahyra. This corresponds to the *Parintintin* culture hero, Bahirá (Nunes Pereira, 1940), and the *Tupinamba* Maira.

Shamans foretold the future and treated sick people. In order to learn about the outcome of a war expedition, the shaman fell into a deathlike trance, during which he spoke with spirits. Upon regaining his senses about midnight, he began to sing and prophesy. People had great respect for him but paid only for his cures. To cure, he blew on the patient and sucked on the affected parts, then washed him with decoctions of crushed herbs which were poured through a sieve. He cured colds by causing the patient to sweat over a fire built around and under his hammock. Cures were undertaken simultaneously by two shamans, who agreed upon the procedure. The treatment always lasted 3 days—2 days for blowing and sucking and 1 for bathing. The shamans never returned to see the patient after the treatment, regardless of its results. As pay, they received the best personal possessions of their client. For the treatment of injuries by sucking and application of crushed herbs, the payment was always lower than for the cure of internal ills. It was with the treatment of wounds that novices were initiated into the medical side of their profession.

BIBLIOGRAPHY

See Cawahíb, Parintintin, and Their Neighbors, bibliography, page 297.

THE TRIBES OF THE UPPER XINGU RIVER

By Claude Lévi-Strauss

TRIBAL DIVISIONS AND HISTORY

The Xingú River was known south only as far as lat. 4° 5' 11" S. through the expedition of Prince Adalbert of Prussia in 1843. When Karl von den Steinen descended it for the first time in 1884, its upper course, the region inland, and the numerous tribes inhabiting the area were entirely unknown. Von den Steinen descended the Batoví River, a branch of the Xingú River, and discovered the *Northern Bacaïri, Custenau, Waura,* and, on the Xingú River, the *Suya* and *Manitsaua.* During a second expedition in 1887, he traveled down the Culiseu River, also a branch of the Xingú River, and saw the *Nahukwa, Mehinacu, Auetö, Yaulapiti, Trumai,* and *Camayura.*

Hermann Meyer made an expedition in 1896 to the Culiseu and Jatobá Rivers, and another in 1889, mainly to explore the Ronuro River. In 1900–1901, Max Schmidt traveled to the Culiseu River. Later, Hintermann (in 1924–25), Dyott (in 1928), Petrullo (in 1931), and Buell Quain (in 1938) studied the upper Xingú River region.

The upper Xingú tributaries form an elaborate comblike system of waterways, about 150 miles (240 km.) wide. After running most of their course parallel to one another, the streams join at about lat. 12° S. to form the Xingú River. The confluent branches are, from west to east, the Steinen (Ferro), Ronuro, Jatobá, Batovi (Tamitoala, Culiseu (Kulisehu), and Culuene Rivers.

Along their upper courses, the rivers are bordered by continuous strips of gallery forest which hardly screen the savanna of the hinterland. Along their middle and lower courses, the forest widens, and lagoons and marshes form dead-water channels which permit communication with the secondary streams. Several tribes live close to one another near the rivers. The more important settlements lie between the Culiseu and Culuene Rivers, in the eastern part of the basin. Few inhabitants dwell along the western rivers.

The native population of the Xingú area is numerous and extremely varied. The tribes belong to all the chief Brazilian linguistic families, but there is no correlation between the linguistic provinces and geo-

321

graphical divisions. The linguistic boundaries are difficult to determine because they freely overlap, crossing valleys and watersheds.

The location of the tribes of the upper Xingú River may be sketched as follows (map 1, *No. 1*; see Volume 1, map 7.) :

(1) Cariban tribes.—Only the eastern portion of a formerly important nucleus of *Cariban* tribes south of the Amazon River falls within this area. It extended west to the Tapajóz Basin, where it is now represented by the *Bacaïri* of the Novo and Parantinga Rivers (lat. 14° S., long. 56° W.). In the south it reached the neighborhood of Cuiabá. The *Carib* of the upper Xingú Basin include: (*a*) The *Bacaïri* of the Batoví River (4 villages in Von den Steinen's time) ; (*b*) the *Bacaïri* of the Culiseu River (3 villages) ; and (*c*) the *Nahukwa* (*Nahuqua, Anauqua*). on the right bank of the Culiseu River (lat. 13° S., long. 53° W.). Between the Culiseu and Culuene Rivers, there were numerous villages, whose inhabitants Von den Steinen called *Nahukwa,* though they bear distinct names, among which *Guicuru* (*Cuicutl*) and *Apalakiri* (*Calapalo*) are mentioned most frequently (lat. 12° S., long. 53° W.). A careful census of the villages between the Culiseu and Culuene Rivers was made by Hermann Meyer, who recorded no less than 15 different groups. In Von den Steinen's time, the *Mariape-Nahukwa* were the northern representatives of the *Cariban* family. The *Bacaïri* language differs in important features from that of the *Nahukwa.* The latter includes several dialects distinguished by phonetics rather than by semantics or morphology.

(2) Arawakan tribes.—The *Arawakan* linguistic family, named *Nu-Aruak* by Von den Steinen, occurs mostly in the country between the Culiseu and Batoví Rivers, even crossing the lower course of the latter toward the Ronuro River. *Arawakan* tribes live north to the *Bacaïri* of the Batoví River, northwest of the *Bacaïri* of the Culiseu River, and east of the *Nahukwa.* From the southeast to the northwest, they include the *Mehinacu* (*Minaco*), on the left bank of the Culiseu River (lat. 13° S., long. 54° W.) ; the *Yaulapiti* (*Yawalapiti*), north of the *Mehinacu* (lat. 12° S., long. 54° W.) ; the *Custenau* (*Kustenau*), on the right bank of the Batoví River (lat. 12° S., long. 54° W.) ; and the *Waura* (*Aura;* not to be confused with the Orinoco Delta *Warrau*), on both banks of that river (lat. 12° 30′ S., long. 54° W.). All the *Arawakan* dialects of the upper Xingú River are similar.

(3) Tupian tribes.—In Von den Steinen's time, the *Tupian* tribes occupied a small area on the left bank of the Culiseu River, opposite the *Nahukwa* and close to the *Yaulapiti.* They include the *Auetö* (*Autl, Auiti*), lat. 12° 30′ S., long. 54° W., the mixed *Arauiti* (resulting from intermarriages between *Auetö* and *Vaulapiti*) to the south, and the *Camayura* (*Camayula*) to the north (lat. 12° S., long. 54° W.). The *Manitsaua* (*Mantizula*) are also *Tupi,* but their language includes many elements from the *Suya* (a *Ge* tribe), on the Xingú River to the north, about lat. 11° S., long. 54° W.

(4) Trumaí.—This isolated linguistic family was in Von den Steinen's time represented by two villages, one on the left bank of the Culiseu River between the *Auetö* and the *Yaulapiti,* and the other on the right bank of the lower Culuene River north of the *Mariape-Nahukwa* (lat. 12° 30′ S., long. 54° W.).

(5) Ge.—The *Suya* (*Tsuva*), who inhabit the Xingú River at about lat. 10° 5′ S., belong to the *Ge* linguistic family, as probably do the unknown "*Cayapó,*" who are said to live to the east on the headwaters of the Culuene River. (See vol. 1, p. 478.)

The history of the area is not well known. The *Bacaïri* say that their first home was on the headwaters of the Paranatinga and Ronuro Rivers. They moved to the great falls of the Paranatinga River, and later to the country between the Ronuro and Paranatinga Rivers. After unsuccessful wars against the *Cayabi* (*Cajabi*), who still occupy the Verde River, they returned to their present dwellings. The *Suya* appear to have moved during the first quarter of the 19th century from the Arinos and Verde Rivers to the upper Xingú River. Similar migrations within a relatively small area are said to have been made by most of the tribes prior to Von den Steinen's visit.

Since 1887 many changes have occurred in the geographical distribution of the different tribes. According to Hermann Meyer's map (Meyer, 1887 b), the southern *Trumaí* village had disappeared in 1896, but it is found again on Max Schmidt's map made in 1900–1901 and on Petrullo's map made in 1931, though situated farther south, between the *Mehinacu* and the *Nahukwa.* The northern *Trumaí* village was also moved south, across the Culuene River. By 1931, the *Arawakan* tribes had made important shifts. The *Waura* had abandoned the Batoví River and settled halfway between the *Yaulapiti* and the *Mehinacu* on the Culiseu River. Thus, the general trend is toward tribal intermixture and concentration of population on the river banks. The *Nahukwa,* however, still hold a continuous territory, clearly distinct from that of other tribes, along the right bank of the Culuene River.

In 1896, Hermann Meyer obtained information on the hitherto unknown upper course of the Paranaiuba River, a left tributary of the Xingú River. His informants named 19 different tribes said to be settled in that area. It appears from small vocabularies that the *Yaruma* speak a *Cariban* dialect and the *Arawine* a *Tupian* dialect (Krause, 1936 b). Nothing is known of the others. Meyer's list of the Paranaiuba River tribes corresponds, except for a few names, to the lists of tribes east of the Culuene River obtained by Petrullo from a *Bacaïri* and an *Apalakiri* informant. These consisted of 10 and 14 names, respectively. An alleged pygmy people is called *Phoi* by the *Bacaïri* and *Tahulgi* by the *Apalakiri.* Several widely separated groups are called *Cayapó* (*Kahaho*).

On the basis of Meyer's map, the whole upper Xingú area, excluding the Paranaiuba River, contained 35 villages. This number agrees reasonably well with Von den Steinen's estimate of 2,500 to 3,000 inhabitants made in the same region 9 years earlier. For more recent times, we possess only partial data. Fawcett counted about 150 *Bacaïri* in 1925, and there were approximately 50 persons in the *Trumaí* village where Quain stayed in 1938. Although the population is apparently much less numerous now than 50 years ago, the Xingú Basin—probably because of its great isolation—did not suffer the same tremendous demographic decline that affected other parts of Brazil.

CULTURE

SUBSISTENCE ACTIVITIES

The economic life of the upper Xingú tribes is somewhat more complex than that of other Brazilian Indians, as it is based upon fishing, hunting, collecting of wild foods, and agriculture. Activities revolve around different products according to the season. Turtle eggs furnish a basic staple during the dry season. Piqui fruits (*Caryocar butyrosum*) and bitter manioc are the main foods during two different parts of the rainy season. Fishing is practiced throughout the year. To some tribes, it is the main source of food (Petrullo, 1932 a); to other tribes, it is the only recourse when other products are unavailable (Quain, ms.). Ants, larvae, and grubs are eaten; crickets are collected to feed pets. Hunts are usually large expeditions in which all the adult men of the village participate; they sometimes continue for days. Taboos on game seem to be rare; it is not certain whether squirrels, which the *Trumai* do not kill, and the sucuri (*Eunectes murinus*) and a certain bird, which are forbidden among the *Bacaïri* (Capistrano de Abreu, 1938), may simply not be killed or whether they may be killed but not eaten.

Fishing.—Fishing is highly organized and is "one of the few examples of group cooperation which transcends the immediate family" (Quain, ms.). Each tribe possesses the privilege of fishing in well-delimited stretches of the rivers and owns fish dams and weirs. Some dams consist of fences of posts (*Bacaïri*), others are made of branches or stones. Strangely, the widespread technique of drugging fish (p. 13) and the hook were unknown in 1884 (Steinen, 1886). Fishing techniques include nets placed across the streams, baskets used mostly in lagoons, and night fishing with torches. Basketry traps, made of tucum fibers, are either long and narrow or short and wide. Some are conical and open at both ends to permit the fish to be removed with the hand. The natives also fish from canoes, throwing wild fruits as bait and shooting the fish with bows and arrows when they come to the surface. Petrullo describes spear fishing from the prow of a canoe (pl. 27, *bottom*), the spear being about 25 feet (7 m.) long and consisting of a wooden shaft, a foreshaft of reed, and a large conical bone point. Quain did not find spear fishing practiced among the *Camayura*, the *Nahukwa*, or the *Trumai;* and he considers it an individual invention. The fish were usually cleaned before being broiled on a pyramidal babracot.

Farming.—According to Von den Steinen, women planted, weeded with the digging stick, and harvested the crops, but men cultivated tobacco. Among the *Trumai*, only men do the planting (Quain, ms.). A *Nahukwa* chief who was seen planting maize (Steinen, 1894) dug holes about 2 or 3 inches (5 or 8 cm.) deep with a stick and put several kernels in each hole. Manioc sprouts are set obliquely in loosened earth, first dug with hoes, and then replaced in the trench (Quain, ms.). Gardens are opened in the forest by felling and burning the trees. Orchards of wild fruit trees are transplanted near the village or are cultivated in their native habitat. Von den Steinen saw avenues of piquí trees leading to a *Bacäiri* village. The *Waura* had mangabeira (*Hancornia speciosa*) orchards and the *Bacäiri* used to irrigate wild urucú trees. Bacaiuva palm trees (*Acrocomia*) and frutas de lobo (*Solanum lycocarpum*) were also cultivated. The best gardeners were the *Mehinacu* (Von den Steinen, 1894).

The species most frequently found in the area are bitter manioc and maize, the former being predominant; two kinds of yams and two kinds of beans; cara (*Dioscorea*), abóbora (*Cucurbita*), mamona (*Ricinus*) ; a small species of peanut; pepper; calabashes (*Crescentia*) and gourds (*Lagenaria*), chiefly among the *Nahukwa;* sweet potatoes, abundant only among the *Mehinacu;* tobacco, flourishing in the gardens of the *Suya* and *Auetö;* and cotton, the best quality being grown by the *Bacäiri* and *Mehinacu*. Other plants are grown for industrial purposes. For instance, a sharp lanceolated grass (*Scleria*), used for shaving the tonsure (p. 327), and the uba cane (*Gynerium sagittatum*), which provides arrow shafts for the *Batovi* (Steinen, 1894), are grown. The banana and guava were wholly unknown in 1887, but in 1938 the *Camayura* consumed quantities of the former and the *Trumai,* of the latter. The foreign origin of most of the agricultural terms of the *Trumai* suggests that they borrowed cultivated plants from their neighbors.

Food storage and preparation.—To store ears of maize, most tribes, especially the *Bacäiri, Yaulapiti, and Mehinacu,* hang them to the roof of the hut with their leaves artistically arranged in the shape of birds and other animals. The *Bacäiri* keep maize flour in large cylindrical baskets lined with sewed leaves and covered with bark sheets. Among the *Yaulapiti; Naravute,* a *Nahukwa*-speaking group (Petrullo, 1932 a) ; and *Trumai* (Quain, ms.), piquí fruits are boiled and placed in cylindrical bark containers about 4½ to 6½ feet (1.5 to 2. m.) in length, sealed at both ends, and placed in a pool of cool water. On ceremonial occasions the containers are opened and the beverage is equally distributed. It is mixed with water and drunk. Other preparations of the piquí include boiled sap (Quain, ms.), rasped and toasted seeds, and a syrup extracted from the leaves (Steinen, 1894).

Game and fish are broiled in the skin, generally on grids of plaited vines. The *Bacäiri* roast several turtle eggs simultaneously on a spindle-shaped griddle made of vines (Hintermann, 1926). Several kinds of wild nuts are eaten roasted. Although boiling is a woman's task, broiling and roasting are always done by men (Steinen, 1894). To prepare manioc (pl. 28), women grate it on thorns imbedded in wooden planks, but the *Camayura* use an *Anodonta* shell. The tipití is entirely unknown; instead, basketry sieves are used to strain off the poisonous juice (Steinen, 1894). Flour and starch, which are prepared from manioc, are dried on large flat baskets. They are cooked and eaten in the form of gruel or of flat cakes (beijú) ; slightly toasted on clay slabs. Manioc and piquí gruel are a basic meal throughout the area. Quain observed that adult *Trumai* never drink water but only gruel. The *Trumai* season the manioc gruel with "iriwa," a shelled, fibrous, unidentified fruit, and prepare a cottonseed-oil paste (Quain, ms.). The *Bacäiri* dip food in oil before eating it. According to Petrullo, salt is unknown, but Von den Steinen mentions salt made from bamboo salt, and Quain describes the preparation of water-lily salt, each *Trumai* making his own supply by burning the plant and sifting the ashes. Although geophagy is rare, Von den Steinen saw dolls made of edible clay being licked by *Bacäiri* children.

VILLAGES AND HOUSES

Villages (fig. 32) are usually established two miles (3 km.) or more from the river, with a path leading to the stream. The only exceptions

FIGURE 32.—A *Bacäiri* village. (After Steinen, 1886.)

were the *Suya* (in 1884) and the *Trumai* (in 1887) villages, both built on a river bank. Villages visited by Von den Steinen had from 2 to 20 huts and from 30 to 200 inhabitants. Dyott saw a *Nahukwa* village of 7 houses arranged in a circle, and Petrullo visited a village where the huts were scattered in an irregular manner. Quain observed a *Trumai* village with

5 houses and 43 inhabitants and a *Camayura* village consisting of 11 houses, each haystack-shaped, with two clean, straight avenues leaving the village at right angles. The avenues of piquí trees of the *Bacaïri* village have been mentioned (p. 325).

Three types of huts have been observed, the first two of which are rare. Von den Steinen (1894) gives a drawing of a *Custenau* hut with a circular ground plan and a huge conical thatched roof erected on a low circular lattice wall. Hintermann (1926, p. 251) reproduces a *Bacaïri* house formed by a pointed arch covered with grass and closed at both ends with two apses of straw, in which doors were placed. All sources agree on the common type of hut (pls. 29; 30, *top*). According to Petrullo, the ground plan is an ellipse, approximately 30 feet (10 m.) by 65 feet (20 m.). In the center, about 16 feet (5 m.) from each end are three main supporting posts (two, and even one, among the *Trumai* in Quain's description) set deep into the ground.

A ridge pole is lashed on top of the supporting posts, which stand 25 feet (8 m.) above the ground. A wall, 5 feet (1.5 m.) high, is made of posts set 6 inches (15 cm.) apart. To these posts are lashed long thin poles, their tops bent inward and lashed together. Heavier short poles are lashed at one end to the ridge pole and at the other to the bent poles, so as to form a false outer roof. The entire structure is covered with a light framework thatched with grass, except for an opening between the false roof and the ridge pole, which is left as a smoke hole. The ends of the ridge pole project and are thatched decoratively.

A house is shared by several families, each of which occupies a section where it keeps its own fire. Hammocks are hung between the central posts and the wall, sometimes in two or three tiers. In the middle of the hut stands a platform where food and implements are kept. Two low doors are on opposite sides of the ellipse.

In addition to these communal dwellings, every village has a guest house, which Von den Steinen and Petrullo described as poorly built and badly kept. In most of these houses two logs running lengthwise provide seats for the men of the village. Guest huts are reserved for the entertainment of visitors and for ceremonial gatherings. Because dance costumes and musical instruments are kept in them, Von den Steinen called them "flute-houses."

DRESS AND ADORNMENT

Hairdressing.—All the upper Xingú River Indians are tonsured. The *Suya* shave their foreheads but the tribes of the Culiseu River wear a circular tonsure which may be 3 inches (7 cm.) in diameter. *Bacaïri* men sometimes use wooden hair curlers. Women's hair is cut only on the forehead, but men's hair is cut all around at the level of the ear lobe (see pls. 27, 30). Piranha-fish teeth are used for cutting, and red-hot embers for singeing, the hair. The hair is frequently groomed with a composite comb, which hangs from the hammock (Culiseu River) or from the shoulder (*Suya*). Plucking all body hair is customary, although *Camayura* and *Nahukwa* men sometimes keep their moustache and beard, and *Suya* men do not pluck pubic hair.

Mutilation.—All men have their lobes pierced, but only *Suya* women wear large bark plugs in the lower lip. The nasal septum is pierced among both sexes of the *Bacaïri* of the Paranatinga and Batoví Rivers and of the first village on the Culiseu River, but only among men in the second village; whereas the custom is completely lacking in the third village (Steinen, 1894). Men wear wooden pegs and women stone spindles in the nasal septum.

Body ornaments.—Smearing the hair and the body with urucú and oil paste is general. Sometimes dots and straight wavy, and zigzag lines are painted on the face or body. True tattooing exists only among the *Arawakan* tribes, whose men and women use semicircular and lozenge patterns traced with soot and taruma (Verbenaceae) juice. All tribes have scratches on the arms or elsewhere, made for medical treatment. Among the *Trumai* a nonceremonial hygienic scarification is frequently performed by adults.

All men slip their penis up under the belt, except the *Trumai,* who formerly tied only the prepuce with a cotton thread and now let it hang free. *Suya* women go naked, and *Trumai* women formerly used a supple belt of fiber with a perineal band (Steinen, 1894) but have now abandoned it (Quain, ms.). All other women of the upper Xingú River wear the "uluri,"—a piece of straw folded in the shape of a triangle, to two corners of which strings are attached to tie around the waist, with the third corner hanging down and held to the back of the belt by a perineal string passing between the legs (fig. 33).

Ornaments.—*Bacaïri* and *Nahukwa* men use armlets and anklets of straw or woven cotton, and *Bacaïri* men put feathers in their ear lobes. Headdresses are fashioned of skin, feathers, and fur diadems (especially rich among the *Camayura* and *Suya*), feathered circlets, and plaited osiers in cylindrical or star shapes (*Nahukwa*). The *Camayura* wear hair nets or caps trimmed with feathers or tufts of human hair. Necklaces are worn by the more developed tribes. They are made of shell (*Bulimus* and *Orthalicus melanostomus*) and nut beads among the southern tribes (*Bacaïri* and *Nahukwa*), and of stone beads among the northern tribes (*Yaulapiti, Trumai*). The cylindrical, circular, spherical, and pear-shaped (*Mehinacu, Auetö*) stone beads were copied in clay and rosin in the south. In 1887, horn, bone, and teeth beads were used particularly by the *Yaulapiti* and the *Mehinacu*. The *Trumai* and *Auetö* have necklaces of jaguar claws. The *Yaruma* were said to use earrings having a metallic sound (Steinen, 1894). More recently, Dyott (1930, p. 223) noticed elaborate

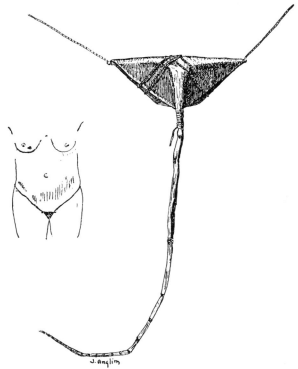

FIGURE 33.—*Bacaïri* pubic covering. (Redrawn from Steinen, 1894, fig. 18.)

stone ornaments among the *Nahukwa,* such as a Maltese cross made of diorite, similar to those worn in the 18th century by the *Paressí.*

TRANSPORTATION

Fishing and intertribal trade make the rivers important communication routes (pl. 27). The upper Xingú canoes, which may be 25 feet (8 m.) or more in length, are made of the bark (pl. 32) of the jatoba tree (*Hymenaea* sp.). A suitable tree is found, and a light frame on which to stand is built against the trunk. A long rectangular piece of bark is stripped off and carefully placed on low trestles above a fire. When the heat has softened the bark, the edges are bent upward and the prow is given a pointed shape, while the stern is bent toward the inside. The *Yaulapiti* curl the edges toward the inside. Holes and cracks are filled with wax and clay. One day's work will make a canoe which can be launched the next morning. When the canoe is completed, several men carry it to the river on their shoulders, protected by a cushion of fiber or bark.

Paddles are cut from solid wood and have a long rectangular blade and shaft, the upper part of which is often carved in the shape of a transverse handle. Decorative designs are sometimes carved or painted on the blade (fig. 34, *a*).

Small streams are crossed on tree trunks.

MANUFACTURES

Raw materials.—Stone, teeth, bone, shells, and feathers are used for manufacturing. Stone, however, is rare, only one quarry, worked by the *Trumaí,* being known to Von den Steinen. On the Xingú River, how-

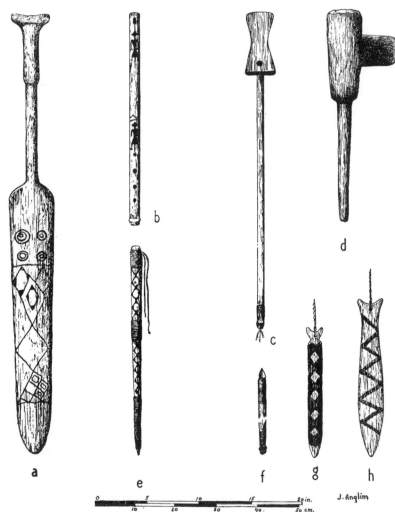

FIGURE 34.—Upper Xingú artifacts. *a, Bacaïri* canoe paddle; *b, Mehinacu* flute; *c,* spear thrower; *d, Trumaí* stone ax; *e, Bacaïri* digging stick; *f,* hafted drill; *g, h, Nahukwa* bull roarers in fish form. (Redrawn from Steinen, 1894, figs. 29, 40, 28, 20, 76, 21, 122.)

ever, the *Suya* had their own stone quarry, and fashioned stone axes. The lower jaw of the piranha fish is used for sawing; and a front tooth of the cynodon fish for tattooing, carving, and piercing. The teeth of the traira fish (*Erythrinus*) and of the aguti (*Dasyprocta aguti*) serve as scrapers; those of the capivara (*Hydrochoerus hydrochaeris*), as graters. Monkey teeth decorate necklaces and belts. The long bones of monkeys and the spikes on skate tails are made into arrow points. Femur bones of deer and jaguars are used as ear borers. Bones also serve to polish wax or rosin surfaces. Jaguar claws and fish vertebrae are often strung on necklaces. Shells are widely used for cutting, rasping, planing, and polishing; the cutting edge is either the external rim or the edge of an irregular hole pierced in the center. A shell is usually tied to a cotton thread and carried slung around the neck to be used as a pry for opening nuts. Feathers are used to ornament the ears, head, and arms, and to feather arrows.

Spinning.—Fibers of wild pineapple (Bromeliaceae), tucum palm, burity palm (*Mauritia flexuosa*), and cotton are prepared by women, who twist the thread on their thighs, previously smeared with white clay, and spin it on a drop spindle. The round whorl is made of tortoise shell or wood and is elaborately carved. Among the *Bacäiri,* the whorl, made of wood, a potsherd, or raw clay, is not decorated.

Netting and weaving.—Fishing nets, carrying nets, and hammocks are netted by women, with a wooden needle.

The *Bacäiri* have twined hammocks of cotton thread, whereas the *Arawakan*-speaking tribes make smaller woven hammocks with burití fiber and cotton. The *Auetö* hammock is woven with a tucum-fiber warp filled with a dense cotton weft disposed in bands alternately white and dark blue. In 1887, the use of the hammock was adopted by the *Suya*, who formerly slept on platforms covered with leaves. Sieves of woven cotton are also made for straining manioc. For weaving cotton armlets, women use a crude loom, made of two low posts fixed in the ground around which a continuous warp is passed.

Basketry.—Basket making is a man's task. Basketry materials are palm leaves, bamboo strips, and vines. The most common techniques are checker, twilled, hexagonal, and open hexagonal weaves. Forms include large flat baskets (*Auetö, Mehinacu*), storage baskets (*Bacäiri*), and narrow, hollow carrying baskets of open hexagonal mesh (*Trumaí,* Schmidt, 1905; and *Bacäiri,* Hintermann, 1926). The natives also make improvised rucksacks and carrying baskets by weaving and knotting two or three freshly cut palm leaves. Small mats used for seats (Petrullo, 1932 a) and to wrap up feathers (Steinen, 1894) are made of bamboo sticks twined with a cotton string and decorated with designs. Square sieves for straining manioc and square and triangular fire fans are also made. In most basketry, part of the material is dyed black, giving diversi-

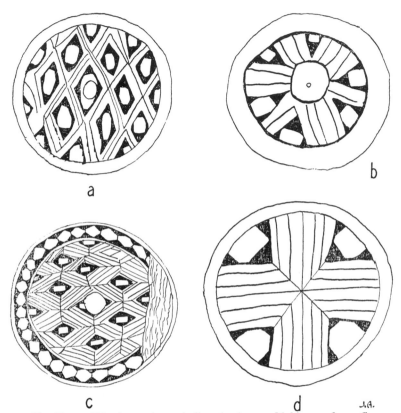

FIGURE 35.—Upper Xingú wooden spindle whorls. *a, Mehinacu; b, c, Camayura; d, Auetö.* (Redrawn from Steinen, 1894, figs. 55, 56, 59, 58.)

fied bicolor patterns (Schmidt, 1905). Dance costumes and *Bacaïri* cylindrical basketry headdresses are elaborately woven of straw.

Containers.—The bark containers for piquí and the bark-covered baskets for flour have already been described. Numerous kinds of containers, such as spoons, bowls, pots, and boxes, are made of gourds and calabashes. The inside of the calabash is varnished with buriti soot mixed with scrapings of rosinous bark; the outside is often carved, pyrograved, or painted with geometric designs. Broken calabashes are repaired by sewing the ends together.

Pottery.—Von den Steinen's statement, so widely commented upon, that the *Arawakan*-speaking tribes were the only ceramists in all the upper Xingú area was probably true as recently as 1938, when Quain noticed that all the pots owned by the *Trumai* came from the *Waura*. Three main types must be distinguished: (1) Large manioc-flour containers with flattened bottom and bell-shaped rim (pls. 28; 31, *bottom*), encountered among the *Mehinacu* and the *Waura*; (2) round cooking pots, already scarce in 1887; and (3) hemispherical bowls about 4 to 8 inches (10 to

20 cm.) in diameter, with a blackened inner surface, an indented rim, and often a modeled, stylized zoomorphic shape representing various animals

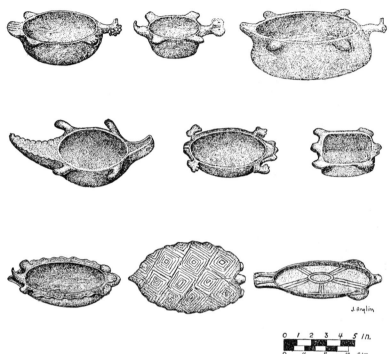

FIGURE 36.—Pottery of the upper Xingú River. (Redrawn from Steinen, 1894, pls. 23 and 24.)

(fig. 36). The last type is most frequently found among the *Auetö, Cama-yura, Trumai,* and *Nahukwa,* and is perhaps made by *Arawak* women who married into these tribes. Earthenware is made only by women and is baked in an open fire.

Wooden artifacts.—Carved zoomorphic benches, used throughout the upper Xingú area and everywhere called by the *Tupi* name, "apüka(p)," have a rectangular, slightly shallow seat supported by two side planks (fig. 37, *a, b*), whose lower edges extend forward and backward to give added support. Many of the seats are carved in the shape of a bird; a few represent quadrupeds (fig. 37, *c, d*) and are provided with four feet instead of the two side planks. Benches have mainly a ceremonial use and are offered to guests and dignitaries (Steinen, 1886, 1894). The *Naravute* use only bark benches (Petrullo, 1932 a).

Miscellaneous implements.—Stone axes are generally of diabase, round or ellipsoidal in cross section, and about 4 to 8 inches (10 to 20 cm.) in length. They are polished on natural rocks. The head is glued into a wooden handle which is shaped like a square club with a short shaft (fig. 34, *d*). Drills (fig. 34, *f*) consist of stone points set in each end of a shaft and fastened with wax and cotton thread. Sand was used in drilling. Gravers are made of a capivara tooth tied tangentially to a handle.

Figure 37.—Upper Xingú artifacts. *a, Camayura* stool; *b, Trumaí* stool; *c, Nahukwa* stool; *d, Mehinacu* stool; *e, f, Bacaïri* cornhusk and wood figures; *g, h, Mehinacu* gum figures; *i, j, Bacaïri* straw and wood figures. (Redrawn from Steinen, 1894, figs. 82, 84, 85, 86, 69, 73, 75.)

Farming implements include digging sticks (fig. 34, *e*), those used by the *Mehinacu* having a carved handle, and hoes made by attaching the claw of a great armadillo (*Priodontes giganteus*) to a stick.

Shovels for turning cakes (beijú) during cooking are half-moon-shaped, with or without an elaborately carved zoomorphic handle, and often have geometric designs painted on the blade.

Combs are always composite; those of the *Nahukwa* and *Mehinacu* have tips carved with zoomorphic figures. Scrapers consist of triangular pieces of calabash imbedded with teeth.

Fire is produced with the drill and bark timber.

Weapons.—Bows and arrows are the only weapons found everywhere. Arrow poison and the blowgun are wholly unknown, although Quain saw the blow gun used as a child's toy among the *Trumai*.

Bows are about 6½ feet (2 m.) long; those of greatest length (8½ feet or 2.6 m.) are found among the *Naravute* and the shortest among the *Waura*. The cross section is generally round, sometimes oval, and occasionally flat (Max Schmidt, 1905; Petrullo, 1932 a). Bows are made of aratazeiro (Anonaceae) or of pau d'arco (*Tecoma*). The *Tupian*-speaking tribes are the only ones who sometimes make bows of palm wood and who decorate them by wrapping the center with cotton. The string is made of twisted tucum fiber. Among the semicivilized *Bacaïri* of the Paranatinga River, Von den Steinen noticed that bows and arrows were smaller than elsewhere.

Arrows, 5 feet (1.5 m.) or more in length, are made of uba cane or camayuva wood, with a thinner foreshaft. The point may be barbed with teeth, with the mandibular sting of the great anteater, with the spike of a skate's tail, or with a tubular monkey bone or a two-pronged bone fragment tied laterally to the foreshaft. Arrows with a barbed point are used only for fishing. Those with a point made of a large splinter of bamboo fastened to the foreshaft in such a way that the point will slip off the shaft or break off and remain in the wound are widely used in warfare. The *Trumai* and *Suya* employ such a point for hunting the jaguar. Von den Steinen described whistling arrows for bird hunting, made with a pierced tucuma nut slipped over the shaft; but those collected by Petrullo have the whistling nut in place of a point, and are used only for sport.

Two halves of feathers spirally twisted and sewed to the shaft are widely called "Xingú feathering." There is often a philodendron wrapping at both ends, plain among the *Camayura* and intricate among the *Trumai*. All tribes use the primary release and direct shooting for short distances, indirect or elevated for more distant targets.

The fishing spear of the *Naravute* has already been described.

The spear thrower, or atlatl (fig. 34, *c*) was known only to the *Camayura, Auetö,* and *Trumai,* but none used it as a true weapon. Although spear throwers were more numerous than bows in Von den Steinen's time and perhaps were formerly employed in warfare, they are used now only in sportive ceremonies (p. 347). The upper Xingú spear thrower is about 2⅓ feet (70 cm.) long and consists of a cylindrical palm-wood shaft, one end carved in the shape of a flattened handle, which is grooved on each side and has a finger hole, and the other end having a hook fastened on it. The spear is of uba cane without feathering or with small, non-spiraled feathers. The wooden or stone point is set on the shaft. It is either blunt (spherical, conical, pear-shaped, or cylindrical) or else sharp (knob-shaped, two-pronged, or flattened). A whistling nut is sometimes slipped over the shaft.

The *Suya* have clubs with a flattened oval head and a short shaft; these are made of siriva palm, a tree of the Cocus family. *Trumaí* clubs are of the same type but smaller and cruder. Both the *Trumaí* and *Camayura* use even smaller clubs for ceremonial dances.

SOCIAL AND POLITICAL ORGANIZATION

Information on social and political organization is extremely scarce. Von den Steinen stated that there were several chiefs; Petrullo, that each house has its headman; and Quain, that the *Trumaí* chief was assisted by two vice-chiefs, who rule in his absence, and by helpers or servants. Chieftaincy was transmitted from father to son, or, if there were no son, to the sister's son or the daughter's husband (Steinen, 1894). In 1938, the *Trumaí* chief was the son of the daughter of the chief whom Von den Steinen had met 50 years before. All sources agree that the power of the chiefs is limited. The *Trumaí* chief, for instance, is not the only medicine man of the group. He does no work and has no garden of his own. His main function is to assign work to men and women and to organize collective gangs for fishing, hunting, and tilling the soil. Petrullo described the exhortation pronounced by the headmen each morning followed by communal bathing in the river.

A division of the members of the group into "elders" and "youths" seems to exist among the *Trumaí*. A sib organization is only vaguely suggested by our sources, except in the case of the *Nahukwan*-speaking villages, each of which has its own name and territory.

The *Bacaïri* are matronymic, and authority inside the family belongs to the maternal uncle. A distinction between the elder brother and the younger brother, the name for the latter being also used for cousin, seems to be made in all the kinship systems of the area (Steinen, 1894). Among the *Trumaí,* residence is patrilocal, and marriage is forbidden between true cousins and some types of classificatory cousins and with the sister's daughter. The latter is permitted among the *Camayura,* who otherwise have the same kinship system as the *Trumaí* (Quain, ms.). Among both groups there is a joking relationship between cross-cousins, and an avoidance and shame relationship between brothers-in-law. Some undefined kinship relations imply homosexual relations (Quain, ms.). Nothing is known of the kinship systems of the other groups, but marriages between natives belonging to different generations among the tribes on the Paranatinga and the Culiseu River (Steinen, 1894) and the fact that Von den Steinen was called "younger brother" by the *Bacaïri* and "maternal uncle" by the *Mehinacu* are strong indications that kinship systems might not be identical throughout the area.

LIFE CYCLE

Birth.—Sexual intercourse is forbidden among the *Trumai* during the last months of pregnancy and until the child can walk (Quain, ms.). Abortion is often practiced, either by manipulating the abdomen or by drinking magic medicines. Women give birth in a sitting position (Quain, 1894) or crouching and grasping a pole (Steinen, 1894). *Trumai* men attend each parturition and smoke tobacco (Quain, ms.). The couvade consists of social and dietary prohibitions accompanied by ceremonial blowing on the baby's body (Steinen, 1894).

The child is given magical drinks to ensure its being strong (Quain, ms.). Its father gives it a name different from his own. A prohibition on the use of personal names seems to have been widespread. Among the *Bacaïri* it is more strict for women than for men. Personal names can be changed several times; an exchange of personal names establishes a special tie of friendship between adults (*Auetö* and *Mehinacu*) (Steinen, 1894).

Puberty.—The initiation ceremony for *Trumai* boys includes scarifying the body with a fish-tooth instrument and rubbing the arms with the claw of the great armadillo. Whenever possible, the boy is given an opportunity to wrestle with a boa (Quain, ms.). During her first menstrual period, a girl is isolated; while tobacco is blown on her, her body is scarified; and she is forbidden to eat (Steinen, 1894). Her ears are pierced and her hair is cut and turned down over her face. During her subsequent menstrual periods, a girl is not isolated; but she is forbidden to have sexual intercourse, to do any cooking, or to eat anything but manioc (Quain, ms.). Leaves are used as an absorbent.

Infant betrothal was observed among the *Trumai* (Quain, ms.) and *Bacaïri* (Steinen, 1894). The marriage ceremony of the *Trumai* is merely the presentation and acceptance of a hammock and other gifts (Quain, ms.). A fishing expedition seems to be connected with the marriage feast. Among the *Bacaïri* there is no ceremony, but the bride's father receives an ax and arrows from the groom and his help in farming (Steinen, 1894). The only form of polygyny practiced among the *Trumai* is sororal. Adulterous relations between a husband and his wife's sisters are not infrequent. Among other tribes on the Culiseu River, a man may simultaneously marry both a mother and her daughter (Quain, ms.). The levirate and some form of fraternal polyandry probably are practiced by the *Trumaí*. The behavior of *Trumaí* women suggests the fear of rape. When adultery is committed, the husband beats his wife, who seeks the protection of her mother. He stands in the center of the village and accuses her lover. Either spouse may bring about divorce (Quain, ms.).

Death.—*Trumaí* behavior faintly suggests that a stigma attaches to old age. All the tribes of the upper Xingú area bury their dead in a recumbent position with the head toward the east, except the *Suya,* who practice a crouched burial. *Trumaí* corpses are wrapped in their hammocks and, with their implements and cooking utensils, interred in the village plaza (Quain, ms.; Steinen, 1894). The *Mehinacu* cover the graves with pebbles and stones; the *Auetö* (pl. 31, *bottom*) and the *Yaulapiti* surround each one with a low fence, which, among the *Camayura,* forms a square, with two of the opposing sides concave. The *Camayura* break the dead man's implements on the grave and express their grief by shaving their hair and fasting (Steinen, 1894). Nothing is known about inheritance rules, except that, among the *Trumaí,* the "ole" songs are transmitted from the maternal uncle to the sister's son (Quain, ms.).

SOCIAL RELATIONS

In social life there is a marked segregation of the sexes. Men have their own meetings. Their custom of smoking in the center of the village— the "evening group"—has impressed all travelers as a fundamental institution of upper Xingú society. Other occupations of *Trumaí* men include trade games, the "ole" dance, and wrestling with visitors, the last an extremely popular pastime among all groups (Steinen, 1894; Quain, ms.). Trade games may last hours, while each man successively offers raw materials, art objects, or implements for sale. *Trumaí* women, in contrast to the women of some of the other tribes (pp. 343–344), do not frequent the center of the village or participate in dances (Quain, ms.).

Trumaí custom forbids a public display of the natural functions, which are performed far from the gardens (Quain, ms.). A *Bacaïri* never eats in public, or else turns his back when eating. Singing in a loud voice is disapproved. Disgust is expressed by spitting quickly (Steinen, 1894). Most of the formalized etiquette is connected with receiving visitors in the guest house, presenting them ceremonial seats, and offering them food and tobacco. Ceremonial wailing was noticed among the *Bacaïri* (Steinen, 1894), *Yaulapiti,* and *Naravute* (Petrullo, 1932 a).

INTERTRIBAL RELATIONS

Although Petrullo emphasizes the homogeneity of material culture, wide variations in tribal customs undoubtedly once existed. A semblance of homogeneity was produced by intertribal trade; for example, ceramics were, and in some instances are now, furnished to the *Bacaïri* and *Nahukwa* by the *Custenau* and *Mehinacu,* and to the *Trumai* and *Tupian*-speaking tribes by the *Waura.* In Von den Steinen's time, the *Bacaïri* specialized in the production of urucú and cotton, and in the manufacture of hammocks, rectangular beads, and other kinds of shell beads. The *Nahukwa* were the best producers of calabash containers, tucumã nut beads, and red shell beads. Stone implements were the monopoly of the *Trumai* and *Suya;* tobacco raising was a specialty of the *Suya;* and the production of salt was, and still is, important among the *Trumai* and *Mehinacu.* The *Arawakan*-speaking tribes exchanged their pots for the calabashes of the *Nahukwa.* In 1938, *Trumai* bows were still made by the *Camayura* (Steinen, 1894; Quain, ms.).

Industrial specialization was accompanied by a difference in living standards. Von den Steinen was struck by the poverty of the *Yaulapiti,* whose food supply was running low and whose manufactured articles were scarce. Such situations could also result from poor crops or from an unforeseen enemy attack, as intertribal relations on the upper Xingú River were not exactly pacific.

Each tribe possesses its own territory with well-defined boundaries, frequently river banks. Though the rivers themselves are unrestricted, the fishing dams which are built at short intervals are tribal property and are respected as such. The distrust between neighbors is shown in the custom by which visitors build a fire as a warning signal several hours or days before reaching a village (Quain, ms.). Tribes designate one another as "good" or "bad," according to the generosity they expect or according to the aggressive spirit of their neighbor. When Von den Steinen visited the Culiseu River, the *Trumai* had just been attacked by the *Suya,* who had also captured a large number of prisoners from the *Manitsaua.* The *Bacaïri* feared the *Trumai* because of their alleged custom of tying up and drowning their war prisoners. In 1887, the *Trumai* were fleeing from the *Suya* (Steinen, 1894), whom they still feared in 1938 (Quain, ms.). These conflicts existed even between groups speaking the same language, for instance among the *Nahukwa.* (Steinen, 1894; Quain, ms.; Dyott, 1930.)

Although visiting strangers were frequently robbed (Steinen, 1894; Quain, ms.), intertribal ties were undoubtedly stronger than rivalries. Quain noticed a general multilingualism. Each village always had visitors. Commercial travels and trade games, intertribal wrestling matches, and reciprocal invitations to feasts offered constant inducements for visits (Steinen, 1886, 1894; Quain, ms.). Extremely significant is Quain's suggestion that initiation ceremonies were perhaps performed jointly by the *Mehinacu (Minace)* and *Trumai.*

Intermarriages resulted from these half-warlike, half-friendly relations. In Von den Steinen's time, marriages occurred between the *Mehinacu* and *Nahukwa*, the *Bacaïri* of the Batoví River and the *Custenau*, and between the tribes of the Culiseu River and the *Nahukwa*. Intertribal marriages could even found new groups, like the *Arauiti*.

ESTHETIC AND RECREATIONAL ACTIVITIES

Toys and games.—*Bacaïri* children play shuttlecock with a maize husk topped with a feather. They spin tops made of a fruit impaled on a stick with cotton at the lower end to prevent skidding. They also have small spear throwers, blowguns, bows and arrows, and zoomorphic toys made of woven and twisted straw (fig. 37, *e, f, i, j*). Woven straw dolls have been found among the *Mehinacu* and dolls of clay and tree gum (fig. 37, *g, h*) throughout the area.

Trumaí adults often wrestle for entertainment (Quain, ms.). The solid rubber balls of the *Auetö* are made by laying latex strips on the chest and rolling them into a ball, then piercing it with a small hole, and painting it red (Steinen, 1894).

Plastic art.—Esthetic activities are especially well developed among the tribes of the upper Xingú River, who tend to cover all their artifacts with painted designs (Steinen, 1894). Painting and drawing are stylized, often with purely geometrical patterns, such as checkerboard, triangles, lozenges, and parallel lines. But even these elements bear naturalistic names, e. g., a checkerboard represents a bee swarm, and recurrent triangles, bats. Quain collected naturalistic drawings among the *Trumaí* far superior to the childish sketches published by Von den Steinen. The "mereschu" pattern is encountered throughout the area and was called after, and said to represent, a small fish of the lagoons (*Myletes*). It consists of a lozenge with four blackened angles representing the head, tail, and upper and lower fins. The *Auetö* seem to have brought the *Xingú* style to its highest level of abstraction. A special hut of the *Auetö* village was named by Von den Steinen "the painters' house," not only because of its numerous decorations but because it was inhabited mainly by artists.

House decorations are not rare. A frieze of bark strips (fig. 38) blackened with soot and painted with white clay extended along the wall of a *Bacaïri* hut for 185 feet (56 m.). Its decorative themes included zigzag lines, dots, circles, lozenges, and triangles, which were said to represent several kinds of fish, feminine sex symbols, palm leaves, snakes, and bats. The *Auetö* apply white clay uniformly to house posts and then paint designs in black soot over it.

Other decorated objects include paddles and pancake (beijú) shovels (all tribes), canoes and drums (*Bacaïri*), and calabashes (*Bacaïri, Nahukwa*). Tortoise-shell whorls are carved and painted with soot, often in a rosette pattern. During ceremonies, they are slung around the neck

FIGURE 38.—*Bacaïri* house wall decorations on bark strips. (Redrawn from Steinen, 1894, pl. 20.)

as ornaments (*Mehinacu, Auetö, Camayura*). Earthenware is painted with straight, parallel lines, angles, half-circles, and sometimes with reproductions of the tattoo patterns of the *Mehinacu.*

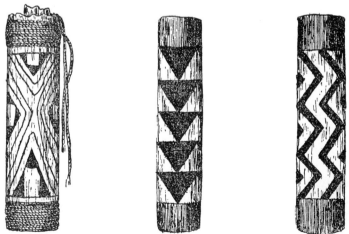

FIGURE 39.—*Bacaïri* wooden dance pendants. (Redrawn from Steinen, 1894, fig. 48.)

Many wooden ornaments, implements, and pieces of furniture are carved in zoomorphic shapes (p. 333). Shell and stone beads are frequently retouched to suggest birds or fishes. In a guest house of the *Mehinacu,* Von den Steinen saw two small mounds modeled in the shape of a lizard, each about 3 feet (1 m.) long and 3 inches (8 cm.) wide. The most remarkable carving of the upper Xingú River is done on trees in the forest. The *Nahukwa* and to a lesser extent other tribes draw large effigies of men, women, and animals on trunks of trees, either by carving an outline of the figure or by removing the bark from the whole silhouette.

Dance costumes and masks.—Costumes of foliage and straw caps ornamented with shells or feathers are widely used in dances. Straw garments like coveralls, with separate sleeves and legs and huge crinolines 30 feet (10 m.) in circumference, are worn by the *Bacaïri*. A two-piece straw costume gives the *Camayura* actor the appearance of a mushroom. Cylindrical blocks of wood richly painted with geometric designs (figs. 39, 40) hang on the back to complete the dance costume (Steinen, 1894).

FIGURE 40.—*Bacaïri* masked dancers. (Redrawn from Steinen, 1894, figs. 98 and 90.)

South of the Amazon, masks were most highly developed on the Upper Xingú River, but are no longer made. They represented animals, but were shaped like human faces, the archetype being suggested only by a pattern painted in the middle of the face. The "mereschu" design was common on all masks. The simplest type of mask might be the fishing net that a *Nahukwa* put on his head (Steinen, 1894). Several elaborate types can be distinguished: (1) Zoomorphic headdresses made of carved wood, woven straw, painted calabashes, furs, or the dry head or skin of some animal. A remarkable headdress of the *Bacaïri* of the Batoví River consisted of seven carved and painted birds mounted on sticks to which cotton is glued (Steinen, 1894). (2) Straw masks woven in the shape of an oval sieve and either without human features or with stylized eyes and nose modeled in wax and attached to the frame (*Bakaïri, Nahukwa, Auetö*). (3) Flat, oval straw masks (fig. 42, *a, b*) with a frame of netting or of woven cotton and features made of plastic wax, cotton tufts, beans, or shells, lavishly painted (*Bacaïri, Auetö, Camayura, Trumaí*). (4) Rectangular wooden masks, often with only the forehead and nose carved and an animal pattern painted in place of the mouth (figs. 41; 42, *c-f*). This type was found among the *Bacaïri, Nahukwa, Auetö,* and *Camayura,* and was the only one found among the *Mehinacu.*

a

b

c

FIGURE 41.—*Mehinacu* and *Bacaïri* masks. *a, b, Mehinacu; c, Bacaïri.* (Redrawn from Steinen, 1894, figs. 103, 102, 94.)

The lower part of the mask usually bears a beardlike fringe of straw. The best carved and painted masks seem to have been made by the *Mehinacu* and *Auetö*. The *Trumaí,* who now use no masks, had only woven cotton ones, probably borrowed from the *Camayura* (Quain, ms.).

Most tribes had "fish" masks and "bird" masks, each probably associated with a dance cycle. Every village possessed its own collection of masks; today these are not worshiped and are willingly sold.

Dances, songs, and music.—*Bacaïri* women are excluded from the guest house during "great feasts" but participate in lesser feasts and in exclusively feminine festivals (Steinen, 1894). Except among the *Trumaí,* women are allowed to dance (Quain, ms.). The *Camayura* have seven different dances. According to Dyott's description (1930, pp. 201–202) of a *Nahukwa* dance, men form two lines lengthwise of the house; the women, two rows at right angles to them. The men hold their hands outstretched and stamp their feet; each woman rests an arm on the shoulder of her companion and swings the right foot back and forth. In another *Nahukwa* dance, witnessed by Von den Steinen, three men stamped and whirled rhythmically while an old woman jumped back and forth. In a *Yaulapiti* dance, the men circled counter-clockwise, stamping the right foot. Chanting, the women danced outside the circle, arm in arm and palm

FIGURE 42.—Upper Xingú masks. *a, Trumaí; b, Camayura; c, Auetö; d, Camayura; e, Mehinacu; f, Bacaïri.* (Redrawn from Steinen, 1894, figs. 118, 112, 314, 113, 104, 44.)

to palm with fingers interlocked, taking three steps forward, pausing, and stepping back (Petrullo, 1932 a, p. 142). During another feast, clowns with big flageolets marched grotesquely from hut to hut, entering each while the women pretended to be frightened (Petrullo, 1932 a, p. 139). Von den Steinen described a *Bacaïri* ceremony that is possibly related to the last. Men gathered in the guest house and each, wearing a dance costume, rushed out in turn to enter some hut, from which he returned with an offering of food. Quain (ms.) says that although *Trumaí* singing was not polyphonic, "its modulations seemed like classical harmony."

Musical instruments.—All Indians dance with rattling anklets or necklaces of shells and seeds. Gourd rattles are common among the *Bacaïri, Nahukwa,* and *Camayura,* and tortoise-shell rattles among the *Nahukwa* (Steinen, 1894). The *Auetö* have rattles made of an egg fastened to a stick. There are also bottle-shaped rattles which are beaten (stamping tube?) against the ground.

Two drums made of hollow tree trunks resting on the ground were found in a *Bacaïri* and a *Camayura* village (Steinen, 1894).

Wind instruments are common. Whistles consist of palm nuts pierced with one or two holes. Several types of small and large panpipes are used. *Suya* "panpipes," which have three tubes and are 5 feet (1.5 m.) long, have air ducts and reeds, and may really be three clarinets bound together. A widely used instrument is the flageolet, about 2½ to 3 feet (75 to 90 cm.) long, with four holes and an air duct through the wax of the mouthpiece, which is sometimes beveled. The flageolet is usually made of a solid piece of bamboo, but sometimes two longitudinal halves are glued together with wax and wrapped with cotton or bark. The *Bacaïri* play two flageolets in unison (Steinen, 1886), and the *Nahukwa* and *Yaulapiti* play three that are attached together and painted red and black (Dyott, 1930; Petrullo, 1932 a). Von den Steinen mentioned a toneless rhythm trumpet made of bamboo without holes and with a calabash resonator at the bottom.

Drinks and narcotics.—Von den Steinen emphasized the lack of fermented drinks as proof of the primitive state of the area. When he was on the upper Xingú River, all men smoked, except those of a single *Bacaïri* village on the Batoví River. Tobacco leaves were dried between two planks and twisted in a spindle-shaped roll. Tobacco rolls similar to those described by ancient travelers are still in use. Cigarettes are rolled in special leaves and are tied with a bit of grass. Although tobacco has a secular use, smoking is frequently associated with magic and ceremonial.

RELIGION AND SHAMANISM

Shamanism.—Shamanism is said to be uncommon among the *Bacaïri* and *Auetö;* more frequent among the *Nahukwa* and *Mehinacu;* and fully developed among the *Trumai*. To become a shaman, one must submit to long and complicated trials, including fasting, remaining awake, and self-punishment, such as knocking one's head against the hut posts and scarifying the body (Steinen, 1894). When curing a disease, the *Trumai* chief produced "blubbering noises . . . healing and blowing upon the patient with tobacco" (Quain, ms.). The belief in the life-giving property of breath is often emphasized by Von den Steinen, who also describes the shooting of "magic arrows," consisting of small sticks or cotton threads which were believed to cause illness and which the shaman sucked out of the body.

The practice of witchcraft ("okei" in *Trumai,* Quain, ms.) both for benevolent and evil purposes, is widespread. A knowledge of poisons is important to the shaman. Some drugs are said to swell the patient's body fatally (Quain, ms.); others consist of lizards mixed with the blood and hair of an enemy (Steinen, 1894). According to the use they make of witchcraft, sorcerers are designated "good" or "evil."

An important culture trait is the magic use of tobacco for "seeing-smoking" (Quain, ms.). This narcotic state enables one to receive messages, warnings, and visions. According to Von den Steinen, narcosis is a privilege of the shaman, who might, in a narcotic state, assume the appearance of an animal and travel far away. Quain witnessed an exoteric use of the process by the *Trumai,* among whom "seeing-smoking" might be practiced by anyone, though only at night. The natives interpret reading as a sort of "seeing-smoking." They also believe in premonitory dreams, which the *Bacaïri* explain as the alleged power of the soul to leave the body temporarily during sleep.

Religious beliefs.—Nothing is known of more elaborate religious beliefs, except that the *Trumai* are afraid of the rain, which "might kill people" (Quain, ms.). They also believe that after death one travels the Milky Way, meets many jaguars in the sky, and at last enters the Village of the Beyond, where one may fish with poison (Quain, ms.). This statement is in contradiction to Von den Steinen's opinion that fishing with poison was unknown on the upper Xingú River (p. 324). The *Bacaïri* distinguish between man's two souls, "ghost" and "cover." When the "ghost" leaves the body it undergoes consecutive transformations, becoming first a wandering soul ("kXadopa"), often in the shape of an armadillo, and later being liberated, when it climbs to the sky on a cotton ladder and joins its ancestors in its final state called "yamüra" (Abreu, 1938).

Supernatural beliefs are probably associated with the custom, followed by most tribes, of raising a harpy eagle (*Harpia harpyja*) in a conical cage of poles erected in the middle of the village (photograph in Dyott, 1930, p. 220). The bird is carefully fed but is not worshiped. Petrullo suggests that it receives its share of all game in exchange for its feathers, which are periodically plucked and divided among the men.

Ceremonials.—The *Camayura* have special ceremonies for warfare, fishing, hunting, and initiation (Steinen, 1894). Among the *Trumai,* the manioc ("ole") ceremony is the most important (Quain, ms.). Several peeled poles, each rubbed with white clay, painted in black and red designs, and decorated with cotton tufts glued to the top, are set up in the plaza so as to form a shrine. Offering of fish cakes (beijú), and other kinds of food are placed before the altar, which is sprinkled at intervals with manioc soup. The ceremonial is reserved for men and includes wrestling matches, songs, and dances, the last similar to those performed at a shaman's cures and on other more profane occasions (Quain, ms.).

Another feast is given after piquí fruit drops, which is the time for piercing boys' ears. It is suggested, though not positively established, that

PLATE 27.—**Yaulapiti Indians in "woodskins," or bark canoes.** (Courtesy University Museum, Philadelphia.)

PLATE 28.—**Yaulapiti women preparing manioc in pottery vessels.** (Courtesy
University Museum, Philadelphia.)

PLATE 29.—**Upper Xingú house frames.** *Top:* Roof of a *Naravute* house. *Bottom: Yaulapiti* frame. (Courtesy University Museum, Philadelphia.)

PLATE 30.—**Naravute and Yaulapiti Indians.** *Top: Naravute* communal house. *Bottom: Yaulapiti* polygamous family. (Courtesy University Museum, Philadelphia.)

PLATE 31.—**Upper Xingú Indians.** *Top: Bacaïri* hunter with carrying basket.
Bottom: Cooking pots and *Auetö* grave. (After Steinen, 1894.)

PLATE 32.—**Auetö carrying bark canoe.** (After Steinen, 1894.)

PLATE 33.—**Upper Xingú Indians.** *Top: Suya. Bottom: Yaulapiti.* (Courtesy University Museum, Philadelphia.)

PLATE 34.—**Fish-net dance of the Nahukwa.** (After Steinen, 1894.)

different tribes are invited to participate in this initiation ceremony.
The Spear Thrower Feast takes place at the beginning of the rainy
season.   The *Naravute* told Petrullo that ceremonial weapons are
divided between two teams which try to strike each other with blunt-
pointed spears.   The spectacle of a similar feast among the *Camayura*
was observed by Von den Steinen.   Quain mentions a "Kuth" ceremony,
with wooden symbols which women are forbidden to see.   These symbols
may be bull roarers, of which Von den Steinen describes several types.
They are swordlike with black and red designs among the *Mehinacu*, and
carved in the shape of a fish among the *Nahukwa*, who have no sexual
prohibitions regarding them.   The *Bacaïri* call their bull roarers "thunder"
or "thunderstorm."

MYTHS AND LEGENDS

The *Bacaïri* tell of their migration to the earth, because of the high
mortality in their first homeland, the sky (Steinen, 1894), and of the
subsequent destruction of the universe by flood and fire and its re-
creation (Abreu, 1938).   The creation myths of the *Trumai* put several
characters on the stage, the Crow, Sun, Moon, "Grandfather," and Jaguar
("Fetde"), father of the Sun (Quain, ms.).   An important body of
Bacaïri myths and tales were recorded by Von den Steinen.   Three groups
may be distinguished.

(1) **The cycle of Keri and Kame.**—Keri and Kame, which designate
two culture heroes, are the *Arawakan* terms for Sun and Moon, borrowed
by the *Cariban* speaking *Bacaïri*, who have reversed their meaning.   Kame,
the less intelligent and more foolish of the pair, got killed and had to be
revived by Keri.   These culture heroes are not identified with the eponymic
celestial bodies; the latter are conceived as balls of feathers, which once had
been united but which the heroes separated.

The numerous legends belonging to this cycle tell of an unsuccessful
attempt by a mythical stranger to make new human beings; of the birth
of Keri and Kame from two human bones swallowed by a woman married
to a jaguar; of the murder of the pregnant woman by her own mother;
of her post-mortem birth of the boys, done by a jaguar who was her
uncle; and of the revenge by the two heroes.   From their "masters," they
received the natural elements, laws and customs, and fundamental items
of *Bacaïri* culture, e.g., the hammock from the lizard, cotton from a kind
of marten (*Galictis*), tobacco from the electric eel, and manioc from the
deer.   After having saved their tribe on a final occasion, the two heroes
disappeared.

The *Trumai* also had tales about the Sun and Moon, in which the Moon
played the foolish part and had to be saved by its companion (Quain, ms.).

(2) **Animal tales.**—The cycle of Keri and Kame is the basis for several animal legends.   Others, such as the *Trumai* Tale of the Crow

(Quain, ms.) and the *Bacaïri* Tale of the Jaguar and Anteater (Steinen 1894), are pure animal tales, rather humorous in character.

(3) Historical legends.—Many details in the cycle of Keri and Kame and in other legends are interpretations of the early history of the upper Xingú River. The *Trumaí* believe their ancestors to have been aquatic animals (Steinen, 1894; Quain, ms.). They explain the cultural diversity of the tribes of the upper Xingú River as having resulted from a choice of things which the Sun once offered people. The *Trumaí* took the beeswax, the *Camayura* the bow, the *Waura* pots, but the White man preferred the ax and hence he built an extensive civilization (Quain, ms.).

LORE AND LEARNING

According to the *Bacaïri,* the sky was once in close contact with the earth. The Sun and Moon, each a ball of feathers, are hidden under a pot when they are not visible and are carried through the sky by animals, either slow or fast, depending upon the hour and season. Sometimes the Moon is hidden by the body of an animal at work, and then an eclipse occurs. Several constellations are identified, chiefly the Pleiades, Orion, the Southern Cross, and Gemini. They are said to represent implements, plants, foods, and other objects. The Milky Way is compared to a drum which contains animals (Steinen, 1894). The *Trumaí* believe that the sky is immortal and that it changes its skin like a snake. They also think that the visible sun is altogether different from, and is the "pet" of, the real sun, which is called by a special name (Quain, ms.).

All tribes draw geographical maps of the area on the sand. Rivers are suggested by zigzags cut by transverse lines for the rapids; circles represent huts, and circles arranged in a ring are villages. As signs to fishermen, drawings of the special kind of fish which is abundant at a certain spot are left on the sand bank of the rivers (Steinen, 1886, 1894).

The *Bacaïri* have distinct words for the numbers one to three. Three is not used frequently, and a combination of the words for one and two is often substituted for it. The counting of the *Trumaí* is not perfectly clear, but they, as well as the *Waura* and *Camayura,* seem to have a distinct word for four. Five is expressed by a special word by the *Trumaí* and *Auetö,* while the other tribes use the same word as for "hand." Counting above five is done with the help of hands and feet, and numbers above five are expressed by combinations of the basic terms.

BIBLIOGRAPHY

Abreu, 1895 (rep. 1938); Dyott, 1929, 1930; Ehrenreich, 1897 a; Fawcett, 1925; Hintermann, 1925, 1926; Krause, 1936 a, b, c; 0000; Lévi-Strauss, 1943 b; Lima Figueiredo, 1939; Meyer, 1897 a, b, c, d, 1900, 1904; Nordenskiöld 1930 b; Petrullo, 1932 a, b; Quain, ms. (n. d.); Ranke, 1906; Schmidt, 1902–04, 1905, 1924, 1928; Steinen, 1886, 1888, 1892, 1894.

PART 2. THE TRIBES OF MATO GROSSO AND EASTERN BOLIVIA

THE PARESSI

By ALFRED MÉTRAUX

TRIBAL DIVISIONS

The *Paressí* of Central Brazil together with the *Mojo* and *Chané* represent the southernmost branch of the *Arawakan* linguistic family.[1] They occupied in the Mato Grosso an area delimited in the east by the Arinos and the Upper Paraguay Rivers, in the west by the Upper Guaporé and Juruena Rivers, and in the south by lat. 40°30′.

They were divided into three main groups that were often hostile but that had a homogeneous culture and few dialectical differences: (1) The *Cashíniti* (*Kachíniti*), scattered along the Soumidoro River, a tributary of the Arinos River, and near the headwaters of the Sepotuba and Sucuriu-na Rivers (lat. 15° S., long. 58° W.); (2) the *Uaimaré* (*Waimaré*), who lived along the upper Rio Verde and Sacre River; (3) the *Cozárini* (*Kozárini*), who occupied the region of the watershed of the Juba, Cabaçái, Jaurú, Guaporé, Rio Verde, Papagaio, Burity, and Juruena Rivers (lat. 15° S., long. 59° W.).[2]

The *Cozárini* seem to be a mixed tribe formed by a nucleus of *Paressí* invaders who absorbed and assimilated Indians from other tribes, mainly *Nambicuara* (*Guayguakuré*). As recently as 1910 when Max Schmidt (1914) visited them, the *Cozárini* still fought the *Nambicuara* and kidnapped the men for slaves and the women for wives. The other *Paressí* looked down on the *Cozárini* as an inferior branch of their nation and called them *Cabishí*, a term also applied to the *Nambicuara* of the Serra do Norte and to numerous Indians of the Guaporé basin. Max Schmidt called them *Paressí-Cabishí*, a name which has been adopted in the anthropological literature.

After 1908, the *Paressí* were collected by the "Commissão de Linhas telegraphicas" in the following settlements: Utiáriti, Barão de Cam-

---

[1] *Paressí* is closer to *Mehinakú* than to *Mojo*.

[2] The *Iranxe* (*Iranche*), who have been classified as a *Paressí* subtribe, belong according to Max Schmidt (1942) to a different linguistic group.

panema, Ponte de Pedra, and Aldeia Quemada. In 1928, most of the remaining *Cashiniti* and *Uaimaré* lived in Utiáriti and São José. The surviving *Cozárini* were settled near Villa de Mato Grosso and at Tapiruapán.

Population.—Pires de Campos (1862) stresses the large population of the *Paressí* and *Uaimaré* in 1718. By 1848, their number had been considerably reduced through slave raids. The *Cashiniti* were then estimated at 250, the *Uaimaré* at 400, and the *Cozárini* (*Cabishi*) at 500. In 1908, according to Rondón's census, there were 340 *Paressí* living in 12 villages of which the largest had 57 inhabitants and the smallest 16. In 1937, there remained about 150 *Paressí*.

HISTORY

The *Paressí*, under the name of *Pareti*, are mentioned in connection with the first Spanish expeditions to Chiquitos and Mojos. At the beginning of the 17th century, some conquistadors reached their territory and even saw the Serra dos Parecis and the Serra do Norte. (See Métraux, 1942, p. 160.)

The first account of their culture was written in 1723 by the slaver Antonio Pires de Campos (1862), who in 1718 had discovered this tribe on the highlands beyond the watershed of the Paraguay River. The *Mahibarez*, undoubtedly identical with the modern *Uaimaré* (*Mahimbaré*), had, according to Pires de Campos, the same culture and the same language as the *Paressí*. Pires de Campos mentions also the wild and cannibalistic *Cavihi* (*Cabishi*), but it cannot be ascertained whether the latter were actually the modern *Paressí-Cabishi* (*Cozárini*).

During the entire 18th century, the *Paressí* region was crossed by slavers and by adventurers in search of gold or diamond mines. In the 19th century, the *Paressí* also were molested by rubber gatherers. Their territory was finally opened in 1908 by General Mariano Candido da Silva Rondón, who was then the chief of the Commission that built a telegraphic line across the Brazilian wilderness. Thanks to Rondón's endeavours, the Indians were well treated and were even given the means to adjust themselves to modern civilization. So rapid was their assimilation, that within a few years the Commission could use some *Paressí* as employees, even as telegraphers. Schools were created in several villages and many *Paressí* received White education. By 1928, the *Paressí* were fully acculturated. It is difficult to account for the sharp decline in population which took place after 1910; Max Schmidt (1943, p. 10), however, states that many *Cozárini* fell victims to an influenza epidemic.

SOURCES

Von den Steinen's chapter about the *Paressí* in his "Unter den Naturvölkern Central Brasiliens" (1894) is especially valuable for the creation myths it contains, but his information is fragmentary, for the author never visited these Indians in their home country. Good data about various aspects of *Paressí* culture appear in Rondón's (1912) reports and in the book "Rondonia" written by the Brazilian anthropologist Roquette-Pinto (1917, 1938). Max Schmidt (1914, 1943) has written two important monographs about this tribe: the first one deals exclusively with the *Paressí-Cabishí* (*Cozárini*); the more recent one includes a detailed history of the *Paressí*, a summary of their culture, an extensive dictionary of their language with grammatical notes, and mythological texts in *Paressí*.

CULTURE

SUBSISTENCE

Farming.—The 18th-century *Paressí*, who probably lived somewhat north of their present territory, had large fields of maize, beans, sweet potatoes, and pineapples. The siliceous plateaus more recently occupied by the *Paressí* are less fertile. Only the thin gallery forests along the rivers are well suited for cultivation, hence the dispersion of the fields and the frequent shifting of villages. The *Paressí* cultivate bitter and sweet manioc, maize (a red and a yellow variety), beans, sweet potatoes, cara, tobacco, and cotton. They supplement their diet with wild food plants, such as cashews, jaboticaba, tarumá, tucum, wild pineapples, and many other species.

Hunting.—Game is scarce and elusive in the open savannas of the territory of the *Paressí;* these Indians, nonetheless, are good hunters. They stalk game with the bow and arrow using portable leaf screens to hide themselves. They also shoot from watchposts or organize communal drives in which they set fire to the bush. They decoy the game by imitating its call or catch it with traps. They have well-trained hunting dogs. According to Pires de Campos (1862), the ancient *Paressí* caught deer, rheas, and other animals in pitfalls which they dug within large enclosures built between two streams. Max Schmidt (1914) reports that hunters destroy the game indiscriminately, but Rondón (1912) states that they spare the female rheas during the breeding season.

Fishing.—Shooting with bow and arrows in flooded areas, drugging with timbó, or angling with European hooks are the main fishing methods of the *Paressí*. However, their deep and clear rivers constitute a handicap which makes fishing less important here than in the other tropical areas.

Domestication.—The *Paressí* are among the few Indians of America who practice a primitive form of apiculture. They put swarms of jati bees (*Trigona jati*) in a gourd with two openings, one for the bees and the other, sealed with wax, for removing the combs.

Modern *Paressí*, besides keeping many wild animals as pets, raise dogs, chickens, pigs, and ducks. In 1910, the *Cozárini* had only dogs which were ill treated and ill fed.

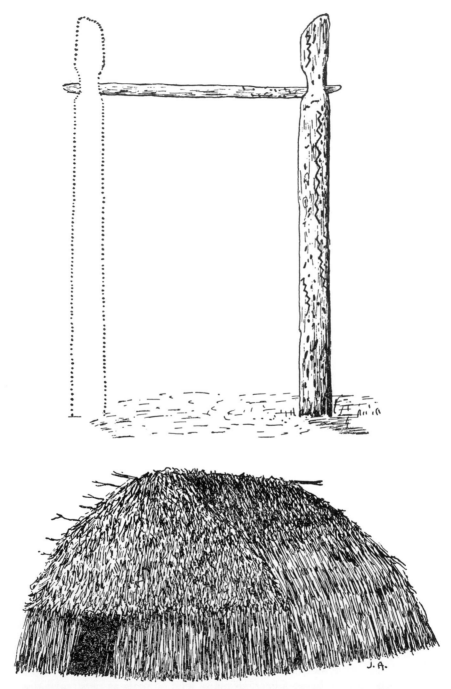

FIGURE 43.—*Paressí* Indians. *Top:* Decorated posts and bar for testing strength. *Bottom: Paressí* house. (Redrawn from M. Schmidt, 1914, figs. 27, 40.)

Food preparation.—Meat is roasted on a four-legged babracot; manioc is grated on wooden graters, strained through sieves, and roasted in clay pans. Maize or manioc is pounded in large, cylindrical wooden mortars with wooden pestles. Gourds of all kinds and sizes serve as bottles, bowls, and cups. Small mats are used as dishes and fire fans.

HOUSES AND VILLAGES

According to Pires de Campos (1862), the ancient *Paressí* villages comprised from 10 to 30 round and oven-shaped huts, from 30 to 40 feet (10 to 13 m.) in diameter.

At the beginning of this century, *Paressí* villages consisted only of one or two communal houses accommodating an average of six families. These huts were dome-shaped with an oval ground plan and a thatched roof which reached the ground. The frame was made of bent rafters attached to a central ridge pole. The lower part of the wall was lined up with large pieces of bark. These huts averaged 25 feet (7.6 m.) in length, 18 feet (5.4 m.) in width, and 12 feet (3.6 m.) in height. Each family occupied a space bounded by the rafters.

Each village had a ceremonial hut, which may be described as a gable roof resting on the ground and closed on all sides but for a single door shut with a leaf screen.

Hammocks, which were made of cotton, but sometimes of tucumã fibers, were suspended from the rafters and from extra posts, which were often decorated with painted motifs (*Cozárini*). Such posts were held to be animated by spirits that protected the families from thieves.

DRESS AND ADORNMENT

Men and women dress today like the Mestizos. Formerly, men went naked, but tucked their penis under a few cotton strings threaded with beads and tied around the waist. Women wore short, cylindrical, cotton skirts, which scarcely covered their lower abdomen (pl. 35, *bottom, left*). Pires de Campos (1862) mentions penis covers (?) and women's skirts covered with feathers. Both sexes wore wide garters and anklets, the men of cotton, the women's often of rubber. Men use also woven bracelets, reinforced with wooden sticks and feather quills. Both sexes took pride in owning a great many beads, which they displayed in the form of bracelets or of heavy necklaces suspended crosswise over the chest.

The only headdresses consisted either of a simple feather circlet mounted on a low frame of bamboo strips or of tufts of feathers attached to the nape. Feathers were passed through the perforated septum of the nose and sticks through the earlobes. In former days, both sexes were tattooed, an operation performed by women. The *Paressí* paint themselves with genipa and urucú.

According to tradition, *Paressí* men wore a tonsure in ancient days;
today they cut their hair around the head. Combs consisted of splinters
inserted between parallel pieces of bamboo.

TRANSPORTATION

Many *Paressí* groups lack canoes. They cross rivers buoyed by a
bundle of burity stems or on tree-trunk bridges.

The ancient *Paressí* seem to have built broad paths or even roads to
connect their villages.

MANUFACTURES

Basketry.—Some circular sieves and concave trays are made with a
plain checker weave of bamboo strands. More complicated diagonal patterns are obtained by using a twilled weave. The finished basket is
smeared with black pigment which, adhering to the rough sides of the
strands, causes the design to stand out sharply. The large cylindrical
carrying baskets represent a third technique: the warp and weft meet at
right angles and are held in position by extra diagonal strands (pl. 35,
top, left).

Spinning and weaving.—Cotton is spun with drop spindles fitted
with a clay whorl or a fruit. Ropes of tucum fibers are twisted on the
thigh.

The loom is of the vertical, or *"Arawak,"* type. Loincloths, baby slings,
and bags are made of the entire cylindrical piece of the finished cloth as
it is removed from the loom. For other objects, such as arm bands and
belts, the warp is cut before the fabric is completed, so that the ends are
always fringed.

Featherwork.—Ancient *Paressí* excelled in making feather fabric,
probably in the same techniques as *Mojo* feather mosaics.

Pottery.—Unlike most *Arawakan* tribes, the *Paressí* have a very crude
pottery, though they might have had a better ceramic in the past. Clay is
tempered with the ashes of the katipe bark and a ferruginous powder,
common in the region.

Rubber.—Rubber balls are made by coating a concave piece of wood
with the latex of the mangabeira (*Hancornia speciosa*). The edges of
the membrane are glued together by pressing them with the fingers. Air
is blown into the ball through a small hole which is patched with a thin
membrane. Several additional coatings of latex give strength to the ball.
The rubber bands which women wore around their legs were made on a
a cylindrical piece of wood.

Weapons.—In 1718, Pires de Campos saw among the *Paressí* bows and
arrows, flat swords of hardwood, and short spears. Bows and arrows fell
into disuse soon after guns were introduced. The bows of the *Cozárini*
have a semicircular cross section and shoulders are cut at both ends for

PLATE 35.—**Paressí life.** (Courtesy American Museum of Natural History.)

the three-ply cotton string. There are three kinds of arrows: those tipped
with a long sharp rod, bird arrows made of a simple bamboo stem with
the root forming the knobbed head, and whistling arrows. The feathering
is of the cemented type. It is lacking on fishing arrows.

Paressí are acquainted with curare, which they extract from shavings
of the bark of a creeper (*Strychnos toxifera*). Other ingredients added to
the poison have magical rather than practical usefulness. Curare is used
on ordinary hunting arrows.

SOCIAL ORGANIZATION

The political unit of the *Paressí* is the independent village, which is
under the direction of a chief and of a shaman. Often one man fills both
roles. Among the *Cozárini,* chieftainship is transmitted to the eldest son,
who enjoys special privileges even when he is only the heir apparent. It
is remembered that in the past some *Paressí* chiefs ruled over minor chiefs
in other villages. The functions of the chiefs are not fully described in
our sources, but we know that they lead all the ceremonies and that they
receive visitors.

Among the *Cozárini,* heads of families control a class of dependents
that includes many adopted captive boys. These servants open clearings,
carry wood to the village, build houses, and give their masters all their earn-
ings (M. Schmidt, 1914, p. 188).

The inhabitants of different villages visit one another frequently and
maintain active commercial relations. The whole territory of these Indians
is crisscrossed by paths leading from one settlement to another.

LIFE CYCLE

Birth.—It is customary for a woman during childbirth to kneel on the
ground and to lean against another woman, generally her mother. Until
the infant's navel cord drops off, both parents remain at home. Moreover,
during his seclusion, the father may eat only manioc wafers.[3] When the
child is about 3 years old, it receives the name of one of its grandparents
(Steinen, 1894, p. 436).

Marriage.—Monogamy prevails now, but formerly sororal polygyny
appears to have been common. When native traditions were still unimpaired, small children were often bethrothed to each other by their parents.
Sometimes an adult man reared a girl from childhood and married her
when she reached puberty.

Marriage was considered sealed after the bridegroom had made a small
present to his bride's parents and after the latter had brought the girl to
his hammock (Steinen, 1894, p. 434). Residence was customarily matri-

---

[3] A father who did not observe the rules of the couvade faced the danger of being killed by bush
spirits.

local, except for chiefs who were privileged to take their wives to their own houses.

Death.—Toward the end of the 19th century, the dead were buried in their huts with food and all their possessions, their heads turned toward the east. Relatives of the deceased remained indoors for 6 days, observing a rigorous fast. On the seventh day, they rubbed their bodies with a plant juice mixed with urucú. The house of the dead was abandoned temporarily or permanently.

The souls of the dead were believed to travel to the sky, but on the way they had to face many ordeals. They passed by a large fire which flared up to burn the "sinners" and by a doglike monster which tore them to pieces. If they succeeded in overcoming these dangers, the souls were received in the sky by Waikomoné and his three brothers, who painted them with urucú (Steinen, 1894, pp. 434–35).

ESTHETIC AND RECREATIONAL ACTIVITIES

Art.—Gourds (fig. 44), dancing sticks, and house posts of the *Cozárini* are decorated with painted, incised or fire-engraved geometrical and real-

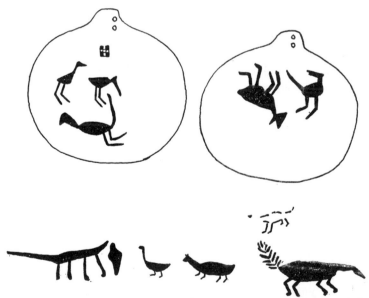

FIGURE 44.—*Paressí* decorated gourds. (Redrawn from M. Schmidt, 1914, figs. 127, 128, and 126.)

istic designs. The geometrical patterns consist of straight or undulating lines, series of dots, triangles, hooks, rows of lozenges, T-shaped motifs, and others. Simple zigzag lines are called "Male serpent spirits"; a group of lozenges represents the "Female serpent spirit." As a rule, however, these design elements are combined according to the fancy of the artist and seem to lack any symbolic or other significance. The realistic decorations are black silhouettes of men and animals. Apparently, there is seldom any attempt to depict a scene. The posts supporting the transverse piece of wood, which young *Cozárini* boys break with their back, are covered with paintings, some realistic, others geometric. These designs are more or less conventionalized representations of the moon, spirits, caimans, and so on. The motifs are haphazardly combined, and cannot be regarded as true pictographs. They show, however, striking resemblances to the petroglyphs of Ponte da Pedra, in *Paressí* territory. (See M. Schmidt, 1940).

Musical instruments.—Many of the musical instruments are highly sacred, and symbolize spirits. In this category are the big flutes with four stops, of which there are several kinds with different tones. Among the *Cozárini,* the Male serpent-spirit, Makunaima, is represented by a clarinet or trumpet formed of two parts, a bamboo tube, and a gourd (resonator bell). The distal end is notched and vibrates when air is blown into the tube.

Men imitate spirit voices by speaking into a bamboo tube, the thin walls of which are slashed. This is not so much a musical instrument as a "tone coloring instrument, somewhat like our mirlitones" (Izikowitz, 1935, p. 235).

Resonator whistles, or flutes made of two halves of gourds and blown with the nose, are also sacred.

The ceremonial musical instruments are kept in the club houses safe from the eyes of women, to whom they are taboo.

Paressí panpipes consist of 5 tubes held together by a simple ligature. Like the gourd rattles which are used as toys, they are profane instruments. Dancers wear anklets of fruit shells. (On musical instruments and on *Paressí* music, see Roquette-Pinto, 1938, pp. 137–140.)

Games.—The *Paressí,* like the *Mojo,* have a rubber-ball game which is played exclusively with the head. The hollow rubber ball is 8 inches (20 cm.) in diameter. The players are divided into two teams, and the ball is placed on the ground on top of a heap of sand. One player runs forward, throws himself flat on the ground, and butts the ball toward the opposite side. The first butt never lifts the ball very high and it rolls and bounces toward the opponents, one of whom throws himself flat on his face and butts it back. After this, the ball flies sufficiently high for the players to strike it with their heads. A score is made by one team when the opponents miss the ball and allow it to fall to the ground. The main rule is that the ball must not be touched with the hands or feet or with any part of the body except the top of the head (Roosevelt, 1914, pp. 198-199).

In a contest of strength, young *Cozárini* men use their backs to break a transverse wooden bar passed through two perpendicular posts (fig. 43, *top*).

Children's games include walking on stilts and throwing shuttlecocks.

Dances.—Ceremonial dancing is restricted to men; women may not even see the performance. Women may, however, join profane dances. Men carrying pipes and trumpets circle slowly round and round stamping their feet, to make their rattles clatter. Dances are led by the chiefs.

Beverages.—*Paressí* prepare manioc chicha in large wooden troughs. They boil the mass in large pots, and add to it chewed manioc cakes (beijú) and an infusion of palm fruits. The main feasts, involving drinking and dancing, take place in October and April and attract many visitors. from far away villages.

RELIGION

Diffuse animism appears to be one of the main features of *Paressí* religion. The Indians people rivers and woods with spirits and demons. The most important deity of the *Cozárini* seems to have been the Serpent spirit, Nukaima, and his wife. The men's club is his temple where he is represented by a trumpet and his wife by a flute (flageolet). According to Pires de Campos (1862, p. 443), the ancient *Paressí* had special huts in which they kept terrifying "idols" and trumpets which belonged to these deities. Women were not permitted to enter the sacred huts where the men assembled in their best outfits to dance and drink.

An unshaped piece of wood is, according to Roquette-Pinto, one of the *Paressí's* main sacred objects. When it becomes old and moth-eaten, a shaman and his assistant go to the forest and get another log, which they carry home while chanting a monotonous duet which women are forbidden to hear.

Drinking bouts are celebrated by the *Cozárini* in honor of the Serpent spirit. At dusk on the day before the feast, beer is sent into the club, where it is received with a curious yell produced in the throat. Men begin the feast by beating the roofs of the huts with a sort of whip to notify the women inside that the Serpent spirits are thirsty and that their anger can be appeased only by offerings of beer. Two dancers, holding the musical instruments symbolizing the spirits, stamp on the ground in front of the houses while other participants sing in deep voices to their rhythm. The chief gives the dancers large quantities of a manioc or chicha beer prepared by the terrified women. The latter remain shut inside the dwelling houses during the entire performance.

The Serpent spirits also demand meat. Large portions of game are set aside and roasted as offerings for them, but actually are eaten by the men in the club house, where they receive the food with deep roars.

Occasionally, lay dances are performed to the accompaniment of musical instruments. Groups of three men dance together while blowing their panpipes. There are also choruses under the direction of some precentor.

SHAMANISM

Shamans are surrounded by apprentices on whom they impose solitary retreats into the forests and severe fasts. Shamans are credited with considerable knowledge and are said to be capable of flying to the sky (Steinen, 1894, p. 435). They treat their patients by blowing tobacco smoke on their bodies, but they use also a great many medicinal plants, judging from the extensive list of them published by Rondón (1912, pp. 15–17). Sorcerers throw poison at their victims or mix it in their drinks.

MYTHOLOGY

The first ancestor was the stone woman Maisö. At the time, there was darkness, and there were neither rivers, earth, nor wood. By introducing a piece of wood into her vagina, Maisö produced first the dirty Cuiabá River and then the clear Paressí River. She put soil in the water and created the ground. Many people issued from her, the first man, Dukavaiteré, entirely of stone. With his wife, Urahiulu, he engendered the sun, the moon, the rheas, the jaguar, the seriema bird, and the deer, all of which he placed in the sky as stars and constellations. Then they procreated several kinds of parrots together with serpents of the same color. For instance, the blue arara, which had a human face, appeared at the same time as the "blue arara serpents." Maisö, concerned by the successive birth of parrots and serpents, made magic on her daughter-in-law, who finally conceived the first *Paressí*. This first man, Uazale, was hairy and had a tail and a membrane between his arms and legs.[4] The other children of the mythic couple became the ancestors of the several *Paressí* subtribes and even of the Portuguese.

Later, the woman, Uarahiulu, produced iron tools, axes, and finally, horses, cattle, and pigs. Everything came from her.

Uazale, the first *Paressí,* was a true culture hero. He discovered manioc in the forest and created cotton by planting his hair. Tobacco grew from the body of a child that he buried. Uazale wanted to kill his children, whom he suspected of incest. The children ran away into the forest, which they accidentally set on fire. Several valuable plants grew from the various parts of their charred bodies. Uazale also taught pottery making to women.

Tshenikauré, Uazale's brother, was the "big jaguar" that devoured Kamazú, the ancestor of the *Cozárini,* and his wife. Waikomoné, Kamazu's son, killed the jaguar. The jaguar's arrows were changed into *Bacaïri* Indians. All the Indians who were hostile to the *Paressí* were believed to be members of the family of the mythical jaguar.

In *Paressí* mythology, Waikomoné is second in importance only to Uazale. Waikomoné and his three brothers receive the souls of the

---

[4] According to the myths recorded by Max Schmidt (1943, pp. 234–235), Uazale and his brothers came from a cave, near Ponta de Pedra. A bird discovered the land outside.

dead when they reach heaven. Waikomoné had a son, whom he created magically of leaves, and who was the husband of all the pretty women who came to heaven. (See Steinen, 1894, p. 435–440.)

In another version of the creation myth (Roquette-Pinto, 1938, p. 133), the Supreme Being, Enore, carved the first men and women out of a piece of wood. This couple had four children, two boys, Zaluiê and Kamaikôrê, and two girls, Hoholaialo and Uhaiuariru. When Enore divided all the good things of the world among his children, Zaluiê refused to accept guns because they were too heavy and horses and cattle because they would soil the plaza of his village. He departed with bows and arrows. Kamaikôrê accepted the objects his brother refused, and the Whites, his descendants, have become prosperous and powerful.

Maize sprouted from the grave of a big chief, Ainotare. Manioc originated from the body of a girl who, despised by her father, asked her mother to bury her alive in the forest.

LORE AND LEARNING

According to the *Paressí*, the sun is a ball of red arara feathers and the moon a ball of yellow mutum feathers. Each belongs to a different master, who stores it away when it must not be seen. Phases of the moon are caused by a spider who gnaws the moon's edge and by four armadillos who hide its disk. Constellations are described as various kinds of animals: A jaguar devouring a deer, a sariema bird, and others. The Coal Sack near the Southern Cross is identified as a rhea. The Milky Way is a path covered with kutá fruits.

Rondón (1912, pp. 40–42) gives the text of four *Paressí songs*. They are short pieces: one describes the meeting with the "Father of the bush"; another tells of the killing of a man; another of the pleasures of dancing and drinking; and the last commemorates a battle.

BIBLIOGRAPHY

Badariotti, 1898; Bossi, 1863; Fonseca, 1880–81; Izikowitz, 1935; Maurtua, 1906; Métraux, 1942; Missão Rondón, 1916; Pires de Campos, 1862; Rondón, 1912; Roosevelt, 1914 (1924); Roquette-Pinto, 1912 a (1917, 1938); Schmidt, M., 1914, 1940, 1942, 1943; Steinen, 1894.

THE NAMBICUARA

By Claude Lévi-Strauss

TRIBAL DIVISIONS AND HISTORY

The *Nambicuara* (*Nambikuara, Mambyuara, Mahibarez*) have been identified only recently. *Nambicuara*, meaning "long eared," was originally a *Tupí* nickname used since the 18th century for the little-known tribes of the western and northern parts of the Serra dos Parecis. These tribes had large ear and lip plugs, like those of the *Suya* and *Botocudo*, and were called Beiços de Pau, "Wooden Mouths," by the rubber collectors and gold miners. About 1830, they began to make hostile sorties from the region of the upper Sangue River. When, in 1907, General Candido Mariano da Silva Rondón discovered important tribes in the Serra do Norte, he identified them with the *Nambicuara* of the old literature. Thus, *Nambicuara* designates a tribe other than the "Long Ears," or "Wooden Mouths," to whom it was originally applied.

Extending northwest from the Papagaio River more or less to the confluence of the Commemoração and the Barão de Melgaço Rivers, branches of the Machado (Gi-Paraná) River, the region of the *Nambicuara* (map 1, *No. 2;* map 2; map 4) is bounded on the south by the right tributaries of the Guaporé River and, farther west, by the whole of the Commemoração de Floriano River. The northern boundary is unknown but probably runs more or less along the 11th parallel between the Theodore Roosevelt and Papagaio Rivers. (Lat. 10°–15° S., long. 57°–61° W.)

The first classification of the *Nambicuara* was made by Roquette-Pinto (1938, pp. 216–217), who listed four main groups. Lévi-Strauss (n.d. b), using linguistic data, distinguishes three main groups. Two of these, which are subdivided into two groups each, clearly belong to the same linguistic family, but the linguistic affiliation of the third group, which is undivided, is doubtful. These groups are: *Eastern Nambicuara* (Roquette-Pinto's *Kôkôzu, Cocozu*) between the Papagaio and Juina Rivers; *Northeastern Nambicuara* (Roquette-Pinto's *Anunze*) in the basins of the Camararé and Doze de Otubro Rivers; *Central* and *Southern*

Nambicuara (Roquette-Pinto's *Uaintaçu*, which includes his *Kabishi*, *Tagnani*, *Tauitê*, *Tarutê*, and *Tashuitê*) between the Guaporé River Basin in the south and the Tenente Marqués, Iké and Roosevelt Rivers in the north and northwest; *Western Nambicuara* (new), closely related to the central and southern groups and living on the headwaters and in the upper basin of the Roosevelt River; and *Northern Nambicuara* (new), speaking its own language and living north of the central group.

The Indians mention other tribes north of the *Nambicuara;* one called *Saluma, Saruma,* or *Solondé* is almost certainly the *Mundurucú;* another may be the *Tapanyuma.*

In 1907, Rondón estimated the total *Nambicuara* population to be 20,000. In 1912 Roquette-Pinto met 1,000 to 1,500. It is doubtful whether the total population, which has been decimated by several recent epidemics, now greatly exceeds 1,500.

The *Nambicuara* language was previously thought to be isolated, but its distinctive trait—the use of classificatory suffixes dividing the universe into about ten categories—is strongly reminiscent of *Chibcha.*

Nambicuara culture, although less primitive than that of the *Sirionó* to the southwest, is strikingly simple in comparison with that of the neighboring *Paressí* to the southeast and of the *Tupí-Cawahíb* to the northwest. Their lack of the hammock, their custom of sleeping on the ground, their crude ceramics (the *Eastern Nambicuara* entirely lack pottery), the nakedness of both sexes, their nomadism, their use of temporary shelters during most of the year, the general poverty of their material culture, and the simplicity of their social organization distinguish them from the higher cultures of the Guaporé River area, to which they nevertheless probably belong.

CULTURE

SUBSISTENCE

The *Nambicuara* habitat is a savannalike plateau about 500 to 1,500 feet (150 to 500 m.) above sea level with an arenaceous soil which comes from disintegrated sandstone bedrock. Except for narrow gallery forests along river banks, the region is infertile, having only shrubs and small trees with thorns or thick bark.

In this unproductive environment the *Nambicuara* have a dual subsistence pattern. They are both seminomadic bush dwellers and incipient farmers. During the dry season, women, accompanied by their children, forage with digging sticks for wild fruits, seeds, and roots, and catch grubs, rats, bats, spiders, snakes, lizards, and other small creatures, while men hunt what large game they can find with bows and arrows and collect wild honey.

When rains come, the *Nambicuara* settle in temporary villages, and the men open circular gardens in the gallery forest by burning and felling the trees with stone (now steel) axes. They till the soil with pointed sticks and raise both bitter and sweet manioc, several kinds of maize which are different from those of their more civilized neighbors (Roquette-Pinto, 1938, p. 297 n.), beans, gourds, cotton, urucú, and a variety of small tobacco with tiny leaves. Despite the difficulty of fishing in the deep, clear tributaries of the Juruena River, they have moderate success using fish arrows, basket traps, and a drug made of a vine.

Food preparation.—Game is usually only half cooked in hot ashes, but it is sometimes smoked on rectangular or pyramidal babracots. Manioc is grated on thorns of the catizal palm (*Iriartea* sp.) imbedded in palm wood plants. To remove the poisonous juice of bitter manioc, the pulp is either squeezed in a strip of bark twisted spirally or buried for several days to allow the juice to drain off. Balls of the pulp are then sun-dried and packed in leaves in baskets or buried at marked places. In times of scarcity, perhaps months later, the half-rotten balls are made into flat cakes, hastily cooked in hot ashes, and eaten.

The *Nambicuara* cannot bear to eat salt, which they do not know how to prepare, or pepper, which they do not cultivate. Even hot food is cooled with water before it is eaten. Wild honey, too, is diluted with water. The only condiment is a variety of cumarú bean which has a strong, bitter almond taste. It is boiled in pots; afterward the liquid is drunk and the beans are mixed with food, especially with grasshoppers crushed in mortars. Armadillo meat is often ground with maize flour.

Domestic animals and pets.—The *Nambicuara* have many pets, especially monkeys, coatis, parrots, and birds. Domesticated animals were unknown until the Rondón Commission introduced chickens and dogs. Although at first extremely afraid of dogs, the Indians quickly adopted them and treated them with the same deep affection they show all their tame animals. Even now they are terrified by oxen seen at telegraph stations, and call them by the name given to the deadly spirits of the water and the bush. They do, however, hunt and eat horses and mules as if they were wild game.

HOUSES

The surprising variety of house types suggests recent borrowing from neighboring tribes. The *Nambicuara*, like the *Sirionó*, may formerly have lacked houses entirely. During most of the year, even at the present time, they build only scanty temporary shelters for a single night. These consist of branches of palms stuck into holes dug in the sand to form a half or quarter circle on the side from which the sun, the wind, or rain are expected (pl. 37, *center, left*). Each individual family builds its own shelter and lights its own fire in the opening.   During the rainy season, villages consisting of one or more beehive huts are built on slight hillocks above the course of a secondary stream.   Some of the *Eastern Nambicuara* build only shelters, although larger and stronger than the ones described. The beehive hut is very light, each about 10 to 20 feet (3 to 6 m.) in diameter.   The frame consists of several long, supple poles, bent so that both ends can be stuck into the ground and tied together at the top, where they cross.   Circular branches running horizontally are tied to the poles at different levels.   The *Central* and *Western Nambicuara* have a more elaborate hut (pl. 37, *top*) whose perimeter is about 50 feet (15 m.). It has a central post from the base of which several forked poles run obliquely to support the bent poles of the external frame.   All types of huts are thatched with horizontal layers of palm leaves, those of *Central* and *Western Nambicuara* exactly like the houses of their southern neighbors, the *Kepikiriwat.*

A gabled house without walls was also observed by Roquette-Pinto, who recorded other kinds of temporary huts.   Some were built by sticking two branches into the ground, bending them over and attaching them to a horizontal pole tied to two perpendicular posts and covering them with bunches of grass.

The *Nambicuara,* although all their neighbors use hammocks, sleep on bare ground or on flat pieces of bark from the paxiuba palm.   Because of this custom, the *Paressí* nicknamed them *Uaikoakôre,* "Those Who Sleep on the Ground."

CLOTHING AND ADORNMENT

Both sexes are naked, except that men sometimes tie a small tuft of buruty straw to their belt to cover the sex organs.   Both men and women wear a thin, cotton-thread belt strung with white or black beads cut from river mollusk shells or from tucumã palm nuts.   Such beads, with larger triangular pieces of mollusk shells, are also used for necklaces, earrings, bracelets, and other ornaments.   Men wear grass or reed pins through their upper and lower lips; and, through their nasal septum, a larger pin made of a jacu (*Penelope*) feather mounted on a stalk covered with plaited cotton thread and porcupine quills and trimmed with a red toucan feather ring.   Both sexes wear armlets and anklets of woven cotton, burity straw, feathers, parts of dried birds, fur, or mollusk or crawfish shells.   Women wear one or more bracelets cut from the tail of the great armadillo and double bandoleers of plaited cotton dyed with urucú and decorated with porcupine quills.   Hair ornaments are confined to men: circlets of plaited straw, of straw and and toucan feathers, or of fur with feather pendants.   War dress consists of a jaguar-skin bonnet (pl. 36, *top, left*) with a long, plaited buriti-straw tail painted with red stripes and dots hanging down from the nape of the neck. A similar but shorter headdress may be worn in daily life.

Hair is groomed with a composite comb. It is cut with a shell, either all around the head at the level of the ear lobe, or only across the forehead, the back and sides being allowed to fall loose. Body painting consists mainly of urucú smeared uniformly, but some groups roughly trace black dots and stripes with genipa juice on the chest and legs. Face and body hair is generally pulled out, especially by women; men often have a sparse moustache and beard.

TRANSPORTATION

Canoes are unknown. Small waterways are crossed on a fallen tree; large ones by swimming, sometimes with the help of large floating bundles of buriti palm stems. Babies straddle their mother's hip supported by a large sling of bark or woven cotton.

MANUFACTURES

Spinning.—Women spin cotton with a crude drop spindle made of grass stalk. The whorl is a wild fruit, a potsherd, or a conical piece of sun-dried clay. Cotton thread is rolled in a ball and, like everything else in a *Nambicuara* household, wrapped in leaves. Women and men twist tucum and buriti fibers on their thighs to make string.

Weaving.—Weaving is limited to cotton bands and belts which men make on small, rough looms of the *"Arawak"* type (pl. 37, *center, right*).

Basketry.—Men make long, open-mouthed, cylindrical baskets using bamboo strips and a hexagonal, open weave. Fire fans are plaited of palm leaves. The *Northern Nambicuara* used palm leaves to weave low square baskets for storing the manioc and maize flour.

Pottery.—Pottery is unknown among the *Eastern Nambicuara*. In other groups, women make coarse pots of varying sizes. They mix the clay with ashes, fire the pot in the open, and wash it while it is still hot in an infusion of resinous bark.

Implements.—Stone ax heads were formerly fixed with wax and strings in the loop of a bent handle. Knives and drills are made of a crude flint chip or piece of iron fastened with wax and thread at the end of a piece of wood or between two pieces of wood, which form the handle. Women hollow small cylindrical mortars in tree trunks by means of fire. Fire is made with a fire drill, crude rubber serving as tinder. The Indians burn almecega (*Tetragastris balsamifera*) resin for light. Knives are thin, sharp-edged pieces of wood.

Weapons.—The *Nambicuara* bow is about 5 to 7 feet (2 m.) long, the section being flat, semicircular, or concave according to the group. The grip is wrapped with cotton. The arrow is released between the thumb and the first finger, the three other fingers being placed on the

string (secondary release). Four types ot arrows are used: (1) featherless fishing arrow with three to five prongs; (2) bird arrow with a blunt
point; (3) big-game arrow with a lanceolate bamboo point; and (4)
poisoned arrow, used chiefly for hunting monkeys, with several barbs
which are attached to the point with cotton wrapping and which break
easily in the wound, being, therefore, usually protected by a bamboo
sheath. The last three have a bamboo shaft and "Arara" feathering.
Sewed feathering is known by the central and northern groups but seldom
used. For warfare, big game arrows with serrated bamboo points are
used.

Nambicuara arrow poison is a curare prepared by grating the root
of a *Strychnos* shrub, and by infusing (*Eastern Nambicuara*) or boiling
(*Central* and *Northern Nambicuara*) it until the water evaporates and
leaves a thick brownish substance, which is smeared on a wax-coated
arrow point. It can be preserved in tiny pots for several months. Among
South American arrow poisons, it is remarkable because it is made of
only one vegetable substance and is prepared openly—in some groups
by the chief or shaman, in other groups by anyone—without magical
practices or taboos. Its great toxic properties were studied by Vellard
(1939 b).

Other poisons of unknown composition are used for amorous or political
revenge. They are in the form of powders and are kept in tubes made
of feather quills, bamboo, or other woods, each ornamented with paintings and cotton or bark wrappings.

Clubs are carved in the shape of a flattened or cylindrical pointed
spade; the handle is often adorned with black and white plaiting of
philodendron bark and bamboo strips. Their purpose is mostly ceremonial.

SOCIAL AND POLITICAL ORGANIZATION

Kinship terms identify parallel-cousins with siblings, and cross-cousins
with potential or actual spouses. Cross-uncles and cross-aunts are called
by the same terms as parents-in-law and grandparents; parallel-uncles
and parallel-aunts are equated with parents. Similarly, parallel-nephews
and parallel-nieces are classed with children, and cross-nephews and cross-
nieces with children-in-law. Marriage is between cross-cousins or between the maternal uncle and his niece. Monogamy is the rule, but
polygyny is the privilege of the chief and other important men. Polygyny
is usually with several sisters (sororal) or with a woman and her
daughters by a former union. The first wife runs the household, subsequent wives being assistants to the husband. The deficiency of available women which results from polygyny is compensated by homosexuality
between adolescent male cross-cousins (Lévi-Strauss, 1943 a).

The village is ruled by a chief, but each of the nomadic bands into
which it splits during the dry season is led by a secondary chief. Chief-

tainship is not hereditary; the chief, when old or sick, designates his successor from the ablest men of the group. The chief's authority is slight; it depends wholly on the good will of the family heads.

Relations between neighboring bands are inspired both by fear and by the desire to exchange goods. Warfare, therefore, is closely connected with barter. Groups not acquainted with each other use ritual speech when they meet.

Before starting a war expedition, a divinatory rite is performed with special songs and dances. An arrow is hidden by the shaman, the outcome of the expedition being pressaged by its appearance the following day.

LIFE CYCLE

Childbirth.—After the delivery of a child, the placenta is buried in the bush and both parents are subjected to rigid prohibitions concerning food, the use of ornaments, and social contacts.

Puberty.—The initiation rite for young men consists of piercing their lips and nose and giving them their adult personal name. At her first menstruation, a girl is isolated for several months in a special shelter outside the village, where she is given ritual food by her mother. At the end of the rite, she takes a long bath in the river; this also constitutes the first step of the marriage ceremony.

Both cross-cousin and avuncular marriages (see p. 367), are often planned by parents for their infant children. Marriage is celebrated by festivals, banquets, and dances. The union is pronounced by the chief. Fish and fishing are important both before and during the ceremony.

Separation is frequent, the chief cause being that the man seeks a younger and prettier woman. There is no social sanction of adultery, except that the seducer is advised by his companion to go away for a while so as to avoid the husband's revenge. A murderer also flees vengeance.

Death.—Some groups of *Nambicuara* bury their dead in a circular pit, the corpse being placed in a crouching position. Others leave the corpse to decompose in an elongated ditch and later wash the bones in the river, put them in a basket, and bury them in the village, which is then abandoned. Weapons, implements, adornments, and other property of the deceased are destroyed, but his garden—if he owned one—is abandoned only for a few months. Later anybody may cultivate it.

ESTHETIC AND RECREATIONAL ACTIVITIES

Art.—Most *Nambicuara* groups are completely ignorant of drawing, although some groups decorate calabashes with dots and straight and sinuous lines. These are conventionalized reproductions of realistic designs found among other groups.

Music and dance.—Music is clearly tonal, with melodic structures easy to identify. The end of a melody is usually marked with several shrill sounds which are repeated after each coda. Music is both instrumental and choral and usually accompanies dances.

Dances are performed under the leadership of the chief. Men and women stamp rhythmically on the ground while turning in a circle. Usually, dancers close one nostril with the left hand to make their singing nasal. Only men perform war dances, forming one or more rows and stepping forward and backward in front of the leader. In the second phase of the dance, they attack a post, a symbolical enemy, with bows and arrows, and clubs. Most of the dances and songs are connected with hunting or seasonal ceremonies, but they may be used at any time for mere entertainment.

Musical instruments.—Flageolets have four holes and an air duct; three are usually played together, accompanied by a rhythm trumpet made of a piece of bamboo with a hollow calabash fixed to its bottom. Nose flutes (pl. 36, *top, right*) are made of two pieces of calabash glued together with wax and pierced with three holes. One hole is blown with one nostril while the other nostril is closed with the thumb; the other two holes vary the notes. Nose flutes are also played in unison. Double and treble whistles have the air duct cut in the middle of the pipe, so that they can be blown at either end. Panpipes (pl. 36, *bottom, left*) are of two kinds: the common type has five pipes; the other type consists of two or three reeds cut obliquely at the mouth-end. All pipes produce approximately the same note in the latter.

Drinks and narcotics.—Drinks are made with crushed manioc or maize mixed with water, or of palm fruits, especially *Mauritia* sp., *Acrocomia* sp., and *Oenocarpus distichus*. A slightly alcoholic beverage is prepared of wild pineapples mixed with water.

The *Nambicuara* are ardent smokers. They cultivate a tobacco with tiny leaves, which they dry between two pieces of wood, crush with their hands, and store in small calabashes. Cigarettes are rolled in special leaves and tied with grass.

MAGIC AND RELIGION

The *Nambicuara* believe in the existence of a diffuse power or substance which may occur in objects and in living beings. It is manifest mostly in poisons, some of which are real (see Weapons, p. 366), some purely magical. To the latter belongs the rosin of the barrigudo tree (a Bombacaceae), which is kept in tubes like the true poisons. When thrown by a special technique at an enemy, it is believed to make him swell like the trunk of the tree and die.

There are also dangerous spirits of the bush and of water, which may appear in the shape of an animal, especially the jaguar, or in a particular form of their own. Death is identified with these spirits. Men's souls are believed to be reincarnated as jaguars, whereas women's and children's souls are taken away by wind and thunder, never to return.

The highest being is the Thunder, with which any man, though usually a shaman, may have personal contact through revelations and visions. Women, however, except when very old, and children are deprived of these privileges. Women are also forbidden, under pain of death, to see the sacred flageolets (see Musical Instruments, p. 368) played at the ceremonies marking the beginning and the end of the dry season.

SHAMANISM AND MEDICINE

The shaman is sometimes distinct from—but more frequently identified with—the political chief. He is distinguished by having the privilege of polygyny, playing the leading role in ceremonial life, and possessing special supernatural powers. He treats patients by sucking out the disease or by fighting it with small ritual arrows called "thunder-arrows."

In addition to magical cures, the *Nambicuara* treat sickness with numerous medicinal plants, which are used externally or internally according to the disease. For eye infection, which is very frequent, they apply the infusion of a special bark with the help of a container made of leaves.

FOLKLORE, LORE, AND LEARNING

The only legend recorded by Lévi-Strauss (n.d. b) is a flood tale relating the destruction of human life and its re-creation through several incestuous marriages between the offspring of an old woman, who was the only being who escaped the disaster.

The only basic numbers used for counting are one and two, but the natives can reckon higher figures by combining these.

Colors are classified differently according to the dialects. The *Eastern, Central, Southern,* and *Western Nambicuara* agree in putting yellow and green in the same category, whereas the *Northern* group identify red and yellow, and class green, blue, and black together.

Some *Nambicuara* groups call stars by the same name which designates the spirits. The year is divided into two seasons and an undetermined number of lunar months. The day includes six main stages, each based on the position of the sun. Space is divided into two sections that are perpendicular to each other, one corresponding to the apparent movement of the sun and the other to the direction of the main waterways.

BIBLIOGRAPHY

Commissão Rondón, 1911 and later; Lévi-Strauss, 1943 a, b, n.d. b; Rondón, 1916; Roosevelt, 1924; Roquette-Pinto, 1912 a (1935, 1938), b, c, 1917; Schmidt, 1929 b; Schuller, 1912, 1921; Souza, A. P. de, 1920; Vellard, 1939 b.

PLATE 36.—**Nambicuara types.** *Top, left:* Man wearing war headdress. *Top, right:* Playing the nose flute. *Center, left:* Young girl. *Center, right:* Portrait of man. *Bottom, left:* Panpipes. *Bottom, right:* Young married girl. (Courtesy Claude Lévi-Strauss, except *center, left,* by courtesy American Museum of Natural History.)

PLATE 37.—**Nambicuara and upper Guaporé Indians.** *Top:* Pimenta Bueno hut. *Center, left: Nambicuara* family shelter. *Center, right: Nambicuara* man weaving an armband. *Bottom, left: Nambicuara* family. *Bottom, right:* Woman drilling a mother of pearl earring. (Courtesy Claude Lévi-Strauss, except *bottom, left,* by courtesy American Museum of Natural History.)

TRIBES OF THE RIGHT BANK OF THE GUAPORÉ RIVER

By Claude Lévi-Strauss

INTRODUCTION

The native culture of the region drained by the right tributaries of the Guaporé River is one of the least known in Brazil. Since the 18th century, explorers, travelers, and missionaries have used the Guaporé River as a thoroughfare, and in more recent times hundreds of rubber tappers have worked along its banks and along the lower course of its tributaries. It is likely, therefore, that a thorough study of the tribes of the Guaporé River will show them to have suffered severely from the effects of that continuous traffic, perhaps almost to the point of extinction.

Unlike most South American rivers, the Guaporé River is not the axis of a homogeneous culture area; it is a frontier rather than a link. The *Mojo-Chiquito* culture area extends from the left bank toward the Andes; the heterogeneous tribes on the right bank have a definitely Amazonian culture (map 1, *No. 2*; map 2; map 4). Geographic factors may partly account for this lack of symmetry. The flat landscape of the llanos merges into the marshy lands of the left bank; whereas the right bank, alternately marshy and steep, marks the farthest extension of the highlands of western Brazil. The highlands and the right bank of the Guaporé River define the limits of the culture area to which probably belong the tribes of the southern part of the upper Madeira River Basin, such as the *Kepikiriwat,* discovered in 1914 by the Rondón expedition (Missão Rondón, 1916).

TRIBAL DIVISIONS

Two areas must be distinguished. One is the right bank of the lower Guaporé River between the Rio Branco and the Mamoré River, which is occupied by the *Chapacuran* tribes (p. 397). The basins of the Rio Branco and of the Mequenes and Corumbiara Rivers comprise the second area, where some of the languages seem to be *Tupian.* The *Arua* (not to be confused with the *Arua* at the mouth of the Amazon) and *Macurap* live along the Rio Branco (lat. 13° S., long. 62° W.); the *Wayoro* on the Colorado River (lat. 12° 30′ S., long. 62° W.); the

Amniapä, Guaratägaja (Snethlage, 1937 a), and *Cabishinana* (Lévi-Strauss, ms.) on the Mequenes River (lat. 13° S., long. 62° W.) ; and the *Tupari* (lat. 12° S., long. 62° W.), and *Kepikiriwat* (lat. 11° S., long. 63° W.) on the headwaters of the southern tributaries of the Machado (Gi-Paraná) River. Linguistically distinct from both *Chapacuran* and *Tupian* are: (1) The *Yabuti* (*Japuti*) and *Aricapu,* on the headwaters of the Rio Branco (lat. 12° 30′ S., long. 62° W.), whose language shows affinities with the *Ge* dialects (Snethlage, 1937 a) but who are strongly influenced culturally by their neighbors; (2) the *Huari* (*Massaca*) on the Corumbiara River, lat. 14° S., long. 61° W., (Nordenskiöld, 1924 a), who are linguistically linked to the *Puruborá* (*Burubora*) of the headwaters of the São Miguel River on the boundary between the two areas, but who, culturally, display strong similarities to their northern and northwestern neighbors, the *Kepikiriwat* (Lévi-Strauss, ms), *Amniapä, Guaratägaja,* and *Tupari* (Snethlage, E. H., 1937 a) ; and (3) the *Palmella,* on the right bank of the Guaporé River between the mouths of the Rio Branco and the Mequenes River (lat. 13° S., long. 63° W.), who, until the late 19th century, were the southernmost representatives of the *Cariban* linguistic family in South America (Severiano da Fonseca, 1895). The unknown Indians who live on the right bank of the upper Guaporé River in the region of Villa Bella, probably belong to the *Southern Nambicuara* (*Cabishí*).

CULTURE

SUBSISTENCE AND FOOD PREPARATION

The tribes of the upper Guaporé River, especially those upstream, rely for food mainly upon maize and peanuts. Manioc is of secondary importance to the natives living between the Guaporé and Machado Rivers. Hualusa, peppers, papaws, gourds, urucú, cotton, and tobacco are widely cultivated. Black beans are grown by the *Guaratägaja* and *Wayoro.* Gardens are tilled with digging sticks and weeded with chonta knives. An exceptional feature of the area is the raising of grubs in the dregs of maize beer, which is kept in long bamboo containers (Snethlage, 1937 a). On the Guaporé River, as on the Pimenta Bueno River, grubs are allowed to breed freely in the trunks of wild palm trees which are left standing for that purpose when forests are cleared for gardens (Lévi-Strauss, n.d. b). Clearing and tilling gardens are cooperative enterprises; helpers are entertained with beer, snuff, and dances. Crops are sometimes stored on large covered platforms. Certain tribes keep peanuts in large bamboo tubes.

Fish are shot with multipointed arrows or are drugged. The natives blow whistles to attract birds and then shoot them from small watchposts. Throughout the area, they either trap game in pitfalls or shoot them with plain arrows. The *Amniapä, Kepikiriwat,* and *Pawumwa,* also use poisoned arrows and the *Pawumwa,* blowguns.

Flat cakes of maize and manioc are grilled on clay plates. Instead of grating manioc tubers, the *Guaratägaja* mash them with a small stone pounder. *Wayoro* mortars are pieces of bark. The *Amniapä* consider boiled mushrooms a special delicacy, a culinary dish noticed elsewhere only among the *Nambicuara.* Game is roasted in the skin on pyramidal babracots.

DOMESTICATED ANIMALS

The Guaporé River tribes keep dogs, hens, and ducks.

HOUSES

The beehive hut, built around a high central post, seems to be common to the area. Each house is divided by mats into several family compartments. *Tupari* houses shelter up to 35 families; those of the *Wayoro* may contain more than 100 occupants. Houses along the Pimenta Bueno River are smaller. In some villages, Snethlage (1937 a) saw a painted woven screen set up in the middle of the hut as a kind of altar. These tribes sleep in hammocks, those of the *Wayoro* and *Makurap* being unusually large. *Amniapä* and *Kepikiriwat* men use small, concave wooden benches.

DRESS AND ADORNMENT

Among the *Huari, Kepikiriwat,* and probably all the southeastern tribes, both men and women cut their hair high above the forehead and depilate the temples and eyebrows (pl. 38, *top*). They wear wooden or rosin labrets in the upper and lower lips and pins of various types in the nasal septum. Women go completely naked except for these and other ornaments—shell beads, cotton necklaces, belts, bracelets, and tight cotton armlets and anklets. *Kepikiriwat, Huari,* and *Guaratägaja* men use a small conical penis sheath of leaves. Men of other tribes, except the *Tupari,* wear a short skirt (pl. 38, *bottom, left*) of buriti fiber. Ear ornaments of tucumã-nut rings strung together like a chain are used by the *Huari* and *Kepikiriwat.* Skin caps (*Wayoro*), feathered circlets (*Huari*), and strips of fiber (*Amniapä*) are worn on festive occasions. Shell disk necklaces (pl. 38) are used by all tribes except the *Tupari.*

Body painting with genipa juice is especially well developed among the *Amniapä,* who, by means of maize cobs, apply elaborate patterns, such as crosses, dots, circles, and hatchings.

TRANSPORTATION

Carrying nets of tucum fiber are used instead of baskets. All the tribes, except, perhaps, the *Huari,* have canoes.

MANUFACTURES

Spinning and weaving.—Both rolled (*"Bororo"*) and drop ("Andean") spindles are known. Fringed bands are woven on looms similar to those of the *Itene* (*Moré*) (p. 402). Hammocks, which seem to reach a record length among some of the upper Guaporé River tribes, are made by extending a single warp between two perpendicular posts and twining it with a double weft. Arm bands are knitted around a circular piece of wood with a bone or wooden needle (*Macurap* and *Aricapu*).

Pottery.—Pottery is generally crude and the clay used for its manufacture is not tempered. Calabash containers are especially common.

Weapons.—To make an ax, the *Wayoro* insert a stone blade into a wooden handle, lash the head, and smear it with wax; the *Huari* use a vine or split branch bent double over the butt and tightened with bast and wax (fig. 45).

FIGURE 45.—*Huari* ax. (Redrawn from Nordenskiöld, 1924 b, fig. 26.)

Arrow feathering is of the "Xingú" (flush) sewn type (*Tupari, Arua*) or of the "Arara" (arched) type (*Huari, Kepikiriwat*). Arrow points are made of plain or indented bamboo splinters, bone points, or spikes of sting rays. The *Tupari* paint arrow feathers. A tribe of the Pimenta Bueno region, known only through some implements found in the possession of the *Kepikiriwat,* paint red, black, and white earth between the feathering of the arrow shaft. The *Amniapä* use three-pointed arrows for birds; the *Kepikiriwat* use similar arrows with less feathering for fishing. Arrows poisoned with curare and the point protected with a bamboo sheath are attributed to the *Kepikiriwat, Amniapä,* and *Pawumwa.*

The *Pawumwa* use blowguns.

Clubs are used only as dance paraphernalia, except among the *Huari,* who fight with large, double-edged clubs, 4 to 5 feet (1.2 to 1.5 m.) long, decorated with a basketry casing around the handle.

SOCIAL ORGANIZATIONS

Sibs which are named after animals but which have no corresponding food prohibitions are found among the *Macurap* and *Yabuti* (patrilineal and exogamous) and the *Arua* (matrilineal).   It is doubtful whether such clans exist among the *Kepikiriwat,* who have moieties that function at ceremonial ball games and probably on other occasions.   Prisoners taken from another tribe are incorporated into the captor's clan, where they pay a small tribute but enjoy great freedom.   Nothing is known about chieftainships, except that *Guaratägaja* chiefs distribute game among the men of the community.   Intertribal commerce seems to be well developed.

A ceremony used by the *Amniapä* to receive a neighboring tribe includes a mock battle, the offer of benches, and a crouched salutation accompanied by ceremonial wailing.

LIFE CYCLE

The couvade, accompanied by abstention from fish, is attributed to the *Macurap*.   They also require that a girl's parents consent to her marriage.   Postmarital residence during the first weeks is matrilocal; later it is patrilocal.   A widow remarries only with the permission of the clan's head.

The *Tupari* bury their dead outside the village in a prone position; the *Amniapä* bury their dead inside their huts in a crouched position. Burial among the *Macurap* is similar to that among the *Amniapä,* but a pottery vessel is placed on top of the grave.   The *Wayoro* practice urn burial, at least for children, and paint their corpses red.   The *Guaratägaja* burn the house of the deceased; the *Cabishiana* burn the possessions of the deceased.

CANNIBALISM

According to Snethlage (1937 a), the *Amniapä* and *Guaratägaja* admit cannibalism and eat not only the barbecued bodies of their enemies but even their own tribesmen and women who are put to death for a crime.

ESTHETIC AND RECREATIONAL ACTIVITIES

Art.—Among many tribes, especially among the *Kepikiriwat* each family possesses many calabashes which are used as beer cups during feasts.   Women decorate the calabashes with incised or pyrograved geometric designs.

Games.—Games, in which a ball is propelled with the head, are played between moieties (*Kepikiriwat*) and between villages or tribes (*Amniapä*).   The *Amniapä* keep score with maize grains; the *Kepikiriwat* play to win arrows.

Dances and masks.—Dancing and singing are generally practiced by both men and women, sometimes, as for instance among the *Arua,* in the form of patterned amorous challenges.   The *Macurap* and the *Amniapä* dance in front of an altar, or round an especially erected ceremonial tree. The *Amniapä* use calabash masks with features attached or painted on.

Masks are kept in the dome of the hut, but they do not seem to be the object of worship or prohibition. Masked dancers costume themselves with a drapery of fibers and hold a stick topped with the wax image of a bird.

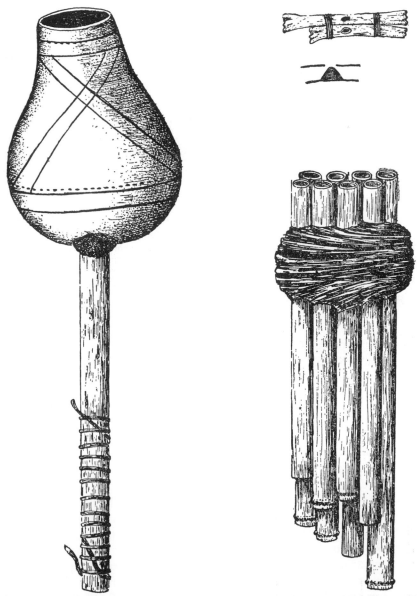

FIGURE 46.—*Guaporé* musical instruments. *Left: Amniapä* trumpet. *Top, right: Guaratägaja* bird imitator's whistle. *Bottom, right: Arua* double panpies. (All ¼ actual size.) (Redrawn from Snethlage, 1939.)

Musical instruments.—Sacred gourd rattles are used only by *Arua*, *Yabuti*, and *Aricapu* shamans, and are unknown among the *Tupari* and *Guaratägaja*, who use jingling belts garnished with fruit shells. The *Yabuti*, *Amniapä*, and *Guaratägaja* use rhythm trumpets with a gourd or bamboo resonator (fig. 46, *left*). The *Amnaipä*, and *Guaratägaia* call the trumpets and also their masks, "gods." Clarinets are played in pairs by a single musician (*Macurap*, *Arua*). True panpipes are made of four closed and four open tubes placed in two rows (*Arua*) (fig. 46, *bottom, right*). A unique type of pseudo-panpipe consisting of a series of two to eight whistles (the latter in two rows), each with a sound orifice and a wax deflector, is used ceremonially among the other tribes (fig. 47);

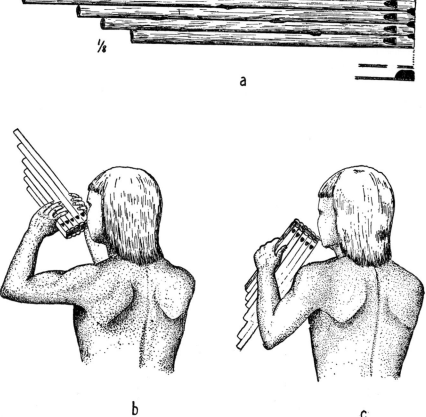

FIGURE 47.—*Macurap* pseudo-panpipes. (Redrawn from Snethlage, 1939.)

two notes may be played at the same time on these instruments. End flutes (fig. 48) of the *Mataco* type with four stops and whistles are used by the *Tupari*, *Guaratägaja*, and *Amniapä*. Snethlage (1939) mentions instrument playing of "disciplined orchestras."

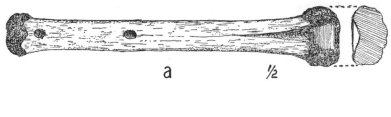

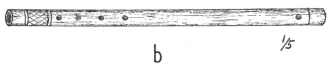

FIGURE 48.—*Huari* bone flutes. (Redrawn from Nordenskiöld, 1924 b fig. 43.)

Narcotics and beverages.—A narcotic snuff of crushed angico, tobacco leaves, and the ashes of a certain bark is blown by the shaman during feasts. For healing purposes he blows it into the nose of the patient, through one or two tubes that terminate in a hollow nut, often shaped like a bird's head. Snuff is carefully prepared with small mortars, pestles, and mixing brushes, and is kept in bamboo tubes.

Beer is made from manioc, maize, and sweet potatoes. The *Guaratägaja* use a special leaf to cause fermentation.

RELIGION, FOLKLORE, AND MYTHOLOGY

Indians of the Guaporé River region seem to believe in the existence of an invisible fluid which may be good or evil. By appropriate gesticulations the shaman captures, manipulates, and incorporates it into food, into the sick, or into the bodies of enemies. On the Rio Branco, the shaman's outfit includes a snuffing tube, a magic board with a handle, and a feathered stick. The board is used as a tablet upon which to mix the snuff; the feathered stick seems to acquire a mystic weight when filled with the magic fluid, which makes it difficult to carry toward the altar. The shaman kneels in front of a plaited screen which forms the altar and is the center of most ceremonies; he speaks to the screen and leaves food and beer near by. The *Wayoro* ceremonies are forbidden to women and children.

Shamanistic cures follow the widespread pattern of sucking, blowing, and spitting on the patient.

Ghosts play a considerable role in the beliefs of the Guaporé River Indians. According to the *Arua*, ghosts are the souls of the dead returning from the Kingdom of Minoiri to harm their enemies and to protect their friends, chiefly shamans. Snethlage (1937 a, p. 141) stated that he distinctly heard the noise which the ghosts are supposed to produce.

The *Amniapä* and *Guaratägaja* attribute the creation of the world to Arikuagnon, who married Pananmäkoza and was the father of the cul-

PLATE 38.—**Indians of the Pimenta Bueno River.** (Courtesy Claude Lévi-Strauss.)

ture hero, Arikapua.   Another culture hero was Konanopo, the teacher of agriculture.   The mythical being, Bäräbassa, is held responsible for the great flood from which only one couple survived to repopulate the world.   Other mythical beings are Ssuawakwak, Lord of the Winds that cause thunder, and Kipapua, Master of the Spirits who play supernatural musical instruments.   Sun and Moon were the first men; together they tilled a garden; Sun burnt his brother and as a punishment was sent to the sky by his father, Sahi.   Two mythical brothers were regarded by the *Arua* as creators of the world and bringers of darkness and of fire.   Disguised as birds, they stole fire from the old man who was its keeper.   When the brothers were old, a flood threatened to destroy mankind, but their sister saved two pairs of children from the best families by putting the children afloat in wooden troughs.

In three tales from the *Arua,* recorded by Snethlage (1937 a), a mother-in-law falls in love with her daughter's husband, a married couple live alternately as toads and as human beings, and a deer brings agriculture (also from the *Bacaïri* of the upper Xingú River).

BIBLIOGRAPHY

Courteville, 1938; Fawcett, 1915; Gonçalves da Fonseca, 1826; Haseman, 1912; Lévi-Strauss, n.d. b; Rondón, 1916; Missão Rondón, 1916; Nordenskiöld, 1924 a; Severiano da Fonseca, 1895; Snethlage, E. H., 1937 a, 1939.

TRIBES OF EASTERN BOLIVIA AND THE MADEIRA HEADWATERS

By Alfred Métraux

THE CHIQUITOANS AND OTHER TRIBES OF THE PROVINCE OF CHIQUITOS

TRIBAL DIVISIONS AND LANGUAGES

It is extremely difficult to obtain a clear picture of the linguistic affiliations or even of the exact locations of the tribes of the region known as the Province of Chiquitos, bordered on the south by the Chaco desert, on the east by the Paraguay River and by the marshes of its upper course, on the west by the Rio Grande (Guapay River), and on the north by a line more or less corresponding to lat. 15° W. (map 1, *No. 2;* map 4).

The chronicles of the Conquest, the official documents and reports of local authorities, and later the letters and accounts of the Jesuits teem with names of tribes and subtribes, but seldom mention their linguistic affiliation and even their location. From the beginning of the Conquest, the Indians of the area just defined have been called *Chiquito,* "the small ones," irrespective of their linguistic family or culture. There is one language, still isolated, called *Chiquitoan,* which is spoken today in that region, but, because several tribes of other linguistic families adopted *Chiquitoan* as a common language when they were collected in the Jesuit missions, it has become impossible to establish the former distribution of the *Chiquitoan* language. Hervás (1800–05, 1:160) lists the following tribes which spoke languages different from *Chiquitoan: Bataje, Corabé, Cuberé, Curucané, Curomina, Ecoboré, Otuque, Paicone, Parabá, Pauná, Puizoca, Quiteme, Tapii, Tapuri, Jarabe,* and *Bauré.* We know, thanks to vocabularies collected by D'Orbigny, that the *Saraveca* (lat. 15° S., long. 60° W.), *Paunaca (Pauna)* (lat. 16° S., long. 60° W.), and *Paiconeca (Paicone)* (lat. 15° S., long. 62° W.) were *Arawakan* (see p. 396), perhaps subtribes of the *Chané,* who are repeatedly mentioned in that area; and that the *Otuke (Otuque)* (lat. 18° S., long. 60° W.), *Coraveca* (lat. 17° S., long. 60° W.), and *Curuminaca* (lat. 16° S., long. 60°–62° W.) formed an isolated linguistic group called *Otukean* (see p. 395), perhaps related to *Bororo.* In 1831, when D'Orbigny visited the Province of Chiquitos, the Indians still remembered that in the past the *Curavé (Corabé),* the *Tapii* (lat. 18° S., long. 60° W.), the *Curucaneca*

(*Curucané*) (lat. 17° S., long. 60° W.), and the *Coraveca* had spoken languages of their own. Créqui-Montfort and Rivet (1913 e) are inclined to include these languages in the *Otukean* group on the basis of their geographical distribution. The *Kitemoca* (*Quitemoca, Quitemo*) (lat. 16° S., long. 62° 30′ W.) and *Napeca* of the Mission of Concepción de Chiquitos (near the headwaters of the Rio Branco) were *Chapacuran;* the *Bauré* (lat. 14° S., long. 62°–63° W.) were *Arawakan,* closely related to the *Mojo.*

The *Gorgotoqui* seem to have been a large tribe extending from the Guapay River toward the San José Range (lat. 18° S., long. 62° W.). They spoke a language apparently different from *Chiquitoan,* but related to *Capaccora* and *Payono.* The Catechism in *Gorgotoqui* written by Father Diego Martinez and a grammar of the same language by Father Gaspar Ruíz seem to have been lost. The linguistic affiliations of the *Anetine,* who were discovered in 1560 by Hernando de Salazar, near the *Mojo,* and of the *Tacumbiacu* and *Nambu,* who lived between the Guapay River and the western part of the Province of Chiquitos, is unknown. The *Tamacoci* were an important tribe on the Guapay River. They must not be confused with the *Zamuco* of the northern Chaco. Other tribes listed by Hervás (1800–05, vol. 1) are meaningless names.

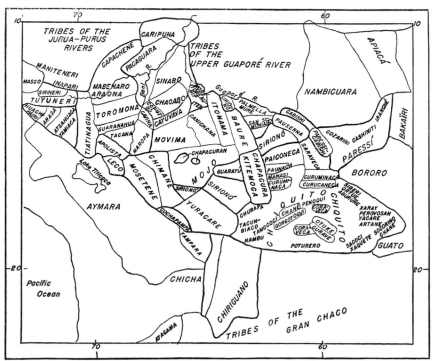

Map 4.—The tribes of eastern Bolivia. Locations are as of first contact with Europeans. (Compiled by J. H. Steward.)

In the south of the Province of Chiquitos, the missionaries had to deal with the *Zamuco* and *Ugareño,* who were closely related to two modern Chaco tribes, the *Chamacoco* and *Tumerehã.*

THE CHIQUITOAN LINGUISTIC FAMILY

Hervás (1800–05, 1:158–159) classifies the *Chiquitoan*-speaking tribes into four subgroups, according to their respective dialects.

(1) Tribes speaking the *Tao* dialect: *Arupareca, Bazoroca, Booca, Boro, Pequica, Piococa, Puntagica, Quibiquica, Tañopica, Tabiica, Tao, Tubacica, Xuberesa,* and *Zamanuca.* The *Tao* dialect was spoken in the Missions of Santa Ana, San Rafael, San Miguel, San Ignacio, San Juan, Santiago, Santo Corazón, and Concepción.

(2) Tribes speaking the *Piñoco* dialect: *Guapaca, Motaquica, Piococa* (in Xavier and not to be confused with the *Piococa* of San Ignacio and Santa Ana, who spoke the *Tao* dialect), *Pogisoca, Quimeca, Quitagica, Taumoca,* and *Zemuquica.* The *Piñoco* dialect was spoken in San Xavier, San José de Chiquitos, and in San José de Buenavista (Desposorios) in Mojos.

(3) Tribes speaking the *Manasí* dialect: *Cucica, Manasí (Manacica), Quimomeca, Sibaca, Tapacuraca* (?), *Yiritua,* and *Yuracareca (Yuracare?).* The *Manasí* dialect, spoken in the Mission of Concepción, was soon discarded in favor of the *Tao* dialect.

(4) The *Peñoqui* dialect was spoken by a single tribe, which was settled in the Mission of San José, where it soon adopted the *Piñoco* dialect. *Peñoqui* was the most differentiated of the four dialects and Father Felipe Suarez, the author of a *Chiquitoan* grammar, was obliged to write a special dictionary for this language and to translate the catechism into it.

According to D'Orbigny (1839, 2:155), the *Cuciquia,* who were split into *Cuciquia, Tapacuraca,* and *Yurucaritia,* used a dialect full of foreign words, mainly *Paiconeca.* The *Cuciquia* came from the northernmost part of the region of Chiquitos, where the *Boxo, Penoto, Tabica,* and *Xamaro* occupied the south of the same province.

HISTORY OF THE PROVINCE OF CHIQUITOS

The first knowledge of the Indians of the region of Chiquitos was brought back by Domingo Martinez de Irala and Nuflo de Chaves, when they ascended the Paraguay River in 1542 as far as lat. 17° S. and discovered the *Surucusi,* the *Orejón,* the *Arencoci,* the *Xaraye* (lat. 18° S., long. 58° W.), and several other tribes. The party journeyed 4 days to the west of the Paraguay River and returned with information given to them by *Guaraní* migrating toward the Andes.

The following year, Alvar Nuñez Cabeza de Vaca organized his big expedition to discover El Dorado and the land of the Amazons, actually the *Inca* Empire as described by the Indians of the upper Paraguay River. From Puerto de los Reyes (lat. 17°57′ S.), Cabeza de Vaca sent an expedition toward the west with *Guaraní* guides. One of his lieutenants, Rivera, arrived at a country where the Indians wore silver disks in their lower lips and gold earrings. They had many metal objects: plates, hatchets, and bracelets of silver. Like the modern *Chiriguano,* they stored their belongings and their provisions of maize in large vessels. These Indians, called *Tarapecosi,* did not understand *Guaraní* and were probably *Chiquito,* as can be surmised from their location and from their use of poisonous arrows, a distinctive weapon of the *Chiquito.* They received the metal objects found among them from the *Payzuno,* who in turn traded them from the *Chané, Chimeno, Caracara,* and *Candire. Caracara* and *Candire* were names used by the *Guarani* of Paraguay to designate the mountain people of the west.

Another reconnoitering party under Hernando de Rivera was sent upstream to the *Xaraye.* They traveled many miles westward until stopped by a flood, and they passed through the land of the *Urtu (Urtues)* and *Aburuñe,* who had metal plates.

The names of a great many tribes of Chiquitos are listed in the brief accounts of the expedition of Domingo Martinez de Irala, who in 1548 left the region of Cerro San Fernando (lat. 21°30′ S.) and marched west, crossing the northern plains of the Chaco and later the southern part of the Province of Chiquitos. He ended his journey on the Guapay River among the *Tamacoci.* The Conquest of Chiquitos was achieved between 1557 and 1560 by Nuflo de Chaves, who, starting from the marshes of Xarayes, also reached the *Tamacoci.* In 1560, Nuflo de Chaves subjugated the *Tamacoci* and *Gorgotoqui* and, in the heart of the Province of Chiquitos, near the San José Range, founded the first city of Santa Cruz de la Sierra in the territory of the *Quibaracoa, Penoqui, Quicme, Parani,* who undoubtedly were *Chiquitoan,* the *Subereca* (probably *Saraveca*), and a few *Chané* who were *Arawakan.* The *Paicono,* also an *Arawakan* tribe, lived 20 leagues from the city.

In 1595, Santa Cruz was transferred to the plains of Grigotá, near the present city of that name. The remaining *Chiquito,* who had been under Spanish influence for 40 years, reverted to their primitive ways and often raided the new Spanish settlements to steal iron tools which had become indispensable to them.

In 1690, the *Zumbiqui, Cozo, Pacara,* and *Pinoco,* defeated by a punitive expedition, sued for peace and consented to receive the Jesuit missionaries. The first mission among the *Chiquito* was that of San Francisco Xavier, founded in 1691 by Father José de Arce among the *Pinoco.* At that time, the *Chiquito* were constantly harassed by the Paulista slavers or mamelucos; entire tribes were exterminated or taken as slaves to the Brazilian coast. The Jesuits, aided by a small Spanish contingent, averted the total destruction of the *Chiquito* by defeating a party of slavers who had occupied the mission.

Between 1691 and 1755, the Jesuits founded 8 missions in the Province of Chiquitos, concentrating representatives of various tribes and subtribes in each. In 1767, the Jesuits were expelled, and soon the populous missions of the Province of Chiquitos slipped back into the half barbarous condition in which they have remained up to the present. A census of the native population in 10 Jesuit missions made in 1766 gave for the region of Chiquitos a total population of 23,788. In 1831, there were 14,925 Indians who spoke *Chiquitoan* (D'Orbigny, 1839, 2:130).

During the three centuries after the Conquest, the Spanish and Portuguese slavers, as well as several epidemics, took a heavy toll of *Chiquito.*

THE CULTURE OF THE CHIQUITO PROPER

SUBSISTENCE ACTIVITIES

Cultivated plants were maize, sweet and bitter manioc, peanuts, gourds, pumpkins, pineapples, tobacco, and, after the Conquest, rice and cacao trees. The staple seems to have been sweet manioc (yuca). Fields were tilled by men with hardwood digging sticks. After the harvest, small groups of men scattered through the bush to fish and hunt. Methods employed in these activities are not described, except for vague references to taking fish by drugging, shooting, and by means of traps. Game was broiled on a babracot in order to preserve it for a few days. At the end of the hunting and fishing season in August, the Indians started work in the fields. In some parts of the province, the Indians dug wells during the dry season.

HOUSES AND VILLAGES

Houses were small, thatched beehive huts with a low entrance as a protection against mosquitoes. Young men slept in large men's houses described as open sheds, where visitors were received and feasts celebrated. Men slept in cotton hammocks, women on mats or on branches.

Villages were protected by thorny hedges and by poisoned caltrops. During the Conquest, the Spaniards had to storm villages defended by strong palisades.

DRESS AND ORNAMENTS

Except for chiefs and persons of wealth, who wore tunics (cushma), men went naked. Before the missionary era, women wore loincloths, later sleeveless shirts (tipoy). Men inserted labrets in their lower lips (after the Conquest, these were made of tin) and feathers in their ear lobes. Their other ornaments were seed and fruit-shell necklaces and anklets, belts of bright feathers and tufts of feathers, and tails of game animals, which they hung on their person. Both sexes let their hair fall down the back and tied it at the nape.

WEAPONS

The principal *Chiquito* weapon was the bow and arrow. Their poisoned arrows were greatly dreaded by both Indians and Spaniards. At close range, the *Chiquito* fought with paddlelike, sharp-edged clubs of hardwood.

SOCIAL ORGANIZATION

Chiefs were selected from distinguished warriors and were assisted by a council of old men. War prisoners were well treated and married within their captors' tribe. Polygyny is said to have been a necessity for chiefs, who, without the help of several wives, could not have organized the feasts which they were obliged to give. Sororal polygyny is indicated.

LIFE CYCLE

Before childbirth, the father refrained from hunting certain animals, mainly serpents. After the birth, he remained idle for a few days. A woman resumed her sexual life after the child was weaned.

Adolescent boys lived in the men's house. A young man who wanted to marry had to prove his skill as a hunter Custom allowed husbands to relinquish their wives to other men in circumstances which are not specified.

The dead were buried with food and with their favorite weapons. Widows remarried after a short time.

ESTHETIC AND RECREATIONAL ACTIVITIES

Musical instruments.—Flutes (with one or two stops), panpipes, and fruit-shell jingles, attached to the ankles, gourd rattles, and whistles (fig. 49, *a*) are the only musical instruments mentioned in our sources. In the pagan era, the *Chiquito* started their daily work by playing their flutes at dawn.

Dances.—In an ancient dance, the boys formed an outer and the girls an inner circle which revolved around two flute players. The mission dances may be survivals of the past. In the "apanaococh" dance, the women dancers placed themselves in two lines and sang while alternately turning from one side to the other. Women danced also in a circle holding each others' hands and making turns to one side and the other. Another dance consisted of a mock fight between two women, one of whom protected a group of dancers behind her from the other woman. The texts of the songs collected by D'Orbigny (1835–47, 3:59–60) are short sentences without special meaning.

Games.—The favorite sport of the *Chiquito* was a ball game played with a complex ceremonialism. Dances and mutual taunts preceded the game itself. A rubber ball was struck back and forth with the head until someone let it fall, thus losing a point to the other team. Scores were kept with maize cobs. The victors were privileged to deride their opponents and to drink all the beer that had been brewed.

Beverages.—The *Chiquito* prepared chicha of manioc, maize, and fruits. The drinking bouts, to which they invited the neighboring communities, lasted for several days and were often the occasions for settling old quarrels.

RELIGION

The moon was regarded as a female deity but was not worshiped. Thunder and lightning were construed as the manifestations of the wrath of spirits. During an eclipse, the people shouted and threw arrows to drive away a celestial "dog" (probably jaguar), which was thought to attack the moon, causing her to bleed.

The *Chiquito* attached great importance to omens and auguries derived from the observation of animals, birds, and plants.

SHAMANISM

Shamans were tribal or community chiefs. Diseases were attributed to witchcraft, to the violation of a taboo, such as that against spilling chicha, or to feeding game flesh to a dog.   In the last case, the game's soul entered the person's body.   The shaman sucked the patient and vomited a blackish substance.   He also beat the ground around the patient with a club to scare away the intruding soul.

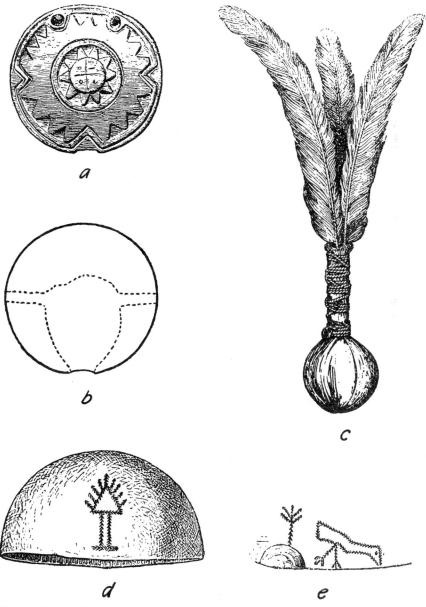

FIGURE 49.—Artifacts from Chiquitos, *Churapa* Indians. *a*, Wooden whistle; *b*, cross section of whistle; *c*, ball of cornhusks and feather for "shuttlecock" game; *d*, incised gourd; *e*, design from other side of *d*.   (After Nordenskiöld, 1922, figs. 3–6.)

The shaman was expected to reveal the name of the witch, whom the patient's family tried to punish. Revengeful feelings were also turned against any woman about whom the patient had dreamed and whom, therefore, he suspected of witchcraft.

At each new moon, the shamans went into seclusion and had long talks with spirits.

THE MANASÍ

LANGUAGE AND HABITAT

The *Manasí* (*Manasica*) (lat. 16° S., long. 62° W.), probably a *Chiquitoan* tribe, were situated in the northwest of the Province of Chiquitos "a two days' walk from the Mission of San Francisco Xavier" (Fernández, 1895, 1:260). Father Lucas Caballero, who discovered the *Manasí* in 1704, considered them a nation formed of *Tapacura* and *Quimemoca*. These two tribes, he adds, spoke the same language with insignificant dialectical differences. The informants, from whom he obtained cultural data on the *Manasí,* came from these two tribes. In his account of the *Manasí,* Caballero always refers to the *Tapacura* and *Quimemoca*. Fernández (1895, 1:265–266), who lists about 50 *Manasí* villages, mentions the *Tapacura* and the *Quimemoca* as the western and eastern neighbors of the Manasí. Hervás (1800–05, vol. 1) classifies the *Manasí* among the *Chiquitoan*-speaking Indians of the Jesuit missions and makes of the *Tapacura* a *Manasí* subgroup. The question is important, because if Caballero is right, the *Manasí* did not belong to the *Chiquitoan* family, but to the *Chapacuran* family, represented by the *Chapacura* and *Quitemoca*. Hervás and Fernández, however, both state that *Manasí* was a dialect of *Chiquito*. Comparisons between the few *Manasí* words recorded by Caballero and the *Chapacuran* and *Mojo* vocabularies did not show any analogies. On the other hand, two *Manasí* words are distinctly *Chiquitoan*: poori (house) and tuu (river).

The habitat of the *Manasí* was crossed by rivers of the Mamoré Basin, probably tributaries of the Río Blanco and Guaporé River. The two names of rivers cited are the San Unalo and the Luquibiqui.

CULTURE

MATERIAL CULTURE

The *Manasí* were proficient horticulturists, hunters, and fishermen. Fishing was especially profitable when the rivers were low. The women were skillful weavers and their pottery was remarkably good, "ringing like metal to the touch."

The bows were long and thick.   Some *Manasí* used poisoned arrows obtained from the *Chiquito*.

The *Manasí* made objects of stone, including stone pendants, carving them with stone tools.   They cut and carved wood with piranha teeth.

SOCIAL ORGANIZATION

Each *Manasí* community was under a high chief and a few "captains," probably lesser chiefs , who were the heads of extended families or households.   The "captains," however, seem to have had less prestige than priests, if the disposition of the different groups at public meetings in the communal halls actually reflected the social ranking.   Immediately behind the supreme chief (cacique) sat the "priests" (sacerdotes de sus dioses) and the medicine men (hechiceros y chupadores) ; the "captains" (capitanes) took their places behind these.   The remaining space was occupied by the common people.

The chief maintained order in the community and represented it in dealing with outsiders.   Personally or through his subordinates, he administered sound thrashings to troublemakers and to those who disobeyed him.   He had several wives, one of whom ruled over the women of the community.   One of his sons, the heir apparent, dominated the youths, and, like his father, chastised delinquents with a stick.   When the heir apparent was old enough to attend to public business, power was transferred to him "with many ceremonies and rites," after he had demonstrated his worth by leading a war party.   It seems, however, that his father lost neither his prestige nor the respect of his subjects.

Hunters and fishermen had to ask the chief for permission to leave the village.   Young people never sat in his presence but stood respectfully at a distance.   Commoners addressed him in a very formal manner.   The subordination to the chief diminished with the age of the subject.   When a boy was old enough to serve the cacique, his father was liberated from many duties.   Drinking bouts were organized by the chief, who sent special messengers to neighboring villages to invite the guests.

The main chief lived in a huge house built by the people in the middle of the plaza ; this house served also as a community hall and as a temple. Each chief had two large fields, which were tilled by his subjects.   He received the first fruits of the crops and a share of all game and fish brought into the village.   Dead chiefs were buried with special ceremonies amid general laments.

RELIGION

There is little doubt that the *Manasí* worshiped real gods with distinct personalities.   The main deity was (O)mequituriqui, known also as Uracozorizo, though perhaps this latter name may apply to some other divinity or may be an epithet.   With the goddess Quipozi, he procreated the god Urasaña.   These three deities were closely associated with Urapo

Stiquitetu, the Thunder God, and altogether these constituted the tini-maa(ka), or major gods. This name was not applied to lesser spirits, among whom were the souls of the dead, who did not sit in the temple "but stood in front" of the gods in a humble position. The River God Ysituu (tuu means "river" in *Chiquitoan*) appears as an independent god, master of fish and water animals, who was worshiped in the sanctuary of the chief's house, but in the description of the afterworld the Ysituu are mentioned merely as river spirits.

(O)mequituriqui (God Father), who spoke in a high-pitched voice, fulfilled the function of judge and avenger of the people. Diseases and deaths were attributed to him, and he appeared to sick people to scourge and torment them. But Urasaña, Urapo Stiquitetu, and especially the goddess Quipozi interceded for mankind.

The goddess Quipozi seems to have enjoyed great popularity. She was ordinarily addressed as "Our mother," and was visualized as a huge woman, clothed in a white floating garment, who protected people against the anger or vengeance of the other gods.

Cult.—Sanctuaries (pooriri) were the large huts which served as chief's residences as well as halls for public assemblies and banquets. When a religious ceremony was celebrated in honor of the gods, part of the hall was curtained off with mats for their reception.

The gods or spirits came down with a sound which filled the air, made the roof of the building shake, and agitated the mats. The people and the priests who were feasting or dancing there bade the god welcome. The oldest man and woman of the community offered the god chicha in a small decorated vase. Only a "high priest" could enter the compartment reserved to the major gods, and lesser shamans were warned that the deities would kill them if they insisted on seeing them face to face. At first, some music was heard. The people accredited it to the god Urasaña, and accompanied it with loud songs. Then, during a long conversation, the "high priest" consulted the gods about future events, such as seasonable rains, bountiful harvests, successful hunting and fishing expeditions, and the issue of prospective war raids. These interviews were carried on aloud. After the consultation, game—but never monkeys—and fish were offered to the gods.

When the ceremony neared its end, the gods fled through the air carrying the shaman with them and shaking the whole building as they ascended. After a while, the goddess Quipozi brought him back to the temple in her arms and held him there sleeping, while she sang in a sweet voice. Chicha and food were presented to the goddess, who then returned to her celestial abode.

The River God, Ysituu (Ssituu), visited the temple if invited to receive food and chicha from the faithful. Before a fishing party, priests went to the river and blew tobacco smoke over the water, reciting charms.

When a new chief's house or sanctuary was inaugurated, no one was allowed to eat meat for 4 days. The diet consisted of fish, fruit, and tubers. People did not sing or dance, and they observed strict silence when entering the temple. Their sole occupation was weaving mats for the sanctuary.

On the fifth day, an old "priestess" received a carved white stone from the chief and gently struck his forehead with it. The priest then performed several ceremonies, which were followed by a banquet and a drinking spree during which the people extolled their prowess in songs.

Priesthood.—Caballero distinguishes the "priests" (mapono) from the "witchs" or "suckers" (chupadores). The latter had a lower status. The difference was based on the specialized activities of the shaman rather than on his training. Priests and shamans underwent the same education and observed the same taboos. Moreover, the whole method used by the mapono to approach the gods followed the shamanistic pattern: The god descended into the tabernacle in the same way as the spirit entered the lodge of the shaman. The cult was essentially a direct and personal interview between the mapono and the gods rather than prayers and sacrifices to an unseen god. The ascent of the "priest" was an old shamanistic trick.

One of the main purposes of a cure was to extract from the patient a blackish substance, like rubber, which some sorcerer or god had injected into his body. Every shaman had some of the same substance in his stomach and used it as a weapon.

During the initiation of the mapono, an old priest became intoxicated and vomited a blackish substance into a calabash. He rubbed the arms and shoulders of the candidate with this substance, and the youth trembled as it penetrated his body. The initiate then drank what was left of the magic stuff.

The training of the young shaman aimed principally to teach him how to fly to the gods.

Among other rites, candidates were exposed to the waning moon while the initiator pulled their fingers to make the joints crack. They were not allowed to cut their finger nails. Their first visits to the gods, whose aspect was awe inspiring, were frought with anxiety and fear.

Full-fledged priests avoided eating various kinds of game and fish, especially granadilla fruit, so as not to lose the faculty of flying and other shamanistic powers. They enjoyed an exalted status within the society and many economic advantages. Like the chiefs, they received part of the crops and game, and they could consume the offerings which were strictly taboo to the rest of the population. The community built their houses, which occasionally were converted into temples or assembly halls. Some priests lived in isolation outside the village. Their property was guarded against theft by the gods, who would have killed anyone who touched their servants' crops.

To address the gods, shamans employed a special language, which according to Caballero, played the same role as Latin did in the Catholic Church. Almost everyone understood it, however, for it was taught to the young people. Several words of their language were transcribed by Caballero (1933, p. 27), who adds: "Thus, in each village there are three tongues: one for the men, another for the women, and a third for the devil."

In each village there were from two to four mapono who served alternately in the "temple." Besides the formal visits of the gods, when they appeared before the whole community, the mapono had private consultations with the deities in his house, which was temporarily evacuated by the women. If no game were found during a hunt, the shaman retired to a small palm-leaf cabin to ask for divine advice, often ascending to the sky to speak face to face with the gods. Many shamans kept serpents in their huts and took them along when strolling around the village.

Treatment of diseases.—Diseases were sent by the gods as a punishment for some transgression, or were caused by an animal spirit that entered the body, or by a witch who mysteriously cast some of his lethal blackish substance into the victim. The treatment consisted mainly in sucking out this substance or some object, such as a small serpent which later grew to larger proportions.

A religious element was combined with the purely magic cure. The sick man could invoke the goddess Quipozi, who came to his bedside and upbraided the gods for afflicting him with illness. She would order the shaman to treat the patient in the usual manner, and, as she departed, she would comfort the invalid with reassuring words.

Funerary rites and the hereafter.—After the funeral, the relatives gathered in the temple where the priests evoked the soul of the dead man. He purified it, and carried it on his back up to the land of the gods. A soul that was not carried by a shaman risked losing its way, and shamans used this fear as a threat against their enemies. The path to the Land of the Dead was alternately rugged and marshy and was crossed by many rivers. The soul finally arrived at a cross road and a bridge guarded by the God Tatusio, who showed it the way to the land of the Gods. Tatusio asked the soul to stop and groom his long disheveled and scabby hair. If the soul refused, he seized it by the leg and threw it into the river, causing rain and floods on earth. The Land of the Dead was an agreeable country abounding with honey, fish, and certain large trees that exuded a rosin which the souls ate. There were also big black monkeys and an eagle, which constantly soared in the sky. The land was divided into different regions to which the souls went according to the place where they had died. Each category of souls had a different name. The Asinecca were those who had perished near a river and who had gone to the land of the water gods (Ysituuca), which teemed with fish, bananas, parrots, and other birds. The Yirituca were those who had died in the bush, and the Posirabca those who had died in their own homes.

Mythology.—The culture hero was miraculously conceived by a virgin. He cured the sick, resuscitated the dead, and performed other difficult things. Finally, to show his superior nature, he ascended to the sky, where he was transformed into the sun.

The sun was a resplendent man and the moon was his sister. Eclipses were caused by celestial serpents which attacked these luminaries, threatening mankind with darkness. This catastrophe was to be followed by the transformation of men into hairy animals and by their mutual extermination. People did everything they could to assist the moon : They shot incendiary arrows into the sky and made all kinds of noises with their musical instruments. They called the sun to the rescue, shouting, "Sun, why don't you protect the moon, your sister? Why don't you help her in her trouble?"

THE MODERN CHURAPA

HISTORY

The acculturated *Churapa* are the only *Chiquitoan* Indians who have been described by a modern anthropologist. In 1908, Nordenskiöld (1922, p. 21) found 500 to 1,000 of them in the Province of Sara, north of the city of Santa Cruz de la Sierra. The ancestors of the *Churapa* had been captured by the Spaniards about 1690, east of the Río Grande (Guapay River) and put under the Jesuit control. Their mission was shifted several times before it was transferred to the town of Buenavista in 1723, where their descendants still live. At the end of the 18th century, their number was 2,017.

CULTURE

Forty years ago very little remained of aboriginal *Churapa* culture. The Indians were good tropical farmers, and they still hunted and fished with the bow and arrow. Their arrows had a cemented feathering, butts reinforced by wooden plugs, and wooden knob and wooden rod tips. They poisoned fish with barbasco (*Lonchocarpus nicou*) and ochohó (*Hura crepitans*).

Houses were of the Mestizo type: A thatched gabled roof rested on walls of palm leaves or of wattle-and-daub. Furniture consisted of palm-leaf mats, hammocks, and platform beds.

The *Churapa* were expert basket makers, and they manufactured Panama hats for sale. Formerly, they made artistically painted pots, but more recently their ware had become plain and crude. They carved wooden bowls and incised realistic motifs on their calabashes (fig. 49, *d, e*).

During Christian feasts, they danced with their faces hidden by cloth masks and their bodies covered with ostrich feathers. Certain masked dancers impersonated the sun. In these festivities, they shot at each other with arrows tipped with a wax lump.

They had wooden whistles similar to those of the *Chiriguano* and of the Chaco tribes: The round, resonator whistle with a blowhole, two stops, and two incised, concentric, toothed circles on one surface (fig. 49, *a*, *b*); and the serere whistles, a long piece of wood with a diamond-shaped cross section perforated from end to end.

They played a ball game with rubber balls, but its rules are unknown. Another game consisted in throwing potsherds at white stones, each man trying to cover the target before his competitor. "Papamkosh" was a kind of bowling game played with palm nuts piled by fours into small heaps, which the players had to knock down with a ball. Children amused themselves by swinging bull-roarers and throwing shuttlecocks made of maize leaves and feathers (fig. 49, *c*).

THE SIXTEENTH-CENTURY ETHNOGRAPHY OF THE CHIQUITOS REGION

The *Xaraye* Indians, who lived around the modern Laguna Maniore (lat. 18° S., long. 58° W.), must have been fairly numerous if one of their villages actually had 1,000 inhabitants.

The *Xaraye* were good agriculturists reaping maize, potatoes, manioc, and peanuts twice a year. Fishing and hunting were important. These Indians raised hens and ducks.

The huts, housing a single family, were grouped around a plaza. The furniture consisted of hammocks and benches.

Men went naked, women wore a tipoy. On festive occasions, they wore cotton mantles with naturalistic paintings. Their main ornaments were stone labrets, wooden "rings" (plugs?) in the ear lobes. They had silver and gold ornaments obtained from tribes near the Andes.

Weapons were the bow and arrow; musical instruments, drums and trumpets.

The chief of the *Xaraye* ruled over four villages.

In his expedition west of the *Xaraye*, Hernando de Ribera met the *Siberi*, who were linguistically and culturally related to the *Xaraye*. He also encountered the *Ortu* and *Aburune*. These Indians wore gold plates on their foreheads and silver bracelets around their arms.

Ethnological data on the western tribes are few: The *Simeno* and *Mayagueno*, mentioned by Schmidel (1903), protected their villages with thorny hedges. The *Siberi* prepared manioc chicha and obtained water from deep wells.

Gorgotoqui men and women wore a stone disk in the lower lip. Their cultivated plants were maize and several kinds of tubers. Weapons were the bow and arrow and tapir-hide shields.

The few data on these tribes are contained in Schmidel (1903), in the "Comentarios de Alvar Nuñez Cabeza de Vaca" (see Hernández, 1852), in Lozano (1873–75) and in the documents published by Mujía (1914).

BIBLIOGRAPHY

Adam and Henry, 1880; Bolívar, 1906; Burges, 1819; Caballero, 1933; Cabello de Balboa, 1906; Charlevoix, 1757; Comentarios de Alvar Nuñez Cabeza de Vaca (*see* Hernández, Pedro, 1852); Créqui-Montfort and Rivet, 1913 e; D'Orbigny, 1839, 1835–47; Fernández, 1895; Finot, 1939; Gandía, 1935 a; Hernández, 1852; Hervás, 1800–05; Lafone Quevedo, 1910–11; Lozano, 1873–75; Maurtua, V., 1906; Métraux, 1942, 1943; Mollinedo, 1906; Mujía, 1914; Nordenskiöld, 1922; René-Moreno, 1888; Sánchez Labrador, 1910; Schmidel, 1903.

THE OTUKEAN TRIBES

The *Otuke, Covareca,* and the *Curuminaca* spoke dialects belonging to an isolated linguistic group, *Otukean,* which shows, according to Créqui-Montfort and Rivet (1913 e), striking lexicographic affinities with *Bororo.*

The *Otuke* (*Otuque, Otuqui*) proper lived in the northwestern part of the Province of Chiquitos, not far from the Bolivian-Brazilian border (lat. 17°–18° S., long. 60° W.; map 1, *No. 2;* map 2). Remnants of the tribe were established in the Mission of Santo Corazón.

The *Covareca,* who formed part of the Mission of Santa Ana de Chiquitos, came from a region near lat. 17° S. and long. 60° W. In D'Orbigny's time, only 50 of these Indians remained in the mission, the other 100 having gone to live in the bush.

The *Curuminaca* were located in the northwestern part of the Province of Chiquitos, around lat. 16° S. and long. 62° W. In 1831, 100 were settled at Santa Ana and 50 at Casalvasco.

BIBLIOGRAPHY

Bach, 1838, 1929; Créqui-Montfort and Rivet, 1912, 1913 e.

TRIBES OF UNIDENTIFIED LANGUAGE, PRESUMABLY OTUKEAN

D'Orbigny (1839, 2:183–186) gives some scanty information on four Indian tribes of the Province of Chiquitos who, although speaking a *Chiquito* dialect, had, according to their own and their neighbors' testimony, once spoken a language of their own. From their geographical position, it may be surmised that they belonged to the *Otukean* linguistic group.

These hypothetical members of the *Otukean* family included: 150 *Curave* in the Mission of Santo Corazón, who had come from the banks of the Tucabaca River, a left tributary of the Otuquis River, and 50 *Tapii* of the Mission of Santiago de Chiquitos, whose former habitat lay between lat. 17° and 18° S. and between long. 59° and 60° W. The *Tapii* might also have been *Zamucoan.* Finally, the *Curucaneca* and *Coraveca,* who numbered respectively 50 and 100 in 1831, had been collected by the Jesuits in the Mission of San Rafael. The *Curuçaneca* came from about lat. 16° S. and long. 60° W., and the *Coraveca* from a region farther south, at about lat. 18° S.

THE ARAWAKAN TRIBES OF CHIQUITOS[1]

TRIBAL DIVISIONS AND HISTORY

The *Saraveca* were an *Arawkan* tribe, split into small groups living in the forests near the Chiquito Mission of Santa Ana and along the hills on the northeastern border of the Province of Chiquitos (lat. 15° S., long 60° W.). In 1831, the number of *Saraveca* at Santa Ana was 250 and at Casalvasco, 100. In about 1886, the bulk of the *Saraveca* tribe, which had remained independent, occupied the course of the Verde River, a tributary of the Guaporé River. The *Saraveca* language is related to *Paressí* and shows close affinities with the *Arawakan* dialects of the Xingú and the Amazon. This relationship may be regarded as evidence that both the *Paressí* and *Saraveca* migrated to their present habitat later than the *Mojo* and *Bauré,* whose *Arawakan* dialect is more differentiated (Créqui-Montfort and Rivet, 1913 f, p. 530).

The original home of the *Paiconeca* (*Paicone*) and of their subtribe, the *Paunaca* (*Pauná*), was the region north of Concepción de Chiquitos between the headwaters of the Río Blanco and the Verde River (between long. 61° and 62° W.). Their *Arawakan* dialect seems to belong to a different subgroup than that of the *Saraveca.*

The *Paunaca* were visited in 1707 by Brother Lucas Caballero and agreed to settle with *Unape* and *Carababa* in the Mission of Concepción. In 1831, 360 *Paiconeca* and 250 *Paunaca* remained in that mission, though some 300 *Paiconeca* had returned to their native forests. During the past century, all the *Paiconeca* retired near the headwaters of the Río Blanco, 20 leagues from Concepción, away from the Whites.

There were isolated *Chané* groups in the western part of the Province of Chiquitos, as stated in several official documents. *Chané* were included among the Indians given as serfs to the first settlers of Santa Cruz, near San José de Chiquitos. (See also Volume 1, pp. 238–241, and this volume, p. 381.)

CULTURE

The *Arawakan* Indians of Chiquitos were undistinguishable in costume and manners from the *Chiquito,* with whom they were in close contact in the missions and whose language most of them adopted. Aboriginally,

---

[1] Map 1, *No. 2;* map 2.

men went naked, but women wore sleevless shirts (tipoy). The *Paunaca* made a beer of flour of carbonized maize grains. They worshiped idols. They placed their dead in shelters made of branches and surrounded by a net to prevent access to the corpse by anyone but the priest and the nearest relatives. Two posts in this hut represented deities to whom they made offerings. Another tribe of the same region burned its dead on pyres and collected the ashes in funerary urns.

THE CHAPACURAN TRIBES

TRIBAL DIVISIONS AND HISTORY

The *Chapacuran* linguistic family includes the following tribes: *Chapacura* proper, *Quitemoca, Rocorona, Moré (Itene), Huanyam, Matama (Mataua), Cujuna, Urunamacan, Cumana, Urupá, Jarú,* and *Torá.*[2]

Most of these Indians live on the lower and middle Guaporé River, on both the Bolivian and Brazilian sides of the frontier (map 1, *No. 2;* map 2; map 4). Until the end of the last century, there were a few isolated *Chapacuran* groups, probably extinct today, who lived on the eastern tributaries of the upper Madeira River. (See also p. 371.)

The culture of the various tribes of this family is very imperfectly known. There are no published cultural data on *Torá, Jarú,* and *Urupá.* The cultural summary presented in this chapter refers exclusively to the *Moré, Cumaná,* and *Huanyam.*

In 1794, the Governor of the Province of Mojos, Miguel Zamora, formed the new Mission of Nuestra Señora del Carmen with *Bauré* Indians and with a group of 185 wild Indians who had been taken from the forests of the upper Río Blanco. The *Bauré* converts, who actively helped to round up and transfer these Indians, called them *Guarayo,* a general term given by civilized Indians and Mestizos to all independent and warlike Indians. These *Guarayo* (also called *Carmelitas*) were later designated as *Chapacura* by the local authorities. A powerful *Tapacura* nation had existed in the 17th century in the region from which these Indians came. The name *Tapacura* occurs in most accounts of Gonzalo de Solís Holguín's journey. They were neighbors of the *Toro (Mojo),* and were friendly to the Spaniards. Some of them took part in the ill-fated Mojos expedition. When in 1630 Gonzalo de Solís Holguín entered the Province of the *Tapacura,* he was accompanied by a priest, who hoped to continue the missionary work among the *Tapacura* started by another priest (Maurtua, V., 1906, 9:193–94). Some *Tapacura* were already yanacona, i.e., serfs of the Spaniards. From these statements, it appears clearly that European contacts with these Indians go as far back as the beginning of the 17th century. The *Tapacuraca* Indians of the Mission of Concepción de Chiquitos, were *Chapacuran* (the ending *ca* is the plural suffix in *Chiquitoan*), though Hervás (1800–05, 1:157) lists them among the *Chiquitoan* tribes. The *Chapacura* from the upper Río Blanco, taken to the Mission of Carmen, spoke the same language as the *Quitemoca* and *Napeca* Indians of the Mission of Concepción de Chiquitos.

---

[2] *Chapacuran Cabishí* are mentioned near the *Huanyam.*

The original home of the *Chapacura* (*Tapacura, Huachi, Guarayos*) was the middle and upper course of the Río Blanco (Bauré), the area around Lake Chitiopa, and that north of Concepción de Chiquitos. The *Quitemoca* and *Napeca* were two subtribes who had been persuaded by the Jesuits to settle with *Chiquito* and other Indians at the Mission of Concepción de Chiquitos. In 1831, *Chapacura* and *Quitemoca* together numbered about 1,350 individuals.

The Indians whom D'Obrigny called *Itene* or *Ite* were those with whom Heinrich Snethlage (1937 a) established friendly contacts in 1935 and to whom he restored the ancient name *Moré* (in 18th century, *Muri*). According to Rydén (1942), these Indians applied to themselves the name *Itoreauhip,* which Snethlage thought designated a distinct tribe near the *Bauré*. They were known among the Mestizos and civilized Indians as *Guarayo*. The *Moré* live in the large triangle formed by the Mamoré and Guaporé Rivers and on the Machupo and Itonama Rivers and the Río Blanco (lat. 12°–13° S., long. 63°–64° W.). On the Mamoré River, the *Moré* reach the vicinity of the Mission of Exaltación. In 1884, a few families had crossed to the left side of that river, where they joined the *Chacobo* and *Sinabo* groups. In 1940, Rydén (1942, p. 84) defines their territory as follows: The confluence of the Guaporé with the Río Blanco, and up this river to a point known as Altura de Nueva Brema, thence in a straight line to the northern edge of Lago Oceano—also called Crespa—and then to the settlement on the Mamoré known as Warnes. Within this area, *Moré* huts are scattered, although many of them are only periodically occupied. Now there are more *Moré* on the Brazilian side of the Guaporé River than in Bolivia. An educational center (Nucleo indigenal Moré) was established in 1938, at about a mile (2 km.) from Puerto Komarek, to pacify the Indians.

In the 18th century, a great many *Moré* resided in the missions of San Simón, San Judas, and San Miguel, which were later destroyed. The 4,000 Indians of the Mission of San Miguel, near the junction of the Guaporé River with the Río Blanco, were mainly *Moré* (Gonçalves da Fonseca, 1826, p. 108). Some of the Indians of the Mission of Santa Rosa de Itenes, destroyed in 1742, were also *Moré* Indians. Snethlage estimates the number of modern *Moré* or *Itene* to be between 3,000 and 5,000.

The *Huanyam* (*Abitona-Huanyam* or *Pawumwa*) had their villages on the San Miguel River, a right tributary of the Guaporé River (lat. 12° 30′ S., long. 64° W.). In 1914, they numbered about 300. The *Cumaná* live on the right side of the Guaporé River, near the ancient fort Principe da Beira (lat. 12° S., long. 64° W.).

The Indians living at the foot of the Serrania de San Simón, and often called *San Simonianos,* are probably *Chapacuran*-speaking Indians who, in the 18th century, were concentrated in the missions near the San Simón River, a tributary of the Río Blanco (Bauré River). There were also two isolated groups of *Chapacuran*-speaking Indians, one (*Moré* and *Ocorono*) in the Mission of San Ignacio, on the Tijamuchi River, a left tributary of the Mamoré River, and the other (*Herisabocono*) in the Mission of San Borja, near the headwaters of the Rapulo River, also a tributary of the Mamoré River. The presence of these *Chapacuran* enclaves in *Mojo* territory may be explained by the shifting of tribes which took place when the Jesuits concentrated the Indians of eastern Bolivia in their missions.

The *Torá* (*Tura, Toraz*) originally lived on the Capaná River and later on the Maicy River, a little below the Machado River (lat. 8° S., long. 63° W.). About 1716, they sent war parties down the Madeira River to attack boats carrying cacao from Solimões to Pará. In 1719, a Portuguese expedition under João de Barros da Guerra destroyed a large number of *Torá*. Many Indians of this tribe were settled at Abacaxi and others were transported to Porto de Moz, at the mouth of the Xingú River, but many remained in or returned to the bush.

These inhabited the Maicy River, the Machado River, the headwaters of the Marmellos River, and the Río Negro, a tributary of the Paricá River.

Their isolation did not protect the *Torá* from the rubber gatherers, who captured them as crews for the navigation of the Madeira River. It was only about 1870 that they, together with the *Arará* and other Indians, were put in the Mission of São Francisco of the Preto River, which flows into the Madeira River near the Machado River. The *Torá* of the Marmellos joined their tribesmen in the Mission but returned to their original home after the mission was abandoned. There they were decimated by various epidemics of smallpox, measles, and influenza and by harsh treatment in the rubber gatherers' camps. In 1923, there were only 12 *Torá* left. (See Nimuendajú, 1925.)

A distinguishing feature of the *Torá* was a tattooed strip running from the corners of the mouth to the ears.

The *Urupá* (*Urupazes*) should not be confused with the *Urupaya* (*Arupaí*) of the upper Xingú River and the *Urupá* (*Uarupá, Ituarupa, Arupá, Gurupá, Urupuya*) of the Tapajóz River. The *Urupá* of the Madeira River (lat. 11° S., long. 62° W.) contributed elements to the population of Borba and Itacoatira, and a few families formed part of the Mission of São Francisco. Toward the end of the 19th century, they lived on the headwaters of the Canaan River, an eastern tributary of the Jamary River. At the beginning of the 19th century, they moved to Bom Futuro and, after they had been decimated by a smallpox epidemic, to the Pardo River. Today the *Urupá* do not exist as a tribe, but a few of them still lived about 1925 at Colonia Rodolfo de Miranda on the upper Jamary.

The now extinct *Jarú* were closely related to the *Urupá*. Their former habitat was west of the Machado River, between its tributaries, the Jarú and Anary Rivers (lat. 10°–10° 30' S., long. 61°–64° W.). About 1915, a few *Jarú* still lived in the Colonia Rodolfo de Miranda.

The language of the *Urupá* and *Jarú* is known through two short vocabularies collected by Nimuendajú (1925, pp. 148–159).

CULTURE

SUBSISTENCE ACTIVITIES

Farming is practiced by all the members of the family on the Guaporé River and has greater importance than collecting or hunting, though wild Brazil nuts are almost a staple in certain periods of the year. Each *Moré* family owns and tills a field which nominally belongs to the family head. As fields continuously yield one crop or another, there are only short periods of scarcity. The cultivated plants are: Maize, sweet manioc, sweet potatoes, cara (yams), pineapples, gourds, bananas, papayas, cotton, and cayenne pepper. Peanuts were probably grown by most of these Indians, though they do appear in our lists.

Wild-plant foods include Brazil nuts, mangaba, wild cacao, and the fruits of various palms. Turtle eggs are also an important food item in September and October; caiman eggs also are eaten. When on a collecting expedition, the *Moré* live in small triangular shelters.

Little information is available on hunting. Peccaries are a favorite game. Deer meat is taboo to both the *Moré* and *Huanyam*. The *Moré* shoot waterfowl from beehivelike shelters built on the flooded plains and constructed so that they could be entered only by diving.

Fish are shot with bows and arrows, caught in conical baskets placed in palm-leaf dams, or drugged with a poisonous creeper.

The staple food is sweet manioc. The tubers are peeled with a bamboo-splinter knife, washed, and grated on the thorny roots of the assahy palm. The pulp is boiled, carefully skimmed with a plaited spoon, strained through a mat made of thin sticks, and roasted on a fire pan. Manioc flour is either consumed at once or kept in a bark-cloth bag. Wafers of manioc are roasted in a pan; manioc buns are baked in ashes. The starchy manioc juice is boiled many times and drunk cold. Maize is ground on the flattened upper side of a horizontal log about 16 feet (3 m.) long, with an oval, flat stone which, with one edge resting on the log, is rocked backward and forward among the grains. The flour is sifted through a special mat. It is baked into thin cakes on a fire pan. (See Rydén, 1942, p. 104.)

Brazil nuts are cracked with a cylindrical stone and the shelled kernels eaten raw, but they are considered a special delicacy when grated to a pulp against the rough inner side of a piece of bark.

Game and fish are broiled on a pyramidal babracot.

These Indians keep many pets, especially birds, for which they make small cages. The *Moré* pluck their tame ara to obtain feathers for arrows.

VILLAGES AND HOUSES

Moré and *Itoreauhip* huts are generally located near the plantations. They are large lean-tos, 15 to 40 feet (about 5 to 14 m.) high supported by two rows of wooden posts. Mats of motacu palm fronds, which form the roof itself, are lashed with liana on poles leaning against the rafters. The open side of the hut is closed in with upright palm leaves as the occasion requires. Some huts are formed by placing two sloping shelters against each other. As many as eight families may live in one hut. (See Rydén, 1942, p. 90.)

The *Moré* and *Huanyam* take refuge from mosquitoes in small conical cabins tightly thatched with patoju leaves. They also build small shelters to be used as workshops and as men's clubs. The temporary shelters erected in the forest consist of a few palm leaves placed horizontally on three perpendicular poles.

Hammocks are usually made of cotton threads, but sometimes also of fibers. To hang them, a loop is attached to a post and passed over a stick that runs through each end of the hammock. *Moré* wooden benches are mainly ceremonial accessories.

DRESS AND ADORNMENT

The dress of both sexes is a long bark-cloth shirt, which, however, is often discarded if it interferes with one's activities or is likely to be damaged by water. The shirts are decorated with sewn or glued strips of bark cloth or are dyed with urucú. Over the shirt, *Huanyam* men often wear a bark-cloth jacket, open in front. Outside their shirts, *Moré* men use a belt of bark cloth adorned with narrow strips of black or brown bark cloth sewn on it. *Huanyam* men tied up the foreskin of the penis with a cotton thread and tucked it under a string belt.

Both sexes among the *Moré* and women only among the *Huanyam* tied plaited cotton ligatures around the fleshy parts of their limbs. Among the *Moré,* both the upper and lower lips are pierced for the insertion of small wooden pegs, feathers, small grass blades, *Astrocaryum* thorns, and sometimes a resin labret. Adult *Huanyam* women thrust large conical quartz labrets in the lower lip and smaller ones in the upper lip; girls used only resin spikes as labrets.

Both sexes among the *Moré* pass a stick through the nasal septum to serve, it is said, as a talisman against diseases. Sticks or feathers are inserted into the ear lobes. A typical *Huanyam* ornament is a fiber band with long hanging fringes, attached around each bicep. Around the upper arm, *Huanyam* women wear a row of triangular shell pendants strung with seeds.

The complete festive attire of these Indians consists of feather headdresses, monkey- or sloth-skin caps, bark-cloth frontlets, feather bracelets, and ear sticks trimmed with feathers and *Astrocaryum* or feather rings. Necklaces were strung with seeds or animal teeth.

Men and women part their hair in the middle and clip it at shoulder level. Some *Moré* tie their hair up in a topknot with a bark-cloth band. Combs are made of bamboo splinters (composite type). These Indians remove all body hair.

Tattooing is not mentioned. Body paintings consisted of various geometrical motifs: Reticulated surfaces, dots, zigzags, stripes, etc.

TRANSPORTATION

Moré dugouts are about 33 feet (10 m.) long, and are propelled with narrow paddles which, characteristically, lack a crutch or knob at the handle. Formerly, the *Huanyam* had bark canoes.

Babies are carried in a bark sling.

INDUSTRIES

Bark cloth.—The *Moré* obtain the bark for their cloth from several species of trees, each yielding a bark of a different color. The inner bark is beaten with the edge of a flat wooden mallet to detach it from the wooden layer; then it is cut to proper size. Patches of bark are hammered on a smooth log, wrung thoroughly, dried, and sewn together. Men are their own and their wives' tailors. Decorative effects are achieved

by glueing or sewing strips or patches of different colors on the surface.
Sewing needles are made of bone or of *Astrocaryum* wood.

Spinning and weaving.—The *Moré* card cotton with small bows.
Thin cotton threads are made with a drop spindle which has a fruit or
a wooden disk for a whorl and a small hook at the proximal end. Thicker
strings are manufactured by the roll method: Cotton is first twisted by
hand, then attached to the toes, and twisted again by means of a spindle
rolled up and down the left thigh.

Arm and leg bands are woven on a small loom formed by lashing two
transverse cross bars to a frame made of a forked branch. The warp
is wound around the two cross bars. The final pattern of the fabric is
obtained by crossing the warp threads and holding them in place with
wooden splinters which are removed as the weft is passed through in their
place. Hammocks are made by wrapping the warp around two vertical
posts and twining it at set intervals.

Pottery.—Potter's clay is mixed with the ashes of a kind of sponge
that floats in flooded forests. The sponges contain calcium spiculae, which
give unusual strength to the clay. Vessels are coiled, then scraped
with shells, and polished with pebbles. After the clay has hardened, the
pot is dried before a patoju-leaf screen that separates it from a fire. The
dried pot is then covered with wood and fired in the open. Painted
decoration is applied after firing. The inside is smeared with a black
waxlike coating. The main vessel types are bowls, large jars which taper
to a point so that they may be stuck into the sandy ground, and other
forms, such as those in figure 50.

Basketry.—*Moré* basketry work includes mats, sieves, fire fans, knapsacks, and rectangular baskets.

A type of basket is constructed by intertwining the leaflets of a palm leaf on
either side of the woody leaf-stalk, whereby something resembling a mat is produced. The woody portion running down the middle of the leaf stalk is then cut
away and the mat doubled, whereupon, along the line where the edges meet, the
leaflets are interwoven so that a cylindrical basket is formed. Around the bottom
there is a raised ring. [Rydén, 1942, p. 106.]

Tools.—The *Moré* and *Huanyam* carve wood with agouti incisors
hafted to a stick, with piranha teeth, or with bird bones and pierce holes
with bone awls.

Weapons.—The *Moré* bow is made of strong palm wood. The back
is flat, the belly convex. The ends have a shoulder for a string. A fine
cotton yarn is wrapped about one third of the bow stave. The rest of
the stave is wound with the surplus length of the bow string. A row
of small red feathers are fastened in the cotton wrapping along both
edges of the stave (Rydén, 1942, p. 97).

War arrows have large lanceolate bamboo heads, sometimes artistically jagged along the edges. The *Moré* often draw conventionalized

"serpent" designs on such heads. Hunting arrows are tipped with a bone splinter serving both as point and barb. Bird arrows consist of a reed with its bulbous root forming the head. Fish arrows have one to three points.

FIGURE 50.—*Huanyam* pottery forms.

The feathering is either of the wrapped (Arara feathering) or of the sewn type (Xingú feathering). The feathering of some arrows consists of three or even four feathers, an unusual number which the *Moré* explain as a device to increase the speed of the arrow. The whistling arrows are provided with a hollow nut near the tip.

The *Huanyam* poison their arrows with curare and carry them with the points in a bamboo sheath to prevent accidents.

The *Huanyam* hunt with simple blowguns made of a section of bamboo about 6 feet (2 m.) in length. Blowgun darts, usually made of thin palm splinters, are kept in a section of bamboo enclosed in a palm spathe. They are poisoned with curare.

For the release, the arrow is held between the index and the middle finger. *Moré* archers use a bark-cloth wrist guard.

The *Moré* and *Huanyam* produce fire by the drill method. Cotton or bark cloth is used as tinder. Basketry fire fans are rectangular in all tribes except among the *Cumaná,* who make them hexagonal. For torches, pieces of bark are dipped in wax.

There are as many chiefs as family heads, and their authority is scant.

LIFE CYCLE

Puberty and marriage.—At puberty, girls' upper and lower lips are perforated by the shaman (*Huanyam*).

In some *Huanyam* settlements, the number of men so far exceeded that of women, that married women were permitted, it is said, to have extramarital intercourse. The *Moré* are, as a rule, monogamous. *Huanyam* parents and children-in-law turn their faces away when speaking to each other; the same avoidance exists between cross-cousins.

Funeral rites.—According to Snethlage (1937 a, p. 66), the *Moré* do not inter their dead, but simply cover them with a heap of leaves and grass. Rydén (1942) states that they are buried in the hut. Both authors agree that sometime after burial the bones are exhumed, but Snethlage says that the bones are kept in a basket suspended from the roof, while according to Rydén, they are burned. After the ashes have been kept for an unspecified period of time, the deceased's relatives prepare a generous supply of maize chicha, pound the calcinated bones into powder, mix them with the chicha, and drink it to the accompaniment of a song (Ryden, 1942, p. 116).

The *Moré* also make a cake of pounded Brazil nuts mixed with ground bones and hair, and the relatives and the guests eat it during a drinking bout. The funerary hut is abandoned, but not the deceased's fields. The *Cumaná* bury their dead in a circular grave over which they sometimes build a roof.

When death approaches, a *Huanyam* distributes his possessions among his heirs. After he has breathed his last, his past deeds are celebrated in a chant. He is then wrapped in his hammock and buried outside the house in a circular grave surrounded by a high fence.

ESTHETIC AND RECREATIONAL ACTIVITIES

Art.—Belts and bark-cloth frontlets are decorated with various geometric figures named after animals; for instance, the favorite pattern, a sinuous line, is a "snake." Designs are often traced or stamped with sticks or pieces of bamboo.

Music and musical instruments.—The *Moré* have an unusually large variety of musical instruments. (See Snethlage, 1937 a.) They are: (1) A drum made of a slit palm spathe beaten with a stick. (2) The "taran," an instrument used only for a special children's dance, consisting of a gourd fitted on a stick. The gourd is allowed to drop so as to produce a thud when it hits the lower and thicker part of the stick. (3) A friction idiophone consisting of a calabash with a semicircular opening which emits sounds when the wax-coated edges of the slit are rubbed with the wet palm of the hand. (4) Gourd rattles. These often have a side patched with a fragment of calabash to modify their resonance. On most rattles, the handle passes through the gourd, but often the gourd is lashed to the end of the handle. (5) Jingles made of small gourds. (6) The musical bow, played by using the mouth as a resonator and striking the two strings with a bamboo splinter. (7) Simple trumpets consisting of a bamboo or soft-wood tube, and composite trumpets made of a tube and a gourd bell. Some *Huanyam* trumpets have a bell modeled of wax and affixed to a long tube of human bone; other trumpets of the same tribe are globular in shape and made of clay; and still others combine a wide bamboo resonator, a slender bamboo tube, and a separate mouth piece. (8) Clarinet mouth pieces provided with a vibrating tongue. (9) Reed tubes with longitudinal slits. (10) Transverse flutes without stops, in which one or both ends of the tube may be open. Several notes are obtained by opening or closing the open end with a finger; if both ends are open, they are alternately opened and closed with the fingers. (11) End flutes. These are sometimes simple tubes with or without notches around the mouth. Others, more complex, have three stops, a sound orifice, and a wax deflector near the proximal end. (12) Panpipes, exceptional in the number of tubes, some having as many as 20. The pipes are held together either by winding a cotton thread around them (simple ligature) or by binding them between two sticks (Uaupés ligature). The *Moré* tie long and short whistles together, thus making an aberrant type of panpipes.

When a group of *Moré* make music, each tends to play for himself without heeding his fellow musicians.

The *Moré* songs heard by Rydén (1942) had as themes the maize crops and the hunting of wild pigs and other game, or they celebrated the Morning Star. Some songs are also dedicated to the dead and to chiefs of early times, whom they call Guá-niám.

Narcotics and beverages.—The *Chapacura* prepare beer by fermenting manioc juice with chewed manioc flour.

SHAMANISM

Cumaná shamans claim to be able to climb to the sky on an arrow chain made by shooting each arrow into the butt of the one previously shot. Upon reaching the sky, they are welcomed by Namakon, the lord of the sky.

Moré shamans treat sick people by blowing on the ailing regions, by making gestures as if they are driving away some obnoxious substance, and by massaging their patients with herbs. They also scarify them with snake fangs attached to a wooden handle.

When effecting a cure, the *Huanyam* shaman reaches a state of trance by smoking a great many cigarettes containing fine powder made of an unidentified substance, and resin fragments. Most of the treatment consists of blowing smoke on the patient.

MYTHOLOGY

A large stone once fell from the sky killing all but two people, a man and a woman. From this couple, all the *Moré* trace their descent (*Moré*).

Aijimo, the first *Cumaná*, had a wife called Zaré and a son called Kumana. Driven by the *Tapoaya* from a mountainous region, they arrived at a large river (the Guaporé), but were driven from its banks by the *Moré*. They settled on the spurs of the Serra do Norte, on the headwaters of the San Domingues River. Zaré was finally killed and eaten by her husband, or, according to another version (*Cumaná*), by her mother-in-law.

The *Cumaná* regard the rainbow as a celestial serpent who, when people looked at him, became angry and threw stones at them.

The *Moré* fear a monster with a big head and bulging eyes. Pains in the side are ascribed to arrows which this monster shoots at people during their sleep (Rydén, 1942, p. 119).

BIBLIOGRAPHY

Burela, 1912; Cardús, 1886; Chamberlain, 1912; Créqui-Montfort and Rivet, 1913 f; D'Orbigny, 1839; Gonçalves de Fonseca, 1826; Haseman, 1912; Hervás, 1800–05, vol. 1; Maurtua, V., 1906; Nimuendajú, 1925; Nimuendajú and Valle Bentes, 1923; Nordenskiöld, 1924 a; Rydén, 1942; Snethlage, E. H., 1937 a, 1939.

LITTLE-KNOWN TRIBES OF THE UPPER MADEIRA RIVER

The Arikêm.—The *Arikêm* have been erroneously classified as *Chapacuran*. Nimuendajú (1925), however, has proved that they belong to the *Tupí-Guaranian* family, even if their dialect contains many foreign elements.

The *Arikêm* (*Ahopovo*) were, until a few years ago, masters of the headwaters of the Jamary and Candeias Rivers and of the Massangana River, a tributary of the former, all of which are right tributaries of the upper Madeira River (lat. 10° S., long. 63° W.). When visited by Rondón, the last 60 *Arikêm* who survived were distributed in four villages.

They cultivated manioc, which they grated on a rough piece of paxiubinha bark. They ground maize in an elongated wooden trough with a semicircular wooden slab.

Each *Arikêm* village consisted of two dwelling houses and an ossuary hut or temple. Huts were constructed in the shape of a low vault, the curve of the ridge pole and of the walls being obtained by bending poles across a central rectangular framework.

Men wore feathers and wooden plugs in their ear lobes and cotton bands around their ankles. They tied fibers on the end of their long hair. Necklaces were strung with river shells and were trimmed with feather tassels.

These Indians spun cotton and manufactured hammocks. Their bows had a semicircular cross section and were decorated at the grip with an artistic cotton wrapping. Arrow feathering was of the wrapped (*Arara*) type.[3]

The *Arikêm* buried their dead in the hut under hammocks. They kept the bones of famous chiefs in a special hut; the skeleton was enclosed in a bark-cloth bag and the skull in a special three-legged, feather-trimmed basket. These relics were decorated with feathers and shells and were hung in a hammock under a jaguar skin. Gourd dippers with trimmed handles, polished stones, stone axes with a hole through the butt, and labrets made of resin—the last probably war trophies—were stored near the roof of the temple. Bundles of arrows, captured from other tribes, were leaned against the walls. Other baskets contained charred human bones.

Itogapuk (*Ntogapid, Intogapid*) and **Ramarama.**—The *Itogapuk* lived on the upper reaches of the Madeirinha River, a tributary of the Roosevelt River (lat. 10° S., long. 61° W.). They were closely related to the *Ramarama,* an almost extinct tribe of the Machadinho River, a left tributary of the Machado River (lat. 9° S., long. 61° W.). Both tribes belonged to the *Tupí-Guaraní* linguistic family.

Matanawí (*Matanaués, Matanaui, Matanau, Mitan(d)ues*).—The *Matanawí* are mentioned for the first time in 1768, near Salto Augusto, on the São Thomé River (lat. 7° S., long. 61° W.). In 1884, they are listed as a tribe of the Rio dos Marmelos and Aripuaná River. At the beginning of the 19th century, the *Matanawí* were attacked by the *Mundurucú* and forced to migrate toward the west, where they joined forces with the *Torá* of the Marmelos. In 1922, there were only 3 *Matanawí* left, from whom Nimuendajú obtained a short vocabulary. Their language is still isolated. Some unknown Indians who live south of the Machadinho River may be remnants of the same tribe.

BIBLIOGRAPHY

Lopes, 1925; Missão Rondón, 1916; Nimuendajú, 1925.

---

[3] Two halved feathers fastened against the shaft by a cotton thread wrapped at regular intervals.

THE MOJO AND BAURE

TRIBAL DIVISIONS

Most of the early literature concerning the Indians of the ancient Province of Mojos, which extended from the Guaporé River to the foot of the Andes, does not always distinguish between the *Arawakan*-speaking *Mojo* and the numerous tribes of other linguistic families, so that the original habitat of the *Mojo* proper cannot be bounded with exactness.

The Mojo.—The bulk of the *Mojo* tribe seems to have been concentrated on the banks of the Mamoré River from its junction with the Río Grande (Guapay River) to about the mouth of the Yacuma River (lat. 9°–12° S., long. 63°–66° W.; map 1, *No. 2;* map 2; map 4).

The *Mojo* were split into small independent groups, which were carefully listed by José Castillo (1906). The southernmost *Mojo* were the *Suberiono,* who had 5 villages on the Río Grande (Guapay), north of Santa Cruz de la Sierra, near the mouth of the Piray River. These *Suberiono,* who numbered 350, were probably an offshoot of another *Suberiono* group of about 300 who lived in the savannas, west of the Mamoré River. A strong group of *Mojo,* including around 500 people, inhabited 10 villages scattered on the Mamoré near its confluence with the Río Grande. The 6 villages of the *Casaboyono* were located at the mouth of the Río Grande. The *Guanapeano* inhabited 1 village and the *Aperucono* 2 villages somewhat east of the river. The *Sebaquereono* lived in 3 villages along the Mamoré River. Seventy people who formed the whole *Moremomo* subtribe were gathered into a single village. Other subtribes along the Mamoré River from north to south were: The *Satirnono, Apereano, Mayuncano, Siyobocono, Cubiquiano, Boseono, Mubocono,* and the *Mopereano.* The *Mariquiono* had 3 villages, 1 on the lower Securé River and 2 in the nearby plains. The *Punuhuana* were the largest subtribe of the *Mojo* and inhabited the region west of the *Mayuncano.* Between the *Punuhuana* and the *Mariquiono* were 3 villages of *Arebocono.*

The Jesuits imposed the *Mojo* language on various small tribes who belonged to different linguistic families. Thus, in 1696, the *Myriana* and other Indians of the Mission of Trinidad had adopted the *Mojo* language. Likewise, *Mojo* became the tongue of the tribes collected in San Ignacio de Loyola and San Francisco Xavier, of the *Churima* of San José de los Maharenos, and of the *Moporoubocono* of San Francisco de Borja.

In 1767, *Mojo* was spoken in the following missions: Loreto (1,200 Indians), Trinidad (100), San Ignacio (1,200), San Xavier (1,500). It also had been spoken in the Missions of San Luis and San José, which had been destroyed before the expulsion of the Jesuits. *Mojo* was still used in the same missions in D'Orbigny's time.

According to D'Orbigny (1839, 2:226), the *Muchojeones* of Carmen de Mojos were a subtribe of the *Mojo* proper.

Hervás (1800–05, 1:248) regards the *Ticomeri* language as a *Mojo* dialect, but elsewhere states that the "majena or maxiena" language of these *Ticomeri* was an isolated language used at San Francisco de Borja.

The Bauré.—The *Bauré* (*Mauré, Chiquimitica*) occupied a fertile country along the Río Blanco, where a village bears their name (Baurés), lat. 13°–15° S., long. 62°–63° W. They also lived along the Itonama (San Miguel) River, along the San Simón River, and in the region between the latter and the Guaporé River. The *Bauré* dialect was in use in the Mission of San Nicolas, San Joaquín, and Concepción (Hervás, 1800–05 1:247–248). There is still a group of presumably wild *Bauré* which lives within two leagues to the southeast of the village of Bauré on Lake Victoria.

Missionaries described the *Bauré* as even more civilized than the other *Mojo* tribes. They lived in large villages, protected by palisades, dressed in cotton garments, and had a well-organized chieftainship (Lettres édifiantes et curieuses, 1780–83, 8:112–113).

Population.—In 1680 the whole *Mojo* nation numbered about 6,000 people distributed among 70 villages, each with an average population of 60 to 80; some contained 100 inhabitants, and 2 or 3 had more than 200. A census taken in 1715 reckons 18,000 inhabitants for the whole province.

HISTORY

Andean influences may have reached the *Mojo* through the channel of the *Mosetene,* who lived between them and the *Aymara. Mojo* merchants visited the former primarily to trade cotton cloth and feathers for metal tools and ornaments. Thus, many Peruvian objects found their way to the plains of Mojos and there, passing from hand to hand, reached the Paraguay River and the Río de la Plata. With these objects traveled tales of the *Inca* Empire and of its wealth. The conquistadors heard them in the marshes of Xarayes at the gate of the Provinces of Chiquitos and Mojos and imagined a fabulous kingdom, the Realm of the Gran Mojo or Paititi, which they located at the source of the rumors, that is, in the plains of Mojos. From 1539 to 1630, countless explorers fought their way across the jungle both from the Andes and Paraguay. In 1580, Lorenzo de Figueroa seems to have reached the land of the *Mojo,* whom he calls *Timbú.* His lieutenant, Juan Torres de Palomino, descended the Guapay River in 1595 and arrived at the country of the *Motilones* or *Torococi,* who undoubtedly were the *Mojo.* A settlement was founded in 1612 in *Mojo* territory. Gonzalo de Solís Holguín attempted in 1617 and 1624 to conquer the *Mojo,* whom he calls *Toro,* but abandoned the undertaking because the land did not correspond to his expectations.

During the first part of the 17th century, the *Mojo* often ascended the Guapay River to obtain from the *Chiriguano* iron tools for which they traded cotton cloth. They formed friendly relations with the Spaniards, which paved the way for the Jesuit missionaries. In 1668, three Jesuit missionaries entered the *Mojo* region but without any great success. In 1675, Fathers José Castillo, Cipriano Barrace, and Pedro Marbán stayed with the *Mojo* for several years, learning their language and planting the first seeds of Christianity. The first mission, Loreto, was founded in 1684, Trinidad in 1687, and San Ignacio in 1689. Father Barrace was murdered by the *Bauré* in 1702. By 1715, there were 15 *Mojo* missions: Loreto, Santa Rosa del Chapare, Trinidad, San Xavier, San Pedro, Exaltación, San Ignacio, San José, San Luis, San Borja, San Pablo, Reyes, Concepción de Baurés, San Juan Bautista de Guarayos, and San Joaquín.

Thanks to the industry of the missionaries and the good disposition of the Indians, the settlements became very prosperous. In 50 years, the Jesuits brought about great changes in the native culture, giving the Indians horses and cattle and teaching them numerous new arts. The silver altars and beautiful carving made by the Indians for the churches still bear witness to the prosperity of the missions.

After the expulsion of the Jesuits in 1767, the missions were given to curates and civil administrators. Thereafter their decadence was rapid. However, the Indians have retained their Christian faith and many of the arts taught to them by the Jesuits. Thanks to their missionaries, the *Mojo* have been able to cope with White civilization.

During the two last centuries, the *Mojo,* ruthlessly exploited and mistreated by the religious and lay authorities, rose on several occasions against the Whites. In 1881, they rebelled at the instigation of a messiah, Andres Guachoco.

At the end of the 19th century and beginning of the 20th century, the *Mojo* were in great demand as boatmen and peons for the rubber companies. A great many were taken into virtual slavery; others died as a result of the mistreatments to which they were subjected.

SOURCES

Our main sources of information on the *Mojo* are the letters and reports of Jesuit missionaries of the 17th and 18th centuries written to their superiors and published in recent years in South American collections or journals, where they have remained buried. Fathers Marbán (1898) and José Castillo (1906) were among the first Whites to settle with the *Mojo,* and they described the culture when it was hardly impaired. Eder's classic work on the *Mojo* ("Descriptio provinciae Mojitorum in regno Peruano," Budapest, 1791) refers to a later period when the *Mojo* were already Christians; yet it contains invaluable material which deserves greater attention. D'Orbigny (1835–47) is our main authority for the postmissionary era.

ARCHEOLOGY OF THE MOJO REGION

The archeology of the *Mojo* region is known mainly through Nordenskiöld's (1913, 1917 b; see also Bennett, 1936) excavations in three mounds (Velarde, Hernmarck, Masicito) near the town of Trinidad, between the Mamoré and Ivari Rivers. In Mound Velarde two stratified layers were discovered. The culture represented by the lower level is characterized by four-footed vessels, modeled rim ornaments, clay ladles and grinders, and absence of handles. The dead were buried in an extended position. A clay seated female figure was also discovered in this stratum. The painted decorations consist mainly of combinations of short spirals, sometimes associated with triangles. The short spiral

PLATE 39.—**Huge trumpets of the Mojos region.** Photographed in La Paz, Bolivia. (Courtesy Grace Line.)

PLATE 40.—**Tiboita and Mojo Indians.**   *Top: Tiboita* man using spear thrower, region of Mojos.   Note cranial deformation.   (After Eder, 1791.)   *Bottom:* Costumes of *Mojo.*   (After D'Orbigny, 1839.)

bears a slight resemblance to the Tiahuanaco Period of Cochabamba and Mizque (Bennett, 1936, p. 396). It is possible, as Nordenskiöld suggests (1917 b), that these cultures were coetaneous.

The material found in the upper layer of Mound Velarde and in Mound Hernmarck, despite great differences in design detail, seems to belong to one culture. It consists mainly of tripod urns, which were used for secondary interment; they were often covered by plain urns or by shallow tripod vessels. In upper Velarde the painted designs are largely geometric, but in Hernmarck there are curvilinear designs which represent stylized faces. Also typical of both are cylindrical clay grinders, ribbed clay grinding platters, three-legged clay stools, clay figurines, and some bone and stone artifacts (Bennett, 1936, p. 405). Some perforated vessels establish a link with the historical *Mojo,* who are known to have used such vessels for preparing chicha.

The culture presented by the finds at Mound Masicito differs somewhat from the other *Mojo* sites.

The pottery is unpainted and decorated by incision stamping, appliqué, pellets and strips, and some modeling. Tripod vessels are again typical. [Bennett, 1936, p. 398.]

The feet are stylized animal feet and possibly heads.

According to Bennett, the chronological sequence is as follows: Lower Velarde (roughly contemporaneous with Mizque-Tiahuanaco, derived Tiahuanaco), upper Velarde, Hernmarck (with Hernmarck possibly somewhat older than upper Velarde), Masicito.

The Masicito pottery resembles somewhat the incised ware decorated with appliqué strips and with modeled rims found by Nordenskiöld at Chimay, below Covendo (Nordenskiöld, 1924 b, pp. 229-234). North of Covendo, at Rurrenabaque, were found three- and four-legged ware, painted and incised, appliqué modeled vessels, and a large effigy urn.

Some light is thrown on the ancient cultures of the region of Santa Cruz de la Sierra by Nordenskiöld's discovery on the Palacios River (Province of Sará) of two groups of urn burials for adults and children. The eight urns unearthed in one cemetery have a conical or ovoid body and a collar decorated with corrugations. They are often covered by urns of the same type. One urn which comes from another site has a conical body, a high collar with corrugations and four quarter-moon side lugs. The mortuary ware consists mainly of bowls with solid bulging tripod legs and with a decoration of appliqué strips. With the exception of the corrugations on the rims, neither the urns nor the bowls show the slightest resemblance to any type of *Guarani* ware. Direct urn burial is not in itself sufficient proof of the *Guarani* origin of the finds. A few specimens of pottery discovered at Guayabas, South of Santa Cruz (Métraux, 1933), suggest with their appliqué decoration and their tripod feet the material of Masicito and of Chimay. (See figure, Handbook, vol. 5.)

CULTURE

SUBSISTENCE ACTIVITIES

Farming.—The *Mojo* were proficient farmers who cultivated sweet manioc (yuca), maize, sweet potatoes, pumpkins, gourds, beans, peanuts, arracacha, pepper, papayas, bananas, sugarcane, tobacco, and cotton. Eder (1791, p. 99) mentions the use of poisonous manioc for food in the Province of Mojos, but his statement is not verified by other sources.

The *Mojo* cleared their fields in forests which were not flooded during the rainy season. The Spaniards who penetrated the country with Solís Holguín were amazed at the size of the plantations and by the wide roads that crossed them. Peanuts were sown preferably along the sandy beaches.

The *Bauré* are said to have cultivated on communal ground the plants from which they made their drinks.

The *Mojo* and the *Bauré* supplemented their vegetable diet with wild fruits, especially those of palms.

Hunting.—Two types of hunting were practiced by the *Mojo;* one was characteristic of the jungle, the other of the open plains. In the first, individual hunters stalked monkeys and birds in the gallery forests along the rivers. In the second, large groups of men led by the cacique, whose authority was absolute for the occasion, hunted deer herds communally. They pursued the animals with dogs trained to obey the command of the hunters, or drove them toward ambushes by means of grass fires.

During the flood season, a very profitable hunting method was to surround an island on which game had taken refuge. Some of the party took vantage positions on high places, others remained in their canoes, and still others invaded the island from all sides making as much noise as possible with trumpets, drums, and packs of dogs. The panic-stricken animals, especially the deer, ran to the shore, where they were killed by the boatmen, who struck them with sticks, lassoed them, stabbed them, or jumped on their backs and drowned them.

Hunters who stalked deer wore white shirts and headdresses shaped like a bird common in the plains; when they were sufficiently close they shot them with bows and arrows.

The *Mojo* attacked jaguars either with two spears or with bows and arrows. However, it was considered safest to lure them to the river bank or into the water by imitating their call with a calabash and then to shower them with arrows from a canoe. They also treed jaguars with dogs and shot them with blowguns. The *Bauré* also caught jaguars in pitfalls. It was the chief's privilege to shoot them. The killing of a jaguar brought unusual honors to the hunter, and the event was celebrated with dancing, drum beating, and other ceremonies.

Traps and snares are mentioned, but not described.

After the *Mojo* had acquired horses, they began to use the lasso to hunt game, even jaguars. They dragged the animal behind their horses and then dismounted to tie it up.

All of those who had participated in a hunting expedition received an equal share of the game.

Bird hunting.—The *Mojo* shot birds, especially ducks, with blowguns from blinds built where the birds roosted. They also threw gourds on a lagoon so that when the ducks had grown accustomed to their presence, the fowler could cover his head with a gourd and approach the birds, seize them by the feet, and twist their necks underwater.

Fishing.—Fishing was one of the most rewarding activities. Annually, the receding floods left millions of fish stranded on the land or concentrated in small pools were the Indians killed them at leisure with cudgels and spears. More commonly, fish were shot with bows and arrows. Fish were also attracted at night by torches fixed to the prows of canoes and were speared with tridents.

The *Mojo* drugged fish with a creeper (*Paullinia pinnata*). Another creeper, even more powerful, was used only after a period of fasting.

Nets were introduced by the missionaries, but the Indians found them of little use, for the rivers were full of branches and trees which tore the meshes. In pre-Columbian times, the Indians made a barrier of weeds in a lagoon and pushed it against the shore, where they caught the trapped fish with their bare hands.

They also attached a cow skin perpendicularly to the gunwale of a canoe, and, by striking the water with poles, they made the fish jump against the hide so that they fell into the canoe.

When a swarm of small fish migrated, the *Mojo* caught them with conical baskets, open at both ends, which they threw over the fish.

The *Mojo* also built weirs across the outlets of lagoons and placed a fish trap in each opening of the weir.

Cooking.—Manioc tubers were boiled or roasted in ashes. Bitter manioc tubers were sliced thin and dried in the sun, or they were grated, dried, and roasted in a clay pan. Large game was roasted.

Eder states that the Indians relished certain worms which they collected during May and June. They crushed them with their fingers, dried them in front of their houses, and boiled them until they formed a blackish mush.

The only condiment was the ash of certain plants mixed with cayenne pepper. Mineral salt was traded from the *Mosetene*.

At meals, the *Mojo* sat on the ground around a single large dish. Meat was served on mats.

Domestication.—At the beginning of the 17th century, the *Mojo* reared native ducks, but had not yet obtained the chickens which later were so numerous in their villages. They ate ducks or chickens only on such special occasions as the end of drinking bouts, or when a man wanted to treat friends who had helped him till his field.

Like many tropical Indians, the *Mojo* changed to bright red the natural color of the wings and tail feathers of the tame parrots by plucking them and filling the wounds with the blood of a frog (*Dendrobates tinctorius*) and then coating the bird's skin with wax (tapirage process) (Eder, 1791, p. 152).

The dog was found by the Jesuits among the *Mojo*. Its resemblance to the Spanish greyhound suggests that it had been obtained from the inhabitants of Santa Cruz, with whom the *Mojo* had active trade relations, or from Indians in closer contact with the Spaniards. These dogs were extremely well trained for hunting and, though they had individual masters to whom they were attached, they obeyed any person during the collective hunting expedition.

Cattle were introduced among the *Mojo* by Father Cipriano Barrace at the end of the 17th century; horses were brought soon afterward. Within 50 years, the *Mojo* became excellent horsemen, as skillful as the gauchos with the lasso. They rode bareback, without a bridle and bit, guiding their horses by a thong attached around the animal's lower jaw. Cattle increased to immense herds and roamed in thousands through the plains and in the forests. Yet, in spite of favorable conditions, the *Mojo* did not become herdsmen as did the *Goajiro*, and even now they do not drink milk. Wild cattle became a favorite game animal.

HOUSES

Some *Mojo* villages must have been unusually large, even allowing for exaggeration in the Spanish claims that some of them contained up to 400 houses. Perhaps kitchens and drinking houses or temples, which were separate buildings, were enumerated with dwellings. Marbán (1898, p. 132) estimated that each village had only 30 to 100 people, only a few having as many as 200.

Floods, which cover the Mojos plains during 4 months, often forced the Indians to build villages on elevated land. These mounds, now covered with potsherds and studded with burials, were not made artificially, although refuse increased their height. If, as was usually the case, *Mojo* settlements were built along river banks, when flood waters invaded their houses, the Indians erected platforms and covered them with soil on which to build cooking fires. Some villages were near lagoons, a considerable distance from the rivers. The houses were grouped around a central plaza.

The villages were connected by large causeways about 9 feet (2.7 m.) wide and about 2 feet (0.6 m.) high, the remains of which Nordenskiöld (1913, p. 225) and Allan Holmberg discovered near Mound Velarde and

Mound Hernmarck and between Baurés and the Rio Blanco and near Mound Ibiato (near Trinidad).

Bauré villages were surrounded by palisades with loopholes for archers and by a ditch; for further protection pitfalls were concealed in the paths.

Mojo dwellings were round; their cook houses were rectangular sheds. The dwellings were about 15 feet (4.5 m.) in diameter and of the same height. The walls were of wattle-and-daub, about 3 feet (1 m.) in height; the conical, thatched roof was supported by a center post. The doorway, which was so low that one had to crawl in, was closed by a skin or by reeds fastened between parallel sticks.

In each hut there were six or seven cotton hammocks, wooden benches, mats on which women sat, and large jars for storage of small objects.

Under Jesuit influence, the *Mojo* adopted gabled houses, with a thatched roof of motacu palms and walls of reeds. Today, only children sleep in hammocks; adults use ox skins as beds.

DRESS AND ORNAMENTS

Long cotton or bark-cloth shirts (cushma), often elaborately decorated, were used by *Mojo* men in the premissionary era (pl. 40, *bottom*), but apparently this garment became longer and was more consistently worn after the Fathers insisted on modesty. Men fastened their shirts around the waist with a string and, in more recent times, with a cotton belt woven with red, blue, or yellow stripes.

Men wore a short silver tube through the septum of the nose, two small silver or tin nails through the alae, a silver labret in the lower lip, and two round tin nails in the ear lobes. They also hung three or four strings of beads from the ears. Before European contact, *Mojo* labrets probably were made of rock crystal like those of the *Bauré*.

Men tied up their long hair with cotton strings which they hid under strips of bark; between the threads, they fixed parrot feathers. Feather headdresses varied from a few feathers attached over the forehead to gigantic diadems of bright tail feathers trimmed with small feathers of various colors, mounted on a basketry frame covered with a mosaic of short feathers. One of these headdresses, used a few years ago, consisted of 300 tail feathers, plucked from 85 birds, mainly *Ostinops decumanus*, ara, and other kinds of parrots. These feathers, to which were attached the wing-shells of multicolored beetles, were fixed to a basketry hat and to a row of bamboo splinters to form a large semicircular screen over the nape. The ends of the long tail feathers were covered with pieces of bird skin.

Men also wore silver circlets and bracelets. Heavy necklaces of small shell disks, seeds, and jaguar or monkey teeth were worn around the neck or over the shoulders. A silver, tin, or shell plate was suspended over the chest. The *Mojo* girded themselves with belts fringed with strings of beads and silver tubes. When dancing they covered their buttocks with a large net to which deer hoofs and shells were attached.

A woman's costume consisted only of a narrow loincloth, similar to that of the *Paressi*. Young girls went naked until puberty. Later, under missionary influence, women adopted the men's shirt, but it was longer and without slits along the legs. Women wore thick necklaces, bracelets, and ear pendants of beads, and, during festivals, covered their shoulders with a netlike shawl or collar made of metal tubes and beads, from which hung bells, medals, and crosses.

Women tied their long hair with cotton thread and trimmed it with ribbons.

Both sexes painted themselves with urucú and genipa. The women traced on their male relatives' bodies elaborate designs in the same style as those decorating their pottery.

Eder (1791, p. 217) reports that some Indians of Mojos tattooed themselves with thorns or fish teeth, using genipa as a pigment. The tattooed patterns, he writes, represented "caimans, monkeys, and fish."

TRANSPORTATION AND COMMUNICATIONS

Some of the wide causeways connecting the *Mojo* villages remained above water level during the annual floods. In the dry season, the ditches from which the soil had been taken to make the embankments formed canals which the natives navigated in canoes, especially at harvest time when they brought home their crops. One of these canals, 2 km. (1¼ mi.) long and 6 to 7 m. (20 to 24 ft.) wide, connects the Mamoré River with the Urupuru River. Another canal 5 km. (3 mi.) long and 2 m. (6 ft.) wide unites the Chumano and the San Juan River, from which another canal leads to the Itonama River.

Ancient dugouts are not described. Modern craft have a sharp bow and a flat stern. Paddles are 5 feet (1.3 m.) long and have a crotch at the proximal end.

Eder (1791, p. 75) also describes balsas or reed rafts with an upturned prow and stern, on which the Indians—he does not say which ones—took long trips. The pelota or bull-boat was also known to the *Mojo*—at least in the 18th century. An ox hide was stretched over a frame of reeds or rods and the sides were folded to stand out of the water.

They built bridges over narrow streams by lassoing bamboos or slender palm trees and bending them until they touched the ground on the opposite side. The arch was then covered with transverse sticks so that the women and children could climb to the other shore.

MANUFACTURES

Bark cloth.—Bark cloth was fabricated from large pieces of bibosi bark measuring 3 by 12 feet (1 by 4 m.) which were beaten with a wooden grooved mallet. The bark strips were then washed, wrung out, and dried in the sun.

Basketry.—The *Mojo* made boxes of reeds twined together with cotton. The modern *Mojo* make flat circular trays and round baskets with overlapping lids in twilled basketry. They also have large carrying baskets with a hexagonal weave (lattice type).

Spinning.—To spin cotton, the woman sat on the ground, rested t. distal end of the spindle between the large and second toe of her left foot, and rolled the spindle with her right hand along her right leg. The skein was held with the left hand.

Weaving.—*Mojo* textiles were of cotton. They used a variety of cotton, naturally reddish, to produce patterns on their fabrics. Modern *Mojo* and *Bauré* weave on the vertical loom.

Wood carving.—Wood carving was probably practiced by the *Mojo* before their contact with Europeans, for it is improbable that they could have developed so suddenly the skill for which the Jesuits praised them.

Featherwork.—Featherwork seems to have been the *Mojo's* greatest artistic accomplishment. Down was plucked from the breast and from under the wings of brightly colored birds and was sewed on cloth so skillfully that it resembled natural plumage. The feather mosaics represented animals and people. When dancing, they held these feather pictures in their hands and shook them as if they were small shields.

Pottery.—Early sources highly praise *Mojo* pottery. It included jars, bowls, dishes, and cooking pots. There is little doubt that the ware found by Nordenskiöld (1913) near Trinidad belongs to the historical *Mojo*.

Clay was tempered with the ashes of sponges (*Parmula batesii*) containing small spiculae, which gave the material a remarkable resistance.

Weapons.—*Mojo* bows made of chonta wood were about 5 feet (1.5 m.) long. They were often trimmed with feathers and wrappings of cotton threads. Arrows were tipped with a lanceolate bamboo blade or with a rod to which a bone head or the spike of a stingray was fastened with wax. War arrows were sometimes provided with a hollow nut which made them whistle when flying. Feathering seems to have been of the cemented type.

The *Mojo* used the spear thrower for hunting and war (pl. 40, *top*). It consisted of a narrow board with a hook to engage the butt of the dart.

The *Mojo* blowgun was, like that of the *Huari,* a long bamboo tube straightened by heating it over a fire. The darts, made of palm splinters, were kept in a bamboo quiver. The poison, undoubtedly curare, was extracted from the coropi creeper. The creeper was shredded, the fibers sprinkled with hot water, and the decoction was slowly filtered through cotton and then boiled on a slow fire until it became quite thick. The mass was dried in the sun. To use the poison, it was moistened with tobacco juice.

Spears seem to have been adopted after European contact, but slings and bolas appear to have been used long before the Conquest. The *Mojo* attacked the first Spanish expeditions with spear throwers, slings, and bolas. By the end of the 18th century, the *Mojo* used bolas of lead. Clay pellets bristling with poisoned thorns are said to have been used as missiles for slings.

In battle, the *Mojo* and *Bauré* carried a shield made of reeds firmly twined together with cotton threads and trimmed with feathers.

Tools.—A few stone axes were found by Nordenskiöld in his excavations.

Metallurgy.—The silver or tin ornaments—diadems, bracelets, disks, and tubes—were made of pieces of metal cut from bowls and dishes traded from the Spaniards. The only tools of the smiths were knives, scissors, and stone hammers. They did not smelt ores, but occasionally melted down the purchased silver or tin. All metal objects were painstakingly polished.

SOCIAL ORGANIZATION

The village community was the basic social unit, though subtribes sometimes consisted of two to three villages. Each village had a chief whose authority did not transcend its limits. Nothing is known about other social groups. A tendency toward class stratification is revealed in the existence of war captives who, though well treated and allowed to marry the daughters of their captors, were regarded with some contempt. The importance of this incipient servile class was perhaps enhanced by the slave trade, one of the first consequences of the establishment of the Spaniards in eastern Bolivia. The colonists of Santa Cruz, who were in need of labor for their fields and for the mines of the Highlands, not only raided the neighboring tribes for that purpose, but also induced Indians beyond their reach to provide them with captives for whom they paid iron tools and glass beads. So great was the desire for metal, which eased the daily struggle for life, that the Indians, lacking other commodities acceptable to the Whites, soon turned into slavers and thus had new incentives for their intertribal warfare.

POLITICAL ORGANIZATION

Chieftainship was probably hereditary, though this has been doubted by some of our early sources.

The authority of the *Mojo* chief (achiaco) depended greatly on his personality. Respect shown to the chief was very conspicuous: "They respect their chiefs," says Castillo (1906, p. 337), "as good children do their fathers, even if the 'cacique' is a young man, as he sometimes is." If he came on a visit with other men, he was immediately offered a bench or a hammock to sit on. Respect did not always imply actual power, and, among the *Mojo*, chiefs could interfere with the activities of the rest of the people only in certain instances. Those chiefs who were at the same time shamans had a far stronger position.

The enforcement of internal peace was one of the main functions of the chief. On one occasion Father Castillo saw the village chief "boxing and kicking" two individuals who, in a drinking spree, had killed a man. The decision to shift the village rested with the chief, who frequently decided to move to another place when some personal misfortune had befallen him.

The chief had greater power during war and communal hunting parties. When the men of the village cooperated in a game drive, the chief assumed complete control and required immediate obedience. He had to insure the success of a war expedition not only by his skill and courage, but also by his strict observance of several taboos. Thus, he had to fast in behalf of the community and could not comb or even cut his hair.

The *Bauré* chief, called "arama," bequeathed his title to his eldest son if he had been born of a noble woman, that is, if his mother were a chief's daughter. His subjects provided him everything he needed, and if he wanted to get rid of somebody, his wish was complicd with immediately. To curtail his power, an old man was selected every year, at harvest time, to remind him of his duties and to warn him against excesses.

LIFE CYCLE

Childbirth.—Pregnant women, shortly before delivery, were confined in special huts outside the village, a precaution supposed to prevent miscarriage (Castillo, 1906, p. 360; Marbán, 1898, p. 155). Those who suffered a miscarriage were immediately drowned lest dysentery epidemics spread through the village (Orellana, 1906, p. 12). If a mother died during or after childbirth, the baby was buried alive, for a child might be nursed only by its own mother. If the delivery was difficult, relatives implored the assistance of a spirit by playing the flute and singing. Normal deliveries were always accompanied by the recital of charms and the sacrifice of ducks.

Of twins, only the first to be born was regarded as the child of a man, and the paternity of the second was attributed to a spirit. The mother of twins was held in such respect that her husband left the house and treated her with the greatest consideration. Twins had to marry other twins or remain single (Eder, 1791, pp. 245–246).

Marriage.—Marriages do not seem to have been celebrated with any ceremony. Residence was patrilocal; according to a single source, it was matrilocal. Polygyny existed but was rare. Infant betrothal is reported for a few unspecified tribes of the region. Marriage with a woman and her daughter is also mentioned.

In commiting adultery a woman endangered her husband's luck in hunting and even his life; she was, therefore, severely punished by her

husband or even by her own relatives. The lover, however, was unmolested until the offended husband in the turmoil of a drinking bout
could pick a fight with him, tear off his ornaments, and thrash him.

Conjugalties were brittle.

Funeral customs.—Little is known about this subject. The *Mojo*
buried their dead in shallow graves on which they placed bows, arrows,
maize, and beer. Secondary burial in urns occurs in the upper levels of
Velarde, Hernmarck and Masicito Mounds (p. 411).

ESTHETIC AND RECREATIONAL ACTIVITIES

Dances.—Dances performed in the missions in the 18th century still
followed the pre-Hispanic pattern. The male dancers, wearing spectacular
feather headdresses or disguised with monkey or bird skins, formed two
facing lines, but each man danced according to his own fancy, moving to
and fro with slow steps, which corresponded to movements of his hands.
Some dancers accompanied themselves with flutes and gourd rattles and
turned their heads from side to side. At times they stamped on the
ground to make their anklets of nuts jingle. The women danced apart
in a house. Holding each other's hands, they turned in a circle, singing
a monotonous song and stooping almost to the ground after each stanza.
Extravagantly dressed clowns, each with a drum slung over his shoulder,
danced at one side.

Modern *Mojo* still execute ancient dances at church festivals. The
most famous of these is that of the macheteros, or sword men, who
brandish their wooden weapons in front of the altar before laying them
down with their feather diadems at the foot of the crucifix.

Musical instruments.—Native *Mojo* instruments as listed by the
ancient sources were: Fruit-shell jingles attached to the ankles, jingle
rattles of deer hoofs, shells hanging from the lower edge of nets worn
around the waist, gourd rattles, a large drum (probably the hollow-log
drum) beaten with a single stick, panpipes consisting of a single row of
reeds held between two sticks, a trumpet or clarinet composed of an
elongated gourd and a "flute," and long funnel-shaped bark trumpets.

The large trumpets, the gourds, and a wind instrument described as "a
big hollow nut into which they blew" were sacred instruments taboo to
women, and they were played in a ceremonial parade, "The jumping of
the caiman."

Modern *Mojo* have transformed their bark trumpets into gigantic panpipes by joining together 11 bark trumpets of various lengths (pl. 39).
Their small skin-headed drums belong probably to the postmissionary
period.

Games and sports.—The favorite sport was a ball game. The rubber
ball was made by coating a clay core with a thick layer of rubber, removing

the clay through a hole, inflating the ball with air, and adding several other layers of liquid rubber.

The ball was struck either with the head or the feet. When the feet were used, the two contesting teams were 25 feet (7.6 m.) apart, but when they butted the ball with the head the interval was about 42 feet (about 13 m.). Players protected their legs with bandages.

Drinking bouts.—Chicha was made of roasted maize pounded and partly chewed. For making manioc beer, the Indians crushed the tubers, sifted them, and allowed the mass to ferment. This beer was sifted through perforated vessels, many of which were discovered by Nordenskiöld (1913) in his excavations at Mound Velarde and Mound Hernmarck.

Fermented drinks were also brewed with all kinds of fruits, especially pineapples. Chicha was served in gourds which, on festive occasions, were trimmed with feathers and decorated with figures. On a long journey, the *Mojo* always took a provision of fermented manioc mass which they mixed with water to prepare a stimulating and nourishing beverage.

Most religious ceremonies were followed by drinking bouts. Each community gave 10 or 12 feasts a year, but its members were frequently invited to those organized by other villages in the region.

A feast, religious or secular, was announced the day before by the beating of a large and a small drum. The guests gathered in the drinking house and sat on wooden benches and on hammocks between rows of large maize chicha jars, buried to the neck. During the party, the intoxicated men boasted about their past deeds or challenged their enemies. Disputes were often settled by a conventional wrestling match. The wronged person grabbed the hair or the ear of the offender and did his best to throw him to the ground; if he succeeded, the quarrel ended and harmony was restored.

Female singers and dancers were admitted in the hall, and married women were allowed to drink beer. When the rejoicing had reached a high pitch, the guests, as a mark of courtesy, seized the host's wife and married daughters, wrapped them entirely in skirts, covered their heads with hoods, and took them to the temple, where these women made their entrance singing and dancing. There they were offered chicha and were allowed to dance for a while with the men.

RELIGION

Mojo religion is imperfectly known except for a few aspects, such as the Jaguar cult and shamanism.

According to the missionaries, "gods"—perhaps spirits—presided over water, fish, clouds, lightning, crops, war, and jaguars, but there is some indication that the *Mojo* had functioning nature gods. The tutelary deity of the village of the *Moremono* was the Star god, Arayriqui. The Rain goddess was the Rainbow and the Sun's wife, and to her tall trees were dedicated. Shamans consulted the moon, who appeared to them in the shape of a woman. Some gods or spirits were closely associated with the territory of a subtribe or a village. The *Saturiano* had a divine protector who lived in a lagoon near their village. The Indians were desinclined to abandon their native district because their ancestors were supposed to have come from some place located within their territory, a belief which was and still is common among the mountain Indians of Perú.

In daily life, the *Mojo* were more concerned with the swarm of spirits (acsane) who pervaded the world than with the higher gods. To these invisible spirits was offered every morsel of food that fell to the ground.

Cult.—In every village there was what the Spaniards called a "beve-dero," a drinking hut in which religious ceremonies and drinking bouts were held. There were kept such trophies as the skulls of enemies and jaguar heads and paws. Very likely, the sacred musical instruments were deposited in this hut, as among the *Paressi* and other *Arawakan* tribes.

The building of a feast hall was surrounded with many rites and taboos. The workers fasted for several months; during the construction no woman could enter the building; and certain foods could not be eaten within the structure.

Castillo (1906, p. 353) regards the offering of chicha to the gods or spirits, who were thought to appear in person and to drink, as the main feature of the cult. The priests or shamans uttered long prayers or charms.

The appearance of the new moon was considered to be a propitious time for religious ceremonies. The crowd assembled in the sacred hall at dawn where they uttered "loud cries to soften the invisible powers." They spent the whole day fasting. At night the priests cut their hair and adorned themselves with red and yellow feathers. Jars of liquor were brought as offerings to the gods; the priests drank and gave the rest to the people who sang and danced through the night.

The jaguar cult.—Jaguars were regarded with religious awe and were the object of a cult. Men who had been wounded by a jaguar formed a special group of shamans called camacoy and performed the rites connected with jaguar spirits. For a year or two before assuming their new status, they observed chastity and various food taboos, particularly those against eating fish and cayenne pepper. Any violation of these rules was punished by the jaguars.

If a jaguar-shaman learned by supernatural means that a jaguar might prey on a community, he warned the people to bring offerings of food and chicha to his hut at night. The jaguar-shaman entered the house alone playing a special type of flute. He pretended to have an interview with the jaguar from which he would come bleeding and with his clothes torn off as if he had been clawed by the beast. Some shamans were credited with the power of changing themselves into jaguars when offerings were not brought to them.

The belongings of a person killed by a jaguar were consecrated to the animal, and it became the rightful owner of them. Whoever kept for himself even a small part of these possessions was sooner or later doomed to be devoured by a jaguar (Eder, 1791, p. 247). The killing of a jaguar gave great prestige to the successful hunter and was followed by elaborate ceremonies. The Indians danced and beat a drum around the slain animal for a whole night and ate its flesh. The paws and cleaned skull trimmed with cotton ornaments were deposited in the drinking hall among other trophies.

The hunter himself retired for several days to the temple, where he observed many taboos. The jaguar-shaman offered libations on his behalf to the Jaguar god and revealed to him the secret name of the jaguar, which the hunter was to bear henceforward. A drinking bout, during which the hunter trimmed his hair, ended the feast and the seclusion.

Priests and shamans.—According to Castillo (1906, p. 352), the *Mojo* had both ceremonial priests and shamans. Actually, it is more likely that individuals with the same training performed different functions in which they might specialize according to their own inclination or the occasion.

The generic term for "shaman" was tiharauqui, a word more aptly translated by "clairvoyant." These tiharauqui, men or women, entered their profession under supernatural compulsion, manifested by some accident which deprived them momentarily of their senses or brought them near death. Unequivocal references to such persons offering beer to the gods or taking the initiative in religious ceremonies makes it more evident that the so-called "priests" were actually shamans. Nevertheless, it is difficult to reconcile the important role of women in religion with the strict prohibition against their seeing the caiman dance or the sacred musical instruments.

Fasting on behalf of the community was one of their functions. During their fasting periods, they had to refrain from eating fish, drinking chicha, and smoking, and they had to observe chastity.

To interview the spirits, shamans drank a decoction prepared from a plant called "marari," similar to our verbena, which caused for 24 hours a general condition of excitement characterized by insomnia and pains.

Besides their function at the temples, shamans had to discover thieves, disclose the whereabouts of stolen objects and reveal secrets (Eder, 1791, pp. 246–247). The consultation of the shaman with the spirits was often conceived of as a fight in which the shaman forced the spirit to answer his question.

Treatment of diseases.—Diseases were ascribed to spirits without whose collaboration they could not be cured. The shaman, when consulted, drank marari in order to discuss the matter with his familiar spirit. Usually the spirit asked for presents before he would reveal the cause of the illness and the appropriate treatment.

A common treatment, if the drugs suggested by the spirits failed to relieve the sick man, was to extract the disease by repeated massages, by tying the body, and by sucking out the pathogenic objects (worms, feathers, tobacco leaves). Blowing tobacco smoke over the patient was also part of the cure (Eder, 1791, pp. 254–255).

Serpents, visible only to shamans—hence their name "clairvoyants"— also were responsible for many diseases, which, if our sources are correct, were treated by rubbing the foam of a root against the chest, shoulders, and stomach of the patient (Castillo, 1906, p. 353; Marbán, 1898, p. 153). Patients who complained of heart trouble received from the shaman a stone to replace the ailing organ (Eder, 1791, p. 255).

MYTHOLOGY

A myth recorded among the *Mojo* a few years ago probably contains references to the Creator and perhaps also has elements of the Trickster cycle. The gluttonous Moconomoco, father of men, ate all the seeds and then drowned in a river. When the eagle told the famished men where Moconomoco's body was, they pulled it out of the water and the "hornero" bird opened its stomach, where all the seeds were found and recovered (Pauly, 1928, p. 160).

In the creation myths of the *Mojo,* the ancestors of each subtribe originated in some spot located within the limits of their own district.

Partial eclipses were interpreted as ailments of the Sun or the Moon, and the total disappearance of these luminaries as their temporary death. The *Mojo* also believed in a celestial Jaguar, father of all the terrestrial jaguars, who ate the moon. Constellations were named after animals: jaguar, deer, alligator, bear, and so on. The *Mojo* had stories in which the celestial Jaguar pursued and attacked the celestial deer. In one of their stellar myths, the rhea, greedy for food on the earth, lost its tail feathers when these were pulled out by another animal at the very moment it was about to jump through a hole in the sky. Ordinary stars were the children of the Sun and the Moon (Eder, 1791, pp. 56–57; Castillo 1906, p. 349).

BIBLIOGRAPHY

Adam and Leclerc, 1880; Almanach de Lima (*see* Southey, 1817–22) ; Altamirano, 1891; Argomosa, 1906; Arlet, 1781; Bennett, 1936; Caballero, 1933; Castillo, 1906; D'Orbigny, 1835–47, 1839; Eder, 1791; Eguiluz, 1884; Garriga, 1906; Hervás, 1800–05, vol. 1; Keller-Leuzinger, 1874; Lettres édifiantes et curieuses, 1780–83; Marbán, 1898; Mathews, 1879; Maurtua, 1906, vols. 9 and 10; Métraux, 1933, 1942, 1943; Nordenskiöld, 1910 a, 1910 b, 1913, 1917 b, 1924 b; Orellana, 1906; Pauly, 1928; René-Moreno, 1888; Rosario, 1682; Southey, 1817–22.

THE CANICHANA, MÓVIMA, CAYUVAVA, AND ITONAMA

THE CANICHANA

TERRITORY AND HISTORY

The *Canichana* (*Canisi, Canechi, Kanisiana*) formed by themselves an independent linguistic group. Before the Jesuits collected them in the Mission of San Pedro on the upper Machupo River, the *Canichana* had lived along the Mamoré River and around the headwaters of the Machupo River and along its lower course down to the mission of San Joaquín (map 1, *No. 2;* map 2; map 4). They had about 70 villages in the region between lat. 13° and 14° S. and long. 64° and 65° W.

The *Canichana* were visited in 1693 by Father Augustín Zapata, who estimated their number at 4,000 to 5,000. In 1695, they expressed their willingness to be gathered in a mission, which was founded two years later with about 1,200 Indians (Arlet, 1781). Even after 100 years of disciplined mission life, the *Canichana* retained their warlike disposition. They rose against the Spanish authorities in 1801 and 1820, and in the last rebellion burned the building containing the Jesuit archives.

A census taken in 1780 put the population of San Pedro at 1,860; another census of 1797, at 2,544. According to D'Orbigny (1839, 2:244), in 1831 there were still 1,939 *Canichana*. Their present number is unknown.

CULTURE

Farming was less important in *Canichana* economy than hunting and fishing. The tribe caught caimans, which they relished, by passing a noose around their necks and dragging them to the shore, where other Indians killed them with axes, or else a man crawled toward the caiman holding a stick sharpened at both ends which he thrust into the animal's gaping mouth. The prey was dragged ashore by means of a cord attached to the stick.

Villages were protected by palisades.

When first visited by missionaries, both sexes went naked, but in the missionary era they were forced to wear cotton or bark-cloth shirts. The *Canichana* were armed with bows and arrows and spears. In all probability, they were acquainted with the spear thrower.

Girls fasted 8 days upon reaching puberty, which was celebrated by a drinking bout. Polygyny was widely spread.

The *Canichana* were feared as a warlike tribe and were the scourge of their neighbors, the *Moré, Cayuvava,* and *Itonama.* Missionaries always refer to the *Canichana* as fierce cannibals.

Drinking bouts were arranged as a reward for those who had helped a man clear a field. Fermented beverages were prepared with various fruits.

Among the *Canichana,* Father Zapata (1906, p. 26) heard a version of the wide-spread myth of the Amazons and of the pygmies.

BIBLIOGRAPHY

Arlet, 1781; Créqui-Montfort and Rivet, 1913 d; D'Orbigny, 1839; Eguiluz, 1884; Heath, 1833; René-Moreno, 1888; Zapata, 1906.

THE MÓVIMA
TERRITORY AND HISTORY

Linguistically, the *Móvima* represent an isolated family. Their primitive home was on the left side of the Mamoré River and along the Yacuma River (map 1, *No. 2;* map 2). They were settled by the Jesuits in the missions of San Luis and Borja on the upper Maniqui River, a tributary of the Mamoré River (lat. 13°–15° S., long. 65°–66° W.). The Mission of Santa Ana, near the junction of the Yacuma and Rapulo Rivers, consisted also of *Móvima.* In one of the early 17th-century accounts of eastern Bolivia, written by Gregorio de Bolívar (1906, p. 218), the *Móvima* (spelled *Moyma*) are placed down the Himana River (Mamoré River). In 1709, they killed Father Baltazar de Espinosa. In the second half of the last century, a few *Móvima* families who had escaped from Santa Ana dwelled on the Apéré (Mato) River. It seems that as late as 1908 a few independent *Móvima* still lived on the upper Rapulo River (Nordenskiöld, 1922, p. 76).

In 1749, there were 1,630 *Móvima* in the Mission of San Luis and 1,300 in the Mission of San Borja. In 1767, the population of Santa Ana was about 2,000; that of San Borja, 1,200; and that of Santos Reyes, 1,200. In 1831, there remained 1,238 *Móvima.*

CULTURE

The *Móvima* were fishermen, hunters, and farmers. In recent times, those of the Yacuma River went in the dry season to the Mamoré River to sow beans and peanuts on the sandy beaches. They traveled in dugouts 30 feet (about 10 m.) long, by 16 to 18 inches (40 to 45 cm.) wide. Their weapons were bows and arrows. The feathering of their arrows was of the wrapped (Arara) type, and the butt of the shaft was strengthened with a wooden plug. Formerly, the *Móvima* seem to have used the spear thrower.

The last *Móvima* seen by Nordenskiöld (1922, p. 76) were well-to-do agriculturists and stock raisers. They had abandoned most of their native culture except for a few items, such as clay pans supported over the fire on three clay stumps, and bows and arrows.

BIBLIOGRAPHY

Balzán, 1894; Bolívar, 1906; Cardús, 1886; Créqui-Montfort and Rivet, 1917–20; D'Orbigny, 1839; Giglioli, 1906; Gonçalves da Fonseca, 1826; Nordenskiöld, 1922.

THE CAYUVAVA

TERRITORY AND HISTORY

The former habitat of the *Cayuvava* was the western side of the Mamoré River, 15 leagues above its junction with the Guaporé River (map 1, *No. 2;* map 2). These Indians were scattered in small settlements along the main course of the Mamoré River and along several of its small left tributaries from lat. 12° to 13° S. and long. 65° to 67° W.

The *Cayuvava* were discovered in 1693 by the Jesuit Missionary, Father Augustín Zapata. They then lived in large villages, each with a population which is said to have varied from 1,800 to 2,000 inhabitants. Father Zapata saw seven such villages. The *Cayuvava* were concentrated by the Jesuits in the Mission of Exaltación, on the Mamoré River, below its junction with the Yacuma River. In 1749, there were about 3,000 *Cayuvava;* in 1831, some 2,073; and in 1909, only 100.

CULTURE

The ancient *Cayuvava* are described as good farmers who raised peanuts, sweet manioc, maize, and other plants. Their weapons were bows and arrows and chonta wood spears, the latter tipped with a sharp bone and trimmed with feathers. At the beginning of the present century, little of the original culture remained, but they still wore bark-cloth tunics and still fished with open-top conical baskets which were thrown over the fish in shallow places. *Cayuvava* men filed their incisor teeth, a custom rare in South America and perhaps of African origin.

In the 17th century, the seven *Cayuvava* villages were apparently under the rule of a single chief. In the Mission of Exaltación, the *Cayuvava* were divided into eight groups, corresponding perhaps to former tribes.

In 1695, Father Zapata found in the region occupied by the *Cayuvava* a large village with streets and a central plaza where the inhabitants, dressed in luxurious cloaks and covered with feathers, were gathered in front of a temple to make a sacrifice to the gods. The offerings consisted of rabbit, rhea, and deer meat placed on trays around a fire which was never extinguished (Eguiluz, 1884).

Only a few fragments of their religion are known. The *Cayuvava* called their good spirit or spirits Idaapa and the bad one Maïnaje. They closed the mouth and nose of dying people to prevent the escape of death, that is to say, of the evil spirit which had attacked the patient. Men refrained from working when their wives menstruated.

BIBLIOGRAPHY

Balzán, 1894; Créqui-Montfort and Rivet, 1914 a, 1917–20; Eguiluz, 1884; Giglioli, 1906; Gonçalves da Fonseca, 1826; Nordenskiöld, 1922; Teza, 1868.

THE ITONAMA

TERRITORY AND HISTORY

Like the *Cayuvava*, the *Itonama* speak an isolated language. In the 17th century, their villages were scattered along both sides of the Itonama River from the great lagoon, Laguna Itonama or Cármen, to the Machupo River (lat. 13°–15° S., long. 63° W.; map 1, *No. 2;* map 2).

About 1720, the *Itonama* were attacked by a party of Mestizos from Santa Cruz, and 2,000 of them were taken as slaves (Maurtua, V., 1906, 10:43–48). The Jesuits collected the *Itonama* in the Mission of Santa Magdalena, on the Itonama River, but in 1792 part of them were moved to the village of San Ramón on the Machupo River. In 1767, there were 4,000 *Itonama* at Magdalena and a few families in the missions of Loreto and Trinidad in the Province of Mojos. In 1831, those of Magdalena numbered 2,831 and those of San Ramón, 1,984. In 1914, Nordenskiöld (1924 a, p. 188) found only 300 of these Indians in the region of San Ramón.

CULTURE

Modern *Itonama*, with a background of 200 years of Christianity, retain little of their aboriginal culture. They live in large villages near the rivers and are agriculturists, hunters, and fishermen. They roast maize meal in large flat-bottomed pans with raised edges.

Both sexes dress in large cotton or bark-cloth shirts, often painted black, but originally women wore a loincloth. Until puberty, children went naked, wearing nothing, but bands below the knees and above the ankles. Little girls wore besides a string of beads around their waists (D'Orbigny, 1839, vol. 2, p. 241).

The *Itonama* spin cotton (fig. 51) by inserting the distal end of the spindle in a notched stick and rolling the proximal end on a log. They are the most famous weavers in the Mojos area. They make circular baskets, some with an hexagonal weave (lattice type); other baskets are twilled.

Their weapons were bows and arrows and the double-edged club. The *Itonama* had slings and bolas long before European contacts, but the lasso was introduced in the 18th century.

Child betrothal was a deep-rooted custom which survived into the Christian era. Children were engaged to each other soon after birth.

The feet of a newly born baby are tied lest it follow its father. The latter observes several taboos, e.g., that on swimming in deep water. The strength of marital ties grows with the number of children that a woman bears her husband; childless women cannot expect much support.

At festivals, the *Itonama* blow a sort of huge panpipes, which actually consist of 11 bark trumpets, varying from 2 to 5 feet (0.6 to 1.5 m.) in

FIGURE 51.—*Itonama* woman spinning. (After Nordenskiöld, 1924 a.)

length and joined together in the same manner as the tubes of true panpipes.

Forty years ago the *Itonama* still preserved some of their old beliefs. They did not till the land of a deceased person and did not exploit trees which had belonged to an ancestor.

They believed that ghosts turned into hummingbirds, butterflies, and serpents, and that they caused death.

Shamans were of both sexes. A shaman summoned his familiar spirit and asked it about a patient's fate. Disease was usually ascribed to a vengeful ghost that had captured the soul.[4] The soul had to be rescued in order to heal the patient. When a shaman wanted to send his soul out of his body to discover hidden things, he took a narcotic, nowadays opium, which put him in a trance. Witches changed themselves into jaguars to kill their enemies.

Every animal was believed to maintain a mystical relationship to a plant which bore a slight resemblance to one of the animal's features. Plants associated with dangerous animals should not be touched. Medicinal plants were thought to be related to men by mystic ties.

---

[4] According to D'Orbigny (1839, vol. 2, p. 241), the *Itonama* were so afraid that death, which overtook a person, might pass into another person's body that they stopped the nose, the mouth, and the eyes of those who were about to breathe their last, so that many sick people died of suffocation.

BIBLIOGRAPHY

Adam, 1897–98; Balzán, 1894; Cardús, 1886; Créqui-Montfort and Rivet, 1916; Eder, 1791; D'Orbigny, 1839; Hervás, 1800–05; Izikowitz, 1935; Maurtua V., 1906; Nordenskiöld, 1915 b, 1924 a; Rivet, 1921; Severiano da Fonseca, 1880–81.

THE GUARAYU AND PAÚSERNA

TRIBAL DIVISIONS

The *Guarayú* and *Pauserna* (*Itatin, Carabere, Araibayba, Moterequoa*) formed a single tribe, but separated when the ancestors of modern *Guarayú* were collected in missions. The *Pauserna* are the descendants of the *Guarayú* who remained independent (map 1, *No. 2;* map 2).

Originally, the *Guarayú* probably lived mainly along the upper San Miguel (Itonama) River and between it and the Río Blanco (approximately lat. 15°–16° S., and long. 63°–64° W.). Most of the *Guarayú* were later distributed among five Franciscan missions: Yotau, Ascensión, Urubichá, Yaguarú, and San Paulo.

The *Pauserna* (*Guarayú-tá*) live on the left side of the upper Guaporé River (lat. 14° S., long. 61° W.), where the pao cerne is abundant; hence their name. Formerly, when they were more numerous, they reached the lower Paraguay River and its tributaries. In 1935, only two groups of *Pauserna* numbering some 50 persons remained, one at Bella Vista and the other on the lower Paraguay River. They had lost most of their ancient culture and lived precariously. Severiano da Fonseca (1880–81, pp. 168–171) found *Pauserna* along the left side of the Guaporé River, from a little north of the Paraguay River to the Rio da Pedra. Their main villages were Pao Cerne, Las Flexas, Jangada, Veados, and Acarisal.

HISTORY

The *Guarayú*, like the *Chiriguano*, are descendants of the *Guaraní* of Paraguay, who, at the end of the 15th and the beginning of the 16th century, crossed the Chaco and the Province of Chiquitos in several groups to raid the borders of the *Inca* empire, and finally settled along or near the Cordillera.

The *Guaraní* migrations took place in several successive waves, the first perhaps during the reign of Inca Yupanqui (1476). Another must have occurred about 1513 to 1518, but apparently met with disaster. According to Felipe de Alcaya (Maurtua, V., 1906, vol. 6), it started from the region of the Xarayes marshes and ended in the plains of Grigotá near the present city of Santa Cruz de la Sierra. A party of the same *Guaraní* stayed in the Province of Itati of Chiquitos (which is not to be confused with the Province of Itati north of the Apa River).

In 1564, Nuflo de Chaves, returning to Chiquitos from Paraguay, brought 2,000 to 3,000 *Itatin* of the Province of Itati, who settled in the new country. Were the *Itatin* of Chiquitos, so often mentioned in the second half of the 16th century, those who migrated in 1513 or were they the followers of Nuflo de Chaves in 1564? The answer will remain undecided, though the second hypothesis seems the more likely.

Early documents often use the name *Guarayú* for all the *Guarani* Indians (both the *Chiriguano* and *Guarayú* proper) who had migrated from Paraguay. (See Métraux, 1927, 1928 c, 1942; Schmidt, M., 1936.)

There are several references to the *Guarayú,* under the name of *Chiriguano, Moperecoa, Pirataguari,* in the accounts of the Spanish expeditions which undertook the conquest of eastern Bolivia at the beginning of the 17th century.

The Jesuits visited the *Guarayú* in the late 16th century. In 1695, Father Cipriano Barrace reestablished contact with them, and a few *Guarayú* were taken to the Jesuit mission of San Xavier. The Mission of Juan Bautista de Guarayos was founded for the *Guarayú,* some of whom were also taken to San José de Buenavista.

In 1793, some *Guarayú* were placed in San Pablo, on the San Miguel River, but they soon returned to the bush at the instigation of a messiah, Luis, who announced that they would soon join Tamoi, the Great Ancestor. In 1822, the *Guarayú* were entrusted to Franciscan missionaries from Tarata. After the independence of Bolivia, the missions were abandoned and the Indians resumed their old ways. In 1840, the Franciscans regained control of the region and founded the missions which exist today.

In 1884, there were 4,439 Indians in the four missions of Yotau, Ascención, Yaguarú, and Urubichá. In 1915, there were 6,364 Indians; in 1919, after the influenza epidemic, only 5,607.

At the end of the 16th century, *Guarayú* culture was still very similar to that of the *Guarani* of Paraguay: They had large communal houses, went naked, tattooed themselves by incision, practiced ceremonial cannibalism, buried their dead in urns, and remembered such mythological characters as Pai Zumé and Pai Tacure and Pai Amandre. (See Métraux, 1928 c.)

When it was observed in 1831 by D'Orbigny, *Guarayú* culture had been modified in many respects under the influence of their neighbors, the *Chiquito* and *Mojo.* The culture of the *Guarayú* visited by Nordenskiöld in 1908 had undergone even greater changes after almost a century of missionary life.

CULTURE

SUBSISTENCE ACTIVITIES

Modern *Guarayú* subsistence is more or less aboriginal. Crops are still those of their ancestors, except that they have given up bitter manioc and have adopted rice and other new plants, such as caripo (*Disocorea*) and hualusa (*Colocasia* sp.). Hunting methods conform to the general pattern of the area. (See *Guarayú* traps, fig. 52.) They shoot fish with single or multiprong arrows, drug them with the sap of the *Hura crepitans,* spear them with gigs, and catch them in baskets set in dams, in small dip nets, and in basket sieves. They take eels with spears and baskets.

Cooking methods and utensils differ little from those of their neighbors, but they are the only Indians in the area who use the cylindrical wooden mortar and the long pestle, both survivals of their old *Guarani* culture. (See fig. 53, *a, Guarayú* fire drill.)

Fields are cleared and tilled collectively. Men sow maize; women plant sweet manioc and carry the crops from the fields.

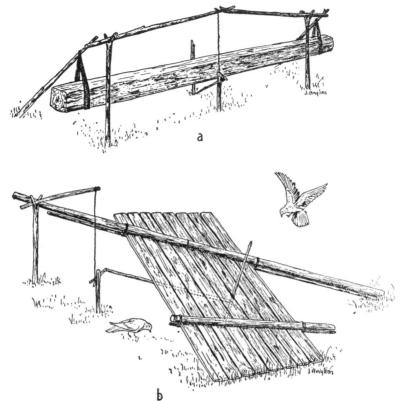

FIGURE 52.—*Guarayú* traps. *a,* For large rodents and armadillos; *b,* for pigeons. (Redrawn from Nordenskiöld, 1924 b, figs. 19, *a, b.*)

HOUSES

The ancient *Guaraní* multiple-family house, which was still used in the 16th century, has been replaced among the modern *Guarayú* by a single-family dwelling with an octagonal ground plan and wattle-and-daub walls and among the *Pauserna* by open sheds. The main pieces of furniture are platforms on which food is stored, cotton hammocks, benches for men, and mats for women.

DRESS AND ORNAMENTS

Guarayú men adopted the long, bark-cloth tunic, characteristic of the *Mojo* area, but women wore only a skirt. In religious ceremonies, people went naked, as formerly. The ornaments were: Feather diadems, feather frontlets, labrets, feather-trimmed sticks passed through the nasal septum, tufts of feathers in the ear lobes, necklaces, and bracelets of aguai fruits. The ancient *Guarayú* also glued feathers to their bodies.

They painted themselves with genipa and urucú. Among the ancient *Guarayú,* women incised their faces, arms, and legs, and rubbed genipa juice or charcoal in the wounds. The *Guaraní* tonsure was still common in the 16th century, but later both sexes wore their hair long. In D'Orbigny's time, *Guarayú* men wore long beards, an unusual feature in South America.

Bark Cloth.—They make cloth of the bark of the bibosi tree (*Ficus* sp.), beaten with grooved wooden mallets.

Basketry.—Basketry (fig. 53) is of the twilled, wicker, hexagonal, or lattice varieties. In the hexagonal weave, the weft passes alternately over a strand of one and under a strand of another of two series of warp elements crossed diagonally. Rectangular baskets made of *Gynerium* stalks,

FIGURE 53.—*Guarayú* carrying basket. (Redrawn from Nordenskiöld, 1924 b, map 21.)

bound together by cotton twine, are used to store personal possessions. The *Guarayú* carry crops and heavy loads in elongated shoulder baskets which are entirely open on top and on the outer side, with only the lateral sides to support the burden.

Pottery.—*Guarayú* pottery was comparatively crude. It consisted of cooking pots, water bottles, and jars, some of them of considerable size. The *Pauserna* tempered the potter's clay with pulverized potsherds. The finished vessel was dried in the sun and heated over a fire before it was exposed to a higher temperature.

Spinning and weaving.—While the *Pauserna* have retained the drop spindle which turns by itself once set in motion, the *Guarayú* have adopted the long spindle which is rolled along the thigh. The distal end of the spindle rests on a lump of clay which keeps it on a level with the thigh. Both the *Guarayú* and the *Pauserna* weave on the vertical loom. The *Pauserna* plait cotton bands on a small loom, the frame of which is a forked branch with two transverse sticks attached to it. The warp threads are crossed by sticks which are removed and substituted by the weft.

Gourds.—Unlike most tribes of eastern Bolivia, the *Guarayú* use gourds (*Lagenaria siceraria*) more readily than calabashes (*Crescentia cujete*) as containers. The gourds of the *Pauserna* are decorated with simple geometric designs which stand out against a red background. To obtain this ornamentation, the outer surface of the gourd is scratched except for the desired patterns. Then the whole surface is smeared with urucú paste, and the epidermis on the unscratched portions is removed. The interior of these containers is painted in black.

Fire making.—The *Guarayú* often use the shaft of their arrows as a drill and the bamboo head as a hearth. The bamboo blade is perforated throughout and the ignited dust falls on a tinder placed underneath it.

Weapons.—The main features of the *Guarayú* bow are: a cross section externally convex, flat on the belly; a central basketry sheath; and a cotton string. Arrows are tipped with (1) lanceolate bamboo blades (2) wooden rods with serrated egdes and sometimes with a bone barb, and (3) conical wooden knobs (bird arrows). Fishing arrows, as a rule, are provided with two barbed prongs. The feathering is of the arched, or eastern Brazilian type. The arrow shafts are of *Gynerium* stems, with a small peg inserted in the butt to strengthen it. *Guarayú* and *Pauserna* arrows bear a striking likeness to those of the *Guaraní* Indians of Paraguay.

The ancient *Guarayú* had long double-edged wooden clubs, which widened from the handle to the distal end.

LIFE CYCLE

Childbirth.—Prenatal food taboos were aimed at preventing the child from acquiring unpleasant features pertaining to some game animals or plants. Women were delivered in a squatting position. Some relative, usually the grandmother, tied cotton threads around the newborn infant's wrists, elbows, knees, and ankles, and, if it were a girl, around her waist.

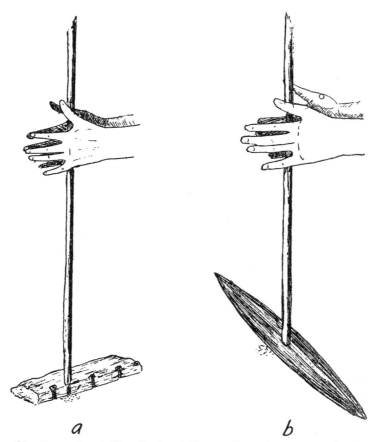

a   b

FIGURE 54.—*Guarayú* and *Chacobo* fire drills. *a, Guarayú; b, Chacobó.*   (Redrawn from Nordenskiöld, 1924 b, map 13.)

The father slashed himself with an aguti tooth, smeared his body with genipa, and lay idle in his hammock for 3 days, eating only small fish. It was a common belief among these Indians that the infant's soul followed its father everywhere, and that it might come to harm if the latter exerted himself too violently.

Among the 16th-century *Guarayú*, a boy was named by his grandfather or another male relative, who handed him a miniature bow.   (See Métraux, 1928 c, p. 922.)

During childhood boys were often scarified or bled with a miniature bow and arrow in order to make them strong.

Girls' puberty.—At puberty, girls were secluded for a month in a corner of the hut and were restricted to a diet of sweet manioc, mush, and bananas.   Afterward their arms and breasts were slashed with an aguti tooth and charcoal powder rubbed into the wounds.   The scars remained as permanent tattoo marks.

Marriage.—The preferred form of marriage was between a girl and her maternal uncle or her cross-cousin. Among the ancient *Guarayú*, girls were often betrothed in early childhood.

The consent of the girl's father, and more especially, of her brother, was absolutely necessary for marriage. The suitor declared himself by leaving a bundle of firewood at the girl's door. (See Métraux, 1928 c, p. 922.) In more recent times, the prospective husband had to walk in front of the girl's hut for a few days, naked and painted with urucú. The wedding was celebrated with a drinking bout. The bridegroom was obliged to work for his father- or brother-in-law or to make them substantial presents. Residence was matrilocal, but sooner or later the new couple went to live in a separate hut. Polygyny was common. The levirate is mentioned in ancient documents.

Death.—At a death, the ancient *Guarayú* expressed their grief by throwing themselves on the ground and by other violent manifestations.

The dead, painted and wearing all their ornaments, were buried inside the hut. The *Pauserna* built a miniature hut on the grave. The body formerly was placed in a large jar, but in more recent times it was wrapped in several mats and interred with the face turned west. After the burial, the mourners slashed their bodies with aguti teeth.

ESTHETIC AND RECREATIONAL ACTIVITIES

Games.—In the 16th century, the ancestors of the modern *Guarayú*, the *Itatin*, played a rubber-ball game in which they struck the ball with the head and elbows.

Musical instruments.—Stamping tubes and gourd rattles played a significant part in religion. The *Pauserna* wear bracelets and belts hung with fruit-shell jingles.

Dances.—Men formed a line and marched forward and backward, thumping their bamboo tubes on the ground.

Narcotics and beverages.—The *Guarayú* smoke tobacco in pipes, the *Pauserna* in the form of cigars.

They made chicha of maize or of sweet manioc fermented with chewed maize.

RELIGION

The *Guarayú* retained many ancient *Guarani* religious features. They seem to have rendered a cult to Tamoi, the Great Ancestor. The data on their religion concern mainly a strong messianic movement which took place at the beginning of the 19th century. Men gathered in their large dancing houses and danced and sung to the rhythm of stamping tubes and rattles, hoping that Tamoi, the Ancestor, would reward their persistence by taking them to his celestial abode. These religious crises offer surprising resemblances to the revivalistic and messianic movements which occurred among the *Guarani* and *Tupinamba* from the 16th to the 19th century.

Journey to the land of Tamoi.—Soon after burial, the soul starts a long dangerous journey to the land of Tamoi, which is located in the west. The soul is ferried across a river on the back of a caiman, jumps on a tree trunk which floats at great speed back and forth between two river banks, passes by the Grandfather of the worms, whose colossal size diminishes as the soul approaches him, then crosses a dark region where it is threatened by huge bats, and runs between two clashing rocks. Finally, it is examined by a gallinazo bird that sees whether its lips and ears have been perforated as is befitting a *Guarayú*. Before reaching the abode of Tamoi, the soul must endure the ordeal of being tickled by a monkey without laughing, must walk past a magic tree without heeding the voices issuing from it, and must look at colored grasses without being blinded by them. After all these ordeals, the soul is received by Tamoi, who washes it and restores its youth and good looks.

MYTHOLOGY

Guarayú mythology presents a strange mixture of confused elements. Its contradictions and obscurities are probably to be attributed to its collector, Father Cors. (See Cardús, 1886, pp. 76–78.)

In the beginning there was only water and bullrushes over which a worm, Mbir, crawled. After assuming human shape, Mbir created the world. He later was known as Miracucha, a name suspiciously suggestive of that of the *Inca* supreme god and culture hero, Viracocha. Next to Miracucha appear two other creators: Zaguaguayu, the god with the brilliant headdress who still lives in the west (the Sun?), and his brother Abaangui. The latter is also a creator and transformer, who changed his shape so often while endeavoring to take human form that he acquired a colossal nose that he had to knock off (the Moon?).

Our mythological text mentions also Candir, a name which in some 16th-century chronicles was applied by the *Guarani* to the Peruvian ruler. Candir probably was a culture hero who later became identified with the *Inca* Emperor. In the first document concerning the *Guarayú*, Candir is presented as a deity. (See Métraux, 1928 c.) Some people fasted and lived in seclusion for his sake and were seized by fits of frenzy which led them to run across the bush indifferent to pain and discomfort. The 16th-century Candir is perhaps the equivalent of Tamoi, or the Great Ancestor.

According to Cardús (1886), Tamoi taught men agriculture and the preparation of chicha. He was also a transformer, for he changed his wife and baby into rocks. Later he departed to a celestial abode in the west.

The two sons of Tamoi (the mythical twins) shot arrows into the sky so that each arrow penetrated into the butt of the other. Thus they formed a chain by which the Brothers reached the sky, where they remained as Sun and Moon.

The spots on the Moon were caused by a girl who had sexual intercourse with the Moon at night. To discover her lover's identity, she smeared his face with genipa juice.

At the end of the 16th century, the *Guarayú* who had left Paraguay a generation before, still remembered Pai Zume, the great culture hero of the *Tupinamba* and *Guaraní*. (See Annuae litterae, 1589; Métraux, 1928 c.)

They retained also a tradition about a Flood from which a few people (probably children) were saved in a pot. In the same Annuae litterae of 1589, there is a passing reference to two mythical characters, Pai Tacur and Pai Amandre, who were undoubtedly Twin heroes. They disappeared after a cataclysm (Métraux, 1928 c).

According to modern *Guarayú* mythology, fire was stolen from the vultures by a hero who, in order to lure the birds, pretended to be dead and snatched a firebrand when they alighted on him. He was assisted by a frog, who swallowed the firebrand to hide it from the vultures.

The *Guarayú* attributed eclipses to a celestial jaguar who attacked the Moon. They came to the rescue of the Moon by yelling and shooting burning arrows into the air.

LITERATURE

The text of a *Guarayú* song was transcribed by D'Orbigny (1839, vol. 2, p. 330). The Indians ask in it that nature don her most beautiful attire, that flowers blossom, that birds appear in radiant plumage and sing joyfully, that trees cover themselves with green foliage, and that everything help attract the attention of Tamoi, who was never supplicated in vain.

BIBLIOGRAPHY

Annuae litterae, 1589; Burela, 1912; Caldas, 1887; Cardús, 1886; Costa Marquez, 1908; D'Orbigny, 1839; Ducci, 1895; Eberlein, 1915; Fernández, 1895; Gonçalves da Fonseca, 1826; Gandía, 1935 a; Herzog, 1913; Hoeller, 1932; Maurtua, 1906; Métraux, 1927, 1928 c, 1942; Nordenskiöld, 1917 c, 1922, 1924 b; Pesciotti, 1904; Pierini, 1907, 1908–12, 1910; Priewaser, 1903; Relaciones geográficas de Indias, 1881–97; Schmidt, M., 1936; Severiano de Fonseca, 1880–81; Snethlage, E. H., 1936 a.

THE TACANAN TRIBES

TRIBAL DIVISIONS

The *Tacanan* tribes and subtribes occupy a continuous territory (map 1, *No. 2;* map 2) which includes the upper course of the Tahuamanú (Orton), Abuná, and Acre (Capechene) Rivers, the Madre de Díos River between long. 67° and 68°35′ W., its tributaries, the Tambopata and Heath Rivers, and the Beni River from lat. 12°–15° S. and its tributaries, especially the Madidi and Tuichi Rivers. The little-known *Tacanan* dialects have been grouped into a single linguistic family by Créqui-Montfort (Créqui-Montfort and Rivet, 1921–22, 13:91–100) on the basis of the available linguistic material. Later, Rivet (1924) proposed the inclusion of the *Tacanan* family within the *Arawakan* linguistic family as a subgroup. Additional material on this linguistic group is to be found in Schuller (1922).

The *Araona* live on both sides of the Manuripe, not far from the Madre de Díos River, and on both banks of the latter, above the Genechiquia River (lat. 13° S., long. 68° W.), which separates them from the *Pacaguara* (lat. 11°–13° S., long. 65°–67° W.). Other *Araona* groups are settled at the headwaters of the Tahuamanu (Orton), Datimanú, and Abuná, on the Karamanu River, a tributary of the Abuná River, and on the Jua River. The bulk of the tribe was on the Tahuamanu (Orton) River. The main *Araona* subtribes are listed by Armentia (1887–88, pp. 53–54) as follows: *Beyuma, Buda, Cahoco, Cama, Camaya, Camoavi, Canamary, Capa, Capanary, Capu, Chumu, Cuesi, Curupi, Dejabai, Ecuary, Eno, Giry, Guajima, Habuwi, Hamapu, Huary, Huarymodo, Ino, Isebene, Jicho, Machuvi, Manipo, Mapumary, Marani, Maru, Masatibu, Mayupi, Moyana, Odoary, Sabatini, Sara, Tade, Taranu, Tuama, Tuno, Uaui, Uranico,* and *Yuma.*

The *Capechene* (*Capaheni*) of the Acre and lower Irariapé Rivers (lat. 11°–13° S., long. 12°–14° W.) and the *Machui* must also be included among the *Araona* subtribes. In the last part of the 19th century, there were about 1,500 *Araona* and 800 to 1,000 *Capechene.*

The *Caviña* (*Cavineño*) (lat. 14° S., long. 67° W.) were moved in 1770 (or 1785) by missionaries from the left side of the Madre de Díos River to the ancient Mission of Cavinas on the Madidi River. Later, the *Caviña* were settled in the new Mission of Cavinas on the Beni River. In 1832, there were 1,000 *Caviña* at Cavinas, but only 153 in 1886. The 218 *Caviña* whom Nordenskiöld (1924 a, p. 266) saw in 1913 in the Mission of Jesús de Caviña on the Beni River had given up all their native culture except for a few isolated objects and customs. A few cultural details suggest that the *Caviña* might formerly have belonged to a different linguistic family and adopted a *Tacanan* dialect in more or less recent times.

The *Guacanahua*[5] on the upper Madidi and Undumo Rivers, the *Chama,* and the *Tiatinagua* are perhaps subtribes of a single large tribe which will be designated here as *Tiatinagua,* following the nomenclature of the early missionaries.

The *Chama* visited by Nordenskiöld on the left side of the Madidi River are a subtribe of the *Guacanahua.*

---

[5] They formed part of the Mission of Santiago de Pacazuaras, abandoned in 1840.

The *Tiatinagua* (*Tambopata-Guarayo, Huanayo, Baguaja, Baguajairi, Quinaqui, Mohino, Chuncho, Echoja*) were to be found on the upper Tambopata River above the mouth of the Távara River between Astillero and Marte (lat. 13°–15° S., long. 69° W.). There are *Tiatinagua* groups between the Inambari and Tambopata Rivers. The so-called *Guarayo* of the Heath River and the *Echoja* at the headwaters of the Heath River are subtribes of the Tiatinagua. Labré (1889, p. 499) mentions "*Guarayú*," related to the *Araona*, on the upper Abuná River.

In 1905, the number of *Tiatinagua* on the Malinowsky River was about 400 to 500. Those of the Tambopata River, from the La Torre River to Echainapa on the Távara River, were estimated at about 300 to 400.

The *Maropa* originally inhabited the banks of the Beni River (lat. 14°–15° S., long. 67° S.), south and west of the *Tacanan* tribes and east of the *Cayuvava*. Later they were transferred to the Mission of Reyes. They probably were closely related to the *Chirigua* (*Chiriba, Chiribi*) of the Mission of Santa Buenaventura, who came from the country adjacent to Reyes and Borja.

The *Tacana* proper are a tribe or subtribe living north of the Tuichi River (lat. 14° S., long. 68° W.), a tributary of the Beni River, but this name is given also to several other groups which are closely related to them and inhabit the same area. These other groups are the *Yubamona, Pamaino, Yabaypura, Pasaramona, Babayana, Chiliuvo, Toromona, Uchupiamona, Saparuna, Siliama, Tumupasa* (whose dialect is also known as *Marakani*), and *Ydiama*, spoken at Ixiamas. Most of these groups were scattered along the Tuichi River. Almost all the Indians settled in the missions of Buenavista, San José de Uchupiamonas, Tumupasa, and Ixiamas came from that region and belonged to these various groups.

The *Toromona*, who occupy the plains of the Carabaya Mountains and the territory between the Beni, the Madidi, and the Madre de Díos Rivers (lat. 13° S., long. 68° W.) are listed by D'Orbigny among the "wild Tacana." It has been impossible to locate exactly the *Guariza* and *Sapibocona*. The first formed part of the Mission of San Antonio de Ixiamas and the second of the Mission of Santos Reyes. The *Sapibocona* probably must be identified with the *Maropa* who lived in the same area. The *Mabenaro* inhabited the forests north of the Madre de Díos River about the headwaters of the southern tributaries of the Manuripe River (lat. 12° 15′ S., long. 68° W.).

POPULATION

When the Mission of San José de Uchupiamonas was founded in 1716, it had 600 Indians. There were 2,500 Indians in the Mission of Ixiamas in 1721. In 1832, 1,028 Indians remained in Ixiamas, 73 in San José, and 1,170 in Tumupasa. In 1886 there were 1,200 Indians in Ixiamas,

1,200 in the Mission of Tumupasa, and 150 in San José. According to D'Orbigny (1839, 1:375), the *Toromona* numbered about 1,000. The same author classifies the 2,033 Indians of the Mission of Atén as *Tacana,* but some might have been *Leco* or from some other tribes. He also puts the total number of *Tacana* in 1831 at 6,304. In the same year, the *Maropa* of the Mission of Reyes numbered 900, but Nordenskiöld (1924 a, p. 160) states that there were approximately 1,500. Hassel (1905, p. 40) undoubtedly exaggerates when he puts the *Tiatinagua* at 3,000.

HISTORY

The first contacts between the *Tacanan*-speaking Indians and the Spaniards go back to the 16th century. In 1539, Pedro Anzules de Campo-redondo entered the territory of the *Tacana* from Ayaviri and Carabaya, and reached the Beni River. The Maldonado expedition in 1567 came in touch with various *Tacana* groups; a Spanish town was founded in *Toromona* territory. In 1593, Miguel Cabello de Balboa went as far as Ixiamas and Tumupasa. In 1621, Fray Gregorio de Bolívar visited the country of the *Tacana* and mentions them under the names of *Uchupiamona, Ayaychuna,* and *Chivamona.*

The natives of the ancient Province of Apolobamba were, with the exception of the *Aguachile* (*Apolista*) and the *Leco,* mostly *Tacanan* tribes. The first town in that area was Nuestra Señora de Guadalupe, founded in 1615. At the end of the 17th century, the Franciscans founded in the region of Apolobamba the following missions:

San Juan Bautista de Buenavista or La Plata, 1680 (*Siliama* and *Pamaino*).
La Concepción de Apolobamba, 1690 (*Leco, Aguachile,* and *Pamaino*).
La Trinidad de Iariapu or Tumupasa, 1713 (*Tacana, Marcani, Saparuna, Paimano. Chiliuvo, Toromona,* and. *Araona*).
San José de Uchupiamonas, 1713 (*Tumupasa, Isiama,* and *Apolista*).
San Antonio de Ixiamas, 1721 (*Tacana, Araona, Marcani, Toromona, Huawayana,* and *Guarisa*).
San Antonio de Atén, 1736 (*Leco* and later *Tacanan*-speaking Indians).

In the region of Carabaya, missionary work started in 1654, but many baptized Indians when left to their own devices returned to paganism. In 1678, the Franciscan missionaries came in touch with *Isiama, Sariona,* and *Pasiona,* and with the *Araona.*

The work of the Franciscans among the *Tacanans* continued with few interruptions up to the present. The best known of their missionaries is Father Nicolás Armentia (1887–88), who explored the Madre de Díos Basin, and is one of the main authorities on the *Araona* ethnography.

Quechua was already spoken in the 17th century by many *Tacanans* who came to Carabaya. In the missions of Apolobamba, the Franciscans favored its adoption, and it has replaced the *Tacanan* dialects spoken in that region.

SUBSISTENCE ACTIVITIES

Collecting wild foods.—The *Araona*—and probably all the other *Tacanan*-speaking groups—depend greatly on wild foods, such as the fruits of several palm trees (*Euterpe oleracea, Jessenia bataua, Attalea humboldtiana, Attalea spectabilis, Bactris maraja*) and Brazil nuts. The last are mentioned in the 16th-century sources as the most important food of the *Tacanan*-groups, especially of the *Toromona,* who not only consumed enormous quantities themselves but traded them to the Indians in the mountains. The *Araona* were also great honey gatherers. During the dry season, the *Tiatinagua* and *Capechene* collected turtle eggs. All the Indians of that area greatly relish the fat abdomens of the cuqui ants.

Farming.—All the *Tacanan*-speaking Indians practice agriculture *Araona* and *Tiatinagua* fields, which average 164 by 66 feet (50 by 20 m.), are scattered, and their owners constantly travel from one to another. In addition to regular plantations, these Indians have plots of bananas and plantains along the rivers, where they hunt and fish during certain seasons.

Tiatinagua plantations have rows of banana and plantain trees, between which grow sweet manioc (yuca), maize, sweet potatoes, hualsua (*Colocasia esculentia*), gourds, tobacco, cotton, cayenne pepper, and sugarcane. The same plants are probably cultivated by all members of the family. The *Araona* raised, in addition to the plants listed above, papayas and two kinds of tubers. Beans and peanuts, though not specifically ascribed to any tribe, are common native foods of the region.

Hunting.—The *Tiatinagua* hunt in large groups, encircling a large area and driving the game toward a center where they kill it with bows and arrows. Dogs are trained to flush various game.

Caviña spring-hole traps have a nose attached to a bent pole and stretched within an enclosure. When a bird alights on a tranverse rod or when a rodent finishes nibbling a tuber fastened to a trigger, the pole flies upward. In another type, the noose is placed in front of an opening into the enclosure, so that the pole springs up when the rodent steps on a peg.

The *Caviña* rub their eyes with vivisapa leaves before hunting. The *Tiatinagua* keep pieces of skin of the slain animals as trophies. Game is shared equally by all members of a *Tiatinagua* community.

Fishing.—The *Tacanan* tribes rely considerably on fishing. At the beginning of the dry season, they capture with their bare hands thousands of fish left stranded by the receding flood. They shoot fish with bows and arrows or capture them (*Araona* and *Tiatinagua*) in rectangular enclosures placed across streams. To catch huge siluroid fish, the *Tiatinagua* use a wooden hook that is unique in South America and consists of a shank with two wooden barbs resembling an anchor. The *Tacanan* tribes also drug fish with the milky sap of the soliman tree (*Hura crepitans*).

Domesticated animals.—The dog was not introduced to the *Tacana* before the 19th century.   The wild *Tiatinagua* have chickens and dogs. Present-day *Maropa* are good horsemen and cattle herders.

Food preparation.—Bananas and plantains, the staple foods of most *Tacana* with the exception of the *Araona,* are usually roasted.   Maize is ground between two stones or in a wooden trough with a big semicircular wooden slab (fig. 55).   As the *Tiatinagua* and *Chama* have little or no

FIGURE 55.—*Tiatinagua* woman making cornmeal.   (After Farabee, 1922.)

pottery, they roast or steam food, especially fish, in green bamboo tubes placed on the fire; the food is cooked before the vessel burns through. The 17th-century Indians of Apolobamba baked game and fish in earth ovens.   Any surplus of meat is roasted and smoked on a rectangular babracot.   Instead of salt, the *Araona* add the ashes of maize stalks to food.   When they travel, the *Araona* eat maize flour mixed with roasted and ground Brazil nuts.   They grind dry fish into a flour which they store for the rainy season.

HOUSES AND VILLAGES

The *Araona* live in large communal huts, which average 60 feet (18.2 m.) in length and 20 feet (6.1 m.) in width, and shelter as many as 20 families.   Such dwellings, covered with skilfully imbricated leaves, endure for many years.   These Indians, however, spend their nights in small conical cabins which are tightly closed to keep out mosquitoes and vampire bats.

In the 17th century, the *Maropa* huts accommodated from 100 to 200 people.

Tiatinagua and *Chama* huts are simple windbreaks, made of a single row of large leaves stuck into the ground, or they are flimsy vaulted structures made of stalks of *Gynerium sagittatum* and covered with leaves and branches.   The size of the hut depends on the number of families using it.

The *Araona, Chama,* and *Tiatinagua* sleep on the bare ground, which they sometimes cover with soft sand.   A stone or log serves as a pillow. The *Araona* use pieces of bark as beds and seats.

DRESS AND ORNAMENTS

If the occasion requires it, men dress in long sleeveless shirts made either of bark cloth or of cotton and generally dyed with urucú.   Women wrap a bark or cotton loincloth around their waists and often throw a square shawl over their shoulders.

The *Araona* and *Tiatinagua* of both sexes wear shell nose ornaments, crescent-shaped among the latter.   Feathers or small teeth inserted in the perforated nasal septum are common ornaments in these tribes.   Some *Tiatinagua* wear a little wooden plug in each corner of the mouth.   Neck-laces are strung with seeds, nuts (which are often trimmed with feathers), snails, and animal claws and bones.   All these Indians array themselves in beautiful feather headdresses.

The *Araona* wear their hair in a queue.   They wash it with a soapy fruit of the susuyo.

Deformation.—Farabee (1922, p. 156) states that the *Tiatinagua* flatten their children's heads by tying a board on their foreheads.

TRANSPORTATION

The *Tacana* travel on water either in dugouts or on rafts.   *Tiatinagua* dugouts are 33 to 50 feet (10 to 15 m.) long and 15 to 28 inches (38 to 70 cm.) wide.   The same Indians have small balsas consisting of two logs fastened together by chonta-palm pins driven through them.

Mothers carry babies straddling on their hip, supported by a sling of bark cloth.

MANUFACTURES

Bark cloth.—Bark cloth was made of the bark of various trees, mainly *Ficus* sp.   The hammered patches were soaked in water several times, thoroughly wrung, dried, and sewn together with a needle.   *Araona* needles were of bone, with large eyes.

Spinning.—*Tiatinagua* and *Chama* spindles are of the drop type.   The whorls are of potsherds or of stone (*Chama*).

Weaving.—A loom collected by Nordenskiöld (1924 b, map 26) at Tumupasa consists of two horizontal sticks around which a thread is wound in such a way that the separate strands are crossed around a series of mesh sticks.   The fabric is obtained by recrossing and tightening the threads with the fingers.

Basketry.—Twilled baskets and fans and ovoid wicker baskets are illustrated by Nordenskiöld (1905, figs. 26–30). The *Tiatinagua* have rectangular baskets of *Gynerium sagittatum* stalks bound together with fine threads.

Pottery.—The *Tiatinagua* and *Chama* have little pottery, in contrast to the *Caviña* who, though decadent, still manufacture beautiful painted, resin-glazed vessels. The *Araona* make many kinds of pottery ranging from huge jars to small vases, which they carry on journeys.

The *Tacanans* use both gourd (*Lagencria siceraria*) and calabash (*Crescentia cujete*) cups and containers.

Tools.—Stone axes were deeply notched near the butt end and lashed to a wooden shaft. Two wooden splinters reinforced the binding. *Araona* stone axes were glued with rosin as well as lashed.

Weapons.—*Tiatinagua* bows are of palm wood, 6½ feet (2 m.) long. The cross section is flat and rectangular, the string of vegetal fiber. Hunting arrows have lanceolate bamboo heads or sharp chonta tips, one side of which has one or two rows of barbs. Fishing arrows have either a simple jagged point or three plain prongs. Arrow feathering consists of two twisted half feathers set spirally against the *Gynerium* shaft and bound tightly with cotton thread smeared with wax (cemented feathering). The arrow is held between the thumb and the index finger, and the string pulled with the other three fingers.

SOCIAL AND POLITICAL ORGANIZATION

Each *Tiatinagua* group consists of from two to eight families, who live together in a communal hut under a chief. Any *Araona* man with a strong personality and many relatives may become a chief and find ready followers among destitute families. People are the more submissive as their leader is also the high priest of the community. His subjects are obliged to work for him. A chief is succeeded by his favorite son, but often the group splits if a brother of the new chief refuses to recognize his leadership.

One of the *Araona* villages visited by Labré (1889, p. 499) was ruled by two chiefs, each of whom had several families under his orders. Among these Indians, descent was patrilineal.

Work requiring cooperation is undertaken for a man by his relatives and friends, who are rewarded with food.

LIFE CYCLE

Childbirth.—*Tiatinagua* women are delivered in the forest, assisted by two other women. The *Araona* have traditional names which they give to their children some time after birth. The couvade is reported among the *Maropa* and *Araona*.

Puberty.—At puberty, *Tiatinagua* boys have the frenum of the penis cut with a bamboo knife; girls, the hymen slit by a woman using the same instrument. At about the age of 15, *Araona* boys go through an ordeal which strongly suggests a specific complex of initiation rites. The priests temporarily blind them by rubbing a powder, made of a poisonous creeper, into their eyes. The initiates are then taken to the local sanctuary, where their sight returns as soon as their eyes have been washed with the priest's saliva.

Tiatinagua groups are said to be exogamous. It is reported also that *Araona* men could marry only *Caviña* women and vice versa. *Caviña* marry at a very tender age; girls are sometimes wed to a boy or a man before puberty. Mothers are said to deflower their daughters by artificial means to prepare them for married life. *Araona* children are married at the age of 9 or 10, but the marriage is consummated only after puberty. Polygyny is a chief's privilege among the *Araona* and *Tiatinagua*. Among the *Tiatinagua,* marriages are easily dissolved by mutual consent.

Funeral rites.—The *Araona* in their eagerness to get rid of the corpses began the funerals before the ailing person had breathed his last. They interred the dead in their huts in a squatting position with a rope round the neck.

The *Tiatinagua* bury their dead in an extended position with all their belongings, somewhere in the bush.

After a death has occurred, the *Caviña* change the place of the house door to confuse the returning soul. It is reported that among these Indians a widower could marry only a widow, and vice versa.

The *Tiatinagua* believe that of the three souls of men, one remains on the earth as a ghost, the second goes to the Great Ancestor, and the third joins other souls in a country crossed by a big river where fish and game may be caught without effort and where fields are covered with big crops (Alvarez, 1941).

ESTHETIC AND RECREATIONAL ACTIVITIES

Musical instruments.—*Araona* women during religious ceremonies played bone quenas, or end-flutes with three stops.

Caviña panpipes are composed of a double row of seven or eight tubes fastened together by a strip of bamboo wound like a band a couple of times around the entire instrument; each pipe is further attached by a thread. The same type of ligature is found also on *Aymara* and *Yuracare* panpipes (Izikowitz, 1935, p. 388). Huge bark trumpets, joined together like the tubes of panpipes, and similar to those of the Christianized *Mojo* and *Itonama,* are in use in the mission of Caviña.

Games.—In their ball games, the *Araona* butt the ball with their stomachs, which are protected with bark belts.

Stimulants.—None of the *Tacanan* tribes is known to brew any fermented drink, though they prepare mush which may easily ferment. This lack of true alcoholic beverages is a curious exception in an area where most tribes enjoy several kinds of beer.

The *Araona* chew coca mixed with motacu palm (*Attalea humboldtiana*) or chameiro (a creeper) ashes. They keep the mixture in special wooden bowls. Several *Tacanan* groups raise tobacco but do not smoke it.

RELIGION AND MYTHOLOGY

Gods and spirits.—When they were visited by Armentia, the main god of the *Araona* was Baba-buada, a wind god invested with the dignity of the creator. He was the master of the seasons, and he set the time for sowing or harvesting crops. Next to him were many inferior gods and spirits: Itzeti Mara Edutzi, the Sun God; Baba Tsutu, the Jaguar God; the God of Health; the Maize God, the Fire God, the God of Houses, the Peccary God, the Thunder God, the God who protects against Caimans, and the Death God. These deities were represented by material symbols, such as carved pieces of wood decorated with feather mosaics (Wind, Sun, and Moon Gods), and manufactured objects, including spears with wooden heads, arrows and axes, pots, or small black pebbles (deities of food: Maize, Yuca, and Banana). These idols were placed in square temples located in the middle of the forest. The interior of the temple was divided into two compartments, one for the symbols of the gods, and the other for the dance paraphernalia. Women and children were not allowed to view the sacred objects and were barred from ceremonies.

Each god had a yanacona or special servant to take care of his image. Priests were obliged to observe chastity. The head of a village was often a priest.

Great feasts were celebrated for the gods at sowing time and before harvest. The members of each family chanted prayers almost every night to ask the deities for favors. The ancient *Pamaino* and *Saparuna* placed in their temples the largest maize ears which they harvested and left them in the sanctuaries for a whole year.

That *Araona* religion has received Andean influences is evidenced by the *Quechua* names of some of the gods of their pantheon. Seventeenth-century explorers found actual Peruvian idols and objects in the sanctuaries of the *Tacana* Indians.

The spirits of the *Tiatinagua* seem to have specialized functions: one is feared because he inflicts diseases, another resides in the rivers and causes shipwrecks. The Sun, the Moon, and the Stars are also personified and in human form come to this earth to harm people. Like the other *Tacanan* Indians, the *Tiatinagua* assign spirits (shahua) to all the plants (Alvarez, 1941, p. 159).

The religious beliefs of the *Caviña* and *Tumupasa* are reflected in their myths and tales, collected by Nordenskiöld (1924 a, pp. 288–305). These Indians distinguish two different kinds of spirits: the ishausa, or nature spirits, and the chokihua, or ordinary ghosts. Every animal species is represented by a special spirit that acts as its protector. These spirits have the appearance of men or of huge animals of the species which they represent. The Caiman spirit has a double tail; the Turtle spirit is a gigantic turtle; and the Frog spirit, a huge frog. The Peccary spirit is fond of kidnapping people to enjoy their company; the Monkey spirit prevents hunters from destroying too many of his people. The Master-of-the-partridges is a serpent who once made a bargain with a hunter stipulating that the latter should be allowed to kill as much game as he wished if he spared the partridges. It was only after the serpent had been killed by mistake that game became elusive.

Some spirits reside in trees, which consequently cannot be felled without danger. There are also river spirits who kidnap and eat women. Rubber trees are inhabited by spirits who punish those who tap their sap unless they are under duress. Meteorological phenomena are caused by spirits. For instance, the wind is a small boy who throws a rubber ball and also causes thunder.

According to *Caviña* mythology, the sun is a man who is married to a jaguar woman but took a spirit woman as his second wife. She bore him a baby so hot that nobody could hold it. The sun also had sexual intercourse with the moon, who had come to steal his vegetables. Fire is a woman, who became insulted because a woman had urinated on her. She withdrew her services to mankind until she found a person whom she liked.

The *Caviña* had a myth based on the motif of the flying heads which, after killing animals and men, go to the sky.

In *Tumupasa* mythology, the former owner of fire was a frog spirit. The first time fire was stolen from him by an old man and woman, the frog succeeded in putting it out. The second time it was stolen, the frog was killed, but was resurrected in various disguises: a woman, a fish, and many other forms. Each time the fire was stolen, the frog spirit was killed again. Finally, the frog poisoned the beer of his adversaries, who died.

Eclipses occur when the sun, in sign of mourning, smears his face with genipa. The spots on the moon are genipa marks put on her face by Venus at a beer party.

The only recorded tale of the *Maropa* is the story of a boy who married a doe, who transformed herself into a woman.

A few *Tiatinagua* myths have been recorded recently by a Franciscan missionary (Alvarez, 1941). According to these stories, the first *Tia-*

tinagua descended from the sky by means of a rope which broke and thus forced many other people to remain in the sky. The other Indian tribes of the region came from holes in the ground. Many animals are transformed people who have suffered various accidents or have been punished for their cruelty. (The jaguar was a man who murdered his wife and children, the peccary was a cruel father, etc.) The motif of the Tree of Life, so characteristic of the Guianas and northwestern South America, occurs among these Indians also.

A great flood was caused by a sudden rise of the rivers, and a huge fish added to the terror by eating people until a young boy killed it. Only one couple succeeded in escaping the disaster by climbing a high mountain.

BIBLIOGRAPHY

Alvarez, 1941; Armentia, 1887–88, 1902, 1906; Brinton, 1892 c; Cardús, 1886; Chandless, 1866 b; Church, 1898; Créqui-Montfort and Rivet, 1921–22; D'Orbigny, 1839; Farabee, 1922; Fawcett, 1911; Giglioli, 1906; Gili, 1902; Groeteken, 1907; Guillaume, 1890; Hassel, 1905; Heath, 1883; Izikowitz, 1935; Labré, 1889; Lafone-Quevedo, 1902; Maurtua, 1906, vols. 6–8; Métraux, 1942; Nordenskiöld, 1905, 1924 a, 1924 b; Perú. Junta de vías fluviales, 1942; Reeves, 1910; Relación y descripción de las misiones y conversiones de infieles (1886); Rivet, 1924; Schuller, 1922; Steinen, W. von den, 1899; Stiglich, 1908; Teza, 1868; Weddell, 1853.

THE SOUTHEASTERN PANOAN TRIBES

TRIBAL DIVISIONS

The *Pacaguará* (*Pacavara*) live on both sides of the Beni, lower Madre de Díos, Mamoré, upper Madeira, and lower Abuná Rivers (lat. 11°–13° S., long. 65°–67° W., map 1, *No. 2*; maps 2, 4). Formerly, they extended father to the south; the Mission of Santiago de Pacaguaras on the Madidi River, above its junction with the Chuini River, consisted of *Pacaguará*. According to Armentia (1887–88, p. 42), there were groups of *Pacaguará* at Sinusinu, San Lorenzo, Biata, Mamorbey Jenechiquia, and Jenesuaya. At Orton, there were three subgroups, two of which were exterminated by the *Araona* in 1885. The southernmost *Pacaguará* were pushed toward the north by the *Tacanan* tribes.

Créqui-Montfort and Rivet (1913 b, p. 21) consider the *Chacobo, Sinabo, Capuibo,* and *Caripuná* as subtribes of the *Pacaguará*. The *Capuibo* reside along the Biata River, a tributary of the Beni River (lat. 13° S., long. 67°W.). The *Chacobo* are split into small units scattered 3 days' walking distance northwest of Exaltación, between Lake Rogoaguado and the Mamoré River (lat. 13°–14° S., long. 65°–66° W.). In 1908, Nordenskiöld visited one of their villages north of Lake Rogoaguado. In 1887 there were two groups of *Chacobo* on the Ivon River, one comprising six families and the other, four. The *Sinabo* (*Gritones*) inhabit the region called Los Armendrales, near the first rapids of the Mamoré

River and along the Bolivian side of the Guaporé River (lat. 11°–13° S., long. 65°–66° W.). The *Caripuná* (*Jaun-avo*) figure among the Amazonian tribes listed by Acuña (1891, p. 45),[6] who places them with the *Zurina* on the Purús River (lat. 10°–11° S., long. 64°–66° W.). Natterer encountered a *Caripuná* subgroup, the *Jacariá* (*Jacaré-Tapuuja*), on the Abuná River, and another subgroup, the *Shenabu* (probably the *Sinabo*) on the Madeira River above the Cachoeira do Pâo. The *Caripuná* had also a settlement near the Caldeirão do Inferno. At the beginning of the 20th century, the few surviving *Caripuná* retired along the Mutum Paraná, a right tributary of the Madeira River. Giglioli (1906, p. 219), on the authority of an Italian colonist, Landi, lists the *Pamá* and *Pamaná* Indians as a subgroup of the *Caripuná*. Their habitat was the Caldeirão and São Lorenzo Rivers, both small tributaries of the Madeira River, and the banks of the Madeira River between the rapids of Caldeirão do Inferno and Girão.

D'Orbigny (1839, 2:262) estimates the number of *Pacaguará* at 1,000; Hassel (1905, p. 49) at 2,000.

CULTURE

Subsistence.—The *Pacaguará* and *Chacobo* are agriculturists who grow the usual crops of the region with sweet manioc, bananas, and maize as staples. They grind the maize in huge wooden troughs with heavy wooden slabs of semicircular shape. They grate the manioc tubers on thorny palm roots and roast the mass in flat clay pans. The *Caripuná* prepare farinha from bitter manioc. The manioc roots are placed in a kind of semicircular trough, made of the split stem of a mirití palm, and are crushed into a pulp. The imperfectly kneaded flour is next put through a sieve made of fiber strings, reduced to a fine dough, and formed into cakes. These are sometimes left for a few hours to ferment. The dough, with water added to it, is placed in a manioc press to eject both the water and the prussic acid. The flour is then put into a pan and moved about with a stick until it is roasted (Domville-Fife, 1924, p. 106).

The *Caripuná* have often been described as inveterate geophagists, a habit which may be attributed to the presence of salty earth in their country.

Houses.—*Chacobo* communal huts are rectangular, with gabled roof and side walls. The clubhouse, where men store their weapons, drink, and sleep, especially if they are unmarried, has an octagonal ground plan with a roof resting on eight wall plates surrounding the central ridge pole, which is supported by two vertical posts. As the sides are entirely open, nothing in the clubhouse can be kept secret, though access to it is forbidden to women. The *Caripuná* have also a men's house,

---

[6] The *Caripuná* mentioned by Acuña may well have been a tribe entirely different from the modern Indians of the same name.

which is an open sunshade. *Pacaguará* huts are tentlike, with no end walls.

The use of cotton hammocks is general among all these groups. Acuña (1891, p. 145) praises the *Caripuná* of the Purús River for their artistically carved benches in animal form. *Chacobo* benches are made of palm stalks nailed on tree stumps.

Clothing and adornment.—*Chacobo* and *Caripuná* men go naked with the penis fastened against the stomach under a cotton belt. A distinctive ornament of the *Chacobo* is a solid, flat broad collar, made of countless monkey incisors and trimmed with tucan feathers. *Chacobo* men also wear a feather tuft or reed with feathers through the nasal septum, pieces of bone or wooden sticks in the ear lobes, and wrappings of long bast strips around the arms and legs. Men cut their hair across the forehead and wrap it with a cotton band into a queue.

Chacobo women cover their pubis with a Heliconia leaf attached to a cotton or fiber string; *Pacaguará* and *Caripuná* women wear a small front flap or apron. *Chacobo* women bore the nasal septum and ears to insert feather tufts. Their other ornaments are seed necklaces, chonta finger rings, armlets of feathers and shells or wrappings of bark around arms and legs, and, occasionally, one or two feathers glued to their long, loose hair.

Transportation.—The *Pacaguará* travel in bark canoes or in dugouts which may accommodate about eight people.

Manufactures.—Industries are the same as those of the neighboring tribes: Twilled baskets, rectangular boxes of *Gynerium* stalks sewn together, and bags of bark cloth for storage of their possessions.

Figure 56.—A "Cascara," or bark canoe of the *Caripuná*. (After Mathews, 1879.)

Pottery is plain; some vessels collected by Nordenskiöld bear imprints of the banana leaves on which they rested during the modeling process.

Cotton is carded with a small bow and spun with a spindle rolled on the thigh.

Their bows, made of chonta palm, have shoulders cut for the fiber string; arrowheads are of the lanceolate and rod types; the feathering is cemented with resin (Peruvian feathering). The *Caripuná* of the Purús River, mentioned by Acuña (1891, p. 145), used beautifully carved spear throwers.

According to Giglioli (1906, p. 225), *Pacaguará* and *Caripuná* stone axes are glued directly to the handle, without any socket or lashing, by means of the rosin of the massaranduba tree, which when it dries, hardens like cement.

The most common tools are bamboo and shell knives, piranha teeth, and planes made of peccary jaws.

Esthetic and recreational activities.—The only *Chacobo* musical instrument described in the literature is a panpipe consisting of five disconnected pipes held in the hand. *Caripuná* drums are said to be made of a pot with a rubber membrane stretched over its mouth.

Chacobo dancers walk in a line to and fro holding short ceremonial clubs.

Chicha is prepared of manioc fermented with the addition of saliva. Tobacco is not grown for smoking, but to kill *Dermatobia* larvae. The *Caripuná* provoke a state of trance by taking parica (*Piptadenia* sp.) in the form of clysters which they administer to each other with rubber syringes provided with a bone tube.

Religion.—According to Armentia (1887–88, p. 43), the *Pacaguará* worshiped their deities in the guise of a jaguar's, a peccary's or some other animal's head. They celebrated magicoreligious ceremonies, which unfortunately are not described, before sowing and harvesting. Acuña (1891) states that the *Caripuná* of the Purús River had wooden idols.

Among the *Chacobo,* practitioners of both sexes use massage and blowing as the basic cure in the treatment of the sick.

The dead are buried in a sitting position in the hut, which is then burned down. Female relatives lament and temporarily discard their ornaments in sign of grief. According to Keller-Leuzinger (1874, p. 124), the *Caripuná* bury their dead in large urns within the huts. Bullroarers are whirled during the funerary ceremonies. (Among the *Chacobo,* bull-roarers are used as toys by children.)

BIBLIOGRAPHY

Acuña, 1891; Armentia, 1887–88; Créqui-Montfort and Rivet, 1913 b; Domville-Fife, 1924; D'Orbigny, 1839; Giglioli, 1906; Grasserie, 1890; Hassel, 1905; Keller-Leuzinger, 1874; Martius, 1867; Mathews, 1879; Nordenskiöld, 1922; Perú. Junta de vías fluviales, 1902; Rivet, 1910 a.

THE SOUTHWESTERN PANOAN TRIBES

TRIBAL DIVISIONS

On the upper reaches of the Madre de Díos River, there are a few *Panoan* groups (map 1, *No. 2*; map 2) which are separated from those of the lower Beni River by *Tacanan tribes*. The *Atsahuaca,* of whom only 20 survived in 1904, lived along the Carama (Atsahuaca) and the Malinowski Rivers, both tributaries of the Tambopata River, and along the Chaspa River, tributary of the Inambari River (lat. 13°–15° S., long. 70°–71° W.). The *Yamiaca,* who live on the Yaguarmayo River, near its junction with the Inambari River, are a branch of the *Atsahuaca.* The *Arasa (Arazaire)* were found on the Marcapata or Arasa River, a left tributary of the Inambari River (lat. 14° S., long. 71° W.). They also belong to the *Panoan* family, though some of them may also speak a *Tacanan* dialect. According to Hassel (1905), their total number was from 500 to 800; according to Cipriani (1902, p. 175), only 20 to 25.

CULTURE

SUBSISTENCE ACTIVITIES

The *Yamiaca* collect fruits in the bush and turtle eggs from the sandy beaches. Both the *Yamiaca* and *Atsahuaca* cultivate fields widely scattered along the rivers. They grow bananas, sweet manioc (yuca), sweet potatoes, gourds, cotton, sugarcane, cayenne pepper, and maize. The *Yamiaca* also raise pineapples and papaya. All crops except sugarcane are communally owned. Staples are bananas and, to a less extent, manioc and maize.

The *Yamiaca* are good fishermen, but the *Atsahuaca* live in a region with only small streams and few fish. The former have harpoon arrows with two removable elements, a head and an intermediate piece of wood between it and the shaft. Both tribes drug fish with poison.

The *Atsahuaca* are skillful hunters with a remarkable knowledge of animal habits and sounds. They hunt with well-trained dogs.

The *Yamiaca* grate bananas on prickly roots. Both tribes cook in clay pots and in bamboo joints and broil game on rectangular babracots. The *Atsahuaca* prepare a sour mead of honey. The *Yamiaca* brew banana and manioc beer.

HOUSES

Atsahuaca huts are simple lean-tos covered with imbricated palm leaves, split along the midrib. Sometimes two opposite lean-tos are brought together so as to form a gabled roof. Each hut accommodated a single biological family. The *Yamiaca* have large communal huts. Originally, the *Yamiaca* slept on the ground, but in more recent times they have adopted platform beds and fiber hammocks.

DRESS AND ADORNMENTS

Men wear a sleeveless shirt of cotton or bark cloth, women a bark cloth or cotton skirt and often a square shawl on their shoulders. The *Atsahuaca* paint concentric circles with dots on their garments.

The *Yamiaca* and *Atsahuaca* put feathers or a stick through the nasal septum or hang shells or other pendants from the nose. Some *Atsahuaca* men insert wooden sticks through the corners of their mouths. A few *Atsahuaca* women thrust sticks or feathers in their ear lobes. All women wear monkey-tooth necklaces. The *Atsahuaca* had beautiful parrot-feather headdresses and cotton frontlets with fringes and feather tassels. Pigments for body paint are urucú and genipa. Combs are of the composite type.

TRANSPORTATION

The *Yamiaca* use both dugout canoes and rafts. The *Atsahuaca* lack any craft, as their territory has no navigable streams.

Contrary to the custom of most Indians of the region, the *Atsahuaca* support ordinary burdens on the back with a band passing across the chest. Children, however, are carried on the shoulders in a baby sling held by a tumpline.

MANUFACTURES

Basketry is little developed. These tribes manufacture boxes and mats, made by sewing *Gynerium* stalks together, and weave a few oval wicker baskets. Spindles are of the drop type.

Clay for pottery is tempered with pulverized potsherds. The finished pots are unornamented.

POLITICAL ORGANIZATION

Both Southwestern *Panoan* tribes have chiefs who enjoy certain authority. The *Atsahuaca* show great respect for their chief, even whispering in his presence.

ILLNESS AND DEATH

Among the *Atsahuaca,* flogging with a nettle and other harsh measures are used in the treatment of the sick.

The *Yamiaca* destroy part of the crops of a deceased person and bury his possessions with him.

BIBLIOGRAPHY

Cipriani, 1902; Grasserie, 1890; Hassel, 1905; Llosa, 1906; Los salvajes de San Gabán, 1902; Martius, 1867; Métraux, 1942; Nordenskiöld, 1905; Perú. Junta de vías fluviales, 1904; Rivet, 1910 a; Steinen, 1904.

THE SIRIONO

By Allan Holmberg

INTRODUCTION

The *Sirionó* (*Mbia*) are an anomaly in Eastern Bolivia. Scattered throughout the high forests of the eastern and northern parts of the Province of Beni (lat. 14°–15° S., long. 61°–62° W.; lat. 16°–17° S., long. 63°–65° W.; lat. 13° S., long. 63° W.; maps 1, *No. 2;* 2; 4), with a culture strikingly backward in contrast to that of their neighbors, they are probably the remnant of an ancient population which was exterminated, absorbed, or engulfed by more civilized invaders. Their language, however, is *Tupian,* elsewhere spoken by tribes of a more complex culture, but here represented only by themselves and the *Guarayú-Pauserna,* whose dialects are closely related. Traditions of friendship suggest that these peoples once may have been linked by a now obscure bond.

The present cultural summary is based largely on the author's field work. For sources, see Métraux (1942, p. 114).

HISTORY

First mentioned by Father Barrace in 1693 (Lettres édifiantes . . . 1780–83, 8 :105), the *Sirionó* have continued to occupy their deep forests until comparatively recently. The Jesuits made several attempts to missionize them, and in 1765 there were a few *Sirionó* in the Mission of Buena Vista; these were later transferred to the Santa Rosa Mission. Up until the present time, however, all other attempts to missionize them have failed, not so much because of the warlike character of the *Sirionó,* but because of their sensitivity to maltreatment and their adherence to nomadic life. In 1925, a band of *Sirionó* was settled at the Mission of Santa María by the Franciscans. Because of bad treatment they left the mission, and traces of the band were encountered wandering in the forests east of the Río Blanco in 1940. In 1937, a small number of *Sirionó* were forced to settle in a so-called government school at Casarabe, about 50 miles east of Trinidad. Population of this school was augmented by periodic expeditions into the forest until 1940, when it reached about 300. Through maltreatment, disease, and death, their numbers had been reduced to less than half by 1944. Some 10 miles east of Trinidad, American missionaries in 1935 established a small group of *Sirionó* at the site of an old *Mojo* mound known as *Ibiato,* but as a result of lack of realistic insight into the culture of the Indian, this attempt has likewise almost perished. The most successful effort to make the *Sirionó* a sedentary group was that of the late Frederick Park Richards, an American cattle rancher near El Carmen, who has had large numbers of *Sirionó* continuously on his place since 1925. These are the most acculturated *Sirionó* in Bolivia.

Many *Sirionó* are also found in forced labor on farms and cattle ranches, along the Río Blanco, Río Grande, Río Mamoré, and Río San Miguel. Only a few bands still wander wild in the forests; they are widely scattered from the Río Blanco to the upper Ichilo, Chapare, and Mamoré Rivers. Probably not over 3,000 *Sirionó* survive today, and these are rapidly disappearing.

CULTURE

SUBSISTENCE ACTIVITIES

In contrast to most other Chiquitos-Mojos tribes, the *Sirionó* are semi-nomadic forest dwellers, who live more by hunting and gathering than by farming. According to the season of maturity, a great variety of wild fruits are collected, among which are the motacu, chonta, totaí, samuque, pacabilla, coquino, pecay, and aguaí. Palm cabbage also forms one of the staples of their diet, being edible the year round and found in all regions where the *Sirionó* wander. Both sexes collect these wild foods, the women more so than the men.

Farming.—A small amount of agriculture is practiced in rude clearings in the forest, which are burned over in the latter part of the dry season (May to November). The following crops are planted: Maize (a soft red variety), sweet manioc, sweet potatoes, papaya, cotton, and tobacco. All planting and tilling are done with a digging stick of chonta palm, the only agricultural implement. Often after planting, the entire band sets out on a hunting and gathering expedition, traveling from place to place as the wild life of each is exhausted, and returning from time to time to note the condition of their crops. After harvest, crops are stored in rude motacu palm baskets. More movement of the band takes place during the dry than the rainy season.

Hunting.—Hunting is the chief economic activity, meat being the most abundant and most desired item in the diet. Hunting is the man's task. On the march, men go ahead with their bows and arrows to hunt, and the women and children follow, gathering vegetable foods. Some 40 varieties of game are taken including tapir, peccary, coati, anteater, forest deer, armadillo, iguana, monkey, jaguar, wild land and water fowl, and about 10 kinds of tropical fish.

Animals are very carefully stalked until they are at close range, or they are brought into range by calls of imitation. Under unusual circumstances, cooperation between hunters takes place. If, for example, an animal, not likely to move, is out of range in a high tree, one hunter will climb the tree to a branch within range of the animal; his companion below then shoots an arrow at half force up to him; he seizes it in flight, puts it in his own bow, and shoots the animal. A form of whistling language is also used in hunting.

The catch is usually divided within the extended family, members of which receive shares according to their rank and status, food and hunting taboos, and abundance of the catch. Although the chief and his immediate family are theoretically entitled to a share of any catch, actually this is rarely the case.

Food preparation.—Food is either roasted in ashes, broiled, or boiled and steamed in clay pots. Game is not skinned for cooking; the hair is burned off in the fire and the skin eaten. All parts of the animal are consumed. The *Sirionó* eat almost all animals of their environment except snakes; food taboos are based largely on age and sex. The food supply is generally scarce and frequently is inadequate.

HOUSES

Sirionó houses are of the rudest and most temporary kind, consisting merely of poles lashed to trees and covered with the long leaves of the motacu palm. These huts sometimes reach considerable dimensions, however, sheltering as many as 80 to 100 people. The entire band sleeps in one hut, the hammocks of the chief and his family being hung in the center. A fire is always smouldering between each hammock, for cooking and to keep off the insects.

ORNAMENTS

The *Sirionó* do not wear clothing, but decorate themselves in a variety of ways. Men, women, and children wear necklaces made of animal teeth, quills, and seeds. Eyebrows and forehead hair are depilated, and everyone paints his body and face, especially on ceremonial occasions, with urucú. The hair is also decorated with toucan, guan, and hawk feathers glued on with beeswax. During a ceremonial drinking feast, which occurs on rare occasions, men and women who have had children are punctured with the dorsal spine of the stingray, women on the upper arm from the elbow to the shoulder and men on the lower arm from the wrist to the elbow. This leaves decorative scars which are a sign of maturity. The practice also has important magical significance in that it gets rid of the old blood.

TRANSPORTATION

The *Sirionó* do not manufacture canoes; all transport is overland. Carrying (chiefly by the women) is done in rude motacu palm-leaf baskets, which rest on the back and are suspended from the head or shoulders by means of a liana. Rivers are crossed by felling trees from either side and putting up a railing of liana. In cases where this is impossible, the people swim.

MANUFACTURES

Textiles.—No true weaving is found among the *Sirionó*. Cotton string, used extensively in arrow making and for the twining of baby slings, is spun with a spindle of the Andean drop type. Hammocks are twined of wood fiber.

Basketry.—Carrying and storage baskets of a very temporary kind are plaited from the leaves of the motacu palm.

Ceramics.—Women make crude coiled cooking pots which are tempered with burned seeds of the motacu palm and baked over the open fire. Women also make the clay pipes.

Weapons.—*Sirionó* bows, made of the black chonta palm, are perhaps the longest in the world, averaging from 7 to 8 feet (2.2 to 2.5 m.) in length, some being even as long as 10 feet (3 m.). Arrows have chuchio reed shafts (in case of scarcity, bamboo may be used) and average from 8 to 10 feet (2.5 to 3 m.) in length. They are tipped either with a lanceolate bamboo blade or with a sharp chonta rod to which a barb is attached. The former type is used to kill the larger game on the ground; the latter for tree game, such as birds and monkeys.

The range of these arrows is not accurate for more than about 30 yards (27.3 m.). One of the reasons bows are so long is that they are pulled to the greatest possible length; a long bow is thus needed so the wood will stand the strain. In shooting the archer's head is put inside the taut bow string so as to aim by sighting along the arrow, then pulled out as the bow string is released. The long arrow affords a means of pulling wounded game out of the trees, and it makes it more difficult for wounded ground game to travel any great distance before falling. Arrows are always retrieved when possible.

Miscellaneous.—Work in stone or metal is unknown, neither of these materials being found in the environment. The only manufactured tools consist of the digging stick and an agouti tooth hafted to the humerus of a monkey. The latter is used to fashion the groove in the nock of the arrow.

Fire making.—The art of making fire now seems to be lost, but formerly it was made by twirling a stick between the palms of the hands.

SOCIAL ORGANIZATION

The *Sirionó* are organized into bands, each made up of matrilineal extended families, the number varying with the size of the band. Some bands may consist of only 30 or 40 people, while the larger ones have as many as 120. Because of the great distances over which the *Sirionó* wander and because of their varying seasonal activities, contact between the bands is rare. As the *Sirionó* are not warlike, relations between bands are peaceful.

Each band is presided over by a chief, who is normally succeeded by his eldest son, provided the latter is a good hunter. Little importance is attached to chieftainship, however. The main prerogative of the chief seems to be that his hammock is hung in the center of the house. He makes suggestions as to migrations, hunting activities, and where to plant crops. But his suggestions are not always followed by others than his immediate family.

The kinship system is highly classificatory. The father and his brothers are included under one term (paba) as are the mother and her sisters (tain). The father's sister and mother's brother's wife are called by one term (ari), and the mother's brother and the father's sister's husband by one term (ami). Grandfathers and grandmothers are also known respectively as ami and ari. No sex distinction is made between siblings and parallel cousins who refer to each other as anoge or between sons and daughters, who are referred to as ečo. Formalized kinship behavior is at a minimum; there are no specific avoidance or joking relationships.

LIFE CYCLE

Childbirth.—The cause of pregnancy is known to the *Sirionó*, and once a woman is pregnant it is believed that intercourse stimulates the growth of the child in her womb. During pregnancy, the woman must observe a large number of food taboos and food preferences in order to insure the birth of a healthy and normal child. It is believed, for example, that to eat the anteater—a forbidden animal—would cause the birth of a club-footed child, while to eat the peccary—a highly desired animal— would cause the birth of a valiant child. The father is not subject to these taboos.

Parturition normally takes place in the hammock within the hut, and is a public event. Generally, the woman receives no help during the birth. Beforehand she ties a rope over the hammock from one end of it to the other with which to support herself during parturition and loosens the earth under the hammock with a digging stick. In most cases, the child when born falls off the strings at the edge of the hammock, which is rarely over a foot off the ground, onto the soft earth below. The mother then gets down on the ground to expel the afterbirth, which is later placed in a basket and after about two weeks thrown deep into the bush. The father uses a piece of bamboo to cut the umbilical cord about 3 to 4 inches (about 7.5 to 10 cm.) from the navel. The part of the cord which falls off from the child is wrapped in a ball of cotton string covered with urucú and worn around the mother's neck as a good luck charm.

The father is seldom present at the birth. As soon as birth pangs are felt he picks up his bow and arrows and goes hunting. The child is named after the first animal he kills. Sometimes, between the time a child is born and the father's return, 8 hours may elapse, thus delaying the cutting of the cord.

During a couvade of about 3 days, the father and mother do not leave the house except for the calls of nature. They are fed by other members of the extended family, and the child when awake is continually given the breast. During this period, the child gets his first hair cut, his eyebrows being plucked and his hair pulled out up to a high line on his forehead—a very painful experience, accompanied by great howling. The father and mother are scarified on both the upper and lower legs with a rat's tooth, they are decorated with toucan, hawk, and guan feathers, painted with urucú, and adorned with urucú-covered cotton string, which is wound around their legs (just below the knees) and around their necks.

After the 3-day confinement, the father takes up his bow and arrows, the mother puts her child in a new baby sling (previously made and covered with urucú), and the couple sets out for the forest, scattering ashes from small palm baskets as they go. This is a purification rite. Not far from camp they stop, gather firewood, and then return to the house. They kindle a new fire and resume normal life.

Technonomy is practiced. After the birth of every child, the father and mother change their names to that of the child plus a suffix indicating father (ndu) and mother (asi). Nicknames, which are given because of some physical characteristic or because of some abnormal event that happened to the individual, are also common. Nicknames are used more frequently than real names in everyday life, but there is no taboo on the use of a person's real name, although a certain reluctance to speak it prevails immediately after death.

Childhood.—Until it is about one year old, a child is constantly with its mother, either in the house or, when on the march, in the baby hammock, which is placed over one of the mother's shoulders, the baby resting in it with his legs astride her hip. Whenever the child cries he is given the breast. All basic habits, such as toilet training, walking, and talking, are instilled very gradually. Young babies, however, are very carefully watched that they do not play with their feces.

Although children are treated indulgently by their parents, the frustrations of the natural environment alone make life a hardship for them. There are always long marches, shortages of food, insect pests, and disease.

Puberty.—There are no puberty rites for boys, but young girls undergo a ceremony known as yuqwa'ki before they are allowed to have sexual intercourse. Sex relations with a young girl who has not undergone this ceremony will result in sickness and death. Girls of about puberty age have their heads shaved and are sent into the forest with a hunter and several old women. They must observe many food taboos and continually take baths to purify themselves. They are also taught songs by the women who attend them. After a month or 6 weeks they return to camp and, when their hair again grows to the length of their chins, they are considered eligible for marriage. Menstruation is not a pre-requisite to undergoing this ceremony.

Marriage.—Assymetrical cross-cousin marriage is the preferred type; a man marries his mother's brother's daughter. And marriages do not occur outside of this type of relationship. There are no marriage ceremonies; the man simply moves his hammock next to that of his father-in-law and mother-in-law (matrilocal residence). Polygyny is practiced, as are the sororate and levirate. Within the bounds prescribed by the kinship system, sex relations are comparatively free. A man has sex rights to the wives of anyone whom he calls brother, and a woman to the husbands of anyone whom she calls sister. Young boys and girls thus readily find sex partners after the age of puberty. Within the polygynous system, wives are placed in a hierarchy, the first wife taken usually being the most influential.

Old age and death.—As people grow older and their usefulness to the band is impaired, they are given less and less attention. When on the march, the aged and very sick are abandoned to die, being left with fire, and a small amount of food and water.

Apart from death by old age, almost all deaths are caused by evil spirits (abačiquaia). The dead are wrapped in a mat, and placed on a platform inside the house; arrows are shot through the house to drive out evil spirits, and it is then abandoned. After several months, when the body has decayed, the bones are buried, but the skull is taken back to the house, where it is placed in a small basket underneath the hammock. When on the march, the skull is carried to the next camping place. When a member of the family is ill, the skull is rubbed over the part of the body which aches.

Most of the possessions of the dead are destroyed, particularly his calabashes. His bow and arrows, however, may be used again and gen-erally pass to his brother. A woman's possessions may pass to a sister or a co-wife.

The period of mourning is very short, generally not more than about 3 days, during which the mourners are smeared with urucú, scarified, and decorated with feathers. Widows and widowers can remarry almost immediately.

RECREATIONAL ACTIVITIES

Drinking bouts.—Accompanying the frustrations of forest life are occasional drinking bouts which vary in frequency with the quantity of wild bee honey available. Chicha is made from a mixture of cooked maize meal (or cooked manioc), water, and wild bee honey which is stored for 3 days in calabashes until it is fermented to about the strength of beer.

At the drinking feast, participants (usually men, but never men and women together) sit in a circle and pass the calabash from one to the other, taking deep draughts of the liquor as it is passed around. Continuous smoking of clay pipes during the drinking soon produces a semi-intoxicated condition. Singing (generally impromptu) by one participant or another starts and others join in. Soon insults are hurled and wrestling begins. Drinking and fighting go on until all the liquor is gone or the participants are too exhausted to continue. Women usually sit on the edge of the circle draining the dregs of the calabashes, but when there is an abundance of chicha, they too have their drinking feasts.

On rare occasions, about once a year or once every two years, all mature members of the band participate in a heavy drinking bout which is a sort of rejuvenation ceremony. Everyone gets very drunk and has his arms pierced with the dorsal spine of the stingray, the blood being run into a small hole in the ground. At dawn the following morning the male participants all go out to hunt, and the female participants to gather palm cabbages, spreading ashes as they go. The *Sirionó* say that after this ceremony they are made more youthful and strong by getting rid of old blood.

Dancing.—Dancing is a very common way of passing parts of the long tropical nights, particularly during the full moon. The men do a circle dance, arms linked, stamping the ground to the accompaniment of songs. These dances usually begin with everyone singing standard songs; later a leader makes up impromptu songs which the others repeat after him. Women likewise dance, but never with the men; instead of stamping the ground, they waddle around in a circle, arms linked, keeping time to the chants of a leader.

MAGIC

Sirionó culture cannot be characterized as magic-ridden, but magical practices especially pervade those aspects of life which have to do with subsistence. Hunters follow certain practices to insure the game supply. The skulls of animals are always hung on sticks near where they are eaten, in order that the same animal will return to be hunted. Feathers of birds are also hung on poles to attract the same bird to return. A hunter is not allowed to eat the meat of a particular animal of certain species that he kills (e. g., the tapir) lest he offend the animal and be unable to hunt another.

Certain hunters are believed to possess special powers to hunt particular animals. Often, when a man of such a reputation is dying, hunters will gather around and ask him to pass them some of his luck. He may tell them to go to a certain place after he dies, where they will find, for example, a band of peccary. They will usually hunt down one of these animals until they find it. Other hunters, cursed with a streak of bad luck, may repair to a spot where bones of a good hunter are buried and ask him for luck.

Black magic, though not unknown, is not practiced to any great extent. In cases of serious quarrels, one man may say to another, "Watch out, or I'll take you with me when I die." Cases are likewise known where a man has said such things to one of his wives, and she has died a few days after his death.

Magic is likewise important in curing. The *Sirionó* have no professional shamans and very few herbal remedies. Practically, all curing is by magical chant and the aforementioned use of a dead person's skull. Pregnant women are said to be better at curing than anyone else. Amulets of cotton string covered with urucú are likewise used to hasten the curing of a wound. Urucú is also considered as a remedy which is both magical and herbal.

RELIGION

The *Sirionó* religious system is highly animistic, and there is no evidence of a belief in a supreme being. Mythology imparts considerable power to the moon, which is believed to have formerly been a powerful person who left most of the things the *Sirionó* now have with them when he went into the sky. He ascended to the heavens after Jaguar killed his son and, because of his anger, has never returned since. It was he who gave the *Sirionó* maize, manioc, and chonta palms; it was he who transferred the animals to the shapes and colors they now have.

Fear of evil spirits pervades the religious system. These spirits are believed to cause sickness and death. The *Sirionó* seldom venture outside of the house at night for fear of these evil spirits. Their whole behavior toward them is one of avoidance.

After death, people can become evil spirits, with the power of harming people. These dead ancestors can also be of some help, as is indicated by the use of skulls in curing. But the *Sirionó* have no well-defined beliefs about life after death. Their concern with the immediate world has dominated all efforts to crystallize an eschatological theory.

In general, the *Sirionó* may be said to be one of the most culturally backward tribes in South America. Their culture, exhibiting as it does a lack of professionalism and complexity, suggests that they have been so occupied with the satisfaction of basic needs that secondary growths within the culture have been reduced to the minimum.

BIBLIOGRAPHY

Barrace (*in* Lettres édifiantes . . ., 1780–83).

TRIBES OF THE EASTERN SLOPES OF THE BOLIVIAN ANDES

By Alfred Métraux

INTRODUCTION

Five tribes live along the slopes of the Bolivian Cordillera from the Argentine border to Perú: The *Chiriguano,* the *Yuracare,* the *Mosetene* and *Chimane,* the *Leco,* and the *Tacana.* The *Chiriguano* belong to the *Tupi-Guaraní* group; the *Yuracare, Leco,* and *Tacana* represent still isolated linguistic families. The *Mosetene* and *Chimane* form a single linguistic group.

CHIRIGUANO AND CHANE

HISTORY

The *Chiriguano* (*Ava Chahuanco*) (map 1, *No. 3;* map 2; map 8, *No. 5*) are the descendants of the *Guarani* who in historic times migrated from Paraguay and crossed the plains of the Chaco in successive waves to settle along the foothills of the Andes from the upper Pilcomayo River to the upper Rio Grande (Guapay River). (Lat. 18°–23° S., long. 63°–64° W.) Seven migrations are alluded to in historical documents.

The first migration (1471 or 1476), reported by Garcilaso de la Vega, took place during the last year of the reign of Inca Yupanqui. Another, between 1513 and 1518, can be surmised from the testimony of a *Guaraní* Indian who spoke to Alvar Nuñez Cabeza de Vaca. A *Chané* Indian captured by the *Guaraní* and brought to Itati told Domingo de Irala in 1542 of a third migration, between 1519 and 1523, which probably came after the 1513–18 invasion and certainly before that in which Alejo García took part. The *Guaraní* migration described by Diego Felipo de Alcaya, curate of Mataca, may perhaps be this third one, though many details are certainly fanciful. According to Gandía (1935 a, p. 24), this was the migratory shift which took the *Guaraní* from the region of Itati to the Province of Santa Cruz and which contributed to the formation of the *Guarayú-Pauserna* tribe.

The fourth *Guaraní* invasion, about which we have the most complete information, occurred between 1521 and 1526. It is famous because a few White men, shipwrecked sailors of the Solís armada, accompanied the invading Indians. One of them, Alejo García, seems to have played a conspicuous part in this migration, although Díaz de Guzmán's (1914, 9:26–30) statement that García was the organizer of the raid may be doubted. With a strong force of *Guaraní* he crossed the Chaco, probably at lat. 13° S., and invaded the borderlands of the *Inca* Empire. The raiders advanced as far as Presto to the northeast and Tarabuco to the southeast of Sucre. Fearing a victorious return of the *Charcas* (*Chicha*), the invaders retreated, carrying their booty. On reaching Paraguay, with *Chané* and *Tarapecosi* (*Chiquito*), Alejo

465

García was killed by the *Guaraní*. The historical character of Alejo García's expedition is amply proved by several passages in documents of the Conquest of Paraguay, mainly in the "Comentaries" of Alvar Nuñez Cabeza de Vaca (Hernández, Pedro, 1852, pp. 579–580). The success of this raid prompted many more *Guaraní* to migrate westward. Those from the Río Paraná followed the Pilcomayo River. Those from the region of Asunción entered the Chaco north of that city. The Indians of Jeruquisaba and Carayzapera, that is to say of the country of Itatí, entered the Chaco near San Fernando (lat. 20° S.). According to Díaz de Guzmán, these Indians were the ancestors of the *Guarayú* or *Itatines,* who lived 90 miles (30 leagues) from Santa Cruz.

In a letter written by Martin González from Asunción in 1556, there is the following passage which confirms the continuous migration of the *Guaraní* toward the Andes: "These Indians [the *Guaraní*] go and come back from the lands of Perú. As they have no roads and avoid their enemies, they reconnoiter the land ahead of them, settle long enough to sow crops and harvest their food, and go on. So went those who for long had been settled in the Peruvian sierras and those who go today to meet the Christians.

"In Asunción are many Indians who with their wives and children have gone there two or three times from opposite that city, along a river [the Pilcomayo] that flows 2 leagues from here and comes from the city of La Plata. The Indians from Paraguay have settled by that river and along the Cordillera, over a space of 100 leagues. Some *Cario* [*Guaraní*] have gone to the mountains along another river, 42 leagues down the Paraguay River, which is called the Ypití [Bermejo River]. *Cario* are established in the mountains near the Ypití River, which also leads, according to what those who came from Perú say, to the city of La Plata." (Quoted by Gandía, 1935 a, p. 37.)

Several thousand *Guaraní,* serving as auxiliaries and porters, accompanied Domingo de Irala and Nuflo de Chaves on their expeditions from Paraguay to the foothills of the Andes. It is historically attested that the 2,000 or 3,000 *Guaraní* of Itatí who followed Nuflo de Chaves in 1564 were in part the ancestors of the modern *Guarayú-Pauserna.*

The *Guaraní* not only invaded and conquered the foothills of the Andes from the upper Bermejo River to Santa Cruz de la Sierra, but certain groups went even farther to the north and settled near the border of the *Mojo* and *Bauré* country. The *Pitaquari* (*Piritaguari*) were a *Guaraní* group established in the Sierras de Chiquitos, north of the first Santa Cruz. There were also *Chiriguano* around the town of San Francisco Alfaro in the Province of Chiquitos, near the Jesuit mission of San Xavier.

The *Guaraní* invasions, which started as plundering raids along the *Inca* frontier, were prompted by the desire to obtain gold and silver ornaments and copper tools from the *Caracara* (*Charcas, Chicha*) and from the *Chané* of the foothills, who were amply provided with these metals. Probably metal objects first reached the *Guaraní* of Paraguay through the *Chané,* whose villages were scattered across the Chaco from the Andes to the upper Paraguay River. Although the prospect of rich loot was certainly the predominant cause of their invasions, the old *Guaraní* dream of a land of immortality and abundance, the abode of the Great Ancestor, also may have played some part in determining their migrations.

The *Guaraní* finally became such a threat to the *Quechua* towns of the Province of Charcas that an *Inca* Emperor, probably Huayna Capac, built fortresses at Samaypata (Savaypata), Saigpuru, and Guanacopampa to halt their inroads. Sarmiento de Gamboa (1906, p. 105) speaks of Huayna Capac's wars against the *Chiriguano,* of the *Chiriguano's* capture of the fortress of Cuzcotuyo (probably Incahuasi), and their defeat by Huayna Capac's general, Yasca. The ruins of these

Inca fortresses were visited by Nordenskiöld (1915 a, 1924 a), who described them under the names of Incallacta and Incahuasi. They bear witness to the accuracy of the various traditions concerning the *Guaraní* invasions, recorded by the chroniclers of Perú and of the Rio de la Plata.

Along the Andes, the *Chiriguano* found a peaceful *Arawakan* population, the *Chané*, a branch of the *Chaná* or *Guana* tribe, which occupied the northern part of the Chaco along the Paraguay River. The western *Chané*, after centuries of close contact with the Andean cultures, had been deeply influenced by them. They dressed like their neighbors, the Andean *Chicha*, produced a pottery which resembled that of Southern Bolivia and of the valley of Humahuaca, wore metal ornaments, and used metal tools. The *Chané* fell easy prey to the *Guaraní*, who slaughtered and ate many of them and reduced the remaining population to a condition of serfdom. The *Guaraní* invaders, having brought few of their own women, however, took *Chané* wives. The fusion of these two tribes produced a civilization in which Andean, *Guaraní*, and some *Arawak* features were intimately blended. The *Chané* did not entirely lose their identity, however, for along the Parapetí River, in the Caipipendí Valley, on the Itiyuro River, and in the Province of Salta (Argentine), *Chané* villages survived under their own chiefs. But even these have adopted the *Guaraní* language and today cannot be distinguished from their conquerors. The *Chiriguano*, nevertheless, consider the *Chané* somewhat inferior, while the latter remember the forays and cannibalistic habits of their former masters. The *Chané* language, probably extinct now, was spoken by a few persons as late as 1908.

The number of *Chané* is said to have greatly exceeded that of the *Guaraní* invaders. They extended from the Rio Grande (Guapay River) to the Argentine along the foothills of the Andes. At the beginning of the 17th century, according to Ruy Díaz de Guzmán, in the region of Machareti, 400 *Chiriguano* ruled over 5,000 *Chané;* in Charagua, 350 *Chiriguano* owned 4,000 *Chané* serfs; and on the Guapay River, 200 *Chiriguano* kept 1,000 *Chané* in subjection.

The first White settlement in the land of the *Chiriguano* was the ephemeral town of Santo Domingo de la Nueva Rioja, founded in 1564 on the upper Parapetí (Cordorillo) River by Manso and destroyed a short time later by the *Chiriguano*. In 1571 the *Chiriguano* attacked the *Chicha* and the natives of the Provinces of Condorillo and Barranca. To punish them for their "arrogance," the Viceroy of Perú, Francisco de Toledo, led an expedition against them. The Indians avoided battle and harassed the troops of the Viceroy until he was obliged to retreat in shameful defeat (1574). San Lorenzo de la Frontera, which became the modern Santa Cruz de la Sierra, was founded primarily to keep the *Chiriguano* at bay.

The first attempt to convert the *Chiriguano* to Christianity was made in 1609, when two Franciscans, Augustín Sabio and Francisco Gonzalez, built a church in the valley of Salinas, but the reduction was soon abandoned because of Indian opposition. The Jesuit fathers founded a college in Tarija in 1690 and undertook the spiritual conquest of the *Chiriguano*. In 1691, Father Arce founded a mission in the valley of Tariquea, which lasted only 3 years; another mission, established on the Guapay River by Fathers Zea and Centeno, met the same fate. At the beginning of the 18th century, the Dominicans founded three missions in the valley of Chiquiacá, Nuestra Señora del Rosario, San Miguel, and Santa Rosa, while the Augustins formed the Mission of Santa Clara in the valley of Salinas. In 1715, the Jesuits reestablished their ancient mission of Tariquea. In 1727, all the missions in the *Chiriguano* country were destroyed by the rebellion of the chief, Aruma, and his followers, who feared being taken into slavery. The revolt was crushed by an armed expedition sent from Santa Cruz and composed of Spaniards, "tame" *Chiriguano,* and *Chiquito* auxiliary troops. The *Chiriguano* had been aroused against the missions by the fear of being taken into slavery.

In 1732, the conversion of the *Chiriguano* was entrusted again to the Jesuits. Fathers Julian Lizardi, José Pons, and Ignacio Chomé entered the southern part of the *Chiriguano* territory and founded the missions of Concepción and Rosario in the valley of Salinas. About the same time, the Franciscans built a missionary center in Tarija and in 1757 they sent missionaries to the *Chiriguano*. In 1767, they reestablished the mission of the Purisima Concepción de Pilipili. After the expulsion of the Jesuits in 1767, the Franciscans continued their work with great success. Between that time and the end of the 18th century, the Franciscans founded many new missions north of the Guapay River (Rio Grande): Abapo, Mazabi, Cabezas, Piray, Igmiri, Tacurú, Iti, Parapetí, Itau, Tapera, Iguirapucuti, Tacuaremboti, Piriti, and Obaig. Some of these were annihilated when the Indians rose in arms in 1796 and 1799. During the war of independence, the Franciscan missions were completely abandoned. In 1845, the Franciscans resumed the conversion of the *Chiriguano,* and built a series of new missions from Itau to the Parapetí River. The more important of these were San Francisco, Tarairi, Machareti, Santa Rosa, San Antonio de Huacaya, Ivu, and San Francisco del Parapetí. In 1886, a messiah called the *Chiriguano* to arms against the Bolivians by assuring the Indians that they had nothing to fear because their oppressors' guns would only "spit water." The messiah and his followers were defeated near Cuevo.

In 1929, the last missions were secularized, and the *Chiriguano* lost the protection of the Franciscans. Many of them migrated to the Argentine where they were employed as skilled workers in the sugar factories. The Chaco war spread havoc in the *Chiriguano* villages at the foot of the Andes. The *Chané* of the Parapetí River then put themselves under the protection of the Paraguayan army, and today they live around the fort of Toledo, intermarrying with Paraguayans, whom they consider to be their kinsmen, "because of the close relationship between both *Guaraní* dialects." These *Chané* are sometimes erroneously designated as *"Guarayos."*

The 16th- and 17th-century chroniclers estimated the *Chiriguano* population at only a few thousand, exclusive of their *Chané* vassals. In 1810, there were 23,936 *Chiriguano* in the Franciscan missions. This figure includes only half the *Chiriguano* tribe, as the pagan members south of the Parapetí River were not reckoned. Cardús (1886, p. 242) gives the following estimate of the *Chiriguano* during the second half of the 19th century: In the province of Acero, 18,000; in the Cordillera and in the region of Izozo, 20,000; in the Chaco, from 5,000 to 6,000. Of these, only 8,000 were baptized and 3,187 lived under missionary care. In 1928, the total *Chiriguano* population was said to be 20,000. Today, after the Chaco war and constant migrations to the Argentine, their number must be greatly reduced.

ARCHEOLOGY

Few archeological finds were made in the region occupied by the *Chiriguano*. Nordenskiöld (1924 a, p. 40) mentions burial urns and ancient sites on the Parapetí River, and similar burials were discovered at Tarupayu. In some graves the dead were seated and were covered with several inverted bowls piled on one another. These bowls have hollow rims filled with pellets. Nordenskiöld refers also to direct burial in urns which show the characteristic corrugations of the *Chiriguano* and *Guaraní* ware.

At Yumbia, in the Province of Tarija, at the borderline between *Chiriguano* and *Quechua* territory, the present author obtained fragments of pots with hollow rims, an anthropomorphic vessel with ring-shaped body covered with a red slip, and a specimen of beautiful stone panpipes with typical *Inca* designs. At Caipipendi (pl. 41, *top, right*), near Charagua, he found a *Chiriguano* cemetery consisting of large, corrugated urns, identical to modern *Chiriguano* chicha jars, covered with smaller jars. Near the surface was found a vessel with incised decoration which has no resemblance to any modern *Chiriguano* ware. The same site yielded a small pot with thin incisions and two suspension holes.

SOURCES

Short descriptions of the *Chiriguano* appear in the early literature. Garcilaso de la Vega's picture of *Chiriguano* culture is on the whole quite inaccurate, but for a few details. Díaz de Guzmán (1914), Barco Centenera (1836, 1912), and Lizárraga (1909) speak briefly of *Chiriguano* culture, but the earliest firsthand account of it is Father Chomé's letter (1819 b). Tamajuncosa's report (1910) about the state of the missions at the end of the 18th century is also an interesting document. Weddel (1853), who visited the *Chiriguano* in the middle of the last century, published a few notes about their culture. The best sources are the reports and books written by the Franciscan missionaries, Cardús (1886), Corrado (1884), and especially Campana (1902). Nino's (1912) much-quoted book is based in great part on Campana's monograph.

Nordenskiöld dedicates several chapters of his "Indianerleben" (1912) and of "Forschungen and Abenteuer" (1924 a) to the *Chiriguano* and *Chané*. His data are accurate though somewhat superficial. Great stress is placed on the economic life and the material culture, but social organization and religion receive only cursory attention. However, the collection of *Chané* and *Chiriguano* myths is fairly large and of great interest. Nordenskiöld made a comparative analysis of *Chiriguano* material culture in one of the volumes of his ethnographical series (Nordenskiöld, 1920). More minute details about *Chiriguano* artifacts may be found in Eric von Rosen's (1924) luxurious publication based on a collection he made among these Indians at the beginning of the century.

Several aspects of *Chiriguano* history and material culture were studied in some detail by the writer (Métraux, 1930 b), who also published new *Chiriguano* myths (1931 a) and two sociological essays (Métraux, 1931 b and 1935).

Several monographs deal with *Chiriguano* pottery, which is today one of the best in South America. (Outes, 1909; Nordenskiöld, 1920; Métraux, 1930 b; Paulotti, 1942.) Recently, Max Schmidt (1938) again published and described *Chiriguano* artifacts and techniques.

Knowledge of *Chiriguano* religious and social life is meager and is limited mainly to Campana's monograph (1902) and to observations made by Nordenskiöld (1912) and the present author (1930 b) at a time when aboriginal *Chiriguano* culture was already decadent. The Paraguayan-Bolivian war accelerated its breakdown and little of it now survives.

The migrations, wars, and the religious conversion of the *Chiriguano* have been the subjects of many historical monographs.   The most important of these are by Corrado (1884), Serrano y Sanz (1898), Dominguez (1918), Gandía (1929 a, and b), Métraux (1930 b), Coni (1925), Moreno (1929), and Finot (1939).   The Jesuit missionary work among the *Chiriguano* has been described by Lozano (1941) and Muriel (1918).

CULTURE

SUBSISTENCE ACTIVITIES

As today *Chiriguano* and *Chané* share in the same culture, the following data may apply to both tribes.

Farming.—The *Chané,* conquered by the *Chiriguano,* were proficient farmers who, though practicing a tropical type of agriculture, were probably acquainted with many of the methods of cultivation of the Andean area.   The *Chiriguano* adopted their traditions.   The new habitat of the *Chiriguano* did not offer the same resources for hunting and fishing as had their homeland.   Therefore, these Indians depend on farming to a larger extent than any other *Tupi-Guaraní tribe.*   The basis of their livelihood is maize, of which they have 11 varieties, all related to those of Paraguay.   Then follow in order of importance: Pumpkins, beans (11 varieties), sweet potatoes, sweet manioc, peanuts, and some Barbary figs (*Opuntia* sp).   Sweet potatoes were grown on a large scale by the *Chané* of the Parapetí River.

These Indians also raise cotton, tobacco, urucú, and, in the Parapetí region, reeds for arrow shafts (*Arundo donax*).   Plants of the Old World adopted by the *Chiriguano* include melons, watermelons, oranges, sugarcane, and sorghum.

Chiriguano men clear the fields and surround them with a tall fence as a protection against the inroads of wild or domesticated animals, a task which is considered to be particularly strenuous.   They also till the soil, but at harvest time they are assisted by the women and children.   The latter, armed with slings, drive away the parakeets and other birds which prey on the crops.   Nordenskiöld (1912, p. 183) observed that among the *Chané* of the Itiyuro region, large maize fields were tended by men while pumpkins and beans were raised by the women.

Collecting wild food.—When their crops fail, the *Chiriguano* subsist on the same species of pods and fruits as those collected by the Chaco Indians: Algarrobo, tusca, mistol, caraguatá, and other plant foods.

Hunting.—Hunting is a very secondary economic activity, at least in modern times.   Peccaries, which are the main game animal, are hunted with specially trained dogs and killed with bows and arrows or with clubs.   Rheas, which are abundant in the Chaco plains, are caught with bolas.   Pigeons are captured with clap nets.   Special arrows with two points are used for hunting yacu birds (*Penelope* sp.).

Fishing.—Fishing is worth while only for those *Chiriguano* and *Chané* who live along the upper Pilcomayo or Bermejo Rivers and, to lesser extent, for the *Chané* of the Parapetí and Itiyuro Rivers. Methods of fishing vary somewhat with the regions. Along the Pilcomayo River, fish are caught with iron hooks, with dipnets, similar to those of the Chaco Indians, with the bow and arrow, and with long two-pronged spears. Fishing baskets are used in combination with stone dams (fig. 57).

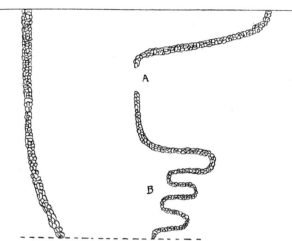

FIGURE 57.—*Chiriguano* fish dam in the Pilcomayo River. *A* is entrance; *B* are pockets where fish are caught. (Redrawn from Nordenskiöld, 1920, fig. 14.)

Among the *Chané* of the Itiyuro, fishing is done almost exclusively by women and children. They use hooks, but more often they capture fish in small ponds which they cut from the main stream by means of weirs. They also catch small fish in narrow-necked gourds into which they place chicha dregs as a bait. The *Chané* of the Parapetí scoop fish with nets or shoot them with arrows tipped with a bundle of cactus thorns (Nordenskiöld, 1912, pp. 184–185).

Domesticated animals.—Modern *Chiriguano* raise sheep, cattle, horses, and chickens. Their dogs are so completely mongrel that their European or Indian origin cannot be ascertained. The *Chiriguano* were probably acquainted with chickens when they arrived in their present territory, for they use a *Guaraní* term for them. Pets are not numerous in their villages; most of them are parrots which were captured by means of a noose attached to the end of a long pole. In order to approach the wild birds, the Indians use tame parrots and decoys.

Cooking.—Maize is prepared in a great many ways. The grains are eaten on the cob, roasted in special pans, boiled in water, or ground into flour, which is served with every meal. One method of preparing maize flour is to steam it in a perforated bowl.

Chiriguano mortars are of the cylindrical type; the pestle is long and heavy. Maize flour is sifted in round basket sieves very similar to those used in the rest of tropical South America. Meat is boiled or broiled on a spit; the babracot is conspicuously absent. Food is served in clay bowls and more rarely in wooden dishes, and eaten with wooden spoons. Salt is extracted from mines near San Luís, or obtained by evaporating the water of salty brooks.

Dwellings.—Until the 17th century, the *Chiriguano* built large communal houses, "150 feet [46 m.] long," in which many families lived together, each occupying the space between two wall posts (Lizárraga, 1909, p. 552). A hundred years later they were lodged, as they are now, in small rectangular houses, with a steep gable roof and wattle-and-daub walls. Sometimes the roof projects in front to form a small veranda. A house belongs either to a single biological family or to two or three closely related families, generally parents with their married children.

The ancient villages were composed of three to five long houses, grouped around the plaza. Modern villages also have a central plaza. A storehouse is built on piles near each dwelling and serves to protect crops against rats and dampness. Like the settlements of their Paraguayan ancestors, some ancient *Chiriguano* villages were protected by a single or double palisade.

Household furniture.—The *Chiriguano* sleep on platform beds of reeds and use their woolen or cotton hammocks to recline on during the day or as cradles for babies. The typical *Chiriguano* hammock is made of long warp threads twined together at set intervals by weft strands; a few caraguatá specimens are made in a net technique. Other items of furniture are benches carved of a single piece of wood, large vessels to store clothes and food, and crude shelves hanging from the roof. A tree trunk with three radiating branches serves as supports for vessels or for piles of corn.

Clothing.—*Chiriguano* men, wearing only a G string (chiripá), were a common sight before shirts and pants came into general use. The cotton tunic (cushma), which was adopted from the *Quechua* after the *Chiriguano* migrations, disappeared long ago, but the poncho, a more recent acquisition, is still popular. As early as the 18th century, *Chiriguano* horsemen, in true Spanish style, wore skin breeches and leather coats. They wear sandals when they have to walk over stony ground or through thorny bush.

Chiriguano women still dress in tipoys, a long, sacklike garment, fastened on both shoulders with thorns or sometimes with luxurious silver pins (pl. 42, *right*).   Some tipoys (tiru) are so long that they need to be folded.

Anciently, *Chiriguano* men shaved their foreheads, as did the *Guarani* of Paraguay.   At a later period, men and women wore their hair long and carefully groomed it with combs.   These were artistically carved from a single piece of wood; some of them were cut into the shape of animals. Men wrapped their hair around the head and kept it in place with a head-band.

Women part their hair in the middle and tie it over the neck with a tasseled fillet, or with a ribbon across the forehead.

Body painting.—Both sexes formerly painted their faces and their bodies with urucú.   In more recent times, women were content to smear their cheeks with urucú before taking part in a feast.   Men stained their teeth black with a special grass.

Ornaments.—The distinctive ornament of the *Chiriguano,* even in modern times, is a tin labret studded with turquoise fragments (pl. 43; fig. 59, *e*).   Originally, labrets were made of rosin, as were those of the *Guarani* of Paraguay.   Wooden labrets or a piece of reed inserted in the lower lip remains common among children and also among men too poor to acquire a metal labret.   Some of the round tin labrets are more than an inch in diameter without including the flanges which hold them on the inside of the lower lip.

Feather ornaments almost disappeared after the migration and were replaced by typical Andean woven frontlets studded with metal plates. Men hung elongated silver plates from their necks; these ornaments probably originated from small metal tweezers worn in the same fashion (fig. 59, *a*).   The most valued necklaces are composed of turquoise or chrysocolla beads which are traded from the Mestizos of Tarija or taken from the sepulchers of the people who preceded the *Chiriguano* in their habitat.   Ordinary necklaces were once strung with shells or seeds, but now consist of glass beads.

Miscellaneous.—The *Chiriguano* have the deserved reputation of being among the cleanest Indians of South America.   Men and women bathe several times a day, washing themselves with crushed fruits containing saponin.   Soap is in great demand throughout *Chiriguano* territory.

Men depilated their faces and bodies with metal tweezers.

TRANSPORTATION

Boats.—The rivers in *Chiriguano* territory are not suitable for navigation; the only watercraft are crude rafts used to cross the Pilcomayo River.

Carrying devices.—In contrast to other *Guarani,* the *Chiriguano* do not have basketry knapsacks; women use large carrying nets with a tumpline. Babies are carried in a woven sling, straddling their mother's hip.

FIGURE 58.— *Chiriguano* and *Chané* pottery decorations. (After Métraux, 1930 b, pl. 32.)

MANUFACTURES

Pottery.—*Chiriguano* pottery is, for the beauty of its painted decoration and the variety of its forms, outstanding in modern South America. The mixed origin of *Chiriguano* culture is reflected in the two types of earthenware vessels. The plain pots for cooking and the large jars for chicha, which did not differ from similar vessels of the Paraguayan *Guarani*, were ornamented with fingernail impressions (pl. 41, *bottom, right*).

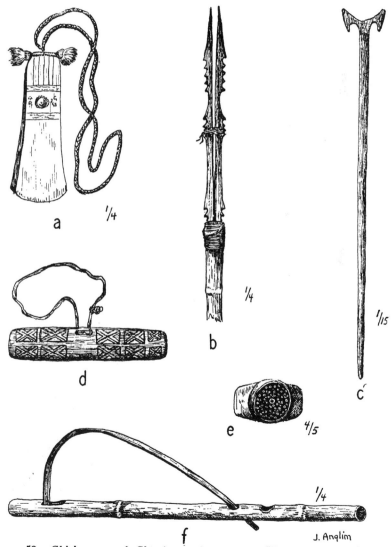

FIGURE 59.—*Chiriguano* and *Chané* manufactures. *a*, Silver pincers used as breast ornaments; *b*, bird arrow point; *c*, handle to wooden spade; *d*, wooden whistle used as ornament; *e*, tin labret with mosaic inlay; *f*, *Chané* pea-shooter. (*a, d, e*, Redrawn from Rosen, 1924; *b, c, f*, from Nordenskiöld, 1920, figs. 29, 15, 5, 34.)

The de luxe vases and dishes, typologically related to vessels in the archeological pottery of southern Bolivia and northern Argentina, were decorated with distinctly Andean patterns (figs. 58, 60). The most common vessel is the yambui, a subglobular vase with ears, in which chicha was served. The motifs are mainly geometrical and most of them

J. Anglim

FIGURE 60.—*Chiriguano* pottery. Specimen at *top, right,* a *Humahuaca* archeological specimen included for comparison. (Approximately 1/7 actual size.) (Redrawn from Métraux, 1930 b, fig. 70, pls. 35, 37, 44.)

are based on a triangle surmounted by a scroll, which is multiplied in countless variations.

Women potters (pl. 41, *top, left,* and *bottom, left*) tempered the clay with crushed potsherds and built up their vases by coiling. They painted them with several kinds of ocher and with black obtained from rosin.

Spinning and weaving.—Among the *Chiriguano,* wool is more commonly used than cotton for textiles, but *Chané* fabrics are generally of cotton. The fibers are spun with a drop spindle weighted with a clay whorl (pl. 42, *center*). Although garments are in part Andean in shape, the loom remains of the vertical type. Formerly, indigo was the favorite native dye; today aniline dyes have entirely replaced it. The ornamentation of the fabrics is limited to a few stripes.

Netting.—Fishing nets and carrying nets are made by means of a wooden gage in a reef-knot technique.

Basketry.—Fans, round baskets with overlapping lids, and sieves are twilled with palm leaves in the best Guiana fashion, but wickerwork basketry is very common. No large baskets for carrying or storing food are made.

Gourds.—The painted, incised, or fire-engraved (fig. 61) gourds (*Lagenaria siceraria*) used as cups are, after pottery, the best expressions of *Chiriguano* art. The motifs are mainly geometrical, with occasional realistic representations.

FIGURE 61.—*Chané* calabashes. *Left:* Specimen with lid (approximately ¼ actual size). *Right:* Pyrograved specimen (approximately ⅓ actual size). (Redrawn from Nordenskiöld, 1920, fig. 50 and Métraux, 1930 b, pl. 62.)

Fire.—For several generations the *Chiriguano* and *Chané* have used steel and flint for making fire. The fire drill is, however, remembered in their mythology.

Weapons.—The *Chiriguano* bow has an average length of 4 feet (1.2 m.) ; the stave is flat on the belly and convex on the back. Both ends are sharpened to prevent the string of twisted hide from slipping.

Arrows are tipped with carefully barbed rods, with two rods barbed along the outer edges, (fig. 59, *b*) with flat lanceolate heads, or with a conical knob (bird arrow). The arrows armed with two diverging rods are used to shoot large birds, such as the yacu (*Penelope* sp.). Fishing arrows of the *Chané* bristle with cactus thorns. Today arrows ending in a sharp wooden rod are rare, as the modern arrows are usually tipped with heavy wires. The shafts are made of cultivated reeds (*Arundo donax*). Formerly, the *Chané* used the uva grass (*Gynerium sagittatum*). Feathering, which is of the cemented type, is sometimes omitted.

The clubs of the *Chiriguano* in the 17th century were short and ended in a flat, oval head, a shape somewhat related to the ancient *Tupinamba* club. These clubs have disappeared (only a single specimen could be obtained in 1929 by Métraux) and have been replaced by simple cudgels that serve only to knock down wild pigs.

Chiriguano in direct contact with the *Quechua* have woolen slings; those living farther to the east have slings made of caraguatá fibers, which they use mainly to chase birds from the fields. The pellet bow is common among the *Chiriguano* and *Chané,* but is merely a toy for boys.

SOCIAL AND POLITICAL ORGANIZATION

Originally, the *Chiriguano* community consisted of a few extended families or lineages, strictly patrilineal. Modern villages are composed of many small biological families bound by relationship ties or by their allegiance to a common chief.

Chiriguano chiefs (mburubicha) of old were men distinguished by their courage, their eloquence, and often by their magic power. They enjoyed considerable prestige and held no little authority. Some of them (tubicha rubicha) extended their influence over a wide area and were recognized as a supreme chief by the local chieftains. The main function of a chief was to settle quarrels within the village, to punish thieves, to see that people worked in the fields at the proper time, to arrange feasts, and to lead his men in war. Chiefs also had right of eminent domain over the land. Sometimes a chief was assisted by an informal council consisting of shamans and of the oldest and bravest men of the community. As a rule, a chief, even if he was powerful, led the same type of life as any of his subjects; in recent time some chiefs had servants. Some aristocratic pride was evidenced by the members of their family.

Chieftainship was inherited in the male line, but the title was bestowed on a chief's son only if he were worthy of it.   There are only a very few cases of women ruling a *Chiriguano* group, but the *Chané* remembered the names of several women leaders.   According to a genealogy of a *Chané* chiefly family recorded by Nordenskiöld (1912, p. 229), power was inherited successively by the brothers and sisters of a deceased chief before it passed to his son.   In the village visited by Nordenskiöld, the brother's son of the chieftainess was the actual ruler, but her son by a commoner was the heir apparent.   This system of succession is probably the same as the one prevailing among the eastern *Chané* (*Guana*).

Chiriguano chiefs of the past wore conspicuous ornaments and were entitled to carry the yanduwa, a pole with a bunch of feathers tied at the end, and a carved stick.

Property.—A plot that had once been cultivated by a man belonged to him and to his descendants, but could not be alienated by him.   In order to insure new ownership rights, a *Chiriguano* would plant a few pumpkins on the land which he intended to clear.

Justice.—Thieves were expelled from the community or sometimes were flogged.   A man convicted of adultery could lose his property. Murderers were sent into exile, unless the victim's family had time to kill him first.   Wronged individuals often took justice into their own hands and challenged the offender to a duel.   The settlement of old accounts occurred generally during drinking bouts.

LIFE CYCLE

Childbirth.—Soon after childbirth, the mother went to the river to wash and smear herself with urucú.   Both parents observed various food taboos.   The father rested for a few days on his bed and refrained from any work, lest he harm the baby.   One twin, as well as any malformed infant, was killed (Campana, 1902, p. 72).

Puberty.—Menstrual flow was attributed to the bite of a mystericus serpent.   At her first menses a girl was hoisted in her hammock to the roof of the hut, where she was compelled to stay for 5 days without uttering a word.   Then she remained for a month or more enclosed in a corner of the hut.   Her hair was clipped short, and she was put on a diet of boiled maize.   During her seclusion, she spun and wove wool and cotton so that she would be diligent for the rest of her life.   Meanwhile, she became pallid, which was greatly admired when she returned to normal life. Henceforth, she used the affirmative "é, é" instead of the childish "ú, ú."

In ancient times, the confinement of a pubescent girl lasted for several months or even for a year[1] (Campana, 1902, p. 86).

---

[1] According to Father Chomé (1819 b, p. 202), the pubescent girl was hoisted in her hammock near the roof.   During the second month, the hammock was lowered, but the confinement ended only in the third month, when a group of old women entered the hut with sticks to start a symbolic hunt for the serpent that had bitten the girl.

Initiation rites.—Some time between the ages of 7 and 12, a boy had his lower lip perforated by a shaman, who used for this purpose a sharp deer horn. The ceremony was performed only when a sufficiently large group of boys in the village was ready for it. Before they underwent the ordeal, the boys were told that they must show fortitude and that subsequently they could give up the affirmative "ú, ú" for the masculine "tà." A short period of fasting followed the operation.

Marriage.—In contrast to the free life led by Chaco girls before marriage, *Chiriguano* girls were expected to keep their virginity and were carefully watched by their mothers.

Chomé (1819 b, p. 202) says that a suitor provided his prospective father-in-law with crops and game. This statement suggests bride service, a custom widely spread among *Guaraní*-speaking tribes and one observed by the *Chané* of the Parapetí River a few decades ago. The bridegroom settled temporarily or permanently with his wife's family.

Polygyny, at least in recent times, was restricted to chiefs or to men of wealth. A man's wives generally lived together in harmony, but in many cases they were kept in separate villages. Polygynous wives were often sisters or a mother and her daughter.

Death.—If the condition of a person was deemed fatal, he was surrounded by a group of women who gave vent to the most spectacular outbursts of grief. This anticipation of the funeral was regarded as a manifestation of affection and respect. The deceased, painted and dressed in his best clothes, was placed squatting in a large chicha jar and was buried, accompanied by his possessions and some food, in the hut where he had lived. The urn was covered with a large jar or plate. The closest female relatives cut their hair and deposited it on the grave. The widow, her head covered with a rag, mourned for a whole year, wailing at certain hours during the day with all the appearance of profound sorrow. She could not resume normal life until a close relative of her dead husband had suggested that she forget her grief. A drinking bout marked the end of mourning.

The soul on its journey to the land of the dead (iwoka) faced many ordeals. It had to walk under a wall of fire, over a boiling lagoon, between two onrushing rocks, and between the blades of gigantic scissors. Finally, the deceased reached a land where the dead lived in abundance and joy. This pleasant heaven was open only to those who had never violated traditional custom.

WARFARE

Intertribal warfare.—Raids to steal crops or cattle or to kidnap women were the main causes of intertribal warfare. The head chief convoked the lesser, i.e., village chiefs, harangued them and listened to their advice. Women performed a special dance and sang to stimulate the courage of the warriors, whom orators constantly exhorted to fight. The main tactic was to surprise and not to be surprised. Scouts were sent ahead of the army and sentries were placed on guard at night. The attack was carried out at dawn. During the battle, the women of the attacked village danced and sang to help their men resist. The victorious party returned with the heads of their slain enemies, which were subjected to all sorts of outrages.

CANNIBALISM

In the past, prisoners were ceremonially killed and eaten. The victims were usually the *Chané,* of whom, according to Lizárraga (1909, p. 552), the *Chiriguano* had eaten about 60,000 during the 16th century. Warriors delivered the captives to their children, who shot them with arrows. Prisoners whom they spared were incorporated into the *Chiriguano* tribe. In more recent times, the prisoners who were not put to death were kept as slaves.

ESTHETIC AND RECREATIONAL ACTIVITIES

Musical instruments.—*Chiriguano* musical instruments are mainly copies of European or Andean instruments, such as the transverse flute. The transverse flute is Spanish, but the quena or end flute (pl. 43, *bottom*) is Andean. Among the most prized possessions of these Indians are round wooden whistles with two stops, and sereres, elongated pieces of wood, perforated lengthwise and blown by stopping the lower aperture (fig. 59, *d*). The clarinet with a slit reed tongue and the cowhorn bell are post-Columbian. The hide-covered drums beaten during feasts is of Spanish origin. Panpipes occur only among the *Chané* of the Parapetí River.

Dances.—Dancers of each sex form a separate line, holding hands with their neighbors. Under the leadership of a master of ceremony who beats time with a feather tuft, men dance on the same spot by bending the knee slightly while women move forward and backward or dance around the men, shaking rattles.

Drinking bouts.—Drinking bouts, in which enormous quantities of chicha are consumed, are attended by friendly communities, which are ceremoniously invited.

Narcotics.—Formerly, tobacco was grown in small quantities by the *Chiriguano* for ceremonial purposes. Today some *Chiriguano* smoke cigarettes, but seldom the pipe. A pre-Hispanic clay pipe was unearthed by Nordenskiöld at Caipipendi. Only a few *Chiriguano* who live near the *Quechua* chew coca, which, however, they do not cultivate.

Fermented drinks.—Maize chicha is the favorite beverage of the *Chiriguano,* who practically subsist on it during the weeks following harvest. Its preparation, entrusted to women, is a lengthy and complicated affair: the grains are crushed in the mortars, and chewed flour is added to the meal, which is thoroughly boiled for many hours in large jars. The *Chané* of the Parapetí River make a fermented beverage of sweet potatoes.

Gambling.—*Chiriguano* and *Chané* are acquainted with the suka game of the Chaco Indians, which undoubtedly has an Andean origin.[2] Another favorite dice game is called chukareta: a bunch of sticks with one face concave and the other convex are thrown to the ground, after one of the partners has chosen one of the sides. If, e.g., the thrower has decided on convex, all the sticks with the convex side up go to him. The one wins who gets most sticks (Nordenskiöld, 1920, p. 99).

European dice games are also known. The dice are of bone or clay and have special markings. Many *Chiriguano* ruin themselves at the famous taba game of the Mestizos. It is played with an ox astragalus, which is thrown in turn by the gamblers, who bet on which side the bone will fall.

Games.—Young boys acquire marksmanship by shooting at a rolling wheel. Boys also play hockey, as do their neighbors of the Chaco. They also hurl darts made of a stick and a corn husk. A popular game among children consists in casting a stick so that it rebounds. The one who throws it farthest scores a point, and the first to score eight points in succession wins (Nordenskiöld, 1912, p. 197).

They also throw at each other a shuttlecock made of maize leaves and strive to keep it in the air as long as possible.

Formerly, the *Chané* of the Parapetí River, like so many Guiana tribes, played a ball game with rubber balls which they butted with their heads. They seem to have used two kinds of rubber balls, black solid ones and white hollow ones which they obtained from the region of Santa Cruz or from the Province of Chiquitos.

Chiriguano women had a game (itarapoa) in which they threw a stone ball or a hollow clay ball filled with pellets at rows of maize grains placed by twos, one above the other.

Small children whirled tops made of a calabash or played with wax or rag dolls.

RELIGION AND SHAMANISM

During 200 years of close contact with missionaries, many Christian concepts have crept into *Chiriguano* religion. Tunpa, or Iandapoha ("Our Creator"), is commonly held to be the "real god." Aguaratunpa, the Fox God, is a mythological trickster with some features of a culture hero. He was regarded by many missionaries as the functioning god of the *Chiriguano*. There is some evidence of a solar cult, just as there is among the *Guaraní*. Aboriginally, the *Chiriguano* were mainly concerned with "iya," nature spirits, and with "ana," the souls of the dead.

---

[2] The dice are made of four pieces of wood, flat on one side and convex on the other. The rules of the game are described in the chapter about Chaco games (Handbook, vol. 1, p. 337).

The shamans (ipaye) enjoyed considerable prestige. When invited by a village to assist its inhabitants in some predicament, they were received with marks of great respect and were lavishly entertained. They served the community as rain makers and as doctors. In the latter capacity, they treated patients or protected the whole village against epidemics. Their curing technique followed the usual South American pattern of blowing and sucking the sick person. They retired to small cabins to communicate with spirits. Blowing tobacco smoke played a large part in the shamanistic ritual. The medicine men were expected to discover the evil charms that threatened the individual or the community as a whole. Shamans were often put to death for their failure to bring rain or to dispel an epidemic. Old women were often called to cure diseases which required the administration of drugs.

During carnivals, which, under the Bolivian influence, have become a period of wild rejoicing, young men wearing masks (pl. 44) of soft wood amuse the spectators by their antics and tricks. As the best masks are those carved by the *Chané*, it is likely that the clown interludes are survivals of dances by masked persons representing nature spirits or ghosts, such as are performed by many *Arawak* tribes. The *Chané* and *Chiriguano* masked characters collect food and depart amid the tears of old people.

MYTHOLOGY AND FOLKLORE

Cosmogony.—The Sun is a man and the Moon is his wife. In the evening the Sun enters a river which he follows until he rises again. An eclipse of the Sun or of the Moon is caused by the attack of a "purple" or "yellow" jaguar. Everybody then makes as much noise as possible to frighten off the celestial feline.

The appearance of the Pleiades, which the *Chiriguano* call "a swarm of bees," announces the harvest season. Their yearly course serves also to reckon time. The *Chiriguano* identify Scorpio with a fenced field, in the center of which is the miraculous spade of Aguara-tunpa. In the black skies near the Milky Way (the road of the rhea), they see a celestial ostrich (rhea), the head of which is the Southern Cross. The Magellanic Clouds are the ashes of a fire built by a couple who went to the sky. (See Lehmann-Nitsche, 1924.)

Folklore.—Most of the *Chiriguano* folklore recorded by Nordenskiöld (1912) was obtained from a *Chané* of the Parapeti River region. The collection of myths and tales made by Métraux (1930 b) in *Chiriguano* villages shows that both groups, in spite of their different origin, share substantially in the same folklore. Certain motifs in the *Chané* version, however, have not been recorded among their ancient *Chiriguano* masters, and may well be *Arawak* traditions which have survived among them. An example is the theme, which is well known in the Guianas, of the "tree-of-life," or "mother-of-all-trees," which was placed by Tunpa on the earth and then disappeared, leaving all food plants as its offspring.

A flood, which once covered the world, was caused by the curse of a young woman who was insulted by her mother-in-law. In another version of this myth, the flood resulted from a storm brought about by a man with wings (Thunderbird). A boy and a girl were placed in a jar with all kinds of seeds and, when the waters subsided, they planted these seeds and repeopled the world.

There are two versions of the myth of the origin of fire. In one, fire was stolen from Sun by the children who escaped the flood; in the other, fire, which was the property of the Vultures, was stolen by a Toad who, pretending to be cold, came near the fire and stole some embers.

The leading characters of *Chiriguano-Chané* folklore are Armadillo (Tatu) and Fox (Aguara), whose names, when mentioned in the various stories, are always followed by the adjective, "tunpa" (sacred). Armadillo is a wise and powerful character, always well disposed toward mankind. Aguara-tunpa (Fox) is a trickster, though in many cases he also plays the part of a culture hero. For instance, Fox steals algarroba seeds from Viscacha (*Lagostomus maximus*), he captures Vulture and forces him to yield the original rubber ball as his ransom. Tatu-tunpa and Aguara-tunpa have several adventures together. On one occasion Aguara-tunpa changes Tatu-tunpa into a repulsive man in order to marry the pretty daughter of a chief while his companion gets the ugly one. Tatu-tunpa shows his greater power by magically tilling a huge field which is instantaneously covered with all kinds of foods. Aguara-tunpa is then unmasked.

Aguara-tunpa kills Tatu-tunpa and puts on his skin, in order to deceive the latter's wife. Again he is unmasked and punished.

The old *Tupí-Guaraní* myth of the Twins was also recorded among the *Chiriguano* (Métraux, 1930 b). A girl is magically impregnated by Tatu-tunpa. She is expelled from her village and wanders in search of the father of the Twins who she bears in her womb and who speak to her. The Twins show her the path to their father's house, but, becoming angry at her, they mislead her to the house of the Jaguars, who kill her. The Twins are brought up by their grandmother. Later they hear about the murder of their mother from a yacu bird. They take revenge on the Jaguars by attempting to drown them when they cross a river by making it wider and wider. Finally, the Twins climb up a chain of arrows to the sky, where they become Sun and Moon.

The *Chiriguano* also have a version of the old *Mayan* and Andean myth of the rebellion of manufactured objects against their masters.

BIBLIOGRAPHY

Alcaya, 1906; Barco Centenera, 1836, 1912; Campana, 1902; Cabeza de Vaca (see Hernández, Pedro, 1852); Cardús, 1886; Cattunar (see Romano and Cattunar, 1916); Chomé, 1819 a, 1819 b; Coni, 1925; Corrado, 1884; Díaz de Guzmán, 1914; Dominguez, 1918; Finot, 1939; Gandía, 1929 a, 1929 b, 1935 a; Garcilaso de la Vega, 1918–20; Giannechini, 1896; Hernández, Pedro, 1852; Kersten, 1905; Lehmann-Nitsche, 1924; Lettres édifiantes et curieuses, 1780–83 (1819, vol. 5); Lizárraga, 1909; Lozano, 1941; Mather, 1922 a; Means, 1917; Métraux, 1930 b, 1931 a, 1931 b, 1935; Moreno, 2nd ed., 1929; Muriel, 1918; Nino, 1912; Nordenskiöld, 1912, 1915 a, 1920, 1923, 1924 a; Outes, 1909; Paulotti, 1942; Romano and Cattunar, 1916; Rosen, 1924; Sarmiento de Gamboa, 1906; Schmidt, 1938; Serrano y Sanz, 1898; Tamajuncosa, 1910; Weddel, 1853.

THE YURACARE, MOSETENE, AND CHIMANE

TRIBAL DIVISIONS

Culturally, the *Yuracare, Mosetene,* and *Chimane* are closely related (map 1, *No. 3;* map 2). The *Leco* probably belonged to the same cultural area, but information on them is scanty and, therefore, it is presented in a special chapter.

The *Yuracare (Conis, Cuchis, Enetes)* territory was defined by D'Orbigny (1839, 1:354–355) as the large zone of Tropical Forest at the foot of the Andes, extending from Santa Cruz in the east to Cochabamba in the west (lat. 16°–17° S., long. 63°–66° W.). In more recent times, *Yuracare* settlements were scattered along the Mamorecillo, Chimoré, Chaparé, Securé, and San Mateo Rivers and their tributaries.

The *Yuracare* were divided into two mutually hostile groups: The *Soloto,* or eastern *Yuracare,* and the *Mansiño* to the west, on the slopes of the Andes. The *Oromo,* though exterminated by the *Mansiño,* seem to have belonged to the latter nation. The *Soloto* of the Mission of San Carlos were called *Mage* by the inhabitants of Santa Cruz.

The contacts of the *Yuracare* with the Whites go far back in time. On several occasions in the 17th century, they raided the Spanish settlements near Mizque and Cochabamba. The first missionary to visit them was Father Francisco Marcos who, in 1776, founded the Mission of Asunción de Maria Santissima on the Paracti River, between the Coni and Chaparé Rivers. This mission was soon abandoned but was restored for a few years in 1784. The Mission of San José on the Coni River was established in 1795 by Father Tomas Anaya, but was deserted by the Indians in 1805, after it had been shifted to the Mamoré River. The Mission of San Francisco, founded on the Mamoré River in 1793, was also soon abandoned. At the beginning of the 19th century, Father Lacueva tried to restore the Mission of Asunción, but it was in ruins when D'Orbigny passed through it in 1831.

The *Yuracare* language is still regarded as unrelated to any other group.

Haenke (1900, p. 182) put the total number of *Yuracare* at the end of the 18th century at about 1,500. In 1831, D'Orbigny (1839, 1:355) estimated that there were about 1,000 *Mansiño* and 337 *Soloto*. A German colonist in 1877 reckoned the whole tribe to be about 1,500 (Holten, 1877, p. 108), and Nordenskiöld (1922, p. 46) estimated their number to be approximately 1,000 in 1908.

The *Mosetene* (*Rache, Amo, Chumpa, Cunana, Aparono, Magdaleno*) lived along the Bopi (Wopi) River to Espia and along the Quiquive and Beni Rivers north to the vicinity of Reyes (lat. 15°–17° S., long. 67° W.) until the end of the 19th century, when they were concentrated in the Missions of Covendo, Santa Ana, and Muchanes. The *Mosetene* of the Beni River are also called *Muchanes;* those at the junction of the Bopi and Beni Rivers are known as *Tucupi.*

The *Chimane* (*Chimanisa, Chumano, Nawazi-Moñtji*), who are closely related to the *Mosetene,* are settled on the upper Maniqui (*Chimane*) and Apere Rivers (lat. 15°–17° S., long. 66° W.).

Mosetene also is classified as an isolated language.

ARCHEOLOGY

In the region inhabited today by the *Chimane,* especially between San Borja and San Ignacio, there are remains of large canals, dikes, and raised earth platforms built to drain and convert the vast marshes into fields. These elaborate works were made either by a large and industrious population which preceded the *Chimane* or else by the original linguistic family from which the modern *Chimane* are descended.

POST-CONQUEST HISTORY

The *Mosetene* are first mentioned in 1588, under the name of *Amo,* when they told Francisco de Angulo (Maurtua, 1906, 9:88–104) of the riches of Corocoro. They informed the Spaniards that the *Inca* were conquering their land when Pizarro landed, and that some *Mosetene* had paid tribute to the Peruvian ruler.

The first missionary to the *Mosetene* was Gregorio de Bolívar, 1621, who also mentioned the *Chimane.* On a second trip, he disappeared on the Sepayco River. In 1666, another Augustin priest crossed the land of the *Rache* (*Mosetene*).

The religious and political conquest of the land of the *Mosetene* was undertaken in 1666 and 1667 by the Governor of Santa Cruz, Don Benito de Rivera y Quiroga. The Dominican Father Francisco del Rosario who, with Father José Morillo, accompanied the expedition as a scout and leader, gave a detailed account of this expedition. (See Meléndez, 1681–82, 3:812–844.) The two priests and a few Spaniards spent the rainy season in a *Mosetene* village planting the first seeds of Christianity. The Indians, who had been decimated by smallpox, were well disposed toward the newcomers.

The following year, the Spaniards reached the Ypati River, where they found the first *Mojo* villages, explored the Cotacaxas River, and finally arrived at the Beni River, near the mouths of the Sopire and Coani Rivers. After raiding a village of *Humuca* Indians near the junction of the Quetoto and Beni Rivers (i.e., the Santa

Elena or Altomachi River), the soldiers deserted, and Quiroga gave up his dream of conquering the mountains of the silver and gold which the Indians had persuaded him he was about to discover.

According to Francisco del Rosario, the *Mosetene* and *Mojo* had active trade relations, especially in salt. The *Mojo* also purchased European knives and beads from the *Mosetene,* who received in exchange cotton cloth, Brazil nuts, and feathers. Many *Mosetene* spoke or understood *Aymara,* a striking evidence of Andean influence on the Forest Tribes.

The systematic conversion of the *Mosetene* began when the Mission of San Miguel de Muchanes was founded in 1804. Santa Ana was founded in 1815 and Covendo in 1842. The first *Chimane* missions were formed by Dominicans at the end of the 18th century, but were destroyed by the Indians. The two Franciscan missions established in this region in 1840 were soon abandoned.

Long contracts with the Mestizos have thoroughly acculturated the contemporary *Mosetene,* but the more isolated *Chimane* still retained much of their aboriginal mode of life 30 years ago.

POPULATION

Father Francisco del Rosario put at 1,000 the total population of six *Mosetene* villages he visited in 1667. In 1831, the *Mosetene* numbered about 2,400. In 1913, Nordenskiöld found only 172 *Mosetene* in the Mission of Covendo. He estimated the *Chimane* to be from 2,000 to 3,000.

CULTURE

SUBSISTENCE

Farming.—The *Yuracare, Mosetene,* and *Chimane,* typical forest dwellers, subsist by farming, fishing, hunting, and, to some extent, by collecting wild foods. The *Yuracare* cultivated a few crops near their houses, but their main plantations were located farther away, in the exceedingly fertile soil of the forest. The surface of one of their fields measured by Nordenskiöld (1922, p. 49) was 33 feet (10 m.) by 1,650 feet (500 m.).

The *Mosetene* cultivate simultaneously several fields distant from their settlements.

The three staple foods of these tribes are sweet manioc (yuca), maize, and bananas. Their other cultivated plants are sweet potatoes, gourds, watermelons, hualusa (*Colocasia esculenta*), papaya, pineapples, cayenne pepper, cotton, and some tobacco. The *Mosetene* grow urucú and plants recently introduced, such as onions, rice, and a very good quality of coffee. Besides the native plants listed here, the *Chimane* also grow a creeper called binca, a big tuber known as chipapa, eight varieties of reed for arrow shafts, creepers for drugging fish, calabash trees, and bamboo for making arrowheads.

Formerly, farming among the *Yuracare* was surrounded by many magico-religious practices. These Indians went to their fields in festive array, playing music. While clearing the fields, both sexes observed several taboos, such as abstaining from eating peccary meat. They never approached a field before the crops were ripe for fear of spoiling them. In fact any house too near a field was vacated until harvest time (D'Orbigny, 1835–47, vol. 3, p. 205).

When the game became scarce around their villages and when no more tembé palms were available in the vicinity, the *Yuracare* migrated elsewhere and opened new clearings. The death of some member of the community also caused them to shift their settlement. As a rule, they chose the season when the tembé-palm fruits were ripe to move to a new site, so that they could wait for their crops without starving.

Gathering wild foods.—The forest provides these Indians with many wild foods, among which the fruits of the tembé (*Guilielma insignis*) and urupa palms are of special importance. To climb the trees in order to pick the fruits, the *Chimane* fasten fiber rings around their legs.

Hunting.—Among the ancient *Yuracare,* hunting besides its economic importance had social significance; it was regarded as a dignified occupation for men and gave prestige to those who were proficient in it.

The hunting weapons are bows and arrows, snares, and traps. The *Mosetene* catch rabbits with springpole traps which are held in position by a trigger passing under a small wooden arch placed in the middle of an enclosure. To kill jaguars and other big animals, they build large fall traps (fig. 62) consisting of a heavy, sloping platform of logs or branches weighted with rocks and propped on two slanting poles. The support is held by a cord attached to a trigger which is maintained in position by a horizontal stick. Smaller animals are caught in a similar trap, but the raised platform is propped by a single stick resting on a horizontal, baited rod which serves as the trigger.

Fishing.—Fishing is of far greater importance to the *Chimane* than hunting. Although all these Indians usually shoot fish with arrows, the *Mosetene* and *Chimane* also use hooks, nets, poison, and weirs. Native *Chimane* hooks were made of bone splinters.

To drug fish, the *Chimane* build two weirs of reeds about 150 feet (50 m.) apart across a stream, throw a crushed poisonous creeper into the water, and shoot the half-drugged fish with arrows. They also catch fish in conical baskets placed in the openings of a weir. When fish migrate to spawn, the *Mosetene* and *Chimane* construct V-shaped weirs which divert them toward slanting platforms placed under the falls, where they become stranded and die in great quantities. The *Yuracare* use dip nets, mainly at night. The mission *Mosetene* dry fish in the sun to store them.

Domesticated animals.—In D'Orbigny's time, the *Yuracare* felt the greatest disgust for the meat of domesticated animals, but they may have changed their attitude. All these Indians keep chickens which they shut at night in conical coops, safe from vampire bats. They also have dogs

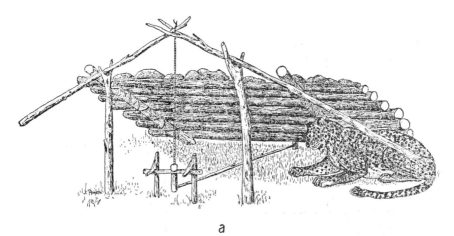

a

b

FIGURE 62.—*Mosetene* traps. *a,* Jaguar and smaller Felinae trap. The animal is crushed by weight of logs and stones. *b,* Similar trap for smaller mammals. (Redrawn from Nordenskiöld, 1924 a, figs. 17 and 18.)

of which they seem to be fond. The *Yuracare* do not allow their hunting dogs to gnaw the bones of game lest they lose their skill.

Food preparation.—Maize was ground on wooden slabs or metates with a stone grinder, meal was strained through a rectangular (*Mosetene*) or concave (*Yuracare*) sieve. Meat was roasted on rectangular babracots. For cooking, these Indians used pots of simple shape. They ate the food with wooden spoons from bowls made of wood or sometimes of palm-leaf midribs (*Mosetene*). *Yuracare* men ate in their clubhouses apart from women. After each meal these Indians carefully buried all the bones or burnt them lest the offended game refuse to multiply.

FIGURE 63.—*Mosetene* hut. *a*, Stool; *b*, fireplace; *c*, grinding stone; *d*, ladder; *e*, shelf for supplies; *f*, hanging shelf for the preparation of foods; *g*, bed; *h*, bench. (After Nordenskiöld, 1924 a.)

HOUSES

The primitive *Yuracare* dwelling consisted of a large, thatched, gabled roof open at both ends and rising directly from the ground (pl. 45, *bottom*). Often, the two sides of the roof rested not on a single ridge pole, but each on its own posts, as if the roof were made of two separate but adjoining lean-tos. The *Yuracare, Mosetene,* and *Chimane* (fig. 63) now live in rectangular huts identical to those of their Mestizo neighbors, but occasionally the *Mosetene* and *Chimane* build temporary huts of the ancient *Yuracare* style.

In the past, each *Yuracare* village had a clubhouse, strictly taboo to women, where men manufactured weapons, ate, and received visitors. Seventeenth-century *Mosetene* villages had also a men's house or council hall in the central plaza. Neither tribe now builds clubhouses. The *Yuracare* cook in special sheds near the houses.

The ancient *Mosetene* arranged their houses in a circle around a plaza. The settlements of the *Chimane* usually consist of a few houses, but isolated single-family huts are fairly common. The Indians prefer to scatter throughout their territory for fear that any large concentration of people at a given point would soon exhaust the available natural resources of the district.

The *Yuracare, Chimane,* and *Mosetene* sleep on mats, the first two under tentlike mosquito nets of bark cloth. Hammocks, generally made of bark cloth, are used only as cradles for babies.

On journeys, the *Mosetene* improvise shelters of palm leaves supported by three vertical poles.

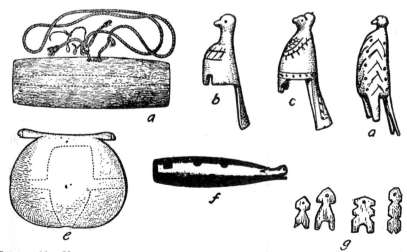

FIGURE 64.—*Yuracare* ornaments, whistles, and flutes. *a,* Wooden whistle, serere type; *b-d,* carved caiman tooth ornaments; *e,* wooden whistle, biria type; *f,* wooden flute; *g,* bone beads. (Caiman tooth ornaments ⅔ actual size.) (*f,* After Mathews, 1879; all others after Nordenskiöld, 1922, figs. 9, *a,* 16, 11, and 10.)

DRESS AND ADORNMENTS

Among the *Yuracare,* both sexes wear long bark-cloth tunics which are often trimmed with tassels and small figures of carved wood and bone (fig. 64, *b-d*). Men's tunics are beautifully decorated with printed patterns (pl. 45, *top*); women's garments are plainer and shorter. Among the *Mosetene* and *Chimane,* bark-cloth tunics were once common, but today are restricted to children, or are worn only as work clothes; both sexes also use long sleeveless cotton shirts or cushmas. Seventeenth-century *Mosetene* women wore only a simple loincloth.

A belt decorated with geometric patterns and long terminal fringes, and a cotton or bark-cloth bag generally form part of the complete outfit of a *Mosetene* Indian.

The ornaments worn by the ancient *Yuracare* included: Semicircular ear pendants (fig. 65, *c*), originally of bone, but later of silver; miter-

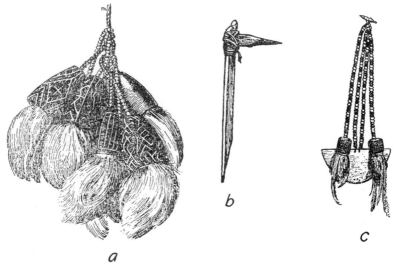

b

c

a

FIGURE 65.—*Yuracare* artifacts. *a,* Woman's pendant of black fruit and red toucan feathers; *b,* instrument for bloodletting; *c,* ear pendant. (Respective approximate sizes: 3/5, 4/5, and 3/5 actual.) (After Nordenskiöld, 1922, figs. 34, 33, and 17.)

shaped feather crowns; and heavy necklaces of seeds, animal teeth, bird beaks, bones, nuts, and other objects. When dancing, girls and boys attached tufts of feathers, strings of beetle wings, or small bells to their shoulders.

The *Chimane* wore headdresses made of the tail feathers of the oropendula (*Ostinops decumanus*). Women's necklaces were strung with the red fruits of the *Cassia fistula;* those of the children with monkey teeth, cocoons, and pieces of bark cut into human shapes. The only other ornaments of these Indians were woven cotton bracelets.

The ancient *Yuracare* pulled out their face and body hair. They clipped their hair across the forehead, but allowed it to hang full length down the back, where it was divided into numerous queues. The *Mosetene* wrapped their hair in a single long queue.

Combs were made either of thin wooden splinters, skillfully bound together with cotton twine wrapped to form geometric patterns, or of series of teeth fastened between two sticks. They were carried around the neck.

Prior to any important activity, such as traveling, visiting, or working in the fields, the ancient *Yuracare* printed elaborate colored designs on their bodies with wooden stamps (fig. 66). *Mosetene* and *Chimane* body painting is rarely mentioned.

FIGURE 66.—*Yuracare* stamps and combs. *a, b, d,* Face stamps of wood; *c,* wooden stamp for bark cloth; *e, f,* bambóo combs. (Stamps approximately 2/5 actual size; combs, ⅔.) (After Nordenskiöld, 1922, figs. 35, 37, 15, 36, 13, *a, b.*)

According to D'Orbigny (1839, 1 : 363), the ancient *Yuracare,* previous to their contacts with the Christianized *Mojo* Indians, had no canoes. Buoyed by a piece of light wood, they swam across rivers. By the beginning of this century, however, the *Yuracare* made extensive river journeys in dugout canoes which were famous throughout eastern Bolivia for their excellent craftsmanship and balance.

The *Mosetene* travel only on rafts, which are better adapted than canoes to the rapid streams of their country. Modern rafts are made of seven logs of palo de balsa, a very light wood, nailed together with chonta spikes and provided with a platform to keep goods dry. The long central logs consisted of two trunks laid end to end. Some rafts have a raised prow constructed of bent pieces of wood attached to three middle logs. The raised bow and platform were introduced in modern times when the *Mosetene* handled most of the river traffic on the upper Béni River. The paddles have a long blade and a plain handle without knob or crutch.

FIGURE 67.—*Chimane* dugout canoe. (Redrawn from Nordenskiöld, 1924 b, fig. 37.)

The *Chimane* have rafts, but usually travel on the rivers in dugouts (fig. 67), which they punt with long poles, using a paddle only to pass rapids. At night they stake their canoes to the sand by means of a stick passed through a hole in the bow.

Women carry loads in nets or in baskets suspended on their backs by a tumpline. Like the Andean Indians, the *Mosetene* always wear a small cotton bag slung over the shoulders.

Among the ancient *Mosetene* mothers often carried small babies on their back in cotton bags. Older children straddled the mother's hip.

MANFACTURES

Bark cloth.—Bark cloth is made from the thick bast layer of the bibosi tree (*Ficus* sp.) and certain other trees (pl. 47, *bottom*). A section of trunk, 8 to 10 inches (20 to 25.5 cm.) in diameter is cut the desired length, and the bark is incised longitudinally with a quartz splinter or a sharp tooth. The stump is heated until the dry bark can be peeled off. The bark is stretched to separate the outer bark from the inner bast, and all the whitish fibers are scraped from the latter. The bast is then beaten with a grooved wooden mallet (fig. 68, *a*) until soft. Several bark-cloth pieces are sewn together with a bone needle to make blankets, shirts, and mosquito nets.

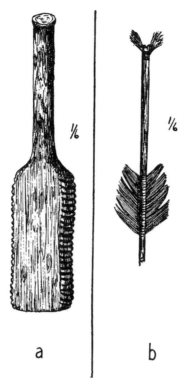

FIGURE 68.—*Chimane* and *Yuracare* artifacts. *a, Chimane* bark-cloth beater; *b. Yuracare* arrow feathering. (Redrawn from Nordenskiöld, 1924 b, map 28 and fig. 8.)

Basketry.—The use of carrying nets limits somewhat the importance of basketry, which, however, seems to be a flourishing industry. The large baskets in which crops are transported and the small containers in which odds and ends are kept, are woven of motacu palm leaves. The large rectangular boxes with overlapping lids in which the *Chimane* store their feather ornaments and amulets are identical to those found in many other tribes of eastern Bolivia. They are made of *Gynerium* stalks joined together with cotton threads (fig. 69). The round and square sieves (pl. 47, *top*) are woven in a simple twilling technique. The *Mosetene* make mats of leaves or reeds cut in strips and crossed within a rectangular reed frame.

Netting.—The carrying nets are made in a reef-knot technique.

Spinning.—Spindles as a rule have small rectangular wooden whorls. To spin, *Mosetene* women sit on the ground with outstretched legs; they place the distal end of the spindle between the large toe and the next toe of the left foot and roll the spindle on the right thigh. This method has been somewhat improved upon by the *Yuracare:* the women set the spindle's distal end in a wooden fork and roll it on a wooden block instead

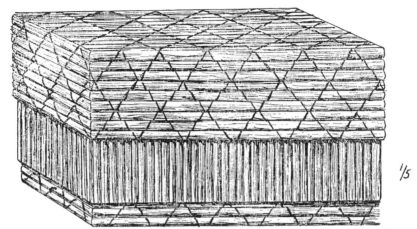

1/5

FIGURE 69.—*Yuracare* twined stick box. (Redrawn from Nordenskiöld, 1922, fig. 26.)

of on the thigh.   (See *Chimane* woman spinning for another variation (fig. 70).)

FIGURE 70.—*Chimane* woman spinning cotton. (After Nordenskiöld, 1924 b.)

Weaving.—The *Yuracare* have the vertical loom. The *Mosetene* know how to make cloth by a method of plaiting which occurs also in the Guianas (see Roth, 1924, chap. 20): Cotton threads are first wrapped around two horizontal bars of the loom. The threads are then crossed over and under the adjoining threads and held in place by transverse mesh sticks until the entire cloth appears to be diagonally woven; then the sticks are withdrawn and strings run in their places to prevent the threads from slipping back to their original position. Patterns are obtained by using different colored threads.

Violet dye is extracted from the leaves of the idzi tree (*Haematoxylon* sp.), and brown from jira or caoba tree bark.

Pottery.—The making of pottery was surrounded among the ancient *Yuracare* by many taboos: clay could not be procured during the harvest season; the potters, who were always women, were secluded in special huts deep in the forest where they could not be seen, especnlly by the Thunder God; moreover, they had to remain chaste and to keep completely silent.

Chimane women sprinkled their pots after they had been fired with banana tree sap to give them a beautiful black color.

Wood carving.—*Yuracare* men are still proficient wood carvers, as evidenced by the complicated designs cut in relief on their wooden stanps, by their small carved wooden and bone pendants, and by their fine wooden bowls.

Tools.—A few years ago, the *Chimane* still used stone adzes. The stone blade was hafted on a forked limb, the longer branch forming the handle and the shorter branch the base against which the blade was lashed.

Weapons.—Bows in these three tribes are from 5 to 6 feet (1.65 to 1.98 m.) long and made of sticks split from chonta palms. The rough staves have a rectangular cross section, with one side slightly convex. This shape is preserved even after the bow has been finished. The string of vegetal fiber is held but sharp shoulders cut at each end.

The various types of arrow heads are: (1) A lanceolate bamboo head; (2) a sharpened rod without barbs (*Mosetene*) or with jags on one side (*Yuracare*); (3) a bone barb is often added to the rod for hunting large game (*Yuracare*); (4) a large wooden knob head or two horizontal sticks lashed at right angle to the rod, for bird hunting (the *Mosetene* often smear heads of bird arrows with rubber); and (5) a long rod point with barbs (*Mosetene*) and without barbs for fishing (*Yuracare*). The feathering is of the cemented type. The feathers are halved, and fastened tightly to the *Gynerium* shaft by means of cotton wrapping smeared with wax. The feathering terminates some distance short of the butt end, as on *Yuracare* arrows (fig. 68, *b*).

When shooting, the *Yuracare* hold the arrow butt between the thumb and index finger and pull the string with the next two fingers.

POLITICAL ORGANIZATION

All these tribes are split into small, independent units, each consisting of one or more biological families. Although some settlements are relatively near one another, each family keeps very much to itself. Each settlement is governed by the family head, whose authority does not extend beyond his own small group.

Revenge.—Quarrels among the *Yuracare* were settled by formal duels with arrows (*pl. 45, top*), which were equipped with heads that could inflict deep wounds but not cause death. The main motives for duels were sex rivalry and revenge for black magic. If a person were bitten by a serpent, one of his relatives donned his best garments and went to the house of the presumed sorcerer, where he challenged him to a duel by striking the roof. The accused, taking his bow and dueling arrows, stood some distance from the challenger, presenting his left shoulder. The accuser shot at the other's arm and then was shot at in turn. Thus they exchanged 8 or 10 shots, until the accuser was satisfied.

Suicide.—Suicide among the *Yuracare* was very common. If a man was afflicted with some incurable disease or suffered some great humilation, he would throw himself from the top of a tree.

Etiquette.—Meetings between strangers were governed by strict etiquette. The *Yuracare* received visitors with elaborate ceremonialism. Standing in front of his house, the family head delivered a speech for several hours in a progressively louder tone. One of the visitors answered in the same manner. At the end, hosts and guests entered the house, and cried for hours, celebrating in stanzas the deeds of their deceased relatives.

Pregnancy and child birth.—During pregnancy, *Chimane* women avoid eating the flesh of several game animals, especially tapir. Formerly, among the *Yuracare,* childbirth occurred in the forest beside a brook; an old woman assisted the mother. Abortion and infanticide were very common among ancient *Yuracare,* who killed illegitimate and crippled children. The *Yuracare* are said to have practiced a kind of birth control, each family limiting the number of its children.

In D'Orbigny's time, children were weaned at 3, but remained with their mothers until 8, when boys were taught to hunt and make speeches. They enjoyed great liberty and were never scolded because harmful magic influences were attributed to reprimands.

Girl's puberty.—The *Yuracare* celebrated a girl's first menses with an elaborate ritual, designed to protect her from various dangers and to make her valiant. The girl was secluded for 4 days in a special cabin. On the fourth day, everyone met for a drinking bout. Each guest cut a lock of the girl's hair and hid it in the forest. The girl was also stabbed in the legs to give her courage and strength. The feast was the occasion for mutual scarifications among the men. After another ceremony 15 or 20 days later, the girl might mix freely among other women and help prepare chicha.

For the next 5 or 6 months the girl had to keep her head covered with a piece of bark cloth and was not permitted to speak to men.

Marriage.—*Yuracare* girls could marry young, but men had first to prove that they were good providers. Either a man negotiated marriage with the girl's parents, or the parents arranged and enforced the marriage on their children. A dubious statement holds that the girl was deflowered by a man who acted as godfather to the couple.

As all *Yuracare* groups were strongly endogamous, marriages were necessarily between close relatives, although marriages between first-degree relatives were forbidden. Marriage with other than a relative required a substantial bride price; a breach of this custom would cause a duel.

Polygyny was very unusual. Divorce was easy, especially if the husband were a poor hunter. Postmarital residence was first matrilocal, but after children were born, the couple set up an independent household.

Chimane girls enjoy sexual freedom after puberty but marry young. To show their willingness to marry, they sit near their suitor on a mat. After a short trial marriage, the couple may separate, but the birth of a child usually strengthens the conjugal tie. A *Chimane* may take only as many wives as he can support.

Death observances.—Among the ancient *Yuracare,* relatives and friends took a dying person to a special cabin in the forest, where he bequeathed his property to his children and received messages from various people to deliver to the ancestors. The corpse was wrapped in bark and buried, with the head toward the east. The mourners expressed violent grief, throwing themselves on the ground and tearing their shirts. Any remaining property was destroyed to prevent the dead's return. Modern *Yuracare* still burn the deceased's house and move their settlement to another locality. They abandon the dead man's fields and do not harvest the crops.

The soul goes to the underworld, where it hunts and lives merrily.

The *Chimane* bury their dead in shallow graves near their huts which, with the deceased's possessions, are destroyed. Mourners occasionally smear their cheeks with ashes.

ESTHETIC AND RECREATIONAL ACTIVITIES

Art.—*Yuracare* art finds its best expression in the painted bark-cloth shirts. The motifs, some rectilinear but most curvilinear, are difficult to analyze. They can be likened to extremely conventionalized leaves and "flames" treated in rococo style.

Games and toys.—For little girls the *Yuracare* make wax dolls and for boys, miniature weapons, including pellet bows and ordinary bows and arrows. Children also play with buzzing disks and tops (fig. 71, *e*).

Musical instruments.—The typical serere whistle—a rectangular piece of wood with a diamond-shaped cross section and a longitudinal hole— is not only a musical instrument but also a prized ornament which men hang around their necks (fig. 64, *a*).

The resonator whistle, closely related to the serere, is a round, flat piece of wood with a blowhole in the edge and two stops in the sides (fig. 64, *e*). Plug flutes (figs. 64, *f*; 71, *a*) with six stops, although made of bird bone, are of European type. The *Yuracare* bone quenas or notched end-flutes (fig. 71, *b–d*) show Andean influence. These have two stops in front and a thumb hole immediately behind the upper stop.

The *Yuracare* panpipes (fig. 71, *g*) average five pipes, which are held together by a strip of bamboo fastened with threads (*Aymara* ligature).

Narcotics and drinks.—The *Yuracare* cultivate, but rarely smoke, tobacco. They used it mainly as a drug against the boro, an oestrid fly (*Dermatobia*) larva.

They prepare beer of pounded and boiled manioc tubers (pl. 46, *top*). The mass is strained and allowed to ferment.

RELIGION AND SHAMANISM

Deities.—Among the ancient *Yuracare,* the Thunder God was Moro- roma, who threw lightning from the top of the mountains. When thunder was heard, men threatened to shoot him. Pepezu was the Wind God, who kidnapped men in the middle of the forest. Chuchu was the War God, who taught the *Yuracare* how to fight. Tele, dressed in white clothes, seems to have been the culture hero. According to Haenke (1900, p. 183), the *Yuracare* believed in a good god, Tantoco, who showed his beneficial power in putting out a big fire caused by an evil deity called Limpelite. Whenever a storm was about to break, women and children were sent into the huts while men shot arrows and recited incantations against this "fiery being" who threatened to destroy their houses and plantations.

The only information on *Mosetene* religion before the introduction of Christianity is Father Francisco del Rosario's statement (Meléndez, 1681–82, 3:821) that their main deity was called Apu, a *Quechua* word meaning "lord," and that Suysuy (a bad spirit), the sun, the moon, and the stars were worshiped; tobacco smoke was offered to them. One night during their sojourn in a *Mosetene* village, the Spaniards heard a noise as if somebody were running away. The Indians explained that it was Suysuy who had died and was going to the underworld.

Mosetene hunters bleed their right arms with an eagle claw and rub their eyes with an eagle eye. They leave the liver of peccaries at the

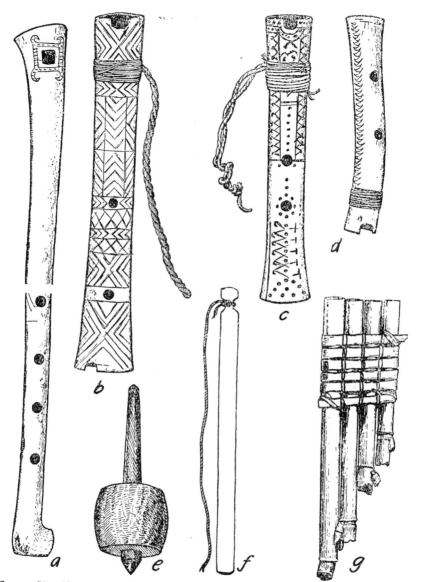

FIGURE 71.—*Yuracare* musical instruments. *a-d*, Bone flutes with engraved designs; *e*, top made of a fruit and wooden stick; *f*, bull roarer; *g*, bamboo panpipes. (Flutes ½ actual size; top, ⅔ actual size; bull roarer, ¼ actual size; panpipes ½ actual size.) (After Nordenskiöld, 1922, figs. 29–32.)

site of the kill, in the hope that they will turn into live animals. Before a hunt, *Yuracare* men paint themselves elaborately and drink a decoction of sumuque bark to insure good luck and prevent accidents. After returning home, they place the slain monkeys on palm leaves and sprinkle them with chicha saying, "We like you and therefore we brought you home." The *Chimane* cut the feet of slain animals lest their ghosts, accompanied by all the remaining game, leave the district. The *Yuracare* burned or carefully buried the bones of slain animals; the *Mosetene* returned them to the forest, lest they prevent the species from being killed in the future. *Yuracare* dogs are not allowed to gnaw bones for fear that they might become unfit for hunting.

Shamanism.—The *Yuracare* attributed diseases to sorcerers and to evil spirits. The wind was believed to bring spirits that caused physical pain and nausea. The rainbow and red clouds in the evening were responsible for many illnesses. Reprimands or scoldings also were considered to be extremely harmful to those who received them.

Because epidemics generally were attributed to visitors, especially to those who complained of some ailment, the *Yuracare* were uneasy when foreigners visited them.

Yuracare shamans examined their saliva in the palms of their hands and summoned their client's soul to diagnose the ailment. They cured by letting blood (fig. 65, *b*) and by blowing tobacco smoke on the patient's body.

Recently, black magic was still rife among the Christianized *Mosetene*. They dread sorcerers, who can kidnap and destroy the souls of their victims. Medical virtues are attributed to the bones of Opo, a gigantic demon (i.e., fossils), which can be found in every hut. Pieces of the body of another demon, Chaumboy, cause a common type of skin disease.

MYTHOLOGY

In *Yuracare* mythology (D'Orbigny, 1835–47, vol. 3, pp. 209–215), an evil demon, Sararuma or Aïma Suñé, set the earth on fire at the beginning of the world, and killed everyone except a man who stayed in a hole. Later, the survivor wandered over the desolated earth; he met Sararuma, who gave him a handful of seeds which he planted. Soon forests again covered the world. He married and had several children. His only daughter transformed an ule tree into a man by painting it with urucú and married him. Ule spent only nights with his wife. She tied him up and forced him to stay with her during the day. Ule was killed by a jaguar, who scatterd the parts of his body. His wife picked up all the pieces and put them together. Ule regained life and said, "I have slept well." Ule then noticed that part of his jaw was missing. This made him ashamed and he refused to return home. He left his wife, telling her that she must not turn her head if she heard a noise behind her and that she should remember that it was produced by her husband's animals. The woman did not heed the advise and lost her way. She arrived at the house of the jaguars. Although the mother of the jaguars tried to conceal her, her sons discovered her and forced her to delouse their heads and to bite the "lice," which were really big ants. The jaguars' mother gave her maize grains, which she cracked with her teeth, as if she were biting the vermin. One of the jaguars that had four eyes exposed the ruse. He killed her and extracted a baby boy, Tiri, from her womb. The jaguars' mother put the baby in a pot as if to boil him, but spared his life and reared him. The child grew rapidly, and hunted game for his foster mother. One day a paca, which he had struck with an arrow, scolded him for pursuing harmless animals while he allowed the murderers of his mother to live. Tiri returned home and shot three jaguars. The jaguar with the two pairs of eyes saw the danger, and, climbing to the top of a tree, cried, "Trees, palm trees, help me! Star, help! Moon, help!" The moon caught him up and kept him with her. The four-eyed jaguar may be seen today on the moon (the spots of the moon).

The hero Tiri opened a big clearing for the mother of the jaguars. He created a companion by breaking off a toenail and changing it into a man, Karu. Tiri and Karu gave salt to a bird that carelessly left it in the open. A heavy rain melted it, and since then the *Yuracare* have had no more salt in their forests.

A bird showed Tiri and Karu a pot which, when emptied, refilled itself. Tiri struck the miraculous pot with his stick and caused a flood which drowned Karu. Later Tiri found his bones and brought him back to life.

Tiri and Karu married pospo birds, by whom they had children. The girls were born with their breasts on their foreheads, but Tiri moved them to their chests.

Karu's son died. Tiri told Karu to look for him and promised that he would find him alive if he did not eat him. On his son's grave Karu saw a peanut plant, which he ate without knowing it was his own son. Because of Karu's rash action, men are mortal.

Karu shook a tree; a duck fell to the ground and was immediately devoured by Karu. When he learned the duck was his son he vomited and from his mouth flew parrots, tucans, and other birds.

The ancestors of the *Mansiño, Soloto, Quechua,* and *Chiriguano* emerged from a cave where they had hidden from a man-killing serpent, which a stork killed at Tiri's orders. Tiri closed the cave to prevent a great chief from coming out, and a serpent has since guarded it. The people scattered. The *Chiriguano* seized arrows which fell from the sky, and people have since quarreled.

Tiri decided to retire to the end of the world. In order to know its extent, he sent a bird to the four directions of the horizon. On the fourth trip, from the west, the bird returned with beautiful new plumage. Tiri went to the west, where he lives with people who, upon reaching old age, rejuvenate.

In *Mosetene* mythology (Nordenskiöld, 1924 a), Dohitt, the creator and culture hero, who attained the dignity of the Christian God, made the earth in the form of a raft supported by spirits and created men from clay dolls. After retiring to the sky, Dohitt and his companion, Keri,[3] the white condor, visited mankind again, descending a rope of mucous. Dohitt reached the earth, but Keri was killed when the rope broke, and Dohitt transformed his head into a fish. Dohitt then traveled about transforming men into animals and birds.

Dohitt is more trickster than culture hero. He borrowed feathers to fly, lost them, and fell on a tree. To get down, he became small enough to ride on a caterpillar, but was dropped and impaled on a bamboo. A wildcat rescued him, but a shaman pinned him to the ground where, struggling to free himself, he caused an earthquake. He made an enormous basket full of water and sent his enemy, the shaman, and other men with similar baskets of water to create rivers in different parts of the world. Even now storms occur when Dohitt orders the shaman to spill water.

As culture hero, Dohitt gave mankind agriculture. Sonyó, following Dohitt, discovered fields of maize, manioc, and other plants.

The *Mosetene* recount that the sky once fell on the earth, but was put back and held up by a serpent. A flood was caused by a man who seduced a woman who was bathing; angered at not finding the child she bore, he made the river flood the world, and only a few people on a mountain were saved.

The Milky Way is a huge worm. Once when it was small, it was picked up by a man as a pet. The worm could be fed only with hearts, first of animals, then of men. After vengeful people had killed his master, it destroyed them and went to the sky. The stars of the Milky Way are arrows which men shot at the worm when he wound himself around their village. The rainbow is the child of a woman and a water man.

Other tales are of monsters and spirits: A man was swallowed by a serpent, but cut its heart and escaped; a man killed by a serpent, was avenged by his son, who transformed himself into an eagle and piled four mountains on top of each other to reach the serpent; a woman married a jaguar who wanted to eat her relatives, but was induced to climb a tree and was killed; a jaguar, the spirit of the chima tree, pursued men for eating the green fruits.

BIBLIOGRAPHY

Adam, 1889, 1893; Bibolotti, 1917; Cueva (*see* Adam, 1893); D'Orbigny, 1839, 1835–47, vol. 3; Haenke, 1900; Herrero, 1834; Holten, 1877; Mather, 1922 b; Mathews, 1879; Maurtua, 1906; Meléndez, 1681–82; Métraux, 1942; Nordenskiöld, 1922, 1924 a, 1924 b; Roth, 1924; Viedma, 1910.

---

[3] Keri is perhaps an *Arawak* mythical hero, for Keri in several *Arawakan* dialects means "moon," and the *Bacáiri* have a culture hero of the same name.

THE LECO

HISTORY

The *Leco* (*Chuncho*) lived along the Kaka (Huanay) River and its tributaries, the Tipuani, Mapiri, Turiapo, and Yuyo Rivers (lat. 16° S., long. 68° W.; map 1, *No. 3;* map 2). That a branch of the Beni River between lat. 13° and 14° S. is called Río de Lecos may indicate a wider distribution.

For *Leco* sources, see Bibliography for *Apolista* (p. 506).

The first reference to the *Leco* figures in Miguel Cabello de Balboa's account (Maurtua, 1906, 8:140–141) written in 1594. In 1621, Fray Gregorio de Bolívar (Maurtua, 1906, 8:214) places them on the Cacamayo River, 25 leagues from Camata. At that time they traded with the Spaniards but occasionally raided them. About 1617, a sergeant of Pedro de Legui Urquiza's expedition attempted to conquer the *Leco*, but was defeated and killed. The *Leco* are often mentioned in the reports of the Franciscans who in 1680 settled in the Province of Apolobamba. They are said to have been distributed in 8 or 9 villages and to have numbered about 800. One of the first missions founded among them at the end of the 17th or beginning of the 18th century was destroyed by the Indians.

Among the 600 Indians of the Mission of Concepción de Apolobamba in 1690, some spoke the *Leco* or *Lapalapa* language. The Mission of San Antonio de Atén was started in 1763 with 380 *Leco* who later were taken to the Missions of Concepción de Apolobamba and of Santa Cruz de Valle Ameno; after clashes with the *Apolista*, they were returned to Atén in 1758. The *Ateniano*, or Indians of the Mission of Atén, were *Leco* according to several documents, but D'Orbigny (1839, 1:374) classifies them as *Tacanan*.

At the beginning of the 19th century, most of the *Leco* were concentrated in the Mission of Huanay at the junction of the Mapiri and Tipuani Rivers. In 1906, they numbered about 500. Their language is still classified as an isolated linguistic family.

CULTURE

Leco aboriginal culture is almost unknown. Maize and bananas formed their staple foods. Fish were shot or were drugged with the sap of the soliman tree (*Hura crepitans*). They prepared a kind of peanut chicha.

The *Leco* are skillful boatmen who specialize in transporting passengers and merchandise on the Beni River. They descend the river on rafts made of light, corky balsa, pinned together with palm spikes. Three of these rafts bound together with stout cross logs tied with strips of bark or vine form a type of craft called callapó.

Modern *Leco* huts have steep pitched roofs and bamboo walls. The main furniture is a sleeping mat.

Formerly, the *Leco* wore the long shirt, or cushma, sometimes dyed with the violet juice of uchuri (*Picramnia lindeniana*) (Weddel, 1853). Today they dress like Mestizos. Sometimes they wear a band necklace of bright beads. Men used to wear their hair long and to paint themselves with urucú and genipa.

In the 17th century, they were armed with bows, arrows, clubs, and shields.

The couvade is reported among the modern *Leco*. Residence probably was matrilocal since parents of a woman are said to have been supported by her husband.

APOLISTA OR LAPACHO

Nordenskiöld collected in 1908, in the Mission of Concepción de Apolobamba, a short vocabulary of a language spoken by a few individuals in a region where *Quechua* was the predominant language. A comparative study of this vocabulary by Créqui-Montfort and Rivet (1913 c) shows that it contains enough *Arawakan* radicals to be classified as a dialect of that linguistic family.

Little is known of the *Apolista*. Their name was coined only a hundred years ago by D'Orbigny when he found 2,775 of them in the Mission of Apolobamba (founded in 1690) and 841 in the Mission of Santa Cruz del Valle Ameno (founded in 1720). Armentia (1887–88, p. 5) states that the *Apolista* language was spoken in the Mission of San José near Tumupasa, but that in 1871 only two Indians still could understand it.

Who were the *Apolista?* The Mission of Concepción de Apolobamba had Indians belonging to three linguistic families: the *Aguachile,* the *Leco,* and the *Pamaino.* The last come from the Tuichi and Béni Rivers and probably spoke *Tacanan,* which, like *Leco,* was supplanted by *Quechua* in the missions.

The *Aguachile* are always listed with the *Leco* as the main tribes of the district of Apolobamba (lat. 15° S., long. 68° W.). In 1678, the *Aguachile* numbered about 1,000 and lived in 16 villages. The limits of their habitat cannot be defined accurately, but seem to have included the region where the Missions of Concepción de Apolobamba and Santa Cruz del Valle Ameno were founded. The bulk of the *Aguachile* probably occupied the mountainous ranges between the Beni and Tuichi Rivers called Altuncama or Chiru Choricha. Judging from their geographical distribution (map 2), the *Aguachile* and the *Apolista* were one and the same tribe.

BIBLIOGRAPHY

Armentia, 1887–88, 1903, 1905; Créqui-Montfort and Rivet, 1913 c; D'Orbigny, 1839; Lafone-Quevedo, 1905; Maurtua, 1906; Post, 1905; Weddel, 1853.

PLATE 41.—**Chiriguano pottery and urn burials.** *Top, left:* and *bottom:* Pottery making. *Top, right:* Urn burials at Caipipendi, Chaco, Bolivia. (Courtesy Alfred Métraux.)

PLATE 42.—**Chiriguano Indians.** *Left:* Granary on piles. *Center:* Woman spinning. *Right:* Woman and child. (Courtesy Alfred Métraux.)

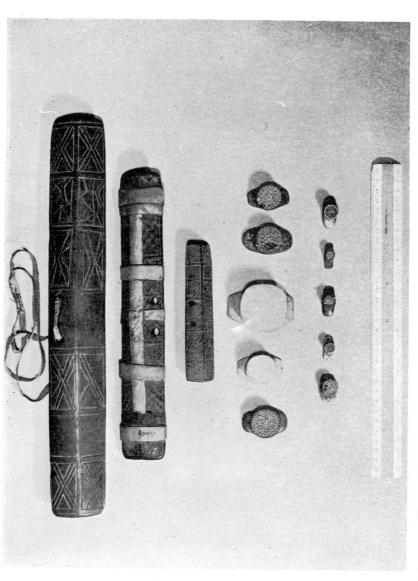

PLATE 43.—Chiriguano artifacts. Three engraved wooden serere whistles and lip plugs of metal with inlays. (Scale, 30 cm.) (Courtesy Museo Etnográfico de la Facultad de Filosofía y Letras, Buenos Aires.)

PLATE 44.—**Wooden masks of the Chiriguano and the altiplano.** *Top: Chiriguano* masks made of a single piece of wood. (The scale is 30 cm. long.) *Bottom:* Painted wooden masks, probably *Chiriguano* in origin. (Courtesy Museo Etnográfico de la Facultad de Filosofía y Letras, Buenos Aires.)

PLATE 45.—**Yuracare Indians of the early 19th century.** *Top:* Combat with dueling arrows. *Bottom:* Thatched house and dance. (After D'Orbigny, 1835–47.)

PLATE 46.—**Modern Yuracare Indians.** *Top:* Chewing yuca for chica. *Bottom:* Women and children. (Courtesy American Museum of Natural History.)

PLATE 47.—**Chimane and Yuracare manufactures.** *Top: Chimane* sieve and fire fan, both plaited from palm leaf. *Bottom: Yuracare* ceremonial clothes of bark cloth for men. (After Nordenskiöld, 1924.)

TRIBES OF THE MONTANA: AN INTRODUCTION

By JULIAN H. STEWARD

INTRODUCTION

The *Chuncho* (Andean name of the peoples of the eastern slopes of the Highlands) occupy the Montaña (the eastern side of the Andes of Ecuador and Perú) and the Yunga (the comparable region in Bolivia) (map 1, *No. 3;* map 5; also map 4). Though by no means homogeneous environmentally or culturally, the *Chuncho* area has sufficient unity and distinctiveness to warrant separate treatment.

Geographically, the Montaña and Yunga are selva or tropical rain forest, but unlike the Amazon Basin have rugged topography and many rapid streams. The environment has isolated the tribes from one another, restricted inhabitable areas, and limited navigation and fishing in the rivers.

Culturally, the *Chuncho* belong with the Tropical Forest peoples. They appear to represent a series of migratory waves that had spent their force against the barrier of the Andes, where representatives of many widely distributed linguistic families—*Arawakan, Tupian, Cariban, Tucanoan*—and members of isolated linguistic families—*Cofán, Jívaroan, Záparoan, Cahuapanan, Panoan, Hibitoan, Cholonan, Tacanan, Lecoan, Chimanean, Yuracarean,* and others—subsided into comparative isolation. No other area of South America has greater linguistic diversity. The *Chuncho* families remained in their valleys, little influenced by the Andean civilizations on the cold heights immediately to their west or even by some of the characteristic Amazonian developments which had spread along waterways of the Amazon Basin.

The contrast between the *Chuncho* and the Andean *Quechua* is as great as that between the environments to which they were conditioned. These cultures correlate to an extraordinary degree with altitude and topography. The jungle culture had spread westward to end abruptly at the sharp escarpment of the Andes and rarely occurred at altitudes of more than 3,000 or 4,000 feet (1,000 or 1,200 m.). But it had penetrated the deep, canyonlike valleys which thrust long prongs into the mountains, for example, the upper Napo, Santiago, Marañón, Huallaga, Pachitea, Perené, and Ené Rivers, and the tributaries of the Madeira River. It was halted only where the mountains rise precipitously above 5,000 or 6,000 feet (1,800 or 2,000 m.) into zones of thick clouds and heavy rains. The Highland cultures clung to the tops of the drier, cooler mountain masses and spread eastward around the deep valleys, sometimes nearly engulfing the lowland peoples, for example, the *Patagón* and their neighbors of the upper Marañón River, but never descending into the low valleys. There seems, in fact, to have been an effective barrier between the Highland and jungle peoples—the Ceja de la Montaña, a rugged, cloud-buried, excessively rainy, precipitous strip between the Puna and the lower hills of the Montaña. This strip was largely unpopulated. Salinas Loyola, for instance, wrote in 1571 (1897) that traveling east into the Montaña of Ecuador, he found the rough mountains entirely without Indians for 20 leagues.

The extraordinarily limited influence of the Highland on the Montaña is intelligible mainly in terms of unlike environmental conditioning of these cultures. Highland civilization rested on intensive agriculture on land that did not need clearing. A dense population underlay elaborate sociopolitical organization; economic surplus permitted religious, artistic, and industrial refinements. The Tropical Forest culture was adapted to an extremely warm, humid, and densely forested region. The hunting, fishing, and slash-and-burn economy produced a low population density and small communities. A Highland economy with its social and political concomitants could not have been introduced. Similarities between Highland and Montaña are largely in items such as clothes and ornaments, which are not functionally part of the socio-economic patterns. Such similarities are actually fewer than has generally been supposed.

The *Chuncho* as a whole also lack common Amazonian traits, such as bitter manioc, the tipití, the vertical loom, trumpets, masks, and clans. Other elements, such as hammocks, fish traps, nets, and large communal houses, have a limited occurance in the Montaña.

But Montaña culture was not uniform. The *Western Tucanoan* tribes are transitional between the *Witotoan* peoples to the north and the more typical *Chuncho* to the south. The *Quijo* and *Cofán* are little known. The *Jívaro* are treated separately because of the relative abundance of information about them. Of the *Záparoan* tribes, we have only fragmentary knowledge. The *Cahuapanan* linguistic group is only slightly better known. Most tribes of the upper Marañón, middle Huallaga, and upper Huallaga groups were assimilated soon after the Conquest. The *Panoan* tribes of the Ucayali River are comparatively well known through Tessmann's research. The *Chiriguano* of Bolivia have been fully described by Giannechini, Nino, Nordenskiöld, and Métraux. The *Arawakan* and *Peban* peoples and the *Panoan Mayoruna* seem, on the basis of scant in-

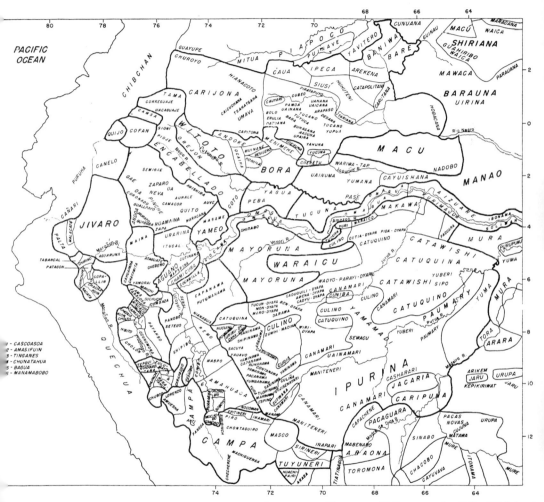

5.—The native tribes of the Montaña and the western Amazon Basin.   Locations areas of first contact with Europeans.   Compiled by J. H. Setward from original sources, but Juruá-Purús area after Rivet, 1924, and Uaupés-Caquetá region based on information from Irving Goldman.)

(Face p. 508)

formation, to possess some distinctive features. The *Arawakan, Panoan,* and *Catukinan* peoples of the Juruá and Purús Rivers were similar to many of the *Chuncho* but are described elsewhere (this volume, pp. 657–686).

HISTORY AND SOURCES

The mountainous terrain, deep jungles, and swift rivers with their many rapids (pongos) make the Montaña difficult of access. Efforts to penetrate the area from the Andes began in prehistoric times, but were rebuffed by geographical as well as cultural and military factors. White soldiers, missionaries, and colonists have encountered such great difficulties that, although the tribes along the main waterways are now greatly acculturated or assimilated, those in the hinterland of the rivers retain more aboriginal culture than is found among most South American Indians. Some of these tribes, like the *Jívaro* and the *Campa*, still present excellent opportunities for studies of functioning aboriginal cultures. Others afford fields for acculturation studies.

Inadequacy of archeological information from the Montaña leaves the question of cultural origins in obscurity and provides no evidence bearing on Tello's (1922, 1942) suggestion that the early Andean peoples came from the Tropical Forests. In Ecuador and Perú, Highland type ruins stop abruptly at the Montaña. In Bolivia, a "Derived Tiahuanaco" influence, seen mainly in pottery, is evident east to the Llanos of Mojos. This is followed by periods with *Arawak*, and then *Inca* influence, the latter manifest in forts built along the historic territory of the *Yuracare, Chané,* and *Chiriguano* (Bennett, 1936, pp. 400–412).

Ethnographic data and *Inca* tradition corroborate archeological evidence. *Arawakan* penetration from the east evidently separated the *Northern Panoan* and *Southern Panoan* groups, perhaps at the time it left an impress on Bolivian archeology. Prehistoric *Inca* conquests, though extending 2,000 miles along the Andes, were halted by the Montaña jungles. Tupac Yupanqui (ca. 1448–82) conquered the Highland *Cañari* but failed against the *Jívaro*, while his expedition to the *Musu* (*Mojo*) and *Chiriguano* did little more than stimulate trade (Means, 1931).

Despite the failure of their expeditions, the *Inca* doubtless had some influence on the *Chuncho*. Metal and other trade objects had reached these people. The *Canelo, Lama, Chasutino,* and *Quijo* probably adopted the *Quechua* language in prehistoric times. Similarly in Bolivia, some of the *Chimane* and *Mosetene* already spoke *Aymara* when first described in 1677 (Meléndez, 1682). The influence, however, was surprisingly slight. The *Campa*, for example, who adjoined the *Quechua* in the region of Cuzco, have few culture elements—the cushma, feather fire fan, satchel, coca chewing—that are indisputably attributable to Highland influence.

In Bolivia, Andean influence extended farther east than in Perú and Ecuador. *Mojo* and *Bauré* pottery from the mounds of Mojos (Nordenskiöld, 1913, 1917 *b*) are Highland (Tiahuanaco) influenced. The culture of the historic *Mojo* (p. 412) has Andean features, and that of the *Chané* of the Andean foothills was even more deeply influenced. The *Guaraní* (p. 69), who invaded *Chané* territory in waves at the end of the 15th century and raided the *Inca* frontier, absorbed many Highland traits. Still farther south in Northwestern Argentina, the cultures had become basically Andean; these are described in Volume 2 of this Handbook.

The post-Contact history brought considerable culture change, even among tribes which today retain a predominantly aboriginal culture (map 6). The 400 years since the Conquest is tentatively divided into three acculturation periods. The dates differ somewhat for the various regions. Future utilization of archival and manuscript material will correct these periods and fill in cultural detail.

(1) Exploration and Conquest, 1532–1643. During this period Spanish contacts had little lasting influence on the Indian. Exploration, 1532–60, seeking El Dorado, brought no settlers. The Conquest, 1560–1600, established towns on the western fringe of the Montaña but these were abandoned by 1600. An interim of comparative inactivity followed to about 1630.

(2) Mission or Colonial Period, 1630–1830. Two subperiods are roughly that of (*a*) Jesuit success, 1640 to 1767, and (*b*) a period of decadence after the Jesuit expulsion.

(3) National Period, 1830–present. After national independence from Spain there was gradual penetration by Whites but no systematic policy. The period brought more regular exploration as well as settlement. The abrupt shock of the rubber boom came about 1890 and lasted to 1915 and, subsequently, the area has been gradually opened to more permanent settlement.

(1) **Exploration and Conquest.**—The first explorations were carried out mainly from the west by adventurers seeking the lengendary empire of fabulous wealth thought to lie east of Perú and variously called El Dorado, Mojo, Sevilla del Oro, Gran Pará, Beni, the Kingdom of the *Omaguas,* and Paititi. In 1532, Gonzalo Díaz de Pineda reached the juncture of the Coca and Maspa Rivers. From 1539–42, Gonzalo Pizzaro explored the region of the Coca and Napo Rivers and Orellana continued on down the Amazon to the Atlantic Ocean. About the same time, Pedro de Candia with Pedro Anzules reached the Beni River, and Almagro visited the Caravaya region. Between 1539 and 1570, nine expeditions from Perú sought El Dorado in vain. Outstanding among these was that of Ursua, 1560, which passed down the Huallaga and Marañón Rivers to the Ucayali River, and Maldonado's, 1567, which reached the upper Madre de Díos River. As the adventurers found neither vast cities, wealth, nor important quantities of gold, the vision of El Dorado faded during the following century. These explorers and con-

querors had had little influence on the Indians and left no important ethnographic sources.

The Conquest began with the establishment of three short-lived towns in the Carabaya region in 1542. By 1560, small towns had been founded in the territory of the *Quijo, Cofán, Canelo, Jívaro,* and tribes of the Huallaga and upper Marañón Rivers. The *Quijo* and their neighbors then numbered 30,000. Indians were enslaved on encomiendas in great numbers. In the *Quijo* region in 1576, for example, Baez had 5,013 Indians; Avila, 2,613; and Archidona, 2,377. Excessive labor in fields, households, and mines, ravages of diseases, especially smallpox, and maltreatment, including use of dogs to track down fugitives, brought a rebellion and abandonment of virtually all these towns by the end of the century, before any lasting influence had been made on the Indians. Because of language difficulties, the missionaries had made slight impression. During the next 30 or 40 years, little was done in the Montaña, though the foundation of Borja, 1619, opened the region for subsequent missionary penetration. The most important source for this period is the journal of Juan de Salinas Loyola (1897), describing his trip in 1556 through *Jívaro* territory, the Province of Mainas, and the Ucayali River.

(2) **Mission Period, 1630–1830.**—Missionary work, carried out from both Ecuador and Perú, was mainly in the hands of the Franciscans and Jesuits, the Dominicans playing a more restricted role. The Franciscans directed their efforts toward the Montaña after the foundation of Huánuco, 1542, but it was not until 1631 that missions were established among the *Tingan, Panatahua, Carapacho,* and other tribes of the upper Huallaga River, and 1632 that the *Ceño (Sunu?),* *Becaba, Encabellado,* and *Omagua* were converted. Missions among the latter group of tribes, however, were abandoned in 1649 and were not renewed until 1686, when efforts were concentrated on the Putumayo and Caquetá regions. Success here was slight, and many converts were lost through slavery and rebellion.

In southern Perú, the Franciscans founded their famous Cerro de la Sal missions among the *Campa* and *Amuesha,* 1635. Later, they reached the *Cholón,* and in 1661 missionized the *Panoan* tribes of the Ucayali River. The foundation of the Colegio de Santa Rosa de Ocopa in 1732 gave great impetus to their work and from 1733 to 1742 they penetrated the Gran Pajonal. At the peak of their success, 1742, when they claimed 10,000 converts in 10 missions, the insurrection led by Santos Atahuallpa brought a serious setback to their work. The Franciscans still have missions on the Ucayali today, but other events have overshadowed their influence on the Indians.

The Dominicans restricted their activities to the *Canelo,* where their missions remained many years.

The Jesuits, with a more vigorous policy than either of the rival brotherhoods, enjoyed 130 years of considerable success until they were expelled in 1767. The foundation of the town of Borja, 1619, on the Marañón River below the Pongo of Manseriche, had provided a springboard for penetration of the more remote areas. About 1638, the Jesuits entered the territory of the *Jívaro, Yameo, Cahuapanans, Záparoans,* and *Cocama* in Ecuador and Perú.

The total converted population of the regions of Mainas and of the Huallaga and Pastaza Rivers in 1660 was estimated at 70,000 (Chantre y Herrera, 1901, p. 202) and in 1663 at 56,000 (by Figueroa), doubtless considerable exaggerations. By 1666, the Jesuits had 13 large missions on the upper Marañón River near the mouth of the Pastaza, Huallaga, and Ucayali Rivers. They missionized the *Tacanan* tribes in 1680, the *Mojo* in 1683, the *Apolista* in 1690, the *Cayuvava* and *Móvima* in 1693, the *Canichana* in 1695, and the *Chiquito* about the same time.

The Indians were profoundly influenced by the missions, even when they did not remain permanently in them. Formerly isolated in extended family groups which frequently moved their homes, they were assembled in large permanent villages. The latter did not wholly allay intercommunity and intertribal hostility, but they created contacts which were a condition for diffusion of native as well as Spanish culture elements. To meet the food problem in these villages, new plants, including bananas, rice, sugarcane, and other Old World species were grown. Steel tools so greatly facilitated farming and technology that they were a major inducement for the Indians to enter the missions. To meet the language difficulty, *Quechua* was made the Lengua Geral, and Highland Indians were even brought in to introduce it (map 6). A *Quechua* school was also founded in Borja to train boys and girls from native tribes.

But the missionary work entailed great difficulties, and the missionaries, with their fanatical zeal, met these with little success. When disease periodically took its devastating toll and created panic among the converts, the Fathers strove to baptize as many as they could of the dying Indians. When the Indians resented being brought into the missions by force of arms and being required to observe Spanish social customs, disciplinary measures were tightened or the Indians were bribed through presents of iron tools. The ban on polygyny, for example, was especially intolerable. The importation of Highland Indians and the presence of Mestizos also served to incite theft and insubordination. The policy of uniting members of different and hostile tribes caused a perpetual unrest and accounted for many desertions. Portuguese slave raids, starting in 1694, and efforts of local colonists to seize Indians for encomiendas continually menaced the missions, although they also tended to force the Indians to seek refuge under the Fathers' protection.

The success of the missions was at best tenuous. Death so reduced the native population that Figueroa (1904, p. 182) thought that two-thirds had died by 1665. Some estimates claim that smallpox took 44,000 in 1660, another 20,000 in 1669, and such numbers in 1680, 1749, 1756, and 1762 that survivors fled the missions into the bush. Converts were also continually lost through desertion. Open rebellion and massacre of the Fathers punctuated the history of every mission. In the Ucayali region, hostility had long hindered the missionaries, and revolts of 1686, 1695, 1704, 1742, and 1767 had made conversion nearly impossible.

The uprising of 1742, led by a remarkable messiah, swept the missions from the area and brought death to 70 or 80 Fathers. The instigator was a Cuzco Indian who had been to Spain and returned calling himself Juan Santos Atahuallpa Apo-Inca and claiming to be the son of God as well as a descendant of the *Inca* Emperor Atahuallpa. Pretending to have the wisdom of Solomon and the ability to make mountains fall, he declared that God had sent him to restore His kingdom. (See also Handbook, vol. 2, p. 385.) There was also a series of revolts in 1660 and 1667 in the lower Marañón-Napo area and among the *Chimane* and *Canichana*. The *Jívaro* had never been successfully converted. Other tribes, such as the *Campa*, resisted so continuously that they became a haven for refugee Indians and a constant menace to the Spaniards. The most serious blow to mission activity was the expulsion of the Jesuits in 1767. Their missions were either secularized or taken over by the Franciscans in the capacity of curates, which greatly handicapped them. The missions declined so rapidly that few survived in the first part of the last century when the wars of independence occurred. The effect on the Indians was directly proportionate to the duration of their missions. In the Huallaga-Ucayali area, there were some 160 Catholic missions in the 18th century, but only 9 remained in 1875. In the Province of Mainas, there had been 12,909 Indians in 24 villages in 1746, and 9,111 in 22 villages in 1787, but only 4,455 remained in these same villages in 1798 (González Suárez, 1890–1903, vol. 6). In 1806, the lower Marañón and Huallaga had 6,525 Mission Indians; Mainas had 3,329 (Izaguirre, 1922–29, 9:1–9). Indians that had been converted earliest, for example the *Patagón, Cofán, Chuache, Cahumari, Quijo, Caliseca,* and *Maparina,* have vanished as tribes. Others, who remained more or less continuously under mission influence, such as the *Mosetene, Itonama, Cayuvava, Móvima, Leco,* and *Apolista,* not only became nearly extinct by the present century, but had lost virtually all trace of their native culture. Some tribes, such as the *Jívaro, Campa, Piro, Conibo, Shipibo, Záparo, Cahuapana, Chébero,* and *Chayawita,* maintained a spirit of independence—revolts occurred as late as 1921—and survive today in some numbers. These especially would still reward investigation of aboriginal ethnology.

The most important sources for the Mission Period are Diego de Córdoba y Salinas (1651); Rodriguez (1684); Figueroa (1904); Laureano de la Cruz (1900); Acuña (1891); "Noticias autenticas del Gran Río Amazonas," compiled by Father Maroni and published by Jiménez de la Espada (1889–92); Escobar y Mendoza, 1637 to 1767 (1769); Fritz, 1686–1723 (1922); Veigl to 1768 (1785); Chantre y Herrera, 1637–1767 (1901); and Amich (1854), written in 1768. Many original accounts and letters by Franciscan missionaries written up to the present century have been reproduced by Izaguirre (1922–29) in his monumental "Misiones franciscanas . . . del Perú." Franciscan and Jesuit reports are also included in V. Maurtua's collection of documents (1906). The first scientific exploration was made by Lacondamine, 1743.

(3) National Period, 1830–present.—Absorbed in internal affairs, the new nations paid less attention to their undeveloped oriente. The missions passed from the Franciscans to the secular clergy, which was poorly trained and which maltreated and exploited the Indians, then back to the Franciscans. Settlers gradually penetrated the main waterways—the Marañón, Huallaga, Ucayali, Napo, and Putumayo Rivers—reducing the more accessible Indians to virtual serfdom on their plantations. Of the *Awishira, Omurana, Amuesha, Chamicuro, Yameo,* and *Záparo,* only acculturated fragments survive today under their patrones. As the settlers came mainly from the Highland and spoke *Quechua,* they served to spread this language even farther into the Montaña. (See map 6.) In general, the tribes living between the main rivers escaped continuous mission influence and best survived White settlement.

Tribes on the fringe of the area suffered the violent shock of the rubber boom after 1890. The lower Marañón, Napo, Putumayo, and Madeira Rivers and all the Juruá-Purús drainage were most affected, but the Ucayali, Pastaza, Curaray, and Huallaga River peoples felt it only indirectly through the dislocation of tribes to their east.

The present century has brought a renewal of missionary activity by both Catholics and Protestants.

The surviving Montaña tribes now appear to be on the threshold of rapid assimilation. Improved travel, especially roads and use of the airplane, and many new and potential commercial developments in the jungles are already bringing Whites in increasing numbers.

The National Period has been one of scientific exploration. The more important traveler's journals are Maw (1829), Pöppig (1835-36), Smyth and Lowe (1836), Herndon and Gibbon (1853-54, vol. 1), D'Orbigny (1839), Armentia (1887-88), Galt (ms. of 1870–74), Castelnau (1851), and Keller-Leuzinger (1874).

Ethnographic monographs date from the present century. Nordenskiöld's collections and studies of the material culture of Bolivia started about 1900. Rivet and Créqui-Montfort classified linguistic families of eastern Perú and Bolivia. The Jívaro were studied by Karsten, Up de Graf, and Stirling. The Tribes of eastern Perú and Ecuador were surveyed by Farabee. The *Masco* and *Yagua* have been

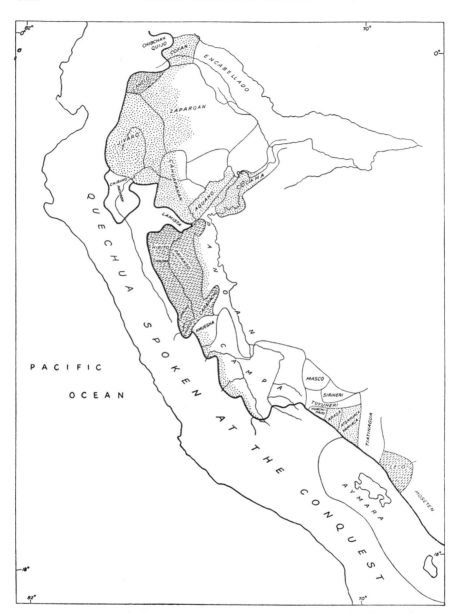

MAP 6.—The post-Conquest expansion of *Quechua* into the Montaña.
(Compiled by J. H. Steward.)

studied by Fejos. The most monumental and important work is by Tessmann
(1930) on the same tribes. Its value to studies of material culture is outstanding,
but its findings on social and religious culture can only be accepted with skepticism
because Tessmann often did not make first-hand observations, relying on poor
informants, and because he lacked interest in modern techniques for social analysis
and was prepossessed with the theory that the Indians had no High God concept.

MONTANA CULTURE AND CULTURE CHANGES

Important recorded changes in Montaña culture during the historic period underline the fallacy of compressing ethnological observations covering four centuries in a single, two-dimensional picture. Post-Contact developments may, in fact, be greater than is known, for without fairly definite records it is difficult to ascertain whether many Indian elements diffused in pre- or post-Columbian times.

Some elements obviously came directly from Europeans: Iron tools and other manufactured objects; new domesticated plants; more complete garments and some European styles of clothing; occasional art styles; some technological processes, such as the roller sugarcane press and the iron smelter; and certain Christian marriage practices, death customs, religious beliefs, and mythology. Other changes probably resulted indirectly from post-European innovations: Greater facility in making canoes, houses, household furniture, weapons, fishing gear, and the like with iron tools; improved agriculture with the iron ax and machete for clearing land; intensification of warfare and slaving expeditions; larger villages and amalgamation of individual families into extended patrilineal families; and decreased isolationism and consequently increased intertribal contacts which furthered trade and diffusion of various cultural elements. Many native elements diffused in the post-Contact period: the blowgun replaced the bow; various aboriginal narcotics and drugs, especially tobacco and cayapi, became more widespread and general; and cushmas, shirts, skirts, hammocks, platform beds, and canoes spread after as well as before the Conquest. Doubtless other features, which cannot be identified with certainty, also diffused or were modified after the Conquest.

SUBSISTENCE ACTIVITIES

The Indians of the Montaña [wrote Skinner (1805, pp. 283–284)] find some difficulty in subsisting without implements of husbandry, which is not owing to any deficiency of soil and rivers, since these are most fertile in fruits, birds, quadrupeds, and fishes; but they cannot dispense with certain roots which require culture. Of these, the principal is the yuca [manioc], with which they made the masato [chicha], their only comfort and drink. They seldom taste water, which, in consequence of the heat and of the innumerable morasses, is of a very noxious quality . . . Their attention is, however, so little occupied by agriculture and manufactures, that it may be asserted that their sole occupations are hunting, fishing, and war.

Although all tribes were horticulturists, the relative importance of hunting, fishing, and collecting wild foods varied with local habitat and with devices used. Thus, fishing outweighed hunting among the *Jivaro* because of scarcity of game, among the *Awishira* because they used only spears to hunt, and among many other tribes such as the *Aguano, Cando-*

shi, Yameo, and *Yamiaca* because of local abundance of fish. Hunting, on the other hand, was a pursuit of prestige to the *Yamiaca*. *Chébero* farming was handicapped by infertile soil, and the *Mayoruna's* swampy habitat made it easier to rely on wild fruits than on farming. June, when shoals of fish swarmed up the Marañón and its tributaries, was a time of intensive fishing for many tribes.

TABLE 1.—*Cultivated plants used by the tribes of the Montaña*[1]

Plant	Quijo	W. Tucano	Záparoans	Jívaro	Pebans	Cahuapanans	Upper Marañón	Middle Huallaga	Upper Huallaga	Panoans	Mayoruna	Arawakans	Tupí Upper Amazon
Sweet manioc or yuca (*Manihot utilissima aypi*)	X	X	X	X	X	X	....	X	X	X	X	X	X
Bitter manioc (*Manihot utilissima*)	X	X	R	O	O	R	....	O	O	O	O	O	(X)
Maize (*Zea mays*)	X	X	X	X	X	X	X	X	X	X	X	X	X
Sweet potato (*Ipomoea batatas*)	X	X	X	X	X	X	X	X	....	....	X	X	X
Peanut, mani (*Arachis hypogaea*)	X	....	X	X	X	X	X	X	X	X	X	X	X
Bean (tuber)	X	X	....	X	X	X	....	X	....	X	....	X	X
Chonta palm	X	X	X	X	X	X	....	....	....	....	....	X	X
Potato (*Solanum*)	X	O	O	O	O	....	X	....	....	....	....	(X)	....
Yam beans (*Pachyrrhizus*)	....	....	....	....	....	....	....	X	....	....	....	....	X
Pepper (*Capsicum*)	X	....	....	....	X	X	....	....	....	....	....	....	....
Papaya (*Carica papaya*)	....	....	....	....	X	X	....	....	....	X	....	....	....
Macabo (*Xantho sp.*)	....	X	X	X	....	X	....	X	....	X	....	X	....
Sicana (*Sicana odorifera*)	....	....	....	....	....	X	....	....	....	....	....	X	X
Pumpkin (*Cucurbita*)	....	....	X	X	X	X	....	X	....	X	X	X	X
Plantain	X	X	X	X	....	X	....	X	....	X	....	....	....
Banana	X	X	X	X	X	X	....	X	....	X	X	X	X
Sugarcane	X	X	X	X	X	X	....	X	....	X	....	X	X
Yam (*Dioscorea*)	....	X	X	X	X	X	....	X	....	X	....	X	X
Taro	....	....	....	....	....	X	....	....	....	X	....	....	....
Tobacco (*Nicotiana*)	....	....	....	X	X	....	....	....	....	X	....	....	X
Cotton	....	....	....	X	X	X	X	X	....	X	X	....	X
Barbasco	....	....	....	X	X	X	....	....	....	....	....	X	X
Bixa (*Bixa orellana*)	....	....	....	X	X	X	....	....	....	X	....	....	....
Coca	....	....	....	....	....	X	....	X	....	(X)	....	X	....
Reeds	....	....	....	....	....	....	....	....	....	X	....	....	....

[1] X, presence; O, known absence; R, rare; blank, no data.

The native staple was sweet manioc, the bitter variety not having spread south of the *Quijo* and *Encabellado,* though it was recently introduced to some *Záparoan* and *Cahuapanan* tribes. Other native crops of general distribution were sweet potatoes, peanuts, pumpkins, beans, the jicama or yam bean, papayas, macabo, pepino and several palms, especially chonta. Maize was grown more for making chicha than bread in 1664 (Figueroa, 1904, p. 206.). Potatoes were restricted to high altitudes—*Quijo,* upper Marañón, and some *Arawakans.*

New crops and implements introduced during the historic period profoundly affected the subsistence pattern through facilitating horticulture. The iron ax made slash-and-burn farming immeasurably easier. The plantain (possibly aboriginal, see Sauer, Handbook, vol. 6), banana, yam, and sugarcane, all well adapted to the Tropical Forests, became more important than most native species and seem to have relegated manioc to use primarily for making chicha. Humboldt calculated that the yield of plantains compared with wheat is 133 to 1 and compared with potatoes 44 to 1. Other introduced plants which attained a more limited distribution are watermelons (Bolivia), pineapples (Bolivia), papaya (*Jívaro, Chébero*), taro (Peruvian *Panoans, Arawakans,* and *Iquito*), and orange, lemon, lime, and fig trees. Rice, though introduced by the missionaries, was not liked by the Indians. Like the Highland Indians, the *Chuncho* apparently adopted no garden vegetables, such as carrots, beets, lettuce, and the like, at least for their own use. Other special plants are mentioned under tribal headings.

The farming pattern seems to be the same everywhere. Families cultivate and harvest their own plots, though men assist one another in felling trees and are rewarded with chicha.

Game animals in the ancient Province of Mainas included 10 kinds of monkeys, punchanas, armadillos, land turtles, lomuchas (burrowing animals caught with nets), peccaries, and birds of all kinds, but neither iguanas, capivaras, nor anteaters. Deer seem generally not to have been eaten, probably because of some notion that they were reincarnated people.

The principal aboriginal devices for hunting had been the bow and spear, but during the historic period most tribes abandoned the bow in favor of the blowgun for hunting small game and birds. Other methods seem to have had a spotty distribution, owing to the incomplete nature of our sources; traps and snares (fig. 72), pitfalls (*Záparoans, Pebans, Panoans, Jívaro*), nets (*Záparoans,* upper Marañón, *Arawak, Panoans*), blinds (*Pebans, Panoans, Cahuapanans, Arawak*), slings (*Cashibo*), deadfalls (*Encabellado*), and sloping sharp stakes planted in game trails (*Arawakans*). The hunting dog was generally used but seems not to have been native.

The main reserves of meat came from manatee, which are huge river mammals, and large water turtles. The former were killed with a harpoon

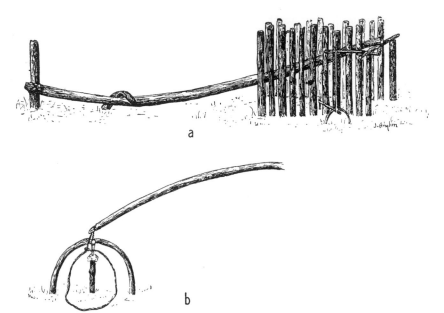

FIGURE 72.—*Coto* traps. *a,* Deadfall; *b,* spring pole. (After Tessmann, 1930, pl. 42.)

to which a wooden float was attached, then dragged to the shore, maneuvered into the canoe, and taken home, where the meat was roasted and placed in a large pot covered with manatee oil, which prescribed it for half a year. Salting meat is a post-Columbian practice. Turtles were caught at any time with harpoons or arrows (pl. 48, *bottom*); or, in October when laying their eggs, they were captured in large numbers by turning them on their backs after which they were taken to the village and kept in penned pools. The meat supply was considerable, for 6 men could take 500 turtles in a short time and each turtle sufficed 30 people for one meal. The eggs were salted, soaked, or the oil extracted by smashing the yokes in a canoe so that it rose to the surface. The oil was preserved in jars for cooking and illumination. Later, it became an important item of trade with the White man (Veigl, 1785 a, pp. 194–198).

The rivers also supplied caimans, dolphins, electric eels, yacu puma or water wolves, and numerous varieties of fish. Fishing methods showed much local variation and some historic change. Nets were of little value in streams filled with driftwood, especially in Bolivia, and were little used despite missionary attempts to introduce them. Hooks evidently had a limited pre-Columbian distribution, but became more general when iron hooks were introduced. Drugging was general, *Tephrosia toxicaria* and *Clibadium vargasii* being used in Ecuador and Perú and the solinan or manuna tree (*Hura crepitans*) in Bolivia. Barbasco (*Lonchocarpus nicou*) was widely cultivated in Perú and Ecuador; *Tephrosia* was sometimes cultivated. The poisonous plant was pounded and put into a lake or into a stream above a wythe fence. People in canoes or wading then gathered up the stupefied fish (Veigl, 1785 a, p. 274). The fish spear was widely used, but the harpoon, thrown usually with an atlatl, had been used mainly by the *Tupí, Záparoan, Quijo,* and *Cahuapanan* tribes. It could be thrown as far as a bow would shoot and was preferred in that it required but one hand, the other being used to manipulate the canoe (Veigl, 1785 a, p. 274). But the bow, which had been used among the Bolivian tribes and the Peruvian *Panoans, Arawak,* and *Tupí,* replaced the atlatl among many of these tribes and was used with harpoon arrows. Arrows, harpoons, and spears were greatly improved with iron points, and the adoption of canoes by many tribes was an aid to fishing.

Among wild foods, palm fruits and terminal shoots predominate. The more important species utilized are chonta (*Guilielma ciliata* and *G. palma*), achua (*Mauritia flexuosa*), *Jessenia bataua, Iriartea ventricosa, I. deltoidea, Scheelea tessmannii, S. bassleriana, Astrocaryum huicungo, A. vulgare,* and *Attalea tessmannii.* Only the *Arawakan* peoples use the climbing ring. Honey, palm beetle larvae, and ants are greatly relished.

The only domesticated animals were the llamas and alpacas on the upper Marañón River, llamas and guinea pigs kept by the *Jívaro,* a few guinea pigs in the Province of Mainas (probably *Záparoan* tribes), and probably the Muscovy duck. The acquisition of pigs and chickens greatly augmented the food supply. By the 17th century, the hunting dog was used by many tribes, but Veigl denies that it was native in the Province of Mainas and it may be post-Columbian everywhere. All tribes kept many tame monkeys, parrots, and other birds and mammals.

Food is most commonly ground in a wooden trough or on a flat wooden grinder with a wooden rocker. Wooden mortars are recorded only from the *Jívaro, Panoans,* and *Tupí;* stone grinders from the *Panoans* and upper Marañón tribes. The babracot is generally used to smoke meat so that it will last a few days, but the pottery stove, which, like the tipití, is used in making farinha of bitter manioc, is unknown. Cooking pots ordinarily rest on three supports.

HOUSES AND FURNISHINGS

House types varied from the single or double lean-to of the *Atsahuaca, Yuracare, Moseten, Chimane,* and *Pacaguara* to large and complicated structures. Some *Tacanan* and *Arawakan* houses are round. Most eastern Peruvian and Ecuadorian dwellings are rectangular, with and without center posts (pl. 49, *top*). More commodious houses were introduced during the post-Columbian period to accommodate the enlarged social groups. Special clubhouses were built only by the *Chacobo* and *Yuracare.* The *Canelo* palisaded village was unique in the area.

All tribes use a men's seat which, in contrast to the well-made product in most of the Amazon, varies from a rough-hewn half log to a stool crudely carved from a single piece of wood. Women sit on mats on the ground. The platform bed was aboriginally used by the tribes nearest the Andes—*Quijo, Canelo, Candoshi, Andoa, Cahuapanan,* upper Marañón, Huallaga, *Yuracare, Chiriguano,* and *Chané.* It subsequently spread eastward to some of the *Panoan* peoples and to the *Yameo, Leco. Mosetene,* and *Chimane.* In native times, the hammock had spread to the western *Tucanoans* and some of the *Záparoans,* the *Mayoruna,* the peripheral *Panoans,* and perhaps the *Southern Panoans,* the *Guarayú* and *Pauserna.* It was later adopted by several *Záparoans, Pebans, Panoans,* and Bolivian tribes.

A tightly-woven mosquito tent or net is used by the *Western Tucano, Záparoans, Yameo, Panoans, Tupí, Yuracare, Araona,* and perhaps Middle Huallaga peoples.

CLOTHING AND ADORNMENT

Complete lack of wearing apparel in native times was not common, though many tribes used only some genital cover. The narrow breechclout, although old in the Highland civilization (Nordenskiöld, 1920, p. 59), was used only by *Chiriguano* and *Chané* men and *Tacanan* women. Elsewhere, the penis was tied (pl. 50) or held up with a string, or men wore a broad breechclout, poncho, or shirt. The broad breechclout, which hung over the belt and virtually surrounded the body like a skirt, was used by the *Quijo, Itucale, Záparoans, Omurana,* and *Cocama.* A wrap-around skirt occurred among the *Jívaro, Panobo,* and some *Záparoan* tribes. The poncho was restricted to the *Western Tucano, Jívaro, Chané,* and *Chiriguano.*

Women used a small apron, shirts, or a skirt that pulled over the head (pl. 50, *left*), the last more characteristic of the Ucayali *Panoans.*

Adoption of a shirt was furthered by missionary precepts of modesty. Some are waist length, but the typical form is a long robe, known as the cushma, or tunic (pl. 50, *top, right*). This is typically a man's garment, though worn in some tribes by women. Poncholike in construction, it is made of a single piece of bark cloth or woven cotton and has a slit for the head. Some *Chama* tribes make it of two pieces. The cushma differs from the Andean woman's mantel in that the latter is wrapped around the body and from the eastern Bolivian and northern Chaco tipoy, which is a single, tubular piece of cloth worn with the warp running horizontally around the body and pinned over the shoulder. The tipoy occurs only among the *Chiriguano* and *Chané.* The *Jívaro* woman's dress supported over one shoulder may be related to the Highland mantel.

Seemingly all the tribes of Perú and Ecuador stain their teeth black by chewing certain herbs and ashes, which produces a stain that lasts several days (Chantre y Herrera, 1901, p. 63).

Two types of head deformation were once practiced. The *Quijo, Peban,* Ucayali *Panoans,* and *Tupí* compressed the forehead against the cradle. The *Awishira* and probably some of the other *Záparoan* tribes lengthened the head by pressing laterally on the temples. The *Pebans* also removed a child's nose cartilage, and the *Iquito* pressed the face and nose to make the face flat.

Tooth filing, perhaps of Negro origin in South America, is restricted to the modern *Aguano, Tupí,* and *Quijo.*

Other mutilations formerly had a wide distribution but seem not to have characterized cultural areas except that the *Western Tucano* and *Pebans* were famous for their large ear disks (whence the name *Orejones*), the *Arawak* for nose ornaments, and the *Remo* and *Mayoruna* for the great number of labrets a person wore (pl. 51).

Tattooing had a wide distribution but seems to have spread farther in post-Contact times.

All tribes formerly painted their faces and bodies, often as much for protection against insects as for ornamentation, but only the *Jívaro* and *Tupí* used a stamp. Chagua juice was used to allay itching.

Hairdress takes many forms, characteristic styles being the *Coronado* tonsure and the custom of shaving the head on the upper Marañón and among the *Iquito.* Depilation is general; the *Záparoans, Pebans,* and *Panobo* pull out hair with melted resin. Composite combs are used to groom the hair; the *Western Tucano* and *Záparoans* also use rosin mirrors.

Ornaments consist of necklaces, arm and leg bands, bands of beads crossing on the chest, and feather crowns. In aboriginal times, a few metal ornaments had come from the Highlands, especially to the *Quijo* and *Tupí.*

TRANSPORTATION

Insufficient data make comparative analysis of carrying devices impossible. Baskets, infant carrying bands, and men's bags seem to have a wide distribution. Nets are reported only on the middle Huallaga River and among the *Arawak.*

In modern times, all the *Chuncho* make canoes except those on small streams, like the peripheral *Panoans,* the *Arawakans* and the middle Huallaga people, who make only rafts. But aboriginal use of canoes is certain only for the Ucayali River *Panoans* and the *Tupí.* It is probable for the *Jívaro* and possible for the *Cahuapanans.* Other tribes learned canoe building and maneuvering from the *Panoans* and *Tupi* under mission influence: the *Western Tucanoans, Záporoans, Mayoruna,* and *Pebans.*

For rafts, the preferred material is palo de balsa (*Ochroma* sp.).

MANUFACTURES

Complete absence of stone everywhere except in the higher altitudes requires use mainly of vegetable and animal products for manufactures.

Baskets.—Baskets seem to conform to the usual Tropical Forest styles, a hexagonal weave being mentioned most frequently. The *Záparo* and *Cahuapanans* make a double-walled vessel. The long "telescope" basketry container is ascribed only to the *Arawak.*

Textiles.—Textiles are made of various fibers, some preference being given even by missionaries to wild-plant fibers over cotton because they lasted better in this hot, humid climate. An excellent cloth called cachibanco is made of achua palm fibers (*Mauritia flexuosa*), especially by the *Záparoan* tribes. Chambira palm is also widely used, being the main fiber of the *Western Tucanoans, Pebans,* and *Mayoruna.* The *Quijo* uniquely used agave and the upper Marañón tribes llama and alpaca wool. Use of *Cecropia* characterizes the upper Ucayali. The *Tupi, Cahuapanan, Panoan,* upper Marañón, and middle Huallaga Indians emphasize weaving in cotton. The *Western Tucanoans* use a little cotton, and the *Quijo* adopted it recently.

A horizontal loom, probably of Highland origin, is used by the *Záparoans, Cahuapanans,* middle Huallaga, Ucayali, and *Arawakan* tribes. A verticle loom is restricted to the *Jívaro* and *Campa.* The peculiar "Ucayali" loom occurs among some of the *Panoans* and *Arawakans.*

Bark cloth.—Bark cloth, made preferably of trees of *Ficus* and *Couratari,* occurs among the *Western Tucano, Záparoans, Jívaro,* and *Arawak.*

Pottery.—All Montaña tribes make pottery, though Spanish wares seem to have been introduced on the upper Marañón and Huallaga Rivers. Tessmann's data (1930) permit only a tentative classification of native wares. Vessel forms of general distribution are large cooking pots, water and chicha jars, and bowls. The first are always unpainted and are ornamented, if at all, only with incised, fingernail impressed or punched geometric figures, usually in bands around the neck. Jars and bowls carry several art styles, some of them coexisting in the same tribe.

The most striking style is a fine geometric polychrome (pl. 52, *a–c*; figs. 73, 74) that is best developed among the Ucayali River *Panoans* but also occurs among tribes bordering the Marañón River (*Cocama, Omagua, Yameo, Aguano, Urarina, Munichi,* and *Jívaro*). The style seems definitely related to that of Marajó and the lower Amazon, having geometric designs formed of widely spaced, heavy lines which are outlined by one

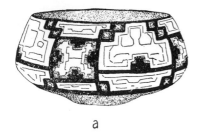

a

b

c

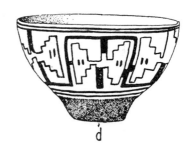

d

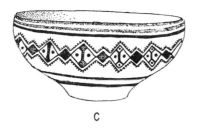

e

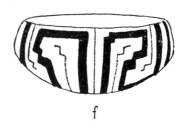

f

Black   White   Red

g

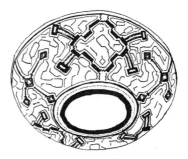

h   J. Anglin

FIGURE 73.—Montaña pottery types. *a, b, Chama; c, d, Cashibo; e, Panobo; f, Piro;*
g, h, Chama. (*f*, Redrawn from Farabee, 1922, pl. 6; *a, b, g, h,* redrawn from
Tessmann, 1928, pls. 4 and 5; *c–e*, redrawn from Tessmann, 1930, color pl. 4.)

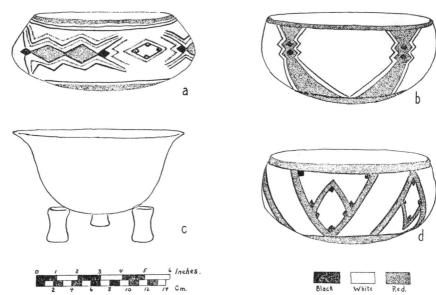

FIGURE 74.—Montaña pottery types. *a, Aguano; b, Chayawita; c, Aguano* (with pot rests) ; *d, Chayawita*. (Redrawn from Tessmann, 1930, color pls. 5, 8, and map. 11.)

or more fine lines. The Montaña style employs red and black on a cream background, and it lacks the incised lines, the occasional zoomorphic motives, and the modeled decoration of Marajó. A few examples of the style are white-on-red (*Cocama, Panobo,* fig. 79).

A second polychrome style, perhaps a modification of the last among the Marañón River tribes (*Jívaro, Chébero, Aguano*), uses a large number of closely spaced parallel lines of equal width to form geometric figures (pl. 52, *d,* fig. 75).

A simpler and cruder geometric style employs white-on-red (*Yameo, Chayawita, Omagua,* pl. 52, *e, f*) or red-on-cream (*Yameo, Coto, Cocama, Jívaro,* pl. 52, *g, h*). This style differs from the first two in having bolder geometric elements and more uncertain brush work as well as in the color combination.

Jars with the lower half red, the upper white, occur also on the Marañón (*Yameo, Chébero, Yamorai, Chayawita, Lama*).

Tribes living away from the main rivers usually had simpler wares (pl. 55). The *Itucale, Yagua, Záparo, Roamaina,* and *Mayoruna* seemingly used no painted designs; their bowls were red outside, smoke-blackened inside. The *Western Tucanoans,* however, were accredited with an elaborately painted ware (fig. 75, *a, b*).

Use of a genipa wash for red and of a copal (payuru) varnish is common in the Montaña.

Calabashes.—Calabashes are painted (*Záparoans*), varnished (*Záparoans*), and incised (*Tupí*).

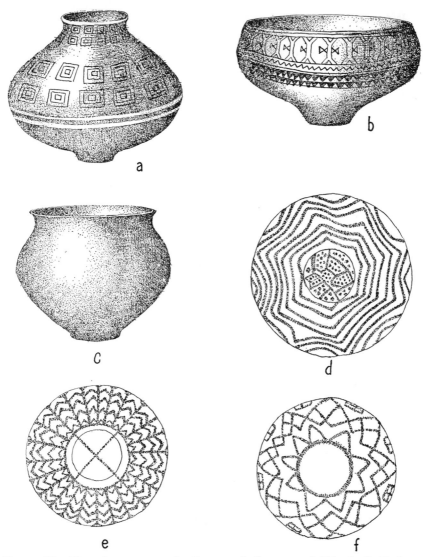

FIGURE 75.—Montaña pottery. *a, b, Coto; c, d, Jivaro; e, f,* "Simaku." (Redrawn, from Tessmann, 1930, pl. 35, color pl. 7, pl. 59, and color pl. 8.)

Metals.—Metallurgy was known in native times only to the *Quijo,* who smelted gold (González Suárez, 1890–1903, 6:59). Post-Contact placer mining in *Jívaro* territory started no important native use of metals, though the *Záparo* collected some gold. Through missionary influence, the *Arawak* adopted iron smelting.

Fire making.—The fire drill was probably used everywhere, although the *Yagua, Cahuapanans, Urarina, Campa,* and *Záparoans* are accredited with use of two stones. The missionaries introduced flint and steel.

Weapons.—At the time of discovery, these tribes used the spear thrown with the atlatl and the bow and arrow in both hunting and warfare. Subsequently, the blowgun and poisoned dart widely replaced the bow and arrow for hunting small game, while the bow and harpoon arrow took the place of the atlatl and harpoon in fishing. The spear is still used in hunting large game and in warfare, but is thrown without the atlatl.

The earliest mention of the blowgun in the area is Saabedra's account of the *Maina* (Stirling, 1938), but it may have been used earlier, for Cieza de León saw it in Colombia in 1540. The number of tribes then using the bow is not known, but several have since abandoned it in favor of the blowgun for hunting: the *Jívaro* during the 17th century; the *Western Tucano,* who once used it with poisoned arrows but now use it only to shoot harpoon arrows at turtles; and perhaps the middle Huallaga tribes, the Ucayali *Panoans,* and the *Mayoruna,* who use it only in fishing; and the *Cahuapanans* among whom it is now a toy. The *Tupí* and Ucayali River *Panoan* tribes, contrary to the general trend, recently adopted the bow for warfare. The *Pebans* never had it.

The blowgun, on the other hand, has become universal among all groups except the *Arawakans,* and peripheral *Panoans,* who continue to use the bow for both hunting and warfare.

The basis for the shift from the bow to the blowgun is unquestionably availability of poison, without which the blowgun is worthless. It is true that some arrows had formerly been poisoned, for example among the *Western Tucanoans,* but it is unlikely that the deadly curare was used. In recent times, in fact, the *Záparoans, Western Tucanoans, Cahuapanans,* and perhaps others imported their poison. The *Lama, Canelo,* and the *Pebans* were main sources; and the last evidently never used the bow. Most of these tribes had a much livelier trade in the historic period, when canoes and mission influence brought about greater intertribal contacts. It seems very possible, therefore, that availability of poison, together with what seems manifest superiority of the blowgun over the hunting bow, brought about the change.

The abandonment of the bow for warfare is more difficult to understand, for the blowgun was never used to kill anything but game. Perhaps a spear for fighting and a blowgun for hunting were all a warrior could carry.

The atlatl was once used by the *Maina,* the *Cahuapanans,* and the upper Marañón tribes for warfare and by the *Jívaro* and the *Panoans* for both warfare and hunting, but all these tribes have given it up. It is now restricted to the *Pebans* and the *Tupí,* who use it only to throw fish harpoons.

All tribes except the *Arawakans* used shields of various materials— wood, basketry, tapir hide. The club once had a wide distribution, but seems to have been used less frequently in recent times. Pitfalls and trenches with sharpened stakes were used everywhere to protect villages; the *Quijo* palisades are unique.

Other weapons attained a more limited distribution. The sling, doubtless of Highland origin, has been reported only among the *Lama, Cashibo, Arawakans,* and *Tupí.* Bone daggers occurred on the upper Marañón River; caltrops are *Arawakan;* weapons planted in the bush with automatic release are limited to the *Jívaro;* and automatic alarm drums are *Tupí.*

SOCIAL AND POLITICAL STRUCTURE

The aboriginal Montaña community typically consisted of one to a few families—15 to 30 persons—each family living in a small house (upper Marañón and Huallaga Rivers, *Western Tucanoans, Pebans, Arawakans, Southern Panoans,* and *Tacanans*). Houses were scattered at intervals of a few hundred yards to a few miles along water courses, or, as among the hinterland *Panoans, Western Tucanoans,* and others, were isolated in the bush for protection from war and slave raids. They were moved every 2 or 3 years. Occasionally, clusters of 5 or 10 houses made small villages. A few tribes, however, had much larger communities: *Tupí* villages numbered several hundred persons; *Cayuvava* settlements averaged 540 per village in 1696; *Mosetene* communities averaged 166 in 1682. These sizes seem to be native, but it is uncertain whether they depended upon greater local resources and an unusually dense population or upon a more developed political sense.

A tendency toward increase in community size occurred in the historic period, though it is remarkable that the mission villages of several hundred to a thousand persons each disintegrated at the close of the mission period when the people tended to resume their native separatism. The *Chébero,* who remained in a single village, and the *Aguano, Chasutina, Chacobo,* and *Araona* are exceptions. Other tribes, such as the *Western Tucanoans,* the *Pebans,* and some of the *Arawakans* began to live in large communities and adopted communal houses. In addition to direct mission influence, it is likely that adoption of canoes, better agriculture, and improved intercommunity relations were factors in the trend toward larger villages.

The social structure of these communities can be described only in general terms. The single-family house contained the elementary family consisting of father, mother, and children. When several families lived together in the molaca, a strong tendency to patrilocal residence, despite bride service, made the community an extended patrilineal family, with the family head as chief. Tessmann (1930) speaks of many of these as "kins," but there is no evidence that they were sibs, nor are there grounds for postulating that they ever had been sibs. In fact, a better case could be made that they represent a condition from which sibs might develop.

They resulted from congregation of patrilineally related families under a single roof. The *Lama*, however, may have had patrilineal moieties. The Ucayali River *Panoans*, in contrast to other Montaña peoples and to the hinterland *Panoans*, were matrilineal and had a hint of totemism which opens the possibility that they had clans.

These communities normally lacked any groupings, such as classes, castes, or societies, although some *Pebans* were alleged to have had some kind of nobles. Until trade with the Whites made slave traffic profitable, captives taken in warfare were incorporated into the local group, except among the *Quijo* and *Tupi*, who aboriginally had kept them in slave status.

Political authority centered in the family head, who controlled travel, warfare, and farm clearing. Chieftainship of greater consequence occurred only during temporary war alliances and in very recent times, when it seems clearly to be an institution imposed by the White man. Shamans often assumed leadership but only the *Quijo* regularly made them chiefs.

WARFARE

The pattern of warfare was very similar among all tribes, differences being found in emphasis and in details of weapons, cannibalism, and trophies. The *Jívaro* are distinctive in their absorbing interest in warfare which, however, may be a post-Contact intensification of a widespread aboriginal pattern.

The "Noticias Autenticas" (Maroni, 1889–92, 27:254–265) described the early war complex of the upper Amazon area in some detail. The motive for warfare was head hunting, and, though the occasion for a war expedition was presumably revenge of some wrong, usually witchcraft, it did not matter whether the foe had perpetrated the supposed crime. The decision to fight was made in a council. To insure victory, the shaman fasted and was chaste and silent; after a victory, he was rewarded with loot. Defeat was attributed to breaking a taboo. Warriors attired themselves in all their ornaments, and the chief whipped their legs to give them courage and put red pepper juice in their eyes to enable them better to see and dodge arrows and to shoot. The main stratagem was surprise attack, though villages were protected by trenches with stakes, by caltrops, and by automatic alarms. Warriors were killed and their heads taken to be shrunken and kept as trophies. Later, the heads were decorated with colored feathers and used in a dance during which the victors boasted and taunted them. Women and children were taken captive and incorporated in the conquering tribe.

Trophy skulls are recorded among the *Quijo, Western Tucano, Záparoans, Cahuapanians* and *Tupi*. The *Jívaro, Chébero, Panoans,* and *Itucale* (?) made shrunken heads (pl. 63). Cannibalism was less widespread: *Encabellado, Záparoans, Cahuapanans,* and *Mayoruna*. The

Peban peoples, who wore human-tooth necklaces, may also have used other trophies. Scalping is attributed only to the *Chama*.

LIFE CYCLE

The life cycle has little of interest. Abortion and infanticide were once fairly common, probably resulting from disturbances of the Contact Period. The couvade has a spotty distribution. The *Western Tucanoans* killed both twins; the *Záparoans* and *Tupí* killed one, probably because one of twins was thought to be a spirit's child. *Záparoans* and *Cashibo* practiced some kind of girl's circumcision soon after birth, and the *Záparoans* also ceremonially flogged girls and put pepper in their eyes.

Girls' puberty observances seem to have been limited to the first menses, when the *Arawakans* isolated a girl for 6 months. Special observances include *Arawakan* and *Chama* circumcision, deflowering, and whipping, *Tupí* removal of the clitoris, the *Jívaro* tobacco festival for strength, and *Awishira* and *Chébero* flogging and putting pepper in the eyes for strength.

No boys' initiation is known, though the *Jívaro* held a cayapi festival for youths.

Homicide of the aged and infirm was formerly practiced by the *Panoans* and *Záparoans*. Disposal of the corpse has taken many forms: Leaving it in the house (*Jívaro, Záparoans*); burial in the house (*Pebans,* sometimes with reburial; *Panoans,* sometimes in a canoe; *Western Tucanoans,* in a hammock); burial outside the house (some *Panoans*); urn burial (*Aguaruna, Tupí,* and *Chébero,* the last both primary and secondary; formerly some *Panoans*); endocannibalism of the cooked corpse (*Panoans, Záparoans*); cremation of the corpse and drinking the ashes with chicha (*Western Tucanoans* and some *Panoans*); mummification of chiefs (*Quijo*). Mission influence increased the use of cemetery burial.

ESTHETIC AND RECREATIONAL ACTIVITIES

Chicha (masato) is a beerlike drink made from manioc or other fruits or vegetables fermented with the aid of a chewed mash and prepared in a wooden trough, e. g., the bulging trunk of paxiuba palm (*Iriartea ventricosa*), or in huge pottery jars. It is consumed by all tribes, and often occasions drunken brawls. The *Canelo* uniquely distilled a hard liquor by means of a pot and bamboo tubes, undoubtedly a post-Conquest innovation.

Several plant narcotics and stimulants were used aboriginally, but gained wider distribution and more general use when culture patterns began to change in historic times. These are of two general classes: intoxicants taken, usually by shamans, to produce visions or a sense of supernatural power; stimulants, taken by anyone, for their effect in anesthetizing or allaying fatigue and hunger. The first class includes cayapi and *Datura,* the second, yoco, coca, and guayusa. Tobacco served both purposes. A species of *Cyperus* is widely used by shamans but its virtue is evidently more magical than physiological.

The use of guayusa, yoco, *Datura,* and perhaps other wild species is less widespread than their natural occurrence.

Tobacco (*Nicotiana* sp.) formerly was largely restricted to shamans but later came into general use. The tribes of eastern Ecuador take it in the form of juice or cigars, several tribes also chewing it. The Ucayali River *Panoans* and *Arawakans* and the *Tupi* smoke pipes and snuff powder. The *Tupi* also smoke cigarettes.

Cayapi (also called yagé, huni, hayac-huasca, and ayahuasca) is probably used throughout the Ecuadorian and Peruvian Montaña except among the *Panoans.* It is mainly a shaman's drink, though its consumption became more general during the historic period. Three very similar species occur in the region: *Banisteriopsis inebrians, B. caapi,* and *B. quitensis.* All are used and all produce the same effect: First, somewhat violent behavior; then deep sleep with vivid visual hallucinations, which among these tribes are usually of animals; and finally, a sense of losing one's body and of seeing distant things. Some people become addicts (Morton, 1931; Reinburg, 1921). Huanto (*Datura arborea*), also called floripondia, campana, and borrachera, is used by the *Záparo, Canelo,* and *Jívaro* to foretell the future. It produces strong intoxication which lasts several days and is so dangerous that anyone taking it is guarded by a friend (Reinburg, 1921).

Guayusa (*Ilex* sp.), anesthetizing and sustaining rather than exhilarating but serving also as an emetic, is used only by the *Quijo, Záparo,* and *Jívaro.* Yoco (*Paullinia yoco*) is also sustaining in its effect, though strong doses serve an emetic (Simson, 1879 a, p. 213). This and related species of the creeper occur widely, but are used only by the *Sioni, Correguaje, Cofán,* and Highland *Quechua* of Ecuador. The Indians make an infusion of the bark and drink it (Schultes, 1942). Coca is limited to the *Quijo,* the middle Huallaga tribes, the *Arawakans,* and some *Panoans.* It is chewed with lime, and is intended only to allay fatigue, except for some ritual use of it among the *Quijo.*

There is considerable uniformity in musical instruments. Transverse and longitudinal flutes and panpipes are used everywhere. The signal drum occurs among all tribes north of the Marañón River except the *Pebans.* Two-headed monkey-skin drums, though probably of Spanish origin, had reached all tribes. Gourd or other hand-shaken rattles are unknown; instead, jingles on the belt and legs are characteristic. The musical bow is fairly general. Trumpets, though of minor importance, are made of a variety of materials: Armadillo shells (*Záparoans*), snail shells (*Jívaro* and *Mayoruna*), wood (upper Marañón), cane (*Panoans*), bark (*Mayoruna*), and human skulls (*Arawakans*). None are sacred or associated with secret men's rites.

Amusements are also comparatively uniform. Maize-leaf ball games, wrestling, and humming tops occur everywhere; rubber balls are restricted to the *Tupi*. Slings of various kinds are used in the Peruvian and Ecuadorian Montaña. A ring-and-pin game is recorded only from the *Panoans*.

RELIGION

Montaña beliefs about supernatural beings are not adequately recorded but seem to be a minor consideration in daily affairs. Most supernatural beings are animistic nature spirits, the most prominent of which are the monstrous water snake (*Záporans, Jívaro, Pebans, Tupi*) and bush demons, often thought to be anthropomorphic and generally somewhat dangerous (*Záparoans, Pebans,* Middle Huallaga tribes, *Panoans*). Concepts other than simple animism are clarified only in the case of the *Jívaro,* who believe in an impersonal supernatural power that resides in certain plants and animals.

The only community religious rites are the puberty observances previously mentioned, certain rites to strengthen warriors, shamanistic performances, and the *Peban* feast of the dead. But various Christian rites were adopted in the historic period (pl. 48, *center*). There are many magical practices, especially the use of *Cyperus* for curing, for increasing fertility, for obtaining hunting and fishing luck and for other purposes. The *Quijo* are unique in divining with zoomorphic images made of coca.

Beliefs about life after death are variable and confused, but a few facts seem to stand out. The *Jívaro, Záparoans, Arawakans, Tupi,* and some *Panoans* believe that souls are reincarnated as animals, the *Arawakans* and possibly the *Panoan* naming the deer. This may explain a very widespread taboo on killing and eating deer. The *Quijo* and *Yameo* believe that souls become guardian spirits; the *Pebans* and *Cahuapanans* that souls merely wander in the bush.

SHAMANISM

The principal function of the shaman is to cause and cure sickness, but among the *Jívaro* and probably other neighboring tribes, he also performs magic for war parties, makes rain, gives love potions, and predicts the future. During a period of instruction, he learns to control a magical substance. Spirit helpers, though indicated for only a few tribes, are probably widespread. The *Jívaro* spirit helper is a blowgun, snake, door, bird, or insect; *Maina,* a bird; *Canelo,* a python; *Pebans,* birds and animals; *Cahuapanans,* birds; *Lama,* plants including *Brunsfelsia grandiflora; Iquito,* a *Cyperus* root. The *Panoan* shaman obtained help from a bird, the *Arawakan* from tobacco and cayapi, and the *Tupi* from the spirit of a deceased shaman in a virola or cottonwood tree and from a bird.

The narcotic or stimulant, particularly tobacco, taken by the shaman seems generally intended to enhance his sense of power, but *Datura* and ayahauasca more specifically produce second sight. Chantre y Herrera (1901, pp. 80–83) said that in the Marañón region the shaman induced spirits to come by fasting or by drinking ayahuasca. In a large hut where people had gathered, he first led singing, then drank ayahuasca to coax the spirit. Another dose of ayahuasca made him first violent, then comatose, when his soul departed and the spirit spoke through him. Later, the shaman revealed what he had learned. A similar account by Jiménez de la Espada (1892, p. 55) states that the shaman and perhaps other members of the community take both *Datura* and ayahuasca to acquire visions of the future or of the identity of a murderer. Words of the intoxicated person are carefully noted.

Sickness is generally attributed to a sorcerer, who injects a magic substance into his victim. This substance is conceived to be a magical "thorn" or "dart" which the shaman keeps inside his body and which returns to him after his victim dies, but the *Western Tucanoans* believe it to be *Cyperus* and the *Cahuapanans* a magic "mass" acquired from an owl.

The *Jívaro* attribute sickness also to the water monster, the *Tupi* to a river dolphin, the *Canelo* to ghosts, and the *Lama* to bush demons. There is a widespread idea that shamans control snakes, jaguars, and other dangerous animals, and the *Jívaro* and *Arawakans* hold the were-jaguar concept.

The soul-loss concept of disease is recorded only from the *Coto* and *Tupi.*

To cure, the shaman takes a narcotic, blows smoke on the patient, and sucks out the "thorn" or other substance. The narcotic helps reveal the sorcerer.

Many substances, including herbs, are accredited with magical properties. *Cyperus,* the most important, is variously thought to cure, to increase female and plant fertility, to serve as love magic, to cause thunderstorms, and to accomplish other desired ends. Tobacco and pepper are common ingredients of magic. Pepper rubbed in the eyes is widely thought to give strength. A deer horn is prepared as an antidote to poison and snakebite; wearing a crocodile tooth is thought to protect against poisons.

MYTHOLOGY

Myth features of comparative interest are legends of the flood (*Záparoans, Pebans*), the theft of fire (*Jívaro, Panoans*), the twins and the jaguars (*Tupi, Záparoans, Jívaro*), and the trickster element in the twin tale (*Záparoans*). There is no clear-cut culture hero, except that certain birds in a *Panoan* myth introduce some customs to mankind; otherwise, the origin of plants and other useful things is variously explained. Creation tales tend to have celestial characters.

There is some indication that myths and folk tales are being forgotten. Biblical themes and other evidence of Christian influence are, however, scarcely discernible.

BIBLIOGRAPHY

Acuña, 1891; Amich, 1854; Armentia, 1887–88; Bennett, 1936; Castelnau, 1851; Chantre y Herrera, 1901; Cordova y Salinas, 1651; Cruz, 1900; Escobar y Mendoza, 1769; Farabee, 1922; Figueroa, 1904; Fritz, 1892, 1922; Galt, n.d.; González Suárez, 1890–1903; Herndon and Gibbon, 1853–54, vol. 1; Izaguirre, 1922–29; Jiménez de la Espada, 1892; Keller-Leuzinger, 1874; Maroni, 1889–92; Maurtua, V., 1906; Maw, 1829; Means, 1931; Meléndez, 1682; Morton, 1931; Nordenskiöld, 1913, 1917 b, 1920; Noticias auténticas . . . (see Maroni, 1889–92); D'Orbigny, 1839; Pöppig, 1835–36; Reinburg, 1921; Rodriguez, 1684; Salinas Loyola, 1897; Schultes, 1942; Simson, 1879 a; Skinner, 1805; Smyth and Lowe, 1836; Stirling, 1938; Tello, 1922, 1942; Tessmann, 1928, 1930; Veigl, 1785 a.

See also pages 509–514.

TRIBES OF THE PERUVIAN AND ECUADORIAN MONTANA

By Julian H. Steward and Alfred Métraux

ARAWAKAN TRIBES

INTRODUCTION

The *Arawakan*-speaking *Amuesha, Campa, Piro, Machiguenga, Chontaquiro, Masco, Sirineri,* and *Tuyuneri,* who inhabit the headwaters of the Ucayali and Madeira Rivers, are a primitive Montaña subgroup (map 1, *No. 3;* map 5). As they lack traits found among most *Arawak* elsewhere, their culture may be proto-*Arawakan* and probably represents an early migration into the Montaña. Like their neighbors to the north, they seem to represent a cultural backwash. The *Campa, Piro,* and *Chontaquiro* on the Urubamba and Apurimac Rivers, however, share traits with adjoining *Panoan* peoples which the more isolated *Machiguenga, Amuesha,* and *Masco* lack.

These tribes are characteristically simple. Social structure is patterned around the individual family, which lives in isolation or with a few related families. There are no clans, large houses, moieties, cults, large festivals, or masked dances. Except for girls' puberty, even crisis observances are simple and essentially practical in nature. Warfare is largely defensive. There is neither exo- nor endo-cannibalism, though the *Machiguenga* attribute cannibalism to the *Masco*. Families support themselves by slash-and-burn farming with sweet manioc the staple, but grow other crops, various drugs including coca, and several plants introduced during the post-Conquest period, especially bananas. Their manufactures are simple. Cotton is gathered wild and woven on the large belt loom or on the "Ucayali" loom. Pottery is inferior, usually unpainted. Houses are generally for single families. People sleep on mats and lack hammocks, platform beds, and stools. They fight and hunt only with bows and spears, lacking blowguns, carved clubs, spear throwers, fishhooks, and harpoons.

TRIBAL DIVISIONS AND HISTORY

Main divisions of the *Arawakan* are difficult to establish, for authors use tribal names with varying degrees of inclusiveness. The *Inca* called these people *Anti* or *Chuncho*. Rivet uses *Tšontikiro* (*Chontaquiro*) as a synonym for *Piro* and *Campa,* and includes among them the *Anti, Camatika, Kimbiri, Pangoa, Catongo, Kirinairi, Matši ganga* (*Machiguenga*), *Pukapakuri, Tampa, Ugunitširi,* and *Ugonino* in the basin of Tambo, Perené, Ene, Apurimac, Urubamba, and Yavero Rivers. Tessmann (1930) includes the *Chontaquiro* and *Simirinche* with the *Piro* and distinguishes them from the *Campa,* the *Amatšenge,* and the *Matshingenga.* Galt (ms.) sees the *Chontaquiro* (*Chunt a quiro*) on the upper Urubamba as *Piro* and regards them as subdivisions of the Brazilian *Masha* (*Maskoo, Mesko, Mosko*). Osambela (1896, p. 220) applies the name *Campa* to all the peoples from the Beni to the Camisea Rivers. García Rosell (1905, p. 5) places *Machiganga,* synonymous with *Campa,* from "the first barrier of the Cordillera and the borders of the Pilcopata River to the Urubamba," and Pio Aza (1923 b, p. 395) uses the name *Machiganga* for all the tribes including the Campa from the Madre de Díos to the Apurimac, Ene, Perené, Tambo, and Alto Ucayali Rivers. Farabee (1922, pp. 1, 53, 77) distinguishes six tribes: the *Campa* of the middle Urubamba; the *Machiganga* of the middle Urubamba; the *Acheyenga* of the Perené, the *Achenega* at San Lorenzo; the *Piro* (*Chontoquiro, Semirentci*) of the headwaters of the Purúa, Mishagua, Camisea, and Manu Rivers and formerly of the Urubama; and the *Mashco* (*Moeno, Masco, Sinineiri*) between the Sutlija and upper Madre de Díos Rivers. Marcoy (1875, 1:572) divided the *Anti* or *Chuncho* Indians of the Gran Pajonal, the Huarancalqui and Yana Rivers, and the Apurimac River to its confluence with the Quillamba River, into a dozen intercommunicating and mutually peaceful tribes: the *Anti, Campa* (*Mesca*), *Pangoa, Menearo, Anapati,* and *Pilcosmi* to the south; the *Satipo, Copiri,* and *Tomiristi* to the north; and the *Cobaro* and *Pisiatari* to the east.

In the face of this conflicting evidence by recent authors, it seems best to base tribal groupings so far as possible on that of early sources. Thus, our main divisions are: The *Campa,* with several subgroups including the *Anti* of the Perené Valley, possibly the *Chicheren* (Izaguirre, 1922–29, 2:89) of the upper Apurimac Valley, and many other local groups named after rivers; the *Piro,* which includes the *Simirich* and *Chontaquiro;* the *Machiguenga;* the *Masco;* and several unclassified peoples. Farabee's linguistic data (1922) for the *Campa* of the Etenes River, the *Piro* at Sutlija and Portilla, the *Machiguenga* of the Paucartambo River, and the *Masco* show a marked difference between these dialects.

Amuesha.—The *Amuesha* (*Amueshua, Amage, Amueixa, Omage, Amajo, Amaje, Lorenzo, Amuetamo*), who are linguistically similar to the *Campa* (Izaguirre, 1922–29, 12:20), lived, during the 17th century, in the Palcazu River Basin and in part of the Pichis River Basin (lat. 11° S., long. 75° W.). The *Lorenzo* between the Chuchurras and Pichis Rivers were, despite their recent *Quechua* language, probably *Amuesha.*

Father Sala (Izaguirre, 1922–29, 12:388) considered the *Panatahua*, an upper Huallaga River tribe (p. 596), to be the *Amuesha*.

It is probable that in prehistoric times the *Amuesha* had been in contact with many tribes who came to the great salt deposits in Cerro de la Sal in their territory (Amich, 1854, p. 19). The first important White contacts started with Franciscan missions founded in the region of Cerro de la Sal for the *Amuesha* and *Campa* in 1635 and Spanish settlements in 1645 and 1649. Indian resentment at the Spaniards' treatment of them and trouble caused by gold seekers soon terminated these settlements (Amich, 1854, pp. 20–25). Another burst of missionary activity in 1671 and in 1673 gathered more than 1,000 Indians in missions on Cerro de la Sal, but soon thereafter the Indians killed several priests in retaliation for their treatment by the lay Spaniards, and activities ceased for another 35 years.

The spiritual conquest of the *Amuesha* was resumed by the Franciscans in 1709 and endured another 40 years. Nearly all the Indians of the Perené Valley were brought into 6 towns, while several missions were established in the Pachitea region with 300 *Amuesha*. The *Amuesha*, however, were evacuated in 1753 as a result of the Santos Atahuallpa revolt (see *Campa*, pp. 537–539), and the Indians moved to Cuchero, where the climate and work as peons killed most of them (Amich, 1854, p. 208). More than 100 years elapsed before the missionaries returned. Meanwhile, the *Amuesha* of the Pozuzo River may have lost their identity, for in 1767 they spoke *Quechua* and were merely called "Indians of Pozuzo." During the last half of the 19th century, the Indians of the Pozuzo and Pachitea headwaters (Herndon and Gibbon, 1853–54, 1:205) and more especially of the Palcazu River were known as *Lorenzo*. (Paz Soldan map of 1880; Ordinaire, 1887, p. 130; Sagols, 1902.)

The Franciscans resumed their labors in 1881 and have continued since. Their missions were established near Chanchamayo and Cerro de la Sal, where the *Amuesha*, who, though decreased by disease, numbered about 2,000 and retained their identity.

In 1906, Farabee (1922, map) mapped the *Amuesha* between the Pachitea and Alto Ucayali Rivers, but in 1925 Tessmann (1930) attributed to them the upper Chuchurras River and Oxapampa region, stating that only 100 survived, partly because of *Campa* attacks. Some were comparatively civilized. The 1940 Census gives 4,000.

Campa (*Kampa, Camba, Tampa, Thampa, Komparia, Kuruparia, Campiti, Ande, Anti, Chuncho, Chascoso.*).—The *Campa* lived along the Ene, Perené, and Apurimac Rivers, but they extended through the Gran Pajonal northward between the Pachitea and Ucayali Rivers (lat. 10°–14° S., long. 72°–76° W.), where they raided the adjoining *Panoan* tribes, and eastward into the Urubamba Valley. Izaguirre (1922–29, 1:226) attributes to them the valley of the Chanchamayo, Perené, Pangoa, Metraro, Ene, and Tambo Rivers and the Gran Pajonal.. The *Campa* were split into small river-named groups. Hervás' *Campa* divisions are: *Amiemhuaca, Curano, Manuá, Nanerua, Nesahuaca, Sepaunabo,* and *Tasio*. Tessmann's (1930) are the *Campa* proper (*Atiri*), the wild *Campa* (*Antaniri*), and, farther south, the *Amatšenge*. Navarro (1924) distinguished four *Campa* groups: *Campa, Machiguenga,* wild *Campa* or *Unconino,* and *Chonta Campa.*

The *Campa* of the upper Perené Valley had already been in touch with White traders when, in 1635, Franciscans came from their headquarters at Ocopa in the Highland to found a mission near the present town of La Merced for the *Campa* and *Amuesha*. A *Campa* chief, resenting enforced monogamy, incited the massacre of a Dominican expedition and burned the Franciscan mission. Nonetheless, the Franciscans had seven centers in this region by 1640. These were finally broken up, however, as a result of trouble caused by Spanish miners who entered the region in 1642.

In 1671, the Franciscans returned, reestablishing the old missions near Cerro de la Sal and founding several new ones along the lower Perené River. Among the Indians pledging allegiance to the missions were the *Pangoa, Menearo, Anapati, Pilcosumi, Satipo, Capiri, Cobaro, Pisiatari, Cuyentimari, Sangireni, Zagoreni,* and *Quintimiri* (Amich, 1854, p. 35), most of them probably river-named *Campa* subtribes, but some perhaps neighboring *Panoans*. But again, in 1674, a chief, Fernando Tarote, rebelled at the prohibition of polygyny. The *Campa* began drifting away from the missions, which were secularized in 1691. A general rebellion in 1694 thwarted new Franciscan attempts to revive them.

In 1709, the Franciscans came again to the Perené region and, despite a rebellion in 1724 by the *Anti*, a subtribe numbering 3,000 in the lower Perené Valley, had 8 missions with 1,239 *Campa* by 1730 (Izaguirre, 1922–29, 2:59). By 1739, 10 more were founded among the *Campa* who were scattered in small groups in the Gran Pajonal (Amich, 1854, p. 158). Skinner (1805, pp. 450–456) gives the incredible figure of 20,000 converts. In 1735, the Franciscans had a total of 38 missions with 8,333 Indians, most of them *Campa*, in the area (Izaguirre, 1922–29, 2:82–83, 752). These figures, evidently based on a careful census, seem entirely acceptable. The total population must formerly have been much larger, for many *Campa* probably remained in the forests and others died of epidemics. For example, of 172 Indians at one mission, 40 died of an epidemic of dysentery. In 1737, 2 of the missions were destroyed by the rebellious chief, Ignacio Torote, son of Fernando Torote (Amich, 1854, pp. 160–170). This period of missionary activity was violently terminated when Juan Santos Atahuallpa, a messiah of some education who claimed descent from both God and the *Inca* Emperors, instigated a general rebellion and massacre in 1742. The remainder of the century witnessed only slow penetration of the Perené area from fortified cities (Skinner, 1805, pp. 450–456), settlers and missionaries working down the Tulumayo River to the Perené in the face of hostility from the *Campa* of the Chanchamayo, Pichis, Pachitea, Perené, Pangoa, and Tambo Rivers and the Gran Pajonal (Izaguirre, 1922–29, 7:111–112). This hostility continued for more than 100 years.

Frustrated in the Perené-Tambo region, the Franciscans turned their attention to southern groups of *Campa*, going from Cuzco in 1743 to the Quillabamba Valley, where in 1753 the one mission had seven "pueblos" (Maurtua, V., 1906, 12:140–143). In 1782, they went to the 300 *Campa* of the Mantaro River (Izaguirre, 1922–29, 5:151), then later to the Apurimac River north of Río Pampas, and in 1790 to Cocabambilla. In 1805 they founded Nuestra Señora de Misericordia de Siapa in the Urubamba Valley, near the *Chontaquiro*. At this time, there were also *Campa* in the Yanatili Valley, tributary to the Urubamba, and on the Coribeni and Cizialo Rivers. But pagan *Campa* remained in the upper Apurimac River region in 1911 (Izaguirre, 1922–29, 12:253).

During most of the last century, the *Campa* of the region of the Perené and Tambo Rivers remained hostile. An exploration of the Tambo River in 1850 was turned back by Campa attacks (Galt, ms.) and the *Chuncho* of the Chanchamayo Valley were hostile in 1851 (Herndon and Gibbon, 1853–54, 1:204). In 1870, numerous and warlike apostate *Campa* held the Gran Pajonal. They were especially bitter toward the Whites and were generally feared by Ucayali River tribes. The greatest number was around Cerro de la Sal and Quiniri, the site of the first mission, where Peruvian criminals had joined them (Galt, ms.). But by 1869, the *Campa* of Chanchamayo were subdued and the city of La Merced founded. These Indians, 100 years after severing intercourse with the Spaniards, still had smithies, using bellows and forges and making machetes, axes, knives, and hammers (Izaguirre, 1922–29, 9:253). A new Franciscan attempt to start a mission on the Pangoa River ended in revolt, caused by the *Campas'* resentment at the colonists' treatment of them (Izaguirre, 1922–29, 12:152).

Recent population estimates show that the tribe survives in great number, though a wide margin of error enters because of census methods and because of differences in tribal classification. Osambela (1896, p. 220) gave 20,000 *Campa* distributed as follows: Carabaya, 4,000; Sandia, 5,000; Madre de Díos, 3,000; Convención, 5,000; Alto Ucayali, 4,000; Alto Madeira, 3,000; Yuruna, 4,000; Purús, 5,000; Pangoa, 500; Tambo, 1,000; Gran Pajonal, 1,000; Perené, 500. The total, evidently including other Indians, is really about 35,000. Navarro's figure of 10,000 (1924, p. 3) and Tessmann's of 3,000 to 5,000 (1930) would seem to indicate a decline, but the 1940 census claims 33,000, although A. F. Reifsnyder (personal communication) estimates 10,000 to 20,000.

These data evidently mean that the relatively resistant and isolated *Campa* have until now largely avoided disastrous contacts. Today, though pushed somewhat down the Perené Valley, they still occupy the Gran Pajonal, most of the region between the Pachitea and Ucayali Rivers, and the country back of the lower Perené, Tambo, and Ene Rivers. Avoiding civilization, though a few obtained occasional farm employment, they have until recently harassed communications over the Pichis trail. But in 1942, when the Gran Pajonal was opened to White settlement, the *Campa* were somewhat more subdued. Many speak Spanish and *Quechua* as well as *Campa*.

Machiguenga.—In 1905, García Rosell placed the *Machiguenga,* (*Machiganga, Matsiganga*) between the Cordillera, the Pilcopata, and the Urubamba, stating that around 1835 they had settled on the Tono and Piñipiñi, expelling the *Tuyuneri.* (Lat. 13° S., long. 72°–73° W.) Navarro (1924, p. 3) gives 3,000 to 4,000 *Machiguenga;* the 1940 census, 1,000. This tribe could be considered a *Campa* subdivision.

Piro.—The *Piro (Pirro, Pira, Simirinche)* occupied the angle between the Urubamba and Tambo Rivers (lat. 12° S., long. 73° W.). The *Simirinche (Simiranch, Semirentci)*, on the right side of the Tambo River, who, at the end of the 17th century were closely associated with the *Mochobo* and *Comobo* on the opposite side of the river (Izaguirre, 1922–29, 1:294), were almost certainly *Piro,* as this region was also the early location of *Piro.* Maroni (1889–92, 30:146–148) distinguished two *Piro* groups in 1690: the *Upatarinavo,* who lived near the *Campa,* and the *Cusitinavo,* between the Pachitea and Ucayali Rivers and neighbors of the *Comava (Combo).* The *Cusitinavo* were perhaps a mixed group, or they may have been the *Simirinche.* Hervás (1800–05, vol. 1) lists three subtribes: *Cusitinavo, Manatinavo,* and *Upatarinavo.* The *Chontaquiro (Chuntaquiro, Chuntaquiru, Chontaders, Chunt a quiro, Tšontikiro),* so named because of their black-stained teeth, are generally known as a *Piro* subtribe.   They occupy the Urubamba River and its tributaries from the Sepahua River to somewhere near the Yavero (Paucartambo) River, and, east of the Ucayali Basin, the Chandless (Araca) River, and the region between the headwaters of the Sepehua and Cujar Rivers.

In pre-Contact times, the *Piro* were said to have been in contact with the *Inca,* whom they helped build the fort of Tonquini (Farabee, 1922, p. 53) and from whom they received gold objects (Chantre y Herrera, 1901, p. 282).

The *Piro* around the Tambo River were the first to be in contact with the Spaniards.   The *Simirinche* and *Piro* participated in the murder of the Jesuit, Herrera, in 1686, and the Franciscan, Biedma, in 1687 (Izaguirre, 1922–29, 1:254–289 passim).   They attacked the *Cusitinavo* to steal iron tools, twice visited a *Conibo* mission to beg them, and threatened to raid the *Conibo* (Maroni, 1889–92, 30:146–148).   But toward the end of the century, Father Ricter visited the *Piro* and wrote a catechism in their language.

In 1790, the *Piro* occupied the Alto Ucayali, extending over 400 leagues along the Paru, Yami (Yanatiri), Tambo, and Cuja Rivers.   The first, unstable *Piro* mission was not founded until 1795.   Another founded in 1809 had 365 *Piro* families and 32 *Pano* families.   At the beginning of the last century, the Franciscans of Moquegua entered *Chontaquiro* country via the upper Urubamba River to establish several missions (Maurtua, V., 1906, 12:192–199).   But the century drew to a close with the *Piro* still largely unmissionized.   Though numerically small, their settlements or trading groups now extended down the Ucayali River as far as Sarayacu in *Setebo* territory (Raimondi, 1862, pp. 116–117).   Still seeking metal tools, they even requested a mission in 1879; but the mission lasted only a year (Izaguirre, 1922–29, 9:214–325; Galt, ms.; Fry, 1889, p. 49).   Early in the present century the *Piro* were victims of enforced labor for rubber gathering.   Farabee (1922, p. 53) thought that 500 to 600 *Piro* remained in 1922; the 1940 census gives 5,000 *Piro,* 1,200 *Chontaquiro.*

Masco.—Fejos (ms.) places the modern *Masco* (*Mashco, Moeno*) between the Madre de Díos, Inambari, and Alto Madre de Díos Rivers and the Cordillera of Caravaya (lat. 13° S., long. 72° W.), a flatish, densely jungled area; the Stiglich map gives the *Inapari* (*Inamari*) as a *Masco* division around the headwaters of the Río de Pejes and the left side of the Madre de Díos to the Tacanti-manu River, with the *Masco* between the Chilive and Abulijá Rivers.   Subtribes listed are the *Careneri* on the Colorado River, the *Puquiri,* the *Toyeri,* and others (Fejos, ms.).

An unsuccessful expedition by the *Inca* Emperor Yupanqui to this region is claimed for 1450.   Expeditions during the 16th century probably did not reach it. After 1862, several parties descended the Madre de Díos River, or visited the region.   (Faustino Maldonado, in 1862; Raimondi, in 1863; Baltazar de la Torre, in 1873; Robledo, in 1879; Fermin Fiscarrald, in 1890; Germán Stiglich, in 1902; Ernesto La Combe Survey and Teniente Olivera Survey, in 1903; Enrique Llosa, in 1906; Leonardo Lama, in 1932; Maxwell Stuart, in 1936; Fejos, in 1940.)

Fejos' report covers the *Careneri,* who are probably the *Arasa* (*Arasaire*), estimated at 800 in 1940.   The *Pariquiri* in 1940 numbered 3,000 and spoke *Quechua.* The *Masco* proper numbered 1,800 and lived on the Manu, Madre de Díos, Colorado, Iuaneari, and Blanco Rivers.

Sirineri.—The *Sirineri* (*Sirineyri, Sireneire*) lived south of the *Masco,* on the Madre de Díos from its great curve to Ccoñecc (García Rosell, 1905), on the Marcapata River (Marcoy, 1875, 1:555), on the upper Pucapuca River, and near the upper Chilive (Pilcopata) River (Stiglich map). (Lat. 13° S., long. 70°–71° W.)   They were estimated at 1,000 in the 1940 census.

Tuyuneri.—The *Tuyuneri* (*Pucapacuri*) adjoined the *Sirineri,* on the Tono, Piñipiñi and Pilcopata Rivers (García Rosell, 1905, p. 7).   (Lat. 13° 30′ S., long. 70°–71° W.).   Cipriani (1902) located them on the lower Inambari River; Marcoy (1875, 1:555), on Río Chaupimayo.

Huachipairi.—The *Huachipairi* (*Huatchipayri*) had settlements on the Coñispata (Ccoñispata) and Pilcopata Rivers (García Rosell, 1905); on the Manu (Manuquia) tributaries (Cipriani, 1902, p. 177); on the lower Inambari and the Madre de Díos Rivers (Stiglich map).   (Lat. 14° S., long. 72° W.)   They are estimated at 1,500 in the 1940 census.

Puncuri.—This tribe lived on the Puncuri River and numbered 15 to 20 in about 1900 (Cipriani, 1902, p. 178).

Pucpacuri.—The *Pucpacuri* lived on the Camisia and Tunkini Rivers, and warred with the *Anti* and *Chontaquiro* (Marcoy, 1875, 1:555).

Several tribes of uncertain affiliation, though probably *Arwakan,* were:

The *Guirineri,* on a right tributary of the Ucayali River below the Ticumbinia River near the mission of Siapa.   They had almost been destroyed by the Masco in 1807 (Maurtua, V., 1906, 12:215; Izaguirre, 1922–29, 8:324).

The *Epetineri* in 1807 were pagans who seem to have occupied the right side of the Urubamba River from the Pijiria River to near the Ucayali River (Maurtua, V., 1906, 12:216–218; Izaguirre, 1922–29, 8:327–328).

SOURCES

The 17th- and 18th-century sources have been mentioned previously pp. 511, 113).

Nineteenth-century travel includes Enock (1908), Herndon and Gibbon (1853–54), Sala (1892), Amich (1854), Exploración de los Ríos Pichis . . . (1897), Fry (1889), Galt in 1870–72 (ms.), Reich (1903), Navarro (1924), and Ordinaire (1887, 1892).

There is no major scientific account of these tribes, Farabee's observations (1922) of 1906 being of uncertain value and Tessmann's (1930) including only a few data from a *Campa* encountered on the lower Ucayali River.   Other sources are García Rosell (1905) on the eastern tribes, Fejos (ms.) on the *Masco,* Cipriani (1902), Fernández Moro (1926–27), and Grain (1942) on the *Michiguenga.*

CULTURE

SUBSISTENCE

Farming.—Farming follows the usual Tropical Forest slash-and-burn pattern with sweet manioc (yuca) the staple (the *Machiguenga* consider it sacred (Grain, 1942)) and bitter manioc absent. Sixteenth-century sources report sweet manioc and bananas among the *Amuesha*. In 1788, *Campa* plants included lima beans, manioc, and sugarcane, the last introduced by Whites. *Campa* crops of the last half century have been yams, peanuts, sweet potatoes, bananas, pineapples, tuber beans, macaba, taro, sicana, pumpkin, *Guilielma* palm, sugarcane, pepper, barbasco (*Lonchocarpus nicou*). But some adaptation to habitat is observable: *Campa* of the Sierra grew coca and potatoes in addition to maize. The *Campa* also cultivate a medicinal narcotic, "hitini" (Navarro, 1924).

Campa clearings usually lie along the river bank, but in times of danger are on hill tops. In the Quiempiric region a chief's plantation was reported to be ¾ league in circumference. But Galt (ms.) observed a *Piro* family in 1872 which had only one stalk of corn, "a dozen or more yuca trees, and a half a dozen banana trees," the produce supplemented by an occasional fish or monkey. The *Careneri* plant circular fields with concentric rings of crops: pineapples, pifáyo, bananas, manioc, maize, and pepper (capsicum) in the center; next, papaya trees; outside, sweet potatoes, peppers, pumpkins, and cocona (Fejos, ms.). The *Campa* and *Amuesha* use paddle-shaped digging sticks; the *Careneri,* plain sticks.

Each *Machiguenga* family has its own clearing, which is made anew every 2 or 3 years. Men help one another prepare these, but subsequently each woman cultivates and harvests from her own plot (Farabee, 1922). A suggestion of nutritional deficiencies is beriberi, which the *Machiguenga* attribute to eating papaya after sungaro fish, roast crayfish, or hipa juice. (See Fernández Moro, 1926–27, for endemic diseases.)

Fishing.—The *Campa* take fish with drugs (barbasco, *Lonchocarpus, Tephrosia, Clibadium*); the *Amuesha* use a wild plant; the *Machiguenga* use one called "kogui," bone hooks (but Farabee denies use of hooks), gill nets, hand nets, large nets with sinkers, fish pots, multiprong spears, and possibly arrows. They also use a weir and some kind of dam to drain a section of river. Notably absent are devices of the lower Ucayali River: harpoons, harpoon arrows, atlatls, weirs, and traps.

Hunting.—Game animals include tapirs, boars, deer, and monkeys, with the last of greatest importance. Sloths, snakes (Tessmann, 1930), deer heads, and corvina fish (Navarro, 1924) are taboo. The *Campa* hunt with bows and arrows, blinds built near water holes, spring-pole traps, sharp sloping stakes placed on animal trails, and recently with some rifles. The *Machiguenga* also smear a glue on tree limbs to catch birds. Neither the blowgun nor hunting nets are known (Tessmann, 1930).

Gathering.—The *Campa* supplement their diet with jungle produce, among it honey, a root called mabe, ants, and several palm fruits (*Euterpe, Iriartea, Scheelea tessmannii,* and *Oenocarpus*). They use the climbing ring to ascend trees.

Domestic animals.—The dog is used for hunting and is bred by the *Piro* for trade. Chickens are kept in coops; they and their eggs are eaten by the *Campa,* but the *Piro* eat only the eggs. Pigs are not kept (Tessmann, 1930). Only the *Machiguenga* have ducks.

Food preparation.—These tribes cook meat on a pyramidal or rectangular babracot; the smoking thus given it may preserve it for a few days. The *Campa* grind food on a "plate-like wooden piece" with a stone mano (Tessmann, 1930); the *Piro* use a hollowed log as a mortar (Farabee, 1922). The sexes eat apart, using wooden spoons, pottery bowls, or monkey skulls (*Machiguenga*). Condiments include rock salt from Cerro de la Sal, and pepper (*Capsicum*).

HOUSES AND HOUSEHOLD EQUIPMENT

Each family erects its own structure; a large communal house is only made by the *Masco* (pl. 54). In 1790, the *Campa* constructed a hemispherical, thatched house—evidently a beehive type—and a special shed in which batchelors slept and men kept their weapons (Izaguirre, 1922–29, 7 :66). Reich (1903) reports similar structures in the present century, but Tessmann believes that beehive houses are for temporary use, the more permanent house being rectangular, with side walls and gabled roof. The recent *Careneri* and *Machiguenga* house is oval, the roof sloping nearly to the ground, but *Piro* houses are rectangular, 20 by 12 feet (6 by 3.6 m.) long and 18 feet (5.5 m.) high, with elevated sleeping storage platforms (Farabee, 1922). The *Campa* are accredited with erecting observation platforms.

Inside the house is a constant fire. The fire fan is woven. Woven or bark sleeping mats are used in place of hammocks.

DRESS AND ADORNMENTS

The standard dress is the cushma (pls. 50, *right;* 53, *top, right*) with a neck opening which runs from front to back for men, from side to side for women. It is made of bark cloth or, among the *Campa, Piro,* and *Machiguenga,* of wild cotton, and is dyed, usually with bixa red, and variously ornamented with feathers, beads, etc. This garment seems to have varied little from the 16th century to the present day (Izaguirre 1922–29, passim; Tessmann, 1930; Farabee, 1822), though missionary influence probably made its use more habitual. Some customary nudity still occurs among the *Antaniri Campa,* whose men pass a cord around the waist and under the genitals (Tessmann, 1930), the *Masco* (pl. 53), the *Careneri,* who use the cushma only for sleeping (Fejos, ms.), and the *Huachipairi* (Gadea, 1895, p. 141). Other garments reported are the *Atiri* man's sleeveless shirt, *Machiguenga* and *Campa* bark shirts, the *Atiri* woman's short fiber apron, and the *Piro* woman's rolled hip cloth (Tessmann, 1930). For dress occasions, the *Machiguenga* now wear European clothes (Grain, 1942).

The most characteristic ornament is a pendant, often of silver, suspended from the nasal septum, but some *Campa* wear a pin through the septum. The *Careneri* and *Machiguenga* place pins through the upper lip and cheeks, the *Campa* and *Piro* through the lower lip. The *Campa* have recently begun to perforate their ears for ornaments (Tessmann, 1930). The *Campa* groom the hair with a composite comb, which the *Careneri* lack. Depilation is not reported. The *Campa* blacken the teeth with Piperaceae. All tribes wear many beads, necklaces, feather headdress, and arm and leg bands, and paint the body with genipa, both as decoration and as protection against sunburn and insects. The *Machiguenga* even paint their animals (Grain, 1942, p. 244).

The only badges of status reported are chiefs' birdskin necklaces and bark headbands with two feathers behind.

TRANSPORTATION

The common carrying devices are tumplines, infant bearing bands, and small bags. The carrying net is ascribed only to the *Lorenzo* (Ordinaire, 1892, p. 162). *Machiguenga* men and women can carry 50 to 75 pounds 15 miles a day.

Tessmann denies that the *Campa* use canoes, but Navarro records cedar dugouts. *Careneri* dugouts are 12 feet (4 m.) long. The *Campa* make pointed balsa rafts held together with chonta nails and cross beams.

Bark cloth.—Bark cloth for cushmas and mats is probably made by all tribes.

Weaving and spinning.—Cords are made of *Cecropia leucocoma* bast. These tribes weave cotton, but whether they grow it is uncertain; the *Machiguenga* and *Piro* gather theirs wild (Farabee, 1922). They rest the end of the spindle in a gourd or pot. The *Campa* are accredited with the vertical, or *"Arawak,"* loom for weaving large pieces of cloth, and with the "Ucayali" loom (see p. 577) for small bands. A horizontal belt loom, varying in size according to the product—cushma, bags, arm and leg bands—is reported among the *Piro, Machiguenga,* and all *Campa* except the *Antaniri,* who do not weave.

The *Piro* make netted bags.

Basketry.—Baskets include twilled sieves and containers, twined telescope baskets of *Gynerium* stalks, and palm-leaf baskets.

Metals.—Some precious metals from the Highland reached these tribes through trade and were made into ornaments. The *Campa,* however, were taught smelting and blacksmithing by the Franciscan missionaries.

They even exploited iron mines in the Cerro de la Sal (Izaguirre, 1922–29, 1:190), and smelted with Catalan type furnaces, making iron knives (Ordinaire, 1892, p. 152).

Pottery.—Ceramics are usually crude, a finer ware being procured from the neighboring *Panoans.* The *Campa* ware is coiled; plates have red designs; pots only fingernail impressions (Tessmann, 1930). The *Machiguenga, Masco,* and *Piro* generally make only crude cooking and water pots, the latter being corrugated in part, but some bowls are painted (fig. 73, *f*). They also make ceramic pot rests, used in threes. The *Careneri* make vessels of lumps of clay, forms being pots and jars and decorative patterns resembling those used in body paint (Fejos, ms.).

Weapons.—The bow and arrow have been used from the 16th century until the present day (pl. 54), but blowguns and atlatls have never been reported. *Machiguenga* bows are 5 feet (1.5 m.) long, flat, 1½ feet (½ m.) wide, and made of chonta palm. The arrows are of *Gynerium sagittatum* and have cemented, spiraled feathers and points of the usual Tropical Forest types, which, however, are never poisoned. The *Piro* shoot left-handed (Farabee, 1922).

Fire making.—The *Campa* make fire with two stones; the *Antaniri* (Tessmann, 1930) and *Machiguenga* (Farabee, 1922) with the drill. Cotton, raw copal, or resin serve as tinder.

Miscellaneous.—Containers are made of calabashes.

The native *Lorenzo* ax had a diorite head fastened to the handle with rosin. The *Campa* stone ax head was slightly anchor-shaped (Fry, 1889, 1:110). Steel axes replaced native types at an early date.

The *Piro* used the dried tongue of a "payshi" fish as a rasp (Herndon and Gibbons, 1853–54, pp. 196–197). The *Machiguenga* still cut with a peccary tooth when they lack steel knives.

ECONOMIC FUNCTIONS

The small village, consisting of one or a few related families, is largely self-sufficient economically. Men hunt and fish collectively and divide the take. They also clear farm lands cooperatively, but women subsequently plant, cultivate, and harvest for their own families.

Intertribal trade has always been conducted. Some *Inca* gold in the form of ornaments formerly passed down the Ucayali River (Chantre y Herrera, 1901, p. 282). In 1806, the *Chontaquiro* were reported to be trading parrots and monkeys for iron tools at Sarayacu, while the *Piro* and others traveled up and down the Ucayali, giving wax for tools, cloth, fishhooks, and beads. It is likely that the excellent painted pots among these tribes came from the *Panoans* downstream.

Social patterns are mainly those based on the individual family. There is no large communal house, no trace of clan or moiety, and no extended family, except as a tendency toward patrilocal residence sometimes brings patrilineally related families into close proximity. These families usually live in separate, neighboring houses. Franciscan accounts of the Apurimac Basin in 1787 reveal small settlements of 3 to 4 houses and 9 to 15 people. Ten *Campa* villages in 1782 averaged 30 persons each. In 1788, a *Campa* village had 3 houses, 16 people (Izaguirre, 1922–29, 6:286). In the present century, Reich (1903; p. 134) reported that each *Campa* community had 8 to 12 huts, hidden some distance from the river. *Machiguenga* families live alone or in small groups. (Farabee, 1922). Some of the modern *Campa* (Tessmann, 1930) and *Masco* (Fejos, ms.), however, have communal houses sheltering up to 6 families.

These tribes frequently take captives in warfare, but absorb them into the local group.

Chieftainship ordinarily falls to the community headman and is inherited patrilineally. A chief's authority is limited to leadership in clearing lands, hunting, fishing, and fighting. Farabee (1922) claims, however, that the *Piro* have a tribal chief, whose authority is absolute. If true, this is probably a recent development.

LIFE CYCLE

Life-cycle observances are, if our scant data are indicative, unelaborate and little patternized, except those at girls' puberty. Childbirth is matter of fact and lacks the couvade; death observances amount essentially to nonritual disposal of the corpse.

Childbirth and childhood.—Possibly because of demoralization through extended White contacts, *Campa* women eat chantini roots for barrenness and *Machiguenga* women practice much abortion (Fernández Moro, 1926–27, pp. 154–155). A *Campa* child is born in the house and the mother confined 1 week (Tessmann, 1930). A *Machiguenga* child is born in the woods, immediately after which the mother returns to routine life (Farabee, 1922). A suggestion of couvade comes from the *Sirineri* only.

A *Campa* child is named when it walks; it acquires a new name at seven. For misbehavior, children are beaten or frightened with a bullroarer, which is said to be the sound of a jaguar (Tessmann, 1930).

Girl's puberty.—The most elaborate girl's puberty rites are those of the *Piro*. The girl is confined in bed and covered to prevent her looking at anyone, even her own family. When leaving the house, she must cover herself and avoid people. After 6 months, she is delivered to her fiancé, who has been chosen years earlier by her family (Fry, 1889). Tessmann (1930) reports some kind of female circumcision among the

Piro but probably mistook this for premarital defloration with a bamboo knife (Farabee, 1922). Fernández Moro (1926–27, 43:156) also mentions ceremonial defloration of girls at a feast; the tribe is not mentioned but may be the *Machiguenga.* Tessmann (1930) claims that the *Campa* confine the girl 6 months, during which she spins; Navarro states that confinement lasts for "some days," followed by an orgy of dancing, drinking, running, washing, and a final whipping of the girl with nettles, which sexually excites the youths present.

Marriage.—There is no evidence of restrictions on marriage except those within the immediate family, i. e., within the community, though the *Campa* are said to permit cousin marriage but not uncle-niece or aunt-nephew unions (Tessmann, 1930). Infant betrothal is ascribed to the *Piro* (Farabee, 1922) and may be more general. Polygyny is not uncommon. Galt (ms.) cites a *Piro* settlement that consisted of an old man and two wives, each bought for a hatchet from a friendly *Campa.* Bride service is reported only among the *Piro,* where the youth may not speak to his father-in-law while serving him (Fry, 1889, 1:51). At a marriage ceremony the *Piro* sacrifice a turkey, tapir, or other animal specially reared for the purpose (Fry, 1889). Postmarital residence is usually patrilocal or independent, but may be matrilocal. Tessman declares that many *Campa* are unmarried and that widows and widowers do not care to remarry. A *Machiguenga* may exchange wives with a friend or lend his wife to a visitor.

The extreme lack of death ritual is found among the *Machiguenga,* who not only throw their dead unceremoniously into the river but similarly dispose of hopelessly ill people. They bury only persons killed in warfare (Farabee, 1922). The *Campa* abandon the corpse in a clearing (Izaguirre, 1922–29, 7:66; Reich, 1903) or, on the lower Apurimac, burn or throw it into a river (Tessmann, 1930). They provision and abandon their seriously sick (Chantre y Herrera, 1901). These tribes give up the settlement after a death, but the *Piro* bury in the house, sometimes in a canoe, under the platform (Farabee, 1922); they cry, cut their skin, blacken their bodies and, if a husband dies, throw his goods into the river, or, under White influence, pay his bad debts! (Fry, 1889, 1:50).

The *Machiguenga* (Farabee, 1922; Pio Aza, 1923 b, p. 379) and *Piro* (Farabee, 1922) believe that the soul enters the red deer, which, therefore, is not eaten. *Campa* belief holds that souls have immortality in a heaven which resembles earth, but wicked magicians hover in the bush to teach their arts to youths. Hence, evil shamans are cremated or thrown into a river.

WARFARE

These *Arawakan* tribes have long been hostile among themselves and toward the Whites. The stronger Ucayali River *Campa* and *Piro* have been friendly with each other and with the downstream *Panoan, Conibo, Shipibo,* and *Setebo,* all of whom victimized the weaker, hinterland tribes— the *Amuesha, Cashibo,* and *Amahuaca*—with slave raids. In the Madeira River headwaters, the *Careneri* are enemies of the *Puguiri, Huachipair,* and others.

Campa weapons of attack are the bow and unpoisoned arrows, slings, and improvised clubs. For defense, the *Campa* fill ditches with sharp stakes, but the *Lorenzo* strew chonta-thorn caltrops on trails.

Navarro states that to acquire courage the *Campa* chew and rub their bodies with ebenque tubers. In 1896, before attacking the Pangoa colony, a shaman chewed coca, sang, and told his warriors that if, prior to the fight, they blew with all their force, enemy bullets would turn into leaves.

RECREATIONAL AND ESTHETIC ACTIVITIES

Art.—Too little is known of art styles to attempt characterization.

Musical instruments.—The following musical instruments are re-ported: A two-headed, monkey-skin drum (*Campa* and *Machiguenga*), 5- to 8-tube panpipes (*Campa*); bone flageolet (*Campa*); 6-hole longi-tudinal flute and 2-hole transverse flute (*Campa*); musical bow (*Campa*); and a trumpet made of a tube inserted in the occipital hole of enemy skulls (tribe unknown, Velasco *in* Maroni, 1889–92, 33:46). The last may be foreign, as no trophy skulls are otherwise reported from these tribes.

Games.—*Campa* games are the humming top, bull roarer, (whirring sticks), maize-leaf balls, and wrestling. *Machiguenga* boys play at archery; girls toss balls made of bladders. Cats' cradles probably occur among all tribes.

Narcotics.—Narcotics include domesticated tobacco and coca, and sev-eral wild species of unidentified plants. The *Campa, Piro,* and *Machi-guenga* smoke tobacco in pipes like those of the *Panoan* tribes, or take it as snuff through **V**-tubes. The *Machiguenga* chew it with ashes (Grain, 1942, p. 242). Shamans, however, imbibe the juice so as to rub it with spittle on their patients or use it while sucking (Navarro, 1924; Tess-mann, 1930). Anyone may put young tobacco leaves on his chest for colds.

The *Campa* grow coca and, when fatigued, chew it with burnt lime and the bark of a creeper called chumayro or chamairo (Ordinaire, 1892, pp. 132–133), which they travel widely to find (Izaguirre, 1922–29, 6:325). The *Machiguenga* chew coca when they can get it (Grain, 1942, p. 242). The *Careneri* take a green powder through the **V**-tubes (Fejos, ms.). Another *Campa* narcotic is naquire, a creeper, which in small doses permits divination but in large doses causes temporary insanity (Navarro, 1924). The *Campa* shaman takes cayapi. A *Piro* hunter and his dog eat the seeds of *Acacia niopo.*

All tribes except the *Careneri* make chicha of manioc, maize, sweet potatoes, bananas, and other produce, the fermentation of which is started by chewing. They intoxicate themselves on festive occasions.

RELIGION

Data on religion are entirely unsatisfactory. There is a hint of a creator god who retired to heaven (*Campa, Machiguenga*). Navarro's account (1924) of an Apurimac *Campa* trinity (Venus as the father, an unidentified star as the mother, and Jupiter as the son), of sacred fires kept by the shamans, and feasts at the new or full moon for Venus seem fanciful. Information on lesser spirits is no more enlightening.

SHAMANISM AND SICKNESS

Farabee gives no information on the *Machiguenga* or *Piro* shaman, indeed denying their existence though his comment that the *Piro* kill witches attests evil shamans. But Ordinaire (1892) describes a *Piro* shaman, who undergoes 2 months of instruction in seclusion, meanwhile eating only bananas, remaining silent, smoking much, and vomiting daily. Tessmann distinguishes good and evil *Campa* shamans. During instruction, the former diets, takes tobacco, especially juice and snuff, until he sees the "mother of tobacco," a white person with whiskers, and finally takes cayapi, whereupon the "mother of cayapi" gives him "thorns" with which to kill sorcerers. The sorcerer is taught at night by the souls of deceased witches, who lurk in the bush. They appear in the form of bats to teach him to throw a "bone" into the victim's body.

These tribes probably recognize natural causes of illness. During epidemics they flee from their villages. Supernatural beliefs are varied. The *Campa* attribute magical disease and death to a "bone" thrown at night by a witch, to a sorcerer who becomes a jaguar, and to snakes ordered by a shaman to bite the victim (Tessmann, 1930). The *Careneri* suppose that a spirit, "He who comes at nightfall," has shot invisible arrows into the sick man (Fejos, ms.).

Many ailments are treated with herbs, but those caused supernaturally are treated by shamans. To ascertain the perpetrator of witchcraft, the *Campa* shaman spits coca into his hand, shakes it, and ascertains the guilty person through its configuration (Ordinaire, 1892, p. 148). To cure, he blows tobacco smoke and rubs coca on the patient, and sucks out the "bone" which the witch has put inside the person. Then, smoking and drinking cayapi, he endeavors to fell the witch by blowing his "thorns" into him. Great supernatural struggles develop between good and evil shamans. It is said that shamans successful in killing witches may develop a lust for killing and turn into jaguars after they die (Tessmann, 1930).

An *Amuesha* designated as a witch is flogged, deprived of food, confined in a room with heavy smoke, then taken to the patient and made to dig up the "bones," "thorns," or other objects he is supposed to have buried. He is then killed and thrown into the river (Izaguirre, 1922–29, 12:22–24). *Amuesha* and *Campa* children are often accused of witchcraft, the *Campa* even torturing and burning them alive (Navarro, 1924). Sala (1905–08) cites a 9-year-old *Campa* girl who was in danger of being killed for witchcraft in 1896.

The *Campa* use a number of magical substances. *Cyperus piripiri* is put on a bow to make it shoot well. It is swallowed with tobacco by a shaman before a sucking treatment, and is used to wash invalids (Tessmann, 1930). Wildcat hearts are taken for courage, gall bladders in order to divine, toad gall for eye trouble, monkey gall for toothache, bear excrement against stoutness, pulverized pitiro (a beetle) against anemia, and cultivated kitini to narcotize oneself and to stop hemorrhages. The *Campa* rub scorched palo de balsa leaves on their heads for aches (Navarro, 1924).

S. García (1942) has recorded several *Machiguenga* myths.

Men were made of palo de balsa by beings called Tasorinchi. The Tasorinchi, who were created from nothing, were very powerful. They changed many *Machiguenga* into animals. One of them tried to drown the Indians by causing a flood. Another nailed him to trees, where he still lives, causing earthquakes by his struggles. A female Tasorinchi is the "mother of fishes." Several Tasorinchi finally became armadillos.

The *Chonchóite,* a legendary cannibalistic tribe; the *Kugapakuri,* a tribe of bowmen; and the *Viracocha,* the people of the Puna, were made by a demon, Kientibákori. The last two were created in the underworld. The *Viracocha* emerged when the spirits, the Inkakuna, who were mining, dug through to the underworld. The hole was plugged and those remaining below became the Kamagárini, or demons. Those who survived above became people when they ate yuca. The people of the Puna came out through a hole dug by a child.

Formerly, people lacked teeth and ate only potter's clay. Kashiri (Moon) brought manioc roots to a menstruating girl and taught her to eat them. He married her and gave manioc, maize, plantains, and other foods to her parents. The girl bore four boys, all suns: (1) the Sun, (2) Venus, (3) the sun of the Underworld, and (4) the sun of the firmament that gives light to the stars. During his birth, the last son burned his mother, so that she died. Kashiri's mother-in-law then made him eat his wife's corpse.

Cultivated crops, especially manioc, are closely connected with Kashiri, to whom they complain if they are not cared for and eaten correctly.

A *Machiguenga* woman had relations with her step-son. Her husband sought another woman for the boy, whereupon the wife became angry and sought to poison him. He thwarted her attempt, and she hid in a tree. When he could not find her, he tied a burning bamboo to himself like a tail and went to the sky, where he became a comet. Meteors are his tears.

LORE AND LEARNING

The *Machiguenga* reckon time by moons, 12 to a year, by moon quarters, and by the blooming of certain flowers. They measure short objects by spans and half spans, and long objects with poles, but have no weights or measures. Travel is estimated by sun positions (Farabee, 1922).

They regard the Milky Way as a river where animals bathe to gain eternal youth (Pio Aza, 1923 b, p. 396).

BIBLIOGRAPHY

Amich, 1854; Chantre y Herrera, 1901; Cipriani, 1902; Enock, 1908; Exploración de los Ríos Pichis, 1897; Farabee, 1922; Fejos, n.d.; Fernández Moro, 1926–27; Fry, 1889; Gadea, 1895; Galt, n.d.; S. García, 1942; García Rosell, 1905; Grain, 1942; Herndon and Gibbon, 1853–54; Hervás, 1800–05, vol. 1; Izaguirre, 1922–29; Marcoy, 1875; Maroni, 1889–92; Maurtua, V., 1906; Navarro, 1924; Ordinaire, 1887, 1892; Osambela, 1896; Pio Aza, 1923 b; Raimondi, 1862; Reich, 1903; Sagols, 1902; Sala, 1892, 1905–08; Skinner, 1805; Stiglich, 1908; Tessmann, 1930.

MAYORUNA

HISTORY

The *Mayoruna* (*Maxuruna, Majuruna, Mayiruna, Maxirona, Mayusuna, Barbudo, Dallus*), who occupy the swamps and forests south of the Amazon River between the lower Ucayali and the Jutahy Rivers (lat. 4°–7° S., long. 70°–74° W.; map 1, *No. 3;* map 5), were seemingly extremely primitive. Fragmentary information from early missionaries and from Tessmann's sketchy report (1930) suggests that they were semi-horticultural and lacked many of the hunting devices, technological accomplishments, musical instruments, rites and religious concepts characteristic of their neighbors. Their culture may, perhaps, be considered proto-*Panoan* or even proto-Montaña.

The *Mayoruna* avoided residence on the large rivers, partly because of hostility with the tribes occupying them. This isolation doubtless accounts for their cultural poverty. Linguistically, however, they are *Panoan*. Their dialect, according to Izaguirre (1922–29, 9:202), resembled that of the *Remo;* according to Figueroa (1904, p. 115), it resembled that of the *Chipeo, Cheteo,* and *Capanahua* of the Huallaga River.

Before the Spaniards came, the *Mayoruna* had raided tribes along the lower Huallaga region, menacing the *Cocamilla* and repelling *Chébero, Maina,* and *Cocamilla* expeditions against them. Later they fought bravely against a Spanish expedition from Moyabamba.

The *Mayoruna's* seminomadic habits thwarted missionary work, but contacts with missionaries and with mission Indians somewhat acculturated this tribe.

In 1654 some *Mayoruna* traded for iron tools near the Mission of Santa María de Huallaga. A *Cocamilla* chief became lay missionary to the *Mayoruna* and initiated peaceful trading, after which Father Raimundo de la Cruz baptized and preached among them. Finally, the *Mayoruna* came voluntarily to the Mission of Santa María on the Huallaga River, which the *Maconagua,* one of their subdivisions, were forced to join. An epidemic in 1655 took a heavy toll, reducing the mission population to 200 warriors (about 1,000 persons). (See Figueroa, 1904, pp. 111–123; Maroni, 1889–92, 28:419–427; Chantre y Herrera, 1901, p. 522.)

Little is known about the *Mayoruna* during the next century. In 1755, a group was taken to the Mission of San Joaquín de los Omaguas but soon escaped (Chantre y Herrera, 1901, p. 503). Later the *Mayoruna* entered a special section of San Joaquín through friendship with the *Omagua. Omagua* children taught *Mayoruna* girls to weave and boys to use canoes and spear throwers. For their part, the *Omagua* welcomed the service of the *Mayoruna* children, especially when through marriage the boys became permanent members of their households. *Mayoruna* girls also married *Yameo* boys. In 1762 additional *Mayoruna* were put in a new mission, Nueva Señora del Carmen, somewhat above Loreto de los Ticunas (Chantre y Herrera, 1901, pp. 521–523).

The majority of the *Mayoruna,* however, continued their seminomadic life in the country crossed by the lower Ucayali and Tapichi Rivers.

Since the expulsion of the Jesuits, in 1767, the *Mayoruna* have occupied the marshes and forests south of the Amazon and east of the lower Ucayali, centering on upper Tapichi and Yavari Rivers. (Izaguirre, 1922–29, 8:130, 160; Skinner, 1805, p. 433; Herndon and Gibbon, 1853–54, pp. 184, 193; Galt, ms.) In 1859 there were also 250 *Mayoruna* at Cochiquinas on the Amazon. The village of Maucallacta, also on the Amazon, was once occupied by 100 *Marubo (Maroba),* a *Mayoruna* subdivision (Raimondi, 1862, p. 100). The *Mayoruna* continued to be more or less hostile to their neighbors and, until recently, were victimized by *Conibo* slave raids. The present century found them still resisting acculturation (Tessmann, 1930). Their number is estimated at 3,000 (Peruvian census, 1940).

CULTURE

SUBSISTENCE ACTIVITIES

The *Mayoruna* have always been seminomadic, living mainly on palm fruits gathered in the marshes (Chantre y Herrera, 1901, p. 521). In native times they fished little because of their remoteness from the rivers, and ate little meat because they lacked the blowgun (Figueroa, 1904, p. 116), but they took turtles with harpoon arrows and kept them in pools (Osculati, 1854, pp. 212–213). In the present century, the blowgun is the main hunting weapon; nets, traps, deadfalls, and the bow and arrow are not used. The *Mayoruna* took fish only by means of baskets and two drugs, one of them a cultivated plant (Tessmann, 1930).

Early sources mention cultivation of some maize and bananas (Chantre y Herrera, 1901, p. 521).   Figueroa (1904, p. 166) adds sweet manioc and some peanuts, and Tessmann (1930) sweet potatoes and pumpkins.

Food was ground in a trough, and meat cooked on the rectangular babracot.

HOUSES AND VILLAGES

Early *Mayoruna* villages consisted of three or four houses (Chantre y Herrera, 1901), each tightly built to keep out mosquitoes (Figueroa, 1904, p. 116).   Tessmann (1930) describes modern gabled houses with supporting posts and auxiliary sheds of similar construction.

People sleep in *Astrocaryum* fiber hammocks.   Men sit on logs, women on mats placed on the ground (Tessmann, 1930).

TRANSPORTATION

Missionary sources remark that the *Mayoruna* learned to make canoes from the *Omagua* at the missions.   Tessmann (1930) describes the recent vessel as merely a hollowed trunk of *Iriartea ventricosa*, propelled by a paddle with a crutch handle.   The *Mayoruna* also use rafts.

DRESS AND ADORNMENT

Both sexes were naked in early days (Figueroa, 1904, p. 117), painted from the head to waist (Izaguirre, 1922–29, 9:202).   Today women wear a *Ficus* bast apron, men a cord to hold up the penis; urucú is the only paint used.   Tessmann (1930) denies tooth filing or blackening, depilation, and combs, but states that men tonsure the hair.

The characteristic ornaments, especially for men, formerly were chonta palm splinters and feathers passed through the ear lobes, the nasal alae, and the upper and lower lips (pl. 51, *top, left*).   The great number worn through the lower lip resembled a beard, hence the name *Barbudo* (bearded).   These ornaments have been abandoned.   The *Mayoruna* also tattooed the face, and wore a shell in the septum of the nose, feather head ornaments, monkey-tooth necklaces, and arm bands (Tessmann, 1930).

MANUFACTURES

The *Mayoruna* make hammocks and bags of *Astrocaryum* or of wild cotton.   The spindle for cotton has a crossed stick attached to it in place of a whorl and is rolled on the thigh.   Cotton is woven into bands and ribbons on a small loom attached in some manner to a stick (Tessmann, 1930).   Weaving was perhaps learned from the mission *Omagua*.   The *Mayoruna* do no netting, but weave palm-leaf baskets (Tessmann, 1930).

Ceramics comprise plain cook pots, bowls, and jugs, the last two with red interiors (Tessmann, 1930).

Early sources list clubs and wooden swords (macanas) (Chantre y Herrera, 1901, p. 527), throwing spears (chinganas) and shields (Izaguirre, 1922–29, vol. 9; Figueroa, 1904, p. 115), and note the absence of the bow and arrow (Izaguirre, 1922–29, vol. 9) and blowgun (Figueroa, 1904). Tessmann (1930) denies use of the shield but affirms use of a blowgun which seems to be made in one piece.

Fire is made with a drill and activated with a feather fan.

TRADE

The *Mayoruna* used to trade with their enemies. They went to the river and blew bamboo trumpets to signal the traders on the opposite side. The latter crossed in canoes and, without landing, held articles for exchange on the points of their spears. The *Mayoruna* gave parrots, hammocks woven of wild cotton, feather headdresses, and various small objects, and received knives and other iron tools. The traders then separated, shooting arrows at each other (Figueroa, 1904, p. 112).

SOCIOPOLITICAL GROUPS

Tessmann's scant data (1930) suggest that the sociopolitical unit is the patrilineal extended family occupying a single house. Marriage is often polygynous, residence patrilocal.

WARFARE

The *Mayoruna* have generally received strangers with hostility. Their main weapons of warfare were the javelin, club, and, formerly if not now, the shield. Castelnau (quoted by Izaguirre, 1922–29, 12:426) accredits them with cannibalism, but this probably refers to funerary cannibalism. (See below.)

LIFE CYCLE

Childbirth.—Birth entails 20 days' confinement and dieting for both parents, the father meanwhile avoiding work (Tessmann, 1930).

Girls' puberty.—At her first menses, a girl is confined where no one can see her and observes a few dietary restrictions (Tessmann, 1930).

Formerly, a man often reared a small girl and married her when she reached puberty (Jiménez de la Espada, 1889–92, 27:79).

Death observances.—Characteristic *Panoan* endocannibalism was practiced at death. Osculati (1854, pp. 212–213) observed that dying people for whom Christian burial was planned were greatly distressed at the prospect of being eaten by maggots instead of by their relatives. The corpse was roasted and, with laments, cut into pieces and eaten. The bones were then ground, mixed with masato, and drunk. (See also Chantre y Herrera, 1901, p. 275). The head was kept until filled with maggots, when the brains were spiced with aji and eaten with great relish (Figueroa, 1904, p. 118). Twenty years ago, the *Mayoruna* buried infants in the house (Tessmann, 1930).

ESTHETIC AND RECREATIONAL ACTIVITIES

The *Mayoruna* had signal drums (Figueroa, 1904, p. 115), bamboo signal trumpets (probably not connected with secret cults), snail-shell signal horns (Tessmann, 1930), and trumpets with a sounding cup and bamboo tube (Tessmann, 1930, table 16, fig. 16). They lacked panpipes, musical bows, and transverse flutes, and used the longitudinal flute only as a child's toy (Tessmann, 1930).

Tops, stilts, ball games, wrestling, and dancing are unknown (Tessmann, 1930).

Tobacco, the only narcotic, was smoked in a pipe made of an *Astrocaryum* fruit shell with a monkey bone stem.

Chicha was originally made of fermented sweet manioc and, later, also of sugarcane.

RELIGION AND SHAMANISM

Tessmann (1930) secured a hint of a sky god, possibly identified with the sun, of an underground deity, and of a belief that souls of the dead lingered in the bush, were feared and perhaps sometimes went into deer, which were taboo. His assertion that the *Mayoruna* have no shamans and attribute all sickness and death to natural agencies is incredible.

BIBLIOGRAPHY

Chantre y Herrera, 1901; Figueroa, 1904; Galt, n.d.; Herndon and Gibbon, 1853–54; Izaguirre, 1922–29; Jiménez de la Espada (Noticias auténticas . . . 1889-92); Maroni, 1889–92; Osculati, 1854; Raimondi, 1862; Skinner, 1805; Tessmann, 1930.

THE PANOAN TRIBES OF EASTERN PERU

INTRODUCTION

A large number of *Panoan* tribes centered in the Ucayali Valley (map 1, *No. 3;* map 5). Along the main river were several large, strong tribes which raided and enslaved their smaller linguistic kin, who kept to the headwaters of the tributaries. The former were the *Setebo, Shipibo,* and *Conibo,* whom Tessmann (1928, 1930) collectively calls the *Chama* (*Tschama*). The *Aguano* may also have been *Panoan.* These river tribes are the best known ethnographically. The hinterland tribes, on whom information is scanty, include the *Chamicura, Cashibo, Capanawa, Puyumanawa, Remo, Mananava, Nianagua, Amahuaca, Maspo, Amenguaca, Ruanagua, Pichobo, Soboyo, Comobo, Mochobo, Nocomán,* and *Mayoruna,* the last treated separately (p. 551). East of these tribes on the headwaters of the Juruá and Purús Rivers were many other culturally similar, *Panoan*-speaking tribes who, for convenience, are described elsewhere (p. 657). Two tribes in the neighborhood of the Ucayali River, the *Carapacho* toward the upper Huallaga River and the *Urarina* (*Itucale*) north of the Amazon River, may have spoken *Panoan*. Many other tribes are merely mentioned in early documents and cannot be classified.

The two common endings of tribal names, "bo" and "nagua" (nahua, nawa), mean "people."

Panoan culture does not differ radically from that of other tribes of the Montaña. Its more distinctive form occurs on the lower Ucayali River. The social, political, and economic unit is the extended family occupying a single, large house and supporting itself by slash-and-burn farming, supplemented by hunting and fishing. But, uniquely, the family is matrilineal, with some clan features. Subsistence is based on sweet manioc, but turtles and river mammals are taken in some numbers with harpoons and spear throwers and with harpoon arrows. The blowgun and spear rather than bow are used for hunting.

The Ucayali *Panoans* lack both the hammock and platform bed and sleep on mats on the ground. They use both the horizontal and the "Ucayali" loom. They have minimal birth and puberty rites, except for subincision and deflowering of girls and *Conibo* circumcision of boys, and they deform infants' heads and blacken their teeth. Warriors' nose deformation (*Urarina*) is unique. These tribes once took trophy heads but did not eat their enemies. They practice urn and earth burial, cremation, and funerary endocannibalism. Beliefs about life after death are varied. The *Panoans* still have a characteristic art style, which distinguishes their pottery and other artifacts. They smoke tobacco as cigars or in pipes or take it through tubes but lack most drugs except cayapi, which is taken by shamans.

The peripheral *Panoan* tribes and the upper Ucayali *Arawakans* are culturally similar to each other, and both groups differ from the Ucayali *Panoans*. They probably have a patrilineal household. They depend largely on hunting and fishing, but their rivers lack turtles and large, aquatic mammals. Bows and arrows, spear throwers and harpoons but not blowguns are their weapons. They make primitive ceramics, have inferior canoes or no canoes, and use simple wooden clubs. They lack circumcision, subincision and head deformation. Unlike the neighboring *Arawakans,* the peripheral *Panoans* practice endocannibalism and use little or no coca.

The *Panoan* tribes of the Ucayali River and those of the Juruá-Purús area have several characteristics in common: dependence on sweet but not on bitter manioc; turtle hunting; harpoons; apparently an extended matrilineal, at least matrilocal, household as the sociopolitical unit, but clans not proven; tooth blackening; cannibalism of their own dead but not of enemies; tobacco snuff taken through tubes; shaman's trance induced by a drug (cayapi?); a variant of the "Ucayali" loom; and domesticated cotton. But, like the peripheral Ucayali *Panoan* peoples, the Juruá-Purús tribes lack the spear thrower and make little use of the blowgun; they hunt instead mainly with the bow and arrow. Also, they do not deform infant's heads. Typically non-Montaña, the Juruá-Purús area uses hammocks, has ceremonies with accompanying purification to celebrate children's tooth blackening and lip piercing, cuts the girls' hymen at puberty, and uses sacred bark trumpets that are taboo to women and children. Some of these traits probably came from the Juruá-Purús *Arawakan* tribes.

TRIBAL DIVISIONS AND HISTORY

Urarina.—The *Urarina* (*Itukale, Itucale, Ytucali, Singacuchusca, Cingacuchusca, Arucui, Arucuye, Ssimaku, Shimacu, Chimacu, Chambira, Chambirino*) lived north of the Marañón River on the tributaries of the Chambira River (lat. 4° 30′ S., long. 75°–76° W.); the *Cingacuchusca*, a subtribe, was evidently on the Tigre River. There were two main *Urarina* divisions: the *Urarina* proper and the *Itucale* (Escobar y Mendoza, 1769; Izaguirre, 1922–29, 12:407), but Hervás (1800–05, vol. 1) gives *Urarina* divisions as *Barbudo, Itucale, Mayoruño* (*Mayoruna?*, see p. 551), and *Musino*.

The *Urarina* are tentatively classed as *Panoan*. Velasco (1842–44, 3:208) states that their language was related to *Mayoruna*, a *Panoan* tongue. (See Tessmann's (1930) *Urarina* vocabulary.) Figueroa (1904, p. 187), however, alleged that the *Itucale* and *Cingacuchusca* spoke the same language as the *Cocamilla*, i.e., *Tupí*. The *Itucale* may have migrated in post-Contact times from near the *Chamicura* and the *Cutinana* on the Samiria River (Maroni, 1889–92, 26:231). The *Itucale* may also have lived south of the Marañón River at one time, for they are very similar culturally to the *Chamicura*.

The *Itucale* were first contacted by Father Majano through friendly *Cocama*. In 1653 a few were taken to Borja, in 1679 several more *Itucale* went to Chamicuros, and, in 1712, others were settled in a mission. As only a few of the mission group remained in 1730, the *Itucale* went to the Huallaga River missions and were known as *Aracui* in 1737 (Maroni, 1889–92, 20:266).

The *Urarina*, having been favorably impressed by the missions on the Marañón River, accepted a mission of their own on the Chambira headwaters in 1738. More than 200 *Itucale* eventually joined them. This mission was moved several times before the end of the century when the population, reduced from its earlier number, was 600. In the present century, although Rivet (1924, p. 674) states that the *Urarina* are extinct, Tessmann (1930) states that 300 largely assimilated *Ssimaku* (*Urarina*) survived.

Aguano.—The *Uguano* (*Aguanu, Awano, Santa Crucino*), consisting of the *Aguano* proper, the *Cutinana*, and the *Maparina* occupied the region of the lower Huallaga and the Marañón (Chantre y Herrera, 1901, p. 60) down to the Samiria River (lat. 5°–6° S., long. 74°–76° W.).

The linguistic affiliations of these tribes is uncertain. The *Aguano* proper had adopted *Quechua* at or soon after the Conquest. But if Rivet (1924) is correct that *Chamicura* is *Panoan,* the whole group must have been *Panoan.* Rivet (1924) does not, however, recognize an *Aguano* group, mapping the *Tupian Cocamilla (Guallaga)* in *Aguano* territory and assigning several *Aguano* subtribes to other linguistic families.

The *Aguano* proper had two main subgroups: one included the *Seculusepa* and *Chilicagua;* the other, the *Meliquine* and *Tivilo.* The *Tivilo (Tibilo)* were *Chébero* according to Beuchat and Rivet (1909), but old sources group them with the *Aguano* (Figueroa, 1904, p. 129; Maroni, 1889–92, 28:435; Chantre y Herrera, 1901, pp. 188–189). The *Aguano* may have been north of the Marañón River when first contacted, for the *Maina* told of *"Aguanu"* living 2 days' east of the Pastaza River (Rel. geogr. Indias, 1881–97, 4:143). The *Tivilo,* however, were on the eastern side of the Huallaga River, opposite the *Chébero.*

Bitter enemies of the *Chamicura* and feared by the Spaniards, the *Aguano* first began trade relations with the *Cocama* in 1653 and the next year, lured by gifts of iron tools, entered a mission on the lower Huallaga River. But they had to live in three separate villages because of disagreement among themselves. After an epidemic, the whole nation numbered about 1,000 persons. The *Tibilo,* continually quarreling with the *Chamicura,* had to be settled separately in San Lorenzo de los Tibilos.

In 1737, San Xavier de los Chamicuros had 237 inhabitants, and San Antonio Abad had 92. In 1758, the *Chamicura* and *Aguano* agreed to occupy San Xavier together. They had been decimated by epidemics and wars against the *Jívaro,* in which they served as auxiliaries of the Spaniards. (Maroni, 1889–92, 28:427–434; Chantre y Herrera, 1901, pp. 188–189; Figueroa, 1904, pp. 124–135.)

In the last century, the *Aguano* were concentrated at Santa Cruz on the lower Huallaga River where there were 350 persons in 1851 (Herndon and Gibbon, 1853–54, 1:170), 300 in 1859 (Raimondi, 1863). At that time there were 80 *Tivilo* at Maipuco on the Marañón River.

In 1925, Tessmann (1930, pp. 253–254) found that 100 *Aguano* survived. They were almost completely acculturated.

The *Cutinana* are classed by Beuchat and Rivet (1909) as *Chébero* which is *Cahuapanan,* evidently on the strength of Veigl's classification (1785 a, p. 36) and because of their later association with the *Chébero* at missions and their subsequent location between the *Chayawita* and the *Chébero.* Figueroa (1904, p. 125), however, identifies them linguistically with the *Aguano* and *Maparina.* They were found to speak the same language as captive *Aguano* brought into a mission.

In 1641, the *Cutinana* were found on what is probably the Samiria River (Figueroa, 1904, pp. 75–78, 382–383), which Maroni (1889–92, 26:292) considers their original home. That year, 100 families went to the *Chébero* mission, then entered their own mission, Santo Tomé. Some, however, evidently remained on the Samiria River in 1738 (Figueroa, 1904, pp. 382–383), while others were near the Urarina and between the Chambira and Pastaza Rivers, having migrated from the Samiria River (Maroni, 1889–92, 26:231). In 1737 most of the *Cutinana* lived with the *Chébero* (Maroni, 1889–92, 26:292).

The *Maparina* were also an *Aguano* subtribe (Figueroa, 1904, p. 187), which probably adjoined the *Cocama.* They apparently fought with the *Chipeo (Shipebo)* in a revolt in 1660 and with the *Cocama* in 1663 (Maroni, 1889–92, 29:93). *Cutinana* prisoners from these wars were put in a Huallaga River mission (Chantre y Herrera,

1901, p. 227). In 1681, they lived on the Huallaga River above Santiago, but epidemics drove them to join the *Cocamilla* in the Santiago mission (Maroni, 1889–92, 28:111). In 1830, they were reported on the Samiria headwaters; in 1881, on the lower Huallaga. They may since have been assimilated.

The *Sicluna* were neighbors of the *Aguano,* but their relationship is unknown (Figueroa, 1904, p. 134).

Chamicura.—The *Chamicura* (*Chamicuro*), linguistically closely related to the *Shipibo,* probably lived originally near the Samiria (formerly the Chamicuro) River (lat. 5° 30′ S., long. 74° W.), where a few pagan *Chamicura* remained in 1737 (Maroni, 1889–92, 26:292).

In 1768, after a smallpox epidemic, 500 *Chamicura* survived on the Samiria River, the others having gone to the Huallaga River (Veigl, 1785 a, p. 57). These were taken with *Aguano* remnants to Santiago de la Laguna on the Huallaga River. In the present century, the *Chamicura* have been dispersed, owing to the rubber boom and to acculturating influences. Only 60 largely assimilated plantation workers live at Pampa Hermosa on the Huallaga River (Tessmann, 1930), though the 1940 Peruvian census gives 1,500.

The *Sicluna* (*Chicluna*) were probably a subtribe of the *Chamicura* (Veigl, 1785 a, p. 57).

Setebo.—The *Setebo* (*Settebo, Shetebo, Ssetebo, Schetibo, Sitibo, Xitipo, Jitipo, Gitibo, Pano, Manoita, Puinahua?,* "turkey hawk people") lived north of the *Cashibo,* centering on the Manoa or Cushabatay River and perhaps extending down the Ucayali to adjoin the *Cocama* (lat. 6°– 9° S., long. 74° W.). In historic times they gradually withdrew from the main river and dwindled in numbers. Meanwhile, the *Sensi, Panobo,* and perhaps *Puinahua* became separate subdivisions of them.

The *Setebo* were first visited in 1657 by Father Alonso Cabellero, who founded a few short-lived missions. In 1661, Father Lorenzo Tineo and 200 *Payanso* established two *Setebo* missions with 2,000 prospective converts, but the *Setebo* plotted a revolt after receiving iron tools. Tineo evacuated the missionaries and 100 *Setebo* followed him to join the *Panatahua, Payanso,* and other upper Huallaga River missions. Further attempts to found missions resulted in more murders of Spaniards and the projects were abandoned. In 1670, smallpox swept the region. The same year, Father Lucero took some *Setebo, Chepeo* (*Shipebo*), and *Cocama* to his mission, Santiago, on the Huallago River (Chantre y Herrera, 1901, p. 251), but many of these died of smallpox in 1680 (Maroni, 1889–92, 28: 105–112).

During the 18th century, the *Shipibo* killed many *Setebo* settled at the mouth of the Manoa River and forced others to take refuge in marshes up the Cushabatay River. Renewed missionary efforts began in 1754 (Izaguirre, 1922–29, 2:209). An expedition in 1757 with 300 *Cholón* participants failed, but by 1760, the pitiful condition of the Indians and their desire for protection from the *Shipibo* and for tools to cultivate their fields induced them to accept a mission. The *Setebo* remembered something of Christianity after 80 years, having crosses everywhere and baptizing babies with lemon juice. The missionaries wrote a *Setebo* grammar and dictionary. The revolt of a division called the *Yambo* (*Yaubo*) led by Rungato in 1767 put an end to this mission and started the general uprising on the Ucayali River.

Franciscans returned during the 19th century, founding Sarayacu (pl. 48, *center*) in 1790 with many tribes, but in 1860 a violent epidemic of smallpox destroyed many of the *Setebo,* and in 1861 the missionaries abandoned Sarayacu because of conflicts with the civil governors and traders. The *Setebo* migrated to the lagoon of Cashiboya on the right side of the Ucayali (Izaguirre, 1922–29, 9:254–264). Galt, traveling up the Ucayali River in 1870 (ms.) "saw nothing and heard very little" about the *Setebo*, some of whom were said to be at Santuaba, at Lake Santuaba, and at Roioboya. Marcoy wrote (1875, 2:47) that the *Setebo* extended from the Cushabatay River, above which lived the *Shipibo*, along the Ucayali to its mouth. In 1925, Tessmann (1928, p. 8) reported that the *Setebo* were the northernmost *Chama*, with their main settlement at Cruz Muyuna, where there were also *Panobo*. The 1940 census records 3,000, though Tessmann estimated 360.

The *Puinahua*, meaning "excrement men" in *Panoan* and called *Hotentot* by the missionaries because of their filth, were a semilegendary tribe who lived "beyond the Isla deseada" on the Marañón River. They were discovered about 1800, but only a few persons were ever seen (Izaguirre, 1922–29, 9:42, 203; 12:437–438). In 1870, Galt (ms.) thought they were largely extinct, but Tessmann (1928) takes them to be the *Setebo* who once lived along the Canal de Puinagua.

Panobo.—The *Panobo* (*Manoa, Pano, Pana, Pelado*) sprang either from *Setebo* who had gone to Huallaga River missions in 1670 or from those of the upper Cushabatay River (lat. 7° S., long. 76° W.). Favoring the former hypothesis was the presence in 1681 of *Pelado* (probably *Panobo*) 5 days above Santiago on the Huallaga River. Even these, however, might have moved west from the Cushabatay River, for in 1682, there were 7,000 *Pelado* in the high arid county 5 days (east) from Laguna on the Huallaga (Chantre y Herrera, 1901, p. 283). Skinner (1805, pp. 407–408) records that the *Panobo* were alleged to have been *Setebo* of the Cushabatay River who fled *Calliseca* (*Shipibo*) attacks in 1686. Fritz even maps *Pelado* on the Marañón River below the Ucayali River.

In 1760 the *Panabo* seem to have formed a separate group in the Cushabatay region (Skinner, 1805, pp. 407–408). Hervás (1800–05, vol. 1) gives *Iltipo* and *Pelado* as *Pano* subdivisions. In 1863, the *Pano* were reported at Lake Cashiboya. In 1925, 100 to 200 were scattered on the Ucayali River, some mixed with *Setebo* at Cruz Muyuna (Tessmann, 1930, pp. 106–107; 1928, p. 8); these spoke mainly *Quechua* and Spanish and were being rapidly assimilated.

Sensi.—The *Sensi* (*Senti, Senci, Ssenssi, Tenti, Mananahua*) separated from the *Setebo* at the beginning of the 19th century to live on the right bank of the Ucayali River, lat. 6°30' S., long. 75° W. (Marcoy, 1875, 2:53–57). The subtribes were the *Ynubu* (*Inubu*), *Runubú*, and *Casca*, their number 3,000, and their habitat between the Ucayali and Javari Rivers, near Lake Cruz Muyuna and its affluent, the Chunuya River (Izaguirre, 1922–29, 8:273; 9:38; 12:436–437).

The *Sensi* originally numbered 3,000 but half of them had died of epidemics by 1800 (Izaguirre, 1922–29, 9:38), most of the survivors being placed in the Mission of Chanaya-mana soon thereafter (Marcoy, 1875, 2:176; Izaguirre, 1922–29, 9:38; Sagols, 1902, p. 364), but others remaining in the forests. Chanaya was abandoned in 1821 (Marcoy, 1875, 2:176). In 1852 it had 37 *Sensi* (Izaguirre, 1922–29, 9:37, 88, 197). In 1851, Herndon (Herndon and Gibbon, 1853–54, p. 205) found the *Sensi* on the east bank of the Ucayali, above Sarayacu. In 1875 (Marcoy, 1875, 2:47, 77, 176), 12 to 15 families (100 people) occupied the forests of Chanayamana, especially the village of Pancaya, and formed a distinct group. Their northern limit was Lake Chanaya (Marcoy, 1875, 2:172). Most of the *Sensi* were absorbed by other tribes, but in 1925, 100 remained on the upper Maquia River (Tessmann, 1930).

Mayo.—The *Mayo*, probably a *Panoan* tribe, were discovered on the Tapiche River near the *Sensi* and *Mayoruna* in 1790 (Izaguirre, 1922–29, 12:429–431).

Shipibo (*Chipeo, Chipio, Chepeo, Shipipo, Ssipipo, Calliseca*).—The *Shipibo* (little monkey people) are identified by Amich (1854, p. 29) with the 17th-century *Calliseca* because the latter lived near the *Setebo* and because their "character" was like that of the 18th-century *Shipibo*. Izaguirre (1922–29, 1:136 ff.) and Skinner (1805) concur, but Herndon and Gibbon (1853–54, 1:184) and Tessmann (1930) identify the *Calliseca* with the *Cashibo*. Both *Shipibo* and *Cashibo* lived east of the *Tingan* in the Pachitea and Aguaytia Valleys, but only the former were neighbors of the *Setebo*. Early accounts relate that trips eastward through *Payanso* country reached the *Calliseca* near the Ucayali. As this *Calliseca* territory is almost certainly that of the *Shipibo*, we accept the *Shipibo* as the 17th-century *Calliseca*.

The *Shipibo* spoke the same language as the *Setebo* (Marcoy, 1875, 2:58). They originally lived on the upper Aguaytia River (lat. 8° S., long. 75° W.), from which they were driven in the 17th century by the *Cashibo*, who in turn had been pressed by the *Campa* of the Gran Pajonal. The *Shipibo* themselves drove the *Conibo* from the region of the mouth of the Aguaytia River southward up the Ucayali River to Pisqui (Izaguirre, 1922–29, 1:303–304). They numbered 1,000 or more (Skinner, 1805, p. 409).

The *Manamabobo* and *Manava* (lat. 10° S., long. 74° W.) were probably *Shipibo* or *Cashibo* divisions.

In 1657, missionaries and soldiers visited the *Shipibo* (then called *Calliseca*) and the *Setebo*, but were killed by the former (Amich, 1854, pp. 26–29). The *Shipibo* joined the *Cocama* in hostilities against the Huallaga River missions in 1660 (Chantre y Herrera, 1901, p. 226). In 1661, 2,000 or 3,000 *Setebo* and "*Calliseca*" were gathered in two towns (Skinner, 1805, pp. 444–449; Izaguirre, 1922–29, 1:136), but they rebelled against their missionaries and, in 1670, attacked the *Panatahua* missions. The same year some *Shipibo* joined the Mission of Santiago on the Huallaga. In 1680, after the *Cocama* fled, many *Shipibo* who remained in order to "go to heaven" died during the smallpox epidemic (Maroni, 1889–92, 28:105–112). From 1686 to 1698, the *Shipibo* were under Jesuit influence, but in 1698 they killed their missionary and overthrew White domination (Chantre y Herrera, 1901, p. 296).

By 1704, all missions were lost in this region and little was done for 50 years. Meanwhile, the *Shipibo* carried on bitter warfare against the *Setebo*, whom they defeated in 1736 (Skinner, 1805, pp. 409, 444–449). In 1764, about 1,000 *Shipibo* lived scattered in family groups (Amich, 1854, p. 239), occupying 20 leagues of the left side of the Ucayali River and extending 10 or 12 leagues into the interior (Izaguirre, 1922–29, 2:237). In 1765 several new missions were founded in the region (Amich, 1854, p. 239) and by 1766, *Shipibo* of 5 towns had been reconverted, but the missions were lost in the Rungato revolt of 1767 (Skinner, 1805, pp. 410, 448).

In 1790, the *Shipibo* were reported on the Pixi, Tamaya, and Aguaytia Rivers, on the Ucayali above the Sarayacu, and on the Cushabatay River. They numbered about 275 families in two main villages, with other scattered families (Izaguirre, 1922–29, 8:223, 239–240, 275, 307). In response to requests, the Franciscans founded two missions (Izaguirre, 1922–29, 8:159, 241). Marcoy (1875, 2:60) attributes to them a mission population of 800 to 900 in 1791. The *Shipibo* were then great travelers and salt traders. Another mission was established for 300 families in 1813 (Izaguirre, 1922–29, 9:36). In 1821, the *Shipibo* inhabited the Pisqui River, from Charasmana to its headwaters and the Aguaytia and Cushabatay Rivers (Izaguirre, 1922–29, 9:42). In 1851, Herndon and Gibbon (1853–54) saw *Shipibo* villages near Sarayacu (23 persons), Sucre (25 persons), and Isla Setico (3 persons). Galt in 1870 saw and heard little of them (ms.), but Marcoy (1875, 2:16, 47) attributed to them 180 miles of the Ucayali from the right bank of the Caponcinia River, where they adjoined the *Conibo,* to the Caxiabatay River, where *Setebo* territory began. In 1925, Tessmann reported (1928, pp. 11, 12) that many *Shipibo* workers had withdrawn from plantations to live scattered between Contamana and the mouth of the Utoquinea River. He guessed their number at 1,300, but the 1940 census records 2,500.

Manamabobo (*Manambobo*)—Though possibly *Cashibo* or *Conibo* (Hervás, 1800–05, vol. 1), this was more likely a *Shipibo* subdivision who in 1680 were called *Chipeo* montareces, "wild" *Shipibo,* and lived near the Pachitea River (lat. 10° S., long. 74° W.) but migrated to the forests near the *Conibo.* In 1687, they were put in the Mission of San Nicolas Obispo, but fled because of epidemics and were later resettled (Maroni, 1889–92, 30:145).

Manava.—Though possibly *Cashibo,* the *Manava* were more probably *Shipibo* who had been taken to Lamas and Laguna after the *Cocama* rebellion. They fled from these towns and, in 1690, attacked the *Conibo* on the Ucayali to steal iron tools. Their mission on the Taguaco River was abandoned in 1695. Some *Manava* on the Cushabatay River were taken to Lamas and Moyabamba in 1703 as slaves (Maroni, 1889–92, 30:148–150).

Mananamabua.—These were listed by Hervás (1800–05, vol. 1) with the *Manabobo* as *Conibo* subdivisions.

Conibo.—The *Conibo* (*Conivo, Cuniba, Cunivo, Curibeo,* "fish people") had their aboriginal settlements on the Pachitea River and up and down the Ucayali River (lat. 9° S., long. 74° W.). The original number at the mouth of the Pachitea was 2,000 (pl. 49, *top*).

When first visited in the 17th century, the *Conibo* were raiding other tribes for slaves and loot and exchanging the slaves to the *Cocama* of the lower Ucayali for iron tools. But they were friendly to the Spaniards, partly because of a desire for iron tools.

The first contact with Whites was probably in 1682 when the *Conibo* visited the lower Huallaga River and left some of their young people at Santiago to learn the language (probably *Quechua*) and Christianity (Chantre y Herrera, 1901, p. 282). In a race to establish the first *Conibo* mission, the Franciscans came down from the Tambo River and the Jesuits ascended the Ucayali River. Father Viedma, a Franciscan, established San Miguel in 1685 at the mouth of the Pachitea River, but the Jesuits won favor and the Franciscans withdrew. A few other Jesuit missions were founded (Izaguirre, 1922–29, 1:273), all evidently sought by the *Conibo* because of the opportunity they afforded for the Indians to obtain iron tools. Resentment at enforced military service on a punitive expedition against the *Jivaro* in 1691 led to revolt and massacre of Spaniards in 1695. The *Conibo* supported by the *Piro, Campa, Shipibo, Manamabobo,* and *Mananamabua* repelled a punitive expedition in 1698 (Maroni, 1889–92, 33:47–54; Chantre y Herrera, 1901, pp. 293–296) and resumed their former mode of life. Thirty years later, other missions were started (Skinner, 1805, pp. 409–410), iron tools again being an inducement for the Indians, though jealousy about the quantities given different chiefs and epidemics led to trouble (Amich, 1854, pp. 171–175). Another revolt occurred in 1767, the year of the Jesuit expulsion, when *Conibo, Setebo,* and *Shipibo* under Rungato massacred all the missionaries and temporarily terminated their work (Skinner, 1805, pp. 409–410).

Franciscans later returned to the region and established two missions in 1790 and 1811 with 556 families (Izaguirre, 1922–29, 8:241; 9:37). Meanwhile, the *Conibo* had spread along the river and conducted slave raids among all tribes from the *Mayoruna* near the Amazon to the *Amahuaca* of the upper Ucayali (Izaguirre, 1922–29, 8:131). This produced considerable tribal intermixture. By 1851, their villages were scattered north almost to the *Cocama* (Herndon and Gibbon, 1853–54, vol. 1) and in 1870 though centering at Sarayacu (which was reduced by smallpox from 1,000 in 1860 to 200 in 1872), they were spread from the Pachitea River to the mouth of the Ucayali (Galt, ms.). Marcoy (1875, 2:21) found 600 to 700 *Conibo* in 10 or 11 settlements along 200 miles of the Ucayali River from the Capoucinia River on the north, beyond which were *Shipibo,* and to the Paruitcha River in the south, where *Chontaquiro* territory began. A nativistic concept, which probably underlay the early revolts, held that the *Conibo* were descended from the *Inca* Emperor and would ultimately return to power. For this reason the people liked *Quechua* names and spurned miscegenation (Galt, ms.). The same idea seems to have persisted in 1925, when Tessmann (1928, pp. 3, 11, 13) found that they avoided White towns and would not marry Peruvians. They lived mainly along the upper Ucayali River from the mouth of the Pachitea to the Sheboya River above Cumaria, although many had settled among neighboring tribes. Tessmann estimates them at 1,200; the 1940 census, at 3,000.

Cashibo (*Cacibo, Caxibo, Casibo, Cachibo, Cahivo, Managua, Hagueti, Capapacho*?).—The *Cashibo* occupied the Pachitea and Aguaytia Valleys, adjoining the *Conibo* (lat. 9° S., long. 75° W.). They probably once reached the Ucayali River (Sobreviela map), but later avoided it, fearing other tribes, and even withdrew in the 18th century from the Pachitea proper to its tributaries, the Inuquira and Carapacho Rivers (Marcoy, 1875, 2:143).

Apparently the *Cashibo* were not visited by missionaries (unless the 17th-century *Carapacho* or *Calliseca* were the *Cashibo*) until 1757, when they killed one missionary and forced others to flee (Izaguirre, 1922–29, 2:205, 229). In 1790, they were hostile to all neighboring tribes and were the main obstacle to navigation of the Aguaytia and Manoa Rivers (Izaguirre, 1922–29, 8:308). In 1820, they had retreated to the hills and to the Pachitea, Shipiria, and Aguaytia Rivers (Izaguirre, 1922–29, 9:42–43) but in 1851 were again on the Pachitea River, though some occupied the Aguaytia and Pisqui Rivers. They were at war with other tribes which attacked them (Herndon and Gibbon, 1853–54, 1:184). In 1870, those on the Aguaytia River were safe, but in the Pachitea Valley they were victims of *Setebo* and *Conibo* raids (Galt, ms.). In 1902 (Sagols, 1902, p. 360), they lived from south of the Aguaytia River to the Sierra of San Carlos, east of the Pachitea River. In 1925, 1,500 to 2,000, divided into three groups, the *Kakataibo, Cashiño,* and *Ruño* (Tessmann, 1930, pp. 124–128, 153–154), still avoided civilization, and lived mainly on the upper Aguaytia River, extending south to the Sungaroyacu, a tributary of the Pachitea, north to the Pisqui River and perhaps to the headwaters of the right tributaries of the Cushabatay River. The 1940 census gives 5,000 to 7,000 but Reifsnyder (personal communication) believes that epidemics have reduced them to only a few hundred families. The *Cashibo* were still relatively isolated in 1925, and retained their native culture (Tessmann, 1930).

Carapacho.—The relation of the *Carapacho* (lat. 9° S., long. 76° W.) to neighboring tribes is obscure. They did not speak *Amuesha* (Amich, 1854, pp. 145–153). Marcoy (1875, 2:143) believes that *Carapacho* is a synonym for *Calliseca,* a 17th-century tribe that may have been the modern *Shipibo* (or possibly *Cashibo*). But the *Carapacho* and *Calliseca* were mentioned in 1631 as tribes east of and adjoining the *Tingán* of the Huallaga River (Izaguirre, 1922–29, 1:81–82), one account stating that the *Carapacho* lived on a small tributary of the Pachitea River in the middle of the Pampa del Sacramento. Sobreviela's map shows them north of the Pozuzo River at about lat. 9° 45′ S. They may have been the *Cashibo.*

They were first contacted in 1631 by Father Felipe Luyando while he worked among the *Panatahua*. The *Carapacho* favored the missionaries, who were threatened by the *Chanatahua* and *Tingán*. Juan Rondón built a mission at their request, but it was abandoned in the latter half of the century, the Indians reverting to their former mode of life. In 1734, Father Simon Jara found them again after 2 years of exploration of the Pampa del Sacramento. He made peace, but did not missionize them. In 1773, the *Carapacho* extended over 60 leagues from Mairo to Huamancot. In 1794, they were still hostile when visited on the Pachitea River near the junction of the Palcaso and Pichis Rivers (Izaguirre, 1922–29, 8:308). Sagols (1902, p. 362) reports them on the Callescas River.

Capanawa (*Kapanahu, Capanagua, Buskipani, Busquipani*).—The *Capanahua* lived east of the Ucayali River toward the Javari River, on the upper Maquea River, and near the headwaters of the Tejo, Gregorio, Libertade, and Breu Rivers, between São Pão and Capoeira Rivers, tributaries of the upper Juruá, and around the headwaters of the Envira River (lat. 6° S., long. 74° W.). Other *Capanawa* were established at the headwaters of the Javary, Tapiche, Blanco and from the Maquea (Alacran) to the Guanacha River. The latter were also called *Buskipani.*

A Franciscan attempt to missionize the *Capanawa* in 1817 was frustrated by an epidemic, and the Indians returned to the bush. In 1925, they lived on the upper Tapiche River under a patron (hacienda owner) and on the upper Rio Blanco, which rubber workers called the Rio Capanawa. Only 100 survived, as they had never been numerous and had been subject to attacks by other tribes during the rubber boom (Tessmann, 1930; Izaguirre, 1922–29; Sagols, 1902, p. 363). The 1940 census figure of 900 must be too high.

Remo.—The *Remo* (*Rheno*), who spoke a *Conibo* dialect, avoided the aggressive *Shipibo* and *Conibo* by living on the headwaters of the eastern tributaries of the Ucayali River between Cerro de Canchyuaya and the Tamaya River (lat. 8° S., long 74° W.). A branch lived on the Jurua-mirin River, a left tributary of the Juruá River.

In 1690, there were said to be 600 family heads, about 3,000 people (Maroni, 1889–92, 30:151). A century later, some *Remo* settled with *Piro* at the Franciscan mission of Sarayacu (Izaguirre, 1922–29, 8:225), but in 1820, most of the tribe was still avoiding the shores of the Ucayali River for fear of the *Conibo*. The *Remo* lived mainly on the Cayaria River. A few of them spoke *Sensi*, a *Setebo* dialect (Izaguirre, 1922–29, 9:38–43, 91, 202).

The first mission in this region was founded in 1859 for the *Shipibo*, who later abandoned it and attacked a *Remo* village. The latter took refuge in the interior of Piyuya (Izaguirre, 1922–29, 9:243–244). In 1862, the *Remo* left the upper Cayaria River to enter a mission at Shunumaná, farther downstream, but within a few years the *Conibo* attacked the mission and captured women and children (Izaguirre, 1922–29, 9:307). In 1870, Galt (ms.) said there were *Remo* remnants at Calleria and above Calleria in the interior, most of the tribe having been killed off or enslaved by the *Conibo* and *Shipibo*. The rubber boom also took a heavy toll. In 1925, Tessmann (1930) reported that most of the surviving *Remo* occupied the sources of the Javari, Tapicho, Ipixuna, and Mos Rivers; others were under White settlers on the Javari and Batan Rivers. The 1940 census figure is 2,500.

Niaragua.—The *Niaragua* (*Niamagua*) lived 12 leagues from the Ucayali River (lat. 7° S., long. 74° W.), east of Mano (Izaguirre, 1922–29, 8:264).

Amahuaca.—The *Amahuaca* (*Amajuaca, Amawaka, Amaguaco, Ameuhaque, Ipitinere, Sayaco*) preferred to live at the headwaters of the tributaries of the upper Ucayali, Juruá, and Purús Rivers because they feared slave raids from the Ucayali proper. *Amahuaca* have been recorded in the following places: Between the Tamaya and Inuya Rivers; between the Chesea and Sepehua Rivers (tributaries of the Ucayali and Urubamba respectively); the Amonya headwaters; between the Guru-maha and Purús Rivers; the Amoaca, Tejo, and São Jão Rivers, all upper Juruá tributaries; and the Tarajuaca Basin. (Lat 9°–11° S., long. 73°–74° W.)

In 1686, a village of 12 huts (150 people) was seen on the Coniguati River. During the 18th and 19th centuries, the *Amahuaca* remained pagans and were hostile to Whites and to other Indians, especially to the *Piro, Conibo,* and *Shipibo,* who enslaved them (Izaguirre, 1922–29, 1:272; 8:160, 308; 9:41; Galt, ms; Herndon and Gibbon, 1853–54, 1:195). The only attempt to missionize them failed, and the missionary was forced to leave. The *Amahuaca* continued to avoid the Ucayali River peoples (Izaguirre, 1922–29, 9:308–315, 325; Fry, 1889, 1:100). In 1925, the *Amahuaca,* numbering about 3,000, were still hostile to Whites and to other Indians, except the *Campa* and *Cashinahua,* the latter their close relatives. They lived at the sources of the Juruá, Purús, and Embira Rivers and on the upper and right tributaries of the Ucayali and Urubamba Rivers, from the Tamaya River in the north to the Sepahua River in the south. They were little acculturated (Tessmann, 1930). The Peruvian *Amahuaca* were estimated at 1,500 in 1940.

Amenguaca.—Possibly *Amenguaca* is a synonym of *Amahuaca.* These Indians lived on the Imiria River. The best known of their many groups and subgroups are the *Inuvaqueu* and *Viuivaqueu.* In 1690, Father Ricter found them hostile (Maroni, 1889–92, 26:234–235; 30:150–151).

Maspo.—The *Maspo,* mentioned only in 1686, were a tribe which, like the *Amahuaca,* avoided the Ucayali River. There were 26 huts with 500 people 2 leagues up the Taco River and others 3 days up the Manipaboro River, right tributaries of the Ucayali River, lat. 9° S., long. 74° W. (Izaguirre, 1922–29, 1:272).

Yuminahua.—This tribe lived on the Riosinho and Tejo Rivers, and in the Tarahuacá mountains near the *Amahuaca* (Villanueva, 1902–03, 12:427).

Ruanagua.—The *Ruanagua* were reported in 1663 on the Ucayali River, above the *Maspo,* especially at the mouth of the Corjuamia (Curahuania) River (Galt, ms.) and in 1686, 1 day up the "Coraguania" River and on the upper Taraba River (Izaguirre, 1922–29, 1:276–277). (Lat. 11° S., long. 74° W.) They were subsequently associated with the *Comobo* at the junction of the Ucayali and Apurimac (probably Urubama) Rivers (Skinner, 1805, p. 429). In 1830 they remained in the same general area.

Pichobo.—The *Pichobo* (*Pichaba*) are mentioned in 1663 and in 1686 as a tribe on the Ucayali at the mouth of the Taguanigua River (Galt, ms.; Izaguirre, 1922–29, 1:276). They were mapped in 1830 in the same region.

Soboibo (*Soboybo, Sobobo, Soboyo, Soyboibo, Bolbo*).—A tribe mentioned in 1686 in the region of the Taguanigua and Cohengua Rivers (Izaguirre, 1922–29, 1:276), where they remained in 1830 (lat. 11° S., long. 74° W.).

Mochobo (*Mochovo, Univitza*).—The *Mochobo* lived in 1663 between the Guanini (Unini?) and Guanie Rivers (Galt, ms.), and in 1686 between the Guarini and Guanué Rivers, left tributaries of the Ucayali (Izaguirre, 1922–29, 1:277). (Lat. 12° S., long. 74° W.) They seem to have been closely associated geographically and historically with the *Comobo.*

Comobo (*Comavo, Comambo, Univitza*).—The *Comobo* and *Mochobo,* according to Maroni, lived between the Unini and Inua Rivers above the *Conibo.* The *Mochobo* were on the Unini River, the *Comobo* on the Inua, Sepa, and Mapoa Rivers (Maroni, 1889–92, 26:234–335; 30:137). In 1686, the *Comobo* were with the *Ruanagua* on the upper Tarabo (Tambo?) River; in 1687, on the right side of the Tambo River (Izaguirre, 1922–29, 1:227, 294). In 1688, they asked for a missionary. In 1693, those on the Sepa River, hard-pressed by the *Piro Upatarinavo,* went to a *Conibo* mission (Maroni, 1889–92, 30:152). The *Comobo* are subsequently unknown.

Nocomán.—This tribe was first identified by Tessmann (1930) as a people who had been confused with the *Cashibo* but who really constituted a distinct but small group, once living near the sources of the Inua River (lat. 11° S., long. 72°–73° W.), thence moving to the Amueya River and later to the Tamaya River, where the *Chama* nearly annihilated them. In 1925, only three survived.

Unidentified tribes of the Ucayali region.—Several tribal names appearing on early maps or in early documents without identification were probably *Panoan.* Many of these occupied the hinterland east of the Ucayali River where, perhaps like the better-known *Remo* and *Amahuaca,* they avoided the predatory river tribes, but also escaped the attention of travelers. In the general region between the Ucayali and Tapiche Rivers were the *Ysunagua, Diabu, Sinabu, Viabu, Puyamanawa,* and *Aguanagua* (Izaguirre, 1922–29; Sobreviela map, 1830). Other tribes, perhaps in the same region or farther south, were the *Chunti, Ormiga,* and *Trompetero* (Izaguirre, 1922–29). East of the Alto Ucayali, above its junction with the Pachitea River, in addition to the *Maspo, Amahuaca, Pichobo,* and *Soboyo* already mentioned, were the *Saninahuaca* on the Chesaya River and the *Camarinagua* on the Cumaria River, both shown on the Sobreviela map of 1830.

SOURCES

The outstanding historical source is Izaguirre's compilation of missionary documents (in 14 volumes, 1922–1929). Other early 17th- and 18th-century records are found in Maroni (1889–92), Escobar y Mendoza (1769), Velasco (1842–44), Rel. geogr. Indias (1881–1897); Figueroa (1904), Raimondi (1862), Veigl (1785 a), Fritz (1922), Hervás (1800–05, vol. 1), Amich (1854), and Jiménez de la Espada (Noticas . . ., 1889–92).

The 19th-century travelers include Skinner (1805), Herndon and Gibbon (1853–54, vol. 1), Galt, 1870–72 (ms.), Marcoy (1875), Fry (1889), and Ordinaire (1892).

The principal work of the present century is Tessmann's general survey (1930) and his monograph (1928) on the *Chama* (i.e., the *Setebo, Shipibo,* and *Conibo*). Farabee (1922) provides some supplementary details. Rivet (1924) has given the most systematic linguistic classification. Other data are contained in Sagols (1902), Villanueva (1902–03, vol. 12), Woodroffe (1914), and Fejos (ms.).

CULTURE

SUBSISTENCE ACTIVITIES

Farming.—Sweet manioc and maize seem to have been the staple crops since earliest records in 1665 (Figueroa, 1904, p. 206; Amich, 1854, p 264; Herndon and Gibbon, 1853–54, vol. 1), though plantain now ranks with them (Tessmann, 1928). Bitter manioc has never been grown. Other cultivated plants that were probably aboriginal are: pumpkins of several varieties, peanuts, cyclanthera, tuber beans (*Pachyrhizus tuberosus*), papaya, red pepper (ají), scitamea (*Calathea*), sweet potatoes, and macabo (*Xanthosoma* sp.). A banana like the eastern Asiatic *Musa cocinea* with fruit that stands erect is thought native by Tessmann (1928, p. 147), but see Sauer (Handbook, vol. 6). Several important plants have been introduced during the historic period: Bananas (*Musa paradisiaca*, subsp. *sapientum*), sugarcane, yams (*Dioscorea trifida*), *Chrysophyllum cainito*, anona, a variety of macobo, pineapples, taro, and beans, the last two in 1791 (Izaguirre, 1922–29, 8:254). Rice, coffee, and onions have become important in the last century. Other crops, the origin of which is uncertain, are cashew (*Anacardium occidentale*), *Inga*, *Matisia cordata*, maranta, and guava. The *Chama* also grow tomatoes, watermelons, and *Passiflora quadrangularis*.

The *Panoans* cultivate cotton for weaving, genipa and urucú for paint, reeds for arrow shafts, two species of fish poison, and tobacco.

Cultivation follows the usual slash-and-burn pattern, men doing the heavy work. New clearings are necessary every 2 or 3 years (Herndon and Gibbon, 1853–54, 1:202). Among the *Pano*, the settlement helped a man clear his fields and was rewarded with a drinking bout (Izaguirre, 1922–29, 8:246). The *Chama* place their main fields on high ground but grow peanuts in sandy soil by the river. They plant sweet manioc, yams, and macabo, in the same field, with various palm trees scattered throughout and a border of bananas, guava, anona, and other fruit trees. Manioc is harvested 7 to 8 months after the shoots are set out (Tessmann, 1928, pp. 137–130).

Fishing.—Fish, turtles, and river mammals are important foods to all Ucayali River peoples, and especially to the *Aguano*. During the historic period, salt fish became an important trade item. About 1850, Herndon and Gibbon (1853–54, 1:197) estimated that 25 Indians could collect and salt 4,000 pieces of fish in 6 weeks, or 4 pieces per day per person.

Fishing devices used on the main stream of the Ucayali are like those of the *Tupian* and other tribes of the lower Marañón River: the bow and arrow with single, multiple, and harpoon points (pl. 48, *bottom*); fish spears with single and multiple points (fig. 80, *d*); and harpoons (fig. 80, *e*), thrown mainly with the atlatl (which has recently been discarded). Tribes like the *Urarina*, living along small streams, seem to lack these methods (Veigl, 1785 a, p. 68). Most *Panoans* drug fish with cultivated plants, such as *Lonchocarpus nicou, Tephrosia toxicaria*, and *Clibadium sylvestre*. The *Sabela* use a wild plant called "mandiko." The leaves and branches of these plants are beaten with a wooden mallet, mixed with water in a canoe, and dumped into a stream, after which whole canoe loads of fish may be picked up (Tessmann, 1928, pp. 132–133, 145–146).

Other fishing devices are of spotty occurrence: the dip net (*Chamicura, Aguano*), hand basket (*Omurana, Cashibo*), and hooks (*Omurana, Aguano,* and *Nocomán*), which are probably recent. Herndon and Gibbon (1853–54, 1:172–173) note that fish of the lower Marañón, though numerous, do not readily take a hook, and Figueroa (1904) said that the *Aguano* first got hooks from the Spaniards. Weirs, perhaps native, are placed across the mouths of lagoons and have openings for canoes to pass through (Tessmann, 1928, p. 116).

Turtles (pl. 48, *bottom*) and turtle eggs, taken during low water in late August, were formerly of great importance, but have recently decreased in numbers and laws now restrict their exploitation. They are mainly a source of grease, an important article of commerce with the White man. The grease is scraped from turtle intestines or rendered from the eggs, which are crushed with water in a canoe-shaped trough. The grease is skimmed off, boiled, and salted down in jars (Marcoy, 1875, 2:33–35). Turtles are sometimes kept in corrals.

The Ucayali *Panoans* spear manatee with iron harpoons which have a wooden float attached (Izaguirre, 1922–29, 8:252). They usually avoid caimans but occasionally kill them with the bow and arrow (Tessmann, 1928, p. 113).

Hunting.—The *Panoans* eat water hogs, pacas, agutis, squirrels, potos, bears, deer, tapirs, peccaries, monkeys, water fowl, parrots, and sometimes water snakes and small caimans, but eschew opossum, bats, ant-eaters, sloths, snakes, and carrion birds. Monkeys, waterhogs, and young bucks are most important (Tessmann, 1928, p. 142), but Woodroffe (1914, p. 79) declares that *Chama* will not kill deer.

The *Nocomán, Cashibo,* and *Amahuaca* use the bow and arrow for hunting, but all lower Ucayali tribes use the blowgun for small game and the spear, formerly thrown with the atlatl, for large game. Other *Panoan* hunting devices are: hunting dogs (wherever the dog occurs), blinds, usually in the form of a small house, pitfalls with sharpened stakes in the bottom, hunting nets (sporadically used), and a variety of deadfalls, spring noose, and box traps. The *Chama* also make animal calls of a hollow caiman or jaguar tooth (Woodroffe, 1914, p. 66).

Collecting wild plant foods.—The *Chama* rarely gather wild plant food in great quantities. The main species are palms, especially chonta, *Euterpe, Astrocaryum, Iriartea, Guilielma, Scheela,* and *Jessenia bataua.* Use of the cabbage palm was introduced (Tessmann, 1928, p. 144). Wild fruits eaten include *Pourouma cecropiifolia, Noyera mollis, Achras sapota,* and *Lucuma lateriflora.* Various nuts were also eaten.

The *Chama* eat snails (*Ampullaria* and *Achatina*), "crabs" or "shrimps," insects, beetle larvae from *Scheelea* palm nuts, termites, and honey (Tessmann, 1928, p. 143).

Food preparation.—The *Chama* and *Aguano* crush manioc with a wooden pounder in a trough and grind maize, manioc, and peanuts on a wooden board with a grooved chopper, but the *Setebo* and *Amahuaca* use a stone grinder. A wooden mortar and pestle is used for plantains (figs. 78, *d;* 80, *h*). The *Chama* food grater is a paddle-shaped board studded with wires—formerly with wooden splinters. The *Amahuaca* employ a thorny root.

Nearly every house on the lower Huallaga and Ucayali Rivers has a roller sugarcane press, but the *Cashibo* and *Nocomán* squeeze the cane with a stick, while the *Amahuaca* and *Urarina* merely suck it.

The *Chama* boil meat, fish, and vegetables in a pot, roast them in ashes, or fry them when sea cow (manatee) fat is available. They smoke meat and fish on a pyramidal babracot or an improvised frame (Tessmann, 1928, p. 146).

These tribes season their foods with several varieties of cultivated pepper (*Capsicum*), spices, and salt, the last obtained from the *Cashibo,* who mine it on the upper Pisqui River and trade it widely (Tessmann, 1928, p. 163). They eat from pottery bowls, using their fingers, shells, or, recently, wooden spoons and drink from incised calabashes or fruit shells (Tessmann, 1928, pp. 172–173).

Drinks, both fermented and unfermented, supply much nourishment. Palm fruits, plantains, manioc, maize, yams, sugarcane, and even peanuts are mixed with water and drunk. Manioc or maize chicha, or masata, fermented with chewed sweet potato, affords both a food and intoxicant. Fermented manioc carried on journeys is diluted in water and eaten.

Domesticated animals.—In aboriginal times, the *Panoan* tamed wild animals, e.g., pigs, parrots (Izaguirre, 1922–29, 8:245), monkeys and agutis (Tessmann 1928, pp. 97–99). They later acquired chickens, the *Chama* believing that theirs came from the *Inca.* At first the *Conibo* ate neither chickens nor their eggs, fearing blindness (Izaguirre, 1922–29, 1:310) ; now they consume both, but more often trade them to the White man. Ducks were seemingly introduced in the early post-Contact Period, though the Muscovy duck may have been native. Domesticated pigs are more recent and are found at only a few villages (Tessmann, 1928, pp. 97–98). The dog may not be native, but it was used for hunting at an early date.

HOUSES AND VILLAGES

A large house sheltering one to several families constitutes the *Panoan* village or community. Tessmann believes that the original *Chama, Amahuaca, Cashibo,* and *Panobo* house had a gabled roof which was supported by two or three center posts and sloped to posts forming side walls (pl. 49, *top*). *Aguano, Chamicura,* and *Urarina* had a dwelling of the

Chébero type, 60 feet (20 m.) by 17 feet (5.5 m.), the roof being supported by beams and rafters instead of by center posts. The *Buiño* and *Huiño Cashibo* made a beehive type house, while the *Nocomán* built a conical hut with 4 central posts to support the roof. Under Spanish influence, the *Chama* and perhaps other tribes have recently adopted the *Chébero* type. (See Tessmann, 1928, 1930.)

The *Mayo* (Izaguirre, 1922–29, 12:430) were alleged to have made a tightly closed structure inside a gabled roof, the customary darkness of which trained their eyes for night fighting!

In addition to dwellings, the *Panoan* tribes construct potters' shacks, storehouses, chicken houses, and a variety of shades and temporary shelters. The 18th-century *Pano* built guard houses where they stored their weapons and kept a sentry to watch for enemies (Izaguirre, 1922–29, 8:247–248).

The *Panoan* tribes used to sleep on a mat on the ground, though the *Aguano, Chamicura, Panobo, Pano, Nocomán, Shipibo,* and *Urarina* have recently adopted platform beds and use hammocks for resting. *Itucale* and *Chamicura* infants sleep in hammocks. Only the *Amahuaca* and *Remo* adults normally sleep in hammocks. To escape mosquitoes, the *Chamicura* use a cover, formerly of mats, now of imported netting, while the *Pano* make a cotton-cloth tent. The *Urarina* sleep under a densely woven bast mosquito net. A wooden stool, made of a half log, is used by men on the lower Ucayali, women sitting on mats.

DRESS AND ORNAMENTS

Garments.—Customary nudity was undoubtedly very common at one time, despite occasional use of various garments, but missionary precepts instilled ideas of modesty, which led first to the spread and more frequent use of native garments (pl. 49, *bottom*), and later to adoption of some White man's clothes. In 1782, the *Carapacho* (Izaguirre, 1922–29, 5:132) and in 1800 the *Capanahua, Sensi,* and *Mayo* (Izaguirre, 1922–29, 9:41; 12:436) were still nude. In 1834, among the *Cashibo,* who were little affected by missions, men continued to go naked but women sometimes wore cotton loincloths (Izaguirre, 1922–29, 9:104). Galt (ms.), however, found these women still nude in 1871 and saw only one woman wearing a loincloth, but in 1925, all *Chama* were fastidious, even newborn babies being immediately clad in shirts, and girls of 5 or 6 changing to skirts. The *Aguano* wore European dress, and the *Cashibo* made a great virtue of modesty (Tessmann, 1928, pp. 66–67, 120).

Nakedness in men had a high correlation throughout the Montaña with some method of tying up the genitals, the distribution of which is, however, spotty. The *Cashibo* and *Nocomán* bound up the foreskin of the penis with a thread (pl. 50), whereas the *Amahuaca, Remo,* and *Setebo* fastened it up with a string of *Astrocaryum* passed around the waist (Tessmann, 1930, plate 10, map 1.).

Garments were known long before they gained everyday use. In 1686, the *Conibo* had painted shirts for men, and shirts and shoulder capes for women; these were embroidered with colored threads (Izaguirre, 1922–29, 1:309). But, like the cushma (pl. 49, *bottom*), which was recorded before 1767 (Amich, 1854, p. 264), it was reserved for special occasions. *Aguano* men wore short skirts (Figueroa, 1904, p. 434); in 1851, Herndon and Gibbon (1853–54, 1:170) found them still unclad above the waist. *Urarina* women wore skirts (Izaguirre 1922–29, 8:106). Herndon and Gibbon (1853–54, 1:198) attributed the cushma to the *Remo, Shipibo,* and other Ucayali River tribes. The *Chama* cushma is made either of bark cloth or of woven cotton. Though mainly a man's garment, *Chama* women also wore it. That of the *Setebo* is distinguished by its short sleeves (Izaguirre, 1922–29, 12:440).

The short *Shipibo* men's shirt with sleeves and the *Nocomán* sleeveless shirt are probably recent.

Women usually wear some form of skirt or apron covering at least their genitals (pl. 50). The *Amahuaca, Remo,* and *Campa* wear an apron suspended from a string. A woman's skirt, consisting of a single strip of cloth sewed together at the ends to form a tube, is used among the *Urarina, Chama, Chamicura, Panobo,* and *Nocomán. Yuminahua* and *Amahuaca* women wear a cotton skirt and nothing else (Villanueva, 1902–03, 12:427).

A woman's shawl or mantle, worn over the shoulders and sometimes over the head, and used to carry children, is characteristic of the *Chama.*

All of these garments often have panels, woven of different colors, in which are painted designs characteristic of the area (pl. 49). *Chama* paints are red, black, purple, yellow, and white, obtained mainly from several plants listed by Tessmann (1928, pp. 157–158). Several other plants are used to perfume shirts (ibid, p. 159).

Head deformation.—The Ucayali tribes—*Chama, Cashibo, Shipibo, Conibo,* and *Nocomán*—compress an infant's head for 4 days after birth under a pad on the forehead held in place by a board and a band passing around the head (figs. 76, 77; Tessmann, 1930, map 2). The *Conibo* of Castañeda's day compressed the head between two boards for a year (Izaguirre, 1922–29, 1:305–306). Skinner also observed this in 1805. In 1851, Herndon and Gibbon (1853–54, p. 199), reporting deformation between two boards, one on the forehead, the other behind, said that the effect was not observable in adults. But Gabriel Sala, observing this in 1896 (Izaguirre, 1922–29, 10:48), said the effect lasted throughout life.

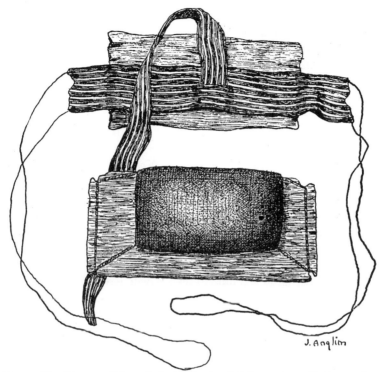

J. Anglim

FIGURE 76.—*Panoan (Chama)* device for head deformation. (Redrawn from Tessmann, 1928.)

FIGURE 77.—*Panoan (Shipibo)* mother and children. The head of the infant is undergoing artificial deformation. (After Farabee, 1922.)

Headdress.—The *Chama* formerly wore their hair long but now cut it medium length, with bangs on the forehead. They dye it with the juice of genipa or of *Justicia inficiens.* The *Capanahua* shave (?) their heads (Villanueva, 1902–03, 12 :426). *Chama* combs are made of small reed stems, the teeth bound between transverse reeds and woven with cotton threads. The *Conibo* use a jagged seed. Hair is cut with a bamboo knife. The *Chama* originally used no head covering but now wear straw hats or handkerchiefs. Festival feather headgear is used by all tribes.

Depilation.—The *Chama* pluck their sparse beards with tweezers made of two mussel shells tied together; the *Nocomán* shave with bamboo knives. The *Panobo* used to smear tree gum on the skin, then remove it with the hair adhering to it.

Ear, nose, and lip ornaments.—The ears, noses, and lips were perforrated, often with many holes, through which ornaments could be suspended (pls. 49, *bottom;* 51). An early observer counted 28 holes in the nose and lips of a *Remo* (Izaguirre, 1922–29, 9 :208). The *Amahuaca* passed a stick through the nasal septum. The Ucayali River *Panoans* preferred to suspend a silver ball or crescent from a cotton thread through the septum but might use sticks, shells, or other materials. Similarly, sticks, feathers, and pendants of various materials, silver preferred, were put in the lips and through several holes in each ear.

Tooth blackening.—Stained teeth occurred among the *Urarina, Chama, Amahuaca, Panobo, Setebo, Shipibo,* and *Conibo.* The *Chama* chewed the stem of a pepper, *Piper pseudochurumayu,* grown specially for this purpose. The *Chamicuro* darkened their teeth by chewing an unidentified fruit. The *Aguano* filed their incisors to points.

Miscellaneous ornaments.—All these tribes wear a wide variety of forehead bands, necklaces, chest bands, bracelets, rings, and leg bands made of seeds, sweet grass, monkey teeth, and other materials. Early *Aguano* wore anklets and garters of human hair (Figueroa, 1904, p. 258).

Paint and tattoo.—Use of paint on the face, arms, legs, and body was common. *Chama* colors were: black (genipa), red from the fruit shell of *Bixa,* and a reddish yellow from the bark of *Bixa.* The *Cashibo* clean their bodies with grease.

The *Amahuaca* tatooed the face, the *Remo* and *Sensi* the face and body, and the *Sensi* even the penis. They performed the operation during childhood, using a thorn and copal soot.

TRANSPORTATION

Canoes and rafts.—Well-made canoes are used on the Ucayali River, but some tribes, such as the *Cashibo* and *Amahuaca* living on smaller or more rapid streams, had no use for boats and used only balsa rafts (Galt, ms.), which consisted of five pieces of wood (Izaguirre, 1922–29, 9 :99).

The *Urarina* learned to canoe and to fish only after they were settled on the Marañón River (Veigl, 1785 a, p. 68).

In 1800, *Conibo* canoes were 50 to 60 feet (about 15 to 18 m.) long and 3 to 5 feet (1 to 1.5 m.) wide, with both the stern and the prow a "pyramidal point." These canoes, which took a year to build, were made of a tree felled with a stone ax. The limbs were burned off, the outside was shaped with fire, the inside was burned out, and the canoe was scraped with flint until the hull was 3 to 4 inches thick. Then, by filling the canoe with water and building a slow fire outside, the cavity was widened and braced with crosspieces (Skinner, 1805, p. 443). Seventy-five years later, these canoes were described as 10 to 20 feet (3 to 6 m.) long (Marcoy, 1875, 2:37–38).

The modern *Chama* and *Aguano* made dugout canoes of *Calophyllum brasiliense,* mahogany (*Swietenia tessmannii*), a species of *Leguminosae,* and, most favored, the soft wood of (*Cedrela longipetiolulata*). The tree is felled, moved to the shore on rollers, and hollowed with an adze, fire being used only to harden the finished vessel. The canoe is trough-shaped, the bow usually having a rhomboid head in which holes are cut and the stern being furnished with a square, flat piece. Holes and cracks are temporarily filled with clay but are permanently mended with resin of the copal tree or of *Clarisia racemosa* (Tessmann, 1928, pp. 123–124).

Ucayali River paddles have a narrow blade and a crutch handle (fig. 78, *i*). *Shipibo* paddles have blades narrower than those of the *Conibo*.

Carrying devices.—*Chama* men habitually carry their pipes and other articles in a small woven cotton bag. The hexagonally woven burden basket is probably in general use. A child may be carried in the mother's shawl, or in a special band (fig. 77).

MANUFACTURES

Basketry.—Basketry products are distinctive neither in weave nor form. They include woven and twined sleeping mats, women's sitting mats, fire fans, round and square food storage containers, chicha sieves, women's trinket and workbaskets, and carrying baskets. The last, made with a hexagonal weave, is produced by most of the tribes, though the *Chama* obtain theirs in trade (Tessmann, 1928, 1930).

Weaving.—Three-ply cord, used for various purposes, is usually made of wild *Astrocaryum* and *Cecropia leucocoma* bast, the former being more abundant on the upper Ucayali River. The *Nocomán* make bast hammocks, and the *Panobo* knit bast bags; the *Urarina* make both, and loom-weave loincloths, mosquito nets, cushion covers, and bast bags.

True weaving is done with cultivated cotton, which is cleaned by hand and spun with a spindle having a clay, bone, tortoise-shell or hardwood whorl, and resting on the ground or in a calabash or pot. It is woven on

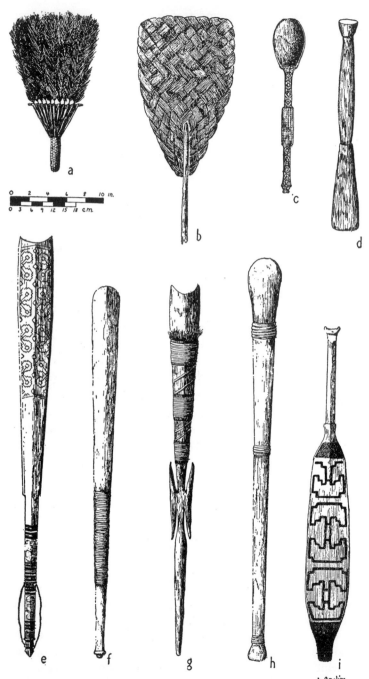

J. Anglim

FIGURE 78.—*Chama* and *Cahuapana* utensils. *a*, Feather fire fan; *b*, woven fire fan; *c*, wooden spoon; *d*, wooden food pounder; *e–h*, wooden clubs (macana type); *i*, canoe paddle. (*f*, *Cahuapana*, all others *Chama*.) (*a–e*, *h*, *i*, Redrawn from Tessmann, 1928, pls. 21, 50, 45, 59, 31; *f*, *g*, redrawn from Tessmann, 1930, map 23.)

two types of loom.   The first, used for cushmas, shirts, loincloths, and large bands, is the horizontal belt loom: the stick holding the warp at one end is attached to the weaver's belt, the other end to her feet, or, if the loom is large, to a house post.   The second, called the "Ucayali loom," consists of a small, oval frame.   The warp runs between one end of the frame and the transverse stick affixed inside the other end.   Fabrics produced on the belt loom have an ordinary in-and-out weave and are made with the help of a weaving sword.   The weave on the "Ucayali loom" is, as in Guiana, accomplished by first crossing over the warp elements and holding them in place with small sticks, then drawing through weft strands to replace each stick.   Textiles have both woven-in and painted-on decoration (Tessmann, 1928, 1930).

Pottery.—An excellent and beautifully painted pottery ware distinguishes the *Panoan* from other Montaña tribes (figs. 73, 74; pl. 52). Rectilinear designs in red-and-black-on-cream are applied to vessels ranging from small bowls and jars to huge chicha vessels 2 or 3 feet in diameter (pl. 52).   These ceramics are best developed among the *Conibo* (pl. 52, *a*), *Shipibo,* and *Setebo.*   The *Amahuaca* and *Nocomán* paint none of their ware, ornamenting merely with punched elements.   The *Cashibo* make only unornamented red bowls and incised cook pots.   The *Chamicura* and *Urarina* make fingernail-decorated cook pots, red and white water jugs,

FIGURE 79.—*Panobo* bowl, white and red.   (Redrawn from Tessmann, 1930, color pl. 6.)

and bowls with smoke blackened interiors.   *Aguano* ceramics include punctate-decorated cooking pots and vessels with Spanish shapes and ornamentation.

The *Chama* vessels are made of various clays mixed with the ashes of *Licania* bark (Rosaceae); construction is by coiling.   Red and black designs are painted with hair brushes over a white slip; small incised lines may provide additional decoration.   A pot is baked inside an old jar filled with ashes; subsequently it is glazed both inside and out with rosin (Burseraceae).   Bowl interiors are sometimes soot-blackened over a fire (Tessmann, 1928).   Marcoy (1875, 2:27) states that a woman was supposed to dance while the *Conibo* baked a pot and that the vessel interior was glazed with copal gum and the exterior painted black (soot), yellow (Guttiferae), blue (indigo), green (pepper leaves), and red (urucú).

The *Amahuaca* make pottery tobacco pipes.

Modeled potsherds with human and animal heads found in the vicinity of Yarino Cocha were disclaimed by modern *Chama* (Tessmann, 1928, p. 26).

Woodworking.—Wood carving is exclusively a man's industry. *Chama* wooden products include bowls, molds, troughs, stamps, stools, sugarcane presses, spoons, and pipes (Tessmann, 1928, p. 95).

Weapons.—For hunting, the principal aboriginal weapon on the lower Ucayali—*Panobo, Setebo, Shipibo, Urarina, Aguano,* and *Conibo*—was the blowgun, whereas the blowgun was lacking and the bow and arrow was used for both hunting and warfare among the hinterland tribes—*Nocomán, Cashibo* (pl. 50, *left*), and *Amahuaca.* The bow and arrow was probably aboriginal also on the lower Ucayali, but gained importance only after the dart and spear thrower were abandoned, when it became chiefly a fishing weapon. Firearms are now increasingly used.

Early *Remo* bows were 7 to 9 feet (about 2.1 to 2.7 m.) long and semicircular in cross section, but in 1834, they were round in cross section (Izaguirre, 1922–29, 9:91, 104). In 1870, the *Cashibo* made bows about 6 feet (2 m.) long of chonta palm (Galt, ms.). *Conibo* also made chonta palm bows (Marcoy, 1875, 2:31). The modern *Chama* bow is of *Guilielma* palm, square or D-shaped in cross section, with a string of *Cecropia* and *Astrocaryum* fibers (Tessmann, 1928, pp. 140–141).

The early arrows (Izaguirre, 1922–29, 9:104; Galt, ms.) were 6 feet (2 m.) long and featherless, having a chonta palm point and various kinds of barbs. The *Cashibo* were distinguished for their long arrows. Modern arrows have four kinds of points for hunting: bamboo blades for large game; barbed palm-rod points for small game and birds; one or two pieces of bone arranged to form a barb for small game; and a knob head for birds. Only the last lacks feathers; the others have flush, wrapped feathers. *Chama* fish arrows have three prongs (*Amahuaca,* four) set in the same plane, the points often tipped with barbed iron, but for swarms of fish, seven palm points are set around the shaft (Tessmann, 1928, pp. 122, 141). The *Chama* also make two kinds of harpoon arrows. One has three detachable parts, the shaft, foreshaft, and wooden point with iron barbs, all three held together with a cord and separating after being shot into a fish. The other, used to shoot turtles, has only two detachable parts; the main shaft and the foreshaft are permanently joined, but the plain iron point is detachable. Both kinds have two feathers (Tessmann, 1928, p. 122). *Cashibo* hunting arrows resemble those of the *Chama,* though they are often featherless, but war arrows are large and beautifully ornamented, often having

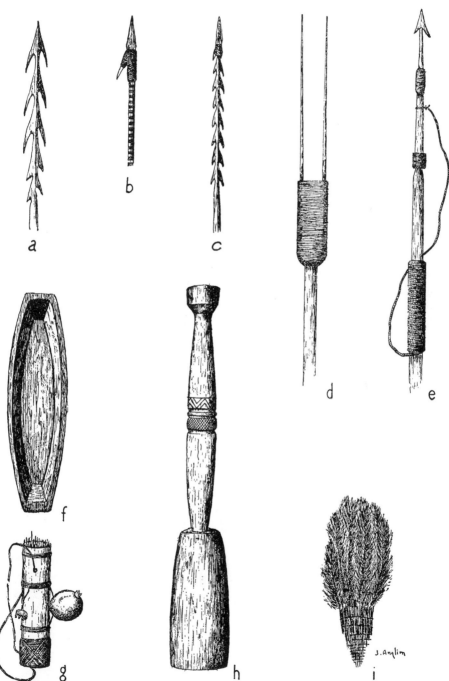

FIGURE 80.—Montaña artifacts. *a-c, Cashibo* spear points; *d, Aguano* two-pronged spear; *e, Aguano* harpoon; *f, Aguano* wooden dish; *g, Aguano* quiver with blowgun darts; *h, Aguano* food pounder; *i, Chébero* feather fire fan. (*a-c,* 1/13 actual size; *d-i,* 1/16 actual size.)   (Redrawn from Tessmann, 1930, pls. 15, 46, 42, 45.)

women's hair attached. These are the center of *Cashibo* art interest (Tessmann, 1930, pl. 15, figs. 1–14).

The *Chama* blowgun is made of two halves of *Iriartea deltoidea* wood, bound together with wrapping covered with copal and equipped with a mouthpiece of two jaguar or crocodile teeth. The largest are 7½ feet (2.5 m.) long. Darts, bearing poison procured in trade from the Huallaga River, are kept in a section of bamboo (fig. 80, *g;* Tessmann, 1928, pp. 138–139).

Tessmann states (1928, 1930) that the *Chama* and *Panobo* formerly used a throwing board to cast fish arrows (darts?), but have given it up. The *Chama* fish spear has one or two barbed iron points and a cord attached to the butt end by which to recover it if it slips from the fisherman's hand (Tessmann, 1928, pp. 112, 115). The *Chama* harpoon has a 9-foot shaft, a foreshaft, and a detachable barbed iron head fastened to a wooden float (Tessmann, 1928, p. 119). Spears have a varying number of barbs (fig. 80, *a*).

The macana, or wooden club, was recorded for the *Sensi* in 1834 (Izaguirre, 1922–29, 9:88) but was probably of general distribution. It was used in duels, especially over adultery, more than in warfare. Recent *Chama* specimens are shown in figure 78, *e–h*. The *Sensi* shield of 1834 had a circular rim of creeper covered with hide (Izaguirre, 1922–29, 9:88). For a scalping knife, the *Chama* carried the upper part of a toucan beak, hung around the neck by a cord (Tessmann, 1928, p. 222). In aboriginal times, stone knives were also used. Recent *Chama* show some skill in metallurgy: they shape the iron knife with heat, burn the blade into the handle, and fasten it with wax and fiber (Woodroffe, 1914, p. 66).

Skinner (1805) stated of the *Chuncho* generally that a missionary

brought from Manoa one of these hatchets [of stone], in shape perfectly resembling ours, but which, instead of a handle, was provided with two ears, with a channel to secure the extremity by the means of cords. The Indians manufacture them with other stones, aided by the chambo, or small copper axe, and then with water and patience proceed to sharpen them.

Fire making.—Tessmann (1930) states that the *Nocomán* did not know how to make fire and that few remembered using the fire drill. Evidently flint and steel supplanted the drill at an early date. The *Urarina,* however, use the drill and, for a stunt, two stones. Fire fans, either woven of feathers or made of matting (figs. 78, *a, b;* 80, *i*) are of general distribution. The *Chamicura* use a rosin torch; the *Urarina* one of beeswax or a bunch of certain seeds on a stick.

ECONOMIC LIFE AND TRADE

The family was evidently self-sufficient for essential wants, though communal assistance in preliminary farm clearing was probably given.

The large house was community property; so, perhaps, was the canoe, chicha jar, and other objects.

Aboriginal trade is little known, though Tessmann's information (1928, pp. 217–218) in 1925 that the *Chama* formerly traveled to procure white earth for painting pots, copal, white clay, varnish, and poison for blowgun darts suggests considerable barter. When iron tools, especially axes, became available during the historic period, a lively trade with the White man for these coveted objects began. The *Pano* took cinnamon, peanuts, parrots, cotton, and shawls to the missions to trade for iron and were willing to exchange a canoe that had required months of work for an ax or machete (Izaguirre, 1922–29, 8:248). In 1791, the *Conibo* were trading "bed coverings" and resin to the *Omagua* for iron tools; a canoe for an iron ax was considered a fair exchange (Skinner, 1805, p. 433; Marcoy, 1875, 2:37–38).

In the last century, several items produced by the Ucayali River Indians became major export products: turtle oil, sarsaparilla, vanilla, canelon, copaiba, sandi (Marcoy, 1875, 2:176), salt fish (peixe), manatee and charipa lard, flor de balsa (for pillows and mattresses), wax, cacao, coffee, honey, tobacco, and cedar. The Urubamba River exported cacao, coffee, cane, and wax. Although prices became standardized (Galt, ms: Herndon and Gibbon, 1853–54), exchange was usually in goods. Products received today from the Whites are axes, machetes, knives, mosquito netting, jackets, pants, handkerchiefs for covering the head, beads, mirrors, and guns. Meanwhile, Indians continue to trade among themselves. The *Campa*, for example, obtain cushmas from the *Piro*. The *Conibo* trade arrows, bows, wax, cotton, and hammocks. The *Panobo* procure blowguns from the *Setebo;* the *Conibo* get theirs from the *Chébero* in exchange for wax.

SOCIOPOLITICAL GROUPS

The aboriginal *Panoan* sociopolitical unit was the household, which evidently consisted of related families, though its precise composition and rules of descent are not known. It was also the political unit, despite the proximity of many houses to one another, and was to a large degree the economic unit. It acted as a group, moving every few years when new farm lands were cleared. It is not known whether the *Aguano,* who now have a single village of 16 houses, formerly conformed to this pattern.

Tessmann calls the *Chama* unit the "kin," meaning sib, but fails to demonstrate sib characteristics. He states that the *Nocomán* and *Amahuaca* lacked the "kin."

The household community has persisted since earliest times. Even mission life, when scores of people were concentrated in large villages, failed to destroy it, for families returned to their aboriginal separatism after leaving the missions. The 1,000 *Shipibo* were, prior to 1800, scattered in communities of a single family each (Skinner, 1805, p. 409). The *Sensi* in 1834 were split into small groups under the leadership of family heads (Izaguirre, 1922–29, 9:88). Herndon's observations in 1851 (Herndon and Gibbon, 1853–54, 1:154, 170, 195–203, etc.), show the difference between missions or trade towns and native communities. The Indian population at some of the former was: Sarayacu, 1,000; Parmari, 30; San Regis, 210; Urarinas, 80; Laguna (mostly *Cocamilla*) 1,044; Santa Cruz (*Aguano*), 350; Chasuta (1,200). Some native communities were: 2 *Remos* houses, 22 people; 2 *Conibo* houses, 15; 4 *Conibo* houses, 33 persons; 3 *Conibo* communities with 30, 25, and 9 persons respectively; *Shipibo*, 25; *Piro* village with 150 persons or 33 families.

Of Indian settlements on the Ucayali in 1835, very few were still occupied in 1850, although the total population was about the same (Herndon and Gibbon, 1853–54, 1:212–213). In 1870, Galt observed that the Indian villages of this area consisted of one, two, or three families.

The *Conibo, Shipibo, Setebo, Piro, Remo,* and *Amahuaca,* wrote Herndon (Herndon and Gibbon, 1854, 1:205), were a roving people who even lived in boats. Small communities were still the rule in 1925, except where encroaching colonists had reduced the Indians to plantation workers. *Chama* houses tended to be grouped 100 to 200 m. (about 300 to 600 feet) apart around lagoons. *Amahuaca* houses were more widely separated.

The community on the lower Ucayali River was inferentially an extended matrilineal family, for the household was said to consist of the headman, his wife, his unmarried sons, and his married daughters with their husbands and children. Marriage was matrilocal and polygyny was sororal (Tessmann, 1928, 1930), or, according to older sources, a man married several women who were bought or captured. These features are consistent with matrilineal sibs or clans, though it is remarkable that the extended family household elsewhere in the Montaña is patrilineal. Tessmann (1930, pp. 127–128, 150) states that the *Cashibo* are divided into three groups, each having several "sibs" bearing animal, plant, or other names. Each "sib" seems to be localized in a scattered village, whose people will not eat their eponym. The *Setebo* have also animal-named sibs (Tessmann, 1928). Tessmann gives, however, no geneological data to indicate the descent, localization, exogamy, or other functions of *Cashibo* or *Chama* "kin," so that it is not certain that the exogamy is more than avoidance of near relatives or that the group name designates more than a community. The peripheral tribes, except possibly the *Urarina,* were less strictly matrilocal and their communities seem to have been extended patrilineal households.

Slaves, captured from the weaker *Panoan* tribes of the hinterland, were evidently an important element in the communities of the stronger Ucayali River peoples. The *Pano* used to capture *Mayoruna, Panatahua, Amahuaca,* and *Shipibo* (Izaguirre, 1922–29, 8:249; Skinner, 1805, p. 433;

Maroni, 1889–92, 30:137). *Shipibo* and *Conibo* took *Cashibo* and had nearly exterminated the *Remo* in 1870. Slaves, wrote Villanueva (1902–03, 12:428), were captured in periodic raids; a 10- or 12-year old boy was worth 500 soles, a *Campa* boy much more; a girl brought 300 to 400 soles. Many captives were sold to the Whites or other Indians, but others were incorporated into the community. Americh (1854, p. 90) remarks that *Piro* taken by the *Conibo* had to cultivate the plantations.

The aboriginal community headman was doubtless the family elder. Recently, the White man created chieftainship and defined its functions (Tessmann, 1928, pp. 217–218).

Division of labor within the household seems to have thrown the burden of productive labor on women: tilling the soil, transporting goods, cooking, weaving, making pottery, and preparing drinks (masato). Tessmann (1928, p. 211) states that a *Chama* man works for his wife's father, but sometimes contributes meat or fish to his own father's family. A pattern of group participation in land clearing and perhaps other labor is suggested, but this does not affect individual family ownership and harvest of farm plots. There is little inheritable property other than the canoe and fields which pass from a man to his son (Tessmann, 1928, p. 223). This arrangement is conceivable in the case of canoes, but in the case of fields, it is quite inconsistent with the matrilineal nature of the community and is largely meaningless, because fields were normally tilled for only about 3 years.

Matrilocal residence threw a man into daily contact with his mother-in-law, whom he had to avoid. In case of divorce, which was easy, the man returned to his own home (Tessmann, 1928, pp. 210–211).

Chama murder and suicide were unknown. Thieves were required to replace stolen goods, physical violence rarely being necessary to coerce them. Theft of a wife entailed a combat with clubs between contenders, but no one was killed, and the thief kept the woman. Adultery was settled by a combat between the husband and paramour during a drinking bout (Tessmann, 1928, pp. 221–222), but the *Amahuaca* might murder in reprisal for adultery (Tessmann, 1930).

LIFE CYCLE

Birth and childhood.—A *Panoan* mother delivers her child in isolation, assisted by other women. All tribes but the *Chamicuro* bury the umbilical cord and afterbirth. The mother is confined for varying periods, the longest being 15 days (*Cashibo*). Dieting lasts much longer. There is no couvade, and few restrictions are imposed on the father, except for a day or two of dieting and avoidance of heavy labor.

The *Chama* baby is painted and receives the head deformation board shortly after birth (fig. 76). Skinner (1805, p. 269) stated that the waist and joints of a male baby were bound to give it strength. When old

FIGURE 81.—*Panoan* (*Chama*) walking aid for infants. (Redrawn from
Tessmann, 1928.)

enough to stand, a *Chama* child plays in a pen (fig. 81). For misbehavior,
children are whipped or threatened with the jaguar. The *Chama* father
frightens disobedient children with a disguise of banana leaves and a
calabash mask. Boys play with toy canoes, bows, arrows, and the like,
and girls with dolls; there are no group games. Every child is taught
adult tasks (Tessmann, 1928, 1930).

Naming involves no ritual, no sib names. The ancient *Conibo*, however, named and baptized children at the age of 1 year, when the head
press was removed, subjected them to dietary restrictions, and gave them
herbs to develop desirable qualities and to protect them from witchcraft
(Izaguirre, 1922–29, 1:305–307).

The *Cashibo* removed an infant girl's clitoris at 2 months (Tessmann),
but the *Chama* performed this rite at puberty. Other *Panoan* tribes lacked
this practice.

Puberty.—None of these tribes have any initiation rite for boys, except
that in 1800 the *Cashibo* were said to circumcize (Izaguirre, 1922–29,
9:42).

Girl's puberty rites are usually minimal. At her first menses, the
Amahuaca do nothing to the girl. The *Cashibo* and *Nocomán* merely
isolate her for a few days, the *Urarina* confine her 10 days, the *Aguano* for
1 month, but the *Cashibo, Conibo, Setebo,* and *Shipibo* have fairly elaborate
ceremonies, featuring subincision. In 1871, Galt (ms.) said that the
Conibo held a 10-day festival, after which the girl was tied to a tree for 3

days and the operation performed, a rite he attributed also to the other three "principal" tribes of the Ucayali—probably the *Chama* group. Tessmann reports that a group of pubescent *Chama* girls were assembled at full moon while men and women danced all night and drank from special zoomorphic pots. Next morning, the girls were painted, stupefied with drink, then each laid on a bench where an older woman cut off and buried the clitoris and labia. Reich (1903) adds that the girl was deflowered with a clay penis representing her fiancé. The girl was then isolated in her hut for one month, wearing an "egg-shaped" piece of pottery as a pubic cover. (Cf. the pottery "fig leaves" of Marajó, Santarém, and the upper Xingú River.)

Cashibo girls were subincised during a feast, which started with a contest of shooting chickens, included dances and a song by women alluding to flowers, stars, etc., and culminated when the neophyte girl, leading dancers, drank herself to unconsciousness, and an old woman cut her clitoris. A wild orgy in which men fought each other followed (Izaguirre, 1922–29, 1:311–114).

Among most of these tribes, sexual relations are prohibited before puberty but condoned subsequently.

Marriage.—Data on marriage restrictions and preferential unions are unreliable. Tessmann states (1930) that the *Amahuaua* permit aunt-nephew and uncle-niece marriages, prohibiting only brother-sister unions, and the *Pano, Nocomán,* and *Chamicura* tolerate even cousin marriage, but the *Cashibo* prohibit uncle-niece alliances. The levirate was accredited to the *Chamicura* (Escobar y Mendoza, 1769, p. 45), and sororal polygyny to the *Conibo* and probably others. Probably all tribes were polygynous which, if not sororal, meant that outside women became part of the wife's family's household because of matrilocal residence. Galt (ms.) cites a *Conibo* man in 1870 who had four wives, each with children, and was on his way to buy more children from the *Piro*. Chiefs, especially, were polygynous, and the missionaries' attempt to abolish it was a major cause of rebellion.

Unions were sometimes contracted through infant betrothal (Skinner, 1805), but usually the man sought the girl's father's permission. The couple went to live permanently with the girl's family, where the man worked mainly for the support of his in-laws.

Adultery brought some punishment of the woman—the *Sensi* flogged her and spread ants on her—and a duel between the interested men (Izaguirre, 1922–29, 1:308; Tessmann, 1930).

Death observances.—Death observances varied considerably, especially in disposal of the corpse: cremation, urn burial, canoe burial, and earth burial both inside and outside the house. The main feature showing functional connection with the total culture is parenticide, that is, the occasional killing of aged relatives who had become a burden on the community. This custom is not uncommon among similar marginal peoples. Endocannibalism coupled with parenticide and with cremation also occurred sporadically.

The *Aguano* accomplished suicide with barbasco (Figueroa, 1904, p. 134). The *Conibo* and *Ruanagua* killed and ate their parents (Izaguirre, 1922–29, 1:277). In 1871 (Galt ms.), the *Cashibo* did the same when their parents were aged and helpless. Endocannibalism, possibly without parenticide, was common. In 1800, the *Capanahua* were said to eat their dead parents (Izaguirre, 1922–29, 9:41; 12:435–436); the *Cobino* and *Setebo* also ate dead relatives (Izaguirre, 1922–29, 9:104; Jiménez de la Espada, 1892, p. 4). The *Remo, Cashibo, Conibo, Yuminahua,* and *Amahuaca* coupled endocannibalism with cremation, first burning the body, then mixing the ashes with masato, and drinking them during a wake (Izaguirre, 1922–29, 12:244–748; Villanueva, 1902–03, 12:427; Maroni, 1889–92, 30:132–133). This was seen among the *Remo* as late as 1912, but the *Amahuaca,* though still cremating in 1925, did not drink the ashes.

There is some indication that urn burial, now usually restricted to children, was once more general. The *Chamicuro* were thought to have substituted cemetery for urn burial (Tessmann, 1930); the *Setebo* abandoned urn burial inside the house under missionary influence (Izaguirre, 1922–29, 8:250); and the *Conibo,* who buried under the house floor in urns in 1875, recently cremated. Burial under the house floor but not in urns is reported for the *Pano* (Izaguirre, 1922–29, 12:474), the *Chama,* in a coffin made of two canoes (Tessmann, 1928, pp. 214–216), the *Piro,* in a canoe (Herndon and Gibbons, 1853–54, vol. 1), and the upper Manay River tribes (Galt, ms.). The *Urarina* bury in the house, which they abandon (Tessmann, 1930). Burial outside the house, not in urns, is attributed to the *Panobo,* and *Nocomán* (Izaguirre, 1922–29, 12:475). The *Sensi* also bury.

Urn burial for infants occurs among the *Panobo* and *Amahuaca.*

Property of the deceased is pretty generally destroyed, leaving little to be inherited. All clothes, utensils, weapons, and personal effects are burned or buried with the corpse. Growing crops are preserved. Whether houses are burned, abandoned, or kept means little because of shifting residence. The chief remaining item, the canoe, is evidently used more and more often as a coffin.

During mourning, close female relatives wail, males maintain ceremonial silence, and both sexes wear old clothes, cut the hair, and do not marry again for some months. The *Remo* even mourn deceased pets.

WARFARE

These tribes have probably always been in a state of strife because of enmities created by slave raids, so that retaliation as well as slaving serve as war motives. The main aggressors were the *Chama, Shipibo, Conibo,* and *Setebo*. Victims were the smaller tribes, away from the main course of the Ucayali River. Of the latter, one of the principal victims, the *Cashibo,* made much of warfare and expended their main art talents on war arrows. Fights consist of sudden, stealthy attacks by expeditions of men.

The spear thrower was formerly used in warfare on the lower Ucayali. but recently the bow and unpoisoned arrow have become the principal weapons. Other weapons are slings (*Cashibo*), thrusting spears (*Cashibo*), clubs (*Cashibo, Amahuaca, Capanahua, Setebo, Nocomán*), and a knife for cutting up victims (*Cashibo*). The *Sensi* formerly used circular hide shields (Izaguirre, 1922–29, 12:436). Caltrops were never employed, but the *Cashibo* and *Nocomán* set unpoisoned stakes in defensive trenches. The *Cashibo* shot from behind palm screens.

An *Urarina* warrior slit the skin along his nose to form an arch of flesh, its length indicating his prowess (Maroni, 1889–92, 27:72).

Cannibalism of war victims has not been reported, but various trophies were taken: scalps (*Aguano, Chama*), heads (*Cashibo, Setebo*), lower limbs and forearms (*Cashibo*). The *Aguano* wore human-hair belts and hung scalps on their leg bands. The *Itucale* in 1665 removed and smoked the skins from enemies' heads, then filled them with grass to form masks (Skinner, 1805, p. 289). A house full of trophy skulls gave a *Setebo* man social status and helped him get many wives. A *Cashibo* preserved his enemy's skull and wore his teeth as a necklace.

ESTHETIC AND RECREATIONAL ACTIVITIES

Art.—A well-defined art style characterizes the *Panoan* tribes of the Ucayali River and extends south among the *Arawakan* people at least to the *Campa*. The style consists essentially of complex angular, geometric designs drawn in rectangular panels. Most characteristically, the design is formed by a heavy line outlined by one or two fine lines. Colors are usually black and red on a cream or white background, but occasionally negative designs, white-on-black, are used. Such decorations are applied to most objects—pots (figs. 73, 86), clothes (fig. 82), pipes, rattles, paddles (fig. 83), body and face (fig. 84), beadwork, weaving implements (fig. 85), etc.

The beadwork has a striking resemblance to that of parts of the interior of the Guiana region and of portions of Central America.

Realism is restricted mainly to animal effigy jars employed in girls' puberty ceremonies.

Musical instruments.—Two-headed skin drums, probably of Spanish origin, are used by the *Urarina, Aguano, Chama, Panobo,* and *Chamicura.* The large signal drum was used by the *Chamicura* and may once have

FIGURE 82.—Decorative design from a *Shipibo* man's cushma. (After Farabee, 1922.)

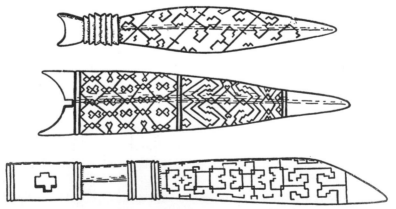

FIGURE 83.—*Shipibo* paddle. The decorations, on both sides, are in black paint. (Length 68 inches (1.7 m.)). (After Farabee, 1922.)

FIGURE 84.—*Shipibo* body painting. Used by both sexes. Lines are in black or red. Usually neck and forehead are painted black. (After Farabee, 1922.)

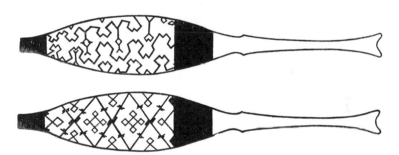

FIGURE 85.—*Shipibo* decorated weaving sword or batters. Used with belt looms. (After Farabee, 1922.)

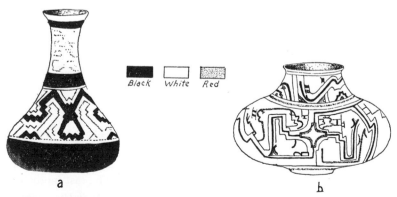

FIGURE 86.—Montaña pottery types. *a, Piro; b, Panobo.* (*a,* Redrawn from Farabee, 1922; *b,* redrawn from Tessmann, 1930, color pl. 6.)

been known to the *Remo*. Amich mentions (1854, p. 262) *Conibo* war drums carried in canoes. Most music is made with wind instruments: panpipes, with 3 to 12 tubes (fig. 87, *b*); longitudinal flutes, with 4 to 6 holes, and among the *Cashibo* made of human bone; transverse flutes; a calabash blown into the hole left by pulling out the stem (*Chama*); trumpets (fig. 87, *c*); and a clay instrument with 2 holes or pipes which gives a double note (*Chama*). Skinner (1805) mentions a *Conibo* "horn" made of thick cane and used to announce the peaceful intention of strangers approaching a village. The musical bow and fruit-shell leg rattles are used by most *Panoan* tribes. A zoomorphic rattle is shown in figure 87, *a*.

Singing seems generally to be done by people intoxicated with chicha.

Dances.—People dance during drinking bouts but dance forms and purposes are not known. "They dance with their clubs on their shoulders, turning around and yelling like mad men" (Izaguirre, 1922–29, 8:245). Tessmann gives three *Cashibo* dances: circle, bow and arrow, and skull.

Games and toys.—Children play individually with miniature implements, weapons, and toys rather than in group games. Even maize-leaf balls, known to most of these tribes, wrestling, and rubber balls (*Nocomán* only) did not involve real group play. Among children's toys were stilts, humming tops, whirring sticks, various slinglike devices for throwing stones and maize grains, and possibly the bull-roarer. The *Conibo* played ring-and-pin (pl. 48, *top*) with a turtle skull (Marcoy, 1875, 2:40).

The only adult game may be of recent origin: laying stones in grooves in the earth and counting them in tens (Tessmann, 1928, pp. 41–43).

Drinking bouts.—Drinking bouts are frequent and entail considerable drunkenness. They provide an opportunity for general release of suppressed aggressions, especially between men who settled their disputes with some violence though without murderous intent (Tessmann, 1928, pp. 106–108).

Intoxicants are made of fermented manioc, maize, sugarcane, and other plants.

Narcotics and drugs.—The *Panoan* tribes used few narcotic and drug plants, despite their proximity to the area of eastern Ecuador and Colombia, which is prolific in such plants as yoco, cayapi, and guayusa, and to the Highland, where use of coca is customary. The *Amahuaca, Panobo,* and *Urarina* drink cayapi; the *Panobo* use coca, drinking it on special occasions; the *Aguano* drink guayusa.

Tobacco has been coming into more general use; the *Cashibo* are said to have borrowed it recently from the *Chama,* but the *Nocomán* still lacked it in 1925. It is smoked in pipes (fig. 87, *d*) or cigars, taken as snuff through tubes (fig. 87, *e*), or drunk as juice. The last method is restricted to shamans, except among the *Itucale*. The modern *Aguano* also chew tobacco.

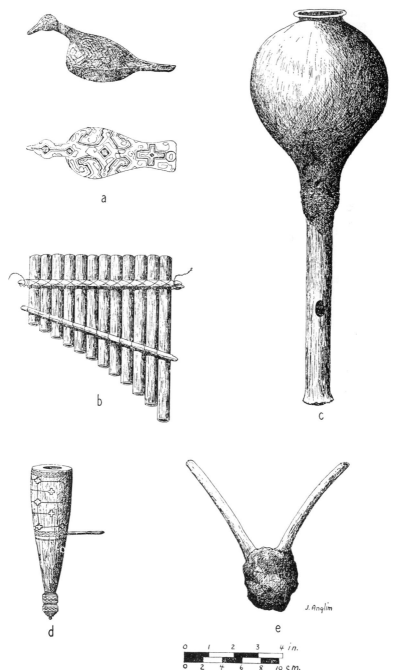

FIGURE 87.—Artifacts of the Montaña tribes. *a, Chama* rattle (2 views) ; *b, Chama* panpipes; *c, Mayoruna* trumpet; *d, Chama* wooden tobacco pipe; *e, Panoan* V-type snuff inhaler.   (*a, b, d,* Redrawn from Tessmann, 1928, pls. 58, 30, 26 ; *c, e,* redrawn from Tessmann, 1930, pl. 16 and map 17.)

The pipe in 1790 consisted of a hollow reed with a small, tubular mouthpiece (Izaguirre, 1922–29, 8:162), but the recent *Chama* and *Panobo* pipe is made of wood and has a stem (fig. 87, *d*). The *Amahuaca* pipe is of clay. The *Urarina* and *Chamicura* formerly smoked only cigars but the latter have borrowed the *Chama* type of pipe. Smoking, once restricted to men, is spreading to women.

Tobacco powder is taken through V-tubes (fig. 87, *e*), one of which is inserted in the nose while an assistant blows through the other. This method has been used by both sexes on the Ucayali River from 1790 to recent times (Izaguirre, 1922–29, 8:162; Tessmann, 1928, 1930) and is also used by the *Amahuaca* and *Panobo*.

RELIGION

Recorded beliefs have some mixture of Christian and native ideology. Tessmann denies that the *Chama* had any concept of a soul, ghost, life after death, gods, or spirits (1928, pp. 183–184).

Galt (ms.) agrees with Tessmann that the *Chama* have no High God concept, but Skinner (1805, p. 274) recorded the belief that God came to earth to count men, causing an earthquake. The *Conibo* held that God, Mueraya, controlled the heavens and the jaguars, and aided shamans (Izaguirre, 1922–29, 1:317). Other myths (below) of a god or creator have an undetermined Christian element.

The Panoan tribes believe in some bush spirits, the *Cashibo* regarding them as anthropomorphic giants and pygmies and as spirit animals, which molest and frighten people at night (Tessmann, 1930).

Beliefs about life after death are so extraordinarily varied that a common denominator is difficult to recognize. Castañeda wrote (Izaguirre, 1922–29, 1:317) that souls of good people went to a sky above the sky, but wicked people roamed until chained for eternity by Mueraya-sent jaguars. The *Conibo* soul (Maroni, 1889–92, 30:131) first lingered near the corpse and was then attracted to heaven by the sun which imparted to it indestructibility. Most *Amahuaca* souls went to heaven where they married and ate, but did not molest the living; others went to the underworld to live with a spirit called Tjaxo. The *Cashibo* soul lived an idyllic existence in heaven, but the *Chamicura* soul remained alone without food or shelter in heaven. The *Panobo, Urarina,* and *Nocomán* believed that the soul remained on earth, immortal, the first two tribes regarding it as harmless; the *Nocomán*, as likely to kill wanderers at night (Tessmann, 1930).

SHAMANISM AND CURING

The shaman's major function is the cause and cure of disease, though Jiménez de la Espada ascribed to *Conibo* shamans the power to foretell the future. Tessmann credits shamans solely with the ability to manipulate a magical substance, usually conceived as a "thorn," but other sources hint at spirit helpers. Castañeda wrote (Izaguirre, 1922–29, 1:313–316) that *Conibo* shamans (mueraya) drank tobacco juice to get in touch with the God or spirit also called Mueraya (see above). The *Shipibo* shaman, called mucroya, entered a hut, covered his head with leaves, chanted, whispered, shouted, and shook himself until a spirit appeared (Ordinaire, 1892, pp. 220–221).

Illness is thought to be caused by a magical substance controlled by a sorcerer; it is generally cured by a medicine man. The sorcerer's art is learned during months of instruction from an experienced practitioner, except among the *Amahuaca*, where the neophyte, insensate with cayapi, travels to receive thorns from the soul of a former magician. The pupil learns to take the magical substance—a "thorn" or splinter (*Chama*), a monkey bone (*Amahuaca*)—into his own body and becomes immune to it. The *Panobo* witch is supposed actually to swallow a bow and four arrows, but the *Nocomán* magician merely learns to use his thorn and thorn thrower. During this period of instruction the neophyte diets (*Chamicura, Shipibo, Urarina, Panobo*), smokes cigars (*Chamicura, Urarina*), smokes a pipe (*Panobo, Chama*), takes tobacco juice (*Chamicura, Panobo, Urarina*), drinks cayapi, observes continence (*Chama*), and learns magical chants (*Chama*).

To cause sickness, the *Amahuaca* sorcerer smokes, vomits his "thorns," and throws them at his victim at night. The *Panobo* magician operates similarly with his bow and arrow. The *Chamicura* and *Urarina* magician spits or blows his "thorns" from a distance; a drunken man is especially vulnerable. The *Chama* sorcerer swallows tobacco juice, coughs up his "splinter," and sticks it in his victim. The *Cashibo* magician coughs up packages of poison, dons a feather headdress, changes into a bird, and flies to his enemy. He turns himself into a small man to enter the victim's house, throws the poison on him, turns again into a bird, and flies home. A *Nocomán* witch soaks his "thorn" in a "poisonous" red herb, waylays his victim, and flips the thorn at him with a short stick. Unless removed, the magical object quickly causes death, after which it returns to its owner.

The *Conibo* attributed illness to animals and stones as well as to sorcerers (Izaguirre, 1922–29, 1:313–316). Tessmann (1930) records that a magician may transform a venomous snake or mice into jaguars and send them to attack a person. These ideas may be in the pattern already described.

The *Nocomán* concede no remedy for illness caused by magic. The *Cashibo* say it can be cured only herbally, not magically. But the *Panobo, Chama, Amahuaca, Urarina,* and *Chamicura* shaman may cure as well as kill. Smoking and massaging, the *Panobo* medicine man withdraws and exhibits the magical "arrows" but the patient usually dies of "internal injuries." The *Chamicuro* and *Urarina* shaman dreams the identity of the sorcerer while smoking, then, blowing cigar smoke over his patient, sucks out the "thorn," exhibits it, and swallows it in order to use it against others. He is paid for a cure, which is rare. The *Chama* shaman smokes and sucks out the "splinter," which he draws into himself. The *Amahuaca* shaman smokes, sings, sucks out the "thorns," and throws them away (Tessmann, 1930).

In addition to these procedures, Galt (ms.) mentions burning leaves as a "conjuring" device to cause sickness. Tessmann adds that a *Chamicura* shaman may send a jaguar not only to kill people but to hunt game.

Tessmann states that magicians are not accused of sorcery because people fear their power. Galt (ms.) cites the murder of a *Cashibo* by a *Conibo*, who suspected him of practicing black magic against his family.

Medicinal practices.—Among nonmagical cures are bleeding, bathing, and administration of herbs.

Father Leceta (Izaguirre, 1922–29, 9:51) wrote that Ucayali River tribes gave the patient a monkey-broth purgative, after which the bleeder bit his arm and sucked his blood.

The *Chama* take cold baths to cure fevers.

Herbal remedies comprise a considerable pharmacopia; some were generally used, some administered only by specialists; many were cultivated. Their true pharmaceutical properties are not known, but some are clearly magical in function. The *Carapacho* cured wounds with cane shoots (*Gynerium sagittatum*) according to Izaguirre (1922–29, 2:71). The *Chama* take *Brunfelsia grandiflora* roots as an aphrodisiac; *Tabernaemontana sananho* for costiveness and constipation; the sap of a *Ficus* for biliousness, anemia, and as a purgative; and various medicines to increase strength when hunting or weaving, to help children learn to walk, and for other purposes. The *Amahuaca* rub leaves of *Dracontium longpipes* into snake bites, but the *Urarina* use *Cyperus*.

MYTHOLOGY

Native mythology is greatly confused with Biblical narratives. Thus, *Cashibo* creation stories in which the Sun (Nokoya) and Moon (Kamu), a man and his wife, create the world and things on it, including people, may be Christian in plot. The *Chamicura* believe that God, Yusi, dwells in heaven; he made the world and everything on it, and retired when the Jews persecuted him, but he still helps mankind in planting and in business (Tessmann, 1930). The *Chama* tale of the origin of cultivated plants is more aboriginal. A couple and their daughter ate only genipa fruit mush. Two birds, Mashentari and Ruirui, visited the daughter alone at the house. Mashentari refused her offer of genipa and told her to strike his knees with a stick. She did so and ripe plantains fell out. Next time he came, she struck plantain plants from one knee, and manioc, sweet potatoes, yams, maize, and other plants from the other knee. The bird then instructed her in planting them. In another tale, an *Inca,* Yoashiko, gave the *Chama* roasted maize and other plants (Tessmann, 1928, pp. 199–200).

The story of the origin of fire is also native. A small parrot belonging to the *Shipibo* asked Yoashiko for food. When a coal was thrown at him instead, he took it home and thereafter had fire. A *Cashibo* version also relates that a pygmy parrot stole fire from the *Inca* (Tessmann, 1930).

An early historic document (Izaguirre, 1922–29, 1:305) records a semihistoric *Conibo* story. The first *Conibo* lived with his family on a mountain in the west. Becoming numerous, his people migrated to the Gran Pajonal, thence to the Ucayali River.

LORE AND LEARNING

Some *Sensi* constellation names are: Canopus, the "thing of the day"; Mars, "forward"; Capella, "spoon"; Southern Cross, "dew fall" (Herndon and Gibbon, 1853–54, 1:205). The *Chama* have names for the Morning Star, Evening Star, and Pleiades (Tessmann, 1930, p. 182).

According to the *Conibo,* the sun (Bari) is the son and the moon (Usë) is the daughter of Habi. The sun smeared the moon's face with genipa (Izaguirre, 1922–29, 1:317). The Pleiades are seeds changed into children who had adventures with a caiman and climbed to heaven. The Southern Cross is the skeleton of a manatee which God killed. The Great Nebulous is a jaguar preying on deer. Various stars are also named (Castañeda, *in* Izaguirre, 1922–29, 1:320).

BIBLIOGRAPHY

Amich, 1854; Beuchat and Rivet, 1909; Chantre y Herrera, 1901; Escobar y Mendoza, 1769; Farabee, 1922; Fejos, n.d.; Figueroa, 1904; Fritz, 1922; Fry, 1889; Galt, n.d.; Herndon and Gibbon, 1853–54, vol. 1; Hervás, 1800–05, vol. 1; Izaguirre, 1922–29; Jiménez de la Espada, 1892, (Notícias auténticas .... 1889–92); Marcoy, 1875; Maroni, 1889–92; Ordinaire, 1892; Peruvian Census, 1940; Raimondi, 1862; Reich, 1903; Relaciones geográficas de Indias, 1881–97; Rivet, 1924; Sagols, 1902; Skinner, 1805; Tessmann, 1928, 1930; Veigl, 1785 a; Velasco, 1842–44; Villanueva, 1902–03; Woodroffe, 1914.

THE SEVENTEENTH-CENTURY TRIBES OF
THE UPPER HUALLAGA RIVER

TRIBAL DIVISIONS

Early sources mention a large number of tribes on the upper Huallaga River (map 1, *No. 3;* map 5), south of the *Hibito* and *Cholón,* but give little idea of their linguistic affiliations and their culture, except that it seemed to resemble that of the Tropical Forests rather than that of the Highland.

These little-known tribes are as follows:

Tepqui.—This tribe adjoined the *Cholón* and occupied the Santa Marta River, a tributary of the Huallaga River (Izaguirre, 1922–29, 1:81–82), lat. 9° S., long. 76° W. Diego de Córdova (Izaguirre, 1922–29, 12:386) states that they may have been related to the *Panoan*-speaking *Mayoruna*.

Muzape.—This was mentioned only as a tribe hostile to the *Cognomona* (Izaguirre, 1922–29, 1:126).

Comanahua.—The *Comanahua* (*Cumanahua*) were 3 days' travel from the *Tepqui* and ajoined an *Inca* tribe (Izaguirre, 1922–29, 1:123–126).

Quidquidcana (*Chuquidcana?*).—This tribe was a neighbor of the *Tepqui* and occupied the Magdalena Valley (Izaguirre, 1922–29, 1:81–82, 123–125), lat. 9° S., long. 76° W.

Chupacho.—The *Chupacho* were said to live in the forests of the Chinchao, Monzón, and other left tributaries of the Huallaga River, almost to Moyobamba (Maurtua, A., 1919, p. 6), which, however, would overlap *Cholón* and *Hibito* territory. (Lat. 9° S., long. 77° W.).

Panatahua.—The *Panatahua* lived on the left bank of the Huallaga River, between the Coyumba and Monzón Rivers, on the lower Chinchao River, which was the center of the upper Huallaga missions, and on the headwaters of the Pachitea River. (Lat. 9°–10° S., long. 76°30′ W.) Izaguirre (1922–29, 12:386) quotes Padre Sala's improbable assertion that the *Panatahua* language seemed to be related to that of the *Amuesha* (*Lorenzo*). Pulgar Vidal (1943) notes that the *Panatahua* were supposed to be related to their various neighbors; their language is, however, not recorded.

This tribe was split into many independent groups.

Chunatahua (*Chinatahua*).—Near the *Panatahua* on the right bank of the Huallaga River and near the mouth of the Chinchao River (Izaguirre, 1922–29, 1:81–82), lat. 9° S., long. 76°30′ W.

Tulumayo and Sisinpari.—On the Tulumayo (modern Azul?) River (Izaguirre, op. cit.), and the right side of the Huallaga River between the Muña and Aguaytia Rivers (Maurtua, A., 1919, p. 6), lat. 9° S., long. 76° W.

Tingan.—Extending eastward from the mouth of the Monzón River (Izaguirre, 1922–29, 1:81–82), lat. 9° S., long. 76° W.

Timayo, Huatsahuana, Ninaxo, Guatinguapa, Mailona, and Muzape.—Somewhere near the *Panatahua* and *Chusco* (Izaguirre, 1922–29, vol. 1).

Chusco.—Many divisions of *Chusco* lived near Huanuco (Izaguirre, 1922–29, 1:81–82), lat. 10° S., long. 77° W.

HISTORY

In 1557, the Franciscan, Arías de Avila, entered *Panatahua* country, but the Indians burned their houses and fled. The *Sisinpari, Panatahua,* and *Chupacho* also resisted him or fled eastward into the forests. But in 1631, a Franciscan mission was established at Tonua at the mouth of the Chinchao River with 1,000 *Panatahua* and *Chunatahua.* The missionaries, though well received by the *Panatahua,* were, at the instigation of an old female shaman, threatened by a war party of 500 *Chunatahua, Tingan, Quidquidcana,* and *Carapacho.* Observing that the *Carapacho* favored the missionaries, the war party became peaceful. Fray Juan Rondón settled the *Carapacho,* and during the next 12 years, Father Luyando founded 8 new missions in the region of the *Panatahua* (Skinner, 1805, pp. 444–449), all controlled from San Francisco de Chusco. Meanwhile visits to the *Quidquidcana* and *Tepqui* accomplished only the baptism of a small number of Indians. The upper Huallaga River missions declined because of heavy mortality caused by epidemics of smallpox, measles, and mumps (papera) in 1662 and again in 1670. In 1691, only 200 Indians remained in 4 small villages in the *Panatahua* region. In 1700, the *Shipibo* or *Cashibo* attacked the *Payanso.* Soon the Franciscans abandoned the region. In 1704, the *Panatahua* mission was declining and the Indians returning to the bush. The last Christian Indians were assembled on the Tulumayo River, but the settlement was attacked by Indians and the survivors moved to Cuchero (Amich, 1854, p. 126).

By 1704, disease and the *Calliseca* had ended missionary work among the *Payanso.* From 1726 to 1755, the missionaries did little in this region. After 1760, the region was crossed by parties en route to the Ucayali via Huanuco and the Panchitea River, but penetration of the Ucayali River was suspended by revolts of 1767 (Skinner, 1805, pp. 444–449). The *Panatahua* tribes seem to have become assimilated to Peruvian national life, while the *Tulumayo, Chunatahua, Tepqui,* and others have blended with the *Cholón* and *Hibito.*

ETHNOGRAPHIC SUMMARY

Brief notes in Izaguirre (1922–29, 1 :99–130, 12 :384–386; Córdova y Salinas, 1651, bk. 1, ch. 25; Pulgar Vidal, 1943) reveal some 17th-century culture.

The *Panatahua* grew maize and sweet manioc, took fish, gathered honey, and drank chicha.

Weapons included clubs (macanas) and lances or spears of chonta palm (*Panatahua*) and bows and arrows (*Panatahua*). The *Tepqui* made good pottery and wove cloth.

Many of these tribes seem to have gone naked, the *Panatahua* painting themselves with genipa. The *Tepqui* wore the hair in bundles down the back. The *Panatahua* wore shell necklaces and breast bands. The *Panatahua* passed a bone splinter through the nose and wore a bone labret. The *Tepqui* and *Quidquidcana* painted the face with stripes.

The *Tepqui* were described as canoe Indians. The *Panatahua* built bridges over the rivers.

The *Tepqui* were monogamous. A newly married couple set up an independent household.

BIBLIOGRAPHY

Amich, 1854; Cordova y Salinas, 1651; Izaguirre, 1922–29; Maurtua, A., 1919; Pulgar Vidal, 1943; Skinner, 1805.

TRIBES OF THE MIDDLE HUALLAGA RIVER

TRIBAL DIVISIONS AND HISTORY

South of the *Cahuapanan*-speaking tribes of the lower Huallaga River lived the *Cholón* and several tribes, whose aboriginal languages were unknown (map 1, *No. 3*; map 5). Among these were the *Lama, Tabalosa, Payanso, Cascoasoa, Amasifuin, Suchichi, Chedua, Alon, Cholto, Huatahua, Nindaso, Pandule, Zapazo, Nomona, Cognomona, Mapari, Cumbazá,* and *Hibito*. Many of these names may be synonyms or subtribes of one another or of better-known tribes. By the beginning of the 19th century, only the *Cholón, Hibito,* and *Lama* survived.

Most of these tribes, especially the *Lama* or *Motilón* (Rivet, 1924, p. 669) and their immediate neighbors, spoke *Quechua* when first discovered. It is possible that they had previously spoken other languages, for *Quechua* quickly supplanted many native languages of the Montaña in post-Columbian times and this region was entered by the Spaniards by the way of Moyobamba in the 16th century. Linguistic diversity is indicated for the *Tabalosa, Pandule,* and *Suchichi* by the fact that the missionaries were handicapped by the different languages when an interpreter who spoke *Quechua* died (Letra anua del Perú de 1635, *in* Rel. geogr. Indias, 1881–97, 4:CLXIII). On the other hand, *Quechua* may, as Tessmann (1930) believes, have been introduced to some of these tribes in pre-Columbian times. We are unaware of the evidence to support Beuchat and Rivet's (1909, pp. 619–620) claim that the *Lama, Lamisto,* and *Tabalosa* spoke *Cahuapanan*. In 1830, Pöppig (1835–36, 2:320) found that all the tribes of the Huallaga Valley between the Huayabamba River and Chasuta, i.e., those listed above, spoke *Quechua* (Izaguirre, 1922–29, 9:80).

Lama.—The *Lama* (*Lamisto, Lamista, Lamano, Motilón,* not to be confused with the "Motilones" of eastern Colombia) occupied the general area of the Moyobamba (San Miguel) River, around Moyobamba Lamas, and Tarapoto, and even extended along the Huallaga River to Chasutino (Pöppig, 1835–36, vol. 2), lat. 6°–7° S., long. 66°–67° W.

In 1554, Pedro de Ursua founded a short-lived town in *Lama* territory. The *Lama, Amasifuin, Cascoasoa, Suchichi,* and *Tabalosa* were finally converted by a Jesuit, and in 1654, brought under the government of Lamas centering in the city of Lamas (Santa Cruz de los Motilones y Lamas), which came to consist of Indians and Mestizos from Moyobama and Chachapoyos. Many of them settled in the Mission of San Francisco Regis on the Paranapura River (Maroni, 1889–92, 29:99–101). In the 18th century, the Indians, all serfs of Lamas, occupied three small pueblos, Cumbazá, Tabalosas, and Pueblo del Río. In 1735, San Francisco Regis had about 100 people (Figueroa, 1904, p. 295), and in 1737, 60 *Lama* fugitives occupied the village of Baradero on the Paranapura River (Zarate *in* Figueroa, 1904, p. 387). In 1767, they passed under Franciscan authority (Amich, 1854, p. 271). At the end of the 18th century, there were only 4 towns in the area: Santa Cruz de Motilones y Lamas, Cumbazá, San Miguel, and Tabalosas (Velasco, 1841–44, 3:248; Skinner, 1805, p. 179). In 1829, only the *Lama* of Chassuta retained their native culture. In 1925, there were 1,000 or more *Lama* (*Lamista*) in the mountains southwest of Yurimaguas on the middle Mayo River and on the upper Cainarache and Sisa Rivers, centering at Lamas. They were partly acculturated but retained some native religious beliefs (Tessmann, 1930, pp. 219, 234).

Tabalosa.—The *Tabalosa* (*Tavaloso*) probably lived on middle Mayo River, a little above Lamas, where the present village of Tabaloso stands, lat. 7° S., long. 67° W. (Beuchat and Rivet, 1909, p. 620).[1] Chantre y Herrera (1901, p. 60) locates them in the Huallaga region. In 1630, the *Tabalosa, Suchichi,* and *Pandule* numbered 11,000.

Suchichi.—The *Suchichi* (*Suchiche, Suriche*) were the Indians of Tarapoto. In the 17th century, a Franciscan missionary, Manuel Casiano visited them. Later came the Jesuits. There were 281 Indians at Tarapoto in 1790. (Izaguirre, 1922–29, 7:175, 251, includes Sobreviela's census.)

Cascoasoa.—The *Cascoasoa* (*Coscanasoa, Chasutino*) originally occupied the right bank of the Huallaga River between the Chapillisa (Chapisa)River—not shown on the recent maps—and Lupuna River at the mouth of the Huayabamba River (lat. 7°30′ S., long. 67° W.). In 1790, there were 262 *Cascoasoa* at Cumbazá Mission (Izaguirre, 1922–29, 7:175, 241).

In 1851, there were 1,000 docile and peaceful Indians, probably *Cascoasoa,* under a priest at Chasuta. They were good hunters and expert canoeists (Herndon and Gibbon, 1853–54, p. 164).

In 1925, several thousand *Chasutino* (*Cascoasoa*) lived in several villages along the middle Huallaga, at Charuta, Yariña, Pucaarca, Chapaja, and lower Sisa River at Boca de Sisa and Buenaparte (Tessmann, 1930). Their dialect is nearly identical with that of the *Lama.* The people were largely assimilated, but independent and quarrelsome.

Amasifuin.—The *Amasifuin* lived on the left bank of the Huallaga, across the river from the *Cascoasoa* (Izaguirre, 1922–29, 7:175, 251) between the *Cahuapanan* and *Cholonan* stocks (lat. 7°30′ S., long. 77° W.)

Payanso.—In the middle 17th century, the *Payanso* (*Payanzo*) were found along the right side of the Huallaga River from the Huayabamba to somewhat north of the Chipurana River (lat. 7°–8° S., long. 77° W.). According to Skinner (1805, pp. 444–449), this was an area of 4 by 25 leagues, lying in the Cordillera and extending from the Huanuco River to the Sacramento Plain. Although numbering 20,000 originally, the *Payanso* have either become extinct or are represented by the modern *Quechua*-speaking peoples. Their original language is entirely unknown.

In 1644, the *Payanso* were first visited by Father Ignacio de Irarraga. By 1650, Franciscan missions among the *Payanso* were: La Santisima Trinidad, 3,000

---

[1] According to the Relaciones geográficas de Indias (4:CLXIII), the *Tabalosa, Pandule,* and *Suchichi* lived around the town of San Miguel de Avisama.

people; La Limpia Concepción, 800; San Luis, 3,000; San Francisco, 200; another village, 150. The total mission population was 7,150. In 1662, the population had decreased through epidemics and infant mortality, but the region had many large villages with streets and churches, and the Indians, a large number of whom spoke Spanish, were expert tailors, barbers, and blacksmiths. A smallpox epidemic occurred in 1670. In 1704, the missions were destroyed by a *Shipibo* (*Calliseca*) invasion from the east, and the Franciscans abandoned the region (Izaguirre, 1922–29, 1:128–139). Later, Skinner (1805, p. 408) listed the *Payanso* as a tribe near the *Setebo*.

Huatana, Nindaso, Nomona, and Zapaso.—These were tribes living in the middle 17th century in the Huallaga Basin, near the *Payanso* (Izaguirre, 1922–29, 1:133), lat. 6°30′ S., long. 77° W. The *Zapaso* were probably on the Saposoa River, a tributary of the Huallaga at lat. 7° S.

Chedua, Alon, and Cholto.—In 1685, these tribes lived on the Huambo River (Skinner, 1805), connected with the Mission of Santa Rosa de Huambo, lat 7° S., long. 77° W. (Izaguirre, 1922–29, 12:391).

Cumbazá.—The *Cumbazá* (*Cumbasa, Belsano*) inhabited Balzapuerto on the Huallaga River (Marcoy, 1875, 2:172) and Tarapoto on the Shilcayo River (Izaguirre, 1922–29, 9:204). The *Mapari* in 1850 were a *Cumbazá* subgroup living between Santa Catalina and Yanayacu, in the mountains between the Huallaga and Ucayali Rivers at the headwaters of the Cuschiabatay River (Izaguirre, 1922–29, 9:204). (See also *Cahuapanan, Yamorai*, pp. 606, 607).

The *Cumbazá* had entered Franciscan missions in the 17th century, then, after a dispute with the *Chébero* in the 18th century, migrated to the Pampa del Sacramento, and, finally, became dispersed in *Setebo* missions on the Ucayali River (Marcoy, 1875, 2:172).

Cognomona.—The *Cognomona*, friends of the *Tepqui* lived 20 leagues from the *Panatahua* and near the *Payanso* (lat. 8° S., long. 76°30′ W.). In 1640, a party of them visited the Franciscan missions (Izaguirre, 1922–29, 1:81–82).

Hibito.—The *Hibito* (*Ibito, Jibito, Zibito, Xibita, Chibito*) had an isolated language, which was spoken from Monte Sión to Lupuna and Pachiza. It still survived in 1834, although *Quechua* had supplanted all native languages farther down the Huallaga River. (Lat. 7°30′ S., long. 76°30′ W.)

Although visited by Jesuits about 1670, the *Hibito* were converted in 1676 by Franciscans. The missionary, José Araujo, founded Jesus de Ochanache and wrote an "arte," vocabulary, and catechism in the *Hibito* language (Izaguirre, 1922–29, 2:197).

In 1767, the *Hibito* were collected in two missions and, in 1789, the town of Pachisa was founded with Indians from Pajaten. The wild Indians who roamed between the Huayabamba River and the Jelache, may have been *Hibito* from Pajaten mixed with *Conibo*. In 1790, there were 205 *Hibito* at Sión and 372 at Del Valle

(Skinner, 1805, pp. 417–418). *Hibito* was spoken in 1834 from Sión to the mouth of the Huayabama River (Izaguirre, 1922–29, 9:80). In 1851, there were 500 *Hibito* at Tocache, Lamasillo, Isonga, and Pisana (Herndon and Gibbon, 1853–54, p. 146).

Cholón.—The *Cholón* occupied the Huallaga Valley above the *Hibito* (lat. 8° S., long. 77° W.) and spoke a distinctive language.

During the 17th century, Indians east of Cajamarquilla, probably including the *Cholón,* had often raided the Highlands and even destroyed the villages of Condurmarca and Collay. But in 1670, they peacefully received a shepherd from Cajamarquilla and later requested a priest. Beginning in 1676, the Franciscans undertook to Christianize the *Cholón.* The Mission of Buenaventura de Apisonchuc was built by Father Francisco Gutierrez de Porres, who wrote a grammar, a dictionary, and several religious books in the *Cholón* language (Izaguirre, 1922–29, 2:197). Apparently some attempt had been made to include the *Hibito* and *Cholón* in the same mission, for quarrels required their segregation, and each was placed in 2 missions (Skinner, 1809, pp. 406–408), the 4 having 1,800 persons in 1767 (Amich, 1854, pp. 75–80), though in the same year Izaguirre (1922–29, 2:198) estimated that the *Cholón* and *Hibito* together numbered 4,800 persons. In 1790, there were 204 Indians at Playa Grande, 205 at Pampa-hermosa, 325 at Pajaten, and 378 at Buenaventure del Valle. In the missions, the Indians were divided into bands and companies and had regular hours of labor. The *Cholón* numbered about 900 to 1,000 in 1829 (228 families in 6 missions (Pöppig, 1835–36, 2:320–321)). Herndon and Gibbon (1853–54, p. 134) reported 188 docile *Cholón* under church influence at Tingo María. In 1925, they occupied the area south of Pachisa between the Huallaga River and Río del Valle (Tessmann, 1930, pp. 546–547). Their language still survives, though many speak *Quechua.*

SOURCES

Some historical information is contained in early mission records compiled by Izaguirre (1922–29), Raimondi (1862), and Maroni (1889–92).

Later explorers adding fragments of historical and ethnographic material are Herndon and Gibbon (1853–54), Skinner (1805), and Pöppig (1835–36). Tessmann (1930) arrived in the area after most of the native culture had disappeared. Miscellaneous compilations include Rivet (1924), who, however, has no linguistic material; Brinton (1892) on language; and Father Pedro de la Mata, who published the first part of a *Cholón* grammar (1923).

CULTURE

SUBSISTENCE

Farming.—The *Payanso* cultivated maize, peanuts, and sweet manioc, and took game and fish. In the 17th century, the *Cholón* and *Hibito* grew bananas, sweet manioc (yuca), peanuts, coca, cotton, and chonta palms. They caught and salted fish, hunted monkeys and peccaries (Izaguirre, 1922–29, 12:395), and gathered wild fruits. The ground kernels of chapaxa palm fruits were a substitute for yuca. In the late 18th century, farming and fishing were essential sources of food (Amich, 1854, p. 75).

Tessmann (1930) listed as 20th-century *Lama* crops: bananas, plantains, maize, yams, sweet manioc, peanuts, sweet potatoes, beans, pumpkins, solanum, macabo, and sugarcane.

Agricultural ceremonialism is suggested by a *Hibito* (?) feast which was held when ground was cleared for the priest at Sión in 1850. People danced, drummed, played fifes, and drank chicha (Herndon and Gibbon, 1853–54, pp. 149–150).

Hunting.—The *Lama* hunted with spears and the blowgun, the darts of which were poisoned with a liana sap (Tessmann, 1930). A century ago the *Cholón* believed that to kill vultures, hawks, and armadillos would spoil their hunting poison; that to kill snakes would make their blowguns crooked; and that to kill caimans would ruin their rifles. Pöppig (1835–36, 2:320) said that these Indians gave their dogs a plant juice (*Tabernaemontana sananho*) to sharpen their scent. *Cholón* hunters of 1830 wore necklaces of Annonaceae and *Achras* seeds and carried amulets in their pouches.

Fishing.—The *Lama* fished with harpoons, spears, bows, multiprong arrows, harpoon arrows, dams, drugs made of *Tephrosia* and *Clibadium,* and, recently, with nets (Tessmann, 1930). The *Cholón* used barbasco (Izaguirre, 1922–29, 6:183).

Food preparation.—The *Lama* ground food on a wooden slab or in a stone mortar, cooked in a pot set on three stones, and smoked meat on a babracot (Tessmann, 1930). Herndon and Gibbon (1853–54, p. 140) observed *Cholón* cooking animals in their skins and eating monkey foetuses. Salt came from the hills of Callana Hacu, up the Huallaga River.

HOUSES

The 20th-century *Lama* house is gabled, side-walled, and thatched. The *Payanso* built rectangular palisaded houses in groups of 6 to 10 forming villages. The houses had loop holes for shooting.

In 1830, the *Cholón* slept on mats and in hammocks purchased from the *Maina*. The 17th-century *Payanso* and the modern *Lama* sleep on platform beds. The *Lama* use no mosquito nets (Tessmann, 1930), though Skinner (1805) described *Hibito* or *Lama* mosquito nets that were rigged on canoes. The *Lama* use footstools.

DRESS AND ORNAMENTS

In 17th-century missions, the *Cholón, Payanso,* and *Hibito* were clad in painted cotton cushmas for everyday purposes, but for dress costume men wore pants and women wore long dresses and shawls, which they procured in trade (Izaguirre, 1922–29, 2:199; 12:391–392). The *Payanso* wore belts sewn with snail shells. In 1851, the *Hibito* painted their faces with red (achote) and blue (huitoc) daubs (Herndon and Gibbon,

1853–54, p. 146). The men of Balzapuerto (*Cumbazá?*) suspended colored feathers from their necks (Maw, 1829, p. 125). Modern *Lama* dress is Spanish in type, but feathers, bracelets, and red (bixa) paint may still be seen (Tessmann, 1930). The 17th-century *Payanso* suspended a bead, bone, or shell from the nasal septum, perforated the ears for bone sticks, and tattooed the nose.

TRANSPORTATION

The 17th-century *Cholón* and *Hibito* used carrying baskets (Izaguirre, 1922–29, 12:393), but Maw (1829, p. 125) reported carrying nets in the Balsapuerto region (*Cumbazá*) and Izaguirre (1922–29, 6:226) mentions them among the *Cholón*. Herndon and Gibbon (1853–54, p. 158) state that an Indian on the lower Huallaga River could carry 75 pounds.

The *Cholón* used pouches, like the Andean chuspa, for small objects.

Tessmann (1930) ascribes to the *Lama* rafts but no canoes. River craft were probably no better developed upstream.

MANUFACTURES

Basketry.—Fragmentary information on baskets seems to indicate the usual Tropical Forest types. Mats were woven of two large palm fronds.

Weaving.—The *Cholón* and *Hibito* probably grew and wove cotton in native times. The 20th-century *Lama* use a drop spindle and horizontal loom; the *Chasutina* had adopted a Spanish type loom.

Ceramics.—Modern wares are: (1) incised cooking pots; (2) "pitchers" with the upper part white, the lower part red; and (3) red or black bowls (Tessmann, 1930).

Fire making.—In recent times, the *Lama* made fire with flint and steel and activated it with feather fans.

Weapons.—All tribes used blowguns (Figueroa, 1904, p. 95; Maw, 1829, p. 125) and spears. The former were made of two half tubes glued together or of one tube inserted in another. The darts were poisoned with a mixture of a liana sap, cayenne pepper, barbasco, sarnango, and other ingredients (Herndon and Gibbon, 1853–54, pp. 135–136), known as "poison of the Lamistas," which the *Hibito* and *Cholón* bought from the *Lama* (Raimondi, 1862, pp. 111–112). Izaguirre (1922–29, 7:251), however, reports that the *Lama* obtained poison from the Ucayali River, near the Manoa River. The *Lama, Payanso,* and *Cholón* use clubs, and the *Lama* is the only tribe in the area to use the sling (Tessmann, 1930). Only to the *Cholón* have been ascribed the bow and arrow (Izaguirre, 1922–29, 6:215). The *Payanso* use lances or spears.

TRADE

In the 17th century, the *Cholón* and *Hibito* traded coca for Spanish garments and iron, making 8-day trips to Cajamarquilla for this purpose (Izaguirre, 1922–29, 2:199; 12:391–392).

By the end of the 18th century, the Huallaga River region had con-
.siderable trade.   Local products were salt fish, woven pouches, bees' wax,
manioc meal, "vegetable bougies" from a tree, feathered hats, container
lids (Skinner, 1805, p. 423), coca, and fish lines.   These were sold or
traded to the Highland peoples.

SOCIAL CULTURE

Information on nonmaterial aspects of the culture of these tribes is
extremely limited.   Social and political patterns and birth, puberty, marriage, and death practices have been obscured if not entirely displaced
by Christian customs.

For the *Lama,* Tessmann (1930) claims an arrangement unique in the
Montaña: patrilineal "sibs" (apparently each a separate settlement),
which are paired into mutually hostile groups.

There is no means of knowing whether the individual family huts of
the *Chasutina* area of 1851 (Herndon and Gibbon, 1853–54, 1:154) were
native.

A century ago, a pubescent *Cholón* boy drank a strong purge and a
decoction of certain creepers, which were kept from his view lest they
lose their power.   He remained for a month fasting in his hammock
(Pöppig, 1835–36, 2:320–321).

ESTHETIC AND RECREATIONAL ACTIVITIES

Games.—Games and toys mentioned are humming tops, maize-leaf
balls, and stilts.

Musical instruments.—Recent *Lama* musical instruments include two-
headed drums, panpipes, and longitudinal flutes.   The *Hibito* had bone
flutes.   In the *Hibito* region, Herndon and Gibbon (1853–54, p. 142) saw
four trumpets, each made of a section of hollowed wood, joined together
with twine wrapping and wax and fitted with a reed mouthpiece.   These
were blown to announce a friendly visit when approaching a settlement.

Beverages.—Chicha made of manioc is an old trait (Izaguirre, 1922–29,
6:185).   The Balzapuerto Indians made chicha of manioc, maize, plantains,
and chonta fruit.   Maize chicha was made of crushed and boiled grains
to which a small quantity of chewed cumal (probably kumara, sweet
potatoes) was added and the mixture boiled again.   It would not keep
longer than a week (Maw, 1829, p. 157).   Banana chicha was brewed
of overripe fruit which was crushed, boiled, and strained through a rush
sieve and boiled again.

Narcotics.—Tobacco was taken as juice and smoked in cigars and pipes.
The latter were formerly of wood with a bone stem and recently of clay.
Coca was chewed with lime (Tessmann, 1930).   It was cultivated along
the Huallaga River from Tingo María to Pachiza (Raimondi, 1862, p.
134).

RELIGION AND SHAMANISM

Data on native religion are lacking. These tribes were all good Catholics in 1830 (Pöppig, 1835–36, 2:321) and probably earlier.

Lama shamanism had some peculiar features. The neophyte sorcerer dieted and took tobacco juice, cigars, ayahuasac, and, uniquely, *Brunfelsia grandiflora* and another liana. He acquired a general power from these plants but no internal "thorns." To cause illness, he impregnated a splinter with his power and cast it at his victim. To cure it, a shaman sucked out the splinter. Anthropomorphic bush demons might also cause sickness.

Cyperus was used only as a curative. The sap of an Apocynaceae and the seeds of *Jatropha curcas* were used to prepare a powerful purgative. The *Cholón* were reputed to be powerful doctors in 1830.

BIBLIOGRAPHY

Amich, 1854; Beuchat and Rivet, 1909; Brinton, 1892 a; Chantre y Herrera, 1901; Figueroa, 1904; Herndon and Gibbon, 1853–54, vol. 1; Izaguirre, 1922–29; Letra anua del Perú de 1635 (*in* Rel. geogr. Indias, 1881–97); Marcoy, 1875; Maroni, 1889–92; Mata, 1923; Maw, 1829; Pöppig, 1835–36; Raimondi, 1862; Rivet, 1924; Skinner, 1805, 1809; Tessmann, 1930; Velasco, 1841–44.

THE CAHUAPANAN TRIBES

TRIBAL DIVISIONS AND HISTORY [2]

Owing to incomplete and often contradictory statements by the earliest observers, to paucity of linguistic material, and to the change of terminology in the course of centuries, the true affiliation of many tribes included in this section can only be guessed. It would only serve to perpetuate possible errors were the doubtful tribes to be pigeon-holed as *Cahuapanan* with the appearance of certainty. Some tribes, which Rivet and Beuchat appear to class as *Cahuapanan* on the basis of geographical position, we list as doubtful. There is linguistic material on the *Cahuapana* language (Beuchat and Rivet, 1909, pp. 622–634; Rivet and Tastevin, 1931), but not for the *Cahuapanan* affiliation of other tribes, such as the *Chébero, Paranapura, Chayawita* (Chantre y Herrera, 1901, p. 93; Zarate *in* Figueroa, 1904, p. 386), and *Munichi* (Veigl a, 1785, p. 37). Early sources, moreover, are not consistent in classifying these tribes.

Cahuapana and Concho (*Chonzo*).—When first described these tribes lived together in the quebradas of the mountains of Chayavitas toward Moyobamba (lat. 5° S., long. 77° W.)

Until 1691, they hid in their mountains, avoiding missionaries and slavers, but obtained iron tools, clothes, and poison from the Indians of Moyobamba and Lamas.

---

[2] See Map 1, *No. 3;* map 5.

Their first mission, 1691, soon failed, but later, when a secular priest attempted to sell them into slavery, they migrated across the Chayavita mountains (probably to the south) and settled in a village under missionary care (Chantre y Herrera, 1901, pp. 300–301, 312–313). About this time, 200 *Concho,* the remnant of a much larger tribe which had been destroyed by the people of Moyobamba, were taken to the Mission of Nuestra Señora de los Cahuapanas y Conchos. In 1737, 518 Indians remained at this mission, and other *Concho* were still in the forests (Maroni, 1889–92, 26:215; 28:413). They moved in 1757 to the mouth of the Cayapanas River (Chantre y Herrera, 1901, pp. 312–313). In 1767, Spanish raids had reduced the *Cahuapana* to 600 (Veigl, 1785 a, p. 42). In 1925, some 150 *Cahuapana* remained in two villages on the Cahuapanas River (Tessman, 1930).

Chébero.—The *Chébero* (*Xévero, Xébero Jébero, Shiwila;* not to be confused with the *Jívaro* or *Hibito,* each a wholly distinct tribe) spoke the same language as the *Chayawita,* which is *Cahuapanan* (Beuchat and Rivet, 1909). Two subtribes are the *Chébero* proper (lat. 5° S., long. 76° W.) and the *Paranapura* (*Chébero-Munichi*), the latter an offshoot of the *Chébero* who settled among the *Munichi* in 1654. It is likely that both the *Cutinana* and *Tivilo* are subtribes of the *Aguano* (this volume, pp. 557–559) who, having moved into *Cahuapanan* territory in historical times, were thought to belong with the latter.[3]

The *Chébero* were originally scattered in the angle between the Marañón and Huallaga Rivers, extending west along the Marañón and to the Sierras of Chayabitas and Cavapanas (Chantre y Herrera, 1901, p. 143; Veigl, 1785, p. 35). When first visited by Father Lucas de la Cueva in 1638, they were 1½ days' travel up the Apeina River (Maroni, 1889–92, 28:393) scattered in small settlements, 2 to 6 leagues apart (Figueroa, 1904, pp. 33–78). The *Chébero,* terrified by punitive expeditions hunting down rebellious *Maina,* readily accepted mission protection (Figueroa, 1904, pp. 33 ff.), and Concepción de Xéveros was founded in 1640 with 2,000 Indians (Chantre y Herrera, 1901, p. 525). In 1643, believing that the baptismal records were a census made to facilitate enslaving them on encomiendas and fearing punishment for their part in assaults against the *Maina,* the *Chébero* abandoned the mission. They warred against other tribes but soon starvation and threats of being taken as slaves to Borja impelled them to return to the mission (Figueroa, 1904, pp. 33–78).

Meanwhile, neighboring tribes were missionized, but, mistrusting one another and attributing deaths to witchcraft, they were placed separately in three annexes to the original *Chébero* mission: San Pablo de los Pambadeques, 1646, for the *Cocamilla;* Santo Tomé, 1641, for the *Cutinana;* and San José, 1648, for the *Ataguate* (Figueroa, 1904, p. 72). It was not until about 1690, when suspicions and hostilities were sufficiently allayed, that these tribes agreed to assemble in a single, new mission, Concepción de Maria, which had 2,500 *Cocamilla, Cutinana, Ataguate, Chébero, Aunale, Jívaro, Ticuna,* and *Mayoruna*—the last three from remote regions.

Subsequently, the *Chébero* were very helpful in supplying sweet manioc and bananas to missionary parties in the region (Chantre y Herrera, 1901, pp. 116 ff.). In 1737, there were 1,757 people in Concepción, which included *Cutinana* and other tribes as well as *Chébero* (Zarate *in* Figueroa, 1904, p. 383). In 1769, the *Chébero* mission included *Alabano, Jívaro, Mayoruna, Yameo,* and *Ataquate.* A census in 1840 showed 5,000 *Chébero.* In 1859, Raimondi (1863, pp. 85–86) estimated that there

---

[3] Beuchat and Rivet also class Velasco's *Ataguate* and Velasco's and Hervás's *Cutinana* and *Tivilo* as *Chébero.* Figueroa (1904, p. 125), a 17th-century source, classes the *Cutinana* as *Aguano;* Veigl (1785, p. 36), as *Chébero.*

were 3,000 *Chébero*. They were peons of the inhabitants of Moyobamba, specializing in making blowguns, torches, and wax candles for trade. In 1925, 600 *Chébero* lived at Concepción. They retained some of their aboriginal culture, but about 80 percent could speak *Quechua* (Tessmann, 1930, pp. 415–416).

The *Paranapura* (*Xévero-Munichi*) were *Chébero* who had fled from Moyobamba slavers to the Paranapura River, where they intermarried with the *Munichi* and adopted their language. They numbered about 150. Father Raimundo de la Cruz assembled them with some *Chayawita* at the Mission of Nuestra Señora de Loreto de Paranapura in 1654; only 192 Indians remained in 1692 (Maroni, 1889–92, 28:435 –443).

Beuchat and Rivet (1909, p. 619) name the *Ataguate* as a *Chébero* subtribe, no doubt because of their proximity to the latter, that is, toward the source of and on the right side of the Aipena River and perhaps at Atagua Lagoon, east of the village of Chébero. The *Ataguate* were placed in the Mission of San José in 1648 by Fathers de la Cueva and Peréz (Chantre y Herrera, 1901, p. 142).

Chayawita.—The *Chayawita* (*Chawi, Tshaahui, Chayhuita, Chayabita, Shayabit*) were thought by Tessman to include the *Cahuapana, Chawi,* and *Yamorai* as *Chayawita* subtribes, but previous usage restricted *Chayawita* to what is probably Tessmann's *Chawi* (*Tshaahui*) subdivision (lat. 5° S., long. 77° W.). The *Chayawita* and *Chébero* languages were so similar as to be mutually intelligible (Veigl, 1785 a, p. 37). Their original home was in the mountains where the Sillay River has its headwaters.

The *Chayawita* had been greatly reduced in numbers by early 17th-century slavers. In 1654, the Jesuit, Raimundo de la Cruz, visited one village of 100 people, but the bulk of the tribe was scattered in the mountains at the headwaters of the Paranapura River. They were placed in a mission that year with *Munichi* and *Chébero* but gradually drifted away after the missionary had departed (Maroni, 1889–92, 28:434– 443). The Mission of Nuestra Señora de la Presentación was later founded and, in 1737, had 442 inhabitants. Veigl (1785 a, p. 37) reports 600 *Chayawita* in 1767. In 1925, a few hundred *Chayawita* (Tessmann's *Chawi*) remained on the upper Sillay and upper Paranapura Rivers and in Balzapuerto (Tessmann, 1930, pp. 378– 382). They retained some native culture.

Yamorai.—*Yamorai* (*Balzapuertino*) is a tribal name used only by Tessmann (1930) to designate 500 to 1,000 Indians living in 1925 on the upper Paranapura River and near Santa Rosa on the left side of the Huallaga River, with a few on the middle Paranapura and Shanusi Rivers. As no early sources mention tribes precisely in this territory, it is impossible to identify the *Yamorai*. Possibly they were related to the *Pambadeque* to the north (p. 608).

Munichi.—The *Munichi* (*Otanave, Otanabe, Munitsche, Munichino*), lat. 6° S., long. 76° W., had, according to Beuchat and Rivet (1909), two subtribes: the *Churitana,* for which Velasco (1841–44) is the authority and which are evidently the *Churituna* mentioned by Chantre y Herrera (1901, p. 60) in the Huallaga River region; and the *Muchimo,* for which Hervás (1800–05, vol. 1) is the authority.

The *Munichi* originally had 3 villages on a small tributary of the Huallaga River, 3 days' journey above the Paranapura River (Maroni, 1889–92, 28:434–443). In

1654, a Jesuit father found only 64 family heads (a total of about 320 persons) in their main village. Chantre y Herrera (1901, p. 60) places them on the Huallaga River. In 1661, the population was 92.

The *Munichi* refused to join the *Chayawita* and *Paranapura* in the Mission of Loreto and held out until two missions of their own were founded in 1652 (Escobar y Mendoza, 1769, p. 52). These missions had been opposed by the settlers of Moyobamba, who regarded the *Munichi* as their slaves. By 1737, the missions were combined, but the total population was only 151 persons (Maroni, 1889–92, 28:435–443; Zarate *in* Figueroa, 1904, p. 387). In 1850, there were 150 to 200 *Munichi* (Raimondi, 1863, p. 82).

In 1925, about 200 *Munichi* remained in 25 houses in a village called Muniches, no doubt the early mission site, on the lower Paranapura River. A few, largely assimilated *Munichi* lived in another village by the same name on the lower Itaya River near Iquitos, where they had moved several decades ago. They retained traces of aboriginal culture (Tessmann, 1930, pp. 303–304, 310).

Pambadeque and Cingacuchusca.—The *Pambadeque* were, according to Beuchat and Rivet (1909, p. 620), *Cahuapanan* living between the upper Aipena and Paranapura Rivers, i.e., between the *Chayawita, Chébero,* and *Yamorai.* Chantre y Herrera (1901, p. 156) mentions them in connection with the *Cingacuchusca* of the lower Huallaga River. Members of both tribes were taken to an annex of the Mission of Concepción de María. There is a possibility that the *Pambadeque* were *Cocama.* (See p. 688.)

SOURCES

Historical material with fragmentary ethnographic information occur in old missionary accounts: Figueroa (1904), Chantre y Herrera (1901), Maroni (1889–92), Izaguirre (1922–29), and Veigl (1785 a). Unless otherwise specified, cultural data which follow come from Tessmann (1930), who found the *Cahuapanan* tribes so acculturated that many aboriginal customs were mere traditions. Many other customs, though native in character, were probably in large part of recent origin, e.g., clothing, use of tobacco, house types, and many foods.

CULTURE

SUBSISTENCE

Farming.—Aboriginal *Cahuapanan* staples were sweet manioc, maize, and bananas (Maroni, 1889–92, 28:408). Other early *Munichi* plants were sugarcane, camarico, and pumpkins (Figueroa, 1904, p. 92). Bitter manioc, though not aboriginal, was introduced to the region at the end of the 18th century to furnish provisions for explorers. Izaguirre (1922–29, 7:238) mentions its cultivation by the *Chébero,* who made farinha for sale. Other *Cahuapanan* plants are listed on page 519.

Tessmann considers *Chébero* land to be very infertile. Figueroa (1904, p. 73) remarked that these Indians cleared new land every 2 years when the soil became exhausted, and Maroni (1889–92, 28:408) observed that fields had to remain fallow for years. The *Chébero* farmed with a dibble and a spatulate cultivating stick.

Hunting.—Game was too remote from the *Chébero* village to be important. Formerly, the blowgun was the main weapon (*Munichi, Chébero, Chayawita*), with spears used for larger game (*Yamorai*). Only the *Chayawita* used the bow and arrow (Tessmann, 1930). Today firearms have largely replaced native weapons. Hunting blinds are ascribed to the *Chébero* and *Chayawita*. About 1800, a box trap of some kind with a dog lure was used to take jaguars (Skinner, 1805, pp. 421–422). Tessmann reports a similar *Chébero* and *Chayawita* trap for birds and a larger one for tapirs.

Fishing.—Drugging fish with *Tephrosia* and *Clibadium* was probably general. The *Chébero* formerly fished with the bow and arrow, but use them now only as children's toys. Spears are used by the *Munichi* and *Chayawita,* harpoons by the *Munichi*. Aboriginal use of hooks is uncertain; importation of iron hooks has certainly extended their use. The *Munichi* and *Chayawita* used nets, the latter a type that was dragged. To take manatee (*Trichechus inunguis*) the *Chébero* stretched a strong net across the opening of a weir. One hunter drove the animal to the opening, where it was caught in the net or speared by a man standing on a platform (Maroni, 1889–92, 26:414).

Food preparation.—The *Cahuapanan* tribes ground food in a wooden trough or bowl (fig. 89) or on a flat wooden slab, and smoked meat on a babracot. Herndon and Gibbon (1853–54, p. 174) described preparation of farinha during the last century by an unidentified tribe in the region. Manioc pulp was put in a sack which was suspended and stretched like the tipití to squeeze out the poisonous juices; then it was roasted and sold. Salt, obtained nearby from Laguna Pilluana near Chapillisa and Cachihuañusca north of Valle Hermoso, was an important trade item on the Huallaga River (Izaguirre, 1922–29, 7:250).

HOUSES AND VILLAGES

The aboriginal house type may have been the gabled, side-walled structure (Tessmann, 1930). The platform bed was used by the *Chébero* (Izaguirre, 1922–29, 12:395), *Munichi* (fig. 88), and *Chayawita* (Tessmann, 1930). Hammocks served the *Chayawita* and *Chébero* only for resting and were used among the *Munichi* by children. Unelaborated footstools were common.

FIGURE 88.—*Cahuapanan* (*Munichi*) low platform bed. (Redrawn from Tessmann, 1930.)

The *Cahuapanan* formerly went nude much of the time, though *Chébero* women sometimes wore a skirt and men a sacklike shirt which was open at both ends and extended only to the waist. Whether naked or not, men held the penis up under a string passed around the waist (Figueroa, 1904, pp. 32, 68; Maroni, 1889–92, 28:405). Similar garments may have been used by the *Chayawita*. Spanish clothing had been adopted by the 18th century, but on festive occasions *Chébero* women wrapped themselves in a large, fringed cloth fastened with a silver pin over the shoulders and tied around the waist; it was dyed blue for married women, and red, blue, and brown for spinsters (Veigl, 1785, p. 40). This costume suggests the *Jívaro* woman's garment. Men wore their hair to the shoulders; women, as long as it would grow. Strings of fragrant seeds and colored tubes, animal-tooth necklaces and perfumed grasses and feathers in the hair band were also worn (Veigl, 1785 a, pp. 32–33). Twentieth century survivals of native costume and ornaments (Tessmann, 1930) include arm and leg bands (*Chayawita*), blackened teeth (*Chayawita*), ornaments in ear perforations (*Chébero, Chayawita*), paint (*Chayawita*), tattooing (*Yamorai* and *Chayawita*, done with a palm needle and rubber soot), and feather headgear (*Chébero, Chayawita*).

TRANSPORTATION

The *Chébero* carried goods both in baskets and knitted bags. Canoes were probably made by all tribes, but those of the *Chébero* were said to be inferior. Figure 89 shows two paddle forms.

MANUFACTURES

Weaving.—Hammocks and bags of *Astrocaryum* fiber were made by the *Munichi, Chébero,* and *Chayawita,* the first also making fish nets of this fiber.

Considerable cotton was grown and woven, and the *Chébero* were famous in Colonial times for the blankets and featherwork which they made for the Whites (Izaguirre, 1922–29, 7:232). Cotton was spun on a spindle suspended in the air (*Munichi*) or twirled on the ground (*Chébero, Chayawita*). The whorl was usually of ornamented tortoise shell. The loom was, according to Tessmann (1930), horizontal like that of the *Chama*.

Basketry.—At least three basket forms are known among the *Munichi, Chébero,* and *Chayawita*: containers, sieves, and carrying baskets, the last having a hexagonal weave (Tessmann, 1930). The *Chébero* also made waterproof containers by weaving a double-wall basket of split creeper strands and stuffing leaves in between (Veigl, 1785, p. 41).

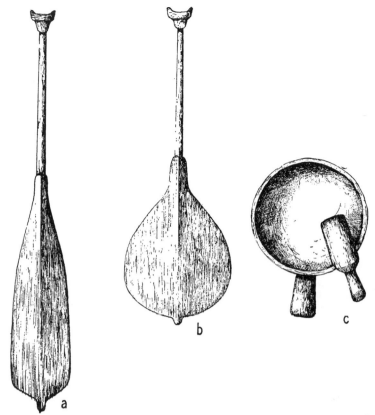

FIGURE 89.—*Chébero* and *Aguano* utensils. *a, b, Chébero* canoe paddles; *c, Chébero* wooden bowl and pounder. (Redrawn from Tessmann, 1930, pl. 76.)

Pottery.—The *Munichi* make pottery bowls (pl. 52, *c*), the upper halves of which are white, the lower red. They also make Spanish-type vessels. The *Chayawita* and *Chébero* make fingernail-decorated and incised cooking vessels (fig. 90), jugs with the upper portion white, the lower red (Tessmann, 1930, table 80, figs. 1, 1a, 7), and ornamented drinking bowls (pl. 52, *d, f*).

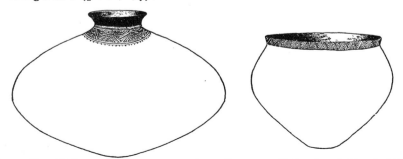

FIGURE 90.—*Chébero* pottery. (Redrawn from Tessmann, 1930, color pl. 10 and pl. 80.)

Weapons.—*Chébero* blowguns were made of two half-tubes and were 10 spans long (Veigl, 1785 a, p. 33). These were sold to other tribes (Izaguirre, 1922–29, 12:355). Some of the *Cahuapanan* purchased their poison from the *Lama*. Both thrusting spears and javelins were used, *Chébero* spears being of chonta wood, 9 spans long (Veigl, 1785 a, p. 33). During warfare of 1661, a tribe of this region, perhaps the *Chébero*, used spear throwers and shields (Figueroa, 1904, p. 265). Clubs were also used, but bows have not been reported, possibly having been replaced by the blowgun at an early date.

Miscellaneous tools.—Veigl (1785 a, pp. 33–34) mentions other *Chébero* implements: a wood-carving tool made of the tooth of a fish, pig, or monkey; a plane or smoother made of the rough bone under the tongue of a large fish called paice; axes with polished stone heads fitted into a socket at the end of a stick.

Fire making.—Fire was made with the drill by the *Chébero* and *Chayawita*. Cotton served as tinder. The *Chébero* fire fan was braided. The *Chébero* use a copal torch. They set their pots on three clay supports, but the *Munichi* use three stones.

SOCIOPOLITICAL GROUPS

Virtually no information on aboriginal social structure, social behavior, or crisis rites is available, as these tribes became almost completely acculturated to Spanish customs at an early date.

Tessmann (1930) believes that the *Chébero* always had a single large village instead of the small "kin" groups found elsewhere in the Montaña, but Izaguirre (1922–29, 12:396) states they formerly were scattered in small groups along the southern bank of the Marañón and were later gathered into their large village. This village, laid out on the Spanish plan with a central plaza and church, is one of the few instances in which Montaña Indians remained in a mission center, whether missionaries were present or not, and did not revert to their aboriginal separatism. *Chayawita* villages consisted of one to several houses.

Recorded chieftainship is probably the result of Spanish influence: the *Chébero* village chief with 10 assistants; the *Chayawita* chief with 4 or 5 assistants. But a reference in 1661 (Figueroa, 1904, p. 265) mentions a war dance, during which high chiefs sat in hammocks and lesser chiefs on stools, while warriors danced.

LIFE CYCLE

The *Chayawita* still confine parents for a few days after a birth.

At puberty, the *Chayawita* seclude the girl for 8 days. Maroni states (1889–92, 29:239) that the *Chébero*, like the *Awishira*, used to flog girls and put red pepper in their eyes to give them strength.

Some survival of the native marriage pattern is recognizable in the *Chébero* requirement that the bridegroom help his father-in-law and in *Chayawita* matrilocal residence which precedes permanent patrilocal residence. The penis bone of the coati is regarded as an aphrodisiac.

The *Chébero* formerly flexed a corpse, put it in an urn, and covered it with another urn (Jiménez de la Espada, 1889–92, 27:85). Christian burial is now general, but the *Chayawita* place the corpse in a hollowed tree trunk and leave it in the bush.

WARFARE

These tribes were remarkably peaceful in late historic times; they had only brawls among themselves, fought with clubs. But warfare must once have been of some importance, for the *Munichi* formerly protected their villages with trenches filled with sharp stakes and the *Chébero* practiced cannibalism. Figueroa (1904, p. 265) recorded a war dance: painted male dancers wearing animal skins on their heads and carrying spear throwers, ceremonial spears, shields, and straw figures pretended to assault a house while chiefs drank chicha. Singing and drinking went on for days. Chantre y Herrera (1901, p. 90) implies that the *Chébero* were unjustly accused of cannibalism because they kept trophy heads, but Father Lucas de la Cueva, their first missionary, states that they ate their victims' livers, entrails, and hearts seasoned with pepper (Maroni, 1889–92, 28:389; Figueroa, 1904, p. 41). Maroni (1889–92, 28:406) recounts that after a war party, the *Chébero* brought back heads, drank chicha, and feasted on the enemy's liver. They evidently made shrunken heads (tsantsas), for Figueroa (1904, p. 263) states that women carried "reduced heads," singing victory songs and praising the excellence of their warrior husbands.

ESTHETIC AND RECREATIONAL ACTIVITIES

Musical instruments include two-headed skin drums, leg rattles, longitudinal and transverse flutes, musical bows, and large and small panpipes.

Figueroa (1904, p. 264), describing a *Chébero* dance of 1661, states that men, women, and children moved in a circle, while the leader in the center, adorned with nose ornaments, urucú, and feathers, lead the singing. The dance often ended in rough play. They also danced in palm-leaf headdresses accompanied by flutes and panpipes (Figueroa, 1904, p. 94). The *Chayawita* now use masks of Spanish origin at their festivals.

The principal toys were humming tops, stilts, maize-leaf balls, and slings.

Tobacco may once have been used only by shamans, who chewed it, but pipe smoking is now general among the *Chébero* and *Chayawita*. The only other narcotic reported is cayapi, also used by shamans.

RELIGION AND SHAMANISM

Native religious concepts are unknown except for a *Chayawita* belief in a mountain demon and an idea that souls of the dead went into the bush and were harmless.

A suggestion of the early reaction to Christianity is contained in a *Chébero* tale. To escape the "evangelic rule," it is said, the *Chébero* took a grass called campana supaya (*Datura*) and went below the water, where they had a good time with their deceased relatives. Taking datura caused one village to change into a lagoon (Maroni, 1889–92, 28:402). On one occasion, the devil kidnapped a *Chébero*. The Indians followed its tracks, which were first those of a man, then of a child, and finally of a jaguar (Maroni, 1889–92, 28:402). Some Indians responded to missionaries so literally that they imitated each gesture, crossing themselves, spreading their arms, yawning, striking themselves, and even opening their mouths each time the missionary did so (Figueroa, 1904, p. 274).

Fragments of the shamanistic pattern recorded by Tessmann (1930) indicate belief in "thorns" and perhaps birds as the source of power. *Chébero* and *Chayawita* shamans received a magic mass with "thorns," which, according to the *Chébero,* was brought by an owl which taught the shaman songs. The shaman took cayapi and chewed tobacco. Disease was caused by injections of these "thorns" into the victim and cured by sucking them out.

The *Chébero* attributed magical virtues to cyperus and used it to prevent snake bites and jaguar attacks, to bring fishing and hunting success, and to increase the fertility of women and of manioc. The *Chayawita* used it only against snake bites. The *Chébero* took Datura to make themselves invisible in addition to the purposes already mentioned.

The *Chébero* believed that earthquakes occurred when God arose in the place where sky and earth meet.

BIBLIOGRAPHY

Beuchat and Rivet, 1909; Chantre y Herrera, 1901; Escobar y Mendoza, 1769; Figueroa, 1904; Herndon and Gibbon, 1853–54; Hervás, 1800–05, vol. 1, Jiménez de la Espada (Noticias auténticas . . . 1889–92); Maroni, 1889–92; Raimondi, 1863; Rivet and Tastevin, 1931; Skinner, 1805; Tessmann, 1930; Veigl, 1785 a; Velasco, 1841–44.

TRIBES OF THE UPPER MARANON RIVER

TRIBAL DIVISIONS

Deep in the Andean valleys of the upper Marañón River in North Central Perú were several tribes which, in contrast to the *Quechuan* peoples, who occupied the higher mountain masses that nearly surrounded them, apparently had diverse languages and Tropical Forest cultures.

They are known only from a sketchy report by Diego Palomino (Relaciones geográficas de Indias, 1881–97, 4:28–33). These tribes were the *Patagón, Chinchipe,* and *Bagua,* who were possibly related to one another, and the seemingly distinct *Chirino, Tabancal, Sacata, Copallín,* and *Chachapoya* (map 1, *No. 3;* map 5).

Linguistic data from these tribes consist of four words each from the *Chirino, Patagón,* and *Copallín,* three from the *Bagua* and *Sacata,* and five from the *Tabancal,* not all of them comparable. On the basis of these, Rivet (1924, p. 664) classifies the *Patagón* as *Cariban.* Disregarding broader affiliations, which seem too tenuous to postulate, *Patagón* and *Bagua* have in common one or two similar words. It was said that the Indians of Perico (probably *Chinchipe*) and of Jaén (probably *Patagón*) spoke the same language, and that the *Chinchipe* and *Bagua* were related. Thus, these three adjoining tribes may have belonged to a single linguistic group. The other brief word lists have nothing in common. Moreover, both the *Tabancal* and *Sacata* were said to be linguistically different. The language of the Indians of Copallín, Llanque, and Lomas de Viento was also said to differ from that of their neighbors. They may have spoken *Quechua,* but as *Quechua* is also mentioned as a distinctive language, this seems unlikely.

Patagón.—The *Patagón* lived somewhat inland from the left side of the Chinchipe River, occupying the territory from Perico or from the confluence of the Chinchipe and Chirinos Rivers down to the Marañón River and a short distance up the Utcubamba River (lat. 5°30′ S., long. 78°30′ W.). According to 16th-century encomienda lists, the Indians of Jaén and of Paco, Chacainga, Olipanche, and Pueblo de la Sal, all villages north of Jaén (Jaén was originally at the mouth of the Chinchipe River) were *Patagón.* (Rel. geogr. Indias, 1881–97, 4:28–29.)

Chinchipe.—The *Chinchipe* (*Chenchipe*) occupied both sides of the lower Chinchipe River from the mouth of the Chirinos River to the Marañón River and lived along the Marañón River to the mouth of the Chamaya River (lat. 5°–6° S., long. 79° W.).

Bagua.—The *Bagua* had a few settlements up the Utcubamba River, just beyond the *Patagón* (lat. 6° S., long. 78°30′ W.).

Chirino.—The *Chirino* lived along the Chirino River and seem to have extended across the mountains north of the *Patagón* down to the Marañón River (lat. 5° S., long. 78°30′ W.) (Rel. geogr. Indias, 1881–97, 4:28–33).

Copallín.—Indians whom we call *Copallín* were those of Llanque, Copallín, and Lomas de Viento, east of the Marañón River and north of the Utcubamba River (lat. 6° S., 68° W.). They differed linguistically from their neighbors.

Sacata.—The *Sacata* were an isolated linguistic group living between the Chamaya and Sacata River, on the Paramos de Sallique and on the Tabaconas River (lat. 6°30′ S., long. 78°30′ W.).

Tabancal.—The *Tabancal* were said to be an independent group between the Chirinos and Aconipa Rivers, tributaries of the upper Chinchipe River.

HISTORY

Juan Porcel, having been granted the privilege of conquering the Indians of the region of Jaén and the Chinchipe Basin, entered the country in 1542. After a brief and abortive attempt at colonization, he left and was succeeded in 1549 by Diego Palomino, who founded the city of Jaén de los Bracamoros[4] near the junction of the Chinchipe and Marañón Rivers. As the subsequent history of these Indians is not known, it is presumed that they became encomienda laborers and soon merged with the rural, *Quechua*-speaking population.

ETHNOGRAPHIC SUMMARY

These people seem to have had simple culture, basically like that of the Tropical Forests but with a few Highland features. Living in deep valleys, rarely above 3,000 or 4,000 feet (1,000 to 1,300 m.) and usually under 1,000 feet (300 m.), they grew maize (the *Chinchipe* had a crop every 4 months), sweet potatoes, sweet manioc (*Chirino*), peanuts (*Chirino* and *Copallín*), many fruits, such as guava, guayaba (guaya-voa?), pears (?), caimito, lucuma, barbarry figs, zapote, and genipa, and such tubers as schiras and aracachas. The *Patagón* and perhaps others even grew potatoes.

Llamas, typical of the Highlands, were kept by the *Chirino,* and alpaca by the *Copallín,* who consequently had wool for garments. Several other tribes used woolen garments, and may have reared these animals, though cotton was more common.

Hunting and fishing devices are mentioned only in the case of the *Chinchipe,* who used fish nets, hunting nets, and hunting snares. Wild honey was gathered.

The *Patagón* ground food with stone grinders (batanes) or wooden troughs (á manera de camellon).

The *Chinchipe* lived in open sheds; the *Copallín* and *Patagón,* in round houses, those of the latter thatched to the ground. *Chirino* and *Patagón* houses held single families. The platform bed was used by the *Patagón* and *Chirino.*

Chinchipe men ordinarily went naked with the penis tied up with a string, whereas Utcubamba River *Copallín* men wore a breachclout (braquero). Probably men of all these tribes wore a shirt, that of the *Chinchipe,* Utcubamba River, Tomependa, and *Chirino* being of cotton, that of the *Patagón* and Lomas Indians of wool or cotton, and that of the *Chirino* and *Copallín* more often of wool. Shirt lengths varied, extending to the navel among the *Patagón* of Perico and to the knees at Jaén. On festive occasions, *Patagón* men wore several shirts, each with tassels.

---

[4] The *Bracamoro* Indians are the *Jívaro* of the Zamaro Valley.

Chinchipe women wore a skirt extending to the calf, and a cotton band around the chest. The more typical woman's garment was a blanket (manta) wrapped around the body, with one arm exposed. *Copallín* men shaved their heads, while women wore their hair long. On the Utcubamba River, the hair was worn in one large braid behind, two small ones on each side.

Ornaments consisted of feathers, a reed through the earlobe, a splinter through the lower lip, a shell or silver plate suspended from the nose, and string of beads around the arms and legs. A *Patagón* chief's ornament was a chest plate of white shells pieced together like armor and a large shell pendant.

All these tribes probably used the lance and spear thrower and perhaps the spear. The *Chirino* lance was of chonta palm, 30 palms long. Clubs and bone daggers were also reported. The *Chirino* shield was of wood, that of the peoples of Lomas de Viento of wood or tapir hide.

These Indians were good swimmers and used rafts.

The only suggestion of social life is that *Patagón* villages were close together and each consisted of 5 to 10 houses with 3 or 4 inhabitants each, so that a chief might rule as many as 10 houses, or 30 to 100 people.

THE JIVARO

INTRODUCTION

The *Jívaro*, (*Chiwaro, Siwaro, Jibaro, Givari, Xivari, Chivari, Givaro, Zibaro, Jivara, Hibaro, Jivira* etc.)—not to be confused with the *Cahua-panan*-speaking *Chébero* of the lower Huallaga River or the *Hibitoan*-speaking *Hibito*—comprise a linguistically isolated group in the Montaña of Ecuador north of the Marañón River (map 1, *No. 3;* map 5). There were formerly three, possibly four, main divisions: the *Jívaro* proper, the *Malacata,* the *Palta* and perhaps the now extinct *Bracamoro.* The *Palta,* aboriginally a Highland type tribe, has been assimilated into the *Quechua*-speaking population of Highland Ecuador, and is described by Murra in the Handbook, Volume 2, page 801.

The *Jívaro* proper are typical of the Montaña except in emphasis. They have little that is directly traceable to the Highland. They practice the rain forest type of farming, hunting, and fishing, but once kept a few llamas and guinea pigs. The principal weapons were formerly the bow and arrow, which were later superceded by the blowgun, spear, and atlatl. Men's dress is typical of the Montaña; women's robes pinned over the shoulder may be of Andean origin. Canoes, baskets, and ceramics are of Tropical Forest types, but men's weaving on a vertical loom is unique in the region. The extended, patrilineal family occupying a single large house is a Montaña feature, especially of the late post-Contact period.

But *Jivaro* preoccupation with warfare is an extreme development of a pattern common to neighboring tribes, and the shrunken head complex, though not unique, is outstanding in its importance and persistence. Crisis rites are distinctive only in the boys' and girls' feast or tobacco ceremony, and in disposal of the dead in hollow logs placed inside houses. The shamanistic complex includes the concept of spirit helpers and magic "darts" as the cause of disease.

TRIBAL DIVISIONS AND HISTORY

The *Jivaro* proper probably now occupy the same territory that they held in aboriginal times (lat. 2°–5° S., long. 77°–79° W., map 5). There are four principal divisions, each split into innumerable communities or jivarías, named after rivers: (1) The *Antipa,* on the right bank of the Santiago River from the Zamora to the Alto Marañón River; (2) the *Aguaruna,* on the right bank of the Marañón between the Nieve and Apaga Rivers (lat. 5° S., long. 78° W.); (3) *Huambiza,* on the right bank of the Morona and Mangosia Rivers and the left bank of the Santiago River from the Cordillera of Cuticu to the Marañón; and (4) the *Achuale* (*Achuare*), between the Pastaza and Morona Rivers, from Lake Puralina to Andoas (Stirling, 1938; pp. 2–4).

The *Palta* and *Malacata* were probably *Jivaro* living in the Highland near Loja (lat. 4° S., long. 79° W.) and speaking closely related languages (Rel. geogr. Indias, 1881–97, 3:213). For their *Jivaro* affiliations, Verneau and Rivet (1912–22, p. 37) cite Benavente's expedition (Rel. geogr. Indias, 1881–97, 4:30). Benavente crossed the Paute and Minas de Santa Barbola Rivers, the latter probably a tributary of the former, and entered what was presumed to be *Jivaro* territory, where the Indians spoke the same language as the *Malacata.*

The *Bracamoro* (*Pacamuru,* "tailed Indians") were the *Jivaro* of the Zamoro River, but the name was also applied to Indians of unknown speech in the region of Jaén de los Bracamoros.

Many attempts have been made to conquer the *Jivaro* because of the placer gold in their territory but none succeeded. Two *Inca* Emperors, Topa Inca and his son, Huayna Capac, both failed to subdue either the *Jivaro* or the *Bracamoro.* The latter, who were nearest Spanish posts in the Highland were, however, conquered in 1542 and the city of Jaén founded in 1549. The same year, the Benavente expedition visited the *Jivaro* proper. Trips by Juan de Salinas, beginning in 1557, led to the founding of several colonies, but the *Jivaro* destroyed them in 1599. The *Bracamoro* subsequently disappeared from the literature, probably having been assimilated, but the *Jivaro* proper retained their independence. During the next century, military and missionary conquests failed. It was not until 1767 that the Jesuits gained a foothold among the *Jivaro,* but they were expelled the same year, and the Franciscans carried on the work from 1790 to 1803. Missionizing subsequently became mainly a subterfuge for treasure seeking until 1850, when it was resumed with greater sincerity. The Jesuits returned in 1869 but there was an uprising in 1873 and the Jesuits were again expelled in 1886. The remainder of the century brought more travelers, missionaries, and military expeditions, but none had a lasting influence. During the present century, Protestant missionaries have entered the field. But the *Jivaro* remain unsubdued and only partially acculturated, though many speak *Quechua*. They showed aggression against the Whites as late as 1915, 1925, and 1928 (Stirling, 1938, pp. 3–28).

POPULATION

On the basis of a partial census of 1580, Stirling (1938; pp. 36–37) placed the aboriginal population at about 30,000. Modern estimates range from Rivet's 20,000 and Karsten's 15,000 to 20,000 to Tessmann's 10,000 to 12,000.

SOURCES

The *Jivaro* have probably received more attention than any other South American tribe; the scientific literature on them is enormous. Nevertheless, many aspects of *Jivaro* culture are imperfectly known.

Old missionary and explorers' accounts contain only fragments of information. (See p. 511 and Stirling, 1938, for a bibliography of these.) Ethnological studies tend to treat only limited aspects of the culture or to reflect strong theoretical views of the authors. Karsten's many publications, which are summarized in his comprehensive work (1935), were based on 3 years of field work, though he only twice spent more than 8 days in a single village. His theoretical interest in religion is very manifest, and it is frequently impossible to distinguish his own or his informant's views from his first-hand observations. Nonetheless, it is the main source on social and religious culture. Rivet's studies are compilations of older sources; he never visited the *Jivaro*. Up de Graf's (1923) work is designed for popular appeal. Tessmann (1930) adds only a few fragments of information from an *Aguaruna* informant. Stirling (1938) is the first to recognize the importance of change in the historic period; he also adds new detailed data on blowguns, preparation of shrunken heads, shamanism, weaving, and warfare.

Present needs include adequate studies of technology (which are now only partially available), clarification of social structure and function and of marriage practice through a genealogical approach, verification of the patterns of religion and shamanism, analysis of property rights, and study of agricultural methods. There is also abundant opportunity for investigation of local variations in this large and widely distributed tribe.

CULTURE

SUBSISTENCE

Jivaro crops of the 16th century were "seeds," maize, and a root, doubtless manioc. Fish, deer, tapir, wild fruits, cacao, nuts, and curassow supplemented the diet. Recently, however, the *Jivaro* have eaten neither deer nor tapir, fearing the spirits in them.

Farming.—Present-century crops appear in table 1 (p. 516). They are cultivated with much ritual (Karsten, 1935) in fields located around the communities. Nonfood crops include cotton, tobacco, mycot, natima, bixa, and barbasco (Stirling, 1938).

Agricultural rites.—Karsten (1920 a, 1935) reports certain agricultural rites of the *Jívaro*. When planting manioc to be consumed during a tobacco feast in her honor, a woman and her companions squat near the cuttings and chant an incantation. Then they address Nungui, the Earth Goddess, who is symbolized by a stone of curious shape. The first manioc cutting is painted red, and the woman to be honored places it against her groin. Each woman who plants the cuttings sits on a manioc tuber. After the field has been planted, a ceremonial digging stick is stuck into the ground and the people pray to Nungui.

The female owner of a field may not paint herself with genipa, or wear a bracelet around the forearm.

When planting banana trees, men observe various tabooes and pray to Shakaema, the husband of the Earth Goddess.

For 5 successive nights after planting their fields, *Jívaro* women dance and chant, asking the Earth Goddess to make their manioc grow. They also practice a magic ceremony to expel rodents which attack the crops. Tubers gnawed by these rodents are covered with ashes and thrown into the forest. The people chant an incantation, requesting the rats not to harm the young plants.

Hunting and fishing.—Aboriginal hunting weapons were the bow and arrow, the spear, and the atlatl. The blowgun has replaced the bow for hunting small game; and spears, thrown without the aid of the atlatl, are used for large game. Firearms are becoming more general (Stirling, 1938). Other devices include deadfalls, spring noose traps, and pitfalls with stakes in their bottoms (Tessmann, 1930). Stirling describes a communal peccary hunt carried on with the aid of dogs; the game is speared from trees or is driven into the water and pursued in canoes. Karsten (1935) gives no data on hunting methods but describes magic: Pepper is put in the eyes of hunters and their dogs to improve their vision; men take tobacco and paint their bodies red for strength; they do the same to their dogs; they keep animal trophies to insure future success; dogs are prevented from eating the bones of game; many charms are used; and hunting dogs are subjected to an elaborate ceremony involving manioc planting, fasting, drinking guayusa, and feasting.

Fish are caught by hand, drugged with barbasco and *Clibadium*, speared, harpooned, and taken with hooks, with traps placed under rapids, and with both hand nets and large casting nets. The antiquity of the hook is uncertain; bone hooks preceded iron. The *Aguaruna* catch fish ascending creeks in weirs (Villanueva, 1902–03, 13:79).

Domesticated animals.—The aboriginal *Jívaro* were unusual among Montaña tribes in keeping a few llama and guinea pigs. It is doubtful whether the dog was native. Chickens and pigs were introduced by the Spaniards and, according to Karsten, were sacrificed in many ceremonies.

Food preparation.—Food is ground on a flat wooden slab and in a mortar. It is seasoned with capsicum pepper and with both a natural and a prepared salt.

The *Jívaro* community is and always has consisted of a single large house (jivaría), usually located for defense on a steep hill at the head of some stream. It is moved at least every 6 years as new farm land is needed.

The house is elliptical, about 40 feet (13 m.) by 80 feet (26 m.), and has a thatched, gabled roof supported by interior posts and a side wall 8 to 10 feet (2.4 to 3 m.) high, made of strong, closely-spaced staves so as to be impervious to attack (pl. 60, *bottom*). One end of the house is occupied by men, the other by women. Furniture comprises sleeping platforms (fig. 91), storage platforms, hooks, and footstools. The *Aguaruna* were ascribed palm-fiber hammocks (Villanueva, 1902–03, 13:81).

FIGURE 91.—*Jívaro* platform bed. (Redrawn from Tessmann, 1930.)

Prior to missionary influence, nakedness was common although two garments seem to have been native: a wrap-around skirt for men (pl. 62, *top, right*) and a full-length robe for women. The latter is pinned over the right shoulder, the left shoulder remaining bare (pl. 62, *bottom, right*). These clothes are generally of brown cotton, but poor people may dress in bark cloth (Stirling, 1938). Some individuals also use ponchos (Tessmann, 1930).

A variety of fashions of coiffure are shown by Stirling (1938, pls. 3–10). Ornaments include fur and feather headdresses, ear pins, women's lower lip labrets, tattoo, red bixa and black (genipa) paint applied with a roller stamp, blackened teeth, wrist and leg bands, and elaborate bead collars and chest bands. Status and other special badges include hunters' ornaments made of tayo bird femora, warriors' girdles with human hair attached, face paint, head rings, and women's upper arm bands.

TRANSPORTATION

Goods are transported in hexagonally-woven baskets held by tumplines. Babies are carried in bands (pl. 60, *top, left*).

Dugout canoes of some size and excellence seem to be aboriginal, but they have never been adequately described.

MANUFACTURES

Basketry.—Hexagonally-woven carrying baskets and mats are mentioned, but basketry techniques have not been analyzed.

Spinning and weaving.—Men do all spinning, weaving, and knitting. Astrocaryum fibers are used to knit bags with an eyed needle and to make fish nets. Cultivated cotton is spun with a kind of drop spindle, the cotton being fed from an elevated container. Belts and clothing are woven on a nearly vertical loom set in a frame. The warp is wrapped continuously around the upper and lower bars, producing a cylindrical piece of cloth. Women color textiles with brown vegetable dyes (Stirling, 1938).

Pottery.—Women are potters. They use a coil technique (pl. 62) and make cooking vessels, bowls, and large chicha jars. Some vessels have incised zigzag decorations. Others are fired, then colored red with copal (Stirling, 1938) or urucú (Tessmann, 1930; Karsten, 1935) (pl. 52, *h*). Some bowl interiors are decorated with white geometric designs representing mythical figures. *Aguaruna* bowl interiors are painted red-and-black-on-white and are varnished with caraña. Some bowls have rattling pebbles inside a double bottom.

Skin work.—Several fur products are made, including head bands and bags. Preparation of shrunken heads (p. 625) also involves techniques of skin and hair preservation.

Metallurgy.—The *Jívaro* have remained very indifferent to the considerable placer gold in their territory. Of Highland metal objects, they acquired only a few copper axes.

Fire making.—Fire is made with the drill and activated with a feather fan.

Weapons.—Weapons of warfare reported in 1540 were lances and round shields; in 1571, spears, spear throwers, round shields of tapir hide and wood, and copper axes; and, in 1582, throwing spears, thrusting lances, and stones (for slings?). The bow and arrow and spear were used in 1582 for hunting.

During the late 17th century, the bow and spear thrower were abandoned, and the blowgun and hand-thrown spear became the principal hunting weapons. In the present century, blowguns, spears (pl. 62), and firearms are used for hunting. Spears are often tipped with iron, but heads of human bone or chonta palm wood are preferred, the latter for their magical potency. The shield is now made of hide or of a single piece of wood to resemble three concentric, superimposed circular slabs.

SOCIOPOLITICAL GROUPS

The sociopolitical unit from pre-Columbian times to the present day has been the household, which formerly consisted of 80 to 300 persons and occupied a single dwelling (jivaría), but today has only 30 to 40 persons. Each house stands in a more or less isolated, defendable site, one-half to several leagues from its neighbor.

The group occupying the jivaría is described as patrilineal, but no analysis of its composition or structure is available. Karsten's assertion (1935) that, after a period of matrilocal residence, a newly married couple established its own house scarcely fits the picture of a patrilineal household which would require ultimate residence in the groom's father's house.

Each community is independent, having its own headman, but half a dozen friendly jivarías may unite temporarily for warfare. After the 16th-century rebellions against the encomenderos, large numbers of jivarías formed alliances against the Spaniards.

LIFE CYCLE

Childbirth.—*Jívaro* women know vegetable abortives. During child birth, a mother is isolated lest she contaminate other people. Afterward, both parents are subjected to food taboos and to various restrictions on their activities in order to protect the infant, but the father does not remain in bed. Unlike many neighboring tribes, the *Jívaro* do not kill one of twins. They practice infanticide only on deformed babies (Karsten, 1920 a).

Puberty.—Tessmann (1930) denies that the *Jívaro* have menstrual observances, but Karsten (1920 a, pp. 13–28) describes measures to protect menstruating women from spirits which seek to make her pregnant and a tobacco ceremony designed to give a girl strength after her first menses and to reinvigorate an older woman. The ceremony begins with a crop fertility ceremony and the slaughter of specially raised pigs and chickens, after which the girl takes tobacco juice to cause vomiting and to produce visions. He also describes a feast to initiate boys into manhood (Karsten, 1935, pp. 237–242), but there appears to be no secret cult.

Marriage.—A man may marry his cross-cousin and his sister's daughter (Karsten, 1935, p. 186). Polygyny is common, especially because of high male mortality in warfare. Stirling describes marriage by purchase, often of pre-pubescent girls (1938), but Karsten states that bride service to the girl's father is given during several years of matrilocal residence in lieu of a price. The levirate is required.

Death.—Archeology indicates some former urn burial in *Jívaro* territory (Stirling, 1938), though recently only the *Aguaruna* have practiced this method (Tessmann, 1930). In the historic period, an ordinary person was placed in a hollow-log coffin in a special hut; a chief's coffin was left in his dwelling, which was abandoned. The deceased was supplied with food and drink for 2 years, at the end of which he was supposed to become an animal or bird (Stirling, 1938). Some children, however, were buried in urns, and occasionally adults were given earth burial (Karsten, 1935, p. 460). Among all *Jívaro,* missionary influence has made earth burial more frequent.

WARFARE

The *Jívaro* differ from other Montaña tribes neither in the causes, methods, nor weapons of warfare but in their extreme zeal for war. Excited to rebellion during their 16th-century reduction on Spanish encomiendas, the *Jívaro* became formidable foes who have never been truly conquered to the present day. But their more absorbing military efforts have always been directed toward other *Jívaro* communities. The desire to avenge the death of members of their own household or to retaliate against imagined sorcery, together with social prestige attached to military success, has, despite intervillage kinship bonds, pitted communities against one another in unending reprisals. Peace, concluded through the ceremony of burying the lance, may readily be broken by serving formal notice on the foe. The chronic danger of attack accounts for the elaborate rites by which peaceful visitors must approach and be received into a village.

Warfare is directed by a special chief of considerable though temporary authority. It begins with a dance of excitation while a shaman drinking cayapi invokes supernatural assistance. The aggressors attempt a surprise attack, using spears but never blowguns. Around their village the defenders have placed lances and firearms, both automatically released by bent poles, and barricades, pitfalls, and trenches filled with sharp stakes. If worsted, the villagers call for help with their signal drums and barricade themselves in their houses, shooting through loop holes. The victors shrink the heads taken from their foe and go home to celebrate a victory dance. The shrunken heads are proof that the ancestors have been avenged.

Shrunken heads.—Shrunken heads (tsantsas) are now most typical of but not peculiar to the *Jívaro* (pl. 63). The skin is cut and removed from the skull, the lips are everted and pinned or sewed together, and the whole head skin is boiled with a plant which somewhat shrinks it and fixes the hair. It is further reduced by placing hot stones and sand inside it; then it is smoked, polished, and kept in a jar. When victim's heads cannot be taken, sloth or other animal tsantsas may be substituted.

Many fraudulent shrunken heads, made from unclaimed dead in city morgues, are on the market and in museums. They generally lack one or more of the following characteristics of genuine *Jívaro* tsantsas: Lips sewn or pinned, the forehead compressed laterally, nostrils dilated, all facial hair except eyebrows removed (mustaches frequently reveal falsified tsantsas), the skin smoked-blackened and polished, and little ornamentation except the lip threads. The *Jívaro,* moreover, never preserve the whole body. (See Stirling, 1938.)

ESTHETIC AND RECREATIONAL ACTIVITIES

Art.—The principal *Jívaro* art products are carved spear handles, feathered head ornaments, and mythological paintings on pots and other objects.

Musical instruments.—*Jívaro* musical instruments include: Hollow-log signal drums used singly (fig. 92; pl. 62); two-headed skin drums

FIGURE 92.—*Jívaro* drum. (Redrawn from Tessmann, 1930, pl. 59.)

played both by dancers and by shamans; transverse and longitudinal flutes; musical bows; snail-shell signal trumpets; and jangles of shell and other materials attached to belts and leg bands. The *Aguaruna* make primitive two-string violins in imitation of Spanish models. Panpipes are merely children's toys.

Drinks and narcotics.—Chicha is made by fermenting manioc and other plants. Narcotics include tobacco, cayapi, *Datura,* and guayusa. Tobacco, the most important, was formerly taken only for magical purposes but is now generally smoked for enjoyment. Karsten (1935) describes the use of tobacco in boys' initiation rites, in women's tobacco ceremonies, in curing, in general magic, and in vision seeking. It is smoked as cigars, or else the juice is drunk or blown up the nose. Placed in the eye, it is thought to counteract bad dreams; painted on the body, it gives protection.

Cayapi is used by shamans or by people wishing to contact ghosts or to provoke divinatory visions.

Datura is drunk or taken as an enema through a straw by warriors desiring to gain power and to foretell the future.

Guayusa is a purgative and emetic and is believed to give strength.

SHAMANISM

The *Jivaro* shaman seems to have a greater variety of functions than his colleague among other Montaña tribes, though the incomparably richer material on the *Jivaro* (Stirling, 1938) may be responsible for this impression. He assists in warfare, makes rain, manufactures love potions, gives miscellaneous advice when under the influence of guayusa, causes disease, and cures illness by both herbal and supernatural means.

A neophyte shaman is instructed for 1 month, dieting for 5 days and taking five drugs, including tobacco juice, cayapi, and three others, one of which may be *Datura*. He learns to control several disease-causing spirits: the spirit of the blowgun; the ray fish, most dangerous of all; snakes; a doorlike spirit causing barrenness; the woodpecker and toucan, which cause stomach trouble; the night bird, which brings various ills; and insects, which cause skin troubles.

To cause sickness, a shaman blows one of the spirits he controls into his victim by means of tobacco smoke (Stirling, 1938) or, with the aid of his spirits, he sends a magical "thorn" or "dart" (Tessmann, 1930; Karsten, 1935) into him. A water monster may also cause illness. To cure, a shaman sings, plays his drum, takes *Datura*, tobacco, and cayapi, and sucks out the "thorn." Shamans may also reveal the identity of a sorcerer. Some shamans may turn into jaguars to attack people.

RELIGION

Jivaro religion is based on the concept of a supernatural essence (tsarutama) that gives power to both objects and spirits. This essence is in the Rain God, who inhabits mountain peaks, in various animals including the Anaconda God, who lives in rapids, in demons, in the sun, the moon, the earth mother (whose importance is repeatedly stressed by Karsten), and, among plants, especially manifest in the chonta palm. It is in many fetishes, such as shrunken heads, fur balls taken from animal stomachs, certain brown stones, seeds, and jaguar teeth (Stirling, 1938). Though feared, these various spirits and demons are the object of no organized cults. The supreme god, Cumbanama, is remote and has no interest in human affairs.

Karsten mentions an ancestor cult, which seems to be linked with ideas of reincarnation. Recorded beliefs about life after death, however, are too varied and conflicting to reveal a clear pattern of ancestor worship. Souls of warriors become, according to the qualities of the deceased man, either ferocious animals, such as jaguars, or innocuous animals, and children become birds. Shamans turn into dangerous monkeys, bears, and deer (Stirling, 1938). Karsten also describes a belief in transmigration of souls to plants as well as to animals. Potential danger from one's ancestors motivates vengeance of their death, but it is not clear that they are propitiated to procure their direct intervention in worldly affairs. No formal ancestor cult with secret initiation, like that of the *Tucano* tribes, is indicated.

There is some hint of a guardian spirit concept in Karsten's statement (1935) that animals, birds, and other spirits seen under the influence of narcotics help the dreamer in various ways. These spirits, called the "old ones," seem to have some connection with the concept of reincarnation.

Karsten describes five ceremonies which employ magic. These, mentioned above, are the victory celebration and the ceremonies for the benefit of children, young men, women, and dogs. It is curious that pigs and chickens, both post-Columbian elements, have a prominent role in these rites.

MYTHOLOGY

Despite the continued vitality of *Jívaro* culture, mythology is being forgotten.

The creation myth recounts that Cupara (Compadre?) and his wife were parents of the Sun. They created Sun's wife, Moon, of mud. Among children of the Sun and Moon were Manioc and various animals, including the Sloth, which was the first *Jívaro*. Ensuing adventures of the parents and children account for a large portion of *Jívaro* culture (Stirling, 1938).

The myth of the star brothers is very similar to the *Tupí* tale of twins. A jaguar killed his *Jívaro* wife, but his mother secretly reared his two sons, who became stars. When adults, they killed the jaguar to avenge their mother, then returned to the sky by means of an arrow chain (Karsten, 1935, pp. 523-526). Other tales recount the flood, the theft of fire by Hummingbird, and the acquisition of salt, potter's clay, and pumpkins (Karsten, 1935).

BIBLIOGRAPHY

Karsten, 1920 a, b, 1921, 1935; Relaciones geográficas de Indias, 1881–97; Rivet, 1924; Stirling, 1938; Tessmann, 1930; Up de Graf, 1923; Verneau and Rivet, 1912–22; Villanueva, 1902–03.

ZAPAROAN TRIBES

INTRODUCTION

Záparoan-speaking tribes occupied a large territory between the Marañón, Napo, and Pastaza Rivers (map 1, *No. 3;* map 5). The main tribes were the *Maina,* the *Coronado* and closely related *Oa,* the *Andoa* and closely related *Gae* and *Semigae,* and the *Pinche, Roamaina (Omurana), Iquito, Awishira, Záparo, Zapa,* and *Canelo.* In addition, there were several tribes of doubtful affiliation in this area: The *Aunale, Alabono, Curizeta, Sucumbio, Coronado* of the Aguarico River, *Neva, Comacor,* and others mentioned below.

Záparoan culture is characterized by considerable variation, the result perhaps of the extreme isolation of the communities, the native lack of canoes for communication along rivers, and the presence of *Witotoan* and *Tucanoan* tribes to the north, the Andean peoples to the west, and the Marañón and upper Amazon tribes to the south and east, which subjected them to diverse influence.

Subsistence was based on sweet manioc, though the bitter variety was introduced to the *Maina* and *Roamaina* at the end of the 18th century. The *Záparoans* did much hunting and fishing, but with simple devices. Blowguns and spears were used for hunting, but poison for the blowgun was imported. The spear thrower was probably aboriginal but was later abandoned. Bows were used little, if at all. Drugs, some nets, and possibly hooks were the main fishing devices.

Early houses and communities were small; the large communal house may be post-European. Mosquito tents and hammocks of cachibana or *Astrocaryum* were well developed. Transportation devices are distinctive only in the aboriginal lack of canoes. Among manufactures, the development of cachibana cloth is outstanding; chambira fiber and cotton products are not unusual.

The aboriginal sociopolitical unit was probably the extended patrilineal family, perhaps smaller than among neighboring tribes. The couvade is strongly developed. The *Awishira,* who adjoined the *Western Tucanoans,* may have initiation rites. Bride service with ultimate patrilocal residence resembles that of other Montaña tribes. The practices of earth burial, urn burial, scaffold burial, and endocannibalism bring widespread features into new combinations.

Wars were fought with spears and shields, the victims eaten, and trophy skulls taken. Musical instruments are remarkable only for the presence of armadillo-shell trumpets, the absence of musical bows, and the near absence of panpipes. The signal drum is a northern feature. Narcotics include tobacco, cayapi, guayusa, and *Datura;* coca is not used.

Religion is typically based on animism, with beliefs in bush and water demons. Shamanism involves spirit powers as well as "thorns."

TRIBAL DIVISIONS AND HISTORY

Rivet (1930, p. 696) classified *Záparoan* as an independent family, with resemblance to the *Tupian Miranya* (*Bora*), and named five dialects—*Záparo, Konambo, Gae, Ando* (*Semigae, Simiga, Shimagai,* or *Ga*), and *Iquito*—and 39 subtribes. Many of these so-called subtribes, such as the *Blanco, Conambo, Curaray, Iginori, Mauta, Meugano, Napotoa, Shiripuno, Supinu, Tiputini,* and *Yasuni* (Beuchat and Rivet, 1908, pp. 237–239) are merely local groups that were named after rivers, a common practice in the Montaña, and consequently merit no further consideration. Grubb (1927, pp. 75–76) lists as modern *Záparoan* subtribes the *Andoa, Yasuni, Pinche, Záparo, Auca* (numbering 2,000), *Nushino,* and *Supinu. Auca,* however, is a generic term in the Montaña for pagan as contrasted to Christian Indians. *Yasuni, Nushino,* and *Supinu,* probably named from rivers, are difficult to equate with the older terms. Ortíz (1940, p. 101) gives the following *Záparoan* dialects: *Gae, Semigae, Iquito, Iginori,* and *Panocarri,* several of which also are evidently river names.

LIST OF TRIBES

The list of tribes included here as *Záparoan* in speech does not entirely correspond to that of Rivet. For the *Záparoan* affinity of *Andoa, Iquito, Gae,* and *Záparo,* Beuchat and Rivet (1908, pp. 241–249) have published linguistic material. Evidence that the *Coronado* and *Roamaina* spoke *Záparoan,* although Beuchat and Rivet (1909) assign them to the *Cahuapanan* family, is cited below. Similarly, we include *Awishira* as *Záparoan,* although Rivet (1924, p. 686) considers them *Tucanoan.*

Maina (*Mayna, Rimachu*).—The *Maina,* the most famous tribe in the ancient Province of Maynas, occupied the lower Morona and Pastaza Rivers down to the Marañón River (Veigl, 1785 b, p. 29), and the Marañón River almost to the Pongo de Manseriche (lat. 4°–5° S., long. 77° W.) (Rel. geogr. Indias, 1881–97, 4:CXL). Their attacks had forced the Indians of Nieva (probably the *Aguaruna*) to retreat from this region toward Nieva. The territory was subsequently occupied by the *Chayawita* and other Indians of the Potro River (Rel. geogr. Indias, 1881–97, 4:CXLII). The *Maina* centered, however, at Laguna Grande de Rimachu (hence *Rimachu*), now called Laguna Rimachuma or Rimachi, west of the lower Pastaza River (Maroni, 1889–92, 26:218).

Tessmann's classification of several tribes in this region must be disregarded, because he states (1930) that *Rimachuma* and *Maina* are synonyms for *Kandoshi,* whom he divides into two subtribes, the *Murata* and *Shapra* (*Chapra, Chapa*). The *Murata,* however, were a subtribe of the *Andoa,* and the *Zapa* a subtribe of the *Roamaina.*

Captain Alonso Mercadillo, descending the Huallaga River in 1538, may have visited the *Maina,* but Juan de Salinas, who found them in 1557 below the Pongo de Manseriche, was the first to describe them. Salinas explored the lower Pastaza River and Rimachuma Lagoon. About 1580, an attempt to build a settlement at the Rimachuma Lagoon apparently failed (Rel. geogr. Indias, 1881–97, 4:34–35). During the 16th century, Spaniards from Santiago de las Montañas on the Santiago River and from Nieva frequently raided the *Maina* to capture slaves or to avenge *Maina* attacks, some of which reached their settlements above the Pongo de Manseriche and even approached Santiago.

After a punitive expedition against the *Maina* in 1616, the Spaniards made peace with several of their chiefs. In 1619, Diego Vaca de Vega took possession of the Province of Maynas, which had been granted to him, established Borja, and sent his son, Pedro Vaca de Vega, to subdue the *Maina* of the Pastaza River and Rimachuma Lagoon (which he called Maracaybo Lagoon). His son brought 4,000 of this tribe from Rimachuma to Borja (Rel. geogr. Indias, 4: LXXI–LXXIII, CXXXIX–CXLV, CLII–CLIV; Figueroa, 1904, pp. 13–33; La jornada del Capitán Alonso Mercadillo, 1895), where, according to Maroni (1889–92, 29:191–203), 600 *Maina* "family heads" (about 3,000 Indians) were distributed among 60 Spaniards as vassals for their encomiendas. Figueroa (1904, p. 15), places the figure at 700 family heads, about 3,500 Indians.

Epidemics and warfare had, by 1636, reduced the *Maina* at Borja to 400 families, or 2,000 Indians (Figueroa, 1904, p. 15). In the general revolt of 1640, the *Maina* killed 34 Spaniards but failed to take Borja (Chantre y Herrera, 1901, pp. 120–122). A new governor, Don Pedro Vaca, pursued them, brought about half back to Borja, and called upon Jesuit missionaries to help pacify them. The Indians were distributed among 21 encomiendas, where the Fathers traveled to baptize them, but the Jesuits estimated that only 1 out of 10 survived the brutal treatment they received. In 1642, the *Maina* were again decimated by epidemics (Maroni, 1889–92), and in 1661, only 200 "tributaries" (about 1,000 Indians) remained at Borja. This number included other Indians more recently brought in but excluded some 500 who had fled (Figueroa, 1904). The total population was about 1,500.

In 1668, Father Juan Lucero founded three *Maina* missions: San Luiz Gonzaga. with 70 family heads (350 Indians); San Ignacio de Loyola, with 110 family heads (550 Indians); and Santa Teresa, with 91 family heads (455 Indians).

There remained in 1737 only one village of *Maina* encomendados, San Ignacio, near Borja, with a population of 63 people (Maroni, 1889–92, 29:191–203). A few pagan fugitives were on the Samiria River (Maroni, 1889–92, 26:292).

In 1752, Christian Indians from Chayawitas helped to found a mission for the *Maina* at Rimachuma. Another mission, San Juan el Evangelista, was established below the mouth of the Pastaza (Chantre y Herrera, 1901, p. 520). In 1768, the *Maina* population had greatly decreased because of revolts, smallpox, suicide, and infanticide, although missionaries had brought in a few more families from the forests (Veigl, 1785 b, p. 30). Izaguirre (1922–29, 12:396–397) considers that the *Maina* are now extinct.

Záparo.—The *Záparo (Curaray, Zápara),* named from their wickerwork baskets, cannot be located with certainty because many *Záparoan* groups seemingly bore this name.

The *Záparo* proper were first found by Father de la Cueva below the junction of the Noxino (Oas) and Curaray Rivers, some distance inland (lat. 2°30′ S., long. 76° W.) (Maroni, 1889–92, 29:230). The mission of Los Santos de Záparas must have contained *Záparo* though it is not so stated explicitly (Chantre y Herrera, 1901, p. 308). In 1848, Father Castrucci found *Záparo* on the Bobonaza River, 7 days' travel from its mouth, and near the Tigriacu and Napo Rivers, the whole tribe numbering 1,000, a sharp contrast to Osculati's estimate of 20,000 persons a few years later.

In the second half of the 19th century, the *Záparo* were divided into two groups: one, the more numerous, between the Curaray, Napo, and lower Arajuno Rivers, the other, centering in a village on the upper Curaray River but including settlements along the Lliguino, Nushinu, Nuganu, Supinu, and other rivers (Pierre, 1889, p. 90; Simson, 1886, p. 166). Of numerous groups named after rivers—*Muegano, Curaray, Tupitini, Matagen, Yasuni, Manta, Shiripuno, Nushino, Andoas, Rotuno,* and others (Villavicencio, 1858, p. 170)—many are probably *Záparoan* subtribes. A large number of these spoke *Quechua* in addition to *Záparo.*

In 1925 Tessmann (1930) guessed that only a few hundred *Záparo* remained; they occupied the sources of the Curaray, Villano, and Cononaco Rivers.

More recently, a small group of *Záparo* has been discovered on the Putumayo River in Colombia at Salado Chico, between Puerto Leguízamo (formerly Caucaya) and Puerto Montclar del Putumayo. These Indians had originally lived on the Napo River, near the *Witoto-Caimito.* The *Záparo* of the upper Napo River speak only *Quechua* (Ortíz, 1940, p. 99).

Zapa (*Cepa, Iñuru*).—The *Zapa,* so-called because the women wore a shell pubic cover, were apparently distinct from the *Záparo,* being linguistically and culturally close to the *Roamaina,* whose history they shared (Figueroa, 1904, pp. 135–136). (Lat. 4° S., long. 76° W.) These are perhaps Tessmann's *Shapera* (*Sapa*), a division of his so-called *Kandoshi.*

Gae and Semigáe.—The *Gae* (*Gaye, Siaviri*) and *Semigáe* (*Semi Gaye, Ssemigáe, Soronotoa?*) were so closely related linguistically, culturally, and geographically that they might be considered a single tribe. (Lat. 2°–3° S., long. 76°–77° W.) Rivet's *Gae* vocabulary is also very similar to that of the *Andoan Murata.*

The *Gae* lived between the Tigre and Bobonaza Rivers, the latter being the home of the *Coronado,* their bitter enemies. They occasionally visited the Bobonaza River, but their villages were some days travel in the interior. (Figueroa, 1904, p. 155, however, placed them on the Bobonaza.) From subsequent historical accounts (below) the *Gae* seem mainly to have occupied the Beleno (present Villano?) and Callana-yacu Rivers, both headwaters of the Curaray River (Maroni, 1889–92, 29:85). Chantre y Herrera (1901, pp. 207, 214, 249, 307–308) locates them near the Bobonaza River between the Pastaza and Napo Rivers, which they visited to fish. Veigl (1785 b, p. 50) states that *Gae* and *Semigáe* territory was between the upper Tigre, Napo, and Curaray Rivers.

The *Semigáe* were east of the *Gae,* on the Curaray River above the *Awishira* and were neighbors of the *Neva* (*Neova*) and *Záparo* (Maroni, 1889–92, 29:229, 261–264). *Semigáe* subdivisions were the *Aracohor, Mocosiohiro, Usicohor, Ichocomohor, Itoromohor,* and *Maithiore,* the last sometimes appearing as an independent tribe (op. cit.). The *Comacor* on the upper Tigre River might, judging by the name, be a *Semigáe* subdivision, but a *Semigáe* informant mentioned them in connection with the *Neva* (Maroni, 1889–92, 26:232). As the *Neva* were neighbors of the *Semigáe,* this might imply that the *Comacor* were either a distinct tribe or a *Roamaina* subdivision, or that *Comacor* was a synonym for the *Iquito,* who were also called *Mamacor* and *Omacacor.*

The *Gae* were first visited by Dominicans on the upper Pastaza River near the *Canelo* in 1581 (Pierre, 1889, p. 135) but subsequently eluded all missionaries and slavers (Maroni, 1889–92, 29:29, 85–86, 231–235, 246) until 1672, when a few of the tribe entered their first mission, San Xavier, on the Gaye River (Maroni, 1889–92, 29:255; Chantre y Herrera, 1901, p. 250). But continued slave raids from the Pastaza River region and intermittent missionary activity prevented complete stability of the mission until Father Nicholas Durango settled at San Xavier in 1696. Meanwhile a *Gae* cacique induced some of the *Semigáe* to enter San Xavier and others to join Mission Santa Cruz on the Pastaza River (Chantre y Herrera, 1901, p. 308).

In 1707, when the Indians killed Father Durango, the *Semigáe* and most of the *Gae* fled from San Xavier. The chief who instigated the murder went to the *Neva* and *Zápara* in the role of a missionary, but was finally killed (Maroni, 1889–92, 29:256). The next year, many *Semigáe* and the *Gae* who had remained at San Xavier went to the *Andoa mission,* Santo Tomé. The *Gae* who stayed in the bush were practically wiped out within 2 years by Spanish slavers from Borja. By 1768, the *Gae* were extinct, while only a few *Semigáe* survived, some in the mission of Andoas, others wild (Veigl, 1785 b, p. 51).

In modern times, Ortíz (1940) found two *Semigáe* dialects, one on the Tigre River, related to *Andoa* and another on the Curaray River.

Andoa.—The *Andoa* were closely related linguistically and culturally to the *Gae* and *Semigáe* (Chantre y Herrera, 1901, pp. 307–308), which led Tessmann (1930) incorrectly to believe that *Semigáe* is merely a synonym for *Andoa.* They lived aboriginally between the Pastaza and Morona Rivers (Veigl, 1785 b, p. 47) above the *Maina* (lat. 3°–4° S., long. 77° W.). Three *Andoan* groups mentioned in early sources—the *Guallpayo* (*Toqueoreo*), *Guasaga,* and *Murata*—appear to be post-Columbian subdivisions, which had separated from the *Andoa* proper.

Andoa was a name applied not only to the tribes of the Pastaza River above the *Maina,* but in 1582 to the Indians of the encomiendas of the Santiago River, who had probably been brought by slavers from the Pastaza River. The *Andoa* taken from the Guasaga River (Maroni, 1889–92, 29:261–263) to the region of Borja on the Marañón River were called *Guasaga.* Those who escaped the encomiendas and returned to their homes became known as *Guallpayo.* A hamlet of 56 *Andoa* remained at Del Alto or Nuestra Señora de las Nieves opposite Borja in 1737.

Toward the end of the 17th century, the *Andoa* remaining in the Pastaza River region were settled by Father Tomas Santos on the Bobonaza River, somewhat above the Mission of San Xavier, but the settlement did not thrive. In 1701, the *Andoa* on the Guasaga River were collected in a mission by Father Nicolas Durango, then they moved to the *Gae* mission, but fled in 1707, fearing the *Semigáe* who murdered Father Durango. Subsequently they joined the *Gae, Semigáe, Guallpayo,* and *Guasaga* in the Mission of Santo Tomé de los Andoas built in 1708 on the Pastaza River near the Bobonaza River. In 1737, this mission had 447 people (Chantre y Herrera, 1901, pp. 307–308, 419; Maroni, 1889–92, 26:227; 29:261–263) and in 1768, 400. There were also *Andoa* at Borja and a few wild families in the bush. In the first half of the next century, the tribe lacked a mission and became a constant victim of *Jívaro* and *Murata* raids. In 1846, however, Father Castrucci gathered 450 *Andoa* into their ancient village. In 1925, only 12 families remained at Andoas (Tessmann, 1930).

The *Murata* (*Murato*), erroneously included by Tessmann (1930) as a *Kandoshi* (*Maina*) subtribe, were not known previous to 1744. The *Andoa* at Santo Tomé had long reported that a tribe called the *Murata* lived near their territory and menaced them when they hunted in the bush and carved canoes on the Guasaga River. They said that the *Murata* were related to them (Veigl, 1785 b, p. 43; Escobar y Mendoza, 1769, p. 58, expresses the same opinion), but a vocabulary supposed to be *Murata,* published in 1928 (see Rivet, 1930) bears no resemblance to any *Záparoan* dialect. The *Murata* fought off Jesuit missionary expeditions in 1748 and in 1754, but the next year a *Murata* was captured and sent back to his tribe with presents, after which they agreed to have a mission. Nuestra Señora de los Dolores was founded on the Guasaga River with 158 Indians (Chantre y Herrera, 1901, pp. 477–482). In 1762, many *Jívaro* joined the *Murata.*

In the first half of the 19th century, the *Murata* were reported attacking the *Andoa* and, about 1846, they and the unidentified *Machine* Indians frequently came from the Manacaro-yacu and Mitu-yacu Rivers to assault travelers on the Pastaza River. These tribes still inhabit the marshy region between the Pastaza, Morona, and Marañón Rivers.

The *Guallpayo* were the *Andoa* who escaped from encomiendas near Santiago de las Montañas on the Santiago River, where they were listed in 1582 (Relación de la gobernación de Yahuarzongo y Pacamurus, *in* Rel. geogr. Indias, 1881–97, 4:34–35), and, to avoid slavers, settled near the *Gae* (Maroni, 1889–92, 29:263) at the headwaters of the Tigre River. They might originally have been an *Andoan* enclave among the *Jívaro* on the Santiago River, but more likely they had been brought from the Pastaza River by slavers who raided the *Maina* and *Gae* in the 16th and 17th centuries (Rel. geogr. Indias, 1881–97, 71–73, 146, 152–154; Figueroa, 1904, pp. 13–33). Some of the *Guallpayo* joined the Mission of San Xavier (founded in 1672), but were subordinate to *Gae.* In 1684, others were reported in the forests pirating on the Asarunatoas River, fighting the *Asarunatoa,* and intimidating other tribes.

The *Guallpayo* were last mentioned in 1708, when a few of them with 100 *Guasaga* were building a mission on the Pastaza River near the Bobonaza River. The mission later included *Gae, Semigáe,* and *Andoa,* and it is presumed that the *Guallpayo* became submerged in this population.

Coronado (*Ipapiza, Hichachapa, Quilinina*).—These Indians were called *Coronado* because of their triangular, crownlike hairdress. Early references variously located their habitat on: the Pastaza River near the mouth of the Bobonaza River, 1656 (Figueroa, 1904, p. 157); the Aarrabima River, a right tributary of the Pastaza somewhat above the Bobonaza (Maroni, 1889–92, 26:216); and the Tigre River, 2 days below its headwaters and 1 day overland from the Bobonaza River (lat. 3° S., long. 77° W.). The *Coronado* of the Aguarico River (Maroni, 1889–92, 29:183) were probably a totally different tribe, perhaps *Tucanoan,* who bore this name because of a similar hairdress.

The *Taroqueo* (probably distinct from the *Toqueoreo,* an *Andoan* subtribe), spoke the same language as the *Coronado.* In 1681, 6,000 *Taroqueo* lived near the *Coronado, Gae,* and *Záparo* (Chantre y Herrera, 1901, p. 273). The *Chudavina,* whom Maroni calls "friends of the Coronado," and whom missionaries wished to unite with them (Figueroa, 1904, p. 158), may also have spoken the same language. The *Miscuara,* mentioned as living near the *Coronado* on both sides of the Pastaza River (Chantre y Herrera, 1901, p. 60), were perhaps also related to the latter.

Beuchat and Rivet (1909, p. 619) classify the *Coronado* as *Cahuapanan*, accepting Chantre y Herrera's statement that the former were south of *Pinche,* between the Pastaza and Tigre Rivers, at about lat 3° 50′ S., adjoining the *Maina.* Earlier references, however, not only place them north of this supposed location, well within *Záparoan* territory, but explicit statements link them with the *Záparoans.* Figueroa (1904, p. 155) calls them "kinsmen" of the *Oa,* while Chantre y Herrera (1901, p. 239) states that the *Oa* spoke the same language as the *Awishira.* Father Lucero wrote in 1676 that the *Awishira* understood the language of the *Coronado* and *Gae* (Maroni, 1889–92, 29:246), the latter unquestionably *Záparoan.*

The *Coronado* were first contacted by slavers who subsequently captured many of them. The tribe remained elusive, however, until 1656, when two *Coronado* slaves sent by a Jesuit, found them at the mouth of the Bobonaza River. Only 43 persons remained of the once large tribe, the others having been killed by the *Gae,* the *Maca* (probably a *Jivaro* subtribe), and the Spanish slavers. Seven families fleeing from the *Gae* had migrated north to join their kinsmen, the *Oa.*

In 1659, Brother Antonio Fernández de Enciso stayed among the *Coronado* 7 months, building the Mission of Jesús de los Coronados, but no other missionary came after his departure and they returned to the bush. In 1702, Father Gasper Vidal brought them back to this mission, hoping to settle them with the *Semigáe,* but as their name disappears from the literature, they probably died off or were assimilated (Figueroa, 1904, pp. 153–160; Maroni 1889–92, 29:88).

Oa.—The *Oa* (*Oaqui, Deguaca, Santa Rosino*), close relatives and neighbors of the *Coronado,* lived near the Aarrabima River near the junction of the Bobonaza and Pastaza Rivers (lat. 2° 30′ S., long. 77° W.). Spanish slavers and *Gae* hostility drove them to the Tigre headwaters, thence to the Nushino (Nonxino) River, where some *Coronado* families joined them. They were put in a mission in 1659, then transferred to a mission on the Ansupi River, and finally placed under secular authority at Santa Rosa (Maroni, 1889–92, 29:118–119). They have since disappeared from the literature.

Roamaina.—The *Roamaina* (*Numurana, Hunurana, Omurana*), totally distinct from the *Maina,* lived at the headwaters of the Chambira River (lat. 3°30′ S., long. 76° W.). The *Zapa* seem to have been an intimately associated tribe or subtribe. The *Pinche, Pava,* and *Araza,* who spoke the same language and lived in the same region as the *Roamaina* (Maroni, 1889–92, 29:264–266), may also have been subgroups of this tribe. The *Habitoa,* found in 1684 with the *Pinche* on a tributary of the upper Tigre above the Asarunatoas River (the *Asarunatoa* might have been an *Andoa* subtribe), may or may not have been another of their subtribes (Maroni, 1889–92, 32:142–143). The *Uspa,* who lived with the *Pinche* and *Araza* in the Pastaza Basin and were taken to the same

PLATE 48.—**Panoan Indians of the 19th century.** *Top: Conibo* playing ring-and-pin game. *Center:* Procession of the Immaculate Conception, at Sarayacu, on the Ucayali River. *Bottom: Conibo* Indians shooting tortoises. (After Marcoy, 1869.)

PLATE 49.—**Conibo Indians.** *Top:* Village on the Pachitea River. (After Castelnau, 1850–59.) *Bottom:* Group wearing cushmas. Some have lip plugs. (Courtesy University Museum, Philadelphia.)

PLATE 50.—**Cashibo and Campa garment types.** *Left: Cashibo* man and wife. *Right: Campo* boy in cushma. (After Tessmann, 1930.)

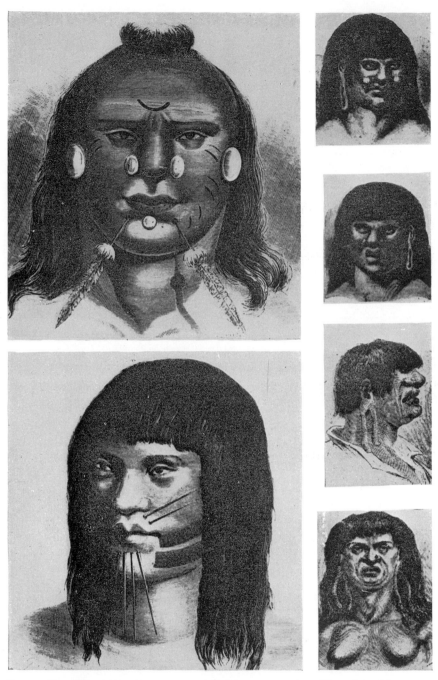

PLATE 51.—**Montaña ear, nose, and lip ormanents.** *Top, left: Mayoruna.
Bottom, left: Marahua.* (After Marcoy, 1869.) *Right:* Types of ear enlarge-
ments for ornaments: *Coto-Orejón,* above; *"Sarayacu,"* below. (After
Ricaurte, 1936.)

PLATE 52.—**Montaña pottery types.** *a–d*, Polychrome: black-and-red on cream; *e*, *f*, white-on-red; *g*, *h*, red-on-cream. *a, Conibo*, fine-type polychrome; *b, Aguano: c, Munichi: d, Chébero: e, Yameo: f, Chayawita: g, Yameo: h, Jívaro.* (*a*, Courtesy University Museum, Philadelphia; *b–h*, after Tessmann, 1930, color pls. 5, 7, 9, 11, and 13.)

PLATE 53.—**Masco Indians.** *Top, left:* Group beside large communal house. *Top, right:* Man dressed in cushma beside small hut. *Bottom, left* and *right:* Men with labrets. (Courtesy Paul Fejos.)

PLATE 54.—**Archers of the Montaña.** *Top: Masco.* (Courtesy Paul Fejos.)
Bottom: Amuescha. (Courtesy James Sawders.)

PLATE 55.—Masco rack of pottery and temporary wind shelters. (Courtesy Paul Fejos.)

PLATE 56.—**Acculturated Canelo Indians.** *Top: Canelo* chief, war captain, and two Barias judges, with canes of authority, a Spanish heritage. *Bottom: Canelo* at Paei Yuca, Ecuador, wearing Spanish dress and ponchos. (Courtesy American Museum of Natural History.)

PLATE 57.—**Canelo Indians.** *Top:* The chicha shampoo in progress on the last day of the feast, Paci Yacu. *Bottom:* The dance around the cross, Paci Yacu. (Courtesy American Museum of Natural History.)

PLATE 58.—Canelo Indians of the 19th century. (After Pierce, 1889.)

PLATE 59.—**Záparo Indians of the 19th century.** *Top: Záparo* in hunting and war dress (at left); *Encaballado* chief and woman (at right). *Bottom:* Communal house (malocca) on the Napo River. (After Osculati, 1854.)

PLATE 60.—**Jívaro Indians.** (*Top*, Courtesy American Museum of Natural History; *bottom*, after Tessmann, 1930.)

PLATE 61.—**Scenes of Jivaro life.** (Courtesy Matthew W. Stirling.)

PLATE 62.—**Jívaro Indians.** *Top, left:* Warrior with European-type drum. *Top, right:* Lances used for hunting and fighting. *Bottom, left:* Pottery making. *Bottom, right:* Woman's dress. (Courtesy Matthew W. Stirling.)

PLATE 63.—**Human heads shrunken by the Jívaro.** (Courtesy American
Museum of Natural History.)

missions, may also have been a *Roamaina* subtribe (Chantre y Herrera, 1901, p. 308).

Beuchat and Rivet (1909, p. 620) classify the *Roamaina* as *Cahuapana*. This is doubtful, because although they adjoined the *Maina,* who conceivably were *Cahuapanan,* they also adjoined the indisputably *Záparoan Andoa* on the north and the *Iquito* on the northeast. To the south were the *Panoan Urarina* and *Itucale.* Moreover, the *Pinche* are thought to be *Záporoan,* even by Beuchat and Rivet.

Beuchat and Rivet (1909, p. 619) include the *Chapa* (doubtless the *Zapa; Rodriguez, 1686, gives *Chapa* as a synonym for *Zapa*) as a *Roamaina* subtribe, but Tessmann, although linking the *Zapa* with the *Roamaina,* divides the *Maina* (*Kandoshi*) into the *Murata* and *Chapa.* But the *Murata* is an *Andoan* subtribe (Chantre y Herrera, 1901, p. 477), and it is very doubtful that the *Chapa* and *Zapa* were distinct peoples.

The first White contact with the *Roamaina* seems to have been in 1641, when a number were captured to serve as interpreters. Plans to missionize the *Roamaina* and *Zapa* in 1656 were postponed by enforced serfdom at the new colony of Santander on the lower Pastaza River and by epidemics of influenza, smallpox, and dysentery, which reduced the population of the two tribes from an estimated 10,000 in 1654 to 1,500 in 1660. Jesuit influence brought the abandonment of Santander and, in 1659, the Mission of Santos Angeles de los Roamainas was established on the Pastaza River. By 1695, however, epidemics and desertion left only five *Roamaina* in the mission.

The *Roamaina* subsequently joined the Mission of San José de los Pinches in 1708, but deserted in a few years at the instigation of a chief who insisted on carrying on sororal polygyny. In 1737, 20 to 40 *Roamaina* families were discovered on the Capirona River. They were ready to accept Christianity but reluctant to go to the Pastaza River (Maroni, 1889–92, 29:265; Zarate *in* Figueroa, 1904, pp. 142–155, 395).

In 1925, only 21 *Roamaina* (*Omurana*) survived. They claimed to have moved from the Marañón or possibly the Pastaza River to the Uritu-yacu, a small, left tributary of the Marañón, where they lived under a patron, spoke *Quechua* in addition to their own language, and were largely assimilated (Tessmann, 1930).

Awishira.—The *Awishira* (*Ixignor, Awishiri, Avirxiri, Abixira, Avixira, Avijira, Abigira, Abijira, Auishiri, Agouisiri, Auhishiri, Auxira, Abira, Ahuishiri, Ashiri*) were classified by Rivet (1924, p. 686) as *Tucanoan* but Father Lucero stated in 1676 that they understood the language of the *Záparoan*-speaking *Coronado* and *Gae* (Maroni, 1889–92, 29:246). Their proper classification must await better linguistic data, which can still be obtained. Their original territory lay between that of the *Tucanoan* and *Záparoan* tribes on the lower Curaray River and extended northward to the Napo River (lat. 2°30′ S., long. 75° W.).

Though the *Awishira* were probably seen by the Orellana expedition of 1540, it was not until after 1620 that visits by missionaries, explorers, and Christianized Indians together with the baptism of a few of their own tribe paved the way for their first mission, founded at San Miguel in 1665. At this time, the *Awishira* were numerous, extending some 50 leagues along the right bank of the Napo River, opposite the *Tucanoan Encabellado* (Cruz, 1900, p. 36), and southward to and along both sides of the Curaray River (Maroni, 1889–92, 28:182–183; 29:224–225). Within two years, the chief, objecting to the missionary's ban on polygyny, instigated the murder of the missionary. A punitive expedition entered their territory in 1676 (Maroni, 1889–92, 29:85–87).

In 1755, 118 Indians called *"Abijira Encabello"* were transferred to the Napo River missions, but most of them escaped.

One hundred years later, the *Awishira* occupied their original territory (Osculati, 1854, p. 183; Pierre, 1889, p. 90) but were definitely hostile to both the *Encabellado* and Whites. Their feeling toward the latter was in part due to Portuguese slave raids (Simson, 1886, p. 152). They lived on the right bank of the Napo River opposite the *Orejón* or *Coto* and were closely associated with the *Iquito* and *Mazane,* but retained their own language and customs (Villavicencio, 1858, p. 175). In 1925, the main group of *Awishira,* reduced through warfare with the Peruvians and neighboring tribes to between 30 and 50 persons but still savage, moved to the Tiputini-Shiripuno River region. Another group of some 25 *Awishira* lived under a patrón at Lake Vacacocha near the lower Curaray River; these had lost most of their native culture (Tessmann, 1930).

Iquito.—The *Iquito (Iquita, Ikito, Amacacore, Hamacore, Quiturran, Puca-uma),* closely related linguistically to the *Gae* (Chantre y Herrera, 1901, p. 345), were evidently unknown before the 18th century. They are not mentioned in the early literature and do not appear on Fritz's map of 1707. They seem to have lived north of the *Yameo,* occupying most if not all of the drainage of the upper Nanay River and its tributary, the Rio Branco (probably Chimbira River), and extending from the Tigre to the Napo River (lat. 3°30′ S., long. 75° W.)

The *Iquito* had three subtribes: the *Iquito* proper, the *Maracano,* and the *Auve.* The *Iquito* proper lived up the Yuracnamu or Yracanamu (probably the modern Yaraca-yacu) River, a tributary of the Tigre, and extended from the Tigre to the Curaray River. Tessmann erroneously classed modern *Iquito* as a distinct language, and named two divisions, the *Iquito* and the *Cahuarano* (Tessmann, 1930), the latter perhaps being the older *Maracano.*

The *Maracano (Moracano)* occupied the Guashchamoa (Necamumu) River, a tributary of the Rio Branco. This may be Tessmann's *Cahuarano* (Chantre y Herrera, 1901, pp. 348–349, 387–389, 486–490, 544–550). The *Auve* lived near the *Encabellado* of the Curaray River.

The *Iquito* proper, first visited in 1737, were eventually enticed by gifts to enter two missions. One of these was abandoned in 1749 and the Indians scattered, some going to other missions and others reverting to a primitive life along the Rio Branco. More *Iquito* later joined missions, and even helped convert their kinsmen (Chantre y Herrera, 1901, pp. 348–349, 544–550; Figueroa, 1904, pp. 379–382). In 1925, there were several hundred *Iquito* on the middle Nanay River and 1,000 *Cahuarano* on the lower Curaray River. The latter still retained some of their native culture (Tessmann, 1930).

The *Maracano* were missionized in 1748, but moved several times. In 1858, Villavicencio (1858, p. 175) reported some *Maracano* on the Amazon River. They had acquired some elements of European culture through contact with the Christianized Indians. The *Cahuarano* are perhaps their descendants.

The *Auve*, who were always hostile to Whites, have not been mentioned since Chantre y Herrera's account (1901, pp. 400–405).

Pinche.—The *Pinche* (*Pintsche*), with its subtribes, the *Pava, Araza* (*Arasa,* not to be confused with the *Arawakan Arasa* of Bolivia), and *Uspa* (*Uchpa, Utschpa, Uchupa, Llepa*), lived in the mountains between the Pastaza and upper Tigre Rivers, (lat. 3° S., long. 76° W.) (Veigl, 1785 b, p. 44; Escobar y Mendoza, 1769, p. 56). It is impossible to distinguish their territory sharply from that of the *Roamaina,* whose language they spoke, or from that of their neighbors, the *Semigáe, Pava,* and *Camacor* (possibly a branch of the *Iquito*), but it is probable that they lived north of the *Roamaina* and south of the *Semigáe* and *Záparo.*

The *Pinche* and *Ilavitoa,* the latter an unidentified tribe, were visited by Father Tomas Santos in 1684 (Maroni, 1889–92, 32:142–143). The *Pinche, Pava, Uspa,* and *Araza* were first placed in two missions in 1698. They numbered about 500 warriors (some 2,500 people) in 1700. The mission was twice moved, most of the *Pinche* and *Pava* dying soon thereafter and others following the *Roamaina* into the bush in 1713. In 1731, 50 *Araza* joined the mission, San José, at the invitation of the *Andoa.* In 1737, the *Pinche* mission had only 136 inhabitants, but wild *Pinche* and *Uspa* were reported in the area between the Chambira and the Pastaza Rivers. Only 100 *Pinche* survived in 1846. (Maroni, 1889–92, 29:264–266; Figueroa, 1904, pp. 297, 395; Chantre y Herrera, 1901, p. 308; Izaguirre, 1922–29, 9:167.) In 1925, there were still savage and hostile *Pinche* on the upper Tigre River.

Canelo.—The native language of the *Canelo* (*Canela, Kanela, Napo, Santa Rosina, Lorreto*) is unknown because they quickly adopted *Quechua* when they, one of the first Amazonian tribes to accept Christianity, were placed in a mission by the Dominicans in 1581. (Lat. 2° S., long. 78° W.) Reinburg (1921) believes the *Canelo* are *Záparo*; Karsten (1935, pp. 9–10) that they are a mixture of *Jívaro, Záparo,* and *Quechua.* The mission, located at the mouth of the Pindo River, a tributary of the Pastaza River, included also *Gae* and three tribes of unknown identity, the *Ymmunda* (*Ynmuda*), the *Guallingo,* and later the *Sante* (*Santi*), none of whom are subsequently mentioned in early chronicles. All of these Indians were indiscriminately called *Canelo* (Pierre, 1889, pp. 106, 135). Other tribes mentioned in connection with the *Canelo,* such as *Penday, Chonta,* and *Canincha,* were probably named from rivers.

Jívaro raids eventually forced the mission to be moved to Chontoa, then to the Pastaza River, where it still exists, though the raids continued through the last century. By 1775, the *Canelo* were decimated by smallpox, but their number was augmented by *Jívaro* converts.

At the end of the last century, the *Canelo* (*Napo*) had lost their identity, being lumped with the *Quechua*-speaking peoples of the upper Pastaza and Napo Rivers. They were distinguished from the *Jívaro, Encabellado, Záparoan,* and other pagan jungle tribes, all called "*Auca,*" by the fact that they ate salt, wore more clothes (pl. 56), were more completely Christian, and would not associate with the latter.

In 1877, they occupied Canelos and Sarayacu on the Bobonaza River, upper Curarai village, the left bank of the Napo River down to the Coca River, the villages of Napo, Aguano, Santa Rosa, Suno, Archidona, San José, Avila, Baez, Papallacta. Tena, Loreto, Concepción, Payamino, and Cotapino (Simson, 1886, pp. 153–154).

Of these villages, Canelos, founded in 1712 (Maroni, 1889–92, 1 :234), had about 30 people in 1730, its population consisting of refugees from encomiendas. In 1780, it had 100 people; in 1870, about 70 *Quechua*-speaking families or 350 persons (Orton, 1870, p. 172). In 1877, when the mission was in ruins, it had only 150 to 200 people, many of whom spoke *Jívaro* (Simson, 1886, pp. 98–100). In 1894, there were 600 people (Rimbach, 1897, p. 372). At the turn of the present century, the *Canelo* were scattered in several villages on the Bobonaza and numbered between 1,000 and 1,300 (Tessmann, 1930). Reinburg (1921) states that they were scattered in isolated families, but gathered twice yearly in missions to observe Christian rites and festivities. About 2,000 now remain at Canelos under Dominican missionaries (Karsten, 1935, p. 10).

TRIBES OF DOUBTFUL AFFILIATION IN OR ADJOINING ZÁPAROAN TERRITORY

Many of the following names may designate little-known tribes:

Alabano.—The *Alabano* lived on the upper Tigre River. They were in the Mission of San Xavier for a while but, decimated by smallpox, returned to the bush in 1764. Some later settled with the *Iquito* in the Mission of Santa Barbara (Chantre y Herrera, 1901, p. 555).

Neva (*Neova*).—The *Neva* lived on the Tiu-yacu, an upper Tigre tributary (lat. 3° S., long. 76° W.) (Maroni, 1889–92, 26 :232), and may have been a *Roamaina* subdivision.

Asaruntoa.—The *Asaruntoa* were situated near the *Roamaina* and *Andoa*, and were perhaps a subdivision of the latter.

Aunale.—The first location of the *Aunale* is shown on Fritz's map of 1691 between the Curaray and Tigre Rivers, south of the Abijira. But Maroni (1889–92, 26 :233) puts them on the right side of the Tigre below the Yuracnamui (the modern Yaraca-yacu?) River. The *Aunale* are first mentioned in 1743 when *Yameo* scouts sent by Father Brentano traveled 2 weeks up the Tigre River and found 11 houses of *Quechua*-speaking *Aunale* who had deserted the *Chébero* mission of Concepción. (Lat. 3° S., long. 75° W.) Nearby lived some *Itucal*. Twenty *Aunale* called on Father Brentano, who sent them back with an invitation for the others to visit the mission. The *Aunale* were at Concepción during the 18th century (Maroni, 1889–92, 28 :412; 31 :70–71).

Curizeta.—The *Curizeta* were Indians who fled from the encomiendas of Archidona on the Napo River near the Curaray to the headwaters of the Cosanga River, a tributary of the Coca River (Maroni, 1889–92, 28 :118).

Coronado of the Aguarico River.—Although, like the *Coronado* of the Pastaza River, these people were probably named for their crown-like hairdress, they were not related to the latter and may have been *Tucanoan.* They were found in 1621, 12 leagues below San Pedro de

Alcalá del Río Dorado.   Their most ancient settlement was at the town of San Francisco de los Coronados.   There were 20 families in 1621, all good boatmen and Christians (Maroni, 1889–92, 28:183).

Inemo dikama.—The existence of this tribe was revealed by a vocabulary collected by M. de Wavrin (Rivet, 1930) from two Indians living between the upper Curaray and Napo Rivers.   It does not have the slightest resemblance to any *Záparoan* dialect and is apparently an isolated language.   According to one informant, his language was called *Tuei* and his tribe *Inema dikama*.   The neighboring tribes were called the *Sapeiné, Tuie, Wau,* and *Eimi,* all unidentifiable names.

CULTURE

SUBSISTENCE

The *Záparoans* were all slash-and-burn farmers, but depended in varying degrees on other foods.   The *Andoa* relied greatly on collecting wild fruits; the *Awishira* in 1858 were primarily hunters and fishermen.

Farming.—The main crops were those common to tropical South America, with sweet manioc the staple.   In post-Columbian times, bananas and plantains were also major foods.   The *Awishira* received bananas even before they came in contact with the Whites.   Bitter manioc had not spread in aboriginal times west of the *Encabellado* and *Quijo,* but it was introduced to the *Maina* and *Roamaina* at the end of the 18th century, so that they might make farinha and sell it to explorers as a traveling ration (Izaguirre, 1922–29, 8:28).   Other crops are listed on page 516.

Fields were cleared with stone axes (which the *Awishira* used until the 19th century), burned, and tilled with a dibble.   Bush and weeds were kept down with a large chonta knife, which was later replaced by the machete.

Hunting.—Hunting weapons had a sporadic distribution.   The blowgun for hunting birds and monkeys has been ascribed the *Roamaina, Záparo, Canelo,* and *Maina,* but the bow only to the *Roamaina.*   The *Awishira* and *Iquito* used neither blowguns nor bows, and hunted only with spears, which placed them at some disadvantage.   Spears were used by all tribes for large game.   The *Záparo* resorted to spears whenever they exhausted their stock of blowgun poison, which they obtained only through trade (Simson, 1886, p. 167).

These tribes used trained hunting dogs.   The *Záparo,* like the *Jívaro,* put tobacco juice in their dogs' throats and noses to improve their scent. *Záparo* hunters used bone whistles to lure monkeys by imitating their calls and to communicate with other hunters by imitating birds (Simson, 1886, p. 168).   Other hunting devices included nets and traps (*Iquito*), pitfalls with pales for taking pigs (*Iquito, Pinche*), and bird snares (*Pinche*).

An *Iquito* hunter who had slain a wild pig took its head as a trophy and left his spear with a few of the animal's hairs at the site of the kill.

Canelo hunting ritual is described in detail by Karsten (1920 a, 36–42).

Fishing.—The principal fishing method was drugging with barbasco (all tribes), *Clibadium* (*Roamaina, Záparo, Awishira*), and *Tephrosia* (*Záparo, Awishira, Iquito*). Fish spears were *Canelo* and *Záparo* weapons, but the harpoon was limited to the *Canelo*. Bows and fish arrows were used only by the so-called *Kandoshi* among whom they were children's toys (Tessmann, 1930). The fishhook may have been native to the *Iquito* and *Záparo*, the latter using a gorge. The *Canelo* and *Záparo* had fish nets; the former placed several nets, each 5 feet (1.5 m.) by 20 to 25 feet (6 to 8 m.), end to end across the mouth of a stream (Simson, 1886, p. 157). The *Roamaina* fished with dip baskets.

The *Awishira* occasionally took turtles in the Napo River (Maroni, 1889–92, 29:85–87).

Collecting.—During certain seasons, wild fruits, especially of chonta and achua palms, were important foods. Fat palm grubs and certain flying ants were also relished.

Food preparation.—Food was grated either on a thorny piece of wood or on a board studded with pebbles and thorns. For grinding, the *Roamaina* and *Iquito* used a wooden trough.

Fermented manioc provided a food as well as an intoxicating beverage. A mass of the tubers was pounded, then slightly fermented with saliva; it was stored in a jar and consumed after adding water. As it kept for a long time, it was always the main provision for a long journey.

Because mineral salt could be obtained only through trade from the Marañón River tribes, most of these Indians used certain plant ashes instead.

Domesticated animals.—Each Indian household was surrounded with pets, but there were no domesticated animals until the missionaries introduced chickens.

HOUSES AND HOUSEHOLD EQUIPMENT

The long communal house predominated in the area. *Awishira* dwellings were about 75 feet (22.5 m.) wide and 300 feet (90 m.) long. The *Coronado* built equally large houses and closed them tightly against mosquitos. In the last century, the *Záparo* lived in open sheds sufficiently large to protect 25 to 30 people from the rain, but now use side-walled houses. The *Canelo* formerly built palisaded villages, with secret entrances (Pierre, 1889, p. 144). In 1894, they had rectangular, palmthatched houses with walls of thin posts (Rimbach, 1897, p. 372). Most houses in the area are built of lathes made from the tarapote tree (*Iriartea ventricosa*), which splits easily.

To avoid mosquitos, the *Roamaina* and *Kandoshi* sleep under tightly woven tents, the former using palm bast or cachibana, the latter, *Astrocaryum*. The *Roamaina* sleep on the ground, the *Canelo* and perhaps *Andoa* on platforms, though some *Canelo* use hammocks. The *Záparo, Awishira,* and *Iquito* sleep in hammocks. Men's log seats are standard equipment of most houses.

The *Awishira* built interior storage platforms, and the *Iquito* had special stands for spears.

DRESS AND ADORNMENT

Complete nakedness was customary among both sexes of *Coronado* and among *Awishira* and perhaps *Gae* and *Semigáe* men. In other tribes, at least the genitals were covered. *Roamaina* and *Záparo* men used a short flap of bark cloth or of cachibanco cloth; the *Iquito* tucked the penis under a belt. On important occasions, *Maina, Záparo,* and *Awishira* men wore a bark-cloth tunic, the *Záparo* decorating theirs with blue, red, and black geometric designs; *Roamaina* men wore capes (capuces) of cachibanco cloth. *Canelo* men, however, used either the breechclout or European drawers or pants and a poncho (Galt, ms; Simson, 1886, p. 154) and both sexes now wear Spanish costumes (pl. 56).

Women of all tribes except the *Coronado* wore some covering. Among the *Záparo,* they used a leaf and, more recently, a belt so narrow as to conceal nothing. *Zapa* women wore a shell pubic cover. Women of other tribes were clad in a wrap-around skirt, those of the *Canelo* and *Awishira* being of cotton, the latter painted and hanging to the ground. *Iquito* skirts were beautifully woven of cachibanco cloth, crudely painted, and trimmed with jingling animal teeth, seeds, and shells. *Maina* women dressed in a short, palm-fiber skirt and sometimes cloaked their upper bodies with a cloth passed over one shoulder and under the other (Veigl, 1785 b, p. 31).

Ear ornaments varied greatly: large shell disks glued to the end of wooden sticks, triangular shell pendants, and bone tubes (*Iquito*), fruit shells and other jingles or colored wooden disks 3 inches (7 cm.) in diameter (*Záparo*), a stick worn by men (*Awishira* and *Andoa*), and reed ear tubes with tufts of feathers (upper Nanay River).

The *Iquito* suspended triangular shell plates from their noses. The *Itucale* and *Urarina* were widely famous for mutilating the nose in a manner unique in South America. They detached a strip of skin along the ridge of the nose and placed a rolled leaf under it. Because of this peculiarity the *Quechua*-speaking Indians called them *Singacuchuscas* (Cut-noses). Only the *Awishira* are accredited with lip ornaments. Galt (ms.) remarked that *Záparo* women stained the lower lip black; this perhaps resulted from blackening the teeth, which was practiced by the *Iquito, Awishira, Záparo,* and *Maina.* The *Maina* accomplished this by chewing a certain grass with ashes; they cleaned their teeth with maize leaves and renewed the stain every day or two (Chantre y Herrera, 1901, p. 63).

Necklaces of teeth, fruit shells, beetle wings, and other materials and bracelets, armlets, anklets, and feather diadems have no striking peculiarities.

The *Coronado* owed their name to a triangular tuft of hair projecting above the forehead, though the *Roamaina* and *Zápora* evidently fixed their hair similarly. The *Iquito* singed the tops of their heads and smeared them thickly with urucú and rosin, which gained them the nickname. "Puca-uma" ("redheads" in *Quechua*).

Tribes on the Nanay River removed eyebrows, eyelids, hair on the front of the head, women's pubic hair, and men's beards. They spread hot gum on the hair, then, after it hardened, pulled it and the hair off (Galt, ms.). In a similar manner, the *Zápora* used resin to pluck their eyebrows, and body hair. Beauty operations were performed with mirrors of black rosin (*Iquito*).

Urucú and genipa paint provided decoration for formal occasions. Status badges are not reported, but *Maina* men were alleged to have worn as many ankle rings as they had wives.

Only the *Awishira* deformed infants' heads; lateral pressure somewhat lengthened the skulls (Tessmann, 1930). The *Iquito* and *Záparo,* however, pressed babies' noses in some way to make the face broad.

TRANSPORTATION

Babies were carried in a sling. A *Záparo* man kept his comb, tinder, poison, and other essentials in a small pouch.

The *Awishira, Záparo, Iquito,* and perhaps other *Záparoan* tribes lacked canoes in aboriginal days, perhaps because they lived away from the main streams. The *Kandoshi* were thought to have learned canoe making from the *Cocama.* Canoes were introduced to the *Awishira* by a tribal member who learned about them from his Spanish captors, but in the last century, this tribe still preferred rafts and made only poor two-passenger canoes of hollowed bombana palm with the ends stopped with clay (Simson, 1886, p. 199). But certain unidentified tribes of the area made canoes that held 20 people. The best canoe material is cedro blanco and cedro colorado (*Icica altisima*).

MANUFACTURES

Spinning and Weaving.—Cordage was usually made of chambira fibers.

Woven and knitted products were of chambira, cotton, and cachibanco (achua palm fibers), the last being preferred despite the greater strength of cotton. The *Iquito* either knitted chambira or wove it for loincloths and bags. The *Iquito, Roamaina,* and *Záparo* made clothes, mosquito tents, and bands of cachibanco cloth. For this they extracted the fibers from terminal palm shoots (cogollo) and spun them to make large skeins. The spindle and loom are not described but may have been similar to those used for cotton. Cachibanco cloth was colored with various vegetable dyes. Most of these tribes also wove cotton, the *Záparo* and *Awishira* using a small, horizontal loom.

Bark cloth.—Bark cloth was made by several of these tribes, probably being used when woven cloth was not available.

Basketry.—Little is known of baskets except that the *Záparo* were named after theirs, which had lids and double wickerwork walls of split creepers and were somehow water-proofed. These were used to store personal possessions.

Pottery and other containers.—The *Roamaina, Záparo, Awishira,* and *Iquito* made chicha jugs, bowls and punctate or fingernail-decorated cooking pots. *Maina* decoration was red, black, and white (Rel. geogr. Indias, 1881–97, 4:cxlvi). Certain *Roamaina* vessels were red outside, black inside. *Iquito* bowls were undecorated. *Canelo* bowls, jars, and cups have geometric and conventionalized black and red designs on an orange or cream background (Karsten, 1935, pls. 19, 20).

The *Maina* made wooden bowls and containers of calabash, the latter painted and varnished with parinari fruit (Izaguirre, 1922–29, 8:117).

Weapons.—The principal hunting weapon was the blowgun. Bows were used for hunting only by the *Roamaina.* The blowgun was made of two wooden half-tubes carefully glued together. One of the earliest records of the use of the blowgun in South America is for the *Maina* in 1571. (See Stirling, 1938, p. 12). Later accounts attribute it also to the *Andoa* and *Záparo,* but deny that the *Awishira* and *Iquito* used it. The *Záparo* imported their poison from the *Tucuna* (Villavicencio, 1858, p. 367) and, when their supply ran out resorted to spears (Simson, 1886, p. 167). The *Canelo* make poison, but obtain a stronger brand in trade (Karsten, 1935, pp. 145, 152).

For war, the *Záparoans* typically carried large bundles of javelins and hurled them in rapid succession. The *Canelo* could throw them 45 to 60 feet (15 to 20 m.). *Iquito* and *Gae* lances were tapered at both ends, tipped with sharp chonta or bone points, and were decorated with feathers and basketry sheaths having alternating black and white design elements. Only *Iquito* lances were poisoned. The *Záparo* used thrusting spears as well as javelins (Villavicencio, 1858, p. 171).

The spear thrower and club (macana) are ascribed to the *Maina* in 1571 but are not mentioned subsequently.

Large shields of palo balsa covering most of the warrior's body have been used throughout the historic period. Some were round, e. g., *Záparo;* others, rectangular, e. g., that of the *Iquito,* which was 6 inches

(15 cm.) thick, 18 inches (45 cm.) wide, and 5 feet (1.5 m.) long
(Figueroa, 1904, p. 380). Basketry shields were also common, those of
the *Iquito* being rectangular and woven of creepers. The *Iquito* used
tapir-hide shields (Jiménez de la Espada, 1889–92, 27:77).

Axes.—Axes had a polished greenstone head inserted in a hole in a
wooden handle.

Metallurgy.—Practice of metallurgy in pre-Columbian times is doubtful, but within the historical period the *Gae* traveled from the Bobanaza to
the Napo River to collect gold dust (Chantre y Herrera, 1901 p. 249).
The *Santa Rosina* (*Canelo*) also produced some gold (Galt, ms.).

Fire making.—The fire drill was native, but flint and steel were
preferred after their introduction. Tessmann's reference to "two stones"
(*Andoa* and *Iquito*) may mean flint and steel. Fire fans were woven
of feathers.

TRADE

There was some local pre-Columbian specialization in manufacture and
trade, though trade increased greatly after the Contact. A main article
of exchange has always been the excellent chambira hammock made on
the Napo River and sought by the aboriginal Indian tribes as eagerly
as by modern Mestizos. Iron knives, which the *Záparo* received for their
hammocks, were traded on to more remote tribes. The *Roamaina* were
a source of palm-fiber mosquito tents (Figueroa, 1904, p. 151).

To obtain salt, the *Canelo* made arduous journeys requiring months
to the Chasuta mines on the Huallaga River. When bartering salt to
the Whites, a man exchanged the amount he brought back for 30 varas
of cloth, of which he made clothes and mosquito tents (Simson, 1886,
pp. 158–160). The *Canelo* also gathered sarsaparilla for sale. All of
these tribes undertook long trips to the lower Napo and Amazon to
purchase curare from the *Tucuna* and *Pava* and went to the Napo River
to obtain signal and dance drums (Pierre, 1889, p. 144).

SOCIOPOLITICAL GROUPS

Aboriginal sociopolitical groups are not adequately described. In
1664, the warlike *Awishira* were dispersed in very small groups, each
occupying a house located 2 to 4 leagues from a river. These households so mistrusted one another that Father de la Cueva's *Awishira* mes-
senger needed a *Chébero* escort when approaching a village to announce
the missionary's arrival (Maroni, 1889–92, 29:85–87).

Within the last century each *Záparoan* community consisted of several
families occupying a single, large house. The *Canelo* village, for example
had only one large hut which sheltered several families, each with its "platform" (bed?) (Pierre, 1889); in addition, each family had a hut in the
bush near its plantations to which to retire from the village but where

people might come to visit, and another hidden hut that was known only to the family (Simson, 1886, pp. 157–158). A *Záparo* settlement had about 100 people, living in the midst of their plantation, but members were not strongly united and continually wandered in "small hordes" (Simson, 1886, p. 172). Orton (1870, p. 171) calls these communities "isolated ranches." Later, Tessmann (1930) found that only about 3 families occupied each house and constituted the community. In 1871, the Nanay River Indians were living in small, peaceful groups of 10 to 14 people each (Galt, ms.). Recent *Iquito* villages had 1 to 4 houses each (Tessmann, 1930).

Every tribe was patrilocal, suggesting the existence of extended patrilineal families, though some villages may have been made up of several extended families.

War captives were incorporated into the social group.

Etiquette.—A *Coronado* or *Gae* who had been away was received by his community with tears and laments.

LIFE CYCLE

Birth and childhood.—The widespread belief that the penis bone of the coati is an aphrodisiac is shared by the *Záparoan.*

During childbirth, women are generally isolated; they are assisted by other women. *Iquito* women gave birth in special huts built some distance from the village. Among the *Záparo,* the oldest woman of the village cut the navel cord. Restrictions of varying rigor and duration are imposed on both parents. *Záparo* parents are confined 10 days, the father avoiding work. The *Murata* father spends 4 days in bed. Both *Awishira* parents remain in their hammocks for 2 weeks, dieting; *Iquito* parents, for 3 days. The *Roamaina* mother is isolated 1 month, and the father does not work for 5 days. *Canelo* parents diet and the father avoids working or hunting for several days.

Abortion is evidently common. One of twins is generally killed among the *Záparo, Roamaina,* and *Canelo,* the *Canelo* burying it alive.

An *Iquito* girl was circumcised one week after birth. The reference to ceremonial flogging and to the *Awishira* custom of putting red pepper in the eyes to make a person "strong, courageous, vigilant, and diligent" may allude to initiation rites. A few Montaña tribes used pepper also to improve hunters' vision. Initiatory whipping occurred among the *Eastern Tucanoan* tribes but not in the Montaña.

The *Iquito* frighten recalcitrant children with masks—the only use of masks in the area.

Puberty.—Girls' puberty is marked by a period of confinement: Two days (*Roamaina*), 1 week (*Iquito*), 8 days (*Kandoshi*). The *Awishira* isolate a pubescent girl from men, the *Iquito* from the view of everyone except her mother. After her confinement, the *Roamaina* and *Záparo* bathe her and hold a chicha feast.

Marriage.—Child betrothal is common among the *Iquito;* a man rears a girl until she is old enough to marry him. To court a girl, the man usually places firewood by her hut, then makes a formal request of marriage to her father or brother. The marriage ceremony is simple : the couple sits in a hammock and drinks chicha. According to the usual marriage pattern, a man works for his father-in-law in return for his bride, either contributing food (*Iquito*), helping on his plantation (*Roamaina, Záparo*), or living with the wife's family in temporary bride service (1 month, *Awishira;* one to two years, *Kandoshi, Andoa*). Residence is patrilocal, either immediately after marriage or following bride service. *Záparoan* marriage ties are loose, there being frequent exchange and theft of wives and promiscuous sex relations (Simson, 1886, pp. 172–173).

Polygyny is a chief's prerogative. Some *Iquito* headmen used to have as many as 12 wives; some *Záparo*, 3 or 4. Maroni (1889–92, 29 :265) mentions a case of sororal polygyny among the *Pinche*.

Death.—The *Záparo* occasionally killed hopeless invalids who had become a burden on the community. They also sometimes buried a child alive with its dead mother (Simson, 1886, pp. 175–176).

Methods of disposing of a corpse varied greatly : earth burial, urn burial, and scaffold burial, various forms of reburial, and endocannibalism. The *Iquito* placed the body, either flexed or vertical, in a round pit and covered the grave with clay. The *Záparo* bury inside the house, placing weapons, utensils, and food with the corpse (Izaguirre, 1922–29, 12 :472; Tessmann, 1930), but they or their predecessors at Aguano had once practiced urn burial (Simson, 1886, p. 135). The *Andoa* and *Kandoshi* put the body in a canoe, place it on a scaffold, and later rebury it in an urn. The *Andoa,* however, sometimes bury the canoe in the earth and later rebury in urns. The *Awishira* leave the deceased in his hammock for 3 days, collecting the fluids of decomposition in an urn, and then bury him in the house. They burn his possessions. In 1664, the *Roamaina* laid the corpse in his hammock and suspended it in a deep pit. When the flesh had rotted away, they collected and cleaned the bones and placed them in an urn decorated with appliqué figures. A year later they buried the urn (Figueroa, 1904, p. 249). According to Tessmann (1930), however, the *Roamaina* recently cremated men and buried the remains in anthropomorphic jars, but buried women directly in the earth inside the house.

The house was not abandoned after death, except among the *Iquito,* who did so only when the owner died.

The *Roamaina* and *Zapa* were said to have eaten their deceased relatives (Figueroa, 1904, p. 150), the practice perhaps being akin to that of the *Panoan* tribes (p. 586).

The *Canelo* play games after a death (below), those of maize grains and die casting serving as a means of distributing the deceased's property (Karsten, 1935, pp. 466–478).

WARFARE

These tribes are now largely pacified, except perhaps the *Awishira*. Accusation of witchcraft used to be the main cause of hostility between the tribes and communities. The general pattern of fighting was to launch a surprise attack, kill the men with spears, capture the women and children, and retreat rapidly. *Iquito* warriors smoked tobacco to make themselves invulnerable. The spear was the principal weapon of attack, though the *Roamaina* used bows and clubs. Shields, previously described (p. 643), were used in defense. Villages were protected by trenches and pitfalls filled with sharp stakes, which were poisoned among the *Murata*. The *Canelo* used palisades.

CANNIBALISM

Cannibalism and trophy taking was formerly common. The *Roamaina* and *Zapa* ate their slain enemies; the *Gae* boiled their flesh and took it home to eat (Figueroa, 1904, p. 150). The *Yameo* and *Encabellado* accused the *Iquito* of cannibalism, but the missionaries found no evidence of it (Chantre y Herrera, 1901, p. 90). Maroni (1889–92, 29:224) attributes cannibalism to the *Awishira*. Funeral endocannibalism has been mentioned.

The *Roamaina* and *Canelo* held trophy skull feasts. The former placed the skulls on **T**-shaped poles, women dancing around them while the men drank (Figueroa, 1904, p. 263). The *Awishira* drank from enemies' skulls. They and probably other tribes made necklaces of their victim's teeth.

ESTHETIC AND RECREATIONAL ACTIVITIES

Musical instruments.—The *Záparoan* tribes used transverse flutes (*Andoa, Kandoshi*), two-headed skin drums (probably post-European), and belts with jingles (*Záparo*). Curiously, panpipes are ascribed only to the *Andoa* and *Iquito* and denied for the *Záparo, Roamaina*, and *Kandoshi* (Tessmann, 1930). The musical bow does not occur. The *Canelo* made signal and dance drums 18 inches (45 cm.) long, 12 inches (30 cm.) in diameter, scooped from a hollow log (pl. 57; Simson, 1886, p. 106). Other tribes including the *Iquito* may also have used the signal drum. The *Záparo* have whistles to lure monkeys and trumpets made of armadillo shells. The *Canelo* carved fiddles, after Spanish models, from a solid block of wood (Simson, 1886, p. 156).

Toys and games.—Amusements included children's humming tops, slings attached to sticks, the maize-leaf ball game, and men's wrestling.

Drinking and dancing.—At festivals, chicha and cayapi were always drunk. The chicha is made principally of various fruits, especially fermented manioc. The *Iquito* strengthened their chicha with a fungus that grows on decayed trees and on manioc stems. The *Canelo* constructed a still of pots and bamboo tubes, a device seemingly unique and surely post-Columbian in South America (Simson, 1886, pp. 162–163).

The *Awishira* dance with a palm-branch costume, flourishing their weapons and accompanied by drums and flutes (Maroni, 1889-92, 29: 236). During a *Záparo* feast, Osculati (1854, pp. 173–174) observed a woman's circle dance, a jaguar dance in which a man raced to and from the plaza with a woman whom he struck with his stomach, a parrot and monkey dance, and finally a circle dance for men whose song was answered by the women. Old men sat apart drinking and singing of the deeds of their ancestors. *Canelo* cayapi and chicha drinking bouts lasted 8 days (pl. 57).

Games.—After a death the *Canelo* play several games, evidently of Highland origin: casting a wooden die; tossing maize grains into holes on a board; blindman's bluff; blowing a ball of burning cotton; seeking a concealed pin; and a game in which one person took a position in a row of people (Karsten, 1935, pp. 466–478).

Narcotics.—Narcotics used in this area include tobacco, *Datura,* cayapi, and guayusca, but not coca.

Tobacco may once have been somewhat restricted to magical use, especially by shamans; in fact, Tessmann (1930) believes that formerly the *Záparo, Awishira,* and *Iquito* lacked tobacco altogether. But Reinburg (1921) affirms that the *Záparo* drank tobacco to produce vomiting and a dream state, its effect being similar to that of cayapi, and Simson (1886, pp. 148, 164–170) mentions it as a general remedy throughout the Napo-Putumayo region. The *Roamaina* also drink tobacco juice. The cigar, formerly used perhaps only by some shamans, recently became general among the *Záparo* and *Andoa.* Tobacco chewing is a recent *Záparo* practice (Tessmann, 1930).

Huanto (*Datura arborea*) is taken by the *Záparo* and *Canelo* to foretell the future.

Cayapi is generally drunk to produce a trance and visions. *Záparo* warriors drink it to foretell the success of warfare, and shamans take it to invoke spirits which reveal the cause of sickness (Reinburg, 1921). The *Awishira* drink cayapi after chicha; *Canelo* drinking bouts have already been mentioned. The *Iquito* wear a special woven headgear while drinking cayapi; they see visions of animals (Tessmann, 1930), the significance of which is obscure.

Guayusa, which is anesthetizing rather than exhilarating, was drunk during dances. The *Pinche* took it to increase their endurance on arduous trips. The *Záparo* plant and drink it as a curative. The *Iquito, Roamaina,* and *Awishira,* however, are said not to have used it.

The *Canelo* and their neighbors are essentially Christian today, but native animism doubtless survives among many *Auca,* or pagan tribes, of the lower jungles. Missionary influence has probably faded among the latter, though Simson (1886, p. 118) found the *Záparo* practicing a meaningless ritual long after they had lost their priest.

To the *Záparo* the monstrous water snake or python was dangerous, but water spirits were harmless. The forest demons were usually conceived to be anthropomorphic and menacing. The *Iquito* believed in bush dwarfs, giants, and other anthropomorphic spirits, and the *Awishira* in a skeletonlike being with a visible heart. According to the *Záparo,* a black spirit, mungia, devoured travelers in the bush.

The souls of brave *Záparo* men were thought to be reincarnated in birds and those of cowardly persons in reptiles (Villavicencio, 1858, p. 371), but shamans were held to become jaguars or pythons. The *Canelo* believed that souls of deceased shamans turned into demons. Other tribes stated that the soul went to the bush and became innocuous (Tessmann, 1930).

Shamanism.—Shamanism in this group of tribes is described on page 650.

Cyperus is or was taken by most of these tribes for hunting and fishing luck, fertility of manioc, female fertility, and as a general curative (Tessmann, 1930). To stop storms, the *Záparo* chewed piri-piri grass and spat it into the air.

We have three fragments of *Maina* flood legends. (1) The flood was caused by a god whom people had thrown into a dirty pit because he was covered with sores; the only survivor was the man who rescued and cleaned him. (2) A man and woman took refuge on a zapote tree, which grew up to the sky. They ate its fruits until the flood subsided. (3) A flood of the Rimachuma Lagoon destroyed all mankind except one man who lived in a hut where he found food prepared daily; he discovered that it came from two parrots who flew to his house and became women, one the mistress, the other her servant; he married the mistress, hence women are now lazy (Rel. geogr. Indias, 1881–97, 4 :xxii–lxxiii).

A *Záparo* tale related that the moon was formerly a man who had sexual intercourse with his sister. To locate her lover, the girl smeared his face with genipa. Moon's wife became a night bird. The *Záparo* creator is called Piietzo (Osculati, 1854, p. 169).

The *Tupi-Guarani* twin story was recently recorded among the *Záparo* (Reinburg, 1921). A woman, apparently the sister of the moon, was pregnant with twins. Her husband abandoned her, but the voices of her unborn babies guided her in her search for him. She was misled to the house of the jaguars who devoured her, but gave the twins to their old jaguar mother. Later, the twins killed the jaguars. One of the twins spoiled everything that his brother attempted to do for the benefit of mankind.

The *Roamaina* thought that earthquakes occurred whenever God raised the hand in which he supported the earth. The *Maina* believed that they signified that God was inquiring the whereabouts of people; in answer, the people stamped the ground and shouted, "Here we are" (Jiménez de la Espada, 1889–92, p. 52).

The *Maina* explained that gods coming from the west and east had opened the Pongo de Manseriche so that they could meet. One god, Innerre, lives with his wife, a large serpent, in a cave above the Pongo. Three Indians once visited this god; two were killed by the large number of bats in the cave but the third obtained medicines from Innerre (Jiménez de la Espada, 1889–92, p. 52).

SHAMANISM

The shaman, probably still functioning among many tribes, is both sorcerer and curer. His power, acquired and utilized with the aid of narcotics, comes from plants and animals, but is materialized in the form of "thorns."

During his instruction, the *Andoa, Awishira, Canelo, Roamaina,* and *Kandoshi* shaman takes cayapi in order to "see better." Tobacco, however, gives the true power. The *Andoa* and *Roamaina* smoke it; the *Roamaina, Záparo,* and *Kandoshi* take it as juice. The *Iquito* and *Canelo* shaman takes *Datura* and *Cyperus* instead of tobacco.

An *Awishira* shaman's power is his breath; the *Iquito's* is *Cyperus* root; the *Kandoshi's,* a magical bird; the *Canelo's,* a python spirit; and the *Andoa's, Roamaina's, Záparo's,* and *Kandoshi's,* "thorns."

Disease is caused by sending the power or "thorn," sometimes by means of a bird, into the victim, but the *Awishira* shaman sent a snake or his breath, and the *Iquito* his *Cyperus* root, whereas the *Roamaina* might make a water demon seize the person. Cure consists of blowing smoke and sucking out the disease substance, that is, the "thorns."

The *Canelo* believe that some illness is caused by ghosts, which they drive away with shouting.

The *Iquito* buried sorcerers alive (Chantre y Herrera, 1901, p. 564).

A shaman made contact with his spirits either by fasting in a small, isolated cabin or by remaining in his hut where he lay in his hammock or sat taking cayapi on a platform surrounded by other people. After long persuasion, the spirits came, took possession of the shaman, and spoke through his mouth. Meanwhile, the shaman's spirit had wandered far away to acquire knowledge of the future.

Miscellaneous cures.—*Cyperus* and tobacco juice were general curatives. Snake bites were treated among the *Záparo* with a creeper, itiningi or Soga de San Pablo (Maroni, 1889–92, 26:420). On the Napo River (*Canelo?*), salt, tobacco, and red pepper were administered and the patient was required to observe taboos, such as not eating grease or toothed fish or passing a pregnant woman (Maroni, 1889–92, 26:420).

BIBLIOGRAPHY

Beuchat and Rivet, 1908, 1909; Chantre y Herrera, 1901; Cruz, 1900; Escobar y Mendoza, 1769; Figueroa, 1904; Galt, n.d.; Grubb, 1927; Izaguirre, 1922–29; Jiménez de la Espada (Noticias auténticas . . . 1889–92); Karsten, 1920 a, b, 1935; La jornada del . . . 1895; Maroni, 1889–92; Ortiz, 1940; Orton, 1870; Osculati, 1854; Pierre, 1889; Reinburg, 1921; Relaciones geográficas de Indias, 1881–97; Rimbach, 1897; Rivet, 1924, 1930; Simson, 1886; Stirling, 1938; Tessmann, 1930; Veigl, 1785 b; Villavicencio, 1858.

THE COFAN

The *Cofán* (*Kofán*) lived in the upper Aguarico River region, near its junction with the Azuela River (Maroni, 1889–92, 26:245). (Lat. 0°–1° S., long. 75°30'–77° W.; map 1, *No. 3;* map 5.) Archidona and San Pedro Alacalá del Río, founded near the Coca River in 1536, were the first Spanish settlements. The Jesuit Father, Rafael Ferrer, visited the *Cofán* in 1599 and founded several missions, especially Bendoa, but the Jesuits left the *Cofán* following disagreement with the Spanish civil authorities. Ferrer returned in 1608, but the Spaniards of Alacalá were enslaving the Indians, and he was killed by the Indians in 1611. In 1635, the Franciscans, Domingo Brieva and Pedro Pecador, visited the *Cofán* at Alacalá de Oro (Maroni, 1889–92, 26:245). Subsequent Jesuits' efforts were ineffective, and the *Cofán* continually decreased.

In 1940, there were 206 Christianized *Cofán* in Konsayá Puerto Asís to Cuembí, Achote (tributary of the Guamués), San Antonio del Guamués, Abusía River, and San Miguel River (Igualada and Castellvi, 1940, p. 97).

BIBLIOGRAPHY

Barnuevo, 1942; Castellvi, 1938; Igualada and Castellvi, 1940; Maroni, 1889–92; Rodriguez, 1684; Velasco, 1841–44.

UNIDENTIFIED TRIBES OF THE UPPER PUTUMAYO-NAPO RIVER REGION

Several tribes in this region which are of uncertain identity are as follows:

Sucumbio.—This tribe was visited by missionaries in 1633 east of Quito (Cruz, 1900, p. 14). Probably the Sucumbíos or San Miguel River, a branch of the Putumayo River, was named from them, and they are the *San Miguel* Indians, who in 1877 lived between the *Macaguage* and *Pioje* divisions of the *Encabellado* and occupied the San Miguel, upper Aguarico, and Santiago Rivers (Simson, 1886, pp. 192–193). Their habitat was close to if not within that of the *Cofán.*

Seño (*Suño*).—A tribe below the *Sucumbio,* north of the Putumayo River near the equator, visited in 1633 by Fathers Anguita and Cararubia (Cruz, 1900, p. 18).

Becaba (*Pecaba*).—A tribe, less numerous than the *Seño,* on the Putumayo River, 8 days downstream from the San Miguel River, living on islands in the river when Fathers Lorenzo Fernández and Juan Cayado found them in 1635. Attempts to missionize them were given up (Cruz, 1900, pp. 18–19).

Several other tribes, the *Andacui* and *Otequa,* are mentioned with the *Encabellado, Macaguage,* and *Payagua* as having had a numerous population in 16 villages in 1700. By 1780, they were decimated to only six reduciones around the headwaters of the Putumayo and Caquetá Rivers. They had raided and destroyed the Spanish towns of Mocoa, Ezija, and Sibundoy along the mountains.

THE QUIJO

INTRODUCTION

The *Quijo* (*Kicho, Quixo, Napo, Santa Rosino*), not to be confused with the *Iquito,* were, according to Rivet (1924), a *Chibchan*-speaking people. They lived in the region of Baeza and Archidona, at the headwaters of the Coca River, and were in close contact with the *Panzaleo* of the Highlands (lat. 0°–1° S., long. 75°30′–77° W.; map 1, *No. 3;* map 5).

Quijo culture has a number of elements which link it with the Highland, especially with other *Chibchan* tribes: potatoes, metallurgy in gold, mummification, bone-bead money, coca divination, dwellings scattered through farm lands with central villages for only temporary occupancy, and great political power of chiefs. Cieza de León observed that the *Quijo* were not very different from the *Panzaleo* (Handbook, vol. 2, p. 795), a *Chibchan* tribe, with whom they maintained close relations. A *Quijo* chief was reported to be related to chief of the *Latacunga,* a *Panzaleo* division.

Many *Quijo* traits, however, are typically selvan: slash-and-burn agriculture, with manioc, sweet potatoes, and other lowland crops as staples, hunting with the blowgun, fishing with drugs, the shamanistic power from "thorns," and belief in nature spirits. Although it is possible that the Highland traits and the *Chibchan* language diffused from the nearby

Andes to replace older Tropical Forest traits, it is more likely that the *Quijo* was a Highland *Chibchan* tribe which moved into the Montaña and adapted certain features of its culture, especially its economic pattern, to the jungle.

HISTORY

Gonzalo Días de Pineda, the first White man to visit the *Quijo* (in 1536), found them hostile. Colonization of *Quijo* territory started with the foundation of Baeza in 1559 and later of Avila on the Suno River. Resentful of the harsh treatment to which they were subjected by the encomenderos, the Indians revolted in 1577. The revolt failed, the priests who led it were either killed or deported to Quito, and many *Quijo* were sent to the coast, where they soon died. The Spaniards estimated the population at about 30,000 in 1559. Deportation, infanticide, and smallpox epidemics after the revolt reduced it in less than 50 years to 2,829 (Rel. geogr. Indias, 1881–97, 1 :CIV).

In the last century, the *Quijo* were reputedly among the Christian Indians who looked down upon the "Auca," the pagan tribes of the lower forest regions. But they still had a native economy, fished with poison, used the blowgun, and wore aboriginal ornaments (Orton, 1870). In 1925, Tessmann (1930) found that several thousand *Quijo* lived on the Tena, Suno, and Payomino Rivers, all left tributaries of the upper Napo River, where they were divided into villages. Prolonged mission and lay Spanish contact had left little of the aboriginal culture; Spanish and *Quechua* had supplanted their previous tongue.

SOURCES

The main source on the ancient *Quijo* is Don Diego de Ortegon's "Descripcíon de la Provincia de los Quijos," written in 1577 (Rel. geogr. Indias, 1881–97, 1 :C–CXII), from which González Suárez (1890–1903, 6:55–60) and Jijón y Caamaño (1940–41, 1 :291–294) took their material on these Indians. These Indians are also mentioned by Rodriguez (1684). Last-century information can be found in Orton (1870) and Simson (1886). Tessmann (1930) has some material on the acculturated *Quijo*.

CULTURE

SUBSISTENCE

Farming consisted of slash-and-burn cultivation of maize, sweet manioc (yuca), potatoes, sweet potatoes, peanuts, beans, pumpkins, *Guilielma* palms, pepper (*Capsicum* sp.), yams, macabo, cocona (*Solanum* sp.), and a Cyclanthaceae (Tessmann, 1930; Ortegon, "Descripción . . . 1881"). Cultivation of bitter manioc is mentioned only in recent sources. Introduced European foods include plaintains, bananas, sugarcane, pigs, and chickens. Other crops are tobacco and barbasco, the latter a fish drug.

Typical of the Forest Tribes, the *Quijo* gather wild fruits, especially palms. In the 16th century, they fished with dams and barbasco; recent sources mention use of drugs (barbasco and *Clibadium*), landing nets, spears, harpoons (?), and bone hooks. The *Quijo* hunt with two-piece, chonta wood blowguns, the poison for which comes from the *Tucuna,* and with spears, darts, and some traps.

The *Quijo* grind food with both a flat and a trough-shaped grinder and smoke meat on the babracot. In the 16th century they prepared a "pan de yuca," probably cassava.

VILLAGES AND HOUSES

Ancient houses were built of posts stuck in the ground and plastered with mud. Settlements had an average of four houses, but were occupied only on market days. Like the modern Indians, the people probably spent most of their time in huts closer to their fields.

Modern Napo River Indian huts are rectangular with a gabled roof, the frame obviously copied from the Whites. The ancient *Quijo* slept on the ground; today they sleep in bedsteads, and use hammocks for resting.

DRESS AND ADORNMENT

In the 16th century, men in the region of Avila and Baeza wore two capes (mantas) knotted over the shoulders. In Archidona they went naked with the penis tied up. In both regions women used cotton loincloths. The most conspicuous ornaments were golden nose ornaments and breastplates. A thin labret, probably of resin, was worn through the upper lip.

Modern *Quijo* dress exactly like the Mestizos, but still wear armbands and place feathered sticks through the ear lobes. Feather circlets were festive ornaments of the last century. The Indians now blacken their teeth, paint themselves with genipa and urucú, and tattoo.

The 16th-century *Quijo* deformed infants' heads fronto-occipitally between two boards, a custom which has entirely disappeared. Some modern *Quijo* have adopted the *Cocama* custom of filing the incisors.

MANUFACTURES

The ancient *Quijo* were expert goldsmiths and good weavers, cotton blankets constituting a large part of the tribute they paid to their encomenderos. The modern people make nets and bags of agave or *Astrocaryum* fibers, crude pottery (fig. 93), and some mats and baskets.

TRADE

Markets played an important part in the economic life of the ancient *Quijo*. At these, they sold clothes, jewels, foods, and slaves. They had a sort of money (carato), consisting of strings of 24 bone beads, which was used to fulfill social obligations and to pay workers.

The modern people undertake long trips to the salt mines of the lower Huallaga and exchange their salt for dress material.

FIGURE 93.—*Quijo* pot on stone rests. (Redrawn from Tessmann, 1930, map 11.)

LIFE CYCLE

Childbirth.—Childbirth occurred near a river, where the mother washed herself and baby, then remained for a certain time, while the husband observed a strict diet, drinking only chicha beer.

Marriage.—Child betrothal is said to have been common. In early times, the suitor paid bone money (carato) to the girl's parents. The marriage was sealed after the bridegroom deposited wood, a bundle of straw, and food at the girl's doorstep, but sometimes a husband had to give several years of bride service before taking his wife to his own home. Caciques and frequently commoners had many wives. Our earliest source records that hospitality required the host to lend his wife to a guest, who repaid him with bone money.

Death.—Common people were buried indoors under the hearth, after which a 1-day wake was held and the widow washed. Chiefs were mummified, the corpse being eviscerated, smeared with tar, and smoked over a fire. The deceased's jewels were placed inside the stomach cavity. Funerals were celebrated with dances and drinking bouts.

Modern *Quijo* bury their dead in the hut in a coffin made of a part of a canoe, but they do not abandon the hut. The night following the burial, the deceased's relatives and friends play several games (Karsten, 1920 a, pp. 92–95): A blindfolded man representing the deceased tries to catch his comrades, who tease him; players blow small burning cotton balls toward each other; a person with closed eyes tries to find a needle hidden in the corpse's clothes; a man representing the deceased stands at the head of a line and must catch the last one of the line, who tries to take his place. At dawn the mourners walk on all fours, barking. They catch and kill chickens. A funeral meal ends the wake.

SOCIAL AND POLITICAL ORGANIZATION

Political power was in the hands of priests or shamans, as among many *Chibchan* tribes. On certain occasions, including market days, chiefs received a tribute of food, fruits, and other presents. They had slaves to work in their fields.

WARFARE

The *Quijo* fought with spears, javelins, wooden swords, and shields (?). For defense, large boulders were placed along mountain slopes and loosened to roll down on the enemy passing underneath. Villages were protected with caltrops. The *Quijo* cut off the heads and hands of their enemies to decorate chiefs' houses. Diego de Ortegon attributes cannibalistic victory feasts to them.

ESTHETIC AND RECREATIONAL ACTIVITIES

Musical instruments.—Musical instruments include panpipes, transverse- and end-flutes, two-headed skin drums, musical bows, and humming tops (Tessmann, 1930).

Narcotics and stimulants.—The *Quijo* chewed both coca, mixed with a substance containing the ashes of several plants, and ground tobacco, mixed with honey. Today they take guayusa infusions, tobacco juice, and cayapi (ayahuasca), which play the same part in their religious life as in other tribes of the area.

Women prepare chicha of boiled yuca. The fermented mass is often the only provision while traveling. Both the ancient and modern *Quijo* prepare a drink of roasted yuca.

Toys.—Tessmann mentions maize-leaf balls, humming tops, and slings.

RELIGION

The early *Quijo* worshiped birds, trees, and other natural objects. In their houses they kept carved stones, in which they ground coca, and figures called coquindes, which they worshiped. They gave great importance to divination, which consisted in examining a coca quid spat in the hand. The modern *Quijo* still believe in dangerous bush demons.

Reincarnated souls of relatives become guardian spirits.

Modern shamans acquire power from spirit helpers and from "thorns," the latter sometimes embedded in a magical substance, which they take into their bodies. They induce a state of trance by fasting and by drinking cayapi, *Datura,* or tobacco water. The last also "feeds" the "thorns" so that they multiply within the body. To kill, a shaman shoots the "thorns" into his victims; to cure, another shaman sucks them out.

BIBLIOGRAPHY

Cruz, 1900; González Suárez, 1890–1903; Jijón y Caamaño, 1940–41; Karsten, 1920 a; Laureano de la Cruz, 1900; Ortegon (Descripción de la . . . 1881) ; Orton, 1870; Relaciones geográficas de Indias, 1881–97; Rivet, 1924; Rodriguez, 1684; Simson, 1886; Tessmann, 1930.

PART 4. TRIBES OF THE WESTERN AMAZON BASIN

TRIBES OF THE JURUA-PURUS BASINS

By ALFRED MÉTRAUX

INTRODUCTION

The basins of the Juruá and Purús Rivers (map 1, *No. 4;* map 5), which drain a large area of lowlands in the southwestern portion of the Brazilian Province of Amazonas, were the habitat of many tribes speaking dialects of *Panoan, Arawakan,* and *Catukinan.* These languages had an irregular distribution within the area, probably because of the easy communication afforded by the many connecting waterways.

Panoan and *Arawakan* dialects also occur in neighboring areas among tribes who are culturally similar to those of the Juruá-Purús Basins, so that the line dividing these areas is somewhat arbitrarily drawn. It is not unlikely that the *Remo, Maspo, Nianagua,* and other *Panoan* tribes on the smaller eastern tributaries of the Ucayali River were even more closely related to the Juruá-Purús tribes than to the *Conibo, Shetebo, Shipibo,* and other large *Panoan* tribes of the Ucayali proper, for they had retreated into the deep forests as fugitives from slave raids and lacked many culture traits dependent on a habitat on the main river. We have, however, drawn the line between the Ucayali area (described p. 555) and the Juruá-Purús more or less along the watershed, and included with the former the *Amawaka, Capanahua,* and *Remo,* which straddled the watershed. The reason for this is historical. The tribes east of the Ucayali River were, like those on the river, visited and described by missionaries, and were even taken into missions long before the Juruá-Purús tribes were known. For similar reasons, the *Arawakan*-speaking tribes have been divided; the *Piro, Campa, Chontaquiro, Masco, Sirineri,* and *Tuyuneri* are included with the Ucayali River peoples, and the *Maniteneri, Inapari,* and the tribes to the north and northeast of them are treated in the present chapter.

The *Panoan*-speaking *Mayoruna,* who live in the hinterland of the Amazon River below its confluence with the Ucayali River, also occupy part of the lower Juruá Basin, but, since their culture is somewhat aberrant, they form the subject of a special chapter (p. 551).

657

The inclusion of the Purús tribes within the same area as those of the Juruá may seem arbitrary. It is very likely that the *Arawakan* Indians and the *Panoans* presented differences which might have justified their separation in two different chapters. Actually, our information is too patchy to allow a sharp line to be drawn between them. Great care has been taken to specify to which tribes the culture data pertain.

The linguistic relationships of the various tribes and subtribes of the Juruá-Purús Basin were the most confused in South America until Rivet and Tastevin (1921, 1919–24) established their classification on the basis of new data. Most of the problems presented by this area resulted from the loose application of the same names to unrelated tribes. The name *Catukina*, for instance, was given to three groups of Indians who spoke entirely different languages. Three tribes known as *Canamari* speak *Arawakan, Panoan,* and *Catukinan* respectively. There are *Curina* (*Culina, Culino*) who belong to the *Arawakan* family and *Curina* (*Culino*) who are *Panoan*.

Although these tribes must once have been numerous, the influx of civilization during the 19th-century rubber boom, which was facilitated by the excellent waterways, left the native population decimated and largely assimilated. Many towns sprang up; the Territory of Acre at the headwaters of the Juruá and Purús Rivers had, in 1920, a civilized population of about 92,000. The present Indian population of the entire Juruá-Purús area is thought not to exceed 10,000.

SOURCES

Tribes of this area are little known historically. Early explorers and missionaries largely by-passed them. The majority of the early accounts of travels and explorations of the Purús and Juruá Basins date from the latter half of the 19th century and contain only fragmentary information on the Indians.

Thanks to Capistrano de Abreu's (1914) collection of native *Cashinawa* texts, we have not only precise and abundant data on the ethnography of these Indians, but also a considerable number of myths and tales. Capistrano de Abreu (1938) has also written a valuable ethnography of the *Cashinawa* based on these texts. More data on these Indians may be found in Sombra's (1913) article.

Ehrenreich's (1891 a) and Steere's (1903) descriptions of the *Arawakan* tribes of the Purús River are useful monographs, as is Wallis' (1886) short but dependable account.

Much ethnographical information is included in Father Tastevin's geographical studies of the Juruá and Tarauacá River Basins. He also recorded several myths. Lange's (1912) description of the *Mangeroma* (*Tucun-dyapa*), however, must be used with a certain caution. Considerable material on the various linguistic families of that area, assembled by

Father Tastevin, has been published in collaboration with Rivet (Rivet and Tastevin, 1919–20, 1921–22, 1927–29, 1938). A detailed ethnic map of the Purús-Juruá area established by these authors was published in 1921.

TRIBAL DIVISIONS

PANOAN TRIBES

Espinó.—On the Curumahá River, above the *Cujigeneri* Indians (lat. 11° S., long. 72° W.).

Marinawa (*Aguti Indians*).—On the Furnaya River, a tributary of the upper Embira River (lat. 11° S., long. 72° W.).

Tushinawa (*Yellow Indians*).—On the Humayta River, tributary of the upper Murú River, and on the Furnaya River, tributary of the upper Embira River (lat. 10° 30′ S., long. 72° W.). A tribe by the same name is also reported on the Jutaí River, above the *Catukina*.

Shahnindawa.—On the right side of the Embira River, along the Riosinho River.

Yura.—Around the headwaters of the Juruá River, on the Piqueyaco and Torolluc Rivers (lat. 10°30′ S., long. 73° W.).

Pacanawa (*Dagger Indians*).—On the headwaters of the Embira River (lat. 10° S., long. 72° W.).

Contanawa (*Jaçy Palm Nut Indians*).—On the upper Tarauacá and Humayta Rivers, right tributaries of the upper Murú River (lat. 9° S., long. 72° W.). These Indians are probably a branch of the *Amahuaca*.

Yaminawa (*Yuminawa, Jaminawa*).—Settlements of this numerous tribe are widely scattered along the Yaminawa River, a right tributary of the Embira River; and on the upper Tarauacá; the Humayta, a tributary of the Murú River; the Igarapé de Besta or Riosinho; the Valparaiso, Amoaca, Tejo, and São João Rivers, all of which are tributaries of the upper Juruá River. (Lat. 9° S., long. 71° W.; lat. 8°–9° S., long 73° W.)

Catukina.—On the left side of the Gregorio River, near the headwaters of the Reconquista River. The *Catukina* of the Javarí-alto River and the *Catukina* on the Katukina River, a tributary of the Tarauacá, and on the upper Embira River (lat. 7° S., long. 73° W.) belong to the same tribe according to Rivet and Tastevin (1921, p. 460). These *Panoan*-speaking *Catukina* should not be confused with the *Catukinan* linguistic family mentioned below.

Cashinawa (*Bat Indians*).—Settlements along the right side of the Embira River and its tributary, the Paraná do Ouro River; on the upper Murú River and its tributaries, the Iboaçu and Humayta Rivers; and on the upper Tarauacá, Gregorio, and Libertade Rivers (lat. 8° S., long. 72° W.). About 1920 there were only 42 *Cashinawa* families left (Tastevin, 1925, p. 413).

Shipinawa (*Monkey Indians*).—Between the upper Libertade and upper Valparaiso Rivers and along the Amoaca and Grajahu Rivers, all right tributaries of the Juruá River (lat. 8° S., long. 73° W.).

Ararawa (*Arara, Shawanawa*).—These *Panoan*-speaking *Arara*, not to be confused with the Madeira River *Arara*, are on the upper Libertade, Humayta, and Embira Rivers.

Yauavo (*Yawabu, Peccary people*).—On the Acuria River, right tributary of the Juruá River (lat. 9° S., long. 73° W.).

Saninawa (*Parrot Indians*).—On the Valparaiso River, right tributary of the Juruá (lat. 8° S., long. 73° W.). They are probably related to the *Saninauacana*, who live between the Coniguati and Oncano Rivers, tributaries of the Ucayali River.

Sacuya.—Between the Tamaya and upper Juruá Rivers (lat. 8° S., long. 72° W.). These Indians are probably a subgroup of the *Remo*.

Cuyanawa.—Between the Môa and Paraná dos Mouras Rivers.

Nucuini (*Inukuini*).—On the upper Môa River, extending to the Sungaru River.

Nawa.—On the upper Juruá River, somewhat above the mouth of the Libertade River.

Curina.—*Curina* are reported by Samuel Fritz (1922) along the right side of the Amazon River, from the lower Javarí River to the mouth of the Jandiatuba (Eneate) River. These Indians are to be identified with the *Panoan*-speaking *Culino*, who lived on the Jutaí River, above the *Arawakan Marawa*, on the lower Jandiatuba and Comatia Rivers, and on the right side of the Javarí River. They should not be confused with the *Arawakan Culino*.

Canamari (*Kanamari*).—On the upper Purús River between the mouth of the Rixalá and the Curumahá Rivers (lat. 11° S., long. 71° W.)

ARAWAKAN TRIBES

Some *Arawakan* tribes of the basins of the Purús and Juruá Rivers form a subgroup within the *Arawakan* linguistic family to which Rivet and Tastevin (1938) have given the name of *Arauá*. Previously, Brinton (1891) had classified the closely related *Arauá* languages as an independent linguistic family. Ehrenreich (1897 b) was the first to suggest their inclusion within the *Arawakan* family.

The tribes of the *Arauá* subgroup are:

Arauá.—On the lower Cheruan River and Lake Jahiruan, on the left side of the Juruá River and on the Igarapé Chiué (right side of the Juruá River). (Lat. 7° S., long. 68° W.) In 1877, this tribe was entirely destroyed by an epidemic of measles.

Culino (*Kulina, Kulino, Kolina, Kollina* or *Kurina*).—The *Culino* Indians are one of the most important tribes of the *Arauá* subgroup (lat. 7° S., long. 68°, 69° W.; lat. 8°–9° S., long. 71°–72° W.). They fall into two groups separated by the *Yamamadi,* but speaking closely related dialects.

The first *Culino* group consists of the *Culina* (*Colina*) scattered on the right side of the Juruá River along the Marary River and the upper reaches of the Tapauá River. They are closely related to the *Arauá.*

The second and far larger group includes the numerous *Culina* or *Curina* "sibs" living between the Erú and the Gregorio Rivers. In recent years, the *Culina* have driven the *Parawa* Indians to the other side of the Juruá River and have settled near the mouth of the Gregorio River. Their former habitat was probably located between the Embira and the Tarauacá Rivers, on the left side of the Murú River (Tastevin, 1925, p. 416).

The *Curia* on the upper Murú and Embira Rivers, the *Curiana* on the Paraná do Ouro River, the *Culiña* or *Karunawa* on the Santa Rosa River, belong to the same tribe. In recent years these groups seem to have migrated to the north and joined forces with their relatives of the upper Erú River. There are also some *Culina* groups on the Purús River.

The *Culina* call themselves *Madihá* (people) and each of their political units is called after an animal and sometimes a plant followed by the word madiha (e.g., *Sinamamadiha,* "The aguti-people"; *Camanui-madihá,* "Paca-Indians" etc.). The *Cashinawa* Indians call the *Culina, Pishinawa,* "The stinkers," or *Chapunawa,* "The rotten ones".

Pama.—On the left side of the Madeira River, above the Maparana River.

Pamana (*Pammana*).—On the Ituxy and Mucuim Rivers, above Lake Agaam.

Paumary (*Pamarí, Pammari, Pamaurí, Kurukurú, Wayai*).—On the islands and banks of the middle Purús River from its junction with the Jacaré River (or with the Tapauá River) up to Hyutanaham (lat. 6°–7° S., long. 63°–66° W.). The *Paumary,* together with the *Yuberi,* were a division of the ancient *Purupurú* tribe whose name has now disappeared. In the 17th century, the ancient *Purupurú* extended to the mouth of the Purús River. Some remnants of this tribe are mentioned in the middle of the 19th century between Lake Jary (Paraná-mirim do Jary) and the Paraná-pixuna, a right tributary of the lower Purús River. Other *Purupurú* are also indicated at the mouth of the Ituxy River.

Sewacu (*Sehuaku*).—On the Pauini River, a left tributary of the Purús River.

Sipó (*Cipó*).—On the Tapauá River, another left tributary of the Purús River.

Yamamadí (*Jamamadí, Jamamandí, Kapinamari, Kapaná*).—The habitat of these Indians lies between the Purús and the Juruá Rivers and is bounded by the Mamoria-mirim, Pauini, and Cheruan Rivers. There are also *Yamamadí* groups on the upper Tapauá River. Rivet and

Tastevin (1938, p. 76) consider the *Amamati* or *Jamamiri* mentioned by Martius in the basin of the Madeira River and the *Anamari* of the Mucuim River to be related to the *Yamamadi.* (Lat. 7°–9° S., long. 65°–68° W.)

Yuberí (*Juberí, Jubiri*).—On the lower Tapauá River, on the shores of Lake Abunini, and on the Purús River below its junction with the Mamoria-asu River (lat. 8° S., long. 66° W.).

According to Rivet and Tastevin (1919–20, 1921–22), the other *Arawakan* tribes of that area belong, together with the *Chontaquiro* and *Campa* (p. 535), to the "pre-Andean subgroup" of the *Arawakan* linguistic family.

Ipuriná (*Hypurina, Hyupurina, Jupurina, Kangütü, Kangite, Kangiti, Kankiti, Kankete*).—On the Purús River from the mouth of the Sepatnyim River to that of the Hyacu River; on the Acre River up to lat. 9°45′ S.; on the Ituxí (Iquirí) River; and on the Entimari and Punicici Rivers, two tributaries of the Ituxí River (lat. 9°–10° S., long. 65°–69° W.).

Cashararí (*Kacharadi, Kacharari*).—The *Casharari* are an *Ipuriná* subtribe living at the headwaters of the Curequeté River, a right tributary of the upper Ituxí River (lat. 10° S., long. 66° W.).

Canamari.—The *Canamari* of the upper Acre and Abuná Rivers speak an *Arawakan* dialect and must not be confused with the *Panoan* and *Catukinan Canamari.* The *Arawakan*-speaking *Canamari* are reported on the headwaters of the Acre River; on the Abuná River; on the upper Irariapé River, a left tributary of the upper Acre River; and on the Hyacú River (lat. 10°–12° S., long. 66°–70° W.). The *Canamari* inhabiting the region between the upper Abuná and the Acre Rivers are closely related to the *Piro* and *Chontaquiro.*

Maniteneri (*Manitineri, Maneteneri, Manetiniri, Manicheneri*).—On both sides of the Purús River from a point between the mouths of the Hyacú and Aracá Rivers up to the mouth of the Curinahá River (lat. 9° S., long. 69°–71° W.). They were also found on the Caspahá River and on the Río de Maloca, a tributary of the upper Acre River. (Lat. 12° S., long. 69°–71° W.)

Cujigeneri.—On the Curumahá and Cujar Rivers.

Catiana (*Kateana, Kathyana*).—On the upper Curumahá River, left tributary of the Purús River.

Cuniba.—They lived between the Juruasinho and the Jutaí Rivers. Formerly, they lived on the left side of the Juruá River, opposite Yainú, on the Igarapé do Pe. Constantino, opposite Soriano; and on the Mapuá River, above Taoca (lat. 7° S., long. 69° W.). These Indians are now extinct.

Marawa.—Chandless (1869 a) found them on the canals of Breo and Tucumán and on the Caapiranga River near its junction with the Juruá River. They are also reported on the lower Jutaí River; on the Rio

Sapo (Içapo), a tributary of the lower Jutaí River; and on the small rivers between the lower Jutaí and the Juruá Rivers. They can still be found on the Jutaí River, extending toward the Cupatana River, on the Caapiranga, and on the Meneru River and its tributary, the Meneruazinho River.

CATUKINAN TRIBES

Tucun-Dyapa (*Tukano-Dyapa* or *Mangeroma*).—Between the Río das Pedras and the Itecoaí River, both tributaries of the Javarí River (lat. 7° S., long. 72° W.).

The territory of the *Tukun-dyapa* corresponds exactly with that of the *Mangeroma* Indians described by Lange (1912). The names are undoubtedly synonyms.

Tawari (*Tauaré, Kadekili-Dyapa*).—Between the headwaters of the Jutaí River and San Felipe on the Juruá River (lat. 6°30′ S., long. 70° W.). The group living near the headwaters of the Jutaí River calls itself *Wadyo-Paraniñ-Dyapa* and is called *Kairara* or *Kayarára* by the *Canamari*. These Indians are probably related to the *Tauaré*, who are located between the Riosinho and the Yaminawa Rivers.

Buruè (*Buruhe*).—On the Jutaí River, above the *Tushinawa;* also on the Biá River, a right tributary of the Jutaí River.

Catukina (*Pidá-Dyapa, Jaguar People*).—On the middle Jutaí River and on its tributaries the Mutum and Biá Rivers (lat. 7° S., long. 65°–66° W.). A group of these *Catukina*, the *Kutiá-Dyapá* (Otter People), is settled on the Preto River, right tributary of the Jandiatuba River. Not to be confused with the *Catukino* cited below.

Parawa.—On the left side of the lower Gregorio River, near San Amaro (lat. 7° S., long. 71° W.).

Beñ-Dyapa (*Bendiapa*).—On the left side of the Juruá River, opposite Bomjardin (lat. 7° S., long. 71° W.). Their name means "Mutum tribe."

Canamari.—From the Tarauacá River to the headwaters of the Pauini River and south to the Purús River (lat. 9° S., long. 70° W.) There is a *Canamari* group on the left side of the Juruá River, from the mouth of the Pupunha River to the mouth of the Tarauacá River (lat. 7° S., long. 68°–69° W.). They extend to the headwaters of the Jutaí River and to its right tributary, the Biá River. There is another *Canamari* group on the headwaters of the Tapauá River (lat. 7° S., long. 67° W.). They came from the region between the Pauini and Jurupari Rivers.

Catawishi (*Hewadie*).—On both sides of the upper Teffé River and on the headwaters of the Coari River. Their territory extended from the Juruá River at the mouth of the Andirá River to the Purús River, opposite Paraná-pixuna. Their southern limit was the Tapauá River. (Lat. 6° S., long. 65°–67° W.) Not long ago there were members of this tribe between Breosinho and the lower Juruá River and near Bacu-ruru, at the mouth of the Andirá River. *Catawishi* also lived between the Purús and the Madeira Rivers; on the Paciá, Mary, and Mucuim Rivers; and on the Içuam River. In the west, they reached the Ituxí River and in the east, the Madeira River, at the junction of the Mamorian and Purús Rivers.

Catukino.—From the right side of the Tarauacá River to the left bank of the Purús River, south of the Tapauá River (lat. 7° S., long. 69° W.). Subgroups were settled on the upper Cheruan River; on the Oiday River, right tributary of the Purús River; and near the headwaters of the Coari River. Not to be confused with the *Catukina,* above.

THE TUPIAN FAMILY

The *Catukina* (*Catukinarú*), who about the end of the last century lived between the Embira and Embyrasú Rivers, two tributaries of the Tarauacá River (lat. 9° S., long. 70° W.), are mainly known for their famous underground telegraphic system. (See p. 679.) The short *Catukinarú* vocabulary collected by Bach (see Church, 1898, p. 64) is mostly *Tupian,* but it seems unlikely that this tribe belongs to that family. Rivet and Tastevin (1921, p. 460) are inclined to classify them with the *Catunikan* or with the *Panoan* tribes. In 1897, the *Catukinarú* numbered **196.**

CULTURE

SUBSISTENCE ACTIVITIES

Farming and collecting wild foods.—All the tribes of the Juruá and Purús Rivers practiced agriculture, but the relative importance of farm crops in their diet varied with the terrain. The *Paumary,* who were proficient fishermen, did not raise manioc, a circumstance which generally indicates unfamiliarity, or very recent familiarity, with agriculture. The *Ipurina* cultivated small gardens, but depended for food mainly on fishing and to a lesser extent on hunting. Geophagy is often reported for the tribes of the Purús.

The Indians drew their sustenance largely from the forest. The fruits of bacaba (*Oenocarpus* sp.), sorva (*Couma utilis*), masaranduba (*Mimusops excelsa*), jaçy, murumu, uricurí (*Attalea excelsa*), wild cacao, Brazil nuts, and the shoots of several palm species gave them a variety of wild-plant food. To a variable extent they cultivated manioc—almost exclusively the sweet species—maize, beans, bananas, plantain, peanuts, sweet potatoes, pumpkins, taiá, cara, pineapples, pupunha palms (*Guilielma speciosa*), papayas, sugarcane, tobacco, cotton, cayenne pepper, timbo creepers (barbasco), reeds for arrows, and coentro for a condiment.

Farming here did not differ greatly from that of the other regions of tropical America, except that sweet manioc was cultivated almost to the exclusion of the poisonous variety. *Cashinawa* fields were of impressive size; over half a mile (2 km.), said one visitor, but 600 to 1,000 feet (200 or 300 m.) seems to have been the maximum length. Before the Indians had iron tools, they killed large trees by hammering a ring around the trunk. Such trees were burned with the underbrush before the planting season. Peanuts were always planted in sandy soil. Among the *Cashinawa*, men planted and sowed; the women planted only cotton trees, but did most of the harvesting.

Hunting.—The *Ipuriná, Cashinawa,* and probably all the other tribes frequently left their villages to go on extensive fishing and hunting trips. The main hunting weapon was the bow and arrow; in addition, the *Yamamadí* and *Tukun-dyapa* (*Mangeroma*) used the blowgun to shoot game in trees.

The *Cashinawa* prepared themselves for hunting by fasting or by rubbing their bodies or weapons with magically potent plants. They made a large supply of new arrows and collected others from those who were not joining the hunt. During their excursions in the forest, the hunters built cabins with large platforms to which they returned every night to sleep and to broil the catch of the day. When they came upon a grove of fruit trees frequented by peccaries or other game, they built small shelters in which to hide while stalking the animals. During the hunters' absence, the women danced and sang songs expressing their craving for meat. When a large number of peccaries, tapirs, monkeys, and armadillos had been killed, the party set out for home, with forerunners announcing their success. Their first night at home was spent in special cabins on the plaza. The following day they feasted their relatives and all those who had contributed arrows.

Fishing.—Drugging fish with timbó and cangui creepers or with assacú sap (Amazonian manzanilla, *Hura crepitans*) was the most common fishing method of the *Cashinawa,* but they also fished with harpoons or with tripointed arrows or caught them in small dip nets mounted on circular frames. The Purús River Indians used multipointed arrows and two-pronged harpoons. A fish trap of the *Ipuriná* and *Yamamadí,* and common in the Guianas, deserves special mention because of its ingenuity. A conical basket (fig. 94), attached to a spring pole and placed between crossed sticks in a stream, was kept in a horizontal position by means of a baited trigger. When the fish touched the bait, the trigger was released and the basket swung up into the air.

Turtles were hunted by the *Paumary* and other tribes of the Purús River more often than any other game. The Indians pursued them in large flotillas of 20 to 30 canoes, and shot at them with harpoon arrows or captured them as they came onto sand bars to lay their eggs. Turtles were stored alive in small corrals "made of stakes placed in the lakes near their villages."

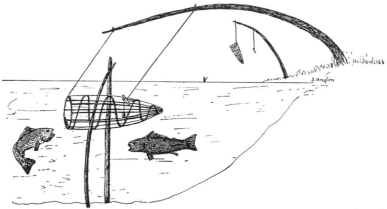

FIGURE 94.—*Yamamadí* fish trap. (Redrawn from Ehrenreich, 1891 a, fig. 35.)

Domesticated animals.—The Purús River Indians, who had had no domesticated animals before the European penetration, were exceedingly fond of their many tame birds and animals. Later dogs became indispensable to hunters, and the *Cashinawa* paid extravagant prices for trained hunting dogs. So great was their affection for dogs that women suckled puppies like babies.

The *Paumary* kept roosters for the sole purpose of using them as alarm clocks.

Food preparation.—Manioc flour, or farinha, was the customary food. All the tribes, even the *Paumary*, prepared a substitute flour with unspecified tubers and the fruit of a legume. Manioc tubers, both sweet and poisonous, were grated on boards strewn with palm thorns and were then squeezed either in an oval mat which was twisted like a rag or in a cylindrical press (tipití). The *Ipuriná* placed the grated mass in baskets lined with leaves and soaked it in water for several weeks until it fermented. Only then did they squeeze it in the manioc press. Manioc was also eaten in the form of wafers (beijú).

The diet of the *Cashinawa* included a diluted mush of manioc, bananas, maize, or peanuts (mingau), cakes of peanuts or maize, roasted maize or peanuts, raw or boiled bananas, boiled manioc tubers, and barbecued meat.

The *Yamamadí* prepared several nonintoxicating drinks from the crushed fruits of the bacaba, assai, and pupunha palms.

Cashinawa and *Ipuriná* mortars were wooden troughs and their pounders heavy semicircular slabs with lateral handles; the *Yamamadí* used vertical hollowed tree trunks with a cylindrical pestle.

HOUSES

During the dry season, the *Paumary* lived on the sandy banks of the river in small oven-shaped huts whose frames of bent rods were covered with palm-leaf mats. When the water rose, they built similar vaulted houses on rafts (fig. 95, *a*) made of light timbers with a floor of palm-wood strips tied with vines. These floating huts were anchored by heavy stones attached to creepers.

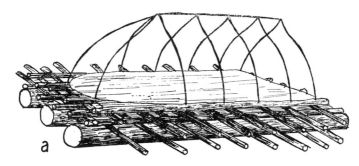

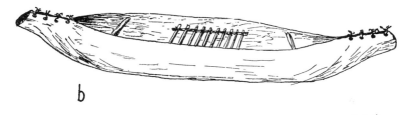

J. Quolim -

FIGURE 95.—Boats of the Juruá-Purús. *a, Paumari* raft; *b, Yamamadí* bark canoe. (Redrawn from Ehrenreich, 1891 a, fig. 24; and Steere, 1903, fig. 12.)

The *Ipuriná* hut must have undergone rapid modification at the end of the 19th century. In 1887, Ehrenreich (1891 a) described it as a vaulted structure 50 feet (15 m.) long and 33 feet (10 m.) wide, with an oval ground plan (fig. 96, *top*). The frame consisted of bent poles leaning against horizontal beams supported by slanting posts. The ridge pole rested on the rafters. A horizontal lath along the inside walls strengthened the frame. The hut was thatched with split palm leaves attached to long creepers. The *Ipuriná* huts seen by Steere (1903) were huge gable roofs with rounded ends resting directly on the ground. Hammock posts were set up inside. The families lived in compartments separated by straw partitions.

Yamamadí and *Tucun-dyapa* (*Mangeroma*) conical huts were among the largest huts known in South America. The dwellings of the former were up to 130 (40 m.) in diameter and 70 feet (22 m.) high; those of the latter were 150 (46 m.) wide and 40 feet (12 m.) high. The framework of the *Yamamadí* huts consisted of two concentric circles of

12 (?) posts which supported the wall plates (fig. 96, *bottom*). These in turn supported long and slender rafters that met in a peak, although there were no king posts. The thatching was made of the leaves of the carandai palms, split and plaited over a narrow piece of wood. The

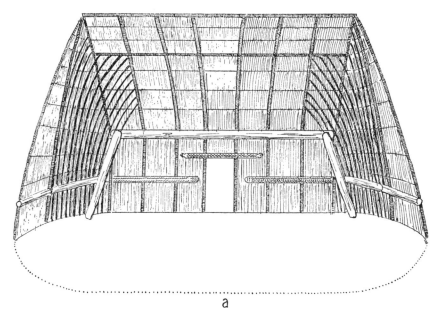

a

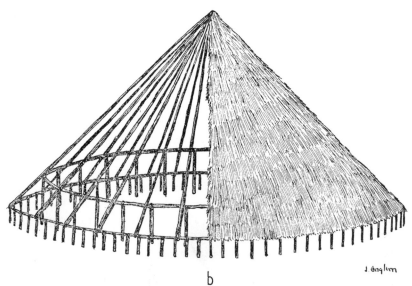

b

FIGURE 96.—Houses of the Juruá-Purú. *a, Ipuriná; b, Yamamadí.* (Redrawn from Ehrenreich, 1891 a, fig. 38; and Steere, 1903, fig. 9.)

intervals between the posts of the outer circle were open. The space between the outer and inner circles of posts was divided by horizontal poles into 25 family compartments. The *Yamamadi* vaulted huts (fig. 97) that were visited by Ehrenreich in 1887 had an oval ground

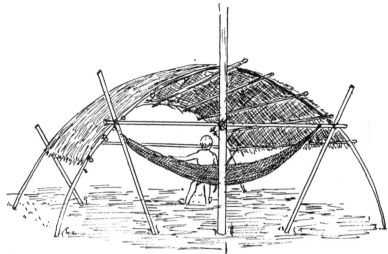

FIGURE 97.—*Yamamadi* shelter. (Redrawn from Ehrenreich, 1891 a, fig. 29.)

plan and were of a very different type from, and far less elaborate than, those described by Steere (1903). Such a discrepancy between the structures attributed to the same tribe is puzzling. The huge conical huts of the *Tucun-dyapa* (*Mangeroma*) sheltered up to 258 people. A low door and a circular aperture in the roof were the only openings.

The large communal *Cashinawa* houses set in the middle of the fields, were open sheds with a gable roof resting on a row of low posts. Houses of the *Canamari, Parawa,* and *Curina* were huge beehive huts in which a whole group lived. Each compartment reserved for a family was separated from the next one by an horizontal bar (Tastevin, 1920, p. 151).

Furniture.—Furniture here too consisted mainly of hammocks, wooden benches, and interior storage platforms for food. *Cashinawa* hammocks were made either in a net technique or of a solid cotton fabric with blue, black, and red stripes. The netted hammocks were made by men and were used for traveling. The hammocks of the *Arawakan* tribes of the Purús River were made of palm fiber. The *Ipuriná* when traveling improvised hammocks from three long, broad strips of bark tied together at both ends. The *Paumary,* who slept either on the sandy beaches or in their small floating huts, had no hammocks.

DRESS AND ADORNMENT

Clothing.—The male attire in most tribes was limited to a belt under which the penis was tucked (*Canamari*) and sometimes hidden by a small hanging fringe (*Yamamadi* (fig. 99, *b*), *Paumary, Ipuriná, Cashinawa*). Women, with the exception of the *Tucun-dyapa* (*Mangeroma*), who were entirely nude, wore a short apronlike (tanga) cotton fringe (*Paumary, Yamamadi, Ipuriná, Canamari, Culina*) or a cotton skirt (*Cashinawa*).

On ceremonial occasions, *Cashinawa* chiefs are said to have donned a short cotton tunic, and to have thrown over their shoulders a cotton cape decorated with feathers and toucan (tucán) skins. A pair of homemade trousers completed an outfit which contrasted so strangely with traditional Indian costumes that its native origin appears doubtful.

Ornaments.—Ear ornaments were mother-of-pearl disks either glued to a stick (*Canamari* women, *Culina*) or fastened to a cord and secured behind the head so that the disks showed in front of the ear lobe (*Yamamadi* women); plugs of reed or rosin (*Yamamadi* men); long sticks with feather tufts (*Cashinawa* men); fruit shells attached to strings of beads and fixed to the upper edge and lobe of the ear (*Cashinawa* women); and large mother-of-pearl triangles suspended from the ear lobes (*Ipuriná*).

The septum of the nose was generally perforated for the insertion of tail feathers (*Tucun-dyapa Mangeroma*) or of bone or reed plugs into which feathers or tufts of feathers were fastened (*Yamamadi*). The *Catukina, Tawari,* and *Cashinawa* suspended large mother-of-pearl crescents, pointing downward, from their noses. *Cashinawa* women were sometimes content to attach a short string of beads to their nose.

Ipuriná women placed **T**-shaped pieces of mother-of-pearl in their upper and lower lips; *Cashinawa* men had both lips studded with thin splinters; and *Cashinawa* women wore a string of beads hanging from the lower lip. The only ornament of the *Tucun-dyapa* (*Mangeroma*) women was a wooden labret in the lower lip.

The best necklaces consisted of various kinds of animal teeth, sometimes combined with fruit shells and seeds. The teeth were perforated and joined with great skill to form heavy collars, some of which covered part of the chest. The *Cashinawa* often sewed their tooth necklaces to cotton bands. It took *Ipuriná* men more than a year to make their long necklaces of perforated animal teeth and bone beads with incised spirals. They traded these ornaments to their neighbors for high prices.

Both *Cashinawa* and *Tucun-dyapa* (*Mangeroma*) men in festive attire attached tufts of tail feathers around their wastes in apron or skirt fashion. *Yamamadi* women wore broad red bark or cotton belts; the men, a narrow cord with a tassel of feathers or with a tapir's hoof at one end. The *Canamari, Culina,* and *Cashinawa* tied strings of white beads around their waists.

Most of the Indians of the area wore arm and leg bands (fig. 99, *a*) of bark strips or knitted cotton, generally finished with fringe and decorated with simple geometric designs. The legginglike ankle bands worn by

Ipurina women were knitted directly on the leg and could not be removed. *Cashinawa* women wrapped long strings of beads around their legs.

Feather headdresses were an essential festive adornment among all tribes of the area. Feathers were often attached to a brim of "palm leaf with a warp of cotton cord." Such brims without feathers were often worn as hats. *Cashinawa,* perhaps to enhance their hunting luck, put on frontlets of jaguar or boa skin. They also had a sort of tiara made of bamboo joints sewn together.

The hair was usually cut across the forehead and allowed to fall down the neck; no hair was tolerated on the face or body.

Painting.—Body painting with genipa and urucú or with rosin mixed with soot and ashes was one of the most striking customs of the *Cashinawa.* The combination of arabesques, frets, undulating lines, and other motifs differed so greatly in the various groups that a person's group affiliation could be discerned at once. The complete decoration was named after an animal, the markings of which were supposed to have served as a model. The characteristic *Paumary* body painting consisted of red stripes of urucú mixed with rosin.

The *Catukina, Ararawa,* and *Tawari* tattooed a solid band around the mouth and from the mouth to the ears.

The *Cashinawa* stained their teeth black with the juice of a plant called nixpo, "to prevent their decay."

NAVIGATION

The *Yamamadi* and *Ipurina* traveled in canoes made of a single piece of bark (fig. 95, *b*), generally jutahy. *Yamamadi* canoes were "about 16 feet [5 m.] long and 3 feet [1 m.] wide, flat on the bottom and the ends were drawn up and tied, thus forming hollow beaks" (Steere, 1903, p. 385). The *Paumary* had dugouts 12 or 14 feet (3.5 or 4.5 m.) long, pointed at both ends. Paddles were long and pointed and had crutched handles.

MANUFACTURES

Basketry.—Twilled baskets showed the usual combination of black and light elements to produce simple geometrical patterns. *Cashinawa* interpreted the lozenge patterns on their rectangular knapsacks as conventional representations of the water serpent.

Cashinawa women made small baskets of embauba bark, in which to keep their small belongings.

The hexagonal weave (lattice type) predominated in carrying baskets and knapsacks. The *Paumary* plaited simple mats.

Pottery.—The few references to the pottery of the *Yamamadi* and *Paumary* stress their lack of any decoration. *Ipurina* vases were oval or elliptic in shape and carefully smoothed with a shell. A mixture of ocher and silicious earth gave the clay various shades of color. The surface of the pot was coated with rosin immediately after it was fired.

Cashinawa earthenware was made of a blackish clay that could be obtained only in a few places and was tempered with crushed potsherds. Vases were ornamented with geometrical designs similar to those of body paintings.

Weaving.—The only loom that has been described is a small one on which the *Ipuriná* (fig. 98) wove armbands. It consists of a triangular frame; the warp threads are wound around a cross bar and two parallel strings. There is no device to maintain the warp crossed.

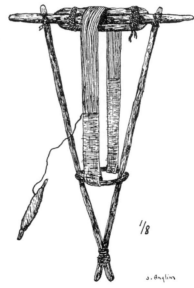

FIGURE 98.—*Ipuriná* loom. (Redrawn from Ehrenreich, 1891 a, fig. 42.)

Tools.—The *Yamamadí* chisel for carving arrows was an agouti tooth hafted to a long bone.

Fire making.—The *Yamamadí* fire drill (fig. 99, *c*) was of the usual type but had a piece of wood lashed to the horizontal stick to permit a firmer grip on the drill during the twirling process. The fire fan was of basketry.

Weapons.—The bow and arrow were without exception the main weapon of all the tribes of the area. In former times the *Ipuriná* had spear throwers, which they discarded during the last century for the bow and arrow.

Bows were carved of palm wood (of pupunha palm among the *Cashinawa*); their section was plano-convex (*Yamamadí*) or elliptical (*Ipuriná*); and the strings were of palm fibers (*Yamamadí*) or of cotton (*Ipuriná*). *Cashinawa* bows were decorated with artistic cotton wrappings.

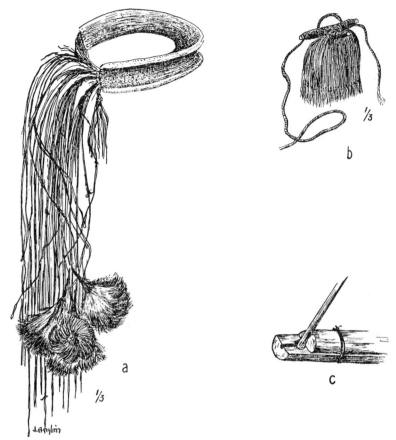

FIGURE 99.—*Yamamadí* manufactures. *a*, Arm band; *b*, man's penis cover; *c*, fire-drill. (Redrawn from Ehrenreich, 1891 a, figs. 28, 25, 32.)

The hunting arrows of the *Cashinawa* were tipped with lanceolate bamboo heads or with vertical rods having bone barbs or toothed edges. The *Ipuriná* bartered arrow shafts for the lanceolate arrowheads of the *Casharari*. The poisoned arrows of the *Yamamadí* and *Ipuriná* were tipped with long rods, notched so as to break in the wound (*Yamamadí*) or grooved longitudinally (*Ipuriná*).

The *Ipuriná* feathering consisted of two halved feathers fastened against the shaft by a cotton thread wrapped at regular intervals ("wrapped," or *Arara* feathering). *Yamamadí* arrows were without feathering but were trimmed around the butt with a few short feathers, devoid of any practical purpose.

The blowgun was used by the *Yamamadí, Tucun-dyapa* (*Mangeroma*), and *Culina*. The *Yamamadí* blowgun was made of a split sapling, the two halves of which were glued together with wax and rosin and wrapped with rattan strips. The sight was an animal tooth glued in a lump of wax.

Darts were needlelike splinters of palm wood, which were carried in a quiver of palm leaves or in a special basket. The cotton which was to be wrapped around the butt of the arrows just before shooting was carried in a separate calabash or in a special basket of wickerwork. In order to increase their lung power, hunters drew a wide bark band tightly around their waist, directly under the ribs.

To protect their villages from attack, the *Tucun-dyapa* (*Mangeroma*) set traps that were provided with blowguns which shot their darts automatically.

The blowgun was placed horizontally pointing at the path. At the "breech of the gun" was a young sapling severed five feet [1.5 m.] above the ground. To this was tied a broad and straight bark strip which, when the sapling was in its normal vertical position, completely covered the mouth piece. A long, thin and pliable climber was attached to the end of the severed sapling which was bent to its extreme position and then led over branches, serving as pulleys, right across the path and directly in front of the mouth of the blowgun and there was tied to some small root covered with leaves. When an enemy passed along the path, he must cut the thin bush rope or climber, thereby releasing suddenly the tension of the sapling. The bark-flap was drawn quickly up against the mouthpiece with a slap that forced sufficient air into the gun to eject the arrow. [Lange, 1912, p. 345.]

The poison of the *Yamamadi,* unlike that of the other tribes of the upper Amazon River, was fluid. When it was heated until it foamed, the points of arrows were dipped into it and passed through the fire to dry. The *Tucun-dyapa* (*Mangeroma*) prepared a thick brownish poison (curare?) by boiling shavings of one creeper with the crushed pulp of the root of another creeper and by adding tocandeiras ants to the mixture. The *Ipuriná* crushed about 10 different barks in a mortar, soaked the pulp in water, drained off the liquid, and boiled it in a pot until it became a thick mass. This poisonous decoction was smeared on arrows with a hair brush. Its action seems to have differed from true curare in paralyzing

Cashinawa men wore a short dagger suspended from the forehead. The dagger, which was their most characteristic weapon, was a piece of the central organs instead of the peripheral nerves,

Tucun-dyapa (*Mangeroma*) clubs of caripari wood were unusual in that six bicuspid black jaguar teeth were embedded in the heavy end of the club and projected about 2 inches above the surface of the wood (Lange, 1912, p. 370). The *Cashinawa* clubs, triangular in shape, were flat with cutting edges; those of the *Nawa* were also of the flat type.

The *Yamamadi* hunted large animals with spears of a single piece of *Tecoma* wood, from 6 to 7 feet (1.5 to 2 m.) long. Spears were used in hunting and war by the *Nawa, Yaminawa,* and *Tawari.*

taquara with deep lateral notches and a handle covered with squirrel-tail skin. A long macaw (ara) feather was fastened along the blade (Reich and Stegelmann, 1903, p. 136).

Circular tapir shields, common among the tribes of the upper Amazon River, occurred only among the *Nawa, Yaminawa,* and *Tawari.*

The *Tucun-dyapa* (*Mangeroma*) protected their villages with surrounding pits, covered by platforms that gave way under the slightest weight. The bottom of the pit was wider than the opening and the top wall slanted inward, so that it was difficult to climb out. The *Tucun-dyapa* (*Mangeroma*) and *Tawari* stuck caltrops, sometimes poisoned with curare, along the paths leading to their settlements.

SOCIAL AND POLITICAL ORGANIZATION

The social unit throughout the area seems to have been the extended family, living in an isolated settlement under the leadership of an old man. Several families formed large groups, generally called after an animal or after a moral or physical peculiarity (the People of the Squirrel, the People of the Jaguar, Frog, etc.; also Bone Eaters, Criers, etc.). Some authors have called these *Panoan* groups "totemic clans," but they have presented no other evidence of a sib system. Animal-named social groups occur also among the *Arawakan Paumary* and the *Culina,* who were split into the Caiman, Paca, Monkey, Vulture, Peccary, etc. people. The *Ipuriná* village consisted of six to eight families, usually living in two large huts separated by fields.

A *Cashinawa* informant described the ideal chief as "an old man who owned many things and many crops," which he generously distributed among his people. His main functions were to remind his subordinates to live together peaceably, and never to commit adultery. He also exhorted them to be active and to fulfill their duties as useful members of the community. Every morning the chief allotted to each his task for the day. He took the initiative in organizing hunting and fishing parties, and told his people when to open their clearings or to plant crops. He was the organizer of drinking bouts and the initiator of the youth. The chief's wife performed similar duties toward the women, prodding them to be industrious and cooperative.

PROPERTY

The hunting ground of each *Cashinawa* family was marked by bunches of hair (capivara, agouti, etc.) set in a cleft stick along the paths leading from the village to the woods.

LIFE CYCLE

Birth.—When a *Cashinawa* woman was pregnant, she and her husband stopped eating various foods. A woman gave birth standing in an enclosure, near her husband, and surrounded by women. She was washed with hot water to prevent abdominal swelling, and was then taken to a hammock in which she lay for 5 days. Both parents observed food taboos. After the confinement, they smeared themselves and the baby with genipa to protect it against fever. The husband did not have sexual intercourse with his wife until the baby could walk. The birth of twins was regarded as inauspicious, and one of them was killed.

Ipuriná women were confined in a special hut in the forest, where they were attended by old women, who named the child. After 5 days, during which the husband fasted, the mother returned home. For a year the father might not eat peccary or tapir meat. If a woman had had intercourse with several men before the birth of her child, all of them had to provide for its care (Ehrenreich, 1891 a, p. 66). A meat taboo was observed by the *Paumary* father and even by his father-in-law. A *Catawishi* father refrained from any work for a whole month after the birth of his child (Tastevin, 1920, p. 149).

Initiations and Puberty.—Two events with magico-religious implications occurred during the childhood of a *Cashinawa*. When still young, he received nixpo fruits which he chewed, thus staining his teeth black to insure a long life. Then his lips and the alae of his nose were perforated. On both occasions, the adults celebrated a feast during which they executed a special dance, called omã.

During the teeth-staining ceremony, the children were assembled on the plaza, seized by the hand, and forced to run to and fro. A fall was considered an ill omen. The children were then ordered to lie in their hammocks within a mat enclosure, where they remained for 5 days without eating or speaking, and with their eyes focused on their feet. At the end of the ordeal, they purified themselves in a river and henceforth were allowed to resume their normal existence.

The perforation of the lips and nose was accompanied by similar rites. The children, decorated with feather diadems and capes, listened to a speech in which the chief enumerated all the ceremonial food taboos which they were to observe. Then, singing, they walked to a house, escorted by the chief, who wore foot jingles and danced. A child who cried during the operation brought himself bad luck. The candidates were put on a diet of boiled manioc, mush, and peanuts, and were forbidden to bathe. Death would inevitably follow any infringement of these rules. From the account of the natives, it seems that the feast ended with a general purification rite: All the fires in the village were extinguished, the people washed themselves in the river, and then built new fires.

Ipuriná boys had their lips perforated at the age of 8. The first time that a *Yamamadi* child ate meat was the occasion for a ceremony, during which the shaman put a piece of meat into the child's mouth.

When *Cashinawa* girls came of age their hymen was cut in the presence of the men, who surrounded them holding weapons. The girls and the women who operated on them refrained from eating game for 2 months and lived on a diet of broth and bananas.

Marriage.—The preferred form of marriage among the *Cashinawa* was between cross-cousins. No man could take a wife without the permission of the chief. A man who intended to marry asked a female relative to make him a large hammock, which he presented to his bride after their first night. For the next few days, "feeling ashamed," he left at dawn to hunt and returned after dusk. Residence was matrilocal if the father of the bride were alive, patrilocal if the girl were an orphan. Only parentless couples built a house for themselves. *Cashinawa* folklore stresses the necessity for a man to be industrious if he wants to marry. Only those with unusual skill and energy could afford two wives.

In the *Ipurina* marriage ceremony, the bride pretended to run away from the bridegroom, who pursued her.

Polygyny was common among chiefs (*Cashinawa, Canamari*). A woman past her prime was often abandoned by her husband, who then would marry a very young girl. The deserted wife was supported by her children or by a very young lover (*Cashinawa*).

Death.—The *Cashinawa* buried the dead and either buried or destroyed all his possessions, lest the soul should refuse to depart for the land of the spirit and haunt those who had retained some of its belongings. On the grave they planted bananas, papayas, and sugarcane.

Male mourners smeared themselves from head to toe with genipa, but women smeared only a portion of their bodies. Failure to observe any of these customs aroused the wrath of the soul.

Many *Panoan* tribes of the Juruá River Basin ate the roasted or boiled corpses of their relatives. They also drank the pulverized bones mixed with chicha (Reich and Stegelman, 1903, p. 137). Tastevin (1925, p. 35) states specifically that the *Cashinawa* also practiced endocannibalism before their contact with the Whites.

The *Paumary* and *Yamamadi* buried the dead in a squatting position in a pit in the bush, and erected a small hut over the grave. The *Ipurina* interred the dead and their belongings in the huts where they had lived. *Yamamadi* and *Ipurina* exhumed the bones, smeared them with urucú, wrapped them in a bundle, and kept them hanging from the roof of their houses. Steere (1903, p. 375) states that the funerary hut was abandoned. The *Ipurina* celebrated a mortuary feast, during which a man held a bone of the deceased while he praised his war deeds.

The hereafter.—The *Cashinawa* believed that when a man breathed his last, his soul was taken to the sky by a spirit. There it "woke up again" and lived forever with the "Great Ancestor" in a pleasant country with no evil and no suffering. The shadow of the deceased remained on earth, where it wandered as a ghost, whistling, frightening the living, and sometimes sucking their blood.

Art.—The esthetic manifestations of the Purús-Juruá River Indians are little known. However, it seems that the *Cashinawa* and other *Panoan* tribes displayed no little artistic skill in tracing geometric patterns on the human body. The style of the motifs used in body painting was the same as that traced on pottery. *Cashinawa* fabrics and basketry were enlivened by geometric figures, with a predominance of the meander. The *Ipuriná* showed some proficiency in carving bird figures of light wood, which were described as dance accessories. The *Ipuriná* also decorated the interior of their houses with straw or bark figures and carved serpents on the ends of the horizontal laths of the hut frame.

Songs and dances.—Judging from the examples recorded by Steere (1903, pp. 378, 387), the songs of the *Ipuriná* refer mainly to war; those of the *Paumary* are melodies sung by canoe paddlers. Their words are short descriptive sentences of trivial events, such as, "The toucan eats fruit in the edge of my garden and after he eats, he sings" (Steere, 1903, p. 387).

The *Cashinawa* had several types of dances, each called by a different name. In all the dances, the men clasped hands and circled or followed winding lines. Certain ceremonial dances were wild displays of vitality, during which the participants jumped, shouted, invoked the spirits, and recited the names of the forest animals.

Musical instruments.—Huge bark trumpets (fig. 100) played the same part in the ceremonial life of the *Arawakan* tribes of the Purús River as they did among the *Arawakan* tribes of Guiana and Bolivia. The *Paumary* made trumpets of clay, probably of the same type as those of the Orinoco River. Panpipes, though probably known to all the tribes of the Purús River, are specifically mentioned only for the *Paumary*.

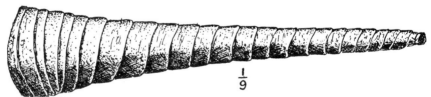

$\frac{1}{9}$

FIGURE 100.—*Ipuriná* bark trumpet. (Redrawn from Ehrenreich, 1891 a, fig. 47.)

The musical instruments of the *Cashinawa* are: A bamboo flute with a wax plug near the mouth and with a lateral stop and four other stops near the distal end; a trumpet with the bell made of the tail of a tatu canastra (large armadillo) ; a musical bow composed of two bows rubbed against each other; and a wooden drum covered with a tapir or deer skin and beaten with two sticks. Such a drum of European type is undoubtedly a recent acquisition.

A most remarkable combination of slit drums was used by the *Tucun-dyapa* (*Mangeroma*) on board their canoes. An upright forked stick was fastened on each side of a canoe, near the middle.

About three and a half feet [1 m.] astern of these a cross-piece was laid on the bottom of the craft. To this were attached 2 shorter forked sticks. Between each pair of upright forked sticks was placed another cross-piece, thus forming 2 horizontal bars, parallel to each other, one only a few inches from the bottom of the boat and the other about a foot and a half [½ m.] above the gunwales. Next 4 slabs of caripari wood of varying thickness, about 3 feet [1 m.] long and 8 inches [20 cm.] wide, were suspended from these horizontal bars, so as to hang lengthwise of these canoes and at an angle of 45 degrees. Each pair of slabs was perforated by a longitudinal slit and they were joined firmly by finely carved and richly painted end-pieces. The operator strikes the slabs with a wooden mallet or hammer, the head of which was wrapped with an inch layer of caoutchouc and then with a cover of thick tapir-skin. [Lange, 1912, pp. 356–57.]

By combining the various tones of their drums, the Indians were capable of sending long messages to the villages along the rivers.

The *Catukinarú* of the upper Juruá River developed an amazing "telegraph" (cambarysú), consisting of signal drums which when struck transmitted vibrations to other drums, sometimes located a mile away, "which respond to or echo the blow." The Indians answered by striking the receiving drum in their hut, and the blow was in turn echoed by the instrument originally struck. The drum was constructed by placing a hollowed palm-wood trunk in a pit on a layer of coarse well-tamped sand. The pit was filled to the surface with fragments of wood, raw hide, and resins of various woods, and was covered with a layer of hard rubber. The drum itself was partly filled from bottom to top with successive layers of sand, wood fragments, bone fragments, and powdered mica. The center of the drum was empty and its upper surface was covered by a hide, a piece of wood, and finally a layer of hard rubber. The Indians beat the drum with a club, the head of which was covered with hard rubber and raw hide. It is likely that in this region there was "a stratum of earth or rock of such composition that it transmitted the vibrations of the blow given upon one of the instruments, which being enclosed and nearly buried in the earth, certainly did not transmit the sound through the air" (Church, 1898, p. 67).

Games.—*Cashinawa* games, which unfortunately have not been described, were named after the animals represented by the participants; for instance, the game of the serpent or of the peccary. In the "turtle game," women tried to release a land turtle which had been bound with a cord, against the opposition of a group of men who fell over them. Other women beat their opponents to free their partners (Tastevin, 1925, p. 33).

Narcotics.—Tobacco was widely cultivated, not for smoking but for snuffing, a habit common to both sexes but predominant among men.

Instead of tobacco, some groups used parica leaves, which are said to contain some nicotine. The tobacco leaves were first dried on a platform or exposed to the fire at the end of a cleft stick or on an upturned pan or a potsherd, and then pulverized in an ash-heated small mortar, generally made of a Brazil nut shell. The powder was mixed in equal proportion with the ashes of a bark or the hull of cacao beans. It was inhaled through two tubes, (fig. 101, b), occasionally through a single tube, made of the hollow leg bones of a bird, wrapped together with cotton

FIGURE 101.—*Ipuriná* tobacco container (a) and inhaler (b). (Redrawn from Ehrenreich, 1891 a, fig. 41.)

thread and wax. One end of each tube was rounded with wax so as to fit the nostrils. The *Cashinawa* snuffing apparatus was V-shaped, permitting the snuffer to blow the powder into his own nose or have it blown in by a companion. Even when using the vertical tube, Indians were often assisted by a friend who held the powder in the palm of the hand.

The *Casharari* took parica in the form of clysters administered with a rubber syringe.

The tobacco or carica (i.e., parica) powder was kept in a snuff box, generally a snail shell (*Pomacea*), furnished with a cockle shell and a small pouring tube (fig. 101, a). The *Cashinawa* looked upon tobacco snuff as a prophylaxis against colds and influenza. The *Ipuriná* were much given to coca chewing and were seldom without a quid in their cheeks.

The *Cashinawa* induced hallucination by drinking a decoction of the bark of an unidentified creeper called honi, probably a species of *Banisteriopsis*. Under the intoxicating effect of the drug, they perspired, trembled, saw dangerous animals, and were seized by homicidal fury. Later they perceived swarms of souls calling them, and felt themselves transported to the land of the spirits, who showered them with presents.

Fermented drinks.—Fermented beverages were prepared from manioc, peanuts, maize, and palm fruits. The *Cashinawa* brewed their chicha in the hollowed trunk of a paxiuba tree that was generally cut for the occasion, an act considered symbolical of an approaching feast.

RELIGION

The *Cashinawa* believe in an "Old Father" who lives in the sky with his wife, the "Old Mother," and is the ruler of the Lightning People. The main function of this deity is to carry to heaven the souls of the dead and to provide them with all kinds of foods and goods. However, he and his wife want them to work and be diligent. The "Old Father" is also conceived of as a Thunder God for thunder is caused by his tears and sobs whenever he remembers his lost children. Capistrano de Abreu identifies the "Old Father" with Pokã (The Good One), who tried to make men immortal and is the father of the culture hero who brought darkness. Though nothing more is known about the "Old Father," it may be assumed that he is the *Cashinawa* equivalent of the Creator and Great Ancestor of other South American tribes.

The folklore of the Juruá and Purús Basins abounds in stories of forest spirits and ghosts who frightened and tormented men, yet could be deceived and overcome by them. It is difficult to decide how far these tales reflect native beliefs and fears. The *Ipuriná* peopled the forest with gruesome bush spirits, but hostile ghosts were of greater concern to them.

Among the *Ipuriná,* certain nature spirits, the Kamutshi or Kamatsha (kamu in many *Arawakan* languages means "sun"), were embodied in flutes and large bark trumpets hidden in a place known only to the shamans. At the feast of these spirits a group of men entered the village dancing and blowing the sacred instruments. The women, who could not look upon the trumpets and flutes without endangering their lives, shut themselves in their houses and expressed their terror in a chant. To placate the spirits they gave food and drink to the men, who seem to have enjoyed greatly the fear which they caused (Ehrenreich, 1891 a, p. 70–71).

The religious life of the *Cashinawa*, as known to us, did not include such elaborate ceremonies. However, dances were often performed to influence spirits, in particular the maize spirit, to secure abundant crops and bountiful game, or simply to guard the community from malignant influences. To bring good luck at hunting, the *Cashinawa* fumigated themselves with the smoke of game hair or bird feathers, inoculated themselves with toad secretions, fasted, and wore frontlets of serpent skin. Those who found a boa and enumerated the names of game by pointing at its spots could rely on abundant catches. Many magically potent herbs were taken internally, applied externally, or were carried as hunting charms.

According to Tastevin (1925, p. 34), the *Cashinawa* distinguished two souls, one of which resided in the eyes and after death went to heaven, and the other, identified with the shadow, became a ghost and tormented the living.

No such duality is suggested in the *Cashinawa* texts collected by Capistrano de Abreu (1914, p. 137–140). Dreams were considered as adventures of the soul, which left the body during sleep. Sometimes the soul reached the land of the spirits, who rejoiced and entertained it. After a bad dream, a person remained at home for a day and refrained from any activity.

Fear of bad dreams forced the *Cashinawa* to keep a vigil before a fishing party or an attack on enemies. After returning from an armed expedition, they drank a decoction of cayenne pepper and observed a strict diet of mush and boiled bananas.

Ceremonies.—Now and then the *Canamari* and the *Curina* organized feasts which began with reciprocal flagellations with manatee thongs. A man or woman would advance with raised arms to receive a lash and then would reciprocate on his partner. Thus the two would turn around a hut until one of them gave up. Father Tastevin (1920, p. 150) interprets the rite as a duel, but actually it was probably a magic flagellation.

SHAMANISM

The *Ipuriná* shaman was a curer and also the leader of religious ceremonies. A candidate shaman swallowed crystals that his instructor had supposedly vomited, and was thus provided with missiles which would bring disease and death to his enemies. Then he lived in seclusion and fasted rigorously until he was consecrated as a full-fledged shaman by a supernatural jaguar. The main object of medical treatment was to extract from the patient's body the crystals shot at him by a sorcerer.

A *Cashinawa* who wished to converse with the spirits and obtain magical power from them first had to consent to the cruel fustigation which the spirits inflicted on him with thorny branches. After he had endured this treatment awhile, the spirits "inoculated" his body with small pellets of "poison" (magical stuff: small chips of wood, iron, beads, etc.). They also warned him, under penalty of losing his magical power, never to eat any game, sweet manioc, sweet potatoes, or yams. The diet of a shaman was broth, bananas, raw peanuts, roasted maize, pumpkin, and fish.

Before summoning the spirits, the shaman drank the sap extracted from the shoots of several palm trees, which provoked a state of intoxication. He also climbed to a treetop and called his invisible friends. They entered the hut, whistling, and people could hear them speak in *Cashinawa*. As the spirits feared light, the shaman ordered all the fires put out, but sometimes he would suddenly light the hut with a torch so that the audience could enjoy the sight of the spirits for a few seconds before they scattered. The persons who were present generally asked the spirits about their future and inquired about their death.

A shaman could use magic stuff to kill his enemy, but the soul of his victim could recognize him and denounce him to the family of the deceased.

The medical science of the Juruá Indians did not rest entirely on shamanism. They had a wide knowledge of herbs, some of which are enumerated by Father Tastevin (1926). Certain herbs had magical prophylactic virtues or were good luck talismans; others were purely medicinal and were administered internally or externally. Before taking a therapeutic bath, the patient had part of his hair shaved, probably to facilitate the penetration of the infusion's virtues. To induce vomiting and to evacuate intestinal contents, toad secretions were introduced into abdominal wounds inflicted with a fire brand.

A shamanistic cure that Ehrenreich (1891 a, p. 58) observed among the *Yamamadí* differs from the usual procedure in the silence of the practitioner and the absence of the customary blowing and spitting. The medicine man pinched the skin around the seat of the disease and rubbed his fingers as if to clean them from obnoxious stuff. He then buried the disease. Tobacco was applied on serpent's bites.

MYTHOLOGY AND LITERATURE

According to *Cashinawa* mythology, sun, night, and cold did not exist as part of the original universe. Sun and night were kept in two jars by a cruel spirit (the trickster), Icã, until Spider succeeded in freeing them. In another version, it is Vulture who steals the sun to warm his bald head. He puts it in a jar next to that containing cold. In another myth, sun, morning, and night were hidden in separate holes guarded by three groups of people. As a result of a quarrel, the owners of night released it so suddenly that everyone fell asleep in the position in which he was caught by darkness. Later, the three groups decided to release the elements at set times. Darkness was said to have been in the possession of a man who agreed to give some away, but the people who came for it brought a very small box and their nights were too short. Later, they carried off so much darkness that the harvest season was long past when they awoke. Finally, they obtained a satisfactory amount of darkness. Sloth, ancestor of the *Ipuriná,* created the sun by throwing fruit kernels into the water of the flood.

There is little consistency in the myths explaining thunder and lightning. When Xexeu birds dance in their house, there is widespread obscurity, thunder, and lightning. Vulture, master of the sun, wants to join them, but his stench chases the birds away, and the sun shines again. Thunder is also caused by the cracking of the sky when the spirits hack at it with their axes. Ants patch the cracks to prevent the collapse of the sky. Some

Cashinawa believe in a thunder spirit who has a bald head and several red-headed children. Whenever he gets angry and beats his children, it thunders; lightning is the blinking of his eyes.

The moon is the severed head of a man (a woman in one version) that rolled across bush and rivers to return home. Unable to enter its own house, the head ascended to the sky by means of a cotton thread which a vulture attached to the celestial vault. There the head became the moon, its eyes, the stars, and its blood, the rainbow. Henceforth, women menstruated when the moon was full.

To the *Ipuriná*, the moon is a young boy who grows alternately fat and lean; Orion is a beetle; the Pleiades, a serpent; the Southern Cross, a partridge; and the Hyades (including Aldebaran), a turtle.

In the sky (*Cashinawa*) is a lake in whose depths is a hole which the stork keeps closed with his foot. When the stork goes fishing, rain falls. The *Cashinawa* attribute the destruction of the world and its first inhabitants to excessive rains, to flooded rivers, and to a general fire caused by a spark fallen from the sky. Some versions add that the sky crashed down and changed places with the earth.

The first men were drowned; they either changed into animals, or continued to live as spirits in the sky. The earth was repopulated by the progeny of the seven children of a sky woman who was struck by lightning. The babies were saved and brought up by a crab. In the *Ipuriná* mythology, a flood of boiling water was caused by the overflowing of the big pot of the sun in which storks cooked all kinds of food.

Stories of the origin of mankind are varied and unrelated. Men developed from maggots growing in the bodies of giants drowned by the flood; they were created by the thunder spirit, Kana, from worms or from the blood of game; they fashioned themselves by magic from jacy seeds, but the coata monkey provided them with hands and feet, teeth, mouth, and nose. The macaco prego monkey taught them to procreate. The first man, Ichan, produced his own life in a calabash. Later, he turned into a fish. The *Cashinawa* descended from a girl who was left alone after the whole commuunity had changed itself into peccaries. She found a baby—the tobacco spirit—whom she took home, and after a few days, when the child became a man, she married him.

Old men might have regained their youth by slipping into a new skin had their ancestors correctly understood the message given them by the first man who died. He said, "Change your skin," but they heard, "It is finished." Only a few animals, such as the serpents and the iguana, understood the message, and for that reason they are periodically rejuvenated.

Culture heroes.—Culture heroes do not appear in the numerous tales collected by Capistrano de Abreu. Tastevin (1925, pp. 23–29), on the contrary, found evidence of such mythical characters.

The *Cashinawa* learned agriculture, as well as arts and crafts, from Kuma, who traveled in the company of a trickster, Icã (Inga). Icã often displayed his ignorance and stupidity and introduced many unpleasant features on the earth.

The *Canamari* identified their culture hero, Tamacuri, and his weaker companion, Kirak, with the moon and sun. The culture hero of the *Cama-nawa* was a personification of the sun.

Ichan, the ancestor of men, created birds by molding them of clay and projecting life into them.

Animals often play the part of culture heroes. Icã, the master of the sun, was the niggardly owner of fire and crops. Fire was stolen from him by a parrot; when he tried to quench the firebrand with rain, all the birds covered it with their wings. Icã was also unable to prevent a swallow, a lizard, a toad, and a jaguar from robbing him successively of a manioc cutting, a grain of maize, a peanut, and a banana, which they gave to the *Cashinawa*. Birds acquired their bright colors by bathing in the blood or gall of Icã. According to another *Cashinawa* story, men learned agriculture from a friendly deer, weaving from a hummingbird, and pottery and house building from a wasp.

Metamorphosis.—The transformation of men into animals or of animals into men is a favorite theme of *Cashinawa* stories. An old woman without teeth became an armadillo; a widow with long hair turned into an anteater; a group of men or children were transformed into a herd of peccaries. A cripple, incapacitated for work, chewed a magic leaf, recited an incantation, and became a turtle. A little boy went after birds, which kidnapped him.

Animals also assumed human shape. A coati-puru married a woman and saved her and her people from famine by magically producing abundant crops. A frog changed itself into a man and called on the people who had tried to kill it. A toad in the guise of a man called on two women and swallowed all their earthenware.

Many stories are concerned only with the animal world. The Jurity fools the Sloth and rubs it with genipa instead of urucú; the Wasp plays tricks on the Vultures; the Turtle by a ruse kills the Tapir, but is in turn devoured by a jaguar angry at his boasting.

Helpful animals.—Animals aid men in distress. A man with a gangrenous wound is restored to health by a rat. A jaguar out of gratitude hunts for a man who had extracted a bone from its throat.

Legends and ghost stories.—Many stories deal with the supernatural power of shamans. Ghost stories were also popular. A man finds the soul of his mistress, who insists on living with him, but he gets rid of her by pushing her into the water.

Hunting adventures sometimes have a comic touch. A successful hunter takes an unlucky one on a hunt and provides him with abundant game;

they exchange wives; then the unlucky hunter plays tricks on his fortunate associate, pushes him into a rapid, and scalps him. A successful hunter became the favorite of women but remained indifferent to their entreaties; finally, a disappointed woman wounds him. A small child kills a jaguar. A man is swallowed by a serpent; he is rescued although his body remains boneless. A man enjoys serpent flesh more than game and forces his wife to eat some of it.

Hero tales.—The adventures of a hero who, after having been betrayed by his wife, dedicates himself to the destruction of monsters forms a sort of epic in prose. This cycle has many analogies to the deeds attributed to the culture hero in other folklores.

Origin of narcotics.—The intoxicating properties of honi (ayahuasca) were revealed to men by a water spirit. A man who had observed her intimate relations with the tapir, managed to capture her. She took him under the water and gave him a decoction of honi, which provoked strange troubles in him, but also made him see wonderful visions. He returned to this world and revealed the secret to his fellow tribesmen. He was swallowed successively by several serpents, but still had time to teach men how to use ayahuasco.

An old man asked to be buried in a deep grave, but always left his tomb until he was nailed in it with five paxiuba sticks. Four plants grew from his eyes, his nose, and his mouth. They were the pati huni that causes visions, the chupa that makes people bellicose and whips up their energies, the yura yuti, which is a violent poison, and the tuku huni, which causes ulcers.

BIBLIOGRAPHY

Abreu, 1914, 1938; Bates, 1892; Brinton, 1891; Castelnau, 1850–59; Chandless, 1866 a, 1866 b, 1869 a; Church, 1898; Labré, 1889; Courboin, 1901; Ehrenreich, 1891 a, 1897 b; Fritz, 1922; Hassel, 1905; Herndon and Gibbon, 1853–54; Koch–Grünberg, 1914; Lange, 1912; Linhares, 1913; Marcoy, 1869; Markham, 1910; Martius, 1867; Masô, 1919; Ordinaire, 1887; Petersen, 1886; Polak, 1894; Reich and Stegelmann, 1903; Rivet, 1920, 1921; Rivet and Tastevin, 1919–24, 1921, 1927–29, 1938; Sombra, 1913; Steere, 1903; Stiglich, 1908; Tastevin, 1914, 1920, 1924 a, 1924 b, 1925, 1926, 1928 a, 1928 b; Verneau, 1921; Villanueva, 1902–03; Wallis, 1886.

TRIBES OF THE MIDDLE AND UPPER AMAZON RIVER[1]

By Alfred Métraux

TUPIAN TRIBES OF THE UPPER AMAZON RIVER

TRIBAL DIVISIONS AND HISTORY

The widespread *Tupí-Guaraní* family was represented on the upper Amazon by two powerful tribes, the *Cocama* and the *Omagua,* the former still numerous, the latter now almost extinct. The material recently collected by Espinosa (1935) on the *Cocama* language has not yet been compared to other *Tupí-Guaranian* dialects, but research based on a few vocabularies seems to indicate close connections between the *Omagua* and *Cocama* dialects and that of the eastern *Tupí.* The *Omagua* and *Cocama* migrated to their present territory in pre-Columbian times, but perhaps in a not very distant past. Like many other *Tupí-Guaraní* tribes, they became rapidly adjusted to their new surroundings. Their culture resembled in its most fundamental features that of their neighbors on the Ucayali and Huallaga Rivers. Living on large rivers with easy navigation and abundant resources, they relied for food to an unusual extent upon turtles, turtle eggs, large fish, and manatees. The river habitat facilitated farming on beaches and flood plains, lessening the labor of slash-and-burn horticulture. It was perhaps these ecological factors that made possible the existence of large villages, which contrasted sharply with the single-house communities found among the Montaña people.

Judging from the few scattered data which exist on their ancient culture, little seems to have linked them with their *Tupian* relatives of eastern Brazil: temporary urn burial (*Cocama*), the marriage of a woman with her maternal uncle, the occasional ceremonial sacrifice of prisoners, the large communal dwelling, the cultivation of bitter manioc, and preparation of casava (*Omagua*).

Cocama.—The *Cocama* were divided into two branches, one, probably the more important, was found on the Ucayali River and the other, on the Huallaga River.

The *Cocama* of the Huallaga River (lat. 5°30′ S., long. 74°30′ W.) were generally designated as *Cocamilla,* the "small Cocama," to differen-

---

[1] See Map 1, *No. 4;* also maps 4 and 5.

tiate them from the Ucayali River *Cocama* of the "Gran Cocama" (lat. 5° S., long. 74° W.). There was practically no difference between the *Cocama* and the *Cocamilla,* except that the latter dressed like their *Chébero* neighbors.

The *Cocama,* or *Ucayali,* lived on both shores of the lower Ucayali River, 12 days by canoe from its mouth. They were discovered in 1559 by the expedition of Juan de Salinas when he ascended this river.

At the beginning of the 17th century, the *Cocama* were greatly feared as river pirates. Each year during the flood season they crossed from the Ucayali River to the Huallaga River by a system of small rivers and creeks and by portages. They sailed up and down the latter river and the Marañón River, and entered their creeks and small tributaries to attack the *Maina* Indians and other tribes of that area. They returned at the dry season with booty and head trophies.

When the *Chébero* revolted in 1644, they found some support among the *Cocama;* for this reason a Spanish expedition was sent to intimidate the Ucayali *Cocama,* who had received *Chébero* and *Cocamilla* refugees. The Spanish party was well received owing to the presence of a Jesuit Father, Gaspar Cujia, and a *Xibitaona* Mestizo whom the *Cocama* imagined to be one of their reincarnated chiefs.

The first Jesuit mission among the *Cocama,* Santa Maria de Ucayali, was founded in 1653 by Father Bartolomé Perez; Father Tomas Majano, who carried it on in 1657, was, however, soon forced to abandon it. He was followed to the Huallaga mission by about 100 families of *Cocama* converts. (See Maroni, 1889–92, 29: 73–84.)

In 1669, the Spaniards sent a punitive expedition against the *Cocama,* who were continually raiding the Indians subdued by the Spaniards, and even their establishments in the upper Amazon. Father Lucero accompanied the armed force and succeeded in winning new converts for the Mission of Santiago de la Laguna, which he founded in 1670 on the Huallaga River. This mission soon became the center of the Jesuit activities in the zone of the Marañón. The *Cocama* of Santiago de la Laguna abandoned the mission during the great epidemic of 1680, and took refuge among the *Omagua,* but later they returned to it.

The *Cocamilla* (*Huallaga, Pambadeque, Pandabequeo*) occupied the land between the lower Huallaga, the Marañon, and the Simbiría Rivers. In 1643, they fled from the Spaniards to the country of the *Cocama,* but returned to their former territory at the request of the Jesuits. In 1649, the Mission of Santa Maria de Huallaga was established among them by Father Bartolomé Perez. It was later in charge of Father Raimundo Cruz, who composed a *Cocama* grammar.

At that time the mission had a population of about 600. About 1655, many *Cocamilla,* who had been forced to join the expedition of Martín de la Riva Agüero against the *Jívaro,* deserted the mission and joined the *Cocama.* In 1663, some *Cocamilla,* who had banded with *Chepeo* (*Shipebo*) and *Maparina,* resumed their piratical operations in the Huallaga-Marañón region; these ceased only when their leader was executed by a punitive expedition. Meanwhile, they had lured away from the missions a great many converts, stormed the Mission of Concepción, and killed Father Francisco Figueroa, a missionary whose writings on the region and its inhabitants are of considerable interest (Chantre y Herrera, 1901, pp. 224–231).

Several smallpox epidemics, in particular that of 1680, decimated the *Cocamilla* of Santa Maria de Huallaga. The survivors were finally shifted to the Mission of

Santiago de la Laguna (founded in 1670), where they resided with *Cocama* and *Pano* until the expulsion of the Jesuits (Maroni, 1889–92, 29:73–84; 30:132).

After 1767, the *Cocama* remained in their native country. Today isolated *Cocama* families are scattered along the Ucayali River as far up as Sarayacu and Cumaria, along the Huallaga River up to the Yurimaguas, and along the Amazon from the mouth of the Pastaza River to Pebas (Tessmann, 1930, pp. 66–67).

The *Cocama* withstood better than most tribes of the area, the Spanish colonial regime, the slave raids, and the disastrous smallpox and measles epidemics. Their number in the 17th century was estimated at 10,000 to 12,000 (Maroni, 1889–92, 29:81). In 1936, it was reckoned at 9,500 to 10,000 (Tessmann, 1930, p. 66, and Peruvian Census).

Most of the *Cocama* work as peons for White or Mestizo patrons on the Ucayali and Amazon Rivers, but many are said to have migrated to Brazil during the rubber boom. They are all Christian in name, but still practice many of their old customs. Shamanism has survived among them almost unimpaired. Most of them speak or understand *Quechua* and Spanish in addition to their own language.

Xibitaona.—The *Xibitaona* (not to be confused with the *Hibito*) were a colony of *Cocama* Indians who had settled on the Santiago River near the town of Santiago de las Montañas, above Borja. At the beginning of the 17th century, they were placed on encomiendas. Their relationship with the *Cocama* was discovered when a *Xibitaona* Mestizo who in 1644 accompanied a Spanish expedition to the *Cocama* could converse with the latter (Figueroa, 1904, p. 100).

Omagua (*Umaua, Cambeba, Campeba, Cambela, Canga-Peba ("Flat Heads"), Agua, Carari ?*).—Orellana's expedition in 1542 passed through the territory of the *Omagua,* but its chronicler, Carvajal, gives the name *Omagua* to a tribe located below the Trinidad River (probably the Juruá River), i.e., to the east of the territory of the *Omagua* as defined by later travelers. According to these sources, the *Omagua* country began at the mouth of the Napo River and extended eastward to the junction of the Jutahy River[2] with the Amazon, lat. 3°–4° S., long. 66°–73° W. (Acuña, 1891, p. 115). Therefore, Carvajal's *Omagua* were probably not the historic *Omagua,* but must be identified with the Indians ruled by Aparia the Great and perhaps by Machifaro. Actually, two native words recorded by Carvajal in Aparia's village are *Guarani* (coniupuyara, "women", and chise, "stars" not "sun") (Carvajal, *in* Medina, 1934, p. 181). The *Omagua* are designated in the accounts of the Pedro de Ursua expedition in 1549 as *Carari.*

Omagua settlements formed an almost continuous line of houses for 200 leagues on the shores and islands of the Amazon. When first discovered, the *Omagua* were in full expansion. Annual war parties followed the innumerable water roads of the Amazon Basin and penetrated remote regions to raid villages or settle as independent tribelets. Early missionaries found *Omagua* colonies far up the Napo, Aguarico, and Quebeno

---

[2] The last *Omagua* village to the east was Mayavara, below the mouth of the Jutahy River (Fritz, 1922, p. 76).

Rivers. Aparia the Lesser, who is mentioned by Carvajal as a chief of the Napo River, may well have been an *Omagua* chieftain. Like the *Cocama,* the *Omagua* seem to have deserved the name of "America's Phoenicians" given to them by Hervás (1800–05).

The Franciscans, among them Father Laureano de la Cruz, made a brief attempt to missionize the *Omagua* in 1647, but a smallpox epidemic wiped out their village of San Pedro de Alcantara, after 3 years' of toil.

The Jesuits started their missions among the *Omagua* at the request of these Indians, who sought protection against Portuguese slavers. During the 40 years following 1641, these slavers had reduced the *Omagua* from approximately 15,000 to 7,000 persons (Velasco, 1841–44, 3:235). After 1686, Father Samuel Fritz spent many years among the *Omagua,* traveling, preaching, and founding the missions of San Joaquín, Nuestra Señora de Guadalupe, San Pablo Apóstol, and San Cristóbal (Maroni, 1889–92, 30:227–35; Chantre y Herrera, 1901, pp. 284, 297).

During the war between Spain and Portugal at the beginning of the 18th century, the Portuguese attacked and destroyed the 33 *Omagua* settlements under the jurisdiction of the Jesuits. In 1710, the *Omagua* who had not been taken prisoners or killed, migrated upstream and formed a new mission, San Joaquín de Omaguas, first on the southern bank, later on the right bank of the Marañón River, somewhat below the mouth of the Ucayali River (Velasco, 1841–44, 3:230–336; Chantre y Herrera, 1901, pp. 313–315). In 1732, the *Omagua,* armed by the Jesuits, repelled a major Portuguese invasion. The Jesuits succeeded in warding off more Portuguese encroachments on their missions until their expulsion in 1767.

The *Omagua* population declined rapidly despite the inclusion of *Cocama, Yurimagua,* and *Yameo* in their mission. In 1737, San Joaquín had only 522 inhabitants, not all of them *Omagua.* A smallpox epidemic further reduced its population in 1751 (Chantre y Herrera, 1901, p. 49). In 1925, there were only 120 to 150 *Omagua* left in the two villages of San Salvador de Omagua and San Joaquín, and they were rapidly absorbed by the *Cocama* (Tessmann, 1930, p. 48).

During the first half of last century there existed another important group of *Omagua* at São Paulo de Olivença. They were the descendants of the ancient *Omagua* who inhabited the islands of Jahuma, Calderon, and Capiahy, and who had been settled by force at Olivença. (Ribeiro de Sampaio, 1825, pp. 72–73; Spix and Martius, 1823–31, 3:1187; and Marcoy, 1875, 2:340.) These *Omagua* seem to have merged with the Mestizo population of the Solimões region.

Omagua-yeté.—The *Omagua-yeté* (*Ariana, Pariana*) had been an *Omagua* colony at the mouth of the Aguarico River. In 1635, they were taken as slaves to the Sunu River, but they revolted, and some migrated to the upper Teputini River, while others joined the bulk of the tribe on the Amazon. The *Omagua-yeté* of the Teputini River were divided into four groups—*Omagua-yeté, Anapia, Macanipa,* and *Yhuata,* comprising about 45 families (Maroni, 1889–92, 26:243–244). They harassed Spanish settlements on the Napo, Sunu, and Payamino Rivers in order to steal iron tools. In 1737, there were still some *Yeté* one day and a half up the Aguarico River, near a lagoon called Cocaya (or Taricaya). In 1735, the *Omagua-yeté* united with the *Omagua* of San Joaquín, but later they returned to the Teputini River, where they seem to have disappeared, as they are not mentioned after that date (Maroni, 1889–92, 27:50).

SOURCES

Carvajal (Medina, 1934) and the chroniclers of the Ursua expedition (Jornada de Omagua y Dorado, 1909, pp. 321–322, and Ortiguera, 1909, pp. 429–430) give us scattered ethnographic data on the *Omagua*. A semi-fabulous account of the "kingdom" of *Omagua* figures in the declarations made to the Spaniards by *Tupinamba* Indians who had migrated from the Brazilian coast to Chachapoyas. (See Carta de Gobierno del marques de Montes-Claros, virrey del Perú A. S.M., *in* Rel. geogr. Indias, 1881–97, 4:cxxiii–cxxxix).

The *Cocama* are lumped together with the *Maina* in the "Relación de la entrada que hizo el gobernador D. Diego Vaca de Vega al descubrimiento y pacificación de las provincias de los indios Maynas, Cocamas y Gibaros" (Rel. geogr. Indias, 1881–97, 4:cxxxix–cl).

Figueroa's "Relación de las Misiones de la Compañía de Jesús en el país de los Maynas" (1904) contains some first-hand data on the *Cocama* and *Cocamilla*. Laureano de la Cruz (1900), the first missionary of the *Omagua,* gives scattered information on the material culture of these Indians. The standard authorities for the ancient *Omagua* are Acuña (1891) and Father Fritz (1922), who describe briefly their puberty rites, warfare, and religion. Very valuable but disconnected details on the *Cocama* and the *Omagua* may be gleaned from the "Noticias auténticas del famoso río Marañón" (see Maroni, 1889–92) and from Chantre y Herrera (1901). Veigl (1785) refers to the already acculturated *Cocama* and *Omagua* of the missions and is content to mention a few of their techniques and artifacts. The history of the *Omagua* during the Jesuit period has been outlined by Velasco (1841–44, 3:230–236).

Fragmentary data on the *Omagua* and *Cocama* may be found in La Condamine (1745, pp. 78–79), Ribeiro de Sampaio (1825, pp. 72–73), Spix and Martius (1823–31, 3:1187), Martius (1867, pp. 433–442), and Marcoy (1875, 2:258–61, 340–345).

On modern *Cocama* and *Omagua,* the best source is Tessmann's "Indianer Nordost-Perus" (1930). Father Espinosa (1935) is the author of a good monograph on the language and culture of the *Cocama.* Rivet (1910 b) has collected and analyzed the linguistic material available on *Cocama* and *Omagua* dialects before the publication of Espinosa's work.

For bibliography, see page 712.

CULTURE

SUBSISTENCE

Farming.—The *Omagua* and *Cocama* cultivated the same plants as the *Maina* Indians, but only the *Omagua* grew bitter manioc in early days. The present-day crops of the *Cocama* are maize, sweet potatoes, several tubers—cara (*Dioscorea*) and taja-cara (*Solanum immite*), beans, yams, sicana, pumpkins, peanuts, pineapples, cayenne pepper, and such fruit trees as pupunha palms, caimitos, avocados, zapotes (*Matisia cordata*), guanábanas (*Annona muricata*), papayas, and guavas (*Inga spectabilis*). Food plants of Old World origin are bananas, which have become a staple, sorghum (*Sorghum vulgare*), sugarcane, oranges, watermelons, mangos, and others.

Plants raised for other than food purposes are cotton, tobacco, barbasco, and *Clibadium,* the last two for drugging fish.

When crops were planted in the forest, the usual slash-and-burn pattern was followed; the main tools to clear the bush were stone axes and chonta knives. The ancient *Omagua,* however, often avoided this labor by cultivating on the beaches, planting in June, and harvesting in January and February between annual floods (Maroni, 1889–92, 30:197).

Hunting and fishing.—The principal resource of the rivers is turtle eggs, laid on sandy beaches in untold thousands during August and September. Indians aboriginally collected these for food and, during the post-Contact Period, they also extracted and sold the oil of the eggs to the Portuguese. Commerce in oil became so heavy that the governments have had to regulate egg collecting. The *Omagua* and *Cocama* killed turtles with spears and arrows or else captured and kept them in corrals by lagoons.

These tribes took fish during low water with spears—some with two prongs—harpoons (formerly propelled by spear throwers), bows and arrows (both multiprong and harpoon arrows), hooks (probably of European origin), weirs, drugs (barbasco and *Clibadium*), and by hand. To catch manatee and large fish, the post-Columbian *Omagua* and *Cocama* used an iron-headed harpoon with a float attached to it (Maroni, 1889–92, 30:415).

Hunting was of limited importance, at least to the *Cocama*. Small animals were killed with the blowgun; peccaries were hunted with spears, generally as they crossed a river, where they were pursued by the Indians in their canoes. The *Omagua* also used log deadfalls for small game.

Wild foods included palm fruits, such as *Euterpe, Oenocarpus,* and *Mauritia*; Brazil nuts; palm grubs; ant eggs; and honey.

Domesticated animals.—Dogs,[3] pigs, and chickens, unknown in the pre-Columbian period, reached these *Tupian* tribes at an early date; chickens were introduced before direct contact with Whites. In recent times, they were kept in special coops, safe from vampire bats.

FOOD PREPARATION

The *Omagua* kept garnered maize in their houses, but buried manioc tubers in leaf-lined pits below river level, often for 1, 2, or more years

---

[3] Dogs, however, are already mentioned among the tribes of *Maina* in the middle of the 16th century. (See Rel. geogr. Indias, 1881–97, 4:cxlvi).

After the river began to fall, they removed what they needed, leaving the rest buried. They considered rotten manioc better and more nutritious than the fresh and from it they made their drinks, flour, and cassava bread (Fritz, 1922, p. 50).

To prepare cassava, the manioc tubers were soaked 4 or 5 days, crushed in a mortar, squeezed in a manioc press, strained, and baked in a pan. The flour was exposed to smoke in a basket and later made up into mush (Maroni, 1889–92, 27:61).

For grinding food, these tribes used both the cylindrical wooden mortar and the wooden trough combined with a semicircular, flat wooden grinder typical of many Forest Tribes of eastern Bolivia and Perú.

HOUSES AND VILLAGES

Omagua villages were generally situated on islands, beaches, or banks of the Amazon River, on lowlands likely to be flooded (Fritz, 1922, p. 50). The thatched, rectangular dwellings were occupied by three to a dozen families. One door of the house faced the water, the other opened toward the jungle. Inside were platforms, made of bark, on which the occupants took refuge from high water. At such times they also moored their canoes indoors (Fritz, 1922, p. 51).

Cocama villages were formed by 30 to 40 huts, each sheltering several families (Maroni, 1889–92, 29:92).

The large *Cocama* house had a gabled roof which descended almost to the ground, where it was supported by a low wall of split palms and longitudinal beams. The ridge pole rested on the crossed rafters rather than on posts. The modern house type with its gabled roof and side walls is probably of recent origin (Espinosa, 1935).

To avoid mosquitoes, the ancient *Cocama* and *Omagua* swung their hammocks inside tents made of cachibanco (a palm-fiber cloth) or of discarded blankets and shirts (Rel. geogr. Indias, 1881–97, 4:146; Laureano de la Cruz, 1900, p. 101). They also used feather fans to drive away these insects. Modern *Omagua* and *Cocama* sleep on platform beds (fig. 102) and use hammocks only for babies. Mosquito nets are imported.

FIGURE 102.—*Cocama* platform bed. (Redrawn from Tessmann, 1930.)

Formerly storage platforms, men's four-legged benches carved from a single piece of wood, and women's mats completed the household furniture. Houses were lighted with copal rosin wrapped in leaves.

DRESS AND ORNAMENTS

Omagua and *Cocama*[4] men originally wore the long, sleeveless cushma, or tunic, woven of cotton and decorated with painted or woven geometrical designs in red, blue, yellow, orange, and green. Women wore knee-length cotton skirts and sometimes a little mantle. Today they dress like the Mestizo population.

Gold ear and nose ornaments, probably of Highland origin, are mentioned by the first explorers in *Omagua* territory, but no reference to them appears in the missionaries' accounts. *Cocama* men of the 17th century perforated the lower lip to hold a piece of leather from which hung beads and pendants. They even made labrets of soldiers' belt buckles and of bullets (Figueroa, 1904, p. 103). Today the only mutilations are the ear perforations among *Cocama* women.

Feather headdresses were formerly the most conspicuous ornaments. Belts, armlets, bracelets, and anklets of thread or braided hair were plain (Rel. geogr. Indias, 1881–97, 2:145).

Women painted large surfaces of their body and even their hair with genipa; men stained part of their face and their limbs with the same pigment. Formerly, wooden stamps were used to decorate the body with elaborate designs. Today, body painting is confined to facial decorations among *Omagua* women and some applications of paint against sunburn. Modern and probably ancient *Omagua* stained their teeth black, as did most tribes along the eastern slopes of the Andes. Tooth filing among modern *Cocama* may be ascribed to Negro influences. Native combs were made of reed splinters bound together.

Deformation of the skull.—The *Omagua* were called "flat-heads" (*Canga-peva*) by their neighbors from the shape of their deformed skull. They compressed their infants' heads between a board or a wattle of reed placed on the forehead and a plank or trough which served as cradle, making the "back and front of the head . . . as flat as the palm of the hand." (See Acuña, 1891, p. 117; Veigl, 1785, p. 68).[5] The practice disappeared after the *Omagua* came under Jesuit rule, but at São

---

[4] *Cocamilla* men, like the *Chébero,* wore a short skirt, and women wore a loincloth (Maroni, 1889–92, 28:416).

[5] Laureano de la Cruz, 1900, p. 99: "Toman la criatura de pocos dias nacida y ciñenle la cabeza por la parte del cerebro con una faja de algodón ancha, y por la frente con una planchuela que hacen de cañas bravas, que les coje desde los ojos hasta el cabello muy bien apretada, y de esta manera lo que la cabeza había de crecer en redonda, crece para arriba y queda larga, chata y muy desproporcionada."

Fritz, 1922, p. 48: ". . . they proceed little by little to flatten the tiny heads of their young children by applying to the forehead a small board or wattle of reeds tied with a little cotton so as not hurt them, and fastening them by the shoulders to a little canoe, which serves them for a cradle."

Paulo de Olivença it seems to have been retained for a longer time. Marcoy (1875, 2:345) unearthed in one of their burials a skull with the above type of deformation.

TRANSPORTATION

For long voyages, warfare, and crop transportation, the *Omagua* made huge dugout canoes of cedar (*Cedrela angustifolia*) taken as driftwood from the river or felled in the forest. These craft were about 45 feet (14 m.) long, 4½ feet (1½ m.) wide. After the log had been hollowed and carved, the whole community dragged it to the river over rollers and pieces of bark. Individual fishermen used small dugouts which they could carry on their backs or drag to and from the river (Veigl, 1785, pp. 83–87).

These tribes carried burdens in large, cylindrical baskets with hexagonal weave, suspended by a tumpline. Babies straddled the mother's hip, supported by a sling.

MANUFACTURES

Basketry.—*Omagua* and *Cocama* basketry forms and techniques were typical of the Tropical Forest: Hexagonal woven (lattice) carrying baskets and twilled sieves, mats, containers, and parrot cages. *Carludovica trigona* was the principal material for basketry.

Spinning and weaving.—Cotton threads were spun by means of a long spindle rolled along the thigh; cords of tucum fibers were rolled by hand on the thigh. The *Omagua* and *Cocama* formerly wove cotton on the Andean-type, horizontal loom. *Cocama* women passed their warp threads around two horizontal sticks, one of which was fastened to two posts or to the house wall, the other to their waist. They wove with the help of a shuttle. Products of their industry were shirts, loincloths, arm and leg bands, and mosquito nets. Designs were either woven into or painted over the completed textile. Like the *Maina* and *Záparo,* the ancient *Cocama* and *Omagua* made cachibanco cloth, that is to say, fabrics of palm fibers.[6] With tucum fibers, the modern *Cocama* make knotted bags, hammocks, and fish nets.

Pottery.—The first explorers of the Amazon praised *Omagua* ware for its varied forms, beautifully painted ornamentation, and smooth glaze.[7] The *Cocama* are still among the best pottery makers of South America (fig. 103).

An *Omagua* potter only worked in a special hut where she felt safe from malevolent charms. She first ground her clay to which she added

---

[6] Rel. geogr. Indias, 1881–97, 4:146: "Su hacienda es mantas, camisetas de algodón blancas y labradas de colores con pincel, y cachibangos (petates) del grandor de tapetes, que los hacen de cogollos de palmas de que hacen cierto modo de hilaza y los texen muy curiosamente, y dellos hacen toldos."

[7] Chantre y Herrera, 1901, p. 68, "un berniz permanente, vistoso y fino de manera que se limpian las piezas con mucha facilidad."

charred apacharama bark to serve as an aplastic. Then she built her vessel with coils of clay, smoothed it with a stick, and polished it with a pebble. After drying it in the sun, she coated it with a white clay slip, on which she applied red and black linear designs. She baked it

FIGURE 103.—*Cocama* pottery. (Redrawn from Tessmann, 1930, color plates 2 and 3.)

in an open fire. While the vessel was still glowing hot, she smeared a glaze of *Vismia guianensis* rosin on the outside and of copal (*Hymenaea courbaril*) on the inside. To decorate the large cooking jars, she merely made fingernail impressions in the soft clay around the neck. The *Omagua* made in this manner bowls, plates, and water bottles, but they were specially expert at manufacturing large chicha jars.

Calabashes and gourds.—*Cocama* and *Omagua* painted calabashes were regarded by both Spaniards and Indians as one of the best expressions of their arts and were an important article of trade in the area. They probably were decorated by the same method as the *Yurimagua* gourds. (See p. 704.)

Rubber.—In the 18th and 19th centuries, the *Omagua* were widely known for the numerous rubber articles which they manufactured. It was even said that the colonists of Pará became acquainted with rubber and its properties through them. Among the rubber objects made by the *Omagua* were waterbottles and pear-shaped enema syringes. They also prepared elastic bands by smearing strips of cauari bark with rubber latex (La Condamine, 1745, pp. 78–79; Martius, 1867, p. 440).

Weapons.—The typical weapon of the *Cocama* and *Omagua* was the spear thrower. It is described as a small board with tapering ends, a bulging central section, and a projecting peg to engage the butt of the dart. The darts had a reed shaft and a barbed chonta head.

There are good reasons to assume that the *Cocama* and *Omagua* discarded the bow after their migration to the upper Amazon, but that they readopted it in more recent times under the influence of their *Panoan* neighbors. In recent times, the *Omagua* used the bow for fishing and hunting, the *Cocama* mostly for fishing. *Omagua* arrows had a lanceolate bamboo blade or a barbed rod point for hunting, a knobbed head for stunning birds, and two to six points for fishing.[8]

Both *Omagua* and *Cocama* were already acquainted with the blowgun in the 18th century. In our day, they obtained their supplies of curare from the *Tucuna*. Spears and harpoons have been mentioned above (p. 692).

In warfare the *Omagua* carried spear throwers, lances, round-headed clubs and round shields, made of "reeds split and closely woven," different from those of the *Tapuya* "which were made of tapir skin, or woven hemp-fiber" (Fritz, 1922, p. 50; see also Chantre y Herrera, 1901, p. 88). Ancient villages, like modern plantations, were probably protected by concealed pitfalls.

Fire making.—Aboriginal methods of fire making are not recorded, since they were displaced at an early date by flint and steel. The *Omagua* and *Cocama* activate fires with the feather fans used also to drive away mosquitoes.

TRADE

The articles which the *Cocama* traded with their neighbors were cachibanco cloth, tunics, and mantles (mantas) (Rel. geogr. Indias, 1881–97, 4:CXLVI). *Omagua* painted earthenware, calabashes, and cotton cloth seem to have been in great demand in Colonial times among neighboring tribes. The *Cocama* and *Omagua* obtained the curare for their blowgun darts from the *Peba* and *Tucuna*. Today these peoples have merged into the Peruvian national economy, working for Whites and purchasing from them industrial products.

SOCIAL AND POLITICAL ORGANIZATION

The *Omagua* and *Cocama* seem to have differed from modern Montaña tribes in the size of their villages (Maroni, 1889–92, 28:416). Each community consisted of several houses, in contrast to the large, single-house communities of the *Pano, Záparo, Witoto,* and *Tucano.* The size of *Omagua* villages may be gaged from population data in missionary accounts. The number of the inhabitants in the 34 villages on the islands

---

[8] According to tradition, the *Omagua* formerly used slings, but such a weapon seems outlandish m an area where stones must be rare.

of the Amazon varied from 16 to 250 (Laureano de la Cruz, 1900, pp. 82, 84–88). An *Omagua* village is said to have been divided into two sections (moieties?), each with 30 houses and an average of 50 to 60 people per house, but not all the houses reached such proportions, for many were occupied only by 3 to 5 families. Like a great many villages along the middle course of the Amazon, 17th-century *Omagua* villages were so close to one another that large stretches of the shores were lined by a continuous row of huts.

As elsewhere in the Amazon, the occupants of a large house seemingly comprised an extended family. This family was presumably patrilineal and patrilocal, though there is no definite evidence on this point. The authority of the *Cocama* chief seems to have been slight, but the statement that the *Omagua* chief (zana) had more authority than in most tribes of the area may mean that he controlled not merely the household but the village.

Each family owned two or three slaves, captured in war or purchased from neighboring tribes. Though required to work hard, these slaves were treated kindly and formed part of the family (Maroni, 1889–92, 30:195). At first, the *Omagua* refused to sell their slaves to the Portuguese, but later they not only become slavers for the colonists but helped the Jesuits to capture wild Indians to be brought up in the missions. *Omagua* slavery may have developed from the widespread *Tupí-Guaraní* custom of keeping prisoners for a long time before eating them ceremonially. The early *Omagua* continued to kill prisoners occasionally, but had abandoned cannibalism. By the incorporation of prisoners into their communities, they began to form a class society. This social stratification may have been furthered by an incipient group of nobles, so designated during childhood (see below).

LIFE CYCLE

Birth.—An *Omagua* woman gave birth squatting on her husband's bed, and assisted by another woman. The naval cord was cut with a bamboo knife and buried with the afterbirth. Both parents were subsequently confined in the house and observed a special diet from which game meat was entirely excluded. These food taboos lasted until the child could sit up by itself (Martius, 1867, p. 441).

Infanticide occurred among the *Omagua* when the mother was already nursing or when the parents had desired a child of the opposite sex. The *Cocama* killed the crippled or deformed children (thought to be the children of spirits) as well as illegitimate or unwanted children. In such cases, unless one of the parents or some relative lifted it from the ground the infant was buried alive with the placenta. Abortion was widely practiced. (Cruz, 1900, p. 97; Figueroa, 1904, p. 111; Maroni, 1889–92, 29:82.)

In both tribes, the birth of twins was deemed to be an evil omen. One of the twins was ceremonially taken to the river in a painted vessel— among the *Cocama* in a basket—and set adrift with the hope that a shaman might somehow retrieve and rear it. Then all the women held a purification ceremony in which they broke their pots, cleaned their fireplaces, washed their clothes, and bathed themselves (Chantre y Herrera, 1901, pp. 74–76).

Chantre y Herrera (1901, pp. 83–85) described a ceremony, called usciumata, which in his opinion conferred nobility on children of both sexes, but which is so strongly reminiscent of the solemn *Quechua* ceremony of cutting children's hair that it may well be a kind of rite of passage performed during early childhood. It took place when the child was about a year old. The parents chose godparents for their children and organized a big drinking feast to which all the neighbors were invited. They placed the children on profusely decorated stretchers, which were carried by a crowd to the chief's house. Dancers marched at the head of the parade, which was followed by four women wrapped in painted capes with feathered sticks in their hands. They danced to the rhythm of a pottery drum beaten by a woman. At the chief's house, each child was taken by his godparents to the chief, who ceremonially clipped the hair and placed it in a vessel. The godparents then cut the child's hair short and brought him back to the chief, who presented him to each person in the audience saying, "Aiquiana ne zana" (This is your chief).

Puberty and marriage.—At her first menses, a girl was hoisted in her hammock near the roof of the hut, where she remained motionless for 8 days and was given only a few yuca tubers and a little water every 24 hours. Her seclusion lasted a month, during which she spun cotton and might not be seen. At the end of her confinement, the girl was taken to the river, washed, and half of her body painted and decorated with feathers. Then she was ceremonially carried home on a stretcher and served chicha by all the women of the community until she vomited. An old man struck her on the shoulder with a stick and gave her a new permanent name. During the next month, she continued to observe several food taboos lest she become sick or be killed by some wild beast. From these rites she was supposed to emerge a strong and industrious woman (Maroni, 1889–92, 30:194–195).

Present-day *Omagua* still shut the girl in a special compartment of the hut, where she stays 3 weeks and eats only bananas and fish. No one, not even her mother, may see her. The confinement of the *Cocama* girls is less rigorous. At the end of the period, a feast is celebrated during which the girl drinks herself into a stupor. She is then taken to a compartment built above the ground, where an old woman cuts the extremity of her clitoris. Ashes are rubbed in the wound to stop the blood. This rite was obviously borrowed from the *Panoan* tribes of the Ucayali River.

After her puberty rites, an *Omagua* girl may freely indulge in sexual life until some young man marries her.

The preferred, aboriginal *Cocama* marriage was between a maternal uncle and his niece. The *Omagua* and *Cocama* bridegroom had to work for his father-in-law, after which he took his wife to his own home. The mission *Omagua,* consequently, sought sons-in-law among converts from other tribes, for, having no homes to which to return, these young men necessarily remained as servants in their wives' house after their period of bride service. Today men pay money for their wives.

It is stated that formerly a *Cocama* man would rear several small girls and later marry them (Rel. geogr. Indias, 1881–97, 4:145). Polygyny was most common among chiefs.

A wronged husband killed his wife's lover only if he surprised him in flagranti; otherwise he challenged him to a duel with a club. No punishment was inflicted on the guilty woman among the *Omagua,* but among the *Cocama* she was thrashed, and the husband engaged his rival in a boxing match.

Death and burial.—After the death of an *Omagua,* his whole family remained in seclusion for a month and was supplied with game by its neighbors (Martius, 1867, p. 441). Three months after the burial, the bones were disinterred, washed, painted, and set adrift in a vase (Maroni, 1881–92, 27:85). The *Cocama* combined primary and secondary urn burial. They first interred the corpse in a huge jar under the hut. When the flesh had rotted, the bones were cleaned and put in a decorated vase, which was kept in the house or was carried on their journeys. At the end of a year, they buried the bones permanently at a feast called "to dry the tears," after which the name of the deceased was never spoken (Figueroa, 1904, p. 250). In the 18th century, both the *Omagua* and the *Cocama* buried their dead in their canoes with all their personal effects (Veigl, 1785, p. 303). Today these Indians have church cemeteries.

Beliefs about the soul are described under Religion.

WARFARE

The *Omagua* continually harassed the *"Tapuya",* i.e., the non-*Tupi* tribes on both sides of the river, while the even more aggressive *Cocama* made annual forays in fleets of as many as 45 canoes to raid tribes of the Huallaga and Marañón Rivers. The attacks of the *Omagua* upon their neighbors were prompted by the desire of bringing back young captives (Fritz, 1922, p. 49). The Spaniards gave loot as the main goal of *Cocama* war parties, but head hunting seems to have been of greater importance than indicated by our sources. So warlike were the *Omagua* that they believed dead warriors continued to assail ghost villages and to behead their adversaries, thus causing thunder and lightning

Among the *Cocama,* the decision to wage war was made during a drinking bout, at which all the men took ayahuasca and went into a trance.   Afterward, their dreams were interpreted as premonitory visions.   Special importance was attached to the visions of shamans.   Before leaving for battle, the men rubbed cayenne pepper in their eyes to sharpen their sight and were whipped on the legs by the chief to become more agile.   After the warriors' departure, the shamans secluded themselves and fasted and were responsible for the outcome of the expedition.

The main strategy was to surprise the enemy at dawn.   The raiders generally killed the adult men but enslaved the women and children, who were later incorporated in the community.   Victorious *Cocama* warriors celebrated their success by drinking and dancing around the trophy heads (Chantre y Herrera, 1901, p. 230).   The Tepuitini River *Omagua* decorated trophy heads with paint and feathers.   The *Omagua,* like the *Tupinamba,* killed some captives of high rank or of outstanding courage (Acuña, 1891, p. 120) and kept their heads, but threw their bodies into the river.   In historical times, neither the *Omagua* nor *Cocama* practiced cannibalism.

ESTHETIC AND RECREATIONAL ACTIVITIES

Games.—Modern *Omagua* children amuse themselves with stilts, wrestling, and tug-of-war.   *Cocama* children play with rubber balls, which they strike with their knees, toy spear throwers, and dolls.   Both tribes have buzzing disks, humming tops, and maize-leaf shuttlecocks.

Musical instruments.—The most conspicuous *Omagua* and *Cocama* musical instrument was formerly the large slit drum.   Among the *Cocama,* four or five drums of different sizes up to 15 feet (4.5 m.) long were beaten simultaneously, producing "diverse and harmonious sounds which were heard far away" (Figueroa, 1904, p. 101).   The modern double-headed skin drum is obviously copied from the Spanish type.   A unique *Omagua* percussion instrument consisted of a paddle placed across the mouth of a pot and beaten with a rubber drum stick.[9]   Other *Omagua* and *Cocama* instruments were: End-flutes of reed or bone with six stops; panpipes, with 12 pipes among the *Omagua,* 10 among the *Cocama;* whistles; and musical bows.   Rattles and jingles attached to the knees are still used by the *Cocama.*

Dances.—There is no information about ancient *Omagua* and *Cocama* dances.   Modern *Omagua* wear gourd masks at carnivals.   The *Cocama* remember a dance performed by men covered with leaves.

Alcoholic beverages.—Masato, or chicha, a beverage of sweet manioc fermented with chewed paste, was a food as well as drink.   Diluted in

---

[9] Chantre y Herrera (1901, p. 84) . . . "Siguen en sus meneos el tono de otra mujer que va dando golpes con una maza de caucho sobre un remo que mantiene en la mano izquierda a la boca de una tinaja que lleva colgada como tambor."

water, it was drunk daily for nourishment; consumed in large quantities, it caused intoxication. Fermented maize, palm fruits (*Euterpe* sp., *Mauritia flexuosa*), sweet potatoes, sugarcane (*Omagua*), and bananas also produced mildly alcoholic drinks.

Narcotics.—Both the *Omagua* and *Cocama* inhaled powdered curupá leaves (*Mimosa acacioides*), to which they ascribed great therapeutic and magical powers. It was blown into the nose through Y-shaped tubes or, with the help of small rubber syringes, administered as a clyster which provoked agreeable visions. (See La Condamine, 1745, p. 72; Veigl, 1785, p. 37.)

In order to induce trances and visions, shamans drank ayahuasca or floripondia (*Datura arborea*).

They cultivated tobacco, and men formerly smoked it in huge cigarettes made of bark of a species of Bignonaceae. Today both sexes smoke pipes. The *Cocama* chewed tobacco powder, which they kept in small calabashes. Modern *Omagua* often chew tobacco while smoking.

RELIGION

Fritz (1922, p. 50) calls the main god of the *Omagua*, Zume Topana. The first name strongly suggests that of the *Tupinamba* culture hero Sumé. Topana is the name of the Thunder-god, and it has been adopted by missionaries for the Christian God. According to a fragmentary myth, "Our Lord" (Yara) created mankind between his big and second toes, and later made the earth before retiring to a heavenly city. The rainbow was conceived to be a huge water serpent dangerous to men.

The *Cocama* attribute natural phenomena to spirits called "mama" (mothers). They regard each river, forest, and even trees of unusual size or shape as the abode of a spirit. Nature is also full of spirits and ghosts that frighten and harm travelers and kidnap the wandering souls of sleeping people (Espinosa, 1935, p. 142). So convinced were the *Cocama* that dead people could be reincarnated in living ones, that the *Xibitaona* interpreter in whom they recognized one of their deceased chiefs, was immediately given authority over the village of the dead man and was visited by his supposed subjects (Figueroa, 1904, p. 102). Souls could also migrate into the bodies of animals; those of virtuous men became noble animals. Therefore, great respect was shown to an animal thought to contain the soul of a relative.

According to the *Omagua*, every man has two souls. One wanders at night and causes dreams, and the other, the "mai," resides in the shoulders and can be projected out of the body only by shamans. The *Cocama* also believe that a man has two souls; after death, one, identified with the shadow, goes to heaven, while the other becomes a wandering but harmless ghost.

SHAMANS

Early shamanistic practices are little known, though the *Omagua* were famous as the most powerful shamans and best druggists in the region. Information comes mainly from the accounts of Tessmann (1930) and Espinosa (1935, pp. 145–151) of the *Omagua* and *Cocama* of the present century.

An apprentice shaman was trained for 5 or 6 months under the guidance of an experienced practitioner. He fasted, smoked tobacco, and, among the *Omagua,* took curupá powder and a decoction of the bark of the virola tree. In both tribes, the instructor summoned the spirit or magic substance belonging to a deceased shaman, which was supposed to have gone into a virola tree (*Omagua*). This power, together with magic "thorns" which issued from the instructor's mouth, were implanted in the novice's body, where they remained for future use against his victims. Today during their apprenticeship, *Omagua* and *Cocama* novices drink ayahuasca (*Banisteriopsis caapi*).

Ancient *Omagua* shamans intoxicated themselves with floripondia (*Datura arborea*) and, like their modern *Cocama* colleagues, with ayahuasca as well, in order to consult spirits from whom they learned the causes of diseases, the whereabouts of stolen objects, and the nature of future events (Chantre y Herrera, 1901).

Diseases were often the result of witchcraft. A sorcerer might transform his magic substance into a bird which flew to the victim and projected the "thorns" into his body, or he might go personally to flip his small magic "arrows" into an enemy. If the victim died, the "thorns" returned to the body of the sorcerer.

Among the *Cocama,* some diseases were attributed to the loss of the soul, which either had gone astray or had been stolen by a demon.

To cure disease caused by "thorns," the shaman blew tobacco smoke on his patient and massaged his body to drive away the illness, then sucked out and destroyed the "thorns." Through dreams, he ascertained the identity of the sorcerers against whom, in the event of the patient's death, his family took revenge. In a case of illness caused by soul-loss, the sick man and his close relatives were put on a diet of thin manioc mush. The shaman and the patient then lay side by side in a small mat enclosure, and the shaman chanted in a high voice and pleaded with the soul, "Do not go away." The audience repeated the appeal. Then followed the customary sucking of the patient's body.

Shamans also administered drugs, mostly plant decoctions with real or fancied virtues. They required a patient to inhale tobacco juice, mixed with cayenne pepper, through his nose or gave an enema made of parica tc relieve general depression.

BIBLIOGRAPHY

For bibliographic references, see page 712.

TRIBES OF THE MIDDLE AMAZON

Yurimagua (*Zurimagua*).—According to Father Fritz (1922, p. 92), who converted the *Yurimagua* to Christianity, they spoke a language "quite different from that of the *Omagua*." Father Veigl (1785 a, p. 54) also states that their language was different from any other in the region. Whatever the affinity of the now vanished *Yurimagua* language, it was certainly not a *Tupí* dialect as has been often stated.

The *Yurimagua* lived on the islands of the Amazon from below the mouth of the Jutahy River to the vicinity of the junction of the Juruá and the Amazon Rivers (lat. 3° S., long. 64°–66° W.).

Father Samuel Fritz collected them in the Mission of Nuestra Señora de las Nieves, soon after starting the conversion of the *Omagua*. Later he established a few more settlements (for instance, San José de Yurimaguas) among these Indians and their neighbors.[10] In 1708, the *Yurimagua* who had escaped from the Portuguese slavers migrated upstream, and were settled by the Jesuits near the mouth of the Paranapura River, on the Huallaga River in a village which still bears their name. Others joined the *Omagua* at San Joaquín. A great many *Yurimagua* perished during the smallpox epidemics of 1760.

Both sexes went naked until they adopted cotton clothes under the pressure of the missionaries. Their staple food was manioc stored in pits covered by the annual floods. Their favorite weapon was the spear thrower. They captured jaguars in corrals where a dog protected by a smaller enclosure served as bait; a trigger touched by the jaguar caused a sliding door to fall (Izaguirre, 1922–29, 7:242).

The *Yurimagua* painted calabashes were famous and were an important trade article. The outer surface of the calabash was first scratched and stained black, and then red and yellow was applied, separated by floral motives. The vessel was varnished with parinari rosin (Veigl, 1785 a, p. 55). The *Yurimagua* women were also good potters. In Colonial times they decorated their vessels with floral motifs, a pattern which still can be seen on vessels from the upper Amazon.

The *Yurimagua* celebrated a cult reminiscent of the "Yurupary feasts" of the *Tucano* and *Arawakan* tribes of the Caiary-Uaupés region (pp. 793, 795; figs. 116–117). It centered around a spirit called Guaricana, whom they worshiped in a special hut barred to women and children. During the ceremony, they played a big "flute" (probably the Yurupary trumpet) and the spirit—actually an old man—whipped the youths with a lash of manatee hide, to make them strong (Fitz, 1922, p. 61).

---

[10] According to Chantre y Herrera (1901, p. 288), the missions founded by Father Fritz among the *Yurimagua* were Coary, Santa Ana, and Tracuatuva de Teffé. This is probably a mistake, because these villages would have been beyond the territory of the *Yurimagua*, further downstream. If the missions correspond to the modern towns by the same name, they were probably occupied by *Aisuare* and *Ybanoma*.

Aizuare (*Aysuare, Aissuari, Azuaro*).—On Father Fritz' map, the *Aizuare* appear on the left side of the Amazon. Their territory began somewhat below the mouth of the Juruá River and extended to the mouth of the Japurá River, lat. 3° S., long. 65° W. (Laureano de la Cruz, 1900, p. 107; Fritz, 1922, passim). Though culturally they resembled the *Yurimagua,* they spoke a different language. They were collected in the Mission of Teffé de Aisuaris in 1688. Harassed by the Portuguese slavers they placed themselves under Jesuit protection and migrated together with the *Yurimagua* to the Mission of Yurimaguas on the Huallaga River.

Among the *Aizuare* men and women were naked. They lived in thatched huts, tightly closed as a protection against mosquitoes. They were excellent potters, and their painted ware and gourds were in great demand among other tribes. They also made shell beads which were highly valued by their neighbors, who traded them for slaves. The *Aizuare* sold these slaves to the *Guaranacua* Indians of the upper Rio Negro for iron tools which the latter obtained from the British and the Dutch of the Guianas.

Ibanoma.—The *Ibanoma* (*Ybanoma*) were a little-known tribe of the right side of the Amazon from the Juruá to the Purús River (lat. 4° S., long. 73° W.). Like the *Aizuare,* they had trade relations with the Guiana Indians.

Curuzirari.—The *Curuzirari* (*Curucicuri*) are reported by Acuña (1891, p. 101) from a point 28 leagues below the Juruá River to another 22 leagues below the Araganatuva River, probably a branch of the Japurá. Ribeiro de Sampaio (1825, p. 56) located them on the southern bank of the Amazon from the Teffé to the Juruá River. Their settlements were so close to one another that they formed an almost uninterrupted line along both banks of the Amazon (Acuña, 1891, p. 101). They manufactured abundant pottery of various shapes (jars, pots, and pans), which they traded to other tribes. They wore in their ears and noses a great many gold ornaments which they obtained from the *Manao* of the Rio Negro (Acuña, 1891, p. 102–103).

Paguana (*Jaguana, Payana*).—A chief named Paguana is mentioned in Carvajal's account. Acuña places these Indians on the Teffé River, but Laureano de la Cruz (1900, p. 109) locates them near the mouth of the Araganatuva, a branch of the Japurá River. (Lat. 4° S., long. 65° W.) Ribeiro de Sampaio (1825, p. 57) listed their name among the Indians of Fonte Boa.

Soliman.—The *Soliman* (*Yoriman*) were once a powerful tribe on the southern bank of the Amazon from below the Japurá River to the vicinity of the Purús River, lat. 4° S., long. 72°–73° W. (Acuña, 1891, p. 103), but they disappeared at an early date. Their villages were of considerable size—one of them is said to have been one league and a half long (7 km.). They consisted of large communal houses accommodating at least four or five families.

Acuña (1891), Laureano de la Cruz (1900), and Fritz (1922) mention two tribes on both banks of the Amazon River from the mouth of the Napo to the Rio Negro. They were: *Guareicu* (*Guarayco, Guaraicu*), near the lower Jutahy; and the *Mayzuna*, south of the *Omagua*. The tribes of the Jutahy River enumerated by Acuña (1891, p. 99) were the *Tipuna* (*Ticuna?*), *Guanaru, Ozuana, Morua, Nauna, Conomoma, Mariana*. The *Juana* are located by Laureano de la Cruz (1900, p. 105) on the northern bank of the Amazon, near the Putumayo River.

On the Tocantins River lived in the 18th century the *Cayvicena* (*Cayuviuna*) and the *Pariana*, who were linguistically related (Ribeiro de Sampaio, 1825, p. 61).

ETHNOGRAPHIC DATA IN CARVAJAL'S ACCOUNT OF THE ORELLANA EXPEDITION (1542)

The account of the Orellana expedition by Carvajal (Medina, 1934) contains a few scattered data on the ethnography of the Indians with whom he came in contact. Unfortunately, it is often difficult to determine the tribe or even the region where his observations were made.

After he left the domain of Aparia, i.e., the land of the *Omagua*, Orellana sailed through the densely populated country of Cacique Machifaro (*Yurimagua?*). Villages here were never more than half a league apart, and some settlements stretched for 5 leagues without intervening space (Medina, 1934, p. 198). In each village there were large pens full of turtles.

In the land of Cacique Omagua, Carvajal (Medina, 1934, p. 201) came upon a house full of "jars and pitchers, very large, with a capacity of more than 25 arrobas, and other small pieces such as plates and bowls and candelabra of this porcelain of the best that has ever been seen in the world, for that of Malaga is not its equal." This pottery was glazed and decorated with all sorts of painted motifs. In the same village there were two idols "woven out of feathers of divers sorts . . . and on their arms, stuck into the fleshy part, they had a pair of disks resembling candlestick sockets, and they also had the same thing on their calves close to the knees; their ears were bored through and very large, like those of the Indians of Cuzco and larger." The conquistadors found there gold and silver.

Below the Rio Negro the Spaniards found a village fortified with a wall of heavy timber (Medina, 1934, p. 204). In the plaza of another village, Carvajal saw two strange wood carvings which he interpreted as the relief plan of a city. Nearby there was a hut containing feather dresses. On the lower Amazon the Spaniards thought that the Indians used poisoned arrows because two wounded soldiers died 24 hours after they had received some light wounds (Medina, 1934, pp. 224, 226).

The description of the Amazon kingdom given to Orellana by an Indian of the lower Amazon River is undoubtedly a mythical account of the *Inca* Empire.

BIBLIOGRAPHY

For bibliography, see page 712.

ARAWAKAN TRIBES OF THE LEFT, MIDDLE AMAZON

TRIBAL DIVISIONS AND HISTORY

Until the beginning of the 19th century, several *Arawakan* tribes, which today are almost entirely extinct, lived between the Rio Negro and lower Içá River. These were the *Manao, Pasé, Cauishana, Jurí,* and *Uainumá.*

Manao.—The most famous tribe was the *Manao* (*Manaus, Manavi, Managu, Manoa*), whose name first appears in Acuña's account (1891, p. 133), lat. 3° S., long. 63° W. The *Curuzirari* near the mouth of the Japurá River told Acuña that the gold objects which reached the Amazon had been traded by the *Manao* (*Managu*) from the Indians of the Yquiari River (Rio Negro). In 1686, Father Fritz met some *Manao* traders among the *Yurimagua* Indians. Their trade objects were "gold, vermillion [urucú], manioc graters, hammocks of cachibanco with various kinds of clubs and shields, that they worked very curiously." Fritz adds (1922, pp. 62–63), "they do not themselves extract the gold, but they go to the river Jurubetts navigating the Yquiari, where they obtain it by barter, and this is the river much famed for its gold amongst these tribes." Thus, these peddlers of the Amazon were intimately connected with the legend of El Dorado and the golden city of Manao on the shores of Lake Parima.

The Yurubeth or Yurubashi River, where the *Manao* lived near a great lake, is the Urubashi River, a left tributary of the Rio Negro, by which one may reach the lakes of the Japurá River. Actually, *Manao* territory was more extensive. Ribeiro de Sampaio (1825) mentions *Manao* in the towns of Lamalonga, Tomar (which he calls the "Court of the Manaos"), Moreira, Barcellos, Poyares (or Camaru), Carvoeiro (Aracary), and Moura. Martius (1867, p. 577) says that these Indians were concentrated between the Xiura and the Uarira Rivers, both southern tributaries of the Rio Negro (from Santa Isabel to Moreira) and on the left side of the Rio Negro along the Padauiry River. The *Manao* of the Padauiry River called themselves Ore or Ere-Manao. Several *Manao* families were settled in the city of Manaos, where, in Martius' time, they showed great receptiveness toward European civilization and were already strongly mixed with the Brazilian population.

In the 18th century, the *Manao* became slavers for both the Portuguese and the Dutch of the Guianas. One of their famous chiefs, Ajuricába, scoured the Rio Negro under the Dutch flag to capture Indians whom he traded for European goods (Ribeiro de Sampaio, 1825, p. 110). In 1757, a *Manao* Indian of Lamalonga rebelled against the Portuguese and destroyed Lamalonga and Moreira. Then he took possession of the island of Timoní and formed a confederacy with the neighboring wild Indians to attack Barcellos, but failed. The *Manao* were converted to Christianity by the Carmelites, who settled them in the aldeas enumerated above.

Pasé.—The *Pasé* (*Passé, Pacé*) were closely related to the *Manao*. They seem to have occupied a large territory from the lower Rio Negro to the Japurá or even the Içá Rivers (lat. 3° S., long. 68° W.). At the beginning of the 18th century, they were reported at Tomar, Santo Angelo de Cumaru, N.S. de Conceição de Mariua, Barcellos, and Manaos. They also formed part of the native population of Fonte Boa on the Solimões River. Ribeiro de Sampaio (1825, p. 35) mentions them on the Içá River in 1775, where Spix and Martius found them also in the beginning of the 19th century. In Bates' time (1864, p. 342), from 300 to 400 *Pasé* lived on the Japurá River 150 miles from Ega. About 1820, Martius (1867, p. 504) estimated their entire population at 1,500. At present, only a few *Pasé* may be found on the lower Içá River (Grubb, 1927, p. 94).

The *Pasé* were considered the most advanced Indians of the middle Amazon and were highly esteemed by the Portuguese for their fidelity, their mild disposition, and their handsomeness. Those who were not killed off by smallpox were rapidly absorbed by the Neo-Brazilian population of the Rio Negro.

Cayuishana.—The *Cayuishana* (*Cauixána, Caishana, Caujána, Cauxána, Caecena, Cujubicena, Cayubicena*) were closely related to the *Pasé*. In the first half of the last century, most of them lived west of Acunauy Lake, on the Mauapari River (Martius, 1867, p. 481). (Lat. 2°30' S., long. 66°–67° W.) Other groups had villages near the ancient *Pariana* (another *Arawakan* tribe), between the lower Japurá and Içá Rivers. Bates (1864, p. 431) gives the forests near Tunantins as their habitat. They numbered 600 in 1820 (Martius, 1867, p. 481), and about 400 forty years later (Bates 1864, p. 432). Around 1920 there were still 13 *Cayuishana* families on the Mapary River, an affluent of the Japurá River.

Jurí.—The *Jurí* (*Yuri, Juru-pixuna,* "Black Mouth") were closely allied to the *Cayuishana* and *Pasé.* They lived between the Ica and Japurà Rivers (lat. 2°–3° S., long. 68°–69° W.). During the first half of the 19th century, a great number migrated to the Rio Negro, where they became settled and partly civilized (Wallace, 1853, p. 510).

Uainumá.—The *Uainumá* (*Uaynumi, Uaypi, Uaima, Uaiuána, Ianuma, Ajuano*) called themselves *Inabishana.* Martius (1867, p. 501) locates them between the Upi River, a tributary of the Içá River, and the Cauinarí River, a tributary of the Japurá River (lat. 2° S., long. 69° W.). About 1820, 600 *Uainumá* still remained independent, the rest of the tribe having migrated to the towns of the Rio Negro and Solimões River where, like the *Jurí* and *Pasé,* they were rapidly absorbed by the local Mestizo population.

CULTURE

SUBSISTENCE ACTIVITIES

All these Indians were good farmers who raised manioc, cara (*Dioscorea*), maize, bananas, sugarcane, watermelons, pupunha palm (*Pasé, Jurí*), and other plants. They ate manioc in the form of wafers (beijú).

HOUSES

The native house of all these *Arawakan* tribes was circular with a conical roof,[11] but at an early date this type was replaced by the rectangular, wattle-and-daub hut adopted from the Neo-Brazilians. The *Jurí* took refuge from the mosquitoes in small ovenlike structures made of earth. They all slept in hammocks made of tucum fibers.

DRESS AND ORNAMENTS

Among the *Manao,* men wore a fringed skirt of mirití, and among the *Pasé,* a kind of apron made of the inner bark of the sapucaia tree. *Jurí* men tucked the penis under a belt. *Uainumá* women used a fringed bark apron, and wore earplugs, long reed or wood labrets, woven bands around the arms and under the knees (also *Cayuishana, Pasé, Jurí*), and feather ornaments. Among the *Uainumá,* both sexes had the sides of the nostrils incrusted with round shell disks.

The distinctive *Uainumá, Jurí,* and *Pasé* ornament was extensive facial tattooing in wide patches which covered the whole mouth region and often reached the eyes. This tattooing was begun in early childhood and increased during life, until in old age it finally reached its perfection. The *Jurí* owe their name, *Juru-pixuna,* "Black Mouth" (in Portuguese, Bocapreta) to their typical tattooing. Among the *Uainumá* and *Pasé,* tattooing varied according to the groups into which the tribe was subdivided.

MANUFACTURES

Canoes.—*Manao* craft were big dugouts made of the large tree trunks of the iacareva (*Calophyllum* sp.) or angelim (*Andira* sp.).

Weapons.—The bow and arrow was used by all these tribes. Poisoned javelins are specifically mentioned as a favorite weapon of the *Jurí, Pasé,* and *Cayuishana.* The blowgun, which the *Pasé* made of two half tubes carefully joined, was the main hunting weapon. The *Jurí* were expert at preparing the curare for blowgun darts. The *Jurí* and *Pasé* had large shields made of tapir and manatee hide.

SOCIAL ORGANIZATION

The *Manao* were divided into groups led by headmen, who were subordinate to a supreme chief, who exercised his authority through delegates.

---

[11] *Cauishana* huts were 4 fathoms high and 6 fathoms wide.

However, the hierarchical system described by Martius (1867, p. 580) seems to be somewhat idealized and, if it existed, it must have come into being only shortly before the downfall of the *Manao,* when chiefs like Ajuricaba mustered important contingents of allied troups against the Portuguese.

The *Uainumá, Juri,* and *Pasé* kept their war prisoners as slaves, who were harshly treated and were required to work hard (Martius, 1867, p. 73).

LIFE CYCLE

Childbirth.—After her delivery, a *Pasé* woman remained in the dark for a whole month on a diet of cassava and manioc mush. The husband, painted black, lay in his hammock and fasted until the baby's naval cord dropped off. The name of an infant was chosen by a shaman. Among the *Manao* and *Cayuishana,* the father remained in his hammock and fasted for a few days. Circumcision of babies is reported among the *Manao.* The *Manao* killed misshapen babies by putting them in a grave pit around which the family and the inhabitants of the maloca moved, knocking soil over the infant until it choked him.

Puberty.—When a *Manao* girl had her first menses, she fasted while wrapped up in her hammock. She was also painted and had her skin incised. *Pasé* girls were hoisted in their hammocks near the roof and fasted for a month.

As in many Guiana tribes, *Manao* and *Cayuishana* boys who had reached manhood were cruelly flogged.

Marriage.—Polygyny, practiced mainly by chiefs, was not common. Levirate is specifically reported only for the *Pasé.*

Death.—Among the *Manao,* the dead were wrapped in their hammocks or in strips of turiri bark and buried with their possessions in a grave dug in the communal hut. After the grave had been filled in, the mourners trampled down the soil amidst ritual laments. A fire was kept burning on the grave of a beloved child. Large funeral urns for direct burial have been unearthened near the city of Manaos (Keller-Leuzinger, 1874).

According to Ribeiro de Sampaio (1825, p. 79), the *Pasé* buried their dead in large urns, but later removed the bones to smaller vessels. The *Cayuishana* also buried their dead in large urns.

NARCOTICS

The *Pasé, Juri,* and *Uainumá* blew parica powder into their noses or took it in the form of an enema.

RELIGION

The *Manao* are credited with the belief in two gods, Mauari and Saraua, the first benevolent, the other evil. They feared several nature spirits, such as Gamainha, the water demon, and Camainha pichene, a forest demon.

The only information on *Pasé* religion comes from Ribeiro de Sampaio (1825, p. 79), who says that they believed in a Creator of all things and in a future state of rewards and punishments. The upper world was divided into several layers in the uppermost of which God resided. The stars were his beams.

CEREMONIES

The *Uainumá* celebrated great feasts when certain foods were abundant, e.g., at the season of the pupunha fruit and when a migrating water bird came to their lakes.

The principal *Manao* feast took place at the first full moon in March. Preparations for it began several months in advance under the supervision of the chiefs, who stored large amounts of crops and fish. At this feast, men and women underwent cruel flogging, a magico-religious rite performed by most Guiana tribes. Men with uplifted arms bore without a sign of pain the blows which their partners inflicted on them. Women with their arms crossed over their breasts, competed with men in stoical endurance. The *Jurí* and *Pasé* had masked dances.

SHAMANISM

Manao shamans enjoyed great prestige. They were trained from an early age by long fasts, by strict continence, by periods of silence, and by frequenting isolated and gloomy places. When, after a year of seclusion, a novice appeared in public, he was painted black and wore scars which a jaguar had supposedly inflicted on him. He then danced until completely exhausted. Afterward, he had to endure the bites of ants without flinching. Tobacco juice was poured in his eyes as a final test. Only then was the novice regarded as a full-fledged shaman capable of coping with snakes and other poisonous animals and of curing diseases.

To cure, the shaman, shaking his rattle and muttering incantations, blew tobacco smoke on the patient's body and, after massaging and kneading it, sucked out the pathogenic objects, such as red mushrooms (*Boletus sanguineus*), bugs, grubs, centipedes, etc. Shamans had some knowledge of herbs, about which they were very secretive. Their medical power, however, was regarded as seriously impaired if they married.

Shamans were also diviners and prophets, who learned about the future through the assistance of spirits who visited them in the guise of frogs, mosquitoes, snakes, and other animals. Mothers bought amulets from them for their children. These consisted of pieces of wood or of claws of several birds, for example, *Polyborys vulgaris,* curajeu (*Caprimulgus* sp.), and cacy (*Coracina ornata*).

Mythology.—The *Manao* had a tradition of the destruction of the world by a big fire which originated in a mountain and spread through the forest. They attributed eclipses to the attempts of a celestial jaguar to devour the sun or the moon. Whenever eclipses occurred, they danced and wailed to put the monster to flight. The *Manao* also believed in the existence of small people with upturned feet (motacu).

BIBLIOGRAPHY

Acuña, 1891; Bates, 1863, 1864; Brinton, 1892 b; Caravajal (see Medina, 1934); Chantre y Herrera, 1901; Espinosa, 1935; Figueroa, 1904; Fritz, 1922; Grubb, 1927; Hervás, 1800–05, vol. 1; Izaguirre, 1922–29; Jornada de Omagua y Dorado, 1909; Keller-Leuzinger, 1874; La Condamine, 1745; Cruz, 1900; Marcoy, 1875; Maroni, 1889–92; Martius, 1867; Medina, 1934; Métraux, 1928 a and b, 1940; Ortiguera, 1909; Peruvian Census, 1940; Relaciones geográficas de Indias, 1881–97; Ribeiro de Sampaio, 1825; Rivet, 1910 b; Spix and Martius, 1823–31; Tessmann, 1930; Veigl, 1785 a; Velasco, 1841–44; Wallace, 1853.

THE TUCUNA

By Curt Nimuendaju

HABITAT, HISTORY, AND LANGUAGE

The *Tucuna* (*Tukuna, Ticuna*), not to be confused with the *Tucano*, occupied the jungle tracts of the tributaries of the northern side of the Amazon-Solimões River from long. 71°15′ (Peruaté Island) to 68° 40′ W., and the upper course of the streams on the opposite side of the watershed of the Putumayo-Içá River (map 1, *No. 4;* map 5). They avoided the banks of the Amazon-Solimões, fearing the *Omagua,* their traditional enemies of the islands. When the latter disappeared, the *Tucuna* spread out over the islands and shores of the Solimões as far as the Auatí-Paraná River (long. 66°30′ W.).

The country is flat, covered by Amazonian jungle. A wide strip bordering on the Solimões River is subject to great periodical floods.

The *Tucuna,* inconspicuous in the history of the Amazon, were first mentioned in 1641 by Cristobal d'Acuña.

Rivet (1912 b) designated the *Tucuna* language as "un dialecte arawak très corropu." Only a part of his list of lexicological similarities appears to be valid, especially as he lacked sufficient reference material on the *Tucuna* language. There is, however, no doubt that the *Tucunan* vocabulary has a number of elements which were borrowed from the *Arawakan* languages, as noted also by Brinton (1901) and Tessmann (1930). *Tupi* influence is greater than Rivet supposed, being revealed in the pronouns, which he noted but did not evaluate. Correspondences with *Yuri* are fewer, but not unimportant. It is regrettable that there is not more phonetic material on this language. The *Tucanan* element, which Tessmann states is second in importance, is, as Rivet also noted, very weak. The *Mura* element postulated by Loukotka lacks absolute proof.

Martius called attention to 11 *Ge* elements in *Tucunan;* Rivet added five more examples. (Both Martius and Rivet include *Camacán* and *Masacarian* in the *Ge* family.) But, of Rivet's 16 *Ge* elements, only 4 are valid, 3 being formed of *Camacán* elements and only one of *Ge* elements.

There is, therefore, insufficient evidence for Brinton's, Rivet's, and Loukotka's inclusion of *Tucunan* in the *Arawakan* family. For the present, it is advisable to follow Chamberlain and Tessmann in consider-ing it a separate language.

CULTURE

SUBSISTENCE ACTIVITIES

Farming.—The main *Tucuna* crops are bitter manioc, sweet manioc (macaxera), cara (*Dioscorea*), and maize. The last is planted with some ceremony. There are also at least three species of edible tubers which are not used by civilized people.

Fishing and hunting.—Fish, of great importance to the *Tucuna*, are taken with four- to nine-pronged javelins, arrows, harpoon arrows, baskets, weirs, traps, and a drug made of timbó. The Indians fish almost daily from childhood. On the Solimões, they are expert fishers of pirarucú, an important article of commerce.

Hunting today is unimportant, since game has been depleted to fill the demand for hides. The *Tucuna* now use firearms, but formerly employed the bow and arrow, spear, and blowgun. They also use pitfalls and several types of snares and traps. The blowgun, once the principal weapon, is disappearing.

Gathering.—The wild burity, bacaba, patauá, and açahy palms are of great economic value. Some *Tucuna* plant Brazil nut trees near their houses. They eat certain frogs, Coleoptera larvae, and female red ants at hiving time. They like wild honey but keep no bees.

Domesticated animals.—The *Tucuna* raise a few chickens, but do not want hogs or other domestic animals because they dirty the premises. They keep young wild mammals and birds uncaged.

Food preparation.—Instead of a mortar, the *Tucuna* use a trough with a half-moon-shaped rocker of thick and heavy wood.

The making of manioc flour, introduced by the Neo-Brazilians, became one of the principal sources of income among the *Tucuna*.

HOUSES

The old houses had a small rectangular central portion with a short ridge pole mounted on props. Each end was semicircular, so that the ground plan was oval or nearly round. The walls were of a man's height, and were made of boards of paxiuba or of straw. The house could be sealed tight against mosquitoes. Families occupied the lateral corridors, the central space being reserved for ceremonies. All houses were spacious and well built.

The introduction of mosquito nets made house walls unnecessary. People slept on bunks along the walls, covered with mosquito nets, instead of in hammocks. Many houses were built without the semicircular extremities but with a longer central part, being like an open rectangular ranch house with a ridge pole. When the tribe occupied the flood plains of the shores and islands, they built houses on piles.

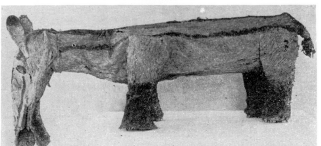

PLATE 64.—**Tucuna objects of bark cloth.** *Top, left:* Jaburú. *Top, right:* Garment with mask. *Center:* Mythological animal. *Bottom:* Jaguar. (Animals are about 4 ft. long; other objects to same scale.) (Courtesy Curt Nimuendajú and Museu Paraense Emilio Goeldi, Belém.)

PLATE 65.—**Tucuna Indians of the 19th century.** *Top:* Part of girl's puberty ceremony. (After Marcoy, 1869.) *Bottom: Tucuna* of the upper Amazon; a *Mundurucú* woman in center. (After Osculati, 1854.)

Each residence has a proper name, given by the owner at a special feast. Houses are usually clean.

Household furniture.—Hammocks are made by a netlike technique of tucum thread of different colors; they are now used only for daytime resting. Clothes are kept in large baskets.

On the struts and rafters of the house one can often see remnants of the paraphernalia of feasts: masks, turury fringes, drums, and dance sticks. Ears of maize hang from the frame of the house or are piled in the loft.

The *Tucuna* never build a fire or eat in the dwelling. The kitchen is always a small separate house. Fire was formerly produced by drilling a horizontal piece of wood, which was placed over two cross pieces. There is, however, a tradition that even in old times they made fire by striking two stones.

Fire fans are made exclusively of large bird wings.

The *Tucuna* have plenty of small four-legged stools, either rectangular or oval, made from a single piece of wood, sometimes elaborately carved in the shape of a chelonian or batrachian.

TRANSPORTATION

Formerly, the *Tucuna* traveled largely on land, although on the small streams they used small primitive canoes made of paxiuba palm. From the *Omagua* they learned to make "ubá" type dugout canoes, and from the Neo-Brazilians to make "casco" type dugouts which were widened by heating them over a fire. These are sometimes provided with round shields (rodellas) and gunwales. *Tucuna* canoes are so well made that civilized people seek them. Paddles have crutch handles and a round blade with a large point. The blade and the crosspiece on the end of the handle, but not the handle, are invariably painted black.

DRESS AND ORNAMENTATION

Formerly, both sexes trimmed their hair slightly over the brows, and used a comb made of twigs held between two parallel sticks.

Both sexes used to pierce their ear lobes; only women do so now. Through the hole they usually wore little plates of white wood; on feast days they inserted small rods with feathers on the front end, from which a small metal plate hung. Women's plates were triangular, men's moon-shaped. Long ago they pierced the nasal septum, through which they had put a little rod of *Gynerium*. They also used to tattoo the face, which at one time may have indicated clans. There are still recollections of circumcision of girls, but not of men, as described by Father Noronha in 1768.

Men formerly wore a belt with one apron of turury inner bark in front and another behind. The penis was stuck under the belt. Women perhaps at first went about entirely nude, but later adopted a short cloth of turury or of woven cotton, wrapped around the hips. Men wore bracelets with long feathers and necklaces of teeth (pl. 65, *bottom*). At feasts chiefs wore a cap of feathers mounted on a cotton or *Bromelia* net, or large diadems.

MANUFACTURES

Bark cloth.—Various masks and zoomorphic figures are made of bark cloth (pl. 64).

Basketry.—Clothes baskets are made of uarumã stalks with a round opening closed with a lid. Four points are drawn up and down over the lid and the bottom, the latter serving as legs. Other baskets have a flat square lid and bottom. Both types of baskets are made in all sizes, from 2 to 16 inches (4 to 40 cm.) in diameter. Burdens are carried in large conical baskets hexagonally woven of liana, or in cylindrical baskets of uarumã stalks. These are supported by an embira-fiber tumpline. The *Tucuna* also use pouches of looped tucum threads.

Pottery.—Women and sometimes men still make bowls, dishes, pans, and pots of clay, which are decorated with painted or modeled ornaments. Potter's clay is gathered according to certain rules so as not to anger its owner, a water demon who appears in the shape of the western rainbow.

Gourds.—Gourds are covered with a black lacquer, and may bear designs in indelible red pigment. Wooden spoons are carved, sometimes in fantastic shapes.

Weapons.—The bow is 6½ feet (2 m.) long with the ends notched to hold the string. It is now rare, even as a fishing weapon. The hunting arrow has a poisoned wooden head and feathering of the arched type. Arrows are 5 feet 4 inches (1⅔ m.) long. Spears have three types of points: (1) a poisoned, wooden point with four corners; (2) an iron point; and (3) a plain pointed stick. The last two are still used to hunt jaguars and peccaries. The *Tucuna* blowgun is over 10 feet (3 m.) long, and the darts 1 foot (30 cm.) long. The poison is the most effective of any made in the Amazon Basin, but its manufacture, which requires much time and care, is now being forgotten. Hunting dogs, which are of little use, are, according to tradition, preColumbian.

SOCIAL AND POLITICAL ORGANIZATION

The *Tucuna* are industrious and hard working, kind to their friends, honest, patient, and hospitable. But they are more liable than other Indians to great outbursts of sudden anger, a trait which sometimes leads them to suicide. This is a manifestation of their individualism and desire to live apart, which is correlated with their lack of social organization other than blood ties. When drunk they quarrel and often cause injuries and death. In their dealings with the Neo-Brazilians, both parties exhibit their worst qualities. Nevertheless, the *Tucuna* are not unsociable and frequently visit one another and hold festive meetings, when they work collectively for their host. They retain tenaciously their original spiritual culture, although hard work has brought important material improvements. They now have good firearms, tools, clothes, and sewing machines, and they live in financial independence. Some, however, enticed to industrial establishments (rum factories) of the civilized people, become proletarian and then degenerate.

Moieties and clans.—The *Tucuna* are divided into two exogamous, unnamed patrilineal moieties, associated respectively with the east and west. One has 15 unlocalized, patrilineal sibs with tree names; the other has 21 sibs with bird names. Neither the clans nor moieties have outward distinguishing features, except for the private use of certain musical instruments on ceremonial occasions. There is no clear relationship between clan members and their eponym, except that a person's name refers obscurely to certain qualities of the animal or plant, thus revealing his clan. A person is named by his maternal relatives the day after his birth.

The *Tucuna* maintain moiety exogamy with strict inflexibility, and in 1941 still punished violations with death. They regard incest as a sin against the goddess Taé, who punishes it by making one insane during his life and by annihilating his soul after his death.

LIFE CYCLE

Birth and childhood.—After coitus, conception depends on Taé, who gives a soul to children. Abortion and infanticide are practiced, especially when the father is a Neo-Brazilian, as the child would be disqualified for sib and moiety membership. Otherwise, it is believed that infanticide is a sin and that Taé punishes the soul of the perpetrator after death.

Childbirth takes place in a temporary shelter prepared in the bush near the house. The newborn child is immediately painted with genipa. Both parents are confined and diet until the umbilical cord drops off. Children are carried in a woven cotton sling passing over a shoulder. Slings are double in part, so that a child sits in one portion while the other supports its back.

When a child begins to crawl, there is a feast in which it is painted with urucú and covered with bits of parrot feathers while the paint is still sticky. At another feast, formerly celebrated when the child was 2 but now when it is 4, its hair is pulled out and its ears pierced. Contrary to certain authors, this operation does not endanger a child's life. About 8 months later there is a supplementary feast when the hair, having grown again, is trimmed, and the relics of the previous feast are burned.

More than among other tribes, *Tucuna* children receive corporal punishment, especially with the external application of nettle flowers that are grown for this purpose at the edge of the yard. They play with dolls carved of muirapiranga, figures of animals, little canoes, small bows and arrows, and buzz-disks of gourd shells.

Boys' puberty observances.—There is a tradition that in former times, young men were initiated when their voices changed, being secluded and then perhaps formally admitted to the secrets of the megaphone (tá/ki) through an application of snuff called ká/vi, which is still used occasionally.

There are no vestiges of homosexuality, as claimed by Tessmann (1930, p. 563).

Girls' puberty rites.—At her first menstruation, a girl is secluded in the house loft. This is not so cruel as certain travelers (Bates, 1863, 2 :406) proclaim. Every girl submits willingly, convinced that her peculiar condition requires it and that its omission would be dangerous, as she is surrounded by invisible "immortals" and demons, who seek contact with her and at times cause extraordinary supernatural experiences. Many stories told to a. girl in seclusion illustrate this dangerous state.

The people hasten to prepare for the girl a circular seclusion room adjacent to the east or west wall of the house, according to her moiety. They decorate the walls with painted bands and lines, and figures of the sun, moon, morning star, and deer, the last a symbol of vigilance and not a "totem."

Preparations for the feast sometimes require months. They prepare roast meat and beverages and make the house ready. The girl's father is host, but her paternal uncle and his wife direct all ceremonies concerning her person, being wholly responsible for her. Friends and acquaintances receive two invitations to the feast; the second, which specifies the date, is issued to the sound of the bark trumpet, which is carried hidden in the canoe.

In the exterior portion of the house, corresponding to the girl's seclusion room, a long fence is made with straw walls to conceal the megaphone (tá/ki), its statues, and the bark trumpet which operate behind it each night of the feast and are removed before daybreak and hidden underwater in the creek. People are chosen and invited to operate these instruments by the head of the house when the time comes; there is no permanent assignment. Inside the fence of the megaphone, snuff (ká/vi) or tobacco powder is taken with several ingredients (but not parica). The snuff is kept in a snail shell and blown into the nose by means of an apparatus made of a tubular bone and two quills of royal sparrow hawk feathers, or by means of a simple taboca (bamboo) tube. Boys of 7 or older customarily are given snuff, after which they may see and touch the instruments within the fence, which are taboo to women and to boys who have not yet had it.

At this feast, as at the feast of children's depilation and ear piercing, masks are used (pl. 65, *top*). These are made, used, and cared for by the guests, who portray anything they wish, such as imaginary demons and fantastic animals. They are in no way associated with individual persons, societies, or other groups. The masked persons customarily remain unidentified until they deliver their masks to the host. About 90 percent of those wearing masks are men, 7 percent boys, and the remainder girls and young women. For costume, clothing is cut and sewn from the bast fiber of certain trees (*Ficus* sp.), sometimes in the shape of pants, sleeves, and fringes, and at other times in the form of a tight gown without sleeves, extending half way down the leg. The face, generally a horrendous caricature of a demon (pl. 64, *top, right*), may be attached to or separate from the costume. The mask representing the storm demon is distinguished by an enormous face and a phallus nearly 18 inches ($\frac{1}{2}$ m.) long. Nearly all clothes are painted with vegetable dyes. Sometimes the motif of the mask is identified by the song rather than by the appearance of the mask, which is entirely a product of the individual's imagination. The masked people, sometimes numbering 40 to 50, gather in a special place in the woods, and go to the house in groups up to 10, some of them running up and down at a furious pace, and others approaching slowly. They come for a drink, then disappear to make way for another group.

At the appointed time the guests arrive at the house with their families, sometimes numbering more than 300 persons. They are received inside along the walls, the center being left open for the ceremonies. When all have assembled, they go to the kitchen to be painted with urucú and to have their faces decorated with royal sparrow hawk down. After everyone receives a piece of roast meat, all return in a solemn procession to the house and put their meat on a stand on the side of the seclusion room. On the other side are the vessels of beverages. The feast now begins. Henceforth, everyone goes around the central space in the house singing to the accompaniment of small drums and carrying his dancing stick on his shoulder.

Early in the morning, the girl is brought through a door from the seclusion room to the fenced place around the megaphone where, with her face turned to the proper cardinal point, she is adorned with genipa and white turury that have been ceremonially prepared. Before sunset, she is decorated in the seclusion room with streamers of royal sparrow hawk plumage, a long macaw feather diadem, feather bracelets with white turury fringes, strings of feathers made of toucan abdomens and tails, shell bells with bone clappers, and ear pegs, which are prepared by skilled persons and tried out by her relatives. The women fan her with broad leaves. She then stands in her room facing the place where the megaphone and trumpet are sounded and scratching herself with a little stick. The guests in the main room are given meat and fish stew and cooked bananas.

Several hours after midnight, half a dozen of the girl's relatives, holding her around the waist while her eyes are covered by the feather diadem, dance back and forth toward the wall, which is cut open with a knife so that they finally pass through into the main room. As she is now more exposed to invisible forces, the relatives dance with her until near dawn, then slowly go outside and circle the house. At sunrise they uncover her eyes and have her throw a burning stick against a pole marked to represent the "enemy." She now walks without assistance and dances freely with the others in the house.

Depilation follows. The girl sits on the tapir hide in the middle of the room while three to six women pull out her head hair in little bunches, accompanied by a small drum (tambor) and rattle. She endures the operation calmly, not even drink being given to alleviate the pain. Her paternal uncle in a vigorous speech then instructs her about her future duties as a marriageable girl.

The masks are now surrendered, each owner receiving a piece of roast meat. The disguises are piled around the girl, until only her head protrudes. The cloth is then ripped and the shreds thrown over the house beams. The turury cloths, which now belong to the host, are wound up and put away.

The seclusion room and roast-meat stand are dismantled. The participants divide the pieces, going in a solemn procession to toss them into the river. The girl is carried on the tapir hide held by five or six men over their heads in the procession. She undresses, and, kneeling in shallow water where a magic arrow protects her against water demons, she is washed by all the men who have magical powers. She then redecorates herself and joins the dancers, who perform in the house until the last drop of beverage is drunk. At the end of the feast, everyone bathes hilariously together, tossing each other into the water.

Formerly, in order to bring a large haul of fish, the girl was washed again after the feast with a solution of timbó at an appropriate spot on the creek.

Six to eight months later there is a supplementary but less ceremonial feast to trim the girl's regrown hair.

Subsequent menstruations entail few restrictions: a woman stays in her yard because the spirits of certain trees may injure her with an arrow and because contact with her would make a man inefficient in any undertaking.

Marriage and adulthood.—Sexual intercourse with prepubescent girls is unthinkable; with young women it brings shame on the whole family. There is no instance of ravishment. Rape is a grave offense to the parents.

A request for marriage is made to the girl's paternal uncle, but if the girl refuses peremptorily, she cannot be forced to marry. Public notice is unnecessary; a boy and girl may meet at a feast and leave married at the end. The wife's parents never renounce their authority over her and do not permit the husband to take her far away, which results in a certain matrilocal tendency.

Polygyny even today is considered licit, but cases of bigamy are rare. In the only case known, a famous man who was both priest and chief had three sisters as wives simultaneously. Other cases of sororate have occurred. The levirate, also formerly frequent, was considered desirable.

Jealousy may cause violent quarrels between husband and wife, but never murder and rarely divorce. Adultery, though causing scenes, is insufficient reason for divorce. Guilt is always placed on the woman. The father's authority in the family is great.

In case of robbery, the offended party requires restitution and sometimes is extremely severe with the thief.

Injuries and death occur almost exclusively when people are drunk during a feast, for alcohol stimulates certain *Tucuna* to fight. Drunkenness absolves the murderer from responsibility, but the victim's relatives always feel resentful and hostile toward him.

A house is the property of its builder, i.e., the head of the family. The clearing belongs to the woman by whom it was made.

The *Tucuna* no longer have chiefs as they are too individualistic to accept authority and as the civilized people have discredited the office by designating chiefs through whom they could exploit and oppress the Indians. Formerly, chiefs of local groups were heads of large families whose magic powers, intelligence, and ability in dealing with foreigners gave them prestige. There was never, however, a chief for the entire nation.

Death.—Until the end of the past century, the deceased and all his ornaments were placed in a large chicha jar which was covered with a vessel, buried in a cemetery, and the site sometimes marked with a rod of muirapiranga. Well-liked people sometimes were buried in the house. They put a little food, beverage, and a fire on the grave, periodically renewing it. Tessmann (1930, p. 564) incorrectly attributed secondary burial to the *Tucuna*.

WARFARE

The *Tucuna* are not warlike. They defended themselves against the *Omagua,* their principal enemies, and drove them to the banks of the Solimões River only when the latter had invaded their lands. They fought with arrows, poisoned spears, and round tapir-hide shields, and protected their paths with poisoned caltrops. They did not take prisoners or keep trophies from slain enemy. They never fought civilized people, except to avenge personal insults.

ESTHETIC AND RECREATIONAL ACTIVITIES

Art.—The *Tucuna* were fine sculptors. Their carved figures on the dancing sticks, stools, and tucumã nut figures in their necklaces are at times very artistic. Painting is restricted mainly to masks and pottery ornamentation.

Music.—During feasts, the *Tucuna* sing in a falsetto voice so low that it can hardly be heard. Three important instruments are: (1) a wooden, tubular megaphone into which they speak and sing and which is 22 feet (6¼ m.) long with an opening 5 inches (12 cm.) wide and a mouthpiece 2 inches (5 cm.) long; (2) a conical trumpet 13 feet to 19½ feet (4 to 6 m.) long made of a strip of bark wound spirally; and (3) a piston whistle made of liana bark. The last is always sounded before the other two. In any ceremony there is always a faithful imitation of the European drum and a *Thevetia*-shell rattle, the latter taking the place of the conventional maracá, which is unknown. The old form of drum was possibly the shell of a chelonium, which now is used only in one ceremonial. There are also panpipes, bone flutes, and bamboo horns.

Adult games.—In shuttlecock, a maize-husk ball is batted into the air with the palm of the hand by men standing in a ring. In a tug-of-war in which a thick liana is used, one team of men competes against another. A ring-and-pin game is played by two men facing each other. Grown girls make cats cradles with threads wrapped around the fingers, toes, and head.

Beverages.—Women make alcoholic beverages from maize, cooked bitter manioc, and half-burned cakes (beijú) of manioc; the last was adopted from the Neo-Brazilians. Today many men are addicted to rum.

SHAMANISM

Even today many Indians possess magic powers to help or harm others. These powers come from intercourse with the spirits of certain trees with which an old shaman puts his disciple in contact. The neophyte shaman receives a magic substance which contains invisible thorns. He throws these into his victim's body, where they reproduce and cause his death unless another shaman sucks them out and completes the cure by applying herbs. The shaman chews tobacco (formerly, he used a tubular wooden pipe with an opening on the side for the mouth) to become possessed of the spirit which supplied the magic pathogenic substance to the witch doctor. Chewing tobacco identifies the evil shaman.

Children fall ill when the spirits of the trees kidnap their souls. Epidemics come from the sun and are spread by the wind.

When the *Tucuna* are convinced that a shaman is responsible for one or more deaths, their revenge even reaches his relatives. In 1942, three *Tucuna* killed a much-feared shaman and his two sons. The avengers undergo a ceremony performed by some competent shaman, who seeks mainly to protect them from the soul of the murdered witch.

RELIGION AND MYTHOLOGY

The upper world.—The upper world, which is much lower than the stars, is divided into two parts. One is inhabited by men, who are like Indians, but live under very different conditions. The other is the residence of the goddess Taé (Our Mother) and of the souls of the deceased (naáe) who have been righteous. On their way to the upper world, souls must pass through a sort of gate made of two wooden posts which move back and forth in opposite directions and exclude the souls of incestuous persons, infanticides, murderers, and evil sorcerers. If, however, an evil soul reaches the residence of Taé, she releases two fantastically shaped monsters which demolish it, or else she throws it back to earth, where it becomes a small frog and eventually dies. Taé orders her monsters to purify the souls of occasional sinners by licking them from head to feet. An infanticide's soul has to appear before Taé with the body of the child across his mouth and eat it as a pap.

Taé is not all-powerful, and makes some careless mistakes. She is not the creator and has no connection with the two culture heroes, who equal her in importance, nor with demons, tree spirits, priests, or shamans. But the *Tucuna* greatly respect her because of her close connection with the punishment of sin, both during and after life, and her role as mistress of that part of the soul called naáë (thought, sense).

The other part of the human soul (natcií) is manifest after death as the "shadow of the deceased." It haunts old house sites and takes a human shape at night but at dawn is transformed into some small animal. It is somewhat feared because of its desire to suck one's blood and eat one's flesh and bones, leaving only the empty skin. Brave and smart people, however, easily fool it.

The lower world.—The oldest beings in the world are the demons of the underworlds (naáe); some are grouped in many clans, and others are unaffiliated. Though mortal, many are superior to or are very dangerous to men. Their appearance, represented in certain masks, is usually strange and horrible, though they sometimes assume human shape. Most of them live in different kinds of underground and subaquatic regions (nápi), which are entered through caves. Certain nápi are inhabited by anthropomorphic beings with strange defects, such as blind men, dwarfs, and men without anuses.

The most important subaquatic demons are the dyévae, who have the shape of gigantic silurides or ophidians. One, the master of fishes, shows itself in the eastern rainbow. Another, the master of potter's clay, appears as the western rainbow. Some cause the dangerous whirlpools of the Solimões River, but can be calmed by the priests.

The culture heroes.—The most outstanding character in *Tucuna* religion is Dyaí, the culture hero, who made people, established all tribal laws and customs, and gave mankind the most important elements of material culture. He was the demons' most feared enemy. At times harsh and cruel, he is never deceitful. Even toward his brother, Epi, an intruder and shameless liar, he is indulgent and kindly, mocking him and punishing him only occasionally. The *Tucuna* avoid using the name Dyaí and call him Tànáti (Our Father), Baiá, or Búi. Sometimes Dyaí is called Téginènapií-va-ya (the one of the right knee), and Epi is called, Tave-napii-va-ya (the one of the left knee).

A long myth cycle recounts the origin of Dyaí and Epi and their deeds. Dyaí, with a blowgun in his hand, and his sister Maváca, with a net pouch, were born from the right knee of Nutapa; Epi, with a spear, and his sister Aikine, with a carrying basket, were born from the left knee of Nutapa, who was later killed by a jaguar. The brothers avenged his death and resurrected him. Afterward, Dyaí acquired daylight, sleep, fire, and cultivated plants, and saved Epi from a series of difficulties into which he had thrown himself. The brothers were joined by Teci-ari-nuí, daughter of Aikine, whom Epi had seduced. Dyaí punished the seducer by compelling him to grate himself when he grated the genipa for painting the son of Teci-ari-nuí. After he again took a human shape, the two companions created men from fish caught with a hook. Finally, they separated, Dyaí going east and Epi west.

On the bank of the upper Igarapé Preto de São Geronymo the *Tucuna* showed the former site of Taivegíne, Dyaí's house; Epi's house, called Déi, is somewhat downstream. There Epi's son, Teku-kirá, lives today with many other immortals (iíne, or má/gita), the men whom Dyaí and Epi fished out of the water. At night during the full moon one can hear them feasting but no one dares approach for fear of becoming insane. Some mortals (dyunati) have become immortal by taking a drink offered by the iíne, whereupon they accompany the immortals to their residence.

The *Tucuna* have a legend of a world conflagration and a subsequent deluge.

The eclipses of the moon are caused by the struggle of a star with a heavenly demon of the Jaguar clan.

Messianism.—The *Tucuna* messianic movement springs from a consciousness of having offended Dyaí, the culture hero, by corrupting their ancient spiritual (not material) culture under the influence of the civilized people, and from a fear that the cataclysms of former times will be repeated. It also involves the tendency of immortals to appear during a person's puberty. In repeated visions, a pubescent man or woman in seclusion sees and talks with the immortals (má/gita), who sometimes may carry his soul (naáe) to their abode and keep it there for a time. The immortals foretell an imminent cataclysm, which threatens to destroy civilized people, and instruct the Indians to save themselves by gathering at a sheltered place and performing certain ceremonies. As soon as the Indians assemble, the civilized people quash the movement, fearing a threat to their interests. This happened in 1941, when the *Tucuna* met in Taivegíne, following the visionary instruction of a 13-year old boy named Naráne.

BIBLIOGRAPHY

Acuña, 1891; Bates, 1863; Barbosa Rodrigues, 1882 c; Berredo, 1905; Brinton, 1901 (1891); Castelnau, 1850–59; Chamberlain, 1910; Cruz, 1879 (1900); Fritz, 1691; Herndon and Gibbon, 1853–54; Loukotka, 1939; Marcoy, 1866; Maw, 1829; Monteiro Noronha, 1862; Nimuendajú, 1930 b, 1932 a, ms.; Orton, 1875 (1870); Ribeiro de Sampaio, 1825; Rivet, 1912 b; Spix and Martius, 1823–31, vol. 3, Atlas; Tessmann, 1930.

THE PEBAN TRIBES

By Julian H. Steward and Alfred Métraux

INTRODUCTION

The *Peba, Yagua,* and *Yameo,* which are the main *Peban* tribes, occupy the region of the lower Putumayo and Napo Rivers, north of the Amazon (map 1, *No. 4;* map 5). They are technologically and socially simpler than their neighbors and seem more affiliated with the *Záparoans* to the west than with the *Witotoans* to the north or with the tribes to the east and south.

The structure and function of *Peban* culture is probably exemplified by the *Yagua* (Fejos, 1943). The *Yagua* practice slash-and-burn farming with sweet manioc the staple, fish only with barbasco poison, hunt only with blowguns and poisoned spears, make rafts but no canoes, dress in simple clothes of fiber, and manufacture unelaborated pots, chambira-fiber bags and hammocks, simple baskets, and mats. The sociopolitical unit is the exogamous, patrilocal, patrilineal, extended family occupying a single communal house. The social pattern allows no individualism or cohesion of special groups within the community. There are no social strata, secret societies, clubs, occupational groups, or other divisions. The main alignments are on a sexual and age basis. There are no prestige activities; except for the shaman and the elective chief, all community members are noncompetitive, equals and conformists. The community is close-knit and strongly cooperative within itself but offish and suspicious of outsiders. The only religious observances are shamanistic rites carried out for curing, for protection against evil, for prognostication, and for weather control. Birth and girls' puberty rites are designed to protect the community by isolating the woman. Warfare is minimal and only for self defense. A woman's pursuits are noncooperative, but are generally carried on in contact with other women. The main integrative force is hunting, which is the predominating interest and the principal cooperative pursuit. Dancing, chicha drinking, house building, and communal fishing are secondary group activities.

It is perhaps this passive integration that has preserved *Yagua* culture against change, despite the mission influence and many subsequent White contacts.

727

TRIBAL DIVISIONS AND HISTORY

The *Yameo, Peba,* and *Yagua* are generally named as the three principal *Peban* tribes, but Fejos (1943) considers the *Peba* to be merely those *Yagua* who live on the Marañón River. Citations of the *Peba* as distinct from the *Yagua* are made in order to preserve all possible information on local differences.

Izaguirre (1922–29, 12:414) stated that the *Peban* and *Tucunan* languages are related, but Rivet (1911 b) groups the *Peba, Yagua,* and *Yameo* in an independent *Peban* linguistic family, and Nimuendajú considers the *Tucuna* to be linguistically isolated (this volume, p. 713).

Peba (*Peva, Pava, Pehua*).—The *Peba,* occupying the Chisita River (lat. 3°30' S., long. 72° W.), are divided into three subtribes: *Cauwachi* (*Caguachi, Cavachi*), *Caumari* (*Caumar, Cahumari*), and *Pacaya.* Izaguirre (1922–29, 12:408), however, lists the first two as *Yameo* subtribes. The *Caumari* lived on the Guerari River, a small tributary of the Napo (Izaguirre, 1922–29, 12:414).

The *Peba* had, through friendship with the *Omagua,* been briefly missionized in 1685, but the *Caumari* continued to be hostile to Whites (Maroni, 1889–92, 30:380, 385). By 1732, the *Caumari* and *Cauwachi* shared a mission village, but in 1753 the former murdered the missionary and fled. Later, 60 *Yagua, Tucuna,* and *Peba* were added to the mission, which eventually had 700 persons. But in 1757 it suffered a smallpox epidemic and by 1768, feuds and disease, especially influenza which the *Peba* blamed on witchcraft and avenged by murdering 30 *Tucuna,* had caused most of the *Peba* to flee to the bush. In 1788, the missionary was assassinated. The *Peba* were subsequently brought into a new mission along with neighboring Indians, but the mission was abandoned early in the 18th century. By 1850, they had largely relapsed to paganism. Their subsequent history is closely linked to that of the *Yagua.*

Yagua (*Yahua, Llagua, Yava*).—The *Yagua* lived on the headwaters of the Yaguas River and the upper Guerari River, lat. 3° S., long. 72°–73° W. (Veigl, 1785 b, p. 94).

In 1769, most of the *Yagua* were still pagans, though a few had been taken to the Mission of San Ignacio during the 18th century. Living remoter from the Amazon, the *Yagua* eluded civilizing influences more than the *Peba* during the 19th century, but both tribes suffered epidemics and the impact of the rubber boom during the present century. The *Yagua* and *Peba* now occupy the region of the Ampi Yacu and Yaguas Rivers, where Fejos (1943) maps 12 villages. Tessmann (1930) estimated the combined population of these tribes at 1,000 to 1,500 in 1925; Fejos states that, after being reduced by about one-third by smallpox in 1932, it numbered about 1,000 in 1941. There is some intermarriage with other tribes, especially the *Tucuna,* but native culture remains comparatively intact today.

Yameo (*Llameo, Zameo, Napeano, San Regino, Camuchivo*).—The *Yameo* occupy the triangle between the lower Napo and the Marañón Rivers (lat. 4° S., long. 74° W.), being separated from the *Peba* and *Yagua* by the *Tucanoan*-speaking *Payagua* (*Coto. Orejon*) of the lower left Napo River.   The neighboring *Arda,* long thought to represent an independent linguistic family, are a small group of Negroes.

The *Yameo* proper occupy the region between the Tigre and Nahuapo Rivers.   Other closely related tribes are the *Nahuapo, Amaono,* and *Masamai (Massamae, Masshama, Mazan, Mazana, Parará)* extending from the Nanay to the lower Mazan River, the *Migueano* and *Napeano* of the Nanay River, and *Parrano, Yarrapo,* and *Alabono* in the mountains near this river, and the *Pativa, Patara, Zamua, Parano, Necaono, Mueno, Maino, Baulin, Molouceo, Nicahala, Mohala,* and *Motayara (Barbon),* all probably so-called "kins," i.e., extended patrilineal families or villages.

The first White men to contact the *Yameo* were slave raiders from Boya, whom the Indians successfully resisted.   The *Yameo* were temporarily missionized in 1682 and again in 1700, but were more successfully converted in 1729, with the help of *Omagua,* who taught them much about fishing.   Within 10 years, 9 new missions had been founded among their more remote villages.   In 1769, the *Yameo* had decreased to 1,000 (Escobar y Mendoza, 1769, p. 47).   In 1851, there were 240 at San Regis (Herndon and Gibbon, 1853–54) ; in 1859, 150 (Raimondi, 1862, p. 97).   In 1925, approximately 50 survived, all of whom had lost their native culture and all but 3 of whom had adopted *Cocama, Quechua,* or Spanish in place of their own language (Tessmann, 1930).

POPULATION

The *Yameo* originally numbered 3,000 to 4,000, according to Maroni (1889–92, 30 :48), 6,000 according to Chantre y Herrera (1901, p. 302). Figueroa (1904, p. 374) estimated them at 8,000 to 10,000 in 1737, Escobar y Mendoza at 1,000 in 1769 (1769, p. 47), and Tessmann (1930) at 50 in 1925.

The original number of the *Yagua* and *Peba,* who were less continuously under missions than the *Yameo,* is not known.   The estimate of 1,000 to 1,500 for the present century must indicate that originally their number was nearly as great as that of the *Yameo.*

SOURCES

Despite frequent mention of the *Pebans,* little ethnographic information was available prior to the Fejos expedition.   Traveler and missionary sources are found in González Suárez (1904), Maroni (1889–92, vol. 30), Escobar y Mendoza (1769), Chantre y Herrera (1901), Figueroa (1904), "Noticias Auténticas" (1889–92), and Izaguirre (1922–29), all of which contain more historical than cultural data.   Travel accounts of the past century are unsatisfactory: Maw (1829), Castelnau (1850–59, vol. 5), Martius (1867), Ordinaire (1892), Raimondi (1862), Marcoy (1866, 1875; also published as Saint Cricq, 1853 a), Velasco (1841–44), Herndon and Gibbon (1853–54, vol. 1), and Orton (1870).   Of works by anthropologists we have only Rivet's linguistic classification (1911 b) and Tessmann's fragmentary data (1930) on *Yameo* and *Yagua* culture.

As Tessmann's data were not collected among these Indians, they are superseded by Fejos (1943), whose general monograph results from one of the few applications of modern concepts and objectives to field work in the area.

CULTURE

SUBSISTENCE ACTIVITIES

The *Pebans* depend on slash-and-burn cultivation, growing sweet but not bitter manioc, maize, yams, bananas, sweet potatoes, pupunha or *Guilielma* palm, pumpkins, and sugarcane. The *Yagua* also grow papayas and pineapples; the *Yameo*, peanuts and tuber beans. Farming is done with plain and spatulate digging sticks.

The more important wild fruits are honey, palm larvae, and palm fruits.

When schools of fish run upstream, the *Yagua* and *Yameo* use barbasco and the *Yameo* also use *Clibadium* to drug great numbers of them. The *Yagua* still refuse to adopt other fishing methods, even iron hooks, but the *Yameo* use not only iron hooks but the bow and fish arrow, multiprong spears, and turtle harpoons thrown with the atlatl, all probably of *Omagua* origin. No *Pebans* use traps or weirs.

Among the *Yagua*, hunting is not only the principal source of food but the activity of most consuming interest. Game animals include peccaries, deer, tapirs, five kinds of monkeys, agutis, anteaters, large sloths, armadillos, river turtles, and dolphins. Deer, tapirs, and peccaries are hunted communally under the leadership of the village chief, the game being subsequently distributed among all families. The *Yagua* use poisoned spears and dogs in deer and tapir hunts, but employ blowguns to kill peccaries. They generally kill smaller game and birds with blowguns, the hunter often concealing himself in a blind. The *Yagua* make many intricate traps (Fejos, 1943) : cage traps for large felines, door traps for monkeys and birds (pl. 72), snares, deadfalls, and pitfalls with poisoned stakes in the bottom. They also use bird lime.

The *Yameo* and a few *Yagua* keep pigs and chickens, and both tribes have many animal and bird pets.

Food is ground in a wooden trough with a wooden rocker (pl. 68). Uniquely, both the *Yagua* and *Yameo* are accredited with the tipití though they grow no bitter manioc. The former drink the juice squeezed from the manioc. The *Pebans* smoke meat on a rectangular babracot (pl. 74) and boil food in pots set directly on the fire without potrests (pl. 68). They originally procured salt on the Huallaga River, but now obtain it from the White man. They flavor food with capsicum; the *Yameo* make a sauce of red pepper, grubs, and maize flour.

PLATE 66.—**Yagua and Peba Indians.** *Top, left: Yagua* chief. *Top, right: Peba. Bottom, left:* Young *Yagua* woman with typical hairdo. *Bottom, right: Peba* family. (*Left*, courtesy Paul Fejos; *right*, courtesy University Museum, Philadelphia.)

PLATE 67.—**Yagua Indians.** *Top:* Masked dance. *Bottom:* Man and woman. (After Marcoy, 1869.)

PLATE 68.—**Yagua village scenes.** *Top, left:* Grinding manioc. *Top, right:* Curing meat. *Center, left:* Cooking pot on fire. *Center, right:* Mother and child. *Bottom:* Hair dressing. (Courtesy Paul Fejos.)

PLATE 69.—**Yagua house construction.** *Top, left:* Lower frame arrangement. *Top, right:* Lashing frame. *Bottom, left:* Plaiting and placing thatch. *Bottom, right:* Finished house. (Courtesy Paul Fejos.)

PLATE 70.—**Yagua cutting and carrying logs for a raft.** Men, at top, are using stone axes. (Courtesy Paul Fejos.)

PLATE 71.—**A Yagua raft.** *Top, left:* Working raft out into stream. *Top, right:* Helmsman. *Bottom, left:* Lashing logs. *Bottom, right:* Raft preparatory to launching. (Courtesy Paul Fejos.)

PLATE 72.—**Yagua traps.** *Top:* Small conical trap. *Bottom:* Cage box trap
(Courtesy Paul Fejos.)

PLATE 73.—Yagua Indians preparing blowgun and darts. *Left:* Scraping gun. *Center:* Preparing dart. *Right:* Poisoning darts. (Courtesy Paul Fejos.)

PLATE 74.—**Yagua blowgun.** *Top:* Manner of holding gun. *Bottom:* Polishing bore. (Courtesy Paul Fejos.)

PLATE 75.—**Yagua textiles.** *Top, left:* A horizontal belt loom. *Top, right:* Plaiting a hammock. *Bottom, left:* Making a netted bag. *Bottom, right:* Making and dyeing the upper garment. (Courtesy Paul Fejos.)

PLATE 76.—**Yagua industries.** *Top:* Pottery making. *Bottom:* Preparing fibers for garment. (Courtesy Paul Fejos.)

PLATE 77.—**A Yagua council meeting.** Men are holding walking sticks.
(Courtesy Paul Fejos.)

PLATE 78.—**Yagua scenes.** *Top:* Dance following capture of jaguar. *Center:* A canoe secured by trade with neighboring tribe. *Bottom:* Memorial statuettes. (Courtesy Paul Fejos.)

PLATE 79.—**Yagua Indians.** *Left:* Shaman in complete costume. *Center:* Playing panpipes. *Right:* Men applying face paint. (Courtesy Paul Fejos.)

VILLAGES AND HOUSES

The *Peban* community consists of a single communal house, which has a thatched roof sloping to the ground and is partitioned with mats into family compartments (Maroni, 1889–2, 30:51; Orton, 1870, p. 320). In 1854, the *Yagua* house was oval and consisted of poles bent over from opposite sides and tied in pairs to form a Gothic arch (Herndon and Gibbon, 1853–54). The modern house is similarly constructed and is covered with mats woven of pinnate palm leaves (pls. 69, 78). The shaman consecrates the house site (Fejos, 1943).

Chantre y Herrera (1901, p. 367) states that each *Yameo* family formerly had its own house, and Fejos (1943) suggests that the *Yagua* substituted communal houses for small "huts" during the historic period.

Chambira-fiber hammocks are now used by the *Yameo*, *Peba*, and *Masamai*, but their antiquity is doubtful. The *Yameo* sleep on a mat-covered platform bed, using their hammocks merely for lounging. The *Yagua* formerly slept on mats but now use chambira-fiber hammocks, though they revert to mats when they can obtain mosquito nets. The tightly closed mosquito tent may have been aboriginal among the *Yameo*. The *Yagua* sit on log stools and mats, the *Yameo* on four-legged stools.

DRESS AND ADORNMENT

Peban men were said to wear a bark belt or girdle, sometimes with a taillike appendage. (Raimondi, 1862, p. 114; Orton, 1870, p. 320; Ordinaire, 1892, p. 254; Figueroa, 1904, p. 273; Maw, 1829, p. 200; Tessmann, 1930.) "Noticias Auténticas" (1889–92, 27:67) also mention a *Peba* shredded bark-cloth skirt with a taillike appendage front and back. This is probably the *Yagua* garment described and pictured by Fejos (1943). (See pls. 66, 70, 76, 79.) It is made of fibers of the shoots of *Mauritia flexuosa* palm, which hang thatchlike from a belt to cover the legs and from a bark band around the neck to cover the chest and the back. A woven palm crown completes normal male attire. Izaguirre (1922–29, 12:415–417) shows a similar *Yagua* garment, stating that they keep off mosquitoes. Maroni (1889–92, 31:66) attributes cushmas to *Caumari* men.

Yameo and *Caumari* women wore painted skirts of cachibanco cloth perhaps similar to the wrap-around cotton cloth skirts (pl. 66, *lower, right*) now worn by *Yagua* women (Fejos, 1943). *Yagua* women also cover the upper body with palm fibers, but wear no head bands.

Bark bands are worn around the arms and legs. At one time, the *Peba* hung a shell pendant from the nose (Figueroa, 1904, p. 273), the *Yameo* stuck feathers through the nasal septum (Maroni, 1889–92, 30:66), and the *Yameo* and *Masamai* wore large wooden earplugs that stretched their lobes down to their shoulders (Chantre y Herrera, 1901, p. 64), but no tribe now practices these mutilations. The *Yameo* formerly also removed the nose cartilage of children (Veigl, 1785 b, p. 73). The *Yameo* (Chantre y Herrera, 1901) and *Yagua* (Fejos, 1943) depilate by means of a resin. Hairdress is shown in plates 66, 68, and 75. A crude wooden comb is used. The *Pebans* paint the body with bixa and genipa; the *Yagua* make horizontal designs across the face (pl. 79). Tessmann (1930) attributes tooth blackening to the *Yagua*. *Pebans* wear necklaces of seeds and, on festive occasions, feathers in the arm and head bands.

The only status badges are warriors' human-tooth necklaces (*Yameo*, but not *Yagua*), hunters' jaguar-tooth necklaces, men's painted staffs (pl. 77), and chiefs' toucan-feather crowns (pl. 66).

TRANSPORTATION

The *Pebans* carry infants in a band (pl. 66), usually astride the hip, and transport burdens in a netted bag. The *Yameo* use a burden basket.

The *Yameo* have recently learned to make dugout canoes (pl. 78), but the *Yagua* employ only dugouts obtained from other tribes. Their main craft is a balsa raft, often huge enough to transport the entire community (pls. 70, 71).

MANUFACTURES

Bark cloth.—The *Yagua* make ground covers of bark cloth from the capinuri tree.

Basketry.—The *Yameo* employ a hexagonal and probably other basket weaves. They make sieves, carrying baskets, and storage containers. The *Yagua* seemingly never made baskets, though they weave mats of pinnate palms for roof covers, screens, and temporary shelters.

Weaving.—The *Yameo* formerly wove cotton on a loom and made a fine cloth (cachibanco) of achua palm fibers. They now make only hammocks and bags of *Astrocaryum* and *Cecropia leucocoma* fibers, apparently finger-weaving them. The *Peba* make chambira-fiber hammocks and bags. The modern *Yagua* use only *Astrocaryum,* twisting the fibers on the thigh. They make loom-woven bands, and netted bags and finger-woven hammocks (pl. 75), crossing over and interlocking the strands (Fejos, 1943).

Pottery.—The *Yagua* manufacture large chicha and water jars, cooking pots, and bowls, all of a coiled construction (pls. 74, 76). The jars and pots are baked but the bowls are merely sun-dried. After being fired, pots and jars are sometimes painted with black or red "parallel rings or a running-V band" (Fejos, 1943). *Yameo* pots resemble those of the *Panoans*.

Calabashes.—The *Yagua* drink from gourds painted black inside.

Skin work.—To make hunters' pillows, the *Yagua* scrape and soften but do not tan feline and beaver furs.

Weapons.—The *Yagua* refuse firearms, preferring the silent blowgun and spear. The spear has a detachable point, which is poisoned and notched so as to break off in a wound (Maw, 1829; Fejos, 1943). In addition to blowguns (pls. 73, 74, 79) and spears, the *Peba* use the spear thrower to cast harpoons, probably having adopted it from the *Omagua*. The *Peba* and *Yagua* manufacture their own poison but the *Yameo* obtain theirs from the *Chasutina*. *Peba* poison is made with considerable ritual of *Cocculus toxicoferus, Strychnos castelnoeana* (Raimondi, 1862, p. 100), and, according to Chantre y Herrera (1901, p. 37), 30 herbs, roots, and fruits. It is in great demand among neighboring tribes. The *Yagua* make blowgun and spear poison of curare (*Strychnos toxifera*). They do not use it in warfare and have no antidote for it. The *Peba* antidote is a solution of urine, honey, and sugar or ripe bananas (Maroni, 1889–92, 26:407). The *Yameo* and *Peba* once used a round shield made of balsa wood or chambira fibers (Maroni, 1889–92, 30:50, 130), but the only modern *Yameo* weapon of warfare is the heavy wooden club.

Miscellaneous implements.—The *Yagua* use an ax with a stone head lashed tangentially to the handle (pl. 70, *top*), a bamboo knife, and a wooden wedge.

Fire making.—The *Yameo* now make fire with flint and steel, the *Yagua* with two flints. Both tribes use the feather fire fan.

SOCIAL ORGANIZATION

The modern *Yagua* sociopolitical unit is the extended patrilineal family— an exogamous, patrilocal group of 5 or 10 families occupying a single communal house 6 or 7 miles from its neighbor. Each group is named after a plant or animal, but there is no taboo on or belief in descent from the eponym nor are there other totemic features (Fejos, 1943). Tessmann (1930) calls these groups "kins" and Fejos calls them "clans." But unlike clans, the exogamy applies only to actual patrilineal relatives (no data are given respecting possible marriage with one's mother's kin), and descent, though necessarily patrilineal when residence is patrilocal, may sometimes be matrilineal, as when a woman returns to her own group after separation from her husband and rears her children as members of her own community.

Each extended patrilineal *Yagua* family has its own roughly delimited territory (Fejos, 1943). But hunting rights are evidently not strictly enforced, for a hunter often claims to be trailing game near a neighboring community as a pretext for visiting. The house, raft, chicha jar, and certain elaborate traps are communal property.

Chantre y Herrera (1901, p. 367) reports that the *Yameo* lived in small single-family houses, whereas Veigl (1785, p. 73) wrote that each local group consisted of blood relatives and was strictly exogamous. Tessmann attributes modern *Yameo* "kins" comparable to those of the *Yagua*. The aboriginal *Masamai* were divided into 129 groups, which were perhaps extended patrilineal families; each was under a chie₁ (Maroni, 1889–92, 30:48–77).

Chantre y Herrera states (1901, p. 83) that the *Peba* and *Cauvachi*, like the *Omagua,* had a class of nobles, whose status was formally proclaimed at a drinking bout during their infancy. No other source alludes to nobles, and Fejos (1943) expressly describes complete equality of all individuals, stating that a lack of competitiveness and of any means of gaining status is the striking characteristic of modern *Yagua* communities.

The *Yagua* have an elective chief who, advised by a council of elders (pl. 77), initiates and directs communal affairs, of which hunting is the most important.

No special forms of behavior nor taboos between relatives are reported, though *Yagua* in-laws are restrained with one another. In part, this may be an aspect of the great embarrassment any *Yagua* feels when visiting a strange community.

LIFE CYCLE

The *Yameo* seem formerly to have had the couvade; today, both parents observe moderate restrictions after a birth. A *Yagua* woman delivers her child in the woods and is afterward confined for one day; her husband stays in his hammock for 2 days and must refrain from any normal activities for several more days (Fejos).

Until they are 6 or 8, *Yagua* children learn largely from their playmates and from experience, with little parental intervention or punishment. Subsequently, each child is instructed in adult pursuits peculiar to its sex. Boys receive painted staves, symbolizing adulthood.

At her first menses, a *Yameo* girl is isolated, especially from men, for 1 week; a *Yagua* girl, for 10 days. Premarital sexual relations within the *Yagua* community are not infrequent.

The *Yagua* and *Yameo* marry outside the community. The *Yagua* husband serves his father-in-law for several months at his wife's home before settling permanently in his own father's house. Maroni (1889–92, 30:50–51) states that a *Yameo* man acquired his wife at a drinking bout, then supported his mother-in-law; divorce was uncommon because he feared the mother-in-law's black magic. A *Yameo* man often reared a young girl until she was old enough to marry him.

A *Yameo* might commit suicide with barbasco or curare because he was unhappy or sexually frustrated (Escobar y Mendoza, 1769, p. 47).

The *Yameo* formerly buried their dead in the house and subsequently reburied. They celebrated the funeral with a drinking bout, while cremating the deceased's possessions (Maroni, 1889–92, 30:51). They now use the church cemetery. In 1870, the *Yagua* buried inside the house, which they burned (Orton, 1870, p. 320; Osculati, 1854, p. 209). Today, they still bury in the house but continue to occupy it. Stereotyped memorial figurines of balsa wood made in honor of the deceased (pl. 78) are kept in the house.

During the historic period, *Peban* communities fought against one another because of witchcraft and against Whites because of slaving and other aggressions. They used poisoned spears, round shields, and probably trenches with stakes in the bottoms. The only war trophies recorded are human-tooth necklaces (*Yameo*).

The modern *Yagua* are entirely peaceful, and recalled having fought only the *Mayoruna*, when they used improvised unpoisoned spears and took no trophies. But shamans wear dried sloth heads, reminiscent of the shrunken sloth heads which the *Jívaro* sometimes substituted for shrunken human heads (tsantsas).

RECREATIONAL ACTIVITIES

The *Yagua* painted designs on their bodies and on men's staves and made carved wooden memorials of the dead.

Games and amusements include humming tops spun with a string, maize-leaf balls (*Yameo* only), wrestling, and slings (*Yagua* only).

The *Peban* tribes drink much chicha made of manioc, maize, or Guilielma palm fermented with chewed sweet potato or manioc. The *Yameo* strengthen their chicha with a mushroom and also drink a narcotic called chaburaza (Chantre y Herrera, 1901, p. 85). When intoxicated, the *Yagua* usually dance (pl. 78).

Tobacco is smoked in cigars. Tessmann states that *Peban* shamans also take tobacco juice, but Fejos writes that *Yagua* shamans only smoke cigars. In recent years, shamans have also used cayapi.

Among musical instruments are panpipes (those of the *Yagua* have 22 to 32 tubes and are played by nearly everyone (pl. 79)), longitudinal flutes, a kind of whistle with a fruit-shell amplifier on the end, hollow sticks to beat rhythm on the ground while dancing, and two-headed skin drums of Spanish origin. The large signal drum is not used.

RELIGION AND SHAMANISM

Maroni (1889–92, 31 :72) describes a *Yameo* belief in an invulnerable parrot which he calls the "devil" and in spirits which, often disguised as parrots, take the ghosts of dead people from their graves to the forests. Tessmann (1930) mentions bush demons that kill people at night and water demons, including a serpent, that upset canoes and drown people. The modern *Yagua,* among whom there is no trace of Christianity, believe in dangerous anthropomorphic bush demons (Fejos, 1943).

The souls of the dead are thought to dwell on a hill and to have no interest in living people except when they return for a chicha feast, at which men wearing *Ficus* bast masks impersonate them and drink the chicha. *Yagua* belief assigns souls a place in the sky, where they do not eat or work but from which they occasionally return unseen to drink chicha and to play tricks on the living (Fejos, 1943). *Yameo* souls were thought to become the guardian spirits of their living children.

The *Yagua* shaman causes and cures disease, prevents snake bites, makes rain, stops bad weather, reads omens, and blows smoke over houses, rafts, cultivated fields, and other things to protect them.

The *Pebans* attribute all sickness and death to black magic and to water demons; they use no herbal medicines. Belief in were-jaguars is seemingly absent. The *Yameo* distinguish good and evil shamans, each with an animal spirit helper. The *Yagua* shaman both kills and cures. The shaman's supernatural power consists of magic "thorns" (*Yameo*) or "darts" (*Yagua*), which are kept in his body. The novice shaman is instructed for a long period (*Yameo*, 1 year; *Yagua*, 5 years), during which he smokes cigars and, recently (*Yameo*), takes cayapi to make his "thorns" or "darts" grow.

MYTHOLOGY

The *Yagua* (Fejos, 1943) recount that people once lived in the sky; when they exhausted their game, a brother and sister were lowered to the earth and became the first *Yagua*. There is also a flood legend. Some tales explain the origin of pottery, of the markings on a peccary, of pitfalls, and of the tapir's long nose. Others relate various adventures of animals.

BIBLIOGRAPHY

Castelnau, 1850–59; Chantre y Herrera, 1901; Escobar y Mendoza, 1769; Fejos, 1943; Figueroa, 1904; González Suárez, 1904; Herndon and Gibbon, 1853–54, vol. I; Izaguirre, 1922–29; Jiménez de la Espada, 1892; Marcoy, 1866, 1875 (also see Saint Cricq, 1853 a); Maroni, 1889–92; Martius, 1867; Maw, 1829; Ordinaire, 1892; Orton, 1870; Osculati, 1854; Raimondi, 1862; Rivet, 1911 b; Saint Cricq, 1853 a; Tessmann, 1930; Veigl, 1785 b; Velasco, 1941–44.

WESTERN TUCANOAN TRIBES

By Julian H. Steward

TRIBAL DIVISIONS AND HISTORY

The *Western Tucanoan* peoples are divided into five groups: The *Coto* (*Orejón, Payagua*) on the left bank of the Napo River, below the Algodón River; the *Encabellado* (*Angutera, Piojé*) on the middle and upper Napo River and on the Aguarico River; the *Sioni* of the upper Putumayo River; the *Correguaje* with a number of villages on the Oretguaza River in Colombia (lat. 1° N., long. 75° W.); and the *Tama* (*Tamao*), apparently closely linked with the *Correguaje,* on the Orteguaza River (map 1, *No. 4;* map 5).

Coto.—The *Coto* (*Koto, Orejón, Oregón, Orechón, Payagua*) are probably the same as the *Tutapischo*. *Orejón,* meaning "large ears" and referring to the huge earplugs (pl. 80), was applied also to a nearby *Witotoan*-speaking tribe as well as to other tribes in South America. *Payagua* is the name most often used for the *Coto* in early literature.

The *Coto* originally lived between the Napo and Putumayo River, from the Tambor-yacu to the Guerari River, near the junction of the Marañón and Napo Rivers (lat. 2°–4° S., long. 73°–74°). A few were brought to missions in 1682. The first *Coto* (*Payagua*) mission was established in 1722 but was soon abandoned because the Indians feared slavery. Another mission attempted in 1729 failed because of epidemics and mistreatment of the Indians. By 1739, however, *Coto* were settled with other neighboring tribes in local missions, though some were taken to the Huallaga River and placed with *Aizuari,* where many died of smallpox in 1761 (Chantre y Herrera, 1901, pp. 283, 321–328, 365–369; Escobar y Mendoza, 1769). A century later, Simson (1886, pp. 209, 236) stated that the *Coto* occupied both sides of the Napo River below Rubio Cocha. He considered that the *Orejón* of the Putumayo region between Tohallo Grande River and Yacare Cocha and Toquella Urca were the same as the *Coto*. In 1925, Tessmann (1930) found some 500 *Coto* surviving on the left side of the Napo River below the Algodón River; today probably but a fraction of this number remains. The aboriginal culture is nearly gone.

The affiliation of the *Jeibo* on the lower left side of the Napo River (Maroni, 1889–92, 26:245–246) is unknown.

Encabellado.—The *Encabellado* or *Piojé* (*Pioché, Icaguate, Ycahuate, Cieguaje, Santa María, Tarapoto, Angutera, Angutero, Ancutere, Anckutere, Ancutena, Sekoya-gai, Ruma, Rumo, Macaguaje*), named *Encabellado* because of their long hair, or *Piojé,* meaning "no" in their language,

737

are *Tucanoan*-speaking (Rivet, 1924, p. 686). In 1635, they lived on the
northern side of the Napo River, probably extending from somewhere
near the Tambor-yacu River upstream to the tributaries of the Aguarico
River (lat. 30'–3° S., long. 74°–76° W.). Maroni (1889–92, 26:245)
gives the Cuyabeno (Cuyabano) River, a tributary of the Aguarico River,
as their northern limit, but they probably extended northeast to the
Putumayo River and perhaps beyond, for "Noticias Auténticas" in 1738
mentioned some near the Caquetá River. Their distribution along the
Putumayo River is uncertain, but some *Encabellado* were taken to a mission at the junction of the San Miguel and Putumayo Rivers. In the
middle of the 18th century, after more than 100 years of intermixture with
other tribes in missions and subsequent redistribution through the country,
Chantre y Herrera (1901, pp. 374–380) attributes to them the area between the Napo and Putumayo Rivers extending from the Cordillera to the
mouth of the Napo River, an area which, however, includes the territory
of their neighbors, the *Cofán* upstream, the *Coto* downstream, and the
Awishira on the south side of the Putumayo River. Toward the end of the
last century, Simson (1879 a, pp. 210–211; 1883, p. 22) found two
groups: one, called *Santa María* or *Piojé,* living on the middle and lower
Aguarico River and along a considerable stretch of the left bank of the
Napo River; the other, called *Macaguaje,* separated from the last by
tribes of other languages and customs, on the Cocaya River, a tributary
of the Putumayo River (lat. 0°., long. 76° W.). Izaguirre (1922–29,
12:412–413) distinguishes *Encabellado, Guaciguaya, Ciguage,* and *Icaguate.* Tessmann (1930, pp. 291–292) found these two groups in the present
century in more or less the same area and called them *Pioché* and *Sioní,*
respectively.

The question of nomenclature is confused by changes introduced during
the historic period and lack of significant cultural or political divisions.
The *Encabellado* were originally divided into independent villages of perhaps 50 to 60 inhabitants each. If Father Pedro Pecador and Captain
Juan de Palacios met anywhere near the 8,000 *Encabellado* claimed in
1635, there must have been more than 100 such villages, each probably
with its own name. Some of the names were taken from the village chief,
e.g., *Paratoa*s and *Curatoas,* and others were probably river names.

The five principal names—*Encabellado, Icaguate, Piojé, Santa María,*
and *Angutera*—are synonyms for the entire group as well as names of
different divisions used at different periods. *Encabellado* in early literature
usually designated the people of the Aguarico River region. *Icaguate,* for
which *Angutera* was later substituted, was often a synonym of *Encabellado,* and applied especially to those along the Napo River below the
Aguarico River. It is said to have been first used for the *Guaciguage* and
Cieguage divisions after they were gathered into a single mission in 1722.
At the end of the last century, Simson, following local popular usage,

applied *Piojé* to the people of the lower Aguarico and Napo Rivers, i.e., the earlier *Encabellado* and *Icaguate* (*Angutera*), using *Santa María,* which had formerly been limited to the peoples of the village of *Santa María,* both as a synonym for *Piojé* and as the designation of the more restricted group.   He called the people of the Cocaya River and at Consacunti, 100 miles below Yasotoarô on the Napo River (Simson, 1886, p. 242), *Macaguaje,* which is perhaps the *Amuguage* (*Amoguaje*) who entered a mission at the mouth of the San Miguel River 150 years earlier (Maroni, 1889-92, 26:251) or the *Macaguage* known during the 18th century near the Highlands.   The *Piojé* appear in the present century as *Pioché* and seem to include all the early *Encabellado,* whereas the *Macaguaje* are evidently now called the *Sioni,* while the Aguarico-Napo *Pioché* are divided into the *Sekoya* and *Campuya* (*Kampuya*), the latter including the *Angotero,* each named after rivers (Tessmann, 1930).

Other names mentioned in the early literature were probably *Encabellado* divisions:

Cunchi, a division named by Veigl (1785 a, p. 99).

Cungi (perhaps the *Cunchi*), a subtribe on the Capoya River or Rio de los Atambores.

Guanvomaya, Indians at San José who may have been *Encabellado.*

Javi (*Yeis?*), an *Encabellado* division on the Capoya River.

Mumu, an *Encabellado* division near the Putumayo River (Chantre y Herrera, 1901, pp. 380–381).

Murcielago (*Oio*), a group of *Encabellado* in 1738 near the Caquetá River.

Ruma (*Rumo*), *Encabellado* on the left bank of the Napo River below the Aguarico River (Laureano de la Cruz, 1900, pp. 78–89).

Vito (*Vitogauge*), *Encabellado* who entered the mission at the mouth of the Curaray River.   The *Vitocuru* between the Napo and Curaray Rivers, near San Miguel, who moved to San Miguel in 1742, may be the same.

Vuencanevi, Indians at San José, who may have been *Encabellado.*

Zapua, Indians at San José, who may have been *Encabellado.*

History of the Encabellado.—Shortly after 1599, the *Encabellado* and their neighbors were visited briefly by the Jesuit Fathers, Ferrer and Fernando Arnulfi. In 1635, the Franciscan Father Pedro Pecador, and Captain Juan de Palacios were well received by an alleged 8,000 *Encabellado* near the mouth of the Aguarico River. The same year the Franciscans abandoned their work among the neighboring *Awishira* to found San Diego de los Encabellados.   But the Captain was soon killed for having offended a chief, the Indians revolted, and the mission was given up in 1638 (Laureano de la Cruz, 1900, pp. 31-35, 46-50; Izaguirre, 1922-29, 1:323-348; 2:187).   The *Encabellado* who did not participate in this murder turned on the rebels, who fled to *Awishira* country, where they were soon nearly exterminated (Maroni, 1889-92; 29:223-324).

The *Encabellado* seem to have returned to their native haunts for nearly a century, although a few may have remained in the Pueblo of San José.   They are mentioned only in connection with the transient visit made by the Jesuit, Raimundo Santa Cruz, in 1654 while seeking a water route between the Marañón River and Quito.

Missionary activity was renewed with brief success at the turn of the 18th century. After the Jesuits regained the parish of Archidona in 1709, Father Juan de Narvaez made several visits to the *Icaguate* (Maroni, 1889–92, 28:117). In 1722, Father Luis Coronado gathered the *Guaciguage* and *Cieguage* into a mission called San Xavier de Icaguate, but the murder of a Spaniard caused them to flee. Later a new mission was established at the mouth of the Curaray River with *Icaguate,* whom the missionaries had rescued with difficulty from their slavery at Lamas and Chachapayas, and with other mission *Encabellado.* The new converts traveled the bush to persuade their kinsmen, who had migrated toward the Curaray River, to join them, but encountered hostile *Masamai.* The ensuing *Masamai* raids forced removal of the mission upstream, where the *Vito* joined it. In 1733, a new *Icaguate* mission, San José de los Nuevos Icaguates, was founded at the mouth of the Aguarico River.

Meanwhile the Franciscan missions met little success. The *Mumu,* probably an *Encabellado* subtribe near the Putumayo River, had in 1719 killed their Franciscan missionaries. After 40 to 50 years of migration, they returned to the Putumayo, where most of them died (Chantre y Herrera, 1901, pp. 380–381). The same year, the *Amuguague* at the mouth of the San Miguel River killed their missionary (Maroni, 1889–92, 26:251). In 1738 there was a temporary flurry of missionary activity in the Aguarico River region, and soon there were nine missions in the vicinity of the Aguarico River, with others on its northern tributaries. Previously independent groups of *Encabellado,* each under a strong chief, however, mistrusted one another in the large mission villages. The fatal blow came in 1744, when Chief Curazaba caused the murder of Father Francisco Real by convincing the Indians at Mission San Miguel that they were destined to be sold as slaves in the Highland. The *Encabellado* deserted eight missions and only five remained, but most of the fugitives perished at the hands of other Indians or else starved because the chonta palms did not bear fruit that year (Chantre y Herrera, 1901, pp. 351–354, 395–398). In 1769 only two *Encabellado* missions remained and few Indians survived (Escobar y Mendoza, 1769, p. 60).

One hundred years again elapse until 1858, when Villavicencio (1858, p. 175) records that only a few *Encabellado* survived, living on turtle and manatee on the lower Aguarico River. The *Angutera* lived on the left side of the Napo River below the Aguarico River, where they cultivated manioc, yuca, and bananas. The *Santa María* were peacefully and industriously growing crops and trading hammocks and sarsaparilla (Villavicencio, 1858, p. 176). In 1879 semicivilized but disease-ridden (colds, smallpox, and carate) groups of *Piojé* lived at San José, Cuembí, Yasotoaró, Montepa, Consacuntí, Cajucuma, Pañacocha, Angoteri, Oritoyacu, and Tarapoto. These, described by Simson (1879 a, 1886), were seminomads who refused to settle in large communities, but were in occasional contact with Whites from whom they had acquired a nominal Christianity, liquor, and occasional trade goods, especially clothing, iron tools, cloth, beads, and a few guns. When not in debt slavery, which was sporadic for most of them but permanent detention as servants for some, they lived on the country, using blowguns and bows as well as guns. Native social, religious, and economic practices seem to have persisted despite a superficial influence of European contacts.

In 1928, Tessmann (1930) found some 200 *Encabellado* (*Pioché*) remaining: the *Sekoya* on the Aguarico River, the *Campuya* on the sources of the Tambor-yacu, Santa María (both tributaries of the Napo River), and Campulla (tributary of the Putumayo) Rivers. They were on the verge of losing their native customs.

Igualada and Castellvi (1940) list 86 baptized *Macaguaje* between Trocha del Mecaya and Puerto Restrepo, Piñuña Negro and San Joaquín, and between Yurayaco (Quinoró) and Puerto Boy (Caquetá) and 30 *Piojé* scattered in the basin of the lower San Miguel (Sucumbíos) River, though others were doubtless elsewhere.

Sioní.—The *Sioní* (*Cioni, Siona,* and *Ceño?*) inhabited the upper Putumayo River, extending downstream from the region of Santiago and Sibundoy with its *Quechua*-speaking peoples, to the equator (lat. 0°, long. 75° W.). The *Ceño* were briefly missionized by the Franciscans in 1632 (González Suárez, 1890–1903, 6:86, 104). Some 1,000, most of whom could speak Spanish, survived in 1912 (Hardenberg, 1912, pp. 78–86, 99–100).

CULTURE

SUBSISTENCE ACTIVITIES

Farming.—All *Western Tucanoans* grew sweet manioc, but only the *Encabellado* cultivated the bitter variety. The *Sioní,* however, gathered the bitter variety wild, and removed the poison by wrapping the pulp in bark and squeezing it (Hardenberg, 1912, p. 83). The *Orejón* and *Coto* made no use of the bitter (Tessmann, 1930). Other cultivated plants were bananas, plantains, sweet potatoes, beans, macabo, *Guilielma* palms, yams, maize, and sugarcane. Peanuts and pumpkins seem not to have been cultivated (Tessmann, 1930).

The *Western Tucanoans* cultivated with large knives and wooden planting sticks.

Hunting.—The blowgun was the main hunting weapon, the bow being limited to the *Encabellado,* who used a poisoned arrow. Nets are not recorded, but the *Encabellado* used bird traps, pitfalls, and deadfalls (Simson, 1886, p. 195). *Coto* traps are shown in figure 72. In the present century, the *Sioní* were using shotguns and machetes as well as blowguns (Hardenberg, 1912, p. 81). The *Encabellado* used hunting dogs.

Species hunted by the *Sioní* include tapir, peccaries, capivaras, deer, monkeys, sloths, armadillos, and other animals and many birds.

Fishing.—The *Sioní* fish with spears, chambira-fiber nets, and hardwood or thorn hooks baited with larvae or with *Cecropia* fruit (Hardenberg, 1912, p. 82). The *Coto* use the bow and arrow and long basketry traps but neither nets nor spears. Nets but not arrows are attributed to the *Encabellado* (Tessmann, 1930). All *Western Tucanoans* fish with poison: barbasco (*Sioní*), cultivated *Tephrosia,* and wild *Leguminosae* and *Clibadium* (*Coto, Encabellado*).

Domesticated animals.—The *Encabellado* adopted dogs and chickens, the latter both for their flesh and their eggs.

Gathering wild foods.—Palm fruits, honey, and larvae were gathered by all tribes. Hardenberg (1912) lists the papaya, lime (*Citrus limon-*

um), cashew nut, *Guilielma* palm, and bread fruit (*Artocarpus incisa*) among wild fruits eaten by the *Sioni*. The *Encabellado* gathered fruits of various palms; *Iriartea, Euterpe, Scheelea tessmannii, Mauritia,* and *Jessenia bataua* (Tessmann, 1930).

Food preparation.—The *Coto* and *Encabellado* grind food in wooden troughs, cook in pots, and smoke meat on rectangular or pyramidal babracots (Tessmann, 1930). The *Encabellado* shred bitter manioc on a thorn-studded grater, squeeze out the juices in a tipití, and bake it on a clay stove. The *Sioni* use such stoves to make farinha of sweet manioc. Food is eaten from calabash vessels with a shell or small calabash. It is seasoned with pepper (*Capsicum*) and salt, the latter obtained on arduous journeys to the Huallaga River.

HOUSES AND VILLAGES

In 1651, the *Encabellado* had villages of four, six, or eight houses, each holding one or two small, biological families (Cruz, 1900, p. 36), a total of some 50 to 60 persons in each community. These villages were one-quarter to one league apart and one or two leagues away from the river. Early *Coto* houses seem also to have sheltered single biological families, though large, rectangular communal dwellings were later adopted (pl. 80). By 1750, the *Encabellado* were building longhouses which accommodated 10 families; 14 or 15 of these houses made up a village, which now consisted of about 300 persons (Chantre y Herrera, 1901, pp. 414, 488). In the present century, the *Sioni* lived in communal houses occupied by several families, each with its own compartment, fireplace, and utensils (Hardenberg, 1912).

This increase in house size and community size may have resulted partly from missionary influence and partly from the adoption of canoes, which, affording better transportation, made greater population concentration possible and, producing greater contact between people, made larger groups desirable.

Construction of the large modern house is described and illustrated in Tessmann (1930, table 36, fig. 1). In addition to dwellings, various wind screens are erected.

The *Western Tucanoans* all sleep in chambira-fiber hammocks. Tessmann (1930) denies use of mosquito shelters, but the small, tightly-closed sleeping houses of the *Coto* may amount to the same thing. Logs or carved wooden stools for men are everywhere standard furniture.

DRESS AND ADORNMENT

The ancient *Western Tucanoans* went naked much of the time, though the cushma was sometimes worn. The *Encabellado* and *Sioni* made the cushma of red bark cloth or chimbira fiber, the neck opening running from front to back for men and from side to side for women. The *En-cabellado* also used the poncho, and women sometimes wore short, painted skirts. In the last century, Simson (1879 a, p. 214) found many of them, especially women, still naked, although European clothing had been introduced. Some men, however, wore knee-length ponchos sewn along the sides to form baggy shirts (perhaps the cushma) and women had chambira-fiber bands, 8 inches (20 cm.) wide, around their loins (Simson, 1886, p. 195). Desire to clothe the body was strong in the present century, when Tessmann (1930) reported that *Encabellado* men who lacked European garments wore sleveless unpainted *Ficus*-fiber shirts, women *Astrocaryum*-fiber hip cloths, and even children some kind of clothing. *Coto* men either used European clothes, or they went naked, with the penis tied up, while women wore a sleeveless bast shirt (pl 80).

The typical *Coto* ornament was a huge earplug up to 5 inches (13 cm.) in diameter (pl. 80). The *Sioni* also pierced their ears and wore nose pins. Although the *Encabellado* formerly made perforations near the corners of their mouths for the insertion of sticks and feathers, Simson (1886) and Tessmann (1930) report only nasal perforations through which thorns and sticks were thrust. In ancient *Encabellado* coiffure, the hair was carefully braided and wound around the head with a piece of cloth—in the present century, a piece of bark—or allowed to fall loose behind. Festive headgear in all periods has consisted of a feather circlet. The *Sioni* groomed their hair with combs. Depilation was general; modern *Encabellado* pluck both eyebrows and eyelashes. The *Coto* and *Encabellado* tattooed the face and blackened the lips; the latter also stained the teeth red. All tribes attached great importance to face and body paint. The *Encabellado* stuck cotton fuzz on their bodies. Only early sources mention mirrors made of copal melted and poured into a shallow dish; travelers carried these along with paint with which to decorate themselves before entering foreign villages (Chantre y Herrera, 1901, p. 63). Arm and leg bands of woven cotton or of bark cloth, necklaces, bracelets, and chest bands of seeds, animal teeth, and other beads were worn in great profusion. *Sioni* necklaces weigh 10 to 15 pounds.

TRANSPORTATION

Carrying devices include burden baskets used by men, bast bags used by women, and bast bands for supporting infants.

Early sources hint and the customary residence of early *Encabellado* some distance from rivers implies that canoes were little if ever used until the missionaries established the people on rivers (Chantre y Herrera, 1901, p. 381). The modern canoe is of wood, never of bark, and paddles are long and narrow. Rafts are unknown (Tessmann, 1930).

MANUFACTURES

Spinning and weaving.—Most textiles were woven of chambira fiber: hammocks, carrying bags, nets, cushmas, women's loin cloths or skirts, and fishnets. Weaving in cotton was seemingly elementary; the *Coto* made cotton string but no cotton textiles, and the *Encabellado* wove only cotton arm bands.

Basketry.—The *Encabellado* made men's carrying baskets, parrot cages, and women's work baskets. Materials used were *Carludovica trigona* and *Mauritia* stems.

Bark cloth.—Probably all *Western Tucanoans* made bark cloth in early times, but its manufacture has been discontinued in the present century. The *Encabellado* prepared it with a wooden pounder.

Pottery.—Wares cannot be defined, but ceramics seem to have reached some development. *Coto* pottery was coiled and painted red-on-cream. *Sioni* pots were said to resemble those of the *"Inca"* and to be skillfully painted. *Encabellado* vessel forms include jugs, bowls, cooking pots, and baking pans (Tessmann, 1930).

Weapons.—The bow and poisoned arrow are old *Encabellado* weapons but, in 1879, were used only to take turtles in the Solimões River (Simson, 1879 a, p. 221) and for warfare. The blowgun, not mentioned in early sources but not necessarily absent, was the main hunting weapon in the last (Simson, 1879 a, p. 221) and present centuries. It is made of two half-tubes with a peccary bone mouthpiece and aguti tooth sight; the darts are poisoned with a liana sap mixed with snake poison.

Spears have been used at all times for hunting and warfare. They have poisoned chonta tips that break off in wounds, and they are carried in bundles of five to seven with their ends sheathed (Simson, 1886, p. 195). War clubs are mentioned in early but not in recent sources, and the use of shields is controversial.

Fire making.—The *Western Tucanoans* formerly used the fire drill and both the woven and feather fire fan. Recently, they adopted flint and steel.

SOCIOPOLITICAL GROUPS

There is some evidence that the sociopolitical unit developed during the historic period. The *Encabellado* community of the middle 17th century was a small, politically independent group of about 60 people living in 4 to 8 houses, each sheltering one or two adult men and their families (Laureano de la Cruz, 1900, p. 36). A century later, the average community consisted of about 300 people, occupying 10 to 15 houses, each of which accommodated some 10 families. The community had a chief of considerable authority. Political separatism was still so strong, however, that *Encabellado* from different groups at missions feared to associate with one another (Chantre y Herrera, 1901, p. 362). Subsequent use of the canoe fostered intercourse which weakened this isolationism (Chantre y Herrera, 1901, p. 381), though strong political cohesion never developed. In 1879, villages were groups of scattered huts, which were readily deserted when disease, ants, or floods beset them (Simson, 1879 a, p. 215). Modern villages also consist of scattered houses, each occupied by 4 families (Tessmann, 1930).

Chieftainship had once developed so that all the *Sekoya* were under a single leader, but this arrangement was abandoned. The modern *Sioní* live in large, multifamily houses, and elect a governador and capitán, both obviously post-Spanish offices. Among the *Coto,* the shaman is community leader.

Fragmentary evidence seem to rule out the existence of patrilineal sibs, like those of the *Eastern Tucanoans* in the Vaupés-Caquetá region (p. 780) and even of extended patrilineal families. Originally, *Encabellado* and *Coto* exogamy probably applied to families, not to villages. The *Coto,* moreover, were matrilocal. For the *Encabellado,* Tessmann (1930) denies restrictions on marriages, except those between near relatives.

LIFE CYCLE

Child birth.—The *Encabellado* and *Coto* confine parents for several days after a birth; the *Coto* father stays in the house, the mother in a special hut; the *Encabellado* father is isolated and fasts for 3 days, even if away, and the mother is confined for 2 weeks, doing no work and bathing daily (Tessmann, 1930; Simson, 1879 a, p. 222).

Twins were formerly buried under the wings of the house roof so that rainwater would drown them (Chantre y Herrera, 1901, p. 434).

Puberty and marriage.—At her first menses, the *Coto* girl is isolated 3 days in the house, dieting. The *Encabellado* girl was confined for 1 day in a special hut.

Aboriginal marriage was probably somewhat unstable. Simson (1879 a, p. 213) states that more binding unions had come into fashion because of church influence and the prestige value of imitating the White man. A marriageable woman must have matured physically; a suitable husband had to have proficiency in hunting, in clearing farmland, and in making hammocks. The *Encabellado* man gave presents to his bride's parents; a *Coto* husband rendered some bride service to his father-in-law. Polygyny occurred mainly among chiefs.

Death.—The modern *Encabellado* clothe a corpse in his garments and ornaments, wrap him in a hammock and bury him under the house floor, and then cremate his possessions and abandon the house. The ancient *Icaguate,* however, cremated the body and drank the ashes mixed in chicha (Jiménez de la Espada, 1889–92, vol. 27).

An *Encabellado* guest sat on a bench, while the host touched him on the shoulder, and asked, "Have you come?" to which he replied, "I have come" (Chantre y Herrera, 1901, p. 418).

The aboriginal *Encabellado* had feast halls holding 300 to 400 persons and furnished with benches. In 1651 these were used for dances and gatherings (Cruz, 1900, p. 40).

WARFARE AND CANNIBALISM

The *Western Tucanoans* were not notorious warriors but nonetheless engaged in both offensive and defensive fighting. The special enemy of the *Encabellado* were the neighboring *Awishira,* a belicose people who continually raided them for loot and women. *Encabellado* warriors fought with spears and bows, *Coto* with spears and clubs; use of the shield is uncertain. Villages were defended with trenches having sharpened stakes in the bottom.

The *Encabellado* took trophy skulls (Chantre y Herrera, 1901, p. 164) and practiced cannibalism (Maroni, 1889–92, 29:224).

ESTHETIC AND RECREATIONAL ACTIVITIES

Art.—Recorded art is limited to body and face painting. Basketry, textile, and ceramic designs are not known.

Games.—Modern amusements include humming tops made of *Astrocaryum* fruit spun with a cord, a toy sling to throw fruit, and wrestling. Such characteristic Montaña toys as maize-leaf balls and dolls were not used (Tessmann, 1930).

Musical instruments.—All tribes made two-headed skin drums. The *Encabellado* but not the *Coto* had large signal drums. Other instruments included panpipes, flutes with four to six holes, transverse flutes, leg rattles, musical bows (Tessmann, 1930), and bamboo tubes blown through one hole while the tone is modulated by placing a hand over the other hole (Simson, 1879 a).

Stimulants and narcotics.—Fifty years ago, Simson (1879 a, p. 213) denied that the *Encabellado* made fermented drinks, though he described much drunkenness on alcoholic beverages obtained elsewhere. Tessmann, however, records use of fermented drinks made of various plants and fruits. Drinking was purely recreational, and, though done at festivals held in large dance houses, had no connection with a secret cult like that of the *Eastern Tucanoans.*

Narcotics include tobacco, cayapi, yoco, and coca; *Datura* was not used. Fifty years ago, tobacco was taken by the *Encabellado* in the form of a thin paste kept in a bottle and transferred to the mouth by means of a feather or stick (Simson, 1879 a). Today the *Encabellado* and *Coto*

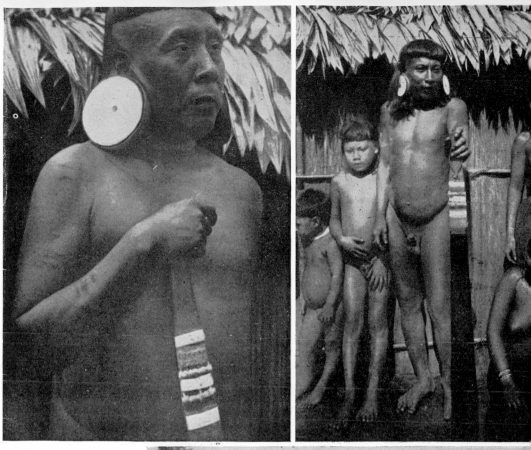

PLATE 80.—**Coto Indians.** *Top, left:* Man. *Top, right:* Family group. *Bottom:* House on Sucusany River. (After Tessmann, 1930.)

drink tobacco juice and smoke cigars; the latter also snuff the powder and chew the leaves.

Cayapi was mainly the shaman's drink, though other persons might take it for its intoxicating effect, which led to broils (Simson, 1886, p 196), and as a malaria cure. Yoco, like coca, was taken for its sustaining and refreshing effect, though in strong doses it is an emetic (Simson 1879 a, p. 213).

The *Correguaje* are the only *Western Tucanoans* to use coca (Schultes 1942).

RELIGION AND SHAMANISM

Tessmann records a modern *Encabellado* belief in a remote supreme being in the heavens, but he found no evidence of ideas of lesser gods or spirits. Concepts of life after death appear to be Christian.

The pattern of shamanism centers around the belief that "thorns" are the cause of disease, although the *Coto* are unique in the Montaña (but linked with the upper Amazon *Tupian* tribes) in holding that soul-loss, that is theft of a dreamer's soul by a ghost, also caused illness. The *Encabellado* shaman received 3 months of instruction during which he drank much cayapi. His instructor put in his body three "thorns," which multiplied themselves. To cause illness, the shaman went, in the capacity of sorcerer, into the bushes to draw the "thorns" from his own body with the aid of tobacco smoke or juice, and to blow or throw them at the victim, who generally died 5 days later. To cure, the shaman sang, drank cayapi and tobacco juice, smoked, blew, and sucked out the "thorns." The *Encabellado* shaman used roots of *Cyperus piripiri* instead of sucking to remove the thorns. This procedure is unclear, but is probably related to the *Záparoan* practice. Shamans sometimes fought each other with "thorns," drinking cayapi to see the adversary better.

Cyperus piripiri was rubbed on the hands and fishing gear for good luck and on tired hunting dogs to restore their strength (Tessmann, 1930). Men scratched their arms with scorpion stings or let ants bite them to acquire skill in shooting the bow (Simson, 1879 a, pp. 221–222).

TRIBES OF UNCERTAIN AFFILIATION IN THE UPPER PUTUMAYO REGION

Several tribes of uncertain affiliation are reported on the right side of the Napo River and along the Curaray River, above the *Awishira* and south of the *Encabellado*.

The *Ssabela,* a *Quechua*-speaking people in 1925, lived on the upper Yasuni, Tiputini, and Chiripuno Rivers, right tributaries of the Napo River (Tessmann, 1930). This is very near the location of a branch of the *Omagua*. The *Ssabela* were divided into the *Tihuacuno* (*Tibacuno*) and *Chiripuno*. In 1925 they were still hostile to the Whites.

Tessmann's notes (1930), though fragmentary, indicate that the *Ssabela* resembled their neighbors. They grew sweet manioc, maize, yams, peanuts, sweet potatoes, beans, and *Guilielma* palms, but not bitter manioc. They took fish with poison but not with nets or hooks, hunted with the blowgun, and lacked dogs, pigs, chickens. They slept in hammocks in gabled houses (Simson says houses were thatched to the ground, 1886, p. 237). People went naked, men tying up the penis, women wearing a leaf suspended from a cord. They wore a stick through the nostrils and ear lobes, blackened the teeth, and had various ornaments, including woven cotton arm bands. They used dugout canoes and carrying baskets. Manufactures included *Astrocaryum*-fiber hammocks and bags, pots that were sometimes painted red, and spears. They did not have poisoned spears, bows and arrows, or shields. For warfare, they used spears and clubs. They buried the dead in the house and abandoned it. They used neither tobacco, coca, nor guayusa, and took cayapi only as a medicine. Musical instruments were limited to a long flute with one hole above and two or three below. Witches produced disease by blowing thorns at the victim.

Several other tribes occupied territory close to the *Ssabela, Omagua,* and certain *Záporoan* peoples and perhaps were related to some of them. These included the *Avacore* and *Parana* on the Curaray River, who were known to but not visited by the early missionaries (Veigl, 1785 a, p. 111), and the *Meguana* on the Tiputini River, enemies of the *Záparo* (Simson, 1886, p. 188).

BIBLIOGRAPHY

Chantre y Herrera, 1901; Escobar y Mendoza, 1769; González Suárez, 1890–1903; Hardenberg, 1910, 1912; Igualada and Castellví, 1940; Izaguirre, 1922–29; Jiménez de la Espada (Noticias Auténticas), 1889–92; Cruz, 1900; Maroni, 1889–92; Rivet, 1924; Schultes, 1942; Simson, 1879 a, 1883, 1886; Tessmann, 1930; Veigl, 1785 a; Villavicencio, 1858.

THE WITOTOAN TRIBES

By Julian H. Steward

INTRODUCTION

The *Tupian*-speaking *Witotoan* tribes occupy the Para-Paraná and upper Caquetá Rivers, splitting the *Tucanoan*-speaking peoples into an eastern and western division (map 1, *No. 4;* map 5). Their culture is typical of the Tropical Forest, but, like most tribes of the upper Amazon, they lack several eastern Amazonian traits, such as the cotton hammock, the vertical or *"Arawak"* loom, bark canoes, and elaborately carved wooden stools. A large number of important features, however, place them with the *Tucanoans* (pp. 764–766) in a distinctive Northwest Amazon culture area, though others distinguish them as a subarea.

Traits in which the *Witotoan* peoples resemble the *Tucanoans* but differ from the *Záparoan, Jivaroan, Cahuapanan, Tupian,* and *Panoan* tribes to the south are: cultivation of bitter manioc and considerably greater use of hunting traps and nets; the use of weirs, baskets, and hollow-log traps instead of harpoons and atlatls for taking fish; fire making with two stones but not with the fire drill; cooking on a pottery stove instead of on a flat plate supported by three potrests; bast hammocks in place of sleeping platforms or mats; nakedness among women and the bark breechclout for men as against the tunic; finger weaving, almost exclusively with wild basts, instead of the belt or horizontal loom and cotton; the rolled (*"Bororo"* type) spindle in place of the dropped (Andean) spindle; the use of coca but not of guayusa; consumption of cigars and tobacco juice but no tobacco pipes; failure to practice head deformation; minimal girl's puberty rites, but the couvade strongly developed; possibly a boy's initiation into an ancestor cult, like that of the *Tucanoan* tribes; cannibalism of enemies rather than of deceased relatives; use of the signal drum and bark trumpets, the latter kept secret from women; use of masks; and possibly patrilineal sibs.

But the *Witotoans* lacked several traits characteristic of the *Tucanoans*: the bow for hunting and warfare; fishing; cayapi (a narcotic); intoxicating beverages; and perhaps aboriginally the dugout canoe.

TRIBAL DIVISIONS AND HISTORY

Ortíz (1942, p. 383) believes that the *Witotoan* tribes may be the ancient *Cambela* (*Cambeba*), but these are more likely the *Tupian Omagua.*

He also identifies them with the *Quiyoya* of the Franciscan missionaries and with the *Cafuane* (not related to *Cofán*) mapped by Codazzi and Pay. Other early names were *Orejón, Orelludo,* and *Mativitana.* Ortíz's three main divisions in this region are:

(1) *Witoto* proper (*Uitoto, Huito, Ouitoto, Huitato, Huitota, Guitoto,* etc.), with the following subdivisions: *Kaime, Xúra, Séueni, Jayruya, Mekka, Menekka,* and *Búe.* (Lat. 0°–2° S., long. 72°–75° W.)

(2) Differentiated dialects: *Bora* (*Boro, Miranha, Miranya, Miraña-Carapana-Tapuyo, Uirauasú-Tapuyo, Mirayo, Marayo, Miragua, Mariana, Miraña, Meamuyna*), lat. 1°–2° S., long. 71°–73°W.; *Nonuya* (*Achote, Achiote*), lat. 1°–30° S., long. 72°–73° W.; *Okaina* (*Ocaina, Dukaiya*), lat. 1°–2° S., long. 73° W.; and *Muenane,* lat. 1° S., long. 72°–30° W. The *Fitita* may be an *Okaina* subdivision.

(3) The Eastern and Southeastern dialects: *Orejón* ("large ear," not to be confused with many other tribes with this name, especially the nearby *Tucanoan Coto,* also called *Orejón*) and *Coëruna* (*Koëruna*), lat. 1°–30° S., long. 71° W.

The affiliation of the *Eraye* and *Soina,* between the *Yagua* and *Bora* (Izaguirre, 1922–29, 12:415) is not known.

Many of these subdivisions may be village or sib names. For example, Pinell recorded 136 *Witoto* subdivisions in 1909, Tessmann gave 50 to 60 in 1928, and Ortíz listed 39 in 1942, a marked decline in the number of local groups.

The place of Tessmann's *Resigero* (lat. 1° S., long. 72° W.) and *Andoke* (lat. 30° S., long. 72°–74° W.), both probably *Witotoan,* in Ortíz's classification is not clear.

The *Witotoans* were little known until the end of the 19th century. Padre Ferrer visited the Putumayo River in 1605, and the *Witoto* were first mentioned by name in 1695, but their first real contact with the White man started about 1886, when rubber gatherers moved into the Putumayo district. This contact was essentially exploitative; the Indians collected rubber in return for machetes, beads, mirrors, fishhooks, tin bowls, cans of sardines and a few guns and ammunition. Exploitation was intensified in the first decade of the present century and these tribes, especially the *Witoto,* victimized by ruthless measures, rapidly declined (Hardenburg, 1912). At the same time, they gradually moved away from their aboriginal habitat.

It is estimated that the population of the Putumayo district declined from an aboriginal total of 50,000 to some 7,000 to 10,000 during the first decade of the 20th century (Casement *in* Hardenburg, 1912, pp. 336-337). This decline has continued despite amelioration of the rubber abuses. In 1910, estimates of the *Witoto* were 15,000 (Whiffen, 1915), 25,000 (Preuss, 1921-23), or 30,000 (Casement *in* Hardenburg, 1912, pp. 269-70). Whiffen also estimated the other tribes as follows: *Bora,* 15,000; *Okaina,* 2,000; *Muenane,* 2,000; *Nonuya,* 1,000; *Resigero,* 1,000; and *Andoke,* 10,000. By 1940, only a fraction of the *Witoto* survived and most of these had moved to new regions. Igualada and Castellví (1940) list 3,652 *Witoto,* including *Mekka, Menekka, Ifikuene* (*Caimito*), and *Búe* in Amazonas, Putumayo, and Caquetá Provinces, Colombia, Ortíz (1942, p. 384) estimates that 1,500 *Witoto* survive on the Caquetá and Putumayo Rivers, with small, separate groups on the Negro, Apáporis, Muritiparaná, Napo, and other rivers. The *Bora* decreased from 15,000 in 1910 to 12,000 in 1926 (Tessmann, 1930) and 427 in 1940. Today both *Bora* and *Witoto* are being further dislocated from their habitat and assimilated. The *Orejón* (*Coto*), estimated at 500 in 1926, and the *Coëruma* are probably extinct.

SOURCES

Fullest accounts of the *Witotoans* come from the present century. Castelnau's account (1850–59) of his visit of 1843–47 and Crévaux (1883) have little of value. The first ethmological accounts are by Koch-Grünberg (1906 a, 1906 b); the fullest are by Whiffen (1915). Preuss (1921–23) studied mythology and religion. Farabee (1922) records some second-hand information. Tessmann (1930) gleaned many fragments of information, much of it flatly contradicting Whiffen. Fejos' investigations in 1941 are not yet published, but he has kindly criticized and augmented the present summary. The great need is clarification of social structure and religious concepts, as both Tessmann and Preuss approached the field with strong theoretical bias. It is probably not too late to record essential data on native cultures.

CULTURE

SUBSISTENCE ACTIVITIES

Whiffen noted that the *Witotoans* seemed chronically on the verge of starvation and that clay eating was a vice. Like the *Tucano,* they subsist mainly on bitter manioc, but the *Witoto* devote much attention to fishing and all tribes to hunting. Today they keep pigs and chickens.

Farming.—Cultivated plants include both sweet and bitter manioc, plantain, bananas, yams, pawpaws, sweet potatoes, pineapples, mangos, *Guilielma* palms, peanuts (*Witoto*), tuber beans, macobo, solanum, cacao (*Theobroma bicolor*), sugarcane, and some maize (*Muenane, Orejón*). Nonfood plants grown are coca and tobacco. Cotton is raised in small quantities by the *Bora*. Cacao is also collected wild.

Fields are usually one-half mile from the village, where a special house stands. A clearing is good for two crops of manioc. Men, sometimes assisted by their friends, who are rewarded with a feast, do the heavy work, clearing the fields by slash-and-burn, in which they formerly used a stone ax. Women plant and cultivate with a wooden digging stick and harvest ground crops. Men, using climbing rings, gather pawpaws and palm fruits.

Wild foods.—Local game animals include peccaries, tapirs, pacas (*Coelogenys paca*), capybaras (*Hydrochaerus capybara*), agoutis, small ant bears, armadillos, deer, sloths, parrots and other birds, frogs, turtles, turtle eggs, and monkeys, the last being the most important animal food. A few species, especially carnivores, are taboo, but it is not known whether there are prohibitions on killing and eating animals because they are sib totems. Game is divided communally by the household head.

For small game and birds, the blowgun and poisoned dart are used; for large game, hunting dogs and poisoned spears. The bow is not used. Other hunting devices are traps, pitfalls with poisoned stakes or with deep mud in the bottom, and deadfalls with logs. Tessmann and Whiffen disagree about the use of hunting nets; Farabee claims that nets 6 feet high and 1,000 or more feet long were used for deer, peccaries, and tapirs.

Fish are taken with dip nets, large drag nets, spears, bows and arrows, long basket traps set in dams or weirs, and hollow-log traps. They are also drugged with *Tephrosia toxicaria, Clibadium sylvestre,* and barbasco. Spear throwers are unknown and fishhooks appear to be recent. Harpoons have been used since the rubber era for obtaining the large payshi fish.

Honey, larvae, and a variety of fruits, especially palms, are the principal wild foods.

Food preparation.—Meat is broiled, i.e., smoked, on a three- or four-legged babracot, but is never preserved. Manioc is grated on a thorn-studded board, sifted, and, among most tribes, squeezed in the tipití. The *Bora,* however, are said not to remove the starch; heating or even drying is sufficient to remove the volatile prussic acid. (See pp. 000.) Cooking is done on a pottery stove, i.e., a flat plate, supported by vertical slabs. Whiffen emphasizes the lack of salt, but Tessmann records that it is made from leaf ashes of *Scheelea tessmannia* and from a bark. Pepper (*Capsicum*) and a spice from bitter manioc are condiments.

Miscellaneous utensils include: woven fire fans, wooden tree-trunk mortars and pestles, pottery, and bark vessels.

VILLAGES AND HOUSES

The typical *Witotoan* community consists of a single large multifamily house (pl. 81), though some villages have several large houses, the *Muenane* as many as 10. A dry site is chosen some distance from the river for protection from enemies and mosquitoes. Communities move to a new site when new clearings are needed or when local game animals have migrated away. Movements are probably within a fairly circumscribed area.

The houses are 30 feet (10 m.) high and either tend to be rectangular in ground plan, 30 feet (10 m.) by 60 feet (20 m.), or circular, 60 to 70 feet (20 to 23 m.) in diameter. They have a sloping thatched roof and a low side wall (pl. 81; fig. 104). The interior is divided into family compartments, in which the hammocks are usually swung to form a triangle around the fire. The dance place is either inside or just outside the house.

FIGURE 104.—*Witoto* house. (After Crévaux, 1891.)

Household equipment consists of rough wooden stools, usually made of a split log, fire fans, palm-leaf brooms, pots, etc. Mats are said to be recent.

Some villages are protected by shallow trenches embedded with poisoned stakes.

DRESS AND ORNAMENTS

Witotoan women are characteristically nude, while men, as among the *Tucano* to the north, wear a bark-cloth breechclout after the age of 5 or 6 years (pls. 85, 86, 87). Other attire consists of ornaments: ear plugs, nose sticks both in the septum and alae, necklaces, armlets, and leg bands or ligatures. For festivals, men are adorned with elaborate feather head-dresses, but women wear dance girdles and glue bird down on their bodies. Leg rattles are also used. Teeth are blackened for esthetic purposes and as protection against "worms." There is a little tattooing but more body painting, colors being black (genipa), red (bixa), yellow (clay or pollen), and white (pl. 88). The hair was formerly worn long and groomed with a composite comb; beards and women's eyebrows are plucked by applying a sticky sap. Head deformation is not reported.

No item of attire seems to be a badge of status, except that men vaunt their hunting and fighting ability by wearing necklaces of animal and human teeth. Farabee, however, states that chiefs wear two extra labrets.

TRANSPORTATION

Burdens are transported in carrying baskets or by means of a bark-cloth tumpline.

Tessmann believes that only the *Muenane* originally had canoes. All tribes now make dugouts. A tree is grooved, felled, and then burned and hewn to shape; manufacture and ownership is communal. There are no bark canoes or rafts. Temporary canoes may be made of the bulging stem of a palm tree.

Bridges consist of trees felled across a stream.

MANUFACTURES

As stone does not occur in *Witotoan* country (the stone axes came from an unknown source), the only materials for manufactures are vegetable and animal products—mainly wood, bark, bone, and teeth.

Basketry and weaving.—The *Witotoans* make containers, carrying baskets, and tipitís or manioc squeezers. The predominating technique is a plain, often twilled, weave. Twining, though known to the *Tucanoans* to the north, has not been reported.

Hammocks and bags are made of twisted *Astrocaryum* fibers, but loom weaving is unknown. Cotton is used only by the *Bora,* who make a few head ornaments of it.

Fire fans are made of feathers, the lower ends of which are braided together to form the handle.

Nets are made for hunting and fishing.

Mats are said to be of recent manufacture, and are made only for trade with the Whites.

Bark cloth.—Bark cloth is used in place of textiles and serves for carrying-bands, masks (p. 83), breechclouts, and girdles.

Skins.—Animal skins are not tanned; they are used only in the form of furs, for pouches and shields.

Pottery.—Each *Witotoan* tribe seems to have a different ceramic technique and ware. The *Bora* and *Muenane* make a monochrome or undecorated ware, which is modeled from a hollow lump (Tessmann, 1930). The *Witoto* made a paddled ware which is smoothed but not decorated. The *Menimehe* apparently make or made red and black pots. Ceramic products include pots and flat plates on which to bake manioc cakes.

Miscellaneous.—Knives are made of hardwood, scrapers of a paca tooth, and borers of a capybara tooth.

Weapons.—Weapons of the hunt include the two-piece blowgun, the darts for which are poisoned with curare (*Strychnos toxifera*), pani (*Cocculus toxicoferus*), and a putrified substance. Spears have various kinds of points, including detachable, poisoned chonta points and blunt ones for birds. They are carried in bundles up to four. The *Witoto* can hurl them 60 to 75 feet (20 to 25 m.).

These tribes lacked bows and arrows and used slings only as toys.

Fire making.—According to Whiffen, fire making is unknown, so that a perpetual fire is kept. Tessmann and Farabee, however, report the use of two stones to strike a spark, and Farabee claims the use of the fire drill. Hardenberg (1912, p. 156) describes maguey or chonta torches impregnated with resin.

ECONOMIC FUNCTIONS

Sexual division of labor is clear-cut: men fight, hunt, clear fields, harvest fruit that requires tree climbing, build houses, and manufacture weapons, poisons, nets, hammocks, wooden objects, and beverages, especially ceremonial drinks; women cultivate crops, keep house, and make hammocks, pots, and baskets.

Intercommunity trade is minimal because of a high degree of self-sufficiency and because of intertribal strife. Trade consists of such items as ligatures, blowguns, *Menimehe* pottery, *Witoto* tobacco and hammocks, *Bora* mats and other woven products, and *Carijona* poisons.

Communal property seems to include the house, dugout canoe, and large, hollow drum. Fields, although sometimes cleared with community help, are individually owned and inherited. There are some kinds of rights to fishing stations. Most personal possessions are buried or cremated when the owner dies; others might be inherited by a man's brother.

SOCIAL AND POLITICAL ORGANIZATION

The sociopolitical unit is the exogamous, patrilocal community which usually occupies a single large house and is divided into family groups. Local exogamy seems to prevail even when the community has several houses, e.g., among the *Muenane,* whose villages may have as many as 10 houses scattered a few minutes' walking distance from one another. The community averages about 100 members among the *Witoto* and *Okaina,* perhaps 300 among the *Bora.* Hardenberg states that the *Witoto* sub-tribe ranges from 25 to 500 persons. Its territory averages about 100 square miles among the *Witoto* and *Okaina,* about 50 among the *Bora.* Whether territory is community-owned is not certain but hunting and fishing rights of some kind are claimed.

If the community were no more than an exogamous, patrilocal, extended family, it would have to be considered a patrilineal band (Steward, 1936). Comparison with the *Tucano,* however, where each community is a sib and where sibs are grouped into three phratries, suggests that the *Witotoan* tribes had similar groups. Whiffen's data throw no light on this problem, but Tessmann describes each *Miranya* community as a "kin" group, stating that the *Witoto* had 50 to 60 "kin." His list of 20 *Bora* "kin" includes such names as Red Arara, Parrot, Palm, Moon, Manioc Meal, Dirt, and Firewood; some of these names occur in several tribes. But there is no hint of phratries, quite explicably because Tessmann did not use the genealogical method in collecting his data. Inconsistent with a true sib organization is the apparent failure of any "kin" to extend beyond a single community and to carry with it exogamy which is more than local exogamy. But individuals retain group (stamme) membership, regardless of locality, as Preuss' census of several villages shows, and a woman continues to feel solidarity with her own as against her husband's group. The presence of an ancestor cult, which the *Tucanoan* tribes link to their sibs, is uncertain, but Preuss (1921) records *Witoto* origin myths, one for each of 31 groups. These designate the group "father" and account for the group name, which is usually a plant or animal. There are also sets of group names, which are given to children (Preuss, 1921–23; Hardenburg, 1912). Whiffen was convinced that initiatory whipping did not occur among the *Witoto*. Careful field work is needed to clarify the nature of the *Witotoan* "kin."

Regardless of whether the *Witotoan* concept of the kin group warrants its classification as a sib, i.e., as a nonlocal group, its function is predominantly localized. Local exogamy coupled with patrilocal residence makes the community consist of the household head, his sons and his son's wives, and unmarried children. Each household is the political unit, the headman only rarely extending his influence beyond the village and then only when communities unite in an emergency, as against the White man. The headman inherits his office patrilineally, from his father or brother, with the approval of the council. He leads his people in warfare, festivals, and work in the fields. His power to punish has been granted only recently, at the insistence of the Peruvian Government. The council discusses hunting, warfare, and wrongdoers. Agreements are sealed by a tobacco ceremony—licking tobacco juice mixed with pepper from a stick.

WARFARE

Considerable hostility has prevailed between the *Witotoan* tribes and even between communities of the *Witoto*. Causes of war are the desire to take prisoners and vengeance against shamans, who are presumed to have caused sickness. Attacks are usually made by stealth. Weapons are flat clubs (macanas), poisoned spears, and thrusting lances, which recently have had iron points. Blowguns are not used. Whiffen states but Tessmann denies that bows and arrows are used. Whiffen records that these tribes use the round tapir-hide shield; Tessmann disagrees with this, but attributes to them a tunic armor of hide. Villages are defended by means of shallow ditches in which sharp poisoned stakes are concealed.

Young persons are taken captive and later merge into the community; old people are eaten. Cannibalism of war victims is attributed to the *Muenane, Witoto,* and *Bora,* alleged motives being, in the order of their importance: (1) to liken the enemy to animals by eating them; (2)

need of food; (3) to acquire the qualities of the victim; and (4) lack of salt. The victory or cannibal feast consists of dancing, singing, and orating. The captive is stretched between two posts and killed with a lance or dagger. Only men eat parts of the body, after putting tobacco juice in their cheeks. After the meal, they make themselves vomit. Preuss describes the use of animal masks in this feast. The victim's skull is cleaned and hung as a trophy, the long bones are made into flutes, and the teeth are used for necklaces.

LIFE CYCLE

Birth and childhood.—Pregnant women are not permitted to eat meat. Birth occurs in the forest. The couvade is practiced by all tribes. According to Preuss (1921–23, p. 164), the *Witoto* mother does not work for 14 days after birth, the father for 5 days. Other sources, however, say that the father remains in the house, avoiding all animal food and refraining from any work until the infant's umbilicus is healed, 3 to 6 weeks later, when the child is given a secret name. Both *Witoto* parents paint their hands and feet red lest the child die. Deformed infants are killed. Children are given a "kin" name, but may be called by an animal nickname.

Children are punished physically, but are not frightened.

Puberty observances.—At her first menses, a *Witoto* or *Bora* girl is merely confined for 1 night. But among the *Okaina* and *Muenane*, a girl is seemingly married at this time, when she is confined with her husband for 2 weeks while both diet and remain silent though the guests dance and feast.

It is possible that the *Witotoan* tribes, like the *Tucano* to the north, combine features of boys' puberty or initiation with a sib cult festival, but inadequate knowledge of social organization and of festivals leaves this matter obscure.

Marriage.—Marriage follows the rule of local, i.e., "kin," exogamy, but Tessmann and Whiffen disagree as to whether a man may marry into his mother's group. Whiffen states that marriage with the mother's sister's daughter is allowed, but, with patrilineal descent, this relative would normally belong to a different "kin" or community than that of one's mother or father. An exception to the rule of local exogamy is that when the chief needs a successor, his daughter weds a man who has been adopted into the community.

Personal preference in the choice of a spouse is ordinarily permitted, thought there is some infant betrothal. The *Witoto* suitor offers the girl's father a load of firewood and a large bag of coca. He must demonstrate his hunting skill and his ability to clear farm land by working for his prospective father-in-law for perhaps one-half year.

Polygyny is usually the privilege only of community headmen and shamans.

Death and burial.—An old or hopelessly infirm person is abandoned on the theory that only those who are useful to the group should survive. After epidemic deaths, the house is burned and the group moves away. Normally, the deceased is wrapped in his hammock and buried in a squatting position in the house. The house is abandoned only when a chief dies. A person's possessions, perhaps including his dog, are either cremated or buried with his corpse. The *Bora* hold a feast of the dead some months after a death.

The soul leaves the body to go into the bush (*Muenane*) or to heaven (*Bora*) or the air (*Witoto*), where it subsequently lives an ethereal and innocuous existence.

An image, purely memorial in purpose, is made of any deceased member of the chief's family. It is always accompanied by a second image of the opposite sex (pl. 82).

ESTHETIC AND RECREATIONAL ACTIVITIES

Art.—Technologically and conceptually, art is limited. Crude carving is done on house posts, dance staves, various utensils, and tooth beads, though some *Witoto* and *Ocaina* incise excellent conventionalized floral designs on gourds and nuts. Baskets have simple rectilinear designs; *Menimehe* and *Orejón* pots carry black and red geometric figures. The most elaborate art is applied to the human body: feather headdresses, bark-cloth masks, complicated geometric painted figures, and a variety of ornaments.

Games and toys.—Adult sports are mainly wrestling (*Witoto, Muenane*) and a festival game in which a rubber ball is struck with the knees (*Muenane*) or the knees, hands, and feet (*Witoto*). The sling is a toy, not a weapon. Stilts, humming tops (*Bora, Witoto*), whirling disks (*Bora, Muenane*), and whirling sticks (*Bora*) also provide amusement.

Music and musical instruments.—The large hollow-wood signal drum, played in pairs of "male" and "female," is a characteristic *Witotoan* trait (pl. 81; fig. 105). It is beaten with rubber-headed sticks and is

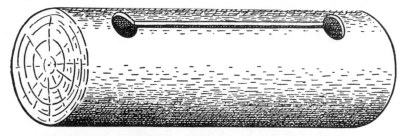

Figure 105.—*Witoto* drum. Five feet (1.5 m.) long and 2 ft. (0.6 m.) in diameter, it is made from a log burned out through the holes and slit. (After Farabee, 1922.)

capable of four notes—two on each drum. By prearranged codes, the *Witoto*, *Bora*, and *Okaina* can send fairly complicated messages 6 to 8 miles (10 to 12 km.). A smaller two-headed skin drum is probably of European origin.

Other instruments are three-tube and many-tube panpipes, bamboo and human- or animal-bone flutes, longitudinal flutes with a hole in the center played in pairs at festivals, rattles affixed to the legs or to sticks, castanets, and sacred bark trumpets.

Dances.—Dances accompany community festivals which seem to be mainly religious in nature, and are occasions for hundreds of people to assemble. These are described below. Others seem to be purely recreational and are accompanied by games, airing of grievances, and drinking nonintoxicating beverages. The celebrants used to go from house to house during several days.

Narcotics and beverages.—Yoco is not used. Coca, grown locally by these tribes, is toasted, pulverized, and taken with leaf ashes. Eaten in lieu of food, it has a sustaining effect. Tobacco is made into long cigars or is mixed with water and drunk; only men use it. The *Orejón* take tobacco powder by mouth. Cayapi is not taken. Some kind of a snuff is taken by an individual using a pair of tubes in V-shape or by two friends using crossed tubes (fig. 106).

FIGURE 106.—*Witoto* taking snuff. Powder is blown up nostril by the partner.
(After Crévaux, 1891.)

Various beverages are made, but no tribes south of the Japurá River ferment them, except the *Orejón* (Tessmann, 1930).

RELIGION

Little information is available on concepts of supernatural beings. The belief in a beneficent creator called "father," who lives above, and a malevolent god, who lives below and causes sickness, may reflect Christian ideas, though there has been little missionary influence on these tribes and a similar high god concept is recorded among the *Tucanoan* tribes to the north.

There is some evidence that an ancestor cult, similar to that of the *Tucanoan* peoples, occurs among the *Witotoan* tribes. Festivals, masks, and sacred trumpets have been described but their meaning has not been clarified.

Among lesser supernatural beings are the sun and his wife, the moon, both benevolent and unimportant; spirits of both animate and inanimate natural objects, which are potentially evil, especially the jaguar and boa; and demons, which formerly inhabited the earth but were killed in a flood and went underground.

SHAMANISM

Witotoan shamanistic practices, though described with some confusion and contradiction by Whiffen and Tessmann, apparently conform to an old Amazonian pattern in general outline and to the practices of neighboring tribes in details. The shaman, probably with spirit helpers, causes and cures disease; the were-jaguar concept is well developed. The supernatural cause of disease is a foreign object sent into the victim by the shaman; the cure is its removal by sucking.

Shamanism is usually inherited from father to son (pl. 87, *top, right*). As hirsuteness favorably predisposes to acquisition of supernatural power, shamans do not depilate themselves. A neophyte undergoes a period of instruction, observing dietary restrictions and taking tobacco and coca. These induce visions, during which the magic substance from the body of a deceased shaman ("balls," *Witoto;* male and female "beings," *Bora;* "thorns," *Muenane*) enters the youth.

The shaman apparently has some spirit helpers, both bird and animal. Whiffen remarks that he controls condors by means of their claws and lizards and snakes by means of their skins, but the role of these animals is unclear. The most important animal is the jaguar. The shaman may change into an invulnerable jaguar to attack his victims.

The *Witoto* and *Bora* recognize natural causes of death, such as snake bite, drowning, warfare, and old age, but the *Muenane* attribute all death to supernatural malpractice. The evil magician always belongs to a foreign group or tribe. Shamans kill their victims by several means: use of actual poisons; turning themselves into jaguars and attacking; sending the the magic substance from their own body into the victim, i.e., a "ball," an evil spirit, a magical "being," or a "thorn." The *Muenane* believe that the shaman sends an animal, which turns into a human being, to throw the "thorn" into the victims. These sickness-producing substances return to the body of the shaman after the victim dies. Sickness is also caused by the evil god living below the earth.

A cure may be accomplished with herbs or by strictly shamanistic means. The shaman—shouting, beating, imitating bird and animal calls, taking coca and tobacco to induce dreams, which he interprets, shaking a rattle, blowing, and performing sleight-of-hand tricks—undertakes to remove the disease object. He massages, breathes on the patient, and sucks out the object, which he may exhibit. The *Witoto* object may be gold, silver, wood, or bone (Farabee, 1922). The shaman is paid for his cure.

In addition to causing and curing disease, the shaman divines who has worked evil, advises on warfare, and forewarns of attacks.

FESTIVALS

Certain *Witotoan* festivals have characteristic features of the *Tucanoan* ancestor cult, especially the sacred trumpets and seclusion of women, and most of them seem linked to an earth god and the original subterranean home of men and animals. Whiffen is explicit in his belief that initiatory whipping is not practiced, for the scars it leaves are unmistakable. Other festivals employ bark masks representing spirits, but their purpose is not clarified (pls. 83, 84).

Apparently all festivals were occasions for dancing and drinking non-intoxicating beverages. The cannibal feast has already been described. Others were held at the harvest of certain fruits. Tessmann lists seven festivals. The Whirling Beam involves dancing on a pivoted log; in it the *Muenane* use masks. Farabee interprets this as a planting festival, when house and fields are protected against destruction. A Renewal feast is held by men blowing trumpets of spiralled bark, which the women, who are confined inside the house, are not permitted to see. This has some connection with house building and is seemingly held at the beginning and completion of construction. All tribes hold this festival, but only the *Witoto* use masks. The *Guilielma* palm feast occurs at the harvest of these fruits; among the *Bora* and *Muenane,* but not the *Witoto,* male dancers wear masks. Another festival features the rubber-ball game. Tessmann believes, without convincing evidence, that a celebration in which men and women dance indoors, using decorated dancing staves with rattles attached, is a feast of the dead. The *Witoto* have two other festivals: in one, various animal masks are used; in the other, masks and the large drum.

MYTHOLOGY

People came through a hole from underground, whence also came animals (Farabee, 1922). The Earth God, below, and these animals and people, "his children," underly *Witoto* festival concepts, songs, and myths (Preuss, 1921–23).

The culture hero, according to the *Witoto,* was the Sky God, who gave people manioc. But means of propagating it were found by the daughter of a virgin whose father had been a manioc plant; the girl instructed the women in planting manioc stalks. There are also tales of the flood, of Amazon women, and of many adventures of animals, each of which has definite characteristics. For example, the capybara or agouti is the trickster.

BIBLIOGRAPHY

Castelnau, 1850–59; Crévaux, 1883; Farabee, 1922; Hardenburg, 1912; Igualada and Castellví, 1940; Izaguirre, 1922–29; Koch-Grünberg, 1906 a, 1906 b; Ortiz, 1942; Preuss, 1921–23; Rivet, 1911 a; Steward, 1936; Tessmann, 1928, 1930; Whiffen, 1915.

PLATE 81.—**Bora drums and Witoto communal house.** (Courtesy Paul Fejos.)

PLATE 82.—Witoto carved wooden memorial figures. (Height approximately 1 m.) (Courtesy Paul Fejos.)

PLATE 83.—**Witoto bark-cloth masks and dance costume.** *Bottom,* *right:*
Pounding stave. (Courtesy Paul Fejos.)

PLATE 84.—**Witoto dance.** (Courtesy Paul Fejos.)

PLATE 85.—**Bora types.** Varieties of body painting. (Courtesy Paul Fejos.)

PLATE 86.—**Witoto men and women in festive decorations.** (Courtesy Paul Fejos.)

PLATE 87.—**Witoto types.** *Top, right:* A shaman. (Courtesy Paul Fejos.)

PLATE 88.—**Witoto body painting.** (Courtesy Paul Fejos.)

TRIBES OF THE UAUPES-CAQUETA REGION

By Irving Goldman

INTRODUCTION

The area designated here as the Uaupés-Caquetá region (map 1, *No. 4;* map 5; map 8, *No. 2*) lies within a rough quadrilateral, bounded on the north by the Guaviare River, separating the Colombian-Venezuelan llanos from the rain forest to the south; on the east by the Rio Negro, and its principal affluent, the Guainía River; on the south by the upper reaches of the Caquetá River; and on the west by the wall of the Andes. Except for some bare stretches of high plateau—sabana (savanna)—the eastward sloping land is heavily wooded and cut by many quick-moving, rapids-blocked streams; westward it is hilly, the shallow streams rock-bedded. The main streams of the area all drain into the Amazon: the Caquetá, Apáporis, Tiquié, Papury, Içana, Vaupés (Caiarí), Cuduiarí, Querarí, Aiarí, Xié, Guainía, and Negro.

Within this network of rivers, draining virtually all of northern South America, live people of diverse linguistic families—*Arawakan, Cariban, Tucanoan, Witotoan (Miranyan)*, and unclassified—but having sufficient cultural resemblances to merit preliminary classification within a single culture area. Primarily for convenience, the *Eastern Tucanoan*-speaking peoples are treated here as the culture center, with the *Arawak* forming a northeastern periphery and the *Carib* a western. The *Witoto-Bora-Miranya* group, which forms a southern periphery, and the *Western Tucanoan* tribes, who live beyond the *Witoto* on the Napo and upper Putumayo Rivers, are each described in a separate chapter. No culture-historical implications are assumed by this treatment. This particular center of gravity has been chosen because more detailed information is available about the *Tucanoan* groups in this area than about any other group.

Among the distinctive cultural features of this area, to which will be noted numerous exceptions, may be listed the following: Primary emphasis upon bitter manioc cultivation and fishing, with hunting of secondary importance; the use of large multifamily houses, each constituting a local kinship group, rather than villages; a complex of men's rites associated with an ancestor cult, inadequately referred to in the literature as yurupary; the existence of patrilineal sibs; painted bark-cloth masks,

763

unevenly distributed in the area; frequent and prolonged chicha drinking, with intoxication common; chewing of powdered coca mixed with leaf ash and use of vision-inducing lianas; shamanism associated with the jaguar; and striking emphasis upon sorcery. Tribal organization is either weak or absent, with authority vested in the leader of the sib or local kin group. Cannibalism has been attributed to most of the tribes in the area.

TRIBAL DIVISIONS

Tucanoan tribes.—The *Tucanoan*-speaking tribes, usually known as *Betoya,* though linguistic affiliations have been established on fragmentary bases, fall into an eastern and western group separated by a *Cariban* and *Witotoan* wedge. From the sparse data on the *Western Tucano* (p. 737), it is clear that they are culturally differentiated from the others. The reputed but not conclusive absence of sibs among them, the absence of such traits as masked dances and coca chewing, their cultivation of cotton, and weaving on a simple loom link them more closely with the neighboring *Panoan* stock. (See pp. 449–463).

The *Eastern Tucanoan* tribes may tentatively be classified into 18 subtribes as follows:

The *Tucano* proper (self name, *Dáchsea;* called by the *Cubeo, Xwévewa,* "Toucan people") are stated to fall into three groups, occupying some 30 to 40 sites on the Vaupés River from the first cataract of Ipanoré to the lower Vaupés River, and along the Tiquié and Papury Rivers, and in the neighboring Curicuiari River region (lat. 0°, long. 70° W.). Some small groups living in single-family huts are found on some of the tributaries of the Rio Negro. Their present population is estimated at around 1,000; Coudreau estimated them in 1883 at close to 2,000.

The *Desana* (self name, *Winá*) occupy sites on the Papury River and on the Tiquié (lat. 0°, long. 69° W.). Their population in 1900 was about 200–300 on the Tiquié River, and 600–800 on the Papury.

The *Buhágana* (*Karauatana-mira,* "Blowgun people") live on the Pirapiraná and Dyi-Igarapé Rivers (lat. 0°, long. 70°–71° W.). Probably *Buhágana* sibs or subtribes are the following Dyi-Igarapé River groups: *Ömöa, Särä, Doä, Tsáina, Tsöloa.*

The *Tuyuca* (*Dochkáfuara,* "Clay people," or *Tejuca,* "Mud people," as they call themselves) live on the upper Tiquié and Cabary-Igarapé Rivers (lat. 0°, long. 70°30′ W.). Their population in 1900 was estimated at 150–200. Whether they constitute a subtribe or a sib of the *Tucano* is not clear.

The *Bará* (medicine) live on the headwaters of the Tiquié River (lat. 0°, long. 71° W.) and in 1900 had a population of about 100. They are closely related to the *Tuyuca* and are probably to be regarded as a *Tucano* sib.

The *Macuna,* represented in 1900 by only two large houses on the Apáporis River below the mouth of the Piraparaná River (lat. 1° S., long. 70° W.), are closely linked with *Buhágana,* and are probably a sib.

The *Cueretú* (*Coretus*) live on the Caritaya River, a tributary of the Miriti-Paraná River, and on the right bank of the Caquetá River, opposite the mouth of the Apáporis River (lat. 2° S., long. 70° W.). Martius located some single families in São João do Principe.

The *Yahuna* occupied some 8 houses on the lower Apáporis River (lat. 1°30' S., long. 69° W.), with an estimated population in 1900 of 150–200. They comprise many subgroups or sibs, among them the *Opaina* (*Tanimboka*) and *Dätuana.*

The *Yupua* (*Japuá, Jupihuá*) were a very small group in 1900 living at Thöta, an arm of the Apáporis River. They are probably a sib.

The *Hobacana* (*Yabahana, Japuana, Chapoannas*) live on the Inabu River, a northern tributary of the Rio Negro. When first encountered by the Brazilians, they occupied the Marauia River, a tributary of the left bank of the Rio Negro, north of Castanheiro Novo. A branch of this tribe was found on the Pacimoni River by Spruce in 1854. They are closely related to the *Macuna,* and may also have been a sib.

The *Arapaso* (*Koreá,* "woodpecker") occupy three house sites on the middle Vaupés River between Yavarete and Ipanoré (lat. 30' N., long. 69° 30' W.). Together with the closely related *Neenoá, Yohoroá* and *Uiua Tapuyo,* they are probably to be regarded as sibs of the *Tucano.*

The *Piratapuyo* (self name, *Uaikena,* "Fish people") live partly on the middle Vaupés River, and along the small tributaries below Yavarete on the Vaupés, but for the most part on the lower Papury River (lat. 1°30' N., long. 70° W.). In 1900 they were estimated at about 600–800. They may be a subgroup of the *Uanana.*

The *Uanana* (*Ananas;* self name, *Kótitia*) consist of two groups: one is above the mouth of the Querarí River; the other, at Carurú, is divided into a number of sibs (lat. 1° N., long. 70° W.). The present population may be close to 500. Martius places them first at the Serra de Maduacaxes near the Orinoco River, from where they presumably moved by way of the Padauri River to Guaracapury on the Vaupés River. They are closely intermarried with *Cubeo* sibs of the Cuduiarí and Querarí Rivers.

The *Uaiana* (*Yuriti-tapuyo,* "Dove people"; called by the *Cubeo, Hülaliua*) live mainly on the Paca-paraná River, and occupy some house sites on the Dyi-Igarapé River (lat. 30' N., long. 71° W.). They are a sib of the *Uanana.*

The *Carapaná* (self name, *Möchda,* "gnats") live between the Yurupary Falls of the Vaupés River and the Paca River, a tributary of the Papury River.

The *Uásona* (*Pisá-tapuyo*, "Net people") live on the Paca-Igarapé River, with one small group at Manapialia, a tributary of the Vaupés River.

The *Pamoa* (*Tatuyo*, *Tatú-tapuyo*, "Armadillo people") live near the Karapanas River (lat. 30° N., long. 71° W.). Their present population may be close to 300.

The *Cubeo* (*Cobbeos*, *Kobeua*; self name, *Pamíwa*, "First people") comprise at present 31 patrilineal sibs grouped into three unnamed phratries occupying a section of the Vaupés River, from the falls of the Guaracapurí River to the small Carurú River, and the Cuduiarí, Pirabaton, and Querarí Rivers (lat. 1° N., long. 71° W.). The present population is about 2,000.

Arawakan tribes.—The *Arawakan*-speaking tribes of the area form a northern and northeastern boundary to the *Tucanoan* groups, and occupy principally the Rio Negro and its tributaries, the Içana, Aiarí, Xié, Guainía, and Inirida Rivers. A small *Arawakan* enclave, the *Cauyari*, is encountered deep in *Tucanoan* territory, between the Vaupés and the Apáporis Rivers (lat. 1° N., long. 71°30′ W.). As in the case of the *Tucanoan* groups, the nomenclature of the *Arawakan* tribes is subject to serious confusion as to distinction between tribe, sib, and local group. They may be tentatively classified into 10 ill-defined groups as follows:

Baniva (*Baniwa*, *Manibas*, *Karútana*, *Korekaru*, *Baniba*) is the term frequently applied to all the *Arawak* of the region (lat. 3° N., long. 67°–68° W.). Following Koch-Grünberg, it is used here to refer only to the *Arawak* of the Guainía River.

The *Carútana* (*Maniba*, *Baniwa*; called *Karútana* by the northern *Arawak*) are a small group occupying single-family huts on the lower Içana River (lat. 1° N., long. 67°–68° W.).

The *Siusí* (*Oalíperi dakeni*, "Star people") comprise three groups: on the lower Caiarí River, on the middle Aiarí, and on the Içana River from the mouth of the Aiarí to its large rapids (lat. 1°30′ N., long. 69°–70° W.).

The *Ipeca* (*Kumata Minani*) occupy sites on the Içana River above the *Siusí*, and at the Yavarate-Paraná River (lat. 2° N., long. 69°–70° W.). They probably are a sib of the *Siusí*.

The *Catapolítani* live primarily at the village of Tunuhy above the Umaca-Igarapé River, a left branch of the Içana River (lat. 1° N., long. 68° W.). They are mostly Christians. The population in 1900 was between 100–150.

The *Cáua* (called *Maúlieni* by the *Siusí*) live along the middle Aiarí River and some of its tributaries (lat. 2° N., long. 70°–72° W.). They are mixed with *Cubeo* and had adopted the *Cubeo* tongue. In 1900 they were returning to the use of *Arawak*.

The *Arekena* (*Uarekena, Arequena, Uerequena, Guariquena*) lived originally on the Içana and Xié Rivers (lat. 2° N., long. 67°–68° W.), but were subsequently removed by missionaries, in the middle 19th century, to Barcellos (Mariua). They have little contact with the *Arawak* of the Içana River.

The *Baré* live on the Guainía River (lat. 2°–3° N., long. 66°–67° W.) and are closely related to the *Arekena*.

The *Huhúteni* live on the lower part of the Aiarí River (lat. 1° N., long. 69° W.).

The *Tariana* occupy some 20 houses in the vicinity of Yavarete on the Vaupés River (lat. 0°, long. 69° W.), and are the only *Arawak* on that river. Koch-Grünberg asserts that they had originally been brought to the Vaupés River from settlements on the Içana and Aiarí Rivers by missionaries. The present population may be close to 500.

Cariban tribes.—The *Carib* in the western part of the area (lat. 1° S.–3° N., long. 72°–75° W.) are called *Umaua* by the *Tucano* and have often been known as *Omagua* or *Omague* (not to be confused with the *Tupian Omagua* of the Amazon River). Martius placed them along the stony savanna in the region east and northeast of the upper Yapura River. Wallace listed them with Vaupés tribes, and Coudreau placed them at the headwaters of the Vaupés and the upper Apáporis River. Koch-Grünberg (1909–10), who groups all these *Cariban* as *Carijona* (*Carihona*, "people" in *Carib*) identifies the following subgroups or "hordes": *Hianacoto* (eagle) with 8 houses on the Cuñary River; *Tsahatsaha* (diving bird) with 3 houses on the Cuñary and Mesay Rivers; the *Mahotóyana* (fire) on the Macaya River; and *Caikuchana* (jaguar) with 4 houses on the Apáporis River. Relatively little is yet known about these people, who, according to Whiffen (1915, p. 59), numbered 25,000 in 1915. According to Martius, they are fierce nomadic cannibals who live in conical multifamily houses. Their attire is characterized by the broad tururi girdle under which the penis is fastened to the body. Both sexes cut the hair short, and the women are naked. They do not have the masked dances found among the *Tucana* and *Arawak* to the east, but use the elaborate feather headdresses of the region when dancing.

TRIBAL HISTORY

The absence of archeological evidence and of early detailed missionary and travelers' accounts prevents the reconstruction of the culture history of the area. A trait comparison with adjacent areas points, however, to the composite character of this northwest Amazon culture. *Tupi* influence would seem to be indicated by the following common characteristics: Large communal houses, a system of fortification, slavery, frequent shifting of village sites, extended patrilineal families, household chiefs, naming a child from an ancestor, and practically the entire manioc and food-gathering complexes. *Tucano* traits of material culture are shared with adjoining *Arawakan* and *Cariban* tribes and unilaterality in reckoning descent is shared with the *Tucana* and with the coastal and Rio Negro *Arawak*. There is evidence to suggest the intrusion of *Arawak* and *Carib* into the area but there is nothing to show the origin of the *Tucanoan* tribes. The elaborate network of large streams draining a vast area of northern South America presumably facilitated a ceaseless movement of peoples. But whether the *Tucanoan* peoples have been moving westward from the slopes of the Andes or eastward cannot be determined at present.

The Vaupés River is first mentioned in the accounts of the expeditions of Hernán Pérez de Quesada (in 1538) and of Phillip von Hutten (in 1541). These sources refer vaguely to a mighty people on the Guapes (Vaupés) River, whom they called the *Uape*. The people are not described.

In 1784, the Portuguese, Manual de Gama Lobo do Almada, ascended the Vaupés as far as Panoré and established mission stations as nuclei for Indian settlements at San Jeronimo, São Joaquim de Coané, Terra Cativa, Jukira-Apecona, and at Yavarate. None of these settlements took root. The Jesuits established contact with the Indians of the Rio Negro in the 17th century, and, at the end of that century, the Carmelites founded missions on the upper Rio Negro and Rio Branco. Indian rebellions in the early and middle 18th centuries, led by chiefs of the *Manao* tribe near the present site of Manaos, virtually destroyed missionary influence in the area for almost a century. A Carmelite mission established in 1852 at Caruru on the Vaupés River lasted a short time only. Between 1852 and 1880 missions were organized on the Vaupés River some three or four times, only to be abandoned. A number of Franciscan missions established after 1881 on the lower Vaupés among *Tucano, Uanana,* and *Cubeo* managed to survive until the present.

Except in the immediate vicinity of mission stations or in regions dominated by intensive rubber gathering activities in the first decade of this century, no profound changes appear to have occurred as a result of White contact. Some interpenetration of Christian ideology in native religious practices and beliefs is, however, evident in all but the most remote tribes; and dependence upon White trade commodities, such as machetes, fishhooks, and firearms, is more or less general. In relatively recent times, the introduction of White-manufactured hunting and fishing implements has uniformly raised the standard of living; the developing trade in farinha, a dry manioc flour, has stimulated increased manioc production, placing a new emphasis upon the economic value of women as the chief agriculturists. The impact of this on social organization cannot be generalized, however. White contact has also diversified agriculture and in varying degrees developed some animal husbandry—chicken and, in a few instances, pig raising. But against the benefits of an improved technology must be weighed the frequently harsh consequences of callous exploitation of Indian labor by rubber gatherers. On the Putumayo River, for example, 80 percent of the Indian population, according to some estimates, died during 10 years of the rubber boom prior to 1920.

The earliest detailed account of Indians of the Rio Negro and Vaupés River is that of A. R. Wallace (1853), who lists the tribes of the region, describes in fragmentary form material culture, social organization, and religion, and adds some brief word lists. Like his successors in the area, Wallace fails to analyze social organization and religion intensively enough to be reliable. The botanist, Spruce (1908), adds little to Wallace's account. More ambitious studies of religion are those of H. Coudreau (1886–87) and Stradelli (1890). The failure of both reports to employ native religious terminology and their ethnocentric evaluation of native institutions considerably diminishes their value. By far the best and most detailed published accounts of Northwest Amazon culture come from the pens of Koch-Grünberg (1905–08, 1909–10) and of Whiffen (1915), the latter an English Army officer. Koch-Grünberg is particularly unreliable on social organization; he is excellent in describing artifacts but not technology. As an amateur's report, the work of Whiffen is outstanding. The present information on the *Cubeo* is based on the unpublished field work of the present author during 1939–40 on the Vaupés and Cuduiarí Rivers.

CULTURE

SUBSISTENCE ACTIVITIES

Farming.—Dependence upon bitter manioc as the basic and virtually unfailing food crop is characteristic of the entire area. In gardens which men clear by the slash-and-burn method, women cultivate manioc and prepare it as food in the form of cakes or dried flour (farinha), as a tapioca porridge, and as a fermented beverage. A nonseasonal crop, manioc may be planted at any time and harvested after 8 months, when the roots have reached maturity. New clearings are usually prepared just before the beginning of the rainy season to take advantage of more rapid growth during the wet months. The *Cubeo* follow a regular pattern of harvesting and replanting from the shoots, so that one cannot really speak of a planting season.

A single *Cubeo* woman produces approximately 5 tons of manioc a year, using a clearing which comprises about one acre (4 sq. km.) ; she harvests an average of 25 pounds a day. Each day's harvest is converted into a single flat circular cake, called beijú in Portuguese, and meets the normal needs of an adult for 2 days if other food is also available. Part of the manioc, the pure starch extract, is consumed as a porridge mixed with fruit or crushed berries.

Not all manioc is produced for home consumption. Where farinha flour is traded to Whites, as much as 10 percent of the manioc is diverted toward the acquisition of cloth, jewelry, and other items of trade. An additional 15 percent goes into the brewing of chicha, a weakly fermented beverage of considerable nutritive value. Variations in social status among the *Cubeo* are linked with surplus manioc production.

The only factor limiting manioc production is labor; land is relatively limitless. Variations in production between families are related to the number and industry of the women in each.

A relatively wide variety of other crops, apparently recently introduced and upon which the Indians do not greatly depend, are also grown. Among these are sweet potatoes, bananas, plantains, squash, pineapples, yams, mangoes, batatas, some maize, papaya, umari, guayaba, *Inga*, urama roots, Marantaceae (arrowroot), and sugarcane. Chili peppers, tobacco, coca, and the pupunha palm appear, however, to be old and well-established crops. The *Cubeo* eagerly adopt any crops that will grow in their soil.

The periodic exhaustion of the soil by manioc produces a seminomadic tribal life. But mobility is limited not only by tribal boundaries but by the necessity of maintaining contact with the gardens nearing exhaustion. To avoid abrupt transitions, the Indians select a new site not too far from the old one and begin to plant it many months before moving. They continue to harvest the abandoned gardens until the entire new crop has reached maturity 8 months to a year later. Abandoned fields are reputedly not replanted, although their owners may continue to harvest the fruit trees for a considerable time. Presumably according to its quality, the soil is exhausted in 3 to 5 years.

Work habits in manioc processing.—The processing of manioc from garden to table normally occupies approximately 75 percent of a woman's working time and, when chicha is being prepared for a drinking festival, all of it. The process follows a very regular rhythm, compared with the more sporadic hunting and fishing pattern of men.

Cubeo women adhere to an alternate work-day cycle. One-half day, starting from sunrise or from shortly after dawn, is spent in the manioc garden, harvesting, clearing, replanting; part of the afternoon is devoted to preparing part of the manioc. The following day is spent entirely at home, when the remaining tubers are processed.

Wild food collecting.—Fullest use of wild foods is made by all tribes in the area. Women gather various kinds of edible ants, grubs, berries, and roots. Wild food gathering is not a regular activity; it is undertaken sporadically, either to make up deficiencies in the fish and game diet, or for variety. The known ripening of fruits and berries is almost invariably an occasion for a gathering expedition.

Hunting.—With some minor exceptions, all tribes in the area hunt, usually selecting the short dry season when animals congregate around the main streams. They take virtually all animals that are not beasts of prey:

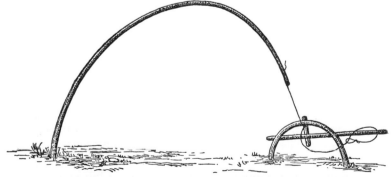

FIGURE 107.—Spring-pole trap, Curicuriarí River. (Redrawn from Koch-Grünberg, 1923 b, p. 135.)

peccaries, tapirs, paca, deer, caimans, monkeys, birds, armadillos, and
agoutis. Where the muzzle-loading shotgun has been introduced, it is the
basic hunting weapon. Formerly, and to a considerable extent today, the
Indians used the lance, blowgun, bow and arrow, snare and fall traps.
(See figs. 107, 108, 109.) Hunting techniques vary with the animal to

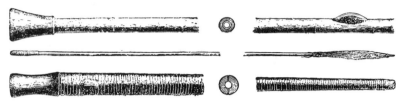

FIGURE 108.—Northwest Amazon blowguns. *Top:* Blowgun (showing cross section)
and dart, Içana-Aiarí region. *Bottom:* Blowgun of the Yapurá region. (After
Koch-Grünberg, 1923 b.)

be hunted. The peccary is usually hunted by a group of men, the paca
is hunted at night with flares, and the tapir, shortly before sunset at a
salt lick. On extended hunts, women accompany the men and maintain

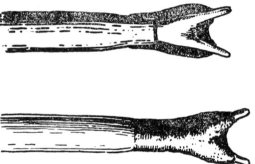

FIGURE 109.—Poisoned arrow point of the *Guariua,* northwest Amazon. Yapurá River
region. Cross section below (actual size). (After Koch-Grünberg, 1906 a.)

camp. Compared with farming and fishing, hunting is a minor activity
and was probably even less important before the gun was introduced.

Fishing.—Everywhere in the area, fishing is a man's chief industry
and the main source of protein. Although all men may fish daily, the
tempo of fishing is seasonal. Its height comes during the dry season, when
fish founder in the drying streams, and at the beginning of the rainy season,
when the fish again ascend the streams. Periods of high water are, on
the whole, seasons of protein deficiency.

The fishing techniques chiefly used are: steel hooks and lines; bows and
arrows; three- or four-pronged spears; weirs set with basket traps; hand
nets (pl. 101, *center*); and poison. The hook and line are often suspended
from boughs overhanging the river's edge and inspected from time to time,
or else dangled from a pole placed alongside the fisherman in his canoe.

Children fish from the river bank. Worms and berries are the usual bait. The bow and long arrow are most suitable in shallow water, especially during the dry season. The arrow, consisting of a reed shaft 5 feet (1.5 m.) long, into which has been set an 18-inch (0.5 m.) hardwood stem with a barbed bone point, is aimed with the point just above the water level and rather close to the fish. For flare-light fishing at night, the pronged spear is used. In almost all small streams and rapids conical basket traps of varying sizes are set, either in a lattice-work weir (pl. 89, *top*) or in rock crevices at rapids. Some basket traps are as much as 3 feet (1 m.) in diameter and about 5 feet (1.5 m.) long. Shallow streams and ponds are saturated with a variety of fish poisons and drugs and the stupefied fish shot with arrows or scooped up with hand nets or with the bare hands. The varieties of fish in the upper Amazon are considerable. A list of nearly 100 edible types was obtained from the *Cubeo*. The most popular variety, however, is the guaracu, known in *Tucano* as boríkakü.

Domesticated animals.—Dogs are universal in the region, and are trained as hunters or as watch dogs, or else are simply kept as pets. Among many of the tribes almost any animal susceptible to taming is eagerly sought. Among the common household pets are monkeys, dogs, chickens, parrots, lemurs, agoutis, toucans, cats, pigs, and ducks. No animals are domesticated for home consumption. Chickens are sold to Whites but rarely eaten by the natives. Dogs are well cared for, being frequently provided with a sleeping platform in the house to protect them from chiggers.

Food preparation.—Manioc is eaten as a flat circular bread, about 2½ feet (0.7 m.) in diameter, that is prepared fresh daily. Although the highly volatile prussic acid in the bitter manioc is readily removed by boiling, by soaking in water, or by desiccation, most tribes practice a highly complex process which simultaneously extracts not only the prussic acid but the starch, which is consumed separately. From the garden, manioc tubers are taken to the river and washed. They are then carried to the house, where the woman peels, grates, pounds, presses, and sifts the manioc until, only slightly moist, it is spread in a flat open oven and roasted into a bread. The process is lengthy and, to a large extent, arduous.

The manioc skin is stripped off, either with a knife or with the teeth, and then grated on a board set with stones. Sitting with her feet stretched straight out and with the board resting on her legs, one end braced against a house post and the other resting against her abdomen, the woman takes up two roots, one in each hand, and scrapes (pls. 89, *bottom*; 90, *bottom*) with alternate arm movements, putting most pressure on the forward stroke. The action is vigorous, involving not only full arm movements but the entire torso. The resulting mash, which piles up at the far end of the board, is next pounded through a shallow, tightly woven basket set on a tripod. Pounding with her fists, the woman drives the liquid starch through the "sieve" and prepares the thickened mash for the long tipití or squeezer (pl. 90, *top*). It emerges almost completely dry from the tipití and, after passing again through a coarse sieve, is ready for the oven. The starch, which has been collected in pottery bowls, is permitted to dry and lose its prussic acid. To facilitate desiccation, ashes are strewn upon the first hardened film.

Farinha is prepared in a similar way, though with minor modifications. The peeled tubers are soaked in water for 3 days, all liquid is removed by squeezing them in the tipití, and the meal is strewn on the stove and stirred with a paddle until completely dry (pl. 90, *center*). If kept well wrapped and off the ground, farinha lasts almost indefinitely. The perpetual manioc harvest, however, does not require storage, so that farinha is prepared only as an emergency ration for journeys or for trade.

Manioc starch boiled with bananas, pineapples, or berries is taken as the first meal of the day.

Fish are usually stewed or boiled with chili peppers, but may also be wrapped in leaves and roasted in hot ashes, barbecued, or smoked. Smoking preserves properly dried fish for about a week. Boiled fish are frequently mixed with powdered chili peppers and pounded into a paste that is spread on manioc bread. Fish are never eaten unless well seasoned. Game is similarly prepared.

VILLAGES AND HOUSES

The large multifamily house is the basic type in the area. A single house frequently comprises the settlement, although it is not uncommon to find one large house and a number of small single-family dwellings at the same site. Settlements are relatively small, having from 20 to a little over 100 persons. On the Vaupés River a single settlement may be occupied by a particular sib. A settlement is abandoned when the house is in poor condition, the soil exhausted, or the chief or headman dies. A well-constructed house may, with proper repairs, last from 3 to 5 years, the average period required to exhaust the soil. Among the *Cubeo*, at the death of the headman—the "owner of the house"—the house is abandoned, the new headman building a new one within convenient distance of the manioc plantations. Besides availability of food and water and safety from floods during the rainy season, social relations of the tribe and defense devices influence choice of house sites. Vaupés River tribes rely for protection on deep trenches set with poles surrounding the settlement. Settlements here are almost invariably upon high banks of streams. Groups hostile to the Whites prefer the smaller, more remote streams.

Houses with both circular and rectangular floor plans occur in the area. (See pls. 91, 92, 93.) Among most tribes of the lower Apáporis River, a conical roof and circular floor plan prevail (pl. 91, *bottom*);

elsewhere, a rectangular floor plan with a roof of two or four eaves is used. The rectangular, sharp-gabled multifamily dwellings most common in the northern section of the area are equally large, often measuring as

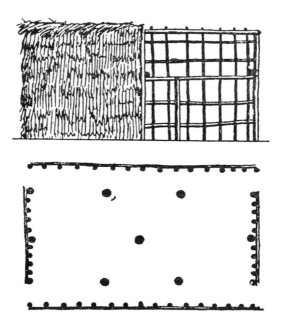

FIGURE 110.—*Cumaca* hut. End, side, and ground plan views. (After Stradelli, 1889.)

much as 50 by 70 feet (15 m. by 21 m.) and about 30 feet (9 m.) high, and accommodating as many as 12 families. Smaller houses in the area are usually square, with four-sided thatched roofs. Among the *Tuyuca,* Koch-Grünberg reported multifamily houses with the rear semicircular in shape, a form observed by Wallace on the Vaupés, but now extinct. A variety of temporary shelters are known, the most frequent type, which can be built in a few minutes, consisting of a narrow, arched, palm-leaf roof set across a pole fastened between two trees.

On the Vaupés River, multifamily houses are designed with a wide central corridor, the dance floor, flanked by narrower aisles, which serve as sleeping quarters. The front, kept free of kitchen utensils, is the reception quarter for guests and the burial ground for house members. Manioc is prepared toward the rear, which is usually known as women's quarters. Many houses have atticlike structures built over the sleeping quarters and used for storing ceremonial paraphernalia and hunting and fishing tools. Small objects, such as fishhooks and arrows, are thrust into the thatch of the sloping roof. Among the *Cubeo*, the headman prefers a central section extending across either side of the house as living quarters for himself and family, but earlier evidence suggests that during the period when houses with the semicircular rear were fashionable, the headman lived in the back portion. The *Cubeo* regard the headman as the house owner, and his wife or wives are responsible for keeping it clean. The small clearing at the front of the house has special significance as the place where dances are prepared, and is always kept very clean. Houses with a rectangular floor plan always have a front and rear door that are swung up and propped up with a pole and one or more small side exits facing away from the river to permit rapid escape.

Single-family residences follow a variety of constructional plans (fig. 110), but are most often square, with four-sided roofs.

Largely because of the spasmodic character of work in the area, the construction of a multifamily dwelling may be prolonged for the better part of a year. Accessibility of building materials, particularly palm leaves for thatching, also affects the construction time. Among the *Cubeo*, and presumably elsewhere, house building is the collective enterprise of the men directed by the local chieftain, referred to as "owner of the house." The headman provides the 3 pairs of central posts, is responsible for drafting the floor plan, and assigns the work. Nonparticipants in the building, it is assumed, will leave the group. Stability of the structure depends greatly upon the accuracy with which the floor plan is laid out. Right angles are estimated, and, as a rule, rather accurately, but distances are carefully measured with special poles. Three pairs of central posts about 6 inches (15 cm.) in diameter, placed about 13 feet (4 m.) apart form the structural skeleton. Cross beams are lashed to each pair, and shorter posts set upon each cross beam to form an inverted **T** support the roof ridge poles. A secondary set of shorter upright posts, set parallel to the central posts, about 13 feet (4 m.) apart, and connected by transverse poles, are then added to support the series of sloping roof poles. The entire structure is secured by temporary lashings of palm-bark fiber; when the framework is complete, a permanent set of lashings is introduced. As an indication of the quantity of material employed in constructing a multi-family dwelling may be mentioned (pl. 91, *center*) six heavy central posts, 10 secondary shorter and lighter posts, 72 roof poles, 76 transverse connecting poles, and 560 bundles of thatching material. About 5 bundles of thatch can be transported in a large canoe. Roofing proceeds from the bottom upward, and, as soon as one side is roofed over, it is immediately occupied. All salvageable material from the preceding house is utilized in the new construction.

Household equipment is relatively meager (pl. 93, *bottom*), the possessions of each family being easily portable. Heavy equipment, owned usually by the headman, consists of a number of large pottery and wooden chicha containers, a flat manioc oven, a sugarcane press, and two long, low guest benches. Each individual family also owns its hammocks, a small collection of cooking pots, water gourds, baskets, trays, manioc presses, manioc grating boards, typical hourglass pot supports, and one or two low stools.

ENGINEERING WORKS

In addition to defensive moats, now going out of fashion since the introduction of the gun and the gradual suppression of warfare, engineering works are limited to narrow time-worn paths, and the occasional bridging of a stream with a convenient tree trunk. Log staircases with handrails are sometimes erected at particularly steep banks leading to the house, and a number of logs may be laid along a swampy approach.

DRESS AND ORNAMENTS

Nakedness among women was apparently universal before White contact, but some pubic covering for men has always been reported. Among the *Carib*, a wide bark-cloth girdle enveloping the body from hip to breast is worn by the men (pl. 104, *bottom, right*), but elsewhere a narrow breechclout of bark or cloth is the conventional attire. Elaborate multicolored feather headdresses of a type similar to that found among coastal *Arawak* are characteristic of the area, and are worn only on ceremonial occasions. Elaborate tapirage is found in the western part of the area. The highly-prized man's dancing costume consists of a woven palm crown set with heron, toucan, and parokeet feathers (pl. 99, *bottom, left*), and with a short thick tail of braided monkey hair appended behind; a necklace of jaguar teeth; a belt of vertebrae; and feathered anklets and wristlets. Heron down is frequently used as a headdress, and is pasted to the body in some pattern. White quartz cylinders, which are very highly prized, are worn about the neck. Men wear woven ligatures just below the knee, and children, both below the knee and above the ankle to make the calf swell (pl. 103, *right*).

Body painting is widely practiced by both sexes, elaborate designs being produced by a roller dye. Women paint the under surface of the jaw and the throat with genipa to achieve a curious sculptured effect for ceremonial occasions, and smear the face with red pigment to ward off danger on working days. Although the back is crudely splattered with genipa (pl. 89, *bottom*), care is taken with painted designs on the legs, thighs, breast, and face. Among the *Cubeo*, individual painted designs for the face have been noted. Geometric designs with frequent use of cross-hatching are most common.

TRANSPORTATION

Canoe transportation is basic throughout the area, but, on short hauls, women carry manioc in large woven baskets. All canoes are hollow-log dugouts prepared by either hacking or charring and widening by dry heat (pl. 94, *top*). Canoe sizes found in any particular settlement vary from the small one-man fishing canoe to the large half-ton type. Paddle shapes are distinctive, the broad elliptical blade being common on the Vaupés River and Rio Negro, and the narrow elliptical blade on the Apáporis River. The crutch handle is, however, universal in the area.

MANUFACTURES

Domestic utensils are manufactured by women among the *Witoto,* but on the Vaupés, Negro, and Içana Rivers men make all the household utensils except pottery.

Pottery.—Vaupés River pottery is rarely decorated. It is prepared by the reduction method, i. e., in a covered fire, and is unglazed. Pebble polishing gives a shiny surface. The black ware is most common in the region. Women mold huge pottery chicha containers, which the men subsequently envelope with an openwork basketry wrapper. Fine ash is a common temper. Pottery from other Northwest Amazon regions is often decorated by painting (figs. 111, 112).

FIGURE 111.—*Baniva* pottery. (Redrawn from Koch-Grünberg, 1923 b.)

Calabashes.—Drinking dishes are made from calabashes, the inner surfaces of which are lacquered with black made by applying urine-soaked manioc leaves to them. Frequently geometric patterns are incised on the outer wall (fig. 113).

a

b

c

d

e   f   J. Anglim

FIGURE 112.—Northwest Amazon pottery types. *a, Desana; b, Tucano; c–f,* Içana River *Arawak.* (Redrawn from Koch-Grünberg, 1909–10.)

Manioc graters.—The stone-set manioc grater, a valuable trade object, is not universally distributed in the area. The more remote groups use a flat stone as a grater; *Arawakan* and *Tukanoan* tribes employ elaborate graters set with quartz embedded in a pitch matrix and arranged in a formalized pattern. The best graters are reputedly made by *Arawakan* women of the Içana River and are traded as far as the Tiquié and Yapura Rivers.

Basketry.—Most basketry in the area is woven, with checkered, twilled, and hexagonal techniques most frequently, but some baskets are twined (pl. 95). Decorative geometrical patterns, produced by twilling with two contrasting colors of warp and weft strands, are most highly developed among the *Arawak* and are either completely absent or reduced to a minimum among the *Cubeo*. Twilled work is employed for shallow serving trays, manioc-flour sifters, and the tipití or manioc press. Large carrying and storage baskets, in which weight saving is desirable, are made with an open hexagonal weave or a loose checkered technique. Small containers for drying hot chili peppers are made of parallel rows of splints bent to form an oblong tube with a narrow opening; the splints are lattice twined, with a maximum of four or five rows of more flexible wefts. Other types of small ovoid containers are similarly made. Manioc carrying baskets, about 20 inches (0.5 m.) tall and of an almost equal diameter, are of checkerwork with straight walls, four-cornered bases, and circular rims, or are twined. Basket rims are rigid, the warps being finished over a circular frame.

Bark cloth.—Bark cloth is widely used in the preparation of ceremonial masks, pouches, breechclouts, and aprons (pl. 94, *bottom*). For masks, white bark cloth is preferred, the darker or reddish type being used for more ordinary purposes. The bark is removed from the tree by chopping the narrow trunk into suitable lengths and then pounding until it is loosened sufficiently to be slipped off. The bark cloth is then paddled until properly stretched. Bark-cloth masks are known only to the *Arawak* and *Tucano* of the area and are not reported among either *Witoto* or the western *Carib* groups.

Weaving and cordage.—Weaving is apparently unknown to the *Tucanoan* groups, but the *Carib* and *Arawak* who use looms weave tight hammocks (pl. 101, *right, center,* and *right, bottom*). A variety of palm-leaf fibers are rolled on the thigh to make fishing lines or are braided into heavy ropes by all the tribes in this region. True textiles are apparently rare, although knitted ligatures, woven hammocks, and knitted wallets are reported to be common among the *Yahuna*. A simple loom, undoubtedly of European origin, is found among the *Tucano, Desána, Tariana,* and *Arawak* of the Içana and Aiarí Rivers, but not among the tribes of the Tiquié and upper Vaupés Rivers. Cotton is unknown anywhere on the Içana or Vaupés Rivers. The characteristic hammock (pl. 101, *right, top*) on the Vaupés River is made of heavy twisted tucuma fiber bound in widely spaced parallel roles with lattice twining at broad intervals. Balls of fiber for hammocks are an important trade item.

SOCIAL AND POLITICAL ORGANIZATION

In the absence of adequate field studies of most tribes no comprehensive areal account of social and olitical organization can yet be given. Investigations by the present author in 1940 among the *Cubeo* of the Cuduiarí River disclosed a social organization based upon patrilineal sibs. Whether careful study of the *Cariban-* and *Arawakan-*speaking peoples of the region would also uncover sib organizations is, of course, uncertain. But, in the light of the *Cubeo* data, the conclusions of Wallace (1853), Koch-Grünberg (1909–10), and Kirchhoff (1931) that sibs do not exist in the area cannot be taken as final. The accounts of Wallace and of Koch-Grünberg on social organization appear to be contradictory: the former reported marriage with blood relatives; the latter asserted that marriage was always outside the tribe. Kirchhoff, attempted to explain this apparent contradiction by attributing "tribal exogamy" to the *Tucano* and marriage with blood relatives to the *Arawak,* but overlooked the possibility that cross-cousin marriage accompanied by sib exogamy avoids the contradiction entirely. His classification of the northwest Brazil area as a region of gross-familien, that is, bilaterally extended families, in this case with patrilocal residence, is contrary to the evidence for the *Tucanoan-Cubeo,* whose social organization has been studied more intensively than that of any other group in the area. The intimate relations between the *Tucanoans* of the Vaupés River and the *Arawakans* of the Içana River and the virtual identity of almost all described traits suggest a parallel social organization among both groups as not at all improbable.

The patrilineal sib among the *Cubeo* is basically a local group, all its male members and their wives inhabiting one or more multifamily houses, each divided into 8, 10, or 12 "apartments." Some large *Cubeo* sibs occupy as many as five such houses, all closely adjoining. In some regions, sib members have individual houses, but these are grouped together. In a few cases, particularly after a serious quarrel, individual families may move some distance away from the sib site, but they never lose membership in the sib nor relinquish sib obligations. *Cubeo* sibs are further grouped into three unnamed exogamous phratries, each occupying a more or less continuous territory, so that in some cases marriage would be with someone at a considerable distance. Thus all sibs on the Cuduiarí River, except for one at its source, constitute a single exogamic unit, and members of these groups choose their wives from among *Cubeo* sibs on the Vaupés River or on the Querarí River. It is presumably this necessity of choosing a wife from a geographically distant branch of the tribe that has given rise to the mistaken impression of tribal exogamy. This phratric system introduces a number of difficult problems of sexual adjustment in view of the broad compass of incest restrictions. While marriage within the phratry is never tolerated, discreetly conducted sexual affairs that are not intrasib are frequently overlooked.

A lengthy *Cubeo* origin myth narrated by the elders at all phratric gatherings formulates the historical background for the sib and phratric arrangement: The first people emerged from three different sites along the lower Vaupés River, thus accounting for the tripartite grouping. These first ancestors emerged in the form of anacondas from the rocks forming the river rapids. As each pair of anacondas shed their skins, they became brother and sister and sought others in marriage. The off-spring of each of the males formed the present sibs. Of course, brother and sister, as well as people emerging from the same site, were forbidden to marry. The first male to emerge, the ancestor of the first ranking sib, named all of the succeeding sibs of his phratry. The names of the sibs describe some characteristic trait, e. g., "Fat people," "Cassava grater people," "Jaguar children people," "Scabby people," "Wasp people," etc. The ancestor of each sib gave the first sets of personal names to his off-spring, many of them being names of birds, animals, and fish. Each sib thus has its own set of names, and no sib member may eat the bird, animal, or fish represented among the list of names of his sib. This taboo is no longer in force. When the population of the sibs had grown, the groups moved up the Vaupés River, and its tributaries, and settled among their present sites. Subsequently, certain readjustments in the composition of the phratries took place. Sibs of different exogamic groups decided to establish a firm friendship by forbidding intermarriage between them and by settling in adjacent sites. Another sib reputedly split to form two sibs, now very closely related. Another that, according to tradition, had come from the Papury River to the Cuduiarí River was admitted to the exogmic group of that river and friendship sealed by forbidding intermar-riage. Koch-Grünberg has stated that one of the "subtribes" of the upper Cuduiarí River was formerly an *Arawakan*-speaking group of the *Baniva* tribe that had become affiliated with the *Cubeo*. He adds that most of the *Cubeo* of the Querarí River were of *Arawak* descent. Unfortunately, he offers no concrete evidence to substantiate the claim. But it does suggest the interesting possibility that the phratric structure of the *Cubeo* may have resulted from a persistent series of intermarriages with other tribes, a possibility enhanced by the absence of reported phratries from the area. As will be seen subsequently, *Cubeo* marriage practices are not incon-sistent with this possibility.

The sib house is composed of a group of brothers, their wives and children. Each individual family occupies its own hearth, prepares its own food; each woman cultivates her own manioc garden. Though pro-duction is based almost exclusively upon the small family, food must be shared within the sib house. Though a man may leave the sib house with his wife and children and set up an independent household, he never re-linquishes his sib affiliations. He continues to bring his portion of manioc chicha to the sib drinking party, chooses his children's names from the sib genealogies, and may at any time resume his rights to sib-owned fishing sites and to a manioc garden. From birth to death, an individual remains a member of the same sib. Property inheritance is from father to son.

Political authority is nowhere very strong. There is no phratric chief. At present, the Colombian authorities are attempting to set up certain Indians as phratric chiefs but with little success. Within the house, the "house owner" has a certain limited authority. He is the man who has first set up main house posts, and those who desire to live in the great house with him assist in building it, their willingness to cooperate being a sign of confidence in the builder. He is the host at drinking parties, the first to welcome guests, and to assign them a portion of the manioc garden if they are going to stay long. His wife or wives are responsible for the cleanliness of the house. He must be the leader of the ceremonies. A war chief is selected as the occasion demands. At the death of the house owner, the house is abandoned. With few exceptions, he is an elderly but vigorous man.

The relationship system stresses sib conditions, residence, and the varying functional degrees of relationship with other sibs, both within and outside of the phratry. In the first ascending generation father, father's real brothers, and all men of the sib of father's generation are referred to by the same term, though they are distinguished in terms of address. Similarly, mother and mother's sisters are equated. Mother's brother and father's sister are called father-in-law and mother-in-law respectively. In one's own generation, cross-cousins call one another "my in-law," a term also meaning sweetheart, but once a cross-cousin has married, he or she is addressed by a more distant term. Parallel cousins are differentiated on the basis of actual sib affiliation, so that father's brother's children are equated with own siblings, but mother's sister's children—unless they should be the same as father's brother's children—fall into another category, that might be called a phratric category. The terms for brother-in-law and sister-in-law depend upon whether the marriage has been legalized by the payment of a bride price or by brother-sister exchange. The term for wife means "my children's mother," but before children are born she is addressed simply by the expression, "listen." After the first child she may be addressed as "child's mother." Children are addressed by their age classification, as baby, grown person, etc., but terms of reference distinguish between lineal descendants and the collateral lines.

Kinship terminology between sibs of the same phratry is based upon actual degrees of friendship, propinquity, and tradition. In closely related sibs, one calls men of his father's generation by the term for father and applies the term for parallel-cousin not of his sib to his own generation level. Where friendship between two sibs is not marked, they call one another simply "relative" or, in other cases, "distant relative." The *Cubeo* refer to all sibs of the same phratry as "the same people," but the affinal sibs are referred to as "her people."

Phratric unity is maintained by ceremonial bonds, by a common origin tale, and by propinquity. The sibs come together at drinking parties to recite the phratric origin saga; they share the secret men's initiation rites. At the latter ceremony, the first phratric ancestors, represented by four sets of flutes called the Ancients, appear in the house. The boys are whipped to the sound of these flutes, after which the men of the phratry take turns in whipping one another. The purpose of the ceremony is to make the boys grow to the reputed size of the Ancestors. Horns representing the Ancestors may not be seen by the women, who flee the house at the first sound as the men bearing them come up the river. In the ceremony of naming a child, the name is sib property but the recitative chanted over the infant by the oldest male of the sib, a grandfather, is the common property of the phratry. The elaborate mourning rites, in which masked dancers representing all the Beings of the universe appear, is also a phratric function. Theories about life after death also reflect the phratric-sib organization. The spirits of the dead are thought to live in the sib house at a site near the villages, but all the sibs of the phratry have houses at the same site, so that there is actually a phratric village of the dead.

Cross-cousin marriage is preferred, and wherever possible brother-sister exchange. Although a bride price is acceptable in lieu of an exchange, it is regarded as undesirable, because it does not make for marital stability. The bride price is never refunded. A study of marriage records shows decided preference for taking a wife from the mother's sib. This is because the men are reluctant to visit an in-law sib in which they have no blood relatives for fear of a hostile reception. An analysis of 40 marriages of one sib shows that 75 percent of the marriages were with other *Cubeo* Indians, that an additional 25 percent were with such closely related *Tucanoan*-speaking peoples as the *Yuriti* and *Guanana*. This was because one of the sibs that reputedly entered the phratry later had had very close ties with these tribes and had taken all their wives from them. But of the marriages within the *Cubeo* tribe, more than one-third of the wives were taken from the mother's sib. This created a particularly close tie between two intermarrying sibs.

ETIQUETTE

Eating, and the reception of guests are subject to the most formalized procedure. Among the *Cubeo*, for whom the most detailed account of social relations is available, the sexes eat separately, the men in a group eating first, after which the women eat what is left. Most meals are of a communal nature. Each woman, having prepared food at her own hearth, brings her offering to the center of the house floor, along with a tray of manioc bread. The men and the young boys gather in a circle and each eats something from each service. The *Cubeo* eat slowly and rarely to repletion. Gorging oneself is definitely in bad taste, particularly as a portion must be left for the women. Courtesy also requires that before the men have finished eating, they pass out among the women small preliminary portions of food, such as meat or fish on small pieces of manioc bread. Sharing food, even when it consists only of a few small sardines, is, though not obligatory, regarded as an essential of proper social behavior. On the other hand, no open criticism is ever voiced of less cooperative individuals. Censure of individuals and invidious comparisons are as a rule avoided, except in cases of extreme breaches of conduct.

The reception of guests is extremely formal at all times, and during ceremonies becomes virtually a ritual. A visitor arriving at a house stands in the doorway until greeted. He takes a few steps within the house and greets each person by the appropriate kinship designation, each occupant replying "You have come, my in-law," etc., depending upon the relationship. A stool is placed near the door for the visitor, while each woman in the house sets out an offering of chili pepper sauce and some manioc at the center of the house. The visitor eats sparingly of each of the offerings and retires to his stool, where he is served a calabash of chicha. When guests are received at a drinking party or at any ceremony, the men visitors form a line outside while the men of the house form a similar line inside; then each guest is greeted with a lengthy harangue, explaining why he had been invited, and the guest replies at length, explaining how pleased he is to come. While addressing a stranger, the gaze is averted, as only a close relative may be looked in the eye. Women are received by the women of the house by way of the rear door, if the reception is formal. A serious breach of etiquette is for a man to enter a house through the rear door. Should this occur accidentally, the visitor is ignored until he notices his faux pas and appears at the proper door.

ECONOMIC ORGANIZATION

The only detailed account of economic organization from this area is for the *Cubeo*. Among these people, property attitudes are dominated by sib considerations. Each sib lays claim, primarily on the strength of the sib tradition of the wanderings of its ancestors, to a definite sib territory, the most important boundaries of which are river frontages. Uncultivated jungle is not claimed as territory. River frontages, traditionally determined, are usually delimited by creeks, and all fishing rights in the sector are jealously guarded, though navigation rights are free. Where weirs are employed along a river occupied by a number of sibs, a definite protocol is maintained regulating the times when the weir may be closed and when it must be kept open. Serious conflict over infringements of river rights are not common. Petroglyphs at rocky sites are stated to be the creation of sib ancestors and are cited as territorial validation. These petroglyphs are renewed from time to time. Travelers must receive permission from the headman to fish on the territory of another sib. Hospitality regulations require that visitors be fed; but guests staying for any length of time are permitted to fish, and their women allowed a section of manioc garden to harvest.

Territory is divided among the adult sib members by agreement of the headman and the informal male council. Individual family ownership comes into play after some labor has been put into the development of a site, planted manioc gardens or prepared clearings becoming the property of the individual family that did the work. Each family can add to its grounds by cutting the clearing deeper into the forest. Older men get preference in the choice of sites for weirs, but each man uses, though he does not own, his preferred spot for fishing by other techniques, but the sib river frontage is never subdivided.

Title to the sib house resides with the headman, called literally "owner of the house." Each male sib member establishes his residence rights by contributing toward its construction. Ownership of a house means that if the headman dies or leaves the house it will be abandoned because no one may occupy that which he does not own. The same principle applies to garden land. Should the cultivator of a garden die, the plot is abandoned and allowed to grow over. But some sib member, a brother or son, inherits both the weir and the site on the river.

Much household and fishing equipment, though individually owned, is shared within the sib, particularly objects that are difficult to make, such as large canoes, sugarcane presses, chicha troughs and jugs, fish nets, and weir screens. As a rule, the headman, assisted by the other men, makes the equipment listed above; it is then spoken of as his property, but may be freely used by any sib member. The one or two manioc ovens in the house serve the entire household. All other objects, such as pots, small fishing canoes, and other hunting and fishing equipment, are individually made and owned, but are freely shared.

Wealth differences are rather insignificant—a rich man is one who has a complete dancing outfit of feathers, quartz cylinder, necklace, and jaguar-tooth belt. Such an outfit, acquired patiently over a long period of time, is very highly valued and suffices as a bride payment. No social distinction, however, accrues to its owner, who is obligated to share his dancing regalia with his poorer sibsmen. Since there is equal access to the means of production for everyone, wealth differentiation arises only from differences in skill and enterprise. Under modern conditions, the harder working men and women acquire a greater share of White trade goods.

On the whole, the *Cubeo* show relatively little attachment to their possessions. Loss of property through theft or otherwise is never viewed with alarm. Often a canoe that has drifted from its moorings is not even sought, the Indians taking it for granted that eventually someone will find and return it.

The sexual division of labor gives women a vital economic role. As producers of manioc, they furnish the basic food supply, the chicha essential for ceremonies, and the highly desired machetes, cloth, matches, ammunition, etc., obtained from the Whites in farinha trading. *Cubeo* women are the potters; men make all the other household implements, such as the hammocks, stools, baskets, and manioc presses.

The basic supply of cultivated food is individually produced, each woman working in her own garden and preparing her own manioc bread or farinha. Fish and game are taken either individually or collectively, depending primarily upon circumstances (see p. 785), but, regardless of the method of food production, the final product is generally shared within the sib. Each woman, cooking over her own hearth in her own pots, prepares the fish or meat her husband has brought in. When the food is ready, each woman sets her pot and tray of manioc in the center of the house, and all the men gather about, each eating some from each woman's pot. If only one man has brought in fish and game, that is also shared. There are times when an entire household will feast on a few sardines stewed with chili peppers—the contribution of one family.

The patterns of food sharing appear to present two difficult problems: hoarding and shirking. There are some persons who, during periods of food shortage, do not share; husband, wife, and children eat in their own "apartment" not looking up, and ignored by the others. No punishment has been devised for such people. Similarly, equal license is allowed the shirkers. But as hostility toward such people inevitably increases, they eventually leave the house and go visiting. Ultimately, it is said, they become such nuisances that someone poisons them.

WARFARE

Wars are waged for revenge and to capture women and children as slaves. Trespass by a distant group or tribe usually precipitates hostilities that continue for generations. Except on the larger streams close to White settlements, wars are frequent even today, though they are rarely very bloody. War parties seem, as a rule, to be small. They are led either by the local headman or by a specially designated war leader. A surprise night attack is the chief tactical weapon and fighting is hand to hand, with heavy war clubs favored over bows and arrows. Dead enemies are eaten at a dance celebrating the victory. The penis and scrotum are cut off, smoked until dry, and worn by a dancing warrior over his own genitals. At the conclusion of the dance, the *Cubeo* warrior's wife eats the penis to become fertile. Men prefer the loins, although arms and ribs are also eaten.

LIFE CYCLE

Birth.—Parturition occurs in the woman's manioc garden, never in the house. In her first delivery, a woman is aided by her mother-in-law and by the other elderly women of the sib. After the first child, she is unassisted; alone, she either cuts or bites off the umbilical cord.

When the expectant mother announces that she is going to the garden to deliver a child, her husband begins the couvade observances that last 5 days. He spends most of his time in the house, scrupulously careful to avoid doing anything that would bring harm to the child. It is believed, for example, that should the father stumble, the infant would also fall. Should he drop something, it would be equivalent to dropping the child. He eats nothing but stale manioc and takes some water. He does not simulate labor pains.

The child is brought home immediately after birth, bathed in warm water, painted with genipa to ward off harm and, a day later, is covered with red spots to make it resemble the jaguar, who will thus spare its life. The woman joins the husband in the couvade. Both submit to the same food taboos, do no work, and avoid accidents. It is stated that the monsters of the earth, angered at the birth of a human child, seek to destroy it and its parents. More dangerous are the river monsters, among them a huge anaconda who lashes the water like thunder. To overcome the anaconda, an old man courageously goes to the river and blows tobacco smoke across the water, thus forming a protective sheath through which the anaconda cannot penetrate. But if the parents go near the river, they are certain to be killed by some water monster.

At the conclusion of the period of couvade, the headman of the sib or some other old man must charm all the fish and game so they would cause no harm to the child. For example, he says to a spiny fish, "You spiny fish, let no spines lodge in the throat of our little one."

At the age of about 6 months, "when it is old enough to know what is going on," the child is given a name from the genealogy of the sib. The "grandfather" holds the child in his lap and chants a recitative referring to the first ancestors of the sib. In one hand he holds a small calabash of milk drawn from the breast of the father's sister. At the conclusion of the chant, he dips his index finger into the milk and touches it to the breast of the child to make it grow. He then asks the child, "What is your name?" and its father replies for it. Then the old man touches the child on the bridge of the nose, whence the soul escapes at death, so that the child's soul might not be imprisoned. A literal translation of the chant recited by the *Cubeo* is as follows:

> Milk of our soil
> That the little ones may grow
> That we may see them grow
> Milk of the calabash he drank.

A child was being born to the "great fat one"
A little child—etc.

Puberty.—No important puberty practices for girls seem to be prevalent. At their first menses, girls remain in the house for 10 days, use the
scratching stick, and paint their faces red. Among the *Cubeo,* an old man
deflowers the girl with his finger and announces that she is now a woman.
It is then declared that she had been deflowered by the moon, which was
responsible for the onset of menstruation. Food taboos are enjoined at
this time.

The cult of the Ancestors or Ancients comes closest to puberty rites
for boys, but initiation begins well before the onset of physiological
puberty. In the dry season, when *Inga* berries are ripe, the elders take
all the young boys (from about the age of 6 to postpuberty) on a berry-
picking expedition, during which they show them the secret hiding place
on the river bank of the sacred Ancestor horns. Each sib has its own
set of three or four pairs of horns, the large ones like trumpets made
of wound bark and the smaller ones flageolets. Each pair of horns bears
the name of one of the sibs' ancestors and is believed actually to represent
the Ancestor. The women, who are forbidden under pain of death to
see the horns, are led to believe, when the horns have been sounded, that
the Ancients have come to visit the sib.

After the horns are uncovered and shown for the first time to many
of the boys, everyone bathes to the music of the Ancients and, toward
dusk, returns to the settlement. As the horns come into earshot, the
women run to their manioc gardens, and the men take over the house.

The essential feature of the ceremony inside the house is the whipping
of the boys and all the men. The child steps to the center of the dance
floor, his hand raised high above his head, and is whipped three times,
once across the back, the abdomen, and the back of the knees. The strokes
are hard and meant to draw blood. This is "to make the child grow."
No concern is shown if the child cries out, but fortitude is greatly admired.
After the children have been whipped, the men take turns in lashing one
another to exhibit their endurance.

When the whipping is concluded, the horns are withdrawn from the
house and the women called back. In a well-darkened house, the women,
seated with averted faces, are also whipped to the accompaniment of the
singing of the Ancients, whom they cannot see.

This is actually a sib cult rather than a puberty rite, but its purpose of
making the young males grow and the adults strong is analogous to that
of "rites de passage." All adults past the age of puberty are expected to
bathe with the Ancestors every morning before dawn to get strength.
(See also p. 795.)

Death and mourning.—Death resulting from illness is always attributed to sorcery, hence the immediate response to a person's dying is

grief mixed with fear and anger at the malevolent sorcerer.   Before burial, all members of the household and all other sib and phratric relatives who can come quickly enough gather about the hammock in which the deceased is laid and each delivers a funeral oration which follows a formal pattern.   First he announces his relationship to the deceased and narrates some incident to illustrate the relationship, then he expresses anxiety that the wicked person who had killed a sib member would probably try to kill others, and finally he utters a curse and a threat of vengeance against the sorcerer.   The headman, last to deliver his funeral oration, usually names the sorcerer, assisted by broad hints given by the medicine man, and promises vengeance.

At dawn, the deceased is wrapped in his own hammock and placed on his back, the legs drawn up, in his own canoe, which has been cut into two equal halves for the purpose, one-half serving as a cover.   With him are laid a calabash, a walking staff, a fishing line, and bows and arrows.   The grave is dug in the house beneath the dance floor and, as the coffin is lowered in place with ropes, a male relative blows tobacco smoke in each of its corners.   The deceased, whose spirit makes a river journey and then a short overland trip, is provided with all necessities, including tobacco.   The calabash is for water.

Between the burial and the mourning rites, which may come as much as 6 months later, only the widow remains in mourning.   She greets all visitors to the house with loud lamentations, leading them to the grave site and weeping over the grave.

The headman prepares for the mourning rites, known in *Tucano* as oyne, "weeping," by requesting all kinsmen to make the bark-cloth masks and other paraphernalia used in the ceremony (pls. 96, 97, 98). These objects are destroyed at the conclusion of the rites.

The mourning ceremonies appear to have a threefold function among the *Tucano*.   They serve, first, to provide the occasion for the expression of grief by all the kinsmen of the departed; second, to have the grief assuaged by the solacing presence of the Ancestors and the Beings of the world, including the forest monsters and all the fish, insects, animals, and birds; and, finally, to drive the ghost of the deceased out of the house, when the ceremony ends.   Henceforth, the deceased is to be forgotten and his name never mentioned.

ESTHETIC AND RECREATIONAL ACTIVITIES

Art.—Art forms in the Uaupés-Caquetá region are developed in the decorative treatment of domestic utensils, in body decoration, and especially in the production of ceremonial paraphernalia.   Lozenges, hatched or solid triangles, and crude frets predominate as art motifs.   *Arawakan-* and *Tucanoan*-speaking peoples in the area have elaborated the symbolic representation of animal, fish, insect, bird, and mythological beings in their bark-cloth mourning masks and in the realistic representation of fish (pl. 102, *center*) and birds, either painted on wood or constructed of palm leaves. Gourd rattles are blackened with genipa dye and are

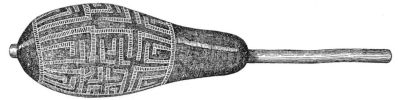

FIGURE 113.—*Cubeo* engraved gourd rattle.

incised; hollow stamping tubes are also incised in elaborate patterns. Geometric and anthropomorphic designs, in white, yellow, and dark red, are painted on house posts in some parts of the Northwest Amazon area (fig. 114).

FIGURE 114.—House decorations of the northwest Amazon. White, yellow, and dark red. (After Koch-Grünberg, 1923 b.)

Games.—Children play a number of games representing mythological incidents and also spin tops; boys use stilts (fig. 115, *right*); and adults play catching games with rubber balls. Gambling is completely absent. Cat's cradles are known but are of no great significance.

Dances.—Frequent dances, at which much weakly fermented but nevertheless intoxicating manioc chicha is consumed, are characteristic of all tribes in the region. Most dances are primarily social, are held as frequently as a sufficient supply of chicha can be prepared, and are attended at times by 200 or more people. Food is rarely served at these gatherings.

Except for the funeral ceremony described earlier, where a specific dance routine portrays a particular being, dances consist of two main types: the circle dance, in which all men, women, and children participate; and

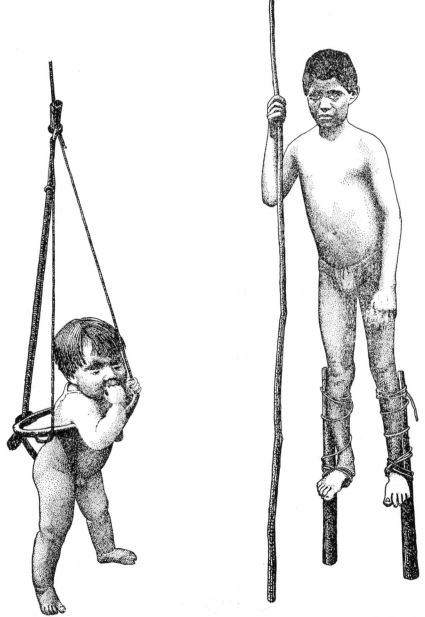

FIGURE 115.—Indian children of the northwest Amazon. *Left: Cubeo* baby in hanging chair, Cudináry River. *Right: Siusí* boy on stilts, Acarí River. (Redrawn from Koch-Grünberg, 1909–10, fig. 87 and fig. 66.)

another dance involving a smaller group.   In the circle dance, the participants line up outside the house in order of size, the tallest in the center.

FIGURE 116.—*Tuyuca* "Yurupary" feast. Bringing wild fruit, with music.
(After Koch-Grünberg, 1923 b.)

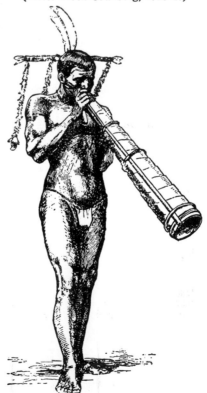

FIGURE 117.—*Tuyuca* "Yurupary" dancer. (After Koch-Grünberg, 1923 b.)

Each places his left arm around the next person's shoulder and in his right hand bears a hollow dance stave for pounding the rhythm. The entire group enters the house and, forming a huge circle, moves sideward a number of steps, then sways backward, then forward, and continues the side step. The dance rhythm is given by appropriate songs and emphasized with the dancing staves. The dance usually ends outside the house. In smaller group dances, the male dancers play panpipes or long flageolets, always with one arm about the partners shoulder. In the dance with the panpipes, a group of five men, constituting an orchestra, dance side by side to the accompaniment of their own panpipes, characteristically with three heavily accented steps and then, after a single step backward, three quick steps forward. Women join the dance by thrusting their heads beneath the yoke formed by the arms of the men placed around the shoulders of their male partners and leave before the men have finished dancing. The flageolet dance has similar dance steps, but involves only two men; women do not participate.

Music and musical instruments.—A wide variety of instruments is known in the area, including panpipes, played individually or as an orchestra of five distinctively keyed instruments; flageolets, ranging in size from small reeds to large paxiuba palm instruments 5 feet (1.5 m.) long; flutes of reed or bone; and huge trumpets 10 feet (3 m.) long (pl. 101, *left*). A European type of drum is also widely known. Men are the only musicians and no woman is even permitted to touch a musical instrument. Songs are all associated with dances.

Narcotics.—Coca prepared as a fine dry powder and mixed with leaf ash is chewed by adults of both sexes and even children, principally during dances (pl. 100, *d, e*). Considerable care is taken to deposit the powder at the side of the mouth with a small wooden spoon or leaf to avoid choking. At more formal and elaborate ceremonies, cayapi is taken to induce color visions and to increase intoxication. The ultimate effect of this extremely bitter drug is a total blackout of vision followed by a brief loss of consciousness.

Intoxicating beverages.—Manioc chicha parties, which are not sacred and in which both men and women participate, are very frequent. They last sometimes for 2 or 3 consecutive days or until all the chicha is consumed, for no drinking party may end until the last drop has been drunk. The addition of sugarcane extract to the chicha produces a relatively intoxicating beverage. Fights and sometimes serious quarrels are an inevitable consequence of these sprees.

RELIGION AND SHAMANISM

Supernaturalism centers about an ancestor cult—mistakenly referred to in the literature as yurupary—and a richly elaborated shamanistic complex. Supplicatory rites to a deity are apparently absent, although two

FIGURE 118.—Wooden cigar-holder, northwest Amazon, Tiquié River. (1/6 actual size.) (Redrawn from Koch-Grünberg, 1909–10.)

deities, known among the *Tucanoan*-speaking groups as Kúwai and Húmé-nihinkü, figure prominently in mythology as creators. Húménihinkü, the Supreme Deity, is possibly an acculturated Christian concept, and is actually so regarded by many Indians. This god has a house in the sky where he lives with his wife, and receives the spirits of the dead, who give presents to enter the house. The creation of the earth and the rivers is attributed to him, but he does not intercede in the affairs of men. The *Cubeo,* who are familiar with the Húménihinkü deity, maintain at the same time the belief that the spirits of the dead retain their sib ties and occupy sites a short distance from the sib territory, where they can be heard talking and singing at night. Kúwai, the culture hero of the *Tucano* groups, is more intimately associated with men and displays trickster and trans-former characteristics. He created some of the rivers, taught the people agriculture, fishing, and all their arts and industries, introduced death and all the dances and ceremonies now practiced, and was in constant difficulties with mortals, who interfered with his plans and even sought to kill him. At present, Kúwai, mortified by the treatment he had received at the

PLATE 89.—**Cubeo fishweir and manioc preparation.** *Top:* Fishweir. At the extreme right a lower section can be opened to pass a canoe. *Bottom:* Scraping manioc. Note the genipa paint on woman's back. (Courtesy Irving Goldman.)

PLATE 90.—**Food preparation, northwest Amazon.** *Top:* A manioc squeezer (tipití). *Center:* Drying farinha on a pan inside a *Baniva* house. (Courtesy American Museum of Natural History.) *Bottom: Cubeo* woman grating manioc. (Courtesy Batista Venturello.)

PLATE 91.—**House types of the northwest Amazon.** *Top: Baniva* house. (Courtesy American Museum of Natural History.) *Center:* Framework of a multifamily *Cubeo* house. (Courtesy Irving Goldman.) *Bottom:* A *Macúna* house, Apáporis River. (After Koch-Grünberg, 1909–10.)

PLATE 92.—A Cawa house.　(After Koch-Grünberg, 1909–10.)

PLATE 93.—**House types of the northwest Amazon.** *Top: Tucano* house of the upper Papony, Colombia. *Bottom:* Interior of a *Baniva* house. (Courtesy American Museum of Natural History.)

PLATE 94.—**Cubeo manufactures.** *Top:* Spreading a dugout canoe by heat. *Bottom:* Making bark cloth. Man in center is pounding log from which cloth will be stripped; man at left has removed cloth; man at right is stretching it. (Courtesy Irving Goldman.)

PLATE 95.—**Cubeo baskets.** *Top, left:* A twined and a twilled manioc carrying basket. *Top, right:* Twilled serving tray resting on an "hourglass" potstand. *Bottom, left:* Twilled serving tray. *Bottom, right:* Twined manioc carrying basket. (Courtesy Irving Goldman.)

PLATE 96.—**Cubeo mourning ceremony.** *Top:* Men lined up for dance with dancing staves. Man in center is headman, having jaguar belt and vertebrate necklace. *Bottom:* Dressing for dance. Man at right is headman of sib. (Courtesy **Irving** Goldman.)

PLATE 97.—**Cubeo mourning dance regalia.** *Left:* Man in dance regalia being checked over by boy. *Right:* Images representing fish spirits used in dance. (Courtesy Irving Goldman.)

PLATE 98.—**Cubeo mourning ceremony.** *Top* and *bottom, right:* Bark dance masks. *Bottom, left:* Women entering rear of a house to attend mourning ceremony. (Courtesy Irving Goldman.)

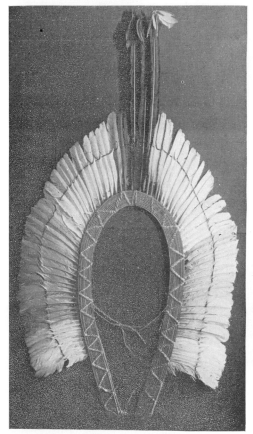

PLATE 99.—**Northwest Amazon drum and ceremonial objects.** *Top: Tucano* drum. (After Koch-Grünberg, 1923 b.) *Bottom, left: Tucano* feather headdress. *Bottom, right:* Effigy of bark dance mask. (Courtesy Museu Paraense Emilio Goeldi, Belém.)

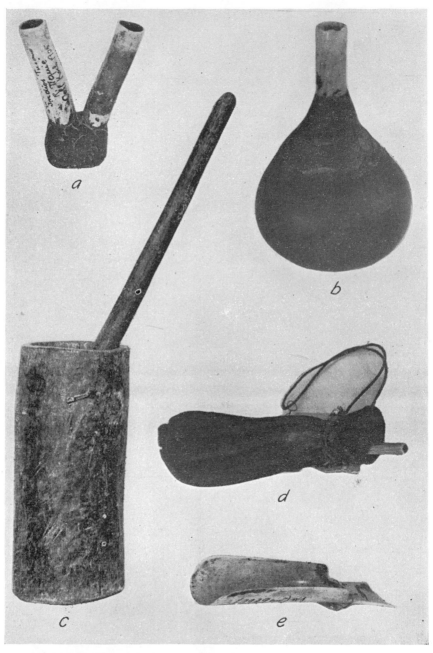

PLATE 100.—**Northwest Amazon manufactures.** *a, Tucano* snuff tube; *b, Tucano*
calabash for snuff; *c*, a wooden mortar and pestle from the Aiarí River (much
reduced); *d, Bora* bark-cloth bag for coca with a bone tube; *e, Bora* bone dipper
for coca. (*a, b, d, e*, Courtesy Museu Paraense Emilio Goeldi, Belém.) (*c*,
After Koch-Grünberg, 1909–10.)

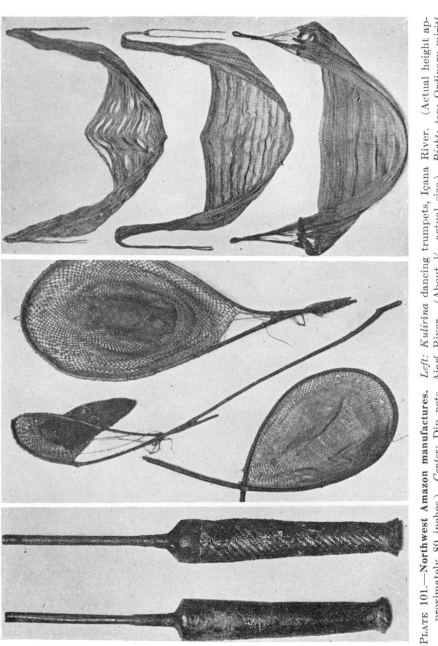

PLATE 101.—**Northwest Amazon manufactures.** *Left: Kulírúna dancing trumpets, Içana River.* (Actual height approximately 80 inches.) *Center: Dip nets, Aiarí River.* (About ⅕ actual size.) *Right: top: Ordinary mirití hammock, Aiarí River. Right, center: Closely woven hammock of tucum, Macáya River. Right, bottom: Heavy tucum hammock, manufactured on loom, Aiarí River.* (After Koch-Grünberg, 1909–10.)

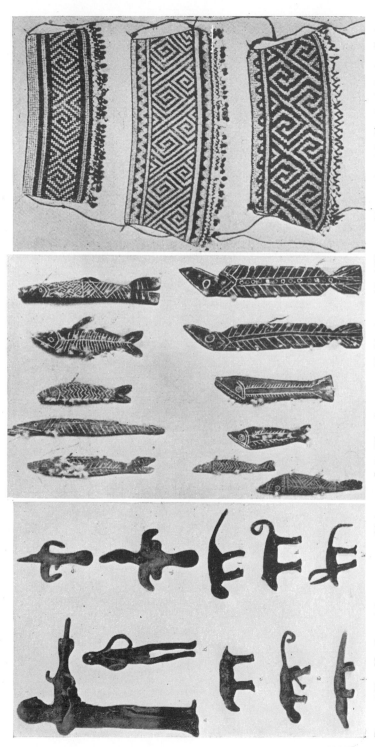

PLATE 102.—**Northwest Amazon manufactures.** *Left:* Wax figures molded by boys, Aiarí River. (Approximately ⅖ actual size.) *Center:* *Cubeo* wooden fish for burial celebrations. (Approximately ½ actual size.) *Right:* Skirts of beads, woven by women at dances, Aiarí River. (After Koch-Grünberg, 1909–10.)

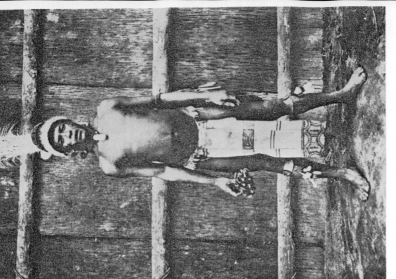

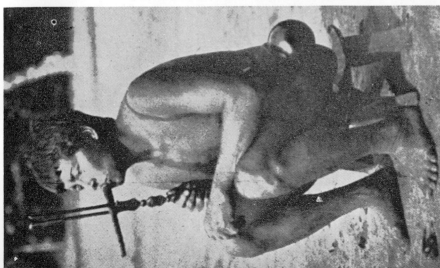

PLATE 103.—**Indians of the northwest Amazon.** *Left:* A *Tucano* with a large cigar. *Center:* *Tucano* with lances and shields. *Right:* A *Tuyuca* in dance dress. (After Koch-Grünberg, 1909–10.)

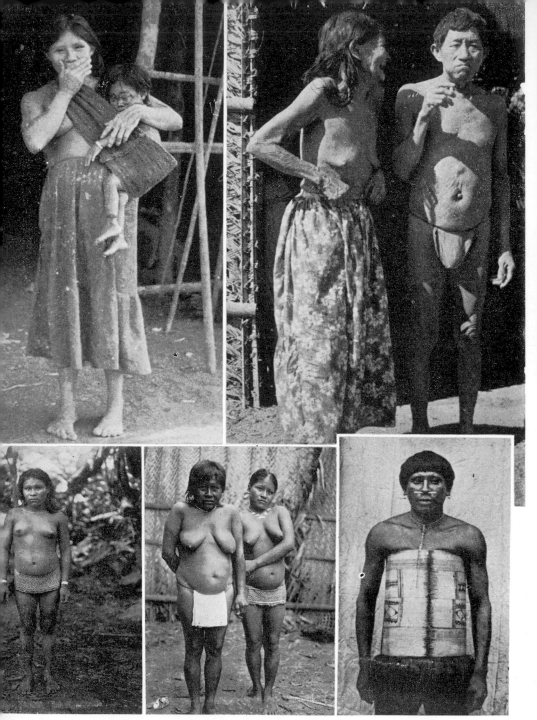

PLATE 104.—**Indians of the northwest Amazon.** *Top, left: Cubeo* mother and child. *Top, right:* Old *Cubeo* couple. (Courtesy Irving Goldman.) *Bottom, left: Guanana* girl. *Bottom, center: Isana* women. (Courtesy Batista Venturello.) *Bottom, right: Hianákoto-Umáua Kauánamu* man, Macáya River. (After Koch-Grünberg, 1909–10.)

hands of the *Cubeo,* is said to have retired to a solitary existence on some distant mountain site. The elders narrate with amusement the difficulties Kúwai had with women. His wives, frequently taken from among the Indians, either deserted or proved faithless. Even when he created a wife out of a tree, she eventually eloped with a fish. An extensive body of folk-lore deals with Kúwai. No moralistic connotations are associated with Kúwai, except among groups subjected to prolonged mission influence.

Besides these two major deities, all peoples in the area believe in the existence of a host of forest and river creatures, usually malevolent. The forest monsters, abuhuwa (also inaccurately designated in the literature as yurupary), invoked by parents to scare children, are generally described as hairy, humanlike creatures with double-faced heads and with cannibalistic tendencies. There are many varieties of these monsters. Some are linked together, like Siamese twins. These are single at first, but when the male monster sees a woman and jumps at her, she sticks to his side permanently and becomes a cannibal. The female monsters seize men in the same fashion. Another group catches children and kills them by tossing them high in the air; others cut a hole in the top of the victim's head and suck him dry while kneading his body to soften it, and then leave the dry skin on a tree. During a lunar eclipse the monsters can be seen by human beings but are visible always to a shaman. Hair from the armpit of the cannibal monster seized during a lunar eclipse is regarded as a potent weapon of sorcery.

Among the river monsters, the white anaconda is most menacing to menstruating and postparturient women. The river men, short fat creatures, seize men who have violated couvade regulations. Other river creatures are harmless, causing only the night fog.

The Ancestor cult.—Major religious activity centers about the cult of the Ancestors or Ancients, the founders of the sibs. These beneficent beings, who are invoked at every sib gathering, are usually represented by trumpets or depicted in ancient petroglyphs, and are regarded as the protectors of the sib and imparters of strength to the men. The trumpets representing the Ancestors may not be viewed by the women. Men and boys who seek strength and courage bathe each morning to the sound of the Ancestor horns. Collectively, the Ancestors are known in *Tucanoan* as Bekwüpwanwa (the ancient people), but each sib venerates its own particular Ancestors. During the mourning ceremonies, the sole female Ancestor in the pantheon comes to assuage the grief of the mourners. (See also p. 789.)

The afterworld.—The human spirit is believed to leave the body during sleep and wander about at close range; toward morning it reenters the head via the mouth and the sleeper awakes. The shaman can capture the spirit and thus cause death. Shortly before death the spirit departs from the body permanently and hovers about the house until driven off by burning dried chili peppers. Such ghosts are troublesome and are believed to be seeking to carry other relatives off with them. When frequent deaths follow one another in the same house the site is abandoned as "haunted." Normally, the ghost finally settles down at the ancestral site and joins all the other sib members. The ghosts of wicked people and of those captured by sorcerers are transformed into birds, insects, or animals, and, under the control of the shaman, are likely to be troublesome. The spirit of a shaman enters a jaguar and never joins his sib ancestors.

Shamanism.—The shaman in the area is generally referred to as a jaguar, and combines the functions of medicine man and sorcerer. Older shamans assume the guise of the jaguar and are particularly feared. Every jaguar who attacks human beings is assumed to be a shaman, and the shaman who is suspected of such an attack is not infrequently put to death. As the spirit of a murdered shaman enters another jaguar, however, little relief is expected from killing them. The shaman is credited with powers to cure, to kill by sorcery, to bring storms and generally to control the weather, to locate lost objects, to divine the cause of death, to affect human, animal, and plant fertility, and to cause dreaded lunar eclipses. Many grades of shamans are recognized, ranging from simple practitioners— old men who can cure a hangover by blowing tobacco smoke at the top of the skull—to those whose powers are virtually limitless. Although the profession is open to both sexes, women shamans are rare. Power is generally associated with length of experience and heredity. The son of a powerful shaman will have greater powers than a newcomer. The power of the shaman derives from his control of a number of animal spirits, to which are added the captured spirits of victims. In addition, the shaman contains within his body quantities of black palm needles, which he "shoots" at his victims.

The shamanistic novice spends a month learning the art from at least two professionals. He obtains tree resin, dupa (*Tucano*), and inhales it in a powdered form for 4 days. Then, under the guidance of his mentors, he "loads" his body with the palm needles. These are placed on the upper forearm and on the chest. Next, he inserts tips of eagle feathers up his nostrils. Thus "loaded," the novice sings with his mentors until a thunderstorm breaks over the house. He then departs for a 5-day solitary vigil in the forest, subsisting on manioc flour and water and practicing his songs. Upon his return, he is tested; when his singing can produce a thunderstorm, he is acknowledged to be a shaman. Thereafter, for a period of months he is abstinent and only gradually arrives at a full diet.

Curing requires the extraction of some intrusive body, either a crystalline substance or black palm needles, and consists of applying the palm of the hand to the affected area or of sucking. The crystalline object thus removed is "blown" away. When the illness is diagnosed as the presence of palm needles, the shaman pours water over the patient. More obdurate illnesses require lengthy sessions of singing and the application of both techniques. The extraction of palm needles is among the shaman's more spectacular demonstrations of power. Filling a deep black pottery bowl with water, the shaman spreads broad banana leaves, within which he has secreted the palm needles, on the surface. When he scoops up water with a calabash, the needles, virtually invisible in the water, are also doused over the patient. The bystanders are then asked to hunt for the needles.

The fear of sorcery constitutes an ever-present threat to the stability of social relations, even within the individual family. All illness and non-violent death is attributed to sorcery, and such an occurrence invariably provokes bitter recriminations and open battles. Among the *Cubeo*, sibs have often been reduced to a mere handful of people following the accusation that they practice sorcery. Fear of sorcery not infrequently interferes with ceremonies and sometimes restricts attendance at drinking parties, which are ordinarily popular, to members of the immediate household. All adults are believed capable of practicing sorcery, and the number of alleged techniques is considerable. Certain persons, whom the *Cubeo* call "powerful monsters," are said to wander about between darkness and dawn, to possess night visions, to be invisible, and to attack the victim in his sleep. When caught, such sorcerers are tortured with fishhooks, tearing the flesh from the limbs bit by bit to insure a slow and painful death. Particularly suspected are persons with long nails on the index finger, under which a "poison" may be secreted to be flicked into the victims food or drink. Among the more common "poisons" are plant substances which cause genital disturbances, abdominal swellings, gastrointestinal disorders, general wasting away, and, in effect, every affliction common to the region. As such "poisons" are accessible to everyone and are very easily utilized, the danger from "poisoning" is ever present. A number of counter charms furnish some security.

Other sorcerers, known as "blowers," are men with shamanistic skill, but who are not shamans. By blowing tobacco smoke at a victim from any distance, they can induce paralysis, illness, and death. Body "dirt" boiled with hot chili peppers is another technique of sorcery and is used especially to avenge a death. Scrapings of skin, callouses, some fingernails, and a bit of hair from the deceased are boiled, while the sorcerer, sitting over the pot, chants a spell and orders the victim to cut off his ear or other parts of the body. Finally, the soul of the victim in the form of a butterfly or other insect falls into the pot, the pot is quickly broken, and the victim dies.

MYTHOLOGY AND LITERATURE

Folklore includes a series of animal tales with the tapir and tortoise as prominent figures, a culture-hero cycle, stories of human experiences with supernatural forest monsters, and lengthy sagas about the adventures of tribal or sib ancestors. Of cosmological significance are tales dealing with the moon, but there are none concerning the stars. A flood tale with a moralistic theme is found among the *Cubeo*. Tapir is usually worsted in encounters with Tortoise. The culture-hero cycle explains the origin of social practices, of techniques, such as agriculture and fishing, of various insects, death, illness, and so on. The *Tucano* culture hero, Kúwai, is frequently worsted in relations with human beings, but overcomes all obstacles when involved with animals or supernatural beings. Moon seeks to copulate with young girls, explores new graves, and prevents the theft of his lamp when it is inadequately covered by the thief. The narration of the Ancestor saga is an important feature of all ceremonies and has something of a sacred character.

BIBLIOGRAPHY

Albis, 1861; Appun, 1871; Aranha (see Figueirêdo Tenreiro Aranha, 1907); Arcaya, 1920; Avé-Lallemont, 1860; Barbosa Rodriguez, 1885; Beuchat and Rivet, 1911; Bollaert, 1860; Brett, 1868; Brown, 1876; Carvajal, 1892; Chaffanjon, 1889; Church, 1912; H. Coudreau, 1886–87; De Goeje, 1928; Ehrenreich, 1904; Fabo, 1911; Farabee, 1916 b, 1918 b, 1922, 1924; Farson, 1938; Figueirêdo Tenreiro Aranha, 1907; Fritz, 1922; Gilij, 1780–84; Grupe y Thode, 1890; Gumilla, 1791; Hamilton, 1934; Hardenburg, 1912; Humboldt, 1852–53; Im Thurn, 1883; Jahn, 1927; Jeménez Seminario, 1924; Kirchhoff, 1931; Koch-Grünberg, 1900, 1905–08, 1906 b, 1906 c, 1906 d, 1907, 1908, 1909–10, 1911, 1913 b, 1913–16, 1922, 1923 b; Marcoy, 1867; Markham, 1895, 1910, 1911; Matos Arvela, 1908; Martius, 1867; Mason, 1940; Medina, 1933; Melgarejo, 1886; Miller, 1919; Mochi, n.d.; Montolieu, 1877; Nordenskiöld, 1924 a, 1930 a, 1931 b; Perez, 1862–63; Pinell, 1928; Preuss, 1914 and 1920–21, 1921–23; Reinburg, 1921; Rivero, 1883; Rivet, 1912 a; Rocha, 1905; Schomburgk, 1848; Schumann, 1882; Speiser, 1926; Spix and Martius, 1823–31; Spruce, 1908; Steinen, 1892; Stradelli, 1890; Tavera-Acosta, 1907, 1927; Triana, 1907; Viñaza, 1892; Wallace, 1853; Whiffen, 1915.

PART 5. TRIBES OF THE GUIANAS AND THE LEFT AMAZON TRIBUTARIES

TRIBES OF THE GUIANAS

By JOHN GILLIN

INTRODUCTION

The area here considered to comprise the Guianas lies in northern South America (map 1, *No. 5;* map 7). Bounded coastally by the Atlantic Ocean to the east and north, its northern interior boundary is the right bank of the Orinoco River where, from the mouth of the Apure River to the ocean, its course takes a general east-to-west direction. The Delta of the Orinoco River is thus not included in our region. The southern boundary is the left bank of the Amazon River from its confluence with the Rio Negro to its northernmost mouth. The islands of the Amazon Delta, including the Island of Marajó, are thus also excluded. The western boundaries of the Guianas, for present purposes, may be described as the right bank of the Orinoco River, upstream from its meeting with the Apure River to its head; an arbitrary straight line from the head of the Orinoco River southeastward to the mouth of the Catrimani River, a right tributary of the Rio Branco; the left bank of the Rio Branco southward to its confluence with the Rio Negro; and the left bank of the Rio Negro southeastward to its meeting with the Amazon River.

The landscape in the region of the Guianas is of four kinds. (1) Coastal plains and deltas, such as border most of the Atlantic shore, are low, somewhat swampy, subject to partially inundating seasonal floods, and covered with thick swamp forest of medium height. Such a landscape, as, for instance, the Pomeroon coast of British Guiana and the Parimaribo coast of Suriname, extends inland from the shore to a variable depth, usually 20 to 30 miles (32 to 48 km.), seldom farther than 100 miles (160 km.). (2) Inland forests cover a large portion of the Guianas. The elevation is somewhat higher than that of the coastal plains, the jungle cover is higher and more pervading, and, because the topography is level or rolling, vistas open only for short distances on the rivers, as on the Barama River drainage and the Oyapock River drainage. (3) The savannas and partially forested regions are level or mildly rolling, and

799

occasionally mountains are visible along their borders. The Rupununi savannas of southern British Guiana and the Gran Sabana of eastern Venezuela are relatively dry, but the savannas intermittently bordering the left bank of the Amazon River and the smaller ones of the lower Oyapock River and the Aruka savanna of British Guiana's Northwest District are semiswampy at all times and during portions of the year may become inundated meadows. (4) A considerable portion of interior Guiana is mountainous, with a rough and broken topography as in the Sierra Pacaraima, Sierra Parima, and the Tumuc-Humac Mountains, but with a fair amount of mountain rain forest, except among the rockier masses, such as Mount Roraima.

In all but the mountain areas, some of the streams or waterways are suitable for intermittent canoe navigation, although rapids or falls break their upper courses. Lakes are rare in the Guianas and most of them lie near the Amazon River or in the coastal region of Brazilian Guiana.

Tribal languages representative of at least 10 aboriginal linguistic families are known to have existed in the Guianas during historic times. These families are *Arawakan, Auakéan, Cariban, Caliánan, Macúan, Muran, Salivan* (or *Macúan*), *Shirianán, Tupian,* and *Warrauan* (or *Guaraunan*). Two of these families, *Tupian* and *Muran,* were apparently intrusive into the region in the post-Columbian period. A list of tribes follows, classified by linguistic family; under family the tribes are listed alphabetically according to the spelling which is used most frequently in modern literature, where that is available. Each tribal name is accompanied by synonyms or variant spellings, if either the synonyms or the variant spellings are significant for the identification of the tribe. The location of each tribe is given and also, in several cases, the location of the tribe at different dates. Such a summary, primarily for identification, should not be considered a chronological record of the movements of the tribe. In many cases a reference or two on the identification and location of the tribe is provided for the convenience of the reader, but these references are not to be taken as a bibliography of cultural information. To the list of tribes of known linguistic affiliation is added another list of linguistically unidentified tribes. These unidentified tribes are mentioned in the literature and geographically located, but linguistic material either does not exist or has been insufficiently studied to permit linguistic identification. When the tribal name is followed by the family name with a question mark (*Apirua (Arawak?)*), the family identification, on the basis of the literature, seems probable, but is not certain.

Three areas of culture may be tentatively distinguished in the Guianas: (1) the coastal area, (2) the inland mountain-savanna area, and (3) the Amazonian area. Not only have migration and mixing of culture elements blurred the distinctions which may have been clearer at one time, but lack of information may also lead us astray. Later studies may well

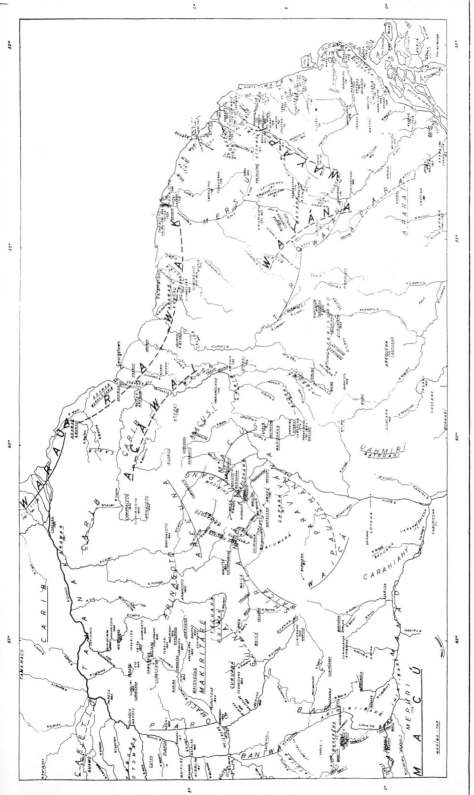

MAP 7.—The tribes of the Guianas. Solid underlining, modern tribes; broken underlining, extinct portions of tribes; otherwise, date of location is given under the tribal name. Tribes not underlined are extinct. (Compiled by Curt Nimuendajú.)

(Face p. 800)

indicate changes and subdivisions. The Amazonian area is so incompletely known that its culture type cannot be accurately described, although evidently it has greater affinities with the southern Amazonian area than have other portions of the Guianas. The inland mountain-savanna area contains many elements which in more elaborated form are native to the Rio Negro region. The coastal area is populated mainly by *Carib* and *Arawak* tribes, but also by some *Warrau* who have apparently migrated from the Orinoco Delta. A special section (p. 870) deals with the Delta culture of the *Warrau,* and the Guiana culture of the *Warrau* has been discussed merely to indicate the extent of their divergence.

Characteristic traits of the inland mountain-savanna region are the lance, blowgun, tobacco-chewing, use of parica, circular houses with walls, sandals, discoid paddle blades, possibly cremation as an earlier trait, nose flutes, dance sticks, turtle-shell friction drums, and more elaborate cere-monial costumes, star lore, and puberty and mourning ceremonies than those of the coastal region. These traits are not all common to all the inland tribes, and, although they are found with greater frequency in the inland area, they are not unknown to all the coastal tribes. Characteristic coastal traits seem to include a more frequent use of the rectangular, wall-less house and of houses built on piles, wooden shields, clay and bamboo trumpets, more emphasis on aboriginal cannibalism, greater elaboration of watercraft, greater dependence upon, and elaboration of, the bow and arrow, and more emphasis upon hunting ceremonials and magic.

Thus, no clear-cut lines of culture dissimilarities are discernible among the various regions of the Guiana area; rather the culture area must be distinguished on the basis of tendencies, emphasis, and statistical averages. Even the Guiana area as a whole is not strikingly distinctive, for it shares many traits and configurations in common with the other tropical regions of South America.

TRIBAL DIVISIONS[1]

THE ARAWAKAN FAMILY

Amariba (*Amaripa,* etc.).—A brother tribe of the *Wapishana,* which lived near the *Atorai* in 1787 in the source region of the Tacutú and Rupununi Rivers (lat. 2° N., long. 60° W.) (Koch-Grünberg, 1922, p. 220; Richard Schomburgk, 1922–23, 2:387–388, reported only one old woman remained in the 1840's).

Apirua (*Arawak?*).—On the Camopi River in 1722 (lat. 3° N., long. 53° W.) (Lombard, 1928).

Aramisho (*Arawak?* but possibly *Cariban* (see p. 805)).—On the Araoua River, upper tributary of the Maroni, and downstream on the Maroni River (lat. 2° N., long. 54° W.) (Lombard, 1928).

---

[1] See map 7.

Arawak (*Aroaqui, Aruac, Aruaki, Aravaco, Arouage,* etc.).—Scattered along the Guiana Coast from the Moruca River in British Guiana to the French-Brazilian boundary region, also between the Rio Negro and Jamundá River. Their own name for themselves is *Locono.*

Arekena (*Arequena, Guariquéna, Uariquéna, Warekéna,* etc.).—On the upper Rio Negro and Atabapo River (lat. 2° N., long. 67° W.).

Arua (*Aruan,* etc.).—Formerly, on the north bank of the lower Amazon River and the Island of Marajó (lat. 1° S., long. 50° W.) ; now extinct (Ehrenreich, 1904, p. 48). A few are said to live on the Uaçá River. They moved northward by migration from the Island of Marajó, gave trouble to Portuguese missionaries in the 18th century, and in 1722 attacked the village of Moribira, giving rise to a French-Brazilian international incident, in which the Brazilians accused the French of supplying the Indians with arms. (Nimuendajú, 1926, pp. 7–17 ; Rio-Branco, 1899, 4 :226, 240, 242, and 3 :53, 67, 101 ; Lombard, 1928.)

Atorai (*Atorya, Attaraya, Attorraidi, Atorad, Daurai, Dauri, Tauri,* etc.).—In southern British Guiana at the sources of the Rupununi and Tacutú Rivers (lat. 2° N., long. 59° W.). Now absorbed by the *Wapishana,* according to Farabee (1918 b).

Baniva (*Vaniva, Baniwa, Abane*).—In the region of the Venezuelan-Colombian border on the Atabapo and Guainía Rivers (lat. 3° N., long. 68° W.) (Gumilla, 1791 ; Crévaux, 1883, p. 531 ; Grasserie, 1892).

Baraüna (*Barauána,* may be same as *Baré*).—On the upper Padauri River and its right tributary, the Marari River (lat. 1° N., long. 65° W.) (Koch-Grünberg, 1922, p. 222; Coudreau, H., 1886–87, 2 :119, 394). Formerly, at the end of the 18th century, on the upper Catrimani River, then in the village of Casmo on the Rio Branco.

Baré (*Barre,* etc.).—On the Casiquiare River (lat. 3° N., long. 67° W.)

Caberre (*Caverre, Cabre,* etc.).—Gave name to the Guaviare, or Guayabero, River; extend along this stream up to the Ariarí River from the Zama and Orinoco Rivers (lat. 4° N., long. 71° W.) (Roth, 1924, p. 725; Gumilla, 1791).

Cariaya (*Carahiahy, Cariai*).—On the Rio Negro, near the mouth of the Rio Branco, where Spix met them (lat. 1° S., long. 63° W.) (Chamberlain, 1910).

Guinau (*Ginyau, Quinhau, Quinhao, Guainare,* etc.).—On the upper Caura River; Robert Schomburgk found them in the 1840's in all villages on the Merevari and Padamo Rivers, also on the Cunucunuma River (lat. 4° N., long. 65° W.) Now they are mostly absorbed into the *Yecuana,* according to Koch-Grünberg. Their own name for themselves is *Temomöyämö* (Gama Lobo, 1903).

Inao.—On the middle Caura River around the Michave, a right tributary. Chaffanjon found an abandoned village near the Island of Chaparro and the portage of Píritu (lat. 4° N., long. 65° W.). They may be the same as the *Guinau*.

Locono (*Lokono*).—The *Arawak* name for themselves.

Macapa (*Macapaí, Makapa, Makapaí; Arawak?*).—Between the Camopi and Yaroupi Rivers, left tributaries of the Oyapock (Oyapoque) River (lat. 2° N., long. 52° W.) (Lombard, 1928).

Maipure (*Maypure, Maypoye,* etc.).—On the Ventuari and Orinoco Rivers, around the mouth of the Ventuari (lat. 4° N., long. 67° W.) (Gumilla, 1791, 1:161).

Maopityan (*Mapidian, Pidian, Moonpidenne*).—Said to be a subtribe of the *Atorai*. In 1884 they lived on the Brazilian slopes of the Acaraí Mountains at the sources of the Apiniwau, or Curucuri, River (lat. 2° N., long. 59° W.), which region they have abandoned to migrate to southern British Guiana.

Marawan (*Maraón, Marauaná?,* etc.).—In the coastal region around the mouth of the Oyapock River (lat. 3° N., long. 52° W.). Rivet identified them with the *Palicur,* but Nimuendajú has shown them to be a distinct tribe, now extinct. Only two words of their language were recovered by Nimuendajú, so that the linguistic classification is not conclusive. Apparently they preceded the *Palicur, Galibi,* and *Arawak* on the Oyapock River.

Marourioux (*Arawak?*).—On the Ouanary River in 1729 (lat. 3° N., long. 53° W.). Taken to the mission of Ouanari with the *Tocoyen* and *Marawan* (Lombard, 1928).

Palicur (*Palikur*).—In Brazilian and French Guiana and the drainage of the lower Oyapock and Uaçá Rivers (lat. 3° N., long. 52° W.) (Nimuendajú, 1926).

Parauana (*Barauana*).—On the Ayarary River, west tributary of the Rio Branco in 1755 (lat. 2° N., long. 63° W.) (Ferreira, 1903).

Parauien.—An extinct branch of the *Tarumá* (q.v.) (lat. 3° S., long. 60° W.) (Rivet, 1924).

Pauishana (*Pauixana, Pauisiana,* etc.).—On the Catrimani River, a left tributary of the Rio Branco (lat. 2° N., long. 62° W.) (Nimuendajú gives this as *Carib.*)

Piapoco.—On the middle course of the Guaviare River (lat. 3° N., long. 70° W.) (Crévaux, 1883, p. 508).

Pino (*Arawak?*).—West of the *Acokwa* (lat. 3° N., long. 54° W.) (Lombard, 1928).

Purui (*Pouroui; Arawak?*).—On the left bank of the Couyary River, across from the *Amicuana* (lat. 2° N., long. 52° W.) (Lombard, 1928).

Tarumá (*Arawak?*).—According to Nimuendajú, the *Tarumá* spoke an independent language. They were formerly in the lower Rio Negro region, west of the small Ajurim River in 1668, according to Pedro da Costa Favella, who also reports *"Aroaqui"* in this region (lat. 3° S., long. 60° W.). By 1808 Governor José Joaquim Victorio found no trace of them. Robert Schomburgk in 1837 heard of the *Tarumá* numbering at that time about 500, at the head of the Essequibo, Kuyuwini, and Cassiquity Rivers. They have also been reported at the head of the Courantyne River. Apparently, they were formerly located in the Amazon Basin and migrated northward to British Guiana in the 18th century.

Tocoyen (*Arawak?*).—On the Ouanary River in 1730 (lat. 3° N., long. 53° W.). Later they migrated southwest (Lombard, 1928). First cited by Fauque, 1729, on the middle Oyapock River; later they were taken to the mission of Ouanari by P. Joseph d'Ansillac. They were mentioned by Lombard in 1730 (H. Coudreau, 1891 a).

Wapishana (*Warpeshana, Mapeshana, Wapisiana, Ouapisiana, Ouapichane,* etc.).—Now located on the savannas of southern British Guiana. Formerly, they occupied the basin of the Tacutú River (lat. 3° N., long. 60° W.). In recent times they have invaded the plains of the middle Rio Branco and absorbed the *Atorai* and *Paraviyana.*

THE AUAKÉAN FAMILY

Auaké (*Awaké*).—An independent linguistic family with representatives located at the head of the Parauá, a left tributary of the Caroni River (lat. 5° N., long. 64° W.) (Rivet, 1924, p. 651; Koch-Grünberg, 1913 a).

THE CARIBAN FAMILY

Acawai (*Akawai, Acawoio, Akawoio, Wacawai, Waïca, Waïka, Capohn, Kapohn, Capong, Kapong,* etc.).—During the 19th century, their center was the Cuyuni River, with outlying groups on the Barama, Barima, and upper Pomeroon Rivers, and elsewhere (lat. 6° N., long. 60° W.).

Acokwa (*Akokwa, Acoquoi, Acoqua,* etc.).—On the Camopi and Approuague Rivers in 1720 (lat. 3° N., long. 53° W.) (Lombard, 1928, p. 123).

Acuria.—Between the Nickerie and Copename Rivers, in Dutch Guiana (lat. 5° N., long. 55° W.).

Amicuana (*Amicwan, Amikwan, Amicouan, Amikonan; Carib?*).—In 1720–30 located between the sources of the Oyapock and Couyary Rivers (lat. 2° N., long. 53° W.), with evidence indicating probable earlier residence southward toward the Amazon (Lombard, 1928, p. 124). Martius (1867, 1:709) places them at the head of the Anauira-pacú River.

Apalai (*Aparai, Arakwayú*).—Now on the Parú River, formerly also on the Jarí and Curuá Rivers (lat. 1° S., long. 55° W.) (Speiser, 1926).

Apurui (*Apouroui, Upurui, Piriou, Pirio, Piriu*).—On the lower Jarí River (Crévaux, 1883, p. 234; Grillet and Bechamel, 1698). Fauque and Lombard mention them about 1730 as on the middle Oyapock River, (lat. 3° N., long. 53° W.). About this time they were placed in the mission of St. Paul d'Oyapock by P. Arnaud d'Ayma (Coudreau, H., 1891 a). In 1830, Leprieur (1834) found a few on the Armontabo Creek and near the mouth of the Camopi River.

Aracaret (*Aracaré, Aricari, Arikari, Racalet,* etc.).—According to Grillet and Bechamel (1698), they were the ancient inhabitants of the Isle de Cayenne, where they were located in 1673 (lat. 4° N., long. 53° W.). They may be the *Racalet* of Biet (1664), who were allied with the *Galibi* (H. Coudreau, 1891 a). According to Lombard (1928), they were the first Indians to contact the Whites and the first to disappear, being extinct by 1730.

Aramagoto (*Armagoto; Carib?*).—West of the Couyary River in 1730–41; reported around sources of the Camopi River in 1731-43, and on tributaries of the Oyapock in 1763 (lat. 2° N., long. 54° W.). Probably mixed with the *Aramisho* during the 18th century, after being attacked and dispersed by *Tupi* slave hunters (Lombard, 1928, pp. 125–126).

Aramisho (*Aramichaux, Aramisa; Carib?*, but possibly *Arawakan,* see p. 801).—On the Ouaqui River in 1742 (lat. 2° N., long. 54° W.); the Araoua River in 1767 (Lombard, 1928, pp. 124–125).

Arebato (*Carib?*).—Reported by Chaffanjon (1889, pp. 94–99) as on the middle Caura River, around the village of Cuchara and the Raudal del Para (lat. 7° N., long. 65° W.).

Arecuna (*Arekuna, Aricuni;* in British Guiana are known as *Taulipáng, Taurepáng, Jaricuna, Jarêcoune,* etc.).—Used to occupy the Uaupés River drainage; now in the mountains and savannas around the sources of the Caroní, Cuyuni, and Mazaruni Rivers, with a branch in the Roraima region (lat. 4° N., long. 62° W.) (Koch-Grünberg, 1923 a).

Arigua (*Carib?*).—Reported by Chaffanjon (1889, p. 82) on the Tauca River, right tributary of the Caura River.

Arinagoto (*Aringoto*).—On the upper Caroni River (lat. 4° N., long. 63° W.) (Rivet, 1924, map).

Atroahy (*Atrohai, Atroahi, Atruahi*).—On the Rio Negro and Jauaperí and Alalahú Rivers (lat. 1° S., long. 62° W.); related to the *Crichana* (Lima Figueirêdo, 1939; Grubb, 1927, p. 96).

Attaraya.—At the bend of the Mazaruni River (Hilhouse, 1834 a, p. 26).

Bonari (*Boanari*).—On the Uatumã River. Language similar to the Jauaperí River Indians (the *Yauoperi*) (Hübner, 1907). Around the mouth of Rio Negro (lat. 3° S., long. 58° W.) (Ehrenreich, 1904, p 50).

Cadupinapo (*Kadupinapo; Carib?*).—On the Erevato River (Koch-Grünberg, 1922, p. 235).

Caicouchiane (*Calcucheen, Caicusian, Kaikusian, Caicuchana, Kaikuchana; Carib?*).—In the region south of the Ouaqui River (Lombard, 1928).

Calina. See *Carib.*

Camaracoto (*Kamarakoto*).—On the upper Caroni and Paragua Rivers (lat. 6° N., long. 62° W.) (Rivet, 1924; Simpson, 1940).

Carabinani (*Carabeana; Carib?*).—On the Rio Negro and Jauaperí River (lat. 0°, long. 62° W.) (Lima Figueirêdo, 1939). Destroyed villages between the Trombetas and Urucurú Rivers in 1727 and lived on the Kixauaú River, a Trombetas tributary; were warlike and attacked the *Purucuato* (San Mancos, 1903).

Caran (*Karan; Carib?*).—(Lat. 4° N., long. 52° W.). In 1663, they were enemies of the *Nourage* and lived to the east of them. In 1738, they were in the mission of St. Paul d'Oyapock (Grillet and Bechamel, 1698; Lombard, 1928).

Caranariu (*Karanariu; Carib?*).—Probably same as the *Caran.* They lived about 1730 in the same locale as the *Maye.* They came from the south and lived as slaves of the *Palicur.* Now they are extinct (Lombard, 1928).

Carib (*Caripuna, Carinye, Karinye, Calina, Kalina, Pure Carib, Calibite, Caribi, Caribice, Galibi,* etc.).—A widespread group of tribes or hordes in British, French, and Dutch Guiana. They are scattered on the Mazaruni, Cuyuni, and Pomeroon Rivers, and are now in exclusive possession of the Barama and Barima Rivers; they were formerly on the Courantyne, Rupununi, and Guidaru Rivers. The *Caribice* of the lower Essequibo River are said to have retreated when the Dutch settled there (Hilhouse, 1832, p. 236). The *Galibi* was the most important tribe of coastal Guiana in Biet's time (1652). In the 1880's the largest groups were on the left bank of the Maroni River (Coudreau, H., 1891 a). Inland groups became slave hunters in Colonial times. (For the Barama River *Carib,* see Gillin, 1936.)

Cariguano (*Carib?*).—At the head of the Trombetas River (Martius, 1867, 1 :708).

Cariniaco (*Kariniako*).—On the Orinoco, near the mouth of the Caura River (lat. 7° N., long. 64° W.) (Rivet, 1924, p. 661).

Cashuena (*Kashuenã*).—On the Casuro (Cashorro) River, right tributary of the middle Trombetas River (lat. 1° S., long. 58° W.).

Catawian (*Katawian*).—On the Katcana River, south of the *Puricoto* (Grubb, 1927, p. 107).

Cereu (*Carib?*).—In 1727 on the Goayhini River, tributary of the Trombetas (San Mancos, 1903).

Chayma (*Sayma*).—Hilhouse (1834 b, p. 331) refers to this group, a subtribe of the *Acawai,* as living on the Waini (Wayena) and Barama

Rivers (lat. 8° N., long. 60° W.). *Sayma* are mentioned by Raleigh (1928, p. 50) as inhabitants of Cumana.

Chikena (*Sikena*).—On the Katcana River, south of the *Puricoto* (lat. 1° N., long. 58° W.) (Grubb, 1927, p. 101).

Chiricoume (*Carib?*).—Supposed to be between the Jamundá and Mapuerá Rivers, but were not found by O. Coudreau (1903 a).

Comani (*Cumani; Carib?*).—On the Aniba River (Martius, 1867, 1:708).

Comayana (*Carib?*).—On the upper Aroué River; allied to the *Oyaricoulet*. In 1780, they were masters of the Itany River, but about that time were driven into the interior by the *Rucuyen* (*Oyana*) (Coudreau, H., 1893, pp. 58, 79).

Conduri (*Cunuri; Carib?*).—Between the Jamundá and Trombetas Rivers (lat. 3° N., long. 57° W.) (Martius, 1867, 1:708; Acuña, 1641).

Coritanahó (*Carib?*).—On the Ajubacálo River, a Trombetas tributary, in 1728 (San Mancos, 1903).

Couryenne (*Carib?*).—At the mouth of the Orapu River in 1722 (Lombard, 1928).

Crichaná (*Krischaná, Kirishaná*).—On the Jauaperí River and the Rio Branco, up to the sources of the Uraricoera River (lat. 2° N., long. 62° W.) (Barbosa Rodrigues, 1885; Coudreau, H., 1886–87, 2·895).

Cuacua (*Kuakua, Mpoyo, Mapoyo*).—Between the Paruaza and Suapure Rivers, right tributaries of the Orinoco (lat. 7° N., long. 67° W.) (Rivet, 1924).

Cunuana (*Kunuana, Cunuara, Kunuara*).—Closely related to the *Decuana* and *Yecuana* (*Maquiritare, Maiongcong*). On the right bank of the upper Orinoco; also on the Cunucunuma, Padamo, and other right tributaries of the upper Orinoco (lat. 4° N., long. 65° W.). Chaffanjon's *"Maquiritare"* (*Yecuana*) vocabulary may have been taken from this group.

Curasicána (*Kurasikána, Curashikiana, Kurashikiana, Curacicana*).— At the sources of the Biehita River, a tributary of the Suapure (lat. 6° N., long. 66° W.) (Koch-Grünberg, 1922, p. 234). See *Yabarana*.

Curcucuan (*Kurkukuan; Carib?*).—On the upper Cassiporé (Cachipoure) River (Lombard, 1928).

Cusari (*Kusari, Coussani*).—*Carib* identification not certain. (Lat. 1° N., long. 52° W.) They began a slow migration about 1720 on the Courouaie River near the coast. Some reached the mission of Kourou; others the Cassiporé River. Eventually, they spread in all directions and were gradually acculturated to the *Tupi*.

Custumi (*Carib?*).—On the upper Oyapock River in 1730 (lat. 3° N., long. 52° W.) (Lombard, 1928).

Decuana (*Dekuana*).—A branch of the *Yecuana*, on the left side of the middle and lower Ventuari River (lat. 4° N., long. 66° W.).

Diau.—See *Yao;* also *Trio.* On the Iliau River, 7 days' above the confluence of the Apiniwau and Trombetas Rivers (lat. 2° N., long. 57° W.).

Gabinairi.—On the Camanaú River, a left tributary of the Rio Negro (Grubb, 1927, p. 96).

Garipon (*Carib?*).—On the lower Oyapock River to the mouth of the Camopi River (lat. 3° N., long. 53° W.).

Guacará (*Guacari*).—Placed by Martius (1867, 1 :708) between the Jamundá and Trombetas Rivers (lat. 2° S., long. 57° W.).

Guaynungomo (*Waiomgomo, Carana-cuna*).—Same as the *Yecuana* and *Decuana.* In the village of Achagua on the right bank of the Caura River, just below the mouth of the Erebato River; also on the Carana Cuna, right tributary of the Caura River (Chaffanjon, 1889).

Guayuno. See *Pariagoto.*—Spanish name for *Carib* of Venezuelan Guiana, the Cuyuni River, etc.; otherwise known as the *Pariagoto* (Burr, 1897, pp. 306–307).

Guimara.—On the upper Maracá River (Gama Lobo, 1903).

Heurá.—On the Trombetas River in 1727 (San Mancos, 1903).

Ichu.—Probably a branch of the *Yauaperi,* on the Camanaú River, a tributary of the Jauaperí (lat. 2° S., long. 60° W.) (Grubb, 1927, p. 96).

Ihuruána (*Ihuduána*).—A branch or horde of the *Yecuana,* living at the head of the Ventuari River (Koch-Grünberg, 1922, p. 230).

Ingarico (*Ingariko, Engarico*).—Neighbors of the *Taulipáng* and *Arecuna,* north and northeast of Mount Roraima (lat. 5° N., long. 60° W.) (Koch-Grünberg, 1922, pp. 211–212).

Ituan (*Carib?*).—On the upper Cassiporé River (Lombard, 1928).

Macuani (*Macouani; Carib?*).—On the upper Oyapock River in 1729 (Lombard, 1928).

Macushí (*Makusi*).—On the savannas of southern British Guiana and adjacent regions (lat. 3°–4° N., long. 58°–61° W.). In 1778 on both sides of the upper Essequibo River, according to Surville's map (Caulin, 1779). In 1787, the Portuguese report places them in the same region "from Macarapan Mountains to sources of the Mahú (Ireng)." They then had five chiefs, were completely wild, and did not come down to the Rio Branco (H. Coudreau, 1886–87, 2: 392). They were visited by Natterer in 1832, at which time they lived on the Pirarara River which falls into the Mahú, a tributary of the Tacutú and thus of the Rio Branco. Robert and Richard Schomburgk were in contact with them between 1835–44. At present their center lies between the Ireng, Tacutú, and Rupununi Rivers in the borderland between British and Brazilian territory. From there they stretch to the Cotinga River and across it, on both banks of the Surumú River, and south therefrom in the hilly savannas near the *Wapishana* to the region of the upper Parimé-Maruá River. On the right bank of the lower Uraricoera River, near its confluence with the Tacutú River, there are only a few settlements mixed, as on the Surumú River, with *Wapishana*. The most western outpost is on the Island of Maracá at the village of Santa Rosa, on the east point of the island (Koch-Grünberg, 1922, pp. 206–208). They are divided into five important and mutually distrustful hordes, according to Koch-Grünberg. According to Roth (1924, p. 734), they are also to be found on the Parima River, and along the Pacaraima and Kanuku Mountains.

Maitsi (*Mauitzi*).—A sister tribe of the *Maiongcong* (*Yecuana*), mentioned by Robert Schomburgk (1840, p. 403, large map) on the upper Paragua and the Ventuari Rivers. Koch-Grünberg (1922, p. 231) was unable to find any trace of them.

Maye (*Carib?*).—On the savannas of the Coupipi River in 1684; near the mouth of the Oyapock River in 1730 (lat. 3° N., long. 52° W.). They lived like slaves of the *Palicur;* they probably originally came from the south (Lombard, 1928).

Mersiu (*Carib?*).—At the sources of the Arataye River, right tributary of the Oyapock River (Lombard, 1928).

Nourage (*Norage, Nolaque*).—On the upper Approuague and upper Cassiporé Rivers in Cayenne (lat. 3° N., long. 52° W.) (Barrère, 1743, pp. 11, 237). Between the Comté River and Arataye in the 1730's (Lombard, 1928).

Ouayeoué.—Probably the same as *Waiwai*. O. Coudreau (1903 a) identifies them as a *Carib* group she met on the Mapuerá River.

Oyana (*Ojana, Ajana, Ouyana, Uajana, Upuri, Oepoeroei, Rucuyen, Orcocoyana, Orkokoyana, Urucuiana, Alucuyana, Alukuyaña*).— In the southern border regions of Dutch and French Guianas and on the upper Parú, Jarí, Marouini, Lawa, Paloemeu, and Tapanahony Rivers (lat. 2° N., long. 54° W.). (De Goeje, 1908 a, map; Rivet, 1924, p. 662; Roth, 1924, p. 735.)

Oyaricoulet (*Oyacoulet, Ojarikoelle*).—On the upper Tapanahony and Oulémary Rivers. H. Coudreau suggests (1893, p. 32) that they may be the ancient *Amibouan*, or "Longears," mentioned by P. Lombard in 1729 and by Thébault de la Monderie in 1819, in the region of the upper Oyapock River. In Dutch Guiana they occupy the region between the Oranje and Tumuc-Humac Mountains, according to De Goeje (1908 b, map).

Palank (*Palonque*).—Now extinct, formerly on the middle Apirua and Yaroupi Rivers, on the left bank of the Unare River, and to the north of the Tamanaco River, according to Rivet (Lombard, 1928).

Panare.—At the sources of the Cuchivero River, a right tributary of the lower Orinoco (lat. 7° N., long. 66° W.) (Koch-Grünberg, 1922, p. 235). On the Mato River, a left tributary of the Caura River, according to Rivet (1924).

Paraviyana (*Parauiána, Paravilhana, Parauillana, Palaquiyang, Para-uana*).—About 1910 on the Catrimani River and north and east of the Rio Branco (lat. 2° N., long. 60° W.). Only a few remained in the border region in Schomburgk's day, and apparently they have wandered south fairly recently (Koch-Grünberg, 1922, p. 214; M. R. Schomburgk, 1847–48, 1:315). Now absorbed by the *Wapishana*, according to Rivet (1924). (For their culture in 1777, see Ribeiro de Sampaio, 1850.) On the Ocahy River in 1755 (Ferreira, 1903); on the Catrimani River (Gama Lobo, 1903); and on the Guanauau River in 1755 (Ferreira, 1903).

Pariagoto.—On the lower Orinoco, in Venezuelan Guiana, and the Cuyuni River (lat. 7° N., long. 62° W.) (Burr, 1897, pp. 206–207).

Pariqui.—On the left bank of the Amazon, between the Rio Negro and Uatumã River (lat. 3° S., long. 58° W.) (Freitas, 1914).

Patamona (*Partamona, Patomana, Paramona, Paramuni*).—Probably a branch of the *Acawai;* Dance (1881, p. 216) mentions them among the tribes he met from Cumapuru Rapids to beyond the Great Falls of the Demerara River. They are mentioned as "mountaineers" by Hilhouse (1832, p. 240). On the Potaro River (Rivet, 1924, map).

Pauxi.—On the right bank of the Cuminá River, a tributary of the Trombetas (lat. 2° S., long. 57° W.) (Rivet, 1924, p. 660).

Peritaua (*Carib?*).—On the Trombetas River in 1727 (San Mancos, 1903).

Pianocoto (*Pianoghotto, Piannocotau, Pianogoto, Pianacoto, Piana-koto*).—On the upper Courantyne (Corantin) River, on both banks of the Cumanaou River (lat. 3° N., long. 57° W.) (Richard Schomburgk, 1847–48, 2:478). Ehrenreich (1904, p. 50) places them on the upper Trombetas and Jamundá Rivers, whither they probably came in recent times from the Guianas to the north. At the source of the Cuminá River (Grubb, 1927, p. 107).

Pirio (*Piriou, Pyrion*). See *Apurui.*—Near the *Acokwa* in 1673, according to Grillet and Bechamel (1698).

Pishauco (*Pischauco, Pischauko, Pshavaco, Pichauco, Pichauko*).—In the Serra Tepequem, north of the Island of Maracá (lat. 3° N., long. 62° W.). Now extinct. (Koch-Grünberg, 1922, p. 215.)

Puricoto (*Ipuricoto, Parukutu, Purucoto, Purukoto, Purucutu, Pro-goto, Porocoto, Porokoto,* etc.).—On the Uraricapara River, tributary of the upper Parima River (lat. 3° N., long. 62° W.). Said to be extinct now as a tribe (Koch-Grünberg, 1913 b, p. 449). Also mentioned on the upper Trombetas and between this stream and the Mapuerá River. Barbosa Rodrigues (1885, p. 135–145) regards them as ancestors of the *Macushi* and *Crichana.*

Purucuato (*Parucuato, Purucutu, Purukutu*).—On the lower Jamundá River in 1728; also reported between the Mapuerá and Trombe-tas Rivers and at the head of the Trombetas (lat. 3° S., long. 57° W.).

Quiri-Quiripa.—On Gumilla's map, at the head of the Caura River. Chaffanjon (1889) places them on the Orinoco, above the Moitaco River at the village of Kamurika; also on the Purguisi, right tributary of the Orinoco, just below the Caura (lat. 5° N., long. 64° W.).

Rouorio (*Carib?*).—On the coast around the mouth of the Oyapock in 1720 (lat. 3° N., long. 51° W.) (Lombard, 1928).

Saluma (*Saloema*).—On the upper Uanabe (Trombetas tributary); south of the Tumuc-Humac Mountains (lat. 1° N., long. 56° W.).

Sapara (*Zapara*).— Along the south side of the Island of Maracá and on the east end of the island (lat. 3° N., long. 61° W.) (Koch-Grünberg, 1922, p. 216). On the Cauamé and Uraricoera Rivers (Monteiro de Noronha, 1903); on the Mucajahy River (Gama Lobo, 1903); in 1755 on the Ocahy River (Ferreira, 1903).

Serecong (*Serekong, Sarracong, Sarrakong, Sericuna, Serikuna*).— On the upper Mazaruni River (lat. 5° N., long. 60° W.). (Schomburgk, O. A., 1841, p. 385; Uhle, 1913; Schomburgk, M. R., 1847–48, 2:237, 253.)

Suppaye (*Sapaye*).—In 1673 on the lower Approuague River, on the Atoroui, and in Suriname (Grillet and Bechamel, 1698).

Taira (*Tayra*).—Between the Moroni and Oyapock Rivers (lat. 3° N., long. 53° W.). According to Patris, in 1762 they drove the *Emerillon* from the Camopi River. They were at war with the *Emerillon* in 1766. H. Coudreau (1893, p. 257) mentions one village at head of the Mana River, another at the head of the Abounami River.

Tamanac (*Tamanak, Tamanaco*).—On the middle Caura River and westward; on the southern bank of the middle Orinoco and southward (lat. 7° N., long. 65° W.). Now extinct.

Taparito (*Taparita*).—On the middle Caura River and westward; between the Caura and Cuchivero Rivers (lat. 6° N., long. 66° W.) (Koch-Grünberg, 1922, p. 235).

Tapicari (*Carib?*).—On the upper Mucajahy River, formerly on the Rio Branco (Gama Lobo, 1903).

Terecumá (*Taracum, Sericumá*).—Between the Auavilhana and Uatumã Rivers (Martius, 1867, 1:708).

Teweya.—Eastern border of the *Taulipáng* area (lat. 4° N., long. 60° W.).

Thuruaná.—On the upper Ventuari River (Rivet, 1924, map).

Tiverighotto.—On the Rio Branco (Roth, 1924, p. 743).

Tonayena (*Tunayana*).—On the Katcana River (lat. 2° N., long. 56° W.) (Grubb, 1927, p. 107).

Trio (*Drio, Diau, Kiliu*).—In the 18th century, lived all along the Tapanahony River; now on the upper Paloemeu River, upper Courantyne River, and upper courses of the Amazon tributaries arising in this region (lat. 3° N., long. 57° W.). Linguistic identification is uncertain, inasmuch as H. Coudreau (1893, p. 79) states that the true language has no resemblance to *Rucuyen* (*Oyana*).

Uassahy (*Carib?*).—On the Jauaperí River (lat. 2° S., long. 62° W.) (Freitas, 1914).

Upurui.—In southwest Suriname (lat. 2° N., long. 55° W.). On the Paloemeu River, they are mixed with the *Oyana* and speak the same language (De Goeje, 1906, vocabulary).

Wai (*Ouay, Ouen*).—Near the junction of the Jamouri and Apirua Rivers (Lombard, 1928).

Waica (*Waika, Uaica, Uaika*).—On the Cuyuni River (lat. 6° N., long. 60° W.); show close linguistic resemblance to the *Arecuna* and *Macushi,* according to Tavera-Acosta (1921–22). Rivet places them in the Yuruari River region of Venezuela and on the Barama River of British Guiana (Rivet, 1924, p. 663); but there were none on the Barama in 1932–33 (Gillin, 1936). Not to be confused with the *Shirianá Waica* (pp. 861–864).

Waimiry (*Uaimiry, U-ah-miri*).—On the Rio Negro and Jauaperí, Mahua, and Campinas Rivers (lat. 1° S., long. 61° W.). (Grubb, 1927 p. 96).

Waiwai (*Woyamana, Waiwe, Ouayeoue*).—On the upper Essequibo River drainage and south (lat. 1° N., long. 59° W.). Probably on the Mapuerá River.

Wayumara (*Waiyamara, Waéamara, Uaiumaré, Wuaiamare, Uaimará, Oyamara, Guimara*).—On the Island of Maracá and its region (lat. 3° N., long. 62° W.) (Koch-Grünberg, 1922, pp. 216–217). Are these the same as the "*U-ah-miri*" (*Waimiry*) placed on the left bank of the Jauaperí River by Payer (1906, p. 219)?

Wöciare (*Uiquiare, Uiquire, Uaiquire, Weciare*).—At the sources of the Paro, or Parú, River, right tributary of the Wanapiari (Koch-Grünberg, 1922, p. 234). Close to, if not a dialect of, the *Yabarana*.

Yabarana.—There are now 20 to 30 *Yabarana* on the middle Ventuari River (lat. 5° N., long. 65° W.); it was formerly the principal tribe, with language very different from the *Maquiritare* (*Yecuana*). They have two dialects, the *Curasicana* and *Wökiarc.* The former is spoken on the upper Biehita River; the latter on the upper Parú River (Koch-Grünberg, 1922, pp. 233–234).

Yao (*Iao, Anacaioury, Caripou-Yao, Yaye*).—Identified as *Carib* by Adam (1890 b). Nimuendajú (1926, p. 17) places them at the mouth of the Oyapock River in the 17th century (lat. 4° N., long. 52° W.), and calls them *Arawak.* Keymis (1811) says that in 1596 they were fighting the *Arawak* who lived on the Barima River and who, in league with the Spanish, drove the *Yao* out of the Moruca (Moruga) River. Harcourt (1613) states that the *Yaio, Arawacca, Sappaio,* and *Paragoto* were allied against the *Carib.* Rivet (1924) places the *Yao* on the

Ivaricopo (Brazil) and Kaw Rivers. Wilson (1906) refers to them as *Yaye*.

Yapacoye.—On the left bank of the Itany River, south of the *Comayana* (lat. 2° N., long. 55° W.). They understand the *Oyana* language and have similar customs (Coudreau, H., 1893, p. 84).

Yauaperí (*Yauapiri*).—On the Jauaperí River (lat. 2° S., long. 61° W.).

Yecuana (*Yekuana, Maquiritare, Makiritaré*).—*Macushi* call them *Maiongking, Maiongcong, Maiongkong, Mayongong, Maingcong, Mayonggong, Maschongcong, Maschongkong*, and *Waiomgomo*. On the Merevari, Paraba, and upper Mazaruni Rivers (lat. 4° N., long. 65° W.). (Roth, 1924, p. 734; Crévaux, 1883, p. 379; Koch-Grünberg, 1913 b, p. 459; R. H. Schomburgk, 1841 b, p. 215; O. A. Schomburgk, 1841, p. 467; Chaffanjon, 1889, ch. 19.) According to L. Williams (1941), they are found on the Erebato and Cunaracuni Rivers, upper left tributaries of the Caura River.

THE CALIANAN FAMILY

Caliana (*Kaliana*).—An independent linguistic family on the upper Parauá River, a left tributary of the Caroni River (Rivet, 1924; Koch-Grünberg, 1913 b, 1922, p. 227). Not to be confused with the *Tupian Calianá* of the Tumuc-Humac Mountains.

THE MACUAN FAMILY

Macú (*Makú, Maca, Maucu, Mahacu*).—An independent linguistic family on the middle Auarí River, a left tributary of the middle Uraricoera River (Koch-Grünberg, 1922, pp. 227–228). Not to be confused with the *Macú* of the Rio Negro and Japurá River, who are of the *Puinave* family; the *Macú* of the Ventuari River, who are of the *Saliva* family; nor with the *Maco* of Lake Cuyabeno (Ecuador), who are of the *Cofán* family (Rivet, 1924, pp. 670–671). (See pp. 864–867.)

THE MURAN FAMILY

Mura.—A small acculturated group is reported on the right bank of the lower Urubú River (Grubb, 1927, p. 96). (See pp. 255–266.)

THE SALIVAN OR MACUAN FAMILY

Ature (*Adole*).—Five leagues up the Orinoco from the mouth of the Meta River (lat. 6° N., 68° W.) (Gumilla, 1791, 1:291). Chaffanjon (1889) states that they have become extinct. (See *Piaroa* below.)

Macú (*Makú*).—Occupy the savannas of the right bank of the middle and lower Ventuari River, from its mouth to several days above the mouth of the Cunucumina River (lat. 4° N., 68° W.) (Rivet, 1924, p. 677).

Piaroa (*Atures*).—On the Sipapo River and the right bank of the Orinoco in the region of Atures and Maipures Falls; on the upper Cataniapo River; also on the lower Orinoco tributaries, Zama and Mataveni, according to Tavera-Acosta and Crévaux. According to Chaffanjon, they extend as far as the mouth of the Guaviare River and on the right Orinoco bank from the Paraguassú River to the Ventuari (lat. 5° N., long. 68° W.). Koch-Grünberg (1922, p. 236) found them on the savannas of middle and lower Ventuari and on the upper courses of its tributaries, the Camani and Mariéte; they are also believed to live on unexplored right tributaries of the Orinoco, above the mouth of the Ventuari, such as the Jáo and Puruname Rivers. Tavera-Acosta (1907, p. 76) identifies them with the ancient *Ature* (q. v.).

THE SHIRIANÁN FAMILY

The *Guaharibo, Shirianá,* and *Waica* are described elsewhere (pp. 861–864).

THE TUPIAN FAMILY

Apanto (*Apoto*).—On the Jamundá River and eastward to the Trombetas (lat. 2° S., long. 57° W.). (Acuña, 1891, p. 176; Martius, 1867, 1:708; Métraux, 1928 a, p. 32.)

Calianá (*Calayoua, Calayona, Kalianá*).—On the southern slopes of the Tumuc-Humac Mountains (lat. 2° N., long. 55° W.), near the *Oyampi*.

Camacom (*Kamakom*).—Around sources of the Paraparantuba River in Brazilian Guiana, west of the *Cusari* (lat. 2° N., long. 53° W.) (Rivet, 1924, map).

Cusari (*Kusari*).—Probably originally *Carib,* now acculturated to *Tupí.* On the Anauira-pucú River, Brazilian Guiana, near the Amazon mouth; at the head of the Araguary River (lat. 1° N., long. 53° W.) (Rivet, 1924, map). On the upper Arawari and Napari Rivers (Leprieur, 1834).

Emerillon.—Along the east Brazilian coast from the Amazon mouth north into French Guiana (lat. 4° N., long. 54° W.). At present they form one nation with the *Oyampi.* They migrated from the south, beginning about 1736–37, into the basin of the Oyapock River, where former residents were *Carib.* Probably preceded the *Oyampí* into the Guianas (Métraux, 1928 a, pp. 33–34; Coudreau, H., 1893, pp. 156, 392, 596).

Guayapi. See **Paikipiranga.**

Oyampí (*Oyambi, Aipí, Aiapí, Uajapí, Oaiapí, Guyapí, Ayapí, Guaiapy, Waiapi, Wayapí, Paikipiranga* (q. v.)).—In French Guiana and on the Brazilian coast north of the Amazon mouth (lat. 2° N., long. 53° W.).

Now a single nation with the *Emerillon*. They came from south of the Amazon about 1736, because of fear of the Portuguese, but, after arriving in Guiana, they aided the Portuguese in slave hunting, their victims being mainly the *Carib*. They entered French Guiana about 1800–20. Those already settled in Guiana pushed northward again in 1828, as a result of an epidemic. Since 1850, they have been strongly influenced by the *Oyana* (Métraux, 1927, pp. 30–34). They are also reported on the Yary (Jarí) and Guarataburú Rivers.

Paikipiranga (*Parichy*).—At the head of the Maracá River (Rivet, 1924, p. 690; Métraux, 1928 a, p. 32; Nimuendajú, 1927; Farabee, 1917 b). Mentioned by Vasconcellos (1859) as being at the head of the Araguary River and wishing to settle in Cachoeira on the Anauira-pucú (Villa Nova) River. They were at Macapá in February 1860. The Indians whom Farabee (1917 b, p. 139) called *Paikipiranga* called themselves *Ayapí* or *Wayapí,* and Nimuendajú considers them to be *Oyampí.* This group disappeared, dying off and intermarrying with rubber workers (Nimendajú, 1927).

Uara-Guaçu (*Araguaju, Uaçu*).—Near mission of Urubuquara, between the Parú and Gurupatúba Rivers. (Métraux, 1928 a, p. 32; Martius, 1867, 1 :708; Nimuendajú, 1926.)

THE WARRAUAN FAMILY

The *Warrau* are described elsewhere (pp. 869–881).

LINGUISTIC FAMILY UNIDENTIFIED

Acarapi.— At the source of the Parimé River (Gama Lobo, 1903).

Aniba (*Anoiüba*).—On the Aniba River (Martius, 1867, 1 :708).

Aramayu.—On the Oyapock River, near Anotaye in 1730 (Lombard, 1928).

Aritarai (*Harytrahe*).—On the Gurupatúba River (Martius, 1867, 1 :708).

Armabutó.—At the head of the Anauira-pucú River (Martius, 1867, 1 :708).

Aturajuz.—On the Guanauau River (Résumé . . ., 1903) in 1755 (Ferreira, 1903).

Axina.—On the Camoó River in 1728 (San Mancos, 1903).

Baenna (*Mbae-una*).—On Lake Saraca (Martius, 1867, 1 :708).

Cabareijo.—On the Hetabú River (San Mancos, 1903).

Calauamái.—In 1727 on the Trombetas River (San Mancos, 1903).

Calcouó.—On the Coromuó River in 1728 (San Mancos, 1903).

Camará.—On the Trombetas River in 1727 (San Mancos, 1903).

Camaré.—On the Camoó River in 1728 (San Mancos, 1903).

Canahaubó.—On the Camoó River (San Mancos, 1903).

Caparanao.—On the Coromuó River in 1728 (San Mancos, 1903).

Chaperú.—On the Caiai River (Monteiro Noronha, 1903).

Guajurá.—On the Ocahy River in 1755 (Ferreira, 1903).

Heno.—On the Camoó River in 1728 (San Mancos, 1903).

Hoaluxa.—On the Trombetas River in 1727 (San Mancos, 1903).

Hureana.—On the Trombetas River in 1727 (San Mancos, 1903).

Japy.—On the upper Mapuerá and Tueréné Rivers (Coudreau, O., 1903 a).

Juhi.—On the Trombetas River in 1727 (San Mancos, 1903).

Macacabo.—On the Cabremen River in 1728 (San Mancos, 1903).

Macorei.—On the Trombetas River in 1727 (San Mancos, 1903).

Makenu.—On the Trombetas River in 1727 (San Mancos, 1903).

Maprouan.—According to Grillet and Bechamel (1698), a few on the Oyac River in 1673, remains of a tribe formerly living in the Amazon; were attacked by the *Arian*.

Maracana.—Along the Uraricapara River (Roth, 1924, p. 735; Koch-Grünberg, 1922, p. 227). On the Uraricoera River (Lima Figueirêdo, 1939). Enemies of the *Shirianá* (Grubb, 1927).

Maruaru.—Koch-Grünberg (1922, p. 235) heard of them north of the Ventuari River.

Matocoxima.—On the Trombetas River in 1727 (San Mancos, 1903).

Maxaro.—On the Trombetas in 1727 (San Mancos, 1903).

Mayoyaná Naucú.—In the interior of the Trombetas drainage; come occasionally to the Urucurin River (San Mancos, 1903).

Moroux.—Between the *Pino, Macapa,* and *Apurui* (Lombard, 1928).

Morulaboca.—On the Camoó River in 1728 (San Mancos, 1903).

Oanaháuhó.—On the Camoó River in 1827 (San Mancos, 1903).

Oanu.—On the Ajubacálo River in 1728 (San Mancos, 1903).

Ojemuna.—On the Ajubacálo River in 1728 (San Mancos, 1903).

Orabaru.—On the Joruá River (San Mancos, 1903).

Orekia.—On the Ajubacálo River in 1728 (San Mancos, 1903).

Paranacori.—On the Ajubacálo River in 1728 (San Mancos, 1903).

Paraugoaru.—On the Cabo River in 1728 (San Mancos, 1903).

Patuo.—On the Coromuó River in 1728 (San Mancos, 1903).

Pujala.—On the Trombetas River in 1727 (San Mancos, 1903).

Seden.—On the left bank of the Amazon, between the Negro and Uatumã River (Figueirêdo, 1939).

Taguari.—Between the Jamundá (Yamunda) and Trombetas Rivers (lat. 2° S., long. 58° W.) (Martius, 1867, 1:708).

Tamocom.—On the Moucourou and Carapanatoube (upper tributaries of the Jarí River); in contact with the *Oyampí* during the rainy season (Leprieur, 1834).

Taucu.—On the Trombetas River in 1727 (San Mancos, 1903).

Tucane.—On the upper Mapuerá and Tueréné Rivers (Coudreau, O., 1903 a).

Tucujú.—On the Tueré River (lat. 2° S., long. 53° W.) (Martius, 1867, 1:709).

Tutumú.—On the Camoó River in 1728 (San Mancos, 1903).

Uariua.—Koch-Grünberg (1922, p. 235) heard of them on the Mariéte River.

Uayoru.—On the Caiai River (Monteiro Noronha, 1903).

Waruwádu.—Koch-Grünberg (1922, p. 235) heard of them living in the high mountains of the watershed between the upper Ventuari and Erebato Rivers.

Xibiliana.—On the Trombetas River in 1727 (San Mancos, 1903).

Xikiana.—On the Huheini River (San Mancos, 1903).

Xumi.—On the Trombetas River in 1727 (San Mancos, 1903).

HISTORY

Historical documents concerning the native peoples of the Guianas prior to the last decade of the 16th century do not exist. The area had been ignored by Europe. Spain, busy with the consolidation and exploitation of her territories in western South America, had made no serious attempt to extend her dominion east of the Orinoco River, other than to found the settlement of San Thomé on the Orinoco River, as the nucleus of the intended province of Spanish Guiana. Portuguese settlements had not reached the mouth of the Amazor River by 1600, and it was only in 1612–15, as defense against the increasing activities of Dutch and English trading posts in the lower Amazon, that the Portuguese outpost of Pará was established. Between Pará and the outposts of the Spanish Main stretched the "Wild Coast," or Guiana, practically unknown.

To the Dutch and English, in fear of the Spanish and Portuguese, the possibilities of Guiana were enhanced by its multiplicity of rivers, which made attack by the Iberian powers difficult. The earliest English explorers were in quest of El Dorado or the fabled city of Manao. Sir Robert Dudley, in 1595, sent a boat's crew 16 days up the Orinoco River, and later in 1595 Sir Walter Raleigh journeyed 400 miles up the river. Besides establishing a lasting reputation for friendly dealings with the Indians, Raleigh wrote the first book, albeit somewhat fanciful, on the region. In 1596, Lawrence Keymis, a companion of Raleigh's first voyage, landed on the west side of the Amazon Delta and proceeded along the Guiana coast to the mouth of the Orinoco River. He surveyed the whole coast, giving the first systematic outline of the location of tribes (Keymis, 1811), rivers, and products. The tribes were apparently moving eastward from one river valley to another in advance of the Spanish penetration of Venezuelan Guiana. Keymis ascended the Oyapock River to the first falls and found the region inhabited by *Arawak*. Leonard Berry, in 1597, penetrated the Oyapock, Marouini, and Courantyne Rivers to the first rapids of each and was well received by the natives. In 1598, the first recorded Dutch expedition arrived on the Guiana coast to be hailed by a party of *Carib* on the Caurora (Cayenne) River, asking if they were "Anglees." In 1604, Charles Leigh planted the first settlement, an English one, on the Oyapock River and a period of English and Dutch exploitation began. The English, Dutch, and French Guiana colonies of the 17th century were under private companies which, with limited means, established trading factories rather than plantations. Their relations with the Indians were good; they did not attempt to enslave the natives nor to seize their lands. On the Oyapock River, the *Arawak* induced Leigh to defend them against the *Carib* on the Wia and the Cayenne Rivers. Leigh's colony on the Oyapock River failed after his death in 1605, and was succeeded in 1609 by Robert Harcourt's colony. Harcourt (1613) gave us the first extensive account of the manners and customs of the Indians of the Guiana coast. With the building of a Dutch factory and fort by Groenewagen in 1616 on the Essequibo River at the mouth of the Mazaruni River (Kyk-over-al) and of another Dutch factory in 1624 on the Berbice River, the Dutch interests in the region were established and have since persisted in spite of many territorial readjustments. The French, who at first suffered a series of massacres at the hands of the *Carib,* obtained a permanent foothold around the Cayenne River during the second quarter of the 17th century.

Although, beginning about 1616, the English and Dutch had established a number of factories and plantations along the right bank of the Amazon River, as far as the mouth of the Tapajóz River, they were cleared out by 1625, after a series of Portuguese attacks from Pará. Relations with the Indians were reported to be friendly, but details are lacking. From 1625 until the middle of the 19th century, Portuguese activity north of the Amazon River was confined largely to missionary explorations, desultory general exploring, and the establishment of a few towns. On the other side of the area, the Spaniards, in what is now Venezuelan Guiana, suffered somewhat from the raids and revolts of the *Carib,* who occasionally allied themselves with the English and Dutch. In the 18th century, Capuchin missionaries reduced to mission status a considerable number of *Carib* living on the right tributaries of the Orinoco River, particularly around the lower Caura and Caroni Rivers. During the same period the Dutch developed a slave-hunting partnership with certain *Carib,* particularly the *Acawai,* whereby the latter hunted members of less warlike tribes in the interior, even as far as the Portuguese territory beyond the head of the Essequibo River. Such slaves, however, were eventually superseded by Negroes, as large sugar and rice plantations developed along the coasts of the English and Dutch colonies. From the first quarter of the 18th century, relations between the Indians and Europeans of these areas were on the whole friendly, the Indians retiring into the interior from such lands as were given over to plantations. Since the interior was not exploited to any extent by Europeans, White culture influences were for the most part confined to trade. Up to the present, Indian contacts with the Whites of interior Guiana have been predominantly with traders, small-scale placer miners, ecclesiastics, occasional ranchers (as on the Rupununi savannas), and explorers. European conquest and direct labor exploitation have not been characteristic of the region.

At the present time all the governments of the region have made some provision for the "protection of the aborigines" of the interior, which places certain restrictions upon their contact with, and exploitation by, outsiders. While the basic outlines of aboriginal culture still predominate among most of the tribes of the interior, numerous borrowings have affected the details of the culture of practically all of the Guiana tribes—borrowings of certain European and African words, occasional Christian religious concepts, a few Africanisms in myth and ritual, and artifacts, such as iron cutting implements, trade cloth, and steel needles.

SOURCES

The ethnography of the Guianas suffers from the lack of systematic modern studies of individual tribes. Roth's publications constitute the standard compilation, but they underemphasize many aspects of nonmaterial culture and fail to cover thoroughly the material of Brazilian and Venezuelan Guianas. Ahlbrinck's "Encyclopaedie der Karaiben" (1931), another compilation of *Carib* material, is useless to much of the scholarly world by reason of its being published in Dutch. Most of the earlier information must be combed out of the accounts of missionaries and explorers. Among the better of these for ethnographic purposes are Barrère, Stedman, Brett, Waterton, Kappler, and Quandt. Among the scientist-explorers, who usually give reliable, if sometimes incomplete and unsystematic accounts, are the brothers Schomburgk, Koch-Grünberg, Farabee, Crévaux, Appun, and H. Coudreau. Modern systematic accounts dealing with single tribes are to be found under the names of Ahlbrinck, Gillin, Nimuendajú, A. P. and T. E. Penard, Simpson, and Speiser. Because of the material, it is difficult to determine precisely the pre-European patterns or even the modern distribution of traits and movements of peoples throughout the area. The literature on the Brazilian portion of the Guianas is of little value, except for inferences regarding the geographical locations and historical movements of tribes. The same is only slightly less true of the literature of the Venezuelan portion.

ARCHEOLOGY

The archeology of the Guianas has not been systematically investigated by planned field surveys and coordinated excavations. Our present knowledge is derived from reports of chance finds by ethnologists and travelers, plus a few exploratory excavations. Perhaps because of the relative paucity of European settlements and travel in the interior, the bulk of the finds have been made around the geographical margins of the area. In the absence of a comprehensive picture of the actual archeological resources of the interior, statements regarding prehistoric distributions of culture and population for the Guianas as a whole must remain highly tentative. Furthermore, chronological determinations are almost entirely lacking. Typological divergence of artifacts from types used by historic tribes implies prehistoric status, of course; but, although typological cross-dating to dated sites outside the Guianas seems to offer an approach to a more refined prehistoric chronology, it has not been accomplished successfully, nor as yet hardly attempted.

We may summarize the principal types of sites from which archeological material has been reported as follows: (1) Caverns or caves, (2) artificial burial wells, (3) shell mounds or sambaquís, (4) open surface sites with scattered artifacts but no structural remains, (5) painted or incised rocks usually found in the interior near rapids or falls of rivers, (6) stones circles or alignments, and (7) graves dug below the surface of the ground.

Cave sites of archeological interest have been reported only in the Amazon River drainage and on the Orinoco River. One of the best known is the group of caves on a small tributary of the Maracá River, which joins the Amazon River from the left, just west of the Island of Marajó. The site was reported by Ferreira Penna (1877) and Hartt (1885). In a number of small natural caverns in the escarpment of the plateau, at some distance above the river, were found numerous funerary urns representative of human and animal forms and of fruits. The urns had been set in regular order about the floors of the caves, indicating that the latter were special mortuary chambers. Hartt discovered that the site was composed of three groups of caves, quite distinct from each other, but all overlooking the same stream. Some jars held a pelvis encircled by long bones standing on end around the inside of the jar with a skull on top, a feature also found by Nimuendajú at the site of Rebordello, Island of Caviána, at the mouth of the Amazon River (Nordenskiöld, 1930 a, pp. 21–22). The urns are mainly cylindrical and are crudely decorated in relief—molded, applied, and incised—with thick elephantine "arms" and "legs" the most striking feature. The style is quite distinct from that of Pacoval (Marajó), and the pottery is inferior in all respects. The paste contains much sand, the walls are thick and irregular, and the surface is poorly smoothed, unpainted, and colored red from imperfect firing, while the interior portions of the paste remain black or greenish.

Other cave sites along the left bank of the Amazon include Miracan-uêra, 14 miles (22.5 km.) upstream from Serpa, and a site near the mouth of the Trombetas River, in the district of Obidos. The first series of caves is 5 miles (8 km.) long; the second stretches along the river bank for 2 miles (3 km.) (Ferreira Penna, 1877). Both sites yielded funeral urns made of fine clay richly decorated. The Miracan-uêra urns are distinguished by a white slip which gives a porcelain effect to the surface. Nimuendajú also found fragments of urns in caves near Ulakte-Uni on Mount Ukupi, near Oyapock River, in Brazilian Guiana. The pottery shows a cream and pinkish background and decorations both in brownish paint and in long, raised relief, representing eyes, noses, and eyebrows (Nordenskiöld, 1930 a, pl. 23).

The one other well-known funerary cavern in the Guiana region is the Cavern of Ataruipes on the right bank of the Orinoco River, near the mission of Atures. Humboldt (1852–53, 2:289), who reported it, thought it a cemetery of the extinct *Atures* (*Piaroa*) tribe. In a large cave under a projecting rock he found 600 human skeletons, each in a quadrangular basket of palm leaves averaging 10 inches (25.5 cm.) by 3 feet 4 inches (100 cm.). The bones were whitened in the sun, dyed red with annatto, or, like mummies, varnished with odoriferous resins, and wrapped in the leaves of the *Heliconia* or plantain. According to the Indians, bodies were exposed for several months and the skeletons then scraped with sharp stones for sepulture. Near the baskets were urns, measuring as much as 5 feet (1.5 m.) in height and 3 feet 3 inches (1 m.) in width, green in color and of a graceful oval outline. Applied handles or lugs in the form of crocodiles and serpents formed the decoration, as well as painted labryinths, meanders, and frets. Unfortunately, much of Humboldt's collection was lost. (See Wickham, 1827, for a later description of the site.)

Near this site, on the Island of Curcurital in the Orinoco River, Crévaux (1883, p. 561) reported finding a cave high in the rocks, containing a large number of skeletons, each enclosed in a pottery vessel, and a number of other skeletons covered with palm matting. Chaffanjon (1889, p. 183) also reported funeral urns in the grotto of Arvina at Punto Cerro near the Atures rapids.

In summary, two centers of the use of natural caverns as mortuary chambers containing funerary urns of pottery, in which bones were secondarily buried, have been reported for the Guiana region, the left bank of the lower Amazon and the right bank of the middle Orinoco. Differences in detail in pottery and burial styles would indicate possible derivation from a common cultural source rather than a close cultural connection between the two centers in the Guiana region itself. Further explorations may indicate that secondary urn burial in caves was more widespread. The trait has not been reported for any Guiana tribe in historical times.

Specially constructed burial wells were discovered by H. Coudreau at the site of Monte Curú, on the small Igarapé da Holanda, a left tributary of the Cunani River, and fully reported by Goeldi (1900) and Pinto Lima Guedes (1896), as the result of an expedition under Goeldi's leadership from the Museu Paraense in 1895. The Igarapé da Holanda enters the Cunani River at the fifth falls, and the Monte Murú, a small hill, rises some 1,300 feet (400 m.), upstream from the creek's mouth. The site was marked by a piece of worked granite in the form of a truncated pyramid on the summit of the hill, somewhat similar to those used as land markers by Europeans. Twenty-six feet (8 m.) on either side were two large granite disks, each about 20 inches (50 cm.) in diameter and 5½ inches (14 cm.) thick, which were found to cover two wells each about 8 feet (2.5 m.) deep. In the bottom of each well was an excavated area, shaped like an imperfect sphere about 3 feet (90 cm.) in radius, opening into the well shaft toward the east. In these vaults were found pots of various forms and sizes, the largest in the center, the smaller ones ranged about the sides. Some were like earthen pans with small cavities in the bottom, others like a tray divided into four quarters; one was like a small cylinder, and two were like large spheres. In addition were several large-bellied urns decorated with modeled face and head, with pierced ears, and small spindly arms and legs. The urns contained fragments of calcined bones in such number that it was thought that each urn was the receptacle for the remains of more than one individual. The pottery was decorated not only in relief but also with dichromatic designs, although the colors are less brilliant and the relief is more rigid and less elaborated than the designs from Pacoval (Marajó).

Disks similar to those covering the wells at Monte Curú were found south of the Amazon River, according to Teodoro Sampaio (1922), in Ceará (Cariri territory); at Carui, with sculptured figures about the periphery; at Coronzo; Sertão de Inhamuns; Icó; and Pirangi; as well as in the States of Piauí, Rio Grande do Norte, Pernambuco, Baía (site of Cachoeira), and Alagoas (site of Riochão, Municipio de Viçosa). The Cunani nucleus, like that of Marajó, is linked by Uhle (1913) to finds on the Napo River (eastern Ecuador) and to the *Chibchan* cultures of Colombia and Costa Rica. Numerous other writers have considered the Marajó pottery, at least, to be the work of *Arawak* who migrated from Central America along the Guiana coast to the mouth of the Amazon River and thence spread upstream into the interior of the continent. (See Nordenskiöld, 1930 a.)

Shell mounds have been reported from the coastal region of British Guiana, particularly in the vicinity of Morawhanna; Akawinni Creek, and the upper Pomeroon River (Roth, 1924, p. 77), and from various sites on the left bank of the Amazon as far as the mouth of the Trombetas River. Among the sites on the Amazon the best known are Pinheiro, some miles north of Belém, and Lago Grande de Villa Franca, near Obidos. Various specialists have advanced varying estimates, based on conchological studies, of the antiquity of the Amazonian shell mounds (or sernambys) without reaching a definitive conclusion. At present we may say that they indicate the presence of a fishing population of some antiquity along the Guiana coast and in the lower Amazon valley.

Open surface sites have been reported in all parts of the area. Some of the principal locations and the type of archeological material found at them follow: Sandhills on the Demerara River: elongated, curved, double-edged celts engraved with head of akuri (Roth, 1924, pl. 3, A, B) and a pestle 7 inches (17 cm.) long. The Demerara and Essequibo Rivers: small celts with trimmed and rounded butts, straight ground cutting edges (ibid., pl. 3, C-E). The Courantyne River: large rounded heavy celts with truncated butt and rounded cutting edge (ibid., p. 75), also a chipped celt of gray limestone with thick ovoid blade. The Kanuku Mountains: flat, side-notched celts (ibid., pl. 4, A, B). Kanuku Mountains and Rupununí River: notched celts of ground technique (ibid., pl. 4, C, D). East bank of Demerara River: ground constricted-neck celts (ibid., pl. 4, E). Barima River: wide-notched ground celt (ibid., pl. 4, F). Dadanawa on the upper Rupununi River: stone knives and fragments with chipped, irregular edge of the same type used by *Waiwai* for cutting cassava (ibid., pl. 6, G). Pacaraima Mountains: chipped stone scrappers (ibid., pl. 6, H-K). Skeldon on the Courantyne River: stone mortars in round, ovoid, and elongated shapes. Potaro River: stone pestles. Demerara River: stone pestle (ibid., pl. 82). Various other sites of this type have been reported, for instance, Kouriabo on the Barima River where the soil "is composed almost entirely of flint utensils, idols of clay, broken ollas, and cinerary urns. Here without doubt existed a native pottery-making shop" (Toro, 1905, pp. 130–132). Although no geological evidence is available, it is doubtful that these open sites antedate European occupation for any considerable period.

Painted or incised designs on rocks occur throughout the Guianas, where rock surfaces are available, usually near rapids or falls of the rivers. Speculation upon whether the designs had religious significance or whether they were applied simply as amusement by canoe men resting at a portage are inconclusive at present. But on the whole, the painted designs are more elaborate and seem more often to be of possible ceremonial importance. Pecking of designs is to this day a favorite occupation of resting canoe travelers, according to the reports of many explorers.

As examples of Guianese pictographs and petroglyphs we may mention the following: Cerro Pintado, 7½ miles (12 km.) south of the Atures rapids on the Orinoco: designs of a lizard, centipede, square-bodied men, a bird, various bizarre figures, and a lizard and a serpeant about 400 feet (120 m.) long pecked in granite porphyry (Chaffanjon, 1889, p. 189, illustration). Cerro Teramoto, between the lower Cuchivero and Caura Rivers: 2 rocks in the middle of a plain inscribed with 2 tangent "suns" and a figure taken to be the moon (ibid.). Urawan River, a branch of the Cuyuni River: painted frogs (McTurk, 1882, p. 129). Curiebrong River, a branch of the Potaro River, at Amailah Falls: red painted human figures on sandstone (Brown, 1876). Monte Alegre, left bank of the Amazon River: red painted figures of caimans, birds, and circles on a high cliff (Wallace, 1889, p. 204). Ihla da Pedra, on the Rio Negro just below its junction with the Rio Branco: numerous engravings of men, birds, animals, 13 men dancing in a row, and 2 ships under sail (Schomburgk, Robert H., 1841 c, p. 261). Casiquiare River, just south of Pomoni, circles and lines on granite (ibid., p. 248; Koch-Grünberg, 1907, figs. 2, 8, 10). Numerous sites in the western Guianas (Rojas, 1878, pp. 176–198). Maroni River, near the Ile Portal (Crévaux, 1883, p. 143). Montagne d'Argent, between the Cayenne and Oyapock Rivers (ibid., p. 145). Oyapock River (ibid.). Rupununi River (Schomburgk, Robert H., 1836 b, p. 275; 1840, 1:320; Im Thurn, 1883, p. 394). Yapore on the upper Essequibo River: a human head incised on rock by rapids (Roth, 1924, p. 605). Camuti or Taquiari Rocks on the upper Essequibo River: pecked designs (Robert Schomburgk, 1841 a, p. 159). Kuyuwini Creek on the upper Essequibo River: pecked designs on blocks of green sandstone (ibid., p. 168). Babumana Creek, upper Essequibo River: monkeys and frogs (Brown, 1876, p. 244). Quitaro River, beyond Ataraipu Rock: rising sun with human face incised (ibid., p. 152). Several sites on the Berbice River (Schomburgk, Robert H., 1837 a); temehri (*"Carib"*) Rock, Courantyne River: gigantic engraved figures, one of which measured more than 10 feet (3 m.) in height (Brown, 1876, p. 314). Rio Branco, 12 miles (19.3 km.) from Marau: incised designs on granite boulders 300 to 400 feet (91.5 to 122 m.) high (Schomburgk, Robert H., 1841 b, p. 213). Suquadie River, a branch of the Ireng River, near Twin Falls: flat jasperous sandstone rocks in the savanna carved with figures of the sun, snakes, spirals, and circles (Brown, 1876, p. 288). To the north of Serro do Panellão, between the Parimé and Surumu Rivers: pictographs made with a sharp pointed stone, as demonstrated by *Macushi* and *Wapishana* Indians (Koch-Grünberg, 1907, p. 28). Upper Parimé River, Pedra Pintada: a large rock completely covered with scratched pictographs (ibid., fig. 18). Various sites on the Rio Negro (Schomburgk, Robert H., 1841, pp. 186 ff.; Wallace, 1853, pp. 151 ff.; Koch-Grünberg, 1906 c, pp. 293 ff.; Netto, 1885). Cuminá River (Coudreau, O., 1901, pp. 33 ff.). Serra do Ereré, west of Monte Alegre (Hartt, 1885, pp. 300 ff.). Near Noura on left bank of Rio Negro (Barbosa Rodrigues, 1885, pp. 168–170). Numerous sites have been reported from the lower Amazon River (Costa, 1938, pp. 125 ff.). As Pinto (1935, p. 58) points out, the majority of the designs represent dangerous animals, such as those which are powerful spirits of the *Carib* medicine man, heavenly bodies, flying or grotesque human figures, or masks. In so far as this is true, the designs may be thought of as mythological, if not ceremonial. On the other hand, numerous more common designs appear, apparently the product of mere whimsy or crude attempts at representation. Neither rock inscriptions nor paintings figure in the ceremonial life of any tribe of the area reported by Europeans, whereas the practice of this form of art as an amusement or time killer has been fairly widely reported.

Several possible stone circles, alignments, or dolmens have been reported from the area. For example, in the Waetipu Mountains on the way from Cara-Cara to the Ireng River is a line of small white quartz rocks set close together in a row 50 yards (46 m.) long, while red painted figures on the walls of a cave nearby are said to commemorate a *Carib* killing of a tiger (Brown, 1876, p. 189). On the Cuchivero River, to the east of the sierra, Chaffanjon reports stone alignments, with the remark that the ancient inhabitants of the region are said to have come here to worship the moon. In a grotto in the Raudal of Chicharra, in the same region, is a stone structure somewhat like a dolmen with a table rock on top and on the interior walls simple designs as well as fantastic figures (Chaffanjon, 1889, pp. 57–58). In the middle of the savanna on the Island of Bouche de l'Enfer on the Orinoco River are three rocks, 20 to 24 feet (6 to 7 m.) distant from each other covered with inscriptions one-third of an inch (1 cm.) deep and several depressions made by polishing stone artifacts. Chaffanjon thought the rocks might have been placed in position by human beings (ibid.).

Finally, in various parts of the area, skeletal material, together with artifacts, has been found in shallow graves in the ground. Since many of the present-day tribes practice burial within the house floor, these finds are not necessarily to be considered of great interest archeologically. However, west of the lower course of the Caura River, near the deserted village of El Benco, Chaffanjon found several rocks placed as if to mark tombs. Skeletons covered by turtle shells, rock, and wood, were found under, or at the foot of, the rocks, 8 inches (20 cm.) deep, with head on knees, arms folded around legs, small vases held between the hands, and accompanied by two figurines.

As to artifacts, other than pottery, the region has yielded chipped stone knives or scrapers but no stone arrowheads or spearheads (Roth, 1924, p. 77). Although the ground-stone ax is commonly found, socketed or perforated heads seem to be absent. One distinctive artifact remains to be mentioned, the muyraquitã, or "stone of the tribal chief" (*Tupi*: Mira, "nation"; ki, "chief"; ita, "stone"). These small, perforated, zoomorphic pendants made of green nephite have been found in a restricted region about the mouths of the Jamundá and Trombetas Rivers and the neighboring lakes and backwaters (Barbosa Rodrigues, 1875 a, b; Heger, 1924). Mello (1924) reported a specimen from Pernambuco which shows that this trait traveled south of the Amazon River, if it was not indigenous there. Nordenskiöld (1930 a, pls. 39, 43) illustrates two statuettes, one in the form of a stylized bird of gray slate from near the confluence of the Igarapé do Nazario and Arapuins River; the other, in the form of an animal in gray greenstone from São Joaquim, between the Igarapé de Franceza and the Couanany River. He also shows a muyraquitã in greenstone and cites Heriarte's (1874) rare description of the *Tapajóz* Indians of the 17th century who used the same type of pendants, called by them buraquitã. According to Heriarte, beads were made in round, oblong, droplet, bird, and beetle shapes from a green clay which later hardened into rock. The same author says that similar objects were made by the Indians of the Trombetas River, who also used a remarkable clay for pottery. The *Araquiz* (*Arawak; Aroaqui,* according to Nimuendajú) between the Tapajóz and the Madeira Rivers had the same types of pendant idols and also pottery which, according to Heriarte, they traded to tribes as far away as the Orinoco River. These indications, together with evidence of a radiation of Santarém pottery forms into the region north of the Amazon (Palmatary, 1939), would speak for some culture interchange between Brazilian Guiana and the region to the south.

Another remarkable type of artifact from the region deserves mention, namely the medium-sized idols of which Nordenskiöld (1930 a, pls. 40, 41) illustrates two. One was found at Sacurujú, on the left bank of the Trombetas River, below the falls. It is 7 inches (17 cm.) high and has the form of a man seated, with mouth wide open, orbits empty, six-fingered hands in front, and head held between the paws of a lizard-like animal mounted on his back. The material is brownish soft stone and the base is perforated by two parallel holes. A second specimen in the same general style came from the shore of Lake Jacupá, between Lake Sapukuá and the Trombetas River, a place called Boa Vista de Santa Anna. This specimen is 11 inches (27.5 cm.) high and represents a woman with mouth open, orbits empty, with an animal similarly mounted on her back and with two parallel perforations in the base. Harcourt (1613, p. 109) heard from a *Carib* Indian that his tribe near the headwaters of the Oyapock River kept such an idol in a special house. Bettendorf (1910, p. 353) speaks of mummies and possibly stone idols among the Tapajóz River Indians, and João Daniel (1840–41, p. 480) definitely mentions stone idols on the Tapajóz River in the 17th century.

A review of our somewhat scattered knowledge of the archeology of the Guianas and an examination of the older records suggest that at least the margins of the area were occupied in prehistoric times by peoples whose pottery, burial customs, and religion were more advanced or elaborate than those of the Indians described in the 18th century and later. As Nordenskiöld remarks, no Indians of modern times in the Amazon River region, with the exception of a few groups such as the *Arawak* and *Betoya* of the Rio Negro, show a culture of the level which seems to have survived in the lower Amazon River as late as the 17th century.

There is only one noteworthy example of the use of archeology to illuminate the post-Columbian movements of tribes in the Guianas.

On the upper Jarí (Iratapuru) River, Nimuendajú (1927) found open sites near a stream which yielded pottery of considerable excellence, bearing both incised and applied relief. One pot was anthropomorphic. The pots had convex bottoms, concave or straight sides, and were decorated in heavy horizontal bands with incised spirals, parallel lines, and quadrangular elements. Nimuendajú attributes these vessels to the *Oyampí,* who, he believes, left them on their journey northward into the Guianas in the early 18th century. The sherds are similar to material from old *Guaiapy* sites of the middle Xingú River, and *Waiapy* (*Guaiapy*) is the *Aparai* name for the *Oyampi*. The *Guaiapy* disappeared from the Xingú River about the same time that the *Oyampi* appeared in Guiana; and the trip from the Xingú River to the Jarí River would be easy because the mouths of these two rivers are opposite each other on the Amazon River.

CULTURE

SUBSISTENCE ACTIVITIES

Farming.—The majority of the tribes farmed by the slash-and-burn method. Bush was usually cleared by the men, each working alone at his convenience, or assisted by relatives, or "peitos" (see p. 849); occasionally, they worked in gangs fortified by drink furnished by the owner of the field (Bates, 1892, p. 221). Stone axes were formerly used to girdle large trees, which were then burned. Now most tribes have iron axes. Large trees generally lie where felled, but the smaller trees and the brush are piled and burned at the end of a dry season. Wood ashes are used to improve the soil, but other fertilizers are not generally used. Soil exhaustion required either a constant cutting of new fields or alternation of planting and fallowing, the latter seldom being reported, because of the rapid regrowth of the forest.

Fields are seldom more than 1 or 2 acres (4,000 or 8,000 sq. m.). Planting is usually done between the stumps and fallen logs of a clearing, immediately after the burning (pl. 111, *top*). Probably the only aboriginal implement was the digging stick, which was used primarily for loosening the soil or for digging holes in the ground in which to plant cuttings or seeds. The "shovels" mentioned by Gumilla (1791, 2:29) were apparently elaborated digging sticks. The soil was rarely cultivated after planting; but the garden was weeded. The machete, or cutlass, introduced by European trade, is now used for weeding and for cutting brush. Possibly clubs were used aboriginally to knock down brush, as Gumilla speaks of them. Although Roth (1924, p. 214) states that planting is women's work, there are numerous tribes in which only the men plant, e.g., *Camaracoto* (Simpson, 1940, p. 387), or in which both sexes cooperate, e.g., *Carib* (Gillin, 1936), *Taulipáng* (Koch-Grünberg, 1923 a, 3:50), and *Acawai* (Hilhouse, 1832). Weeding, however, is generally women's work, as is harvesting the crops, except for kraua grass, of which men make cords and baskets.

Manioc, which is planted from cuttings, is everywhere the basic crop. Both "sweet" and "bitter" varieties, especially the latter, are grown. Other aboriginal cultivated plants include the pineapple, papaya, coconut(?), calabash, sweet potato, arrowgrass, cotton, tobacco, pepper, avocado, and maize. Practically all the tribes now cultivate one or more of the plants introduced by the Europeans, such as the banana, plantain, yam, edo, sugarcane (pl. 112, *top*) and, sporadically, citrus fruits. Beans do not seem to have been cultivated aboriginally nor are they common now. Although squashes and pumpkins are now common, we hear little about them in earlier times.

A number of tribes seemed to have practiced no horticulture, but maintained themselves on a hunting-gathering-fishing economy. Among these were the *Waica* (the more backward tribe of the *Shirianán* family), the *Macú* (who may now have some cultivation but were traders in Koch-Grünberg's time), and the *Caliana*. These groups live in the mountainous interior and may be regarded as refuge groups. Several other tribes which seem to have acquired horticulture from their neighbors in recent, if not post-Columbian times are the *Warrau* of the coast and the *Shirianá* and *Auaké* of the mountainous interior. These tribes are described elsewhere (pp. 869–885, 861–867, 862).

Collecting.—Wild fruits, honey, insects, and reptiles are collected by all the tribes, although invariably such sources play merely an accessory role in the food supply. Among the vegetable foods collected are hog plums, fruits of various palms, and palm cabbage (along the coast and near the Orinoco Delta), guava, mushrooms, sapodilla, custard apple, Brazil nut, various berries, sweet tree beans, and wild bananas. No special collecting methods are used, although trees are sometimes felled for their fruit. Tree climbing is reported, with loops pinning the feet and supporting the back. Certain trees are especially useful. For example, Schomburgk and Gumilla state that the buriti palm (*Mauritia flexuosa*), provided the *Warrau* leaves for roofing houses, fibers for thread, and rope used to make hammocks, edible pith, material for sandals from the leaf sheath, conelike fruits regarded as a confection when soaked in water, sap for the manufacture of an alcoholic drink, and the edible larvae of a beetle. According to Gumilla, wild rice was used on the Orinoco River. In case of famine, the seeds of the mora, greenheart, dekamballi, and pario trees are grated and baked into cakes on the cassava pan. Honey is collected by smoking out the bees and is usually eaten in the comb, along with any larvae which may be present. Occasionally, honey is mixed with water, but is neither fermented nor stored.

Among the more usual animal foods collected are the turtle and tortoise, iguana, lizard, caiman, frog and toad, crab, mollusks, worms, caterpillars, beetles, ants, wasps, bees, and tree grubs. Frog eggs are taken by hand from streams, and frogs are sometimes trapped in small pits dug in the bottom of ponds. Snakes are seldom, if ever, eaten, but are captured with a noose or sticks to sell to traders. Shellfish and snails, gathered from rocks in river beds and elsewhere, formed a large item in the menu of the coastal peoples, to judge by the middens. Neither worms nor any available insects are despised as a food.

On the whole, however, the resources of the Guiana region are not such as to make a life which depends primarily upon food collection a satisfying one even to people of very low culture.

PLATE 105.—**Guiana house frames.** *Top: Mapidian. Bottom: Waiwai.*
(Courtesy University Museum, Philadelphia.)

PLATE 106.—**Guiana houses and villages.** *Top: Taruma* Indians and house. (Courtesy University Museum, Philadelphia.) *Bottom:* Arabupu, an *Arecuna* village on the savannas at the jungle border. (Courtesy T. D. Carter and the National Geographic Magazine.)

PLATE 107.—**Guiana houses.** *Top: Macushi. Bottom: Waiwai* house interior with three tiers of hammocks. (Courtesy University Museum, Philadelphia.)

PLATE 108.—**Guiana house construction.** *Top: Yecuana-Ihurana* cone-shaped roof. The roof is covered from the inside out with palm leaves. *Bottom:* Completed hut. (After Koch-Grünberg, 1923 b.)

PLATE 109.—**Fishing in the Guianas.** *Top: Waiwai* crushing a vegetable fish drug. *Bottom: Wapisiana* shooting fish. (Courtesy University Museum, Philadelphia.)

Plate 110.—**Panare blowgun.** *Top:* Using the blowgun. *Bottom:* Preparing curare dart poison. (Courtesy Llewelyn Williams.)

PLATE 111.—**Growing and preparing manioc in the Guianas.** *Top: Tarumá* cassava field. *Center: Tarumá* woman squeezing manioc in tipití. *Bottom: Macushí* woman grating cassava. (Courtesy University Museum, Philadelphia.)

PLATE 112.—**Guiana industries.** *Top: Macushi* cane-press. *Bottom: Waiwai* pig traps. (Courtesy University Museum, Philadelphia.)

PLATE 113.—**Guiana Indians in the late 19th century.** *Top, left:* Hunting a sloth (man on trunk using climbing ring). *Center, right: Oyampi* making a bark canoe. *Bottom: Galibi* making pottery. (After Crévaux, 1891.)

PLATE 114.—**Rucuyen Indians fishing and hunting.** Late 19th-century drawings. *Top:* Killing fish. *Bottom:* Shooting birds from a blind. (After Crevaux, 1891.)

PLATE 115.—**Guiana women weaving and spinning.** *Top: Wapisiana. Bottom: Waiwai* spinning. (Courtesy University Museum, Philadelphia.)

PLATE 116.—**Guiana weaving and woodwork.** *Top: Wapisiana* woman weaving a hammock. *Center: Macushi* woman weaving a skirt of beads. *Bottom, left: Yecuana* man painting a manioc grater after the stone splinters have been set. *Bottom, right:* Smoothing the manioc board with an adze. (After Koch-Grunberg, 1923 b.)

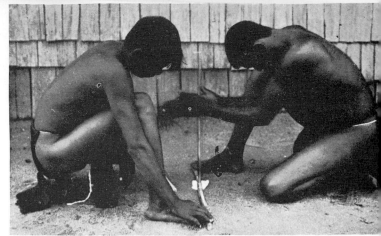

PLATE 117.—**Guiana household and camp scenes.** *Top: Wapisiana* making fire by drilling. *Center, right:* Eating. *Bottom, right:* Smoking monkeys on babracot. *Left:* Interior of *Macushi* house. (*Center* and *bottom, right,* after Farabee, 1918 c; others, courtesy University Museum, Philadelphia.)

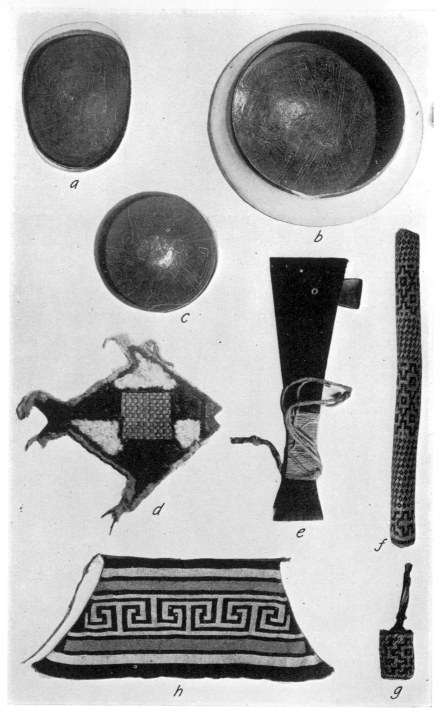

PLATE 118.—**Guiana artifacts.** *a–c*, Pottery vessels of the *Aparaí*. (Courtesy Carlos Estevão.) *d, Aparaí* basketry device, in shape of a fish, for holding ants. It is applied to the body during certain ceremonies. *f, g, Yauaperí* maracás, or basketry rattles. *h*, Tanga, or bead apron, worn by women. (Courtesy Museu Paraense Emilio Goeldi, Belém.) *e*, Stone ax hafted in hardwood, Dutch Guiana. (Courtesy Museo Etnográfico de la Facultad de Filosofía y Letras, Buenos Aires.)

PLATE 119.—**Guiana religion, dances, and burial.** *Top: Macushi* Christian service. *Center: Mapidian* dance. *Bottom:* Urn burial from the *Macushi* area. (Courtesy University Museum, Philadelphia.)

PLATE 120.—**Guiana cremation, curing, and ceremonialism.** *Top: Rucuyen* cremation. *Center: Apalai* shaman curing by blowing cigar smoke. *Bottom: Rucuyen* feast of the dead. (After Crevaux, 1891.)

PLATE 121.—**Guiana costumes and transportation.** *Top, left: Apalai* festive dress. *Top, right: Wapisiana* carrying wood. *Bottom, left: Parikutu. Bottom, right: Parikutu* chief. (Courtesy University Museum, Philadelphia.)

PLATE 122.—**Guiana women.** (Courtesy University Museum, Philadelphia.)

PLATE 123.—**Guiana types.** *Top: Wapisiana* dancers. *Bottom: Waiwai* dancer in festive costume. (Courtesy University Museum, Philadelphia.)

PLATE 124.—**Guiana types.** *Top: Panare* women. *Bottom, left: Waiwai* men. *Bottom, right: Mapidian* men. (*Top,* courtesy Llewelyn Williams; others, courtesy University Museum, Philadelphia.)

Hunting.—All tribes hunt with a variety of weapons: blowguns (pl. 110, *top*), bows and arrows, spears, harpoons, traps (pl. 112, *bottom*), and dogs. The blowgun has a spotty distribution, and centers in the west-central part of the area, among the *Macushi, Taulipáng,* and *Arecuna.* The bow and arrow has a more general occurrence. Arrows have barbed points for game, blunt points for birds, and sometimes poisoned points for monkeys. Clubs are perhaps used to dispatch wounded animals. Traps include arrow traps, deadfalls, nooses, and spring snares; some are baited, some unbaited.

Usually, only one or two men hunt with dogs although encircling drives for deer and even monkeys are not infrequent. Grass burning to drive deer in the savanna country is practiced by the *Macushi.* Blinds made of leaves and branches are used in hunting accouri and certain birds (pl. 114, *top*), such as the powis (*Crax* sp.). "Calls" for attracting game animals are common but the apparatus consists merely of folded leaves. In hunting nocturnal animals, such as labba, torches are used to blind the animal when it is surprised on the trail or at the water hole. Stealth and trailing ability mark Guiana hunting methods, and large organized hunts with special officials are not reported.

Dogs are trained to assist in hunting and receive special care; burrowing insects are removed from their feet and skin and, to sharpen their olfactory powers, preparations such as pepper juice or mashed caterpillars are injected into their nostrils.

Hunters usually prepare to protect themselves magically for the hunt. Most widespread is the use of binas, plant or animal substances, or species intimately associated with the individual hunter and believed to charm the game. Taboos of various types are likewise frequent; somewhat less common is purification through biting ants held in special triangular basketry frames, as reported for the *Macushi* (Roth, 1924, pp. 178–179). Hunting magic is further discussed under Religion.

Among the commonly hunted game animals in most parts of the area are the accouri (*Dasyprocta aguti*); armadillo, usually dug out of its burrow; anteater (*Myrmecophaga*), hunted for its hide but seldom eaten; peccaries (*Tayassu pecari* and *T. tajacu*); deer of several varieties; manatee, or sea cow, usually hunted with arrows from a canoe; monkeys, usually taken with blowgun or arrows; otter, hunted from canoes, but seldom eaten; the three-toed sloth, hunted, at least by *Acawai;* tapir, (pl. 113, *top, left*), or bush cow, the largest animal of the region; the capybara, or water hog, usually found feeding in the grass and reeds along stream banks; and many types of birds, of which powis, wicissi ducks, and tinamou are most preferred for food, and parrots and macaws for feathers. Ducks are occasionally seized by underwater swimmers (Dance, 1881, p. 233). Water turtles are hunted with arrows shot into the air, by diving, and by turning them on their backs when ashore.

Land turtles are occasionally hunted with dogs. Iguana are shot with bows and arrows or caught with slip-noose traps (Pomeroon River *Carib*). Iguana eggs are also collected. Caimans are captured with loops or lassos or heavy traps, or shot in the eyes with poisoned arrows. The tail and eggs of the caiman are particularly prized.

Domesticated animals and pets.—Dogs were the only aboriginal domesticated animals of the Guiana region, although most tribes kept smaller wild animals and birds as household pets. At present chickens are found in many Indian settlements; they are admired for their fighting qualities and appearance but they and their eggs are seldom eaten. Turtles are sometimes kept alive in ponds for future food.

Fishing.—In this region of many rivers, fishing is of first importance to a almost all tribes. In general the methods may be classified as follows: (1) Hook and line; (2) poisoning; (3) traps; (4) nets; (5) killing with arrows or spears of various types; and (6) miscellaneous methods. Although the methods are arranged in the order of their frequency of use, certain methods cannot be assigned exclusively to certain tribes. In modern times metal hooks have become ubiquitous through trade, but the aboriginal hook seems to have been of the gorget type, baited, and used on a throw line, drop line, rod, spring line of several types (Roth, 1924, pp. 197–198), or on a set line, although the last may be a European introduction. Lashing the water with a rod is also effective seasonally in certain regions (pl. 114, *top*). Poisoning (pl. 109, *top*) is usually done in relatively quiet water and necessitates building a fence across the stream against which the dead or stupified victims may be caught. The commonest poison throughout the area is derived from the roots of various species of *Lonchocarpus,* the active ingredient of which is the chemical compound, rotenone. Leaves, seeds, and fruits of various species of *Clibadium* are used either to poison the water or to poison the fish directly when they swallow the poison in the form of balls. *Tephrosia toxicaria* is reported used by the *Macushi.* Other fish poisons include the juice of the leaves of *Phyllanthus conami,* nebi ("bush rope," liana), chips of moraballi wood, roots of the sinapou, and wild agave seeds.

In addition to spring lines and set hooks, the Indians caught fish in a variety of enclosing and holding traps, such as fence weirs, enclosing baskets, and cone-shaped wicker baskets which are usually used with fences although occasionally they are rigged into a spring trap which hoists the basket out of the water after the fish has entered it. Dip nets of kraua fiber appear to be a western (Rio Negro, Rio Uaupés) trait, as they are reported only from the interior and not along the coast. Harpoon arrows (pl. 109, *bottom*) and throwing spears, often with multiple heads, are a secondary method employed only in clear water. The modern *Warrau* use a harpoon. Miscellaneous methods mentioned in the literature include the use of bait, such as insects, cast on the water to entice fish to the surface, where they can be clubbed or killed with cutlasses; catching by hand; the building of dams, the impounded water of which is bailed out and the fish captured; and the muddying of the water to force the fish to the surface.

Food preparation.—Throughout most of the area, manioc is peeled, grated (pl. 111, *bottom*), squeezed in a basketry tube press (pl. 111, *center*) and baked in thin discoid cakes on pottery disks (now iron) over the fire.   Manioc graters (pl. 116, *bottom*) were formerly made of a block of wood set with chips of stone; the stone is usually imported from the mountainous interior.   Their manufacture has deteriorated of late years, however, and the block of wood is now covered with a sheet of perforated tin.   Certain of the central tribes used to carry on a considerable trade in graters which they manufactured.   In Brazilian Guiana, farina, instead of cakes, is prepared by drying the pressed mash on plates over the fire.   Except in Brazilian Guiana and among the non-horticultural groups, cassava bread constitutes the staff of life and may be smoked, wrapped in leaves, and stored under the roof of the house. Maize is eaten green, either boiled or roasted, or is made into a fermented drink; it is never ground dry.   Surplus meat is dried and smoked over a low fire on platforms (pl. 117, *bottom, right*) of green saplings, with or without being previously salted.   Fish after being split dorsoventrally in the sagittal line, are similarly heated.   Meat and vegetables are usually boiled together in the "pepper pot," which is kept constantly simmering over the fire and seasoned with peppers and the expressed juice of the bitter manioc.   Pieces of meat and fish are also roasted over the fire, impaled on pointed sticks.

Fermented drinks are described elsewhere (p. 854).   Nonintoxicating beverages are made from various cultivated plants as well as from berries and the sap of the ite palm and the fruits of a number of other palms (*Oenocarpus, Euterpe edulis, Astrocaryum tucumoides, Bactris minor*). Nonfermented drinks are usually taken as fresheners upon arising.   Red pepper and the boiled juice pressed from the bitter manioc were the standard aboriginal condiments; salt was available on the surface in some parts of the savanna, was boiled out of sea water by coastal groups, and was obtained from the ash of certain palm trees, particularly the central rib of the kokerit leaf.   Many tribes, however, used no salt.   Earth eating is occasionally mentioned (*Trio, Macushi*), but it seems to be an individual peculiarity.

VILLAGES AND HOUSES

Relatively small settlements, seldom if ever containing more than 200 individuals, oftener 30 to 40, are the rule; this size is presumably determined by the limitations of the food-producing techniques. Guiana settlements tend to be impermanent because of the exhaustion of the soil, intertribal wars, the exigencies of trade, and customs demanding the abandonment or destruction of dwellings upon the death of their owner or residents. In forested country, the settlement is usually located at some distance from the navigable river bank, often as protection. Other means of protection are rare. Palisades are mentioned occasionally: two *Arawak* villages on the Demerara River, an *Arecuna* village, and an *Acawai* village on the upper Mazaruni River. Poisoned spikes in the paths approaching the village are mentioned in the early accounts of the *Acawai* and among the *Carib* (?) on the Oyapock River. House building everywhere seems to be primarily a male occupation.

The men of all tribes build temporary shelters of a number of different patterns for overnight protection on the trail and on hunting and trading expeditions. These consist essentially of a framework of saplings supporting a hastily thatched roof, and can be erected within half an hour. In form they may be described as lean-to's, triangular flat-roofed (fig. 119, *a*), gable-roofed (fig. 119, *b*), or some combination of these forms.

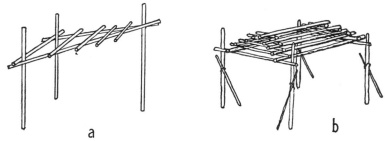

FIGURE 119.—Guiana banabs, or temporary shelter frames. *a*, Simple, triangular form; *b*, rectangular form. (Redrawn from Roth, 1924, figs. 69, 68.)

Small structures for the shelter of the hollow-log drinking trough are present in most villages.

The basic type of permanent dwelling seems to be the single-family house, grouped into small settlements. The beehive type, round in ground plan, conical-roofed, and thatched down to the ground on a frame of saplings bent over and tied together at the top without interior support, may have been an early type, but now has nearly disappeared. The *Rucuyen* sleep in such structures as protection from mosquitoes. These huts have a single low entrance. More common is the rectangular house with pitched roof and supported horizontal ridge pole (fig. 120, *a*). Possibly the older form of this type was provided with sapling rafters inserted into the ground along the sides and bent over to the ridge pole at the top (fig. 120, *c*), providing basis both for thatched roof and wall.

This type is reported among many eastern *Carib* groups. Simpler is the wall-less rectangular house with pitched roof, supported on four or six upright posts (Barama River *Carib,* coastal *Warrau*). The rectangular type is widespread throughout the area. Large circular houses occur in the central area among such groups as the *Arecuna* (pl. 106, *bottom*), *Taulipáng, Wapishana, Macushi,* etc. This type is structurally different from the simple beehive type, having a central supporting post and a circular wall frame with uprights, rafters, and tie-beams (pl. 105; fig. 120, *d*). Large houses of this type, 50 feet (15 m.) in diameter and 70 feet (21 m.) high, are apparently confined to the westerly reaches of the area, again indicating influence from the western Amazon region (pl. 108).

Walls are relatively rare among forest tribes but more common among savanna dwellers. The aboriginal pattern made use of wattle, closely-set poles, and thatch or bark. The daubed and adobe walls found in the Caroni and Rupununi River savanna country appear to be influenced by European prototypes. Rectangular pile houses with floors are reported from the early coastal *Warrau* and from the *Galibi* of Cayenne (French Guiana) and Suriname; otherwise only earth floors were seen. Many transitional house forms occur, such as the rectangular ground plan with

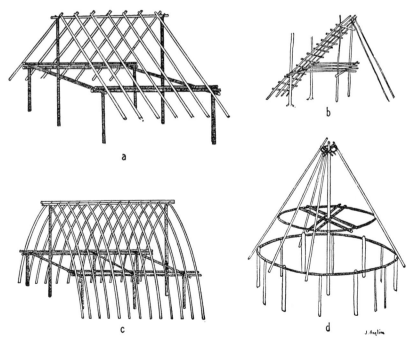

FIGURE 120.—Guiana house frames. *a,* Permanent house, rectangular, 2-post type; *b,* permanent house, lean-to type; *c,* permanent house, arched type; *d,* circular house. (Redrawn from Roth, 1924, figs. 75, 70, 71, 72.)

apsoidal ends used by the *Camaracoto* (fig. 121), *Arecuna,* and Barama River *Carib.* Several types of houses were sometimes used by a single tribe, the *Camaracoto* having three, the *Macushi* four, and the *Arecuna* (pl. 106, *bottom*) three. From few tribes do we have any mention of house decoration although painted designs on posts or walls are reported from the *Rucuyen, Apalai,* and *Macushi.*

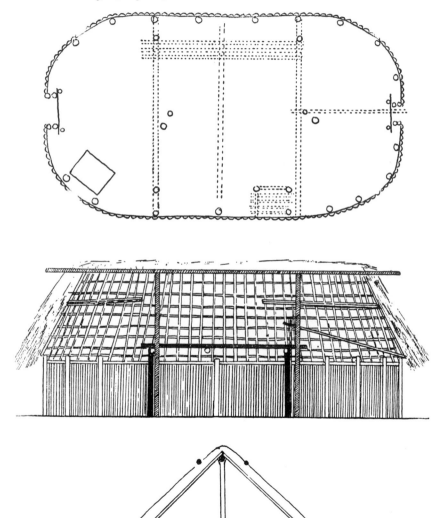

FIGURE 121.—*Caramacoto* house. (Redrawn from Simpson, 1940, fig. 6.)

What appeared to be a bachelor house is mentioned in early accounts of the Cayenne *Carib*. A special house for dances and assemblies is also mentioned.

Household furniture is sparse (pl. 117, *left*), consisting essentially of hammocks used for sleeping and daytime lounging (pl. 107, *bottom*); wooden benches of the elongated, four-legged type (fig. 122), often carved

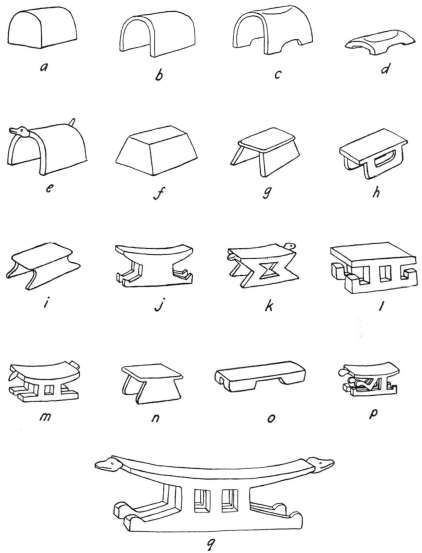

FIGURE 122.—Guiana wooden seats. *a, c,* Common form for *Arawak, Carib, Warrau; b, d, Acawai,* and *b* i- also an *Oyana* type; *e, Macushi; f,* common *Arawak* and *Carib* form; *g, Macushi; h, Baniva; i, Patamona, Macushi; j, Arawak; k, Arecuna; l, Macushi; m, Arawak; n, Macushi; o, Barama; p, Macushi; q, Warrau.* (Redrawn from Roth, 1924, fig. 81.)

into stylized animal shapes; logs smoothed for sitting purposes; and fire-places consisting of two or more stones around a pile of ashes. Numerous domestic implements are usually found in the houses. Telescoping baskets are commonly used as containers, although many objects are stored under the roof thatch, hung by strings from the rafters, or placed on the tie poles under the roof.

ENGINEERING WORKS

Paths or trails, rather than roads, are characteristic of this region. Streams are bridged, if at all, simply by felling a log across the water. Occasionally a handrail of wood or of bush rope is provided.

DRESS AND ORNAMENTS

Permanent ornamentation by deformation of the head is mentioned occasionally among the Cayenne and Suriname coastal *Carib, Tarumá,* and *Maopityan,* although the evidence is not clear that the deformation was intentional. Frontal deformation occurs on the coast, and fronto-occipital and side-to-side in the interior. Filing of teeth is also not universal, being mentioned for the Cayenne *Carib, Wapishana,* and *Guajajara.* Perforation of the lower lip and the insertion of a pin or pendant ornament (pl. 121, *bottom, right*) may be an original *Carib* trait, for it is almost universally practiced among these people and to some extent among *Arawak* groups (the *Wapishana*). *Mura* men perforate both lips. Piercing of both cheeks and the insertion of parrot feathers is practiced among the *Acokwa* of the Cayenne River, certain unspecified Suriname River coastal groups, and the *Tarumá.* Perforation of the nasal septum and the insertion of bars or pendant ornaments was formerly very general, being repeatedly reported from *Arawak, Carib,* and *Warrau* groups. Perforation of the ear lobe is widespread while the perforation and decoration of the helix is limited to the *Tarumá,* Berbice River *Arawak,* and some other groups. Depilation of eyebrows and of the face generally is almost universal, although many *Carib* groups favor the preservation of the mustache and beards in the men. Eyelash removal is rare but has been reported in two instances. Pubic hair is removed by both sexes among most *Arawak* and *Warrau,* by neither sex among the *Rucuyen,* by females only among the *Shirianá* and Barama River *Carib,* and variably among the *Carib* tribes. Tattooing is widely practiced, but its application by the individual is restricted. Facial tattooing is more prevalent among the *Arawak* and *Warrau* and among some *Carib.* Tattooing is most commonly found on the forearm, where it is often associated with magic, such as the puberty ordeals and the use of hunting binas and other charms. The method was either incision with animal teeth or pricking.

Impermanent ornamentation includes the use of body unguents and oils of various kinds to give a shiny appearance and to protect the body against insects. Body and face painting occurs widely (pls. 121, *bottom;* 122, *bottom*). The *Arawak* emphasize painting the total body, and the *Carib* and *Warrau* only the face. Annatto, urucú, and genipa provide vegetable stains, usually black or dark red. Women are often expected to paint the designs on the men's bodies. Designs are applied for ceremonies, dances, and war parties. Sticking tufts of down or feathers on the body is common, with the *Carib* groups preferring the forehead thickly covered with white down. The use of crab oil for dressing the hair is ubiquitous among the coastal peoples. Hair dressing styles are varied and show no regularity of distribution. One of the more common styles is a center part with the hair in the middle enclosed in a wrapping which hangs down the back; another is a straight fringe across the forehead with a "high-bob" around the head. The *Carib* of the Caroni River region shaved their heads, leaving a topknot. Two-bar single-type combs of palm splinters were used among the central and southern groups. Headdresses include peaked palm-leaf hats; crowns of wickerwork decorated with multicolored feather patterns; net caps covered with feathers; filets of cotton decorated with tassels, knots, feathers, and insect wings; and forehead bands similarly decorated. Chiefs and others of distinction among some tribes wear specially elaborate ceremonial headdresses (pl. 121, *top, left*). True masks, either for face or body, are unknown, except for a full-length costume worn by the *Rucuyen* in their whipping dance. Arm and leg bands of cotton and liana fiber, sometimes decorated, are common, especially among *Carib* tribes. The *Carib* of both sexes frequently produce abnormally bulging muscles by wearing tight ligatures above and below the calf and bicep. Necklaces of all kinds of available materials, but not of metals, are worn by all tribes. Rings carved from nutshells and girdles made of cotton, hide, hair, or bark are ubiquitous. The *Patamona* and *Macushi* produce hollow-cylinder plaited belts of vine fiber.

Accounts of absolute nakedness among the *Carib* are so common in the early literature as to raise doubt as to whether the use of loincloths or aprons, now so general, was ever an aboriginal custom. The use of an apron of trapezoidal shape by women may have originally been an *Arawak* trait; the beaded aprons (pl. 118, *h*) of the *Wapishana* and other tribes are a late improvement. Materials used for loincloths or aprons in early days appear to have been bark cloth, unwoven cotton threads, and possibly woven cotton textiles of small size. Bark cloth used for sleeveless shirts was formerly made, at least in Venezuelan Guiana, from the inner bark of the same trees which furnished cigarette wrappings. Sandals of palm fiber and of hide are worn by the present-day Indians of the savannas, but, as the term for sandal frequently seems to be a corruption of Spanish "pisar," or of "zapato," they may be a recent introduction.

TRANSPORTATION

Carrying devices.—No domestic animals are used for transport in this region. On land, all transport is by human beings; on water, by a number of types of boats. The principal carrying device is the rimmed carrying frame—a wickerwork or basketry container attached to a rectangular frame and suspended on the back by means of a tumpline over the head (pl. 121, *top, right*). The container is typically open at the top end and on the rear side, and closed on the bottom end and on the right and left sides. The load is kept in position by lashings running back and forth across the open rear side between the right and left edges. (See Roth, 1924, pp. 375–377, for descriptions and illustrations.) The load is usually protected from rain by a covering of leaves or occasionally by specially prepared mats. Such carrying baskets show a number of minor variations from the basic pattern and in fineness of workmanship. For carrying small objects, "satchels" or "handbags" of matting, often showing elaborate twilled designs, are used. These look somewhat like a modern woman's handbag in shape and size and are suspended from the shoulder by a cord or strip of hide. Baby slings, woven cotton bands about 9 to 12 inches (22 to 30 cm.) in width, are usually worn over the right shoulder and passed under the left arm, which is used to steady the infant, who rides in the sling against, usually not astride, the mother's left hip.

A good deal of attention is given to tracking and to marking trails, particularly by the jungle-dwelling tribes. Among trail-blazing techniques are the breaking of branches in a given direction as one passes along, notching or slashing trees along the trail, setting up pointers in forked sticks, and laying stones in piles or on the ground to indicate direction. Possibly some of the pictographs and petroglyphs usually found either at rapids or along trails were formerly used as direction markers. Aside from the crude bridges, mentioned above, no labor is expended on the improvement of trails, which are usually narrow and are traveled by groups walking in single file.

Boats.—Water transport is by dugout canoes, bark canoes (pl. 113, *center, right*) or "woodskins," and rafts. A number of tribes, like the small independent linguistic families of the Parima Range and surrounding area, had no water transport. The *Shiriana* now have dugouts, a recent acquisition according to Koch-Grünberg. Certain tribes of the Savanna, like the *Camaracoto,* used their boats almost solely for ferrying across streams (Simpson, 1940, p. 514). Dugouts are made in a variety of sizes and patterns, the larger and more elaborate being reported from the Cayenne coast. Usually the tree is hollowed by burning, is spread

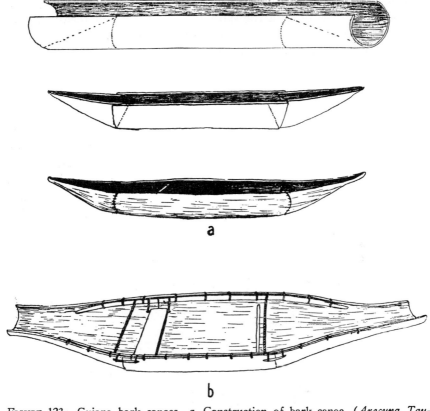

a

b

FIGURE 123.—Guiana bark canoes. *a,* Construction of bark canoe. (*Arecuna, Tau-lipáng,* etc.) ; *b,* canoe of Barama River *Carib.* (Redrawn from Koch-Grünberg, 1923 a, fig. 5; and Roth, 1924, fig. 336.)

with hot water, and wooden braces are inserted. On the Cayenne coast among *Carib* and *Arawak* (*Palicur:* Nimuendajú, 1926, pp. 39–40) we hear of apparently aboriginal gunwhales being raised by attaching planks, and of the bow and stern occasionally being made of separate insets of wood or of lumps of clay. A tent of thatch or leaves is often built amid-ships for the protection of cargo. Rectangular lug sails made of split palm-leaf stems are reported in very early accounts from the Cayenne coast, Suriname, and the Antilles.

The crutch-handled paddle is everywhere in use and the elongated, leaf-shaped blade is most common. The circular, or discoid, blade is confined to the western Guianas and the margin of the Amazon River.

The woodskin canoe is of very shallow draft, made of a single piece of bark stretched on a rectangular frame with the ends folded up a few inches above the water (fig. 123). It is used mainly in the upper reaches of the rivers, where its shallow draft and light weight are particularly adaptable. Rafts, propelled by poles, are used in this region, primarily as emergency craft or as a transport for heavy loads in relatively calm water. Various savanna- and swamp-dwelling tribes, for instance the *Palicur,* use poles for propelling canoes.

<h2 style="text-align:center">MANUFACTURES</h2>

Bark cloth.—The making of bark cloth has been mentioned (p. 835).

Basketry.—The Guiana Indians reach their highest technical proficiency and artistic virtuosity in the making of basketry and matting. A great variety of products and designs are produced, but the basic techniques are confined to wickerwork, checkerboard, and twilled weaving, with a little twining in the making of "roll up" mats of parallel lathes. No coiled, sewn, or imbricated basketry is known to have come from this region.

FIGURE 124.—*Rucuyen* woman spinning. (After Crévaux, 1891.)

Technically the most complicated achievements are shown in edging, in changing diameters of the basket, and in drawing three-dimensional into two-dimensional shapes. (See Roth, 1924, ch. 18, for complete illustration of the various techniques.) Among the products are tubular manioc presses (tipitís), cassava and farinha sifters, fire fans, plated rectangular boxes, wicker pot stands, sitting mats, carrying baskets, handbags, rectangular telescoping two-piece containers for household goods, trays for holding cotton with or without supporting wooden legs, rectangular and round hanging trays, deep bucket-shaped utility baskets, bottle-necked farinha baskets, fish traps, conical landing baskets for fish, hourglass-shaped containers, rattles for babies (pl. 118, *f*, *g*), cover nets for the suspension of pots, knapsack covers, and hollow-woven belts. All of these articles are carefully decorated either by creating designs from the surface texture of the weaving or by using elements of various shades of color. Painting or pitching baskets to make them waterproof is not practiced. Basketry is usually a man's work.

Spinning and cord making.—Raw stock of single-ply cotton thread is first ginned by hand and then spun on a hooked spindle with a bone or calabash whorl (fig. 124). The spindle is rolled against the thigh and then allowed to spin freely in the air (pl. 115, *bottom*). The whorls are occasionally decorated with engraving. Two-ply yarn is spun on spindles, but three-ply is first looped around the toes, twisted around the leg, and then spun. Multi-ply yarn is usually spun on the thigh without a spindle, although the *Wapishana* spin it with a bow-driven spindle. Various types of cording (see Roth, 1924, ch. 2, for full illustrations) are made by a series of braiding techniques (fig. 125). Multi-strand yarns, cords, and braids are used as leading lines of hammocks, and for belts, girdles, fish-lines, and tying cords.

Fabric making.—Among fabricating techniques of the Guiana Indians are one-, two-, and three-string cording; strand plaiting, simple and overcast; loop plaiting with four and five loops; needle plaiting with a single flat needle (said to be exclusively *Carib*) and with two flat needles; crotcheting with a single hooked needle and with two hooked needles; and "knitting" of a sort, with four and six rounded split-eye needles and with two long sticks. Plaited cotton bands seem to be an original specialty of the *Carib* tribes. Possibly loom techniques (pl. 115, *top*) were introduced into the area by the *Arawak*. Miniature two-bar looms are used by tribes of both families for weaving very narrow cotton bands used as belts and forehead bands.

Twine is made from other substances than cotton: *Mauritia flexuosa* (palm), leaves, *Bromelia*, or silk grass ("kraua"), and a variety of other grass and tree fibers available in various districts. The outer sheath of

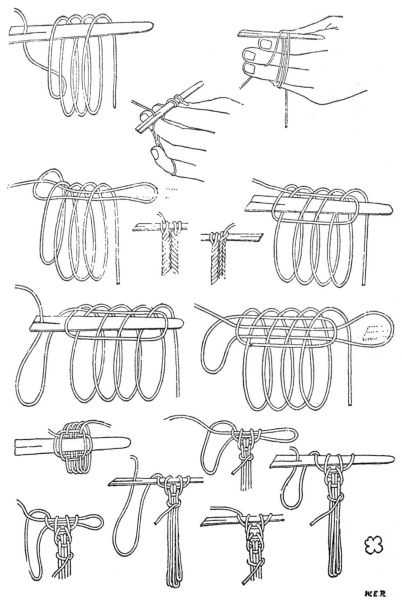

FIGURE 125.—Guiana cotton cord making. Using a single flat split-eye needle.
(After Roth, 1924, pl. 8.)

the *Bromelia* leaf is removed by pulling the leaf roughly through a loop of cording. Twisting is done by rolling the fibers on the thigh or by twisting them in the hands after looping one end around a post or tying both ends to uprights. Two- and multi-ply cords are made for hammock ropes, fish lines, carrying straps, and "bina strings," knotted cords which are pulled through the nose and out of the mouth.

True loom weaving is confined to the making of bands, aprons, and hammocks (pl. 116, *top*). Materials for hammocks include primarily cotton and *Mauritia* fiber, with a number of lianas and other "bush straps" used for temporary purposes. The *Warrau* (fig. 130), who probably did not aboriginally have cotton, specialize to this day in *Mauritia* hammocks. All hammocks in this area are woven on a continuous warp which is crossed at regular intervals by "bars" of weft, each consisting of two weft threads twined on each other or of four weft threads alternately intertwined in passing through the warp to produce a series of semiloops. The loom itself appears in three forms: (1) two vertical bars with warp horizontal and weft vertical (fig. 126); (2) two horizontal bars supported on vertical bars, warp vertical and weft horizontal (fig. 127); and (3) two horizontal bars or ropes equidistant from the ground with warp horizontal (fig. 130). In the third type, which is confined to the *Warrau*, the hammock is actually made by a netting technique, for the "weft" is one continuous strand which is passed over and under the warp elements with a needle in a series of loops which progressively locks them. The

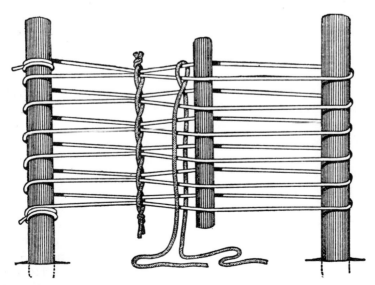

FIGURE 126.—Guiana hammock making. Frame of two vertical posts with horizontal warp and vertical weft; each weft bar consists of two threads. (After Roth, 1924, fig. 195.)

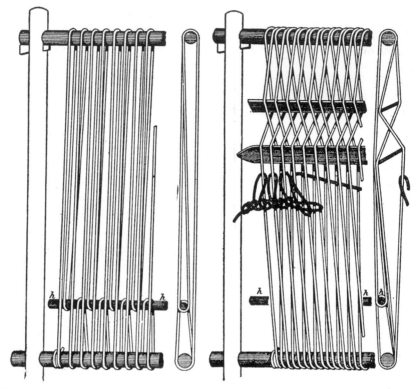

FIGURE 127.—Guiana hammock making. Frame of two horizontal timbers. *Left:* Vertical warp is run indirectly over a head stick (*h*) which, when finally pulled out, allows the article to be removed whole. *Right:* Separator is inserted below the permanent one in order to bring forward the posterior layer (of the front set) of warps, so as to get plenty of space. (After Roth, 1924, figs. 199, 202.)

second type of loom has a number of improvements used by various tribes (figs. 128, 129): (*a*) a headpiece, around which the warp passes at the lower end, rather than being directly attached to the lower bar, permitting the whole fabric to be rotated around the main bars and removed without cutting; (*b*) shuttle spools for carrying the yarn; (*c*) shed rods for separating layers of warp; (*d*) heddles of string loops; (*e*) wooden laminae for keeping bars of weft horizontal and equidistant; (*f*) leveling strips for keeping bars of weft even; and others. Miniature looms of the same continuous warp type, usually of the vertical-bar variety, are used for such weaving as bands and baby slings. The weft is double twined at each end of the fabric but is continuous between the ends. A sword beater is used for consolidating the weft. Beaded aprons (pl. 116, *center*) are made on a loom consisting of a bent switch with a bar tied across the open ends to make a **D**-shaped frame (fig. 131, *g*). The straight side forms the lower bar of the loom, and a series of cotton cords tied in one

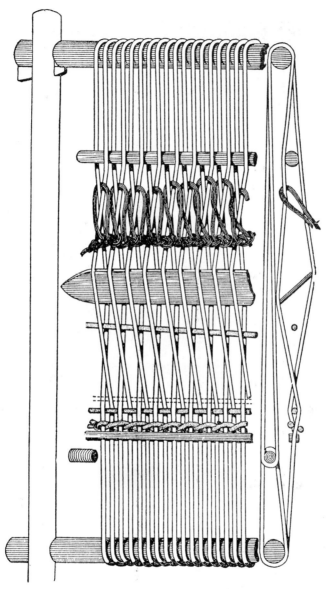

FIGURE 128.—Guiana hammock making. The temporary separator being removed, the posterior layer of (front set of) warps resumes original position, but is now under control of the raiser. The level is next attached and the first chain-twist made by taking up every alternate warp at a time. (After Roth, 1924, fig. 204.)

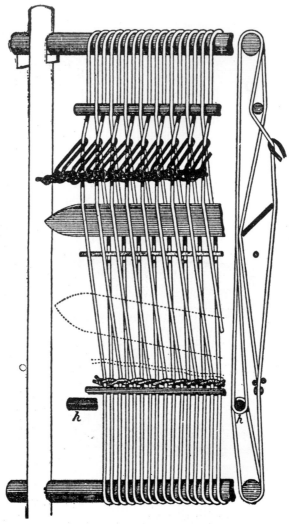

FIGURE 129.—Guiana hammock making. The raiser, on being pulled upon, drags forward the posterior layer of (front set of) warps, and in this position the temporary
separator, heater, or presser, is inserted behind it. (After Roth, 1924, fig. 205.)

strand between the curving sides, at a proper distance from the bar, forms
the other "bar." Into this bar are twined the warp threads (fig. 132),
which are then attached to the straight wooden bar. Each element of weft
consists of two threads, one of which passes over and one under each warp
thread. Between the warp threads, they are held together by the beads
which are strung on them (fig. 133).

Skin preparation.—Hides are used sporadically for sandals, the heads
of drums, pubic coverings, pouches for carrying small articles (probably

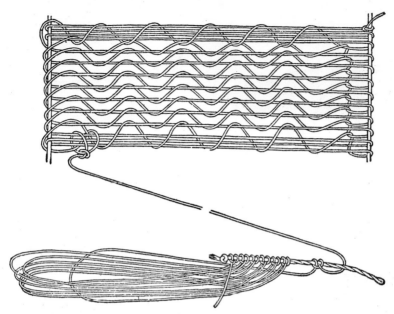

FIGURE 130.—Manufacture of a Guiana (*Warrau*) ite (sensoro) hammock.
(After Roth, 1924, fig. 209.)

post-Columbian, because they require sewing), and straps. Hides are not
tanned, and leather working, properly speaking, does not exist.

Pottery and calabashes.—Pottery (pl. 113, *bottom;* 118, *a–c*) made
by the aborigines of the Guianas since the time of European contact is
less distinguished both technically and artistically than is much of that
recovered from archeological sites. (See pp. 819–825.) Ash or crushed-
shell (rarer) temper, coiling, firing in the open, and glazing with vegetable
resin occur throughout the region. Crude and unsystematic decoration
with vegetable paints and incising are occasionally used. Pottery is
primarily utilitarian. Most tribes have a variety of shapes, such as large
containers for liquids, cooking pots, and the like. The scarcity of smaller
pottery vessels may be due to the universal use of calabashes for drinking
cups and water bottles. These, too, are often decorated with incised
designs. In recent times, the coastal *Arawak* and *Carib* have taken to
making zoomorphic (fig. 131, *a, b*) and other shapes of highly decorated
pottery (fig. 131, *c*) for sale to Europeans.

Weapons.—Only one type of the blowgun (pl. 110, *top*) has been
reported—that with an inner and outer tube. The inner tube is made
from the *Arundinaria schomburgkii*, which seems to grow only in the
Parima River region. Although the blowgun is reported among some
Arawak tribes (e. g., *Guinau*, Pomeroon and Demarara River *Arawak*),
it is more common among the westerly *Carib* (*Yecuana, Camaracoto,*

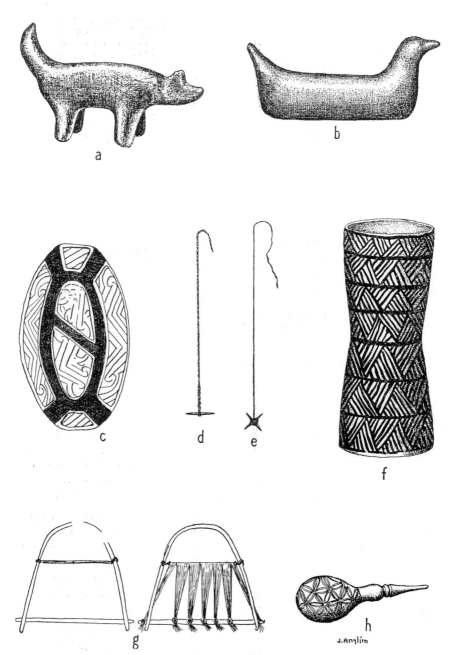

FIGURE 131.—Guiana manufactures. *a, b,* Modern Suriname *Carib* pottery figurines; *c,* pottery plate, same Indians; *d, e, Waiwai* fish gorges made of palm spines; *f, Waiwai* (?) wooden mortar; *g, Acawai* bead apron, frame, and warps; *h,* rubber syringe. (Redrawn from Roth, 1924, pls. 22, 46, pl. 17, fig. 4; *b,* redrawn from Roth, 1929, pl. 92, *a.*)

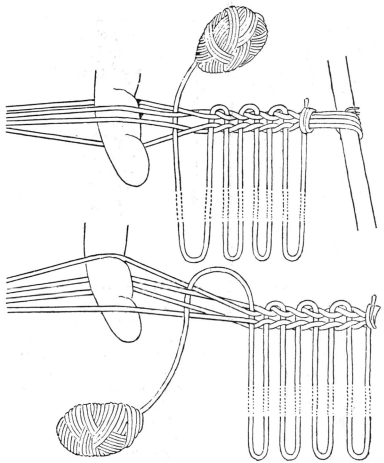

FIGURE 132.—Guiana bead-apron technique. Close up of technique of making warps.
(After Roth, 1924, pl. 17.)

Taulipáng, Arecuna, and *Acawai*), which suggests that it was introduced into the Guiana area from the Rio Negro and western Amazon region, perhaps by *Carib* movements or trade. The weapon is unknown among many of the easterly groups, such as the *Warrau,* Barama River *Carib,* and Suriname *Arawak.* In the central area, a considerable trade is carried on in blowguns and poison. The *Yecuana* and *Guinau,* according to Koch-Grünberg (1923 a, 3:338-342), obtain their poison from the *Piaroa* of the lower Ventuari and middle Orinoco Rivers; however, the *Guinau* and *Yecuana,* controlling the source of supply for the inner tubes, carry on a thriving trade with neighboring tribes. The principal dart poison of the area is curare, of which *Strychnos toxifera* is the most important toxic ingredient (pl. 110, *bottom*). A number of other poisons have been reported (Roth, 1924, pp. 151–152).

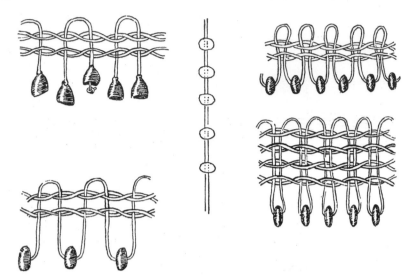

FIGURE 133.—Guiana bead-apron technique. Method of threading beads for *Acawai* apron. (Redrawn from Roth, 1924, pl. 16.)

The bow, made from a variety of woods, is generally long. It is either a self bow or is strengthened by several lengths of surplus bowstring carried in a groove along the back. Arrows—generally made of reeds, which are sometimes cultivated—were formerly tipped with wood or with animal or fish bone, but are now tipped with iron. Use of stone points on arrows is doubtful, although they were used by some tribes on lances. A variety of point shapes is made for different types of game: single, double, and multiple-barbed, blunt-ended (for birds), and harpoon-point (for fish). Primary and secondary releases have been reported, probably others are in use.

The spear or lance, with wood or bamboo head, has a westerly distribution in the Guianas, a fact which, as in the case of the blowgun, suggests introduction from the upper Amazon. Clubs, although formerly widely used in war and ceremonies, were employed little in hunting.

Miscellaneous.—Drilling seems to have been the only pre-European method of fire making (pl. 117, *top*).

A wide variety of gums, glues, and resins are obtained from the forest trees and widely used for fastening points to arrows, for calking boats, and for other purposes. Most pigments used in the area are vegetable. Rubber was made into balls, rings, and syringes (fig. 131, *h*) by a number of *Carib* tribes mentioned in the literature.

SOCIAL AND POLITICAL ORGANIZATION

Beyond the immediate family, the settlement is everywhere the basic social unit, a group usually of 15 to 50 members, sometimes as large as

200. Typically, a group of blood relatives with their spouses constitutes the kernel of a settlement, if not its entire membership. Among the Barama River *Carib,* individuals and families may be drawn to a settlement solely by reason of friendship, fear, or a desire for economic opportunity (Gillin, 1936, pp. 99, 101–140). Politically, the settlement is under the supervision of a headman, who receives informal advice from the mature married men of the group, frequently through the mechanism of uninhibited discussions at drinking sprees. Formal councils and constituted officers are not typical. The headman is usually only nominal head of the settlement, and true tribal chiefs are everywhere absent.

Three configurations of social organization are present in the area (Kirchhoff, 1931) : (1) Society organized into matrilocal, matrilinear, and unlocalized clans is characteristic only of the Locono, or coastal *Arawak,* but not, so far as is known, of the *Wapishana* and *Guinau,* or "Central *Arawak.*" Coastal *Arawak* tribes are the only ones in the area having sib organization of any kind, and the matrilinear pattern is characteristic also of the *Arawak* of the Antilles. It should be noted however, that one *Arawak* tribe, the *Palicur,* according to Nimuendajú (1926), have seven existing and four extinct patrilinear gentes. This may be an eastward extension of the second configuration. (2) A patrilinear influence is seen in the patrilocal marriage and patrilocal settlements of the *Aparai* and *Wapishana.* In patrilocality the *Wapishana* belong with the *Arawak* of the Rio Negro region, rather than with the coastal *Arawak,* a fact which suggests their relatively recent migration from the southwest into their present location. In patrilocality the *Aparai* differ from all other *Carib* tribes of the Guianas, a fact which, likewise, may indicate their former connection with the west. The *Tucanoans* of the Vaupés River region have patrilocal, patrilinear, and localized gentes (p. 780). (3) The composite type of settlement organized on a permanent or temporary matrilocal basis is characteristic of the remainder of the known tribes of the region.

Among the matrilocal tribes, as well as most of the others, the bride is won through service of some sort to the future father-in-law, or at least through a preliminary residence under his control. Among the *Rucuyen* and Orinoco River *Carib,* at least, the relationship has generalized into the peito institution. Peito includes not only servile sons-in-law but among a number of *Carib* tribes it includes war captives and unattached men who have placed themselves under the direction and protection of a headman. This institution represents an incipient system of graded status, the only indication of this sort of thing in the area. Cross-cousin marriage is preferred in all tribes, but is not regularized. Among the *Carib* tribes, it is widely permissible to marry a sister's daughter, a usage reflected in the kinship terminologies. Such a marriage frees the groom from the service features of marriage and the peito status, since the father of the bride is already under the control of the groom's father in matrilocal tribes.

Polygyny is permissible everywhere, so far as data go, with the sororal type generally preferred, but it is not widely practiced. Certain tribes, for instance, the *Macushí,* are comparatively monogamous. Usually plural wives live in their husband's house, although in individual cases they may continue to live in their father's village. Tribal exogamy is not generally prohibited; among a number of *Carib* tribes it was used as a technique of political domination and absorption. The levirate is also common, as is marriage with the stepdaughter. Both child betrothal and independent courtship occur, with no significant regularity of either.

The village headman is either chosen by acclaim or else inherits his position. In the matrilocal tribes the son-in-law is frequently the heir; but in certain matrilocal tribes (*Macushí*) the oldest son is the heir and does not move away from the settlement. Inheritance is paternal among the *Aparaí, Rucuyen,* and *Galibi.* Among the *Warrau,* according to Richard Schomburgk (1922–23), the daughter's son is heir, a unique usage in this area. Among the *Locono,* the headman has a number of wives and is economically supported by their families.

Complete kinship terminologies are too rare to permit generalizations. Those available are bifurcating in type.

The tribe nowhere appears to be more than a loose, unorganized linguistic, territorial, and cultural unit.

ECONOMIC ORGANIZATION

Money or other universal media of exchange are unknown; likewise surplus goods are not valued as wealth, nor is there any other concept of economic wealth per se. Nevertheless, considerable barter formerly took place, with certain tribes specializing in trade. However, no market institution existed among the tribes; traders traveled singly or in groups and bartered during irregular visits. The *Taulipáng* specialized in making blowpipes or the inner tubes for them; the *Macushí,* manioc graters and curare poison; the *Guinau* hammocks, cassava graters, aprons, and feather decorations; and the coastal *Warrau,* dugout canoes. The *Acawai* were everywhere known as traders and made extensive expeditions from Manaos through the interior to the coast and the mouth of the Orinoco River. In Colonial times they made their trading experience available to the Dutch and became the principal slave hunters and traders of the interior. No formalized immunity for traders developed and it seems often to have been necessary for trading expeditions to fight. European trade with the Indians of the interior is still carried on by barter. In addition to new goods the Europeans have introduced the practice whereby Indians give their labor in return for goods.

LIFE CYCLE

Childbirth.—Accouchement takes place in the bush, in a temporary room of palm leaves in the house, or in a separate house.   Mechanical abortion is probably known among all tribes, most of whom claim vegetable abortifacients although these have not been scientifically identified. The umbilical cord was reported to be bitten off among the *Warrau*; elsewhere a knife is used. *Arawak* mothers keep the cord to be passed on to the child when it grows up.   The after-birth is buried immediately. Food and action taboo are required of both parents before and after birth. The couvade is well developed, at least among the *Arawak, Carib,* and coastal *Warrau* tribes.   The essential idea is that a connection exists between the soul or spirit of the child and its father, and that harm will befall the child if the father goes into the bush or leaves the settlement for a given length of time after the child's birth.   Babies are nursed for a year or two and are carried in baby slings.   There seems to be no taboo on intercourse during lactation. Although cradles are unknown, the infant sometimes has a small hammock of its own for night use.   Clothing is usually not worn before puberty. Instruction in adult activities is informal and imitative. Toy tops, weapons, household utensils, and wooden and fiber dolls combine amusement with the formation of adult habit patterns. A hanging chair, or "walker," is used in some tribes when the child begins to walk.   Personal names, which are usually given at the end of the couvade and are often bestowed by the medicine man, are of the nickname type and refer to the child's appearance or to his resemblance to an animal or plant. Names are not used in direct conversation and are taboo after death.

Puberty ordeals are usually phrased as preparation for marriage.   The Maraké ceremony for boys among the *Rucuyen* (Crévaux, 1883, p. 307) subjects them to stinging ants held in frames against the skin. Work ordeals, such as hunting, cutting a field, or building a house, are common. Girls are secluded either in the bush or in a special structure during their first menstruation and are required to observe certain food taboos. Among the *Macushí,* girls are whipped during their seclusion.

Mourning is generally observed by the family's cutting their hair, deserting the hut or village, and foregoing the use of ornaments.   Burial in the floor of the house in a hammock or in a hollowed log or old canoe was common among historical tribes.   Cremation is rare.   However, among the *Rucuyen* the corpse is cremated (pl. 120, *top*) in a sitting position, and the ashes are kept in a pot by the widow; and among the *Atorai,* the corpse is cremated and the ashes buried.   From archeological evidence, it appears that cremation and urn burial were formerly common along the Orinoco River and in Brazilian Guiana.   Exhumation and redistribution of the bones among relatives or reburial is mentioned for some *Arawak*. Mummification is mentioned for the *Piaroa* and for the medicine men of the *Rucuyen*. The final mourning ceremonies, known as mukuari, seem to have been typical of the *Arawak*, although historical coastal *Warrau* also practiced them, and the pono and toulé dances of the *Rucuyen* have what may be borrowed makuari features. The makuari ceremonies drove away evil spirits by the systematic whipping of the participants with sacred whips (pl. 120, *bottom*). An effigy of a white crane, which gave the ceremony its name, was carried in the burial procession and interred. A drinking spree concluded the ceremonies.

WARFARE

The *Carib* were the most warlike of the tribes. According to early accounts (Fermin, 1781, for Suriname *Carib*), a warlike expedition was preceded by a council called by the headman. The participants boasted to stimulate their courage, invoked the jaguar spirit in an exciting imitative dance, and imbibed manioc drink mixed with worms from the putrid brains, heart, and liver of jaguar, camudi snake, and slain enemies. Arms and weapons were likewise smeared with the putrid stuff. Calls were sent to outlying warriors by shell trumpets or by setting up signs, such as a barbed arrow on a trail. Although the Island (Antillean) *Carib* had special war captains, evidence for them in the Guianas is conflicting. The usual tactics were to attack an enemy village at night by stealth. Defense included the concealment of the village, sunken logs to impede enemy navigation, traps along the trail, and, rarely, the use of stockades. Coastal tribes, both *Arawak* and *Carib,* used light wooden shields. The blowgun was not usually used in war. The principal weapons were arrows, sometimes poisoned; spears; and, for close fighting, clubs of hardwood in a variety of shapes. The *Acawai* had a wooden dagger-shaped club. Motives for war seem to have been revenge, captives, and, in Colonial times, slave raiding. It is doubtful whether scalping was aboriginal in the region, although it was practiced by coastal tribes in historic times. Cannibalism was practiced not only by the *Carib* but also by the *Arawak*. Although reports on cannibalism in the Guianas are confused, it appears to have been based primarily upon revenge rather than upon an appetite for human flesh. Cayenne *Carib* are reported to have kept the head temporarily as a trophy and to have made thigh and arm bones into flutes. Disarticulated human bones are found in the shell heaps of the coast, indicating probably prehistoric cannibalism. Slaves were taken in war and constituted the peito class among the *Macushi* and certain other *Carib* tribes. The captive men often married the daughters of their captors. Among some *Carib* tribes, "peito" (see p. 849) is used for both "captive" and "son-in-law." Central *Arawak* use the term "maku" in the same way. The *Macú* Indians themselves seem to have been singularly peaceful and furnished many captives to more war-like tribes. The war pattern has now practically disappeared from the area.

Art.—Decorative art is little developed in this region, except for woven designs on baskets and feather ornaments, and headdresses. Painting and incising of pottery and carving on wooden clubs are crudely done.

Dances and music.—The most ubiquitous social amusement is the drinking spree combined with singing, dancing (pl. 119, *center*), and sex play. Long cycles of highly formalized dances are not typical in historical accounts but among the more structuralized dances are the "humming-bird dance" of the coastal *Arawak* and *Carib* (Penard, F. P. and A. P., 1907–08, 1:167–170), the Aruhoho dance of the *Warrau* (Roth, 1924, pp. 471–472), and the parishara dance of the *Macushi, Patamona,* and *Wapishana* (Roth, 1924, pp. 475–580). The parishara is a variety of the hummingbird dance. Other dances imitative of animals and birds are mentioned. Special dance houses or assembly halls are accredited at least to the Suriname *Carib*. Miniature clubs and other weapons are used in some of the dances. The *Macushi* men engage in foot races before certain dancing and drinking sprees (Im Thurn, 1883, p. 325). The singing is usually done to an accompaniment of flute, drum, and (in modern times) fiddle music, played by specially recognized musicians. A few simple tunes are typical, to which a variety of words may be improvised or well-known verses repeated. We do not hear of long, stylized sets of words which must be carefully repeated on pain of punishment.

Games and miscellaneous amusements.—Other recreation includes informal and semidramatized storytelling in the camp or house during the evening, and playing practical jokes. There are a number of ball games (sporadic distribution), team wrestling, a pushing game with shields (*Warrau*), making of highly developed string figures and cat's cradles (widely distributed), and the children's games already mentioned. Swimming and diving amusements are notably absent, except among coastal *Warrau* children. Gambling, perhaps because of a typical lack of emphasis on wealth, is not mentioned in the literature.

Musical instruments.—Aerophones include: clay trumpets (*Carib?* and Pomeroon and Morka River *Warrau*); wooden flageolets (?) inserted in wooden animal effigies (used in *Macushi* parishara dances: Roth, 1924, p. 454); bamboo, wooden, and bone flageolets (general distribution); side flutes of bamboo and wood (general), sometimes nose-blown (*Central Carib* and *Oyana*); voice flutes made of large-diameter bamboo (Roth, 1924, fig. 235: *Carib* of Moruka); ocarinalike instruments of gourd, clay, or wood (general); simple whistles of nut shells and wood (general); panpipes of reed with from 3 to 10 pipes (general); and compound clarinet-trumpet (seróre) with interior vibrating reed (*Warrau* only).

Cordophones, probably introduced by Europeans or Negroes, occur in several forms: self-cord fiddles, the strings (usually three) of which are raised over bridges and are cut from, and are still attached to, the bamboo or ite palm stalk forming the body of the instrument (wide distribution); monochord of ite stalk, with a cord of kraua twine, bridge, and revolving peg (*Warrau*); compound fiddle of bamboo section with tail piece, three kraua or cotton strings, bridge, and three revolving pegs; and cheap violins obtained in trade, usually played with three strings.

Idiophones include: rattles of wood, clay, bamboo, seeds, gourds, and insect wings, either used as pendants, which are usually worn on strings in dances, or placed on handles and universally used by medicine men; and dance sticks tamped on the ground in time with dance rhythm. The latter are hollow and sometimes have skin stretched across one end and rattles attached (*Wapishana, Macushi, Arecuna, Patamona*). It is probably a western (Rio Negro) trait.

There are three kinds of membranophones. The double-headed skin drum is probably of European origin. It is played on only one head with one or two sticks; the other head is used as a resounder and has a tightening cord stretched across it. The frame is a piece of hollow wood; the heads are attached with hoops and tightened with European-type drawstrings. Wooden drums, though widely used in upper Rio Negro, are not found in the Guianas. The foot drum consists of a hole in the ground covered with a sheet of bark which is stamped on (*Rucuyen*). The friction drum is made of turtle shell and has a hole through which a notched stick is rasped (*Wapishana, Macushi*); it is probably a Rio Negro trait.

Intoxicating beverages.—Fermented drinks are made from manioc bread, maize, sweet potatoes, pineapple juice, wild cashew, and, since their introduction, sugarcane and bananas. Except in the case of pineapple and cane juice, the substance is chewed, left to ferment or mold, mixed with water, and allowed to "work." These drinks are usually consumed at community parties, which may continue, with singing and dancing, for several days. Intoxication is the rule.

Narcotics and stimulants.—In addition to alcoholic drinks, tobacco is universally used. It is grown in crop fields, and smoke-cured, and preserved either in the leaf or in rolls or plugs. Most commonly it is smoked in cigarettes wrapped in' thin tree bark or leaves. True cigars of the upper Rio Negro and Uaupés River type were not used aboriginally, nor were the associated cigarholders or forks. Tobacco chewing seems to have been restricted aboriginally to a few of the central tribes (*Patamona, Acawai, Arecuna*). Tobacco is mixed either with the pulverized, salty-tasting shell of the freshwater alga, *Mourera fluviatilis*, and baked on cassava pans into a cake (*Patamona*), or it is mixed fresh with a black niter-containing earth (*Arecuna*). An infusion of tobacco leaves is commonly drunk by medicine men to induce séance. Pipe smoking is sporadic and appears to have been introduced by the Whites.

The use of parica in snuff, paste, or cigarette seems to be another western trait which had barely reached the fringe of the Guiana area at the time of our earliest knowledge. Its use is mentioned for the *Mura*, the *Maué*, and the Parima River tribes. The use of pepper juice as a cure for congestion and possibly as a stimulant is widespread. The *Macushí* pour pepper water into the nostrils from long-necked gourds, and the Pomeroon River *Arawak* administer it as an enema by means of an animal-bladder syringe.

RELIGION

A lack of formalism, as in other aspects of Guiana culture, is typical of religion. The cosmogony of the known tribes follows certain patterns. A deity or "boss spirit" is usually recognized but not worshiped. This individual is mentioned in myths, but is not clearly conceived as the creator of the universe. The world as it is known to man is usually thought to have been created by a culture hero (e. g., *Arawak* Yaperi-Kuli, Haburi; *Warrau* (?) Kororomanna; *Carib* Macunaima, Amalivaca; etc.). A number of mythological themes in which such heroes figure are found throughout the Guianas. The hero frequently creates animals or their distinctive peculiarities from a magical tree, often a silk-cotton tree. Various parts of the tree are broken off and turn into animals, or the animals develop their present characteristics through trying to pick the fruit from the tree. The hero in some cases has a twin brother, both of whom are children of the sun or of some other heavenly body (e. g., Macunaima and Pia of the *Macushí*). Another frequent figure, especially in *Carib* mythology, is a supernatural snake, which is usually killed by the hero. However, from the snake's body develop men, animals, or binas (hunting charms). In addition to these figures, the mythology of all the tribes contains numerous incidents in which animals and birds figure as creators or as teachers of man. For example, among the *Carib* the bunia bird is frequently credited with teaching the Indians the use of cultivated plants and other culture traits.

Animism and magic characterize the religion of the whole area. Practically everything or class of things or beings is credited with spirits; for example, each tree, manioc, etc. In addition, a number of general classes of spirits are recognized. The jaguar spirit exercises a general and more powerful influence over the affairs of men. Familiar spirits are characteristic only of medicine men whose social influence depends largely upon their ability to contact spirits intimately for the benefit of laymen. While fetishes are known in the form of beeswax, clay, and wooden images, they are used either privately or as part of the equipment of the medicine man. In historical times, there seem to have been no true cults in the Guianas, although stone images (see p. 824) seem to have been well developed earlier in Brazilian Guiana, and we have at least one historical account of a stone god venerated in a special cult house or temple among *Carib* (?) of the upper Oyapock River (Harcourt, 1613, p. 109). It could thus be argued that the religious systems of the area have suffered a decline during the last 400 years.

There is universal belief in bush spirits, "kanaima," which some tribes thought of as debased human beings, others as semisupernatural creatures who roam the bush seeking to torture and annoy unwary human beings. They stupify and torture their victims by supernatural means and are everywhere feared. There is some evidence that ordinary men use "kanaima" as a means of revenge (Gillin, 1934).

Contagious and homeopathic magic enters almost all phases of the individual's life in the Guianas. The practices are too numerous to list here.

Although ghosts of the dead are considered annoying and for this reason the house of the deceased is usually abandoned, systematized concepts concerning their ultimate disposition or the general picture of the afterlife are lacking.

Clownish spirits, the "hebu" of coastal tribes, appearing in the mythologies of most tribes, are usually grotesque in appearance and serve as the stupid butts of tricks played upon them by mortals.

SHAMANISM

The medicine man, or shaman, a specialist in all things supernatural, is found in every community. The *Carib* designation is "piai" and its derivatives, or "mariri" (Caroni River); the *Arawak* root seems to be derivatives of these terms. In historical accounts, no distinctive functions or status differentiated a *Carib* medicine man from an *Arawak* one. Their stock in trade consists of a carved bench, a rattle containing stones or crystals representing the medicine man's familiar spirits, a doll or manikin, a specially built hut or cubicle usually of palm leaves in which séances are held, a prepared drink (usually the juice of green tobacco) which induces visions, and a cigarette whose smoke, when inhaled by the operator, has magical properties. The training of a Suriname *Carib* shaman is typical of the Guiana pattern (Andrés, 1938; Penard, A. P., 1928–29; Ahlbrinck, 1931), although variations occur among different tribes. Good spirits are introduced into the shaman, so that he can work with them, and he learns how to go into trances, so that he may enter the world of spirits and converse with them. Six or more candidates are initiated in a special house by an established medicine man, assisted by an old woman and a pubescent virgin for each candidate. The course lasts

24 days and nights, and involves various ordeals, such as drinking tobacco water, putting pepper water in the eyes, fire jumping, and dancing without sleep.

Medicine men conduct a few communal ceremonies, such as magical rites to encourage the growth of tobacco or manioc, but on the whole they serve in an individual capacity as advisers, seers, and curers of disease. Not infrequently the headman of a settlement is a medicine man, but the curer, as such, has no constituted political power other than that of an adviser to war parties and the like. He usually preserves myths and traditions. Among the *Arawak* there seems to be a stronger tendency than among the *Carib* for medicine men to band together, but even this tendency is rare.

Some tribes possess sorcerers (e.g., Barama River *Carib;* Gillin, 1936), who have no relations with spirits, but who specialize in discovering offenders and in directing the use of black magic in reprisal. They are consulted by individuals on a fee basis.

To effect a cure, the medicine man holds a séance with the patient in a special hut, consulting with the spirits, blowing tobacco smoke over the patient (pl. 120, *center*), massaging him, sucking, and placing taboos on certain food and actions. Nonreligious medical treatment is also practiced in all tribes. Treatment may be ordered by a medicine man, but, as often as not, laymen on their own initiative use purgatives, emetics, enemas (using syringes of rubber or bladders), cold and warm baths, bleeding, and medicinal leaves as "plasters" to ulcers and sores. Anyone may also remove chigoes and other boring insects. (See Roth, 1924, Ch. 36.)

Binas and hunting charms have been discussed (p. 827).

LORE AND LEARNING

Star lore is better developed among the savanna tribes than among those living in dense forests. The seasons of the year are reckoned by the stars or by the appearance of fruits or leaf changes in the forest. The month is reckoned by the moon. For keeping track of future dates, the knotted cord (an eastern version of the Peruvian quipu idea?) is universal; a knot is tied for each day intervening between the present and the event to be remembered, and untied as the proper time intervals elapse. Similar time counting is done with notches cut in sticks (*Macushi*), or holes bored in sticks from which a peg is removed for each day, or bundles of sticks from which one is removed for each day. Distances are usually reckoned in terms of the number of days required to travel between them, or in terms of the change in position of the sun. Houses are measured and laid out with poles cut to proper length by eye estimate. Writing is, of course, entirely unknown.

ETIQUETTE

Hospitality toward friendly persons is common, although unformalized. Newcomers usually announce their arrival with shouts or by pounding the trunks of trees, and pause at the outskirts of a settlement until inspected by the men of the settlement, whereupon they are escorted to a house. A man does not enter a house nor stay in a settlement where only women are present. Once in a house, the guest is given drink from a gourd, tobacco with which to make a cigarette, and a place to hang his hammock. During drinking sprees, the drink is usually served by women, and a refusal to partake is regarded as an insult. Among the matrilocal tribes, at least, avoidance and respect tinge the relations between in-laws, although rigid toboos are unknown. Respect is also accorded a headman, although informally. Most reports indicate that the normal relations between members of a settlement are friendly and even playful. Teasing and joking is common, but formalized "joking relationships" are not reported.

BIBLIOGRAPHY[2]

Acuña, 1641 (1682, 1859, 1891) ; Adam, 1878, 1879 a, 1879 b, 1890 b, 1892 a, 1892 b, 1893, 1897, 1905; Aguerrerere (see Exploración de la . . ., 1939) ; Ahlbrinck, 1922–25, 1924, 1925–26, 1931; Aldenburgk, 1627, 1930; Alexander, J. E., 1832, 1833; Altolaguirre y Duvale, 1908 [1909?] ; Alvarado, 1912, 1921, 1925; Amador de los Rios (see Oviedo y Valdés, 1851–55) ; Anderson, 1909; André, 1904 [1938?] ; Angyone Costa, 1934 (1938) ; Appun, 1868–69, 1871; Armellado, 1936; Bakhuis, 1902, 1908; Balen, 1930; Ballet, 1875; Bancroft, 1769; Barbosa Rodrigues, 1875 a, 1875 b, 1875 c, 1875 d, 1879, 1885, 1892 a, 1899; Barrère, 1743; Bates, 1892; Baumgarten, 1882; Bauve, 1833–34; Bechamel (see Grillet and Bechamel, 1698, and Labat, 1730) ; Beebe, 1910; Bellin, 1763; Benjamins, 1924–25; Benoit, 1839; Berkel, 1695, 1789; Bernardino de Souza (see Souza, Conego Francisco Bernardino de) ; Berneau, 1847; Bettendorf, 1910; Beyerman, 1934–35; Biet, 1664, 1896; Blanchard, 1882; Blanco-Fombona, 1915–16; Boddam-Whetham, 1879; Boekhoudt, 1874; Bolingbroke, 1807; Bonaparte, 1884; Bosch, 1829–43; Bosch Reitz, 1886; Brazil e Guyana Franceza, n.d., 1899, 1899–1900; Breton, 1665; Brett, n.d. a; n.d. b; 1900–02 (1849), 1851, 1852, 1880; Briceño-Iragorry, 1930; Brinton, 1871; Broekhuijsen, 1926; Brown, 1873, 1876; Bueno, 1933; Burr, 1897; Bushnell, 1910; Caitano da Silva, 1861; Campbell (see Holmes and Campbell) ; Capitan, 1882; Capelle (see Van Capelle) ; Carrocera, 1935; Caulin, 1779; Cerqueira e Silva, n.d.; Chaffanjon, 1887, 1889; Chamberlin, 1910; Cisneros, 1912 (1764) ; Cohen (see Meillet and Cohen) ; Coll (see Van Coll) ; Constant and Gras, ms.; Cooksey, 1912; Copazzi, 1841; Coreal, 1722; Costa (see Angyone Costa) ; Costambert, 1861; Coudreau, H., 1883, 1886 a, 1886 b, 1886–87, 1891 a, 1891 b, 1892, 1893, 1899; Coudreau, O., 1900, 1901, 1903 a, 1903 b, 1903 c; Crévaux, 1879, 1880–81, 1882, 1883; Cruls, 1930; Currier, 1897; Dalton, 1855; Dance, 1876, 1881; Daniel, 1840–41; Darnault, 1934; De Goeje, 1906; 1908 a, 1908 b, 1910, 1924, 1924–25, 1928, 1929, 1929–30 a, 1929–30 b, 1930, 1930–31, 1931–32, 1932–33, 1934–35, 1935, 1937; De Laet (see Laet, Joannes de) ; Denis, 1823; Denis and Famin, 1837; Deuber, 1926; Deyrolle, 1916; Dixon, 1895; Duff, 1866; Dumontier (see Focke, Landre, van Sypestein, and Dumontier) ; Dupont,

---

[2] Dates in parentheses after a date signify other editions. Queries are in brackets. Cross references are in parentheses.

1875; Dutertre, 1654 (1667–71) ; Ehrenreich, 1891 a, 1891 b, 1904, 1915; Emmerich-Högen, 1922; Endriss, 1911; Ernst, 1870, 1886–87, 1888, 1889; Exploración de la Gran Sabana, 1939; Famin, 1839 (also see Denis and Famin) ; Farabee, 1916 a, 1917 a, 1917 b, 1917 c, 1918 a, 1918 b, 1921 a, 1921 b, 1924; Febres, 1931; Federmann, 1557; Fehlinger, 1925; Fermin, 1765 (1769, 1781) ; Fernandes de Souza (see Smyth, 1836) ; Ferreira, 1903; Ferreira Penna (see Penna) ; Figueirêdo (see Lima Figueirêdo) ; Flu, 1911; Focke, 1858; Focke, Landre, van Sypestein, and Dumontier, 1855; Fogg, 1927; Franssen, 1917–18; Freitas, 1914; Friederici, 1929; Frödin and Nordenskiöld, 1918; Froidevaux, 1894; Furlong, 1915; Galard de Terraube, 1799 (1800) ; Gama Lobo de Almada, 1903; Gilij, 1780–84; Gillin, 1933, 1934, 1935, 1936; Glasenapp, n.d., 1937; Gli, 1934; Goeldi, 1896, 1897, 1900; Goreaud, 1934; Goslings, 1935; Gras (see Constant and Gras) ; Grasserie, 1892; Grillet (see Labat, 1730) ; Grillet and Bechamel, 1698; Grubb, 1927; Grupe y Thode, 1890; Guedes, 1896; Guianas Boundary, 1890; Gumilla, 1791; Hancock, 1835 (1840) ; Hanson, 1933, 1938; Harcourt, 1613 (1626, 1928) ; Harlow, 1928; Hartsinck, 1770, 1893; Hartt, 1885 [1886?] ; Heger, 1916, 1924; Heriarte, 1874; Herrera y Tordesillas, 1601–15; Herskovits (see Panhuys, Mordini, and Herskovits, 1934) ; Hervás, 1800-05; Heshuysen, 1925–26; Hilhouse, 1832, 1834 a, 1834 b; Hitchcock (see Tate and Hitchcock) ; Holden, 1938; Holdridge, 1931, 1940; Holmes and Campbell, 1858; Hornbostel, 1923; Hübner, 1898, 1907 (also see Koch-Grünberg and Hübner, 1908) ; Humboldt, 1814, 1852–53 (1881) ; Ignacio de Oliveira, n.d., 1935; Ihering, 1904; Im Thurn, 1882, 1883, 1884, 1890[?], 1892, 1934; Jahn, 1929, 1935, 1939; Jansen, 1931; Jenman, 1907; João Daniel (see Daniel) ; Joest, 1893; Josselin de Jong, 1919–20, 1919–21; Joyce, 1912; Kappler, 1854, 1881, 1887; Kemys, 1811; Kessler, 1930–31, 1936–37; Keye, 1672; Keymis (see Kemys) ; Kirchhoff, 1931; Kirke, 1898; Klüpfel, 1859; Koch-Grünberg, n.d., 1900, 1905, 1906 c, 1905–08, 1907, 1908, 1913 a, 1913 b, 1920, 1922, 1923 a, 1934; Koch-Grünberg and Hübner, 1908; Krieger, 1935; Labat, 1730, 1931; La Borde, 1704; Lacerda e Almeida, 1841; La Condamine, 1745; La Croix, 1904; Laet, 1625 (1630, 1633, 1640), 1644; Landre (see Focke, Landre, van Sypestein, and Dumontier) ; Lans, 1842; Lasch, 1910; Lawner, 1930; Leblond, 1813, 1814; Leigh, 1906; Lelyyeld, n.d.; Leprieur, 1834; Lettres édifiantes et curieuses, 1819 (1780–83) ; Level, 1850, 1873; Lima Figueirêdo, 1939; Linné, 1925, 1937; Lisandro, 1921; Lodares, 1929–31; Lombard, 1928; Lopez Borreguero, 1875; Lopez de Aranjo, 1884; Lovén, 1924, 1928; Luquet, 1933; Lutz, 1912 a, 1912 b; McTurk, 1882; Manouvrier, 1882; Marcano, 1889 b; Marcgraf (see Piso and Marcgraf) ; Martin, 1886; Martius, 1863, 1867 (also see Spix and Martius) ; Massa, 1936; Matallana, 1937; Matos Arvelo, 1903, 1912; Maurel, 1882; Meillet and Cohen, 1924; Mello, 1924; Mello Moraes, 1858–63; Mentelle, 1782; Métraux, 1927, 1928 a; Michelena y Rojas, 1867; Miller, 1917; Milthiade (*in* H. Coudreau, 1893) ; Mocquet 1645; Monteiro Baena, 1870; Monteiro Noronha, 1903; Montezon, 1857; Morais, 1924; Mordini, 1931, 1934 (also see Panhuys, Mordini, and Herskovits) ; Moura, 1922; Navarrete, 1895; Nelson (see Rippy and Nelson) ; Netto, 1885; Niemeyer, 1885; Nieuhoff, 1707; Nimuendajú, 1926, 1927; Nordenskiöld, 1930 a (also see Frödin and Nordenskiöld) ; Normand, 1924; Noronha (see Monteiro de Noronha) ; Nuñez, 1936; Oramas, 1917; Ounque, 1906; Oviedo y Valdés, 1851–55; Palmatary, 1939; Panhuys, 1897, 1897–98, 1904 a, 1904 b, 1904 c, 1906 a, 1906 b, 1910, 1912, 1913, 1920–21, 1921–22, 1922, 1924–25, 1925, 1931–32, 1933–34, 1934, 1934–35; Panhuys [Paniuijs?], Mordini, and Herskovits, 1934; Pareau, 1898; Passarge, 1933; Pauwels, 1903; Payer, 1906; Pelleprat, 1655; Penard, A. P., 1925 a, 1925 b, 1926 a, 1926 b, 1926 c, 1927 a, 1927 b, 1927 c, 1927 d, 1928–29; Penard, A. P. and T. E., 1917, 1925–26 a, 1925–26 b, 1926, 1927; Penard, Ph., 1927; Penard, F. P. and A. P., 1907–08, 1913; Penna, 1877; Pereira da Silva, 1922; Perkins, 1885; Perret, 1933 a, 1933 b; Pinto, 1935; Piso and Marcgraf, 1648; Pistorius, 1763; Pitou, 1807 (1805) ; Plassard, 1868;

Pons, 1806; Prudhomme, 1798; Quandt, 1807, 1900; Raimondo, 1934; Raleigh, 1928; Regueira, 1894; Reinburg (see Rivet and Reinburg); Reise . . ., 1930–32; Résumé . . ., 1903; Ribeiro de Sampaio, 1825, 1856 (1839), 1872 (1850), 1903; Rice, 1921, 1928; Riemer, 1833; Rio-Branco, 1899; Rippy and Nelson, 1936; Rivet, 1923, 1924; Rivet and Reinburg, 1921; Robertson, 1822; Robinson, 1918; Rodrigues Barata, 1903 (1798–99); Rodrigues Ferreira, 1885–88; Rodway, 1891–94, 1894, 1895, 1897, 1912; Rojas, 1878; Roop, 1935; Rosny, 1884; Roth, W. E., 1908, 1909–12, 1911, 1912, 1915, 1920, 1924, 1929; Rousseau, 1901; Roux, 1936; Sack, 1810, 1821; Saegham, 1663–70; St. Clair, 1834; Salas, 1908, 1920 (1921); Sampaio, A., 1933; Sampaio, T., 1915, 1922; Sanderson, 1939; San Mancos, 1903; Sanson, 1856; Schmeltz, 1897, 1910; Schomburgk, M. R., 1847–48; Schomburgk, O. A., 1841; Schomburgk, Richard, 1879, 1922–23; Schomburgk, Robert H., 1836 a, 1836 b, 1837 a, 1837 b, 1840, 1841 a, 1841 b, 1841 c, 1841 d, 1842, 1843, 1845, 1848; Schuller, 1911; Schultz, 1850; Scott, ms.; Shaw, 1940; Shedd, 1933; Sievers, 1887; Sijpesteijn [Sypestein?] (see Van Sijpesteijn); Silva, 1861; Simon, 1861; Simpson, 1940; Smyth, 1836; Souza, Conego F. B. de, 1873; Speiser, 1926; Spix and Martius, 1823–31 (1846); Staelhelin, n.d.; Stahel, 1921–22; Stampaert, 1924–25; Stedman, 1796; Steere, 1927; Stockum (see van Stockum); Stoel, 1937; Stradelli, 1889; Strickland, 1896; Surville, 1778; Tate, 1930 a, 1930 b; Tate and Hitchcock, 1930; Tavera-Acosta, 1905–13, 1906, 1907, 1913, 1919, 1921–22, 1923, 1927, 1930; Tello (see Zuloaga and Tello); Ten Kate, 1887, 1888, 1924; Tibiriça, 1936; Tony, 1843; Toro, 1905; Uhle, 1913; Van Capelle, 1903; Van Coll, n.d., 1909; Vasconcellos, 1859, Van Sijpesteijn [Sypestein?], 1854 (also see Focke, Landre, van Sypestein, and Dumontier); Van Stockum, 1905; Viegl, 1785; Vellard, 1931; Veness, 1875, Venezuela-British Guiana, 1898; Verrill, 1918, 1925; Vidal, 1862; Vincke, 1935; Voyages et avantures . . ., 1749; Voyages et travaux . . ., 1857–61; Waldeck, 1939; Wallace, 1853, 1889; Waterton, 1891; Weiss, 1915; Whitley, 1884; Whitney, 1912 a, 1912 b; Wickham, 1827; Williams, J., 1924, 1928, 1928–29, 1932, 1936; Williams, L., 1941; Williamson, 1923; Wilson, 1806; Winter, 1881; Zanten, 1925; Zuloaga and Tello, 1939.

THE HUNTING AND GATHERING TRIBES OF THE
RIO NEGRO BASIN

By Alfred Métraux

THE SHIRIANA, WAICA, AND GUAHARIBO

TRIBAL DIVISIONS

On the upper reaches of the Orinoco and along the Uraricoerá River extend vast unexplored regions in which roam many groups of forest nomads (map 1, *No. 5;* map 7). These little-known bands are surrounded with mystery and legends. Judging from short vocabularies recorded by Koch-Grünberg, the *Shirianá* language is isolated. In many respects, the *Shirianá* and *Waica* have the same relation to the sedentary tribes of the Guianas as the *Macú* of the Rio Negro and Caiarí-Uaupés River, the *Sirionó* of eastern Bolivia, and the *Guayakí* of Paraguay. They represent a very ancient population which in some places has been destroyed or assimilated, but in other areas has succeeded in surviving.

Shirianá.—The *Shirianá* (*Shiliana, Shilianaidya*) are mentioned for the first time by Schomburgk (1847–48), who places them in the region of the Parima Mountains and identifies them with the *Guaharibo.* (Lat. 3° N., long. 64° W.) He calls them *Kirishana,* a term which has caused them often to be confused with the *Cariban Crichaná* of the *Jauaperí* River.

In 1911–12, Koch-Grünberg (1923 a) met two *Shirianá* groups, one from the upper Uraricapará River, a left tributary of the Uraricoerá River, and the other established on the right side of the Uraricoerá River, opposite the Marutani Mountains, on the Motomotó River. Though Koch-Grünberg was able to obtain a vocabulary only from the first group, he is convinced that it is closely related to the second.

The *Shirianá* of the Uraricapará River obtain European goods from *Cariban* tribes of the Paragua River by the intermediation of the *Auaké,* who are true peddlers. The *Shirianá* also maintain relations with the *Taulipáng, Macushí,* and *Wayumará.*

The *Shirianá* of the Motomotó River have been influenced in many respects by the *Macú* of the Auarí River who, among other things, taught them agriculture.

The *Shirianá* are very warlike people who succeeded in dominating several weaker tribes.

Waica.—The *Waica* (*Waiká, Oiaca, Uaica, Guaica*), who roam in the same region as the *Shirianá,* are regarded as fearsome savages. (Lat. 2° N., long. 65° W.) They are even less known than the *Shirianá,* to whom they seem to be linguistically and perhaps culturally related. According to Koch-Grünberg, the *Waica* formerly extended more to the east, for they are mentioned on the sources of the Parimé-Maruá River and on the upper reaches of the Rio Branco. Koch-Grünberg heard that they lived in the Marutani Mountains. There are also *Waica* at the headwaters of the Orinoco River, where they are mentioned together with the almost unknown *Guaharibo.*

Guaharibo.—The term *Guaharibo* (*Uariba, Iaribu, Uajaribo, Uaharibo*), like *Macú* and *Tapuya,* is a collective designation for any wild Indians and, therefore, it is very likely that *Waica* and *Guaharibo* are closely related and perhaps are the same tribe. *Carib* tribes call all these Indians *Shirishana.* On the Matacuni River, a tributary of the Padámo River, the *Yecuaná* succeeded in settling a group of these nomads. (Lat. 3° N., long. 65° W.)

Auaké.—On the upper Paragua River, there are still a few remnants of the once more numerous tribe of the *Auaké* (*Oewaku, Uakys, Aoaqui*), who lived on the Uraricapará River (lat. 5° N., long. 63°–64° W.). Today they are held in a state of vassalage by the *Shirianá,* who have occupied their former territory. Their simple culture has been greatly modified by influences from their *Cariban* neighbors.

Calianá and Maracaná.—Koch-Grünberg (1922, p. 227) was told of the existence of two small tribes speaking isolated languages: the *Calianá* (*Cariana, Sapä, Sahä*) of the upper Paragua River (lat. 4° N., long. 63° W.), and the *Maracaná* (*Maracaña*), who were driven away from the Uraricapará River (lat. 3° 30′ N., long. 62°–63° W.) by the *Shirianá* and migrated to the south of the Uraricoerá River, where they constantly attack other Indians.

CULTURE

SUBSISTENCE ACTIVITIES

The *Shirianá, Waica,* and *Guaharibo* are forest nomads who subsist mainly on hunting, fishing, and collecting, but the two *Shirianá* groups seen by Koch-Grünberg (1923 a) raised manioc, *Dioscorea,* bananas, and sugarcane in large clearings. They admitted, however, that they had learned farming from their more advanced neighbors. Hunting was done mainly with the bow and arrow and, very rarely, with the blowgun. The only fishing method which could be ascertained was shooting with bow and arrow.

Every year at the season of the Pará, or Brazil, nuts the *Guaharibo* descended below Guaharibos Creek to collect them. This was the time chosen by the civilized Indians to attack these Indians and enslave them.

The *Shiriand* grated manioc on rough stones, and, instead of using the manioc press found among their *Cariban* neighbors, they squeezed it in a mat twisted with both hands. They prepared a beverage made of bacaba fruits, and ate a fat, whitish clay kneaded in the shape of balls.

HOUSES AND VILLAGES

An informant told Spruce that *Guaharibo* huts

were annular, the low roof sloping slightly outwards and being only 2 or 3 varas [yards] in width, while the whole of the center was open to the sky. The roof and outer wall were made of the long, broad, simple leaf of a palm, apparently like the Bussú of Pará. [Spruce, 1908, 1 : 397.]

In an abandoned *Guaharibo* village, Chaffanjon (1889, p. 305) saw a few flimsy conical huts made of poles, about 8 to 10 feet (2.5 to 3 m.) high, stuck in the ground and fastened together on top. These dwellings were said to have been only 32 inches (80 cm.) in diameter.

The *Shiriand* village visited by Koch-Grünberg (1923 a, 3 :300, pl. 43) consisted of nine open sheds built in a circle around a plaza. The huts, which perhaps were only temporary shelters, were simple lean-tos supported by four and sometimes by only three vertical posts (pl. 125, *bottom*). The *Shiriand* are said to have rectangular communal huts, which they might have copied from the *Taulipáng* sheds.

These Indians sleep in hammocks made of a bundle of fibers loosely joined by transverse twined cotton threads.

DRESS AND ORNAMENTS

Koch-Grünberg's *Shiriand* had partly adopted *Carib* costume, but among the Motomotó River *Shiriand,* men still wore a belt of threads under which they tucked the penis. In both *Shiriand* groups, women use a small fringed apron, which also seems to be a recent acquisition. Men tie cotton threads or woven bands around the upper arms and under the knees; the women wear the distinctive *Carib* bands around the ankles.

The Motomotó River *Shiriand* had their ear lobes, nasal septa, and lower lips perforated for the insertion of sticks. Women wore as many as three sticks through the nose, and they passed sticks through the corners of their mouth. In the same group, men wore a tonsure smeared with urucu, but this fashion was unknown to the *Waica* and the Uraricapará River *Shiriand.* Women cut their hair along the forehead and the nape. Both sexes painted themselves with urucú and genipa.

TRANSPORTATION

Originally, neither the *Shiriand* nor the *Waica* had boats. To cross streams, the *Guaharibo* built ingenious bridges, which have been carefully described by Chaffanjon (1889, p. 311). At short intervals they stuck poles crossed in the form of an **X** in the river bed. On these, they laid poles on which to walk, while holding to a railing made of other poles. The bridge was supported by lianas attached to trees on both shores. Today the *Shirianá* of the Uraricoerá River have long dugout canoes (pl. 125, *top*) with raised and pointed ends, which they propel with paddles like those of the *Taulipáng* and *Macushí*.

MANUFACTURES

Shirianá baskets (carrying baskets and deep trays) are carefully made and are very strong, but, unlike most basketry work in the area, they are twined.

The pots collected by Koch-Grünberg were plain and had perhaps been traded from some *Carib* tribe. On the other hand, the *Yecuaná* and *Guináu* told the German explorer that they obtained their best pots from the *Shirianá* of Parimá Mountain.

Shirianá bows are 1.9 to 2.3 m. (about 6 to 8 feet) long. They are flat on the back and somewhat convex on the belly, with shoulders cut at both ends for a *Bromelia* string.

Arrows are of three main types: war and hunting arrows, with a large lanceolate bamboo head; hunting and fishing arrows, tipped with a simple barbed rod or with a bone spur; and arrows with a poisoned wooden head. The poison used is curare. There are no blowguns, except those obtained in trade from the *Yecuaná* and *Taulipáng*.

Musical instruments are transverse flutes with three stops and a whistle with three stops made of a fruit.

DISPOSAL OF THE DEAD

From an Indian who had visited a *Guaharibo* village, Spruce learned that,

they burn the bodies of their dead, collect the calcinated bones, and pound them in a mortar, and keep them in their houses in globular baskets of closely woven mamuri. When they move their residence or travel, they carry with them the bones of their ancestors. [Spruce, 1908, 1:398.]

THE MACU

The name *Macú* is given to three different tribes of Indians who linguistically are completely unrelated: (1) A group, by far the most numerous, which includes a large number of bands which roam between the Rio Negro and the Japurá River (lat. 1°–3° S., long. 64°–69° W.); (2) a little-known tribe of the Uraricoerá region (lat. 3°–4° N., long 64°–65° W.); and (3) a subdivision of the *Piaroa* tribe of the Orinoco River (lat. 4° N., long. 67° 30′ W.). Each group will be treated here separately.

THE MACU OF THE RIO NEGRO AND CAIARÍ-UAUPÉS RIVER

Tribal divisions and history.—The name *Macú* is given by the *Tariana* and other *Arawakan* tribes of the Rio Negro· and the Caiarí-Uaupés River basin to various groups of forest nomads whose culture is practically unknown. The Brazilians call them "Indios do matto." It is yet uncertain whether all these *Macú* are linguistically related or not, but the vocabularies recorded by Koch-Grünberg (1906 b, 1922) and Fathers Tastevin and Kok (see Rivet and Tastevin, 1920; Rivet, Kok, and Tastevin, 1924–25) from *Macú* of the Curicuriarí, Tiquié, Papury, and Jurubaxy Rivers, show, despite considerable dialectal differences, affinities which justify their inclusion into a linguistic group related to *Puinave.* (See Rivet and Tastevin, 1920.)   The differences between the Jurubaxy and Papury dialects are particularly great.   The isolation of the *Macú* and the strong influences to which they are subject explain the disintegration of their dialects, which are being replaced by the language of their *Tucanoan* and *Arawakan* neighbors.

The *Macú* of the area defined above are divided into several groups named according to the specific region where they have been seen or mentioned by travelers or by other Indians.   One large group occupies a vast territory between the Japurá River, the middle and lower Rio Negro, and its tributary, the Curicuriarí River.   These *Macú* are generally designated as *Guariba,* a *Guaraní* word meaning "the howling monkeys." Undoubtedly, they are closely allied to another group of acculturated *Macú Mansos* ("tame" *Macú*), who live between the sources of the Cumapi, a tributary of the Japurá River, and the headwaters of the Alegria (Arirahá) River, an affluent of the Rio Negro.   Most of these "tame" *Macú* are settled on the left banks of the Jurubaxy River, which is also a tributary of the Rio Negro.   The "tame" *Macú* call the *Guariba, Nadöb,* and themselves, *Nadöpa,* a word meaning "people."

Another group of *Macú* is found between the upper Caiarí-Uaupés River and its tributaries, the Papury and Querarí Rivers.   These Indians must probably be identified with the so-called *Yapóoa.*

Koch-Grünberg (1922, p. 261) considers the *Bahúna, Balöaúa,* and other groups who today speak *Cubeo* to be former *Macú* who had been assimilated by the *Cubeo.* He also assigns the same origin to the *Huhúteni* of the lower Aiarí River and to the *Catapolítani* of the middle Içana River, who now belong to the *Arawakan* linguistic family.

At the beginning of the present century, there were on the Tiquié River many *Macú* who were bondsmen of the *Tucano* and the *Tuyuca.*

The Rio Negro *Macú* are generally considered to be the last representatives of an ancient people who occupied vast areas of the Amazon Basin before they were exterminated or assimilated by the *Carib, Arawak,* and *Tucano,* the carriers of a more advanced culture based on farming.   Even today the territory assigned to the *Macú* is still considerable and their number seems to be high.

The recent history of the Japurá and Rio Negro *Macú-Guariba* has been told in great detail by Father Tastevin (1923 b). It consists of a series of stealthy attacks on the rubber stations, each followed by a punitive expedition. The "tame" *Macú*, though not actually a group distinct from the *Macú-Guariba*, have remained at peace with the Whites, and, for their own security, disclaim any connection with their warlike brothers.

The *Arawakan* and *Tucanoan* tribes of the upper Rio Negro, Caiarí-Uaupés, and Tiquié Rivers have since time immemorial waged merciless war against the *Macú*, whom they enslave or reduce to serfdom. Some small groups of *Macú* come to work for the sedentary *Uanana* and *Desana* and, after a few months, disappear again into the bush. The *Tucano* of the Tiquié River subjected a large group of *Macú* to their rule, but on the slightest suspicion of sorcery, they were prompt to attack them and to sell their captives to the Whites.

Culture.—Anthropological data on the Rio Negro *Macú* are meager. Those of the Caiarí-Uaupés River are described by Koch-Grünberg as forest nomads subsisting on hunting, fishing, and collecting. Some of their abandoned huts were flimsy pyramidal structures covered with branches and leaves.

The *Macú-Guariba* of the regions between the Rio Negro and the Japurá River seem to differ from the Caiarí-Uaupés *Macú* in a very important respect: they are good agriculturists who live in large, permanent communal houses (pl. 126). A *Macú* settlement found on the Igarapé Preto de San José by a punitive expedition, consisted of two large huts surrounded by 15 small cabins. In the huts were numerous hammocks slung at different heights. The village was surrounded by large plantations of manioc, bananas, pineapples, and pupunha palms.

The "tame" *Macú* are in many respects culturally inferior to the wild *Macú-Guariba,* but their miserable dwellings and their small, ill-kept fields may be the result of decadence following their contact with the Whites. The "tame" *Macú* are, however, skillful basket makers. They weave mats for roofing their huts and fine baskets in which alternate yellow and black arumã strips produce geometrical patterns.

Their blowguns, about 6 feet (2 m.) long, are made of two palm tubes, one inserted into the other and firmly glued together with rosin. The inner tube projects a centimeter at the opening. The blowgun has no sight. The darts are splinters of palm wood smeared with curare (Tastevin, 1923 b).

The *Macú* of the Curicuriarí River have long bows and several kinds of arrows, some of which are tipped with rods of palm wood and are poisoned. They also have blowguns and clubs. The tribes of the interior still use stone axes. They make pots and bowls. They sleep on leaves

PLATE 125.—**Shiriana Indians.** *Top: Shiriana* in a dug-out, Uraricoera River. *Bottom: Shiriana* screen for protection against weather. (After Koch-Grün-berg, 1923 b.)

PLATE 126.—**Macú** malloca and plantation. (After Rice, 1928.)

on the ground.   They lack canoes and cross rivers by swimming or wading
(Koch-Grünberg, 1906 b, p. 879).

THE MACU OF THE URARICOERA BASIN

In 1912, Koch-Grünberg (1922, p. 227) collected a short vocabulary
from a *Macú* tribe on the middle Auarí River, a left tributary of the
Uraricoerá River, in Brazilian Guiana.   Their language is entirely isolated.
These Guiana *Macú* (*Maca, Mahacu*), who were first mentioned in the
18th century, are famous traders.   Every summer they descend the
Uraricoerá River to reach the villages of the *Taulipáng* and *Macushí*,
where they barter their products for European goods.   They are on
friendly terms with the *Shirianá* of the Motomotó River, whom they have
greatly influenced (Barboza Rodríguez, 1885, pp. 139, 145).

THE MACU-PIAROA

The Uraricoerá *Macú* must be carefully distinguished from other *Macú*
(*Maco*) who are a subgroup of the *Piaroa*.   The latter, mentioned by
Humboldt on the headwaters of the Cataniapo River, live today in the
savannas between the lower course of the Ventuari and the Orinoco Rivers.
They may be found on the upper Camani and Mariéte Rivers.

BIBLIOGRAPHY

Barboza Rodriguez, 885; Chaffanjon, 1889; Koch-Grünberg, 1906 b, 1922, 1923 a;
Rivet and Tastevin, 1920; Rivet, Kok, and Tastevin, 1924–25; Schomburgk, M. R.,
1847–48; Spruce, 1908; Tastevin, 1923 b.

THE WARRAU

By Paul Kirchoff

LOCATION, HISTORY, AND SOURCES

The *Warrau* live in the intricate Delta of the Orinoco and the area between it and the Pomeroon River (lat. 7°–10° N., long. 60°–63° W., map 1, *No. 5;* map 7). Except for a few patches of higher land, these regions are inundated many months every year.

Nothing is known of localized differences in *Warrau* culture. The *Warrau* of the main part of the delta, especially the western section, are known only through a few short paragraphs left us by Gumilla (1791). The area best known is that east of the delta toward the Pomeroon. This, however, seems to be precisely the area in which *Arawak* and, to a lesser extent, *Carib* influences made themselves felt most strongly. Aruacay, the famous 16th-century *Arawak* (?) town, located a little above the delta, on the banks of the Orinoco, may have influenced the *Warrau*. Unfortunately, lack of knowledge of the *Warrau* closest to this *Arawak* center makes it impossible to clarify this matter. Until a study of the *Warrau* of the western delta has been made, our reconstruction of original *Warrau* culture must remain inadequate.

The *Warrau* (*Araote, Farute, Guarau, Guaraon, Guaraunan, Guaraúna, Guarauno, Guaraune, Guaraounoe, Guaranu, Guarano, Guararini, Guaraoun, Guaraouno, Guaranne, Houaroux, Uarau, Uarao, Uarauno, Uarow, Oraw-it, Ouavaous, Varaa, Warrau, Warow, Warraw, Warrow, Warran, Warouwen, Warray, Waraweete, Tibitibi, Tivitivi, Tivitiva*) are divided into subtribes, some 20 according to Plassard (1868). Among them are the *Mariusa*, between the Imataca, the Macareo, and the Manamo Rivers; the *Chaguane* (*Ciawani*) on the right bank of the Orinoco from the Caño Piacoa to the Sierra Imataca; and the *Warrau* proper on the banks of the Orinoco from the Caño Piacoa to the sea.

There is a possibility that in times not far back the *Warrau*, or tribes closely related to them, occupied certain regions to the north and the west of the delta. Trinidad may have had originally a *Warrau,* or a *Warrau*-like, population.

At the end of the 16th century, the region was visited by Sir Walter Raleigh, and missions were founded in 1682. During the 18th century various governors, Spanish and English, tried to pacify the *Warrau* and reduce them to settlements.   This caused many *Warrau* to migrate to Suriname, where they made friends with the Dutch and where some of them still live along the Courantyne River.   Our only data on demography is Gumilla's (1791) statement that there were from 5,000 to 6,000 *Warrau* in his day (the middle of the 18th century).

Gumilla (1791), Crévaux (1883), Plassard (1868), Schomburgk, M. R. (1847–48), Hilhouse (1834 b), and Roth (1915, 1924) are our most important sources on the *Warrau.*

LANGUAGE

The *Warrau* language constitutes an independent family.   In Spanish times it was used as lingua franca by the neighboring tribes as well as by the Spaniards.

CULTURE

SUBSISTENCE ACTIVITIES

Farming.—Manioc cultivation is probably due to *Arawak* influence. The *Warrau* call the starch derived from manioc by the same term they use for the starch extracted from the *Mauritia* palm.   On the Barima River they mix it with greenheart seeds (*Nectandra rodiaei*) and the pith of the *Mauritia* palm.   Today, plantains, chile pepper, sugarcane, and watermelons are cultivated in addition to bitter manioc.   Felling trees is the collective work of the men, who celebrate afterward.   The rest of the farming is done by the women.

Fishing.—The most important subsistence activity is fishing.   The *Warrau* fish with unfeathered arrows, some having the point attached so as to form a barb, and others with three hardwood prongs.   They also use harpoon arrows (a double-barbed, detachable point fastened to the shaft by a cord), harpoons thrown like spears, light spears, hooks, including triangle spring hooks, and cylindrical fall-traps made of the bark or a hollowed-out branch of the trumpet tree and used for the haimara fish.   With vegetable poison (*Phyllanthus conami*) they stupefy the fish, which are then taken out of the water with a scoop.   Formerly, they used a hook made of a palm spine sharpened at both ends, with a line tied to its center; a double type was made by crossing two spines. Low-low (*Silurus* sp.) are caught with several baited hooks connected with a strong cord which is tied to a float made of empty calabashes. When fishing with bow and arrow, the *Warrau* throw fruits into the water as bait.

Hunting.—Hunting is not as important as fishing.   The bow and arrow seems to be the only weapon used.   The arrows have two feathers, attached with two or three sets of wrappings.   Arrow poison is unknown. The peccary was formerly caught in simple creel traps placed behind

hollow trees out of which the animals were driven with sticks or fire.
Rats are trapped and eaten. Small birds are captured, mainly by boys,
in multiple snare traps fixed over the nest. Dogs are used in hunting.
To carry a slain peccary and deer, the hunter ties the legs together and
passes his arms through them as if they were shoulder straps. He
leaves his game at some distance from the house, and the women bring
it in. The men cut up larger animals such as the tapir, peccary, and
deer, while the women clean and prepare the entrails. Women also
cut up and clean small game.

Gathering wild foods.—The vegetable staple of the *Warrau* is the
Mauritia palm (ite). Gumilla (1791), who deals at length with the
uses of this tree for building, manufacturing, and food, gives the following description: A tree is felled and a tunnellike opening is made in it
for the sap to collect. The sap is gathered every evening and made
into a fermented drink (according to Roth it is also sometimes drunk
fresh) ; after a few days, it turns to vinegar and is used in the preparation
of fish and palm worms. When all the sap has been taken out, a spongy
mass remaining in the trunk of the tree is washed, strained, dried, and
ground into a starch called yuruma to be used for making bread. Roth
(1924, pp. 215–216) gives a somewhat different description:

When an ite tree begins to fructify it is cut down, a large slice is cut off one side,
and the stringy substance of the interior is cut into shreds, the remainder of the
trunk serving as a trough, in which it is triturated with water, by which is disengaged
a considerable quantity of starch. The fibrous particles are then extracted, and
the sediment, or aru, formed into molds like bricks. This is spread out on stones
or iron plates over the fire, and makes a very nutritive but at the same time un-
masticable bread.

Both the meat and the kernels of the *Mauritia* palm fruit are eaten.
The former is beaten and prepared as a refreshing drink.

The *Warrau* presumably collect greenheart seeds, sweet potatoes, yams,
and pineapples, although some of these are only mentioned in myths.
Crabs and the larvae of certain beetles are collected, the latter in holes
made in trees.

Resin (*Protium heptophyllum*) is saved for lighting fires. Gum derived from the *Tabebuia longipes* is obtained by making incisions in the
tree. Mixed with beeswax and finely powdered charcoal, it is used for
fastening arrow points, for waxing thread and fishing lines, and for
chalking canoes and cordage.

Food preparation.—The principal method of preparing food is the
barbracot: horizontal sticks supported by four upright posts. Meat and
fish seem to be eaten mainly, or exclusively, smoked. For the preparation of cassava the same methods are used by the *Warrau* as by the
neighboring *Arawak* and *Carib* (tipití, strainer, sifter, etc.). Greenheart seeds are grated, put into fresh water to separate a starchy sub-

stance, repeatedly washed to lessen the bitterness, and mixed with rotten wood, previously pounded and sifted.

VILLAGES AND HOUSES

Rectangular pile dwellings are typical of the delta, while farther east on higher ground rectangular huts without piles are built. In Gumilla's time, the *Warrau* constructed their houses, streets, and plazas upon a common platform, which rested on poles sunk through the mud until they reached firm ground. In the 19th century, Hilhouse (1834 b) described a village, probably smaller, in which the house platforms were built on the trunks of *Mauritia* palms left standing, with a resulting irregular distribution of piles. The platform or floor of the houses consisted of two layers of tree trunks and an additional layer of clay. Some of these houses could hold 150 people. On the Barima River, M. R. Schomburgk (1847–48) mentions a settlement consisting of miserable huts 7 to 8 feet (2 to 2.5 m.) long. Although in Gumilla's time settlements in the delta must have been large, today the eastern settlements (not on poles) are small, consisting of 6 to 8 houses.

Houses have a gabled roof thatched with palm leaves, and two central forked posts supporting the ridge pole. Ends and sides are open, but the roof slopes nearly to the ground.

Household furniture includes hammocks of *Mauritia* palm fiber (today only the warp is made of this fiber, the weft being of cotton), used for sleeping, and little wooden stools. The last often have a concave seat and in some cases are zoomorphically carved.

DRESS AND ADORNMENT

Men go naked except for a bast penis sheath or a string around the waist to tie up the prepuce. They wear high pointed caps of the spathe of the truli palm, moistened and stretched. Jaguar-skin caps, on the other hand, may have been restricted to chiefs. On festive occasions, men wear feather crowns on a basketry foundation or rings made of the fiber of the *Mauritia* palm.

Women wear aprons of *Mauritia* palm fiber strings or of bark cloth, which are tied to a string around the waist (Gumilla, 1741).

Men and women tie broad woven cotton bands below their knees. Adults wear necklaces, and children use armlets made of fruit kernels and seeds.

Both sexes remove all hair from the face, including the eyebrows, and also all pubic hair. As soon as a child starts crawling around its hair is shorn. Both sexes wear bangs. Men wore their hair to their shoulders; women tied theirs with a palm-fiber string. On the Essequibo

River, men shave the hair off around the ears, while women wear it very long (Bancroft, 1769).

Widowers, widows, and, occasionally, other close relatives of a dead person cut their hair short.

Men and women paint their faces with the juice of *Bignonia chica,* *Bixa orellana,* and *Homalium* sp. Men paint lines ending in dots on their faces; women paint two bands around the forearm and one below the knees.

Men and women tattoo the face with a palm thorn and the juice of the korowatti fruit. Tattoo designs take the shape of a curled-up moustache and eye brows.

Formerly, the *Warrau* perforated their ears, but it is not known what, if anything, they wore in the holes. Both sexes wore oval silver plates hanging from a hole made in the septum and covering the upper lip. The holes in the ears and nose were made soon after birth and were kept open with bits of wood.

Rain protectors, partly woven of big palm leaves, were carried over the head.

TRANSPORTATION

The *Warrau* have two kinds of canoes. One, made of bark, is flat bottomed, with a capacity of not more than 3 persons. The other, a dugout, is made from the silk-cotton tree; it holds up to 50 persons and lasts for 10 years. While dugouts have been characteristic of the *Warrau* for a long time, having earned such fame that *Arawak* Indians sometimes go to remote *Warrau* villages to buy them, the original absence of stone axes (see below) makes it likely that the truly native *Warrau* craft is the bark canoe, notwithstanding that one of their cultural heroes is said to have been the inventor of the dugout.

MANUFACTURES

Basketry.—Artifacts woven out of palm leaves, plaited, or twilled, include: mats, baskets, and boxes of many shapes and techniques, circular concave trays, fire and mosquito fans, the tipiti, the "finger-catcher," and frames for the application of ants in ordeals. Some baskets are woven out of a single leaf. Baskets are usually made by men, but also occasionally by women. Plaitwork is also used to keep together the two calabashes used as floats in fishing (p. 870).

Weaving.—Hammocks and cotton bands used as anklets, forehead and waist bands, and baby slings are today woven by women on a loom similar to that of neighboring tribes. Thirty years ago men did the weaving. Rope and string were made by the women with one, three, or eight strands.

Axes.—Axes were originally absent, the felling of a tree having been accomplished in Gumilla's time exclusively by the use of fire. Double-edged stone celts were sometimes imported from other tribes.

Calabashes.—Calabashes are boiled for about an hour, scraped out, and used for receptacles.

Ceramics.—Pottery is made, but the details are unknown. According to M. R. Schomburgk (1847–48), the *Warrau* dry their pottery in the sun and smear it with a varnish prepared from the soot of old pots mixed with the sticky gum of the *Mimosa*.

Large drinking troughs have handles at both ends. These sometimes crudely represent a caiman's head.

TRADE

In Gumilla's time (middle of the 18th century), hammocks and the starch of the *Mauritia* palm were the main articles of trade. More recent sources mention, in addition, smoked fish, canoes, cassava sifters, and cotton hammocks.

There seems to have been a special ceremonial for bartering. First there is bargaining, then conversation, and, finally, drinks to confirm the deal, the whole ending up with a general dance. It appears as if trade goods were stored in some villages.

SOCIAL AND POLITICAL ORGANIZATION

Little is known on this subject. Each settlement had a headman, whose authority was greatest in time of war. If settlements were larger in the past, as Gumilla's data suggest, the headman's authority may also have been greater.

According to M. R. Schomburgk (1847–48), the daughter's son succeeds the headman, but a nonrelative could assume power upon the death of a chief if he possessed the courage and ability to hold his own against the deceased's family.

Polygyny seems to be the rule, and the *Warrau* are considered the most polygamous tribe of the Guianas. Most men have two or three wives, and chiefs have four or five, generally sisters.

A widow and her children are inherited by the brother or nearest relative. If she rejects him, the provoked blood relatives revenge themselves by forcing their way into her house and thrashing her, whereafter she is free to live as she pleases. There are special ceremonies for the remarriage of a widow. She is beaten with a whip by her future husband and by other men; after this the husband is whipped in a similar fashion; during the procedure both stand with their hands joined above their heads.

Sexual relations between certain kinds of cousins (probably parallel) were forbidden.

In cases of intertribal marriage only the children of *Warrau* mothers were considered *Warrau*.

To splash a woman with water during the communal bathing is an indication of courting. A man who aspires to marry must show his fitness, by clearing a certain piece of land within a given time.

The parents of a girl choose a bridegroom at a very early age and hand her over to him at a later period without any further ceremony. From the day of the betrothal, the boy must work for her parents until he reaches manhood, when he takes the girl to the hut he has built. A man may ask a father for his daughter and, if he is accepted, he removes his property to his father-in-law's hut and hunts, fishes, and clears a field for him. The second and third wives are obtained by purchase. When his wife becomes old (20 years), a man takes a little girl of 7 or 8, and his wife instructs her in household duties until she is old enough to marry him.

A mother-in-law and son-in-law never communicate their orders or requests directly to each other but use intermediaries.

As a proof of friendship between members of the same sex, the younger person adopts the name of the older.

Kanaima (p. 856) is sometimes found among the *Warrau*.

When a man considers his, or his wife's, reputation injured, he becomes so angry that he kills the offender and even the offender's whole family.

A *Warrau* chief greets his visitor, while sitting on a low stool surrounded by his men, all armed with war clubs.

At drinking parties held on special occasions, as upon the clearing of a field, the Indians never leave their seat or hammock.

LIFE CYCLE

There are indications that sexual intercourse is not always considered necessary for pregnancy. A miscarriage is thought to be the result of pregnancy caused by water spirits. There is a belief that in the past women did not bear children, but that they were sought and found in the woods. A myth explains the origin of childbirth.

Childbirth.—During childbirth, a woman is isolated in a hut that is distinguished by bunches of ite shreds. Other women help her only in difficult cases. The umbilical cord is bitten off and tied with a strand. During confinement she is considered impure and a dangerous influence. Her confinement ends with a bath. After the birth the father goes into seclusion and refrains for some time from eating deer, from various customary activities, and from intercourse with his wife or any other woman. Otherwise the child will die. Children suckle up to 3 or 4 years.

On the Pomeroon River children are named after creeks of the Orinoco region, where the *Warrau* originally came from.

Puberty.—At the time of her first menstruation, a girl's hair is shaved by her mother, or occasionally by her father. The girl is secluded in the confinement hut, already mentioned, and lies in a smaller hammock than usual. She must neither speak nor laugh during the 2 or 3 days of the period or she will lose all her teeth at adulthood. The first thing she is allowed to eat is a little cassava flour wrapped in a leaf.

During a celebration, probably at the end of the confinement, the girl is adorned with strings of beads and with white feathers glued to her shaved head, arms, and legs. Originally women seem to have been secluded during every menstruation. While menstruating they must never eat the flesh of large animals, such as tapir or turtle, nor of certain fish. The meat of animals caught with the help of dogs is specially forbidden them lest the dogs never again be good for the chase. Menstruating women must cook their own food in special small vessels, but may not prepare any food for others and must never extinguish a fire. Finally, they may not touch boats, fishing gear, or anything else connected with water. During this time women are especially open to sexual attacks from the spirits of the bush and of the water.

At puberty, boys are subjected to severe trials. They have to slash their chest and arms with a tusk of a wild hog or the beak of a toucan. They can take this test a second time if they have failed in the first.

Young people of both sexes may not marry until they have gone through the ant ordeal. The ants are placed on the body, either directly or by means of special plaited frames, while the subject is resting in a hammock. If a boy cries out he is condemned to celibacy; if a girl cries out it means that she cannot work and, therefore, does not deserve a husband.

Death.—Several kinds of burial have been reported. In the case of high chiefs, i.e., of a subtribe (?), the body is allowed to putrefy and the skeleton is then suspended in the chief's house. The skull is decorated with feathers and the dead man's gold plates (not mentioned otherwise) are hung around the bones. Or else, the body is tied to a rope and left a whole day hanging in the river until the fish have cleaned it to the bones.

The bones are then put in a basket, placed in order from the smallest to the largest with skull on top, and the basket is hung in the house.

In some cases, a coffin made of hollowed tree trunk or a canoe is placed on two forked sticks thrust into the ground (fig. 134) near the hut, or on several sticks placed together in an abandoned hut. It is not clear if this method is reserved for chiefs, shamans, and other important people or is used during inundations when burial in the ground seems hardly feasible. In other cases, the corpse, rolled up in a hammock, is buried in a sitting position in a grave 3 feet (1 m.) deep.

The corpse is always disposed of on the spot where the person expired. On one occasion, a shaman was buried in the house where he had died and the whole village was burned down.

In one instance, an old woman's grave was dug by four young women, and, in another, the earth of the half-closed grave of a man was trampled down by the wailing widow and sisters. In the case of important people, a fire is kept burning close to the grave for several days, or even weeks.

FIGURE 134.—*Warrau* burial. (After Crévaux, 1891.)

In some cases the dead person's belongings, including his ornaments, weapons, utensils, and dog, together with dried fish, fruit, and bread, are buried with him, either in the hollowed tree, canoe, or in the ground. Sometimes the dead man's belongings are burned, but no case of cremation of the body has been reported. In other cases the dead person's belongings are buried separately several days after the body.

The women sit by the grave and direct sad songs to the dead.

According to Crévaux (1883), among the *Warrau* near the mouth of the main branch of the Orinoco, the widower lies down in front of the dead body, crying and singing, whereupon, all men who once have had relations with the dead woman must step forward and do the same.

Women sit by the grave and direct sad songs to the dead. In some cases the widows pull up all plants from the dead man's fields. When a person dies, a drink may be prepared immediately by others than the deceased's relatives, but the drinking bout may occur several days later, when the wife's hair is cut and the dead man's belongings are buried. Or the festival may be postponed until the manioc planted by the deceased, or that planted after his death on his behalf, has grown sufficiently to furnish drink for the guests. At this festival the widow or widower is given permission to remarry. On the Wani River, about a week after

death a dance is held inside the house, attended exclusively by men. At
this dance, one of the dancers may whip the ground at intervals.

The *Warrau* believe that every man has a soul in his heart, in his saliva,
in his shadow, and in his footprints. At death, that of the heart leaves
the body and becomes a hebu, or anthropomorphic bush spirit. There is
no known account of the fate of the other souls.

WARFARE

In 1596 Sir Walter Raleigh found two chiefs of *Warrau* subtribes warring with each other and with neighboring tribes, especially the *Caribs*.

Weapons are the bow and arrow and both a paddle-shaped and block-
shaped club. Rectangular "shields" are used in a sport (p. 879), but
probably not in warfare.

ESTHETIC AND RECREATIONAL ACTIVITIES

Dances.—There are several kinds of dances. The most important
imitate the movements of the bush hog. Women participate only occasionally in some dances, but they are essential to others. All dancing is
accompanied by singing, drinking, and sexual laxity.

The Aruhoho festival is probably of foreign origin, although the only
description of it comes from *Warrau* sources. When the manioc is ripe,
the men go to sea and catch crabs while the women prepare special cassava
cakes which, upon the return of the men, they eat together. Then a young
man and woman are placed in the center of a circle, separated by an arrow
stuck in the ground with the tip pointing upward, upon which is stuck a
wooden doll. The man has a new hammock tied around his neck and
folded behind the buttocks; he locks his fingers together across the lower
part of his chest while the girl has hers folded over her little apron. The
dance consists of a few single steps on the spot, different for men and for
women. Both have to stare at each other without any movement whatever of eye or mouth. The slightest sign of laughter disqualifies either
one, who is thereupon bundled out of the ring and the crowd shouts, "That
man (woman) is no good. He (she) will never get a wife (husband)."
Music is supplied by two oboe players, who are the only ones to wear
special feather headdresses. All others wear the ordinary cotton forehead
band.

Music and musical instruments.—Musical instruments include reed
flutes, ocarinas made of calabashes, a special kind of oboelike flute (with
glotis, vibrator, and gourd resounder), and two kinds of signal trumpets,
one made of pottery in the shape of an **8,** and another of bamboo sections.
Drums, beaten with a stick, are made of hollowed logs covered with the
skin of the peccary, acouri, monkey, deer, or sloth. The silent skin is
crossed by a string with a small wooden resounder or tongue in its center.

Every *Warrau* settlement has its own music master, who teaches the young boys and men to blow on a kind of oboe. Almost every evening the young men hold a concert in the middle of the settlement under their teacher's guidance. The musical tone varies in pitch according to the size of the bamboo stem and its reed. Although each instrument only gives one note, the musical director knows the tone of the combined instruments so exactly and gives his directions so correctly that "a basis of harmony rules the sound" (M. R. Schomburgk, 1847–48). Certain stringed instruments (both monochord and violin type) made by raising the fibers of the rib of an ite leaf and placing a bridge under it, must be of European or Negro origin.

The rattle is the shaman's instrument.

Miscellaneous.—Children's and adult's playthings include tops (sometimes of the buzzing type), buzzers, "finger catchers" woven out of palm leaves, and a great variety of string figures.

Girls have wooden dolls made by their fathers and miniature hammocks. Boys play "fishing": A boy dives, takes a cord thrown at him between his teeth, and is hauled out.

Rectangular "shields" made of the leafstalks of the ite palm lashed together across a frame are used today in "pushing matches" played by pairs of opponents. The champions, especially dressed for the game, stand behind their respective shields and, firmly grasping its edges with both hands, try to push their opponents off the playground. Each champion comes to the contest with two backers. Today these matches are mainly for sport, although they are used occasionally to settle personal disputes. Possibly they may be a survival of a former mode of warfare consisting of a series of individual duels, as found in some other tribes of this cultural level.

Intoxicating beverages.—In addition to the fermented drinks made from the *Mauritia* palm, the *Warrau* prepare intoxicating beverages from cultivated plants, such as manioc (the drink is prepared from toasted cassava bread), maize, and, today, sugarcane. Fermented drinks are prepared and preserved in large wooden troughs.

RELIGION AND MYTHOLOGY

A belief in a supreme being has been reported. Competent students doubt whether this is an original *Warrau* belief, but no details are known. According to the *Warrau,* the moon is a male who used to be a human being. The stars and constellations are thought of as living beings who, together with plants, animals, and men, are the actors in *Warrau* mythology.

The most important figures in *Warrau* mythology are the two tribal heroes: Abore, the father of all inventions, and Korroremana, the **creator** of the male half of humanity. Women are thought to have been created by another deity.

The most directly important supernatural beings in the life of the *Warrau* are the hebus, who are the spirits of the bush, the water, and the sky (Gumilla, 1791). The spirits of the bush are hairy, with such prominent eyebrows that they can look up only by lying on their backs. They have teeth on their stomachs, and hearts of fire instead of rumps. One of them, called Maihisikiri, is specially attached to women but remains invisible to men; women who have relations with him die after a short time. The spirits of the water, which are divided into those living in rivers, those living in the ocean, and those living at the very bottom of the water, are also prone to ravish women; such relations always end in abortions.

The spirits of the bush cause illness and death to human beings and may transform them into animals; they are also blamed when fermented drinks do not turn out well.

Plants, animals, and human beings all come out of a silk-cotton tree, except the neighboring *Carib,* who are thought to have descended from animals. At one time the *Warrau* lived in the sky, from where they descended through a hole, on a cotton rope; at the very last a woman got stuck in the aperture, so that they were unable to return. The woman is recognized as the morning star.

Men once were immortal, but lost their immortality as a punishment. They received fire from the two sons of the sun, whole stole it from Nayobo, the big frog.

SHAMANISM AND SORCERY

The shaman (wishidatu or wisedaa) is an important personage. Sometimes the headman is also the shaman. Female shamans seem to be rare. The shaman has a little hut built of kokerite leaves, where he keeps his insignia. It is called the spirit house and is taboo. Shamans carry around with them, in a special basket provided with a lid, a ceremonial stool (ornamented with a jaguar, turtle, macaw, or caiman head), a crudely carved figure, a rattle (sometimes double), and quartz crystals. Sometimes such crystals were put in the rattle instead of the usual pebbles. Tobacco has a special relation to the shaman; it was brought to this world by a colibri (hummingbird) from an island inhabited by women, and, therefore, the colibri is considered to belong to the shaman.

At the ordeal of initiation, a novice shaman has to fast and then drink an enormous quantity of tobacco juice, which reduces him to a deathlike state of sickness. His death is loudly proclaimed. About 10 days later he recovers sufficiently to come out of the sacred hut. For the next 10 months the new shaman can eat only the smallest kinds of fish, and he abstains from intoxicating drinks. In the Pomeroon district, he wears a special cotton headdress at the initiation ceremony.

Shamans do not eat meat or any other food from outside their area. No details are available on curing methods. When a shaman imposes a diet on a patient, the latter's parents and brothers and sisters join him in it. The shaman has control over spirits that harm mankind; he can foresee the future and interpret dreams. If a sick person dies, the shaman's rattle and crystals lose their power and are buried. At the anniversary of the death of the headman, the shaman blows over the grave in the direction of the person who is thought to have caused the death. Evil spirits are driven from the dancing grounds by blowing a small flute. Blowing, as a magic procedure, may be used by others than shamans. To drive away clouds, people will blow into one closed hand and dash it upward toward the clouds. Parents blow on the face or the hand of their children when they cry or when, as adults, they start out on a hunting trip.

Rain may be caused by burning the carcass of a certain snake (camuchi).

A hunter must never bring an animal to his house or he will lose his hunting luck. Hunters call their dogs by the names of animals known to be good hunters, such as sharks, wild dogs, a certain crab, and a species of wasp.

Certain words must not be used while one is traveling by canoe. Travelers must never wash the pot spoon in the river or ocean, lest big squalls or storms arise.

When looking at a mountain for the first time, a *Warrau* shuts his eyes to avoid attracting the shadow of the Spirit toward him. When one person looks at another, he draws the other's shadow toward himself.

People can transform themselves into animals simply by dressing in their skins. Parts of plants or animals are used as charms to obtain the fulfillment of certain wishes, including the love of the desired one or pregnancy. This whole complex, according to the *Warrau* themselves, is of *Carib* origin. When a *Warrau* woman wants a baby, she pounds up a certain fungus in water and drinks the infusion.

In contrast to many other of the Guiana and Orinoco tribes, the *Warrau* are said to care well for their sick. In cases of rheumatism, some of the *Warrau* let a certain species of ant bite the painful spot a few times.

LORE AND LEARNING

The new year begins with the rise of the Pleiades at sunset.

Strings with knots, one to be untied each day by each party, serve to keep appointments.

BIBLIOGRAPHY

Bancroft, 1769; Crévaux, 1883; Gumilla, 1791; Hilhouse, 1834 b; Plassard, 1868; Roth, 1915, 1924; Schomburgk, M. R., 1847–48.

Part 6. Culture Areas of the Tropical Forests

By Julian H. Steward

INTRODUCTION

In the present state of knowledge, the features which distinguish the various subdivisions of the Amazon Basin have to be presented geographically, in terms of their distribution in areas, rather than anthropologically, in terms of their integration in cultural structures. To a very large extent, their occurrences seem random and capricious, inexplicable in environmental, historical, or functional terms. Nonetheless, the present article undertakes to recognize the general forms suggested by many small fragments and to present a broad picture which is frankly hypothetical, sketchy, and preliminary. The present tense is used, but the data refer to aboriginal cultures.

The distribution of culture elements and complexes reveals at least one broad pattern. The basic Tropical Forest cultures occur mainly in the areas accessible by water routes, both the coast and the great rivers, whereas simpler or Marginal cultures tend to be distributed in a vast **U** around the periphery of the Amazon Basin. Significantly, this **U**, which includes the Amazon-Orinoco watershed, the eastern slope of the Andes, parts of Mato Grosso, and some of the Highlands of eastern Brazil, has today the greatest number of unacculturated Indians. The country is remote and the streams are small, making it difficult of access in pre-Columbian times no less than in modern times to essentially riparian peoples. The inference is clear that what is thought of as a typical Tropical Forest or selvan culture—a developed agriculture and a technology manifest in twilled and woven baskets, loom weaving, cotton, hammocks, ceramics, and other material traits—flowed along the coast and up the main waterways, stopping where streams were less navigable and leaving the hinterland tribes on a more primitive level. Some of these tribes, such as the *Shiri*, *Guahibo*, *Macú*, and *Sironó* remained preagricultural nomads. Others, such as the *Mura* and the groups herein designated the Northwestern Marginals, Western Marginals, and South Amazon Marginals, adopted some agriculture but otherwise acquired few of the basic Tropical Forest traits. Some of these traits, such as manufactured items, simply did not reach them; others, such as canoes and devices for taking fish and aquatic game in the large rivers, were precluded by the environments. On the other hand, the Marginals more

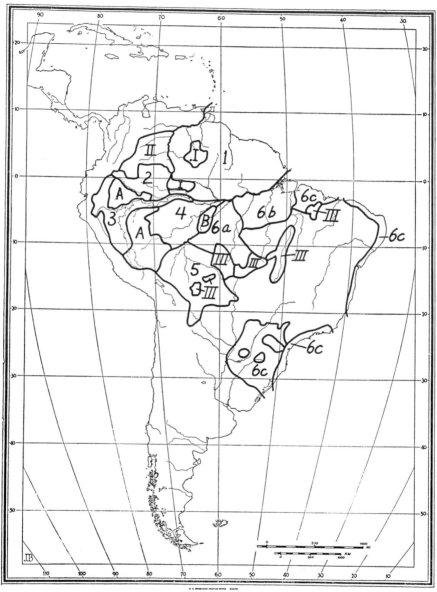

MAP 8.—Cultural divisions of the area included in the present volume. *1-6*, Basic Tropical Forest cultures: *1*, Guianas, *2*, Northwest Amazon, *3*, Montaña, *4*, Juruá-Purús, *5*, Mojos-Chiquitos, *6*, *Tupían* (*a*, Madeira-Tapajóz; *b*, lower Xingú-Tocantins; *c*, *Tupinamba* and *Guaraní*). *A*, *B*, Submarginal tribes: *A*, Western Marginals, *B*, *Mura*. *I-III*, Marginal tribes: *I*, Guiana Internal Marginals; *II*, Northwestern Marginals; *III*, Southern Amazon Marginals.

often than the developed Tropical Forest peoples have sibs, moieties, and other social elaborations.

A further inference of these distributional data is that the developed Tropical Forest culture spread southward along the Atlantic Coast to the Amazon and along the Amazon tributaries, predominantly upstream. There was relatively little cultural diffusion overland, either from the Orinoco Basin or from the Andes, though a few traits may have spread from Colombia via the upper Orinoco. The Guianas and the lower Amazon are postulated as the center of dispersal on the evidence of the probable direction of cultural flow within the Tropical Forest and of the rich archeological remains in these centers rather than on the ethnography of the historic tribes, who, unfortunately, became extinct or absorbed before their culture was described. In Volume 4 of the Handbook, the ultimate source of the Tropical Forest culture will be traced to the Circum-Caribbean area. The Tropical Forest technology spread up the Amazon to the Andes in Perú, passing around the less accessible Western Marginal peoples and reaching the very border of the *Inca* Empire. Some Highland influence is recognizable in isolated material items, but the fundamental economic, social, political and religious patterns of the Montaña are those of the Guianas and eastern Amazon rather than of the Highland. A significant number of basic Tropical Forest traits was also adopted in the Northwest Amazon which, however, is distinctive for its patrilineal sibs and ancestor cult. South of the Amazon, the Tropical Forest culture spread up the Juruá and Purús Rivers, but largely failed to reach the Western Marginals situated on the watershed between the sources of these rivers and of the Ucayali and the Madre de Díos. It may have been carried by *Arawakan* tribes up the Madeira River through the lowlands at its headwaters to the llanos and forests of eastern Bolivia in the Provinces of Chiquitos and Mojos, where again it bordered the Andean civilizations. The culture of this area, however, has a few Andean traits of material culture, a tendency to a class-structured society, and a god cult with priests, all of which are characteristic of the Sub-Andean cultures found in northern Colombia and Venezuela rather than of Tropical Forest culture. A Tropical Forest culture also reached Bolivia in a very roundabout manner, being carried by the *Tupí,* in part down the Atlantic Coast to the mouth of the Río de la Plata, and inland from some point on the coast across Paraguay to the foot of the Andes. *Tupian* peoples are notable for their skill in navigation and for their warlike nature and their extreme cannibalism.

From a technological and ecological point of view, the basic Tropical Forest culture is strikingly uniform so far as present data reveal. In fact, its distribution coincides almost exactly with that of tropical rain forests. (Compare with vegetation map, Handbook, vol. 6.) The greatest differences are between shore lines and interfluvial areas. Tribes on the main watercourses and sea coast could exploit fish and aquatic game as well as forest resources; in addition, they had easier means of travel and transportation. Unfortunately, however, these tribes were the first to succumb to the Conquest. It is known that their villages were large and numerous, but the social and political concomitants of a dense population are not recorded. So far as agriculture, hunting, and gathering are concerned, important local differences have not been indicated. Sweet manioc was general, and bitter manioc became the staple throughout the area of its distribution, but no local cultural features seem to correlate with the cultivation of these or other species under the universal slash-and-burn farming. Similarly, general patterns of hunting and gathering appear to have been fairly uniform, regardless of local exploitative devices, such as blowguns, bows, traps, or climbing rings. In short, the important ecological differences were those between water-front and hinterland peoples, and these were little effected by specific exploitative devices. The differences were in resources, and these partly determined population density and community size, which in turn conditioned the sociopolitical patterns.

The more conspicuous and the most often mentioned differences between the Tropical Forest peoples are such readily observable items as dress, ornaments, body painting, tattoo, and featherwork. These external features, however, distinguish tribes and individuals even more than major areas; the culture elements involved have highly diversified distributions. The same is probably true of ornamentation, form, and other secondary features of bows, basketry, ceramics, and the like; if these features do characterize culture areas, their correlations will probably have to be shown statistically rather than through any inner, logical relationships between them.

In drawing lines between the main cultural subdivisions of the basic Tropical Forest cultures, therefore, we are brought to sociological and religious patterns, which, though recorded with annoying incompleteness, are often clearly discernible.

THE BASIC TROPICAL FOREST CULTURES

THE GUIANAS

Because the Guianas have the greatest number of traits regarded as characteristic of the Tropical Forests, they may be postulated as a center of dispersal, though not necessarily of all items. The Guianas were not culturally homogeneous, but it is impossible at present to establish their subdivisions with certainty. It would be profitable to examine further the distinctions between the coastal area, the inland mountain-savanna area, and the Amazon area, which Gillin (p. 800) has sketched. Systematic comparisons of *Arawakan* and *Cariban* culture would also be helpful.   From the point of view of dispersal of these cultures, more knowledge of the coastal and Amazon tribes is essential.   As these disappeared before their culture was recorded, the problem is thrown squarely to archeology.   For the present purposes, the Guianas are considered as a whole.

The Guianas have a long list of cultivated plants, including both bitter and sweet manioc and the typical processes for utilizing the former.   They have fish drugs, traps and weirs, probably aboriginal fishhooks and nets, the bow and arrow, blowgun (northern, especially among the *Carib*), climbing ring, pepper juice and ants used in hunting ritual, the pepper pot, and the domesticated dog.   Bark canoes are used on the smaller streams, but well-developed dugouts, even with planked gunwales, are found on the coast.

Characteristic Tropical Forest manufactures are all present: plain and twilled basketry highly developed and in profusion; many basketry forms, such as pack baskets, "telescoping" storage baskets, various containers, sifters, and manioc squeezers (tipitís) ; twined mats; developed netting; a large variety of plaiting techniques (perhaps attributable to the *Carib*) ; true weaving on the vertical loom (perhaps attributable to the *Arawak*) ; bark cloth; rubber work, including balls, syringes, and rings; hammocks; and elaborately carved wooden benches.

Both round and rectangular houses are found, and some settlements on the coast were protected by palisades and poisoned stakes.

Bodily ornaments occur in profusion and head deformation is reported from the coast.

The Guianas tend to be strongly matrilineal, although patrilocal and presumably exogamous settlements occur among the *Aparaí* and *Wapishana*.   The common pattern is one of matrilocal, extended families, each probably constituting the village, and there is strong bride service.   The coastal *Arawak* have matrilineal, nonlocalized, exogamous clans.   Chieftainship is basically patrilineal, but some features are adjusted to matrilineal descent.

The communities have not been accredited with age groups or social classes, except that *Carib* chiefs may have a following of sons-in-law, unattached men, and captives, called "peito," who comprise a kind of lower class.   *Arawak* captives, called "macu," form a similar class.

Crisis rites include the couvade, girl's seclusion at puberty, and earth burial.   Distinctive are *Arawak* work ordeals (hunting, cutting a field, building a house, etc.) for boys, *Rucuyen* ant ordeal for boys, whipping of girls (*Macushi*), cremation (*Atorai, Rucuyen*), mummification (*Piaroa*), and a whipping ceremony at burial to drive away evil spirits (*Arawak*).

Warfare is especially developed among the *Carib,* who formerly fought to avenge wrongs and to take captives, but, since the Conquest, have also taken slaves to sell them to Whites.   They have a dance of excitation, and fight with arrows, which are sometimes poisoned, and with spears, clubs, and shields. Both *Carib* and *Arawak* practice cannibalism as a means of revenge, make flutes of their victims long bones, and keep heads as temporary trophies. Captives are incorporated into the tribe, and are not, as among the *Tupi,* subsequently killed and eaten.

The Guianas have foot races, rubber-ball games, and many dances, especially those imitating animals. Numerous musical instruments are recorded (p. 853), including dancing staves, clay and bamboo trumpets, turtle-shell friction drums, hollow wooden drums (western), and foot drums. Fermented drinks are in general use, but the only narcotics are tobacco, which is smoked in cigarettes or chewed (central tribes), and parica. Pepper juice is used as a curative; the Pomeroon *Arawak* take it in an enema syringe.

The most important supernatural beings are nature spirits, particularly the jaguar spirit, and dangerous bush demons. Only shamans have familiar spirits. There is a culture hero and creator who, in many tales, makes animals from different parts of a magical tree or who kills a supernatural snake and makes men and animals from it (*Carib*). In some legends, the Hero has a twin brother, both of whom are children of the sun or other celestial body. In public festivals, the mourning ceremony is distinctive. There are also prayers to nature spirits for more abundant foods.

The shaman obtains power from supernatural spirits and uses a rattle, a bench, tobacco juice, and cigarettes. Shamans both cause and detect black magic. They cure by sucking, massaging, and blowing smoke. They also conduct rites for tobacco and maize growing and act as seers and advisors. The were-jaguar concept is predominent in shamanism.

The *Manao* and other *Arawakan* tribes of the left, middle Amazon (p. 707) apparently belong to the Guiana area. They have the blowgun, bow, parica, flogging of boys (evidently not in connection with an Ancestor cult), harvest festivals rather than puberty or cult feasts, war prisoners kept as slaves, and some form of simple social organization without sibs.

NORTHWEST AMAZON

The *Eastern Tucanoans* and their neighbors on the Vaupés and Caquetá Rivers, the *Witotoans*, the *Tucuna*, and probably the *Yurimagua*, form a block of tribes which are somewhat marginal in their technology (particularly the *Witotoans*) but are sharply distinguished from their neighbors by their well-developed sib system and initiation rites.

Subsistence is based on farming, with bitter manioc staple. These tribes have the blowgun, the bow and arrow (except *Witotoans*), bark cloth, the dugout canoe, fish weirs, traps and drugs, carrying baskets, pottery stoves, twilled baskets (twining also survives among the *Tucanoans*), the Amazon type rolled spindle, and weaving, mostly of bast without a loom. The *Carib* and *Arawak* have looms, but make only hammocks on them. *Tucuna* hammocks are netted. *Tucuna* pottery is modeled and painted; that of most of the other tribes is painted, but among the *Tucanoans* it is plain.

The village generally consists of a large, communal house. The *Tucanoans* and possibly also the *Arawak* and *Carib* of the Vaupés-Caquetá area and the *Witotoans* have patrilineal sibs, those of the *Tucanoans* being totemic and grouped into three phratries, each with an origin myth. Each sib tends to be localized and to form an exogamous, patrilocal household. The *Tucuna* have patrilineal, exogamous sibs grouped into moieties, but they are not localized and households even tend to be somewhat matrilineal. Each sib has musical instruments for its private use.

The *Tucanoan* boy is initiated into an Ancestor Cult, really a sib cult, when he is whipped and is shown the sacred trumpets, which are identified with the Ancestors. A pubescent girl is deflowered and uses the scratching stick. The *Witotoan* sacred trumpets may also have been connected with an initiation and an Ancestor cult. *Tucuna* children pass through stages signaled by hair trimming, ear piercing, and the like, and at puberty boys take snuff and are initiated into the secret of the megaphones and the bark trumpets. Girls are first secluded, then feasted and made to dance while the secret trumpets and megaphones are sounded and masked dances are performed. Their hair is pulled out, and they are bathed. The *Yurimagua* seem to have a similar initiation in which spirits are represented by sacred trumpets and youths are whipped.

These tribes have rubber-ball games, pounding staves (*Tucanoans*), hollow-log drums (*Witotoans*), maize-leaf shuttlecocks (*Tucuna*), cigars, and taking of tobacco juice and chicha (except *Witotoans*). Coca (*Witotoans*) and cayapi are used on the Uaupés-Caquetá.

Warfare is less emphasized than elsewhere. Slavery of captives and cannibalism are found among the *Witotoans* and in the Vaupés-Caquetá region, but neither trophy taking nor cannibalism occur among the *Tucuna*.

There is a general belief in upper and lower worlds, each with its gods. Missionary influence has been suspected in this belief, but, as little missionary work has been carried on among the *Witotoans, Tucanoans,* and *Tucuna,* it may be native.

The principal public religious festivals are the initiation rites and the *Tucanoan* and *Witotoan* masked mourning ceremonies. These contrast with the harvest and fertility rites of the lower Amazon, but the mourning ceremonies may be connected with those of the Guianas.

Shamans among the *Tucuna* acquire power from a tree spirit. Among the *Witotoans* and *Tucanoans,* they are associated with the jaguar and are accredited with power to transform themselves into jaguars. Magic "thorns" are the source of shamans' power to cause disease and must be sucked out of sick patients.

THE MONTAÑA

Crowded against the Andes in Perú and Ecuador but extending down the Marañón, Huallaga, and lower Ucayali Rivers is a large number of linguistic groups with the basic Tropical Forest culture. The more important and best known of these are the *Panoans, Cahuapanans,* and *Jivaroans.* Their fundamental economy, technology, and social and religious patterns are those of the Tropical Forests; Highland influence is observable only in particular items, which have a limited distribution among the tribes.

The economy is based on slash-and-burn farming, without bitter manioc, and on river resources. There is much use of hunting blinds, traps, pitfalls, harpoons, spear throwers, blowguns, and nets, the last perhaps of Andean origin. Highland influence is observable in the cultivation of the potato among only a few tribes at higher altitudes, in llamas and alpacas on the upper Marañón, and llamas and guinea pigs among the *Jivaro.* Muscovy ducks were general. The mortar is the main utensil in food preparation among the larger tribes.

Highland influence was greatest in dress and ornaments: the breechclout, cushma, woman's skirt and apron, poncho (some tribes), head deformation, and a few metal ornaments. Tooth blackening is a trait limited to the Montaña.

Houses are of the Tropical Forest communal type, but platform beds and special mosquito-proof sleeping enclosures are used.

Manufactures are also of Tropical Forest types: dugout canoes, carrying baskets and carrying bands, woven baskets, cotton weaving on the "Ucayali" loom, a modified Guiana type (p. 841), calabash work, and pottery. All these, especially the pottery, suggest a derivation of the main items of Montaña culture from the lower Amazon rather than from the Highland. But Andean influence is seen in such things as the horizontal loom, drop spindle, and feather fire fan.

Socially, Montaña tribes have the extended, patrilineal household, except that the *Panoans* are strongly matrilineal and perhaps have clans. They devote considerable energy to warfare and take prisoners; captives acquire a slave status among the *Tupí* and *Quijo.* Trophy heads, skulls, and shrunken heads are characteristic, and there is some cannibalism.

Crisis rites are not well developed, and girl's puberty is variously marked by removal of her clitoris, a tobacco festival, flogging, or putting pepper in her eyes. Urn burial marks the *Tupí* and their immediate neighbors, but endocannibalism—either eating the corpse or drinking the cremated remains with chicha—is found in most other tribes.

There is a variety of musical instruments, but handshaken gourd rattles and sacred instruments connected with secret rites are absent. Maize-leaf shuttlecocks, humming tops, and slings are common toys. Tobacco is the only narcotic.

No clearcut god concepts, group worship, or other organized religion are reported; even culture heroes are in doubt. The supernatural being most widely reported is a monstrous water serpent. Bush spirits, however, are generally feared, and the *Jívaro* believe in a magical, mana-like power. Belief that souls are reincarnated in animals is common. Ritual is for warriors, pubescent girls, and weather control, and not for food resources, ghosts, or boys' initiations.

The shaman has a spirit helper, that of the *Tupí* being a dead shaman. A magical "thorn" or "dart" is the shaman's inner power; such objects are projected into a person to cause disease and must be sucked out. This concept occurs also to the east, south of the Amazon, but receives greatest emphasis here. Magical virtues are widely attributed to various plants, especially to *Cyperus piripiri*. The werejaguar concept prevails.

THE MURA

The *Mura* have been sometimes described as nonhorticultural nomads, but Nimuendajú (p. 258) believes they did some farming. In any event, they are essentially rivermen and fishermen with a somewhat meager material culture and with certain distinctive social and religious traits, especially those connected with taking parica snuff and with whipping.

The *Mura* travel and almost live in bark canoes, fishing with the bow and arrow and taking large aquatic species with harpoons. They have palm-frond baskets and ornamented gourds, but lack blowguns, pottery (the *Pirahá* certainly, the *Mura,* possibly), hammocks, and perhaps weaving.

Several poorly built houses, each sheltering a single family, constitute a village. Social structure is based on the simple monogamous family, and bride service is not recorded. Natively, the *Mura* were fairly peaceful. Pubescent girls are confined; boys are allowed to take parica snuff and are whipped. People are buried wherever they die.

Great emphasis is placed on parica, which is taken both as a snuff and as an enema, being used especially during feasts, when men whip each other. Flagellation is also the central rite of a ceremony to promote manioc growth. Stinging ants are used for fishing success.

THE JURUA AND PURUS RIVER TRIBES

Three main linguistic families—*Panoan, Arawakan,* and *Catukinan*—are described in the article on the tribes of the Juruá-Purús region (p. 657), but cultural comparisons show a great difference between the *Panoans* and *Arawakans*. Data on *Panoan* technology, however, are inadequate, and this group seems to be set off from the *Arawakans* most in social and religious customs. The *Panoan* puberty rites with tooth staining, lip and nose piercing, and deflowering of girls, the anthropophagy of the dead, and the religion involving belief in a high god, ghosts, and bush spirits, use of magical herbs, and fertility ceremonies are all unlike recorded *Arawakan* features. Although the *Panoan Cashinawa* are intensive farmers, as contrasted to the gathering and fishing *Arawakans,* they lack the blowgun, spear thrower, and perhaps other traits of the latter. Thus, so far as we know, they belong with the Western Marginal tribes rather than with the Juruá-Purús area.

The *Arawakans,* on the other hand, have most elements of the developed Tropical Forest culture and are thus also distinguished from the Western Marginal *Arawakans* farther south at the headwaters of the Jurús, Acre, and Madre de Díos Rivers. As the tribes of the latter area, especially the *Canamari* and *Maniteneri,* are virtually unknown, it is difficult to say precisely where the line should be drawn.

The *Catukinans,* though covering a large area immediately south of the Amazon, are classed with the Juruá-Purús *Arawakans* for lack of knowing where else to place them.

Information on the *Arawakans* of the Juruá-Purús area comes mainly from the *Paumari* of the Purús River and the *Ipurina* southwest of them. These tribes are fishermen on the large rivers, using dugouts (*Paumari*) or bark canoes. They hunt with the bow, blowgun, and spear thrower, and make twilled baskets, plain pottery, hammocks, and loom-woven bands. They live in large communal houses, the social group evidently being some sort of animal-named, patrilineal household. Crisis rites include boy's lip perforation (*Ipurina*) and the exhumation and preservation of bones of the dead in the huts. Parica is used and tobacco is taken as snuff. Religion centers around a feast of nature spirits, with sacred flutes and bark trumpets which women and children are not permitted to see.

THE MOJOS-CHIQUITOS AREA

The Mojos-Chiquitos area of eastern Bolivia has material culture of the Tropical Forest type but its social and religious patterns are Sub-Andean. Socially, it is distinguished by a tendency to a class system and by a religious cult with a priesthood rather than one connected with initiation rites. The typical tribes are the *Mojo,* the *Chiquito,* and the now-extinct *Manasí* and *Xaray.* The *Canichana,* the *Movimá,* the *Tacanans,* the *Guarayú* and *Pauserna,* the *Southeastern Panoans,* and the *Chapacurans* belong to this area, though several of their tribes preserve certain primitive features resembling the Marginal tribes. The *Chiriguano* may also be included, though their culture is fundamentally *Tupian* with Andean additions. The southern half of the area described in "Tribes of the Right Bank of the Guaporé River" (p. 371) seems to belong with Mojos-Chiquitos, the northern half with the Tapajóz area.

Subsistence is based on intensive slash-and-burn farming (though bitter manioc is little grown), but combines hunting methods of the jungle with types found on the open savannas to the south: the bow and poisoned arrows and the blowgun for hunting in the forest; game drives, surrounds, disguises, and bolas in the savanna. The post-Columbian development of cattle raising among the Mojo is a plains feature. Of special interest are the strong development of jaguar hunting and ceremonialism, the aboriginal domesticated duck, and incipient apiculture (*Paressi*).

Villages are unusual for the fairly consistent arrangement of houses in streets and for a central plaza with a temple or men's club house in it. Some villages are protected by palisades.

The Chiquitos-Mojos area has the main Tropical Forest diagnostic material traits: cotton, hammocks, loom weaving, bark cloth, carved wooden stools, mats, pottery, bow, poisoned arrow, blowgun, hollow-log drum (*Mojo*), large trumpets (sometimes combined in rows, *Mojo*), ear, lip, and nose ornaments, featherwork, and rubber balls. In addition, it shows Highland influence in the cushma or tunic, coca (*Araono*), ornaments of precious metal traded from the Andes, head deformation (*Tiatinagua*), carrying nets as well as carrying baskets, pottery metates as well as wooden troughs and mortars for grinding food, feather fire fans, bolas, spear throwers, slings, and clay missiles with poisoned spikes embedded in them. Pottery is varied in fineness but attains some excellence in the *Mojo* area.

Communities are characteristically large. Each has a chief, and stratified classes, some of which suggest castes. Among the *Mojo, Bauré,* and *Paressi,* and especially among the *Manasí,* the relative rank of classes is: chiefs, priests, commoners, and slaves (war prisoners). Social structure reveals neither sibs, moieties, nor unilinear descent, though the *Tiatinagua* have some degree of community exogamy.

Warfare is emphasized, with capture of slaves the primary motive. The *Paressi* are unique in the Tropical Forest for their wars of conquest. In contrast to the *Tupí,* there is no cannibalism, except among the *Canichana.*

Religion is somewhat distinctive in having elements of wide distribution patterned in the temple cult with its sacred god symbols (images and musical instruments), a distinction between priestly and shamanistic functions, and ceremonies held in the men's club or temple and restricted to men who dance, sing, and become riotously drunk. The *Mojo* and *Manasí* keep all persons from the inner sanctum where the priests consult the gods, but the *Paressi-Cabishi* only exclude women and the *Tacanans* merely prevent women and children from seeing their god symbols. There is suggestion of a *Tacanan* men's cult to which boys are initiated. The purposes of the temple cults are obscure, but evidently differ among the tribes. The *Mojo* cult features the jaguar, and its rituals are conducted partly for slain enemies.

The shamanistic pattern is that of the Tropical Forest, the only feature of interest being the belief that the intrusion of an evil spirit as well as a foreign substance into the body may cause sickness.

TUPIAN TRIBES

The *Tupian*-speaking peoples, who spread over a large area, partly through comparatively recent migrations, form three cultural subgroups: (1) the *Tupinamba* and *Guarani*, scattered along the Atlantic Coast and some of the interior from near the mouth of the Amazon to the Río de la Plata; (2) the block of small tribes along the lower Tocantíns; and (3) the tribes of the Tapajóz and the lower Madeira Rivers. The *Tupi* of the upper Amazon are classed with the Montaña. The primitive enclaves of *Tupian*-speaking *Guayaki* among the *Guarani* have been described in Volume 1 of the Handbook (p. 435).

The *Tupian* tribes have slash-and-burn farming. All were exceptionally good canoemen, except for tribes between rivers. The *Parintintin, Tupi-Cawahib,* and *Cayabi* in the Madeira-Tapajóz area make only bark canoes; the others also dugouts.

Technology is simple, with not all basic Tropical Forest traits present. Twilled basketry is general, though the *Parintintin* and *Tupi-Cawahib* make only palm-leaf baskets. All tribes make pottery, but only the *Tupinamba* and *Guarani* ornament it elaborately. Hammocks and other articles are twined, though cotton is generally used; weaving on the vertical loom is restricted to the *Guarani* and *Tupi-Cawahib*. Weapons are the bow, lance, spear, some clubs, and, in eastern Brazil, the shield. Blowguns and spear throwers are not found. The *Guarani* acquired the tipoy and loincloth for men and the breechclout for women from the west, but other tribes have only the usual Tropical Forest profusion of featherwork, body paint, and ornaments.

Communities generally consist of several multifamily houses, the largest being on the coast, but among some interior tribes, such as those of the lower Xingú and the *Maué,* they are made up of only a few, single-family houses. The lack of a ceremonial or men's house, except among the *Mundurucú,* evidently correlates with the absence of cult religion and of a men's tribal society.

These tribes are strongly patrilineal, possibly a consequence of a predominantly aquatic life, which is a masculine concern. Among the coast *Tupi,* the 50 or more families occupying each house probably constitute an extended patrilineal family. The *Mundurucú, Parintintin,* and *Tupi-Cawahib* have patrilineal, exogamous sibs, those of the first two nonlocalized, and those of the *Mundurucú* assigned to exogamous moieties. Bride service is general, regardless of descent or postmarital residence.   There is always a secular village chief and often additional house chiefs, but shamans exercise much political power, especially among the *Guarani*, whose chiefs are always shamans.

The couvade occurs throughout these tribes.   Pubescent girls are usually isolated, and the coastal tribes cut or shave their hair, whereas the *Arapium* and *Tupinamba* may also scarify or bleed them.   Differences appear in boys' maturity observances: youths are subjected to the ant ordeal near the Amazon (*Maué, Arapium, Amanayé, Parintintin*), receive labrets (*Tupinamba, Guarani*), or are tattooed and go to the men's house to live (*Mundurucú*).   Earth burial in the house is usual, but the *Mundurucú* and *Apiacá* often rebury, and the *Arapium* eat the flesh and consume the bone ashes mixed with drinks, a practice more characteristic of the upper Amazon.

All these tribes are outstanding warriors and the greater number of them are trophy-takers and cannibals, often killing and eating even children whom they have captured and reared.   Trophies are most often made of heads or skulls, but other parts of the body may be used and flutes of human bones are commonly found.

The principle musical instruments are gourd rattles, trumpets, flutes, panpipes (except *Tupinamba* and *Guarani*), and clarinets, with drums very rare.   Tobacco is recorded only among the peoples of the coast and the Tocantíns-Xingú region, where it is smoked.   Chicha is made by most though not all *Tupians*.   Narcotics include maté (*Guarani*) and parica snuff taken by the *Maué*.   Wrestling and footraces are the main sports.   Group singing and dancing is a favorite diversion as well as ceremonial exercise.

In *Tupí* religion, the prominent supernatural beings are a creator or culture hero, many bush demons or spirits which are feared, and ghosts. The creator or culture hero, who is variously associated with the sky, sun, moon, and thunder, is the object of something of a cult among the *Guarani, Tupinamba, Parintintin,* and *Apiacá*.   Ceremonies are devoted to ghosts among the lower Xingú peoples and to bush spirits among the *Tupinamba, Mundurucú,* and *Guarani*.   Festivals for better harvests or for more abundant wild species are held by the *Tupinamba, Guarani, Maué,* and *Mundurucú*.

These religious patterns have no features of secret societies with their initiation rites, such as are found in other areas, except that the *Mundurucú* have men's festivals with sacred trumpets for sib ancestors, as in the Northwest Amazon.

The shamans have familiar spirits in most tribes, but the *Guarani* medicine man obtains power from chants given him by dead relatives.   Disease is thought to be caused by the intrusion of a foreign object, which the shaman sucks out of the victim.   Shamans also lead ceremonies, prognosticate, control nature, and perform other functions.

THE MARGINAL CULTURES

GUIANA INTERNAL MARGINALS

In the mountainous, savanna region on the southern headwaters of the Orinoco and the northern headwaters of the Río Negro are several little-known hunting and gathering tribes—the *Shirianá, Waica, Guaharibo, Auaké, Calianá*, and the *Maracaná*.

In native times, these tribes had no horticulture. They hunt with the bow, most of them lacking the blowgun, and fish only with the bow and arrow. Houses are small, and flimsy, but in some groups they are furnished with hammocks. There are no canoes. *Shirianá* basketry—the only reported—is twined. *Shirianá* pots are said to be well made.

Little is known of religious customs except that the *Guaharibo* preserve the cremated bones of their dead.

NORTHWESTERN MARGINALS

The Northwestern Marginal tribes do not all fall within the areas described in the present volume, but may be mentioned here as they form part of the pattern of marginal tribes around the Amazon Basin. They include the *Cariban Carijona* (p. 767), the *Cabarre, Guahibo, Yaruro*, and several *Arawakan* tribes near the Andes, which will be described in Volume 4. Perhaps also with them belong the *Catapolitani, Huhuteni*, and some of their neighbors, who may originally have been *Macú*, but who are now more or less assimilated to *Arawakan* culture.

All these tribes are little known. The *Carijona* are merely described as fierce nomadic cannibals who live in multifamily houses, lack masked dances, and have elaborate feather dance regalia.

THE WESTERN AMAZON SUBMARGINALS

Two groups of tribes preserving many primitive features occupy isolated portions of the western headwaters of the Amazon. One, which includes the *Záparoans, Pebans*, and *Western Tucanoans*, lives north of the Marañón and extends to the Putumayo River; the other, which consists of various *Panoans* and *Arawakans*, dwells in the back country which forms the watershed between the Ucayali, the Juruá-Purús, and the Madre de Díos Basins. These two groups would form a continuous block but for the *Tupians, Cahuapanans*, and *Panoans*, who are typical Tropical Forest tribes of the upper Amazon and Marañón Rivers. The southern group extends into the Andes and immediately adjoins the *Inca* on the upper Ucayali and the *Aymara* nearer Lake Titicaca. Some of the tribes are somewhat transitional, particularly the *Záparoans* and the *Pebans*, who absorbed some culture from the tribes along the lower Marañón.

Although farmers, these tribes rely more than the Montaña peoples on hunting, fishing, and gathering. *Arawakan* farms are very small and the *Mayoruna* subsist mainly on wild fruits in their swampy habitat. The *Pebans* fish only with poison, and most of the tribes lack harpoons and spear throwers. The bow is the principal weapon, except north of the Marañón, where the blowgun is of great importance, the *Pebans* being particularly famous for their manufacture of blowguns and curare.

In contrast to the Montaña tribes, the Western Submarginals use grinding troughs or slabs instead of mortars, hammocks in place of platform beds, bark-cloth and wild palm-fiber textiles rather than cotton cloth, the vertical instead of the horizontal loom, palm-leaf baskets often in place of woven ones, ceramics that are much cruder than the Montaña polychromes, and in some instances carrying nets instead of baskets. Until the historic period, they lacked canoes altogether.

Their social structure is based on the extended patrilineal family, but the communal house is smaller than in the Montaña. In warfare, these tribes are generally victims rather than aggressors. Esthetic and recreational activities, religion, and shamanism, on the other hand, seem to conform rather closely to Montaña patterns, except in a few traits wherein the tribes north of the Marañón River differ from the southern group. The former not only smoke but chew tobacco and drink the juice; in addition, they take *Datura*, cayapi, guayusa, and yoco. They also have the signal drum.

MARGINAL TRIBES OF THE SOUTHERN AMAZON PERIPHERY

Several tribes living on the small tributaries at the headwaters of the Tocantins, Xingú, Tapajóz, and Guaporé Rivers are so isolated that they received few traits diagnostic of the Tropical Forest cultures and retain an extremely primitive mode of life, especially on a technological level. These peoples include the *Carajá*, the *Tapirapé*, the tribes of the upper Xingú, the *Bacaïri*, and the *Nambicuara*, the last the most backward of all. The *Tenetehara* (*Guajajara*) and *Guajá*, nearer the Brazilian Coast to the northeast, also may be classed as marginal. To the west, a Tropical Forest culture spread westward through the low regions of the Madeira headwaters to form the eastern Bolivian culture, but enclaves of *Sirionó* retain the more primitive practices. To the north, a few small tribes living between but not on the large rivers also retain certain backward characteristics.

All of these tribes but the *Sirionó* adjoin the *Bororo*, *Guató*, and *Ge* tribes to the south and east (these are described in Volume 1), and the *Tapirapé* and *Carajá* are really an enclave within the *Northern Cayapó*, a *Ge* division. In a sense, therefore, they are part of the huge area of Marginal peoples who occupy the greater part of eastern Brazil and the southern third of the continent. The justification for including them in the present volume is largely their linguistic affiliation with the Tropical Forest tribes (especially, *Tupians* and *Arawakans*) and their possession of a few Tropical Forest traits.

None of these tribes except the *Guajá* entirely lacks farming, but the nomadism of the *Nambicuara* and *Sirionó* contrasts sharply with the intensive farming of neighbors such as the *Apiacá* and *Mojo*.

Dwellings and villages reflect nomadism. The *Nambicuara* build no houses; the *Sirionó,* structures which, though large, are crude and temporary; the *Guajá,* small temporary shelters.

No *Nambicuara* and few upper Xingú tribes have hammocks.

The *Sirionó, Nambicuara,* and *Tapirapé* lack canoes altogether. Those of the upper Xingú are made of bark; only the *Carajá* have dugouts. Basket making, weaving, and ceramics are technologically primitive. The *Sirionó,* like the *Mura, Mundurucú,* and *Tupí-Cawahíb,* make only plaited palm-leaf baskets and the *Carajá* only twined ones, though the other tribes make twilled forms of Tropical Forest types. True loom weaving occurs among most of these tribes, but tends to be secondary to twining and netting. Loom weaving on the upper Xingú is limited to the *Arawakans;* among the *Nambicuara* it is used only for belts and bands, and among the *Sirionó, Tenetehara,* and *Tapirapé* it is lacking. Pottery is either crude or absent. The eastern *Nambicuara* and the upper Xingú tribes, except the *Arawakans,* make none, while the remaining tribes make a plain ware. *Sirionó* pottery is tempered with burned seeds.

Weapons are restricted to the bow and unpoisoned arrow and club. The blowgun is absent except among a few tribes on the upper Guaporé. Former use of the spear thrower is indicated for the upper Xingú and for the *Carajá.*

Chicha is lacking on the upper Xingú and among the *Tapirapé* and *Carajá,* and the only narcotic is tobacco, usually smoked in a pipe.

Social organization presents a variety of forms, distinguishing the several Southern Marginal tribes from one another. The *Nambicuara* seem only to have a simple family organization and the *Sirionó* extended, matrilocal families, but on the upper Xingú, there are some indications of patrilineal sibs in certain tribes and of matrilineal sibs in others. The *Tapirapé,* the *Tenetehara,* and the *Carajá* have patrilineal, nonexogamic, ceremonial moieties, the last two along with matrilineal, extended households. By contrast, the neighboring Tropical Forest *Tupí* have patrilineal, extended households (*Tupinamba, Tupí-Cawahíb, Mané,* lower Xingú, etc.) or exogamic, patrilineal sibs (*Mundurucú, Parintintin*).

There are no secret cults with formal initiatory rites, but the *Nambicuara* have ceremonies to the Thunder god, with sacred flageolets which are taboo to women and children, and the *Carajá* restrict their ceremonies to men. Stages of child growth are marked by lip piercing for labrets, cutting the hair, scarifying, painting, etc., as among the *Tupí*. There are no ordeals, in contrast to the ant ordeal of the *Tupian* tribes nearer the Amazon.

On the whole, these tribes are peaceful. They lack the cannibalism which is so characteristic of the *Tupi.*

Religious and shamanism beliefs and practices are not unusual. The concept of a creator or culture hero, who is identified with the sky, sun, or moon, the fear of bush spirits, especially of the jaguar spirit, and fear of ghosts are basic. Masks occur among the *Carajá* and some upper Xingú tribes. There are ceremonies for plant or game fertility (upper Xingú, *Tapirapé, Tenetehara*). The Sirionó, however, are outstanding for their primitive religious concepts: lack of any god, except the mythological culture hero, Moon; fear of bush spirits; and a belief that the dead become spirits and that their bones are useful in magic.

It is remarkable that the *Sirionó* lack shamans, performing curing magic with human bones; that the *Bacaïri* have few shamans; and that the *Carajá* shaman only mediates between the living and ghosts, curing being a secular function. Other tribes have highly developed shamanism. The *Tenetehara* and *Tapirapé* emphasize the shaman's control of spirits, a *Tupian* concept. The *Nambicuara* and upper Xingú tribes feature the magic "arrow" as the cause of disease (the source of the shaman's power is not stated).

GLOSSARY[1]

(Sp., Spanish; l.g., Lingua Geral, which is largely *Tupian*)

Achiote. See **Bixa.**

Aldeamento. A settlement about the same size as an aldea.

Atlatl. See **Spear thrower.**

Aturá. A large cylindrical basket used for transporting Brazil nuts.

Babracot. A wooden grill supported by three or four posts for smoking and drying foods, especially meat.

Bahia, baia. A drainage canal; a small lake connecting with a river.

Balsa. (1) A raft on which the Indians live; (2) timber, palo de balsa. used in the construction of small rafts used for navigation on the upper rivers of the Amazon Basin.

Beijú. (1) A kind of cassava (manioc); (2) a kind of biscuit or cake made from manioc.

Bixa. A red paint or dye made from *Bixa orellana.*

Bugre. A name applied to the savage Indians by the seringueiros.

Caboclo. A backwoodsman; a rural Brazilian or mixed White and Indian blood; a generic term for Mestizo, including curiboca and mameluco.

Cabra. A Mestizo who obviously has Negro blood in him; a dark mulatto.

Cachibanco. A fine cloth woven of palm fiber.

Cachirim. (1) A native beer made by fermenting boiled manioc; (2) a kind of food prepared with beijú soaked in water.

Cachoeira (Sp., *cachuela*). A series of small drops in a section of a river; a cascade, a rapids.

Cafuso, cafus. A person of mixed Negro and Indian blood.

Caiçuma. A porridge of tucupí thickened with manioc flour.

Campestre. A small high campo surrounded by forest.

Campina. A treeless plain; a natural pasture.

Campo. (1) A natural prairie or savanna; a broad, flat plain without forest cover, or having only a few trees; (2) an encampment. Campo cerrado—savanna with scattered thickets of deciduous scrub forest. Campo limpo—a treeless savanna.

Caxiri. See **Cachirim.**

Chicha. Native beer made by fermenting various fruits and vegetables.

Climbing ring. A loop placed around the feet to assist in climbing tall, clean trunks of trees.

Cipo. Any kind of vine or liana, used for a great variety of purposes.

Coxo. A wooden vessel constructed of unhewn logs in which manioc decays and ferments under water so as to produce manioc starch (farinha).

Curare. Blowgun dart poison made from *Strychnos toxifera.*

Curiboca (Sp.). A dark-skinned person between a caboclo and a Negro in color.

Farinha. A starchy food made from bitter manioc (see p. 450).

Genipa. A black dye or paint made from *Genipa americana.*

Gentio (Sp., *gente*). Approximately synonymous with bugre.

---

[1] This glossary has drawn heavily upon the "Glossary of Brazilian Amazonian Terms" compiled from the Strategic Index of the Americas by the Research Division of the Office of the Coordinator of Inter-American Affairs.

Ig. (l.g.) Water.

Igarapá. (l.g.) A wide canal; a very long branch of a river; see **Igarapé.**

Igarapé. A narrow natural channel between two islands or between an island and the mainland; a canoe passage.

Ipadu. A substance which the caboclos chew to ward off hunger, made from coca leaves (*Erythroxylon coca*), mixed with tapioca and other substances.

Juruti. A dove or pigeon.

Lingua Geral. A lingua franca based on the *Tupí-Guaraní* language.

Macana. A flat, swordlike wooden club.

Maloca (Sp., *maloca*). (1) A hut, a small and poorly built house; (2) an Indian camp or village, a large communal dwelling of certain Indian tribes; (3) herded cattle on a fazenda; (4) a gang, e.g., of gypsies.

Mameluco. In Brazil, a Mestizo; esp., the offspring of a White man and an Indian woman.

Maqueira. Hammocks manufactured with tucum fiber.

Maracá. A gourd rattle.

Mato. (1) Uncultivated land, ground covered with brush; (2) a clearing; (3) the country, as opposed to the city.

Mestiço (Sp., *mestizo*). Any person of mixed blood, often a Negro-White cross; contrast **Mameluco.**

Mutum, hocco. A forest turkey of the genus *Crax.*

Paraná. An oxbow in a river.

Peçonho. Climbing ring.

Pepper pot. A stew of pepper, meat, and vegetables to which new ingredients are added from time to time.

Piassava. A fiber used for mats, ropes, and brushes, derived from the leaf sheaths of the palms, *Attalea funifera* and *Leopoldinia piassava.*

Piracu. A flour made from dried fish—especially pirarucú and tambaquí—which have been ground with a mortar and pestle; it keeps for a long time and hence is a favorite food for fishermen, hunters and travelers.

Pirahem. (l.g.) Dried fish.

Piranha. A river fish of the genera *Pyrocentrus* and *Serrasalmo,* feared because of its extreme voracity and tendency to attack animals of all sizes in great numbers.

Pirarucu (Sp., *paiche*). A very large Amazonian fish (*Arapaima gigas*), of the family Osteoglossidae.

Sertão. Inland country; the thinly peopled wilderness beyond the frontiers of concentrated settlement.

Spear thrower. A short stick, one end of which is grasped in the hand while the other engages the butt of a spear or harpoon, serving as an extension of the arm when throwing.

Ticuna. See **Curare.**

Tipití. An elongated basketry tube which is pulled lengthwise so as to compress its diameter and squeeze the juice from manioc (pl. 90).

Tucum. Fibers of tucumã (p. 10) used for making rope and thread.

Ubá. A fire-hollowed wooden canoe.

Urucú. See **Bixa.**

BIBLIOGRAPHY TO VOLUME 3

ABBREVIATIONS

Abhandl. K. Bayer. Akad. Wissensch. München.	Abhandlungen der Königlichen Bayerischen Akademie der Wissenschaften. München.
Abhandl. Königl. Gesellsch. Wissensch. Göttingen.	Abhandlungen der Königlichen Gesellschaft der Wissenschaften zu Göttingen. Berlin, Germany.
Acta Acad. Åboensis..................	Acta Academiae Åboensis. Åbo, Finland.
Amer. Anthrop.	American Anthropologist.
Amer. Geogr. Soc. Spec. Publ.	American Geographic Society, Special Publications. New York, N. Y.
Amer. Journ. Phys. Anthrop.	American Journal of Physical Anthropology. Washington.
An. Bibl.	Anales de la Biblioteca Nacional. Buenos Aires, Argentina.
An. Bibl. Archiv. Púb. Pará.	Annaes do Bibliotheca e Archivo Público do Pará. Belém do Pará, Brazil.
An. Bibl. Nac. Rio de Janeiro..........	Annaes do Bibliotheca Nacional. Rio de Janeiro, Brazil.
An. Fac. Cienc. Ed. Paraná............	Anales de la Facultad de Ciencias de la Educación. Paraná, Argentina.
An. Inst. Etnogr. Amer.	Anales del Instituto de Etnografía Americana de la Universidad Nacional de Cuyo. Mendozo, Argentina.
An. Mus. Nac. Buenos Aires...........	Anales del Museo Nacional de Buenos Aires. Buenos Aires, Argentina.
Ann. Rep. Bur. Amer. Ethnol.........	Annual Report of the Bureau of American Ethnology, Smithsonian Institution. Washington, D. C.
An. N. Y. Acad. Sci.	Annals of the New York Academy of Sciences. New York, N. Y.
An. Soc. Cient. Argentina.............	Anales de la Sociedad Científica Argentina. Buenos Aires, Argentina.
An. Univ. Central Venezuela..........	Anales de la Universidad Central de Venezuela.
Anthrop. Pap. Amer. Mus. Nat. Hist. ...	Anthropological Papers, American Museum of Natural History. New York, N.Y.
Anthrop. Rev.	Anthropological Review. London.
Anthrop. Ser. Catholic Univ.	Anthropological Series, Catholic University. Washington, D. C.
Anthropos	Anthropos. Ephemeris Internationalis Ethnologica et Linguistica.
Archiv. Antrop. Etnol.	Archivio per l'Antropologia e la Etnologia. Florence, Italy.
Archiv Anthrop.	Archiv für Anthropologie. Brunswick (Braunschweig), Germany.
Archiv. Soc. Amér. France............	Archives de la Société Américaine de France.
Archiv. Mus. Nac. Rio de Janeiro......	Archivos do Museu Nacional. Rio de Janeiro, Brazil.
Baessler-archiv	Baessler-archiv, Berlin, Germany.
Bibl. Boliv. Geogr. Hist.	Biblioteca Boliviana de Geografía e Historia. La Paz.

Bibl. Cienc. Pol. y Soc. .... Biblioteca de Ciencias Políticas y Sociales. Madrid.

Bibl. Ling. Amér. Paris............... Bibliothéque Linguistique Américaine. Paris, France.

Bibl. Pedag. Brasil.................. Biblioteca Pedagogica Brasileira. São Paulo and Rio de Janeiro, Brazil.

Bol. Acad. Nac. Hist. .... Boletín de la Academia Nacional de la Historia. Buenos Aires, Argentina.

Bol. Acad. Nac. Hist. Quito........... Boletín de la Academia Nacional de Historia. Quito, Ecuador.

Bol. Acad. Venezolana................ Boletín de la Academia Venezolana. Caracas, Venezuela.

Bol. Bibl. Nac. Quito................. Boletín de la Biblioteca Nacional de Quito. Quito, Ecuador.

Bol. Bibl. Nac. Venez. .... Boletín de la Biblioteca Nacional. Caracas, Venezuela.

Bol. Hist. Antig. .... Boletín de Historia y Antigüedades. Academia Colombiana de Historia. Bogotá, Colombia.

Bol. Inst. Geogr. Argentino............ Boletín del Instituto Geográfico Argentino. Buenos Aires, Argentina.

Bol. Mus. Goeldi.................... Boletim do Museu Paraense Emilio Goeldi de Historia Natural e Ethnographia. Belém do Pará, Brazil.

Bol. Mus. Nac. Rio de Janeiro......... Boletim do Museu Nacional. Rio De Janeiro.

Bol. Serv. Geol. Min. Brasil........... Boletim do Serviço Geologico e Mineralogico do Brasil.

Bol. Soc. Ecuatoriana Estud. Hist. ..... Boletín de la Sociedad Ecuatoriana de Estudios Historicos. Quito, Ecuador.

Bol. Soc. Geogr. Hist. Santa Cruz...... Boletín de la Sociedad Geográfica e Histórica de Santa Cruz. Bolivia.

Bol. Soc. Geogr. Italiana.............. Bollettino della Società Geografica Italiana. Rome, Italy.

Bol. Soc. Geogr. La Paz.............. Boletín de la Sociedad Geográfica de La Paz. Bolivia.

Bol. Soc. Geogr. Lima................ Boletín de la Sociedad Geográfica de Lima. Perú.

Bol. Soc. Geogr. Madrid.............. Boletín de la Sociedad Geográfica Nacional. Madrid.

Bol. Soc. Venezolana Cienc. Nat. .... Boletín de la Sociedad Venezolana de Ciencias Naturales. Caracas, Venezuela.

Bull. Amer. Ethnol. Soc. .... Bulletin, American Ethnological Society. New York, N. Y.

Bull. Assoc. Franc. Adv. Sci. .... Bulletin de l'Association Française Pour l'Avancement des Sciences.

Bull. Bur. Amer. Ethnol. .... Bulletin, Bureau of American Ethnology, Smithsonian Institution. Washington, D. C.

Bull. Mém. Soc. Anthrop. Paris......... Bulletins et Mémoires de la Société d'Anthropologie de Paris. France.

Bull. Pan Amer. Union................ Bulletin, Pan American Union. Washington, D. C.

Bull. Soc. Amér. Bel. .... Bulletin de la Société des Américanistes de Belgique. Brussels, Belgium.

Bull. Soc. Anthrop. Paris.............. Bulletin de la Société d'Anthropologie de Paris. Paris, France.

Bull. Soc. Geogr. Commerciale Paris ... Bulletin de la Société de Géographie Commerciale de Paris. Paris, France.

Bull. Soc. Géogr. Paris .... Bulletin de la Société de Géographie. Paris, France.

Bull. Geogr. Soc. Philadelphia.......... Bulletin, Geographical Society of Philadelphia.

Bull. Soc. Normande Géogr. .... Bulletin de la Société Normande de Géographie. Rouen, France.

Col. Hist. Chile..................... Colección de Historiadores de Chile. Santiago, Chile.

Comp. Ethnogr. Stud. .... Comparative Ethnographical Studies. Gothenburg (Göteborg), Sweden.

Congr. Int. Amer. .... Congreso Internacional de Americanistas; International Congress of Americanists; etc.

Contrib. Mus. Bot. Amazonas.......... Contribuiçãos do Museu Botanica do Amazonas. Rio de Janeiro, Brazil.

Cultura Nacional .... Cultura Nacional; Revista Literaria y Cientifica. Caracas, Venezuela.

Das Ausland....................... Das Ausland, Wochenschrift für Erd- und Völkerkunde. Stuttgart.

Dic. Hist., Geogr., Ethnol. Brasil..... Diccionario Historico, Geographico e Ethnographico do Brasil. Rio de Janeiro, (Imprensa Nacional, 1922), Brazil.

Doc. Hist. Bolivia................... Documentos Históricos de Bolivia. La Paz.

Ethnol. Stud. .... Ethnological Studies; Ethnologiska Studier. Gothenburg (Göteborg), Sweden.

Etud. Ethnog. Soc., Ethnol. .... Etudes d'ethnographie, de sociologie et d'ethnologie. Paris, France.

Geogr. Journ. .... The Geographical Journal. London, England.

Geogr. Rev. .... Geographical Review. New York, N. Y.

Globus .... Globus. Illustr. Zeitschrift für Länder- und Völkerkunde. Brunswick (Braunschweig), Germany.

Göteborgs Kungl. Vet. Vitt. Handl. .... Göteborgs Kungliga Vetenskapsch Vitterhetssamhälles Handlingar. Gothenburg (Göteborg), Sweden.

Harper's Mag. .... Harper's Magazine; Harper's Monthly Magazine. New York, N. Y.

Ibero-Amer. Archiv. .... Ibero-Amerikanischer Archiv. Berlin, Germany.

Inca .... Inca; Revista Trimestral de Estudios Antropológicos. Organo del Museo de Arquelogía de la Universidad Mayor de San Marcos de Lima. Lima, Perú.

Ind. Notes Monogr. .... Indian Notes and Monographs, Museum of the American Indian, Heye Foundation. New York, N. Y.

Int. Archiv. Ethnogr. .... Internationales Archiv für Ethnographie. Leiden, Holland.

Int. Journ. Amer. Ling. .... International Journal of American Linguistics.

Journ. Amer. Folk-lore............... Journal of American Folk-lore. New York, N. Y.

Journ. Ethnol. Soc. London........... Journal of the Ethnological Society of London. England.

Journ. Geogr. .... Journal of Geography.

Journ. Ornithol. .... Journal für Ornithologie. Berlin.

Journ. Roy. Anthrop. Inst. Gr. Brit. Journal of the Royal Anthropological Institute of Great Britain and Ireland. London, England.
Ireland.

Journ. Roy. Geogr. Soc. .... Journal of the Royal Geographical Society. London, England.

Journ. Soc. Amér. Paris.............. Journal de la Société des Américanistes de Paris. France.

Kansas City Rev. Sci. Industry........ The Kansas City Review of Science and Industry. Kansas City, Missouri.

Kosmos .... Kosmos. Revista Artistica, Scientifica e Litteraria. Rio de Janeiro, Brazil.

La Geogr. .... La Geographie. Paris, France.

L'Année Ling. .... L'Année Linguistique. Paris, France.

L'Anthrop. .... L'Anthropologie. Paris, France.

Le Muséon........................... Le Muséon. Louvain, Belgium.

L'Ethnogr. .... L'Ethnographie. Paris, France.

Le Tour du Monde................... Le Tour du Monde, Nouveau Journal des Voyages. Paris, France.

Mededeelingen König. Akad. Wetensch. Mededeelingen Königlichen Akademie van
Afd.   Wetenschappen, Letterkunde. Amsterdam.

Mem. Anthrop. Soc. London.......... Memoirs of the Anthropological Society of London.

Mém. Soc. Anthrop. Paris............ Mémoires de la Société d'Anthropologie de Paris. France.

Mém. Soc. Ling. Paris............... Mémoires de la Société de Linguistique de Paris. France.

Mitt. Anthrop. Gesell. Wien. .... Mitteilungen der Anthropologischen Gesellschaft in Wien. Austria.

Mitt. Gesell. f. Völkerkunde........... Mitteilungsblatt der Gesellschaft für Völkerkunde. Leipzig, Germany.

Monatsschr. f. Kriminalpsychol. u. Straf- Monatsschrift für Kriminalpsychologie und
rechtsreform.   Strafrechtsreform. Heidelberg, Germany.

Mus. Journ. Univ. Pennsylvania........ Museum Journal, University of Pennsylvania. Philadelphia, Pa.

Nat. Geogr. Mag. .... National Geographic Magazine, National Geographic Society. Washington, D. C.

Nat. Hist. .... Natural History. The Magazine of the American Museum of Natural History. New York, N. Y.

Pap. Peabody Mus. Arch. Ethnol. Har- Papers of the Peabody Museum of Archae-
vard Univ.   ology and Ethnology, Harvard University. Cambridge, Mass.

Petermanns Mitt. .... Petermanns Mitteilungen. Gotha. J. Perthes.

Physis .... Physis. Revista de la Sociedad Argentina de Ciencias Naturales. Buenos Aires, Argentina.

Proc. Amer. Antiq. Soc. .... Proceedings of the American Antiquarian Society. Worcester, Mass.

Proc. Amer. Philos. Soc. .... Proceedings of the American Philosophical Society. Philadelphia, Pa.

Proc. Pan Amer. Sci. Congr. .... Proceedings of the Pan American Science Congress.

Proc. Roy. Geogr. Soc. .... Proceedings of the Royal Geographical Society. London, England.

Publ. Univ. Nac. Tucamán............. Publicaciones de la Universidad Nacional de Tucumán. Argentina.

Rel. Geogr. Indias................... Relaciones Geográficas de Indias. Madrid, Spain.

Rel. Soc. Arg. Antrop. .... Relaciones de la Sociedad Argentina de Antropologia. Buenos Aires, Argentina.

Rev. Americana..................... Revista Americana. Rio de Janeiro, Brazil.

Rev. Anthrop. .... Review Anthropologique. Paris, France.

Rev. Archiv. Bibl. Mus. .... Revista de Archivos, Bibliotecas y Museos. Madrid, Spain.

Rev. Arq. Mun. São Paulo............. Revista do Arquivo Municipal de São Paulo, Brazil.

Rev. Fomento (Venezuela)........... Revista de Fomento. Caracas, Venezuela.

Rev. Ethnogr. Paris................... Revue d'Ethnographie. Paris, France.

Rev. Gén. Sci. .... Revue Générale des Sciences. Paris, France.

Rev. Hist. Lisbon................... Revista de Historia. Lisbon, Portugal.

Rev. Inst. Antrop. Univ. Nac. Tucumán. Revista del Instituto de Antropología de la Universidad Nacional de Tucumán. Argentina.

Rev. Inst. Arch. Hist. Geogr. Pernambu- Revista del Instituto Archeologico, Histó-
cano   rico e Geographico Pernambucano. Recife, Brazil.

Rev. Inst. Etnol. Univ. Nac. Tucumán.. Revista del Instituto de Etnología de la Universidad Nacional de Tucumán. Argentina.

Rev. Inst. Hist. Geogr. Brasil..........Revista do Instituto Histórico e Geographico do Brasil. Rio de Janeiro, Brazil.

Rev. Inst. Hist. Geogr. São Paulo...... Revista do Instituto Histórico e Geographico de São Paulo. Brazil.

Rev. Inst. Hist. .... Revista do Instituto Histórico. Rio de Janeiro, Brazil.

Rev. Ling. Paris .... Revue de Linguistique, Paris.

Rev. Mar. Coloniale.................. Revista Maritime et Coloniale. Paris.

Rev. Mus. La Plata.................. Revista del Museo de La Plata. Argentina.

Rev. Mus. Paulista.................. Revista do Museu Paulista. Brazil.

Rev. Soc. Cient. Paraguay............. Revista de la Sociedad Cientifica del Paraguay. Asunción, Paraguay.

Rev. Soc. Estud. Paraenses........... Revista da Sociedade de Estudos Paraenses. Belém do Pará, Brazil.

Rev. Soc. Geogr. Rio de Janeiro........ Revista da Sociedade de Geografia do Rio de Janeiro. Brazil.

Rev. Trim. Hist. Geogr. Brasil......... Revista Trimensal de História e Geographia *or* Jornal do Instituto Histórico e Geographico Brasileiro. Rio de Janeiro, Brazil.

Rev. Trim. Inst. Ceará................ Revista Trimensal do Instituto do Ceará. Fortaleza, Ceará, Brazil.

Rev. Univ. Buenos Aires.............. Revista de la Universidad de Buenos Aires. Argentina.

Rev. Univ. Cuzco.................... Revista Universitaria del Cuzco. Perú.

Roy. Soc. Antiquaries................ Royal Society of Antiquaries of Ireland. Dublin.

Scot. Geogr. Mag. .... The Scottish Geographical Magazine. Edinburgh.

Smithsonian Misc. Coll. .... Smithsonian Miscellaneous Collections, Smithsonian Institution. Washington, D. C.

Soc. Sci. Fennica.................... Societas Scientiarum Fennica. Helsingfors. (See Finska Vetenskap Societeen. Helsingfors.)

Texas Agr. Exper. Station, Bull. .... Texas Agricultural Experimental Station, Bulletin.

Tijdsch. Ned. Aardr. Gen. .... Tijdschrift van het Konink. Nederlandsch Aardrijkskundig Genootschap. Amsterdam.

Timehri .... Timehri. The Journal of the Royal Agricultural and Commercial Society of British Guiana. Demerara.

Trans. Ethnol. Soc. London........... Transactions of the Ethnological Society of London. England.

Trans. Amer. Phil. Soc. .... Transactions of the American Philosophical Society. Philadelphia, Pa.

Verhandl. d. Gesell. f. Erdkunde zu Berlin. — Verhandlungen der Gesellschaft für Erdkunde zu Berlin.

Verhandl. d. Berliner Gesell, f. Anthrop., Ethnol., u. Urgeschichte. — Verhandlungen der Berliner Gesellschaft für Anthropologie, Ethnologie, und Urgeschichte.

Verhandl. Gesell. Deutsch. Natur. u. Arzte. — Verhandlungen der Gesellschaft Deutscher Naturforscher und Ärzte. Leipzig.

Verhandl. Schweiz. Naturf. Gesell. ..... Verhandlungen der Schweizerischen Naturforschenden Gesellschaft. Zurich.

Washington Acad. Sci. .... Washington Academy of Sciences.

Welt u. Wissen...................... Welt und Wissen. Berlin

Ymer .... Ymer. Tidskrift utg. af Svenska Sällskapet för Antropologi och Geografi. Stockholm, Sweden.

Zeit. Ethnol. .... Zeitschrift für Ethnologie. Berlin, Germany.

Zeit. f. Rassenkunde................. Zeitschrift für Rassenkunde. Stuttgart.

Zeit. f. Sexualwissenschaft........... Zeitschrift für Sexualwissenschaft und Sexualpolitik. Leipzig.

Zeit. Gesell. f. Erdkunde.............. Zeitschrift der Gesellschaft für Erdkunde zu Berlin.

Zeit. Missions. u. Religion. .... Zeitschrift für missionswissenschaft und Religionwissenschaft.

ABBEVILLE, CLAUDE D'.
1614. Histoire de la mission des pères Capucins en l'isle de Maragnan et terres circonvoisines. Paris.

ABENDROTH, ROBERT.
1871 a. Beiträge zur Kenntniss des Ucayali. Globus, vol. 19, No. 24, pp. 377–379.
1871. b. Ein Menschenhaupt als Götterbild bei den Jivaros-Indianern in Ecuador. Globus, vol. 19, No. 20, pp. 317–318.

ABREU, JOÃO CAPISTRANO DE.
1895. Os Bacaeris. Rev. Brasil., 1st anno, Nos. 3 and 4. (Reprinted in "Ensaios e estudos," 3a Serie, Rio de Janeiro, 1938.)
1914. Rã-txa hu-ní-ku-ĩ, a lingua dos caxinauás do rio Ibuaçu, affluente do Maru (prefeitura de Tarauacá). Rio de Janeiro.
1938. Os Caxinauás. In "Ensaios e estudos (critica e historia)," 3a Serie, pp. 275–357. Rio de Janeiro.

ACCIOLI DE CERQUEIRA E SILVA, IGNACIO.
1833. Corografiá paraënse, ou descripção, fisica, historica, e politica, da Provincia do Gram-Pará. Bahia.

ACUÑA, CRISTÓBAL DE.
1641. Nuevo descubrimiento del gran rio de las Amazonas por el padre Christoval de Acuña . . . Al qual fue, y se hizo por orden se Su Magestad, el año de 1639. Por La Provincia de Quito en los reynos del Perù . . . Impr. del reyno. Madrid.
1682. Relation de la riviere des Amazones. Traduite par feu M. de Gomberville de l'Academie françoise. 2 vols. Paris.
1698. A relation of the great river of Amazons in South America. Containing all the particulars of Father Christopher d'Acugna's voyage, made at the command of the King of Spain. Taken from the Spanish original of the said Chr. d'Acugña, Jesuit. In Voyages and discoveries in South America . . . London.
1891. Nuevo descubrimiento del gran rio de las Amazonas . . . Colección de libros que tratan de América, raros o curiosos, vol. 2. Madrid.

ADALBERT, PRINCE OF PRUSSIA.
1849. Travels of His Royal Highness Prince Adalbert of Prussia, in the south of Europe and in Brazil, with a voyage up the Amazon and Xingú. Trans. by Sir Robert H. Schomburgk and John Edward Taylor. (Trans. of author's "Aus meinem reisetagebuch, 1842–43," 1847.) 2 vols. London.
1857. Reise Seiner königlichen Hoheit des prinzen Adalbert von Preussen nach Brasilien. Nach dem tagebuche Seiner königlichen Hoheit mit höchster genehmigung auszüglich bearb. und hrsg. von H. Kletke. (Second edition of author's "Aus meinem reisetagebuch, 1842–43," 1847.) Berlin.

ADAM, LUCIEN.
1878. Examen grammatical comparé de seize langues américaines. Paris. (Extrait du Compte-rendu des travaux du Congr. Int. Amer., sess. 2, Luxembourg, 1877, vol. 2, pp. 161–244.)
1879 a. Examen grammatical comparé de seize langues américaines. Congr. Int. Amer., sess. 3, Bruxelles, vol. 2, pp. 309–366.
1879 b. Du parler des hommes et du parler des femmes dans la langue caraïbe. Paris.
1889. Notice grammaticale sur la langue mosetena. Rev. Ling. Paris, vol. 22, pp. 237–246.

1890 a. Arte de la lengua de los indios antis o campas; . . . conforme al manuscrito original hallado en la ciudad Toled por Charles Leclerc con un
vocabulario metodico i una introducción comparativa por Lucien
Adam. Bibl. Ling. Amér. Paris, vol. 13.

1890 b. Trois familles linguistiques des bassins de l'Amazone et de l'Orénoque.
Congr. Int. Amer., sess. 7, Berlin, 1888, pp. 489–497.

1892 a. Langue Oyampi. Congr. Int. Amer., sess. 8, Paris, 1890, pp. 610–612.

1892 b. Langue Roucouyenne. Congr. Int. Amer., sess. 8, Paris, 1890, pp. 612–
614.

1893. Matériaux pour servir à l'établissement d'une grammaire comparée des
dialectes de la famille caribe. Bibl. Ling. Amér. Paris, vol. 17.

1896. Matériaux pour servir à l'établissement d'une grammaire comparée des
dialectes de la famille Tupi. Bibl. Ling. Amer. Paris, vol. 18.

1897. Esquisse grammaticale et vocabulaire de la langue guaraouno. Congr.
Int. Amer., sess. 11, Mexico, 1895, pp. 479–489.

1897–98. Pronoms et indices personnels de l'Itonama. Journ. Soc. Amér. Paris,
vol. 2, pp. 48–52.

1905. Grammaire de l'Accawai. Journ. Soc. Amér. Paris, n.s. vol. 2, pp. 43–90,
209–240.

    See also Crevaux, Jules, Sagot, P., and Adam, L., 1882; and Cueva, R. P.
de la, 1893.

ADAM, LUCIEN, and HENRY, VICTOR.

1880. Arte y vocabulario de la lengua chiquita con algunos textos traducidos
y explicados compuestos sobre manuscritos inéditos del XVIII° siglo.
Bibl. Ling. Amér. Paris, vol. 6.

ADAM, LUCIEN, and LECLERC, CHARLES.

1880. Arte de la lengua de los Indios Baures de la Provincia de los Moxos
conforme al manuscrito original del P. Antonio Magio. Bibl. Ling.
Amér. Paris. vol. 7.

AGUERRERERE, S. E. *See* EXPLORACIÓN DE LA GRAN SABANA, 1939.

AGUIAR, FAUSTO AUGUSTO DE.

1851. Relatorio do Presidente da Provincia de Gram Pará . . . on August 15,
1851. Pará.

AHLBRINCK, W.

1922–25. De Karaib en zijn taal. Onze Missien in Oost en West-Indie, No. 5
(1922), p. 233; No. 6 (1923), pp. 241, 392; No. 7 (1924), pp. 33,
159; No. 8 (1925), pp. 20, 100, 177.

1924. Carib life and nature. Congr. Int. Amer., sess. 21, The Hague, pt. 1,
pp. 217–225.

1925–26. Over de Geesten en geestenberzweerders bij de Karaïben. Het Mis-
siewerk. 's-Hertogenbosch. Vol. 7, p. 144 ff.

1931. Encyclopaedie der Karaïben, behelzend taal, zeden en gewoonten dezer
Indianen. Verhandelingen der Koninklijke akademie van wetenschappen
te Amsterdam, Afdeeling letterkunde, n.s., vol. 27, No. 1.

ALBIS, MANUEL MARÍA.

1861. The Indians of Andaquí, New Granada. Bull. Amer. Ethnol. Soc., No. 1,
pp. 53–72.

ALBUM GEOGRAPHICO DO ESTADO DO MATTO GROSSO, 1914.

ALBUQUERQUE LACERDA, ADOLFO DE BARROS.

1864. Relatorio apresentado à Assembléia Legislativa da Provincia do Amazonas, etc., 1° de Outubro de 1864. Pernambuco.

ALCAYA, DIEGO FELIPE DE.
1906 a. Relación del Padre Diego Felipe de Alcaya, Cura de Mataca. *In* Juicio de límites entre el Perú y Bolivia, vol. 9, pp. 124–144. *See* Maurtua, Victor M., 1906.
1906 b. Informaciones hachas por Don Juan de Lizaraza sobre el discubrimiento de las Mojos. *In* Maurtua, Victor M., 1906, vol. 1, pp. 124–144.

ALDENBURGK, JOHANNES GREGORIUS.
1627. West-Indianische Reisse, und Beschreibung der Beläg- und Eroberung der Statt S. Salvador in der Bahie von Todos os Sanctos im dem Lande von Brasilia. Welches von anno 1623. bis ins 1626 verrichtet worden. Coburgk.
1930. Reise nach Brasilien, 1623–1626. Neu herausgegeben nach der zu Koburg bei Friedrich Gruner im jahre 1627 erschienenen originalausgabe. (Vol. 1 *in* Reisebeschreibungen von deutschen beamten und kriegsleuten im dienst der Niederländischen west und ost-indischen kompagnien, 1602–1797, hrag. von S. P. L'Honoré Naber.) Haag.

ALEMANY, AGUSTÍN.
1906 a. Castellano-shipibo; vocabulario de bolsillo. Lima.
1906 b. Castellano-piro; vocabulario de bolsillo. Lima.

ALENCASTRE, JOÃO MARTINS PEREIRA D'.
1857. Memoria chronologica, historica e corographica da Provincia do Piauhy. Rev. Inst. Hist., vol. 20, pp. 5–164.

ALEXANDER, [CAPT.] JAMES EDWARD.
1832. Notes of two expeditions up the Essequibo and Mazaroony rivers in 1830 and 1831. Journ. Roy. Geogr. Soc., vol. 2, pp. 65–72.
1833. Transatlantic sketches comprising visits to the most interesting scenes in North and South America, and the West Indies. 2 vols. London.

ALMANACH DE LIMA. *See* SOUTHEY, ROBERT, 1817–22, pp. 199–210.

ALMEIDA PINTO, ANTONIO RODRIGUES.
1906. O Bispado do Pará. Annaes do Bibliotheca e Archivo Público do Pará, vol. 5.

ALMEIDA PRADO, J. F. DE.
1939. Primeiros povoadores do Brasil (1500–1530). Bibl. Pedag. Brasil., Serie 5a, Brasiliana, vol. 37, São Paulo.

ALMEIDA SERRA, RICARDO FRANCO DE.
1869. Navegação do Rio Tapajóz para o Pará (1779). Rev. Inst. Hist., vol. 9, pp. 1–16.

ALTAMIRANO, DIEGO FRANCISCO.
1891. Historia de la mission de los Mójos. Publicado por M. V. Ballivian. Doc. Hist. Bolivia, La Paz.

ALTOLAGUIRRE Y DUVALE, ANGEL DE.
1908. Relaciones geográficas de la gobernación de Venezuela (1767–1768). Con prólogo y notas de D. Angel de Altolaguirre y Duvale. Madrid.

ALVARADO, LISANDRO.
1912. Ensayo sobre el caribe venezolano. Bol. Acad. Nac. Hist. Caracas, vol. 1, No. 1, pp. 43–67.
1921. Glosario de voces indígenas de Venezuela. Caracas.
1925. Venezuelan ethnology. Bull. Pan Amer. Union, vol. 59, pp. 223–231.

ALVAREZ, JOSÉ.
1941. Mitología, tradiciones y creencias religiosas de los salvajes huarayos. Congr. Int. Amer., sess. 27, Lima, 1939, vol. 2, pp. 153–161.

ALVAREZ VILLANUEVA, FRANCISCO.
1892. Relación historica de todas las misiones de los P. P. Franciscanos en las Indias. Madrid.
AMADOR DE LOS RÍOS, JOSÉ (EDITOR). *See* OVIEDO Y VALDÉS, GONZALO FERNÁNDEZ DE, 1851–55.
AMBROSETTI, JUAN BAUTISTA.
1893. Sobre una colección de Alfarerías Minuanes, recojidas en la Provincia de Entre-Ríos. Bol. Inst. Geogr. Argentino, vol. 14, pp. 242–265.
1894. Los Paraderos precolombianos de Goya (Provincia de Corrientes). Bol. Inst. Geogr. Argentino, vol. 15, pp. 401–422.
1895 a. Los Indios Cainguá del Alto Paraná (Misiones). Bol. Inst. Geogr. Argentino, vol. 15, pp. 661–744.
1895 b. Los cemeterios prehistóricos del Alto Paraná (Misiones). Bol. Inst. Geogr. Argentino, vol. 16, pp. 227–257.
1896. La leyenda del Yaguareté-abá (el Indio tigre) y sus proyecciones entre los Guaraníes, Quíchuas, etc. An. Soc. Cient. Argentina, vol. 41, pp. 321–334.
1903. Cabeza humana preparada según el procedimiento de los indios jívaros, del Ecuador. An. Mus. Nac. Buenos Aires, ser. 3, vol. 2, pp. 519–523.
AMEGHINO, FLORENTINO.
1880–81. La antigüedad del hombre en el Plata. 2 vols. Paris and Buenos Aires.
AMICH, JOSÉ.
1854. Compendio histórico de los trabajos, fatigas, sudores y muertes que los ministros evangélicos de la seráfica religión han padecido por la conversión de las almas de los gentiles en las montañas de los Andes, pertenecientes a las provincias del Peru . . . Paris.
ANCHIETA, JOSÉ (JOSEPH) DE.
1812. Epistola quamplurimarum rerum naturalium, quae S. Vincentii (nunc S. Pauli) provinciam incolunt, sistens descriptionem. Collecção de noticias para a historia e geografia das nações ultramarinas que vivem nos dominios portuguezés, ou lhes são visinhas. Lisbon, vol. 1.
1846. Informação dos casamentos dos Indios do Brazil. Rev. Trim. Hist. Geogr. Brasil, vol. 8, pp. 254–262.
1876–77. Cartas ineditas. An. Bibl. Nac. Rio de Janeiro, vol. 1, pp. 44–75, 266–308; vol. 2, pp. 79–127.
1877–78. Carta del Hermano Joseph que scriuio del Brasil a los padres y hermanos de Jesus en Portugal. An. Bibl. Nac. Rio de Janeiro, vol. 3, pp. 316–323.
ANDERSON, C. WILGRESS.
1909. The aboriginal Indians. Handbook of British Guiana (G. D. Bayley, ed.), pp. 105–114. Georgetown; London; Boston.
ANDRÉ, EUGÈNE.
1904. A naturalist in the Guianas. London; New York.
ANGYONE COSTA, JOÃO.
1934. Introdução á arqueologia brasileira. Etnografia e historia. (Bibl. Pedag. Brasil., ser. 5, Brasiliana, vol. 34.) São Paulo. (Second edition, Rio de Janeiro, 1938.)
ANNAES DO BIBLIOTHECA E ARCHIVO PÚBLICO DO PARÁ.
Vols. 1 and 2: Cartas Regias, etc.
ANNUAE LITTERAE, 1589.
ANONYMOUS.
MS. a. Illustração necessoria e interessante relativa ao gentio da nação Murá.
1826. Documentos para a historia e ethnographia do Pará copiados no Rio de Janeiro (Bibliotheca Nacional) pelo Dr. R. R. Schuller.
1912. MS. no Museu Paraense. Part 2: Observações addicionais.

MS. b. Vocabulario Portuguez—Lingua geral—Maué. Fragmento. Bibliotheca Nacional. Rio de Janeiro. (The author is probably the geologist Charles Frederick Hartt.)

1856. Nova navagação.

ANTHONY, H. E.

1921. The Jivaro Indians of Eastern Ecuador. Nat. Hist., vol. 21, pp. 146–159.

APARICIO, FRANCISCO DE.

1923. Un nuevo tipo de representaciones plásticas. Rev. Univ. Buenos Aires, vol. 51, pp. 94–106.

1925. Un nuevo documento relativo a la colocación de las asas zoomorfas en la cerámica del litoral paranense. Physis, vol. 8, pp. 244–249.

1928. Notas para el estudio de la arqueología del sur de Entre Ríos. An. Fac. Cienc. Ed. Paraná, vol. 3, p. 126.

1928–29. Noticia sobre el hallazgo de cuentas de vidrio en un paradero indígena, caracterizado por la presencia de representaciones plásticas. Physis, vol. 9, p. 456.

See also Frenguelli, Joaquín, and Aparicio, Francisco de, 1923.

APPUN, KARL FERDINAND.

1868–69. Unter den Guaraúnos-Indianern. Das Ausland, vol. 41, pp. 793–796 (Auf dem Orinoco), pp. 891–897 (In Zacupana) ; vol. 42, pp. 175–179, 204–208 (El Rey de los Guaraúnos).

1871. Unter den tropen. Wanderungen durch Venezuela, am Orinoco, durch British Guyana und am Amazonenstrome in den jahren 1849–1868 2 vols. Jena.

ARANHA, BENTO DE FIGUEIRÊDO TENREIRO. See FIGUEIRÊDO TENREIRO ARANHA. BENTO DE.

ARAUJO BRUSQUE, FRANCISCO CARLOS DE. See BRUSQUE, FRANCISCO CARLOS DE ARAUJO.

ARCAYA, PEDRO MANUEL.

1920. Historia del estado Falcon. Caracas.

ARGOMOSA, DON MANUEL ANTONIO DE.

1906. Informe de Don . . ., Governador de Santa Cruz de la Sierra, sobre el estado de las misiones de Mojos y Chiquitos. 6 de Febrero de 1737.

ARLET, STANISLAS.

1781. Lettre du P. . . ., de la Compagnie de Jésus, au Révérend Père Général de la même Compagnie. In Lettres édifiantes et curieuses, vol. 8, pp. 39–51.

ARMELLADO, CÉSAREO DE.

1936. Bellezas del dialecto taurépán (lengua caribe). Bol. Acad. Venezolana, vol. 3, pp. 208–223.

ARMENTIA, NICOLÁS.

1887–88. Navegación del Madre de Dios. Bibl. Boliv. Geogr. Hist., vols. 1 and 2. La Paz.

1902. Arte y vocabulario de la lengua Tacana, manuscrito del R. P. Fray Nicolas Armentia con introducción, notas y apéndices por Samuel A. Lafone Quevedo. Rev. Mus. La Plata, vol. 10, pp. 63–172, 297–311. (See also Gili, Antonio, 1902.)

1903. Relación histórica de las misiones franciscanas de Apolobamba, por otro nombre, Frontera de Caupolicán. La Paz. (Nicolás Armentia is supposed author.)

1905. Descripción del territorio de las misiones franciscanas de Apolobamba, por otro nombre Frontera de Caupolican. Ed. Oficial. La Paz. (Nicolás Armentia is supposed author.)

1906. Arte y vocabulario de la lengua Cavineña, manuscrito del R. P. Fray
. . ., ordenado con notas por Samuel A. Lafone Quevedo. Rev. Mus.
La Plata, vol. 13, pp. 1–120.

ARQUIVOS DA DIRECTORIA DE INDIOS. 1848. Cuyaba.

ARQUIVOS DA INSPECTORIA DO PARÁ. *See* SERVIÇO DE PROTECÇÃO AOS INDIOS, . . .
1942.

ATLAS SHOWING MISSION FIELDS OF THE CHRISTIAN AND MISSIONARY AILIANCE.
Revised ed., New York, 1924.

AUGUSTO MARQUES, CEZAR. *See* MARQUES, CEZAR AUGUSTO.

AVÉ-LALLEMANT, ROBERT CHRISTIAN BERTHOLD.
1859. Reise durch Süd-Brasilien im jahre 1858. 2 vols. Leipzig.
1860. Reise durch Nord-Brasilien im jahre 1859. Leipzig.

AYRES CARNEIRO, JOÃO ROBERTO.
1910. Itinerario da viagem da expedição exploradora e colonizadora ao Tocantins em 1849. An. Bibl. Archiv. Pub. Pará, vol. 7.

AYRES DE CASAL, MANOEL.
1817. Corografia brazilica, ou, Relacão histórico-geográphica do reino do
Brazil . . . 2 vols. Rio de Janeiro. (Other editions 1845, 1943.)

AYROSA, PLINIO.
1943. Apontamentos para a bibliografia da língua tupí-guaraní. Universidade
de São Paulo, Boletim 33.

AZA, JOSÉ PÍO.
1923 a. Tribus florestales del oriente peruano. Inca, vol. 1, No. 2, pp. 394–397.
1923 b. Vocabulario español-machiguenga. Lima.
1924. Vocabulario español-machiguenga. Bol. Soc. Geogr. Lima, vol. 41, pp.
41–78.

AZARA, FÉLIX DE.
1809. Voyages dans l'Amérique Méridionale . . . 4 vols. Paris.
1904. Geografía física y esférica de las provincias del Paraguay, y misiones
guaraníes. . . . En la Asunción del Paraguay. Ano de MDCCXC.
(Manuscrito en la Biblioteca nacional de Montevideo.) Bibliografía,
prólogo y anotaciones por Rodolfo R. Schuller. Montevideo.

BACH, MORIZ.
1838. Das land Otuquis in Bolivia. Nach einem originalberichte des herrn
Moriz Bach . . . mit beziehung auf allgemeine südamerikanische
verhältnisse beschrieben von Dr. Georg Ludwig Kriegk. Frankfurt am
Main.
1929. Descripción de la nueva provincia de Otuquis en Bolivia. (3rd ed.)
La Paz.

BADARIOTTI, NICOLÁO.
1898. Exploração no Norte do Matto Grosso. Região do Alto Paraguay e
planalto dos Parecis. Apuntamentos de Historia natural, Ethnographia,
Geographia e impressões. São Paulo.

BAENA, ANTONIO LADISLAU MONTEIRO. *See* MONTEIRO BAENA, ANTONIO LADISLAU.

BAENA, MANOEL.
1839. Ensaio Corographico sobre o Pará. Pará.
1885. Informações sobre as Comarcas da Provincia do Pará. Pará.

BAKHUIS, L. A.
1902. Verslag der Coppename-Expeditie.
1908. De sde wetenschappelijke Expeditie naar het binnenland van Suriname.
Tijdsch. Ned. Aardr. Gen., vol. 25, pp. 94–113.

BALDUS, HERBERT.
    1929. Ligeiras notas sobre os indios Guaranys do littoral paulista. Rev. Mus.
        Paulista, vol. 16, pp. 83–95.
    1935. Ligeiras notas sobre os Indios Tapirapés. Rev. Arq. Mun. São Paulo,
        vol. 16.
    1937. Ensaios de etnologia brasileira. São Paulo.
BALEN, WILLEM JULIUS VAN.
    1930. Inca's in Suriname? De West-Indische Gids, vol. 12, pp. 353–359. Amster-
        dam, s'Gravenhage.
BALLET, J.
    1875. Les Caraïbes. Congr. Int. Amer., sess. 1, Nancy, vol. 1, pp. 394–438.
BALLIVIÁN, M. V. *See* EXPLORACIONES Y HIDROGRÁPHICAS DE LOS RÍOS DEL NORTE
    DE BOLIVIA; *also* RELACIÓN Y DESCRIPCIÓN DE LAS MISIONES . . . DE APOLOBAMBA.
BALLÓN LANDA, ALBERTO.
    1917. Los hombres de la selva; apuntes para un ensayo de sociología aplicada.
        Tesis doctoral, Universidad mayor de San Marcos. Lima.
BALTASAR DE LODARES, PADRE. *See* LODARES, BALTASAR DE.
BALZAN, LUIGI.
    1894. Un po' più di luce sulla distribuzione di alcune tribù indigene della parte
        centrale dell'America meridionale. Archiv. Antrop. Etnol., vol. 24,
        pp. 17–29.
BANCROFT, EDWARD.
    1769. An essay on the natural history of Guiana, in South America . . .
        London.
BARBOSA RODRÍGUES, JOÃO.
    1872. Os Indios Tembé. Revista da Exposição de Anthropologica Brasileira.
        Rio de Janeiro.
    1875 a. Exploração e estudo do valle do Amazonas. Rio de Janeiro.
    1875 b. Exploração do Rio Jamundá. Rio de Janeiro.
    1875 c. Exploração dos Rios Urubu e Jatapo. Ministerio de Agricultura,
        Commercio, e Obras Publicas. Rio de Janeiro.
    1875 d. Idolo amazonico, achado no rio Amazonas. Rio de Janeiro.
    1879. Antiguidades do Amazonas. Rio de Janeiro.
    1882 a. Mundurucú. Revista de Exposição de Arthropologica Brazileira.
        Mello Moraes Filho, ed. Rio de Janeiro.
    1882 b. A Emancipação dos Mauhés. Revista da Exposição Anthropologica
        Brazileira dirigida e collaborada por Mello Moraes Filho. Rio de
        Janeiro.
    1882 c. Tribu dos Ticunas. Revista da Exposição Anthropologica Brazileira
        dirigida e collaborada por Mello Moraes Filho. P. 52. Rio de
        Janeiro.
    1882 d. Muirakitan precioso coeva do homem anti colombiano. Rio de
        Janeiro.
    1885. Rio Jauapery. Pacificação dos Crichanás. Rio de Janeiro.
    1892 a. Antiguidades do Amazonas. Velloria. Contrib. Mus. Bot. Amazonas,
        vol. 2.
    1892 b. A Necropole de Mirakanguera. Velosia, II. (2nd ed.) Rio de Janeiro.
    1899. O muyrakytã e os idolos symbolicos; estudo da origem asiatica da civili-
        zação do Amazonas nos tempos prehistoricos. Rio de Janeiro.
BARCO CENTENERA, MARTÍN DEL.
    1836. La Argentina, o la conquista del Rio de la Plata, poema histórico . . .
        In Angelis, Pedro de. Colección de obras y documentos relativos á la
        historia . . . del Rio de la Plata, vol. 2. Buenos Aires.

1912. La Argentina; poema histórico. Reimpresión facsimilar de la primera edición, Lisboa, 1602; precedida de un estudio del doctor Juan María Gutiérrez y de unos apuntes bio-bibliográficos de Don Enrique Peña. Buenos Aires.

BARLAEUS, CASPAR (KASPAR VAN BAERLE).
1647. Casparis Barlaei rerum per Octennium in Brasilia et alibi nuper gestarum, sub praefectura illustrissimi comitis I. Mauritii Nassoviae, etc. . . . historia. Amstelodami. (Dutch tr., 's Gravenhage, 1923; Portuguese trans., Rio de Janeiro, 1940.)

BARNUEVO, RODRIGO.
1942. Relación apologética, así del antiguo como nuevo descubrimiento del río de las Amazonas hecho por los religiosos de la Compañia de Jesús en Quito . . . Quito.

BARO, ROULOX.
1651. Relation du voyage de . . ., interprète et ambassadeur ordenaire de la compagnie des Indes d'Occident, de la part des illust. seigneurs des Provinces unies au pays des Tapuies dans la terre ferme du Brasil. Traduit d'hollandois en françois par Pierre Moreau de Paray . . . Paris. Ed. by M. Morisot. (This relation forms the second part of "Relations veritables et curieuses d'isle de Madagascar et du Brasil . . ." Paris.)

BARRACE, FATHER. In LETTRES ÉDIFIANTES ET CURIEUSES . . ., 1780–83.

BARRÈRE, PIERRE.
1743. Nouvelle relation de la France équinoxiale, contenant la description des côtes de la Guiane; de l'isle de Cayenne; le commerce de cette colonie; les divers changements arrivés dan ce pays; et les moeurs et coûtumes des différents peuples sauvages qui l'habitent. (Piget) Paris.

BATES, HENRY WALTER.
1863. The naturalist on the river Amazons . . . London. (Other editions published in 1864 and 1892.)

BAUMGARTEN, JOHANNES, COMP.
1882. Abenteurerleben in Guyana und am Amazonas nach selbsterlebnissen von Emíl Carrey, Bouyer, Jusselain, Agassiz u. a. 2., bedeutend erweiterte und vollständig umgearb. aufl. von Robin Jouet's fahrten und erlebnisse in den urwäldern von Guyana und Brasilien. Stuttgart. (Originally published under title: Robin Jouet's abenteurerliche fahrten und erlebnisse in den urwäldern von Guyana und Brasilien . . . Stuttgart, 1877.)

BAUVE, ADAM DE, and FERRÉ P.
1833–34. Voyage dans l'interieur de la Guyane. Bull. Soc. Geogr., 1st ser., vol. 20, pp. 201–226, 265–282; 2nd ser., vol. 1, pp. 105–144, 165–178.

BAYERN, THERESE PRINZESSIN VON.
1908. Reise studien aus dem Westlichen Südamerika. Vol. 1. Bringt einiges über die Chíwaro, auch Abbildungen. Berlin.

BÉCHAMEL, FRANÇOIS. See LABAT, JEAN BAPTISTE, 1730, vol. 3, pp. 134–350, and vol. 4, pp. 345–424.

BÉCHAMEL, FRANÇOIS, and GRILLET, JEAN. See GRILLET, JEAN, and BÉCHAMEL, FRANÇOIS.

BEEBE, MARY BLAIR, and BEEBE, CHARLES WILLIAM.
1910. Our search for a wilderness; an account of two ornithological expeditions to Venezuela and to British Guiana. New York.

BELLIN, JACQUES NICOLAS.
1763. Description géographique de la Guiane . . . Paris.

BENJAMINS, H. D.
1924–25. Iets over den ouden handel met de Indianen in Guiana. De West Indische Gids, vol. 7, pp. 179–186.

BENNETT, WENDELL CLARK.
1936. Excavations in Bolivia. Anthrop. Pap. Amer. Mus. Nat. Hist., vol. 35, pp. 329–507.

BENOIT, PIERRE JACQUES.
1839. Voyage à Surinam; description des possessions néerlandaises dans la Guyane. Bruxelles.

BERKEL, ADRIAAN VAN.
1695. Amerikaansche voyagien, behelzende een reis na rio de Berbice, gelegen op het vaste land van Guiana, aande wilde-kust van America, mitsgaders een andere na de colonie van Suriname, gelegen in het noorder deel van het gemelde landschap Guiana. Amsterdam.
1789. Beschreibung seiner Reisen nach Rio de Berbice und Surinam. Memmingen.

BERNARDINO DE SOUZA, CONEGO FRANCISCO. *See* SOUZA, CONEGO FRANCISCO BERNARDINO DE.

BERNAU, JOHN HENRY.
1847. Missionary labours in British Guiana . . . London.

BERREDO, BERNARDO PEREIRA DE.
1905. Annaes historicos do estado do Marahaõ, em que se da' noticia do seu descobrimento, e tudo o mais que nelle tem succedido desde o anno em que foy descuberto até o de 1718. Maranhaõ. (1st ed. 1749; 2nd ed. 1849.)

BERTONI, MOISÉS SANTIAGO.
1920. La lengua guaraní como documento histórico . . . Puerto Bertoni, Alto Paraná, Paraguay.
1922. La civilización guaraní. Alto Paraná, Paraguay.

BETTENDORF, JOÃO FILIPPE.
1910. Chronica da missão dos padres da Companhia de Jesus no estado do Maranhão. Rio de Janeiro.

BEUCHAT, HENRI, and RIVET, PAUL.
1908. La famille linguistique Zaparo. Journ. Soc. Amér. Paris, n. s., vol. 5, No. 2.
1909. La famille linguistique Cahuapana. Zeit. Ethnol., vol. 41, pp. 616–634.
1909–10. La langue Jíbaro oü Siwora. Anthropos, vol. 4, pp. 805–822, 1053–1064; vol. 5, pp. 1109–1124.
1911. La famille Betoya ou Tucano. Mem. Soc. Ling. Paris, vol. 17, pp. 117–136, 162–190.

BEYERMAN, J. J.
1934–35. De Nederlandsche Kolonie Kerbice in 1771. De West Indische Gids, vol. 15, pp. 313–317.

BIBOLOTTI, BENIGNO.
1917. Moseteno vocabulary and treatises, . . . from an unpublished manuscript in possession of Northwestern University library, with an introduction by Rudolph Schuller. Evanston and Chicago.

BIET, ANTOINE.
1664. Voyage de la France equinoxiale en l'isle de Cayenne, entrepris par les François en l'anne'e MDCLII . . . Paris.
1896. Les Galibis, tableau véritable de leurs moeurs, avec un vocabulaire de leur langue. Rev. et pub. par Aristide Marre. Paris. (Extrait de Rev. Ling., July and Oct. 1896, and a reprint of part 3 of author's "Voyage de la France equinoxiale en l'isle de Cayenne," Paris, 1664.)

BIGORRE, FRANÇOIS.
1916. Les Missions catholiques. Lyon. Vol. 48, pp. 414–416, 430–432, 441–442, 448–450, 465–466, 478–480, 488–490, 501–504, 513–516, 524–527.
1917. Chez les sauvages Tapirapés. Annales de la Propagation de la Foi, vol. 89, No. 531, pp. 110–122.
BINGHAM, HIRAM.
1914 a. Along the uncharted Pampaconas. Harper's Magazine, August 1914.
1914 b. The Pampaconas river. Geogr. Journ., vol. 44, No. 2, pp. 211–214.
BLANCHARD, M. R.
1882. Flute des Galibis. Bull. Soc. Anthrop. Paris, 3rd ser., vol. 5, pp. 652–653.
BLANCO-FOMBONA, RUFINO.
1915–16. Tribus del alto Orinoco. Las Americas, vol. 1, No. 5, pp. 26–28.
BLANCO, JOSÉ MARÍA.
1931. Los mártires del Caaro e Yjuhí; compendio de la historia de los padres Roque Gonzáles de Santa Cruz, Alonso Rodríguez y Juan del Castillo, primeros mártires de las misiones guaraníticas. Buenos Aires.
BODDAM-WHETHAM, JOHN WHETHAM.
1879. Roraima and British Guiana, with a glance at Bermuda, the West Indies, and the Spanish Main. London.
BODE, KLAUDIUS.
1918. Die Tupistämme und ihre Sprache in der Capitania S. Vincente (São Paulo). Korrespondenz-Blatt der Deutschen Gesellschaft für Anthropologie, Ethnologie und Urgeschichte. Braunschweig, 49 Jahrg, pp. 51–58.
BOEKHOUDT, W.
1874. "Uit mijn verleden." Bijdrage tot de kennis van Suriname. Winschoten.
BOLINGBROKE, HENRY.
1807. A voyage to the Demerary, containing a statistical account of the settlements there, and of those on the Essequebo, the Berbice, and other contiguous rivers of Guyana. London.
BOLÍVAR, GREGORIO DE.
1906. Relación de la entrada del Padre Fray Gregorio de Bolívar en compañía de Diego Ramírez de Carlos, á las provincias de indios Chunchos, en 1621. In Maurtua, Victor M., 1906, vol. 8, pp. 205–237.
BOLLAERT, WILLIAM.
1860. Antiquarian, ethnological, and other researches in New Granada, Equador, Peru and Chili, with observations on the pre-Incarial, Incarial, and other monuments of Peruvian nations. London
1863. On the idol head of the Jivaro Indians of Ecuador exhibited. . . . Trans. Ethnol. Soc. London, n.s., vol. 2, pp. 117–118.
    See also Raimondi, Antonio, 1863.
BONAPARTE, ROLAND NAPOLÉON, PRINCE.
1884. Les habitants de Suriname: notes recueillies à l'exposition coloniale d'Amsterdam en 1883. Paris.
BONPLAND, A. *See* HUMBOLDT, ALEXANDER VON, and BONPLAND, A.
BORBA, TELEMACO MOROCINES.
1904. Observações sobre os indigenas do Estado do Paraná. Rec. Mus. Paulista, vol. 6, pp. 53–62.
BORJA, ANTONIO.
1881–97. In Rel. Geogr. Indias, vol. 3, pp. 120–126.
BOSCH, GEVARDUS-BALTHASAR.
1829–43. Reizen in West-Indië . . . 3 vols. Utrecht.

Bosch Reitz. *See* La Borde, Père de, 1886.

Bossi, Bartolomé.
  1863. Viage pintoresco por los ríos Paraná, Paraguay, S^n Lorenzo, Cuyaba y el Arino tributario del grande Amazonas; con la descripción de la Provincia de Matto Grosso . . . Paris.

Brazil e Guyana Franceza.
  1899. Frontières entre le Brésil et la Guyane Française. Atlas contenant un choix de cartes antérieures au traité couclu à Utrecht le 11 avril 1713 entre le Portugal et la France . . . Paris.
  1899–1900. Frontières entre le Brésil et la Guyane Française. Mémoire présenté par les Etats Unis du Brésil au gouvernement de la Confédération Suisse . . . Vol. 6, Paris.
  n.d. Mémoire contenant l'exposé des droits de la France dans la question des frontiéres de la Guyane Française et du Brésil . . .

Breton, Raymond.
  1665. Dictionaire caraibe-françoise, meslé de quantité de remarques historiques pour l'esclairoissement de la langue. Auxerre.
  1666. Dictionaire françois-caraibe (with Dictionaire caraibe-françois). Auxerre. (A facsimile copy of this edition was published in Leipzig in 1900.)

Brett, William Henry.
  1851. Indian missions in Guiana. London.
  1852. The Indian tribes of Guiana . . . New York. (Second edition published in London in 1868.)
  1880. Legends and myths of the aboriginal Indians of British Guiana. (In metrical form.) London.
  1900–02. A short grammar of the language of the Arawâk Indians, British Guiana. Guiana Diocesan Magazine, Georgetown.
  n.d. a. Acawòio Indian language: First part of Genesis and the Gospel of St. Matthew, with supplementary extracts from other Gospels, including the parables of Our Lord. Society for Promoting Christian Knowledge. London.
  n.d. b. Simple questions on the historical parts of the Holy Bible for the instruction of the Acawòio Indians at the Missions in Guiana. Society for Promoting Christian Knowledge. London.

Briceño-Iragorry, Mario.
  1930. Notas sobre argueología venezuelana. Caracas.

Brinton, Daniel G.
  1871. The Arawack language of Guiana in its linguistic and ethnological relations. Trans. Amer. Phil. Soc., n.s., vol. 14, pt. 3, Art. 4, pp. 427–444.
  1891. The American race: a linguistic classification and ethnographic description of the native tribes of North and South America. New York. (Second edition published in Philadelphia in 1901.)
  1892 a. Further notes on the Betoya dialects; from unpublished sources. Proc. Amer. Philos. Soc., vol. 30, pp. 271–278.
  1892 b. Studies in South American native languages. Proc. Amer. Philos. Soc., vol. 30, pp. 45–105.

Broekhuysen, W. N., and others, Editors.
  1926. Van Nieuw-Guinee tot Curaçao. Wageningen.

Brown, Charles Barrington.
  1873. Indian picture writing in British Guiana. Journ. Roy. Anthrop Inst., vol. 2, pp. 254–257.
  1876. Canoe and camp life in British Guiana. London.

BRÜNING, HANS H.
1928. Reisen im Gebiet der Aguaruna. Baessler-archiv., vol. 12, pp 46–85.
BRUSQUE, FRANCISCO CARLOS DE ARAUJO.
1862. Relatório apresentado á Assembléa Legislativa da Provincia do Pará em 1° de Setembro de 1862. Pará.
1863. Relatório apresentado á Assembléa Legislativa da Província do Pará . . . pelo Sr. Presidente da Província, . . ., em 1° de novembro de 1863. Pará.
BUENO, RAMÓN.
1933. Apuntes sobre la provincia misionera de Orinoco e indígenas de su territorio, con algunas otras particularidades. Los publica, con un prólogo, Mons. Nicolás E. Navarro. Caracas.
BURELA, J. BENJAMÍN.
1912. Contribución al estudio de la etnografía boliviana; distribución geográfica de los indígenas actuales del departamento de Santa Cruz. Congr. Int. Amer., sess. 17, Buenos Aires, 1910, pp. 447–458.
BURGES, FRANÇOIS.
1781. État des missions des pères Jésuites de la province du Paraguay, parmi les Indiens de l'Amérique méridionale appellés Chiquites, et de celles qu'ils ont étabiles sur les rivières de Paraná et Uruguay dan le même continent. Tiré d'un mémoire espagnol envoyé à Sa Majesté Catholique par le père François Burges, de la Compagnie de Jésus, procureur-général de la province du Paraguay. In Lettres édifiantes et curieuses . . . vol. 8, pp. 337–373. Paris. (Also in Lettres édifiantes et curieuses, vol. 5, pp. 205–227, Lyon, 1819.)
BURR, GEORGE LINCOLN.
1897. Report of the evidence of the Dutch archives as to European occupation and claims in Western Guiana. U. S. Commission on Boundary between Venezuela and British Guiana, vol. 1, Historical. Washington.
BUSCHAN, GEORG.
1914–16. Die Sitten der Völker . . . 3 vols. Stuttgart. See also Krickeberg, Walter, 1922.
BUSHNELL, DAVID I., JR.
1910. The bows and arrows of the Arawak in 1803. Man, vol. 10, No. 2, pp. 22–24.
CABALLERO, LUCAS.
1933. Relación de las costumbres y religión de los indios manasicas, . . . Estudio preliminar y edición del ms. de 1706 por Manuel Serrano y Sanz. Madrid.
CABELLO DE BALBOA, MIGUEL.
1906. Carta del P. . . . al Virrey, Marqués de Cañete, sobre la conversion de los indios Chunchos. 11 de setiembre de 1594. Published in Juicio de límites entre el Perú y Bolivia, vol. 8, pp. 140–146. See Maurtua, Victor M., 1906.
CABEZA DE VACA, ALVAR NUÑEZ. See HERNÁNDEZ, PEDRO, 1852 and 1891.
CAITANO DA SILVA, J.
1861. L'Oyapoc et l'Amazon. 2 vols. Paris.
CALDAS, JOÃO AUGUSTO.
1887. Memoria historica sobre os indigenas da Provincia de Matto-Grosso . . . Rio de Janeiro.
CALTUNAR, HERMANN. See ROMANO, SANTIAGO, and CALTUNAR, HERMANN, 1916.
CALVO, VIC. See PALLARÉS, FERNANDO, and CALVO, VIC.

CAMPANA, DOMENICO DEL.
    1902. Notizie intorono ai Ciriguani. Archiv. Antrop. Etnol., vol. 32, pp. 17–139.
    1904–06. L'arte plumaria dei Mundurucú (Brasile). Archiv. Antrop. Etnol.,
        vol. 34–36, pp. 177 ff.
CAMPBELL, W. H. See HOLMES, SIR W. H., and CAMPBELL, W. H., 1858.
CAPELO, JOAQUÍN. See ZAVALA, MIGUEL J., 1895 b.
CAPISTRANO DE ABREU, JOÃO. See ABREU, JOÃO CAPISTRANO DE.
CAPITAN, L.
    1882. Sur les procédés qu'emploient les Galibis pour la fabrication de la
        poterie. Bull. Soc. Anthrop. Paris, 3rd ser., vol. 5, pp. 649–651.
CAPPELLE, HERMAN VAN.
    1903. De biennenlanden van het district Nickerie. Baarn.
CARDIEL, JOSÉ.
    1900. Declaración de la verdad. Buenos Aires.
CARDIM, FERNÃO.
    1939. Tratados da terra e gente do Brasil. (Bibl. Pedag. Brasil., Serie 5a,
        Brasiliana, vol. 168.) Rio de Janeiro.
CARDUS, JOSÉ.
    1886. Las misiones Franciscanas entre los infieles de Bolivia; descripción del
        estado de ellas en 1883 y 1884 . . . Barcelona.
    See also Lafone-Quevedo, Samuel A., 1905.
CARRASCO, FRANCISCO.
    1901. Principales palabras del idioma de las cuatro tribus de infieles: Antis,
        Piros, Conibos y Sipibos. Bol. Soc. Geogr. Lima, vol. 11, pp. 205–211.
CARROCERA, CAYETANO DE.
    1935. Las lenguas indígenas de Venezuela y su classificación por familias.
        Revista de Españas, vol. 10, pp. 316–321. Madrid.
CARTAS ANUAS DE LA PROVINCIA DEL PARAGUAY, CHILE Y TUCUMÁN DE LA
    COMPAÑIA DE JESUS. (Vol. 1, 1609–14; vol. 2, 1615–37.) Documentos para la
    historia argentina, t. 19–20. Iglesia.
    1927–29. Publicadas por el Instituto de investigaciones historicas. Buenos
        Aires.
CARTAS REGIAS. See ANNAES DO BIBLIOTHECA . . .
CARTILLA Y CATECISMO NOVÍSIMO DE LA DOCTRINA CRISTIANA EN EL IDIOMA DE LOS
    INDIOS DE GUARAYOS, CON EL CASTELLANO AL FRENTE, POR EL R. P. PREFECTO DE
    AQUELLAS MISIONES. SUCRE, 1889.
CARVAJAL, GASPER DE. See MEDINA, JOSÉ TORIBIO, 1934.
CARVAJAL, JACINTO DE.
    1892. Relación del descubrimiento del río Apure hasta su ingreso en al Orinoco
        . . . León.
CASEMENT, ROGER.
    1912. The Putumayo Indians. The Contemporary Review, vol. 102, pp. 317–
        328. London.
CASTELLVÍ, MARCELINO DE.
    1938. La lengua Kofán. Journ. Soc. Amér. Paris, n.s., vol. 30, pp. 219–233.
    See also Igualada, Francisco de, and Castellví, Marcelino de, 1940.
CASTELNAU, FRANCIS DE.
    1850–59. Expédition dans les parties centrales de l'Amérique du Sud, de Rio
        de Janeiro à Lima, et de Lima au Para; exécutée par ordre du
        gouvernement français pendant les années 1843 à 1847. 14 vols.
        in 16. (Part I, Histoire du voyage. 6 vols., 1850–51.) Paris.
CASTILLO, JOSEPH.
    1906. Relación de la provincia de Mojos. Documentos para la historia geográ-
        fica de la República de Bolivia compilados y anotados por Manuel V.

Ballivián. Serie primera. Epoca colonial, vol. 1, Las Provincias de Mojos y Chiquitos. La Paz.

CASTRO, MIGUEL JOÃO DE, and FRANÇA, TOMÉ DE.
   1868. Diario de viagem que fizeram os capitães . . . Rev. Inst. Hist., vol. 31, pt. 1, pp. 107–160.

CASTRUCCI [DE VERNAZZA], GUISEPPE EMANUELE.
   1849. Viaje practicado desde el Callao hasta las misiones de las dos tribus de infieles Záparos y Jívaros. Lima.
   1854. Viaggio da Lima ad alcune tribù barbare del Pe₍₎ e lungo il fiume delle Amazoni. Genova.

CATALOGUE OF CONTRIBUTIONS TRANSMITTED FROM BRITISH GUIANA TO THE LONDON INTERNATIONAL EXHIBITION. Georgetown, Demerara. 1867.

CATECISMO DE LA DOCTRINA CRISTIANA EN GUARAYO Y CASTELLANO. Yotau. 1916.

CATHREIN, VICTOR (VIKTOR).
   1914. Die Einheit des sittlichen Bewusstseins der Menschheit. Vol. 3, pp. 49–55. Freiburg.

CATTUNAR, HERMANN. See ROMANO, SANTIAGO, and CATTUNAR, HERMANN.

CAULIN, ANTONIO.
   1779. Historia coro-graphica natural y evangelica de la Nueva Andalucia, provincias de Cumaná, Guayana, y vertientes del rio Orinoco. Madrid. (Another edition published in Caracas in 1841.)

CAZAL, MANOEL AYRES DE. See AYRES DE CASAL, MANOEL.

CERQUEIRA E SILVA, IGNACIO ACCIOLI DE. See ACCIOLI DE CERQUEIRA E SILVA, IGNACIO.

CHAFFANJON, JEAN.
   1887. Sur quelques peupladre de la región de l'Orénoque. Archiv. Soc. Amer. France, n.s., vol. 5, pp. 189–203.
   1889. L'Orénoque et le Caura; relation de voyages exécutes en 1886 et 1887.

CHAMBERLAIN, ALEXANDER F.
   1907. South American linguistic stocks. Congr. Int. Amer., sess. 15, Quebec, 1906, vol. 2, pp. 187–204.
   1910. Sur quelques familles linguistiques peu connues ou presques inconnues de l'Amérique du Sud. Journ. Soc. Amér. Paris, n. s., vol. 7, pp. 179–202.
   1911. Recent literature of the South American Amazons. Journ. Amer. Folklore, vol. 24.
   1912. The linguistic position of the Pawumwa Indians of South America. Amer. Anthrop., n. s., vol. 14, pp. 632–635.

CHANDLESS, W.
   1862. Notes on the rivers Arinos, Juruena, and Tapajós. Journ. Roy. Geogr. Soc., vol. 32, pp. 268–280.
   1866 a. Ascent of the River Purûs. Journ. Roy. Geogr. Soc., vol. 36, pp. 86–118.
   1866 b. Notes on the River Aquiry, the principal affluent of the river Purûs. Journ. Roy. Geogr. Soc., vol. 36, pp. 119–128.
   1869 a. Notes of a journey up the River Juruá. Journ. Roy. Geogr. Soc., vol. 39, pp. 296–311.
   1869 b. Ascent of the River Purûs. Journ. Roy. Geogr. Soc., vol. 39, pp. 86–118.
   1870. Notes on the rivers Maué-assú, Abacaxis, and Canumá, Amazons. Journ. Roy. Geogr. Soc., vol. 40, pp. 419–432.

CHANTRE Y HERRERA, JOSÉ.
   1901. Historia de las misiones de la Compañía de Jesús en el Marañón español. (1637–1767). Madrid.

CHARLEVOIX, PIERRE FRANÇOIS XAVIER DE.
1757. Histoire du Paraguay. 6 vols. Paris. (Other eds. of this work published in London in 1769 and in Madrid in 1910–11.)

CHOMÉ, IGNACE.
1819 a. Lettre du Père Chromé, missionaire de la Compagnie de Jésus, au Père Vanthiennen, de la même Compagnie. *In* Lettres édifiantes et curieuses . . . Lyon, vol. 5, pp. 143–149.
1819 b. Lettre du Père Ignace Chomé, missionaire de la Compagnie de Jésus, au ɪ re Vanthic nen, de la même Compagnie. *In* Lettres édifiantes et curieuses . . . Lyon, vol. 5, pp. 180–204.

CHURCH, GEORGE EARL.
1898. Notes on the visit of Dr. Bach to the Catuquinarú Indians of Amazonas. Geogr. Journ., vol. 12, pp. 63–67.
1901. Northern Bolivia and President Pando's new map. Geogr. Journ., vol. 18, pp. 144–153.
1912. Aborigines of South America. London.

CIBEZZA, MARCELLINO DA. *See* LAUREANO DE LA CRUZ, 1900.

CIPRIANI, CÉSAR A
1902. Exploración del Bajo Inambari por el ingeniero César A. Cipriani. *In* "Vias del Pacífico al Madre de Dios," pp. 153–189. Lima.

CISNEROS, JOSEPH LUIS DE.
1912. Descripción exacta de la provincia de Benezuela. Reproducción de la edición de Valencia, 1764. Madrid.

CLARK, HYDE.
1879. Note on the Zaparo vocabulary. Journ. Roy. Anthrop. Inst. Great Britain, Ireland, vol. 8, p. 227.

CLAUDE D'ABBEVILLE. *See* ABBEVILLE, CLAUDE D'.

COELHO, JERONYMO FRANCISCO.
1849. Falla dirigida á Assembléa Legislativa Provincial no dia 1º de Outubro de 1849. Pará.

COHEN, MARCEL. *See* MEILLET, A., and COHEN, MARCEL, 1924; and RIVET, PAUL, 1924.

COLETI, GIOVANNI DOMENICO.
1771. Dizionario storico-geografico dell'America Meridionale. Venezia.

COLINI, GIUSEPPI ANGELO.
1883. Collezione etnografica degli indigene dell' alto Amazzoni . . . Roma. (*Also in* Bol. Soc. Geogr. Italiana, ser. 2, vol. 8, anno. 17, pp. 287 ff.)

COLL, C. VAN.
1903. Gegevens over land en volk van Suriname. Bijdragen tot de taal-'s-Gravenhage, land-en volkenkunde van Nederlandsch-Indie, vol. 55, pp. 451–640.
1907. Contes et légendes des Indiens de Surinam. Anthropos, vol. 2, pp. 682–689.

COLONEL LABRÉ. S LABRÉ, COLONEL.

COMENTARIOS DE ALVAR NUÑEZ CABEZA DE VACA. *See* HERNÁNDEZ, PEDRO, 1852.

COMMISSÃO RONDÓN, PUBLICACÃOES. 1911 and later. Rio de Janeiro.

CONDAMINE, M. DE LA.
1778. Relation abregée d'un voyage fait dans l'intérieur de l'Amérique méridionale. Maestricht. (Paris edition, 1745.)

CONI, EMILIO A.
1925. Los Guaranies y el antiguo Tucumán. Rev. Univ. Buenos Aires, 2a serie, sec. 2. vol. 2, p. 17 ff. (Reprint No. 27.)

CONSTANT and GRAS.

MS. Journal du voyage que les Sieurs Constant et Gras ou fait par l'ordre de Monsieur Dorvilliers, Gourveneur de Cayenne et que nous avon exémté sout celui de Monsieur La Motte Aigron, Major el Commandant dudit lieu . . . Archivs Coloniales Collection Moveau de Sait-Mery. Paris.

CONTRERAS, FRANCISCO.

1924. Prefectura Apostólica del Ucayali. Lima.

COOKSEY, FATHER.

1912. The Indians of the Northwest District. Temehri, 3rd ser., vol. 2, pp. 327–335.

COPAZZI, AGUSTÍN.

1841. Resumen de la geografía de Venezuela. Paris.

CÓRDOVA Y SALINAS, DIEGO DE.

1651. Corónica franciscana de la religiosissima provincia de los Doze Apostoles del Perú, de la Ordén de N.P.S. San Francisco de la regular observancia. Lima.

COREAL, FRANÇOIS [FRANCISCO].

1722. Voyages de François Coreal aux Indes Occidentales, contenant ce qu'il y a vû de plus remarquable pendant son séjour depuis 1666. jusqu'en 1697. . . . 2 vols. Paris. (Other eds. Amsterdam, 1722, 3 vols.; Amsterdam, 1738, 3 vols.; Bruxelles, 1736, 2 vols.)

CORNEJO, MARIANO H., and OSMA, FELIPE DE.

1905. El Perú admite al agente diplomático del nuevo Estado del Ecuador.— Año 1831. Documentos anexos a la Memoria del Perú, vol. 1, pp. 207–208. Anexo 28.

CORRADO, ALESSANDRO MARIA.

1884. El Colegio franciscano de Tarija y sus misiones. Noticias históricas recogidas por dos misioneros del mismo colegio. Quaracchi.

    See also, Giannecchini, Dorotéo.

CORREA DE MIRANDA, MANOEL GOMES.

1852. Falla dirigida á Assembléa Legislativa Provincial . . . em 5 de Setembro de 1852. Manaus.

CORTAMBERT, M. E.

1861. Coup d'oeil sur les productions et sur les peuplades géophages et les autres populations des bords de l'Orénoque. Bull. Soc. Géogr. Paris, ser. 5, vol. 1, pp. 208–220.

COSTA, ANGYONE. See ANGYONE COSTA, JOÃO.

COSTA MARQUEZ, MANOEL ESPERDÃO DA.

1908. Região oriental de Matto-Grosso. Rio de Janeiro.

COSTA PINHEIRO, MANOEL THEOPHILO DA.

1915. Exploração do Rio Juruena. Commissão das Linhas Telegraphicas Estrategicas de Mato Grosso ao Amazonas. Relatorio 3. Annexo No. I. Rio de Janeiro.

COUDREAU, HENRY ANATOLE.

1883. Les richesses de la Guyane Française. Cayenne.

1886 a. L'Amazonie. Bull. Soc. Géogr. Commerciale Paris, vol. 8, pp. 122–164.

1886 b. Voyage au Rio Branco, aux montagnes de la Lune, au haut Trombetta, mai 1884–avril 1885. Extract "Bull. Soc. Normande Geogr.", Rouen.

1886–87. La France équinoxiale. 2 vols. and Atlas. Paris. (Vol. 1. Études sur les Guyanes et l'Amazonie. 1886. Vol. 2. Voyage à travers les Guyanes et l'Amazonie. 1887. Atlas.)

1891 a. Notes sur 53 tribus de Guyane. Bull. Soc. Géogr. Paris, 7th ser., vol. 12, pp. 116–132.

1891 b. Dix ans de Guyane . . . Bull. Soc. Géogr. Paris, 7th ser., vol. 12, pp. 447–480.

1892. Vocabulaires méthodiques des langues Ouayana, Aparaï, Oyampi, Émérillon. Bibl. Ling. Amér. Paris, vol. 15.

1893. Chez nos Indiens; quatre années dans la Guyane Francaise (1887–1891). Paris.

1897 a. Voyage au Tapojóz, 28 juillet 1895–7 janvier 1896. Paris.

1897 b. Voyage au Tocantins-Araguaya, 31 décembre 1896–23 mai 1897. Paris.

1897 c. Voyage au Xingú, 30 mai 1896–26 octobre 1896. Paris.

1899. Voyage au Yamunda, 21 janvier 1899–27 juin 1899. Paris.

COUDREAU, OLGA.

1900. Voyage au Trombetas, 7 août 1899–25 novembre 1899. (Apres des notes de carnet d' Henri Coudreau.) Paris.

1901. Voyage au Cuminá, 20 avril 1900–7 septembre 1900. Paris.

1903 a. Voyage à la Mapuerá, 21 avril 1901–24 décembre 1901. Paris

1903 b. Voyage au Maycurú, 5 juin 1902–12 janvier 1903. Paris.

1903 c. Voyage au Rio Curuá, 20 novembre 1900–7 mars 1901. Paris.

COURBOIN, ALBERT.

1901. Chez les Indiens, notes et souvenirs d'un séjour dans l'Amazonie. Anvers. (Extrait du "Bulletin de la Societé royale de Geographie d'Anvers.")

COURTEVILLE, ROGER.

1938. Le Matto-Grosso. Paris.

COVINA, JOACHIM JOSEPH. See RODRIGUES FERREIRA, ALEXANDRE, n.d.

CRÉQUI-MONTFORT, GEORGES DE, and RIVET, PAUL.

1912. Linguistique bolivienne. Le groupe Otukè. Journ. Soc. Amér. Paris, n.s., vol. 9, pp. 317–337.

1913 a. La famille linguistique Capakura. Journ. Soc. Amér. Paris, n.s., vol. 10, pp. 119–171.

1913 b. Linguistique bolivienne. Les dialectes pano de Bolivie. Le Muséon, n.s., vol. 14, pp. 19–78.

1913 c. La langue Lapaču ou Apolista. Zeit. Ethnol, vol. 45, pp. 512–531.

1913 d. La langue Kaničana. Mém. Soc. Ling. Paris, vol. 18, pp. 354–377.

1913 e. Linguistique bolivienne. Les affinités des dialectes Otukè. Journ. Soc. Amér. Paris, n.s., vol. 10, pp. 369–377.

1913 f. La langue Saraveka. Journ. Soc. Amér. Paris, n.s., vol. 10, pp. 497–540.

1914 a. Linguistique bolivienne. La langue Kayuvava. Le Muséon, n.s., vol. 15, pp. 121–162.

1914 b. Linguistique bolivienne. La langue Mobima. Journ. Soc. Amér. Paris, n.s., vol. 11, pp. 183–211.

1916. La langue Itonama. Mém. Soc. Ling. Paris, vol. 19, pp. 301–322; vol. 20, pp. 26–57.

1917–20. Linguistique bolivienne. La langue Kayuvava. Int. Journ. Amer. Ling., vol. 1, pp. 245–265.

1921–22. La famille linguistique Takana. Journ. Soc. Amér. Paris, n.s., vol. 13, pp. 91–102, 281–301; vol. 14, pp. 141–182.

CREVAUX, JULES NICOLAS.

1879. Voyages d'exploration dans l'intérieur des Guyanes. Le Tour du Monde, vol. 37, pp. 337–416.

1880–81. De Cayenne aux Andes. Le Tour du Monde, vol. 40, pp. 33–112; vol. 41, pp. 113–176.

1882. Sur les Indiens Roucouyennes. Mém. Soc. Anthrop. Paris, 2nd ser., vol. 2, pp. 250–258.

1883. Voyages dans l'Amérique du Sud. Paris.

CRÉVAUX, JULES NICOLAS, SAGOT, P., and ADAM, LUCIEN.
  1882. Grammaires et vocabulaires roucouyenne, arrouague, piapoco et d'autres
      langues de la région des Guyanes. Bibl. Ling. Amér. Paris, vol. 8.
CRULS, GASTÃO.
  1930. A Amazonia que eu vi, Obidos-Tumucumaque. Rio de Janeiro. (1938
      ed. in Bibl. Pedag. Brasil, ser. 5a, Brasiliana, vol. 113. Rio de Janeiro.)
CRUZ, GUILHERME FRANCISCO DA.
  1874. Relatorio com que . . . passou a administração da Provincia do Pará
      ao exmo Sr. Dr. Pedro Vincente de Azevedo. 17 de Janeiro de 1874.
      Pará.
CRUZ, LAUREANO DE LA. See LAUREANO DE LA CRUZ.
CUADRO ESTADÍSTICO DE LAS TRIBUS DE LA MONTAÑA DEL PERU, según los informes
    enviados a la comisión central del censo, por los maestros de escuela y jefes de
    las guarniciones militares. Baluarte. Junio, 1940, pp. 8–9. Lima.
CUERVO MÁRQUEZ, CARLOS.
  1893. Prehistorica y Viajes. Tierradentro, Los Paeces, San Agustín, El Llano,
      etc. Bogotá.
CUEVA, R. P. DE LA.
  1893. Principes et dictionnaire de la langue yuacare ou yurujure composés par
      le R. P. de la Cueva et publiés conformement au manuscrit de A.
      d'Orbigny. Bibl. Ling. Amér. Paris, vol. 16.
CUNHA, JOSÉ JOAQUIM DA.
  1852. Falla que . . . dirigiu á Assemblea Legislativa Provincial . . . no dia de
      10 de Outubro de 1852. Pará.
  1853. Falla que o exmo Snr. . . . Presidente da Provincia dirigiu á Assemblea
      Legislativa Provincial . . . no dia 15 de Agosto de 1853. Pará.
CURRIER, CHARLES WARREN.
  1897. Origine, progrès et caractères de la race carïbe. Congr. Int. Amer.,
      sess. 11, 1895, Mexico, pp. 504–511.
DALTON, HENRY G.
  1855. The history of British Guiana. 2 vols. London.
DANCE, CHARLES DANIEL.
  1876. Recollections of four years in Venezuela. London.
  1881. Chapters from a Guianese log-book . . . Georgetown, Demerara.
DANIEL, JOÃO.
  1840. Second part of the Treasure discovered on the Amazon River. Rev.
      Inst. Hist., vol. 2, pp. 329–364, 447–500. (Ed. in Portuguese pub. in
      1858.)
  1840–41. Parte segundo do thesouro descoberta no Rio Amazonas: Noticia
      geral dos indios seus naturaes, e de algumas nações em particular
      . . . Rev. Trim. Hist. Geogr. Brasil, vol. 2, pp. 329–364, 447–500;
      vol. 3, pp. 39–52, 158–183, 282–297, 422–441.
DARNAULT, P.
  1934. [Note on Galibis Indians of Guiana]. La Geogr., vol. 61, pp. 49–51.
DE GOEJE, C. H.
  1906. Bejdrage tot de ethnographie der Surinaamsche Indianen. Int. Archiv.
      Ethnogr., Supplement to vol. 17.
  1908 a. Verslag der Taemaekhoemak-expeditie. Tejdsch. Ned. Aard. Ge-
      nootsch., vol. 25, pp. 945–1168.
  1908 b. Beiträge zur Völkerkunde von Surinam. Int. Archiv. Ethnogr.
  1910. Études linguistiques Caraïbes. Johannes Müller. Verhandelingen der
      Koninkly ke Akademie van Wetenschappen te Amsterdam, Afdeeling
      Letterkunde, Nieuwe Reeks, deel 10, No. 3.

1924. Guayana und Carib tribal names. Congr. Int. Amer., sess. 21, The Hague, pt. 1, pp. 212–216.

1924–25. Karaiben an Guiana. De West-indische Gids, 's Gravenhage Martinus Nijhoff, vol. 6, pp. 465–471.

1928. The Arawak language of Guiana. Verhandelingen der Koninkly ke Akademie van Wetenschappen te Amsterdam, Afdeeling Letterkunde, Nieuwe Reeks, deel 28, No. 2.

1929. Mysterie-wijsheid bij de Karaïben. Rep. Kol. Wkbl., Maart 14, 1929, p. 121.

1929–30 a. A Ph. Penard, over Inwijding En Wereld-beschouwing der Karaiben. Overdruk uit "De West-Indische Gids," vol. 11, pp. 275–286. (Elfde Jaarang, No. 6, 's Gravenhage Martinus Nijhoff.)

1929–30 b. Het Merkwaardige Arrawaksch. Iverdruk uit "De West-Indische Gids," vol. 11, pp. 11–28. (No. 1, March 1929, 's Gravenhage Martinus Nijhoff.)

1930. The inner structure of the Warau language of Guiana. Journ. Soc. Amér. Paris, vol. 22, pp. 33–72.

1930–31. Het merkwaardige Warau. Rep. "De West-Indische Gids," 12 Jr. No. 1. 's Gravenhage Martinus Nijhoff. Vol. 12, pp. 1–16.

1931–32. Ouheden uit Suriname. Op zoek naar de Amazonen. De West-Indische Gids, deel 13, afl. 10–11, pp. 449–530.

1932–33. Het merkwaardige Karaibisch. (Een ethnologisch verhaal voor den gewonen lezer). De West-Indische Gids, vol. 14, pp. 99–123.

1934–35. Curiositeiten uit Guyana. De West-Indische Gids, vol. 16, pp. 72–76.

1935. Fünf Sprachfamilien Südamerikas. Mededeelingen Konig. Akad. Wetensch., Afd. Letterkunde, deel 77, Ser. A, No. 5.

1937. Laut und Sinn in Karibischen Sprachen. Särtryck source "Melanges de linguistique et de philologique offerts a Jacq. van Ginneken a l'occasion du soixantième anniversaire de sa naissance" (21 avril 1937), pp. 335–339.

DELGADO, EULOGIO.
1896–97. Vocabulario del idioma de las tribus Campas. Bol. Soc. Geogr. Lima, vol. 5, pp. 445–457; vol. 6, pp. 96–105, 230–240, 347–356, 393–396.

DELGADO, EVARISTA. See VERGARA Y VERGARA, JOSÉ MARÍA, and DELGADO, EVERISTA.

DELGADO O., E. See EXPLORACIÓN DE LA GRAN SABANA, 1939.

DENGLER, HERMANN.
1926–32. Das Haar-Ausreissen bei den Ticuna-Indianer West-Brasiliens. Der Erdball. 6 vols. 1 year.

n.d. O desenhista Hermann Dengler vizitou os Parintintin do Rio Madeira em 1927 ou 1928.

1928. Eine Forschungsreise zu den Kawahib-Indianern am Rio Madeiro. Zeit Ethnol., vol. 59.

DENIS, FERDINAND.
1823. La Guyane, ou histoire, moeurs, usages et costumes des habitans de cette partie de l'Amérique. 2 vols. Paris.

1851. Une fête brésilienne célébrée à Rouen en 1850. Paris.

DENIS, FERDINAND, and FAMIN, STANISLAS MARIE CÉSAR.
1837. Brésil, Colombie et Guyanes. Paris.

DESCRIPÇÃO GEOGRAPHICA DA CAPITANIA DE MATTO GROSSO. ANNO 1797.
1857. Rev. Inst. Hist., vol. 20, pp. 185–292.

DESCRIPCIÓN DE LA PROVINCIA DE LOS QUIJOS.
1881–97 (Written in 1577 by Don Diego de Ortegon.) Rel. Geogr. Indias, vol. 1, pp. C–CXII.

DESCRIPCIÓN DE LAS MISIONES DE APOLOBAMBA, pertenecientes al obispado de La Paz, 1771.

DESCRIPCIÓN DEL TERRITORIO DE LAS MISIONES FRANCISCANAS DE APOLOBAMBA, por otro nombre frontera de Caupolicán. La Paz, 1905.

DES FOREST, JESSE. *See* FOREST, JESSE DES.

DEUBER, ARNOLD.
  1926. Musikinstrumente und Musik der Aparaí. *In* Speiser, Felix, Im Düster des brasilianischen Urwalds, pp. 320–322. Stuttgart.

DEYROLLE, ÉMILE.
  1916. Notes d'anthropologie guyanaise. Les Indiens Maraouanes. Bull. Mém. Soc. Anthrop. Paris, ser. 6, vol. 7, pp. 153–164.

DIAZ CASTAÑEDA, CESAR.
  1923. Kunibo. Inca, vol. 1, No. 2, pp. 398–409.

DÍAZ DE GUZMÁN, RUI.
  1914. La Argentina; historia de las provincias del Río de la Plata . . . An. Bibl., vol. 9.

DICCIONARIO HISTORICO, GEOGRAPHICO E ETHNOGRAPHICO DO BRASIL . . . introducção geral . . . vol. 1, Rio de Janeiro, 1922.

DIECK, ALFRED.
  1912. Die Waffen der Naturvölker Süd-Amerikas. Mit 1 Karte. Inaugural-Dissertation zur Erlangung der Doktorwürde bei der Philosophischen Fakultät der Albertus-Universität zu Königsberg i. Pr. Stallupönen, 1912.

DINWIDDIE, HOWARD B.
  1924. Ecuador: a missionary survey. New York.

DIXON, GEORGE G.
  1895. Four months of travel in British Guiana. Geogr. Journ., vol. 5, pp. 337–345.

DOBRIZHOFFER, [DOBRITZHOFER], MARTIN.
  1784. Historia de Abiponibus equestri, bellicosaque Paraquariae natione . . . 3 vols. Vienna. (Also pub. London, 1822.)

DOCTRINA CRISTIANA EN LA LENGUA JIVARA. Lima, 1903.

DODT, GUSTAVO LUIZ GUILHERME.
  1873. Descripção dos rios Parnahyba e Gurupy. Maranhão. (Later edition pub. in 1939 in São Paulo and Rio de Janeiro.)

DOMÍNGUEZ, MANUEL.
  1918. El alma de la raza. Asunción.

DOMVILLE-FIFE, CHARLES WILLIAM.
  1924. Among wild tribes of the Amazons . . . London.

DORSEY, GEORGE AMOS.
  1898. A bibliography of the anthropology of Peru. Field Columbian Museum, Anthrop. ser., vol. 2, pp. 55–206.

DUCCI, ZACARÍAS.
  1895. Diario de la visita a todas las misiones existentes en la república de Bolivia-America Meridional, praticada por el m.r. P. Sebastian Pifferi. Asis.

DUFF, ROBERT.
  1866. British Guiana. Glasgow.

DUMONTIER, F. A. C.
  1858. Iets over de bereiding van het Wourali-vergift door de Indianen. West-Indie, Part 2, pp. 286 ff.
    See also Focke, H. C., Landré, Dh., Sypestein, C. A. van, and Dumontier, F. A. C., 1855–58.

Dunha, José Joaquim da.
1853. Falla que o exmo. snr. . . . Presidente da Provincia dirigiu a Assembléa Legislativa Provincial . . . August 15, 1853. Pará.

Dupont.
1875. Les indigènes de la Guyane française. Congr. Int. Amer., sess. 1, Nancy, vol. 1, pp. 392–394.

Dutertre, Jean Baptiste.
1654. Histoire generale des isles de S. Christophe, de la Guadeloupe, de la Martinique, et autres dans l'Amérique. Paris.
1667–71. Histoire generale des Antilles habitées par les François. 4 vols. Paris. (Revised ed. of 1654 ed.)

Dyott, George M.
1929. The search for Colonel Fawcett. Geogr. Journ., vol. 74, pp. 513–542.
1930. Man hunting in the jungle. Indianapolis.

Eberhardt, Charles C.
1910. Indians of Perú. Smithsonian Misc. Coll., vol. 52, pp. 181–194.

Eberlein, Baldomero.
1915. La onomatología corográfica del Departamento de Santa Cruz. Bol. Soc. Geogr. Hist. Santa Cruz, 12th year, vol. 5, No. 19.

Eder, Ferencz [Francis] Xaver [Xavier].
1791. Descriptio provinciae Mojitarum in regno peruano, quam e scriptis . . . e Soc. Jesu . . . (annis XV. sacri apud eosdem Curionis) digessit, expolivit, et adnotatiunculis illustravit abb. et consil. reg. Mako. Budae [Budapest].

Edmundson, George.
1922. Journal of the travels and labours of Father Samuel Fritz in the river of the Amazons between 1686 and 1723. London.

Eguiluz, Diego de.
1884. Historia de la Mision de Mojos en la republica de Bolivia, escrita en 1696 . . . Lima.

Ehrenreich, Paul.
1891 a. Beiträge zur Völkerkunde Brasiliens. In Veröffentlichungen aus dem königlichen Museum für Völkerkunde, Berlin, vol. 2, pp. 1–80.
1891 b. Die Einteilung und Verbreitung der Völkerstämme Brasiliens nach dem gegenwärtigen Stande unsrer Kenntnisse. Petermanns Mitt., vol. 37, pp. 81–89, 114–124. (Portuguese ed. in Rev. Soc. Geogr. Rio de Janeiro, vol. 8, 1892.)
1892. Beiträge zur Geographie Central-Brasiliens. Verhandl. d. Gesell. f. Erdkunde zu Berlin, vol. 28.
1895. Materialien zur Sprachenkunde Brasiliens. V. Die Sprache der Apiaká (Pará). Zeit. Ethnol., vol. 27, pp. 149–176.
1897 a. Anthropologische Studien über die Urbewohner Brasiliens vornehmlich der Staaten Matto Grosso, Goyaz und Amazonas (Purus-gebiet). Braunschweig.
1897 b. Materialien zur Sprachenkunde Brasiliens. Vokabulare von Purus-Stämmen. Zeit. Ethnol., vol. 29, pp. 59–71.
1904. Die Ethnographie Südamerikas im Beginn des XX Jahrhunderts unter besonderer Berücksichtigung der Naturvölker. Archiv. für Anthrop., n.s., vol. 3, pp. 39–75.
1905. Die Mythen und Legenden der Südamerikanischen Urvölker und ihre Beziehungen zu denen Nordamerikas und der alten Welt. Zeit. Ethnol., Supplement to vol. 37.

1915. Distribuição geográfica das tribus indígenas na época do descobrimiento. Rev. Inst. Archeol., Hist. e Geogr. Pernambucano, vol. especial, 2nd part, p. 493.

ELÍAS ORTÍZ, SERGIO. *See* ORTÍZ, SERGIO ELÍAS.

EMMERICH-HÖGEN, FERDINAND.
1922. Die Kariben in Guayana. Regensburg.

ENDRISS, G.
1911. Die Corantijnexpedition von Leutn. Kayser. Petermanns Mitt., vol. 57, No. 5, p. 250.

ENFORMAÇÃO DO BRAZIL, E DE SUAS CAPITANIAS (1584).
1844. Rev. Inst. Hist. Geogr. Brazil, vol. 6, pp. 404–435.

ENOCK, CHARLES REGINALD.
1908. The Andes and the Amazon; life and travel in Peru. London.

ERNST, ADOLF.
1870. Anthropological remarks on the population of Venezuela. Mem. Anthrop. Soc. London, vol. 3, pp. 274–287.
1886–87. Ethnographische Mitteilungen aus Venezuela. Verhandl. der Berliner Gesell. für Anthrop., Ethnol., u. Urgeschichte, vol. 4, pp. 514–545; vol. 5, pp. 295–296; and *in* Zeit. Ethnol., vols. 18 and 19.
1888. Praehistorische und ethnographische Gegenstaende aus Venezuela. Verhandl. der Berliner Gesell. für Anthrop., Ethnol., u. Urgeschichte, Jahrg. 1888, p. 467.
1889. Petroglyphen aus Venezuela. Verhandl. der Berliner Gesell. für Anthrop., Ethnol., u. Urgeschichte, Jahrg. 1889, pp. 650–655.

ESCOBAR Y MENDOZA, FRANCISCO DE.
1769. Noticia de las misiones de Maynas.
See also Osma, Felipe de, 1908(?).

ESPINOSA, LUCAS.
1935. Los Tupí del Oriente peruano, estudio lingüístico y etnográfico. Publicaciones de la Expedición Iglesias al Amazonas. Madrid.

ESTADO DE LAS MISIONES Y EXPLORACIONES DEL PADRE PALLARES POR LOS RÍOS PISCHQUI, CHUNYA Y TAMBO. 1852–1854. *See* IZAGUIRRE ISPIZUA, BERNARDINO, 1922–29, vol. 9, pp. 196–218.

ETRÉ, GUILLAUME D'.
1819. Lettre du père Guillaume d'Etré, missionnaire de la Compagnie de Jésus, au père Joseph Duchambre, de la même Compagnie. *In* Lettres édifiantes et curieuses, Lyon, vol. 5, pp. 150–171.

L'ÉVANGILE.
1861. Une Expédition. Scènes et paysages dans les Andes. 2nd ser. Paris.

EXPLORACIÓN DE LA GRAN SABANA. Rev. Fomento (Venezuela), 1939, Año 3, No. 19, pp. 501–730. (By S. E. Aguerrerere, Victor M. López, E. Delgado O., and C. A. Freeman.)

EXPLORACIÓN DE LOS RÍOS PICHIS, PACHITEA Y ALTO UCAYALI Y DE LA REGIÓN DEL GRAN PAJONAL. Lima. 1897.

EXPLORACIONES Y NOTICIAS HIDROGRÁFICAS DE LOS RÍOS DEL NORTE DE BOLIVIA.
1890. Primera parte. Traducciones, reproducciones y documentos inéditos publicados por M. V. Ballivian. La Paz. (Folletines de "El Comercio," No. 2.)

FABO, PEDRO.
1911. Idiomas y etnografia de la región oriental de Colombia. Barcelona.

FAMIN, STANISLAS MARIE CÉSAR.
1839. Columbien und Guyane. *In* Welt Gemaelde-Galerie oder Beschreibung aller Laende und Voelker, ihrer Gebraeuche, Religionen, Sitten usw. Stuttgart.
See also Denis, Ferdinand, and Famin, Stanislas Marie César, 1837.

FARABEE, WILLIAM CURTIS.
1909. Some customs of the Macheyengas. Proc. Amer. Antiq. Soc., Oct. 1909.
1915. Conebo pottery. Penn. Univ. Mus. Journ., vol. 6, pp. 94–99.
1916 a. Some South American petroglyphs. *In* Holmes Anniversary Volume, pp. 88–95. Washington.
1916 b. The Amazon expedition of the University Museum. Mus. Journ. Univ. Penn., vol. 7, pp. 210–244.
1917 a. The Amazon expedition of the University Museum. To the head waters of the Amazon. Mus. Journ. Univ. Penn., vol. 8, pp. 61–82.
1917 b. The Amazon expedition. The Tapajós. Mus. Journ. Univ. Penn., vol. 8, pp. 126-144.
1917 c. A pioneer in Amazonia: the narrative of a journey from Manaos to Georgetown. Bull. Geogr. Soc. Philadelphia, vol. 15, No. 2, pp. 57–103.
1918 a. The Arawaks of northern Brazil and southern British Guiana. Amer. Journ. Phys. Anthrop., vol. 1, pp. 427–441.
1918 b. The central Arawaks. University of Pennsylvania, The University Museum, Anthrop. Publ., vol. 9.
1919. Mummified Jivaro heads. Mus. Journ. Univ. Penn., vol. 10, pp. 173–183.
1921 a. Explorations at the mouth of the Amazon. Mus. Journ. Univ. Penn., vol. 12, pp. 142–161.
1921 b. The central Arawaks: A reply to Dr. Roth. Amer. Anthrop., n.s., vol. 23, pp. 230–233.
1922. Indian tribes of eastern Peru. Pap. Peabody Mus. Arch. Ethnol. Harvard Univ., vol. 10.
1924. The central Caribs. University of Pennsylvania, The University Museum, Anthrop. Publ., vol. 10.

FARSON, NEGLEY.
1937. Transgressor in the tropics. London. (Pub. in New York, 1938.)

FAWCETT, P. H.
1911. Further explorations in Bolivia: the river Heath. Geogr. Journ., vol. 37, pp. 377–397.
1915. Bolivian exploration, 1913–1914. Geogr. Journ., vol. 45, pp. 219–228.
1925. Letter received from Colonel Fawcett. Geogr. Rev., vol. 15, p. 696.

FEBRES CORDERO, TULIO.
1931. Mitología Venezolana. An. Univ. Central Venezuela, vol. 19, pp. 387–396.

FEDERMANN, NIKOLAUS.
1557. Indianische historia. Ein schöne kurtzweilige historia Niclaus Federmanns des jüngern von Ulm erster raise. Hagenaw. (*In* Klüpfel, K., ed., N. Federmanns und H. Staden reisen in Südamerica 1529 bis 1555. Stuttgart, 1859, pp. 1–86. Reprinted in "Bibliotek des Litteriarische Vereins in Stuttgart, 47.")

FEHLINGER, H.
1925. Die Ehe bei den Guiana-Indianern. Zeit. f. Sexualwissenschaft, vol. 12, fasc. 9, pp. 274–278.

FEJOS, PAUL
n.d. MS. on Mascho of Peruvian Montaña.
1940. Mimeographed report of the Wenner-Gren Scientific Expedition to Hispanic America, 1940, to his Excellency Gunnar Reuterskiöld, Envoy Extraordinary and Minister Plenipotentiary of Sweden. Lima.
1943. Ethnography of the Yagua. Viking Fund, Publ. in Anthrop., No. 1.

FERMIN, PHILIPPE.
  1765. Histoire naturelle de la Hollande équinoxiale. Amsterdam.
  1769. Déscription générale, historique, géographique et physique de la colonie de
        Surinam. 2 vols. Amsterdam. (Revised and enlarged ed. of the
        author's "Histoire de la Hollande équinoxiale.")
  1781. An historical and political view of the present and ancient state of the
        colony of Surinam, in South America. London. (An abridged
        English ed. pub. by W. Nicoll.)
FERNANDES DE SOUZA, CONEGO ANDRÉ.
  1870. Noticia geographica da Capitania do Rio Negro no grande Rio Amazonas.
        Rev. Inst. Hist. Geogr. Brazil, vol. 10.
        See also Smyth, Lieutenant (Wm.), 1836.
FERNÁNDEZ, JUAN PATRICIO.
  1895. Relación historial de las misiones de indios Chiquitos que en el Paraguay
        tienen los padres de la Compañía de Jesús. (Colección de libros raros
        o curiosos que tratan de America, vols. 12–13. 2 vols. Madrid.)
FERNÁNDEZ MORO, REV. P. FRAY WENCESLAO.
  1926–27. Estudios de etnografía y medicina salvaje. Bol. Soc. Geogr. Lima,
        vol. 43, pp. 1–29, 149–164; vol. 44, pp. 75–90.
FERRE P. *See* BAUVE, ADAM DE, and FERRE P., 1833–34.
FERREIRA, ALEXANDRE RODRIGUES. *See* RODRIGUES FERREIRA, ALEXANDRE.
FERREIRA, FRANCISCO.
  1903 (1755). Renseignments sur le Rio Branco. Limites entre le Brésil et
        la Guyane Anglaise. Annexes au premier mémoire du Bresil,
        vol. 3, Paris. (Fin Ach. du Conseil et Outre-mer, Bibl. Nat.,
        Lisbon.)
FERREIRA PENNA, DOMINGOS SOARES. *See* PENNA, DOMINGOS SOARES FERREIRA.
FERREIRA PENNA, HERCULANO.
  1853. Relatorio do Presidente da Provincia do Amazona.
FESTA, ENRICO.
  1909. . . . Nel Darien e nell' Ecuador; diario di viaggio di un naturalista.
        Torino.
FIGUEIRÊDO, LIMA. *See* LIMA FIGUEIRÊDO, JOSÉ DE.
FIGUEIRÊDO TENREIRO ARANHA, BENTO DE.
  1907. Archivo do Amazonas. Anno I, vol. 1, No. 4, Manaos.
FIGUEROA, FRANCISCO DE.
  1904. Relación de las misiones de la Compañía de Jesús en el país de los
        Maynas. Madrid.
FINOT, ENRIQUE.
  1939. Historia de la conquista del oriente boliviano. Buenos Aires.
FISHBACH, AGNES IRENE.
  1929. The Guarani Indians of Paraguay: A description and historical study.
        Master of art thesis. Kennedy School of Missions. Hartford.
FLORENCE, HERCULES.
  1941(?). Viagem fluvial do Tietê ao Amazonas de 1825–29. São Paulo.
        See also Steinen, Karl von den, 1899.
FLU, PAUL CHRISTIAN.
  1911. De filaria-ziekte in Suriname . . . 's-Gravenhage, Algemeene lands-
        drukkerij.
FOCKE, H. C.
  1858. De Surinaamsche Negermuzijk. West-Indie., 2nd section; by A. C.
        Kruseman, Haarlem. Pp. 93–108.

FOCKE, H. C., LANDRE, DH., SYPESTEYN, C. A. VAN, and DUMONTIER, F. A. C.
  1855–58. West-Indie. Bijdragen tot bevordering van de kennis der Neder-
    landsch West-Indische Kolonien. 2 vols.
FOGG, PH. M.
  1927. Die Wai-Wai Indianes am unteren Amazonas. Welt u. Wissen, vol. 14,
    pp. 57–61.
FONSECA COUTINHO, ANTONIA CARLOS DE.
  1873. Noticias de voluntaria reducção de paz e amizade de feroz nação do
    gentio Múra nos annos de 1784, 1785 e 1786. Rev. Inst. Hist., vol. 36,
    part 1, pp. 323–392.
FONSECA, JOÃO SEVERIANO DA.
  1880–81. Viagem ao redor do Brasil, 1875–1878. 2 vols. Rio de Janeiro.
    (Another ed. 1895, Rio de Janeiro.)
FOREST, JESSE DES.
  1899. Description de la coste d'west de la Rivière des Amazones—Rio Branco:
    Frontières entre le Brésil et la Guyane Française. Vol. 2, Memoire.
    Berne.
FRAGMENTO DA VIAGEM DAS AMAZONAS E RIO NEGRO.
  1906. Rev. Inst. Hist., vol. 67, 1st part, pp. 272–281.
FRANÇA, CARLOS.
  1926. Ethnographia brasilica, segundo os escriptores portugueses do seculo 16.
    Rev. Hist. Lisbon, vol. 15, Nos. 57–60, pp. 129–152.
FRANÇA, TOMÉ DE. See CASTRO, MIGUEL JOÃO DE, and FRANÇA, TOMÉ DE, 1868.
FRANCISCO DE NUESTRA SEÑORA DOS PRAZERES.
  1891. Poranduba Maranhense. Rev. Inst. Hist., vol. 54, pt. 1, pp. 92–77. Rio
    de Janeiro.
FRANSSEN, J.
  1917–18. Indianen. Onze Missien in Oost en West, vol. 1, pp. 99–149.
FREEMAN, C. A. See EXPLORACIÓN DE LA GRAN SABANA, 1939.
FREITAS, AFFONSO ANTONIO DE.
  1914. Distribução geographica das tribus indigenas na época do descubrimento.
    Rev. Inst. Hist. Geogr. São Paulo, vol. 19, pp. 103–128.
FRENGUELLI, JOAQUÍN, and APARICIO, FRANCISCO DE.
  1923. Los paraderos de la margen derecha del Rio Malabrigo (Departmento
    de Reconquista, Prov. Santa Fé). An. Fac. Cienc. Ed. Paraná, vol. 1,
    pp. 7–112.
FRIEDERICI, GEORG.
  1925. Göttingischer gelehrter Anzeiger.
  1929. Bemerkungen zur Entdeckungsgeschichte Brasiliens. "Sonderdruck aus
    In memoriam Karl Weule. Beiträge zur völkerkunde und vorge-
    schichte," pp. 335–354. Leipzig.
FRITZ, SAMUEL.
  1691. Mapa Geographico del Rio Marañon. Amazonas.
  1892. Karte von Maynas. Bol. Soc. Geogr. Madrid, vol. 33, p. 72.
  1922. Journal of the travels and labours of Father Samuel Fritz in the river
    of the Amazons between 1686 and 1723. (Trans. from the Evora ms.
    and edited by the Rev. George Edmundson.) The Hakluyt Society,
    2nd series, No. 51. London.
FRÖDIN, OTTO, and NORDENSKIÖLD, ERLAND.
  1918. Über Zwirnen und Spinnen bei den Indianern Südamerikas. Göteborgs
    Kungl. Vetenskaps-och Vitterhets-Samhälles Handlingor (Fjörde
    Füljden), No. 19. Göteborg.
FROES ABREU, SYLVIO.
  1931. Na terra das palmeiras; estudos brasileiros. Rio de Janeiro.

FROIDEVAUX, HENRI.
    1894. Explorations françaises à l'intérieur de la Guyane pendant le second quart du XVIII° siècle (1720–1742). Bulletin de géographie historique et descriptive, pp. 218–301. Paris.
FRONTIÈRES, SECOND MEMOIRE. See RIO-BRANCO, BARÃO DE, 1899.
FRY, CARLOS.
    1889. La gran región de los bosques; o riós peruanos navegables: Urubamba, Ucayali, Amazonas, Pachitea, y Palcazu. Diario de viajes y exploraciones por Carlos Fry en 1886, 1887 y 1888 . . . 2 vols. Lima.
FUENTES, HILDEBRANDO.
    1908. Apuntes geográficos, históricos estadísticos . . . de Loreto 1906. Larrabure, vol. 17, pp. 3–277. Lima.
FUENTES, MANUEL ATANASIO.
    1861. Antiguo Mercurio Peruano, Bibliotheca Peruana de Historia, Ciencias, y Literatura. Colleción de escritos del anteriór y del presente siglo de los más acreditados autores Peruanos. Lima.
FURLONG, CHARLES W.
    1915. The red men of the Guianan forests. Harpers Mag., vol. 131, pp. 527–537.
FURTADO, FRANCISCO JOSÉ.
    1858. Relatorio que a Assembléa Legislativa Provincial apresentou . . . em o dia de 7 de Setembro de 1858. Manaus.
GABB, WILLIAM M.
    1875. On the Indian tribes and languages of Costa Rica. Proc. Amer. Philos. Soc., vol. 14.
GABRIEL SALA, R. P. FRAY.
    1905. Diccionario gramatico y catecismo Castellano, Inga, Amuexia y Campa. Lima.
GADEA, ALBERTO L.
    1895. Arbol del damajuhato. Bol. Soc. Geogr. Lima, vol. 4, pp. 132–143.
GAFFAREL, PAUL. See LERY, JEAN DE.
GALARD DE TERRAUBE, LOUIS ANTOINE MARIE VICTOR DE.
    1799. Tableau de Cayenne ou de la Guiane française. Paris. (Published anonymously.) (1799, German ed., Leipzig; 1800, Dutch ed., Leyden.)
GALT, F. L.
    n.d. Diary of F. L. Galt, doctor to the expedition exploring the headwaters of the Amazon in eastern Peru. MS. in Manuscript files, Bureau of American Ethnology, Washington, D. C.
    1878. The Indians of Peru. Smithsonian Ann. Rep. for 1877, pp. 308–315.
GAMA LOBO DE ALMADA, MANUEL DA.
    1903 (1787). Description relative au Rio Branco et Son territoire . . . Limites entre le Brésil et la Guyane Francaise. Annexes au premiere mémoire du Brésil, vol. 3, pp. 271–290, Paris.
GAMA MALCHER, JOSÉ DA.
    1878. Relatorio com que . . . passou a administração da Provincia do Pará ao exmo. Snr. Dr. João Capistrano Bandeira de Mello Filho em 9 de Março de 1878. Pará.
GANDÍA, ENRIQUE DE.
    1929 a. Historia del Gran Chaco. Buenos Aires.
    1929 b. Historia crítica de los mitos de la conquista americana. Buenos Aires.
    1935 a. Historia de la Provincia de Santa Cruz. Buenos Aires.
    1935 b. Historia de Santa Cruz de la Sierra. Buenos Aires.

GANZÁLEZ RUIZ, FELIPE.
  1937. Geografía e histoiia del Amazonas. Bol. Soc. Geogr. Lima, vol. 54,
    pp. 3–31.
GARCÍA DE FREITAS, JOSÉ.
  1926. Os Indios Parintintin. Journ. Soc. Amér. Paris, n.s., vol. 18, pp. 67–73.
GARCÍA ROSELL, RICARDO.
  1905. Paucatambo; sinópsis, exploraciones y descubrimientos. Lima.
GARCÍA, SECUNDINO.
  1942. Mitologia de los salvajes machiguengas. Congr. Int. Amer., sess. 27,
    Lima, 1939, vol. 2, pp. 229–237.
GARCÍA Y MERINO, MANUEL.
  1893. Los nombres vulgares de nuestras plantas. Bol. Soc. Geogr. Lima, vol.
    5, pp. 294–301.
GARCILASO DE LA VEGA.
  1918–20. Los comentarios reales de los Incas. 5 vols. Lima. (Colección de
    historiadores clasicos del Peru, vol. 1, 3–4.)
GARRIGA, ANTONIO.
  1906. Linderos de los pueblos de las missiones de Mojos, declarados y con-
    firmados por el Padre Provincial . . . en su visita de 10 de octubre de
    1715. Juicio de límites entre el Peru y Bolivia, vol. 10, Mojos II, pp.
    34–42. Madrid.
GENNEP, ARNOLD VAN.
  1914. Études d'ethnographie sud-américaine. Journ. Soc. Amér. Paris, n.s.,
    vol. 11, pp. 121–133.
GHINASSI, JUAN.
  1938. Gramática teórico-práctica y vocabulario de la lengua Jíbara . . . Quito.
GIANNECCHINI, DOROTÉO.
  1896. Reglas elementares de la lengua Chiriguana. Obra postuma del R. P.
    Alejandro Maria Corrado. Lucca.
  Also see Romano, Santiago, and Cattunar, Hermann, 1916.
GIBBON, LARDNER. See HERNDON, WILLIAM LEWIS, and GIBBON, LARDNER.
GIGLIOLI, ENRICO HILLYER.
  1906. Appunti sulle condizioni attuali delle tribù indigene dell'alto Madeira e
    regioni adiacenti (Brasile e Bolivia). Raccolti dal Dott. Andrea Landi.
    Archiv. Antrop. Etnol., vol. 36, pp. 219–228.
GILI, ANTONIO.
  1902. Arte y vocabulario de la lengua Tacana (continuación). Catecismo
    Tacana por el R. P. Fr. Antonio Gili . . . Rev. Mus. La Plata, vol. 10,
    pp. 297–311.
  See also Armentia, Nicolás, 1902.
GILIJ, FILIPPO SALVADORE.
  1780–84. Saggio di storia americana; o sia, Storia naturale, civile e sacra de'
    regni, e delle provincie spagnuole di Terra-Ferma nell' America
    Meridionale descritto dall' abate F. S. Gilij. 4 vols. Rome.
  See also Veigl, Franz Xavier, 1785 b.
GILL, RICHARD C.
  1940. White water and black magic. New York.
GILLIN, JOHN.
  1933. Die Strafe bei den Cariben des Barama-Flusses in Britisch-Guyana.
    Monatsschr. f. Kriminalpsych. u Strafrechtsreform, Jahrgang 24, pp.
    654–667. Heidelberg.
  1934. Crime and punishment among the Barama River Carib of British Guiana.
    Amer. Anthrop., n.s., vol. 36, pp. 331–344.

1935. Social life of the Barama River Caribs of British Guiana. Scientific Monthly, vol. 40, pp. 227–236.

1936. The Barama River Caribs of British Guiana. Pap. Peabody Mus. Arch. Ethnol. Harvard Univ., vol. 14, No. 2, pp. 1–274.

GLASENAPP, HELMUTH VON.

1937. Die Inder in Trinidad und Guayana. Zeit. f. Rassenkunde, vol. 6, pp. 307–311.

n.d.   Die Indianer in Guayana und West Indien. Ibero. Amer. Archiv., vol. 7, pp. 295–305.

GLI ABORIGENI DELLA GUIANA INGELESE.

1934. L'Universo, Florencia, vol. 15, pp. 452–453.

GOEJE, C. H. DE.

See DE GOEJE, C. H.

GOELDI, EMILIO A.

1896. Estado atual dos conhecimentos sobre os indios do Brasil. Bol. Mus. Paraense, vol. 2, pp. 397–418.

1897. Eine Naturforscherfahrt nach dem Litoral des südlichen Guyana zwischen Oyapock und Amazonenstrom. Petermanns Mitt., vol. 43, pp. 59–68, 107–113.

1900. Excavações archeologicas en 1895. Executadas pelo Museu Paraense no Littoral da Guayana Brazileira entre Oyapock' e Amazonas. Pt. I. Memorias do Museu Paraense de Historia Natural e Ethnographia. Pará. (*Rev. in* Globus, Sept. 8, 1900, pp. 136–140.)

See also Guedes, Aureliano Pinto L.

GOLDMAN, IRVING.

n.d.   Field notes on the Cubeo. MS.

GÓMARA, FRANCISCO LÓPEZ DE.

1852. Primera parte de la historia general de las Indias. Historiadores primitivos de Indians, vol. 1, pp. 157–294. Madrid. (Bibl. de autores expañoles, vol. 22.)

GOMES, VICENTE FERREIRA.

1862. Itinerario da cidade da Palma, em Goyaz á cidade de Belém no Pará. Rev. Inst. Hist., vol. 25, pp. 485–513.

GONÇALVES DA FONSECA, JOSÉ.

1826. Navegação feita da cidade do Gran Para até a boca do Rio de Madeira . . . Collecção de noticias para a historia e geografia das nações ultramarinas que vivem nos dominios portuguezes ou que lhes são visinhas, vol. 4, No. 1, pp. 1–141. Lisbon.

1874. Primeira exploração dos rios Madeira e Guaporé . . . em 1749. *In* Mendes de Almeida, Candido, editor, Memorias para a historia do extincto estado do Maranhão, vol. 2, Rio de Janeiro.

GONDIM, JOAQUIM.

1938. Etnografia indígena (estudos realizados em várias regiões do Amazonas, no periodo de 1921 a 1926) . . . Ceará.

GONZÁLEZ SUÁREZ, FEDERICO.

1890–1903. Historia general de la república del Ecuador. 9 vols. Quito.

1904. Prehistoria ecuatoriana: Ligeras reflexiones sobre las razas indígenas, que poblan antiguamente el territorio actual de la República del Ecuador. Quito.

GOREAUD, JEAN.

1934. Les derniers Indiens guyanais. Regards sur le monde, No. 25, pp. 15–17 (17 mai 1934).

Göring, Eulogio.
1877. Informe al Supremo Gobierno del Perú, sobre la expedición á los valles de Paucartambo en 1873, al mando del coronel D. Baltazar La Torre. Lima(?).

Goslings, B. M.
1935. De Indianen en Boschnegers van Suriname. Gids in het Volkenkundig Museum XIII, Koninklijke vereeninging Koloniaal Instituut. Amsterdam.

Gosse, Philip. See Labat, Jean Baptiste, 1931.

Grain, José Ma.
1942. Pueblos primitivos—Los Machiguengas. Congr. Int. Amer., sess. 27, Lima, 1939, vol. 2, pp. 239–244.

Gras and Constant. See Constant and Gras.

Grasserie, Raoul de la.
1890. De la famille linguistique Pano. Congr. Int. Amer., sess. 7, Berlin, 1888, pp. 438–449.
1892. Esquisse d'une grammaire et d'un vocabulaire baniva. Congr. Int. Amer., sess. 8, Paris, 1890, pp. 616–641.

Grillet, Jean, and Béchamel, Francis.
1698. A journal of the travels . . . into Guiana in the year 1674. In Voyages and discoveries in South America, pt. 3, London.
See also Labat, Jean Baptiste, 1730, vol. 3, pp. 134–350, and vol. 4, pp. 345–425.

Groeteken, Autbert.
1907. Bischof Armentia O. F. M. und die Erforschung des Rio Madre de Dios. Anthropos, vol. 2, pp. 730–734.

Grubb, Kenneth G.
1927. The lowland Indians of Amazonia; a survey of the location and religious condition of the Indians of Colombia, Venezuela, the Guianas, Ecuador, Peru, Brazil, and Bolivia. London.

Grupe y Thode, G.
1890. Ueber den Rio Blanco und die anwohenden Indianer. Globus, vol. 57, pp. 251–254. Reprinted from Rev. Mensual Soc. Geogr. Rio de Janeiro.

Guajará, Barão de (Raiol, Domingos Antonio).
1896. Historia Colonial do Pará. Rev. Soc. Estud. Paraenses, vol. 2, Belém.

Guedes, Aureliano Pinto Lima.
1896. Relatoria sobre uma missão ethnographica e archeologica aos rios Maracá e Anauerápucú, dirigido ao Dr. E. A. Goeldi, Director do Museu. Bol. Mus. Goeldi, vol. 2, pp. 42–64.

Guianas Boundary.
1890. The Guayana boundary dispute official report. Washington.

Guillaume, H.
1890. Recent explorations in Peru and Bolivia. Scot. Geogr. Mag., vol. 6, pp. 234–245.

Guimarães, Conego José da Silva.
1865. Memoria sobre os usos, costumes, linguagem dos Appiacás, e descobrimento de novas minas na Provincia de Mato Grosso. Rev. Inst. Hist., vol. 6, pp. 305–325. (2nd. ed.)

Gumilla, Joseph.
1791. Historia natural, civil y geografica de las naciones situadas en las riveras del rio Orinoco. 2 vols. Barcelona. (1st ed., Madrid, 1741.)

HAENKE, THADDÄUS (THADEO, TADEO).
1900. Noticia de la vida y trabajos científicos de Tadeo Haenke . . . Descripción geográfica, física é histórica de las montañas habitadas de la nación de Indios Yuracarées. Parte más septentrional de la Provincia de Cochabamba. An. Bibl., vol. 1, pp. 172–185.

HAMY, E. T.
1873. Nouveaux renseignements sur les indiens jivaros. Rev. Anthrop. ser. 1, vol. 2, pp. 385–397.

HANCOCK, JOHN.
1835. Observations on the climate, soil and productions of British Guiana . . . London. (2nd ed. 1840, London.)

HANSON, EARL. P.
1933. Social regression in the Orinoco and Amazon Basins. Geogr. Rev., vol. 23, pp. 578–598.
1938. Journey to Manáos. New York.

HARCOURT, ROBERT.
1613. A relation of a voyage to Guiana. London. (2nd ed. 1626, London; also in works issued by the Hakluyt Society, 2nd ser., No. 60, 1928, London.)

HARDENBURG, WALTER E.
1910. The Indians of the Putumayo, Upper Amazon. Man, vol. 10, pp. 134–138.
1912. The Putumayo, the devil's paradise; travels in the Peruvian Amazon region and an account of the atrocities committed upon the Indians therein. London.

HARLOW, VINCENT T.
1928. El Dorado and the way thither. Introduction to Raleigh, Walter, The discoverie of the large and bewtiful empire of Guiana, pp. XIV–XCVI. London.

HARTSINCK, JAN JACOB.
1770. Beschryving van Guiana, de wilde kust, in Zuid-America. 2 vols. Amsterdam.
1893. The Indians of Guiana. Timehri, n.s., vol. 7, pp. 44–74.

HARTT, CHARLES FREDERICK.
1871. The ancient Indian pottery of Marajó, Brazil. The American Naturalist, vol. 5, pp. 259–271.
1876. Notas sobre algumas tangas de barro cosido da ilha de Marajó. Archiv. Mus. Nac. Rio de Janeiro, vol. 1, pp. 21–25.
1885. Contribuições para a ethnologia do Valle do Amazonas. Archiv. Mus. Nac. Rio de Janeiro, vol. 6, pp. 1–174.
    See also Anonymous, MS. b., Vocabulario Portuguez—Lingua geral—Maué.

HASEMAN, J. D.
1912. Some notes on the Pawumwa Indians of South America. Amer. Anthrop., n.s., vol. 14, pp. 333–349.

HASSEL, JORGE M. VON.
1902. Vocabulario Aguaruna. Bol. Soc. Geogr. Lima, vol. 12, pp. 73–86.
1905. Las tribus salvajes de la región Amazónica del Perú. Bol. Soc. Geogr. Lima, vol. 17, pp. 27–73.

HEATH, EDWIN R.
1883. Dialects of Bolivian Indians. A philological contribution from material gathered during three years' residence in the Department of Beni, in Bolivia. Kansas City Rev. Sci. Industry, vol. 6, No. 12, pp. 679, 687.

HEATON, W. C. ED. *See* MEDINA, JOSÉ TORIBIO, 1934.

HEGER, FRANZ.
 1916. Sonderbar stilisierte Menschenfigur auf der Innenseite einter seltlichen Endplanke eines Holzkanus aus Franzosisch Guayana. Mitt. Anthròp. Gesell. Wien, Rep. vol. 46 (3rd series vol. 16).
 1924. Muyrakitãs. Congr. Int. Amer., sess. 20, Rio de Janeiro, 1922, vol. 1, pp. 255–260 and 7 plates.

HENNEPIN, LOUIS. *See* LA BORDE, SIEUR DE, 1704.

HENRY, VICTOR, *See* ADAM, LUCIEN, and HENRY, VICTOR, 1880.

HERIARTE, MAURICIO DE.
 1874. Descripção do estado do Maranhão, Para, Corupá e Rio das Amazonas. Vienna.

HERMESSEN, J. L.
 1917. A journey on the Río Zamora, Ecuador. Geogr. Rev., vol. 4, pp. 434–449.

HERNÁNDEZ, PABLO.
 1913. Misiones del Paraguay. Organización social de las doctrinas guaraníes de la Compañía de Jesús. 2 vols. Barcelona.

HERNÁNDEZ, PEDRO.
 1852. Comentarios de Alvar Nuñez Cabeza de Vaca. Biblioteca de autores españoles. Historiadores primitivos de Indias. Vol. 1, pp. 549–599. Madrid.
 1891. The commentaries of Alvar Nuñez Cabeza de Vaca. The Hakluyt Society, No. 81. London.

HERNDON, WILLIAM LEWIS, and GIBBON, LARDNER.
 1853–54. Exploration of the valley of the Amazon. . . . 2 vols. (Vol. 1 by Herndon; vol. 2 by Gibbon.) Washington.

HERRERA Y TORDESILLAS, ANTONIO DE.
 1601–15. Historia general de los hechos de los castellanos en las islas i tierra firme del mar océano. 4 vols. Madrid.

HERRERO, ANDRÉS.
 1834. Doctrina y oraciones cristianas en lengua mosetena . . . traducidas en español palabra por palabra. Rome.

HERSKOVITS, M. J. *See* PANHUYS, L. C. VAN, MODRINI, A., and HERSKOVITS, M. J., 1934.

HERVÁS Y PANDURO, LORENZO.
 1800–05. Catálogo de las lenguas de las naciones conocidas, y numeración, división, y clases de estas según la diversidad de sus idiomas y dialectos. 6 vols. Madrid.

HERZOG, THEODOR.
 1913. Vom urwald zu den gletschern der Kordillere; zwei forschungsreisen in Bolivia. Stuttgart.

HESHUYSEN, F. VAN.
 1925–26. Mémoire sur les Indiens à Suriname, 22 sept. 1800. Uit he Surinamer-chief in London (Surinam, 1801 to 1804, vol. 2, Colonial office transmissions No. 71. Miscellaneous). De West-Indische Gids, vol. 7, pp. 346–349.

HESTERMANN, FERDINAND.
 1910. Die Pano-Sprachen und ihre Beziehungen. Congr. Int. Amer., sess. 16., Vienna, 1908, vol. 2, pp. 645–650.
 1913. Nachtrag zur Quellenliteratur der Panosprachen, Bolivien. Anthropos, vol. 8, p. 1144.
 1914. Die Schreibweise der Pano-vokabularien. Journ. Soc. Amér. Paris, n.s., vol. 11, pp. 21–33.

HILHOUSE, WILLIAM.

1832. Notices of the Indians settled in the interior of British Guiana. Journ. Roy. Geogr. Soc., vol. 2, pp. 227–249.

1834 a. Journal of a voyage up the Massaroony in 1831. Journ. Roy. Geogr. Soc., vol. 4, pp. 25–40.

1834 b. Memoir on the Warow land of British Guiana. Journ. Roy. Geogr. Soc., vol. 4, pp. 321–332.

HINTERMANN, HEINRICH.

1925. Beitrag zur Ethnographie der Kuluena- und Kulisevu- Indianer. Verhandl. Schweiz. Naturf. Gesell., vol. 106. Hanresversammlung vom 8 bis II, 1925, Aarau, II Teil, pp. 176–178.

1926. Unter Indianern und Reisenschlangen. Zürich and Leipzig.

HITCHCOCK, C. B. *See* TATE, GEORGE HENRY HAMILTON, and HITCHCOCK, C. B.

HOEHNE, FREDERICO C.

1937. Botanica e agricultura no Brasil no seculo XVI. Bibl. Pedag. Brasil., ser. 5a, Brasiliana, vol. 71.

HOELLER, ALFREDO.

1932. Grammatik der Guarayo-sprache. 1. Aufl. Guarayos . . . Guarayo-deutsches wörterbuch . . . 1. Aufl. Guarayos . . . Stuttgart.

HOLDEN, W. H.

1938. Civilization and sudden death.

HOLDRIDGE, DESMOND.

1931. Notes on an exploratory journey in Southeastern Venezuela. Geogr. Rev., vol. 21, pp. 373–378.

1939. Feudal Island. New York.

1940. Scientific exploration of the Gran Sabana, Venezuela. Geogr. Rev., vol. 30, pp. 319–320.

HOLLOWAY, H. L.

1932. Por la región del río Napo. Bol. Soc. Geogr. Lima, vol. 49, pp. 221–233.

HOLMES, SIR. W. H., and CAMPBELL, W. H.

1858. Report of an expedition to explore a route by the rivers Waini, Barama, and Cuyuni, to the goldfields of Caratal, and thence by Upata to the Orinoco. Proc. Roy. Geogr. Soc., vol. 2, pp. 154–157.

HOLTEN, HERMANN VON.

1877. Das Land der Yurakarer und dessen Bewohner. Zeit. Ethnol., vol. 9, pp. 105–115.

HORNBOSTEL, ERICH MARIA VON.

1923. Musik der Makuschi, Taulipáng und Yekuaná. *In* Koch-Grünberg, Theodore, Vom Roroima zum Orinoco, vol. 3, pp. 397–442. Stuttgart.

HÖRSCHELMANN, WERNER VON.

1918–20. Die Brasiliensammlung Spix und Martius. Berichte des Museums für Völkerkunde (Ethnog. Mus.) in München, vol. 8, *in* Münchner Jarhbuch d. bildenden Kunst.

HORTA BARBÓSA, NICOLAU BUENO.

1916. Exploração e levantamento dos rios Anary e Machadinho . . . Commissão de Linhas telegraphicas estrategicas de Matto-Grosso ao Amazonas. Publicação 48. Issued as Annexo No. 2 to the Relatorio of the Commission. Rio de Janeiro.

HÜBNER, GEORG.
1898. Reise in das Quellgebiet des Orinoco. Deutsche Rundschan für Geograpie und Statistik, vol. 20, pp. 14–20, 55-65.
1907. Die Yauapery. Zeit. Ethnol., vol. 39, pp. 225–248. Kritisch bearbeitet und mit Einleitung versehen von Theodor Koch-Grünberg.
See also Koch-Grünberg, Theodor, and Hübner, Georg, 1908.

HUMBOLDT, ALEXANDER VON.
1814. Researches, concerning the institutions and monuments of the ancient inhabitants of America; with descriptions and views. (Tr. from the French by Helen Maria Williams.) 2 vols. London.
1852–53. Personal narrative of travels to the equinoctial regions of the New Continent, 1799–1804. 3 vols.
1881. Personal narrative of travels to the equinoctial regions of America, during the years 1799–1804. 3 vols. London.

HUMBOLDT, ALEXANDER VON, and BONPLAND, A.
1807–35. Voyage aux régions équinoxiales du nouveau continent, fait in 1799, 1800, 1801, 1802, 1803, et 1804. 23 vols. Paris.

HYAZINTH, P.
1911–12. In Katholische Missionen, pp. 297–299.

IDIOMA SCHIPIBO. (Vocabulario del idioma shipibo del Ucayali.) Bol. Soc. Geogr. La Paz, vol. 1, pp. 43–91, 1898.

IGNACIO DE OLIVEIRA, AVELINO.
1935. Atraves da Guiana Brasileira pelo rio Erepecurú, Estado do Pará. Bol. Serv. Geol. Min. Brasil, No. 31.
1929. Bacia do Rio Branco (Estado do Amazonas). Bol. Serv. Geol. Min. Brasil, No. 37.

IGUALADA, FRANCISCO DE, and CASTELLVÍ, MARCELINO DE.
1940. Clasificación y estadística de las lenguas habladas en el Putumayo, Caquetá y Amazonas. Amazonia Colombiana Americanista. Centro Investig. "Cileac," vol. 1, Nos. 2–3, pp. 92–101. Sibundoy.

IHERING, HERMANN VON.
1895. A civilisação prehistorica do Brasil meridional. Rev. Mus. Paulista, vol. 1, pp. 33–159.
1904. Archeologia comparativa do Brasil. Rev. Mus. Paulista, vol. 6, pp. 519–580.
1906. The anthropology of the State of São Paulo, Brazil. São Paulo.

IM THURN, EVERARD FERDINAND.
1882. On the animism of the Indians of British Guiana. Journ. Roy. Anthrop. Inst., vol. 11, pp. 360–380.
1883. Among the Indians of Guiana. London.
1884. Notes on West Indian stone implements; and other Indian relics. Timehri, vol. 3, pp. 103–137.
1890. Primitive games. (Reprinted from Timehri.)
1892. British Guiana; the North-Western District. Proc. Roy. Geogr. Soc., vol. 14, pp. 665–687.
1934 Thoughts, talks and tramps. London.

IRAZOLA, F. FRANCISCO.
1916. Viaje de exploración por la zona central de infieles: Apurimac, Ene, Perené, Pangoa. Bol. Soc. Geogr. Lima, vol. 32, pp. 183–196.

IRIBARNE, EVA A.
1937. Algunos vasos indígenas de las margenes del Paraná inferior. Rel. Soc. Arg. Antrop., vol. 1, pp. 181–190.
ITINERARIO DEL VIAJE DE IQUITOS AL RIO CURARAI I AL RIO NAPO . . .
1904. Larrabure, vol. 17, pp. 535–543.
ITINERARIOS DE LOS VIAJES DE RAIMONDI EN EL PERU.
1905. Bol. Soc. Geogr. Lima, vol. 17, pp. 241–263, 361–447.
IZAGUIRRE ISPIZUA, BERNARDINO.
1922–29. Historia de las misiones franciscanas y narración de los progresos de la geografia en el oriente del Perú . . . 1619–1921. Lima.
1927. Descripción histórico-etnográfica de algunas tribus orientales del Perú. Bol. Soc. Geogr. Lima, vol. 44, pp. 5–36.
IZIKOWITZ, KARL GUSTAV.
1932. Les instruments de musique des Indiens Uro-Chipaya. (Tr. from Swedish by A. Métraux.) Rev. Inst. Etnol. Univ. Nac. Tucumán, vol. 2, pp. 263–291.
1935. Musical and other sound instruments of the South American Indians: a comparative ethnographical study. Göteborgs Kungl. Vetenskaps— och Vitterhets—Samhälles Handlingar, 5th följden, ser. A, Band 5, No. 1. Göteborg.
JAHN ALFREDO.
1927. Los aborígenes del occidente de Venezuela, su historia, etnografía, y afinidades lingüísticas. Caracas.
1929. Aspecto físico y orígenes etnicos de Venezuela. Sevilla.
1935. Las exploraciones etnológicas de Venezuela y sus problemas. Cultura Nacional, vol. 1, pp. 89–97.
1939. Nombres geográficos indígenas de Venezuela. Bol. Soc. Venezolana Cienc. Nat., vol. 6, pp. 1–4.
JANSEN, PIETRO GERARDO.
1931. Gli indios del Venezuela. La vie d'Italia e dell' America latina, vol. 8, pp. 1269–1274.
JARQUE, FRANCISCO. See XARQUE, FRANCISCO.
JENMAN, GEORGE SAMUEL.
1907. To Kaieteur. Georgetown.
JIJÓN Y CAAMAÑO, JACINTO.
1919. Contribución al conocimiento de las lenguas indígenas que se hablaron en el Ecuador interandino y occidental con anterioridad a la conquista española. Bol. Soc. Ecuatoriana Estud. Hist., vol. 2, No. 6, pp. 340–413.
1940–41. El Ecuador interandino y occidental antes de la conquista Castellana. 2 vols. Quito.
JIMÉNEZ DE LA ESPADA, MARCOS.
1892. Una antigualla peruna. (Tipografia de Manuel Genes Hernández, Impresor de la Real Casa.) Madrid.
1896. Revista geografica de Madrid.
1897. La jornada del capitán Alonso Mercadillo à los indios Chupachos é Isacaicingas. Impr. de Fortanet, Madrid. (Reprinted from Boletín de la Sociedad geográphica de Madrid, vol. 37, 1895.)
    See also Noticias auténticas del famoso Rio Marañon y Mision . . . de la provincia de Quito . . . 1889–1892; Relaciones geográphicas de Indias; and Vocabulario general de la Lengua . . .
JIMÉNEZ SEMINARIO, AUG.
1924. Bemerkungen über den Stamm der Bora . . . am Putumayo. Trans. from Spanish by K. Th. Preuss. Zeit. Ethnol., vol. 56, pp. 83–93.

JIVAROS DI MENDEZ E GUALAQUIZA ECUATORE. TORINO. 1906.

JOEST, WILHELM.
1893. Ethnographisches und verwandtes aus Guayana. Int. Archiv. Ethnogr., Suppl. to Band 5.

JOHNSON, GEORGE R.
1930. Peru from the air. Amer. Geogr. Soc. Spec. Publ. No. 12.

JORNADA DE OMAGUA Y DORADO.
1909. Nueva biblioteca de autores españoles, vol. 15. Historiadores primitivos de Indias, vol. 2. Madrid.

JOURNAL OF A TRIP FROM ST. THOME DE ANGOSTURA, IN SPANISH GUAYANA, TO THE CAPUCHIN MISSIONS OF THE CARONI.
1820. Quart. Journ. Sci., vol. 8, pp. 260–287; vol. 9, pp. 1–32 and map.

JOSSELIN DE JONG, JAN P. B. DE.
1919–20. Karaiben. Indie, vol. 3, pp. 243, 272, 291, 307.
1919–21. Arowakken. Indie, vol. 3, pp. 403, 451; vol. 4, pp. 3, 19, 35, 83, 99, 131, 451, 467, 483, 499, 515, 547, 563, 579, 595, 611, 723.

JOYCE, THOMAS ATHOL.
1912. South American archaeology. London.

KAPPLER, AUGUST.
1854. Sechs jahre in Surinam. Stuttgart.
1881. Holländisch-Guiana. Erlebnisse und Erfahrungen während eines 43 jährigen Aufenthalts in der Kolonie Surinam. Stuttgart.
1887. Surinam, sein Land, seine Natur, Bevölkerung und seine Kultur-verhältnisse mit bezug auf kolonisation. Stuttgart.

KARSTEN, RAFAEL.
1920 a. Contributions to the sociology of the Indian tribes of Ecuador. Acta Acad. Åboensis, Humaniora, vol. 1, No. 3.
1920 b. Beiträge zur Sittengeschichte der südamerikanischen Indianer. Acta. Acad. Åboensis, Humaniora, vol. 1, No. 4.
1921. La lengua de los Indios Jibaros (Shuara) del Oriente del Ecuador. Gramática vocabulario y muestras de la prosa y poesía. Helsingfors.
1935. The head-hunters of Western Amazonas; the life and culture of the Jibaro Indians of eastern Ecuador and Peru. Soc. Sci. Fennica, Commentationes Humanarum, Litterarum, vol. 8, No. 1.

KATE, HERMAN FREDERIK CAREL TEN. See TEN KATE, HERMAN FREDERIK CAREL.

KATZER, FRIEDRICH.
1901. Zur ethnographie des Rio Tapajós. Globus, vol. 79, pp. 37-41.

KELLER-LEUZINGER, FRANZ.
1874. The Amazon and Madeira rivers. London.

KEMYS, LAWRENCE.
1811. A relation of the second voyage to Guiana, performed and written in the yeere 1596. In Hakluyt, Richard, Collection of early voyages, travels and discoveries. London, 1809–12, vol. 4, pp. 160–188.

KERSTEN, LUDWIG.
1905. Die Indianerstämme des Gran Chaco bis zum Ausgange des 18. Jahrhundert. Ein Beitrag zur historischen ethnographie Südamerikas. Int. Archiv. Ethnogr., vol. 17, pp. 1–75.

KESSLER, C. K.
1930–31. De Bevolking van onze west. De Indianen. Tropisch Nederland, pp. 275–323. Amsterdam.
1936–37. Zwarte en roode bewoners der binnenlanden van Suriname. Tropisch Nederland, pp. 232–237, 247–251. Amsterdam.

KEYE, OTTO.
1672. Kurtzer Entwurff von Neu-Niederland und Guajana. (Tr. from the Dutch ed. of 1659.) Leipzig.
KEYMIS, LAURENCE. See KEMYS, LAWRENCE.
KILLIP, ELLSWORTH P., and SMITH, ALBERT C.
1931. The use of fish poisons in South America. Smithsonian Ann. Rep. for 1930, pp. 401–408.
KINDER, P. LEOPOLDO VON.
1936. Introducción a la gramática y vocabulario de la Lengua Huitota. Pasto.
KIRCHHOFF, PAUL.
1931. Die Verwandtschaftsorganisation der Urwaldstämme Südamerikas. Zeit. Ethnol., vol. 63, pp. 85–193.
1932. Verwandtschaftsbezeichnungen und Verwandtenheirat. Zeit. Ethnol., vol. 64, pp. 41–71.
KIRKE, HENRY.
1898. Twenty-five years in British Guiana. London.
KISSENBERTH, WILHELM.
1912. Über die hauptsächlichsten Ergebnisse der Araguaya-Reise. Zeit. Ethnol., vol. 44, pp. 36–59.
KLETKE, H.
1857. Reise Seiner Königlichen Hoheit des Prinzen Adalbert von Preussen nach Brasilien. Berlin.
KLÜPFEL, KARL AUGUST, EDITOR.
1859. N. Federmanns und H. Staden Reisen in Südamerica 1529 bis 1555. Stuttgart.
KOCH-GRÜNBERG, THEODOR.
1900. Zum Animismus der südamerikanischen Indianer. Int. Archiv. Ethnogr., Suppl. to vol. 13.
1902. Die Apiaká-Indianer (Rio Tapajós, Mato Grosso). Zeit. Ethnol., vol. 34, pp. 350–379.
1905. Anfänge der Kunst im Urwald. Indianer-handzeichnungen auf seinen Reisen in Brasilian gesammelt. Berlin.
1905–08. Indianertypen aus dem Amazonasgebiet. 3 vols. Berlin.
1906 a. Die Indianerstämme am oberen Rio Negro und Yapurá. Zeit. Ethnol., vol. 28, pp. 166–205.
1906 b. Die Makú. Mit fünf Abbildungen nach Aufnahmen des Verfassers. Anthropos, vol. 1, pp. 877–906.
1906 c. Die Maskentänze der Indianer des oberen Rio Negro und Yapurá. Archiv. f. Anthrop., n.s., vol. 4, pp. 293–298.
1906 d. Les Indiens Ouitotos: étude lingustique. Journ. Soc. Amér. Paris, n.s., vol. 3, No. 2, pp. 157–189.
1907. Südamerikanische Felszeichnungen. Berlin.
1908. Die Hianákoto-Umáua. Anthropos, vol. 3, pp. 83–124, 297–333, 952–982.
1909–10. Zwei jahre unter den Indianern. Reisen in Nordwest-Brasilien, 1903–1905. 2 vols. Berlin.
1910 a. Die Miránya (Rio Yapurá, Amazonas). Zeit. Ethnol., vol. 42, pp. 896–914.
1910 b. Die Uitóto-Indianer. Weitere Beiträge zu ihrer Sprache nach einer Wörterliste von Hermann Schmidt. Journ. Soc. Amér. Paris, n.s., vol. 7, pp. 61–83.
1911. Aruak-sprachen Nordwestbrasiliens und der angrenzenden Gebiete. Mitt. Anthrop. Gesell. Wien, vol. 41 (ser. 3, vol. 11), pp. 33–143.

1913 a. Meine Reise durch Nord-Brasilien zum Orinoco, 1911–1913. Zeit. Gesell. f. Erkunde, pp. 665–694.

1913 b. Abschluss meiner Reise durch Nordbrasilien zum Orinico, mit besonderer Berücksichtigung der von mir besuchten Indianerstämme. Zeit. Ethnol., vol. 45, pp. 448–474.

1913–16. Die Betóya-Sprachen Nordwestbrasiliens und der angrenzenden Gebiete. Anthropos, vol. 8, pp. 944–977; vol. 9, pp. 151–195, 569–589, 812–832; vols. 10–11, pp. 114–158, 421–449.

1914. Ein Beitrag zur Sprache der Ipuriná-Indianer (Rio Purus, Brasilien). Journ. Soc. Amér. Paris, n.s., vol. 11, pp. 57–96.

1918. Ueber die Kultur der Indianer Guayanas. Jahrbuch des staetischen Museums für Völkerkunde zu Leipzig, vol. 7, pp. 63–66.

1920. Indianermärchen aus Südamerika. Jena. (Also 1927 ed. Jena.)

1922. Die Völkergruppierung zwischen Rio Branco, Orinoco, Rio Negro und Yapurá. Festschrift Eduard Seler, pp. 205–266. Stuttgart.

1923 a. Vom Roroima zum Orinoco, Ergebnisse einer Reise in Nordbrasilien und Venezuela in den jahren 1911–1913. Vol. 3. Stuttgart. (5 vols. pub. Berlin, 1917–28.)

1923 b. Zwei Jahre bei den Indianern Nordwest-Brasiliens. Stuttgart.

1932. Wörterlisten "Tupy," Maué und Purúborá. Journ. Soc. Amér. Paris, n.s., vol. 24, pp. 31–50.

1934. Am Roroima bei meinen Freunden, den Indianern vom rosigen fels. Leipzig. (This is a reprint of vol. 1, chs. 1–8, of Vom Roroima zum Orinoco . . .)

See also Snethlage, Emil Heinrich, and Koch-Grünberg, Theodor.

KOCH-GRÜNBERG, THEODOR, and HÜBNER, GEORG.

1908. Die Makuschí und Wapischána. Zeit. Ethnol., vol. 40, pp. 1–44.

KOENIGSWALD, GUSTAV VON.

1908. Die Cayuás. Globus, vol. 93, pp. 376–381.

KOK, P. See RIVET, PAUL, and FATHERS KOK, P., and TASTEVIN, CONSTANT.

KOPPEL, B. See STÜBEL, ALFONS, REISS, W., and KOPPEL, B.

KOSERITZ, CARLOS VON.

1885. Bilder aus Brasilien. Leipzig and Berlin.

KRAUSE, FRITZ.

1911. In den wildnissen Brasiliens; Bericht und Ergebnisse der Leipziger Araguaya-Expedition, 1908. Leipzig.

1936 a. Die Waura-Indianer des Schingu-Quellgebietes, Zentral-Brasilien. Mitt. Gesell. f. Völkerkunde, No. 7, pp. 14–31.

1936 b. Die Yaruma- und Arawine-Indianer Zentralbrasiliens. Baessler-archiv., vol. 19, pp. 32–44.

1936 c. Forschungsaufgaben im Schingu-Quellgebiet, Zentrallbrasilien. Tagungsberiche der Gesellschaft für Völkerkunde in Leipzig. Bericht über die 2 tagung, pp. 160–172.

1939. Gegenstände der Waura-Indianer, Schingu-Quellgebiet, Zentral Brasilien. Mitt. der Deutschen Gesell. f. Völkerkunde, No. 9, pp. 25–40.

KRIEGER, HERBERT W.

1935. Indian cultures of northeastern South America. Smithsonian Ann. Rep. for 1934, pp. 401–421.

KRIEGK, GEORG LUDWIG. See BACH, MORIZ, 1838, 1929.

KRICKEBERG, WALTER.
  1922. Die Völker Südamerikas. *In* Illustrierte Völkerkunde, George Buschan,
        ed. Stuttgart.
KRUSE, ALBERT.
  1934. Mundurucú moieties. Primitive Man, vol. 7, No. 4, pp. 51–57. (Correc-
        tions and additions to this paper are in vol. 10, No. 1, p. 16.)
  1935. Über die Wanderungen der Mundurucú in Südamerika. Anthropos, vol.
        30, pp. 831–836.
        See also Missionarios Franciscanos.
KRUSEMAN, A. C. *See* FOCKE, H. C., 1858.
KUNERT, AUGUST.
  1890. Rio grandenser Alterthümer. Zeit. Ethnol., vol. 22, pp. 31–37.
  1891. Das Alter der im Gegiete des Rio Cahy und Forromecco gefundenen
        Steinwaffen. Zeit. Ethnol., vol. 23, pp. 339–345.
  1892. Südbrasilianische Höhlen und Rückstände der früheren Bewohner. Zeit.
        Ethnol., vol. 24, pp. 502–504.
KUNIKE, HUGO.
  1911. Ethnographisches und Archäologisches aus der Guayaqui-Region.
        Amtliche Berichte aus der königlichen Kunstammlung, 22 Jahrgang,
        No. 7. Berlin.
LABAT, JEAN BAPTISTE.
  1730. Voyage du chevalier Des Marchais en Guinée, isles voisines, et à Cayenne,
        fait en 1725, 1726 and 1727. 4 vols. Paris.
  1931. The memoirs of Père Labat 1693–1705. Tr. and abridged by Philip
        Gosse. London.
LA BORDE, SIEUR DE.
  1704. Voyage qui contient un relation exacte de l'origine, moeurs, coûtumes,
        réligion, guerres et voyages des Caraibes, sauvages des isles Antilles
        de l'Amerique, faite par le Sieur de la Borde, employé à la conversion
        des Caraibes, et tirée du cabinet de Monsr. Blondel. A. Leide, Chez
        P. van de Aa, 1704. *In* Hennepin, Louis, Voyage ou Nouvelle
        decouverte, pp. 517–604. Amsterdam.
  1886. History of the origin, customs, religion, wars, and travels of the Caribs,
        savages of the Antilles in America. Tr. by G. J. A. Bosch-Reitz.
        Timehri, vol. 5, pp. 224–254.
LABRÉ, COLONEL.
  1889. Colonel Labre's explorations in the region between the Beni and Madre
        de Dios rivers and the Purus. Proc. Roy. Geogr. Soc., n.s., vol. 11,
        pp. 496–502.
LACERDA E ALMEIDA, FRANCISCO JOSÉ MARIA DE.
  1841. Diario da viagem do Dr. Francisco José de Lacerda e Almeida pelas
        capitanias do Parà, Rio Negro, Matto-Grosso, Cuyabà, e S. Paulo,
        nos annos de 1780 a 1790. São Paulo.
LA CONDAMINE, CHARLES MARIE DE.
  1745. Relation abrégée d'un voyage fait dans l'interieur de l'Amérique Méridio-
        nale. Paris. (1st English ed., 1747, London.)
LA CROIX, ABBÉ DE.
  1904. Déscription . . . de la Guyane Française. Journ. Soc. Amér. Paris, n.s.,
        vol. 1, pp. 133–151.

LAET, JOANNES DE.
1625. Nieuvve Wereldt, ofte Beschrijvinghe van West-Indien, wt veelderhande Schriften ende Aen-Teeckeninghen van verscheyden Natien by een versamelt door Ioannes de Laet. Leyden. (2nd Dutch ed., 1630, Leyden; Latin ed., 1633, enlarged; French ed., 1640, Leyden, tr. from 1633 Latin ed.)
1644. Historie of te Iaerlijck Verhael van de Verrichtinghen der Geoctroyeerde West-Indische compagnie. Leyden. (Portuguese tr. pub. in "Officinas graphicas da Biblioteca nacional," 1916–25, Rio de Janeiro.)
1899. Mapa. Rio Branco: Frontières entre le Brésil et la Guyane française. Atlas. No. 60. Paris.
    See also Rio-Branco, Barão de, 1899.

LAFONE-QUEVEDO, SAMUEL A.
1905. La lengua Leca de los ríos Mapirí y Beni según los mss. de los PP. Cardús y Herrero. An. Soc. Cient. Argentina, vol. 60, pp. 5–20, 49–64, 97–113, 168–180.
1909. Etnología argentina. La Universidad Nacional de La Plata en el 4th Congreso científico (1st Panamericano), pp. 176–215. Buenos Aires.
1910–11. Las lenguas de tipo guaycurú y chiquito comparadas. Rev. Mus. La Plata, vol. 17 (2nd ser., vol. 4), pp. 7–68.
    See also Armentia, Nicolás, 1902 and 1906; *and* Schmidel, Ulrich, 1903.

LAGO, ANTONIA F. P. DO.
1822. Estudo historico e geografico da Provincia do Maranhão. Lisbôa.

LA JORNADA DEL CAPITÁN ALONSO MERCADILLO. *See* JIMÉNEZ DE LA ESPADA, MARCOS, 1897.

LANDRÉ, DH. *See* FOCKE, H. C., LANDRÉ, DH., SYPESTEYN, C. A. VAN, and DU-MONTIER, F. A. C., 1855–58.

LANGE, ALGOT.
1912. In the Amazon jungle; adventures in remote parts of the upper Amazon River, including a sojourn among cannibal Indians. New York and London.
1914. The lower Amazon. New York and London.

LANGLOIS, LOUIS.
1940. El Valle del Utucubamba. Mus. Nac., Lima.

LANS, W. H.
1842. Bijdrage tot de kennis der Kolonie Suriname. 's Gravenhage.

LAS CASAS, ENRIQUE DE.
1935. Monografía de la provincia de Huallaga. Bol. Soc. Geogr. Lima, vol. 52, pp. 335–354.

LASCH, R.
1910. Zur südamerikanischen Amazonensage. Mitt. Anthrop. Gesell. Wien, vol. 2, pp. 278–289.

LAUREANO DE LA CRUZ.
1900. Nuevo descubrimiento del rió de Marañon llamado de las Amazonas (1651). Madrid. (From a ms. in the Biblioteca Nacional, Madrid, written in 1653.) ("Saggio di Bibliografia geografica storica etnografica Sanfrancescana por Fr. Marcellino da Cibezza," in edition of 1879.)

LAWNER, HANS N.
1930. Die Cuiapo-Pihiki. Ein neuent deckter Indianerstamm am Orinoco. Der Erdball, vol. 4, pp. 304–306.

LEBLOND, JEAN BAPTISTE.
1813. Voyage aux Antilles, et a l'Amérique meridionale. Commencé 1767 et fini en 1802. Paris.
1814. Description abrégée de la Guyane Française. Paris.

LECLERC, CHARLES. *See* ADAM, LUCIEN, and LECLERC, CHARLES, 1880; and ADAM, LUCIEN, 1890 a.

LEHMANN-NITSCHE, ROBERT.
1924. La astronomía de los Chiriguanos. Rev. Mus. La Plata, vol. 28, pp. 80–102.
1936–37. El avestruz galaxial de los Guaraní. Obra del cincuentenario del Museo de la Plata, vol. 2, pp. 201–205.

LEIGH, CHARLES.
1906. Captaine Charles Leigh his voyage to Guiana and plantation there. *In* Purchase, Samuel, Hakluyt's posthumus or Purchase his pilgrimes . . ., vol. 26, pp. 309–323. Glasgow.

LEITE, SERAFIM.
1943. História da Companhia de Jesus no Brasil. Vol. 3. Rio de Janeiro and Lisbôa.

LELYVELD, TH. VAN.
1919. De kleeding der surnaamsche bevolkingsgroepen in verband met aard en gewoonten. De West-Indische Gids, vol. 1, pp. 247–268, 458–470; vol. 2, pp. 20–34, 125–143.

LEPRIEUR, M.
1834. Voyage dans la Guyane central. Bull. Soc. Géogr. Paris, 2nd ser., vol. 1, pp. 201–229.

LÉRY, JEAN DE.
1880. Histoire d'un voyage fait en la terre du Brésil. Nouvelle édition avec une introduction et des notes par Paul Gaffarel. 2 vols. Paris.

LETTRES ÉDIFIANTES ET CURIEUSES, ÉSCRITES DES MISSIONS ÉTRANGÈRES, PAR QUELQUES MISSIONNAIRES DE LA COMPAGNIE DE JÉSUS. 1780–83. 26 vols. Paris. (Lyon ed., 1819, also cited in this volume.)

LEVEL, ANDRÉS EUSEBIO.
1850. Informe sobre el estado actual de los distritos de reducción de indíjenas Alto Orinoco, Central y Bajo Orinoco, y medidas que reclaman. Caracas.
1873. El Delta del Orinoco tornado de la Esploración al alto bajo Orinoco y central en 1850. Memoria de la Dirección General de Estadistica al Presidente de los Estados Unidos de Venezuela. Vol. 3.

LÉVI-STRAUSS, CLAUDE.
1943 a. The social use of kinship terms among Brazilian Indians. Amer. Anthrop., June.
1943 b. Guerre et commerce chez les Indiens de l'Amerique du Sud. Renaissance, No. 1. New York.
n.d. a. Notes on the Tupí Indians of the Upper Gy-Paraná. MS.
n.d. b. Tribes of the Machado-Guaporé hinterland. MS.

LIMA FIGUEIRÊDO, JOSÉ DE.
1939. Indios do Brasil. Bibl. Pedag. Brasil, ser. 5a, Brasiliana, vol. 163.

LINHARES, MAXIMO.
1913. Os indios do territorio do Acre. Journal do Commercio, domingo 12 de Janeiro. Rio de Janeiro.

LINNÉ, SIGVALD.
1925. The technique of South American ceramics. Göteborgs Kongl. Vet. Vitt. Handl., 4 földjen, vol. 29, No. 5.
1928 a. Archäologische Sammlungen des Gotenburger Museums vom unteren Amazonas. Congr. Int. Amer., sess. 22, Rome, 1926, vol. 1, pp. 583–597.

1928 b. Les recherches archéologiques de Nimuendajú au Brésil. Journ. Soc. Amér. Paris, n.s., vol. 20, pp. 71–91.

1936. A sepulchral urn from Paraguay. Ethnos, vol. 1, pp. 133–136.

1937. Notes on the archaeology of Venezuela. Ethnos, vol. 2, pp. 21–32.

LISANDRO, ALVARADO.
1921. Glosario de voces indígenas de Venezuela. Caracas.

LISTER MAW, HENRY. *See* MAW, HENRY LISTER.

LIZÁRRAGA, REGINALDO DE.
1909. Descripción breve de toda la tierra del Perú, Tucumán, Río de la Plata y Chile. *In* Nueva Bibliotéca de Autores Españoles, vol. 15. Historiadores de Indias, vol. 2, pp. 485–678. Madrid.

LIZER, CARLOS.
1918. Presentación de objetos hechos por los mestizos e indígenas reducidos del oriente boliviano. Physis, vol. 4, p. 128.

LLOSA, ENRIQUE S.
1906. Tribu de los Arazaires. Algunas voces de su dialecto. Bol. Soc. Geogr. Lima, vol. 19, pp. 302–306.

LLOYD, H. E. *See* SPIX, JOHANN BAPTIST VON, and MARTIUS, KARL FREDERICK VON, 1824.

LODARES, BALTASAR DE.
1929–31. Los franciscanos capuchinos en Venezuela. 3 vols. Caracas.

LOHMANN, CHRISTOPH WILHELM, TR. *See* PRUDHOMME, LOUIS MARIE, 1799.

LOMBARD, JESUIT PIERRE AIMÉ.
1928. Recherches sur les tribus indiennes qui occupaient le territoire de la Guyane française vers 1730, d'après les documents de l'époque. Journ. Soc. Amér. Paris, n.s., vol. 20, pp. 121–155.
See also Labat, Jean Baptiste, 1730, vol. 4, pp. 424–681.

LOPES, RAIMUNDO.
1925. Les Indiens Arikêmes. Congr. Int. Amer., sess. 21, Göteborg, 1924, pt. 2, pp. 630–642.

1934. Os Tupis do Gurupy. (Ensaio comparativo). Congr. Int. Amer., sess. 25, La Plata, 1932, vol. 1, pp. 139–171.

LÓPEZ BORREGUERO, RAMÓN.
1875. Los Indios caribes, memorias interesantes de Venezuela. 2 vols. Madrid.

LOPEZ DE ARANJO, FRANCISCO XAVIER.
1884. Relatoria apresentado á assemblea geral legislativa pelo ministro dos negocios estrangeiros . . . Rio de Janeiro.

LÓPEZ, VICTOR M. *See* EXPLORACIÓN DE LA GRAN SABANA, 1939.

LOS SALVAJES DE SAN GABÁN.
1902. Bol. Soc. Geogr. Lima, vol. 11, pp. 353–356.

LOSE BLÄTTER DO CURURU. *See* MISSIONARIOS FRANCISCANOS.

LOTHROP, SAMUEL KIRKLAND.
1932. Indians of the Paraná delta, Argentina. An. N. Y. Acad. Sci., vol. 33, pp. 77–232.

LOUKOTKA, ČESTMÍR.
1929. Le Setá, un nouveau dialecte tupi. Journ. Soc. Amér. Paris, n.s., vol. 21, pp. 373–398.

1932. La familia lingüística Kamakan del Brasil. Rev. Inst. Etnol. Univ. Nac. Tucumán, vol. 2, pp. 493–524.

1939. Linguas indígenas do Brasil. Rev. Arq. Mun. São Paulo, vol. 54.

LOVÉN, SVEN.
1924. Über die Wurzeln der tainischen Kultur . . . Göteborg.

1928. The Orinoco in old Indian times (economy and trade). Congr. Int. Amer., sess. 22, Rome, 1926, vol. 2, pp. 711–725.

LOWE, F.   *See* SMYTH, WILLIAM, and LOWE, F., 1836.

LOZANO, PEDRO.
1873–75. Historia de la conquista del Paraguay, Río de la Plata y Tucumán. 5 vols. Buenos Aires.
1941. Descripción corográfica . . . del Gran Chaco Gualamba. Publ. Univ. Nac. Tucumán, No. 288, pp. 89–103. (Also pub. 1733, Córdova.)

LUBBOCK, JOHN.
1874. Note on the Macas Indians. Journ. Anthrop. Inst. Great Britain, Ireland, vol. 3, p. 29.

LUQUET, G.-H.
1933. Exposition d'ethnographie guyanaise au Trocadéro. La Nature, vol. 61, No. 2896, January, pp. 30–32. Paris.

LUTZ, FRANK E.
1912 a. String-figures from the Upper Potaro. Timehri, 3rd ser., vol. 2, pp. 117–127.
1912 b. String-figures from the Patomana Indians of British Guiana. Anthrop. Pap. Amer. Mus. Nat. Hist., vol. 12, pp. 1–14.

McTURK, MICHAEL.
1882. A journey up the Cuyuni. Timehri, vol. 1, pp. 126–132.

MACEDO COSTA, D.
1875. Der Volkstamm der Apeiacas im Stromgebiet des Amazonas. *Ref. in* Globus, vol. 27.

MACIEL PARENTE, BENITO.
1874. Memorial para conservar y augmentar la conquista y tierra del Marañon. *In* Candido Mendes de Almeida, ed., Memórias para a história do extincto Estado do Maranhão. Vol. 2, Rio de Janeiro.

MAGALHÃES, COUTO DE.
1876. O Selvagem. Rio de Janeiro.

MAGALHÃES DE GANDAVO, PEDRO DE.
1922. The histories of Brazil. (Tr. into English for first time and annotated by John B. Stetson, Jr., with a facsimile of the Portuguese original, 1576.) The Cortes Society. New York.

MAGIO, P. ANTONIO.   *See* ADAM, LUCIEN, and LECLERC, CHARLES, 1880

MAIZ, MORENS.
1862. Tête d'Indien jivaro (Pérou oríental) conservée et momifiée par un procédé particulier, avec quelques renseignements sur les Jivaros. Bull. Soc. Anthrop. Paris, vol. 3, p. 185.

MANGELSDORF, P. C., and REEVES, R. G.
1939. The origin of Indian corn and its relatives. Texas Agr. Exper. Station, Bull. No. 574.

MANOUVRIER, M. L.
1882. Sur les Galibis du Jardin d'acclimation. Bull. Soc. Anthrop. Paris, 3rd ser., vol. 5, pp. 602–643.

MARBÁN, PEDRO.
1898. Relación de la provincia de la virgen del Pilar de Mojos. Bol. Soc. Geogr. La Paz, vol. 1, pp. 120–137; No. 2, pp. 137–161.

MARCANO, G.
1889 a. Ethnographique station precolombienne des vallées d'aragua republique du Venezuela. Bul. Soc. Anthrop. Paris, 3d ser., vol. 11, pp. 225–234.
1889 b. Ethnographie precolombienne du Venezuela. Region des raudals de l'Orenoque. Bul. Soc. Anthrop. Paris, 3d ser., vol. 12, pp. 391–402.

MARCGGRAVI DE LIEBSTAD, GEORG. *See* PISO, GULIELMUS, and MARCGGRAVI DE
LIEBSTAD, GEORGE, 1648.

MARCOY, PAUL.
1866. De l'océan Pacifique à l'océan Atlantique à travers de l'Amérique du Sud.
Le Tour du Monde, vol. 14.
1867. Voyage de l'océan Pacifique à l'océan Atlantique à travers l'Amérique du
Sud. Le Tour du Monde, vol. 15.
1869. Voyage à travers l'Amérique du Sud de l'océan Pacifique à l'océan Atlantique. 2 vols. Paris.
1875. Travels in South America from the Pacific Ocean to the Atlantic Ocean.
2 vols. London.
See also Saint-Cricq, Laurent.

MARIA, JOSÉ DE
1918. Gramatica y vocabulario jibaro. Bol. Soc. Ecuatoriana Estud. Hist.,
vol. 1, p. 171.

MARKHAM, CLEMENTS ROBERT.
1856. Cuzco: A journey to the Ancient Capital of Peru; with an account of
the history, language, literature, and antiquities of the Incas. And
Lima: A visit to the capital and provinces of modern Peru; with
a sketch of the Viceregal Government, history of the Republic, and a
review of the literature and society of Peru. London.
1895. A list of the tribes in the valley of the Amazon. Journ. Anthrop. Inst.
Great Britain, Ireland, vol. 24, pp. 236–284.
1896. Recent discoveries of the basin of the River Madre de Dios (Bolivia and
Perú). Geogr. Journ., vol 7, pp. 187–190.
1907. Bibliography of Peru. A.D. 1526–1907. Publ. Hakluyt Soc., ser. 11,
vol. 22.
1910. A list of the tribes of the valley of the Amazons, including those on the
banks of the main stream and of all the tributaries. Journ. Anthrop.
Inst. Great Britain, Ireland, vol. 40, pp. 73–140.
1911. Expeditions into the valley of the Amazons. Hakluyt Soc.
See also Sarmiento de Gambóa, Pedro, 1907.

MARONI, PABLO. *See* NOTICIAS AUTENTICAS DEL FAMOSA RÍO MARAÑÓN . . . ,
1889–92.

MARQUES, BUENVENTURA.
n.d. Vocabulario de la lengua camba, escrito en favor del Colegio de Ocopa.
MS.
1903. Vocabulario de los idiomas índicos; conocidos por Cunibos y Panao ó
Setebos. La Gaceta científica, año 14. Lima.

MARQUES, CEZAR AUGUSTO.
1864. Apontamentos para o diccionario historico, geographico, topographico e
estadistico da Provincia do Maranhão. Maranhão.
1870. Diccionario historico-geografíco da Provincia do Maranhão. Maranhão.

MARRE, ARISTÍDE. *See* BIET, ANTOINE, 1896.

MARTIN, K.
1886. Berichte über eine Reise ins Gebiet des oberen Surinam. Bejdrage tot
de taal- land- en volkenkunde van Nederlandisch-Indië, vol. 35, pp. 1–76.

MARTIUS, KARL FRIEDRICH PHILIPP VON.
1823–31. Reise in Brasilien. 3 vols. Munich. *See also* Spix, Johann Baptist
von and Martius, Karl Friederich Phillipp von.
1863, 1867. Beiträge zur Ethnographie und Sprachenkunde Südamerika's, zumal
Brasiliens. 2 vols. Vol. 1, Zur Ethnographie. 1867, Leipzig.
Vol. 2, Zur Sprachenkunde. 1863, Erlangen.

Masô, João Alberto.
    1919. Os Indios Cachararys. Rev. Soc. Geogr. Rio de Janeiro, vols. 22–24
        (1909–11), pp. 98–100.
Mason, Gregory.
    1940. South of yesterday. New York.
Massa, Pietro.
    1936. Prélature du Rio Negro et du Port-Velho. Aprés vingt ans d'apostolat.
        Bull. Salésien, vol. 58, pp. 236–239; vol. 60, pp. 231–235. Turin.
Mata, Pedro de la.
    1923. Arte de la lengua cholona. Inca, vol. 1, No. 3, pp. 690–750.
Matallana, Baltazar de.
    1937. La Gran Sabana. Tres años de misión en los confines de Guayana. Bol.
        Soc. Venezolana Cienc. Nat., vol. 4, No. 29.
Mather, Kirtley F.
    1922 a. Along the Andean front in southeastern Bolivia. Geogr. Rev., vol. 12,
        pp. 358–374.
    1922 b. Exploration in the land of the Yuracarés, eastern Bolivia. Geogr.
        Rev., vol. 12, pp. 42–56.
Mathews, Edward Davis.
    1879. Up the Amazon and Madeira rivers, through Bolivia and Peru. London.
Matos Arvelo, Martín.
    1903. Algo sobre tenografía del Territorio Amazonas de Venezuela. Ciudad
        Bolivar. (Another edition, 1908.)
    1912. Vida indiana; usos, costumbres, religión, industria, gobierno, ceremonias
        y supersticiones de los Indios. Barcelona.
Mattos, João Wilkens de.
    1874. Diccionario topographico do Departmento de Loreto na republica do
        Perú. Pará.
Maurel, Dr.
    1882. Etude anthropologique et ethnographique sur deux tribus d'indiens vivant
        sur les rives du Maroni : les Araconquennes et les Galibis. Mém. Soc.
        Anthrop. Paris, 2nd ser., vol. 2, pp. 369–396.
Maurtua, Aníbal.
    1919. La provincia de Pachitea. Lima.
Maurtua, Victor M.
    1906. Juicio de límites entre el Perú y Bolivia. 12 vols. Barcelona.
Maw, Henry Lister.
    1829. Journal of a passage from the Pacific to the Atlantic. London.
Mayntzhusen, F. C.
    1912. über verkolumbianische Siedelungen und Urnenfriedhöfe der Guarani am
        Alto Paraná. Congr. Int. Amer., sess. 17, Buenos Aires, 1910, pp.
        459–469.
Mead, Charles W.
    1907. Technique of some South American feather-work. Anthrop. Pap. Amer.
        Mus. Nat. Hist., vol. 1, pp. 1–17.
Means, Philip Ainsworth.
    1917. A note on the Guarani invasions of the Inca empire. Geogr. Rev. vol. 4,
        pp. 482–484.
    1931. Ancient civilizations of the Andes. New York.
Medina, Elisio.
    1933 a. Monografia sobre el descubrimiento del rio Amazonas . . . Bogotá.
    1933 b. Monografia sobre Amazonas y las tribus (1540–1640). Bogotá.

MEDINA, JOSÉ TORIBIO.
1908. El veneciano Sebastián Caboto, al servicio de España . . . 2 vols. Santiago.
1934. The discovery of the Amazon according to the account of the Friar Gaspar de Carvajal and other documents as published with an introduction by J. T. Medina, tr. from the Spanish by T. Lee, and ed. by W. C. Heaton. Amer. Geogr. Soc., Spec. Publ. No. 17.

MEERWARTH, H.
1904. Eine zoologische Forschungsreise nach dem Rio Acará im Staate Pará (Brasilien). Globus, vol. 86, pp. 289–296.

MEILLET, A., and COHEN, MARCEL.
1924. Les langues du monde. Paris. *See also* Rivet, Paul, 1924.

MELÉNDEZ, JUAN.
1681–82. Tesoros verdaderos de las Yndias . . . 3 vols. Roma.

MELGAÇO, BARÃO DE.
1884. Apontamentos para o diccionario corographico da Provincia de Matto Grosso. Rev. Inst. Hist. Geogr. Brazil, vol. 48.

MELGAREJO, SIXTO.
1886. Vocabulario Guahibo en resumen de las actas de la Academia Venezulana Correspondiente de la Real Española de la Lengua. Caracas.

MELLO, MÁRIO.
1924. Um mirakitã pernambucano. Congr. Int. Amer., sess. 20, Rio de Janeiro, 1922, vol. 1, pp. 251–253.
1929. Os Carnijós de Aguas Bellas. Rev. Mus. Paulista, vol. 16, pp. 793–846.

MELLO MORAES, ALEXANDRE JOSÉ DE.
1858–63. Corographia historica, chronographica, geneologica, nobilitaria, e politica do imperio do Brasil. 4 vols. in 5. Rio de Janeiro.

MEMORIA DA NOVA NAVAGAÇÃO DO RIO ARINOS. Rev. Inst. Hist., 1856, vol. 19. (*Also* 1898 ed., vol. 19, pp. 99–118.)

MENDES DE ALMEIDA, CANDIDO.
n.d. O Tury-assú. Rio de Janeiro.
See also Gonçalves da Fonseca, José, 1874; and Maciel Parente, Benito, 1874.

MENESES, JOÃO MANOEL DE.
1919. Diario da Viagem do Governador D. . . . do Pará a Goiaz. Subsidios para a história da Capitania de Goiaz. Rev. Inst. Hist., vol. 84, pp. 41–294.

MENSE, P. HUGO. *See* MISSIONARIOS FRANCISCANOS.

MENSE, P. H. VON.
1935. Der Hochgottglaube der Mundurukú-Indianer. Zeit. Missions. u. Religion., vol. 25, pt. 1, pp. 21–36.

MENTELLE, SIMON.
1782. Voyage géographique dans l'intérieur de la Guyane française allant de Cayenne par la riviere de l'Oyapock aux Indiens Araunchaux aux Indiens Emerillons et redescendant par l'Araona et par le Maroni pour regagner Cayenne par la côte d'traconbo, en mars et trois mois suivantes, 1767. Feuille de la Guyane française.

MERCADILLO, CAPITÁN ALONSO. *See* JIMÉNEZ DE LA ESPADA, MARCOS, 1897.

MESONES MURO, MANUEL ANTONIO.
1903. Vias al Oriente del Perú. Bol. Soc. Geogr. Lima, vol. 13, pp. 54–89.
1914. La tribu de los Bracamoros. Bol. Soc. Geogr. Lima, vol. 30, pp. 25–26.

MÉTRAUX, ALFRED.
1927. Les migrations historiques des Tupí-Guarani. Journ. Soc. Amér. Paris, n.s., vol. 19, pp. 1–45.

1928 a. La civilisation matérielle des tribus Tupí-Guaraní. Paris.
1928 b. La religion des Tupinamba et ses rapports avec celle des autres tribus Tupí-Guaraní. Bibliothèque de l'école des hautes études, sciences religieuses, vol. 45. Paris.
1928 c. Un ancien document peu connu sur les Guarayú de la Bolivie orientale. Anthropos, vol. 24, pp. 913–941.
1930 a. Contribution à l'étude de l'archéologie du Cours supérieur et moyen de l'Amazone. Rev. Mus. La Plata, vol. 32, pp. 145–185.
1930 b. Études sur la civilisation des Indiens Chiriguano. Rev. Inst. Etnol. Univ. Nac. Tucumán, vol. 1, pp. 295–494.
1931 a. Mitos y cuentos de los Indios Chiriguanos. Rev. Mus. La Plata, vol. 33, pp. 119–184.
1931 b. Observaciones sobre psicología de los Indios Chiriguanos. Solar, vol. 1, pp. 89–122.
1932. Les hommes-dieux chez les Chiriguano et dans l'Amérique du Sud. Rev. Inst. Etnol. Univ. Nac. Tucumán, vol. 2, entrega 2a, pp. 61–92.
1933. Contribution à l'archéologie bolivienne. Journ. Soc. Amér. Paris, n.s., vol. 25, pp. 279–291.
1935. La mujer en la vida social y religiosa de los indios Chiriguanos. Rev. Inst. Etnol. Univ. Nac. Tucumán, vol. 3, entrega 3a, pp. 145–166.
1940. Los Indios Manáo. An. Inst. Etnogr. Amer., vol. 1, pp. 235–244.
1942. The native tribes of eastern Bolivia and western Matto Grosso. Bur. Amer. Ethnol. Bull. 134.
1943. The social organization and religion of the Mojo and Manasi. Primitive Man, vol. 16, Nos. 1 and 2, Jan. and April, pp. 1–30.

MEYER, HERMANN.
1896. Muschelhügel (Sambaki) und Urnenfeld bei Laguna (Brasilien). Globus, vol. 69, pp. 338–340.
1897 a. Tagebuch meiner Brasilienreise. 1896. Zweites Heft.
1897 b. Im Quellgebiet des Schingu. Landschafts- und Volkerbilder aus Centralbrasilien. In Verhandl. Gesell. Deutsch. Natur. u. Arzte, Allgemeiner Teil.
1897 c. Über seine Expedition nach Central-Brasilien. Verhandl. d. Gesell. f. Erdkunde zu Berlin.
1897 d. Meine Reise nach Brasilien. Verhandl. Deutsche Kolonial-Gesellschaft. Abteilung Berlin-Charlottenburg. Heft 5. Berlin.
1898. Carta a Virchow de 16 de Junho de 1898. Zeit. Ethnol., vol. 30, pp. 258–259.
1900. Bericht über seine zweite Xingú-Expedition. Verhandl. d. Gesell. F. Erdkunde zu Berlin, Nos. 2 and 3, pp. 112–128.
1904. Über die Kunst der Xingu-Indianer. Congr. Int. Amer., sess. 14, Stuttgart, pp. 455–471.
    See also Krause, Fritz, 1936 b.

MICHELENA Y ROJAS, FRANCISCO.
1867. Exploración oficial por la primera vez desde el norte de la America del Sur siempre por rios, entrando por las bocas del Orinoco, de las valles de este mismo y del Meta, Casiquiare, Rio Negro ó Guaynia y Amazónas, hasta Nanta en el alto Marañon ó Amazónas arriba de las bocas del Ucayali bajada dél Amazonas hasta el Atlántico. Brussels.

MILLER, LEO E.
1917. Up the Orinoco to the land of the Maquiritares. Geogr. Rev., vol. 3, pp. 258–277.
1919. In the wilds of South America. New York.

MILLIET DE SAINT-ADOLPHE, J. C. R.
1845. Diccionario geographico, historico e descriptivo do imperio do Brazil. 2 vols. Paris.

MISSÃO RONDÓN.
1916. Apontamentos sobre os trabalhos realizados pela Commissão de Linhas Telegraphicas Estrategicas de Matto Grosso ao Amazonas. Rio de Janeiro.
See also Rondón, Candido Mariano da Silva.

MISSIONARIOS FRANCISCANOS.
Information from Fathers Mense and Kruse, partly published in "Lose Blätter do Cururú" and partly furnished directly to Curt Nimuendajú.

MITRE, BARTOLOMÉ. *See* SCHMIDEL, ULRICH, 1903.

MOCHI, ALDO BRANDINO.
1903. I popoli dell' Uaupé e la famiglia etnica Miranhà. Archiv. Antrop. Etnol., vol. 33, pp. 97–130.

MOCQUET, JEAN.
1645. Voyages en Afrique, Asie, Indes Orientales, et Occidentales. Rouen. (English ed., tr. by Nathaniel Pulku, 1896, London.)

MOLLINEDO, ANDRES DE.
1906. Información hecha por el Licenciado Don . . ., en virtud de la Comisión del Ilmo. Sr. Obispo del Cuzco sobre el estado que tiene la misión de los indios infieles contiguos á la provincia de Carabaya. *In* Juicio de límites entre el Perú y Bolivia, vol. 12, pp. 68–94.
See Maurtua, Victor M., 1906.

MONTANÉ, LUIS.
1903. Chanchas y Jibaros. Cronica médico quirurgica de la Habana, vol. 29, No. 22.

MONTEIRO BAENA, ANTONIO LADISLAU.
1843. Observações ou notas illustrativas dos primeiros tres capitulos da parte segunda do Theszouro descoberto no Rio Amazonas. Rev. Inst. Hist., vol. 5. (3rd ed., 1885, vol. 5, pp. 275–311.)
1870. Resposta ao illmo e exmo Snr. Herculano Ferreira Penna, Presidente da Provincia do Pará sobre a communicação mercantil entre a dita provincia e a de Goyaz (1847). Rev. Inst. Hist. Geogr. Brazil, vol. 10.

MONTEIRO NORONHA, JOSÉ.
1862. Roteiro da viagem da cidade do Pará até as ultimas colonias dos Dominios Portuguezes em os Rios Amazonas e Negro. 1768. Pará.
1903. Fragments de l'Itinéraire . . . Limites entre le Brésil et la Guyane Anglaise: Annexes au premier mémoire du Brésil, vol. 3, pp. 192–203. Paris.

MONTEZON, M. F. DE.
1857. Voyages et travaux des missionnaires de la compagnie de Jésus publiés par les pères de la même compagnie, pour servir de complément aux lettres édifiantes I. Mission de Cayenne et de la Guyane française. Paris.

MONTOLIEU, F.
Viaje al Inirida—el Tiempo 1877.

MONTOYA, ANTONIO RUÍZ DE. *See* RUÍZ DE MONTOYA, ANTONIO.

MORAES, JOSÉ DE.
1860. História da Companhia de Jesus na extincta Província do Maranhão e Pará. Rio de Janeiro.

MORAIS, LUCIANO JAQUES DE.
1924. Inscripções rupestres no Brasil. Rio de Janeiro.

MORDINI, ANTONIO.
    1931. Lo spartiacque Guiano-Brasiliano. Roma.
    1934. Les cultures précolombiennes du bas Amazone et leur développement artistique. Congr. Int. Amer., sess. 24, Hamburg, pp. 61–65.
    See Panhuys, L. C. van, Mordini, A., and Herskovits, M. J., 1934.
MOREIRA PINTO, ALFREDO.
    1894. Apontamentos para o Diccionario Geographico do Brazil. "Anambé," vol. 1. Rio de Janeiro.
MORENO, FULGENCIO R.
    1926. La ciudad de la Asunción. Buenos Aires.
    1929. Cuestión de límites con Bolivia, negociaciones diplomáticas, 1915–1917. 2nd ed., vol. 2. Asunción.
MORTON, C. V.
    1931. Notes on yagé, a drug plant of southeastern Colombia. Washington Acad. Sci., vol. 21, pp. 485–488.
MOURA, IGNÁCIO BAPTISTA DE.
    1910. Viagem de Belém a São João do Araguaya. Rio de Janeiro and Paris.
    1922. Etnografia estática. Dic. Hist., Geogr. e Etnol. do Brasil, vol. 2, p. 134.
MURATORI, LUDOVICO ANTONIO.
    1754. Nouvelles des missions du Paraguay.
MUJÍA, RICARDO.
    1914. Bolivia-Paraguay. Exposición de los títulos que consagran el derecho territorial de Bolivia, sobre la zona comprendida entre los ríos Pilcomayo y Paraguay. 4 vols. La Paz.
MÜLLER, FRANZ.
    1934–35. Beiträge zur Ethnographie der Guaraní-Indianer im östlichen Waldgebiet von Paraguay. Anthropos, vol. 29, pp. 177–208, 441–460, 695–702; vol. 30, pp. 151–164, 433–450, 767–783.
MURATORI, LUDOVICO ANTONIO.
    1754. Nouvelles des missions du Paraguay.
MURIEL, DOMINGO.
    1918. Historia del Paraguay desde 1747 hasta 1767, obra latina del . . . tr. al castellano por el P. Pablo Hernández. *In* Colección de libros y documentos referentes á la historia de America, vol. 19. Madrid.
NARCISSO Y BARCELO. *See* SKINNER, JOSEPH, 1809.
NAVARRETE, RODRIGO DE.
    1895. Excerpts of his voyage of 1544, entitled, "Account of the Provinces and Nations of the Aruacos . . ." Arch. de Indias; Patronato. *In* Rodway, James, 1895.
NAVARRO, MANUEL.
    1903. Vocabulario castellano-quechua-pano con sus respectivas gramáticas Quechua y pana. Lima.
    1924. La tribu campa. Lima.
NAVARRO, MONS. NICOLÁS E. *See* BUENO, RAMÓN, 1933.
NELSON, JEAN THOMAS. *See* RIPPY, JAMES FRED, and NELSON, JEAN THOMAS, 1936.
NETTO, LADISLAO.
    1885. Investigações sobre a archeologia Brazileira. Archiv. Mus. Nac. Rio de Janeiro, vol. 6, pp. 257–555.
NIEMAEYER, CONRADO JACOB.
    1846. Carta corographica do Imperio do Brazil . . . Rio de Janeiro.

NIEMEYER, OLYMPIO.
1885. Os Indios Crichanas. Noticia ethnographica com uma introducção de Melo Moraes Filho. Rio de Janeiro.

NIEUHOF, JOHAN.
1682. Joan Nieuhofs Gedenkwaerdige zee en lantreize door de voornaemste landschappen van West en Oostindien. 2 vols. in 1. Amsterdam.
1707. Voyages and travels into Brasil . . .

NIMUENDAJÚ, CURT.
1914 a. Die Sagen von der Erschaffung und Vernichtung der Welt als Grundlagen der Religion der Apapocúva-Guaraní. Zeit. Ethnol., vol. 46, pp. 284–403.
1914 b. Vokabular der Pariri-Sprache. Zeit. Ethnol., vol. 46, pp. 619–625.
1914 c. Vocabularios da Lingua Geral do Brazil nos dialectos dos Manajé do Rio Ararandéua, Tembé do Rio Acará Pequeno e Turiwára do Rio Acará Grande, Est. do. Pará. Zeit. Ethnol. vol. 46, pp. 615–618.
1915. Sagen der Tembé-Indianer (Pará und Maranhão). Zeit. Ethnol., vol. 47, pp. 281–301.
1919–20. Bruchstücke aus Religion und Überlieferung der Šipáia-Indianer. Anthropos, vols. 14–15, pp. 1002–1039.
1921–22. Bruchstücke aus Religion und Überlieferung der Šipáia-Indianer. Anthropos, vols. 16–17, pp. 367–406.
1923–24. Zur Sprache der Šipáia-Indianer. Anthropos, vols. 18–19, pp. 836–857.
1924. Os Indios Parintintin do Rio Madeira. Journ. Soc. Amér. Paris, n.s., vol. 16, pp. 201–278.
1925. As Tribus do Alto Madeira. Journ. Soc. Amér. Paris, n.s., vol. 17, pp. 137–172.
1926. Die Palikur-indianer und ihre Nachbarn. Göteborgs Kongl. Vet. Vitt. Handl., vol. 31, No. 2.
1927. Streifzug vom Rio Jary zum Maracá. Petermanns Mitt., vol. 73, pp. 356–358.
1929 a. Zur sprache der Maué-Indianer. Journ. Soc. Amér. Paris, n.s., vol. 21, pp. 131–140.
1929 b. Wortliste der Šipáia-Sprache. Anthropos, vol. 24, pp. 863–896.
1930 a. Zur sprache der Kuruáya-Indianer. Journ. Soc. Amér. Paris, n.s., vol. 22, pp. 317–345.
1930 b. Besuch bei den Tukuna-Indianern. Ethnologischer Anzeiger. Vol. 2. Leipzig.
1932 a. Idiomas Indigenas del Brasil. Rev. Inst. Etnol. Univ. Nac. Tucumán, vol. 2, pp. 543–618.
1932 b. Wortlisten aus Amazonien. Journ. Soc. Amér. Paris, n.s., vol. 24, pp. 93–119.
1938. Rapports entre les Mundurukú et les Tupí. Anthropos, vol. 33, pp. 975–976.
1939. The Apinayé. Tr. by Robert H. Lowie. Anthrop. Ser. Catholic Univ., No. 8.
MS. Erkundungsreise zu den Górotire-Kayapó (1939–40).
MS. Os Indios Tukuna. (Data supplied to the Inspectoria of the Indian Protection Service in Amazonas and Acre.) Manaus. MS. Archives of the Inspectoria.
MS. Os Tukuna. Pará. 1943. MS. of 147 pages given to the Dept. of Anthropogy of the Univ. of California.
MS. Some unpublished material on the Múra and Pirahá.
MS. Texts of legends and songs in the Tucuna language. Unpublished ms. Belém. 1943.

MS. Results of a 15-day visit in 1929 to the Tucuna of the Igarapé de Belém, of the Cajary Lake, and of the Igarapé Preto de Sáo Jeronymo.

MS. Tucuna vocabulary.

MS. The results of 6 months of study in 1941 and 5 months in 1942 in intimate living with the Tucuna in different places in the Brazilian territory.

MS. Unpublished notes—Turiwára vocabulary.

MS. Verwandschaften der Yurúno-Sprachgruppe.

NIMUENDAJÚ CURT, and VALLE BENTES, E. E.

    1923. Documents sur quelques langues peu connues de l'Amazon. Journ. Soc. Amér. Paris, n. s., vol. 15, pp. 215–222.

NINO, BERNARDINO DE.

    1912. Etnografía chiriguana. La Paz.

NORDENSKIÖLD, ERLAND.

    1905. Beiträge zur Kenntnis einiger Indianerstämme des Dio Madre de Dios-gebietes. Ymer, vol. 25, pp. 265–312.

    1910 a. Archäologische Forschungen im Bolivianischen Flachland. Zeit. Ethnol., vol. 42, pp. 806–822.

    1910 b. Antropogeografiska studier i östra Bolivia. Ymer, vol. 30, pp. 275–284.

    1912. Indianerleben, El Gran Chaco (Südamerica). Leipzig.

    1913. Urnengräber und Mounds im bolivianischen Flachlande. Baessler-archiv., vol. 3, pp. 205–255.

    1915 a. Incallacta, eine befestigte und von Inca Tupac Yupanqui angelegte Stadt. Ymer, vol. 35, pp. 169–185.

    1915 b. Die religiösen Vorstellungen der Itonama-Indianer in Bolivia. Zeit. Ethnol., vol. 47, pp. 105–113.

    1917 a. Die Bevolkerungsbewegung unter den Indianer in Bolivien. Peter-manns Mitt., vol. 63, pp. 109–112.

    1917 b. Die östliche Ausbreitung der Tiahuanacokultur in Bolivien und ihr Verhältnis zur Aruakkultur in Mojos. Zeit. Ethnol., vol. 49, pp. 10–20.

    1917 c. The Guarani invasion of the Inca empire in the sixteenth century: an historical Indian migration. Geogr. Rev., vol. 4, pp. 103–121.

    1919 a. An ethno-geographical analysis of the material culture of two Indian tribes in the Gran Chaco. Comp. Ethnogr. Stud., No. 1.

    1919 b. Sydamerika-Kampen om guld och silver 1498–1600. Uppsala.

    1920. The changes in the material culture of two Indian tribes under the influence of new surroundings. Comp. Ethnogr. Stud., No. 2.

    1922. Deductions suggested by the geographical distribution of some Post-colombian words used by the Indians of South America. Comp. Ethnogr. Stud., vol. 5.

    1923. Indianer und Weisse in Nordostbolivien. Stuttgart.

    1924 a. Forschungen und Abenteuer in Südamerika. Stuttgart.

    1924 b. The ethnography of South-America seen from Mojos in Bolivia. Comp. Ethnogr. Stud., No. 3.

    1924 c. Finds of graves and old dwelling-places on the Rio Beni, Bolivia. Ymer, vol. 44, pp. 229–237.

    1930 a. L'archéologie du bassin de l'amazone. Ars Americana, vol. 1. Paris.

    1930 b. Karl von den Steinen. Journ. Soc. Amér. Paris, n.s., vol. 22, pp. 221–227.

    1930 c. Modifications in Indian culture through inventions and loans. Comp. Ethnogr. Stud., vol. 8.

    1931 a. Ancient Inca lacquer work. Comp. Ethnogr. Stud., vol. 9, app. 2, pp. 95–100.

1931 b. Origin of the Indian civilization in South America. Comp. Ethnogr. Stud., vol. 9.
  See also Frödin, Otto, and Nordenskiöld, Erland, 1918.

NORDENSKIÖLD, OTTO.
  1927. Südamerika. Ein Zukunftsland der Menschheit. Stuttgart.

NORMAND, GILLES.
  1924. Au pays de l'or, Récit d'un voyage chez les Indiens inconnus de la Guyane française. Paris.

NOTICIAS AUTÉNTICAS DEL FAMOSO RIO MARAÑON Y MISION APOSTÓLICA DE LA COMPAÑÍA DE JESUS DE LA PROV. DE QUITO EN LOS DILATADOS BOSQUES DE DICHO RIO. Enscribíales por los años de 1738 un misianero de la misma compañia y las publica ahora por la primera vez Marcos Jiménez de la Espada.
  1889–92. Bol. Soc. Geogr. Madrid, vols. 26–30.

NUNES PEREIRA.
  1939. Ensaio de Etnologia Amazonica. Terra Imatura, vol. 3, No. 12.
  1940. Bahira e suas experiencias. Belém.

NUÑEZ, ENRIQUE BERNARDO.
  1936. Una ojeada al mapa de Venezuela. Bol. Bibl. Nac. Venez., 2nd ser., No. 42, pp. 164–175.

NUÑEZ DE PINEDA Y BASCUÑAN, FRANCISCO.
  1863. Cautiverio feliz y razon de las gucrras dilatadas de Chile. Col. Hist. Chile, vol. 3. (Captivity 1669; written 1673.)

O'BRIAN DEL CARPIO, BERNARD.
  MS. In Bibliotheca Nacional, Rio de Janeiro. Est. 147. Caj-5-Leg. 21.

OLEA, BONIFACIO MARÍA DE.
  1928. Ensayo gramatical del dialecto de los indios Guaraúnos . . . Caracas.

OLIVEIRA MIRANDA, OSCAR.
  1890. Conferencia sobre a expedição do capitao Telles Pires ao Paranatinga. Rev. Soc. Geogr. Rio de Janeiro, vol. 6.

OMAGUA Y DORADO. *See* JORNADA DE OMAGUA Y DORADO. *Also* SERRANO Y SANZ, MANUEL, 1909.

ONFFROY DE THORON, ENRIQUE.
  1895. Arte de la lengua campa, por M. I. Zavala. Lìma.

ORAMAS, LUIS R.
  1917. Apuntes sobre arqueología venezolana. Proc. 2nd Pan Amer. Sci. Congr., vol. 1, pp.138–145. Washington.

ORBIGNY, ALCIDE DESSALINES D'.
  1835–47. Voyage dans l'Amérique Méridionale . . . 9 vols. Paris
  See also Cueva, R. P. de la, 1893.

ORDINAIRE, OLIVIER.
  1887. Les suavages due Pérou. Rev. Ethnogr. Paris, vol. 6, pp. 265–322.
  1892. Du Pacifique à l'Atlantique par les Andes péruviennes et l'Amazone. Paris.

ORELLANA, ANTONIO DE.
  1906. Carta del Padre . . . sobre el origen de las misiones de Mojos. *In* Judicio de límites entre el Perú y Bolivia, vol. 10, Mojos. II. Madrid
  See Maurtua, Victor M., 1906.

ORTEGON, DON DIEGO DE. *See* DESCRIPCIÓN DE LA PROVINCIA DE LOS QUIJOS, 1881–97.

ORTIGUERA, TORIBIO DE.
  1909. Jornada del Río Marañon. (Nueva series bibloiteca de autores españoles, vol. 15, pp. 305–422.) Historiadores de Indias, vol. 2. Madrid.

Ortíz, Sergio Elías.
1940. Lingüistica colombiana. Familia Zaparo o Gae. Univ. Catolica Bolivariana, vol. 5, No. 15, pp. 97–108.
1942. Lingüistica colombiana. Familia Witoto. Univ. Catolica Bolivariana, vol. 8, pp. 379–409.
Orton, James.
1870. The Andes and the Amazon; or across the continent of South America. London. (New York editions 1870, 1871, 1875, 1876.)
Osambela, Claudio.
1896. El Oriente del Peru. Bol. Soc. Geogr. Lima, vol. 6, pp. 193–223.
Osculati, Gaetano.
1850. Esplorazione delle regioni equatoriali . . . Milano. (Another ed. 1854, Milano.)
Osma, Felipe de.
1908 (?). Según las relaciones de los jesuitas, hasta dónde son navegables los afluentes septentrionales del Marañon. Madrid.
Ounque, Jacques.
1906. O valle do Rio Branco. Manaos.
Outes, Félix F.
1909. La ceramica Chriguana. Rev. Mus La Plata, vol. 16, (ser. 2 vol. 3), pp. 121–136.
1912. Craneos Indígenas del departmento de Gualeguaychu (Provincia de Entre Ríos). An. Soc. Cient. Argentina, vol. 73, pp. 5 ff.
1917. El primer hallazgo arqueológico en la isla de Martin Garcia. An. Soc. Cient. Argentina, vol. 82, pp. 265 ff.
1918. Nuevos rastros de la cultura guaraní en la cuenca del Paraná inferior. An. Soc. Cient. Argentina, vol. 83.
Oviedo y Valdés, Gonzalo Fernández de.
1851–55. Historia general y natural de las Indias, islas y tierra firme de la mar océano. 4 vols. Madrid. José Amador de los Rios, ed.
Pallarés, Fernando.
1883. Historia de las misiones de fieles é infieles del Colegio de propaganda Fide de Santa Rosa de Ocopa por los PP. Misioneros del mismo Colegio. 2 vols. Barcelona.
Pallarés, Fernando, and Calvo, Vic.
1870. Noticias históricas dellas misiones de fieles é infieles del Colegio de Propaganda Fide de Santa Rose de Ocopa. Barcelona.
Palmatary, Helen C.
1939. Tapajo pottery. Ethnol. Stud., No. 8, pp. 1–138.
Palomino, Diego.
1897. Relación de las provincias que hay en la conquista del Chuquimayo que yo el Capitan Diego Palomino tengo por Su Magestad y por el muy Ilustre Señor Pedro Gasca, presidente de la Audiencia Real destos reynos del Peru por su Magestad. In Rel. Geogr. Indias, vol. 4, pp. xlvii–lxv.
Panhuys, L. C. van.
1897. Bemerkungen über ein caraibisches Ruder. Int. Archiv. Ethnogr., vol. 10, p. 156.
1897–98. Proeve eener verklaring van de ornamentiek van de Indianen in Guyana. Met affeeldingen. Int. Archiv. Ethnogr., vol. 10, pp. 118 ff.; vol. 11, pp. 51–72.
1904 a. Indian words in the Dutch language and in use in Dutch Guiana. Congr. Int. Amer., sess. 13, New York, 1902, pp. 205–208.

1904 b. Beiträge zur Ethnographie, Linguistik und Entdeckungsgeschichte Amerikas. Haag.

1904 c. Are there pygmies in French Guiana? Congr. Int. Amer., sess. 13, New York, 1902, pp. 131–133.

1906 a. Über die letzte niederländische Expedition nach Surinam. Congr. Int. Amer., sess. 14, Stuttgart, 1904, pp. 427–435.

1906 b. Näheres über die Ornamente der Naturvölker Suriname. Congr. Int. Amer., sess. 14, Stuttgart, 1904, pp. 437–439.

1910. Mitteilungen über surinamische Ethnographie und Kolonisations-geschichte: Trommelsprache; Tätowieren; Zauber- und Heilmittel; Kurze Bemerkungen über Zahlmittel und ein merkwürdiges Buch über das Geistesleben der Indianer. Congr. Int. Amer., sess. 16, Vienna, 1908, pp. 521–540.

1912. Les chansons et la musique de la Guyane néerlandaise. Journ. Soc. Amér. Paris, n.s., vol. 9, pp. 27–39.

1913. A few observations on Carib numerals. Congr. Int. Amer., sess. 18, London, 1912, pp. 109–110.

1920–21. De toekomst van de Indianen in Canada en in Suriname. De West-Indische Gids, vol. 2, pp. 513–516.

1921–22. Het aantal en de woonplaatsen van de Boschnegers en Indianen in Suriname. De West-Indische Gids, vol. 3, pp. 83–99.

1922. De afkomst der Roodhuiden. De Ster der Christelijke Weekbladen, No. 4, pp. 307–331.

1924–25. Boekbespreking: Dr. Gerhard Lindblom. Afrikanische Relikte und Indianische in der Kulture der Buschneger Surinams. De West-Indische Gids, vol. 6, pp. 419–426.

1925. Observations on the name Bacove. Congr. Int. Amer., sess. 21, Göteborg, 1924, pp. 321–332.

1931-32. Uitstervende Arowakken? De West-Indische Gids, vol. 13, p. 537.

1933–34. Folklore in Suriname. De West-Indische Gids, vol. 16, pp. 17–32.

1934. Quelques chansons et quelques danses dans la Guyane néerlandaise. Congr. Int. Amer., sess. 24, Hamburg, 1932, pp. 207–211.

1934–35. Het Kikvorschmotief in Suriname en Elders. De West-Indische Gids, vol. 16, pp. 361–366..

PANHUYS, L. C. VAN, MORDINI, A., and HERSKOVITS, M. J.
1934. Un manuscrit de 1690 sur la Guyane francaise. Congr. Int. Amer., sess. 24, Hamburg, 1932, pp. 26–31.

PAREAU, A. H.
1898. Onze-West. Reisschetsen.

PASSARGE, SIEGFRIED.
1933. Wissenschaftliche ergebnisse einer Reise im Gebiet des Orinoco, Caura und Cuchivero im Jahre 1901–02. Hamburg. Univ. Abhandl., vol. 39, ser. C, Naturwissenschaften, vol. 12.

PAULOTTI, OSVALDO L.
1942. Alfarería guarayo. Rel. Soc. Arg. Antrop., vol. 3, pp. 173–188.

PAULY, ANTONIO.
1928. Ensayo de etnografía americana. Viajes y exploraciones. Buenos Aires.

PAUWELS, W.M.I. BORST.
1903. Over de Wijze van wisschen met het surinaamsche vishvergift Koema-parie. Int. Archiv. Ethnogr., vol. 16, pp. 42–43.

PAYER, RICHARD.
1906. Reisen im Jauapiry-Gebiet. Petermanns Mitt., vol. 52, pp. 217–222.

PAZ SOLDÁN, MATEO, See RAIMONDI, ANTONIO, 1862.

PEIXOTO DE AZEVEDO, ANTONIO.
     1885. Expedição ao Rio Paranatinga. Rev. Soc. Geogr. Rio de Janeiro, vol. 1.
PELLEPRAT, PIERRE.
     1656. Introduction à la langue des Galibis. *In* his Relation des missions des
         pp. de la Compagnie de Jesus dans les isles, et dans la Terre Ferme
         de l'Amerique meridionale. Paris.
PENARD, ARTHUR PHILIP.
     1925 a. Iets over den Caraibischen Pujai. De Periskoop, 21 and 28 November,
         5 and 12 December. Paramaribo.
     1925 b. Iets over de geboorte en de opvoeding van het kind bij onze Caraiben.
         De Periskoop, No. 41. Paramaribo.
     1926 a. Surinaamsche volksvertellingen. Bijdragen van het Koloniaal Institute,
         vol. 80, p. 325.
     1926 b. Iets over onze Caraibischen Pujai. De Periskoop, Nos. 66, 68, 69,
         71-79, 87, 88, 91, 93, 96, 98, 103-105. Paramaribo.
     1926 c. Iets over de feesten bij onze Caraiben. De Periskoop, Nos. 82, 83.
         Paramaribo.
     1927 a. De Wraak van een Masowijnschen Pujai Meester. De Periskoop, No.
         127. Paramaribo.
     1927 b. De Zondvloed, of het ontstaan der vrouw uit den trouwen hond. De
         Periskoop, No. 133, 3. Paramaribo.
     1927 c. De oorzaak van het uitsterven onzer Indianen of het onstaan der
         Ackornigesknollen. De Periskoop, No. 130, 2. Paramaribo.
     1927 d. De Scalparing van het eerste individu, of het ontstaan der Werusi
         (Pasduif) uit de hersenen van den Tijdegeest Kulupi. De Periskoop,
         No. 128. Paramaribo.
     1927 e. De overtreding der couvadewet of het ontstaan der palmen in Suriname.
         De Periskoop, Nos. 132-133. Paramaribo.
     1928-29. De Caraibsche Taal. De Periskoop, Nos. 175, 178, 182, 184, 191, 198,
         203, 209, 213, 214, 224. Paramaribo.
PENARD, ARTHUR PHILIP, and PENARD, THOMAS E.
     1925-26. Uit de pers. Iets over het huwelijk bij onze Caraiben. De West-
         Indische Gids, vol. 7, pp. 189-191.
     1927. Wejumakon-Zoonekinderen of het onstaan der tweelingster. De Peri-
         skoop, No. 129. Paramaribo.
.PENARD, FREDERIK PAUL, and PENARD, ARTHUR PHILIP.
     1907-08. De menschetende aanbidders der zonneslang. 3 vols. Paramaribo.
         (1908 ed., The Hague.)
     1913. Surinaamsch bijgeloof. Iets over Wintie en andere natuurbegrippen.
         Bijdragen tot de Taal-, en Volkenkunde van Nederlandsch-Indië, Deel
         67, pp. 157-183.
PENARD, THOMAS E., and PENARD, ARTHUR P.
     1917. Popular notions pertaining to primitive stone artifacts in Surinam. Journ.
         Amer. Folklore, vol. 30, pp. 251-261.
     1925-26. Birdcatching in Surinam. De West-Indische Gids, vol. 7, pp. 545-566.
     1926. Four Arawak Indian songs. Rep. De West Indische Gids, vol. 7, pp.
         497-500. Martinus Nijhoff. The Hague.
PENNA, DOMINGO SOARES FERREIRA.
     1877-78. Apontamentos sobre os ceramios do Pará. Archiv. Mus. Nac. Rio de
         Janeiro, vol. 2, pp. 47-67.
     1881. Algumas palavras da lingua dos Aruans. Archiv. Mus. Nac. Rio de
         Janeiro, vol. 4.

PEREIRA DA SILVA, LUCIANO.
 1922. Etnografia. Dic. Hist., Geogr., e Etnol. do Brasil, vol. 2, p. 34.
PEREZ, FELIPE.
 1862–63. Geografía física y politica de los Estados Unidos de Colombia. 2 vols.
  Bogotá.
PERKINS, H. I.
 1885. Notes on a journey to Mount Roraima. Proc. Roy. Geogr. Soc., vol. 7,
  pp. 522–534.
PERRET, JACQUES.
 1933 a. Observations et documents sur les indiens Emerillon de la Guyane
  française. Journ. Soc. Amér. Paris, n.s., vol. 25, pp. 65–97.
 1933 b. Nouvelles observations ethnographiques sur la Guyane française. Bull.
  Assoc. Franc. Adv. Sci., n.s., No. 111 (April), pp. 101–105.
PERU. JUNTA DE VÍAS FLUVIALES.
 1902. Vías del Pacífico al Madre de Dios. Publ. de la Junta de Vías Fluviales,
  Lima.
 1904. El istmo de Fiscarrald; informes de los Señores La Combe, Von Hassel,
  y Pesce. Publ. de la Junta de Vías Fluviales, Lima.
PERU-BOLIVIA BOUNDARY COMMISSION 1911–1913. Reports of the British officers
 of the Peruvian Commission. Diplomatic memoranda and maps of the boundary
 zone. Edited for the government of Peru by the Royal Geographical Society of
 London. Cambridge. University Press. 1918.
PERUVIAN CENSUS. 1940.
PESCIOTTI, BERNARDINO GIUSEPPE.
 1904. Devocionario del néofito guarayo (America merid., Bolivia). Genova.
PETERSEN, P.
 1886. Die Paumarys aus G. Wallis' Nachlass. Das Ausland, vol. 59, pp.
  261–266.
PETRULLO, VINCENZO (VINCENT) M.
 1932 a. Primitive People of Matto Grosso, Brazil. Mus. Journ. Univ. Penn.,
  vol. 23, pp. 84–179.
 1932 b. The fate of Colonel Fawcett. Geogr. Journ., vol. 80, pp. 151–154.
 1939. The Yaruros of the Capanaparo River, Venezuela. Bur. Amer. Ethnol.
  Bull. 123, Anthrop. Pap. No. 11, pp. 161–290.
PHILLIPS, RICHARD. See PONS, FRANÇOIS RAYMOND JOSEPH DE, 1806.
PICO, PEDRO P. See ZEBALLOS, ESTANISLÃO SEVERO, Y PICO, PEDRO P.
PIERINI, FRANCESCO.
 1907. Dos asuntos de actualidad en Bolivia. Buenos Aires.
 1908–12. Informe anual que presenta al supremo gobierno el R. P. Prefecto
  sobre el movimento de las Misiones de su cargo.
 1910. Mitología de los Guarayos de Bolivia. Anthropos, vol. 5, pp. 703–710.
[PIERRE, FATHER, DOMINICAN MISSIONARY.]
 1889. Voyage d'exploration d'un missionarie dominicain chez les tribus sauvages
  de l'Équateur. Paris.
PIGORINI, L.
 1878. Di una collezione etnologica della Repubblica dell' equatore. Bol. Soc.
  Geogr. Italiana, fasc. 3, del anno 12, vol. 15.
PINELL, GASPAR DE.
 1928. Excursion Apostólica por los ríos Putumayo . . . Caquetá . . . Etno-
  graficos, Filológicos. Bogotá, Colombia.
PINTO, ESTEVÃO.
 1935–38. Os Indigenas do nordeste. 2 vols. São Paulo. (Bibl. Pedag. Brasil.,
  ser. 5a, Brasiliana, vols. 44 and 112. Rio de Janeiro.)

Pio Aza.   *See* Aza, José Pio.

Pires de Campos, Antonio.
 1862. Breve noticia que dá o capitão . . . Rev. Trim. Inst. Hist. Geogr. Ethnogr.
          Brasil, vol. 25, pp. 437–449.

Piso, Gulielmus (William, Guilherme), and Marcggravi (Marcgraf) de
  Liebstad, George.
 1648. Historia naturalis Brasiliae . . . Lugd. Bat. et Amsterdam.

Pistorius, Thomas.
 1763. Korte en zakelijke beschrijvinge van de colonie van Zuriname. Amster-
          dam.

Pitou, L. A.
 1807. Voyage à Cayenne. 2 vols. Paris. (First ed., Paris, 1805, 2 vols. in 1.)

Plagge, C.
 1857. Reise in das Gebeit der Guajajara-Indianer in der Brasilionischen Prov-
          inz Maranhão. Petermanns Mitt., vol. 3, pp. 206 ff.

Plassard, Louis.
 1868. Les Guaraunos et le delto de l'Orénoque. Bull. Soc. Géogr. Paris, vol. 15,
          pp. 568–592.

Platzmann, Julio.
 1896. O Diccionario Anonymo da Lingua general do Brasil. Publicado de novo
          como o seu reverso. Leipzig.
       See also Quandt, Christlieb, 1900.

Polak, J. E. R.
 1894. A grammar and vocabulary of the Ipurina language. London.

Pombo, José Francisco da Rocha.   *See* Rocha Pombo, José Francisco da.

Pons, François Raymond Joseph de.
 1806. Travels in parts of South America, during the years 1801, 1802, 1803 and
          1804. *In* Phillips, Richard, Coll. of modern and contemporary voyages
          and travels, vol. 4. London.

Pöppig, Eduard Friedrich.
 1835–36. Reise in Chile, Peru und auf dem Amazonenstrome während der Jahre
          1827–1832. 2 vols. Leipzig.

Portillo, Pedro.
 1914. Departamento del Madre de Dios. Bol. Soc. Geogr. Lima, vol. 30, pp.
          139–187.

Post, Charles Johnson.
 1905. An ethnological paradox. Harper's Mag., vol. 110, pp. 910–916.
 1912. Across the Andes. New York.

Preuss, Konrad Theodor.
 1914. (Letter to Berliner Gesellschaft für Anthropologie, Ethnologie und
          Urgeschichte reported at meeting October 17, 1914.) Zeit. Ethnol.,
          vol. 46, pp. 748–751.
 1920–21. Bericht über meine archäologischen und ethnologischen Forschungs-
          reisen in Kolumbien. Zeit. Ethnol., vol. 52/53, pp. 89–128.
 1921–23. Religion und mythologie der Uitoto. Textaufnahmen und Beobach-
          tungen bei einem Indianerstamm in Kolumbien, Südamerika. 2 vols.
          Leipzig and Göttingen.
 1923. Stücke einer ethnographischen Sammlung. Zeit. Ethnol., vol. 55, pp.
          91–93.
 1929. Die Darstellung des zweiten Ich unter der Indianern Amerikas. In
          memoriam Karl Weule. Beiträge zur Völkerkunde und Vorgeschichte.
          Herausgegeben von Otto Reche. Leipzig.
       See also Jíménez Seminario, Aug., 1924.

Prieto, A. S.
  1885. Descripción de la provincia de los Jivaros. Compte Francisco Maria. Varones ilustres de la orden Seráfica en el Ecuador. 2nd ed., vol. 2. Quito.
Priewasser, Wolfgang.
  1903. Compendio de la gramática del idioma Guarayo. Tarata.
Prince, Carlos.
  1905. Idiomas y dialectos indígenas del continente hispano sud-americano con la nómina de las tribus indianas de cada territorio. Lima.
Prudhomme, Louis Marie.
  1798. Voyage à la Guiane et a Cayenne, fait en 1789 et années suivantes . . . Paris.
  1799. Reise nach Guiana und Cayenne. German tr. by Christoph Wilhelm Lohmann. Hamburg.
Pulgar Vidal, Javier.
  1943. La Tribu de los Panatahuas. El Comercio, August 31, p. 5. Lima.
Purchas, Samuel. See Leigh, Charles, 1906.
Quandt, Christlieb.
  1807. Nachricht von Suriname und seinen Einwohnern; sonderlich den Arawacken, Warauen und Karaiben . . . Görlitz.
  1900. Des Herrnhuter glaubensboten Christlieb Quandt Nachricht von der arawackischen Sprache, besonders und unverändert hrsg. von J. Platzmann. Leipzig.
Questions on the Apostles' Creed, with other simple instruction, for the Warau Indians at the missions in Guiana. London. 1870(?).
Quain, Buell.
  n.d. The Trumai. MS. 2 vols.
Raimondi, Antonio.
  1862. Apuntes sobre la provincia litoral de Loreto. In Mateo Paz Soldan's Geografía del Perú, vol. 1, pp. 593–713. Also, Estudio de la provincia litoral de Loreto in Larrabure, vol. 7, pp. 118–278.
  1863. On the Indian tribes of the Great District of Loreto in Northern Peru. (Tr. from the Spanish by William Bollaert.) Anthrop. Rev., vol. 1, pp. 33–43, 85–86.
Raimundo, Jacques.
  1934. Vocabularios Indígenas de Venezuela. Rio de Janeiro.
Raiol, Domingos Antonio. See Guajará, Barão de.
Raleigh, Sir Walter.
  1928. The Discoverie of Guiana. The Hakluyt Soc. London. (First issued in 4 editions, London, 1596.)
Ramírez, Luis.
  1888. Carta, de . . . do Rio de Prata, a 10 de Julho de 1528. Rev. Inst. Hist. Geogr. Brasil, 2nd ed., vol. 15, pp. 14–41. (Also in Medina, L. T., 1908.)
Ranke, Karl Ernst.
  1906. Anthropologische Beobachtungen aus Zentral-brasilien. Abhandl. K. Bayer. Akad. Wis. München, Kl. 2, vol. 24, Abt. 1, pp. 1–148.
Ratzel, Friedrich.
  1894. Völkerkunde. I. Leipzig und Wien. Abb. p. 509: Geräte der brasilianischen Indianer zum Reiben und Schnupfen der Samen des Paricá-Baumes, später auch des Tabaks. Ethnographisches Museum, München.
Read, Charles Herules.
  1904. On two pottery vases from the upper Amazon. Man, No. 32, p. 49.

REEVES, E. A.
 1910. Note on a map of South Peru and North Bolivia. Geogr. Journ., vol. 36, pp. 398–404.
REGUEIRA COSTA, JOÃO BATISTA.
 1894. O Brasil prehistórico. Rev. Inst. Arq. Pernambucano, vol. 45, pp. 3–4.
REICH, ALFRED, and STEGELMANN, FELIX.
 1903. Bei den Indianern des Urubamba und des Envira. Globus, vol. 83, pp. 133–137.
REINBURG, P.
 1921. Contribution à l'études des boissons toxiques des Indiens du Nord-ouest de l'Amazone, l'ayahuásca—le yajé—le huánto. Journ. Soc. Amér. Paris, n.s., vol. 13, pp. 25–54, 197–216.
 See also Rivet, Paul, and Reinburg, P.
REISE BECHREIBUNGEN VON DEUTSCHEN BEAMTEN UND KRIEGSLEUTEN IM DIENST DER NIEDERLANDISCHEN WEST- UND OST-INDISCHEN KOMPAGNIEN, 1602–1797. L'Honoré Naber, Samuel Pierre, ed. 13 vols. Haag. 1930–32.
REISS, W.
 1880. Ein Besuch bei den Jivaros-Indianern. Verhandl. d. Gesell. f. Erkunde zu Berlin, vol. 7, pp. 325–337.
 See also Stübel, Alfons, Reiss, W., and Koppel, B.
RELAÇÃO ABREVIADA DA REPÚBLICA QUE OS RELIGIOSOS JESUITAS DAS PROVINCIAS DE PORTUGAL E HESPENHA ESTABELECERAM NOS DOMINIOS ULTRAMARINOS DAS DUAS MONARCHIAS. Rev. Inst. Hist., 1842, vol. 4. (*Also* 1863, 2nd ed., vol. 4, pp. 265–294.)
RELACIÓN DE LA ENTRADA QUE HIZO EL GOVERNADOR D. DIEGO VACA DE VEGA AL DESCUBRIMIENTO Y PACIFICACIÓN DE LAS PROVINCIAS DE LOS INDIOS MAYNAS . . . Rel. Geogr. Indias, 1897, vol. 4, pp. CXXXIX–CLXII.
RELACIÓN Y DESCRIPCIÓN DE LAS MISIONES Y CONVERSIONES DE INFIELES VULGARMENTE LLAMADAS DE APOLOBAMBA, . . . Written in 1747; published by M. V. Ballivián, 1886. La Paz.
RELACIONES GEOGRÁFICAS DE INDIAS, 1881–1897. Published by M. Jiménez de la Espada. 4 vols. Madrid.
A RELATION OF THE HABITATIONS AND OTHER OBSERVATIONS OF THE RIVER MARWIN AND THE ADJOINING REGIONS. *In* Purchas, Samuel, Hakluytus posthumus or Purchas his Pilgrimes . . . 20 vols. Glasgow. 1905–07.
RENÉ-MORENO, GABRIEL.
 1888. Biblioteca boliviana. Catálogo del archivo de Mojos y Chiquitos. Santiago de Chile.
RENGGER, JOHANN RUDOLPH.
 1835. Reise nach Paraguay in den Jahren 1818 bis 1826. Aarau.
RESTREPO TIRADO, ERNESTO.
 1903. Las invasiones caribes autes de la conquista española. Bol. Hist. Antig., año 1. Bogotá.
RÉSUMÉ DE QUELQUES NOTIONS GÉOGRAPHIQUES FAISANT CONNAÎTRE LES RIVIÈRES DONT LA NAVIGATION PERMET AUX DOMAINES DE LA COURONNE PORTUGAISE DE COMMUNIQUER AVEC CEUX D'ESPAGNE ET DES PROVINCES—UNIES D'AMÉRIQUE. 1764. Limites entre le Bresil et la Guyane Anglaise: Annexes au premier mémoire du Brésil, Paris, vol. 3, pp. 94–100. 1903.
REVISTA DE ARCHIVOS Y BIBLIOTECAS. 3 vols. in 4. 1899–1900. Lima, Perú.
REY DE CASTRO, CARLOS.
 1914. Los Pobladores del Putumayo. Barcelona.

RIBEIRO, FRANCISCO DE PAULA.
    1841. Memoria sobre as nações gentias que presentemente habitam o continente
        do Maranhão (1819). Rev. Trim. Inst. Hist. Geogr. Brasil, vol. 3, pp.
        184–197, 297–322, 442–456. (2nd ed. 1858.)
    1870. Roteiro da viagem que fez o capitão . . . as fronteiras da capitania do
        Maranhão e da de Goyaz . . . (1815). Rev. Trim. Inst. Hist. Geogr.
        Brasil, vol. 10, pp. 5–80. (First ed. 1848.)
RIBEIRO DE SAMPAIO, FRANCISCO XAVIER.
    1812. Roteiro da viagem da cidade do Para até ás ultimas colonias do dominio
        portuguez em o Rio Amazonas e Negro. Collecção de noticias para
        a historia e geographia das nações ultramarinas, vol. 1, No. 4. Lisboa.
    1825. Diario da viagem que em visita, e correição das provoações da capitania
        de San José do Rio Negro fez ó ouvidor, e intendente geral da mesma
        Fr. X. Ribeiro da Sampaio no anno de 1774 e 1775. Lisbon.
    1856. Extracto da viagem, que em visita e correição das provoações da capitania
        de S. José do Rio Negro, fez o ouvidor e intendente geral da mesma
        . . ., no anno de 1774 3 1775; a qual viagem existe manuscripta no
        Archivo de S. M. o Imperador. Rev. Inst. Hist. Geogr. Brasil, vol. 1,
        pp. 109–122. (Another ed. 1839.)
    1872. Relação geographica historica do Rio Branco da America Portugueza.
        Rev. Inst. Hist. Geogr. Brasil, vol. 13, pp. 200–273. (Another ed. 1850.)
    1903. Journal du voyage que fit l'auditeur et intendant général de la captainerie
        de S. José do Rio Negro . . . en 1774–1775. *In* Limites entre le Brésil
        el la Guyane anglaise: annexes au prémier mémoire, vol. 4, pp. 3–88.
        Paris. (Vols. 1 and 2 contain the Portuguese text.)
RICE, A. HAMILTON.
    1921. The Rio Negro, the Casiquiare Canal, and the Upper Orinoco, Sep-
        tember 1919–April 1920. Geogr. Journ., vol. 58, pp. 321–344.
    1928. The Rio Branco, Uraricuera, and Parima: surveyed by the expedition
        to the Brazilian Guayana from August 1924 to June 1925. Geogr.
        Journ., vol. 71, pp. 113–143, 209–223, 345–357.
    1934. Quito to Iquitos by the River Napo.
RICH, JOHN LYON.
    1942. The face of South America; an aerial transverse. Amer. Geogr. Soc.,
        sp. publ. No. 26.
RICHTER, ENRIQUE.
    1685. Vocabulario y catecismo de la lengua campapira i cuniba. Quito.
RIEMBER, JOHANN ANDREAS.
    1833. Missions-Reise nach Surinam und Barbice zu einer um Surinamflusse
        im dritten Grad der Linie wohnenden Freiernationen. Zittau.
RIMBACH, A.
    1897. Reise im Gebiet des oberen Amazonas. Zeit. Gesell. f. Erdkunde, vol. 32,
        pp. 360–409.
RIO-BRANCO, BARXO DE.
    1899. Frontières entre le Brésil et la Guyane francaise. Second Mémoire.
        Berne.
    See also Laet, Joannes de, 1899.
RIO-BRANCO, JOSÉ MARIA DA SILVA PARANHOS.
    1897. . . . Mémoire sur la question des limites entre les Etats-Unis du Brésil
        et la Guyane Britannique. London.
RIPPY, JAMES FRED, and NELSON, JEAN THOMAS.
    1936. Crusaders of the Jungle. Chapel Hill.

RIVERO, JUAN.
    1883. Historia de las misiones de los llanos de Casanare y los rio Orinoco y
        Meta. Escrita el año de 1736. Bogotá.
RIVERO, VICTORINO.
    1897. Breve resumen historico de la fundación de San Lorenzo el real, hoy Santa
        Cruz de la Sierra, seguido de un apéndice que contiene algunas otras
        apuntaciones historicas. Santa Cruz.
RIVET, PAUL.
    1907–08. Les Indiens Jivaros. L'Anthropologie, vol. 18, pp. 333–368, 583–618;
        vol. 19, pp. 69–87, 235–259.
    1910 a. Les langues guaranies du haut-Amazone. Journ. Soc. Amér. Paris, n.s.,
        vol. 7, pp. 149–178.
    1910 b. Sur quelques dialectes Panos peu connus. Journ. Soc. Amér. Paris, n.s.,
        vol. 7, pp. 221–242.
    1911 a. Affinités du Miránya. Journ. Soc. Amér. Paris, n.s., vol. 8, pp. 117–152.
    1911 b. Le famille linguistique Peba. Journ. Soc. Amér. Paris, n.s., vol. 8,
        pp. 173–206.
    1912 a. Les familles linguistiques du Nord-ouest de l'Amérique du Sud.
        L'Année Ling., vol. 4, pp. 117–154.
    1912 b. Affinités du Tikuna. Journ. Soc. Amér. Paris, n.s., vol. 9, pp. 83–110.
    1920. Les Katukina, étude linguistique. Journ. Soc. Amér. Paris, n.s., vol. 12,
        pp. 83–89.
    1921. Nouvelle contribution à l'étude de la langue des Itonama. Journ. Soc.
        Amér. Paris, n.s., vol. 13, pp. 173–195.
    1923. L'orfèvrerie précolombienne des Antilles, des Guyanes, et du Vénézuéla;
        dans ses rapports avec l'orfèvrerie et la metallurgie des autres régions
        américaines. Journ. Soc. Amér. Paris, n.s., vol. 15, pp. 183–213.
    1924. Langues de l'Amérique du Sud et des Antilles. In Meillet, A., and Cohen,
        Marcel, Les Langues du Monde, Coll. Ling., Soc. Linguistique Paris, vol.
        16, pp. 639–712.
    1930. Contribution à l'étude des tribus indiennes de l'orient équatorien. Bull.
        Soc. Amér. Bel., Mars, 1930, pp. 5–19.
        See also Beuchat, Henri, and Rivet, Paul; Créqui-Montfort, Georges de,
        and Rivet Paul; and Verneau, René, and Rivet, Paul.
RIVET, PAUL, and FATHERS KOK, P., and TASTEVIN C.
    1924–25. Nouvelle contribution à l'étude de la langue Makú. Int. Journ. Amer.
        Ling., vol. 3, pp. 133–192.
RIVET, PAUL, and REINBURG, P.
    1921. Les Indiens Marawan. Journ. Soc. Amér. Paris, n.s., vol. 13, pp. 103–118.
RIVET, PAUL, and TASTEVIN, CONSTANT.
    1919–24. Les langues du Purús, du Juruá et des régions limitrophes; 1. Le
        groupe arawak pré-andin. Anthropos, vols. 14–15, 1919–20, pp. 857–
        890; vols. 16–17, 1921–22, pp. 298–325, 819–828; vols. 18–19, 1923–24,
        pp. 104–113.
    1920. Affinités du Makú et du Puináve. Journ. Soc. Amér. Paris, n.s., vol. 12,
        pp. 60–82.
    1921. Les tribus indiennes des bassins du Purús, du Juruá et des régions limi-
        trophes. La Geogr., vol. 35, pp. 449–482.
    1927–29. Les dialectes Pano du haut Juruá et du haut Purús. Anthropos, vol.
        22, pp. 811–827; vol. 24, pp. 489-516.
    1931. Nouvelle contribution à l'étude du groupe Kahuapana. Int. Journ. Amer.
        Ling., vol. 6, pp. 227–271.
    1938. Les langues arawak du Purús et du Juruá (Groupe arauá). Journ. Soc.
        Amér. Paris, n.s., vol. 30, pp. 71–114, 235–288.

ROBERTSON, J. H.
1822. Journal of an expedition 1400 miles up the Orinoco and 300 up the Aranca. London.

ROBINSON, (REV.) ALBAN.
1918. Some figures in string from the Makushis on the Ireng and Takutu Rivers. Timehri, 3rd ser., vol. 5, pp. 140–152.

ROBUCHON, EUGENIO.
1907 a. En el Putumayo y sus afluentes. Lima.
1907 b. Kurze Mitteilung ohne Titel. Larrabure, vol. 13, pp. 431–465.

ROCHA, JOAQUÍN.
1905. Memorandum de viaje . . . regiones Amazonicas. Bogotá.

ROCHA POMBO, JOSÉ FRANCISCO DA.
1905. Historia do Brazil. Vol. 6. Rio de Janeiro. (10 vols.)

RODRIGUES BARATA, FRANCISCO JOSÉ.
(1798–99), 1903. (French translation) Journal de voyage que fit dans la colonie hollandaise de Surinam le porte-enseigne de la 7e companie du régiment de la ville de Para . . . Limites entre le Brézil et la Guyane anglaise: Annexes au prémiere mémoire, vol. 4, 62 pp. at end. Paris.

RODRIGUES FERREIRA, ALEXANDRE.
1841. Propriedade e posse das terras do Cabo do Norte pela corôa de Portugal . . . Rev. Inst. Hist. Geogr. Brasil, vol. 3, pp. 389–421.
1885–88. Diario da viagem philosophica pela capitania da São José do Rio Negro, com a informação do estado presente. Rev. Inst. Hist. Geogr. Brasil, vol. 48, 1885, pp. 1–234; vol. 49, 1886, pt. 1, pp. 123–288; vol. 50, 1887, pt. 2, pp. 11–141; vol. 51, 1888, pt. 1, pp. 5–104.
n.d. Explicação das aquarelas de Joachim Joseph Covina. MS. (Watercolors and text in the Museu Nacional, Rio de Janeiro.)

RODRÍGUEZ, MANUEL.
1684. El Marañon y Amazonas. Madrid.

RODWAY, JAMES.
1891–94. History of British Guiana. 3 vols. Georgetown, Demerara.
1894. In the Guiana forest. New York. (Other editions, 1897, London, and 1911, London.)
1895. Some Spanish accounts of Guiana. Timehri, June, 1895, pp. 1–20.
1912. Guiana: British, Dutch, and French. London.

ROJAS, ARISTIDES.
1878. Estudios indígenas. Caracas.

ROMANO, SANTIAGO, and CATTUNAR, HERMANN.
1916. Diccionario Chiriguano-Español y Español-Chiriguano compilado teniendo a la vista diversos manuscritos de antiguos misioneros del Apostolico colegio de Santa Maria de los Angeles de Tarija y particularmente el Diccionario Chiriguano etimologico del R. P. Dorotéo Giannechini, Tarija.

ROMERO, CARLOS A. See URTEAGA, HORACIO, H., and ROMERO, CARLOS A., EDS.

RONDÓN, CANDIDO MARIANO DA SILVA.
1912. Comissão de Linhas Telegráficas estrategicas de Matto-Grosso ao Amazonas. Relatório apresentado á Diretoria geral dos telégrafos e á divisão geral de engenharia (G.5) do departamenta da guerra. Estudos e reconhecimentos, vol. 1. Rio de Janeiro.
1913(?). Ethnographia. Comissão de Linhas Telegráphicas estrategicas de Matto Grosso ao Amazonas. Annexo 5. Rio de Janeiro.

1916. Lectures delivered by . . . Publications of the Rondón Commission, No. 43, pp. 192 ff. Rio de Janeiro. (Portuguese text published under No. 42.)

    See also Comissão Rondón, 1911; and Missão Rondón, 1916.

Roop, Wendell Prescott.
1935. Watercraft in Amazonia. Woodbury, New Jersey.

Roosevelt, Theodore.
1914. Through the Brazilian wilderness. New York.
1924. Works . . . Vol. 6. London.

Roquette-Pinto, Edgar.
1912 a. Rondonia. Rio de Janeiro. (Reprints, 1917, Archiv. Mus. Nac. Rio de Janeiro, vol. 12; 1935, São Paulo; 1938, Bibl. Pedag. Brasil, vol. 39.)
1912 b. Os Indios Nambikuara do Brasil Central. A communication to the International Congress of Americanists held in London in 1912.
1912 c. Die Indianer Nhambiquára aus Zentral-Brazilien. Brasilianishe Rundschau, Rio de Janeiro.
1917. Os Indios da Serra do Norte. A communication to the Pan-American Congress of Washington in 1917.

Rosario, Francisco del.
1682. Carta de relación del Padre . . . de todo lo sucedido en la conquista espiritual de los Andes del Peru, por la parte de Cochabamba. *In* Meléndez, Tesosoros verdaderos de los Yndias, vol. 3, pp. 812–844. Roma.

Rosell, Enrique.
1905. Conquista de la Montaña. Lima.
1916. Los Machigangas del Urubamba; estudios etnográficos. Rev. Univ. Cuzco, año 5, No. 15, pp. 39–48; No. 16, pp. 2–18.

Rosen, Eric von.
1924. Ethnographical research work during the Swedish Chaco-Cordillera-expedition, 1901–1902. Stockholm.

Rosny, L. de.
1884. De la mort et des funerailles chez les anciens Caraibes. Archiv. Soc. Amér. de France, n.s., vol. 3, pp. 268–278.

Rossi, C. Bartolomé.
1863. Viaje pitoresco por los rios Paraná, Paraguay, San Lorenzo, Cuyabá y el Arinos. Paris.

Roth, Henry Ling.
1920. A loom from Iquitos. Man, vol. 20, pp. 123–125.

Roth, Walter Edmund.
1908. Catch cradle in British Guiana. Etud. Ethnol. et Soc., Nos. 4–5.
1909–12. Some technological notes from the Pomeroon District, British Guiana. Pt. I, Journ. Roy. Anthrop. Inst., vol. 39, 1909, pp. 26–34; pt. II, Journ. Roy. Anthrop. Inst., vol. 40, 1910, pp. 23–38; vol. 41, 1911, pp. 72–82; vol. 42, 1912, pp. 529–540.
1911. Narcotics and stimulants of the Guianese Indians. British Guiana Med. Annals.
1912. On the native drinks of the Guianese Indians. Timehri, 3rd ser., vol. 2, pp. 129–134.
1915. An inquiry into the animism and folk-lore of the Guiana Indians. 30th Ann. Rep. Bur. Amer. Ethnol. 1908–09, pp. 103–386. Washington.
1920. Comments: "The Central Arawaks." Amer. Anthrop., n.s., vol. 22, pp. 291–293.

1924. An introductory study of the arts, crafts, and customs of the Guiana Indians. 38th Ann. Rep. Bur. Amer. Ethnol., 1916–17, pp. 25–745.

1929. Additional studies of the arts, crafts, and customs of the Guiana Indians, with special reference to those of Southern Guiana. Bull. Bur. Amer. Ethnol., No. 91.

See also Schomburgk, Moritz Richard, 1922–23.

ROUSSEAU, GEORGES.
1901. Les richesses de la Guyane française et de l'ancien contestè franco-brésilien. Paris.

ROUX, HENRI D.
1936. Les néo-Amérindiens en Guyane française. Rev. Gen. Sci., vol. 47, pp. 225–226.

RUÍZ DE MONTOYA, ANTONIO.
1876. Arte bocabulario, tesoro y catacismo de la lengua Guarani. Leipzig. (First ed. 1640.)

1892. Conquista espiritual hecha por los religiosos de la compañia de Jesus en las provincias del Paraguay, Paraná, Uruguay y Tape. Bilbao. (Earlier ed. 1639, Madrid.)

RYDÉN, STIG.
1942. Notes on the Moré Indians, Rio Guaporé, Bolivia. Ethnos, vol. 7, Nos. 2–3, pp. 84–124.

SAABEDRA, CRISTÓBAL DE.
1620. Suerte y calidades de los indios y modo de vivir que tienen; frutos y sustentos que da la tierra de los Maynas, que está reducida al servicio Real. Lima. (Rel. Geogr. Indias, vol. 4, 1897, pp. 39–48.)

SABATÉ, LUIS.
1877. Viaje de los padres misioneros del convento del Cuzco a las tribus salvajes de los Campas, Piros, Cunibos, y Sipibos en el año de 1874. Lima.

SABIN, JOSEPH.
1868–92. Dictionary of works relating to America from the discovery to the present time. 20 vols. New York.

SACK, ALBERT (BARON) VON.
1810. A narrative of a voyage to Surinam. London.

1821. Beschreibung einer Reise nach Surinam. 2 vols. Berlin.

SAEGHMAN, GILLIS JOOSTEN.
1663–70. Comp. Verscheyde Oost-Indische voyagien. Korte en wonderlijcke beschryvinge (28 pts. in 2 vols.), pt. 2, No. 9.

SAGOLS, FRANCISCO.
1902. Los habitantes de la Pampa del Sacramento. Bol. Soc. Geogr. Lima, vol. 11, pp. 357–366.

SAGOT, P. *See* CREVAUX, JULES, SAGOT, P., and ADAM, L.

ST. CLAIR, THOMAS STAUNTON.
1834. A soldier's recollections of the West Indies and America. 2 vols. London.

SAINT-CRICQ, LAURENT.
1853 a. Voyage à travers l'Amérique du Sud de l'Océan Pacifique à l'Océan Atlantique. Paris.

1853 b. Voyage du Pérou au Brésil par les fleuves Ucayali et Amazone. Indiens Conibos. Bull. Soc. Géogr. Paris, 4th ser., vol. 6, pp. 273–295.

SALA, F. R.
1892. Du Pacifique à l'Atlantique par les Andes Peruviennes et l'Amazone Paris.

SALA, GABRIEL.
1905–08. Diccionario, gramatica y catecismo castellano, inga, amueixa y campa.
Bol. Soc. Geogr. Lima, vol. 17, pp. 149–227, 311–356, 469–490; vol. 19,
pp. 102–120, 211–240; vol. 21, pp. 311–341; vol. 23, pp. 81–101.
SALAS, JULIO C.
1908. Etnología e historia de Tierra-Firme (Venezuela y Colombia). Editorial
—América. (Soc. Esp. Libr.) Bibl. Cienc. Pol. y Soc. Madrid.
1920. Los indios Caribes, estudio sobre el origen del mito de la antropofagia.
Talleres Graficos Lux. Madrid. (1921 ed. Barcelona.)
SALINAS LOYOLA, JUAN DE.
1897. Descubrimientos, conquistas y poblaciones de Juan de Salinas Loyola.
Five letters. Rel. Geogr. Indias, vol. 4, pp. 65–101 (Peru).
SAMPAIO, A. J. DE.
1933. A flora do Rio Cuminá (E. do Pará-Brasil), Resultados Botanicos da
Expedição Rondón á Serra Tumuc-Humas an 1928. Archiv. Mus.
Nac. Rio de Janeiro, vol. 35, pp. 9–206.
SAMPAIO, FRANCISCO XAVIER RIBEIRO DE. See RIBEIRO DE SAMPAIO, FRANCISCO
XAVIER.
SAMPAIO, TEODORO.
1915. Os naturalistas viajantes do séculos XVIII e XIX e o progresso da
etnografia indígena no Brasil. Rev. Inst. Hist. Geogr. São Paulo,
Tomo especial, pt. 2a.
1922. Arqueologia Brasileira. In Dic. Hist., Geogr., e Etnol. do Brasil ,vol. 1,
pp. 847–856.
SAN MANÇOS, FRANCISCO DE.
1903. Rapport présenté au Roi par le Frère Francisco de S. Manços, religieus
de l'Ordre de la Pitié et Missionnaire dans le village de Nhamondás,
sur son voyage par la rivière Trombetas, au cours duquel il catéchisa
les Indiens en les soumettant au vasselage de sa Majesté—6 Janvier 1728.
Limites entre le Brésil de la Guyane Anglaise: Annexes au premier
mémoire, vol. 3, pp. 42–52. Paris.
SÁNCHEZ LABRADOR, JOSÉ.
1910. Noticia de las misiones de los indios Chiquitos. In "El Paraguay
Católico," vol. 1, pp. 75–88. Buenos Aires.
SANDERSON, IVAN.
1939. A journey in Dutch Guiana. Geogr. Journ., vol. 93, pp. 468–490.
SANSON, NICOLAS.
1856. Partie de Terre Ferme où sont Guiane et Caribane. Paris.
SÃO JOSÉ, JOÃO.
1847. Viagem e Visita do Sertão em o Bispado do Grão Pará em 1762 e 1763.
Rev. Inst. Hist., vol. 9. (2nd ed., 1869, vol. 9, pp. 43–107, 179–227, 328–
375, 476–527.)
SARMIENTO DE GAMBÓA, PEDRO.
1906. Geschichte des Inkareiches. Abhandl. Königl. Gesellsch. Wissensch.
Göttingen, Philologisch-historisch klasse, Neue-folge, vol. 6, No. 4.
1907. History of the Incas. (Translated by C. Markham.) London.
SCHMELTZ, JOHANNES DIEDRICH EDUARD.
1897. Geräthe der Caraiben von Surinam (Niederländisch Guayane). Int.
Archiv. Ethnogr., vol. 10, pp. 60–68.
1910. Die niederländische Tumac Humac Expedition in Surinam. Congr. Int.
Amer., sess. 16, Vienna, pp. 51–54.

SCHMIDEL, ULRICH.
1903. Viaje al Rio de La Plata (1534–1554). Notas bibliográficas y biográficas por Bartolomé Mitre. Prólogo, traducción, y anotaciones por Samuel A. Lafone Quevedo. Buenos Aires.

SCHMIDT, HERMANN.
1910. Die Uitóto-Indianer. Journ. Soc. Amér. Paris, n.s., vol. 7, pp. 60–83.

SCHMIDT, MAX.
1902–04. Aus den Ergebnissen meiner Expedition in das Schingúquellgebiet. Globus, vol. 82, 1902, No. 2, p. 22; vol. 86, 1904, pp. 119–125.
1903. Nachrichten über die Kayabí-Indianer. Zeit. Ethnol., vol. 35.
1905. Indianerstudien in Zentralbrasilien; Erlebnisse und ethnologische Ergebnisse einer Reise in den Jahren 1900 bis 1901, pp. 135–159, 175–317. Berlin.
1907. Besondere Geflechtsart der Indianer im Ucayaligebiet. Archiv. für Anthrop., vol. 34, pp. 270–281.
1914. Die Paressi-Kabishi. Baessler-archiv., vol. 4, pp. 167–250.
1917. Die Aruaken; ein Beitrag zum problem der kulturverbreitung. Leipzig.
1924. Unter Indianern Südamerikas; Erlebnisse in Zentralbrasilien. Berlin.
1929 a. Ergebnisse meiner zweijährigen ethnologischen und archäologischen Forschungsreise nach Matto Grosso. Forschungen und Fortschritte, vol. 5, No. 9, pp. 104–105. Berlin.
1929 b. Ergebnisse meiner zweijährigen forschungareise in Matto Grosso, Sept. 1926 bis August, 1928. Zeit. Ethnol., vol. 60, pp. 85–124.
1932. Nuevos hallazgos prehistóricos del Paraguay. Rev. Soc. Cient. Paraguay, vol. 3, No. 3.
1936. Los Guarayú. Rev. Soc. Cient. Paraguay, vol. 3, No. 6, pp. 158–194.
1938. Los Chiriguanos e Izozós. Rev. Soc. Cient. Paraguay, vol. 4, No. 3.
1940. Nuevos hallazgos de grabados rupestres en Matto Grosso. Rev. Soc. Cient. Paraguay, vol. 5, No. 1, pp. 63–71.
1942. Los Iranche. Rev. Soc. Cient. Paraguay, vol. 5, No. 6, pp. 35–39.
1943. Los Paressís. Rev. Soc. Cient. Paraguay, vol. 6, No. 1, pp. 1–294.
    See also Koch-Grünberg, Theodor, 1902.

SCHMIDT, WILHELM.
1905. Diccionario Sipibo . . . herausgegeben von Karl von den Steinen. Mitt. Anthrop. Gesell. Wien, vol. 35, pp. 127–130.
1913. Kulturkreise und kulturschichten in Südamerika. Zeit. Ethnol., vol. 45, pp. 1014–1124.

SCHOMBURGK, MORITZ RICHARD.
1847–48. Reisen in Britisch-Guiana in den Jahren 1840–44. 3 vols. Leipzig.
1879. On the urari: the deadly arrow-poison of the Macusis, an Indian tribe in British Guiana. Adelaide.
1922–23. Travels in British Guiana, 1840–44. Tr. and ed. by Walter Roth. 2 vols. Georgetown.

SCHOMBURGK, O. A.
1841. Robert Hermann Schomburgk's Reisen in Guiana und am Orinoko Während der Jahre 1835–39. Nach seinen Berichten und Mittheilungen an die Geographische Gesellschaft in London, hrsg. von O. A. Schomburgk. Leipzig.

SCHOMBURGK, ROBERT HERMANN.
1836 a. On the religious traditions of the Macusi Indians who inhabit the upper Maku and a portion of the Mocaraima Mountains. Roy. Soc. Antiquaries.

1836 b. Report of an expedition into the interior of British Guiana. Journ. Roy. Geogr. Soc., vol. 6, pp. 224–284.

1837 a. Diary of an ascent of the River Berbice. Journ. Roy. Geogr. Soc., vol. 7, pp. 302–350.

1837 b. Diary of an ascent of the River Corentyn. Journ. Roy. Geogr. Soc., vol. 7, pp. 285–301.

1840. A description of British Guiana. London.

1841 a. Journey to the sources of the Essequibo. Journ. Roy. Geogr. Soc., vol. 10, pp. 159–190.

1841 b. Journey from Fort San Joaquim . . . to Roraima. journ. Roy. Geogr. Soc., vol. 10, pp. 191–247.

1841 c. Journey from Esmeralda . . . to San Carlos. Journ. Roy. Geogr. Soc., vol. 10, pp. 248–267.

1841 d. Geographisch-statistische Beschreibung von British-Guiana. Magdeburg. (German version of 1840 ed.)

1842. Expedition to the lower parts of the Barima and Guiana Rivers. Journ. Roy. Geogr. Soc., vol. 12, pp. 169–178.

1843. Visit to the sources of the Takutu. Journ. Roy. Geogr. Soc., vol. 13, pp. 18–75.

1845. Journal of an expedition from Pirara to . . . Demerara. Journ. Roy. Geogr. Soc., vol. 15, pp. 1–104.

1848. On the natives of Guiana. Journ. Ethnol. Soc. London, vol. 1, pp. 253–276.
    See also Adalbert, Prince of Prussia, 1849.

SCHULLER, RODOLFO R.

1907. Sobre el supuesto autor del Arte de la lengua de los indios campa y antis. Bol. Ministerio Agr. Colonización. La Paz.

1911. La lenguas indígenas de la cuenca del Amazonas y del Orinoco. Rev. Americana, vol. 5, pp. 622–661; vol. 6, pp. 25–84.

1912. Die Bedeutung der bezeichnung Njambiquára für südamerikanische Indianer. Petermanns Mitt., vol. 58, pt. 2, p. 207.

1916. Discovery of new materials of the Moseten idiom. Amer. Anthrop., n.s., vol. 18, pp. 603–604.

1921. The linguistic and ethnographical position of the Nambicuára Indians. Amer. Anthrop., n.s., vol. 23, pp. 471–477.

1922. The ethnological and linguistic position of the Tacana Indians of Bolivia. Amer. Anthrop., n.s., vol. 24, pp. 161–170.

1927. Wo sassen die Čupačo-Indianer? Anthropos, vol. 22, pp. 997–1000.
    See also Anonymous, MS. a.

SCHULTES, RICHARD EVANS.

1942. Plantae Colombianae II. Yoco: a stimulant of Southern Colombia. Harvard Univ. Botanical Mus. Leaflets, No. 10, pp. 301–324.

SCHULTZ, THEODOR, REV.

1850. The Acts of the Apostles translated into the Arrawack tongue. New York.

SCHUMANN.

1882. Arawakisch-Beutsches Worterbuch. Bibl. Ling. Amér. Paris, vol. 8, pp 69–165.

SCOTT, MAJOR JOHN.

n.d. The historical and geographical description of the great river of the Amazones . . . and of the several nations inhabiting that famous country, or rather mightier Realm, or empire of above three thousand leagues in compass, part of which I have seen myself (circa 1670). Rawlinson MSS., A. 175, No. 356, p. 18.

SELER, EDUARD.
 1922. Museumsnotiz. Präparierte Feindesköpfc bei den Jivaro-stämmen des
 oberen Marañon und bei den alten bewohnern des Departements Ica an
 der Küste von Peru. Baessler-archiv., vol. 6, pts. 1–2, pp. 82–86.
SEPP, ANTOINE.
 1819. Lettre du père Antoine Sepp, missionnaire de la Compagnie de Jésus, au
 père Guillaume Stinglhaim, provincial de la même Compagnie dans la
 province de la Haute-Allemagne. *In* Lettres édifiantes et curieuses, vol.
 5, pp. 476–491. Lyon.
SERRANO, ANTONIO.
 1936. Etnografía de la antigua provincia del Uruguay. Paraná.
SERRANO Y SANZ, MANUEL.
 1898. Los Indios chiriguanaes. Rev. Archiv. Bibl. Mus., vol. 2, pp. 321–339,
 410–421, 514-526, 568–574.
 1909. Relación verdadera de todo lo que sucedio en la jornada de Omagua y
 Dorado. (Nueva biblioteca de autores españoles, vol. 15.) Historiadores de Indias, vol. 2, pp. 423–484.
  See also Caballero, Lucas, 1933.
SERVIÇO DE PROTECÇÃO AOS INDIOS, ARQUIVOS DA INSPECTORIA DO PARÁ. 1942.
SETCHELL, WILLIAM ALBERT.
 1921. Aboriginal tobaccos. Amer. Anthrop., n.s., vol. 23, pp. 397–414.
SEVERIANO DA FONSECA, JOÃO. *See* FONSECA, JOÃO SEVERIANO DA.
SHAW, EARL B.
 1940. The Rupununi savannahs of British Guiana. Journ. Geogr., vol. 39,
 pp. 89–104.
SHEDD, MARGARET.
 1933. Carib dance patterns. Theater Arts Monthly, vol. 17, pp. 65–77.
SIEVERS, WILHELM.
 1887. Bemerkungen zur Karte der Venozolanisch-Brasilianischen Grenze. Zeit.
 Gesell. f. Erdkunde, vol. 22, pp. 1–5 and map.
SILVA, JOAQUIM CAETANO DA.
 1861. L'Oyapoc et l'Amazone. 2 vols. Paris and Rio de Janeiro.
SIMON, PEDRO.
 1861. The expedition of Pedro de Ursua and Lope de Aguirre in search of El
 Dorado and Omagua in 1560–1. Tr. from Pedro Simón's "Sixth Historical Notice of the Conquest of Tierra Firma." Hakluyt Soc., vol.
 28. London.
SIMPSON, GEORGE GAYLORD.
 1940. Los Indios Kamarakotos: Tribu Caribe de la Guyana Venezolana. Tr.
 from English by J. Villaneuva-Ucalde. Rev. Fomento (Venezuela),
 Año 3, Nos. 22–25.
SIMSON, ALFRED.
 1878. Notes on the Zaparos. Journ. Anthrop. Inst. Gr. Brit. and Ireland, vol. 7,
 pp. 502–510.
 1879 a. Notes on the Piojes of the Putumayo. Journ. Anthrop. Inst. Gr. Brit.
 and Ireland, vol. 8, pp. 210–222.
 1879 b. Vocabulary of the Záparo language. Journ. Anthrop. Inst. Gr. Brit.
 and Ireland, vol. 8, pp. 223–226.
 1883. Notes on the Napo Indians. Journ. Anthrop. Inst. Gr. Brit. and Ireland,
 vol. 12, pp. 21–27.
 1886. Travels in the wilds of Ecuador, and the exploration of the Putumayo
 River. London.

SKINNER, JOSEPH.
1805. The present state of Peru: comprising its geography, topography, natural history, etc. London.
1809. Voyages au Pérou, faits dans les années 1791 à 1794 par les pp. Manuel Sobreviela et Narcisso y Barcelo . . . Paris.
SMITH, A. C. *See* Killip, E. P., and Smith, A. C.
SMYTH, LIEUTENANT (WM.).
1836. Account of the Rivers Amazon and Negro, from recent observations. Journ. Roy. Geogr. Soc., vol. 6, pp. 11–23.
SMYTH, WILLIAM, and LOWE, F.
1836. Narrative of a journey from Lima to Para. London.
SNETHLAGE, EMIL HEINRICH.
1913. A travessia entre o Xingú e Tapajóz. Bol. Mus. Goeldi, vol. 7.
1920–21. Die Indianerstämme am mittleren Xingú. Im besonderen die Chipaya und Curuaya. Zeit. Ethnol., vol. 52, pp. 395–427.
1927. Meine Reise durch Nordostbrasilien. I. Journ. Ornithol., vol. 75, pp. 453–484.
1931 a. Unter nordostbrasilianischen Indianern. Zeit. Ethnol., vol. 62, pp. 111–205.
1931 b. Ein figurliches Ikat-Gewebe aus Peru. Sonderdruck: Der Weltkreis, z.f. V., Kulture geschichte u. Vulksdunde. 2 Jr., heft 3–4. Berlin.
1936 a. Nachrichten über die Pauserna-Guarayú, die Siriono am Rio Baures und die S. Simonianes in der Nähe der Serra S. Simon. Zeit. Ethnol., vol. 67, pp. 278–293.
1936 b. Tagungsberichte der Gesellschaft für Völkerkunde in Leipzig, Bericht über die 2 tagung. Pp. 172–180.
1936 c. Uebersicht uber die Indianer-stamme des Guaporegebietes. Sond. aus dem Tagungsbericht der Gesell. fur Völkerkunde. 2 Tagung. Leipzig.
1937 a. Atiko y :meine Erlebnisse bei den Indianern des Guaporé. Berlin.
1937 b. Forschungen und Abenteuer.
1939. Musikinstrumente der Indianer des Guaporé-Gebietes. Baessler-archiv., vol. 10.
SNETHLAGE, EMIL HEINRICH, and KOCH-GRÜNBERG, THEODOR.
1910. Zur Ethnographie der Chipaya and Curuahé. Zeit. Ethnol., vol. 42, pp. 609–637.
SNETHLAGE, EMILIA.
n.d. The linguistic material of the second trip, on Sipáyas and Kuruáyas (of which Nimuendajú has a copy). MS.
SOARES DE SOUZA, GABRIEL.
1851. Tratado descriptivo do Brasil em 1587. Rev. Inst. Hist. Geogr. Brasil, vol. 14, pp. 1–423. (2nd ed. 1879, vol. 14, pp. 1–374.)
SOBREVIELA, MANUEL, and NARCISSO Y BARCELO. *See* SKINNER, JOSEPH, 1809.
SOMBRA, LUIZ.
1913. Os Cachinauas. Ligeiras notas sobre seus usos e costumes. Jornal do Commercio, January 11. Rio de Janeiro.
SOTOMAYOR, JOSÉ ANTONIO.
1901. Relación de los infieles del Ucayali. Bol. Soc. Geogr. Lima, vol. 10, pp. 171–178.
SOTTO MAYOR, JOÃO DE.
1916. Diario da jornada que fiz ao Pacajá no anno de 1656. Rev. Inst. Hist. Geogr. Brasil, vol. 77, pt. 2, pp. 157–179.
SOUSA, ANDRÉ FERNANDES DE.
1870. Noticias geographicas da Capitania do Rio Negro. Rev. Inst. Hist., vol. 10, pp. 411-504.

SOUSA, PERO LOPES DE.
    1839. Diario da navegação da armada que foi á terra do Brasil em 1530 . . .
        Publ. por Francisco Adolfo de Varnhagen. Lisboa.
    1927. Diario da navegação . . . (1530–1532). Edición Eduardo Prado, Rio de
        Janeiro.
SOUTHEY, ROBERT.
    1817–22. History of Brazil. 3 vols. London.
    1862. Historia do Brasil. Vol. 5, p. 90; vol. 6, pp. 248–249. Rio de Janeiro.
SOUZA, ANTONIO PYRENEUS DE.
    1916. Exploração do Rio Paranatinga. Comissão de Linhas Telegraphicas
        Estrategicas de Matto Grosso a Amazonas. Publicação No. 34.
        Annexo No. 2. Rio de Janeiro.
    1920. Notas sobre os costumes dos indios Nhambiquaras. Rev. Mus. Paulista,
        vol. 12, pt. 2, pp. 389–410.
SOUZA, CONEGO FRANCISCO BERNARDINO DE.
    1873. Lambranças e curiosidades do valle do Amazonas. Pará.
    1874. Comissão do Madeira. Pará-Amazonas. Rio de Janeiro.
SOUZA FRANCO, BERNARDO DE.
    1842. Fal la dirigida á Assemblea Legislativa Provincial. 14 de Abril de 1842.
SPEISER, FELIX.
    1926. Im Düster des brasilianischen Urwaldes. Stuttgart.
SPIX, JOHANN BAPTIST VON, and MARTIUS, KARL FRIEDRICH PHIL. VON.
    1823–31. Reise in Brasilien . . . 1817 bis 1820 . . . 3 vols. München.
    1824. Travels in Brazil - . 1817–1820. Trans. by H. E. Lloyd. 2 vols.
        London.
    1831. Atlas. München.
    See also Hörschelmann, Werner von, 1918–20.
SPRUCE, RICHARD.
    1908. Notes of a botanist on the Amazon and Andes. 2 vols. London.
STADEN, HANS.
    1557. Warhaftige Historia und beschreibung eyner landtschaff der Wilnen /
        Nacketen / Grimmigen Menschfresser Leuthen / in der Newenwelt
        America Gelegen / vor und nach Christi geburt im Land zu Hessen
        vnbekant / bisz vff dise y. neehstvergabgene jar / Da sie Hans Staden
        von Homberg ausz Hessen durch sein eygne erfarung erkant / vnd
        yetzo? durch den truck an tag gibt. Getruckt zu Marpurg. (Edición
        facsimilar por Richard N. Wegner bajo el título: Hans Staden,
        Warhaftige Historia etc. Frankfurt a. M. 1925, en la Biblioteca de
        GAEA Sociedad Argentina de Estudios Geográficos.)
    1928. . . . Hans Staden, the true history of his captivity. (The Broadway
        Travellers.) London.
STADEN, HANS, and FEDERMANN, NIKOLAUS. See KLÜPFEL, KARL AUGUST, 1859.
STAELHELIN, F.
    n.d. Die Mission der Brudergemeine in Suriname und Berbice in achtzehnten
        Jahrhundert. Teil II, III: 2. Herrnhut.
STAHEL, GEROLD.
    1921–22. Een Indiaansche rotsteekening aan de Kabalebo-rivier (Coranti jn).
        De West-Indische Gids, vol. 3, pp. 100 ff.
STAMPAERT, G.
    1924–25. Een bezoek aan de Indianen te Suriname. Zaire. Orgaan der
        Vlaamsche Kolonialen, No. 1, p. 39.

STEDMAN, JOHN GABRIEL.
   1796. Narrative of a five years' expedition against the revolted negroes of
       Surinam in Guiana, on the wild coast of South America; from the
       year 1772 to 1777. 2 vols. London.
STEERE, JOSEPH BEAL.
   1903. Narrative of a visit to Indian tribes of the Purus River, Brazil. Ann.
       Rep., U. S. National Mus., 1901, pp. 359–393.
   1927. Archaeology of the Amazon. Univ. Michigan Official Publication 29,
       No. 9. Ann Arbor.
STEGELMANN, FELIX. See REICH, ALFRED, and STEGELMANN, FELIX.
STEINEN, KARL VON DEN.
   1886. Durch Central-Brasilien. Leipzig.
   1888. Über seine zweite Schingú-Expedition. In Verhandl. d. Gesell, f. Erdkund.
       zu Berlin, vol. 15, pp. 369–387.
   1892. Die Bakaïrí Sprache. Leipzig.
   1894. Unter den Naturvölkern Zentral-Brasiliens. Berlin.
   1899. Indianerskizzen von Hercules Florence. Globus, vol. 75, pp. 5–9, 30–35.
   1904. Diccionario sipibo. Castellano-deutsch-sipibo. Apuntes de gramática.
       Sipibo-castellano. Abdruck der Handschrift eines Franziskaners, mit
       Beiträgen zur Kenntnis der Panostämme am Ucayali. Berlin.
   1906. Der Verfasser der Handschrift "Arte de la lengua de los indios antis ó
       campas." Congr. Int. Amer., sess. 14, Stuttgart, vol. 2, pp. 603–605.
   1940. Entre os aborígenes do Brasil central. São Paulo.
STEINEN, WILHELM VON DEN.
   1899. Steinbeile der Guarayo-indianer. Ethnologisches notizblatt herausgegeben
       von der Direktion des Königlichen Museums für völkerkunde in Berlin,
       vol. 2, pp. 35–37.
STETSON, JOHN B., JR. See MAGALHÃES DE GANDAVO, PEDRO DE.
STEWARD, JULIAN H.
   1936. The economic and social basis of primitive bands. In Essays in Anthro-
       pology, pp. 331–350. Univ. Calif. Press, Berkeley.
STIGLICH, GERMÁN.
   1908. La región peruana de los bosques. In Colección de leyes, decretos, reso-
       luciones i otros documentos oficiales referentes al departamento de
       Loreto formada de orden suprema por el doctor Carlos Larrabure i
       Correa. Vol. 15, pp. 308–495. Lima.
STIRLING, MATTHEW WILLIAMS.
   1938. Historical and ethnographical material on the Jivaro Indians. Bull. Bur.
       Amer. Ethnol., No. 117.
STOCKUM, A. J. VAN.
   1905. Een ontdekkingstocht in de binnenlanden van Suriname. Dagboek van
       de Saramacca-expeditie. Amsterdam.
STOEL, G.
   1937. Over de veelvuldigheid van Kanker bij vershillende rassen in Suriname.
       Geneeskundig Tijdschrift voor Nederlandsch-Indie (Batavia), pp. 2292–
       2304.
STOPLE, HJALMAR.
   1927. Collected essays in ornamental art: South America; Atlas. Stockholm.
STRADELLI, E.
   1889. Rio Branco. Bol. Soc. Geogr. Italiana, vol. 26, pp. 210–228, 251–266.
   1890. Leggenda dell' Jurupary. Bol. Soc. Geogr. Italiana, vol. 26.

1929. Vocabularios da lingua geral portuguez-nheêngatú e nheêngatú-portuguez, precedidos de um esboço de Grammatica nheênga-umbuê-sáua mirî e seguidos de contos em lingua geral nheêngatú poranduua. Rev. Inst. Hist. Geogr. Brasil, t. 104, vol. 158, pp. 9–768.

STRAUSS, FRITZ.
1926. Schiggi-Schiggi; abenteuer des Leo Parcus in den urwäldern Boliviens. Berlin and Leipzig.

STRELNIKOV, I. D.
1928. Les Kaa-îwuá de Paraguay. Congr. Int. Amer., sess. 22, Roma, vol. 2, pp. 333–366.

STRICKLAND, JOSEPH, ED.
1896. Documents and maps on the boundary question between Venezuela and British Guayana from the Capuchin archives in Rome. Rome.

STRÖMER, C. VON.
1932. Die Sprache der Mundurukú. Anthropos: Coll. Int. de Monographies Linguistiques. II. Wien.
1937. Unter den Mundurukú in Nordbrasilien. Die Katholischen Missionen, 65 Jahrg., pp. 87–90. Düsseldorf.

STUDART FILHO, CARLOS
1927–32. Antiguida des indigenas do Ceará. Rev. Trim. Inst. Ceará, vol. 41, 1927, pp. 167–221; vol. 46, 1932, pp. 105–118.
1931. Notas historicas sobre os indigenas cearenses. Rev. Trim. Inst. Ceará, vol. 45, pp. 52–103.

STÜBEL, ALFONS, REISS, W., and KOPPEL B.
1889–90. Kultur und industrie südamerikanischer völker; nach den im besitze des Museums für völkerkunde zu Leipzig befindlichen sammlugen . . . 2 vols. Berlin.

SUÁREZ DE FIGUEROA, LORENZO.
1914. Relación de la ciudad de Santa Cruz de la Sierra por su Gobernador don . . . Anexos, vol. 1, pp. 532–554. See Mujía, 1914.

SURVILLE, D. LUIS DE.
1778. Mapa coro-grafico de la Nueva Andalucia provincias de Cumaná, y Guayana, vertientes del Orinoco, etc.

SWANTON, JOHN REED.
1931. Source material for the social and ceremonial life of the Choctaw Indians. Bull. Bur. Amer. Ethnol., No. 103.

SYPESTEYN, CORNELIS ASCANIUS, jonkheer VAN.
1854. Beschrijving van Suriname. Pp. 160–162. 's Gravenhage.
See also Focke, H. C., Landré, Ch., Sypesteyn, C. A. van, and Dumontier, F.A.C.

TAMAJUNCOSA, ANTONIO.
1910. Descripción de las misiones, al cargo del Colegio de Nuestra Señora de los angeles de la villa de Tarija . . . In Angelis, Pedro de, Colección de obras y documentos relativos á la historia antigua y moderna de las Provincias del Rio de la Plata, 2nd ed., vol. 4, pp. 187–223. Buenos Aires.

TASTEVIN, CONSTANT.
1910 a. La langue Tupihiya dite Tupi. Denkschriftten der Kaiserlichen Akademie der Wissenschaften in Wien, vol. 2. Vienna.
1910 b. La lengua tapihiya dite tupi ou neenge tu (belle langua). Grammaire, dictionnaire et textes. Vienna.
1914. En Amazone. Les missions catholiques. Vol. 46. Lyon.

1920. Quelques considérations sur les Indiens du Juruá. Bull. Mém. Soc. Anthrop. Paris, vol. 10, 6th ser., pp. 144–154.

1923 a. Les indiens Mura de la région de l'Autaz (Haut-Amazone). L'Anthrop., vol. 33, pp. 514–533. Paris.

1923 b. Les Makú du Japurá. Journ. Soc. Amér. Paris, n.s., vol. 15, pp. 99–108.

1924 a. Les études ethnographiques et linguistiques du P. Tastevin en Amazonie. Journ. Soc. Amér. Paris, n.s., vol. 16, pp. 421–425.

1924 b. Chez les Indiens du haut Jurua. Les missions catholiques. Vol. 56, pp. 65–67, 78–80, 90–93, 101–104. Lyon.

1925. Le flueve Murú. Ses habitants. Cropances et moeurs kachimaua. La Geogr., vol. 43, pp. 403–422; vol. 44, pp. 14–35.

1926. Le Haut Tarauacá. La Geogr., vol. 45, pp. 34–54, 158–175.

1928 a. Le "Riozinho da Liberdade." La Geogr., vol. 49, pp. 205–215.

1928 b. Sur les Indiens Katukina. L'Ethnogr., n.s., Nos. 17–18, pp. 130–132.

See also Rivet, Paul, and Fathers Kok, P., and Tastevin, C.; and Rivet, Paul, and Tastevin, Constant.

TATE, GEORGE HENRY HAMILTON.

1930 a. Through Brazil to the summit of Mount Roraima. Nat. Geogr. Mag., vol. 58, pp. 585–605.

1930 b. Notes on the Mount Roraima region. Geogr. Rev., vol. 20, pp. 53–68.

TATE, GEORGE HENRY HAMILTON, and HITCHCOCK, C. B.

1930. The Cerro Duida region of Venezuela. Geogr. Rev., vol. 20, pp. 31–52.

TAVERA-ACOSTA, BARTOLOMÉ.

1905–13. Anales de Guayana. Vol. 1, 1905; Vol. 1 and 2, 1913. Ciudad-Bolívar.

1906. Rionegro; reseña etnográfica, histórica y geográfica del Territorio Amazonas. Ciudad-Bolívar. (2nd ed. pub. 1927 Maracay.)

1907. En El Sur (Dialectos Indígenas de Venezuela). Ciudad de Bolívar.

1913. A traves de la historia de Venezuela. Vol. 1. Ciudad-Bolívar.

1919. Páginas historiales. Ciudad-Bolívar.

1921–22. Nuevos vocabularios de dialectos indígenas de Venezuela. Journ. Soc Amér. Paris, n.s., vol. 13, pp. 217–232; vol. 14, pp. 64–82.

1923. Las provincias orientales de Venezuela en la Primera República. Caracas.

1930. Venezuela pre-coloniana; contribución al estudio de las analogías míticas, idiomáticas y religiosas de los aborígenes venezolanos con los del continent asiático. Caracas.

TAYLOR, JOHN EDWARD. See ADALBART, PRINCE OF PRUSSIA, 1849.

TECHO, NICOLÁS DEL.

1673. Historia provinciae Paraquariae Societatis Jesv. Leodii.

1897. Historia de la provincia del Paraguay de la Compañia de Jesús. Madrid. (Two ed. pub. in 1897, one in 2 vols., the other in 5 vols.)

TEJEDOR, P. SENEN F.

1927. Breve reseña histórica de la Misión Agustiniana de San León del Amazonas-Peru. El Escorial.

TELLO B., MANUEL. See ZULOAGA, GUILLERMO, and TELLO B., MANUEL.

TELLO, JULIO CÉSAR.

1922. Introducción a la historia antigua del Perú. Lima.

1923. Wira Kocha. Inca, vol. 1, No. 1, pp. 93–320.

1942. Origen y desarrollo de las civilizaciones prehistóricas Andinas. Lima.

TENAN, L.

n.d. Relatorio da segunda exploração a Tapajonio. 20 de Novembro de 1943. MS.

TEN KATE, HERMAN FREDERICK CAREL.

1887. Observations anthropologiques recuellies dans la Guyane et la Venezuela. Rev. Anthrop., 3rd ser., vol. 2, pp. 44–68.

1888. Beitrag zwi Ethnographie von Surinam. Int. Archiv. Ethnogr., vol. 1, pp. 223–227 and plate 21.

1924. Notes d'anthropologie sud-américaine. Journ. Soc. Amér. Paris, n.s, vol. 16, pp. 183–193.

TENREIRO ARANHA, JOAO BAPTISTA DE FIGUEIREDO.

1852. Relatorio que . . . sobre o estado da Provincia do Amazonas. 30 de Abril de 1852.

TERNAUX-COMPANS, HENRI.

1837. Bibliothèque américaine; ou, Catalogue des ouvrages relatifs à l'Amérique qui ont paru depuis sa découverte jusqu'à l'an 1700. Paris.

TESSMANN, GÜNTER.

1928. Menschen ohne Gott. Stuttgart.

1929. Die Tschama-sprache. Anthropos, vol. 24, pp. 241-271.

1930. Die Indianer Nordost-Perus. Hamburg.

TEXEYRA, JOÃO.

1640. Descripção de todo o martimo da Terra de Santa Cruz. Bibliothèque Nationale. Paris.

TEZA, E.

1868. Saggi inediti di lingue americane. Appunti bibliografici. Annali delle Università toscane. Parte prima. Scienze noologiche, vol. 10, pp. 117–143. Pisa.

THERESE, PRINZESSIN VON BAYERN.

1897. Meine Reise in den brasilianischen Tropen. Berlin.

THEVET, ANDRÉ.

1575. La Cosmographie universelle. Paris.

1878. Les singularitez de la France antarctique, autrement nommée Amerique: et Isles decouvertes de nostre temps. Nouvelle édition avec notes et commentaires par Paul Gaffarel. Paris. (Paris ed., 1557; Anvers ed. 1558.)

THORON, ENRIQUE ONFFROY DE. See ONFFROY DE THORON, ENRIQUE.

TIBIRIÇÁ, RUY W.

1936. Arqueologia brasileira. Rev. Arq. Mun. São Paulo, vol. 24, pp. 137–140; vol. 30, pp. 131–142.

TOCANTINS, ANTONIO MANOEL GONÇALVES.

1877. Estudos sobre a tribu Mundurukú. Rev. Inst. Hist., vol. 40, pt. 2, pp. 73–161.

TONY, CLAUDE.

1843. Voyage dans l'intérieur du continent de la Guyano. Nouvelles annales des voyages, vol. 97, 4th ser., vol. 1, Paris.

TORO, ELÍAS.

1905. Por las selvas de Guayana. Caracas.

TORRES, HELOISA ALBERTO.

1929. Ceramica de Marajó; Conferencia realizada na Escola de belles artes, Rio de Janeiro, 1929, e Rev. do Inst. Arch. de Pernambuco. Rio de Janeiro.

1930. Ceramica de Marajó. Kosmos, No. 1. Rio de Janeiro.

1940. Arte indigena da Amazonia. Publicações do Serviço do Patrimonio Histórico e Artistico Nacional, No. 6. Rio de Janeiro.

TORRES, LUIS MARÍA.

1913. Los primitivos habitantes del delta del Paraná. Buenos Aires.

TRIANA, MIGUEL.

1907. Por el sur de Colombia; Excursión pintoresca y científica al Putumayo. Prólogo de S. Pérez Triana. [Preface, 1907.] Paris.

TYLER, CHARLES DOLBY.
1894. The River Napo. Journ. Roy. Geogr. Soc., vol. 3, No. 6, pp. 476–484.
UHLE, MAX.
1889–90. Kultur und industrie südamerikanischer völker. Berlin.
1923. Toltecas, Mayas y civilizaciones Sudamericanas. Bol. Acad. Nac. Hist. Quito, vol. 7, No. 18, pp. 1–33.
UHLE, E.
1913. Unter den Indianern am Rio Branco in Nordbrasilien. Zeit. Ethnol., vol. 45, pp. 278–298.
ULLRICH, C. O.
1906. Die Tapes. Congr. Int. Amer., 14th sess., Stuttgart, 1904, vol. 2, pp. 473–506.
UP DE GRAFF, FRITZ W.
1923. Head-hunters of the Amazon; seven years of exploration and adventure. Garden City, New York. (Also 1923 ed. London.)
URQUHART, D. R.
1893. Among the Campa Indians of Peru. Scot. Geogr. Mag., vol. 9, pp. 348–359.
URTEAGA, HORACIO H., and ROMERO, CARLOS A., EDS.
1916–19. Collección de libros y documentos referentes a la historia del Perú. Vol. 12. Lima.
VAAS DE CAMINHA, PEDRO.
1812–13. Carta de . . . a El Rei D. Manoel, sobre o descubrimiento da terra de Santa Cruz, vulgarmente chamada Brasil. Collecção de Noticias para a Historia e Geografia das Nacaes Ultramarinas que vivem nos dominios portuguezes, ou les são visinhas. Vol. 2. Lisbon.
VACAS GALINDO, ENRIQUE.
1895. Nankijukima. Ambato, Ecuador.
VALLE BENTES, E. E. See NIMUENDAÚ, CURT, and VALLE BENTES, E. E.
VAN STOCKUM, A. J. See STOCKUM, A. J. VAN.
VAN SYPESTEYN, C. A. See SYPESTEYN, C. A. VAN.
VASCONCELLOS, SIMÃO DE.
1865. Chronica da Companhia de Jesu do Estado do Brasil (1663). Lisbon. (First ed., Lisbon, 1663.)
VASCONCELLOS, V. P. See RONDÓN, CANDIDO MARIANO DA SILVA, 1916.
VEIGL, FRANZ XAVIER.
1785 a. Gruendliche nachrichten ueber die verfassung der landschaft von Maynas in Sud-amerika, bis zum Jahre 1768. In Murr, Christoph Gottlieb von. Reisen einiger missionarien der gesellschaft Jesu in Amerika, pp. 1–324. Nürnberg.
1785 b. Nachricht von den sprachen der völker am Orinokoflusse. Aus dem Saggio di Storia Americana . . . des herrn abbate . . . Gilíj. Ins deutsche übersetzt mit einigen verbesserungen . . . In Murr, Christoph Gottlieb von. Reisen einiger missionarien der gesellschaft Jesu in Amerika, pp. 325–450. Nürnberg.
VELASCO, JUAN DE.
1841–44. Historia del Reino de Quito en la America Méridionale. 3 vols. Quito.
VELLARD, JEHAN ALBERT.
1931. Pétroglyphes de la région de l'Araguaya. Journ. Soc. Amér. Paris, n.s., vol. 23, pp. 139–149.
1934. Notes sur la céramique pré-colombienne des environs d'Asunción. Journ. Soc. Amér. Paris, n.s., vol. 26, pp. 37–45.

1937. Textes mbwihá recueillis au Paraguay. Journ. Soc. Amér. Paris, n.s., vol. 29, pp. 373–386.

1939 a. Une civilisation du miel; les Indiens Guayakis du Paraguay. Paris.

1939 b. A preparação do curare pelos Nambikwaras. Rev. Arq. Mun. São Paulo, vol. 59, pp. 5–16.

VENESS, WILLIAM THOMAS.
1875. Ten years of mission life in British Guiana. London.

VENEZUELA-BRITISH GUIANA BOUNDARY ARBITRATION, 1898. 3 vols. and atlas. New York.

VERGARA Y VERGARA, JOSÉ MARÍA, and DELGADO, EVARISTO.
1860–61. The Indians of Andaquí. Popayán, 1885. Tr. from the Spanish and published in Bull. Amer. Ethnol. Soc., No. 1, pp. 53–72.

VERNEAU, RENÉ.
1921. Contribution à l'étude ethnographique des Indiens de l'Amazone. L'Anthrop., vol. 31, pp. 255–278.

VERNEAU, RENÉ, and RIVET, PAUL.
1912–22. . . . Ethnographie ancienne de l'Equateur. 2 vols. Paris. (Mission du Service géographique de l'armée pour la mesure d'un arc de méridien équatorial en Amérique du Sud sous le contrôle scientifique de l'Académie des Sciences, 1899–1906, vol. 6.)

VERRILL, ALPHEUS HYATT.
1918. A remarkable mound discovered in British Guiana. Timehri, 3rd ser., vol. 5, pp. 21–25.

1925. Indians of Surinam. Ind. Notes Monogr., vol. 2, No. 4, pp. 309–313.

VIDAL, GOMER ÉLIZABETH JULIE.
1862. Voyage d'exploration dans le haut Maroni, Guyane française (Septembre à novembre, 1861). Rev. Mar. Coloniale, vol. 5, pp. 512–548, 638–662.

VIEDMA, FRANCISCO DE.
1910. Descripción geográfica y estadística de la provincia de Santa Cruz de la Sierra. In Angelis, Pedro de. Colección de obras y documentos relativos á la historia antigua y moderna de las provincias del Rio de la Plata. 2nd ed., vol. 2, pp. 413–542. Buenos Aires.

VIEIRA, ANTONIO.
1735–46. Cartas. 3 vols. Lisbôa. Especial ref. to vol. 1, Carta XLIX.

VILLANUEVA, MANUEL PABLO.
1902–03. Fronteras de Loreto. Bol. Soc. Geogr. Lima, vol. 12, pp. 361–479; vol. 13, pp. 30–92.

VILLA REAL, TOMAZ DE SOUZA.
1848. Viagem de . . . pelos Rios Tocantins, Araguaya e Vermelho. Rev. Inst. Hist., vol. 4.

VILLAVICENCIO, MANUEL.
1858. Geografía de la republica del Ecuador. New York.

VINAZA, CIPRIANO MUÑOZ Y MANZANO, CONDE DE LA.
1892. Bibliografía española de lenguas indígenas de América. Madrid.

VINCKE, GASTON.
1935. Avec les Indiens de la Guyane. Avant-propos de Gaston Monnerville. Paris.

VOCABULARIO GENERAL DE LA LENGUA DE LOS INDIOS DEL PUTUMAYO Y CAQUETÁ.
1898. Publicado por primera vez con indagaciones preliminares por el Dr. Marcos Jiménez de la Espada. Madrid.

VOGT, (P.) FR.
1904. Die Indianer des Obern Paraná. Mitt. Anthrop. Gesell. Wien, vol. 34 (der dritten folge, 4 band), pp. 299–221, 353–377.

VOYAGES ET AVANTURES DU CHEVALIER DE . . . 4 vols. in 2. London and Paris. 1749.

VOYAGES ET TRAVAUX DE MISSIONNAIRES DE LA COMPAGNIE DE JÉSUS. 1857–61. Paris. Vol. 1: Mission de Cayenne et de la Guyane française, 1857, pp. 1–180. Paris.

WAGLEY, CHARLES W.
1940 a. The effects of depopulation upon social organization as illustrated by the Tapirapé Indians. Trans. N. Y. Acad. Sci., ser. 2, vol. 3, No. 1, pp. 12–16.
1940 b. World view of the Tapirapé Indians. Journ. Amer. Folk-lore, vol. 53, No. 210, pp. 252–260.
1942. O estado de extase do page Tupí (Tenetehara e Tapirapé). Sociologia, vol. 3. São Paulo.
1943 a. Notas sobre Aculturação entre os Guajajara. Bol. Mus. Nac. Rio de Janeiro, n.s., Antropologia, No. 2.
1943 b. Tapirapé shamanism. Bol. Mus. Nac. Rio de Janeiro, n.s., Antropologia, No. 3.

WAGNER, HENRY RAUP.
1926. Sir Francis Drake's voyage around the world; its aims and achievements. San Francisco.

WALDECK, JO BESSE MCELVEEN.
1939. Back of beyond in British Guina. Travel, vol. 73, (Oct.), pp. 30–34, 43.

WALLACE, ALFRED RUSSEL.
1853. A narrative of travels on the Amazon and Rio Negro. London and New York.
1889. Travels on the Amazon and Rio Negro. London, New York.

WALLIS, G.
1886. Die Paumarys. Das Ausland, vol. 59, pp. 261–266. Stuttgart and München.

WATERTON, CHARLES.
1891. Wanderings in South America. London.

WAVRIN, ROBERT, MARQUIS DE.
1927. Investigaciones etnográficas. Leyendas tradicionales de los Indios del Oriente ecuatoriano. Bol. Bibl. Nac. Quito, n.s., No. 12, Sept.–Oct., pp. 325–337.

WEDDELL, HUGUES ALGERNON.
1853. Voyage dans le nord de la Bolivie et dans les parties voisines du Pérou; ou, Visite au district aurifère de Tipuani. Paris.

WEEKS, JOHN H.
1913. Among Congo Cannibals. Philadelphia.

WEISS, H.
1915. Vier Maanden in Suriname. Nijerk.

WERTHEMAN, ARTURO.
1877. Informe de la exploración de los ríos Perene y Tambo. Lima.

WHIFFEN, THOMAS W.
1913. A short account of the Indians of the Issá-Japurá district (South America). Folklore, vol. 24, pp. 41–62. London.
1915. The north-west Amazons: notes of some months spent among cannibal tribes. London and New York.

WHITELY, HENRY.
1884. Explorations in the neighbourhood of Mounts Roraima and Kukenam, in British Guiana. Proc. Roy. Geogr. Soc., vol. 6, pp. 452–463.

WHITNEY, CASPAR.
 1912 a. Adventuring along the upper Orinoco. Harper's Mag., vol. 125, pp. 528–538.
 1912 b. The flowing road: a sportsman's adventures on the Rio Negro and the Upper Orinoco. Philadelphia and London.
WICKHAM, HENRY ALEXANDER.
 1872. Rough notes of a journey through the wilderness from Trinidad to Pará, Brazil, by way of the great cataracts of the Orinoco, Atabapo, and Rio Negro. London.
WIENER, CHARLES
 1880. Pérou et Bolivie. Paris.
WILKENS DE MATTOS, JOÃO.
 1856. Alguns esclarecimentos sobre as missões da Provincia do Amazonas. Rev. Inst. Hist., vol. 19.
WILLIAMS, HELENA MARIA, TRANS. See HUMBOLDT, ALEXANDER von, 1814.
WILLIAMS, JAMES.
 1924. The Arawak Indians and their language. Congr. Int. Amer., sess. 21, The Hague, pt. 1, pp 355–370.
 1928. The aborigines of British Guiana. The Church Overseas, vol. 1, pp. 220–227. London.
 1928–29. The Warau Indians of Guiana and vocabulary of their language. Journ. Soc. Amér. Paris, n.s., vol. 20, pp. 193–252; vol. 21, pp. 201–261.
 1932. Grammar, notes, and vocabulary of the language of the Makuchi Indians of Guiana. Linguistische Anthroposbibliothek, vol. 8, pp. 389–408. St. Gabriel-Mödling.
 1936. The aborigines of British Guiana and their land. Anthropos, vol. 31, pp. 417–432.
WILLIAMS, LLEWELYN.
 1941. The Caura valley and its forests. Geogr. Rev., vol. 31, pp. 414–429.
WILLIAMSON, JAMES ALEXANDER.
 1923. English Colonies in Guiana and on the Amazon, 1604–1668. Oxford.
WILSON, JOHN.
 1906. The relation of Master John Wilson of Wansteed in Essex, one of the last ten that returned into England from Wiapoco in Guiana 1606. In Purchas, Samuel, Hakluytus posthumus; or Purchas his pilgrimes, vol. 16, pp. 338–351. Glasgow.
WINTER, A.
 1881. Indian pictured rocks of Guiana. Written in aid of the funds of the Potaro Mission, New Amsterdam, Berbice.
WOOD, JOHN GEORGE.
 1868–70. The natural history of man. 2 vols. London and New York.
WOODROFFE, JOSEPH FROUDE.
 1914. The upper reaches of the Amazon. London.
XARQUE, FRANCISCO.
 1900. Ruiz Montoya en Indias (1608–1652) . . . Colección de libros raros y curiosos que tratan de América, vols. 16–19. (Reprint of original edition of 1662 edited by P. Vindel.) Madrid.
YÉPEZ, JACINTO M.
 1927. El Puyu y sus costumbres. El Oriente dominicano. Canelos, 1st year, pp. 6–7.

Yves d'Évreux, (Pere).
1864. Voyage dans le nord du Brésil fait durant les années 1613 et 1614. Introduction and notes by Ferdinand Denis. Leipzig and Paris.

Zanten, J. H. van.
1925. Domografie van de in Suriname levende volken. Mensch en Maatschappij, 201.

Zapata, Augustín.
1906. Carta del Padre . . . al Padre Joseph de Buendía, en la que da noticias del Paititi. 8 Mayo, 1695. In Maurtua, Victor M., 1906, vol. 10, pp. 25–28.

Zárate, Andrés de.
1904. Informe que haze á Su Magestad el Padre . . ., de la Compañía de Jhesús, Visitador y Vizeprovinzial que acaua de ser de la provinzia de Quito, en el Reyno de el Perú, y de sus Misiones del río Napo y del Marañon. In Figueroa, Francisco de, Relación de las misiones de la Compañia de Jesús, pp. 341–418. Madrid.

Zárate, Augustín de.
1577. Historia del descubrimiento y conquista de la provincia del Perú. Sevilla. (Also in Bibl. de autores españoles, vol. 26, Historiadores primitivos de Indias, vol. 2, pp. 459–574, Madrid, 1853.)

Zavala, Miguel J.
1895 a. Arte de la lengua campa. Lima.
1895 b. Vocabulario de la lengua campa. In Capelo, Joaquín, La vía central del Perú, vol. 2, pp. 155–164. Lima.

Zeballos, Estanisláo Severo, y Pico, Pedro P.
1878. Informe sobre el tumulo prehistorico de Campana. An. Soc. Cient. Argentina, vol. 6, pp. 244–260.

Zuloaga, Guillermo, and Tello B., Manuel.
1939. Exploración preliminar de la Sierra de Imataca. Rev. Fomento (Venezuela), año 3, No. 19, pp. 397–430.